Standards in Public Life

First Report of the Committee on Standards in Public Life

Chairman Lord Nolan

Volume 2 : Transcripts of Oral Evidence

Presented to Parliament by the Prime Minister
by Command of Her Majesty, May 1995
LONDON : HMSO
£38.00 net
Cm 2850–II

TABLE OF CONTENTS

VOLUME II
LIST OF WITNESSES

Page

THE COMMITTEE ON STANDARDS IN PUBLIC LIFE

TRANSCRIPTS OF ORAL EVIDENCE

LIST OF SUPPLEMENTARY MEMORANDA RELATING TO TRANSCRIPTS OF ORAL EVIDENCE

VOLUME II

The principal documents necessary to understand evidence given by witnesses in the transcripts of oral evidence are included at the end of this volume. Copies of all other submissions received by the Committee may be consulted at the Public Records Office in Kew, the Public Record Office of Northern Ireland in Belfast, the Scottish Public Records Office in Edinburgh, and the National Library of Wales in Aberystwyth.

LIST OF PERSONS OR ORGANISATIONS SUBMITTING WRITTEN EVIDENCE

TUESDAY 17 JANUARY 1995

Members Present:

The Rt. Hon. The Lord Nolan (Chairman)

Sir Clifford Boulton GCB
Professor Anthony King
The Rt. Hon. Tom King CH MP
The Rt. Hon. Peter Shore MP

The Rt. Hon. The Lord Thomson of Monifieth KT DL
Sir William Utting CB
Dame Anne Warburton DCVO CMG
Diana Warwick

Witnesses:
Ivor Crewe, Professor of Politics, University of Essex
Simon Jenkins, columnist and former Editor of *The Times*
Lord Blake, constitutional historian
Rt. Hon. Roy Hattersley MP

1. LORD NOLAN: We welcome you all, witnesses, public and press, to this, the first of our oral evidence hearings. These hearings are important because we want to carry on in public the debate about what changes may be needed in our institutions if we are to safeguard standards in public life and restore public confidence. There can be no doubt that there has been a fall in public confidence in the standards of behaviour of people in public life. If changes are needed to restore that confidence, we must recommend them without delay, no matter how drastic they may be.

We have had more than 1,400 written submissions. These we propose to make available for public inspection. Time permits us to hear only a very small number of people to give evidence here, so in choosing our witnesses we have concentrated on people who have close knowledge of our institutions and of the events which have given rise to concern. We expect to hear a wide range of forcefully expressed views.

Today we begin with four distinguished witnesses, Professor Ivor Crewe, academic and expert commentator on political developments, Simon Jenkins, journalist, former editor of The Times, columnist and member of quango boards, Lord Blake, constitutional historian and author, Conservative, and Mr Roy Hattersley, senior practising politician and journalist, former Cabinet Minister and former Deputy Leader of the Labour Party.

Over the next six weeks we shall take evidence on each of the three main themes set out in our "Issues and Questions" paper—that is to say, Members of Parliament's financial interests, Ministers and civil servants and their relations with business organisations, and appointments to quangos, in that order. The first two weeks will be devoted to examining the area of Members of Parliament's financial interests. The Members of Parliament at the House of Commons to which they are elected represent the centre of our democracy, and that must be the focus of our initial inquiry.

Many members of the public who have written to us have argued that being a Member of Parliament is a full-time paid job and that no paid outside interests should be permitted. I think it is fair to say that most active politicians would disagree with that view and would argue that some outside interests increase the expertise of Members of Parliament and that, without some scope for these, fewer good people would enter the House. But even among politicians there is very considerable disagreement about where the boundaries on outside interests should be drawn. The rules of Parliament appear to suggest that Members may not accept a fee for advocating a cause; yet it seems reasonably clear that a blind eye has been turned to those rules in practice. We want to explore this with our witnesses. We want to see if we can make recommendations both about what is acceptable and about how it should be declared and monitored.

Parliament's present procedures of dealing with breaches or alleged breaches of the rules require close examination. We shall want to talk to our witnesses about those procedures and consider whether there are ways in which they can be made more open, fairer and more effective, and whether there is a role for some independent element in the investigation and adjudication of alleged offences.

Finally, I want to emphasise that all the witnesses whom we shall be examining have volunteered to come here, to give their views and to answer questions. None of them have been summoned or made to come and none of them are under investigation by us. Some have suggested that we should investigate individual cases. We have neither the time nor the means to do so, and in any event we do not think it is necessary to do so. The systems and rules that we are concerned with can be quite adequately examined without reference to individual cases where the existing rules may or may not have been broken.

With that preliminary, may I come straight to our evidence? I would like first, please, to invite Professor Ivor Crewe, the Professor of Government at the University of Essex since 1982, to help us with his views on the current situation. Professor Crewe will be taken through his evidence by Sir Clifford Boulton on my left, who recently retired as Clerk to the House of Commons. Yes, Professor.

PROFESSOR IVOR CREWE

IVOR CREWE (Professor of Government, University of Essex): Thank you. I shall confine myself to public concern about politicians. This is partly because your committee has, I believe, chosen to focus on MPs and Ministers, and also on quangos, at this stage of your deliberations, but it is also because there is some evidence from polls and academic surveys about the public's perception of politicians that there is very little about their perceptions of holders of other public offices. I very much doubt in fact whether the ordinary citizen has a well-

1

formed view of the behaviour of civil servants or of appointees to quangos.

As regards elected politicians, the British public have always displayed a widespread and, some would say—I would say—healthy cynicism. They have simply taken it for granted, in a fairly good-humoured way, I should add, until recently, that most MPs are self-serving impostors and hypocrites who put party before country and self before party. Over 50 years ago, in August 1944, Gallup asked people whether politicians were merely out for themselves, for their party or to do the best for their country. Bear in mind that this was a time when party politics was suspended for the duration and when the war was clearly being won, but even then barely over a third—36 per cent—answered that politicians put the country first and as many answered that politicians put themselves first.

Since then public opinion has been more sceptical. In the late 1960s, for example, a period when politics was free of scandal, the majority of voters told polls that they believed that people become MPs for their own gain and that most politicians are in it for what they can get out of it. Whenever surveys have asked people to compare various occupations for honesty or trustworthiness or a moral example, MPs have been at or near the bottom of the league, competing with estate agents and journalists to avoid the wooden spoon. In other words, the public have never held MPs and Ministers in as high a regard as politicians themselves might like to think.

However, the recent spate of revelations about politicians' financial and sexual conduct has produced, I think, two important changes in public opinion. Firstly, there is no doubt that distrust and alienation has risen to a higher level than ever recorded before. It was always fairly prevalent; it is now, in many regards, almost universal. We can put some precision to that on the basis of a fairly recent Gallup survey, which repeated questions about MPs' standards of behaviour that had originally been asked in 1985. Here are some examples of the changes. The proportion believing that "MPs care more about special interests than about people like themselves" increased from 67 per cent to 77 per cent. The proportion believing that MPs will tell lies if they feel the truth will hurt them politically increased from 79 per cent to 87 per cent. The proportion agreeing that most MPs have a high personal moral code fell from a not very high 42 per cent to a pretty low 28 per cent. It is always tempting, I think, for politicians to comfort themselves by saying that voters have always been cynical. They have always been cynical, but they are much more cynical now than ever before.

Secondly, public scepticism about one aspect of politicians' behaviour, namely their financial integrity, has risen particularly sharply. Until recently people did not believe that the typical MP was engaged in what the Americans call "graft"—milking political office for private financial gain. They believed that MPs went into politics for status and power, they believed that MPs told lies for political advantage, but they did not believe that more than a small minority of MPs saw Parliament as a means of lining their own pockets, and here the movement of opinion has been very pronounced. In the same Gallup survey that I referred to a moment ago, fully 64 per cent of the public agreed that "Most MPs make a lot of money by using public office improperly", and only 22 per cent disagreed. That 64 per cent figure is up from 46 per cent nine years ago. And I think it is worth noting the wording

of that statement with which 64 per cent of the public agree: "Most MPs make a lot of money by using public office improperly." I myself do not believe that for one moment. I think that kind of behaviour is confined to a small—I would say tiny—minority of MPs. But the fact is that the public agree, by a ratio of three to one, with a blunt statement of that kind. I think that is something that should alarm the committee; it certainly alarms me.

So public distrust is evidently widespread; it has evidently grown. The depth of public concern, however, is a little more difficult to gauge. I do not think it could be described yet as a burning issue. The question of public standards does not figure in people's answers when polls ask them to say what they consider to be the most important problems facing the country or, for that matter, facing themselves. Clearly job insecurity, crime, drug abuse amongst the young are all matters that seriously and persistently worry ordinary people, whereas standards in public life are not in that category.

One indicator of deep public concern in a democratic society about the standards of politicians is the existence of an anti-corruption or a clean government movement that itself puts up candidates in elections of the kind that emerged in the United States in the first quarter of this century or in Japan in the 1960s and 1970s or indeed in Italy today, and I think Britain is very far from that, so far. But there is undoubtedly growing unease. There is distaste bordering on contempt. Genuine alarm that the system of government and public service has become or is in the process of becoming corrupt on a Mediterranean scale may still be confined to a small minority, but, I repeat, especially amongst those who are politically active or active in local communities I do not think there is any doubt that there is very considerable unease of a kind that has not existed at any other time since the war.

Finally, let me just make a general point. Many people in the public think in very general terms. They do not make fine differentiations between different types of public office; they do not distinguish between current Ministers and ex-Ministers or between Ministers and their relatives or between Government and Opposition or between parliamentarians on the one hand and civil servants or the chief executives of hospital trusts on the other. All are regarded as part of an undifferentiated "Them". Media disclosures of breaches of trust or standards by one part of the establishment undoubtedly affect public attitudes towards the whole establishment, and certainly, I think, the reputation of MPs has partly been damaged by revelations of conflicts of interest, nepotism and so forth elsewhere in the public sector, notably in quangos, and some of these revelations may be of breaches of standards that are more serious than anything that has yet been alleged, let alone proved, of MPs or Ministers. But MPs and Ministers are the most visible element of those who hold public office. There is no doubt that the public do have particularly high expectations of the standards of MPs and Ministers, so even relatively minor breaches by MPs and Ministers are likely to affect public trust in the democratic system as a whole. Therefore, I think the committee is quite right to be focusing at this early stage on the standards of conduct of MPs and Ministers.

2. CLIFFORD BOULTON: Thank you very much for a very wide opening statement, which I think has covered many of the points that we were interested in hearing about. Obviously we are more concerned, basically, with

what is actually happening rather than with what people think is happening or what used to happen, but nevertheless I do not think we shall be regarded as a great success if at the end of the day we cannot make recommendations which have the effect of allaying genuine public concern. So it is very relevant to us to establish what is genuine and what is perhaps more temporary, due to other local or passing circumstances.

So having accepted what you say that in the public mind there is not a very clear distinction between Members of Parliament and public officials generally, can I ask you this in general terms: is it not a fact that at the moment there is a general disgruntlement which is producing a "fed-upness" in answer to the question "Is everybody happy?" and there is a general malaise or hangover from an unfortunate economic position or something like that which is producing at least some effect at the moment on what people are saying?

IVOR CREWE: I do not believe that the declining confidence of the public in politicians is simply a function of the lack of what is called the "feel good" factor—that is to say, people's sense of economic insecurity and economic pessimism. Indeed, I think there is reasonably hard evidence to establish that. For example, at the European level a question has been asked in a European-wide survey twice a year going back to 1976 about how satisfied people are in each of the EU countries about the way democracy is working in their own country. If you look at the trend for Britain, the trend, although inevitably it goes up and down from one year to the next, has gone downward. If you go back to the mid-1970s, something like 60 per cent-65 per cent said they were satisfied; in the last two years it dipped for the first time below 50 per cent; this year it is at its lowest ever: it is at 45 per cent. For the first time more people say they are dissatisfied than satisfied.

Obviously there are a number of factors that explain this. The behaviour of politicians—breaches of standards of behaviour—is only one factor, and the economy could well be another factor, but if you look at the trend, it does not follow the ups and downs of the economy. The degree of trust in the way democracy has been working has been very high at times of recession and it has been quite low in times of prosperity. It is clear that this does follow people's sense of the integrity and the propriety of politicians. So although a general sense of fed-upness, as you put it, may make some contribution to public attitudes to politicians at the moment, I am quite convinced that the main factor has been revelations of financial impropriety and other improprieties.

3. CLIFFORD BOULTON: Given that, as you say, people consider politicians in very, very general terms, if, having asked "What do you think about politicians?", you ask your second question "What do you think of your own MP?", that switches the question very much in an individual's mind and he is made to answer what kind of performance his own Member puts in. Is it not a fact that you get a very different answer when you ask that question?

IVOR CREWE: Yes. It is perfectly true that people do make a distinction between their local MP and politicians in general. Unless they have some evidence of either incompetence or impropriety on the part of their local MP, they are likely to give their own MP, irrespective of party and their own views, a relatively clean bill of health.

If I could just answer a question which you did not ask but which may have been implied by that, I am not sure that that should necessarily be of much comfort, because if one is concerned with the public's trust in the working of the political system as a whole, I suspect that their views of their own MP will have very little bearing on that.

4. CLIFFORD BOULTON: I was just thinking that in fact if you asked the question in 650 different parts of the country and added up all the answers, you would get a very different answer than if you simply asked "What do you think about MPs?" As I say, we are simply exploring the reality of the concern.

You said yourself, I think, that you personally did not feel what one might call a great deal of despair about standards or that you did not accept that Members were "on the make" in a general way. What factors do you attribute to this growth? We hear in general terms about institutions that are having a rocky time, "Oh, it's the new behaviour of the media. They say things now in a damaging and irresponsible way which they didn't say about institutions in days gone by." Is there some sea-change in the presentation of facts and news to the public, who, as you say, are not specialists in these matters and tend perhaps to be influenced by the tone of voice taken by the news media?

IVOR CREWE: I do not think that the main change in the way the media have covered the behaviour of politicians has contributed all that much to changes in public opinion, because the main change has been the much greater intrusiveness of the media in the private lives of politicians. The media have mainly been concerned, I think, with some exceptions in the quality press, in revealing a great deal more about the sexual lives of politicians, and this has been something that the public enjoy, it greatly entertains the public; it is not, however, something, as far as one can tell, that greatly exercises them. The public are fairly tolerant actually about MPs' private behaviour. I do not think the press have been very much more intrusive, or very much more investigative, about financial improprieties by MPs on the whole. I think that the press are not very adventurous in that area. Yet it is quite clear that what concerns the public is financial misbehaviour by MPs.

5. CLIFFORD BOULTON: Obviously we simply want to hear your views about this and we are not looking at individual cases, but there are some individual cases under examination at the moment which involve words like "entrapment", "bogus faxes" and all the rest of it, so I think that some people would say that there is an element of change in practice to bear in mind.

Have you any more specific things that you could say about comparisons with other countries? Are there examples of different ways of handling these matters in other countries by the use of the courts? Has self-discipline of Parliament been abandoned more fully in some countries than is the situation here?

IVOR CREWE: Comparisons with other countries are very difficult. On the whole I think that the standard of public behaviour of politicians in this country does compare well with many comparable democracies, certainly with the United States, certainly with much of Mediterranean Europe. On the other hand, if we were to compare Britain with Germany, for example, I am not at all sure now that the standards of public life in Britain are higher than those in Germany, and I am quite sure they are lower than those in Scandinavia and the low countries, so I think that Britain comes probably somewhere in the middle of the European league table, as best one can judge these things, rather than, as I think politicians and indeed the public would have assumed 10 or 15 years ago, at the top of the league.

It is extremely difficult to disentangle the different factors that make for more corruption in some countries than others. I think one of the factors is the way in which political parties are financed and the way in which election campaigns are financed: the greater the dependence of parties on non-government funding, the greater the opportunity and the incidence of certain kinds of corruption. That is something that appears to be emerging from comparisons. But beyond that you have to go deep into the history and culture of different countries to come up with an explanation, and such explanations are not necessarily very satisfactory.

6. CLIFFORD BOULTON: But you are saying that you do sense an emerging public concern about the sources of financing of political parties. Did you say that?

IVOR CREWE: Yes. Well, I think the concern of the ordinary public is with such things as the donation of very large sums of money by individuals to a political party and the statistical relationship between the donation of funds and the receipt of honours, even if one could not possibly establish that there had been any explicit understanding on the part of donor and party. Amongst those who take a much more active specialist interest in political affairs in Britain I think for a long time there has been considerable concern about the dependence of the main parties on institutional funding.

7. CLIFFORD BOULTON: Yes, but of course this does not directly relate to the individual financial interests of Members as such, it is a wider question, but we are obviously interested to know what the general reaction is to that.

Then can I just check that you said that you think the public's concern is principally about financial matters ——

IVOR CREWE: Absolutely.

CLIFFORD BOULTON: ——and they are not so concerned about private behaviour?

IVOR CREWE: Yes. I would say—this is a personal view of course—having looked hard over the last week or so at all the survey evidence that exists, that the public are surprisingly tolerant about MPs' personal lives and I think surprisingly puritan about MPs' financial behaviour. They do not think that having illegitimate children or being homosexual or having an affair are in any sense matters for resignation on the part of MPs, but they are very strict about the receipt of even quite small gifts. They even have mixed views—very mixed views: they split 50-50—about whether MPs should accept a free lunch or a bottle of whisky at Christmas. I imagine that the great majority of MPs—indeed, I imagine, the great majority of ordinary people—would not think twice about accepting a free lunch from someone or a couple of bottles of wine at Christmas, or whatever. Anything beyond that,

overwhelming majorities, majorities in the 80 per cent-90 per cent league, object, and object strenuously, to MPs making any kind of financial gain by virtue of the position that they hold.

8. CLIFFORD BOULTON: But I take it from what you said generally that, although large numbers of people think that a Member's salary should be his only source of income, they are not at the same time saying "And it should be higher"?

IVOR CREWE: They do not think that MPs' salaries should be their only source of income. A recent poll suggests that the public accept that MPs should be able to earn additional income from outside interests, so long as those interests are declared. What they do not think is that their salaries should go up. In other words, if MPs are to earn more money than their parliamentary salary, that should not be provided directly by the taxpayer.

9. CLIFFORD BOULTON: That is a point, following your earlier answer to that question, that I am glad we have elicited, because I had failed to take note of the fact that you think that there is a general acceptance of other forms of income for Members of Parliament in addition to their salary.

IVOR CREWE: There is majority acceptance of the view that it is legitimate for MPs to have outside interests from which they earn money, so long as those interests are fully declared.

10. CLIFFORD BOULTON: And as a sort of general summing-up of what you have told us, you think that there is greater cause for concern now by a committee such as ourselves than at almost any period in the past that you can think of as far as public confidence and satisfaction with politicians is concerned?

IVOR CREWE: I think that is very clear. Wherever it is possible to make comparisons, the comparisons suggest that the public are more dissatisfied now with the conduct of MPs than they have been in the past, and that includes those occasions, and there have not been very many of them admittedly, when there have been a number of scandals and revelations in the media. Clearly it has been the incessant nature of the exposures in the press that has produced that level of public dissatisfaction, but then equally one might argue that the reason for the incessant exposure is that there has been more to expose.

CLIFFORD BOULTON: Thank you.

11. LORD NOLAN: I wonder, Professor, if I could ask one or two questions before bringing in the other members of the committee. In most of the professions in this country—the law, accountancy, medicine—there are clear rules governing the financial transactions that Members can carry out and there are disciplinary procedures for enforcing the rules, and commonly in recent years the disciplinary procedures have involved some outside element. There is nothing comparable in Parliament, is there?

IVOR CREWE: There is nothing comparable in Parliament, and the public are very sceptical about the idea that MPs are capable of regulating themselves. Under 10 per cent believe that the monitoring of the Register of Interests, for example, should be left to

Parliament alone. The rest believe that it is a matter that should be monitored either by an independent committee of some kind or possibly by the law courts. But of course it may well be the case that, with so many more people belonging to occupations and professions which have been subjected to external audit and external scrutiny over the last 10 to 15 years, they believe that MPs should be subject to the same regime. If you think of the number of people who are now affected by citizen's charters of various kinds or who find that what they once regarded as their professional autonomy has, at least to some extent, been dented by the powers that outside bodies, often bodies established by governments over the last 10 to 15 years, have over them, then it may well be that there is just a degree of piquancy and revenge in the public sense that MPs should be subject to similar constraints.

12. LORD NOLAN: But going beyond piquancy, do you think there is a genuine, constructive argument for looking at the present parliamentary procedures and seeing if they can be improved?

IVOR CREWE: I do think that if it was recommended that Parliament should continue to regulate itself in this regard or if Parliament ignored a recommendation that scrutiny should now be in the hands of an outside body, the public would find such a position less incredible. I think they would now take it for granted that if the breaches of standards that have been alleged over the last year or so were to be remedied, MPs would have to be subject to some independent scrutiny and monitoring.

LORD NOLAN: Thank you very much. May I go round the table? Professor King, have you any questions you wanted to ask?

13. PROF A. KING: Just one very general one. If one looks at scandals, and you have used the word "scandal", I think very probably most of them fall under one or more of three headings: those involving sex—one thinks of Profumo and all that—those involving money—one thinks of the Marconi scandal before the first world war—and those involving abuse of power—to take an American case, the whole Watergate business. Is it your impression that either the number or the pattern of such scandals has tended to change in Britain over time? In other words, quite apart from the quantity of allegations of sleaze of one kind or another, do you think that the character of those allegations has changed?

IVOR CREWE: Even though there appear to have been an awful lot of examples of misbehaviour by politicians in the last year or two, one is still dealing with fairly small numbers if one is looking for trends. I do not think that the amount of sexual scandal, if one can use that broad term, has probably changed very much over the years, but there have been incidents in every decade. I suspect that the abuse of political power is the category of impropriety that has increased the most, although I would stress that one is still dealing with fairly small numbers. I do not think there has been any precedent for the allegations, and I stress they are only allegations, that have been made about Westminster Council, for example—I know that here one is talking about local councillors and not about national politicians—and I do not believe that there has been any precedent for the kind of allegations that are being made about the packing of quangos. For example, I understand that the number of Conservative MPs' spouses, usually wives, who have got paid

appointments on quangos at the moment is something like 34 and in the case of the Labour Party it is something like two. That is clearly a discrepancy that could not possibly be accounted for by any meritocratic criteria. I do not think that we have had examples of that degree of bias in political appointments in the past, but that is where I think probably the changes have been.

14. PETER SHORE: You said, in reply to an earlier question, that opinion seemed to accept that it was legitimate for MPs to have outside interests, presumably outside jobs, but is that a holus-bolus acceptance or does public opinion differentiate between MPs having some engagements and employment and receiving income and MPs who are prepared to act as consultants, as agents really, for public relations and other bodies?

IVOR CREWE: I doubt if the general public makes fine distinctions between jobs that lie wholly outside the parliamentary activities of an MP—journalism, for example, or a certain amount of legal practice or whatever—and acting as a consultant for a company or a trade association or whatever. The public are quite clear that they do not think that MPs should earn additional income either from asking questions in Parliament or from using their privileged position in Parliament to assist a particular interest. I think there are examples of MPs acting on behalf of an organisation and declaring that they are doing so and being known to do so which the public would accept as legitimate. I do not think the public had any difficulty with Jim Callaghan acting as an advocate for the Police Federation, because this was something that he made very clear and it was something which was very widely known, but I think that acting for an individual company is probably something that would be regarded rather differently.

15. WILLIAM UTTING: I would like to ask one question. If an independent element were introduced into the regulation of MPs' interests, would this have any serious constitutional implications? Would it affect the independence of parliamentarians in any fundamental way?

IVOR CREWE: I think the answer to that must be yes. Of course it must be an indentation in the sovereignty of Parliament and the independence of MPs if their behaviour is subject to the scrutiny of a body that itself is not part of Parliament, but then MPs are subject to the courts, and I do not think this has been regarded as in breach of any important constitutional convention.

16. DIANA WARWICK: You seem to have told us that the incidence of such events has not increased in very substantial terms or at least, if it has increased, the absolute numbers are small, and you seem to conclude that abuse of political power was the main issue. Taking the collective of public service, you almost seem to be telling us, with the dates of the statistics that you were giving us, that people seem to have slipped into habits or actions that perhaps they would not have contemplated 15, 18 or 20 years ago. Has this anything to do with what is often alleged to be a common explanation, that when there is one party in power for a very long period of time this affects people's comfort factor, their sense of complacency or their willingness to adopt a set of rules? I would apply that not just to national level but to local level. You used Westminster as an example. I can think of others.

IVOR CREWE: I think the particular example that I gave, which was the absolutely evident increase in partisan appointments to quangos, is not necessarily a function of the length of time that a party has been in office. The Conservatives were in power for 13 years from 1951 to 1964, and I do not believe that that particular problem occurred then. This time I think the problem began very early on in the 1979-83 government, because the government quite deliberately wished, as is, I think, quite legitimate, to break what it regarded as the consensus corporate political culture of the country and thought that if it was to make radical changes in certain areas of policy then it needed to make sure that key appointments in quangos and in public offices should be of people who thought in the same way as the government did then. That, I think, has now somehow spread to appointments in lots of areas where there is no reason to believe that that kind of wish on the part of the Government is necessary. So I don't think that what one might describe as partisan nepotism is necessarily a function of the length of time in which a party has been in office. Your reference to local government, I think, is well-taken. I think there has always been a much longer tradition of political nepotism in local government than there has been in national government—indeed, I think that is an area that I would hope the Committee might look at sometime in the future, and that is clearly related to those local authorities which have been in the hands of one party for a very long time.

LORD NOLAN: Thank you very much indeed, Professor, that has been very helpful and clear. I am most grateful to you for coming and we can now ask our next witness, who is Mr. Simon Jenkins, to come forward.

LORD NOLAN: Good morning, Mr. Jenkins.

SIMON JENKINS

SIMON JENKINS (Columnist and former Editor of *The Times*): Good morning.

17. LORD NOLAN: You were described in my opening as journalist, former editor of *The Times*, Columnist, member of quango Boards. Is there anything else you would like to say by way of introduction?

SIMON JENKINS: I would like to exclude the last reference nowadays!

18. LORD NOLAN: Are you a member of a Board of a quango?

SIMON JENKINS: The question of whether the Millennium Commission is a quango is moot!

LORD NOLAN: I see. Possibly and possibly not. Mr. Jenkins, I am very grateful to you indeed for coming along—we look forward with great interest to hearing what you are going to say. I a going to ask on this occasion Mr. Tom King, on my left, to take you through your evidence. Tom, would you like to start off?

19. TOM KING: Do you want to say anything by way of——

SIMON JENKINS: No.

TOM KING: Well, why are you here? (Laughter)

SIMON JENKINS: I was written a letter about two weeks ago and asked to come. It may have arisen out of an

article or two I've written but I think that's all I can do by way of explanation.

20. TOM KING: Well, what motivates you to feel the need to be here today?

SIMON JENKINS: I think I share the same concern that the Committee shares about the standards of conduct in public life. I've seen it as a working journalist over many years. I've also served in the past on a number of boards and watched the manner in which both they were appointed and they conducted their business, and I think I am concerned, as you are, that at least the public perception is that there has been a decline in standards, and interested in the structures that you might put in place to correct that.

21. TOM KING: You are talking about public life in the broad. As you know, we have given three first priorities; one is MPs, the second is Ministers and the third are quangos and appointments to quangos. If we can start on MPs. Ivor Crewe has just said to us that the public perception is, by I think quite a significant majority in one of his polls, that most MPs make a lot of money by using public office for private advantage. But Ivor Crewe does not believe that is true. Do you believe it is true?

SIMON JENKINS: I think it is clearly true that many people think that. If you ask do I share Ivor Crewe's general view as to whether it is the case I think I agree with him that it is not substantially the case.

22. TOM KING: You know a lot of MPs by virtue of your profession and background and would you say that in fact overwhelmingly it is not actually true?

SIMON JENKINS: I think overwhelmingly it is not true. I think they are, given the temptations to which they are open and compared with legislatures abroad, relatively speaking incorrupt. There is petty corruption and grand corruption, I know. I don't share the view that things have got worse in terms of grand corruption. I think that if you go back and scratch the surface of almost any Parliament this century, and further, you will see as bad (if not worse) things that took place. I think there is a greater concern now about an accurate increase, or a factual increase, in the extent to which MPs are subject to what might be called petty corruption and since petty corruption is often more visible, or at least more publicizable, I think that is one of the reasons why you are here.

23. TOM KING: The issue about the public perception—if I can just deal with that—what we have really established then from both yourself and Ivor Crewe is that the public perception is wrong. If it is unfair to MPs how do you actually correct that, because it is obviously very undermining to public confidence which is important in standards in the public eye—if people believe that people are all on the make it is undermining if those are people who, as Clifford Boulton made in his intervention—people in the individual category—I am not sure if you remember the point he made, he asked a question about "Did the public perception of MPs in the mass—was it similar to the individual question as asked in the individual constituencies?" and certainly my impression—I think it is true—is that you get a very different reading when you ask individual constituents what they think of their MP. as opposed to "what do you

think of all those MPs up there?" Now, if the perception is unfair and it is undermining in public confidence generally in the integrity of our institutions, what can be done about it?

SIMON JENKINS: Well, let me be slightly less complimentary about MPs than my last answer implied. One of the reasons why I think it is unfair is that I think most members of the public have an unrealistic impression of the influence that MPs have over what matters, which is the conduct of Government business. One of the consequences of that is that MPs are more of a target of lobbying activity and pressure from outside than probably is justified by their actual power. By the same token, they attract to themselves publicity, the publicity attaches both to themselves as people and to the work they do in Parliament and I think the result of that is that when they do stray from what is considered the correct cannons of behaviour, it is more publicized and it is more undermining. But the remedy for that lies with MPs.

24. TOM KING: Well, does it entirely? I mean one of the ways in which people obviously form their impression has to be through the media and that is one of your main qualifications, obviously, clearly, for being a distinguished witness here today. If you look at your own newspaper, or the one which you previously edited, that used to have a full page of Parliamentary report. It now has nothing. It now has Matthew Parris writing most engaging and very entertaining articles, but of a sketched, somewhat caricature nature, which certainly form their part and I certainly enjoy them enormously, but on many days that is the only report of what is happening in Parliament. Do you think that is right?

SIMON JENKINS: Yes, I took the decision to stop it. I stopped it because I couldn't find who read it apart from MPs. We are not there to provide a public service for a particular profession or, for that matter, for a particular legislative chamber. The House of Lords had always felt hard-done-by in the same respect. Newspapers are about providing people with news. If you are asking a slightly different question, which is ——

25. TOM KING: Sorry, newspapers are about writing good news, is that it?

SIMON JENKINS: Providing news. Up to a point news that people want to read. But if you are asking a slightly different question, which is "Is the coverage of politics in newspapers an accurate reflection of the shifts of power within Government?" I think I'd agree with you that it probably isn't—it isn't—because it focuses too much on what happens in Westminster and too little on what happens in Whitehall. And one of the consequences of that is that an excessively searching spotlight is fastened on MPs. You can't have it both ways. I believe myself that the centre of gravity of political journalism still tends to be too much focused on the corridors of Westminster and not enough over the road in Whitehall.

26. TOM KING: But you think, therefore, it is a responsible position for a newspaper to take—a journal of record—I mean, I am not talking, obviously, about tabloid journalism who work by rather different rules—but the major newspapers of the country and compare them with newspapers of other countries—to give no reporting whatsoever factually, of what actually happens in Parliament on the grounds that people don't read it? Can I

put this point: have newspapers lost out in a sense against the electronic media? I am struck—and others may comment on this—I am actually struck by the amount of people who actually watch the morning programme on BBC2 and others, reporting on Parliament—a half-hour programme every day, which obviously carries much more than the normal Parliamentary Report, and the significant audience that that actually has. An audience which you feel actually doesn't exist?

SIMON JENKINS: Well, people who want to read, not watch or hear, but read, what goes on in Parliament can subscribe to Hansard. The extent to which they appeared to want to read very large amounts of material of MPs making speeches in the House, I believed was limited. And that was my judgment and it is the judgment, I think, of other editors, too.

27. TOM KING: I don't think — I mean, do you think the answer about subscribe to Hansard is a satisfactory answer for a former editor of the major journal —— Can I take you back to the European comparison and to the United States comparison? How would you compare that with the major serious newspapers in those countries, in terms of their reporting of their own Parliaments?

SIMON JENKINS: Well, in the case of France it would be compared quite well. I mean, we do report Parliament—and in the case of Germany we compare well. Congress is more extensively reported, at least in the Washington Post, but Congress, if I may say so, has much more power. The issue here is what matters in terms of the coverage of politics. Traditionally the dignified, rather than the efficient, as Bagehot would say, aspects of politics were heavily covered in the daily press—Parliament was covered. Nothing was written about the mechanics of Government. There has been a shift in the opposite direction over the past ten/twenty years. I happen to think it is a correct shift.

28. TOM KING: So how would you answer my question about how MPs can actually recover the ground that is—I think we generally agree—lost in public perception, unfairly lost in public perception, as is your judgment and Ivor Crewe's, if there is no reporting of what they are actually doing?

SIMON JENKINS: Well, there is reporting of what they are doing, first. Secondly, I think ——

TOM KING: I mean of a serious and more detailed nature.

SIMON JENKINS: There is quite a lot of reporting even of that, but, I mean, there is not verbatim reporting of speeches, I grant you—this is a somewhat arcane point. The question of increasing the public's view of the reputation of individual MPs and MPs collectively I think does have to do with their own conduct of their business. I think that the Prime Minister was right to try and change the theatricals of Question Time. Unfortunately he hasn't changed it. I think that the Government, or Parliament, was right to try and adjust the rules governing private interests of MPs of which you are a manifestation. I think most Members of the public were genuinely shocked to learn of the ease with which MPs could be suborned for what, I have to say I regard as relatively trivial tasks, but nonetheless it was amazing how easily they could be suborned. I thought that campaigns by certain major companies to recruit MPs to their cause were so serious that at one point I and, indeed, the editor of another newspaper seriously considered, somewhat facetiously, putting after the names of MPs, not their constituencies but their companies. I am sure that would have enraged MPs but if MPs are not prepared to adopt higher standards in these matters, I think a certain amount of press comment and even cynicism is in order.

29. TOM KING: May I then lead you on to the next point: do you actually think that MPs should have any outside interests, involvement, activity at all?

SIMON JENKINS: I think I have got a very straight forward view. I think it is perfectly in order and often useful and advantageous for an MP to do another job. I think that public scepticism is total when that job clearly relates to the work of being an MP and I cannot believe there is not a clear distinction to be drawn there. I think for an MP to be a paid-up lobbyist is outrageous and I am amazed, if I may so, that your confreres ever tolerated it.

30. TOM KING: Can I explore the point about lobbyists? You would therefore see nothing wrong with somebody being a farmer, being a barrister, being a journalist, being director perhaps of a family business that he had been involved in before he came into Parliament and continued to be involved in? Those are what you feel would be acceptable activities, but there are some activities that you would prohibit?

SIMON JENKINS: Yes.

31. TOM KING: And just drawing the line on lobbyists. I mean, lobbyists is one. Acting for a company where — I mean, public relations or lobbyists — where you actually don't quite know which client he is speaking for now, that would be your concern. What about trade associations where you cannot be quite sure which company they may be talking for?

SIMON JENKINS: Well, this is why, on a wider point, I believe very strongly in an organisation such as yourselves, because there has to be some judgment made as to where the line should be drawn. But if the purpose of having an MP on a Board or employed by a company is quite clearly for him to use his position as an MP to the advantage of that company, he should not be on that Board or with that company.

32. TOM KING: But could work for that company if, for instance, they were a company in his constituency?

SIMON JENKINS: I suppose so. I mean, you are asking me where to draw the line. But I suppose so. I would have said that he or she ought under no circumstances to play any part in Parliamentary business where that particular activity is involved.

33. TOM KING: I am actually distinguishing between being on a Board or lobbying for a company in the constituency without any financial connection with them. You would see no objection to that?

SIMON JENKINS: These are all grey areas but I think there is a distinction that can be drawn between an MP working outside Parliament in such a way that it is clearly intended that he should use his position in Parliament to

the advantage of that company and what is merely his other job.

34. TOM KING: I think that is very helpful and I think it is a view that I know many share. And you have made clear that there are some activities you think should be prohibited and some that — I mean, of course, there are some prohibited now, prohibited for Ministers, as we know—what about dealing with problems when they arise for MPs, when there are concerns? I mean, do you think the Press Complaints Commission has anything to teach us? Should we have a Parliamentary Complaints Commission? It may be a rather derogatory remark—you don't have to reply to it if you ——

SIMON JENKINS: I hope I am as robust about my own profession as I would be about yours. I think that there is a role—not just nowadays but there always has been—for external oversight of professions. I think nowadays the public in particular expect it of professions that involve or affect their daily and working lives or the conduct of Government and that clearly applies both to journalists and to MPs. You can argue as to whether the extent to which a Press Complaints Commission has adequate teeth to enforce its adjudications and at what point those teeth acquire legal bite. I think there are differences between the press and Parliament—I think Parliament is, in an important sense of the word, sovereign, and I think someone asked earlier as to whether there would be an infringement of constitutional freedom were an exterior body to enforce decisions on Parliament in some way. And as Ivor Crewe said there clearly would be an infringement. The question is whether it is worth it. I think now you have reached a state of affairs where it is to everyone's advantage for there to be an independent commission which does oversee the standards of conduct in public life, including MPs, and I think that body, while I don't happen to think it should have legal status over MPs, should be wholly independent of them.

35. TOM KING: On the Ministerial side, concern has been expressed about people after some interval of time—I think the minimum was two years, but I stand to be corrected on that—people joining the Boards of companies in which they were involved in privatisation. Are you aware of any other concerns—do you have other concerns about Ministerial conduct or abuse of Ministerial position and power? I mean, I am coming on to quangos later, but on the ——

SIMON JENKINS: I think less so. But the one you have mentioned is the most important one. It is noticeable in the—I think it is called QPM—I mean, the procedures for this—that the two-year rule can be waived with the permission of the Government. I think that is the sort of thing that incurs public cynicism. I think if you have a two-year rule it is a two-year rule. You should not see Ministers, however pure as the driven snow their reputations may be, immediately slipping out of public office into a private company, particularly one with which their previous job may have been connected. It looks bad.

36. TOM KING: Can we move on to quangos? Would you like—I know you've served, certainly on British Rail and other—Heritage field as well—what about the method of appointments to quangos?

SIMON JENKINS: I think it should not ultimately be in the hand of Government. I think it should be in the hand of an alternative hierarchy of patronage which should be wholly outside the realm of Downing Street, the Whips office, the Public Appointments Unit—it should be the concern of a body of people who are not in any sense beholden to the Government of the day and I think that the Public Appointments Unit should be switched over to be run by such a Commission. Now, it is perfectly open to Government to be a nominator of names to that commission, names for quangos, I mean, and I think it would be odd if Government didn't take a strong interest in who was appointed to public bodies that it itself has set up. But I do think that it is wrong that there should be any suspicion of partisan bias in appointments to public bodies which are not necessarily, or in many cases, clearly not political.

37. TOM KING: What would you see it as—a permanent standing commission, staffed by and run by what—by the Civil Service?

SIMON JENKINS: Well, in so far as one can achieve total independence of Government, when the estate is Government here, it would be independent of Government and the members of the commission should not, I think, possibly even be politicians. But they should be outwith the Government.

38. TOM KING: That commission would be required, in the interests of balance, if necessary to appoint people to quangos who were diametrically opposed to the very existence of the quango itself?

SIMON JENKINS: It would be entirely a matter for the Government to make representations to the commission of appointments, or whatever it might be called, on the appropriate composition of that particular public body, yes.

39. TOM KING: But, I mean, what would be the terms of reference of the quango, or whatever it is, who is going to appoint the other quangos?

SIMON JENKINS: Parliament would draw up the terms of reference of a public body. Parliament can lay down, if you like, what it wishes, but the actual appointment should be made by an outside body.

40. TOM KING: Yes, but you know the point I am obviously on. One of the reasons, as I see it—others may disagree—why we have some distortion at the present time is one of the significant elements in the present situation are the introduction of a number of new policies and new bodies which follow from quite controversial policies which are strongly opposed on the other side of the political field and obviously National Health Service Trusts would be one, some of the Grant Maintained School situations would be another and those are illustrations that one would give. Now, total balance at all times will invite that situation.

SIMON JENKINS: Well, I wasn't talking about total balance, but if you take the quango packing of health and education bodies, which I think causes widespread public disquiet. I mean, you can't brush it away—it is something that people find, in many cases, offensive. I am trying to find a mechanism for avoiding that sense of public offence. I think the only way you can do it is to declare, if you like, an alternative appointments hierarchy to that controlled by Government and you can then establish

a tension, if you like, between Government and that body. It is clearly the case that it is unreasonable and I hope that such a commission would regard it as unreasonable to appoint to a new Health Authority people who wish to demolish the Health Authority. But that is a decision for the commission to take, it is not a justification for packing with Government supporters.

41. TOM KING: And from your own experience—and I think you have made certain comment—what are your observations actually about the practical realities of the present system? Would you agree with me that one of the problems that Ministers face is actually the inefficiency of part of the system in producing so few names and the fact that the same names keep going round and keep coming up. You have referred to that in some of your writing on this subject.

SIMON JENKINS: I am sure you are as aware as anyone else of the panic that tends to surround the last-minute appointments to public bodies. It is undignified and frantic and people telephone round and say "do you know anyone who is sound?" and the thing goes down to the constituency level and people are asked left, right and centre, and people saunter up to people at parties. It is, I have to say, a procedure that brings public office into disrepute. There must be a better way of doing it than relying on names out of people's heads. Now, a partial system has been introduced through the P.A.U. and I understand that it is at least improving the supply of names, but there is still a horrendous lack of oxygen in this process. It is, I think, conditioned by two things: one is a nervous desire on the part of Ministers not to have anyone who might be at all risky or unsound on a public body, which might cause them trouble, and I think, secondly, it is the fact that the people who are making these appointments don't know so many people as they used to, and that is a change. I think the sphere of social activity (if I can put it that way) of people in public life has, often by virtue of their busy-ness, contracted. It is extraordinary to me how few people from certain walks of life find their way onto public bodies and I think the reason is, frankly, people didn't know them. It was very noticeable in the—I don't want to ramble—but it was noticeable in the biography of Oliver Franks that came out a couple of years ago, how the effect of the war was suddenly to open up public life to a wholly new range of people who were traumatised out of their original careers and I think one of the reasons why there was a feeling that public life was somehow refreshed by war was because of the opening up of these conduits of names.

TOM KING: Thank you.

42. LORD NOLAN: Thank you very much. I wonder, Mr. Jenkins, if I could take you back to the Members of the House of Commons? You have been inclined to say that their influence is over-rated and that one should concentrate more on what happens in Whitehall than what happens in Westminster. But would this be right; that in our democracy the ultimate power in this country—ignore Brussels—rests with the majority of individual Members of Parliament, that people do have high expectations of those Members, of their standards of behaviour and are shocked when they find what they see as lapses in those standards? Are those standards clearly enough laid down for the incoming Member of Parliament to know what kind of approaches from the commercial world he can properly take up and which he should drop like a hot potato?

SIMON JENKINS: Apparently not, is the only answer I can give. I think many incoming Members of Parliament are surprised and sometimes dismayed at how little "power" they appear to have and I think to that extent they are more susceptible to other approaches, to other ways of filling their time, than simply sitting on the Benches in the House of Commons. I think the public, rightly, has an exalted idea of what an MP does all day. I see the MP nowadays as essentially an electoral college for the Government and once that electoral college has declared itself, the job of the MP is to wait until he gets a job. If he doesn't get a job with Government he'll get a job with somebody else and that is wholly natural, it is not a point of criticism. But it does mean, I think, there is tremendous confusion in the mind of an MP as to what is appropriate and certainly a confusion in the mind of the public as to what an MP ought to be doing.

43. LORD NOLAN: Would you think that an attempt should be made to draw up further rules or provide some further machinery for guidance for Members of Parliament?

SIMON JENKINS: I was always attracted to Enoch Powell's thesis that MPs ought to be trusted to be straight, honest and above-board—I used to feel that about athletes and dope testing but I suppose we can't go down that line any more.

44. LORD NOLAN: Well, why is that, if I may interrupt you? Is it just that people are now saying "You have been telling us all along that you are honourable and straight and no doubt you are, but prove it"—is that the stage we have reached?

SIMON JENKINS: I think to that extent we are more open. Our scrutiny procedures are better and we are more democratic. I think it is also the case that in the absence of a body such as yourselves it has been left to the press to exercise scrutiny over the work that politicians do and the way in which they perform their business. It is very noticeable, particularly lately, I think, that the basis upon which a Minister is forced to resign is on the whole his capacity in his job to cause public embarrassment to the Government. Now, embarrassment to the Government, as opposed to incompetence or dereliction of duty, is the function of media coverage, so it immediately establishes a relationship between the media and the Government which I think is unhealthy but inevitable. If nobody else is going to say whether it is right for a Minister to accept a particular gift or particular trip, the press will. As a form of scrutiny the press is, in all sorts of respects, inadequate—it is extremely crude, it can be very unfair, it can go way over the top, but it is all we have got and as long as that has been the case I think you have got an understandable sense of frustration and outrage with the way in which the press perform this function, but it is a necessary function.

45. LORD NOLAN: Yes. If Parliament were to set up a reporting body to report to Parliament, if you like, not some totally independent organisation, but some independent body, something comparable to the Ombudsman which could independently report to Parliament which might, no doubt, have Members of Parliament not only giving evidence but taking part in its liberations, do you think that would provide an alternative to the media as the outside critic of Parliament?

SIMON JENKINS: A version of that was supposed to be the Committee of Privileges and it hasn't worked.

LORD NOLAN: That has not got any outside Members and it is a committee of the House, as I understand it.

SIMON JENKINS: There is a general point in your question, which I accept, which is that professions nowadays are expected to be answerable in some sense to bodies not solely composed of their own members but including an outside element. For what it is worth, my view is that it needs to be a more substantial outside element than an Ombudsman within the Palace of Westminster. But broadly speaking I think it is necessary to get on that route, yes.

LORD NOLAN: Thank you very much indeed. I wonder if I could ask the other members, starting this time with Lord Thomson. Have you any questions you would like to ask this witness, Lord Thomson?

46. LORD THOMSON: Could I ask a question simply for clarification in case I misunderstood. I thought when you were asked about Ministers retiring from Ministerial office and going into industries associated with their previous office, you talked about the document, the procedure for Ministers laying down a two-year rule. As I understand the position there is no such requirement in the procedure for Ministers and there is a very significant difference between the procedure applying to senior civil servants who move out of their post on retirement into industry, and Ministers. If my reading of it is correct, as I believe it is, the question I really want to ask is do you think the same rules ought to apply to cabinet Ministers leaving office and going into the private sector that apply to senior civil servants?

SIMON JENKINS: Yes, I was wrong, thank you. The reference—the two-year rule for civil servants—is self-waivable. In the case of Ministers they are merely expected not to take a position which might have compromised their previous activity or the Government in general. The answer to your question is yes, I do, I think you do need some such rule. I have to say it is very hard. You can suddenly find yourself out of office and you need a job, but I do think we are now in a state of affairs where the public expects there to be published standards and those standards to be adhered to, and one such standard, I think, should include a two-year rule, unwaivable.

47. LORD THOMSON: Could I just follow it up for one moment? The two-year rule, as it applies to civil servants, as you have said—the extreme is two years. Normally conditions are applied that are a good deal less than two years. Are you saying there ought to be a rigid two-year rule?

SIMON JENKINS: I think I am, yes. I mean, the problem with this whole area is it is bounded by discretion. If you are going to inject discretion into these rules the rules don't apply.

48. TOM KING: If you did that, would you compensate civil servants who were prohibited from taking employment in the fields in which they were most qualified for two years and would you pay them accordingly?

SIMON JENKINS: No.

49. TOM KING: So they would be expected to be without pay for two years and if they retired at 58 or 59

they would not be allowed to work in the area where they had experience?

SIMON JENKINS: Yes.

50. TOM KING: May I take you into another view, because obviously I declare an interest in the sense of having been Secretary of State for Defence and having to advise on retirement of some very senior serving officers. Now, one or two of those joined Defence contractors and play a very valuable part in helping British export sales in these fields in countries where they are well-known and which have been benefiting our country. For instance France, certainly, ensures very easy transfer between, perhaps, Government service—and, as you know, in the French system that is pretty easily facilitated to the benefit of France. Do you believe that the concern that has arisen over these issues is bound to be of such a scale that that should never be permitted?

SIMON JENKINS: I think so, yes.

TOM KING: Thank you.

51. DIANA WARWICK: I wonder if I could ask you something. It does strike me very forcibly the difference between the statistics that Professor Crewe gave us that 64 per cent, I think it was, agree that most MPs make a lot of money by using public office improperly and the fact that both of you do not share the perception that there is this dramatic increase in graft. I think we have faced this problem of actuality and perception. But you then went on to say "Hang on a minute, I don't really mean that because what I mean is that they are much more subject to petty corruption" and that being the case, having identified some areas that you would like to see changes—you have dealt with Ministers and so on—but in what areas would you like to see much more strict rules established in this area of petty corruption and how would you match penalties and the seriousness of penalties to the seriousness of the offence?

SIMON JENKINS: I think in the case of MPs I am not sure about penalties. I mean, there are penalties built into the rules as Tom King is implying, but I think they would chiefly concern the jobs that MPs could do and I answered that question before. I simply think that there should be categories of job that should be banned from MPs. I also think that you need—and we haven't discussed this—but I think you need to embrace in my alternative structure of patronage the Honours system and financial donations to political parties, which is one of the substantial areas, to my mind, of public cynicism.

52. DIANA WARWICK: The donations to political parties?

SIMON JENKINS: And its relationship to the Honours List.

DIANA WARWICK: And Honours, yes.

53. WILLIAM UTTING: I wanted to ask a question about the payment of Members of quangos. It seems to me that many more of these appointments are salaried now than was the case twenty years ago. The sums of money may not be large as far as the individual recipient is concerned, but they can certainly appear to be big to

people who are unemployed or living on state pensions. I wonder if you thought this was a significant matter in the public's perception of public office and patronage and improper use of political power?

SIMON JENKINS: I am not sure the actual payment is a source of public concern because, as you say, the payments are not high. What I think is a source of public concern is you have now a situation in which Ministers have constructed an alternative Civil Service which is within their own pocket. There are something like 40,000 people—there are more people now appointed by Ministers to serve on these quangos than are elected in the whole of local government. This is a huge bureaucracy which is not subject to Civil Service Commission Rules, or is only tangentially subject to it.

54. TOM KING: How many of those are paid?

SIMON JENKINS: Very few.

55. TOM KING: The point you are making is that a very considerable number of the appointments—which is Sir William Utting's point—was about unsalaried posts. You could have given an impression that all those are paid a salary. A considerable number of those are people who work for nothing in the fields in which they are and I am not sure — do you think there is public concern about people who are willing voluntarily to serve on quangos without pay?

56. WILLIAM UTTING: I was stimulated, I think, by information that non-executive directors of Health Trusts were paid, whereas my recollection is in the old days members of regional health boards did it for nothing out of a sense of public service. That sort of question.

SIMON JENKINS: I can't answer the question how many of them are paid—an increasing number are paid and an increasing number expect to be paid, and they are not appointed under normal Civil Service rules. They are exercising functions which probably would once have been performed by middle-rank civil servants. This is a good thing to the extent that an external element has been brought into public administration—to that extent I support the concept of the quango. But there is no doubt at all that these quangos are not appointed according to the standards traditionally expected of the Civil Service and to that extent I think it is subject of public concern.

57. WILLIAM UTTING: Do you think this is eroding traditions of unpaid public service in this country?

SIMON JENKINS: I wouldn't worry unduly about that. I mean, I think the fact that people do expect to get some money for spending often a very considerable amount of time sitting at often very tedious meetings is reasonable, but it needs to be the more severely monitored because of that—that is what I am saying.

WILLIAM UTTING: Thank you.

58. CLIFFORD BOULTON: You have told us quite fairly that it was our job to think of the distinction between acceptable and unacceptable financial interests of Members, but could I just ask a supplementary question about your own views. Professor Crewe seemed reasonably comfortable with the idea of a paid adviser to

the Police Federation so long as everybody knew about it and it was declared and registered. There is also, for instance, sponsored Members of Parliament, sponsored by trade unions who, as part of the sponsorship, receive financial benefits to the constituency—not into their pockets but, of course, it is a useful contribution which presumably is only paid so long as they remain sponsored and doubtless part of the sponsorship understanding is that they take opportunities to speak up for the interests of the union. Are you comfortable with examples of that kind?

SIMON JENKINS: No, I am not, they would fall fair and square into the category I would want to exclude. I think there is a contingent problem here because what one is saying is that you increasingly centralise the sources of money for political activity on the party and on the sources that that party gets money from centrally, and I worry about the increasing centralisation of politics and Government. But I do think—going back to the original question—a source of public disquiet that people sit in Parliament, apparently as delegates, for an external point of view.

59. CLIFFORD BOULTON: But you wouldn't stop your farmer voting on issues that concerned farming while he happened to have a farm?

LORD THOMSON: Or working on matters affecting the——

SIMON JENKINS: If somebody came up with a fool-proof rule which prevented people from taking part in legislation in matters that specifically concerned them I'd vote for it. I think there are great difficulties with people—I mean, if an MP is a dentist, or if a Minister is a dentist, is he banned from voting on the NHS? I think there you have to trust to the good sense of the MP concerned, frankly, but there is a line and the line must be drawn.

60. ANNE WARBURTON: I would like to ask a question about the commission with a supervisory role in the House of Commons because I think when you spoke of it yourself, Mr. Jenkins, you said that you saw it as being independent of MPs, having a supervisory role but not having a legal position, and I would really like to ask you to elaborate a bit on how its influence is felt, how you would see it as making its position clear, and perhaps linking that with what would the role of the media be at that point?

SIMON JENKINS: Well, there are two things. One is the extent to which you have a Parliamentary Commission which is exercising the sorts of functions that you are exercising and I think the slightly grander body that I would have envisaged, which would be a Royal Commission for Appointments, or a body with some such name, which would frankly embrace a huge range of public sector patronage. It would embrace the Honours system, it would embrace, I think, the financing of political parties and donations to political parties and it would embrace all appointments to public bodies. The constitution of that body I am not sure about but it would have to be Parliamentary in the sense in which Parliament would have to vote for it, but it should be given constitutional status outside the ambit of Government. I think a body of that sort is now necessary because as your existence shows, we have now scratched the surface of

areas of the public sector which have traditionally remained secret. You have opened a can of worms. Once you open that can of worms you find it very difficult to put the worms back in the can. You cannot, I think, confine it to conduct of MPs, Ministers or quangos. You will inevitably be drawn into the Honours' List, which is a very difficult area, and I think in all these areas you are now going to find it necessary to move the resolution of the questions that you are going to be asked out of the realm of Government itself into some other realm and the realm I would propose, awkward though it might be, is an independent commission.

61. ANNE WARBURTON: Without legal authority, and I wondered whether you were rather relying on the media in general to put in the sanctions as you suggested previously.

SIMON JENKINS: The reason for proposing it is that at the moment you have the most highly centralised government system in any western democracy. The only serious check to that is a frequently irresponsible media, and I do not think everyone is particularly happy with that. I think they would like to see other checks and balances somehow built into the British constitution, however inappropriate checks and balances are to the constitution, than simply almost weekly nuclear explosions from Fleet Street.

LORD NOLAN: We are running short of time, Peter, have you a question to ask?

62. PETER SHORE: Just a very brief one about quangos. You told us your views about appointments of quangos and that is very clear. What do you think about the more or less independent powers that so many quangos seem to have, certainly with regard to their own self awards as well as the administration of their empires? Do you think that something should be done to strength accountability?

SIMON JENKINS: I think I said I was broadly speaking if favour of quangos. They are a worthwhile innovation into previously secret and hierarchical government departments. Although they are not elected they are, at least, new faces and they diversify and pluralise the administration of public services. The mechanism for accountability has to be clear. I think we have been discussing a way in which the appointments themselves can be made more accountable. The quangos themselves are accountable through Ministers to Parliament. If you want my personal view I think they there should be far fewer quangos and far more power delegated back to local government. In other words there should be more elected and fewer appointed officials, but that is because I think that local democracy has atrophied and is, with all its inadequacies, a valid form of local accountability.

63. PROF. A. KING: At the risk of repetition, can I just make clear about one thing. Is it your view that no Member of Parliament at any time should lobby on behalf of a foreign government, a firm, a trade union, a trade association, a PR firm for which he receives remuneration?

SIMON JENKINS: Yes.

64. LORD NOLAN: Thank you very much indeed, Mr Jenkins. As we might have expected, your evidence

has been very crisp, very clear, and extremely helpful. Now we are to hear from Lord Blake.

Lord Blake, amongst your many other abilities and achievements, you are a Constitutional Historian, author of many books, and, I think, almost by inclination a supporter of the Conservatives. Is that right?

LORD BLAKE

LORD BLAKE (Constitutional Historian): That is correct. I take the Conservative Whip in the House of Lords.

LORD NOLAN: Thank you very much. I will ask Dame Anne Warburton if she would be kind enough to go with you through the evidence which you propose to give us based on your experience and opinions.

ANNE WARBURTON: Good morning, Lord Blake.

LORD BLAKE: Good morning.

65. ANNE WARBURTON: I think that the background to this discussion has been set quite clearly. My reference is to the figure of 64 per cent of the public last October thought that MPs were in it for gain. I mention that really because I would like to start off with asking you what your perception is of the state of public life today, perhaps, as you are a Constitutional Historian, with reference to earlier periods. I do not know where you want to start—Victorian or earlier times still if you wish.

LORD BLAKE: Yes, I could say something about that, I think. I have recently been reading a book, the only one I think that has been written on this as an historical subject, called *Corruption in British Politics* by Professor G.R. Searle of the University of East Anglia, and he takes the period 1895 to 1930, those 35 years. It struck me in reading this that there were similarities to the situation today. It seems to me these kind of troubles about malpractices, if you wish, or mistrust of Ministers and Parliament rather go in cycles. From about 1860—1895 there was very little trouble of that sort, but from 1895 onwards there was a lot. The most outstanding episode was the Marconi Scandal, and I should say in passing that the things that have been alleged today pale into insignificance compared with the Marconi Scandal. That really was a scandal in a very big way and I do not think anything of that sort quite is being alleged

66. ANNE WARBURTON: Can you outline that for us?

LORD BLAKE: Briefly speaking, the Attorney General, Sir Rufus Isaacs, and the Chancellor of the Exchequer, who was then Lloyd George, speculated in shares in a company which was not actually a Government contractor but it was so closely associated that its fortunes rose or fell with it. They speculated in the Marconi Company of America which was not actually a Government contractor but the Marconi Company of Great Britain was, and they speculated on the strength of insider information. Ironically they actually lost money in the end, but the morality of it is not, I think, affected by that. There was a great row about it in Parliament, a Select Committee investigated it and divided very much on almost totally partisan lines, but Asquith, who was Prime Minister, felt that the Liberal majority which whitewashed them really was over doing it and the two of them were obliged to make a sort of apology in the debate in the House of Commons. My view is that if a comparable

situation had arisen today in the case of the Attorney General and the Chancellor of the Exchequer, or other Ministers for that matter, I do not think they would have survived in public life for a moment, so our standards may perhaps be a bit better.

From 1895—1930 was a period when a lot of financial scandals were going on, but it was succeeded by a period of relative quiescence. I do not think you could write an interesting book about British corruption from 1930—1965, or, for that matter, from 1860—1895. Thirty-five years is an arbitrary period, but both before and after were relatively quiescent. But something has happened more recently, and I think it may be partly connected—I hesitate to make a sociological remark—with a sort of get rich quick mentality which very much prevailed in the Edwardian era, and I think has been prevailing quite a lot in the last 20 years, and this has a kind of spreading affect. So we are in a period which I think is nothing like as bad as the Edwardian and early Georgian period but is, nonetheless, one which does give rise to a good deal of unease.

67. ANNE WARBURTON: So that would be your first choice of a pressure on public figures as something which pressed them into reducing their idea of how bound they are by high standards. What other pressures would you see? Are there other factors too?

LORD BLAKE: I think partly the length of time that this Government has been office; I think that has had an adverse effect. I would not entirely agree with Professor Ivor Crewe on that point; he thought that the longevity of a party being in power did not matter very much. Once again with my parallel, the same situation arose with the Liberals from 1906 onwards, and I think there was a feeling that they were almost irremovable at the time.

68. ANNE WARBURTON: If we talk particularly about MPs, you have said you thought our standards, standards expected by the public, may be higher today than previously and yet public figures are perhaps not setting themselves such high standards, would you apply that specifically to MPs?

LORD BLAKE: Yes perhaps I would. I think these revelations which have been going on, a thing like the alleged cash for questions, is almost outrageous, it is an extraordinary thing to have happened, so I think possibly that is so.

69. ANNE WARBURTON: If we are going to be talking mostly about Parliament I should perhaps ask if you see the committee's inquiry as properly covering also the House of Lords?

LORD BLAKE: I certainly feel it should cover the House of Lords, yes. My own view, which would probably be rather unpopular in the House of Lords, is that if you have a register of interests for Members of the Lower House you ought to have one for Members of the Upper House as well. I can see no real argument against it. The only argument might be that the House of Lords has so little power that it does not really matter either way. On the other hand, I know your Committee is concerned not just with what is actually happening in public life but also with the public perception of what is happening, and this I am sure you will take very seriously because I think that is an extremely important aspect of the whole matter. It looks bad, I think, if the House of Lords remains exempt from the register of interests which is required by Members of the House of Commons. Whether that in itself is adequate is another matter, but I think the Lords and Commons ought to be treated on the same basis, though, as I say, I doubt if that will be a very popular view in the House itself.

70. ANNE WARBURTON: What about the register of interests? It exists already in the House of Commons in terms of saying the name of a firm, for example. Would you have any ideas of what should be the content of a register of interests?

LORD BLAKE: Yes I do actually. I think that in addition to registering the interests, the firm you represent or whatever it may be, the Member of Parliament should reveal the actual income that he gets from it. I say this because it might well reassure public opinion if they did that. They may be quite wrong but there is no means of knowing for certain as things now stand, but a lot of people think that MPs are making very large sums of money by taking on additional jobs and posts and positions. This may not be true, but if it is not true all the more reason for the actual figures being revealed, and I think it does make a difference. For example, if I may take a purely hypothetical case, the wellknown firm of Ladbrokes. Supposing you have an MP taking some sort of emolument from Ladbrokes, £5000 a year, say, along with £5000 a year for a lot of other things he is doing, that is one thing. But if he is actually being paid £50,000 a year he may then be almost a spokesman for a sort of delegate of the betting industry, or might be suspected of being so. I think no harm could be done, and good could be done, by insisting that the actual figures should be disclosed.

71. ANNE WARBURTON: Would the interests include only those for which you get remuneration?

LORD BLAKE: Yes, only the ones for which you get remuneration, direct or indirect.

72. ANNE WARBURTON: What about other administrative techniques—perhaps that is not quite the right phrase, but code of conduct is talked about quite a lot.

LORD BLAKE: I think that a code of conduct would be a good idea. I would very much hesitate to lay down its exact provisions at this moment, but a great many professions and activities do have a code of conduct. MPs do not as things now stand; they declare interests and that is that. There is no code of conduct as to how they should behave after having declared their interests, and the point was made by Madam Speaker in the House of Commons that MPs should regulate their conduct on the assumption that there was more to acting with probity than simply declaring your interests.

73. ANNE WARBURTON: So it would be a kind of ethical framework.

LORD BLAKE: Yes, what you should or should not do in general. I would have thought if it could be devised for other professions it could be devised for the profession of politics.

74. ANNE WARBURTON: You heard Mr Jenkins just now, as we all did, talking about perhaps an independent commission which would have a role in this sort of thing insuring that things once laid down were actually observed for example. As a Constitutional Historian, would this be an innovation?

LORD BLAKE: I think it would be an innovation, but I rather deprecate the expression "infringing the sovereignty of Parliament". The sovereignty of Parliament is a different concept, I think. The sovereignty of Parliament is Parliament's capacity to pass an Act—Queen, Lords and Commons, so to speak—and that Act cannot be challenged in any way. That is the sovereignty of Parliament. What this is concerned with is a rather different issue, that is the autonomy of the separate Houses of Parliament. At the moment they are largely self-regulating, that is the point. If you had a commission looking at it, or if you had statutory provisions—another matter which I would like to come on to—I do not see that that would be a bad thing to do at all. It is not unknown historically. There was the Contractors Act 1782, if I may go back rather a long way, which obliged Members of Parliament to resign their seats who were partners in a firm which was concerned with government contracts. If there was a By-Election they could fight it again if they wished, but they were obliged to resign their seats and this actually happened as late as 1904 in the case of Anthony Gibbs and Company—the great South American firm. There were two brothers there and they did resign their seats, one of them lost it and the other one got re-elected. I only mention this rather esoteric point because there are precedents for statutory regulation of MPs.

75. LORD NOLAN: Is this still in force, Lord Blake?

LORD BLAKE: I do not know.

LORD NOLAN: I have a note saying that it is thought to have been repealed in 1957.

LORD BLAKE: This may be so, yes, but my point is a precedent does exist. Sorry, I should have looked that up before I spoke, but it does not alter my point.

ANNE WARBURTON: As you say, the precedent is there.

LORD BLAKE: The precedent is there, yes.

76. ANNE WARBURTON: Have you thought at all about what sort of remit an outside, or partly outside, scrutiny committee might have?

LORD BLAKE: Would I be partly answering your question if I said what I thought the limits should be to MPs taking outside occupations which would come under the scrutiny of such a commission if it were set up? I would say straight away that I agree with Mr Simon Jenkins. I think that paid representation of an interest is an undesirable practice. I would try to forbid that, I think, and I would certainly, at the very least, forbid any MP taking money from a firm of lobbyists. I think that seems to me quite inexcusable. If an MP wants to influence the House of Commons, he or she should do so by speaking in the House of Commons not by operating through pressures of that sort. That would be a minimum, so to speak, change that I would make under the prohibitions made in the register.

77. ANNE WARBURTON: Presumably part of the fee from the lobbyist might well be precisely for speaking in the House of Commons.

LORD BLAKE: Yes, it might.

78. ANNE WARBURTON: Some of the evidence which we have read has brought out quite clearly that people tend to think that you should be able to defend your own professional interests, or commercial interests, but not of those of other people. Is that the sort of distinction that you have in mind?

LORD BLAKE: Yes I think it is.

ANNE WARBURTON: Not secondhand.

LORD BLAKE: Not secondhand, no, exactly. That is why I think I would object to an MP being a director or a consultant to a firm of lobbyists whose job was precisely to influence Parliament in that way

79. ANNE WARBURTON: In the period that you have covered in broad sweeps have there been material changes in the balance between the different organs of state of Government and Parliament, of the Civil Service, of the new Civil Service if I can call quangos that?

LORD BLAKE: I think the creation of quangos is a change, though it is interesting again historically that there was a row about the equivalent of quangos as early as about 1909/1910, that time. The Conservatives were of course out of office and I am sure in many cases their attacks on the Liberals were exceedingly unfair, but nevertheless the extension of non-governmental organisations of one sort or another connected with health, insurance, was very much under attack, and there were debates in the House of Commons and strong representations made. Of course, the scale of it was a great deal smaller than the present scale.

I want to say I am not an expert on quangos, but it clearly is a new element in the body politic on the scale that it exists today. I think that is true, and again over the whole period we have developed a system in which the House of Commons is virtually the sovereign body, and the majority in the House of Commons decides everything to a degree that was not so, I suppose, one hundred years ago.

80. ANNE WARBURTON: I think it was Mr Jenkins who was being rather dismissive of the role of MPs; he saw them as an electoral college for the Government and not much more. Would you disagree with that?

LORD BLAKE: No I do not think I would. I think that is probably true, and he made the point partly arising from the exaggerated notion that the public has of the power of MPs, and I think he is probably right on that. The power of any individual MP to do anything is not very great, but the public may think it is a lot greater than it is and that may be part of the trouble about the public perception of what is going on with which your committee is, of course, very much concerned.

81. ANNE WARBURTON: But you are not suggesting that a major part of what comes out of our study should necessarily be the denigration or the downing of public respect for MPs?

LORD BLAKE: No, I hope not. I hope that the result of your deliberations may show, as I think, that the public alarm, although well placed to some extent, is greatly exaggerated. I think there is a great exaggeration, and people think, as I was saying earlier, that this is all new when a great deal if it occurred 70 or 80 years ago.

If I may come on to another point here. One of the troubles about the public attitude is that the public is inclined to think that the House of Commons is a rather cosy body, it regulates itself, it has a Select Committee to do things, and it is all a little bit too much like a private club. That is a reason why I think that some degree of statutory regulation would be desirable if only because I think it would give the public greater confidence—those Members of the public who understand at all what this is all about.

82. ANNE WARBURTON: When you say statutory regulation, what particularly would you want to make statutory?

LORD BLAKE: I think the register of interests at the moment is a non-statutory, as I understand it. It must be because Enoch Powell has always refused to register and I do not believe he is breaking the law in doing that. I would prefer to see that under a statutory law so that it would be an offence against the law of the land if you failed to carry out the provisions.

83. ANNE WARBURTON: I only have one last question before asking you for a summing up view, and that is do you have any impression or knowledge of how we now compare with other countries in matters of standards in public life or what we do about them?

LORD BLAKE: I think my knowledge really must be only anecdotal in that respect. I have never made a close study, a certain study of America but not really of French, Italian and Spanish Parliamentary systems, but you only have to read in the press what has been going on in Italy, France, Spain, Portugal and Greece to see that, however much worried we are about our standards of public life at the moment, they have, or ought to have, a great deal more to worry about in those countries than we have. I hope that is not too chauvinistic a remark.

84. ANNE WARBURTON: Would you like to end our part of the conversation by recapping on your ideas for ways of reassuring public opinion about standards?

LORD BLAKE: It would seem fair if the House of Lords had to register their interests as well as the House of Commons. In the House of Commons, I agree with what Mr Simon Jenkins said, I do not think anybody should be a paid consultant for an interest, and I think a fortiori he or she should not be a paid consultant for a firm of lobbyists, I think that should be forbidden. I think that the rules regulating the conduct of MPs ought to be enshrined in statute rather than simply by resolutions of the House which tends to give a slightly kind of private club cosiness which people rather resent. I think that in the general sense, although there is cause for anxiety and obviously people who think about these things are worried, they should not get it out of all perspective. Probably Mr Jenkins was right when he talked about petty corruption rather than any major scandals. I think that is about it.

ANNE WARBURTON: Thank you very much.

LORD NOLAN: This time I will leave any questions I may have to the last. May I start with Professor King.

Have you any questions you want to put, Professor, to Lord Blake?

85. PROF. A. KING: At least one, possibly a couple. Could I ask you about the implications of your assertion that paid representation of an outside interest is an undesirable practice and your suggestion that it should be banned. Reference was made earlier on to the sort of locus classicus of Mr Callaghan representing openly the Police Federation in the House of Commons. Would you want that banned?

LORD BLAKE: I think actually I would, yes. I agree with Simon Jenkins on that. I am not suggesting for a moment that Mr Callaghan, as he then was, did anything remotely improper by the rules of the time. Nor do I suggest that an MP should not, as it were, make a particular field a special study of his. He might make the interests of the police a special study, a matter that he was concerned with. It is being paid for it which I jib at I think.

86. PROF. A. KING: What about Age Concern?

LORD BLAKE: In what sense?

87. PROF. A. KING: You spoke of an outside interest, but one can imagine a charitable organisation, or an organisation of that character, wanting to have a parliamentary representative. I simply want to know whether you would prevent that as well?

LORD BLAKE: I would not prevent it but I would prevent him being paid for it, that is my point. There is a difference actually.

88. PROF. A. KING: Can I ask you to focus just for a moment on the question of the number of scandals, the number of allegations of impropriety, leaving aside their importance for the moment because I entirely agree with you about Marconi which would have caused an enormously greater storm now than it did then and probably would have deprived Britain of its First World War Prime Minister in passing. When do you think there were last as many of the kinds of scandals involving MPs and Ministers and money as there are now? Can you just cast your mind back: when did we last have this really very considerable number of such scandals?

LORD BLAKE: I think the Edwardian era was it. I do not think there was much, as far as I remember, in the 1930s. In wartime nothing. In the 1950s there were one or two things: although it was really not very important there was the Linskey Tribunal, the inquiry into the conduct of the Under Secretary of State for War whose name was Belcher. I do not recollect anything very much in the 1960s and it was a good point made that, although the Conservatives were in office all that while, it is rather a point against my own view that longevity in office matters, I do not think very much happened in the Eden/Hume/MacMillan period.

89. PROF. A. KING: So we have to go about 85 years?

LORD BLAKE: Yes. Of course the big scandal which I suppose is not quite the sort of thing you are concerned with was the Poulson scandal in the 1970s. That was really much more concerned with local government and I think you are not concerned are you mainly with local government.

LORD NOLAN: Not at this stage, we shall be later.

LORD BLAKE: You shall be later, yes. It was a pretty good scandal at any rate on a rogue scale.

90. PROF. A. KING: Finally, can I ask you under the same heading, there have been a number of allegations in recent months and years about governmental abuse of power. One thinks of Pergau Dam, the Arms for Iraq, appointments to quangos which we have talked about, the business of the Westminster Council and so on. Again, can you cast your mind back and say when there were last a spate of allegations of a government or a local authority abusing its power in this kind of way?

LORD BLAKE: No, I do not think I could answer that. It is possibly a phenomenon of the very much greater extent to which government intervenes in British life generally. I do not remember a spate of anxiety about that particular kind of thing, that is a fairly recent development.

91. PETER SHORE: Lord Blake, you gave us your view about the sponsorship by the Police Federation of Members of Parliament. Do you have the same opposition to the sponsorship of Members of Parliament by Trade Unions?

LORD BLAKE: I think it is wrong actually. It is a bit different, of course, because I do not think, and you can probably correct me on this, that MPs who are sponsored by Trade Unions are actually paid by them, they do not receive emoluments as I understand it. So I suppose that really makes the thing considerably safer really and less liable to be a cause of scandal. It is open, people know if Trade Unions are sponsoring a particular MP, and he is not receiving financial benefit from it. To that extent I would be prepared to leave that alone in my reformist zeal.

92. CLIFFORD BOULTON: I was interested when you talked about the desirability of moving the register over to it having a statutory basis rather than it depending on the power of the House both to make rules for its own Members and then subsequently disciplining them. I think the missing factor in Mr Powell's case was that the House never proceeded to exercise its undoubted right to discipline him. Of course, if it was on a statutory basis it raises the question of enforcement. Enforcement of the law is a matter for the police. You are actually contemplating a criminal offence, are you, of failing to complete the register, and how would you envisage it being enforced? What kind of penalties do you have in mind?

LORD BLAKE: I suppose a fine. Imprisonment I think not, that would be rather drastic probably unless it was something very bad indeed. Statutory law does affect MPs as it is; I think I am right in saying that it is a criminal offence to bribe an MP or for an MP to accept bribes, or is it?

93. CLIFFORD BOULTON: That is a very difficult legal question I understand depending on the legal definition of the position a Member holds. Members of Parliament have no exemption from the ordinary criminal law for things which they do outside Parliament, but the internal proceedings of Parliament are supposed to be, thanks to the Bill of Rights, safe from questioning by

courts, so it would be to that extent a constitutional innovation to have the things that Members actually do in the House as Members subject to the criminal law. You would accept that as having been demonstrated as being necessary, would you?

LORD BLAKE: I think I would accept it. I do realise, of course, that it certainly would be an innovation and it probably would be deeply resented in the House of Commons, though that is just guesswork on my part. I should think it would not be at all a popular step to take. There are occasions when you do have to make constitutional innovations. I do not think the constitution can remain in aspic for ever, and I believe that public concern, which is what we are partly considering, would not be relieved a bit if they felt that the House of Commons was self-regulatory and there was no other check on it.

94. TOM KING: You expressed your concern about everybody being paid for any outside involvements that they might have. One of the things which I notice about the change in Parliament is that when I first came into Parliament there were far more people who had practical experience which they brought to Parliament from their own career activities, and one of the concerns looking at Parliament now is how you continue to make Parliament a place which people are keen to serve in and are willing to make their contribution, and therefore not to build too many obstacles to them coming to Parliament. I look at people who come from business, from industry—one of the frequent complaints is that very few people in Parliament have ever been involved in industry. We have a lot more people who have done nothing but politics. They have been in research departments, in research associations, political advisers of one sort or another, lecturing or students and then moving on to the political field. I do not think it has been to the benefit of Parliament in terms of drawing on the range of experience in debate and in judgment, and I sense that one of the ways in which your proposals might work is that people who actually could contribute to Parliament but are continuing to be involved in whatever their previous activities were would in some way be seen to be less acceptable than a full time politician who had never been anything but a politician and therefore could not possibly be accused of being tainted with any outside interest or knowledge from some particular sphere of interest.

LORD BLAKE: I agree with you about the danger, and I also agree with you that the House of Commons has changed in that respect; you do have far more people coming up from research institutes in that sort of way. I do not think I ever said, at least I hope I did not, that I objected to people being directors of companies or taking outside interests. I would not wish to abolish outside interests all together. What I am against, as I say, is receiving emoluments for representing a trade interest of some sort. I think it is a good thing to have people who are directors of family firms or public companies, farmers, whatever you may have. I am not against that at all. I think they ought to plan it but that is not the situation as it now is.

On the general point you make I should have thought that was very difficult for any recommendations that this committee could make to alter the sort of people who get elected to Parliament. That is just something that has changed socially and politically, and I am not sure that there is much you can do about it.

TOM KING: We could certainly make requirements and recommend requirements that would be a major disincentive to quite a range of people from becoming involved.

LORD BLAKE: I do not think it would be the requirement which Ivor suggested, which is that they should not represent trade or particular interests and be paid for it, and also that they should not be members of firms of lobbyists and be paid for it. I do not think that is a great inhibition. I would have thought that left a very wide field of things open to MPs, and as long as they declare it it is all right.

LORD NOLAN: We are running very short of time, I am afraid. Sir William, have you any questions you want to ask?

95. WILLIAM UTTING: Two brief points about Members' interests. First, the statutory regulation does not necessarily lead to criminalisation, for example, of a failure to register an interest. It could stop short at establishing an independent statutory body, and we could have prescribed powers of investigation and a certain tariff of disciplinary measures that stop short of criminal offences.

LORD BLAKE: Yes I think that could be so, I would agree.

96. WILLIAM UTTING: Secondly about the code of conduct. Like you I am not in the business of attempting to draft a code of conduct at this stage, but I would wish to see it not restricted to financial interests but to cover other aspects of MPs' performance as well. Would you accept that?

LORD BLAKE: Yes I think I would, but I would put some limits on codes of conduct. A great many scandals that have hit the newspapers recently have not been to do with financial interests. They have been to do with sexual conduct. I do not think I would want that to be enshrined necessarily in a code of conduct. In fact my own views on that are that we really ought to be like the French and not bother about it.

WILLIAM UTTING: Things like conscientious performance of certain Parliamentary duties, for example, might be susceptible to inclusion in the code of conduct.

LORD BLAKE: Yes I think that might be.

97. DIANA WARWICK: Could I ask a brief question. I was very interested in the historical comparisons that you drew and the point also made that the public perception of MPs' power is greater than it is. Do you think that the public perception of accountability, particularly of Ministers, has changed? I think of the comment that Simon Jenkins made about why do Ministers resign. They resign because they are pressurised to do so by the press, whereas there are those who argue in that earlier times there was a sort of code of honour about it and then people rehabilitated themselves. Do you think there has been a change in the perception of the public of accountability?

LORD BLAKE: Yes I think there has. I do not know whether this is part of the subject you are going to discuss, but it is a very obvious fact that Ministers are exceedingly reluctant to take responsibility for things that go wrong. I do not think this was true in the past, I think people were more ready to resign on issues where their department was criticised or something had gone wrong. I am thinking of Lord Carrington over The Falklands, and further back the Crichel Down affair.

98. DIANA WARWICK: I asked because when Professor Crewe was giving his evidence he said that in the public mind there is one establishment, there is one group, it is not Ministers or MPs or the Civil Service, and I wondered how far if that was an issue and public perception had changed that was influencing the perception of MPs just as much as it did of Ministers.

LORD BLAKE: I think that might be true, yes.

LORD NOLAN: Lord Blake, we are all extremely grateful to you. Your evidence has held us so enthralled that we have gone rather over the time that we had allotted, but I have no regrets at all for that. Thank you very much indeed for coming.

LORD BLAKE: Thank you for listening.

99. LORD NOLAN: Now we are going to hear please from Mr Roy Hattersley. Mr Hattersley you need no introduction but for the record a thousand years hence, if anyone is reading it, would it be fair for me to describe you as a senior practising politician and journalist, former Cabinet Minister and former Deputy Leader of the Labour Party, amongst your other achievements?

You very helpfully prepared a written submission for this morning's purposes and I believe that you have copies available for the media, which is extremely useful. Would it be best if we begin by my asking you to read that out to us.

RT HON ROY HATTERSLEY MP

RT HON ROY HATTERSLEY MP: Certainly. The brief, and I fear discursive, comments which follow are my personal opinions. Before I set them out, may I offer a view on the timing of the Committee's work? I believe that it is essential that you make speedy progress towards positive recommendations as distinct from interim comments. In both the worlds which I inhabit—politics and journalism—there is a cynical suspicion that you exist to postpone and prevent action rather than ensure the swift elimination of abuse. I hope that you are going to prove the cynics wrong.

I begin, My Lord, with the assumption that we do not want and cannot have a wholly full time House of Commons. Some Members will wish to devote themselves exclusively to Parliament and politics. But an increasing number will expect to work outside Westminster as well. That is the result of the MPs' changing profile. In general, they are more able and better qualified than they were thirty years ago, when I was first elected. Their ambitions and material expectations have increased, and the view that public service is an aim in itself is not so widely held. It would be undesirable to attempt, and impossible to achieve, a total prohibition on outside employment. We could and should prohibit a series of improper activities.

Principal amongst them is lobbying—the most common form of abuse because it does not require any talent. It is the duty of an MP to lobby on behalf of three causes; constituency, party and conscience. But there are a number of ways in which other, in my view, improper lobbying is carried out. Speaking to the House and asking questions (which assist the employing company or damage its competitors) are not the most insidious or dangerous aspects of the lobbyist's work. A House of Commons select committee has reported that "a company which is able to call directly on the services of Members, particularly in arranging meetings with Ministers and Civil Servants, has a perceived advantage over its competitors". The advantage is actual as well as perceived. It is intolerable that MPs arrange introductions in return for payment.

The time has come to prohibit MPs from taking part in all forms of commercial lobbying. That would require:

1. Formal prohibition by resolution of the House.

2. The requirement of Members to register both the names of companies which employ them and the tasks which they are paid to perform.

3. An independent authority which monitors MPs' conduct.

The independent authority is right in principle and necessary in practice. The conduct of MPs is the proper concern, not of the House of Commons alone, but for the whole country which the House of Commons serves. Self regulation, in this as well as other areas, can easily become no more than a protection against real scrutiny.

The system which I propose will give real meaning to the Register of Members Interests—which is now often used to justify behaviour which ought to be unacceptable. It was intended to shame Members into proper conduct. But politicians are notoriously shameless. It is too often assumed that as long as a job is recorded—often in opaque and general terms—it is an acceptable activity. That is not my view.

There should be a second prohibition. There are, I know, strong constitutional arguments against preventing a Member from voting on any issue before the House. Our rights derive from our election. The powers given to us by our constituents should not be limited lightly. But the power to suspend from Parliament—which already exists—is the power to disenfranchise our constituents during the period of suspension. I see no reason why that principle should not be extended to include a ban on voting when a Member has a direct pecuniary interest. Indeed I advocate that prohibition.

It may not have been possible to prevent some Members from pressing for the privatisation of hospital services and then setting up private laundry catering and cleaning companies. But it is clearly wrong for Lloyds "names" to dominate the debate on the regulation of that institution and the nature of compensation which might be received by participants in the system who incur losses. MPs should not be allowed to vote for personal financial advantage.

The prohibitions which I have proposed are very limited. Many MPs would continue their legitimate involvement in outside activities. Some would actually do real professional or executive work. Others would be there to add what some companies seem to believe is a little class to official notepaper.

One hundred and twenty years ago, Trollope, in "The Prime Minister", wrote "a seat in Parliament assists a man in getting a seat as a director of certain companies. People are such asses that they trust a Board of Directors made up of Members. So Members are welcome upon them". I regard it as demeaning for a Member to receive two or three thousand pounds a year for doing not very much. But I would not prohibit it.

Nor would I place any limitations on the relationship between Members and trade unions. I want trade unions to assume a diminished political role. But I do not believe that the small sums, which they provide to subsidise some MPs constituency activities and re-election, are a threat to democracy. The unions' interest in political debate usually concerns generalities, let us say less unemployment, as distinct from specific projects, let us say planning permission for a new factory. The people who make the decision to pay an MP a few hundred pounds, rarely benefit personally from their investment.

I am conscious that whatever rules this Committee may propose and the House of Commons may accept, much will still depend on self-discipline. That needs to be encouraged. When I was a young MP, Sir John Osborn—Member for Sheffield Hallam and part of a famous industrial family—said that steel, the subject about which he knew most, was also the subject about which he spoke with most reluctance. He was afraid that his Honourable Friends would suspect him of feathering his own nest. I think there are few Members who feel similar inhibitions today.

That is, I fear, partly because of the spirit of the age—and the fashionable theories of human conduct. If an internal market in health care, why not an internal market in MPs? I know that, today, you are principally concerned with Members' Interests—the commercial activities of back-bench MPs. But they cannot be wholly separated from the behaviour of governments. If Private Members believe that Ministers are on the gravy train, they will want tickets for the same journey.

That being said, constraints on Ministerial powers of patronage are right and necessary in themselves. I propose two easy and necessary reforms.

First, major appointments should be subject to a nominee's appearance in front of a select committee. I do not suggest that the Committee should have Congressional powers to approve or reject. But having to describe qualifications and experience, in public, will prevent the most unsuitable candidates from accepting nomination.

Secondly, I believe all Ministerial paid appointments to semi-autonomous and regulatory bodies should be printed in an annual report to Parliament which includes explanations for each choice.

The limitations on what Ministers can give should be matched by limits on what they can receive. The present rules, (governing ex-Ministers' employment) were meant for a different age. The problem, and the abuse, has been increased by fifteen years of privatisation. I therefore suggest that:

1. Ministers involved in privatisation should be prohibited from taking employment in those industries for ten years.

2. Ministers' employment in companies with which they have done official business should be prohibited for five years.

I regard the proposals I have made as modest. Others may find them stringent. Whatever their level of severity, they are right in themselves and essential to the rehabilitation of Parliament's reputation—never high but now lower than ever before. Thank you very much.

100. LORD NOLAN: Thank you very much. If I may take you back to a passage you will find on the second page of your note, which for the benefit of those listening to us is the point at which you list a number of undesirable activities, of which the principal one is lobbying. You say, a little later, "there are a number of ways in which lobbying is carried out" and you deplore "arranging meetings with Ministers and Civil Servants" if done as an aspect of lobbying for an employing company. This is a relatively minor point but one that has been put to us by a number of people. Members of Parliament have amongst their other abilities the use of that beautiful building and its entertainment facilities. Is that something that is abused do you think, in commercial interests:

ROY HATTERSLEY: Yes, I share the judgment of your preamble and I share the judgment that you come to in the end. I do not think it is a crucial point. It is, as you say, a relatively minor point, but I would certainly prohibit the use of those downstairs dining rooms or wherever else it may go on, for purely commercial activities. That is not what they were intended for and it does encourage Members to get involved in the sort of practices which I deplore.

101. LORD NOLAN: Coming on to more substantial matters and if I may take you up please on your first prohibitions, those include the requirement of Members to register both the names of companies which employ them and the tasks which they are paid to perform. Is there any reason why the actual contract should not be written out and registered?

ROY HATTERSLEY: I am not a lawyer and I cannot give a really adequate answer to that but instinctively my answer to your question is no, I can see absolutely no reason. The implication of the description of the actual task, is that there are some jobs outside Parliament which it is wholly legitimate for Members of Parliament to do and if they can convince the House, or the authority, that those jobs are the only jobs they perform, then bravo, I share Mr King's point in his question to Lord Blake. We want some outside experience. By nominating and denominating and describing the actual jobs, I hope we would encourage the outside experience without allowing abuse.

102. LORD NOLAN: Yes. Setting out the whole terms of the contract but also include the amount paid?

ROY HATTERSLEY: I would have no objection to that. I know there is a feeling in some parts of the world, in some parts of the country, that a man's or woman's salary is secret information to them but it does seem to me that if you are a Member of Parliament, with certain public obligations and if you are taking on extra duties, you will probably have an obligation to specify what that should be. But before the newspapers telephone me this afternoon, that is a duty that has to be performed in general. There is no reason why anyone should do it particularly until the rule is encompassing us all.

103. LORD NOLAN: Thirdly, and this is a matter which is of great interest and difficulty, you suggest an

independent officer of the House who monitors Members of Parliaments' conduct. Who would that be?

ROY HATTERSLEY: In the end he or she has to be appointed by the House. Since you asked me to come here this morning I have considered how such an authority should be obtained. I cannot think of any way which does not open my proposals and the eventual scheme to the criticism that man, that woman is still employed by the House. I cannot think of any other authority who could be employed to make such an appointment. But what I would have hoped, there would be a person of such independent reputation and status, who would demonstrate by the way he or she proceeded with the job, that he or she were wholly independent of House of Commons pressures and that there was a feeling that our club was not setting its own club rules for the convenience of club members. It has to be somebody who is perceived to be an outsider, otherwise I do not think the public would be satisfied and I think their dissatisfaction would be legitimate.

104. LORD NOLAN: I do not know whether this is your impression. As it seems to me, just as a single individual, the Parliamentary Commissioner, or the Ombudsman seems to have been a very useful and generally successful invention. He is an Officer of Parliament, I think, but has considerable powers and of course authority and clout. Could it be someone of that sort, someone with comparable powers?

ROY HATTERSLEY: I think you are right and there could be comparable status in the form of appointment. Looking back I have been sending cases to the Ombudsman since the Ombudsman was appointed and whilst I have had many complaints about his adjudication, I cannot recall one occasion when people have to said to me, he would say that would he not, he is appointed by Parliament and really is one of you. I have never had that complaint so I guess he would work in the same way.

105. LORD NOLAN: Or perhaps it could be more than one person, possibly a Committee?

ROY HATTERSLEY: Yes.

106. LORD NOLAN: Possibly with some Members of Parliament on it but perhaps with a strong outside representation? These are perhaps fine tuning points.

ROY HATTERSLEY: I ducked the question by calling it an authority because I was not sure whether it should be one, several or a committee. If you ask me that question Lord Nolan, I think, instinctively, I am against having Members of Parliament on it; I think that will pollute the purity in the public mind if we had Members of Parliament.

107. LORD NOLAN: Thank you very much. Then you come on to your second prohibition which would give the House the facility, or the power, to prevent the Member from voting on matters in which he has a direct pecuniary interest.

At the moment the sanctions available to the House—is this right?—are to suspend, for the Speaker to rebuke, or for the House to imprison. I do not remember when it last did, but I think those are the available sanctions. Correct me if I am wrong. If it were something like failure to register an interest in defiance of what, let us assume, had

become a firm rule, should the House have power to impose a fine?

ROY HATTERSLEY: I have no objection to fines. I assume that the penalties will be parliamentary penalties.

LORD NOLAN: Yes.

ROY HATTERSLEY: As in the case of the unhappy Mr John Browne in a previous Parliament, having erred in the terms of what I regard as the adequate declaration of Members' interest, he was censured and suspended. That carries with it a financial penalty in that during the period of suspension the salary was not paid, but I certainly thought of the shame, which I think is important in this context, of a parliamentary censure and a parliamentary penalty like suspension.

108. LORD NOLAN: One can envisage people, speaking in the abstract, who are fairly impervious to rebuke. They are rare and I am sure that a rebuke to most Members of Parliament, and their constituents, is a very grave matter indeed. But it is not at any rate something that you would entirely rule out, to extend the range of possible penalties and indeed you do so by suggesting a ban on voting. Yes.

ROY HATTERSLEY: I do not know how severe a penalty the rebuke is, having only seen one formal rebuke in the sense that Mr Tam Dalyell, many years ago, when I was a much younger and perhaps more sensitive Member of Parliament, was rebuked in a very formal fashion. I regard that as a hideous thing to behold and if it had happened to me I would have found it very near to intolerable. To be perfectly frank, Lord Nolan, I am not sure I would now but I felt that then.

On the other hand, suspension can have enormous consequences. I think Mr John Browne, whose problems I do not want to rake over today any more than necessary, would certainly argue that the reason he is not a Member of Parliament today—there may be other reasons but a reason—was that his constituency party was so unhappy by the rebuke that some people turned against him. So I think the formal parliamentary censure can have very severe consequences.

109. LORD NOLAN: One other point you touched on towards the end of your submission, was the question of trade union sponsorship. We covered this, to some extent, with Lord Blake. It was put to him, I think by Sir William, that relatively small sums are involved and this I think is your point too, that the Member gets no cash in his pocket but, would this be right, it customarily takes the form of the payment of part of his election expenses?

ROY HATTERSLEY: Yes, I think it varies from union to union. The union that has sponsored me is, strangely enough, USDAW. They pay a very small amount towards my election expenses and a comparatively small amount to the general running of my constituency during the year; that amounts to little more than postage and things of that sort. They do not pay as much for my constituency as I pay under the agreement which the Labour Party expects me to make with my own constituency party. These are very small sums and at least in my experience I have never had any pressure brought to bear on me; I have had recommendations about what I should do but if you take an issue very sensitive to USDAW, Sunday trading, to which USDAW are profoundly opposed and to which I was strongly in favour, there was no attempt to be unpleasant to me or threaten me about that. They thought I was slightly strange but they would go on paying for my constituency affairs whilst I needed it.

110. LORD NOLAN: I have no doubt that there are very easily understood historical reasons too why certain sections of society were too poor, they had not got the money to pay election expenses, they needed some help from somewhere and why this might have been thought of as a benevolent attitude for unions to take. But must it not create some feeling of loyalty, of dependence, by the Member, on the union, even if it is not explicit or put into any practical form?

ROY HATTERSLEY: Even if I believed that I could not possibly answer no to that question. I think it does not make the Member feel connected with the union, but I believe the loyalty a Member feels for the union is greater than and precedes and is independent of the small amount of money. If you take the obvious case, the archetypal trade union MP, Mr Dennis Skinner—I guess he is officially sponsored by the National Union of Mineworkers. I guess they put a small amount of money into his constituency, but fairly obviously Mr Skinner's loyalty to the miners is hardly anything to do with £500 a year. It is to do with his background, beliefs, emotions and convictions.

111. LORD NOLAN: To sum up as far as I am concerned, you would be in favour of strengthening the rules on outside interests in the two ways that you have proposed. Is there more to be done in the way of guidance to, particularly new, Members of Parliament about the standards of conduct which they should observe when they are approached by outside organisations and asked for help?

ROY HATTERSLEY: This is what I meant when I said self-restraint ought to be encouraged. Putting aside the Register of Members' Interests, about which I am critical, as I tried to make clear, I think over the last 10 years, as I say, it is something to do with the attitudes of society. People have taken jobs of all sorts for granted. One of the great purposes of your Committee, if I may say so without impertinence, is to establish the idea in people's minds and therefore in MPs' minds, that there are some things that MPs should do and some things they should not do. Your task in creating a climate of opinion, amongst those 650 Members who will be in the House next year after the Election, is in my view very important. The simple idea that there are standards just has to be broadcast rather more fiercely than it has in the recent past.

112. LORD NOLAN: We want people to be proud of being Members of Parliament, we want the public to be proud of their Members.

ROY HATTERSLEY: Yes, I think the first already applies. The second I fear does not.

113. LORD NOLAN: Would there be anything to be said for an addition to the Oath of Allegiance which Members take when they first come to the House, rather like the broad lines of the Judicial Oath, to do justice to all manner of men without fear or favour, affection or ill-will. These words mean something and if you stand up in public

and take an oath to uphold the standards of Parliament, would it register with people?

ROY HATTERSLEY: I do not think it would make a material difference; it would not do any harm. But I think most Members of Parliament, if there is a clear path charted for them, will follow it; a few will transgress. But if it is assumed, if it is thought, that the thing to which I take the greatest exception, as I understand it Lord Blake too, the active commercial lobbying, if it is established that that is wrong, most Members of Parliament will not do it. In the problems over the last 10 years it has been assumed that commercial lobbying was right and some people have been very proud to announce their commercial lobbying achievements in the hope that they might acquire more. It is establishing that it is wrong that is important.

LORD NOLAN: Thank you very much. Now I am going to ask the other Members of the Committee if they would like to put questions to you. Lord Thomson.

114. LORD THOMSON: I want to take up with Mr Hattersley the question of the trade union side of things. In the days when I was an MP and had to declare an interest, like Roy, I had a modest contribution from a union to the running of my constituency office and my election expenses. Now that these issues are raised I frankly find it difficult to make the distinction of principle that Mr Hattersley has made and I want to press him a little on that and to link it up with his other point about which I have practical doubts, that is the ban on voting, where you have a pecuniary interest, as indeed happens very properly in local authorities. I have always assumed that the protection for Members of Parliament who took on outside interests was that the whipping system in the House of Commons provided a protection against them voting improperly but in practice, given the realities of government and perhaps narrow majorities, it is practicable to have a ban on voting where there is a pecuniary interest? If I may put it more precisely, if in fact there were proposals for trade union reform, would all those Members of Parliament who get even modest financial assistance from trade unions, be compelled to abstain from voting and would any Labour government support such a view?

ROY HATTERSLEY: I thought Lord Thomson was going to take me up on the point that the quality of Members of Parliament had improved over the last 30 years and I was going to tell him there were of course exceptions to that rule.

The two points he makes. First of all on trade unions. I say it with some reluctance but I think it is important to be frank with this Committee. The reason I do not believe that trade union association is a threat to democracy, is that most trade union members are not required to do very much for their money. The money is paid to them whether they do the things which might be regarded as providing pressure, whether they are done or not. They are provided to sustain the person in his or her normal existence. Trade unions do not say, look here is the money, why did you not do this? Why cannot you do that? We want to get in here. Lobbying organisations, whether they are lobbying organisations per se or whether they are private companies who employ lobbyists, actually expect some return for their money. That I think is a very substantial difference.

On the prohibition of voting, I was careful to say, admittedly not terribly explicitly because of the brevity of my introduction, but things like supporting privatised hospital services and then immediately going into that industry oneself, probably you could not do anything about that. The Lloyds Names debate is one of the things that concern so many of us. If you read, as I am sure you will, if you have not already, if the Committee does before the end of its deliberations, that debate it is almost embarrassing the way that Lloyds Names were speaking for themselves. Now that would not have brought the government down. Again this is the imperfect scheme I propose but you and I George (Lord Thomson) have both been in politics long enough, we are not going to be trapped into a requirement to provide a perfect alternative for something which is already very imperfect. My scheme is just better than the one that is operating at the moment. It will be fuzzy at the edges but it is an improvement.

115. DIANA WARWICK: I wonder if I could just return to the question of penalties. It does seem to me that we have been talking a lot about the role and probity of MPs and of Parliament and it does seem to me that people's perceptions are very much conditioned by their own experience, and the employment experience of most people these days is that employers are a great deal harsher, that unemployment is more likely, that they face considerable penalties if they offend against the firm's rules or whatever. We are not the first inquiry to be looking into this whole area. Looking back at the inquiries and the recommendations that have been made, either the penalties that have been recommended have not been accepted by Parliament or the penalties are not themselves seen or perceived to be particularly severe. I wonder what you feel about that perception. You seem to get the same kind of penalty for waving the mace around as for concealing the fact that you are accruing a good deal of income that you should not be accruing. I just wonder whether the time has not come for a much greater severity of penalty to be applied to severe infringements.

ROY HATTERSLEY: Well there can be degrees of severity even within the Parliamentary system. Suspension for two or three days, which I think is the normal procedure for simple bad behaviour in the House of Commons, is very different from what happened to Mr Browne. You can have suspension for substantial periods. I repeat, I have got no instinctive opposition to fines, though I think there will be some complicated decisions to be taken as to who should determine what they should be and it is not a job I would want to perform myself. But I have no instinctive opposition to fines. I simply thought perhaps we could have limited imagination, that there would be penalties within the Parliamentary system, but I do not want to give the impression that I am so much part of the club that I think we must have our own penalties our own way. I have no necessary objection to fines.

116. DIANA WARWICK: Yes I was just trying to get at the problem of perception, that if Parliamentary internal sanctions do not appear to be very severe, how do you get over the public perception of that?

ROY HATTERSLEY: I do not know, is the answer. Can I just say one other thing, in terms of public perception, I believe it is hugely necessary for rules to be constructed which stop such bad behaviour rather than punish it after it has occurred because if our concern is the reputation of Parliament I do not know what is worse, the suspicion that one or two things of this sort are going on, or a couple of Members of Parliament being arraigned,

prosecuted and sent to prison for malpractice. I can remember when a very senior Officer of State, not of my Party, was thought likely to be prosecuted and I can remember the more responsible senior Members of my Party saying this will be a bad day for Parliament if he had been and if the Home Secretary was to go to prison this would be a bad day for politics. I think probably your task, if I may put it in this way, is to try and produce rules which stop people doing it, rather than rules which punish them after it has been done.

117. WILLIAM UTTING: Sorry to hop about, this one is on quangos. Your two recommendations you say are easy as well as essential. Is this where you would stop? You do not feel that the power of the Secretary of State to make these appointments should be modified or changed in any way, or that we need an independent commission to oversee salaried appointments?

ROY HATTERSLEY: I am in favour of many of the institutions which are now run by quangos being democratised and being run by some sort of elected body. So that half answers your question. I tried to look for what I regarded as moderate, workable solutions, rather than perfect solutions and I think the problem with quangos is very often the most senior of the officials. As I say I do not believe we can have the House of Commons making a judgment and voting in the way that Congress would do. But I do believe there are some people and I will not give examples today, but there are many examples I could give, who had they been nominated and discovered they then had to sit in front of a body rather like this, and Members of all political parties have said, why is it you think you could possibly become whatever it is, would have felt better to say to the Secretary of State, I do not want to accept nomination, would prefer that rather than justify their rather peculiar qualifications for the job they have been nominated to do.

118. TOM KING: Just a point. I am less sanguine about the impact of trade union support and certainly I can recall in the sort of cross-party, cross-Parliament way, a background where, although not very substantial, quite clearly it is a very useful contribution to the problem of fund raising which we all face and where people are mindful that it would be unwise to step too far out of line. I am conscious also of an important point that Mr Hattersley made, that we have got to deal with perceptions that things are not as they are and yet I am concerned about his remedy because if one took that to its logical conclusion, he states that effectively, and I am not putting words into your mouth, that Dennis Skinner, for example, should not vote on any coal issues. Now that is, I think, unrealistic and I would not like to be the one who tried to prevent him going into the lobby. I think that it is the extreme illustration of my concern, which I think Lord Thomson had, about this prohibition on voting. It is also I think, as you made clear in your paper, does have certain constitutional implications.

ROY HATTERSLEY: Could I just correct that, with respect. I said no such thing that Dennis Skinner should not vote on coal; I said quite the opposite. I see absolutely no objection to Dennis Skinner voting on coal because the trade unions are concerned, as my paper said, with generalities. If Dennis Skinner were a Member of Lloyds, or a name at Lloyds, I would not think he had the right to vote for his own level of compensation, that is a direct, slightly wild, hypothesis but it is a direct financial interest as compared with a general interest and that is the distinction I tried to draw.

119. TOM KING: Well the point I am making for instance, let us go back to John Osborn, do you think John Osborn should have been allowed to vote on matters affecting steel policy? Not his own remuneration?

ROY HATTERSLEY: Yes I do.

120. TOM KING: As a paid director of a family steel business?

ROY HATTERSLEY: Yes I do.

TOM KING: I thought your paper said that he should not.

ROY HATTERSLEY: No. My paper says that he should not be allowed to vote on matters in which he or she have a direct financial interest. Now I cannot believe that the House of Commons is going to vote on the levels of remuneration of Osborn's steel works. I actually believe that John Osborn probably was entitled to vote on public ownership of steel or privatisation of steel. I certainly believe he was entitled to vote on matters affecting the steel quotas which were or were not allowed in the European community. Now you can say Mr King that this may have had an effect on his income, that if the steel quota was bigger Osborn's would make more steel and if Osborn's made more steel the director would get a slightly higher income, but this is so vicarious I think you can get away with it. It is the direct voting to which I am objecting.

TOM KING: Thank you very much.

121. CLIFFORD BOULTON: I just want to follow up one or two of the details of this because I think it is a subject which the public are anxious about; Members' personal benefits from voting. It is a fact, is it not, that there is already a ban on voting in the House of Commons on the matter in which you have a personal pecuniary interest which is not part of general public policy; for instance a private Bill going through, if your house is going to be knocked down for a road, you cannot vote. So there are already rules in the House about that. What you are saying is, by analogy, you thought that the Lloyds Names should have regarded that business going through, although it was a public Bill, as being on the same basis and not voted because they were Lloyds Names. So to that extent it is an extension of the private Bill principle, is it not?

ROY HATTERSLEY: Yes it is. I was going to say Sir Clifford it is an extension which in a sense is more than that because what I want is effective and what we now have I think is not. I do not know if you can tell me how often during your time as Clerk Members did not vote on issues because they felt they were personally involved. I think not very many.

122. CLIFFORD BOULTON: Not many because virtually all the votes were on matters of public policy and we now get the reduction to the absurd that if it was an absolute rule Members would not be able to fix the level of Income Tax because they would have a direct personal interest because they all pay Income Tax. So all I was asking really was, it is a difficult one to draw the line and we have got to distinguish between special private cases, where you have got a direct interest and where they come as close as perhaps local government to having a kind of executive decision-making power and voting on matters of public policy where you also said in your paper, the electorate is entitled to have the use of their vote. If you are an agricultural constituency and you elect a farmer, the last thing you want is for him not to vote whenever there is a farming issue where he is going to benefit from a calf subsidy or something.

ROY HATTERSLEY: As I also said in my paper, knowing the enthusiasm of Parliamentary authorities for precedence, if you were a farmer and farming was to be debated in the House of Commons two days after you have been moved to the Speaker, the Speaker would not hesitate from disqualifying you to vote on this issue because she would suspend you during the time that your matter was going on. So it can happen. But the other point of this against, though you do not need me to tell you, that it is the sort of last refuge to say we have problems of definition here. We always have problems of definition and again you do not need me to tell you because you were doing it on purpose. To take the example of Income Tax is really taking it into its illogical conclusions. There are issues and I think Lloyds is an example, where people should not have been allowed to vote and were allowed to vote and it is up to your successors to help the House of Commons make the definition.

CLIFFORD BOULTON: We have simply got to define something which will stand up because people do not like it and therefore it has got to be pretty practical and I was only trying to get you to agree that it is not going to be easy for us.

ROY HATTERSLEY: You have that agreement.

LORD NOLAN: I think if it is all right with you we can allow ourselves another five minutes Mr Hattersley because you started a little late.

123. ANNE WARBURTON: I would like to come back to your suggestion that Ministers involved in privatisation should not be employed by industries for 10 years and those who have done official business should not be employed for five years. Is that another way of saying that they should not take such employment?

ROY HATTERSLEY: No. I believe that there is sufficient talent in Cabinets, most Cabinets anyway, when they come to the end of their political life for there to be reasonable, remunerative, interesting and rewarding work for them outside the areas in which they have actually operated. Most Cabinet Ministers have operated in two, or three at most, areas of the economy and there are very many others in which they could legitimately operate. Again it is the length of paper that prevented me from doing this but I would like to make some exceptions for Ministers who had real expertise. I mean if you had a Minister who had been a doctor and had worked in the Ministry of Health, it would, in my view, be preposterous to stop him from working for a health company. If there was a real expertise that would make the difference. What I do not believe is right is that having been intimately concerned with the workings of an industry, you then go to work for one company within the industry, knowing what you do about its competitors, its organisation and having the influence you still probably have through knowledge and acquaintance with the Civil Servants who were doing a different job when you were the Secretary of State.

124. ANNE WARBURTON: For Civil Servants the time limit at present is two years. Would you want to change that?

ROY HATTERSLEY: I think I would; certainly some senior Civil Servants. I think some secretaries and deputy secretaries who have moved from the Department of Industry and Trade as it was, into industry, are getting very near to the margins that I would want to avoid and I would extend it to them as well.

LORD NOLAN: Well thank you very much indeed Mr Hattersley. That has given us a fitting finale to our first and most interesting morning. We are most grateful to you for coming.

WEDNESDAY 18 JANUARY 1995

Members Present:

The Rt. Hon. The Lord Nolan (Chairman)

Sir Clifford Boulton GCB   The Rt. Hon. The Lord Thomson of Monifieth KT DL
Professor Anthony King   Sir William Utting CB
The Rt. Hon. Tom King CH MP   Dame Anne Warburton DCVO CMG
The Rt. Hon. Peter Shore MP   Diana Warwick

Witnesses:

Maureen Tomison, Chairman, Decision Makers Ltd.
Dame Angela Rumbold MP
Stewart Steven, Editor, and Mira Bar-Hillel, The *Evening Standard*
Alex Carlile QC MP

125. LORD NOLAN: Good morning. Today we will be taking evidence from three witnesses who have been concerned with the decision on the location of the intermediate stations on the High Speed Rail Link to the Channel Tunnel.

Maureen Tomison is the Chairman of Decision Makers who were engaged as lobbyists for the promoters of the station at Ebbsfleet.

Dame Angela Rumbold, Member of Parliament, Deputy Chairman of the Conservative Party, and was a director of Decision Makers but resigned in the aftermath of criticisms from our third witness, the *Evening Standard*, represented today by its Editor, Stewart Steven and the Journalist, Mira Bar-Hillel.

Now, while Ebbsfleet links these witnesses, I should emphasise that we are not investigating the decision to site a station at Ebbsfleet, or indeed the circumstances surrounding their position. But in many ways the issue encapsulates some of the grey areas we are exploring, the role of lobbyists, the involvement of politicians with lobbyists, especially when they hold some form of office, and the part played by the press in these matters.

I hope, therefore, that by exploring for a little the part each witness has played in the Ebbsfleet case, we can then move on with them, to consider whether any general lessons relevant to our inquiry can be extracted.

We shall also be seeing John MacGregor who, as Transport Secretary at the time, was a main target of lobbying in this case. We had hoped that he could be here today but he cannot. He is, however, going to come and give evidence next Tuesday and no doubt will say then whatever he wants to say about the matter.

Our fourth witness today, Alex Carlile, Member of Parliament, is a Liberal Democrat Front Bench spokesman.

Having heard from senior Labour and senior Conservative figures yesterday, that is to say Mr Hattersley and also, of course today, Dame Angela Rumbold, it will be our first chance to hear a view from the Liberal Democratic Party. But as far as we know he was not involved with Ebbsfleet.

Now Maureen Tomison you have been told, I think, that the questions will come to you this morning from one

Member of our Committee, Diana Warwick. Am I right in thinking that you would be happier if you started with a statement which you have prepared?

MAUREEN TOMISON

MAUREEN TOMISON (Chairman, Decision Makers Ltd.): Yes My Lord, I would like to make an opening statement if I may.

LORD NOLAN: That will be very helpful. Please do so.

MAUREEN TOMISON: My Lord, Members of the Committee, I would like to thank you very warmly indeed for accepting our offer to give evidence. I hope we will be able to offer a useful contribution to the work of the Committee. I have already submitted detailed evidence about good lobbying practice and the role of Members of Parliament.

I have been working in and around Westminster for some 30 years, including 10 years as one of the first women lobby correspondents and the last seven years as Chairman of Decision Makers.

Part of my training to be a lobbyist stemmed from my involvement in a Granada Television film. I think it is the only one ever made, of the progress of legislation, the Fair Trading Act, through all the progresses of its political system.

While filming the programme, I was struck by how Ministers and officials, who were very open to new ideas, reacted to some of the lobbying. Often the lobbyists were ill-prepared. They did not have a coherent strategy and therefore failed to get across important information and I determined, My Lord, that my company would provide information and research of the highest quality in its lobbying.

I believe that lobbyists—and I include professional lobbying companies such as my own, trade unions, trade associations, industry and pressure groups—provide a vital alternative source of information for Ministers and officials. Often a Minister or a civil servant cannot be expected to know all the relevant information for a particular decision, and so must rely upon knowledgeable organisations to present their case.

In my view, lobbying increases the democratic flow of information and better informs the decision-making process. As long as it does, there will be a place for companies such as Decision Makers, who can provide political experience and expertise.

To take the case of Ebbsfleet as an example, my company was originally approached by the MP for Mid Kent, Andrew Rowe, whose constituents were unhappy with all four routes proposed by BR for the Channel Tunnel Rail Link. We were subsequently employed by Ove Arup to find a more acceptable route.

Having walked the proposed routes five times and spoken to many local people, we concluded that all four British Rail routes would cause severe environmental problems for the residents of Kent, especially around the site of the BR proposed intermediate station at Bluebell Hill, and for the residents of South London where the route would cut through densely populated suburbs.

We believed that a better route had to be found. After some 90 local meetings, mainly on-site, we had a major revelation standing on a hill above the proposed British Rail station. We saw how the route could be diverted East to enter London through Dartford and Stratford. We were welcomed extremely warmly by both Gravesham and Dartford local councils, who talked about the creation of major industrial regeneration and the vital job prospects that would come with the station. Subsequently, all independent economic surveys agreed that Dartford—and Ebbsfleet is part of Dartford—was the most logical site for the intermediate station.

During our campaign for the route, we met 360 all-party Members of Parliament, including all the relevant Ministers and Shadow Ministers, with tremendous support from John Prescott and Joan Ruddock, the Labour transport team. We also wrote to every Member of Parliament three times, and I topped and tailed each one of them with a specific paragraph about each one. It was a huge job but this massive weight of informed discussion eventually succeeded in overturning government thinking. In October 1991 our route was adopted and at that stage most politicians had been convinced of the merits also of locating the intermediate station at Dartford.

At this stage Dame Angela Rumbold was still a Government Minister and therefore had not worked for Decision Makers and I had never even met Blue Circle.

Blue Circle asked us as late as March 1993 to work with them to conclude our task and locate the intermediate station at Ebbsfleet on the Dartford Gravesham borders. This was for a small fee and there was no success bonus. To our minds the major part of the lobbying had already been done.

The most important work which remained to be done was to persuade the client to produce a credible package in response to the Government's criteria. Dame Angela was an extremely important element in relating to the client the political realities and the necessity for attempting to produce an acceptable solution for Government.

Local MPs, Bob Dunn (Dartford) and Jacques Arnold (Gravesham), liaised with Ministers and officials to ensure that the Blue Circle presentation was viable. Both have stated that Dame Angela was not involved in the lobbying. They were both extremely well capable of doing this themselves and they would not have welcomed any interference from Dame Angela on their patch.

The confirmation of Ebbsfleet as the site for the station in August 1994 was the logical conclusion to our original work on the Channel Tunnel Rail Link.

Dame Angela joined Decision Makers as a director in April 1992, after a distinguished career as a Minister. She has been one of my closest friends for years, we have always worked very well together and we share the same sense of humour.

Her role with Decision Makers was strategic—she explained and corroborated my experience of politics. She was mainly involved in team meetings at our offices where her experience was very valuable, or in client meetings where she would help explain to clients what was politically possible and how the parliamentary system worked.

Her role was not to lobby Ministers on behalf of clients. Not only would I never ask an MP retained by Decision Makers to do such a thing, that is not how the political system works. It is ridiculous to suggest, as some reporters have done, that any Member of Parliament, however distinguished, could have had anything more than a negligible result on a decision of such importance as the site for a Channel Tunnel Rail Link station. Furthermore, there is simply no evidence whatsoever to suggest that Dame Angela ever lobbied Ministers.

The commodity in which my company deals, and the reason for having Dame Angela as a Director, is political and governmental experience and expertise not influence, and in this case the local Member of Parliament, Bob Dunn, who is an ex-Minister, had all the necessary contacts and influence anyway.

At all times while Dame Angela was with Decision Makers, she displayed the utmost probity, as she always does. Her entry in the Register of Members' Interests was one of the longest because we were both determined that her work for us would be totally above board. She therefore listed all our clients, even when she had done no work for them. It is that openness and honesty which allowed the media to print so much about Dame Angela and Decision Makers.

At the height of the media controversy about sleaze, the *Evening Standard* published a report on 24 October 1994 based on a leaked document, dated 20 May 1993, and this had been written for our client only—and bear in mind our client understood what was going on. I think in my written evidence I said May 1992. It was May 1993.

The first article by the political correspondent, and the leading article, was fairly well balanced and indeed the leader read:

"no constituent part of this case, no individual or single action can be taken in isolation and identified as unlawful. Procedures were kept to. The principals went by the book. Interests were duly registered. Furthermore it has to be restated that there is nothing wicked about lobbying."

The real problem occurred on the following day, when a second *Evening Standard* journalist, who had been campaigning for Stratford, jumped to totally inaccurate conclusions about a meeting that Dame Angela had attended.

The journalist spoke to Brian Wilson, then Labour Transport Spokesman, and apparently reported to him her quite mistaken view that Dame Angela had been meeting Ministers and lobbying them. The journalist had no evidence for this assertion. On the basis of this totally misleading information, Mr Wilson said that this "appears" to have been "grossly improper behaviour" on Dame Angela's part. The article further said that Mr Wilson had already reported Dame Angela to a Commons Committee. In fact Mr Wilson had done no such thing and nor have any of his colleagues.

The leader of Dartford Council has confirmed in a letter to you, which I hope you have My Lord, that that meeting was a day visit to Kent in April 1993 at the invitation of local Conservative leaders. I have the itinerary for this meeting, which makes clear that Dame Angela herself was being lobbied and one of the issues on which she was being lobbied was over the location of a Channel Tunnel station in Dartford.

If there had been any foundation for any of the allegations, one can imagine the opposition quite rightly making hay. Significantly, the opposition leadership held back. It was well known in Westminster that Dame Angela had not intervened and that the local MPs had been actively lobbying. Unusually we took the step of reporting the journalists and we volunteered our assistance to all relevant authorities, including your Lordship's Committee, the Select Committee on Members' interests, the Committee of Privileges.

The *Evening Standard* made a further elementary mistake and suggested that Stratford had lost the battle for a station while Ebbsfleet had won. Stratford was never, and could never have been, in contention with Dartford as an intermediate station. Stratford is in London and we ourselves had recommended it as the site for a London station. That may still happen, as Dr Mawhinney confirmed to the House of Commons on Monday.

Furthermore, by the time that we had started working for Blue Circle, there was very wide acceptance that Dartford was the best commercial, industrial, and environmental solution for the intermediate station and that was in local, regional, national and European terms.

It was the failure of this one journalist to check the facts that led to her misleading the rest of the media—they only had her interpretation of the leaked document. This in turn may I say My Lord, led to a Kafkaesque experience in which the reputation of Dame Angela and my company was threatened by a whole series of unrelated accusations.

I believe that MPs should be allowed to have outside paid interests, providing that they are very strictly scrutinised. The register should be tightened up to include the details of fees paid and for what purpose. I have made some suggestions in my written submissions.

I believe that lobbying should continue as an essential ingredient of the democratic process but I would like to see professional lobbyists regulated and registered in Parliament and by Parliament. That is why I have drawn up suggestions for a Register of Professional Lobbyists in my written submissions.

I am very proud indeed of my company's reputation and am not afraid to submit our actions to scrutiny. I welcome your questions My Lord. Thank you.

May I introduce my colleagues?

On my left is Colin Stannard, who is the former Joint Chief Executive of Eurotunnel and is one of Britain's experts on that kind of issue. He is a merchant banker, he was a consultant to Ove Arup and was very much involved in that process, and he can give evidence about Dartford.

On my right-hand side is David Sandford. I may say that we carried out such extensive research in Kent, My Lord, and we spoke to so many people, we spent so much time doing this, that I ended up marrying David Sandford and buying a house in Kent.

126. DIANA WARWICK: Thank you very much indeed. I wonder if I might start off the questioning. Our concern is not, as Lord Nolan has said, with the Ebbsfleet decision itself but with the characteristics of all the participants as they affect the perception of the public about the role of MPs and those in Parliament. To give them that background, I wonder if you could tell me how specifically you went about influencing the decisions of Ministers and in particular did you distinguish, in seeking to influence their decisions, between official meetings, unofficial meetings, hospitality and so on?

MAUREEN TOMISON: Yes. I believe that the decision-making process is extremely complex and on something as important as an international station you have obviously got to get that right. We decided that you could not get that right unless you spoke to a very large number of people. So in the bulk of my evidence I said that we spoke to 360 Members of Parliament and we broke them down in this way: those Members of Parliament with a local interest—Kent, Essex, South London for example; those Members of Parliament who might have an interest in the location of the station in that if you locate it to the East of London you have much more chance, as soon as possible, of taking the route up to the North. Therefore we spoke to those Members of Parliament with a specific interest in trade and industry and with a regional interest, as for example Midlands Members of Parliament, Scottish Ministers, Welsh Ministers, whatever. We spoke to all the Select Committees because we believe in speaking to these Committees, information which you give to them will be passed on to Ministers.

We spoke to a huge range of people in the view that they would speak to one another if you actually told them something sensible and useful, on something we thought was of national and European consequence and they would all come to a conclusion based on that very large discussion.

Yes, of course, there is a difference between formal meetings and informal meetings. I am in the House of Commons a very large percentage of my time but I do not simply bang into a Minister and say I would like a station; that is not how it happens. I would go to a meeting with the Minister and explain the arguments about the station.

As far as entertaining is concerned, one of the great problems is that because lobbyists do not have a registration or a real entity—they are not recognised—you actually have got a difficulty in meeting people and one of the better places to meet people is actually over lunch.

One of the suggestions I would like to make today is that lobbyists are registered, that they are given a very small access to the House of Commons but they are given an access and that, for example, the kind of privileges which exist to lobby correspondents—of which I am formerly one—should be allowed so that there should be a dining room set aside for lobbyists. There should be a meeting room set aside for lobbyists, all of which they pay for but which would give them an ability to talk to Members of Parliament, to Minsters, within the Houses of Parliament. I think that should be jealously guarded. I do not think I want to see lobbyists in the Members' Lobby because I think that would be a great burden to Members of Parliament; I do not think they should be allowed to loiter along Committee corridors but I think there should be a place where they can go, as lobbyists, and be recognised as such.

127. DIANA WARWICK: Could I just pursue on the business of meetings with Ministers though? How did you actually approach Ministers to obtain those meetings? Did you use MPs? Did you contact the civil servants? How did you go about that?

MAUREEN TOMISON: I phoned up the Minister's Private Office, I think in almost every single instance, explained to the Private Office what it was about, then would send them a note which they could show to the Minister, asking for the meeting. In some cases I think I probably spoke to the Political Advisers as well.

128. DIANA WARWICK: But these would all be fairly formal, I mean in the sense of known to the people who were working with the Minister, these were not informal corridor meetings?

MAUREEN TOMISON: No, I do not think you can press the location of a station of that importance in a corridor; you cannot do it like that.

129. DIANA WARWICK: Could I then ask you how, after having various meetings and lunches and so on with MPs and possibly also with Ministers, did you then monitor the influence of your activities so that you learned of the impact of your work?

MAUREEN TOMISON: Because this was an issue of such importance that in fact MPs were writing to us to say, we would like to have more information about this. When we met we had a large number of meetings, all of which were formal in the House Commons and MPs would come back to us and say, we want more information. Or they would even get in touch with us and say, now you have spoken to the Midlands Members of Parliament, the Scottish Members of Parliament would like to talk to you as well.

130. DIANA WARWICK: Could I move on to ask you about the way in which you involve MPs in your work? We have mentioned Dame Angela as actually being involved in your firm and you have told us that you have rules about the way in which you would expect her to behave and indeed, presumably, other MPs as well. Is there a written contract between you and any MP who works with you, setting out what you expect of them, and indeed possibly what you do not expect of them?

MAUREEN TOMISON: No, we do not have a contract but before I came to this Committee I sat down and on page 18 in my written evidence—I have written out the rules which in fact Dame Angela and I accepted as implicit. We are both old hands, we both know exactly where the line to draw is and I have tried to help this Committee by setting out the lines which we believe were important to draw. I have set them out on page 18 if you wish me to read them out.

131. DIANA WARWICK: No, there is no need. I just wonder, given the number of inquiries that have been made into the role of lobbyists and the comments made by the recent Select Committee, and indeed the fact that certain professional organisations of lobbyists have chosen to ban using or employing, MPs. I am interested in why you did not enter into such a contract given the sensitivity of the relationship.

MAUREEN TOMISON: Well by the time this discussion had happened, as far as we were concerned it was all over. We had had no problems before and we have actually got a very, very good reputation in Parliament. People do talk about the fact that we have such a high reputation. Perhaps from hindsight we might have written a contract for Dame Angela. In fact, Dame Angela has said, on a number of occasions, that we asked her to do rather less than many other people asked her to do for whom she did not work. I have a huge respect for Parliament. I have spent virtually all my working life working in and around Parliament and there are no rules that I would break. Indeed there are no unwritten rules that I would break, and I felt it was very important that Dame Angela registered every single interest that she had, including those clients for whom she did not work. I would never ask an MP working for my company, for example, to ask questions or to get involved in any debate on behalf of our clients. We have a very tough unwritten rule.

132. DIANA WARWICK: What is your opinion about the role of lobbying firms in employing MPs? Do you feel that it continues to be proper, or do you share the view of those professional lobbyist organisations who have chosen to ban employing MPs?

MAUREEN TOMISON: No, I do not share their view because I think that that is a cop-out. I think that they are doing that as an easy option and that if the whole business is properly registered and scrutinised there are no problems. The fact of the matter is that where controversies have arisen, they are on an ad hoc basis; they are not relating to Members of Parliament working for an organisation. We have been criticised on the basis of a mistaken assertion by journalists but until that time we had never been criticised. Everybody knew that Dame Angela worked for us; they knew that she did not ask questions; she did not intervene in debate; she did not lobby on our behalf. They knew precisely what she did and we spelled it out extremely clearly. It is because we have been so open and so frank and filled the register that in fact the media have had a whole wealth of information to go on.

133. DIANA WARWICK: Given your experience and you have many friends in Parliament and amongst Ministers, is it a little ingenuous to say that somebody in the sort of influential position that Dame Angela was, would not be providing a considerable service. If she was

doing what you yourself are capable of doing so eminently, obviously, why was she on your books?

MAUREEN TOMISON: Well I do not have the monopoly of wisdom—oh that I did. I have worked in Parliament for a very long time. I have never been a Member of Parliament. I have not taken a Bill through Parliament. I have not been in the bars at one o'clock in the morning where people have been discussing how things have gone on. My knowledge of government and parliamentary procedure is, I hope, quite good but I certainly think it would be bettered by somebody who had been a Minister, who had been within the processes of government, who had taken Bills through Parliament, who had sat with, who had listened to civil servants' opinion and who had a huge range.

Now Dame Angela was able to offer an invaluable service to our clients because she would say, well this is the political reality and she would have much greater authority in saying that to a client than I would have. I have learned a great deal from Dame Angela, actually working with her.

134. DIANA WARWICK: So you would argue that you were using her for advice about the organisation and running of Parliament and the parliamentary process, rather than to pull strings?

MAUREEN TOMISON: There was no question of using Dame Angela to pull strings. If to pull strings was ever necessary Bob Dunn, who was the MP for Dartford, was a former Minister, he is the Chairman of the Conservative Transport Committee, a man who is very well liked round the House, if there was ever a question of pulling strings, then Bob Dunn would certainly have been extremely able to do it and would surely well have resented Dame Angela being on his patch. It is not the sort of thing MPs do, they do not interfere in another Member of Parliament's patch. I know that. Dame Angela knows that. Bob Dunn would have been extremely cross and shouted at me if I had allowed Dame Angela to do it.

135. DIANA WARWICK: I think you have said that in your presentation there was a very much more detailed statement than we have had from you, that you do not think either your firm or your clients behaved in any way improperly in relation to the particular Ebbsfleet episode. Can I then ask you whether you think it is possible, perhaps moving on from that and from the reaction to the allegations that were made about the role of lobbying in this particular case, to draw a dividing line between what is proper and what is improper lobbying because patently there is great concern about this?

MAUREEN TOMISON: Yes. I think we were the victims actually of jolly bad timing. It was interesting that the *Evening Standard* had a document leaked to them which was 18 months old and suddenly published it in the middle of all sorts of discussions about sleaze. I found that very interesting and the coincidence quite remarkable. I have attempted to put forward my thoughts on page 18 and further on I talk about a much stricter control of Members of Parliament. I think that we ought to know how much Members of Parliament are paid and we ought to know why precisely they are paid. But I have made an attempt, without being too presumptuous, to set down my own views about what Members of Parliament should and should not do, and it is a fairly austere code. I think that

when I say that MPs should be allowed to work for lobbyists, I am suggesting they work for lobbyists but with a very restricted code indeed. It is a tough code—I am a Scot—it is a fairly calvinistic code indeed.

136. DIANA WARWICK: So whatever you have paid an MP you think it is proper first of all to pay an MP to lobby, either for specific assistance or on behalf of a company, but in doing that you believe they should always declare the amount of money that they obtain for that purpose?

MAUREEN TOMISON: Yes, I think that there should be one rule for all Members of Parliament. We know that it has been traditional that some Members of Parliament are sponsored by trade unions. Nobody has questioned that very seriously before. If it is proper for MPs to get some sponsorship from trade unions, I see no reason why other voices should not be represented. But as I said, I think there should be an extremely strict code. I have an enormous respect for Parliament and I believe that Parliament should be respected by the world but I think this code should be open—transparency is the great word in Brussels and I think it should be the great word in Britain too—MPs should be seen to be transparently honest and doing a good day's work.

137. DIANA WARWICK: Could I just ask perhaps my final question. One of the arguments is that lobbying provides privileged access for those who can afford to pay and therefore disadvantages those who cannot. What are your views about that?

MAUREEN TOMISON: I do not think there is any doubt about that, that in an ideal world everybody should have their own lobbyist or should be able to be their own lobbyist. I have to tell you that we do a very great deal of work for free, or for some small sum for charities, for causes which we support. I may also say that we never work otherwise because we have to support it even if it is a client's cause.

Yes, that is certainly true. We do not live in an ideal world and we try, where we can, to do this "pro bono" work. The problem is that where you are making legislation, if you do not have as a Minister sufficient information you will make less well-informed decisions. It is necessary often to find a different point of view, an alternative point of view. It is important to speak to the person working for the charity or for the business, to say to them, would this suggestion work or might it be counter-productive, perhaps we have not thought it through. You are the ones who understand what this will do to your company, to your charity, to your trade union. Please give us your informed knowledge. I think that this improves the democratic flow but of course it is not an ideal situation.

DIANA WARWICK: Thank you very much.

138. LORD NOLAN: I wonder if I could just ask you this. In the courts it is often said that justice must not only be done, justice must clearly be seen to be done and this is an aspect of the problem before which we have to have very much in mind. You made it clear that Dame Angela's role lay in helping to explain the Parliamentary and governmental process to clients and I think in your suggested guidance for the proper limits on what you would ask paid lobbyists, paid members of your organisation, to do if they were Members of Parliament,

you would include asking for clarification from Ministers but without advocacy of a particular case.

MAUREEN TOMISON: Yes.

139. LORD NOLAN: Would it not still be so that if I wanted to promote a particular cause I have the choice of two organisations, yours and another, that I as a normal businessman would be affected by the fact that on your board was a member of the final umpiring body, the elected Members of the House of Commons. It must be must it not, a very good, so to speak, selling point for the organisation?

MAUREEN TOMISON: Well it would certainly be much more useful than if I were to say I have got a plumber or an electrician on my board. Obviously what we are able to offer is experience and guidance and I am not ashamed of that. I think that is extremely important.

140. LORD NOLAN: And you do not think that you could offer it to the same extent without having a Member of Parliament in the company?

MAUREEN TOMISON: Before Dame Angela joined us I think that we were doing a good job and indeed I have suggested to you that we were able to conclude the Channel Tunnel rail route without a Member of Parliament on board. But I find that when I can share my ideas with somebody who is experienced and knowledgeable, it takes an awful load off me. As Chairman of the company I have many things to do and I often say, have I got that right? And Dame Angela would be on hand to say, yes, you are right, or you are not right, and that is a very great help to me.

LORD NOLAN: I am going now round the table and ask the other Members of the Committee if they have got questions they would like to put to you. Dame Anne.

141. ANNE WARBURTON: I would like to ask Mrs Tomison please, have you any other Members of Parliament on retainer in your firm, or have you had?

MAUREEN TOMISON: We have had but we do not have any at present.

ANNE WARBURTON: Thank you.

142. TOM KING: From all parties?

MAUREEN TOMISON: Yes and perhaps I should go back one step because perhaps I misled Dame Anne. One of the original friends, advisers, in my company was Lord Mulley, who is still associated with us. He has never received a penny piece—I am not sure if I have ever even given him lunch—he is a dear friend. He is very wise, very statesmanlike, he remains with us and simply from time to time he will advise me on the Labour Party. But as I say he has never received a penny from me, he is just a dear, very wise statesman. So I think that answers your question.

TOM KING: That is the only one.

MAUREEN TOMISON: Lord Mulley remains associated with us. I have no paid parliamentary consultants associated with my company.

143. TOM KING: There are two ways in which this can work it seems to me. One you either have somebody like Dame Angela, who is obviously experienced and wise as you say and can give you general guidance, who might be on your board or working for the company. Then there are the specific clients who come up, particular problems, where you think particular MPs could give you good advice. Do you then have some special arrangement where, if they work for you and help you on a particular project, you will give them money?

MAUREEN TOMISON: Not at present. No we do not.

144. TOM KING: But you have done that?

MAUREEN TOMISON: We have done. We have paid three other Members of Parliament over the course of seven years—I beg your pardon, we have not paid them all, they have been consultants to the company and been involved in ad hoc projects. One of them was paid nothing at all. One of them was paid £2,000 a year and one of them was paid a total of £530 for two years. So it was not exactly a very lucrative job. They were friends and they were advisers. But I have been involved in politics since I was 17 and I have a wide range of friends over all parties and I go to all my friends and pick their brains when a project that would be of specific interest to them would come along.

145. TOM KING: And if they go to particular trouble or do particular work, you would remunerate them for the time they expended?

MAUREEN TOMISON: No we would not.

TOM KING: I thought you had.

MAUREEN TOMISON: The three people were associated with my company and their names were on this piece of paper.

TOM KING: Right. Okay thank you.

MAUREEN TOMISON: But if I go to a friend I would not dream of paying a friend.

146. PROF ANTHONY KING: You said you appointed Dame Angela because she was an old mate of yours and shared the same sense of humour. Would you have appointed her had she not been a Member of Parliament?

MAUREEN TOMISON: I hope that if ever the time comes when Dame Angela is not a Member of Parliament—I am making a job offer to her now through Your Lordship.

147. PROF ANTHONY KING: But would you have appointed her initially had she not been an MP?

MAUREEN TOMISON: It is difficult to answer this one because she was an MP but as soon as she stops being an MP I will employ her.

148. PROF ANTHONY KING: Right. Would you have appointed her had she not been formerly a Member of the present administration?

MAUREEN TOMISON: I appointed her because she and I got on extremely well together, we are very comfortable together and when I have asked her in the past for advice she has been extremely forthcoming.

149. PROF ANTHONY KING: But would you have appointed her had she not been formerly a Member of the present government?

MAUREEN TOMISON: If she had been a Member of the Labour Party, if she had been Dame Angela and had been a Member of the Labour Party, I would still have appointed her.

150. PETER SHORE: Yes, you have made it clear that Dame Angela was not involved in the particular Ebbsfleet decision, but you also say in your written evidence that even had Dame Angela intervened with Ministers there are no rules that say this would be inappropriate.

MAUREEN TOMISON: Correct.

151. PETER SHORE: Do you think there should be rules that would aim to declare that such interventions were inadmissible?

MAUREEN TOMISON: Yes, I think so. That is why I have done my best to say what we ask Members of Parliament to do and obviously I would be very happy to see our code become a code. I have suggested that these are the things that are appropriate. I choose, and Dame Angela chose, not to ask her to lobby Ministers. That was our code and if Your Lordship's Committee would like to adopt that as a code, then it is at least a starting point. I think that what MPs are allowed to do for lobbying companies should be codified.

152. PETER SHORE: So you do believe that while it is legitimate to use MPs in the sense that you have described, it is wrong for MPs, in your judgment, to be actively engaged in lobbying Ministers and using, presumably, other parliamentary facilities like asking questions and so on?

MAUREEN TOMISON: Yes, provided—my colleague says—they are not doing this on behalf of their constituents and obviously on behalf of their constituents they can do a huge range of things but in there capacity as working for a lobbying company, I do not believe that MPs should ask questions, I do not believe that they should intervene in debates, I do not think they should be actively engaged in the lobbying process. I engaged Dame Angela to share her knowledge and experience with me and with my clients.

153. PETER SHORE: In your choice of Dame Angela, apart from the personal friendship that you have, were you at all influenced, not just by the fact that she is a respected Member of Parliament, but by the fact that she is also a Deputy Chairman of the Conservative Party? Does not that aspect, as it were, of Dame Angela's activities, open up a range of contacts with the senior people in the Conservative leadership?

MAUREEN TOMISON: I do not really think so because Dame Angela's job was choosing candidates and looking at the extension, the changes in constituency boundaries, she was not involved in policy making. I wanted Dame Angela to join the company because she was my best chum, we got on well together and we worked well together.

154. PETER SHORE: Thank you. Just one small question—I would like to be clear about this—in this whole question of getting access to Ministers, very obviously the heart of lobbying is getting access to Ministers, do you, as an organisation, or any of your employees, have research passes in the House of Commons that enable them to move more freely and to meet people than would otherwise be the case?

MAUREEN TOMISON: Yes. One of my staff has because he remains a committee member of a Member of Parliament's staff—beg your pardon I will re-phrase that. He is still a Chairman of a Ward of a Member of Parliament and he writes the magazine for that Member of Parliament.

155. PETER SHORE: And he is employed by that Member of Parliament in other words?

MAUREEN TOMISON: No because he is an unpaid volunteer.

PETER SHORE: An unpaid volunteer but he received a pass and you are able therefore to use him in that sense.

MAUREEN TOMISON: All that we use him for is that he is able to go through the whole process of security checks. We do not use it to collect papers, we do not use it to use the facilities of the House at all. This is for his own private use to write a constituency magazine.

PETER SHORE: Thank you.

MAUREEN TOMISON: What I have suggested, if I may further respond to this, is that I have suggested that lobbyists should be registered and should have, once they are registered, a pass to go into the House of Commons so that that silly problem does not occur but I suggested that that access should be very restricted and I think it should be jealously guarded. I suggested, and perhaps this is fanciful, that before you can be registered you have some number of Members of Parliament who are prepared to say, this person is okay, I have some trust in this person. I have said number, twelve, and I have said of whom, at least a quota should be from a second party, so that you are not allowing anybody to have a pass to come into the House of Commons, you are allowing somebody who is well known to a number of Members of Parliament in at least two parties. I think then you avoid the problem of who is the lobbyist, does the lobbyist have any access at all to a Member of Parliament, because I think that is an embarrassing and difficult situation and I would like to see that regulated.

156. PETER SHORE: One further question. Obviously, as I said earlier, access to Ministers is extremely important and I gather really from what you are saying that you rely upon your own personal relationships to be a very important ally in your attempts to meet Ministers and to lobby them?

MAUREEN TOMISON: It is obviously important to know a Minister or a Member of Parliament. What the Minister and the Member of Parliament at the end of the day is concerned about is, here is this woman, I knew her at university, can I really be bothered seeing her, is she going to waste my time? What matters in getting access to a Minister or to a politician is, do you offer something which is useful? Do you have something credible and well researched? If you are going to produce fairly poor information and embarrass the Minister, you do that only once. A Minister will not see you again. So of course it is important that I have been brought up in the political system. I have been involved in politics all my adult life, for better or worse. I know politicians in all parties and I think I have pretty good access to all parties but it is only because they actually trust me. I have known people at university and they would be the last people that could ever influence me because I would not respect their judgment. It is judgment and a good reputation that is our passport to being allowed to speak to Ministers and because that is so important for us I would do nothing to damage our reputation.

157. CLIFFORD BOULTON: May I just explore a little the distinction you see yourself between a Member being a consultant to an agency such as yourself, and being a consultant to a direct interest group? You say that you think it only proper to make use of Members' expertise in a most general sense and you would not allow a Member, who was on your staff who was at the moment taking an interest in a particular client of yours, you would think it improper for him, having declared that interest, to stand up in the House of Commons and try and in open debate convince his colleagues about that interest. Now, there are many Members, as we know, who have a direct relationship and they may have a consultancy with university teachers or the Scotch Whisky Association, or whatever it might be, and it is perfectly proper under the present rules for them, having registered and declared, to advance what they see as the proper interests of that group in open debate. But do I gather from what you are saying that you think that that is wrong?

MAUREEN TOMISON: I have touched on this because it is a difficult area and as I go on further to talk about the regulation of lobbyists I note my own concern about this issue. I think that if I were to suggest to your committee that trade union sponsored MPs should not be allowed to ask questions or to indulge in a debate or to give evidence as Members of Parliament sponsored by a trade union, that would be extremely controversial. I understand the difference. I am simply saying to you that I, in my capacity employing a Member of Parliament, said to that Member of Parliament "I do not expect you to ask a question". There is a conflict in my mind. I would actually like to be able to say that about all Members of Parliament paid for by anybody, but you've put your finger on the problem that if an MP is a sponsored MP or is representing the Scotch Whisky —— Well, I think the Scotch Whisky Association has to adhere to the same sort of rules as we do. I think there is perhaps a difference between a trade union sponsored Member of Parliament or somebody directly paid for by a trade association. My Lord, that is a dilemma. On the other hand I think all Members of Parliament should be treated in the same way and drawing up your code I suggest this is one of the problems you are going to face. I don't have a clear answer and I apologise for that—I have thought about it a great deal. I can only tell you what I think and what I would tell my own Members of Parliament if they were involved with my company.

158. CLIFFORD BOULTON: Can I just very quickly ask you another question, simply to get your opinion on the record, really, because having advocated a properly regulated and strict and open system of permitted paid interest you then said on the top of page 19:

"If there is any form of ban on the remunerated outside interests of Members of Parliament we believe that the practice will continue but underground, which will make regulation even more difficult than at present."

I just want you to confirm that is your opinion.

MAUREEN TOMISON: I am only being realistic. I wish that I didn't have to be cynical. I am just slightly cynical of humanity. I think there is very very little corruption in this country, I've seen a very very great deal more of it in other countries. I think there is a tiny amount of so-called sleaze in the British Parliament, but I think one has to recognise that it might exist and I do believe that it would be very dangerous to push lobbying underground—I think we have to be transparent, I think we have to be overt, I think we have to have tough rules. I set tough rules for Dame Angela and I think that's the appropriate way to deal with it. That is why I have asked to come to your committee to tell you what our rules are.

159. WILLIAM UTTING: You mentioned the Minister's political adviser as one of the officials you had contact with. Was that because there was a specifically party political angle to this approach or some political advantage that you wished to urge?

MAUREEN TOMISON: I am not sure if I suggested it in this particular case. I was asked who I approach in asking to speak to a Minister and political advisers are one of a number of people who would talk to a Minister if he wanted to speak to the Minister. I think it is very much horses for courses and it may be that the Minister's private office is a private office where you've spoken to them before and they know who you are, it may be that the political adviser is somebody that perhaps has some understanding of that particular problem. But it is very much horses for courses and that is just one of a number of people that one might talk to. One might equally well talk to the Minister's Parliamentary Private Secretary.

160. WILLIAM UTTING: I think not equally well. The point is that a political adviser does have a distinctive role and what I was after really was whether there are circumstances in which it is proper to target the specifically party political aspect of a situation like that and make use of those. That is all.

MAUREEN TOMISON: I don't think that this campaign was ever a party political campaign. Should there be an occasion when we were involved in some party political occasion then certainly the political adviser would be the most appropriate target.

WILLIAM UTTING: Thank you.

161. LORD THOMSON: Could I just ask a brief factual question relevant to the evidence we shall be having from the *Evening Standard* later on? In your very full submission to us you lay a good deal of stress on a leaked document and that is also mentioned a good deal, I think, in the Standard reporting. We don't have the leaked document—can we have it on the record?

MAUREEN TOMISON: Ah, nobody has leaked it to this committee! Yes, of course. I haven't brought it with me ——

162. LORD THOMSON: I think that would be very helpful to us. And could I just ask whether the assertions

that are made in the *Evening Standard* report out of a leaked document about meetings with the Prime Minister, of a party at No. 11 Downing Street—are they true or not true?

MAUREEN TOMISON: All political parties have functions for which they charge slightly over the odds for people to attend. There is no expectation that anything comes out of those. I have attended such functions for the Conservative Party just recently—one of my colleagues came back from Brussels having attended a similar function in Brussels held by the Labour leadership. So there are these kind of functions which are open for people to attend and for which from time to time perhaps £500 is ——

163. LORD THOMSON: Would you therefore allow me ask one related question, relating to generally lobbying practice, it is not particularly like Ebbsfleet, or anything like that, but do you think that it is right and proper that Ministerial residences, such as number 11 Downing Street, should be open for hire?

MAUREEN TOMISON: I think where there is no expectation of anything from the lobbyist or the person attending the meeting, I think that while all parties do it it is appropriate. Whether it should be appropriate that a Ministerial residence should be used —— I have attended such functions during the time of the Labour Government. I am old enough to remember the previous ——

LORD THOMSON: I am not putting that political point across, I am asking whether you feel it is an appropriate thing in terms of the role of lobbyists in our political system.

MAUREEN TOMISON: All parties do it. It obviously should be a question that is raised, but certainly all parties to it and I have gone to Labour Party functions in their term of government and I have gone to Conservative Party functions in their term of government also.

164. TOM KING: I don't know what is meant by "available for hire". What do you understand by it?

MAUREEN TOMISON: It wasn't my question.

165. TOM KING: That was Lord Thomson's question. He said that—what is the suggestion? May I ask that question through Lord Thomson? If, as I believe all parties do, in an official residence—it might be number ten, it might be number eleven—the occupants of those wear different hats. They are the Chancellor of the Exchequer, they are also a senior Member of the Conservative Party. Now, if the Chancellor of the Exchequer gives a party which may have a political flavour, am I right in understanding that he would carry all the expenses himself, he would be responsible for all the costs involved and simply has the facility—which, as far as I know, is done in every country in the world—of actually using the building which he is in? That, I think, has been done—I agree with Lord Thomson, it is not a party political point—by every party. It is, as it were, one of the conveniences of Government. But, I mean, there is no suggestion in any way that there is public funding of political activity, is that right? I mean, you have had considerable experience over a number of years and had friends in all parties, is that correct?

MAUREEN TOMISON: That is correct and I have attended such functions under the aegis of both major

political parties and I believe you are right that the costs of the party are defrayed against any money which is raised.

166. LORD NOLAN: Was that the kind of function you had in mind, Lord Thomson?

LORD THOMSON: As I understand it, there has been a development over recent years—I would not like to say what span of years—under which the residences of Ministers are available, not on a public refunded basis but on some sort of charitable basis, for activities which may be charitable or may be party political. Personally I would regard it as an unhealthy development and I just wondered to what degree in terms of lobbying activities there ought to be some rule to prevent that sort of thing happening for lobbying purposes. That was the motive behind my question.

MAUREEN TOMISON: I don't think there is any increase in the number of these activities. During the government of Harold Wilson I attended many such functions. I remember meeting the Chelsea Football Club on one occasion. I don't think there has been any increase in the number of that kind of function. But it is certainly a question which your Lordship might want to look at.

LORD NOLAN: Do you have anything, Diana?

167. DIANA WARWICK: Well, perhaps if I can just follow up on that. In the list of activities that you would draw up for your client as being those which you could offer to prosecute their case and cause, would you say "we anticipate a reception, a dinner" and so on—I didn't know about this position of residences, but are you offering access of that kind to your client as a means of prosecuting their case?

MAUREEN TOMISON: I think it is extremely important that clients should understand as much as possible the thinking of Government Ministers and Shadow Ministers. There has been a recent function in Brussels—and I don't think this was subject to any criticism—where businessmen were invited to attend for the sum of £500 and presumably to share their thinking and to hear the thinking of the Labour Party leadership. Such things happen in the Conservative Party, too. I think that it is appropriate that there should be a sharing of understanding. I think it is appropriate that our clients should attend such meetings, providing—and this is terribly important—providing that there is no expectation of any favour from it. It is a genuine sharing of ideas and it is as important for the Government to understand what businessmen are saying as it is for businessmen to understand what Government and Shadow Ministers are saying.

168. DIANA WARWICK: The answer to my specific question is "yes"?

MAUREEN TOMISON: The specific question is that we would advise clients to attend such meetings—we don't necessarily have special access to them.

169. TOM KING: I took the question to be "Could a lobbyist say to their client 'we can arrange a party for you in number 10, number 11 [whatever it might be, number 12 or the House of Commons attic] and we can arrange it and get all the right people there", that is what I took to be the phrase about "for hire" and I would like to know quite

categorically from you, are you aware of that ever happening?

MAUREEN TOMISON: Absolutely not, no.

TOM KING: It never happened, because I thought that was part of the question and certainly I have never known it happen and if it did happen it is quite clearly totally wrong.

170. DIANA WARWICK: So if it is offered to a client as a possibility, that is not something that can be delivered, is that right?

TOM KING: No, it is not offered at all, no. Well, I took the question ——

MAUREEN TOMISON: We would not offer the client—these opportunities are offered to business people or to whatever kind of interests. We don't offer them.

171. LORD NOLAN: Could you offer to a client an opportunity to meet a Member of Parliament at a lunch organised by you and paid for by you?

MAUREEN TOMISON: Certainly. Well, paid for by the client.

172. LORD NOLAN: Paid for by the client eventually, of course. And might that take place in the House of Parliament?

MAUREEN TOMISON: It could take place in the Houses of Parliament. We would be able to offer that only if we felt that the MP was actually going to be interested in what the client had to say. We wouldn't just say "come and have a jolly lunch with a Member of Parliament". We would feel that it was appropriate for that Member of Parliament to meet the client because of the specific interest that that Member of Parliament might have in the client's business.

LORD NOLAN: Thank you very much.

173. LORD THOMSON: I am sorry to labour this but I think in fairness to Miss Tomison I wouldn't like there to be any misunderstanding. One has to come back to the immediate focus of our questioning which is the Ebbsfleet affair and I am simply asking the question on the basis of what the *Evening Standard* alleged, allegedly on the basis of this leaked document, that there was a dinner with the Prime Minister, there was a reception at number 11 Downing Street as part of the campaign that Miss Tomison organised. What I want to know is is that true or not, or is that a false statement by the *Evening Standard*?

MAUREEN TOMISON: There are opportunities and there were opportunities to attend a dinner with some 400 other people at which the Prime Minister was present. My client took that opportunity but I am not sure that that client took any opportunity to discuss his particular case with the Prime Minister. It generally is that sort of event, where there are 400 to 500 people sitting in the same room as the Prime Minister and your ability, actually, to influence the Prime Minister would, I would have thought, be minuscule.

174. LORD THOMSON: And the reception at number 11 Downing Street?

MAUREEN TOMISON: There was a reception at Downing Street which we were not able to offer the client access to. The client, I believe, paid for that in the way that they would have paid for it and in the same way as we paid for the meeting in Brussels.

LORD THOMSON: I do, I must say, draw a distinction between the public home of a Minister and a meeting in a hotel in Brussels or a hotel in London organised by any political party.

175. ANNE WARBURTON: I have in my hand a piece of paper which tells us that Hansard of 2nd November contains a statement that no such event took place—that is in relation to a reception at number 11 Downing Street on 28th June and similarly Hansard, with regard to a claim that there is a dinner with the Prime Minister on 28th May, says the Prime Minister attended a function in his constituency that night. Perhaps there were 400 people there, I don't know, but Hansard does actually touch on these things.

LORD NOLAN: Those were answers given by the Prime Minister.

ANNE WARBURTON: Yes.

LORD NOLAN: Thank you very much, Miss Tomison, for coming along and helping us. You have been very interesting and given us a lot of useful information.

MAUREEN TOMISON: May I say, my Lord, I have left little bits of further information which might be useful to you in blue folders there. I am most grateful to you for allowing me to come. Thank you very much.

176. LORD NOLAN: Dame Angela, first of all, let me thank you very much indeed for coming along to talk to us. You have come, like all of our witnesses, as a volunteer. I hope it has been made plain—if not I make it plain on behalf of the committee—that we are not here to criticise in any way the actions you took or didn't take in the Ebbsfleet affair or your conduct in relation to the company of which you were then a director. The relevance of the questions to our enquiry, as you know—the questions relating to Ebbsfleet—are whether there should be rules, clearer rules than at present, regulating the relations between Members of Parliament and lobbying organisations, and that is the line we would like to take, please. But may I say this: what we were hearing from Miss Maureen Tomison was so interesting that we have overshot her time by about twenty minutes. Now, as it happened we had a missing witness this morning so we are not embarrassed by having taken that much longer, but our later witnesses have been warned of times rather earlier than they are now going to be, in particular Mr. Stewart Steven and Alex Carlile. I do hope they are not inconvenienced if we go rather later than we had anticipated. We shall certainly expect to finish all the evidence by one.

Now, did you want to make any opening statements?

DAME ANGELA RUMBOLD MP

DAME ANGELA RUMBOLD MP: Yes, I would just like to say a couple of things before we throw it open because I think it is quite important to indicate to the committee—and I am grateful for this opportunity to come and talk to the committee, Lord Nolan. I think the most important thing that I need to put on record is the decision that I took to leave Decision Makers when I did and in order to set it in context I would ask the committee to cast their minds back to the time when a great deal of press and media attention was focusing on Members of Parliament and other people in public life. I, as Maureen Tomison has very clearly made plain to you, had been a long-standing friend of hers and when she invited me to work with her and offered me a salary of £8,000 a year after I had left Government office, I accepted—I thought it would be an interesting addition to the work that I do in Parliament and I thought it would enhance my understanding of business. So I accepted that and I enjoyed working with her very much indeed. As she has said, we set out very clear rules about how I would behave in relation to being a director of a Parliamentary Affairs organisation, which I adhered to and which she has made absolutely plain to you she adhered to as well.

At the time that we were under such immense pressure because of the *Evening Standard* articles I felt—and I may be wrong, I am perfectly willing to accept that I might have been wrong—but I felt that because I was a high-profile Member of Parliament, I had been a Minister, people knew who I was, I am still Deputy Chairman of the party, although that had no bearing whatsoever on my work for Maureen Tomison, I felt that my presence in her firm was quite likely to cause damage to the firm. Now, this is a firm which was set up by a friend of mine whose livelihood depended on its success and if I, by my presence there, was going to cause damage to that firm I actually felt that it was the honourable thing to do to extricate myself from that and leave the firm to work and to operate, as I knew it perfectly well could, without my presence there. I believe that subsequent events actually proved me to have made the right judgment and I think, although press interest continued, it did not continue in quite the same way because I had removed myself. So I am comfortable with that decision, although I quite understand that a lot of people found it quite hard to believe that anyone would take that view.

Can I make it also absolutely plain to everybody in this room what the task of being a Deputy Chairman of the Conservative Party is? There is a misunderstanding about this. It is obviously an office which carries a certain amount of public interest, but it is not a paid office, it is not an office where one has any access to the workings of Government. The minute you leave Government you leave all of that behind you. I have no access to Ministerial papers, I have no access to the process of decision-making within Government. I have exactly the same access as every other Back Bench Member of Parliament to my colleagues, I use that perfectly properly on behalf of my constituents but I endeavour, because of my own views, not to use it for any other reason. So I think it is plain and clear that my work at Conservative Central Office is related to tasks which are entirely party-based and which have no bearing whatsoever on my role as Member of Parliament.

I think Maureen Tomison has made it absolutely plain to you in your evidence—in the evidence that she has submitted to you—the role that I did not have as far as Ebbsfleet was concerned. She has made it quite plain to you that I regard—as all my colleagues on all sides of the House do—issues which concern individual Members of constituencies as completely out of balance as far as other Members of Parliament are concerned. I would be very angry if people came in to Mitcham & Morden and started lobbying Ministers, or anybody else, about issues which

are properly my concern and I treat my colleagues of all parties in exactly the same way and happily, I have to say, all my colleagues from all parties treat me in the same way. And I think that is a clear understanding that has to be made plain.

As far as the press are concerned, I want to make a couple of observations. I think the majority of Members of Parliament, particularly those of us who have held Government office, have a very good relationship with the press. We work with the press because we know that in a democracy and in an open society like ours there is a duty and a clear need to have a good, investigative press, journalists who behave properly and who can examine issues and put their point of view forward, and I think that is absolutely proper. I have always co-operated. I regard a number of the people in the press as friends of mine, I have always co-operated with them fully on that basis and never at any time, when a journalist has come to speak to me and we have laid the ground rules of whether this is on the record or off the record, have I ever been let down. I have always had total probity on behalf of journalists.

What I did find very difficult to handle was that allegations were made about me and my association with a company which were not based on the truth, that there had not been the proper investigations done and that there had not been the courtesy offered to me of answering the allegation. That I found rather difficult to handle. I also have to say that when you are a public figure, as everyone who has been a public figure knows, if the finger is pointed at you, rightly or wrongly, you have no way of coming back, other than to take recourse in the courts. The courts, as most people in public life know—and I am sure, your Lordship, you will understand the point I am going to make—are a bit of a lottery as far as being able to be certain that the way you see it can come through in the court case, quite apart from the fact that anyone who has recourse to the law has to be substantially wealthy in order to sustain an action like that, and I would never embark on that course simply because I do not believe it is proper. But I do say this: it is then somewhat unfair that you have been pointed at and you have no recourse, because people will not believe you, to come back and say "Excuse me, but that wasn't quite correct". This is why I welcome so much the opportunity this morning to say one or two things that I hope in answer to questions will clarify my position. Thank you very much.

LORD NOLAN: Thank you very much. Now I will ask Professor King to take up the questioning.

177. PROF ANTHONY KING: Our Chairman said right at the beginning and I would like to emphasise that you are in no conceivable sense on trial. You followed the rules and, indeed, I have in front of me your entry in the register of Members' interests and it is, indeed, very full. It not only refers to your association with Decision Makers but to all of Decision Makers' clients, including, I gather, ones you were not involved with. It is an impressive list—it goes from cement to hamburgers. What we want to do, however, is see whether your experience, precisely because you've played by the rules, throws some light on what the rules ought to be. So can I begin by asking you, from your own side of the fence, as it were, how you thought you became an executive director of Decision Makers?

ANGELA RUMBOLD: Well, yes. I mean, as I have said already, I was invited by Maureen, whom I had known for a number of years, when I left Government and when she knew that I was essentially a Back Bencher, although still clearly with the party office. She invited me to join her company, would I be interested, was it something that I would enjoy doing? I am bound to say that I thought it would be very interesting and I could see at that time, as indeed she could see, that it was very important indeed to define the areas that it would be proper for me to work in and those areas where it would perhaps be difficult for me to work in. And I must say this: at no time in my association with Decision Makers was I ever asked to breach what I considered to be the confidence of my relationship with my colleagues in the House of Commons. In other words, nobody ever said to me "Could you just sidle up to somebody in the lobby and ask them a question?" Had they done so I have to tell you the answer would have been "no", I am just not that sort of person. I can't bring myself to ask people favours.

178. PROF ANTHONY KING: Had you had any previous experience in the world of public relations or lobbying, or whatever?

ANGELA RUMBOLD: Yes, of course I had. I had been a Member of Parliament for the best part of eleven years at that time.

179. PROF ANTHONY KING: But on the other side of the fence, actually engaged in this kind of activity?

ANGELA RUMBOLD: No, no, no. I have never been employed by a Parliamentary Lobbyist before, but I have vast experience of Parliamentary Lobbyists, as every Member of Parliament does have. On many occasions I have been approached by lots of different firms. In the case of last year when I was pressing from my own point of view for a certain solution to the question of Sunday trading, I was advised by a series of different Parliamentary groups, not for any money, but simply because they wanted to ensure that I saw their point of view. This happens on a daily basis. Indeed, when I opened my post this morning, as I guess most Members of Parliament will have done, they will have found a considerable amount of material which comes as a direct part of the lobbying process.

180. PROF ANTHONY KING: But presumably you supposed that you were being approached by Maureen Tomison, partly as a friend of hers but partly as a Member of Parliament on the Government side of the house, and a recent former Minister—your usefulness lay largely in those facts?

ANGELA RUMBOLD: Of course. But, I mean, that is the essence, is it not, of any kind of employment. You are employed because you have skills that people think are worth having access to. I find it very difficult to believe that a newspaper would have offered me a job since I have no particular journalistic skills. I might be able to learn them but I don't actually have them on the plate, so to speak.

181. PROF ANTHONY KING: When you were first approached at that time did you think that this new job had an ethical dimension in the sense that you might conceivably unwittingly be in breach of some rules or problems of conflict of interest might arise?

ANGELA RUMBOLD: I was always very conscious that it was extremely important to ensure that I didn't breach the contract one has with one's colleagues in their constituency interests, yes. I thought that was very important, which was one of the reasons why the rules that we chose to work under were much more on the basis of my giving the experience that I had of the internal workings of Government rather than how to lobby or who to talk to. To be fair and to be frank I think Maureen Tomison knew more about that than I did.

182. PROF ANTHONY KING: Maureen Tomison has said—and you have just repeated—that there was a code, that there were rules, but she said that they were not written down, and I take it they were not. In retrospect do you think they should have been?

ANGELA RUMBOLD: I think it would have been helpful for everyone if they had been, yes, and I actually think that perhaps that is one of the ways forward, that anyone who works for a generalist organisation, such as a Parliamentary Lobbying organisation, it is helpful if there is a contract which specifies precisely what the limitations of your expertise are.

183. PROF ANTHONY KING: And should that contract be registered, do you think?

ANGELA RUMBOLD: Yes, why not? I think there is no reason why that contract should not be registered because it then sets out very clearly what the codes are and how people can behave. And people will feel much more comfortable with that on all sides of society.

184. PROF ANTHONY KING: You volunteered a moment ago—rather to my surprise—what you were paid by Decision Makers. Would you have minded registering that if that had been part of the original agreement. Would you have put that in the register?

ANGELA RUMBOLD: Not at all, not at all. I have no difficulty with that. As I say, I started with them, I was paid £8,000 a year to begin with and it went up subsequently to £12,000 a year. I think it is very important that this should be known.

185. PROF ANTHONY KING: You and Maureen Tomison have both laid a good deal of emphasis—quite rightly, and I am not objecting to this—on what you didn't do for Decision Makers. Could you say in a little more detail what exactly you did?

ANGELA RUMBOLD: Yes. I, as Maureen actually did indicate, spent a lot of time talking to Maureen and talking to her staff. My task was very much to explore with the company their approach to certain issues, to issues where they had been asked by clients to investigate the possibilities, to put their point of view—and I spent a great deal of time advising them on how best, in my view, to put those points of view across. I did not at any time say "You must go and see", or "you must contact", I simply said "This would be my advice about the strategy, planning the campaign", if you like. But most of that was done in the office during working hours, during mornings and so on. Sometimes it was accompanied by a ham sandwich, but that was the great extent of it.

I did, of course, as you would expect, and as I do with a number of other companies, I did go occasionally to dinners and to lunches outside the House of Commons. If they were in the House of Commons it was not unknown for me to pick up the tab in the House of Commons and pay out of my own pocket for such meetings, so I did from time to time meet with them and talk to them, but again, very much on the basis of offering advice about how to proceed and the kind of information that I thought needed to be identified and brought forward.

186. PROF ANTHONY KING: Who is "them"—you spoke of lunches and various meetings outside the House of Commons, and so on. I mean who on these occasions would you have been seeing?

ANGELA RUMBOLD: Well, I might well have been talking to people who were clients of Maureen's. I might well have been talking to Maureen herself in the evening, when it was possible for both of us to meet, so we did have a number of meetings like that, both in ——

187. PROF ANTHONY KING: Specifically not Ministers and not fellow MPs?

ANGELA RUMBOLD: No. I think only on a couple of occasions did I have an evening meal with someone who happened to be a Minister at the time present.

188. PROF ANTHONY KING: You said something a moment ago that sounded a little odd. You said that you advised Decision Makers on general strategic questions and how Government worked and so on, but that on no occasion would you say what Minister or person in the Government they ought to make contact with. It sounds a rather odd distinction.

ANGELA RUMBOLD: I didn't need to. I didn't need to. I mean, I think it is important to remember that Maureen herself has extremely good contacts—she already knows that. I didn't need to tell her that at all. I needed, in essence, to say "I think if that is how you are going to run the campaign, these are the points that you need to draw out".

189. PROF ANTHONY KING: But another person in your position, perhaps working for somebody less knowledgeable than Maureen Tomison, might have felt that it was part of his or her role to give specific advice about who to lobby.

ANGELA RUMBOLD: That may well be the case.

190. PROF ANTHONY KING: To take up a point that Peter Shore has raised on a couple of occasions I infer from what you have said so far that at no point were you in any way involved in securing access either for Decision Makers or its clients with Ministers or officials?

ANGELA RUMBOLD: No. I think I have made it quite plain that that was something I wouldn't have cared to have done. I personally would not choose to do that. I can't speak for others. Again I make the point that Maureen Tomison knew the ropes, knew how to get access and preferred, in any event, to secure meetings at her own behest and with the people that she thought were the people to meet.

191. PROF ANTHONY KING: Could I just draw you out on something you were quoted as saying in the *Financial Times*? You said, in the midst of all this business "I am very open about it, I have absolutely nothing to hide

at all, everyone knows perfectly well where I was coming from, I wasn't going into meetings as Deputy Chairman of the Party, I was going in as a representative of Decision Makers." Can one, in practice, sustain that distinction, because people who meet you may well know you are there in the role as a representative of Decision Makers but they cannot "un-know" that you are an MP, a former Minister and Deputy Chairman of the party?

ANGELA RUMBOLD: No, of course they can't. I mean that was precisely the reason why I withdrew from Decision Makers, that I felt that it was just because of the baggage that I carried that it was unfortunate for the people who were trying to run a business and that if anything it was incumbent upon me to make the decision—it was very unlikely that Maureen was going to say to me "Look, you know, you are a bit of an embarrassment to us, would you please go away". On the other hand, it was perfectly possible for me to say "I like you a lot, my dear, I don't want to wreck your business and I'll go because of the baggage I carry". It is true to say that if you are a public figure you always carry baggage so if people, if companies, if the commercial world, if the trade union world—if anyone—wants to have access and believes that individuals, because of who they are and what they are, can help to promote their cause, then if that is the decision I think it is going to take us down a very difficult logical route to preventing Members of Parliament having access to anything or doing anything.

192. PROF ANTHONY KING: On a point you alluded to a moment ago—you have made it clear on several occasions that you resigned from Decision Makers because you didn't want to damage the company. At the time you resigned, or possibly in retrospect, have you considered that maybe you should not have got involved in the first place in the sense that a person in your position, playing that kind of role as an adviser to an outside lobbying firm, even if you obeyed the rules might nevertheless look rather peculiar.

ANGELA RUMBOLD: Well, of course I considered that. I mean, it was one of the questions that I agonised over, because I felt that my role and the person that I was had, in fact, quite unfortunately brought about something that I would have wished could never have happened. So of course I thought about that afterwards and I think all of us think very carefully about how we proceed and what we do. But on the other hand I think it is important to say this: I cannot imagine—and I still don't believe that this is right—I cannot imagine a situation where a Member of Parliament simply has to concentrate on the legislative procedures and the concerns within their constituency once they become elected, because if that happens I do not understand how they can advance and develop as individuals, unless they have an opportunity to secure information and knowledge about the rest of the world working.

One of the things that is constantly said about people in public life but about Government Ministers in particular, is that they are cut off from the real world, the real world being the world where people go out to work and earn a living and are in totally different circumstances. Now, it is true that Members of Parliament will meet a limited number of their own constituents but they are a limited number of their constituents. It is much more likely that they will get the knowledge that they are required to have to have a broad view of what is happening, or the legislation that is coming before them, how best to deal with the issues that are arising, if they actually have some experience of the outside world.

193. PROF ANTHONY KING: But would I be right in inferring from what you have just said in rather general terms that you continue to hold the view that it is all right for a Member of Parliament to be paid to work for a general lobbying firm?

ANGELA RUMBOLD: Of course I do.

194. PROF ANTHONY KING: You do?

ANGELA RUMBOLD: Yes, absolutely.

195. PROF ANTHONY KING: There is no problem about that at all?

ANGELA RUMBOLD: Absolutely no problem at all, provided there is a code of conduct, provided it is clearly demonstrated to everyone who wishes to know exactly what that role entails.

196. PROF. ANTHONY KING: Yet from what you have said so far one has to infer that the code of conduct was quite clear enough for your purposes and that you did not breach it.

ANGELA RUMBOLD: Absolutely, that is quite correct. And, indeed, I think you have to draw parallels about how other people in public life conduct themselves. Most Members of Parliament do, in fact, declare their associations with companies. There has been a bit of an argument put to me about is it not more difficult to be on the board of a generalist company which spans a wide range of things rather than a specific company—Scotch Whisky or whatever. Had I been lucky enough to be a non-executive director of, say, Unilever—Unilever has a huge number of interests—am I to say that I have to limit my conversations in Parliament in the House to Omo, or do I have to list every single thing that Unilever does? The answer is 'no' because people feel that because it is a company they know what it represents. The difficulty is that people do not feel they know what are Parliamentary affairs or what a lobbying firm represents, and that is the area which I think we need to clarify.

197. PROF. ANTHONY KING: You say an area that needs to be clarified, but you seem to be saying, at least as far as your own experience was concerned, that the present rules were perfectly adequate, you might be right to say that, I am not disputing that, and that there was really nothing that this committee could recommend that would improve the position.

ANGELA RUMBOLD: I feel that that is the situation otherwise I think I would automatically put myself into a different situation. I actually believe that that is exactly right.

198. PROF. ANTHONY KING: Can I then come back to the point that Lord Nolan made earlier on in talking to Maureen Tomison: is there not a problem about public perception, and although everything you say may well be true, is there not a real problem that people find it odd that somebody should be paid to be a Member of Parliament, should be a senior figure in a political party, yet, at the same time, working for an organisation whose express and stated function is to lobby the institution of which he or she is a Member. Is that not rather hard to get over even if it is, in fact, in substance satisfactory?

ANGELA RUMBOLD: I think that the mystery that surrounds that particular issue is something that I rather hope your Lordship and his committee is going to produce resolution and answer to. I suspect that that is one of the areas that we have great expectations will be clarified, and I think that Members of Parliament, having had the opportunity to give evidence, will undoubtedly respect whatever comes out of this committee. I hope and wish you great success.

199. PROF. ANTHONY KING: My last question then is, do you have any suggestions?

ANGELA RUMBOLD: I do have suggestions that I think are very clear. I think it is important for Members of Parliament to understand that there is a legitimate interest in what they do and how they conduct their lives. I have always thought that if you are in public life you are there not because of some accident of birth but because you have made a conscious decision that this is what you want to do. Your family has to put up with that, you have to put up with it, and therefore the only way in which you can protect yourself is to live by a code of conduct which was open and very very clearly transparent. I have no problems at all with Members of Parliament having outside interests. I do not believe that it would be healthy or in any way detrimental to the work they do both as part of the legislature or, indeed, as Members of Parliament for them to have other interests. I think they should, if anything, be encouraged to do so, but I do think that when they do that they should register those interests, the exact nature of those interests should be transparently clear, and that, if necessary and if it is felt in the public interest, the amounts of money that they receive for those interests should also be openly declared.

200. LORD NOLAN: Thank you very much. May I just follow up that point about the look of the thing. If there were two companies both involved in lobbying, one has a distinguished Member of Parliament on its board and the other does not, does not the one with the distinguished Member of Parliament have an attraction in the eyes of the cynical Member of the public?

ANGELA RUMBOLD: In the eye of the cynical member of the public it may well do, I do not think there is anything one can do about that. I do think the point needs to be made that if a company is trying to put a point of view across it does not depend on the name of the individual who is part of the board; it depends on the excellence of the work that is being done on behalf of the client by the company.

201. LORD NOLAN: Yes, and you resigned because you had been put in an impossible position, you felt, and had become, in effect, an embarrassment to the company, quite unjustly because you were behaving perfectly, but because there was an apparent conflict of interest in the eyes of the public, is that right?

ANGELA RUMBOLD: I felt, as I have said, that it was extremely important from the company's point of view not to have further embarrassment. I felt that that was very detrimental to their potential livelihood. I was all right; I already had a livelihood and I could survive without it, but I did feel that it was the honourable thing to do. It is not fair to say that it was not perceived as that because it was perceived as that, and a very large number of journalists and people that had been part of the original exercise came to me afterwards and apologised and said that they thought that it had been misjudged.

LORD NOLAN: Yes, thank you very much. I am only concerned, and no doubt we will hear more about this, that it is a sort of conflict of interests that, in the nature of things, may arise when Members of Parliament take up their position. Lord Thomson, what do you think?

202. LORD THOMSON: Dame Angela, you have explained your own position, if I may say so, very frankly to us with great honesty. I just wondered in codifying behaviour for Members of Parliament who accept paid employment of one kind or another with lobbying firms, would you have in that code the kind of provisions that you yourself were telling us you practised? That is a prohibition on either speaking or asking questions in support of the interest which was providing you with some pecuniary reward?

ANGELA RUMBOLD: Not necessarily. I think that it is quite legitimate for people who have a specific interest in a subject, and there are many of my colleagues whose views are widely respected simply because they have spent a lifetime either being employed or working in a particular profession or with a particular interest. I think it would be a great mistake if we were to write in any way that those people with that expertise are not allowed to advise Parliament, to make enquiries, to investigate through their own expertise, some of the things that were being put forward by the executive. It would be a terrific loss to the whole system to prevent that expertise from being used.

203. LORD THOMSON: I am just asking about a narrower question. I do not necessarily disagree with what you have just been saying, but if somebody is paid by a lobbying firm, either as a member of the board or to do a particular job, lobbying firms have clients and the clients come and go, but during the period when someone who is a Member of Parliament is being paid in Parliament to represent a particular interest at that time of a particular client, do you feel that the code ought to lay down the prohibitions that you accepted for yourself in terms of speaking and asking questions?

ANGELA RUMBOLD: No I do not think so but the only reason I put the prohibitions on myself was because there was no other mechanism whereby I could actually declare the interest openly. It would be perfectly proper if Members of Parliament were able to declare that this is a question that is put because I am interested at the present time in this particular aspect of one or other subject.

204. DIANA WARWICK: Both you and Ms Tomison have placed an enormous amount of emphasis on the need for transparency. It seems to me we have a real problem here because throughout our discussions and in other evidence that we have heard we are constantly revealing a difference between perception and actuality. I wonder if I can take you back to your statement where you said, slightly "flip" I think when Professor King asked you about the public perception, you could not do anything about the cynical eye of the public, there was nothing that could be done about that. It seems to me this is the dilemma that we face that, if we are to address what is an apparent broad distrust of the probity of MPs, we must

look to perception as well as to actuality. In the light of that, do you think that it would be more sensible for MPs to recognise that this is very murky water, that influencing Ministers, influencing MPs, can be seen to be done in a way that might affect their Parliamentary interests and their Parliamentary integrity, and therefore it is rather better to err on the side of caution than to err on the side of your own clear sense of integrity and honesty which, even you, I think, have admitted you do not know whether that is shared by your colleagues.

ANGELA RUMBOLD: In a sense, if I might say so, this is a judgment you will have to come to rather than I am because I am here simply to advise you of my own personal perceptions. I simply cannot speak on behalf of anyone else because I do not know how they react. I am incredibly anxious that the public perception of people in public life like myself should be raised. It has been lowered to a dangerous level and it is very, very important that we regain in the eyes of the public a certain amount of esteem. It is a great pity that people who come into public life cannot be recognised in the way that perhaps they have been in the past, that what they are doing is not actually something for their own personal gain but is for the greater good. The understanding in this modern age appears to be that people cannot possibly do something because they really want to give something back to society; they can only do it if there is some underlying and less honest reason for doing it. In other words they are trying to put themselves into a position where they will get some paid remuneration. That is not actually true of people, but it is very difficult indeed to dispute the perception.

205. CLIFFORD BOULTON: I noticed when you were casting round in your mind as to what else you might have been asked to do you mentioned the possibility of a non-executive directorship. That, of course, is a job rather than a consultancy. I think that industry and commerce have demonstrated they feel a big need for them to establish relationships with Members of Parliament. We also had an opinion earlier that if consultancies were banned things might grow up in a different way because this need is there and it is not likely to go away. Do you think, in fact, that if paid consultancies for all Members of Parliament were banned we might simply get more direct offers of employment and that would open up the whole business of whether Members should be allowed to earn money outside their Parliamentary salary and would be more disguising the facts of life rather than helping transparency?

ANGELA RUMBOLD: Yes I think it will. That is very likely to happen. If the committee were to say we in principle have no objection to Members of Parliament being employed by outside organisations, professions, companies and so on, but this is the one area where we are going to prevent them from having access. I think that leads into some further scrutiny and it will be quite difficult to draw that fine line. There is a big decision which has to be arrived at and that is whether or not Members of Parliament should not be paid at all outside their Parliamentary salaries. If that is to be the case, clearly Parliamentary salaries have to be looked at (that is another issue) or whether the present system can be so designed that Members of Parliament and their actions are so transparent that Members of the public feel that they now have better confidence that their Members of Parliament are behaving in a way that they think is right and proper.

206. PETER SHORE: It is very difficult for distinction to be made between a Member of Parliament who is receiving a salary or award by being employed by a PR agency, to draw the line between different kinds of conduct in relation to Ministers, to Parliament itself and its procedures. You have defined the line in relation to the organisation which you have been employed in, and also in terms of your own personal conduct, but I find it difficult to envisage that in practice one could really draw a line as sharply as that which you have suggested. There is such a range, a nuance, of parliamentary activities all of which are concerned with the two things—access and influence. Do you think in practice it is possible to sort out that conduct which is permissable and that conduct which is not for MPs who are employed by PR firms?

ANGELA RUMBOLD: I think it is possible, yes. I honestly believe that it is possible. I share and understand your concerns about the difficulty of that, but I would say that I think that people who are in public life ought to be able to adhere to a code of conduct which is clear and that there should not be a question of whether or not they are able to, or whether this line is murky or not murky. It does not seem to me that the sort of people that we are talking about would have a difficulty with that, and I do question the implication that Members of Parliament for some obscure reason are different from other people and therefore need to have the rules of behaviour written out in words of one syllable, whereas it may be perfectly possible for others to do all kinds of things that are not as explicit. I think there is a question mark in my mind about that.

PETER SHORE: I am grateful for that reply. I think I will desist at this point, thank you.

207. PROF. ANTHONY KING: I would like to ask just one more question having to do with line drawing. In your work for Decision Makers you drew a very sharp line which you found quite easy to enforce between, as it were, consulting to Decision Makers on the one hand and actually acting as an advocate of Decision Makers or its clients on the other. Do you think that that distinction should be written into the rules of the House of Commons—Thou may consult but thou may not advocate.

ANGELA RUMBOLD: I think it would be perfectly possible to do that and it might help my colleague Peter Shore's concern about that line being drawn, so I would not have a problem with that on a personal basis.

208. TOM KING: Professor King has been making a point that you have a position and was it not therefore a considerable advantage to impressing your case. I just wondered whether your own experience does not point in a slightly different direction because you actually felt at one stage that you were a liability to the company that you were with. Drawing on your Ministerial experience, is your experience similar to the experience that I have had that if there is somebody involved in seeking a contract, bidding for an opportunity, whatever it may be, who might be in a privileged position, actually their position and that bid will be that much more crawled over by officials and by Ministers anxious and aware of what people will say. In many cases it is not an advantage, it is actually a liability.

ANGELA RUMBOLD: Exactly so, and I am bound to say in my own experience—I was seven years a

Minister—I had a great deal to do and a great number of people who lobbied me in particular instances. That is precisely my experience that I would be much more cautious of someone who was trying to promote an interest whom the outside world knew I had other connections with, or was in fact professionally associated with.

209. ANNE WARBURTON: Could I just briefly say that I share the concern which has been evident from the questions which have been put about the special nature of the indirect activities which are involved in being a consultant to a PR firm. I have noted various things have been said and I will not ask Dame Angela to repeat them, but just to emphasise that if one is going to try to make lines, to draw lines, from where I sit at the moment it does look difficult to draw the same line for consultants to PR firms, for example the Scotch Whisky was mentioned earlier, as for somebody who is connected with Scotch Whisky, one being direct and indirect, and it may be that this question of thou shalt consult, thou shalt not advocate may perhaps bridge that particular gap. I just want to signal that it is difficult and if you can say anything which will help to clarify that particular relationship I would be grateful.

ANGELA RUMBOLD: Yes, Sir Clifford raised the whole business of non-executive directorships. It is important to remember that a number of people who are concerned with large companies do not actually declare every single aspect of that company's work, so in a sense you are talking about the same thing, that you are in general the non-executive director of Scotch Whisky. It may not be known that Scotch Whisky also makes oatmeal biscuits and when you talk about oatmeal biscuits you are actually talking about the Scotch Whisky firm. They do not, but that is an instance of where there could be a confusion, so I think it is important to recognise that you are talking about generalist firms but you are also talking in the larger remit of how do you identify precisely which bit of whatever the interest is you are representing. This is true of all forms of outside connections.

LORD NOLAN: Thank you very much, Dame Angela. We have taken up a lot of your time and you have been extremely helpful and clear. Thank you.

210. LORD NOLAN: Mr Steven, thank you very much for coming along to see us this morning. I apologise for the fact that we are running a good deal late, I hope this will not interfere with the early editions of the *Evening Standard*.

STEWART STEVEN AND MIRA BAR-HILLEL

STEWART STEVEN (Editor, the *Evening Standard*): We have got that out of the way already.

211. LORD NOLAN: As you know, we have been hearing from Dame Angela Rumbold and Maureen Tomison about the Ebbsfleet affair and broadening out from that into the role of lobbyists and their relationships with Members of Parliament. This is a subject which I am sure has occupied your mind over many months and years in your long experience. Would you like to start by addressing us with a clear statement? Have you got one?

STEWART STEVEN: I would just like to make one or two very brief comments about some of the things which have been said this morning already. There does tend, I fear in these circumstances, to be a tendency among some people to assume that when there is a problem of this nature that part of the problem is the press reporting of it. One could not help but note this morning that to a certain extent the *Evening Standard*'s reporting of these events was seen as being part of the problem. I would say that this document we are discussing came into our possession during the so-called sleaze debate. It seemed to me to be an astonishing document and I understand that the committee actually does not have copies of it. As I thought that may be the case, before I came I prepared documents for you, and I have also made one available for the press room if Members of the press wish to have it. Once you see this I think it will indicate very clearly indeed, certainly in the very first article, all I was concerned to do. Having been a Member of the lobby as long ago as 1962 when there was one parliamentary lobbyist allowed in the House of Commons and that was Sir George Crisp who represented the Lord's Day Observance Society, and there is no other lobbyist in the country who is famous for that, I was so astonished to see the tentacles of the lobbying firms, how deep they had apparently sunk into the political fabric of Whitehall and Westminster that we ran the document virtually as is. We made no comment about it. I gave instructions to those people working on it that there should be no editing for comment in it at all, except for speaking to some of the principals. Dame Angela said in her approach to you that she had, in fact, never been asked for an opinion by the *Evening Standard* and had not been spoken to by the *Evening Standard*; of course she had an opportunity because we spoke to her and she is quoted in that document. We also spoke to Maureen Tomison about that approach and Maureen Tomison sent me a fax about Dame Angela's involvement and we refer to that fax in the article too, so she was given an opportunity to reply.

The document is remarkable. It is remarkable because it seems to suggest—of course we are dealing here with a PR company so one has to remember there are obviously elements of hype which could be involved as well—that indeed they are deep into the government of this country so that when they say in this document, as they do on page 3,

"The following lists details of the key meetings and briefings of senior Ministers and officials"

There is, indeed, a long list—

"No. 10 Downing Street, the Prime Minister has already been briefed on a proposed East Thames Corridor in an informal and private presentation."

Later it goes on to say that Dame Angela as deputy chairman of the party has been able to keep the party fully appraised of Blue Circle's plans of the East Thames Corridor. She told you today that, of course, she did not involve herself with the constituency. It also says here, —

"Dame Angela has recently visited the project site and met local authority leaders."

It then goes on to say that, timetabled, there was a dinner with the Parliamentary Labour Party.

"28th May a dinner with the Prime Minister".

It does not mention here that 400 other people were allowed to be present too.

"18th June Evening for Ministers at Hampton Court 28th June Reception No.11 Downing Street"

If there is any hype at all I do wish to emphasise that that hype is not *Evening Standard* hype, it is the hype by Decision Makers. That is really all I wish to say at this particular point.

LORD NOLAN: Thank you very much. I am going to ask Lord Thomson if he would carry on with your evidence.

212. LORD THOMSON: First of all, thank you very much for leaking to us this leaked document which has so far not reached us, because it is, as I suspected, rather relevant to our discussions.

Can I start by saying that, as Lord Nolan has indicated, we are not making a fresh investigation into the pros and cons of the decision about the siting of this particular station on the Channel Tunnel high speed line. The advantage of this particular affair is that, in a sense, it is over; the decisions have been taken, the dust has settled, there does not seem to be much controversy, and it is a very interesting case study for us about the more general issues that arise from it.

It is very clear that the problem that we have to address of standards in public life and the distrust that has, I think, grown over recent years about the way people in public life have behaved, a very important element of that is the so-called "Fourth Estate", the media. Indeed, it is investigative journalism that has a very important role to play in all this and we recognise that. Without that many of these issues would not be before the public and there would not be the public perception that is one of the aspects that we are dealing with.

I therefore wanted to ask you as editor of a major newspaper engaged, as in this example that is now passed and we are examining, in a piece of investigative journalism, do you lay down any rules for your staff about standards of fairness in dealing with it?

STEWART STEVEN: I think that the rules of standards of fairness are rules which apply to every case as it comes along. The function of editing must be first of all to talk to the journalists—the editor is not somebody who necessarily is the person who brings in the story—to learn about the story which is about to be investigated, to discuss the general parameters which the investigation will bank it up. Then the most important thing of all is when the copy comes in from all sources for the editor himself, or the senior assistants, for those editors then rather than the reporters to take it upon themselves the responsibility of making sure that copy is fair and proper and honest and straightforward by asking of the journalists hard and searching questions. That process can often take several days. That is really, I think, what editors have to do. Therefore if there is a mistake in a newspaper, if investigative journalism has not been properly conducted, that is entirely the fault of the editor who has not gone through that process properly.

213. LORD THOMSON: I perhaps ought to declare an interest. Apart from my real journalistic claim to fame with the *Dandy* comic, I was once in an earlier incarnation a crusading political journalist, and then later on in life I had the task of administering statutory due impartiality as

chairman of the Independent Broadcasting Authority. So I read the file of this particular story with very great professional interest. I am bound to say in terms of due impartiality, what struck me and I would be grateful for your comment or the comment of your colleague, was that there did not seem to be, along with the critique of the Decision Makers' approach to the Ebbsfleet site, any comparable information given to your readers about the efforts being made for the Stratford station through Newham. Let me put it this way. The Stratford group are not a small local London Labour council overawed by the great world in which they are living; they are part of a general grouping that included people like P&O with Lord Sterling who is well known with links to the present government party; Tarmac Mowlem and Laing. Any of these had at least equal, I would have thought, ability as against Decision Makers and their friends to lift the telephone and get access to the private office of a Minister. I did not find any record of that in the cuttings.

STEWART STEVEN: That would be a fair criticism if we had not, in fact, done that. Mira Bar-Hillel here who wrote most of the story will confirm that we did speak to Stratford quite extensively about all of this. Stratford made it plain to us, and I think the copy does say it, that they had on several occasions asked for meetings with Ministers to discuss this and they had always been turned down. They did not get the Minister or the meetings which they requested. Decision Makers apparently managed to achieve that. That seemed to us to be an important point of the story, that one of these two competing consortiums did have privileged access, was able to peddle influence rather than information, and the other did not have that ability to do so, or if they did have the ability they certainly did not use it in this particular case. That was, in fact, the kernel of the story. Stratford, incidentally since then, do have problems. Stratford still feel that they are, as they would put it, "in with a shout" for a smaller station, so Stratford are, as you will observe through diligently reading the cuttings, being rather quiet about things. They do not want to make a public fuss; they still want to be regarded as being in there with some chance.

214. LORD THOMSON: As you know, we shall be hearing evidence next week from Mr MacGregor who was the Secretary of State at the time. What I find striking now that the dust has settled and we are able to examine this in a detached way is, in a sense, the "Sherlock Holmes dog that didn't bark". There is no further controversy. We have submissions here from Stratford saying they did not feel ill-treated or left out in the way that is suggested. In fact the case for Stratford is a different argument from the case for what to do in mid-Kent. Against that background—we all of us have to take our decisions day by day—I just wondered now with hindsight whether you feel that if you knew what you know now the story would have been written differently.

STEWART STEVEN: No, on the contrary. I think that the first story, as I said at the very beginning, was written in a non-argumentative way. It said at the very beginning in the introduction to the story, and I was clear that this should go in, that -

"A review of the lobbyists planned a campaign of persuasion to influence everyone from the local newspaper to the Prime Minister. There was nothing illegal about their activities. They were plying their lawful trade."

What our story shows is how lobbyists have become the essential oils within the wheels of government. It does not suggest this is illegal, improper or that anybody behaved badly. What it suggests is that this is something which I believe the public ought to be aware of. These are hidden persuaders at work; people do not know about it.

215. LORD THOMSON: Well that is a more general question I think we want to concentrate on. I just want to ask whether, arising out of this particular investigation that you did, your criticisms at the end of the day were primarily about lobbyists or were they about Ministers? What conclusions did you draw as a major opinion-forming paper?

STEWART STEVEN: We drew two conclusions from it. First of all we did feel that, when Members of Parliament get involved in this sort of thing, at the very least their activities are likely to be misrepresented. It is possible, I suppose, that one could argue that the people who have the greatest reason to complain about the activities of Decision Makers are Blue Circle Cement who received the document called *The Campaign Update* which may be a load of "tosh". Maybe these meetings did not take place at all. Maybe this influence which Decision Makers tell the directors of Blue Circle Cement they have, they do not have at all. That, of course, we do not know. I also think there is a subsidiary issue which is actually of very considerable importance, which is whether we are sure that the government service is sufficiently immune to the activities of lobbyists or not. That also, of course, we cannot know. There are people who tell me off the record from Stratford (they do not say this on the record because there is still a continuing issue there) that they were disturbed about what Blue Circle was up to.

216. LORD THOMSON: My outstanding point is that lobbying is a legitimate occupation in a democracy. The question we are wrestling with is how it should be conducted and whether there need to be changes in the way it is conducted. Lobbyists face two ways; they face, of course, to the political decision makers in Parliament and in Government and perhaps elsewhere depending on the campaign. They also, of course, have relations with the press and I wondered what your considered view after your experience was about the present state of the lobbying industry and whether you have any ideas about how it might be better regulated.

STEWART STEVEN: I think that is a very, very difficult question and I must say I do not have many ideas about that because I think we have to remember—the word "lobbying" is, I suppose, a smart word for "PR" which is a word which has fallen a bit into disrepair these days.

217. LORD THOMSON: Presumably the *Evening Standard* engages in PR?

STEWART STEVEN: Exactly, people do engage in PR, but PR people are regarded as being rather reprehensible, so we have this modern phrase "lobbyist". What one does know, and maybe this matter has just been caught in time in this country, is that if one looks at the United States of America and looks at the activities of lobbyists in Congress, one can see how far and how dangerous this process can become if allowed to go entirely unchecked. I suspect that we are in this country in the very early stages of that. I think we are nowhere near down that road. But therefore I think that probably rules have got to be laid down now before we do go as far as the

Americans can go. As I said at the very beginning, I thought I understood, having been a lobby correspondent as far back as 1962, the political processes in this country and that there were few things that would surprise me. When I read this document I must say I was fairly astonished by it.

218. **LORD THOMSON:** As a foreign lobby correspondent and a present editor, do you have a view as to whether Parliament would be healthier if Members of Parliament were entirely full-time Members of Parliament and paid only as Members of Parliament?

STEWART STEVEN: No, I don't believe Members of Parliament should be full time.

219. **LORD THOMSON:** You don't believe that?

STEWART STEVEN: No. I think to make them full time would be to restrict the kind of people who become Members of Parliament. I don't think there is necessarily an issue of the money they get when they get into Parliament. I think it is perfectly possible to argue that people are prepared to sacrifice some financial gain on becoming Members of Parliament. I do think, however, that you need to draw Parliament from as wide a cross-section of the community as possible and I think that if you did insist that it is a fully professional occupation, I suspect you would get an advancement of what the situation is today, that there are a large number of Members of Parliament who have done nothing else in their lives other than be politicians, who have gone straight from university into Tory Central Office or some trade union and from there straight into Parliament, people who actually have never experienced the real world.

220. **LORD THOMSON:** There are some who have been giving evidence to us who draw a distinction between a Member of Parliament who is part of a general lobbying firm with a whole range of clients and a Member of Parliament who is acting as a consultant or an advocate for one particular firm or one particular industry or trade association or a trade union, for example. There are of course some occupations that a Member of Parliament is not allowed to have even at present. Would you feel in support of the idea that Members of Parliament should not be a paid part of general lobbying firm with a whole range of clients?

STEWART STEVEN: I think that is philosophically very difficult, if you allow them to remain members of all sorts of other things but not lobbying firms. But the problem with the lobbying industry, it seems to me, is that in itself it has got into a bit of a mess. There are no real standards of conduct laid down for lobbyists. We don't actually really know what they do. If you take this document which I find so fascinating, we don't know whether any of this actually happened. We don't know whether the boasts made here were justified or not. We don't know, therefore, what lobbyists really do. It is fanciful, I believe, to imagine that lobbyists would take on their staff people who have no influence, who have no friends. Maureen Tomison herself of course is a person who is known for the extent of her political contacts. You just need to look at her wedding list to see who attended recently.

221. **LORD THOMSON:** On page 7 of the document that you have based your stories on, which we now have,

we see "28th June—Reception at No 11 Downing Street". It has subsequently been said to us that no such thing ever took place. Did you check on that and can you throw any light on the nature of what happened on 28th June?

STEWART STEVEN: I have no idea what happened on 28th June. What I did check, for example, was 28th May, the dinner with the Prime Minister: did that occur? I remember looking at cuttings from *The Times*. Did the Prime Minister that day have an official dinner? Well, there wasn't one. Did he have an unofficial dinner? I don't know. What our story was about was the document, however—what the boast was, what the claim was. There is this perception that members of the public have about the House of Commons and Members of Parliament. A director of Blue Circle Cement or anybody in Blue Circle Cement who saw this document would think to themselves "Wow, what the hell is going on here in this country that these people are able to have dinners with the Prime Minister, summon the chairman of the Parliamentary Labour Party to meetings, arrange receptions at No 11 Downing Street?" It seems on the face of it to be amazing. You therefore have got to say "Did it happen?" I don't know. I don't know how much of this is fact, how much is fantasy. I don't know what the bill was that Blue Circle Cement paid, for what—fact or fantasy?

222. **LORD NOLAN:** Has that answered Lord Thomson's question? You haven't got a view—is this right?—as to whether or not Members of Parliament should be paid -

STEWART STEVEN: I think they cannot be paid Members of lobbyists because we do not actually know what lobbyists themselves do. It's a sort of secret society.

223. **LORD THOMSON:** One final question of a very general character. As I said earlier, the investigative role of the media is a very important element in our society and has certainly been a very important element in the state of opinion about standards in public life. Since we are continuing wrestling with what Diana Warwick a few minutes ago called "the gap between perception and actuality"—the perception that the public have comes so much to us from the media's reporting—and I just wondered what, with all your experience, your general view is about standards in public life. Do you feel that in this country we are in a serious situation or is it an exaggerated situation? Do you have any feel as to how it compares with the situation in other democracies?

STEWART STEVEN: As a matter of fact I don't think it is a serious situation. I think the situation is worse than it was. I think that the standards of the House of Commons, and of Members of Parliament I suspect, have fallen in the last 10 or 15 years, but I still believe—I am willing to be proved wrong on this, but I hope I never am—that the standards of public life in this country are as high as any in the world. I also believe that sometimes newspapers personalise events and stories when they ought not to do so, when political debate is discussed in purely personal terms rather than in policy terms, and I think that does happen too much. So I think there is some responsibility upon newspapers for a sense of deterioration. On the other hand, I go back to what I say here, and that is that, if you were anybody working for Blue Circle Cement and you read this, you would have a view of Members of Parliament which is very, very low indeed, worse than anything the media could ever say about them.

LORD NOLAN: I am afraid we haven't got quite so much time as we would like. I am going to go round the table. Dame Anne first, please. Have you any questions for Mr Steven?

224. ANNE WARBURTON: Chairman, yes, thank you. I would like to ask this. The editor has said to us that he thinks that lobbyists should be regulated—controlled. There is another aspect to all this. I am sure you have heard that we have two people who say that the media should be controlled. That is not what I am wanting to ask you about. What I want to ask you is this. Do you as an editor, does the media, take it as part of their responsibility not to depress the regard in which parliamentarians and others in public office are held? The reason I ask this is because we were yesterday thinking against the background of that Gallup poll, which said that 64 per cent of the nation thought that MPs went into it for personal gain. I think most of us think that that perhaps is not the right answer. But what attitude does the media take to public confidence in public figures?

STEWART STEVEN: I don't think it is the function of the media, Dame Anne, or of newspaper editors, to take a position that they feel that they have a duty to the public good to depress or impress the public with regard to anybody. I think that the great historic function of a newspaper is to report, to report what we see, to tell the world what is going on, to seek to discover those things which people do not wish to have discovered. It was said by a famous editor of the past "Why is it that journalists spend so much time in the gutters?" and the answer was "Because that is where the ruling class throw their secrets". That may be an exaggeration of the case, but the truth is that that seems to me to be our function—simply to report what is happening, not to take a position upon that initially; subsequently, yes, but initially to report. In so far as that reporting is accurate and, if you like, generous, but accurate, that must fulfil a public function. The moment the media start saying "You'd better not report that, because that is going to demean this person in the eyes of the public" or "demean this institution in the eyes of the public", then I think you are on a very dangerous path indeed. You then start having a conspiracy between an elite, which is the media and the political establishment, and the public, and I think that would be very unhealthy.

ANNE WARBURTON: I think we all are very much impressed, as Lord Thomson said, of the importance of an investigative press, but there must be—and you answered a question on this earlier, I realise—rules within which the function that you have described is carried out.

STEWART STEVEN: I think those rules are ones of honesty and decency. I would add another rule which I suspect the press has forgotten, and that is generosity—generosity of spirit—and that is sometimes, I fear, lacking in some press reporting.

225. TOM KING: I don't hold with your last comments. They don't absolutely square with this argument, which I now understand you say you don't know if it is true or not.

STEWART STEVEN: I don't say that.

226. TOM KING: Well, in terms of the matters that are alleged within it, that this may be over-hyping by Decision Makers, and you don't know if it is true or not. Reading this article, and the point keeps coming back about "What is the perception of the behaviour of MPs?",

do you think on reflection that this does give an impression? It moves from some allegations to some sort of past tense—how the web of influence developed from the Blue Circle board, which is the picture here, which goes right through to the Prime Minister. That is not whether it is alleged; it is how it developed. There is no evidence that it did actually develop—I think you have accepted that—and I believe the Stratford promoters themselves believe that there is no evidence that that is true. I just worry. You have expressed some admirable sentiments, if I may say so: you must tell people what is actually happening, facts are sacred, and I just wonder how that reflects in this article.

STEWART STEVEN: The facts in this particular case are the document. This is a document, 20th May 1993, headed "Strictly private and confidential, Update on activities carried out by Decision Makers on behalf of Dartford Borough Council & Blue Circle Properties Ltd". Once we had proved that this was a genuine document, that it was not a forgery, which we managed to do fairly quickly, it seems to me that it would have been intolerable if we hadn't printed it. This is a document which purported to show what a major PR company was doing, or was proposing to do, on behalf of its client who, at the time when we published this document, we knew had won a great victory.

In retrospect, looking at the document and hearing Maureen Tomison say at this table today "When that document says that we arranged a meeting with the Prime Minister, actually 400 people were present and we are not even sure whether our lobbyist actually managed to address the Prime Minister", all I can say is that didn't appear from the document. I imagine that Maureen Tomison tells all of her clients what you, Mr King, suggested this morning, that it is actually not in the interests of a lobby firm to have people who know Ministers and so on on their books. I imagine that if they told their clients this quite straightforwardly, the PR firms would lose business. Of course there is an element of hype in what they claim, but the claims themselves have to be taken at face value. That is the claim that they make. We put it in the paper; it is up to others to say "Actually that didn't happen that way". The fact that this committee today has decided to give a morning to discussing this document indicates to me that my editorial decision to publish it was correct.

227. DIANA WARWICK: I would like to press you, because it is clear, I think, both from your article and from the document itself, that this is a public relations presentation, and I think you said that you were astonished by it. What I want to press you on is what precisely astonished you and made you think that this was a dangerous document or indicated something rotten in the state of British politics, because quite a lot of the activities that are listed in considerable detail are what one would normally expect from every-day lobbying—targeting MPs, providing accurate information and so on and so on. So what was it about some of these activities that you felt crossed the bounds of normal, acceptable lobbying? What was it that you focused in on and said "Hang on, there's something really peculiar here'?

STEWART STEVEN: I don't think I ever said that. As I said earlier, when I read it my jaw dropped. I knew that lobbyists were around, as lobbyists from time to time come and see me. I know that Members of Parliament have used lobbyists and of course I knew that Members of

Parliament work for lobbying firms. What astonished me was the extent of these claims. On page 3: "Ministerial Meetings, No 10 Downing Street" is the portentous heading. "The Prime Minister has already been briefed on the proposed East Thames Corridor Project in an informal and private presentation by the campaign team." Then it says: "The Prime Minister showed a keen interest in the project and would like more detailed information." I found that incredible.

As a matter of fact I have to say that the following day we approached No 10 Downing Street for an on-the-record statement, which they were not prepared to give us before publication. It wasn't clear if the meeting had happened, but the Prime Minister was aware of the lobbying: he was aware of the issue and had been made aware of the issue. Quite what had gone on between the Prime Minister and the lobbying firm I think is a bit murky. All I can say is that here it specifically states that he had been briefed by his lobbying team at No 10 Downing Street and that he had shown a keen interest—

228. DIANA WARWICK: What I am getting at is: what is the specific area that you feel is worthy of identifying as of concern? If it is lobbying an MP or a Minister, we have got at the fact that this goes on all the time; then Angela said when she was a Minister, Tom King has said when he was a Minister, "you get this all the time." So what is it about these activities that should give us cause for concern, because it seems to me that that is what we have to address. We are talking about a line, and I am trying to get at what that line is.

STEWART STEVEN: I think that line is as I said earlier. I think there is a genuine cause of concern about how far Whitehall and the political establishment can control the activity of lobbyists and, in effect, keep them at arm's length. In this particular case, assuming that this meeting at No 10 Downing Street took place, which nobody knew about at the time—the other side presumably did not know about it—I suspect that that is going way over the top. I think that if the Prime Minister did have a formal meeting with one group of lobbyists, then it should have been absolutely straightforward and with no argument about it that the other side would also be allowed in to put their case. These are very, very, very important issues at stake, and you just can't have, it seems to me, people wandering around the back corridors of Whitehall getting these private meetings, private dinners and so on, and pitching.

229. LORD NOLAN: Am I to understand that you did take steps to check the facts in the leaked document?

STEWART STEVEN: In so far as we were able to check the facts. We had no reason to believe that the document was false. Our first determination of course was to ensure that the document was an accurate and proper document, that it was a real document.

230. LORD NOLAN: Thank you very much, Mr Steven. We have taken up a lot of busy day and we are very grateful to you for your help.

Good morning, Mr Carlile. Thank you very much for coming to talk to us. Although there is no need to introduce you, for the record a thousand years hence may I say that you are a Liberal Democrat Front Bench spokesman. You have been kind enough to send us a letter submitting views on a number of the matters which concern us. I am going to ask in a moment Sir William Utting if he will, so to speak, take you through your evidence. Would it help you to begin by reading out that letter or by reading from it and summarising it?

ALEX CARLILE QC MP

ALEX CARLILE QC MP: It would help to summarise it, if I may, Chairman. May I start by giving the preface that I am part of a dying breed—the practising lawyer MP. We are a dying breed because the increasing demands of the House of Commons are making more difficult outside activities which involve real working time.

In my letter of 12th December I set out a number of issues which I think are worthy of comment. The first dealt with MPs' salaries and allowances. In my view MPs' salaries and allowances are inadequate having regard to the Membership of the House of Commons which, despite popular opinion, is of a high quality by and large, and most people who become MPs suffer a very considerable cut in their earnings. Of course it is a great honour and privilege to be an MP, but that does not feed, educate or clothe one's wife or husband and children.

Secondly, the principle of outside work by MPs I think is a valuable principle to hold to. An MP cannot abandon his experience when he enters the House, and I hope that nobody would wish him or her to do so. The contacts which have been built up outside politics remain valuable within politics and can assist in providing a continuing stream of information which make the Member more useful to Parliament, and indeed to political party.

If, however, consultancy and other outside earnings are to continue, it seems to me to be an important responsibility for MPs to ensure that they are proportionate. It is, I suppose, a reasonable principle that if what an MP does involves real work and not too much payment, it is OK; if it involves practically no work and very substantial payment, then one can assume, subject to contradiction, that it is not OK.

The rules about outside interests are of great concern to me, and I hope that your committee, Sir, will draw up broad rules rather than narrow and prescriptive ones, but rules which MPs and others will be able to understand clearly. I share Diana Warwick's view that we are talking about a line here. It is difficult to define the line, and I appreciate that drawing up the rules is very challenging.

Finally, in my letter I included a paragraph on the policing of MPs' conduct. I think that it is in the nature of the House of Commons inevitable that the policing will have to be done by Select Committees of the House. However, it is quite clear from the current controversies before both the Committee of Privileges and the Committee on Members' Interests that those committees, because of political whipping, are inadequate to deal with issues of credibility. I believe that it would be very valuable to those committees, where issues of credibility as between witnesses arise, to be able to call upon an outside body such as this committee to consider and advise in what would probably be rare appropriate cases.

231. WILLIAM UTTING: I think I am right, Chairman, in saying that the question of MPs' salaries isn't central to our terms of reference, but it is obviously highly relevant to the conduct of MPs, with which we are concerned. I don't actually think we have got the present

salaries of MPs on record since we started oral evidence. Perhaps Mr Carlile would like to tell us what an MP's salary is.

ALEX CARLILE: In round figures it is £32,000 per year for a Member of Parliament—I am sure that Sir Clifford carries the pence in his head from his very recent experience as Clerk of the House—and we do have allowances which, again in broad terms, are just over £42,000 and permit us to employ the equivalent of three not very well paid staff.

232. WILLIAM UTTING: It is simply that the sums of money involved to some members of the public may appear to be large. They appear much less large, and perhaps unreasonable, when they are placed in the context of what people of MPs' general ability can earn, if they so wished, in other walks of life and what in fact other people do earn. There is an implication in your letter that you may have found it necessary at some times actually to subsidise your political activities from your own earnings, in that both the salary you drew and the expenses allowable were too small to allow you to perform all your political duties conscientiously.

ALEX CARLILE: I suppose it is worth putting on record that when one becomes a Member of Parliament one is hopefully already reasonably mature. I had three children by the time I became a Member of Parliament and a certain lifestyle, like I owned a house and had a mortgage. My earnings as a Member of Parliament are still, in cash terms, significantly less than when I entered the House 11½ years ago. That meant that, like many new MPs, I needed income to live on, and also I found that to run a proper political office I needed income from which to pay my staff for the equipment and all the facilities I need. For those 11½ years I have substantially subsidised my parliamentary and constituency office from my own earnings. I don't begrudge that for one moment, but I believe that my constituency association know and appreciate that that is a fact, and it is a useful fact from their viewpoint.

233. WILLIAM UTTING: You obviously would not agree with the concept of enforcing whole-time devotion to parliamentary duties by MPs, but you would agree that an MP's salary and expenses need to be at such a level that people could devote themselves whole time to parliamentary work if they and their constituents wished them to do so.

ALEX CARLILE: I agree entirely, Sir. I would be opposed to the development of what I would regard as an unsavoury political class, because I think that an unsavoury political class, and there are examples of that in many countries in the world, would damage the quality of our democracy. Having said that, I think that it is important that MPs should have the choice as to how they run their lives, how they view their political ambitions. There are those who expect or want to become Ministers; there are those who are content to approach their life as an MP in other ways, but still do an extremely, sometimes a very much more valuable job than by being Ministers. The diversity has to be there, and a political class would kill it.

234. WILLIAM UTTING: Yet you also spoke about the increasing demands that parliamentary work makes upon individuals. Again I think one of the difficulties that people have in understanding this is that the way in which Parliament works is still quite often obscure to them. I wonder if you would like to say something more about the nature of an MP's work and the way in which demands on MPs have increased in recent years.

ALEX CARLILE: Speaking for myself, my work as an MP falls into three broad categories. First and foremost, I have to deal with my constituency work. That is both time and staff-consuming. Secondly, as a spokesman for an Opposition party, I have to deal with my spokesmanship duties. Those involve a great deal of reading and understanding what are often new and unfamiliar concepts. That is very time-consuming and requires the assistance of research staff. In the nature of things one is able to find able but very inexperienced research staff to help one with it. The third part of one's life I suppose is the icing on the cake—all the outside bodies one takes an interest in. But, taking myself as an example, my own interest in the political affairs of Central and Eastern Europe has made a contribution not just to my own understanding of international politics but I hope has made some contribution to their understanding of our democracy and how to develop democratic life, and I believe very strongly that it is entirely legitimate for MPs to have that third part of their political lives to make them better parliamentarians in both the domestic and the international sense.

Quite apart from that, of course, one has the committee duties of the House, which fall broadly into the second category I mentioned, which are very demanding. For example, my baptism of fire was as a Member of the Standing Committee on the Police and Criminal Evidence Bill, upon which you, Chairman, have adjudicated, I believe, from time to time. That committee took 59 meetings. I recall it well because I was presented with a badge at the end of the 59th, recording that it was a record, but I have been on other committees that have run to many meetings, and they are intellectually demanding.

235. WILLIAM UTTING: You said also that MPs' earnings from their outside activities shouldn't be disproportionate. I think that it is quite difficult to define what would be reasonable in that respect. You also indicated in your letter, however, that you felt that MPs were entitled to privacy in relation to disclosing the level of those earnings. Do you think that those two positions are really compatible? If things are going to be left in fairly general terms to the judgment of individual MPs, should they not also be obliged to disclose the level of their earnings from outside interests?

ALEX CARLILE: I think they are compatible. The fault is mine for a lack of clarity in what I sought to make a reasonably short letter to the committee. I believe that an MP's earnings from outside activities should not be publicly disclosed. I think that that is an invasion of the individual's privacy. As you say, proportionality is a difficult concept. If an MP has an especially valuable expertise which commands a high market price, I don't think that it is right that he should undercut the market and I think it is right that he should be properly paid for the advice which he gives, as long as it falls within the rules of legitimacy. But when doubts are thrown, as they often are, by the press, I think that it is proper that those who investigate should then be able to demand to know the level of earnings involved, so that they may make a proper judgment as to whether there has been proportionality.

236. WILLIAM UTTING: We have had some discussion already this morning about the difficulty of

drawing the line between what is acceptable as an MP's paid employment outside parliamentary duties and what is not. Do you have any sense in your own mind of where that line, if such a line is necessary, could be drawn?

ALEX CARLILE: I have a qualitative sense. I believe that any employment which seriously interferes with the independence and discretion, as a Member, of that Member of Parliament is illegitimate, but if it does not interfere with his independence and discretion, it may be legitimate, but then moral questions arise, questions of standards and ethics, which are obviously going to vary from individual to individual, and I think that is where we look to you, Sir, and the members of your committee to help us.

237. WILLIAM UTTING: And questions of whose judgment is exercised in making those decisions, whether it does fall entirely on the shoulders of the individual MP or whether there is an external group of reference or an external scrutinising group that would help either to give advice or to clarify those issues.

ALEX CARLILE: In the first instance I would argue that nobody is fit to be a Member of Parliament if they are not capable of that kind of judgment, but one has to recognise that there are no qualifications for becoming a Member of Parliament, save for having the support of the electors in any given constituency, and therefore a good deal is left to chance. I think the primary responsibility, therefore, has to rest with the Member of Parliament, but it would be helpful to MPs to be able, as we do all the time, to pick up a telephone or to go and see somebody for advice. I do believe, however, that that is possible to an extent. I would have no compunction about going to seek advice from Sir Clifford when he was Clerk of the House, or his successor now, or to ask the Registrar of Members' Interests, and I believe that Sir Clifford would confirm that many Members have asked him for all sorts of advice, ranging from the public to the extremely private.

238. WILLIAM UTTING: Yes, I am sure that the advice is available and readily and expertly given. The problem is whether people always recognise the need for them to go and seek advice. It is not those who go and get it; it is those who don't go and get it about whom one would—

ALEX CARLILE: I think it is very difficult to legislate against obduracy. But I think that the existence of this committee and the fact that this committee will produce reports will concentrate the minds of many who perhaps would have been willing to gloss over the moral and ethical issues concerned.

239. WILLIAM UTTING: Yes. You spoke about our producing some general principles of guidance. Would it not make the situation clearer and be more helpful for MPs if these were codified in some written form that included guidance on conduct, certainly on financial interests but also on such other matters as the way in which they apply themselves to parliamentary and constituency duties?

ALEX CARLILE: I think that would be very helpful. We are in need of something which is more specific and clear than the current rules on the registration and declaration of financial interests, which I have before me, which are issued by the Registry of Members' Interests.

240. WILLIAM UTTING: I think that your last section was about self-regulation by the House and I will

conclude on that subject as well. At first sight, to the person who doesn't know Parliament, the processes for dealing with a complaint against a Member of Parliament seem rather slow and not necessarily likely to produce an outcome that does justice to everybody concerned, even to the Member of Parliament who is complained about. I won't rehearse the processes as I understand them, but they are obviously time-taking, and in the end what happens appears to depend upon action by the whole House, which may not have the full facts of the situation before it. Do you think that this remains a satisfactory process for regulating the conduct of Members of Parliament? Do you think that a greater independent element than the one that you have suggested should be brought into this process? Do you think that the heavens would fall if there were some statutory regulation of MPs' conduct?

ALEX CARLILE: If I may answer your three questions in series, no, yes and no. The present system does not work well, for the reasons which I gave earlier. It simply cannot deal with issues of credibility, where A says that he paid money or money's worth and B, the Member, denies ever receiving money or money's worth. It is not satisfactory for that to be resolved on party political lines, and it is resolved. It is being resolved, I am given to understand, at this moment on party political lines in at least one committee. That cannot be sustained; it is not satisfactory to the public. The insertion, therefore, of an element of independence would be valuable, albeit that one has to recognise that the House of Commons is the ultimate self-regulating authority. Constitutionally there is nothing anyone can ever do about that. It's an old constitutional argument on many fronts. But thirdly I would say that the introduction of a less tentative element of independence than I have suggested might be valuable. I would prefer to see it done by rules of the House than by statute, for the constitutional reason to which I adverted a moment ago.

WILLIAM UTTING: Thank you very much.

241. LORD NOLAN: This may be taking you back over ground which really you have just about covered, but am I right in thinking that, just as at the Bar you have a code of conduct, anyone being called to the Bar undertakes to abide by that code? If he doesn't do so, he may be hauled up before a disciplinary committee, which will have lay members on it as well as barristers. Now that is an open system and fair.

ALEX CARLILE: Yes.

242. LORD NOLAN: And you, allowing for all the differences between the Bar and the House of Commons, would welcome similarly a clear, preferably simple and not too detailed code and some independent element in the regulation and enforcement of that code, in particular as regards the finding of facts.

ALEX CARLILE: I agree entirely. Fortunately I have never been hauled up before the General Council of the Bar, but I have spent five years as a lay Member of the General Medical Council. I think the lack of complexity of the Bar system is an advantage and, perhaps perversely, the legalism of the General Medical Council as compared with the Bar is a disadvantage. A system rather like the Bar's would be clearly understood, with the lay element.

243. LORD NOLAN: Yes. That comes on one matter, perhaps of detail: the lay element is a minority; the

majority are barristers. It might seem difficult to combine an independent tribunal with membership of the House. It might be better perhaps for it to be wholly independent, would you think?

ALEX CARLILE: I think that would be difficult to sustain or to pass through the House itself. My experience on the General Medical Council is valuable in this context: I find that, though the lay members on the GMC are a minority, we are a significant minority and our views are paid the closest attention.

LORD NOLAN: Often, in my experience, rather more lenient than those of the professionals.

ALEX CARLILE: That is absolutely true— sometimes, not always.

LORD NOLAN: I won't trouble you any further for my part. Dame Anne, have you questions for Mr Carlile?

244. ANNE WARBURTON: I just wanted to ask Mr Carlile whether he feels that his clear understanding of the problem of public appreciation, or lack of appreciation, of parliamentarians is widely felt in the House. I suppose I am really asking whether, if we come forward with proposals—obviously you can't forecast—will the House be disposed to do something about it?

ALEX CARLILE: There are more experienced Parliamentarians than myself on the committee, but I believe that there is a wide perception in the House that MPs and politicians of all kinds are extremely unpopular, held in mistrust and suspicion by members of the public and that we have to do something about it. The impetus behind the formation of this committee was strong, and I believe that the House will pay very close attention to your conclusions.

245. PROF. ANTHONY KING: A couple of questions. One of the things that have intrigued me about the answers given by a number of people who have been before us and the impression also given by a good deal of the correspondence is that Members of Parliament themselves are rather at sea on all these issues. I was struck a few moments ago. You were asked by Sir William Utting what ought to be done and you said that that was really the committee's problem. Am I right in inferring from all this that most Members of Parliament probably haven't thought a great deal about these issues, at any rate in detail—they may have general views—but that to some extent we will be, in our report, addressing an audience which, oddly enough, isn't terribly well informed on precisely this matter? Is that correct?

ALEX CARLILE: I think you are absolutely right, Professor King. MPs by and large are totally demand-led, and I think we spend very little time thinking about more abstract and esoteric matters. Most MPs only face these issues when they are slapped across the face by them.

246. PROF. ANTHONY KING: Could I ask you to go into a little bit more detail on a question that Sir William Utting did raise with you, and it refers to paragraph 3 of your letter. I have to confess that in the course of this morning I have gone from confusion to mystification on this. You begin by saying: "Consultancy earnings should not be disproportionate", and I felt sure you were then going on to say that there should be a tariff and that

people's earnings should be revealed, but you then say "It would be impossible to lay down pay scales" and "Members should be entitled to privacy". Then you say: "However, this heightens the responsibility of MPs to obey a strict code of conduct." I would infer from this that the code of conduct would simply say something like "You mustn't earn too much and it's up to you to decide how much too much would be". I am genuinely baffled as to what you have in mind here.

ALEX CARLILE: If I may respectfully put it in this way, I think there is a world of difference between saying that professors who take part in outside activities shouldn't earn too much and that what they earn should be proportionate to their skill. They are very different propositions, and I think the latter proposition is much easier to define in terms which might endure.

247. PROF. ANTHONY KING: But even if that were true, surely the world would need some way of knowing whether that was indeed what the MP was being paid, and no more.

ALEX CARLILE: What I have suggested is that, if the whistle is blown, those who investigate should have the right to know what the MP has been paid and to decide whether that is proportionate. There is therefore a two-stage process: first the MP has to decide for him or herself whether it is proportionate and then, if the whistle is blown, there is an independent scrutiny, including an outside element, as suggested by Lord Nolan.

248. PROF. ANTHONY KING: But what would the strict code of conduct say?

ALEX CARLILE: It is not for me to write the code of conduct. I'm afraid that is your job. But I think that it would make it absolutely clear, amongst other things, that consultancy earnings should be proportionate to the work done and the advice given; and another very important part of it would be that no consultancy or advice given by a Member of Parliament should in any way impinge upon his independence as a Member of Parliament and his ability to act with broad discretion.

249. PETER SHORE: But, following from that, you are clear obviously about MPs being able to—indeed you feel it positively desirable that they should—have other employment, but are you clear that being employed by a public relations firm should be prohibited?

ALEX CARLILE: I haven't dealt with that in my letter, but I do have a clear view on the matter. It is my view that an MP should not be employed by a public relations firm with a broad range of clients so as to be a mouthpiece for that selected group of clients—it is a self-selecting group of clients—who might go to that public relations firm. In the absence of a much better code of conduct covering the way in which lobbying is carried out, I do not believe that lobbying could be sufficiently controlled to make it acceptable for an MP to be employed by a group of consultants in that way.

250. PETER SHORE: The point was put to us earlier on by other witnesses—I don't know whether you were here then—that it is possible to distinguish the two functions of advice and advocacy by a Member of Parliament who is employed by a PR firm. Do you think that such a division, as it were, of activities is really feasible?

ALEX CARLILE: It is feasible for some people but not for others, and I think that maybe some Members of Parliament are good at one but totally incapable of doing the other in an objective way. I think we have to err on the side of caution. I would draw a very clear distinction between a consultancy activity like my own membership of the Bar, which is entirely independent because it is subject only to the instructions you receive, and working for a lobbying organisation, where the instructions you receive have a much more specific applicability to the political arena.

251. LORD NOLAN: But are members of the Bar retained by lobbying firms to present cases?

ALEX CARLILE: I have never been asked if I would be willing to be retained in that way. If I could get away with it under the "cab rank" rule, then I would refuse. I can't answer the question beyond that.

252. CLIFFORD BOULTON: Can I, really just for my own sake, return to the business about registering earnings in addition to interests, because I want to be absolutely clear that you are not wishing to distinguish between earnings that a Member might have in his private capacity for his professional or other work and receipts that he might have for work which provides a parliamentary service. I think what we were trying to get clear is that you would have an objection, would you, to actually declaring those sources of income that a Member had which were actually for parliamentary services? If a Member got £2,000 a year for acting as a consultant to a trade group, so that, from the point of transparency, the public could see that a reward wasn't disproportionate, you would not want that £2,000 a year to be something that had to be registered?

ALEX CARLILE: I think it would be difficult to draw the distinction you posited, because the nature of the professions has changed. As a lawyer I might be instructed in cases on the one hand, and on the other I might be asked to act as a legal adviser of some kind to some company or organisation. One of my constituency predecessors, Clement Davies, who was much respected in the House, was legal adviser to a very large company for a time whilst a Member of the House. I think the difficulty of drawing the distinction would make it impossible to have the type of system you have suggested. I also think that MPs are entitled to a degree of privacy over the earnings which they have, just as they should have a degree of privacy over their private lives. It is more important to have a way of policing the system than to have a register of earnings over which a prurient press and public would swarm like leeches.

253. CLIFFORD BOULTON: Oh, yes. I think the House has always taken the line that there is no public need to know how well off Members are or what their market value is, but if they were receiving payment for a parliamentary service, that could be held to be so closely connected with their public service that the public had a right to know. That is the distinction that I was trying to make.

Can I just mention something which I happen to know we shall agree about, because we have both been concerned with the Industry and Parliament Trust? That is a charitable, non-profit-making body, chaired by the Lord Chancellor and the Speaker as presidents, which exists to meet the perceived need of increased knowledge and information mutually between parliamentarians and commerce and industry, that it is held across the House that it is a good thing that those two should feed each other with information and knowledge. Summing up what you say, you see no objection, so long as it is clear and properly regulated, to Members, in the course of providing that service to industry which can be mutually beneficial, receiving some payment for that, so long as it is according to some properly regulated rules. That is your position.

ALEX CARLILE: That is correct. So long as it doesn't affect their independence and their discretion, and as a trustee and fellow of the Industry and Parliament Trust I regard it as one of the most valuable institutions which have been created in recent years. I wish that it were better funded, so that it could do a greater amount of work.

254. DIANA WARWICK: I rather heard stable doors closing when you were responding to Professor King, and it seems to me that part of the reason for us being set up is that the horse has already bolted. The information on the latest opinion polls is that 64 per cent of the population agree that most MPs make a lot of money by using their public office improperly. It seems to me that quite a lot of the correspondence coming in as evidence to this committee has made a very clear judgment that MPs should only have one job: they are an MP and that is what they should rely on for their income, and I think a lot of that correspondence is actually about money. I don't agree with the fact that money isn't the key issue or that it isn't something that doesn't influence people or isn't perceived to influence people. In those circumstances I think it is very likely that there will be a lot of pressure on this committee to suggest that we ought at least to be identifying what MPs earn. We have learnt what they earn in Parliament, but we should also know just how much money they get from those activities outside. I think it is quite difficult to argue that, given their responsibility to their constituents and to Parliament, only privacy is an issue that will convince people that their income should not be disclosed.

ALEX CARLILE: I think the conclusion that you quoted from the survey is a false and misleading conclusion, because I am absolutely sure that it is based on an entirely false premise. Most MPs do not line their pockets from their public office—very far from it. I am absolutely sure that that is the case.

255. DIANA WARWICK: But why do you think the public have that perception?

ALEX CARLILE: I was reading part of Pepys's diary over the holiday and I think it is a perception that has continued ever since Parliament was created. Horses bolt daily, and I don't really think that's an issue. My view is that this committee has a role to play in enhancing the public view of Parliament if, as I believe it should, it comes to the conclusion that most MPs do not line their pockets from their public office and that what we are dealing with here as a residual problem is the few MPs who may have done so in the past and who have created a situation in which, rightly, suitable codes of practice and rules should be set down to apply to all of us.

LORD NOLAN: It may be as well, on that note, for you to conclude, and a very clear note. Thank you very much for coming along, Mr Carlile. We have been very much helped by your information and advice.

THURSDAY 19 JANUARY 1995

Members Present:

The Rt. Hon. The Lord Nolan (Chairman)

Sir Clifford Boulton GCB
Professor Anthony King
The Rt. Hon. Peter Shore MP

The Rt. Hon. The Lord Thomson of Monifieth KT DL
Sir William Utting CB
Dame Anne Warburton DCVO CMG

Witnesses:

Chris Moncrieff, former Political Editor, Press Association
Rt Hon Lord Callaghan
Harry Barnes MP
Nigel Forman MP

256. LORD NOLAN: Good morning. Our first two days of evidence have helped to clarify the issues. It seems plain from what we have heard so far that the rules for Members of Parliament on connection with lobbyists need to be tightened up, that Members of Parliament need much better guidance on what is and what is not acceptable and that the declaration of certain interests at least should be made in more detail. It also seems reasonably clear that we need to consider in detail the possible introduction of an independent element into Parliament's current arrangements for self-regulation.

What is much less clear is where the boundaries for paid outside interests should lie. This is one of the key issues which we shall wish to explore with today's witnesses. These are Chris Moncrieff, for many years Chief Lobby Correspondent of the Press Association and doyen of political reporters, Lord Callaghan, who needs no further introduction, Harry Barnes, a senior Labour Back Bencher and Nigel Forman, a Conservative Back Bencher and former Minister.

Mr Moncrieff, thank you very much for coming along to join us today. I know this is not your first experience of giving evidence by any means and I hope that you, as we do, can look forward to it. I will ask Mr Shore to put some questions and take you through your evidence.

257. PETER SHORE: Thank you. Mr Moncrieff, how long have you been a Lobby or Parliamentary correspondent?

CHRIS MONCRIEFF

CHRIS MONCRIEFF (Former Political Editor, Press Association): Thirty-three years.

258. PETER SHORE: That is a very substantial period. Thinking over that time as a whole, what key changes have you noticed in both the behaviour of Members of Parliament and in the standards of conduct which are expected of them?

CHRIS MONCRIEFF: What has happened is that, as far as the standards of Members of Parliament are concerned, it is now far more exposed to us than ever it was before. Over the past four or five years there has been a massively increased influx of commercial lobbyist activity in the House of Commons and I think MPs are far more vulnerable now than they have been ever before to outside and commercial pressures. This is certainly very noticeable in the Press Gallery and is something which seems suddenly to have happened.

The lobbyist industry seems to have unexpectedly and suddenly struck a rich vein, which they are exploiting for all they are worth.

259. PETER SHORE: What are the principal ways in which you think these interests are exploiting their new found influence?

CHRIS MONCRIEFF: One way is of course by mail. I was speaking to a Labour MP the other day (not a person of very high profile) and she told me that one third of her very hefty daily mailbag is from commercial lobbyists. That excludes the environmental and so-called "do gooding" lobbyists. I would imagine that her experience is probably repeated throughout the Palace of Westminster.

260. PETER SHORE: I think everyone would accept that there has been a vast increase in mail from commercial lobbying interests and, indeed, from lobbying interests generally, but has there been , in your judgement, a great increase in the actual use of MPs and arrangements between MPs and commercial lobbyists?

CHRIS MONCRIEFF: Yes. It seems to me that there is far more lunching and dining going on in recent years than there ever has been before, involving professional lobbyists and MPs who they think can be of assistance to them. There has been a considerable increase in that activity.

261. PETER SHORE: Yes. Do you think it is possible to say, looking back over this period, that standards of conduct are better or less good than they were when you started as a correspondent in Parliament.

CHRIS MONCRIEFF: That is difficult to answer. I do think that MPs are now more exposed to publicity than before. In recent years the press, including television, has become far more aggressive in its approach to MPs to seek out what they consider wrong doing. Indeed, in some cases, as we know, the press has resorted to acting as an agent provocateur (even, perhaps, as an imposter) to find out what they consider to be the truth. They say that the end justifies the means.

262. PETER SHORE: There certainly has been more aggressive and active scrutinising of parliamentarians and, indeed, of public life generally. But do you think that that is the only reason why there is greater public anxiety about standards of behaviour, or is there cause objectively for concern?

CHRIS MONCRIEFF: I think there is cause objectively for concern; I agree with that. The aggressiveness on the part of the press has arisen to a certain extent from uprated concern. What astonishes me is that some MPs seem to be so gullible in the way they handle people who approach them. I take the view that MPs, generally speaking, are not corrupt and are well intentioned. They fight like Kilkenny cats to get into the House of Commons. Sometimes it takes 10 years to do so and I do not think the money that is offered to them by way of salary and expenses enters into their thinking at all. They are interested in getting into Parliament to do what they think is right for the country. I am astonished by their naivety, some would even say downright stupidity, in handling lobbyists when they have gone to such enormous trouble to get into the House of Commons and sometimes they could foolishly destroy their entire career just by being so naive or even dim.

263. PETER SHORE: To be specific about this, do you think it is naive for a Member of Parliament to engage himself in a commercial relationship with a lobbying firm?

CHRIS MONCRIEFF: I certainly do. If I was an MP I would steer clear of the lobbyist industry like the plague.

264. PETER SHORE: You do not take the view, as I understand it, that MPs should be, as it were, forbidden to do jobs other than being a Member of Parliament?

CHRIS MONCRIEFF: No.

265. PETER SHORE: But you would presumably put a severe limit on what employment they could undertake?

CHRIS MONCRIEFF: Yes. There is an immediate problem because if you happen to be a lawyer and an MP, you can legitimately earn a lot of money on the side. If you happen to be a coal-miner and an MP, you cannot do that at all. There is that problem, but I think that because of the perils of the job—an MP can be thrown out every five years—he ought to be able to pursue his previous career. I also think it should be separated from his political and parliamentary duties.

266. PETER SHORE: That is the crux is it not—that it should be separated from his political and parliamentary duties?

CHRIS MONCRIEFF: Yes.

267. PETER SHORE: Thank you very much for that. Can I ask what reflections you have on the introduction of a Register of Members' interests. Has that helped generally with the question of standards of conduct, or the opposite?

CHRIS MONCRIEFF: I do not think it has made any difference at all, except for causing a certain amount of aggravation. People put down their legitimate earnings from outside and then they get denounced as being greedy or for not doing their parliamentary job properly because they have too many outside interests.

In a way I take the Enoch Powell view (although I accept that it is none of my business), that it is probably best not to have it at all. If you continue to call MPs "honourable" and "right honourable", that should be enough and you should expect them to announce their interests before they speak in a debate or table questions and so on (and I think they do, by and large). Those rules

are by no means so stringent in the House of Commons as they are in local authorities.

268. PETER SHORE: That is a very clear view about the Register of Interests, but given your obvious doubts about its efficacy, do you think it could be improved in some way so that it could serve a more useful purpose and be more effective than it is now?

CHRIS MONCRIEFF: No doubt it could be improved, but I cannot think exactly how. If I was an MP I would resent its existence at all.

269. PETER SHORE: Thank you for that. Let me turn to almost my ultimate question—the business of how the House today investigates and punishes what it believes to be wrong doing, or prima facie cases. Do you think that those procedures are effective or that they need change?

CHRIS MONCRIEFF: As far as we can see, they probably are effective, but from what we hear there seems to be conduct in which MPs engage that is not covered by any rules at all at present. I am not a code of conduct man—generally speaking that is simply a pious list of hopes and aspirations and leaves people content that they have done something about it.

I often think that one way of curbing MPs would be to almost 'wet-nurse' them. When they arrive, new and green, in the House of Commons, they always complain that no-one tells them how to go about it. Somebody should come up and say "You do not talk to lobbyists and if you do, you have to be very careful what you do." A 'wet-nurse' or 'agony aunt' would probably be more effective, certainly than a code of conduct which I would not myself recommend.

PETER SHORE: Perhaps wet-nurses could be combined with codes of conduct.

CHRIS MONCRIEFF: Yes, they might be.

270. PETER SHORE: Lastly, when transgressions of parliamentary rules have taken place, do you think that the punishments available to the House of Commons in judging and dealing with these cases are effective?

CHRIS MONCRIEFF: Where the punishment includes possible expulsion, there is nothing that concentrates the mind more than that. Temporary suspension is a lesser form, but I should imagine that the punishments that are available to the House of Commons authorities may well be adequate.

PETER SHORE: Thank you, Mr Moncrieff.

271. LORD NOLAN: Mr Moncrieff, I wonder if I could take you a little further on that point. Expulsion is a very drastic remedy and it disenfranchises the Member's constituents for ever.

CLIFFORD BOULTON: The suspension would need to be followed by a by-election.

LORD NOLAN: It would need to be followed by a by-election, but so far as he is concerned, the constituents have lost him forever.

CHRIS MONCRIEFF: Not necessarily.

LORD NOLAN: They could re-elect him.

CHRIS MONCRIEFF: Yes.

LORD NOLAN: Subject to that, he is out and disgraced.

CHRIS MONCRIEFF: Yes.

LORD NOLAN: Suspension, again, disenfranchises the voters while it is in force. Those are very severe penalties.

CHRIS MONCRIEFF: Yes.

272. LORD NOLAN: Is there room, do you think, for the introduction of some lesser penalty such as a fine for failure to declare an interest when it should be declared?

CHRIS MONCRIEFF: Yes, I would certainly think there is room for that. But if I may refer to your own remarks, as in the case of a criminal who goes to prison, it is his family who suffers and therefore the MP should think equally of his constituents as a criminal does of his family.

LORD NOLAN: Yes. You were talking about the desirability, as you see it, of having some form of guidance for new Members of Parliament.

CHRIS MONCRIEFF: Yes.

273. LORD NOLAN: What had you in mind? Guidance from senior Members of the House as a body or from Members of their own Party?

CHRIS MONCRIEFF: Yes, I think so. We are constantly being told by MPs in private conversations that they learn the ropes themselves—they stagger around in the dark and sort it out alone. I am sure that there is a case for senior Members of all political parties to groom their newcomers and, as I said, wet-nurse them, so that they do at least know the perils that confront them. As an MP you can destroy your whole career almost by accident. You can do something wrong without realising it and these perils should be drawn to their attention. It is really dereliction of duty for senior MPs not to do this for new arrivals.

LORD NOLAN: Yes. There are of course many others beside senior MPs, for example, the Clerk of the House and no doubt the Speaker who could advise them.

CHRIS MONCRIEFF: Indeed.

274. LORD NOLAN: I realise it would be difficult, but would it be helpful to have some uniform notes for guidance that could be handed to a new MP when he arrived?

CHRIS MONCRIEFF: I think it would, but I am a great one for the personal touch and a homely chat is probably more useful. A little document pointing out the perils, obstacles and minefields that lie ahead would obviously be helpful.

LORD NOLAN: Thank you very much. I am now going to ask other Members of the Committee if they would like to put questions to you. Lord Thomson?

275. LORD THOMSON: Mr Moncrieff, in view of the increased pressures that have arisen over the past few years and which you have been describing so vividly, do you think that the rules in regard to making declarations of interest require to be more stringent? For example, I think I am right in saying that there is no obligation to declare an interest when you are putting down or asking a Parliamentary question. I am told, although it is now 20 years since I was in the House of Commons, that declarations of interest in speeches are less frequent than they used to be because people feel that once they have entered their interests in the Register, they have done their job and there is no need for a verbal declaration. What is your comment on that?

CHRIS MONCRIEFF: I agree. If I had anything to do with it, I would abolish the Register of Interests straight away and resort to Members having to declare their interests orally (or possibly in writing in the case of tabling a question) on each relevant occasion, subject to some sanction if they do not. That is enough and a Register of Interests is actually an insult to MPs.

276. LORD THOMSON: I can see that there is a practical problem about a verbal declaration of interest when asking an oral question, but would it be practicable, for example, to ensure that Members putting down questions, either for oral or written answer, make a declaration of interests when they do so and that it should have some kind of asterisk or symbol attached to it on the order paper so that everybody knows that this is a question asked in relation to a declared interests?

CHRIS MONCRIEFF: Yes, I agree with that, but particularly during Prime Minister's questions, in the case of supplementary questions there might be perhaps just a form of words—"I have an interest to declare in this."—and then you have made that point and afterwards you can expiate on it.

LORD THOMSON: Yes, that is a very important point for supplementaries, which are spontaneous, or semi-spontaneous anyway.

CHRIS MONCRIEFF: Yes.

LORD THOMSON: There may be some way of declaring an interest there.

CHRIS MONCRIEFF: Yes.

LORD NOLAN: Sir William?

277. WILLIAM UTTING: Thank you, Chairman. I want less to put a question than to carry on with a point you raised for discussion about the Register of Interests and codes of conduct. I am sympathetic to your view that it is a shame to have to introduce systems like that, but I am sceptical about the feasibility of doing away with them and going back to an honour system in a situation in which the honour of individual MPs is being consistently impugned. In other words, if we have a Register, we are probably stuck with it. There is a case for saying that if you are dealing with 600 individuals, it may be safer to continue to rely on a system, say of a register and a code of conduct, than to go back to an honours system.

The point really was, do you think it is feasible to go back to something that puts the onus entirely on the honour and judgement of individual Members of Parliament?

CHRIS MONCRIEFF: I am afraid I do.

WILLIAM UTTING: Don't be afraid about it! I think it is a commendable view.

CHRIS MONCRIEFF: The very existence of the Register of Interests implies that you might think some MPs are not as honourable as others. In the world in which we live, that may well be true, but everybody is called an honourable Member or a right honourable Member and they should have the opportunity to exhibit that honour in the way they declare it before making speeches on subjects in which they have an interest. I think that the Register of Interests should be consigned to the flames.

WILLIAM UTTING: I am delighted to hear that and reassured by your conviction about the goodness of individual human beings. I have to say that I retain some scepticism about its feasibility.

CHRIS MONCRIEFF: Yes.

278. WILLIAM UTTING: Could I move onto something that is of more direct professional relevance to you. You said earlier that in some respects the press might have contributed to the problems we have at the moment, by the way in which it reports certain issues, or by certain forms of investigative journalism that amount almost to operating as agents provocateurs.

CHRIS MONCRIEFF: Yes.

279. WILLIAM UTTING: Have the standards of press reporting and interest changed in a worrying fashion over the past 30 years or so? One wants the press to be investigative in an ethical way, because it is one of our bulwarks against the misuse of political power. Is what you said something that we ought to be seriously worried about?

CHRIS MONCRIEFF: I do not necessarily think you should be seriously worried about it (or worried about it at all), it is simply something that 30 years ago would never have happened—a move by a newspaper or any other part of the media to try to entrap an MP into doing something which he should not do.

It is for other people to argue the morality of all that, but it is a new development which I think is here to stay. It is an added peril for MPs, but I do not think it is anything to worry about; it is something for MPs to worry about and, of course, we know that another body is examining a certain case and, no doubt, will come up with a view about that. It is not something that I like.

As a reporter, all I am interested in is finding stories that will sell newspapers. I am not interested in going beyond that, but other papers are and they make it their business now to act in some cases almost like the CID.

280. WILLIAM UTTING: Yes, but you would not go so far as some extreme views put to us, that what people are concerned about now is something that has been manufactured by the press and does not have much basis in reality?

CHRIS MONCRIEFF: If I understand you, there is certainly an exaggerated view in the press (and therefore, probably, in the country as a whole) about the scale of alleged corruption among MPs. I believe it is virtually non-existent. This exaggerated view can be fanned by certain press activities and that does go on.

WILLIAM UTTING: Thank you very much.

281. CLIFFORD BOULTON: Can I just come back to your view of the Register because you said earlier that you did not feel Members should touch money if it is for a parliamentary service. You had no objection to them carrying on with their trade, profession or making money privately, but you thought they should not take money in connection with the provision of a service as part of their parliamentary work. Is that right?

CHRIS MONCRIEFF: Yes.

282. CLIFFORD BOULTON: In that case, if it were banned, there would be a case for throwing away the Register, because that would be about private activities and nothing to do with anybody else. Therefore you would be content that so long as they declared, if they were a farmer or something, that they were a farmer when they got up to speak on agricultural matters, you would be content with that without a Register?

CHRIS MONCRIEFF: I would, certainly, yes.

283. CLIFFORD BOULTON: The present situation is that they are allowed to take on remunerated employment which involves a parliamentary service.

In a note that you sent us you mentioned the activities of lobbyists, how prevalent and active they were and what a nuisance they were. You then said, "But there is no way, whatever rules are devised, of keeping them at bay, even if access to the Commons was restricted, which would anyway be impossible to monitor and be unfair." Are you saying that if we came up with some accepted rules to ban payment for parliamentary services, that would end up by being evaded and that there is so much money around and so much pressure from industry, commerce and other interests that other ways would be found that were not regulated and open, of remunerating or giving money's worth to Members?

CHRIS MONCRIEFF: Yes. Every time there is a budget, there is a whole army of accountants abroad who find loopholes almost the next day. Obviously if bans and embargoes were applied to one part of the system, someone would think of new idea and it would flourish elsewhere. I do not think you can stop that, but I do not know how you can diminish the activities of lobbyists at Westminster at all. You cannot keep them out of the building so I do not know how you can do it.

284. CLIFFORD BOULTON: If it is going to go on, there might be something to be said at least for having some rules about it and having it in the open and known about?

CHRIS MONCRIEFF: Yes, but there will be cases of underhand activities whatever sanctions are imposed or brought in by Parliament. The way to attack this problem is through the MPs, by warning them of the perils and making sure that they do not act as stool pigeons for the lobbyists.

285. CLIFFORD BOULTON: Yes. I was thinking less of people who were thought of as stool pigeons, and more of those who actually speak on behalf of whatever it might be (the Police Federation or the University Teachers) and get a fee for that. Are you saying that you would ban that?

CHRIS MONCRIEFF: I find that difficult to answer. I am not sure. I have a feeling that if you are representing the Police Federation, you should probably do it voluntarily.

286. WILLIAM UTTING: You would be minded to say, on balance, that it is not appropriate to take a fee for that service?

CHRIS MONCRIEFF: Yes.

287. WILLIAM UTTING: Can I touch briefly on another point you mentioned, which is what some people see as an anomaly between members of local authorities and MPs as far as expenses and ability to vote is concerned.

CHRIS MONCRIEFF: Yes.

WILLIAM UTTING: The classic defence or explanation of the present situation is that councillors are more like Ministers: they are doing an executive job, giving contracts, employing people and doing things, whereas MPs are just talking and that therefore there is a valid distinction.

CHRIS MONCRIEFF: Right.

288. WILLIAM UTTING: Do you think it is not really valid?

CHRIS MONCRIEFF: There is certainly an aura of unfairness about it and the point you have just made has not actually been driven home. A lot of councillors are aggrieved at what they consider to be an anomalous position. They can be brought to personal financial ruin, even accidentally, in wrongfully incurring expenditure of public funds. Although as you say MPs just do the talking, there seems to be no sanction on them.

There was a specific case a few years ago involving salmonella and eggs. I know that involved a Minister, but if that had been a councillor, he or she would have been in Carey Street by now I should have thought.

WILLIAM UTTING: Yes, but it does make the case about it being a Minister.

CHRIS MONCRIEFF: Yes, it does.

WILLIAM UTTING: As you are aware, Members have a rule that they cannot vote on anything where they have a personal interest which is not a matter of public policy.

CHRIS MONCRIEFF: Yes.

289. WILLIAM UTTING: It is just possible that a bit of educating needs to be done on the difference between the Back Bencher and the Minister?

CHRIS MONCRIEFF: Yes, but this was a Minister and she lost her job, but suffered no personal financial loss, as far as I understand.

290. WILLIAM UTTING: Yes, but what we are saying is that perhaps the rules for Ministers ought to be more in line with those for councillors?

CHRIS MONCRIEFF: Yes.

291. WILLIAM UTTING: Not the Back Benchers?

CHRIS MONCRIEFF: Yes, thank you.

LORD NOLAN: Dame Anne?

292. ANNE WARBURTON: Thank you. I was also interested in that point and perhaps I might just follow up on one aspect of it, Mr Moncrieff—the voting question. You are not the only person who suggests that MPs should not vote where they have personal interests, but the point that was made against that is that this disenfranchises their constituents.

CHRIS MONCRIEFF: I agree that it does, but I do not see how you can overcome that. That happens in local authorities now. Somebody has to give somewhere, and if an MP is not allowed to vote on a particular issue, then his constituents will just have to suffer on that particular issue.

293. ANNE WARBURTON: Good. I wonder if I might go back to a point on lobbying. Yesterday we were making a distinction (which has perhaps not been made quite so clearly this morning) between lobbying by people who are known to represent the brewing industry or something of that nature and lobbying by people who have a whole portfolio of different issues which they support.

CHRIS MONCRIEFF: Yes.

ANNE WARBURTON: In your dislike of lobbyists, do you make a distinction?

CHRIS MONCRIEFF: As far as I know, I am innocent in the sense that nobody bothers to lobby me, so I do not know what precisely they do. But, if this is your point, there are occasions when I think MPs are not necessarily told the whole, unvarnished truth by the lobbyists about their game. Frankly, I do not know how that can be overcome.

294. ANNE WARBURTON: I think some people feel that in this complicated world in which we live, you need to be lobbied from all directions in order to find out your core of truth and where you want to stand. Because you are lobbied by one person or point of view does not mean that you have only that view.

CHRIS MONCRIEFF: No, but the scale of lobbying that goes on now is a fairly recent phenomenon and as far as I know, in years gone by, MPs got by quite happily without being lobbied at all.

295. ANNE WARBURTON: That perhaps is all I want to ask. I hesitate a bit on your last point, because it could simply be said to be a result of the more high speed world we live in that you have no time to do your own research and therefore count on other people to do it for you and to present a case.

How do you define lobbying? If a firm or representatives of a particular interest put on a presentation and invite all Members to come, is that lobbying?

CHRIS MONCRIEFF: It is and this is a point that has occurred to me. How small does it have to be? You can be taken out to lunch (and that happens every day, I have no doubt), but that is part of it. I suppose one cannot go to ridiculous levels and condemn everything, but certainly the large scale, high powered lobbying that goes on now is far different from an odd lunch a few years ago.

ANNE WARBURTON: Thank you, Mr Moncrieff.

296. PETER SHORE: Just one further question, if I may come back. In your long period of being associated with the Parliamentary Lobby, would you say that there has been a considerable growth of public relations activities, not just of the general kind that you mentioned—ie circulating all MPs with letters, bombarding them with this and that, having them to lunch—but actually MPs being engaged in a paid relationship with public relations firms? Have you been aware that that is on the increase in recent years?

CHRIS MONCRIEFF: Yes.

297. PETER SHORE: And if so, what do you put it down to?

CHRIS MONCRIEFF: I put all these things down to the fact that the lobbyist industry has suddenly discovered this rich seam at Westminster. They suddenly realised what they had not before and therefore a lot more of it goes on. You only have to look at Vacher's to see the number of lobbying firms that are sprouting up and this is, as you know, where they advertise.

298. PETER SHORE: Not only the firms are multiplying and increasing, but the number of Members of Parliament who have a commercial business relationship with them?

CHRIS MONCRIEFF: Yes. I have to contradict myself in a way now, because this is evident from the Members' Interests Register, which I attacked.

PETER SHORE: Yes, thank you.

299. LORD NOLAN: One final question from me, Mr Moncrieff. The press has a system of self-regulation, as does the House of Commons.

CHRIS MONCRIEFF: Yes.

LORD NOLAN: In other organisations, in the professions, for example, in recent years it has been found better to have an element of independent inquiry into complaints against members of the profession. Do you think this would be helpful? I do not ask you about the press, but would it be helpful in speeding up, making more open and fair the inquiries into what is said to have gone wrong in the House of Commons?

CHRIS MONCRIEFF: I am not sure that it would. By creating that, you are inventing another quango really. I sometimes think that MPs are old enough to go out on their own. They should be able to look after themselves better without a whole new body independently overseeing them.

300. LORD NOLAN: Yes. Thank you, that is very clear. From what you were saying about naive and sometimes, with respect, even dim, MPs, I wonder whether it might concentrate their minds if, when first coming into Parliament, they had to take, as well as the Oath of Allegiance, some simple, additional form of oath, saying that they would at all times uphold the honour and dignity of Parliament. Judges take an oath to "do justice to all manner of men, without fear or favour, affection or ill will" and it means something.

CHRIS MONCRIEFF: Yes.

LORD NOLAN: Do you think that might concentrate the mind of a new Member on the standards of good sense as well as good behaviour that he is expected to maintain?

CHRIS MONCRIEFF: Yes, I think that is a good idea. I would applaud that, if I may make so bold.

LORD NOLAN: You have been very helpful and interesting. We are all extremely grateful to you for coming along, Mr Moncrieff. Thank you very much.

CHRIS MONCRIEFF: Thank you.

301. LORD NOLAN: I am very glad to see that Lord Callaghan is now here. I would be grateful, Lord Callaghan, if you would please come and sit in the chair in front of me.

If I may start with your entry into the House of Commons, this I think was in the year 1945, just after you had left the Royal Navy at the end of the war, and you became the Member of Parliament for Cardiff South in the Labour cause. That is 50 years ago. In what ways since then have the pressures, and especially the commercial pressures, on public figures, Members of Parliament and Ministers changed?

RT HON LORD CALLAGHAN

RT HON LORD CALLAGHAN: May I say how much I welcome the appointment of this Committee. Time is overdue to redefine what is acceptable conduct by a Member of Parliament and I hope that you will be able to do that, because the situation has changed very considerably. There is much more wooing of Members of Parliament by business than there ever was in 1945.

Companies have found that this is a useful way of informing Members and much legitimate work goes on to inform them. Members of Parliament can be better informed than they ever were in my day about the needs of industry and what it requires from government. That is all absolutely legitimate and proper, but following up what I heard Mr Moncrieff say, when he talked about a rich seam for lobbyists, the number of which has grown very considerably in the past 20 years, I think a number of companies are naive in believing that it is necessary to have some kind of contact man in order to have their case put properly. A lot of money has been made by public relations firms and lobbyists quite unnecessarily in getting information across to Members of Parliament when there is no need to do anything of the sort. A company can find its own way around perfectly properly.

The short answer to your question is, yes. There is much more wooing of Members of Parliament now. When I first came into the House, I knew of only one gentleman who did that. He wore a frock coat; he had a top hat; he used to sit on the horsehair sofas in the Central Lobby and see the occasional Member. If I may continue for one moment, it was so unknown, that when the Garry Allighan case came up in 1946, the Prime Minister, who introduced the report, said that he understood that there were such people as contact men. He had to say that for himself he had never heard of the phrase until the Garry Allighan case. That reflects entirely the difference between then and now.

302. LORD NOLAN: Yes. We heard from Mr Moncrieff of one Member of the House (who, he said, was fairly junior) who got a third of her mail from commercial lobbying organisations. How should Members of Parliament coming fresh to the House handle that?

LORD CALLAGHAN: This has increased very much. For myself, I hate (I daresay, in company with a great many other Members of Parliament) the arrival of those very large, brown envelopes. We know what rubbish they are going to contain and one dare not put them into the wastepaper basket unopened, much as one would like to. How can that be dealt with?

I wrote down nine or ten suggestions for the Committee, but I do not want to bore you by going through them.

LORD NOLAN: Indeed you will not.

LORD CALLAGHAN: Could I then take two or three minutes to do it?

LORD NOLAN: If you please.

LORD CALLAGHAN: First, the obvious thing: as you will understand and I have already made clear, I hope you will be able to draw up a set of principles of conduct that will govern Members' financial interests.

Secondly, I would suggest that the code, when drawn up and accepted by the House, should be adopted afresh by the House of Commons at the beginning of every Parliament after a general election, preferably not on the nod—in the way so many sessional orders go through—but perhaps after a debate, so that every new Member would understand what was expected of him and what was the normal code of behaviour for a Member of Parliament in relation to his interests.

303. LORD NOLAN: If I may interrupt you there, at the risk of taking a little more time over the oath, would it help if each Member, or at any rate each new Member, undertook to subscribe to the code of conduct?

LORD CALLAGHAN: I am not very strong on that.

LORD NOLAN: No.

LORD CALLAGHAN: I think what we have to encourage is a sense of the dignity of the House in a Member—a phrase that you have used—and a sense of the honour of being a Member of Parliament, so that I would not regard that as adding very much to it. But if it were thought to be right, I would not disagree.

Thirdly, I think that this code ought to be handed to every new Member after a by-election, so that he is aware of what is expected.

The Privileges Committee should be restored to the awe in which it was held when I first came into Parliament. It has slipped very badly in the eyes of Members of the House in recent years. It is used less often than it was when I first came into Parliament. I do not think they should wait to be told by the House, as they are now, before they start an investigation into a possible breach. The Privileges Committee ought to take the initiative itself if it feels that there is a case, but it should sit in private, in fairness to the Member concerned.

Next, I would add an independent element to the Committee. On the Committee itself, Members should be a majority, but I would not object at all to an independent element being added, if only to satisfy the perception of the public about the integrity of what is being done.

I am not sure about the present membership of the Privileges Committee, but I have a feeling that it is not now composed wholly of the most senior Members of the House. It was so in my day and that gave it the sense of dignity and superiority which is necessary for a Committee of this sort.

My next point would be that Members should deposit copies of any agreements and contracts they have made with outside bodies and they should declare the remuneration they receive for the work they do. This is not a new thought on my part; I took part in a debate on 15 July 1947, 48 years ago, when I made exactly this point—that agreements and contracts made with outside bodies should be reviewed by the House of Commons.

304. LORD NOLAN: Is this agreements relating to their work as Members?

LORD CALLAGHAN: No, to their work for outside bodies, especially where there is paid remuneration. I draw a distinction between a Member who is particularly interested, say, in the King George's Fund for Sailors, any other charity of that sort or the National Children's Bureau and paid remuneration for acting as a director or as a trades union secretary or anything of that sort. Indeed, I was referring to trades union agreements in 1947 when I made this proposal myself. I was not alone at the time, but nothing happened.

My seventh point is that the Privileges Committee should not be hesitant, as I have a feeling it is a bit now, to use its powers to recommend disciplinary action. What it does should obviously relate to the gravity of any small offences. You might have the formality of naming a Member, which is not taken very seriously but ought to be taken seriously, or something of that sort, up to a suspension from the service of the House. Suspension from the House would involve loss of pay as well as the ignominy that would accompany it and I believe it would help to remind Members of the way in which they should act in these matters.

My eighth point is that Members should not act as consultants to represent a firm's interest to Ministers—that should be debarred as a practice—but I draw a distinction with a Member who has a specialised professional knowledge that is drawn from his past experience. He should certainly be free, without any feeling that he is doing something wrong, to advise a company from his specialised experience, but he should not be free to carry that to the point of representing their affairs to Ministers. I do not know whether I am making that point clear but I feel it would be wrong for a Member not to be able to use his professional knowledge in order to assist a firm if he feels it is right to do so, but not to take part in any transaction or to represent it to Ministers in relation to the work of that company.

Quangos—I am appalled by what is happening and has happened and I hope that you will make a very searching enquiry into the method and type of appointments. I have no particular recommendations to make but I know from anecdotal evidence that there has been an abuse of patronage in that area.

My tenth point is the use of the facilities of the House by lobbyists. This is getting almost to the point of abuse where, because lobbyists seem able to get hold of rooms, and this sort of thing, the interests of the ordinary Member, especially a Member who has interests that are not commercial, are very difficult to satisfy. There is only a limited number of rooms and dining facilities, and the rest of it, and the use of the facilities by these lobbying firms should certainly be curtailed. Finally, on the appointment of Ministers to firms with whom they have had dealings, a very firm restriction should be put on that. I think privatisation has emphasised that point.

As regards civil servants: I would suggest, if I may, that you should look at what the practice was about retired civil servants. I have the impression that there was a much longer period a few years ago before civil servants were able to join a firm with whom they had had dealings or not as the case may be. I believe that period has been shortened over a period of years from, perhaps, two years right down now to a matter of months before they can join. This is especially the case because of the privatisation of the Civil Service, if I may call it such. I think you will know what I mean. I use that as a shorthand.

May I conclude by saying that having made these points I think most people who join the House of Commons as Members are as animated with the idea of public service as they were 50 years ago. Although public service has been scorned during the 1980s and the ideal of public service needs to be enthroned again, nevertheless most Members of Parliament feel that very strongly and I trust you would find that is so in your investigations. That is where I start from.

305. LORD NOLAN: Thank you very much. You know the old saying in the courts that it is not enough for justice to be done, justice must also clearly be seen to be done and this is an aspect of the problem which has been brought home very forcibly to us by the media and by our correspondence. If I may speak for a moment of my own profession, the Bar. In the past we reckoned that we were pretty straight and if we had any black sheep we could sort them out ourselves. This was not good enough and so there is now a published code of conduct. Every new barrister undertakes to abide by it. If he fails to do so he is hauled up before a disciplinary committee on which there is outside representation. Would you agree that that has been a good thing for the professions to adopt that kind of approach to the greater openness of their internal discipline?

LORD CALLAGHAN: Yes, I think that is implicit, if not explicit, in some of the things I have already said. I do not think we need a separate body. If the Privileges

Committee acts with sufficient determination and with a proper sense of the dignity of what is required of a Member of Parliament there are sufficient people there to handle it. In order to satisfy the public I would say that the perception would be improved if there was an outside element. I think many Members of the House of Commons will object to it but I still think it would be in their interests to accept it.

306. LORD NOLAN: I wonder if one possible approach might be to appoint an Officer of the House, if you like, somebody with the status of the Ombudsman, the Parliamentary Commissioner, who would carry out an independent and, no doubt, initially private investigation into matters of fact, whether that would produce a quicker and, apparently, fairer form of enquiry than individual Members busy with other matters having to do the enquiry themselves. Would you think there might be scope for that?

LORD CALLAGHAN: I am not very much in favour of an Officer of the House doing it. They are servants of the House and should be regarded as such. It is somewhat analogous in my mind to asking the Permanent Secretary to the Treasury to investigate Ministers, which I think was a very improper way of behaving. If we are going to do that I would have somebody separately from the Officers of the House outside in order to conduct such a preliminary investigation.

LORD NOLAN: I was not suggesting somebody who was an existing Officer but somebody from outside who would be given this job by the House.

LORD CALLAGHAN: Yes, that could be done. In that case he should be paid from the Consolidated Fund.

307. LORD NOLAN: So far as this vexed problem is concerned of defining the permissible types of outside interest, Sir Clifford Boulton has researched for us a resolution of the House in 1695—300 years ago—prohibiting Members from accepting—

"any fee, compensation or reward in connection with the promotion of, or opposition to, any Bill, resolution, matter or thing submitted, or intended to be submitted, to the House or any Committee thereof."

In other words, you cannot be paid for anything you do that is going to come before Parliament. That is a clear rule, is it not?

LORD CALLAGHAN: I think it is.

LORD NOLAN: It has been altered, of course, since. When the Register of Members' Interests was introduced that contemplated that Members could be paid for matters connected with their duties in Parliament.

LORD CALLAGHAN: Yes. I think also before that, if I may say so with deference to Sir Clifford Boulton. When I was in the House in 1947 we passed a similar resolution in the very debate to which I referred before in which I took part. If I might read it to you. I will not read the whole lot but it states:

"It is inconsistent with the dignity of the House ..."

I think that is a very important phrase that Members ought to be more aware of—maintaining the dignity of the House—because if that is not maintained then democracy itself is undermined and maintaining the dignity of the House is extremely important. This resolution states that it was inconsistent with the dignity of the House—

" ... for any Member of this House to enter into any contractual agreement with an outside body controlling or limiting the Member's independence and freedom of action in Parliament or stipulating that he shall act in any way as the representative of such outside body in regard to any matters to be transacted in Parliament."

That is a slightly fuller definition than 1695 but, to me, that meets the case.

308. ANNE WARBURTON: Was the resolution adopted?

LORD CALLAGHAN: Yes. That was a report from the Privileges Committee that was adopted at the time.

309. LORD NOLAN: But that, I am told, does not stop you from taking money for acting for outside interests as, indeed, people do, do they not? There are lobbyists for organisations and you, yourself, were, in a sense, a representative, is this right, of the Police Federation in your early days. What did that involve?

LORD CALLAGHAN: I am not against Members having outside paid interests if it can be reconciled with their duty to the House and their constituents. I think it can add something to the House. We will come on to the pressure on Members later if you care to. It stipulates that he shall not act in any way as the representative of such outside body in regard to any matter to be transacted in Parliament. That is where the difference comes. If he acts as a director of a company then he is using his interests there and I regard that as a very different thing from acting in their interests in relation to a matter to be transacted in Parliament.

With regard to my own position on the Police Federation, and I think there is another aspect too that you would like to talk about. I certainly was not a lobbyist. I was their leader. You may be interested to know what the point was. The police were badly underpaid and morale was very low. They had one Metropolitan constable who was seconded in order to be able to handle their wage negotiations. They were quite incapable of doing so. They went to the TUC and said that they had a big wage claim coming on would the TUC help and the General Secretary of the TUC said he did not think they could but why did they not go to that man Callaghan who had great experience of arbitration and arbitration procedures. So, they came to me and asked me to tell them what to do and how to do it. I did and, indeed, I wrote the evidence.

I found myself up against Gerald Gardiner QC representing the employers. With all respect to the Metropolitan constable on loan, I had a tough enough job with a future Lord Chancellor. That was their staff—one Metropolitan constable on loan and a shorthand typist—so I took over the Police Federation for the time being and I told them that my task was to put them into a position where, when I left, they would be able to handle

their own affairs. That is true. I believe they now have relations with Members of Parliament who do not do that sort of thing. I used to go round the country addressing great meetings of a thousand constables at a time. It was a most exhilarating period. I was a keen trade unionist and I built them up into a position where they were certainly capable of getting all the information, knowledge and representation they want today. I was very proud of doing that. To some extent it cut across transactions in Parliament. I never thought about the theory of this at the time but I think that can be justified on the grounds that their remuneration and their conditions of service were determined by the Home Office as well as by the local authorities jointly. If I were asked to do it today I would justify it on those grounds.

310. LORD NOLAN: It involved speaking up for them in the House, did it?

LORD CALLAGHAN: No, they never asked me to do so. I had no contract, no agreement, with them. Some former Tory MP said in the newspapers I was paid £20,000 a year but my recollection is that it was £500. I would have done it for nothing, I so enjoyed it. Never did they attempt to put any restriction on me, in fairness to them and, indeed, to myself. For example, they were very much in favour of hanging. They never asked me to be in favour of hanging; they knew I would not have done it. I was very much opposed to hanging and they never questioned me on that when I voted consistently in the House of Commons in favour of the abolition of hanging, of capital punishment. There is a second point I think you wish to make about this, is there?

311. LORD NOLAN: There is a second point concerned with the existing Register of Interests and the fact that it is not statutory, it is not fully observed. Enoch Powell, as a matter of principle I think, refused to go by it. Mr. Moncrieff says he thinks it is a great mistake but, by and large, it is observed. One journalist has drawn our attention to a newspaper report last report that you, it is said, failed to register a payment to you for secretarial services. Would you like to deal with that?

LORD CALLAGHAN: I had some sympathy with Enoch Powell. He had what is perhaps an old fashioned approach to the dignity of Parliament and the dignity of a Member of Parliament and his honour and I have sympathy with this. I happened to be holding a Ministerial post and I thought I had better follow the general rule. I am sorry if this is old fashioned but in the end I regard the sense of propriety of a Member of Parliament himself as to what he should do as being the ultimate test.

As regards this payment that was made to me, with respect, for the reason I am going to give, I do not think it is germane to your own enquiry. During the whole of the time I was in Parliament I did not accept that kind of money but when I reached the last few months of my 42 years in the House of Commons I was faced with the situation that I would have no secretarial assistance afterwards at all. At that time no payment was made to a former Prime Minister for that sort of thing. It was, I think, six or seven months before I left Parliament that I was engaged in an international examination, under the chairmanship of the former President of Switzerland and with its headquarters in New York, an examination of how we could relieve the Third World of its debt problems. It became known that I would, obviously, not have financial assistance after I left Parliament and I accepted this in order to enable me to employ a secretary and a research assistant. I would not have been able to do so otherwise. I emphasise to you, and this is why I do not think it is germane to your enquiry, that this was in the last few months; it was when I was looking ahead to the time when I left Parliament and, frankly, it did not occur to me whether I should have put it on the register or not because I was looking to the period when I left, which happened to be the following May, or something.

312. LORD NOLAN: We have, I hope, made it clear all the way along that all our witnesses come alone here as volunteers to help us to look at the rules and see if they can be improved and we are not concerned to investigate individual cases, still less to criticise people who come along and tell us about them. Thank you, Lord Callaghan, you have dealt with it very clearly.

On the subject of the register as we have it, your ten principles involve quite a substantial variation of it, do they not?

LORD CALLAGHAN: Yes, they do.

313. LORD NOLAN: I was not quite clear about the registration of outside contracts; were you limiting it to contracts affecting the Member's work in Parliament?

LORD CALLAGHAN: No, I do not think so. I think that anybody who has an outside paid employment, it would be no hardship to him to deposit it, not just register it but to deposit it. If the idea that you yourself have put forward, Sir, were adopted then they could easily be reviewed by whoever was acting.

314. LORD NOLAN: But am I not right in thinking that you are a farmer. You have been a farmer as well as your other activities. A farmer cannot register all his outside contracts, can he, there would be no point in his doing so unless they were connected with the House?

LORD CALLAGHAN: I must say I had not thought of it. You get very little income from being a farmer.

315. LORD NOLAN: Or any business or professional man entering into contracts in the course of his business?

LORD CALLAGHAN: No, this is where the committee is going to have a lot of difficulty in defining what should be registered and what should not.

316. LORD NOLAN: Perhaps if we go back to those old resolutions we would get a clearer line? If we were to say that there should be no pay for doing the work of an MP that would be clear?

LORD CALLAGHAN: Yes. I think a farmer would claim that he does not get paid anyway. His income goes back into the farm. You know what they say about them, that they are always cash poor—they live poor and die rich because most of their wealth is in the capital and farm. They do not really get incomes. It varies so much from year to year. I am afraid I am going to leave this problem with you. I do not think I have a suggestion to offer off the cuff. If I have one, I will communicate with you.

317. LORD NOLAN: To sum up, Lord Callaghan, because I know others will wish to take advantage of your

presence with us, do you think that there has been a change for the worse in standards in public life over the years in which you have taken part in it and have you any general thoughts on the way forward?

LORD CALLAGHAN: Yes. The values of society have changed so much in the past 20 years as to be almost unrecognisable. Parliament does not exist in a social vacuum. It is almost inevitable that if the standards of society change that Parliament is going to reflect that for better or worse and I think it has done so and, in my view, that has meant that it is rather worse. New younger Members come in imbued with the doctrines of the marketplace—the necessity to make a profit margin on everything you do. One reason why firms have been welcomed into the hospitality of the House of Commons—it helps to lessen the subsidy that is paid to the House of Commons for using the facilities. It may be a small illustration but it is an illustration of what has happened.

I think the demands on Members are very much greater than they were when I came in. They have to work very much harder. I talked to my successor about this in Cardiff South and he has given me a breakdown of his correspondence, he kept it for me. I should say that it is at least two or three times as big as when I left the House even seven years ago. The demands of constituents are much greater. I am slightly appalled at the amount of time Members have to spend on their constituents. Members of Parliament have other responsibilities than that. Now we have all these charters and everybody has all these rights, and so on. I am going to use these terrible terms that we all use—middle class, working class—it is the middle class who have begun to articulate their problems and their difficulties much more than they did and they are much more prolific with the pen. This is one reason why I think it was very important, and is very important, that Members of Parliament should hold regular constituency surgeries because it is the people who are not as articulate, cannot write as well, who I used to prefer to spend my time on rather than those who could articulate well but wanted to use their Member of Parliament in order to save themselves a certain amount of trouble. I think Members of Parliament have a much tougher time than when I entered 50 years ago and it has become much harder even during the past 10 or 20 years. If democracy is to work satisfactorily then this must be recognised and they must have adequate facilities to do their job.

318. LORD NOLAN: I think you say that there has been a decline in standards generally and Members of Parliament have not escaped it. Is that a fair way of putting it?

LORD CALLAGHAN: There has been a change in standards. The word "decline"; I suppose one has to define it. I am not absolutely sure about that. For example, in matters of personal morality which you are not particularly concerned with but certainly the public is concerned with it. Whether the change in standards is better or worse. Twenty-five years ago no one would have thought of young people living together and having children without marriage. Now, is that better or worse? I think many people would argue that it is worse but, certainly, it is a change that seems to have been accepted by society.

LORD NOLAN: Thank you very much. I am going to go round the table, if I may, and ask the others if they would like to raise matters. Dame Anne?

319. ANNE WARBURTON: Thank you, Chairman. Most of the points which came up during the discussion have been followed up already, but there is one question I would like to put. How about the House of Lords? We have been talking entirely about the House of Commons.

LORD CALLAGHAN: Yes, I would certainly think there is a strong case for some kind of arrangement in the House of Lords that would follow the House of Commons, although it would not be exactly the same because it could be argued that Members of the House of Lords are not paid and, therefore, they are not expected to derive their living there. I do not know how strongly I would push that forward but, subject to that, yes, there is a committee of the House of Lords looking into it at the present time and I would hope that they would come down in favour of registration.

320. ANNE WARBURTON: A register of interests, again, with an outside element?

LORD CALLAGHAN: I had not thought about it. Yes, yes, a modified yes.

ANNE WARBURTON: Thank you very much.

321. PETER SHORE: I shall not take advantage of your presence to ask you questions across the whole field because you really have provided us with an enormous amount of very interesting suggestions. But, Lord Callaghan, I would like to go back to what I thought was a very fundamental point that you made when you quoted, I think it was the 1947 resolution of the House which, in many ways, seemed to me to restate the 1695 resolution to which Lord Nolan had himself referred.

Why is it that the 1947 resolution and approach has not been reiterated in Parliament and, perhaps, developed to deal with any matters which were not really covered by it. Do you think that Parliament has, as it were, deliberately turned its back on the 1947 approach?

LORD CALLAGHAN: No, I think we have slipped into an easing of these sorts of arrangements rather than taken a deliberate decision about it and our own standards, I think, have fallen into disuse in some ways because we do not have a constant reiteration, as you say, and that is why I proposed, among other things, that this should be a very formal part of the opening of every new Parliament when a number of new Members come in.

322. PETER SHORE: Looking back over the period, I recall one Select Committee report—I think it was an ad hoc one rather than a Privileges Committee—the Strauss Committee in 1969. It was given this sort of broad remit about the standards of conduct of Members. It came to the conclusion that the House should adopt a resolution which forbad paid advocacy of proceedings in Parliament—paid advocacy was to be forbidden—and tried to draw a distinction between "paid advocacy" and simply "paid advice". That was never debated but governments change. I wonder what your reaction to that proposal is?

LORD CALLAGHAN: I think it is true not only of Strauss but of other areas, and this is not confined to this issue alone. You get something that happens, you get a paroxysm of public interest, media hysteria. It is then referred to a committee which produces some sensible results but by that time the interest has died down and everybody passes on. I think this is one occasion where this committee has the opportunity of putting something formally on paper—you are going to have great difficulty in doing it, I think, in defining all these different areas—but putting it on paper, forcing it upon Parliament really to take note of it and then, if we have the proper structure, it can be regularly reviewed at the beginning of every Parliament. I think this is perhaps the best opportunity we have had for some years.

Of course, I have been out of the House now for seven years but I think perhaps senior Members—and I must take my share of responsibility—senior Members have been rather remiss in not accentuating what they think standards in the House should be. In some ways that is due to the fact that every Jack is as good as his Master and every backbench MP who comes fresh to the House of Commons knows as well as the most senior Member who has been there for 40 or 50 years what the standards should be that should be adopted. I think the Privileges Committee has been slow to exert its authority in this particular way so there has been a slackness for which, I suppose, all of us have been partially responsible—perhaps including the Clerks of the House.

323. PETER SHORE: In that context again, do you think that that slackness, as it were, the failure to insist upon and repeat the necessity for high standards, etcetera, do you think that has been affected itself by appointing a Select Committee on Members' interests? Do you think the fact that people can now simply declare their interest has been taken as a kind of substitute for forbidding certain kinds of activities?

LORD CALLAGHAN: I think that is quite likely. I think there is a certain overlap between the work of the Privileges Committee and the work of the Members' Committee—whatever they call that now—on Members' interests. I would like to see the authority vested much more in the Privileges Committee provided it will do its job properly. I do not think it has been doing it properly and I hope one of the things you will investigate is to see whether you agree with that view and, if so, say so very clearly and also insist that not every newcomer to the House is entitled to sit on this committee. I am not saying they are but you should always go for the experience of people who know what has been the practice in the past. People may want to revise that practice in the light of changed social conditions but you should always have these senior people here who are ready to remind Parliament that Members enjoy privileges in order to ensure freedom of speech and not for any other purpose and that this is a privilege. I think all these things have been rather overlooked in recent years.

I do not wish to make unnecessary political points here but the change in recent years about what I call scorning public service as an ideal—I think it was Lord Blake who told you that we lived in a "get rich quick" society and I think this has had an adverse impact on the standards that people automatically would have adopted years ago.

PETER SHORE: Thank you.

324. CLIFFORD BOULTON: May I just confirm your recollection, Lord Callaghan, that the Privileges Committee used to be a smaller and very distinguished body; in fact, up to and including the time of Mr. Attlee

the Prime Minister took the Chair and, to an extent, that was a hangover from the fact that the Prime Minister was also Leader of the House until that sort of period, but certainly the Leader of the Opposition remained a Member of the committee until well into the seventies and it was a smaller and more senior committee. I think it is a 17 sort of size now.

LORD CALLAGHAN: Forgive me, I have to ask you a question. Is the Leader of the Opposition or the Prime Minister on it?

325. CLIFFORD BOULTON: No, the Leader of the House and the Shadow Leader of the House and the Attorney General, and Shadows, are on it.

LORD CALLAGHAN: I do not think that is good enough.

326. CLIFFORD BOULTON: I was simply opening in that way in order to go back to what was being prohibited in 1947. I am simply asking you whether you accept this. It was, at the time, two sides of the same coin. There were examples. For instance, the Civil Service Union trying to put obligations on Members, sponsored Members or Members who had a relationship with them, was complained about—Mr. Browne's case. He said, "I appear to be being given orders". The House said that a Member must not be given orders, that limits his freedom of speech but, per contra, nor must he put himself in a position where he is accepting or receiving orders and nobody must take a fee or put themselves in a position where their freedom of speech in the House is limited. Therefore, it is obvious, to become a paid agent of any outside interest is a breach of privilege because you are undermining freedom of speech.

What has happened since is that so-called consultancies and advisory positions which do gather remuneration have grown up which, nevertheless, avoid in their terms and contracts any obligation on the Member to say a particular thing or vote in a particular way. Do you think that may be the explanation of how the present situation has been arrived at despite the 1947 resolution?

LORD CALLAGHAN: Yes, it could well be. I think, with respect, you stated only one aspect of this matter in 1947. The other aspect which you will have to take into account is whether a contractual arrangement that has been entered into by both sides, whether you are saying that one side, which is not the Member of Parliament, is not free to withdraw from that engagement. The case of the Civil Service Clerical Association was that Mr. Browne was so out of sympathy with everything they were doing they wished to end his contract with them. They would give him a number of years pay—an example of the golden handshake—they would give him the use of the car until he retired and they would ensure that he was all right up until the time of retirement. That presents a difficulty because you must be able to say—and this is particularly true in the case of certain organisations—"Look here, we are no longer in sympathy, you are saying all the things that we do not agree with and do not believe in and so we would really like to bring this to an end." You can argue that is putting pressure on him, although it was not much financial pressure in the case of W.J. Browne, he was doing rather well out of it. It throws up a problem which you are going to have to face.

327. CLIFFORD BOULTON: Yes, certainly. We must accept that the present position is that you must not

threaten a Member that you will withdraw his sponsorship, or whatever it is, if he does not behave in a certain way but, retrospectively, you can part company with him because his services do not come up to scratch. I think that is the distinction but it is not one that would necessarily be readily understood and we must think about that.

LORD CALLAGHAN: I think the trades unions are a special case because I would argue that without the assistance of the trades unions in supporting Members of Parliament at a time when they were very ill-paid it is quite possible that the Labour Party could never have become a major political force in this country. After all, Members of Parliament in my day, and for the first 20 years, had no pension arrangements, nothing to look forward to in later life when their constituencies would have finished with them. They had no secretarial payment of any sort. Their travel facilities were limited to having a ticket to the constituency and back. They had no London living allowance; they were supposed to live in London on the £600 a year, later raised to £1,000 a year, that we had. All those circumstances were very different.

If you look at it from the point of a young Member coming in in those days, with perhaps a young family, he had no prospect at all if he represented a marginal constituency especially as he would have left his own occupation. For example, I was an Assistant Secretary at the Inland Revenue Staff Federation, although I was in the navy at the time, but I had been on leave from it in 1945. My post in my unit was filled in about 1950. Quite rightly. Why should they keep me on if I was going to be a Member of Parliament. They were kind enough to wait until I had won a second election and so it looked reasonably certain that I would be staying there. The circumstances are very different today from what they were then.

328. CLIFFORD BOULTON: Do you think the time has perhaps now come when the personal sponsorship of Members by certain trades unions, which is accompanied by a payment to their constituency expenses, should be discontinued?

LORD CALLAGHAN: No, I do not think that. What do I think? What I notice as the difference nowadays is that the payment, as you say, is not made to the Member—he is able to live on the various allowances that he now gets—it is paid to his constituency. I suppose that might influence a constituency in the selection of its candidate. If somebody can offer to pay £600 a year to the constituency and the next young man comes along and says, "I have nothing I can offer you", that might influence it and I think there are certainly cases where it has but there are also converse cases where it has certainly not. For example, I think of a number of what one regards as mining constituencies where the offer of a substantial subsidy has not succeeded in getting their candidate selected so, no, I would not rule it out.

329. CLIFFORD BOULTON: You do not think it affects the conduct of the Member once he gets elected in not wanting to lose his sponsorship?

LORD CALLAGHAN: Yes, I do. I think all these things are possible and we are never going to have a perfect world in these affairs. I think you could make out a case for what you are saying because I find that nowadays, from anecdotal evidence talking to Members, that a number of them are setting up their own offices in the constituencies. I heard of one case of somebody paying £4,000 a year for offices in his constituency—quite inconceivable in my day. Then we used to get volunteer secretarial assistance, some shorthand typist in your constituency who, having done her day's work, would then volunteer to type your letters for you. We never used to pay a rent to a trade union, or to anybody else for offices. We were reliant on a trade union itself to, very kindly, give us a room although that later weakened when we found that local authorities were able—not all of them were willing—to supply a schoolroom for this purpose on a Saturday morning, or something of that sort, although it did not give you an office. So I think you could make a recommendation to that effect. I would not think that this would be vital to raising standards in Parliament.

CLIFFORD BOULTON: Thank you.

330. WILLIAM UTTING: I was interested, Lord Callaghan, by your proposal to introduce an independent element into the Committee of Privileges. I wondered if you would agree that there might be additional advantages arising from that? Firstly, in that a group of independent people might act as a counterweight if the proceedings of the Committee appear to become dominated by short-term party political interests and, secondly, that a group of outside people might have a valid contribution to make in their own right—particularly in offering a lay view of the conduct of Members of Parliament.

It sometimes seems to people outside Parliament that Members are somehow self-absorbed in their own traditions and rituals and unaware of the way in which ordinary people might regard their behaviour. Would you think that an independent element would help in those areas as well?

LORD CALLAGHAN: Yes I would. I would agree with everything that you have said on that and it could be an additional reason for proposing it. I do think Members of Parliament tend to become self-absorbed. I think so would Members of this Committee if they felt that at the end of a certain period, with a small majority in favour of them in whatever it was they were serving, they were likely to be left. So I think all these things are right.

Let me, however, say one thing which I think touches on what you are saying about Professor Crewe who, according to the newspaper reports, said that all Members of Parliament are regarded as impostors and misfits by the general public. In general, in the abstract, that may well be true. But I believe, if you go to a Member's own constituency and ask what his constituents think about him, they will say: "Oh yes, they are all in it for what they can get out of it—but, you know, our chap's not bad! He's pretty good." That is because they know him, because they see his work in the constituency. Obviously, not all his opponents will say that about him. But I think you will find if you asked a constituency about its own Member, each constituency about its own Member rather than getting a general view, I think you would find that perhaps Members of Parliament would come rather higher up than they see to do at the moment.

WILLIAM UTTING: I think to be fair to him, Professor Crewe made that point also in his evidence, but of course it was not as well reported as the earlier comment.

LORD CALLAGHAN: I am very conscious of that now—that all the odd things I shall say will be fully reported but none of the substance!

331. WILLIAM UTTING: If I could just raise a related point in what you have just said and also in some of your earlier comments, you implied that the demands made upon a Member of Parliament may almost now amount to its being required to be a whole-time occupation if those responsibilities are to be discharged satisfactorily. But that would seem to limit pretty severely the time that Members of Parliament actually ought to be prepared to devote to outside interests. I wonder if you would like to develop that?

LORD CALLAGHAN: I absolutely agree with that. I think that it was far easier when I was first in Parliament to have an outside occupation than it is now. On the other hand, I do not want to rule it out if Members can combine the two, precisely to avoid the over-emphasis on self-absorption that you have referred to. I think it is a valuable outside element, provided Members can fulfil it. But I am concerned about the pressure on Members of Parliament—and also, I may say, upon Ministers to some extent. Although that cuts both ways. Ministers have now the additional burdens of Europe and I think those are quite substantial: travelling to and fro, taking part in the many committees that exist, and the rest of it. That is not an argument, I may say, for leaving the European Community but it is an added burden on them. On the other hand, Ministers have got rid of so many of their functions that sometimes I wonder what they do have to do. Indeed, we have seen something recently that I found quite incredible!—I could not believe it! That is one Minister practising his profession part-time! It would have been inconceivable when I went into Parliament that such a thing should have happened, and I am not sure, frankly, that it adds to the dignity of the House.

I will not go on about Ministers because I think that Ministers have been quite as culpable as backbench Members of Parliament in the change in standards. I will go on for a moment, I think. For example, it was quite clearly beneath the dignity of the House that a Minister should accept his legal costs in relation to an affair which had no bearing on his official duties. That would have been also inconceivable 20 or 30 years ago. I think it is improper—or certainly not consonant with the dignity of the House—that Ministers who have been associated with privatisation should immediately join the Boards of such companies afterwards.

These are all ways in which standards are different and the conception of a Member about his duty to Parliament and to his constituency has changed in my life in Parliament.

WILLIAM UTTING: Thank you.

332. LORD THOMSON: Lord Callaghan, in terms of declaring the Register of Interests. You have put forward what is really a very radical proposal, that people should put in the Register all their outside contracts and all the details of the remuneration that goes with that. It seems to be almost like literally depositing your Income Tax Return in the Register of Interests.

I just wondered two things: I fully understand and have sympathy with the motive that lies behind it, but would it begin to deter people from seeking to become Members of Parliament, and would you demand a similar obligation from those who seek to become Members of Parliament?—So that the sitting MP, having inserted his 'Income Tax Return' in the Register of Members' Interests, at least when an election came had the satisfaction of seeing all those who wished to compete for the seat making a similar detailed return to the electorate!

LORD CALLAGHAN: I am afraid I have not thought about this so the answer is off the top of my head. I think the answer to your first question is that it is still a very great honour to become a Member of Parliament. I think that most people feel this when they stand and when they are successful. I therefore do not think it would deter anyone who has any sense of public service in his bloodstream and I think that this is something that does exist in some people. They do want to contribute in this way. That is why voluntary service is so popular, I think, in this country and it works so well. As to the second: no, I do not think candidates should be required to do it. But I think that Members of Parliament after they are elected should be expected to declare all their income. I cannot think that it would be too difficult for them to do so and if it means reproducing their Income Tax Return, I see no reason why not. I think, after all, many people do have all their income made known and I think this could be added.

333. LORD THOMSON: Could I just ask a second question associated with what one does inside the House of Commons itself. Do you think the rules for the declaration of interest should be made more stringent? One has the impression that the fact that the Register is there—this came up in our evidence from Chris Moncrieff—that people feel because they have given some account of their outside activities in the Register, that they no longer need to make what used to be the normal declarations of interest. Should there be a declaration of interest with a parliamentary question? Should a parliamentary question that relates to an interest carry some sort of sign on the Order Paper?

LORD CALLAGHAN: I think provided the Register is complete enough and that contracts and agreements have been deposited, then I think that would be sufficient. I think that we might stick to the old rule about declaring it during a debate. I am not sure about it. I would not think it was necessary on parliamentary questions, but then of course it was inconceivable in my days that anybody should take a fee for asking a parliamentary question! We had never thought of such a thing! I do not think it ever entered our minds! But of course with the modern development of the public relations and the lobbyists, this has changed. No doubt.

334. LORD THOMSON: Would you prohibit certain kinds of outside interests? It has been put to us in the evidence that we are getting that perhaps one could draw two kinds of distinction. First of all, the distinction between those who are employed by general public relations firms who have a list of candidates that changes as their services are no longer required. Anybody paid on that basis ought to be a prohibited occupation for a Member of Parliament. But if somebody is representing a single interest, provided it is properly declared, that might be all right. Do you think there is validity in that distinction?

LORD CALLAGHAN: Yes, I think you could make a distinction on that basis. Certainly, I would be strongly

opposed to the Member of Parliament who acts as a general lobbyist for people in whom he has no interest at all and no concern. It is different from somebody who is, perhaps because of his previous background, strongly attached to one particular area. So, yes, I would think you might be able to draw up a distinction of that kind. I hope you could. I am not anxious to deny outside experience to Parliament. I think it is very valuable, at all levels. So I think you have got to try and walk a tightrope in this particular thing.

335. LORD THOMSON: The other distinction that has been canvassed with us in fact in some ways relates to your experience with the Police Federation, which of course was an experience that took place in entirely different circumstances from now and when it was regarded not merely as valid but something to be rather proud of, if I recollect it correctly. But the distinction that has been canvassed with us is the distinction between being a consultant on an outside interest—helping them to understand how they should conduct their affairs and make their case professionally and that sort of thing. But not to be an advocate of their affairs in Parliament. Do you think that is a sustainable distinction?

LORD CALLAGHAN: Yes I do. I think that if one tries to walk the line, a person who has a professional interest in a particular company because of his past experience should certainly say to them: "Well, look here, I think you've got to get hold of x or y in order to put your case properly". But not do it himself. I think he can advise the firm but not himself represent the firm to the Minister, because that is where I think undue influence can come in. But, for example, if one goes back to the case of the police. Being an enthusiastic young man, I was anxious to advise them on everything and tell them what they needed to do. I could have stopped at that, you see. But it would, I think, have certainly weakened their position very much if I had: a proper position of an underpaid service whose salaries were in the control of the Home Office. I think this is where the distinction has got to be drawn somehow—if you can find the right formula.

336. LORD THOMSON: Finally, with the distinction between the senior Members of Parliament—whom you have been laying some emphasis on as having some awareness of the dignity of Parliament, and the new MPs coming in fresh and brash and unfamiliar with the way things are done. Apart from your opening debate in the new Parliament, would there be a case for a much better system of some kind of training for new MPs when they came in—on how the House of Commons works and what are the real proprieties?

LORD CALLAGHAN: I thought that happened now. It certainly did not happen in my day. We did not think it was necessary. But I believe now that it does take place.

LORD THOMSON: Not very adequately, we understand. The Whips, you will not be surprised to know, are rather reluctant about it. They think they are the best people to do it.

LORD CALLAGHAN: Oh, I see. I am out-of-date on all these things. I do not think we felt the need. We were so self-confident. We came back out of the war, and I think that because of the experience of the war it was a very different House of Commons. We came back in order to change Britain. We did not come in for a living. I think that it is true of all of us, whoever we were. We intended to have the houses built. We were not going to have any unemployment. We were going to have a decent medical service. There was going to be equality of opportunity in education.

All these things were at the top of our mind. Now I am sure that is at the top of the mind of many candidates now. But I do see, and have seen, a growing element of those who regard being a Member of Parliament as being a job. I think that if you regard it as being a job, I am not at all sure that you are going to fulfil the task of a Member of Parliament properly. You may then tend to get into the position where you put your own interests first, your party second and the country third. That is the reverse of the order in which it should be. I am talking about an ideal situation, naturally. But at the final test, people—and I think Ministers—would be capable, and are capable, of putting the country's interest before the party interest and putting their own interests last. That is where we should aim at the whole time.

LORD NOLAN: Professor King.

337. PROF. ANTHONY KING: Could I just be quite clear, Lord Callaghan, what you think about the distinction between consulting and advising? Outside interests on the one hand and actually advocating their cause or acting as a facilitator for them on the other. When you were working for the Police Federation, perfectly properly, in the late 1940's, I take it you did both of those things?

LORD CALLAGHAN: Absolutely. Yes, yes I did. They were quite incapable. I hope none of them serving today will think I am casting reflections on them! But they knew they were incapable of handling a very difficult arbitration case, followed by a Royal Commission under the awesome chairmanship of Sir Henry Willink, and when we went to the Royal Commission they asked for written evidence. I wrote the written evidence for them. I led the team in front of Sir Henry Willink at the Royal Commission. Rather like this, I was surrounded by two or three police constables and an inspector here and there. But I dealt with the Commission. So that I was not a lobbyist or a consultant. At that time, because of the weakness of their position—I think they paid threepence a week, that's old money not new!, threepence a week or threepence a month or something for subscription—they were in no position to do this.

I regarded myself, with my background and experience, as putting them on an equal position with their employers to ensure that they got fair play—and they did get fair play.

338. PROF. ANTHONY KING: But am I right in thinking that you were saying in response to Lord Thomson that not only can the distinction between pure consultancy and advocacy be sustained, but that probably in present circumstances it ought to be sustained in the sense that Members of Parliament ought no longer to be allowed to act as paid advocates, what you did perfectly properly nearly half a century ago?

LORD CALLAGHAN: Yes, I would say that certainly. I see no particular difficulty in drawing a line between a Member of Parliament—let us say sitting in a company with company directors, and saying to them, "Well, look here. If you want to get this particular area of yours properly understood, the way in which you go about it is to do a, b and c." Take as an illustration the shipping industry. Then somebody who represents a shipping port, or a shipbuilding port—they should be free to sit down, and indeed to be paid for the advice. If he sits down with them and says: "Look here, I think the thing you ought to do is to see the Chancellor of the Exchequer first, before he draws up his next Budget. I can't be part of that delegation." That's where the distinction comes. I am not part of the delegation. I think this is the right way to do it: "If you really want to influence him then the way in which you should put your case is to say a, b, c and d. This is what will appeal to him. It is no use you saying to him e and f, because that will have no appeal at all."

Now I think if that is done with a company, that is perfectly proper. But he should stop at that stage. He should not himself represent anything to the Chancellor of the Exchequer or to anybody else. That is for them to arrange, somewhere else.[1]

339. LORD NOLAN: Or speak on it in the House?

LORD CALLAGHAN: Or speak on it in the House? No—I do not think he should. He should not do that. I broke that rule in the 40's, but that was because there was a question of pensions for the police which were wholly inadequate for widows and so on. The only person who could put it right was the Home Secretary. I was the only person who knew about it, as it were, and I said to them: "Look here, this is wrong," I said to the Police Federation. "This is wrong. We must really get a debate in the House of Commons." But everybody knew what I was doing, and of course the House of Commons was the only place where it could be raised.

But I think that nowadays I would have to argue logically that that should not be done. But this was forty years ago or more.

340. PROF. ANTHONY KING: On a completely different point. You said, in response I think to a question from Lord Nolan, that in fairness to Members the proceedings of the Privileges Committee when dealing with the case of an individual Member should be held in private. Could you explain why you hold that view?

LORD CALLAGHAN: In fairness to the Members who are being investigated. This is not a court of law. It is something that is germane to the Member himself, and I think that with the way in which the Press behave today, people can be "hung out to dry" by the Press quite improperly on the basis of very flimsy information. If some sections of the Press were to behave with more propriety, I am not sure that it would be so strong. But certainly today I think it would put Members quite unfairly under pressure if proceedings were to take place in public. There might come a time when the Privileges Committee would want to go public, but I think that should be a matter for them to decide.

341. PROF. ANTHONY KING: You say it is not a court of law, but presumably an outsider could take the view that if a pretty serious charge has been brought against an MP, such as accepting money to ask a question in the House of Commons, it is as much a matter of public interest that the disposition of that case should be known publicly—that the proceedings should be public, as would be the case in a court of law?

---

[1]This should be read with the second and third paragraphs of Lord Callaghan's letter to Lord Nolan of 31 January, see Evidence p. 505.

LORD CALLAGHAN: I do not think that is so until the case has been decided. I have no difficulty in publishing the evidence afterwards. The Press always loses interest after a certain time anyway. But I think that during the hearing itself, it should not be in public. Then, I think, afterwards of course the results are always published and recommended to the House. I see no reason why minutes of evidence should not be published. But I think then the whole story becomes known at once, instead of bits dribbling out from time to time.

342. PROF. ANTHONY KING: Well presumably there could in principle be restrictions placed on reporting the proceedings of the Privileges Committee in some way analogous to the restrictions that the courts impose—or tried until recently to impose!—on the reporting of court proceedings?

LORD CALLAGHAN: That is the difficulty that you yourself make. It is what the courts try to impose and what would happen in the Privileges Committee. I fear that, again, standards have changed so much. For example, in the Allighan case in 1946, he was found guilty of a contempt of Parliament and indeed resigned his seat because he had disclosed to the Press for a remuneration. He was a journalist but he was on somebody's list and had a regular remuneration for disclosing what went on at party meetings. That was thought to be improper in those days. I do not think it would be thought improper now because I think the parties themselves were driven, even though they wanted private discussions, they were driven to disclose it formally because of their own Members giving the information out and therefore they wanted it to go out accurately.

LORD NOLAN: Well, Lord Callaghan, you have given us much powerful encouragement as well as helpful and practical advice. We, as you know, are appointed for a period of three years and even after we have made our first Report I am sure we are not expected to sit back silent in the face of developments after that Report has been made. We are very grateful to you indeed for coming along and it has been most interesting to hear you. Thank you.

LORD CALLAGHAN: Thank you very much.

LORD NOLAN: Mr Barnes, good morning to you.

HARRY BARNES MP

HARRY BARNES MP: Good morning.

343. LORD NOLAN: I am very sorry we have had to keep you waiting, but as you will have heard it has been in a good cause. I hope it has not disturbed your timetable. Now, a number of our witnesses have preferred to begin by making a prepared statement and that is often very helpful. Are you in a position to do that?

HARRY BARNES: Yes, that is what I would like to do. Copies are being distributed to the Members of the Committee.

LORD NOLAN: Certainly. Well perhaps you would like to do that, and when you have done that I am going to ask Dame Anne Warburton to take you through the rest of your evidence.

HARRY BARNES: Thank you.

In the area of Members' interests, I feel that we need a few straightforward principles to guide the actions of MPs, rather than a whole series of complex and confusing rules. I recognise, however, that such principles can be aided by the operation of a few clear rules of behaviour. Ideally, in a democracy, people should be able to expect that their elected representatives will seek to act on their behalf. We should, therefore, set systems in motion which encourage MPs to act more from a sense of duty than out of their own self-interest. The personal well-being of an MP—in terms of hours of work, remuneration and access to the good things in life is secondary to the furtherance of the well-being of his or her electorate. If a motive is required to attract suitable people into Parliament then it should be that of job-satisfaction rather than access to wealth—or careerism. Through numerous and persistent links with differing groups and individuals in his or her constituency—and beyond, an MP will tend to grow to understand the issues he or she needs to pursue. Many of these links will be sacrificed if an MP receives personal payments for employment services from specific—and thus limited—interests outside of Westminster.

There is a distinct advantage to an MP in understanding the concerns and interests of his or her constituents when he processes the correspondence, talks face-to-face and regularly by phone to constituents, attends local meetings and gatherings and does not just pay others to do this work on his or her behalf. This is not to deny, however, that MPs need more and better back-up facilities and support than they currently receive: again, in the interests of their constituents. The availability and scope of such formal avenues is, therefore, of vital importance to MPs whilst a low level Parliament is likely to attract and hold a lower level of MPs.

A time-tabled parliamentary year which allowed MPs to move regularly between the Commons, their constituencies and other outside activities, and which avoided excessively long parliamentary recesses, would allow MPs to exercise more effective controls over the Executive and to have a more balanced political lifestyle. A regular pattern could be four or five week sessions at the Commons interspersed by single 'Constituency weeks' which would allow MPs to fulfil constituency engagements. MPs should also be allowed to submit written questions and table motions during any recess to enhance parliamentary scrutiny over the Executive.

A Parliament which can attract Members who might be able to earn more money outside but who are attracted to what they see—and find to be—a worthwhile performance of duties on behalf of others, would be healthy for democracy. A rule banning MPs from taking outside jobs would do more than anything else to advance the case I have presented.

LORD NOLAN: Thank you. Yes, Dame Anne.

344. ANNE WARBURTON: Mr Barnes, I was just rather wishing I had been able to look at your points before hearing them as you spoke them, because I think that they deserve reflection. I was also thinking what an interesting discussion we would have if you and Lord Callaghan before you and Mr Forman after you were all talking to us at one time, because I think you take opposite views from the other two today.

I would like, I think, to start you off, if I might, on the reasons you have set out on why you think that Members should only be Members. May I quote to you the phrase which Lord Callaghan used. He said that he thought that

> "MPs with no outside jobs risked an over-emphasis on self-absorption."

I wonder if I can get you to talk a little bit more about your reasons for thinking that outside interests really should be banned?

HARRY BARNES: Well, although some people have a very wide area of outside interests, nevertheless I believe that generally if people are taking paid employment, consultancies etc., then they are liable to be concentrating a great deal upon the areas that they are receiving the payments for. This in fact restricts the areas that they should be involved with in Parliament. An MP, in many ways—although they can develop various specialist interests in certain areas—will be something of a generalist turning into all sorts of areas that interest constituents and are before the country. Therefore, he does not need, I think, to be distracted from those avenues. Now there are many alternative avenues of connections in which people can gain experience of the problems that their constituents have and are problems more widely in society, without them having paid positions. But associations with various voluntary organisations may be quite important, At the moment I have the Civil Rights Disabled Persons Bill in front of Parliament through a Private Member's Bill, and obviously there are a whole host of outside interests that I am in contact with and whose services to a large extent I am dependent upon, or increasingly going to be dependent upon as time goes by as I am facing the Executive with all the authority and power that it has who are proposing their own alternative Bill in front of mine and therefore have all the backing of the Civil Service on it.

So I think that it actually detracts from an MP's ability to act in areas if there are paid outside interests.

345. ANNE WARBURTON: And it is specifically paid outside interests, not outside interests, that you would like to—?

HARRY BARNES: Well I think there has got to be a wide area of outside interests. There have got to be outside interests that are very much in the constituency, connections with all forms of bodies, and therefore people will specialise in particular areas that they are going to push. It may be that various voluntary organisations and many connections with industry and with trade unions are going to be things that are quite fruitful for a person—as long as they are not paid by those organisations.

346. ANNE WARBURTON: You said in the letter that you wrote to Lord Nolan that you thought that this Committee should draft new rules barring MPs from taking any other jobs. Have you drafted such rules yourself—"had a go"?

HARRY BARNES: No, I think generally that is part of your purpose, I would have felt! I think that what we should be doing is that we should be concentrating rather clearly upon the principles which should operate. I think that is fruitful for Members of Parliament to offer. Therefore, to me, it is very much at the end of the exclusion of outside interests that those rules should be drawn up.

347. ANNE WARBURTON: I wonder again, I think from your previous letter we thought it would be interesting to know whether you include trade association contacts—you have said not paid—but if somebody has a particular interest, either with trade associations or with trade unions, do you worry about that as a outside interest?

HARRY BARNES: No, the more understanding about people's links with organisations even on a voluntary basis, then the better. It might be that the Register of Members' Interests in some way could declare what those were, although I see it is quite difficult if it is sort of a voluntary connection or relationship that takes place. It is much easier to record contracts and connections in terms of areas such as consultancies. Then I think that there could be procedures by which those were also recorded by lobbyist and other organisations that would be helpful for people to understand what people's interests were.

348. ANNE WARBURTON: I think there is one more question I would like to ask you on this general point. You seem to be saying in your statement just now that you think that MPs who do the work themselves—in terms of opening envelopes and talking to everybody—that this makes them able to make a better contribution than if they have other interests. I think some people might think that if they have too much of the day to day routine, that it might—I almost said "make them a dull boy", from the nursery rhyme!—but in any case might perhaps reduce the attraction to certain useful Members of the House of becoming Members of Parliament. That it rather limits their ability to use their time, which must be an individual characteristic, an individual thing.

HARRY BARNES: I am in favour of the contacts initially coming through the Member of Parliament, so that the Member sees the daily mail that is sent to him and has the connections with constituents. I am very much aware that that is a great deal of hard pressure upon Members. Therefore they need considerable back-up facilities in order to direct the work to be done on behalf of their constituents as long as they are in charge of that. I would like to see a great extension of the provisions that are available for Members of Parliament. I do not like the current system in which there are allowances for Members of Parliament to determine, both in terms of their accommodation in London under a London allowance and in terms of other work they do, that they have control of those amounts and determine who they employ and generally how that money is to be used.

It also is taken very much on trust by the House authorities when people fill in forms to say they are using money in various ways without a great deal of checking taking place, on the grounds that everyone is an Honourable Member and therefore to be trusted in what they do. I think it would be much better if there were specific areas of facilities that were supplied by the Commons authorities, both in a Member's constituency and in the Commons itself. So that it should determine the size staff that a Member of Parliament should have. That staff should have to have suitable qualifications in order to do that job. But then the Member should be able to select, because he has got people who have political interests that he wishes to be associated with, as to who it is who does that work on their behalf. But I do not think that the business of filling in allowance forms and therefore having control of the finances oneself within a restricted area is something that it is useful for MPs to be involved in. Some MPs make very good use of those arrangements and extend them very very considerably. But a system that you can use can also be rather abused and used very very fully. I think it would be better if there were systems that were put into operation that would help to run MPs as well. It might be that some MPs actually emerge with rather limited experience in terms of running office facilities and organisations. If there are structures that are expected to operate, people who are appointed to them, then to some extent initially they may begin to run the MP but the MP then should come to be in control of that situation. The more they are in touch with their constituents' concerns or interests, then the better they are at knowing what to do.

349. ANNE WARBURTON: Mr Barnes, I think I must leave it to colleagues who know that life in Parliament to ask further about your ideas of the organisation of work. But you have, in your letter, used the word "abuse", that you think the allowance system—I think as you said—"is" rather than just be "can be" abused. I think that, it seems to me, to come within the heading of—I don't like the word—"sleaze". So I feel I ought to ask you a little bit more on that front. Are you saying that you actually are aware of abuse which does take place?

HARRY BARNES: No. Maybe I have worded it rather strongly. It is just that the system is such that the forms are filled in and the claims are made. Some areas require specific backing because money has been spent on a copying machine or something of that nature and the information has to be put forward. On other occasions it is claims for allowances for accommodation etc. and I know of no arrangements by which that is checked as to whether it operates, or any receipts begin to be required. That seems to me to be problematic and puts some temptation in people's way. Given that we are talking about a random sample of human beings, it is likely to be succumbed to in various cases. It sometimes surprised me that Members who do not live in London and are subject to the allowance, sometimes seem to travel quite considerable distances where I assume that the accommodation is somewhat cheaper.

350. ANNE WARBURTON: Thank you very much. I do not think that I am the person to take you through the ideas you have on the structure of Parliament. I am not even sure how much that falls within our remit. We are very ambitious about what we are tackling, but perhaps that might be a little beyond us. But can I just ask you then a final question about the arrangements in the House for disciplinary control. Do you think them adequate?

HARRY BARNES: Well I think that perhaps more facilities and provisions could be given to Members' Interests Committee and to Privileges Committee. I generally feel that it should be the House, because of the problem about parliamentary privilege, that should have a say in these areas. I welcome the work of this Committee in order to set frameworks for Parliament itself to respond to. But I would be a bit worried about external bodies being established in order to take over some of the functions in which those committees have previously been involved.

I do feel however that on bodies such as the Privileges Committee, there should be an attempt to make arrangements by which the Members of those committees are often people who might be thought of as being Parliamentarians: people who take some considerable interest in the procedures of the House, and are not necessarily people who are the "good and the great" who have emerged into Ministerial positions and then are later senior Members of the House and who would be added to those bodies. I think there is a whole tradition of people such as Ian Mikardo and, although he temporarily had a short Ministerial job, the late Bob Cryer who had a great interest in parliamentary provisions and arrangements and it would serve the House well to use some of that knowledge in the committees. He was a Member of Members' Interests.

351. ANNE WARBURTON: Lord Callaghan, I think you probably did not hear him, took the view that those committees, particularly the Privileges Committee, should have on it very senior persons: Prime Minister, Leader of the Opposition.

HARRY BARNES: Well, there might need to be different Members on and people with different areas of experience, but I think it would be a very bad idea if it was to be dominated by those people who are held to have great experience in terms of the positions they have achieved. Because there are many other people who have great experience in terms of what it is that they have done in Parliament and understand well the operations of Parliament and the problems of Parliament. I think their services should begin to be drawn from. There is a problem always about appointments to the committees and the considerable control that the Executive has over Parliament itself, and a need to try and break through that. But it might be that we could at least have certain reserved positions for people who did not fall into the categories that Lord Callaghan was talking about.

352. ANNE WARBURTON: Thank you. Mr Barnes, you said you would not want an outside body. We have been asking various of our witnesses what they would think about having an external element in an internal body. That is to say, for example, the Privileges Committee has somebody who is not a Parliamentarian.

HARRY BARNES: I would have thought that it is quite useful to have outside involvement and connections and expertise that maybe could be there alongside the people who were finally making the decisions. So I suppose it would be possible to have two tiers of membership of committees, those that in the end were the ones that were making the decisions and voting on it because I think it is quite important that votes in Parliament are done by Members of Parliament. I think others have elected them to vote on their behalf and that's what we should do, and a record of what we do should then be seen. But having avenues of expert advice from outside is quite a fruitful notion and is something that I think should generally be extended into Parliamentary procedures, so that something that's a bit more like select committee activities should influence the nature of standing committees and general procedures in the House.

353. ANNE WARBURTON: I am not sure that expert advice is quite the role which perhaps we have been having in mind in our putting this question, I would think of it more in terms of a "Jiminy Cricket" presence, having regard to the fact that our sitting here is in large measure because of the public view of what happens in Parliament, if Parliament regulates itself in every detail.

HARRY BARNES: Well, I suppose the problem is this committee has rather sort of grown in size, if we add all different elements to it, because I've suggested that a Privileges Committee should not just be made up of people with former Ministerial experience but should include active Back Benchers and likewise I suppose there could be an argument that amongst the people who come from outside, expertise in certain areas is looked for, but also the Jiminy Cricket activity, the stimulation, the fact that there is a different viewpoint that begins to be produced that is an external viewpoint, could be of use.

354. ANNE WARBURTON: Have you given any thought to a statutory form of regulation, well interests, presumably, fall away under your...

HARRY BARNES: Yes, under my arrangements then what needs to be declared becomes less because certain areas begin to be excluded from the register. I would not favour, as far as the regulation of Members of Parliament was concerned, statutory provision—I would prefer that to be given by the rules of the House—but then there is the other element which is within the survey of the committee at the moment in terms of lobbying arrangements and I think that those lobbying arrangements and who it is that people have contact with and have as clients is information that should generally be available. And, of course, the way I am arguing that should exclude MPs being involved. If, however, that argument is not being accepted then I think that is a useful way of discovering as to who it is that has particular interests in different areas.

ANNE WARBURTON: Yes, I would like to leave it there. Thank you very much.

355. LORD NOLAN: May I take up, Mr. Barnes, one thing you were saying, about the abuse of the allowance system? We have heard, as I expect you have, anecdotal evidence of a number of Members coming up, as you say, in the same cars and it is suspected, though plainly not known, that they each claim reimbursement of the cost of a car. That is the kind of thing that you were talking about, is it not?

HARRY BARNES: Yes, travel allowances which needs to be looked at carefully, because I don't have a car so my travel allowances are claimed in terms of taxi journeys within the constituency. I am allowed to go up to a certain number of miles in it and beyond that have to then start to record the details of those arrangements. I don't need to produce any receipts from taxi drivers—in fact had this been done it might be that some greater check in those areas would be fruitful—and certainly those who have cars, then when they go over that limit in terms of travelling, and travelling to London, have to give some record of what it is that they are doing. Again anecdotal, it sometimes seems that MPs who have travel allowance by car are involved in train travel, sometimes second class, and sometimes one wonders as to whether they are actually claiming the road travel as being somewhat greater. It is easy for me not having a car in that I am therefore dependent upon rail travel and therefore I am issued with vouchers in order to do it. That keeps me in control to some extent, but it is just that when you look at what the situation is you think "Well, it wouldn't be as easy to make the application and to receive the funding in any other walks of life and therefore why should it be so open for us, when there are 651 of us and therefore there

are going to be all sorts of different circumstances that arise." I wouldn't want, however, it to be a sort of witch hunt area that was involved and that is why I was very strong in suggesting that what should begin to occur is that facilities should begin to be supplied. It always seems to me to be quite ridiculous in terms of London allowances that when they closed the offices of the London County Council opposite Parliament, that that was not made use of by Parliament itself and that would have provided fantastic office space and bedroom space and all the facilities, instead of people having to shunt around in other different areas.

356. LORD NOLAN: Thank you. I wonder if I could just bring you back to the point of principle: it must be generally recognised that fiddling your expenses, dishonestly claiming the reimbursement of expenses you have not in fact incurred is fraud, it is a crime whether it is done by a Member of Parliament or anybody else, and if there is evidence of that, well, the rules there are strict enough and would be applied. I think your point is that it is difficult to check, is that right?

HARRY BARNES: Yes. It is impossible for me to give any evidence of a solid nature to back up what I am saying and all I am saying is that it would be nice if it was tightened and it would be fruitful for MPs generally and it would be better guidance, just as in terms of the Members' Interest Recorded provision, that the Members' Interest did fruitful work in terms of its last report, that produced an actual form that had to be gone through and details had to be completed, to be filled in, and it is just that greater guidance, therefore, would ensure that that problem wasn't there.

357. LORD NOLAN: Thank you. May I ask you just two, I hope, much shorter questions? In your letter to us saying that being a Member of Parliament is a full-time job, you say the salary is perfectly adequate. Now, what concerns me is this: what about the pension? And may I elaborate a little? "I am a civil servant aged 35, I am invited to stand for Parliament, I have a growing family. I give up my job as a civil servant, I go into Parliament, I am in for five years, I am out". Is it really fair to expect people to give up all outside interests with that possibility in mind?

HARRY BARNES: Yes, I think if people were giving up all outside interests then the case you've quoted is something that would need to be better catered for, so that someone who had disrupted their career and had moved into Parliament and had then found that avenue cut off from them, should have some form of recompense for doing that. That doesn't mean that the salary itself needs particularly to be advanced, but it does mean that the period in terms of qualifying, in terms of pension, or various severance payments, need to be taken into account. So I think that the way it operates at the moment is that actually the amount of pension begins to be greater if a person has stood in an election and lost the seat than if they decide that they should go elsewhere. That doesn't seem to me to be reasonable and it means that some people may therefore be tempted to stand for Parliament, realising that they stand little chance of winning, in the hope that it will improve their pension position, and I don't think that that should be part of the consideration of whether someone stands for Parliament or not.

358. LORD NOLAN: Thank you. One final thing—I think this is really a question expecting the answer "no".

One line that has been suggested is that the limit should be this: that you do not accept any pay for your work or services as a Member of Parliament but beyond that you can accept outside interests, can carry on as an engineer or a dentist or a farmer, or whatever it might be, but I think you say that is not good enough?

HARRY BARNES: Yes, I think it should be entirely the other way round and it shouldn't be that arrangement. I know there are suggestions that if people have various outside payments they should sort of deduct that from their MP's salary and obviously that doesn't come into the area of analogies that I am suggesting, because I do feel that this is a position that should be a commitment to a various form of public duty and therefore it is payment from the body that you are giving that duty towards.

LORD NOLAN: Thank you very much. I am going to go round the table. Professor King, have you any questions?

359. PROF. ANTHONY KING: Just a couple. Suppose your proposal that people are barred from accepting outside jobs is not accepted, therefore we go on having a register of Members' interests on more or less the same basis as at present, do you think there is a problem—and it has been suggested to us that there is—that the mere existence of the committee on the Register of Members' Interests gives MPs the impression that if they properly register their interests then it doesn't really matter what their interests are and that were the Members' Interests Committee to be merged in some way with the Privileges' Committee, this might give Members the impression that registering wasn't the whole of the story, that they had other standards of conduct that they had to uphold?

HARRY BARNES: I am not sure whether that is the best method in order to achieve that objective. But certainly I feel that Members need to be alerted to the fact that a declaration of interests doesn't cover everything and excuse all forms of action. There are two ways in which people look at the register; some look at the register in the way you've suggested and others look at the register looking at other people's registrations and say "Ah, this shows that when this person is acting they are in the pocket of these other organisations". So there is a differing attitude that is there about the register and I think that generally what it is that you are aiming for needs to be faced up to and something needs to be done about it. I don't know whether I have the right procedural arguments in connection with it, partly because I am evading that question to some extent by setting other standards that should operate.

360. PROF. ANTHONY KING: Expanding on something that Lord Nolan put to you, is there not a danger that if Members of Parliament had no paid outside interests at all not only would there be problems about recruitment because people would be reluctant to go into the House fearing the loss of their seat in a few years' time, but might there not also be problems arising out of the fact that they would be that much more dependent on the goodwill of the party Whips, the party machine, the local constituency organisation? At the moment and putting it very simply, people who do have outside interests, or many of them, are to that extent immune from pressures?

HARRY BARNES: Yes. I mean I would also think a lot needs to be done in order to try and loosen the control of party Whips and because people's futures are not entirely tied-in to the MP activity and there aren't any other career options that begin to be open to them. Then they may then feel quite restrained in those type of circumstances. So I agree that that is something of a problem but it just seems to me to be outweighed by the type of considerations I had about public duty and the nature of work of an MP and I think that if those standards were adopted it would have some knock-on consequences to the way that MPs operate and function. I did have some suggestions at the end of the initial letter I sent in, which again might be going beyond your area, about how we needed to alter the timetabling and arrangements at the Commons itself and I think that if we are allowed to move in and out between constituency activities, other visits and Parliamentary work itself, and continuously to have Parliament available for us and never to be away long in order that we can check the executive, would be starting to create a different culture that would have an impact in some of the areas that concern you.

361. PROF. ANTHONY KING: The final point I want to enquire into is how total you want the ban on MPs' paid outside jobs to be. There is a long tradition in Britain of the MP as novelist—one thinks not merely of Edwina Curry and Julian Critchley, but of Douglas Hurd, earlier on, and Disraeli before that. Are MPs to stop writing novels and indeed doing other forms of writing for which they receive royalties?

HARRY BARNES: It always astonishes me that MPs do so much writing and write so many books. I often say that I'd rather like the opportunity to read a book now and again and be given the time to do it. I think it is a problem because it is another area of paid employment and it can mean that some people are not just writing books that are about the political process and on advancing their own political ideas, but are generally novels and for entertainment, and I would have thought that one area that could be looked at in that is as to where the funds that are received from those areas go to and should it be the case that that is a matter of another "nice earner" that MPs have got themselves involved in, or should it be that that money goes to charities or campaigns or other bodies that the person is concerned with that have objectives, which are that of trying to influence and persuade people within the political process.

LORD NOLAN: You have made your points extremely clearly, if I may say so. We are running a little short of time but I will ask the other Members of the committee if there is anything we feel has not been covered that they wish to raise. (Pause) I think then we can just record our sincere thanks to you, as to all our witnesses, for coming along, giving up your time and giving us the benefit of your clear and helpful advice. Thank you very much, Mr. Barnes.

HARRY BARNES: Thank you very much.

362. LORD NOLAN: Hello, Mr. Forman. Some of our witnesses have preferred to begin by making a short prepared statement. Are you in that position or would you rather go straight into being questioned?

NIGEL FORMAN MP

NIGEL FORMAN, MP. Thank you for your invitation, Lord Nolan. When I got the letter from the secretary, on behalf of the committee, I was very struck by the fact that prominent stress was put on four key questions and so in the memorandum which I have sent to the committee a few days ago I sought really to direct most of the memorandum to my best attempts to help the committee in answering those four questions. But in the course of doing it and in the interests of brevity it follows that I didn't write as much about the present situation as I might ideally have wished and, therefore, with your permission I will just make a few brief opening remarks if I may to elaborate really what I am saying in the first two paragraphs of my memorandum.

LORD NOLAN: Yes, we have all got your memorandum and are very grateful for it. It would be very helpful to us all if you could elaborate and summarise in the manner you propose. Please do.

NIGEL FORMAN: Thank you. So far as a schematic presentation of what 651 MPs do with their lives once they are MPs, I think it is perhaps helpful, if it does not sound too simplistic, just to sketch out the main headings as I see it and the nature of the duties and opportunities which they are involved in from a sort of analytical point of view. I would suggest to the committee that, first of all, MPs have a duty to their constituents and on certain issues to their consciences as well. One thinks, for example, of the classic issue of capital punishment, but there will be others, and I would say that all MPs, without exception, recognise that duty and perform it to the very best of their ability.

Secondly, MPs owe loyalty—and that is not quite the same thing as duty—they owe loyalty to their parties in Parliament and in the constituency, that is to say the associations which support them, because without that loyalty the modern House of Commons could not function satisfactorily because party loyalty and party discipline is an essential prerequisite for a reasonably well-functioning House of Commons. Equally, without that sense of loyalty reciprocated towards their supporters in the constituency they would not be in Parliament in the first place, because all of us have to go through selection procedures of one kind or another in order to be selected to have the opportunity and the honour to fight for a seat.

Thirdly, MPs, I would suggest, are free to pursue their own outside interests and professional skills and qualifications with which they entered the House of Commons in the first place, because if you look down the list of Members of Parliament in any Parliament, you will find that a great number of them have skills of one kind or another—they may not all be professional skills but they are multiple skills, they may be farmers, they may be lawyers, they may be doctors, they may be dentists—I think I heard you mention dentists earlier in your remarks, Lord Nolan. You can't just wish that away and nor would it be sensible to do so, partly for reasons to do with the prospect of supporting your family in the event that you lost your seat, but partly, also, because presumably you gravitated in that direction in the first place because you had a real interest and skill in that area. So that is the third point.

The fourth point—and this is more germane to your enquiry, I think, at this stage—MPs obviously have opportunities, not duties but opportunities, to act as paid or unpaid advisers to outside interests. Now, they may do this in a variety of ways, as directors, consultants, or they may do it as other professionals do, in other words just pursue their professional career. Or they may do it, as is the case with many members of the Labour Party and a few Members of my own party, as advisers to trade unions, or trade associations, as Dame Anne Warburton was saying earlier.

Fifthly—and, again, as part of that—MPs are sometimes invited to act also as advocates in Parliament for outside interests. There is an important distinction which I make in my paper between advice and advocacy and as long, under the current rules, as this is properly declared it is not prohibited—there is nothing which is against the current House of Commons' rules for MPs to act as advocates as well as advisers. Everybody can think of prominent examples of this which are sort of time-honoured; those who make speeches in transport debates, the burden of their notes having been typed out for them and written by some very clever young man in a trade union research department, which might be — in the old days it was the NUR, it has got a different name now, but something of that kind. Or in the case of the Police Federation there is a tradition that there is always, as it were, a spokesman or an advocate for the Police Federation point of view in most home affairs debates, and so on.

Sixthly and finally in my list, in some cases MPs are directors or paid officials of lobbying firms, are they not, if one looks down the list in the Registry of Members' Interests, in addition to their other duties? And, again, I put it to you, I think it is important for you and the public to remember this, that this is not prohibited under current rules, so we must always keep clear in our minds what is the case and what might be the case in future in the light of your recommendations, Lord Nolan, when you come to make them.

So what I suggest in my memorandum is that, of those six categories I have just schematically set out, probably it would be sensible to rule out the last two in any recommendations you might see fit to make for changes in the rules or tightening up of the rules. The effect of that—to put it in simple English—would be to leave lobbying on behalf of sectional interests to the lobbyists—to registered lobbyists at that—and I think that would be a healthy outcome if you were minded to do that.

If I may turn your attention then, Lord Nolan, to para.2 of my memorandum, I would just like to say a word or two more, if I may, about the present arrangements so far as they relate to Members' interests, because I think I was a bit too cryptic in that paragraph for clarity. The essential point is that the present arrangements rely on self-regulation by Members of Parliament of Members of Parliament and we all know that in recent years self-regulation has fallen into some disrepute as a principle in all sorts of other spheres and I think it is naive to assume that it has not also, as it were, got a bit tarnished in the political sphere as well. So I think we must take that as a premise.

Secondly, the current arrangements rely on timely disclosure and declaration by Members of Parliament and I stress "timely", because all sorts of difficulties can arise when people say they either overlooked or were too busy or forgot about something which actually was germane to the situation and would have constituted a conflict of interest, perhaps.

Thirdly, they rely on good judgment by individual MPs—that goes without saying. I mean, without good judgment and, indeed, in certain recent cases where I don't want to name names, but we can all think of them, I think the failures derive principally from poor judgment rather than outright venality or really malicious intent.

Fourthly—and this, I think, has not been spoken about very much, at least when I have read the reports of your proceedings—the present arrangements rely critically upon very good advice from the Registrar of Members' Interests and even under the existing system it is always open to Members of Parliament to check and double-check in advance with the Registrar, who will give fair, accurate and helpful advice, in my experience, whenever there is a grey area and goodness knows there are quite a few grey areas in this matter.

Finally—and perhaps most portentous of all—the current arrangements make the assumption that Members of Parliament (all of them) will show integrity and honourable behaviour, because that is why we go through the traditional courtesy of describing each other as Right Honourable or Honourable Ladies and Gentlemen.

So, Lord Nolan, I thank you for your invitation and I think those might be helpful to the committee by way of explaining slightly more fully paragraphs 1 and 2 of my note. I think the rest of the note perhaps speaks for itself and I will be very glad to answer questions on that.

LORD NOLAN: Thank you very much indeed. I have asked Professor King if he would please lead the questioning.

363. PROF. ANTHONY KING: I suddenly realise I don't know whether I should address you as Mr. Forman or Dr. Forman. Which do you prefer?

NIGEL FORMAN: I think "Mr." in politics.

364. PROF. ANTHONY KING: "Mr." in politics, right. You say in your memorandum right at the beginning "In certain respects I believe the experience I have gained from my outside interests has enhanced my contribution as a Member of Parliament." That is a very widely held view, but the view is also very widely held that that is really a lot of tosh, that it is just a cover story for people wanting to earn money outside. Can you give some examples of the ways in which you think your pursuit of your paid outside interest has enhanced the doing of your job as an MP?

NIGEL FORMAN: Indeed I can. You will presumably have in front of you, all the Members of the committee, or you will have had drawn to your attention, the entry in the register which applies to me in any case and so I can speak to that to a degree in answering your question, and I can also speak historically. When I was a paid consultant to Kleinwort Benson Securities some years ago before becoming a Member of Government and more recently a paid consultant to Salomon Brothers International, I had derived considerable knowledge and understanding of financial markets and of international financial questions which I did not have before I was performing those self-employed tasks of consultancy for those particular firms. Therefore I am so bold as to say that my contributions, for example, to economic debates and my understanding of the issues was a great deal improved as compared with the position that would have pertained if I had not had that knowledge and those contacts, quite apart from the reasons why they saw fit to pay me a fee for my advice on political and Parliamentary matters.

Again, to give you another example, when I was a temporary part-time lecturer at Essex University, Professor King, which you will know about, in the nineteen eighties, I found that not only, I hope, did Essex University benefit from my particular angle when lecturing and teaching but also I certainly benefited from a broader understanding of the nitty-gritty of the problems facing universities in general and Essex University in particular. So that was useful whenever the House was debating or considering educational policy and particularly higher education policy. So I give you that as two examples, but I could give you others as well.

365. PROF. ANTHONY KING: You have mentioned the register of Members' interests and your own entry in it. Could I just pursue that very briefly? When you entered "Consultant to Gavin Anderson & Company, a firm involved in corporate public relations", did it occur to you that you might have gone on to give a list of the firms that that PR firm was acting on behalf of?

NIGEL FORMAN: It did indeed occur to me and I put that very question to the registrar at the time on the telephone, not in writing—because most of this advice is given on the telephone—and I talked him through exactly what was the nature of the services that I provide on a part-time basis for that firm and having listened to my explanation of what I did precisely he gave me the advice that the entry that you see there was the appropriate way to enter it in the register. And that is why I stressed in my opening remarks the importance of the objective advice one gets from that official.

366. PROF. ANTHONY KING: Do you think in retrospect, in view of what has happened in recent weeks and months, that that advice was necessarily, as it were, politically, from your point of view, the best advice? Might you when you register that interest, if it continues, in the 1995 register, might you want to expand on that a little bit?

NIGEL FORMAN: I don't think I would unless something came out of this committee of such great import relating to this point, that we all felt, or indeed Parliament decided, that things had to be presented in a different way. The reason is this: that in that particular case that you have highlighted I am not in any sense in direct contact day to day on a sort of managerial basis with the clients that that firm has. I give advice to them, as it happens, on a monthly basis, I am advising their firm and it is then up to them to decide what sense or otherwise they make of my advice.

367. PROF. ANTHONY KING: Could I ask you an additional question about the register? It has been suggested to us now quite frequently that not only should people say something like "Consultant to Gavin Anderson" or "Political Consultant to de Montfort University" but that they should register or possibly deposit the terms of their agreement and if they don't have any written terms of their agreement they should have?

NIGEL FORMAN: I think there would be no harm in that at all and it would build up a satisfactory file for the future which anybody who was seriously interested or concerned could consult, yes.

368. PROF. ANTHONY KING: And their remuneration?

NIGEL FORMAN: I am less sure about that. I anticipated that this question might arise because obviously it has been in the public discussion. I think in the interests of privacy—we must not forget the cause of privacy—it is not self-evident to me that there are conclusive arguments as to why people in this sort of position should reveal in pounds and pence exactly what they are deriving. There are various reasons for that; partly that those earnings by their very nature are self-employed and, therefore, will vary and will only be known retrospectively because that is the way the tax system works so far as Schedule D is concerned, partly because it is a nice question as to how far you should go with people in public life in insisting that everything to do with their personal circumstances, financial and otherwise, should be a matter of public record. Of course, you know, Professor King, as an expert, that in the United States it is very open indeed, but I would suggest to you that parallels with the United States are potentially misleading because our political system is, as you know, very different in relevant ways.

369. PROF. ANTHONY KING: But taking up that last point you referred to everything having to do with an MP's personal circumstances, but suppose that one were to try the following distinction; between those kinds of outside employment that in a sense had nothing to do with Parliament or at least didn't have anything to do with the MP's role in acting in Parliament, vis a vis Ministers or whatever, and those outside interests that did have that effect. If I can take your own case, you list here "Modest royalties from previous publications"—I am sorry they are modest ——

NIGEL FORMAN: Blame my publishers!

370. PROF. ANTHONY KING: You probably know that Dr. Forman is the author of one of the standard textbooks on British politics of Government. Now, clearly, although you have learned a good deal through being an MP that was relevant to the book, I mean, clearly writing that particular book does not really have anything to do with your activities as a Member of Parliament, whereas I take it, being Parliamentary Adviser to the Institute of Chartered Accountants does. Would it be reasonable to suggest that while it would be inappropriate for you to list your book royalties or your occasional fees from lecturing and broadcasting, it might be appropriate to ask you to list what you are being paid by De Montfort and the Institute of Chartered Accountants?

NIGEL FORMAN: I think I take the view that it is difficult to draw a provisional line in these matters between those outside interests or activities for which one is being paid where one should under any changed rules declare the figure and those where one should not. For example, take a lawyer, a point which applies to quite a few Members of Parliament, they derive considerable income, as they are perfectly free to do so, from being advocates in courts or from work as solicitors, and in many ways that colours their approach to a number of political issues. Quite rightly—I don't criticise that because they bring to those political issues the experience of practising lawyers, whether it is barristers or solicitors. The same would be true of people who own farms and there are a number of Members of Parliament who own farms, which is bound to colour and to influence the opinions they hold on, shall we say, issues to do with the Common Agricultural Policy, or anything like that. So I think that it would be a natural injustice if one were to single out particular categories of outside paid activity and I think it should be comprehensive or not at all. If you wanted to

compromise I think you could consider following the model that you see in some company annual reports where directors' remuneration, including non-executive directors, is very often given in a bracket rather than in a precise sum and that might be one possibility.

371. PROF. ANTHONY KING: Could I ask you to say a little bit more about what you actually do for Gavin Anderson & Company?

NIGEL FORMAN: In that case I have monthly meetings with their key executives and I give them the benefit of my advice as to what is happening in Parliament, what is likely to happen in the political realm that might be of interest to them and their clients, and I answer their questions to the best of my ability when they seek my judgment as to what this might mean for this or that commercial interest with which they are involved as a company in that realm.

372. PROF. ANTHONY KING: What do you do for De Montfort University?

NIGEL FORMAN: For De Montfort University I give advice, principally to the Vice-Chancellor and to some extent to his senior executives, about issues of concern to them, which are principally the development of higher education policy and also the political context within which that is happening, because obviously these things are influenced by what the House of Commons thinks about, shall we say, public expenditure in general.

373. PROF. ANTHONY KING: Suppose the Vice-Chancellor of De Montfort said that he was a little bit worried about the image of universities or of his particular university in the world of Westminster, would you arrange a reception in the House of Commons for, say, the Leicestershire Members of Parliament. Would that be something you would do?

NIGEL FORMAN: That might be something one would do, yes, and there has been a practice in recent times of having, shall we say, an annual dinner for example, at the House of Commons which provides an opportunity for him and his senior management team to meet interested Members of Parliament, who would include obviously Members of Parliament from Leicestershire, but also those who are known to have a keen interest in higher education matters, who would come from other parts of the country as well.

374. PROF. ANTHONY KING: Do you have any residual qualms about that because I can't imagine that De Montfort University raises anywhere serious problems, but I can imagine kinds of organisations, kind of lobbying organisations, making use of Members of Parliament's access to these facilities in a way that many of us in the outside world would think did not smell terribly good?

NIGEL FORMAN: I should stress that De Montfort University is not a lobbying organisation, it is De Montfort University, and my personal prejudice is that on the whole those who consult with outside interests do much better to respond to invitations, because it usually is a matter of responding to invitations rather than going out and, as it were, selling oneself to anybody who might wish to use one's services. Responding to invitations—it is better really to do that for an individual corporate body or an individual corporation than it is to do it, as it were, for a range of clients which would be the position with lobby organisations. That is why I make a suggestion, both in my memorandum and in what I said earlier, that maybe this committee should look again at the role of Members of Parliament who are either paid officials of lobbying firms or who work directly for them.

375. PROF. ANTHONY KING: Do I take it from your memorandum and from what you said earlier on that you believe that a distinction can be in force between consultancy and advice on the one hand and advocacy and facilitating on the other and that that line should be drawn—the former is allowed, the latter should be disallowed?

NIGEL FORMAN: Yes. I mean, I think—you have taken three categories there in your question and in my memorandum I focus very much on two. I focus on the one hand on consultancy and advice which is a matter essentially of going out to the interest concerned and giving them the benefit of your knowledge and wisdom and views, and on the other hand acting, almost as a barrister might in court, if you like, in Parliament and in Parliamentary proceedings, to argue a narrow case for or against a proposition which would be suitable or advantageous to the interests of that particular outside body. In that latter category I am suggesting to the committee that it might consider ruling that out in any recommendations that it made to Government, whereas in the former category I think it is perfectly respectable—and, indeed, has various benefits for public life which I think we are aware of.

376. PROF. ANTHONY KING: What about acting on behalf of a firm or an interest or a university or whatever in, for example, seeking to gain access to a Minister or to officials in a department—which side of your line does that fall on?

NIGEL FORMAN: I think that it is something which is squarely in between the two positions that I have sketched out and I think it would be a matter for this committee, on taking further evidence from other people, to come to its own conclusion as to whether it should belong in the category of activity which you would recommend should be ruled out, or should be ruled in. My own view, since you ask me, is that on the whole one is acting on those occasions as a facilitator. It is almost like a master of ceremonies and you are merely providing an opportunity for people in the outside world to talk directly to people who have an interest or who have some real power of decision in that area.

377. PROF. ANTHONY KING: Yet if a Member of Parliament is acting on behalf of such a firm or interest or whatever, it might be thought that that firm or interest had a very considerable advantage over a similar firm or interest that didn't have an MP facilitating for it in the same way.

NIGEL FORMAN: I think that is where the public understanding of this is at fault because in fact my experience of both being in Government and being connected with Government leads me to say that if an outside interest, whether it is a firm or a trade union or a trade association, has a good case to make on a point which is on the then current political agenda, it merely has to get in touch with the department concerned and while in the first case the matter might be dealt with or fielded by officials, if it has obviously a political content or a political importance, it is not difficult at all for the strength of the argument itself to determine the fact that they get to see Ministers and so on. In fact, Ministers spend a lot of their lives, I can tell you, just meeting outside delegations of people who have legitimate interests in areas of policy, either prospective or current.

PROF. ANTHONY KING: I am going to stop there. I have a lot of other questions, but I can see the clock and I think in fairness to my colleagues I ought to leave it there.

378. LORD NOLAN: May I just chip in with one question: do I understand you to say that in your role as a consultant to De Montfort you would, for example, accompany them if they wanted to see a Minister about something affecting them?

NIGEL FORMAN: I might well accompany them. As it happens the occasions when I've been present hitherto, when they have met Ministers, have tended to be in a more social framework, that is to say over lunch or dinner, that kind of thing, rather than at Ministerial offices. But they could just as easily be at Ministerial offices if that was what was convenient to the Minister.

379. LORD NOLAN: Yes. That is therefore part of the advice and help you give them and services you give them in return for your consultancy fee, whatever it is?

NIGEL FORMAN: Yes.

380. LORD NOLAN: Did I understand you to say earlier that it is very hard to distinguish between that and the position of a professional lawyer or farmer or engineer raising matters in Parliament in which he had an interest?

NIGEL FORMAN: I think what I was trying to say, Lord Nolan, was that the experience and the knowledge—and, indeed, the financial interest, too, in sort of capital terms—which, say, a farmer (to take that example) has in matters of agricultural policy is in my view qualitatively in no way different to the interest in financial terms which a consultant or a non-executive director would have in the well-being of the firm or the body for which he was consulting.

381. LORD NOLAN: Yes. I suppose the farmer or the lawyer might say that he was not being paid for his role in Parliament—he actually lost money by giving up his professional time to work in Parliament whereas you would be paid for your time?

NIGEL FORMAN: Yes, he could draw that distinction but it doesn't alter the interest. I mean, there is a different question here of vocabulary and the financial interest remains just as it does with large shareholdings as, for example, we see in the register they have to be declared if they are over a certain percentage.

382. LORD NOLAN: You say in both cases they plainly must be declared but that is sufficient?

NIGEL FORMAN: Yes.

LORD NOLAN: Thank you. Now I am going to go round the table. Lord Thomson?

383. LORD THOMSON: Just pursing this point—it is very central, I think, to the judgment we are trying to

make—first of all, do you feel that the fact that quite a number of Members of Parliament are in fact employed by lobbying firms either in individual cases or a lobbying firm with a range of clients—do you feel that there is a serious degree of abuse in Parliament at the moment arising from this?

NIGEL FORMAN: I feel uncomfortable with that. I am not happy when I see it happening. I think that in a sense Parliament is already rather sort of overwhelmed with lobbying groups of one kind or another. I know a bit about the American political system, having lived in that country, and I know the consequences that can flow if that tendency goes too far ——

384. LORD THOMSON: Given that starting point, do you think there ought to be —— there are various things that Members of Parliament are not allowed to do at the moment, or there are various kinds of people who are not allowed to become Members of Parliament—do you think there should be an absolute prohibition on a Member of Parliament being a paid employee or a paid director of a lobbying firm just with a range of clients that come and go but looking after their interests in so far as they exist at any particular moment in terms of Parliamentary legislation?

NIGEL FORMAN: I think if this committee were to recommend a ban on that category of activity as being inconsistent with Membership of the House of Commons I would support that recommendation.

385. LORD THOMSON: Then do I understand that you feel that this distinction between consulting—giving advice, as you have been describing it very clearly to us, to an outside person with a perfectly legitimate interest in legislative prospects—and actually advocacy in Parliament of their interests, is a sustainable distinction?

NIGEL FORMAN: It is difficult to define because when I have discussed this with others, as naturally one does from time to time, the more you look into it the more difficult it is. The devil is in the detail. But nonetheless I think this committee is admirably qualified to attempt that task.

386. LORD THOMSON: Yes. I mean, the difficulty I find with it, if I may say so—and it is an attractive proposition if it would work—is Parliament depends, both Houses of Parliament depend to some extent anyway on the people who are making argument, are engaged in advocacy in Parliament, knowing something about the things that they are advocating, and if you go too far down the road of a prohibition will it not—well, to take an example, the large number of lawyer MPs—if they are to be prohibited from engaging in advocacy on changes in relation to the legal system, legal aid or whatever, it deprives the House of Commons, does it not, of people with actual practical experience of these issues? I am in a dilemma and I just wondered if you could help me.

NIGEL FORMAN: Yes, you put your finger on one of the greatest difficulties in this modest proposal and I think the way to come to terms with it is to say that outside interests, whether they are previous to your Parliamentary career or during your Parliamentary career, are likely to inform and to enhance your Parliamentary contribution, as I said earlier. Therefore if, for example, a farmer is speaking on matters of

agricultural or European policy he is going to be listened to much more carefully and he is going to speak with more authority "cateris paribus" than somebody who has never been near a farm, and that is to the good—and Parliament should cling to that tradition. It always has been thus. But if, on the other hand, somebody is merely standing up as, shall we say, a paid official of either a trade union (and that has been known in the past in Parliament) or of a firm or of a trade association or of an outside interest and more or less reading out the brief, as it were, and then ending his speech with specific recommendations that this tax relief should be granted, or that should be denied, or whatever it is, that, in my book, is outright straightforward advocacy of the kind which I think is probably unhealthy.

387. LORD THOMSON: That is very helpful. And finally, do you think we should get more stringent rules about declarations of interest? At the moment one has the feeling that simply because you have registered in the register you don't even need to declare an interest now because if anybody cares to look you up—I am not talking about you personally—but if anybody cares to look up the register they can find out ——

NIGEL FORMAN: Yes, I think there is a need for, as I said, both tighter and more binding rules. I think I said that in my memorandum and I stand by it.

LORD THOMSON: Thank you very much.

LORD NOLAN: Sir William?

388. WILLIAM UTTING: I wondered if there had ever been any examples of your outside interests proving a handicap to the performance of your Parliamentary duties, or obstructing them in any way?

NIGEL FORMAN: Well, I cannot recall any such instances. Indeed I would turn the argument the other way round, really, and I would reiterate what I said earlier. I think it has actually made me a better and more effective—and certainly more knowledgable—MP than I would otherwise have been. One of the things I slightly deplore, Lord Nolan, if I may be allowed a slightly broader observation, as Mr. Barnes had a few broad observations, is the secular trend in British politics towards the full-time professional MP, very often one who has come from a kind of political background in the first place, so they are on a sort of closed loop, and if we criticise teachers and dons and people for going from school to university, back to school again, and all that sort of thing, so equally we could apply a similar criticism to the tendency for too many politicians to go through those loops as well. If you study the figures you will find it is borne out by the evidence.

389. WILLIAM UTTING: You have gone a long way to answering my next question, but there is still a little bit of that that I would want to put to you, and that is observing the performance of Parliament there may be a case for saying that we should actually look for more professionalism on the part of our politicians instead of less. I am not making that point frivolously because I am wanting to go on to try and establish whether there is a genuine relationship between the conduct of Members of Parliament and the effectiveness and efficiency with which Parliamentary business is done. Points have been put to us that there is a need actually for Parliament to improve the way it does its business. I mean, do you see

any very direct relationship between the conduct of individual MPs and the effectiveness with which Parliamentary business is done? Does direct advocacy really affect Parliamentary competence?

NIGEL FORMAN: No, I don't think it does. In fact I think it is probably neutral but if there were a relationship I think outside involvement of the kind we have been discussing is probably more likely to be positive than negative. If you ask me, therefore, for an explanation as to why Parliament is seen to be and thought to be slightly inefficient, or sub-optimal in the way that it deals with legislation or political questions, you need look no further than the rather archaic procedures which on the whole we are still lumbered with, as Sir Clifford will know far better than any of us, most of which stem from Balfour's reforms of the 1880s.

WILLIAM UTTING: Good, thank you.

LORD NOLAN: Clifford?

390. CLIFFORD BOULTON: Can I just chip away a bit further about this business about permitted and forbidden advocacy? You refer to the long-standing guidance in Erskine May about advocacy, effectively that the Member should not give away or sell his total freedom of action in Parliament, that you shouldn't sign any agreement or come to an understanding with anybody which puts you under an obligation to speak under instruction or to vote under instruction, and I think that is where we get close to the analogy with a barrister and why it was banned originally in respect of barristers in the 17th century and you mustn't take on clients for whom you become a spokesman, you must guard your own freedom of speech. I think there is no dispute about that.

NIGEL FORMAN: Yes.

391. CLIFFORD BOULTON: It is simply a question then of to what extent you should be able to maintain your freedom of choice of what you say and what you do while nevertheless having a financial relationship with a broad interest group. I can understand your diffidence about getting up and speaking specifically about the interests of Gavin Anderson & Co., I am a little more puzzled though about your diffidence about speaking up on behalf of the profession of chartered accountants and I think that very often a body which feels that it can benefit—a two-way benefit—from a Member associating with them, educating him about their problems and letting him educate them about politics —— it very often might be an appropriate Member who had got constituency interest as well or had got personal knowledge —— the idea that he can do everything about tipping them off about the best way of getting things done in Government but is consequently silenced in the House of Commons and he can't get up having declared his interest and say "The profession is very worried about this and I feel I ought to say this about it". You are gagging some of the best people who know about it, aren't you, by your rule?

NIGEL FORMAN: Well, that highlights the difficulty for a body like the Institute of Chartered Accountants of England and Wales which is absolutely impeccably reputable and what it means is in the circumstances I sketched out they would have to rely upon the considerable number of Members of Parliament who have accountancy backgrounds, who knew about accountancy

and would speak from their own personal experience and authority and they would simply not, if you followed my recommendation, be able to rely on the one person, as it happens—because they only ever retain one person for this person at any time—putting the case as well. Now, that might be a loss for them but on the other hand they could fall back on a considerable body of knowledgeable accountants who would be sympathetic to their arguments. And not just accountants, either, because I may say—going back to the point that was made about laymen in earlier testimony—we have to be generalists, Mr. Barnes is right about that, we have to be laymen, almost professional laymen, if you like, and we have to have the ability to understand technical and professional points of view. And that is what I think experience in Parliament teaches one.

392. CLIFFORD BOULTON: So you accept, in fact—perhaps you indicated that at the beginning—this would be a very big change from the current position where many bodies, Institute of University Teachers, or whatever it might be, would expect the person that they had this relationship with from time to time to speak up on their behalf or speak up for them? But entering into these relations with a particular individual Member you would be switching him off, also someone who is free to speak, or vote, of course—we can't talk about motivation of voting, that is not very easy to distinguish, and there is no such thing as declaring your interest on voting, but speaking you would say you must recognise you are silencing that Member?

NIGEL FORMAN: Yes, I think it would be a two-way recognition. The Member of Parliament would have to recognise that in a sense he would no longer have the opportunity to speak in the way that he perhaps does now—for example on behalf of the Police Federation, to take another case in point—but equally the outside interest would have to recognise that in so far as they thought they would continue to benefit from the contact with such a person, the paid contact, it would be benefit derived from the advice that he could give on the basis of his experience and knowledge as a Parliamentarian.

CLIFFORD BOULTON: Thanks.

LORD NOLAN: We are running short of time but I don't think that matters ——

393. PETER SHORE: I haven't many questions. I am also much interested in the distinction between advocacy and advice—and this goes back to the Straus Committee of '69, a report incidentally the Government and opposition decided raised too many complex problems to be pursued any further and it was simply not debated in Parliament and just left on one side. But coming back to the distinction; in order to separate the function of paid advice from the business of paid advocacy, you have already had to concede that in order to make it effective you have got to give up the right to speak in the House on that interest. That indicates, I think, some of the complexities involved, but is there not a really even more difficult one? When we think of advocacy who are we trying to influence? It is above all Ministers, is it not? Sometimes colleagues, I agree, are important as well, but Ministers, and is not really the crux of the matter being paid for providing access to Ministers? That leads you into that difficulty, does it not, when you discussed your functions for one of your consultancies, where you would arrange, if possible, access to Ministers, whether in an

informal setting or a formal setting? I put the problem to you and I would like to have your comment.

NIGEL FORMAN: Yes, I mean, if the rules were changed and one would, of course, abide by the new rules—that goes without saying—then that would rule out certain things which now are ruled in as it were, now legal and possible and acceptable, that is true. But just to take up your earlier point, Mr. Shore, about advocacy, you will know that it is not in every Parliament, goodness knows, that the Government has an overwhelming crushing majority and therefore can just steam-roller things through. We can both remember times, both in recent times, in the last few weeks and months, and back in the 1970s, when the state of Parliamentary opinion, particularly among Government Back Benchers, becomes a critical consideration for any Minister. And so, you know, we would be naive if we ran away with the Governmental view entirely, which is all you have got to do is wheel people into the Whitehall office and Bob's your uncle, things happen. It is not like that.

The other thing is, the important thing about the present position is don't forget the word "disclosure" and so when somebody says something or writes a letter or makes a speech and prefaces his remarks as he is duty-bound to do and he does, with the remark "As you know, I am a paid consultant to this", or "I am a non-executive director of that", any sensible Minister and the civil servants advising him will immediately in their mind's eye, as it were, aim off somewhat to a degree for that fact, because it puts it in a different category to constituency representation or even party political representation. I am sure you would accept that, with your Ministerial experience.

PETER SHORE: Thank you.

394. ANNE WARBURTON: I think it would be right to take the extra time to go back to a slightly different point in Mr. Forman's paper. You said, Mr. Forman, "the time has come to consider carefully whether there is a case for introducing more of an independent and external element into the procedure for investigation in enforcement, such as this committee". It is going rather further, I think, than most of our witnesses have gone because it is rather saying, I think, that something like this committee—which I take it is what you mean by an independent standing committee—would have the right to regulate behaviour in Parliament. You have suggested it so I take it you are happy with that. I am particularly interested to know whether you think that the idea would be well received amongst your colleagues in Parliament, but would you care to develop that thought?

NIGEL FORMAN: Well, I do know, Dame Anne, that it would be very controversial among my colleagues because they have told me so. And it would be controversial because there is a long tradition, as we heard from Mr. Barnes and perhaps others, of Parliamentary self-regulation, partly on the old constitutional grounds of Parliamentary supremacy, and so on, and partly because the House of Commons is sometimes described as the best club in London and it has got still a bit of a sort of club atmosphere about it. But what I prefaced my remarks on at the beginning was that I felt that the world around us, you know, outside Parliament, outside the villages of Whitehall and Westminster, has changed and is changing and public expectations—what the public will put up with is changing—and that is part of the reason, Lord Nolan, why I think the Prime Minister invited you to do this committee in the first place. So taking account of that, that is why I believe on mature reflection that complete self-regulation, which is roughly speaking what we have got now, is no longer tenable and that is why I am driven, not with any great pleasure, to the sort of proposal I make at the end of my memorandum and, indeed, you will notice in paragraph 9 I say very clearly "It appears that there is no ideal solution". I am sure you will agree with that and all there is really is a least-bad solution and I think the most difficult issues of all, which I covered in the memorandum and which you covered in your questions, are the issues to do with investigation and enforcement. I think they make some of these other questions look quite easy by comparison. I don't know whether that answers your question.

ANNE WARBURTON: Yes, thank you.

LORD NOLAN: A very clear answer like all your answers. Thank you very much indeed, Mr. Forman.

TUESDAY 24 JANUARY 1995

Members Present:

The Rt. Hon. The Lord Nolan (Chairman)

Sir Clifford Boulton GCB
Sir Martin Jacomb
The Rt. Hon. Tom King CH MP
The Rt. Hon. Peter Shore MP

The Rt. Hon. The Lord Thomson of Monifieth KT DL
Sir William Utting, CB
Dame Anne Warburton DCVO CMG
Diana Warwick

Witnesses:
Rt. Hon. John MacGregor MP
Andrew Gifford (Chairman) and Charles Miller (Secretary), Association of Professional Political Consultants
John Witherow (Editor) and Michael Jones, *Sunday Times*
Colin Thompson FCA (Director) and Leigh Mendelsohn (President), Public Relations Consultants Association
Emma Nicholson MP

395. LORD NOLAN: As we begin our second week of oral evidence, it is interesting to note that, as from tomorrow, we shall be three months into our work. It was on 25 October last that the Prime Minister gave us our task, so we are more or less halfway through our work on the first report, which was asked for in about six months.

Already we are finding that the oral evidence is yielding useful insights to complement the mass of written submissions we have received. We have of course already set out our priority areas for study in the Issues and Questions paper. We must keep our eyes firmly on those priorities and resist the temptation to follow down every interesting alley which opens up, at least during the first phase of our work.

I am sure that our witnesses today will be able to help us in this. We have five witnesses, or sets of witnesses, today and we shall need to proceed pretty briskly. We have two Members of Parliament, we have the editor of the *Sunday Times* and we have representatives of two organisations covering lobbying and public relations firms.

First, I would like to welcome Mr John MacGregor MP, who has had a distinguished career both as a Cabinet Minister and as Leader of the House of Commons. Following up last week's case study on Ebbsfleet, Mr MacGregor has volunteered to tell us about that decision and the role of the lobbyists, as seen from the epicentre, but we will also be most interested to hear his views on the wider issues we are examining.

Mr MacGregor, am I right in thinking that you have helpfully prepared an opening statement?

RT HON JOHN MacGREGOR MP

RT HON JOHN MacGREGOR MP: I have on the wider issues, but I would also like to say something, if I may, on the first issue you raised, my Lord Chairman, and that is Ebbsfleet and the lobby firms, which may be helpful to kick us off.

LORD NOLAN: Yes, indeed, by all means. Take your own course and then, when you have made your statement, I am going to ask Diana Warwick to continue with your questions.

JOHN MacGREGOR: Thank you very much. Could I make two points in particular at the outset on that set of issues? First, on Ebbsfleet, the decisions on the stations, as on the rest of the line, were taken entirely on their merits and after all, and I repeat "all", representations had been received. In fact Union Railways did by far the bulk of the work, and their report was published, excepting of course matters of commercial consideration. Their recommendations on the transport benefits were absolutely clear cut, and our decisions were based upon them. I can say quite categorically that Decision Makers had no influence on the result: their work added nothing.

Second, I think the role and so-called influence of lobby firms needs to be put into its proper perspective. In my experience and judgment it is greatly overstated. They do not have preferential access to and influence with government. Presumably if such claims are made, they are made to potential clients for marketing purposes and to win business. On the other hand, lobbying firms do have a legitimate role. For those companies, organisations and pressure groups who do not have their own resources they can provide a proper and useful information service, just as some PR firms provide news cuttings services and so on, and that is a service about what is going on in Parliament effectively. They can provide technical knowledge on how government and Parliament work, and they have experience in knowing how best to present a case.

No doubt we are coming on to the question of whether MPs should have remunerated employment of one sort or another with lobbying firms. Can I start by saying that I have never accepted, nor ever would accept, such a position. Some firms, as I understand it, through an association to which you refer in your Issues and Questions, have committed themselves to not employing MPs, but the question, I think, for you and for us is whether Parliament should debar MPs from having connections with lobbying firms. I have to confess to you that I have some difficulty with this. I have been wrestling with this quite a lot since you raised the issue in your Issues and Questions. I can see some force in the point that a prime purpose of such organisations is to lobby Parliament or government for causes, and sometimes they may be causes which MPs may not actually believe in, just as barristers take on cases of advocacy, but MPs are supposed to use their individual judgments as to the arguments they advance and the causes they espouse.

The problem, however, is this: where do you draw the line? Lobbying is a natural and inevitable part of the democratic process. Like other MPs, I am lobbied constantly every day of the week and most Saturdays and Sundays by my constituents, and quite often they are doing so as part of a straightforward national lobby, whether it be an animal welfare group—there is a great deal of that going on at the moment—the Royal College of Nurses, the BMA, the Police Federation or, quite frequently, public sector trade union groups; and every day, too, our mailbag contains plenty of non-constituency lobbying material. That is the first point.

Then it has always been regarded as a perfectly legitimate, indeed useful, role for individual MPs to act as consultants to such interest groups, of course provided they declare it. So the question is: can you draw a distinction between an MP advising a trade association or a body like the Police Federation and a firm which acts for them as well as for others? I rather doubt it, but that is the point you will have to address. It would be all too easy of course for you to respond to certain public pressures, but what is the logic, where are the principles, and I think you must make your recommendations on the basis of logic and principles.

Two very quick final points, on which I am clear. The activities of all sorts of pressure groups at Westminster have increased greatly, as indeed they have, and perhaps even more so, in Brussels. You said you didn't want to go down other by-routes at the moment. Can I just, as a sort of footnote, say that I assume that the committee is looking at experience there in relation to lobbying firms, and indeed at MEPs. I can't see how you can exclude the European Parliament from consideration of questions of MPs, and therefore MEPs come into it as well as the lobby firms at Brussels.

LORD NOLAN: They are in our terms of reference.

JOHN MacGREGOR: They are in your terms of reference, but I notice they are not in your priorities at the moment, and I think there is some interrelationship, between them.

However, back to the point about the activities at Westminster. I am concerned at the extent to which parliamentary facilities are increasingly being booked for such organisations through MPs and I see there was a suggestion put to you that lobby firms should have some limited direct access. That seems to me to be wholly wrong and should be rejected. I think there needs to be a close look at just how much use is made of parliamentary activities directly by lobby organisations.

The other point is this, and it is a point that did worry me as Leader of the House and in some of my Ministerial capacities. MPs who advise lobby groups, trade associations and the like I think have to be extremely careful about the actions they take in Parliament—i.e. what amendments they put down, what Questions they ask, what Early Day Motions they put down or sign as top signatories. This is, to my mind, the key area of concern. I note that you have quoted a point in your Issues and Questions from the Select Committee on Members' Interests, which reported in March 1992, and I think that it is a very relevant quotation:

"Members who hold consultancy and similar positions must ensure that they do not use their position as Members improperly'. A financial inducement to take a particular course of action in Parliament may constitute a bribe and thus be an offence against the law of Parliament."

It then goes on to quote "Erskine May", as I think you did. I just wonder whether one ought not to consider prohibiting MPs with lobby interests directly of that sort from taking those actions, putting down amendments, asking Questions or tabling Early Day Motions particularly related to the lobby group they are advising.

DIANA WARWICK: I wonder, Mr MacGregor, if I could ask you questions in the order in which you have presented your views to us.

JOHN MacGREGOR: Certainly, yes.

396. DIANA WARWICK: Can I deal first of all with the Ebbsfleet affair? The lobbying firm to which we have all referred, Decision Makers, claim to have created "a massive weight of informed discussion which eventually succeeded in overturning government thinking". It is not our job to comment on what might be the hyperbole of lobbying firms, but the editor of the *Evening Standard* gave us a leaked report from Decision Makers to their client, which listed things they had organised—Ministerial meetings, Back-Bench meetings, political party meetings, dinners, receptions, even an evening at Hampton Court. You yourself were said to have had a private meeting and briefing and your special adviser was a key target for the campaign. You have said that they have no influence at all, but do you think the actions of Decision Makers gave the promoters of Ebbsfleet an advantage?

JOHN MacGREGOR: No. I will be as quick as I can, because I know we want to get on to other issues, but I shall deal with all the points you made. First of all, it is not correct that they either had particular influence on the decision or overturned any decision we were thinking of making, because in fact at the time we were receiving all representations, not just from Ebbsfleet interests, and there were a lot of other Ebbsfleet interests apart from Blue Circle. At the time we were doing that we hadn't actually made up our minds. We made up our minds when we got the Union Railways report. I took a view myself and then we discussed it as Ministers generally. I am absolutely clear that I took my decision and my views on the basis, above all, of Union Railways' report. I say "above all", because there were other environmental and economic regeneration issues, but Union Railways were looking at the transport benefits. We had other consultants and others, and of course our officials, looking at those wider aspects. When you put them in, the choice of Ebbsfleet at the end of the day between Ebbsfleet, Rainham and Nashenden as the M25 Parkway station—there is still a question as to whether there should be two stations, and that is where Stratford comes in—was, I thought, absolutely clear on the merits of a very, very well-assembled case, taking into account all representations.

Second point: we deliberately asked to have representations from all the station interests—the local authorities, local business, lots and lots of people—and we indicated that one key consideration was going to be the financial contribution that the promoters would make to the development of the station. So it was obviously right and proper that there should be a lot of representations to us, and indeed we wanted that.

I then come to your third point.

DIANA WARWICK: That means that you did have a meeting with Decision Makers, but it was one among many.

JOHN MacGREGOR: I will come to that actually. It was one of very many.

The third point is that the document that you mentioned in the *Evening Standard*—I haven't seen the full document; I only saw the *Evening Standard* report—seemed to me to be a marketing document to get the business originally, quite frankly, and I can say that much of what was in it didn't happen: I did not visit Ebbsfleet. I went to a Blue Circle site just on the edge of the second Dartford crossing as part of a ministerial visit. I was opening a motorway service station and looking at tolling on the bridge and just below that there was a Blue Circle site which I visited at the request of Bob Dunn MP, but that was done in September 1982, well before any of this came up, and I did not go to Ebbsfleet at all to look at it as part of this process. My Minister of State, who spent two and a half years going up and down the line—I spent a lot of time going up and down the line, but he spent two and a half years—did do so, and he had meetings with all the promoters, just about in equal number. I had one meeting on Ebbsfleet, and that was at the request of Bob Dunn and Jacques Arnold, the two MPs. Miss Tomison did come as Decision Makers to that meeting, but it was requested by the MPs, and I did it with the MPs themselves, but I hope I have made it clear that everything that was done was done absolutely properly with representations, and I am 100 per cent certain that the decisions were taken on the basis of the merits of the argument. I would certainly never think of doing otherwise.

397. DIANA WARWICK: Could I then ask you a general question that arises from what you have just said? You agreed to a meeting at the request of the local MPs and they invited a lobbyist to come with them. Have you ever agreed to a meeting because an MP has lobbied you rather than, normally, leaving it to officials or a junior Minister? Have you had a meeting because you have been lobbied by an MP?

JOHN MacGREGOR: Oh yes, on a whole range of issues. All my ministerial life I have had meetings with MPs. I think that is part of the job of the Minister. But we get a huge number of requests. For example, just about every MP asks to see a Minister of the Department of Transport on his local road project. There is a huge amount of that. I can't do them all, in fact I can do very few, so I normally did one or two—I can hardly recall doing one on a road—with Privy Councillors, but we share it out, and we shared out the other one. So we are doing that with MPs a great deal.

I think one of the points that is missing in the public comment on this debate at least is that the role of the MP is taken by Ministers as being the key issue here, and if a lobby group is involved in the same representation, please remember that it's the MP that one sees; it's the MP that is the critical person. But of course Roger Freeman was seeing a lot of others. I think he saw the Stratford promoters, who actually did one of the most extensive lobbies, probably rather more than any other station. So we are all doing that.

398. DIANA WARWICK: Could I perhaps move on? Others of my colleagues may want to pursue one or two of those points, but if I can move on to the general question of invitations to MPs, I imagine that, as a Minister, you received a very large number of invitations. It is not always easy to distinguish between different forms of invitation—entertainment, lunches, dinners and so on. What I would like to ask you is: when you have accepted invitations, have you ever concluded afterwards that your position was either substantively or even, on reflection, in appearance compromised as a result of it?

JOHN MacGREGOR: I don't think so. You are quite right: one of the jobs of a Minister, and I have always believed this very strongly, is to get out from under his desk, and not just in Parliament but around the country all the time. I think that is very important. Frankly, civil servants don't have enough opportunities, and perhaps that is inevitable, to get round the country, and that is not entirely their role. It is very important that Ministers go and find out about whatever it is that concerns them and make themselves available to people who want to put points of view to them. So I spent a large part of my ministerial life in every job I did meeting people over breakfasts, lunches and dinners, discussing issues with them, because that is how I get my feeling and judgment about what are good cases and what are not, what is really going on and what I should be concerned about as a Minister. Then it must be your judgment as to what views you take as a result of the representations you receive.

399. DIANA WARWICK: But in all that time you don't ever feel even that there might have been an appearance of compromise? I say that because ——

JOHN MacGREGOR: Because I did it so widely.

DIANA WARWICK: ——we are trying to distinguish between the real and the apparent in some of the evidence that we are receiving.

Can I ask you about MPs as paid consultants? You raise that. One assumes that they do have privileged access to Ministers. You seem to be suggesting that in your view they don't, and yet lobbyists seem to be suggesting to us that this is one of their main functions. Could you tell us whether you think that having an MP associated with a company gives that company an additional advantage?

JOHN MacGREGOR: I don't think it does. I can't speak for every Minister and the way that they operate in making sure they are well informed, but it would certainly not be the case with me, and I would think that is true of most of my colleagues, if not all of them.

400. DIANA WARWICK: Do you think that there should be any financial restrictions on the financial connections with MPs to lobbyists?

JOHN MacGREGOR: I have already, I think, outlined my difficulty on this. My difficulty is that I don't see quite where you draw the line. What is the distinction? I can't quite see it myself, but it is for you to recommend to Parliament. Let's take an animal welfare group, or whatever you like. What is the distinction between an MP who works advising the group directly and one who works for a group which wants to work through a firm because it perhaps doesn't have the full resources to employ someone indirectly or thinks it might get a wider range of information and service from a firm for whom an MP works? I can't see where you draw the line. Do you therefore want to say that all MPs should be excluded from working for things like the Police Federation and so on? You can try and draw a line there, if you wish, but that probably means that one is excluding a lot of worthwhile activity. So that is why I come back to being very, very clear about what an MP should do, if it has a relationship with either a lobby firm or a trade association, perhaps debarring them from putting down amendments which directly affect that organisation, putting down Early Day Motions, putting down Questions.

401. DIANA WARWICK: So do you think it would be useful to have more detailed guidance to MPs on what is and what is not acceptable?

JOHN MacGREGOR: The first issue is to decide what is and what is not acceptable, and that is really what I have been trying to address. If that leads to the conclusion that things like curtailing the activities directly of actions in Parliament of the sort I have been describing, then clearly guidance would have to be given on that.

402. DIANA WARWICK: Can I come on to the final point that I would like to raise, which is the question of Ministers moving from office into parts of the private sector where they have had an official dealing? This is something that has come up in relation to your case, and I would like to raise that, and I would like to approach it in this way. The rules which govern the conduct of civil servants are quite clear. Would you suggest that if a Permanent Secretary in your Department, having been involved with a company like Hill Samuel, with which you are involved, were to move to Hill Samuel, do you think the rules would then apply to a civil servant in your Department?

JOHN MacGREGOR: I was actually going to deal with this in the second part of the evidence that I am giving today. I have a reference to it there, but perhaps I will just deal with it now.

I don't think the analogy with the Civil Service is appropriate. There is a problem, I think, for Ministers, and I will be coming on to this later. One of the main thrusts of my argument is going to be the importance of Parliament having real experience and knowledge and also not debarring good people from coming into Parliament, because there is a real issue there, which I shall touch on later. The difference between civil servants and Ministers is this. Civil servants, when they retire as Permanent Secretaries—I was going to say that until very recently there has been very clear job security—or perhaps when they are made redundant, have either substantial pensions or very considerable redundancy payments. Ministers have very little indeed when they are suddenly ousted from office. In fact very many of them face a big drop in salary immediately. If you make the restrictions on what you can do after you cease being a Minister very severe, you will discourage a lot of good people from becoming Ministers, so there is a distinction there.

As far as Hill Samuel is concerned, I was of course employed with Hill Samuel before I entered Parliament and before I became a Minister. Because of that I made it clear throughout my ministerial career that I would not get involved at all, but would absolutely shut myself away from, any tendering for jobs that came from anyone in the

City. In fact it only arose when I went to the Department of Transport, I think, but I was certainly clear about that, and that is well minuted. So I had nothing to do at all with the choice of Hill Samuel for one advisory role that they did for the Department of Transport, and I was very, very keen to make that clear.

403. DIANA WARWICK: But can I pursue you on the question I asked, which was: would a senior civil servant, having had that association, be barred from going to Hill Samuel under the normal rules that exist now?

JOHN MacGREGOR: I don't know, but I think there is a difference, as I have just explained.

404. DIANA WARWICK: We have colleagues who can advise me better, but where civil servants have a close and commercial expertise because of the work they have done for government, they are automatically debarred for, I think it is, two months and then there is an independent review of whether or not there should be a further barring of them moving into the commercial sector. Do you think that that would have applied in this case, should such a case have arisen?

JOHN MacGREGOR: I agreed to go to Hill Samuel more than two months after I left the Government anyway, so I did do that by choice, as it happens. I think if you wanted to be absolutely sure that Ministers were straightforward about this—and I am clear we are; we have to exercise our own judgment—then you could consider something of that sort, but I think it is important to put into the consideration the fact that you have to take account of the fact that Ministers usually face quite a big drop in salary immediately, and you don't want that to be a disincentive to their taking up ministerial appointment in the first place.

405. DIANA WARWICK: I am trying to get at this distinction between the influence that a senior civil servant can bring to bear and the influence that a Minister can. I did wonder if your comment about pensions was a bit disingenuous.

JOHN MacGREGOR: No, I don't think it is, because my later case is going to be the difficulty, I think, which will be increasingly a problem if there are barriers to outside interests, of recruiting good people into Parliament and to ministerial positions. We have certainly got to take that very much into account. I will develop that case later, if I may, but I am quite clear in my own mind that Ministers who use the broad thrust of experience that they have had in both business and government later in the careers exercise their judgment very carefully in so doing, and I would certainly wish to do so.

406. DIANA WARWICK: May I just make a final point, Lord Nolan? Just coming back to my point about appearance and reality—I have obviously pinpointed you, because you are here, but there have been several accusations that there have been ministerial moves of this kind—do you think it would be helpful to have similar rules for Ministers as for civil servants, so that the position is absolutely clear?

JOHN MacGREGOR: It would have to be clear that they are in different positions, and different considerations would have to be taken into account in framing those rules. Could I just say this? You have addressed things to me, but—I don't want go go into my personal position too much—I have actually turned down quite a number of opportunities because I thought they were inappropriate, and I was very careful in what I did.

DIANA WARWICK: And I think under the current arrangements that is a judgment that you as a Minister would make ——

JOHN MacGREGOR: Yes.

DIANA WARWICK: ——rather than it being referred elsewhere.

JOHN MacGREGOR: Yes.

DIANA WARWICK: Thank you.

407. LORD NOLAN: Mr MacGregor, I wonder if I could take you back to the difficulty you mentioned about drawing an acceptable line between the interests which Members might take up with outside bodies. In 1947, Lord Callaghan reminded us, the House passed a resolution that it was inconsistent with the dignity of the House for any Member to enter into any contract with an outside body

"controlling or limiting the Member's independence and freedom of action in Parliament or stipulating that he shall act in any way as the representative of such outside body in regard to any matters to be transacted in Parliament."

That virtually rules out any form of paid advocacy. We know that that was altered later when the Register of Interests was brought in. What is wrong with that as a principle that you shouldn't be able to pay a Member of Parliament for work he does as a Member of Parliament?

JOHN MacGREGOR: I don't think that is quite the principle, is it, that he shouldn't be paid to act as an advocate in Parliament for a paid interest, and that's what it is, and I entirely agree with that, and that's why I raised the last point I did. It seems to me perfectly legitimate for a Member of Parliament to advise bodies on how Parliament works and those sort of issues. Particularly if it is a cause that he feels very strongly about, he may well wish to advise them how best to present the case. But if he is in an employment relationship of one sort or another, I really do worry if he or she then starts to put amendments down to Bills or Early Day Motions, which we all know are only expressions of view but are regarded as rather more than that and do actually galvanise parliamentary support in themselves, and Questions directly. These are, I think, quite difficult issues on which to establish the logic and the principles, but when I have been thinking a lot about this recently that seemed to me to be where you possibly could draw the line.

LORD NOLAN: Paid advocacy you should rule out.

JOHN MacGREGOR: Advocacy, yes.

LORD NOLAN: Thank you. I can see there might then be difficulties distinguishing between the adviser and the advocate, but there it is.

JOHN MacGREGOR: I actually think there are a lot of difficulties in drawing the line in some of these

questions and exactly where you do draw the line, but that seemed to me to be one that was logical.

408. LORD NOLAN: Another area which much concerns us and which you dealt with is the movement of Ministers into posts in industry with companies with which perhaps long ago they had connections or with which they have new connections. Would it be sensible to introduce an umpire, who could act rather as I think the Permanent Secretaries act in relation to civil servants, to look at the contract—the proposed engagement—and say "I am satisfied that there is going to be no advantage to the employing company that it wouldn't otherwise have got, so this is a perfectly proper case" or, conversely, "This is really very unwise. Either there may be a preference, or it will look as if there is." Could there be, do you think, some machinery for doing that?

JOHN MacGREGOR: Machinery or an outside umpire?

LORD NOLAN: Yes.

JOHN MacGREGOR: I can see why the case is being argued, in order to demonstrate, which I think is the case, that Ministers are extremely careful in what they do. There may be some advantage in that, but the rules would have to be clear. I don't think it should just be left to the discretion of the umpire. He would have to be very clear about the considerations that he would have to take into account.

409. LORD NOLAN: Certainly, but you think some independent mechanism of that sort might be helpful for all concerned, given, as you say, that the rules were clarified and were agreed to be sensible.

JOHN MacGREGOR: Yes. It would have to be within a certain period of time as well, obviously.

LORD NOLAN: Yes.

JOHN MacGREGOR: A limited period of time, because I think that if it were a restriction for all time or for an unreasonably long time, for reasons I will come on to later, that would really cause me concern, because that might well prevent very good people nowadays from being willing to take on a parliamentary career, because they will have come from whatever business, profession or whatever it is they have been in. I think it is quite difficult to draw up rules, for example, in relation to professions, but certainly if the rules were satisfactory, I can see that it does give some—what is the right word to use?—some comfort almost. It is not a very precise word, but you see what I am getting at.

410. LORD NOLAN: I do. Thank you very much. Mr MacGregor, you have mentioned more than once that there is a second part of your evidence, and I am not quite clear about what that is.

JOHN MacGREGOR: This is on the question of outside interests generally. I thought we were merely talking about lobbying in the first part.

411. LORD NOLAN: Yes. Have you a prepared statement on that?

JOHN MacGREGOR: Yes, indeed. Would you like me to move into that now?

LORD NOLAN: Yes, please.

JOHN MacGREGOR: If I may say so, Mr Chairman, I noticed with some surprise in the press at the end of last week that the committee seems to have reached some provisional conclusions. I say "with some surprise" because that seems to me highly unusual when you have only just started to take the oral evidence. It is for that reason that I really wanted to concentrate on only one aspect of the extremely important wider issues in my opening remarks.

LORD NOLAN: If I may correct you straight away, there was nothing said that suggested that a conclusion had been reached.

JOHN MacGREGOR: I am absolutely delighted to hear it. I really am very pleased to hear that. I am glad we got that clear, because some of the press reporting didn't indicate that, and I think that is very helpful.

LORD NOLAN: It was an indication of matters that we felt we should consider and which I felt should be raised early, so that subsequent witnesses could deal with them.

JOHN MacGREGOR: That suits me very well, if there are no conclusions already drawn.

I wanted really to concentrate on only one of the important issues, because it seems to me, judging from press reports, to have had too little recognition so far, and it is this. I am not going to look, when we come on to this, at the sanctions and procedures in relation to outside interests. I just wish at the moment to argue very strongly for the continuation of the outside interests of Members of Parliament and that the committee needs to be extremely careful about any further bar or barriers that they put in their way, for four reasons.

First, all my political lifetime there has been growing concern about the increasing lack of knowledge and experience in Parliament as a whole of the world outside Parliament, and I don't mean knowledge of constituency matters or of the situations people face in their everyday lives. Because of our direct constituency Member system and the close connection that that engenders between Members and their constituents, that knowledge is usually very strong, and that is one of the great merits incidentally, I believe, of our direct Member constituency system. What I mean is real, practical knowledge of business and financial sectors, of the professions, of international affairs and so on. That is why the Industry and Parliament Trust was formed, for example, and I hope and I am sure you will be looking at some of the documents at its creation which underline these concerns. Parliament should be a place of knowledge, expertise and experience. We need to strengthen Parliament in this respect, not weaken it. That is my first point.

Second, under our system it is not just Parliament which would be much the poorer if people of quality and experience, leaders or high-fliers in their fields, were discouraged from entering Parliament. Crucially under our system it would be government too, and that would have a seriously detrimental impact. I have no doubt that my business experience was invaluable to me in most of my ministerial jobs. In the United States and France this problem does not arise, because of the ready and immediate interchange of Ministers between their ministerial and their outside careers.

Third, many MPs, and certainly Ministers, face substantial cuts in their income when they get elected or appointed, and I don't mean just those from business and the professions. MPs and Ministers have heavy responsibilities; yet, taking the public sector alone, there are many in the public sector in each of our constituencies who earn more than MPs. We all know the kind of starting salaries that qualified solicitors are now obtaining in, for example, London and no doubt other major provincial centres. I know of journalists who would not consider now entering Parliament because of the substantial reduction in their remuneration that would be involved. That may even apply now to some trade union officials, and certainly many Officers of the House earn a good deal more than Members of Parliament. So there is a problem.

I don't think a substantial increase in salaries alone, if it ever happens, which I actually doubt, would solve the problem, because for many MPs, and certainly for all Ministers, it is a highly precarious career with a limited shelf-life. Few MPs now have substantial private income. For most, the parliamentary pension at the end of the day is small in comparison with what it would have been if they had not entered public life. I believe that maintenance of outside interests helps to mitigate all of these points too.

Fourth, there is increasing evidence that high quality people are being discouraged from entering Parliament. MPs often take substantial cuts in salary, there are long hours and heavy pressure on family life, and great job insecurity. We do it because we believe in public service, but if we add to the present pressures severe restrictions on or further intrusions into outside interests, we will only have ourselves to blame if the high calibre young people of the future are not prepared to make a contribution to public affairs as Members of Parliament at some point in their lives.

I hope you will take evidence on this from leaders of the business community and perhaps from some of the professions and others, because to me it is a matter of great concern. I don't want the Parliament of 15 years' time to be composed extensively of full-time politicians who have done nothing else in their lives. I think Parliament and government would be much the poorer, and I think you bear quite a heavy responsibility in ensuring that we avoid that situation coming about.

LORD NOLAN: Sir Martin, would you like to ask any questions of Mr MacGregor?

MARTIN JACOMB: No, I think he has covered all the ground I wanted, and the next witnesses follow on from that.

LORD NOLAN: Thank you. Lord Thomson?

412. LORD THOMSON: Could I ask Mr MacGregor on one point that arose from what he was saying—the question of access to Ministers, which is of course very important? He made the point that Ministers offer ready access and ought to offer ready access to Members of Parliament. I just wondered whether, in your ministerial experience, who else a Minister would feel that he would offer access to. Would he in fact offer access directly to a lobbying firm? He would, would he not, offer access in

certain circumstances to a major company that had major interests in impending legislation? What are the broad judgments that one makes about the right of access, because that is what lobbying companies tend to market a good deal and is one of the justifications for their relations with MPs? They are a cover for their access to Ministers.

JOHN MacGREGOR: That is an absolutely correct point. One of the problems Ministers face is the length of their diaries every day, and one of the reasons for that is the considerable number of meetings you have with outside bodies of all sorts. So it is impossible to categorise. It ranges from, obviously, MPs to peers, if I may say so, to organisations that are directly relevant to your departmental work—there is a very large amount of that—what you might call the trade associations, for example, and various of the organisations which exist, like road federations, bus operators and so on that are relevant in your chosen field, or the NFU, the Countryside Commission and heaven knows what else when you are Minister of Agriculture, and then of course you are quite right: there are the individual companies, people who really have something to say to you, sometimes just the businessmen themselves or the professional people themselves. I always tried to go to people who I knew had good experience and good knowledge of an issue and who would have a very strong and well-based point to bring to my attention; or where I wanted advice sometimes I would go out and seek it. Then it is up to you to make your own judgment on the basis of that. So it is absolutely enormous, but I think you are right on the point that some lobbying firms, for marketing reasons, claim to be able to get access which they don't actually. I wouldn't put my hand on my heart completely and say I've never done it, but I don't actually recall responding purely to a lobbying organisation for a meeting, and I made the case on Ebbsfleet. But, having knocked them down on that score, that I don't think they have this kind of privileged access, I just remind you of the points I have made where I think they have a legitimate role to play and where it is perfectly right for them to go and seek clients.

413. LORD THOMSON: Could I just ask one thing on Ebbsfleet, to draw a line under it as far as I am concerned? Doesn't it come down to this? You had a case of rather extreme lobbying firm hype and then a rather extreme form of media hype on the basis of the PR hype, and in the meantime the real decision was taken on its merits. Is that the case?

JOHN MacGREGOR: Oh, absolutely. I confirm that. Absolutely. The amount of listening to representations that was done by Union Railways in making their recommendations to us was simply enormous. In six months they must have taken views at over 600 public meetings for a start, taken views from all over the place, from every possible person, and we did actually encourage the organisations wishing to promote the particular station to come and see us, because we positively invited that and said "You have got to put some financial input into it. Come and discuss this with us." So there was complete openness about that process. Interestingly, I wasn't aware of the media hype about one particular lobbying firm until well after the event, after the decision had been taken and when I suddenly saw this article in the *Evening Standard*.

414. TOM KING: When we came into the House there was a complaint then that hardly anybody in the House knew much about industry or had had any practical experience. In your judgment has it got better or worse?

JOHN MacGREGOR: I think it has got worse, and I understand why. It has got worse partly because the pressures on Members of Parliament and their responsibilities have got much heavier, their hours and everything else have got very much longer, and therefore you have to be well organised and prepared to work very long hours to fit in other things, and partly, I think, because of the perception by a lot of people in the outside world that they have to take into account their families and so on, the pressures on family life, the intrusion into family life and then the discovery that they are going to take a substantial cut in salary and may not be able at any point to recuperate it, and then they look at the pensions at the end of the day, and it causes some to take a decision never to enter Parliament. So I think it has actually got worse and I think it's a great pity.

415. TOM KING: Does it have the effect of channelling the likely sources of people who are able to take the political route and to be MPs into much narrower limitations? I don't want to make a party political point, but I was just looking at the backgrounds of the Labour MEPs, the number of new MEPs in the big wins that Labour had in the last European elections. I think I am right in saying that about 75 per cent of them were further education lecturers. I stand to be corrected if anybody knows the answer, but that appeared to be the origins that they claimed. It seems to me that that is a very worthy profession, but what we do need in Parliament is a spread of people, and it should be possible under the system, whatever the basis of remuneration and whatever the opportunities for outside activities, to be able to draw as widely on background. Do you agree with that?

JOHN MacGREGOR: Yes, I do. I very much agree with that. I have certainly found in my experience, both as a Back-Bench Member and then as a Minister, that the colleagues that you tend to take most notice of are those that you know actually know something about what they are talking about, based on either extensive work they have done as a Member of Parliament, and that is very often based on what they have done before entering the House, or based on that outside knowledge, because of the outside interests they continue to have.

416. TOM KING: Can I make this point, which did not come out in your exchange with Diana Warwick. You are not in the same position as certain other Ministers who have joined companies, about which there has been criticism, with which they have had no previous connection. How long were you with Hill Samuel?

JOHN MacGREGOR: Eleven years.

417. TOM KING: The point that you raised was whether you were forbidden then, having once stood for Parliament—goodness knows how long you will stay—from going back. I have great sympathy with that, but is there a limit at which stage you have to say "I can't do my job if I have to forswear any involvement in this section of it". I will embarrass you now by saying that I always thought that you ought to have been Chancellor of the Exchequer. That being the case, could you have maintained that position as Chancellor of the Exchequer of saying, "Anything involving the City I shall have to leave to somebody else'?

JOHN MacGREGOR: The point that occurs to me—we must be sensible about these matters—is that if you want people in government who have no knowledge of the issues they are dealing with which is what your example would lead to, it is absolutely crackers—and all through my political lifetime people have complained that we are going in that direction. If you want people who know something about what they are doing or who are keen to make a lot of contacts with people whom they think are knowledgable in these matters, you are more likely to get better Ministers and better informed decisions. They are not subject to individual pressures: we are all pretty good at spotting the obvious lobby and the self-interest. Any Minister who has been in post for only a short time quickly spots the self-interest and makes his own judgment on the issue. But we should be going out and discussing the matter with people. One might even reach the point where, if one is spending a lot of time discussing important financial and economic matters with people in the City, one is thought to be compromising oneself. That is ludicrous. One must rely on the judgment of the individual. Therefore I fully take your point that a Minister can bring experience to his job both by past knowledge and interest and by current contacts. A Minister must not regard that as something that he ought not to do.

418. DIANA WARWICK: With respect, that was not the point that I was making. I was suggesting that under the present rules senior civil servants would not have been able to do what you did, therefore drawing the conclusion that perhaps we should have similar rules for the civil service and for Ministers.

JOHN MacGREGOR: I am not sure that that is right anyway, but I accept your point.

419. TOM KING: The point is, civil servants will tend to have been civil servants all their life. I came out of industry; if someone had told me "You can't get back", it would have been a major disincentive. Not all civil servants are the same. One of the strengths of the Government recently has been the enlistment of people at a mature age, with considerable experience, to do specific jobs. In your judgment, will they come if they are told they they cannot go back? It is a five-year assignment.

JOHN MacGREGOR: I agree that this is an important area. I have always felt that there has not been enough interchange between the civil service and the outside world.

TOM KING: I am thinking of Derek Rayner from Marks & Spencer.

JOHN MacGREGOR: Absolutely—which we have tried to promote. Could I be a bit more specific on the issue? The only issue, as far as I can see, that has arisen in relation to my position in Hill Samuel is that they were appointed as financial adviser to one particular operation in the Department of Transport; otherwise, Hill Samuel is not a transport organisation.

DIANA WARWICK: Yes, exactly.

JOHN MacGREGOR: I have already made clear in the Department that I would not take any part in any of those processes. If you take the position that there should be a change in that, you are either saying that a Minister who has had previous experience in a sector will disadvantage all firms competing for government contracts in his area, in which case he may decide that he cannot be unfair to his company and will not take on a ministerial role, or that a Minister must not have had any previous outside experience at all. This is where you have to exercise sensible judgment. You are getting into a really difficult area.

LORD NOLAN: Thank you. I am anxious to give the others a chance. Peter Shore, have you some questions?

420. PETER SHORE: I have a number of questions. Following directly on what you have been saying in the past few minutes, Mr MacGregor, surely external advisers who are experts are available to Government. They are called in, like Lord Rayner, to advise. In other words, there is no great problem in the Government obtaining expertise. Previous industrialists who are brought straight from the outside into Cabinet are not normally a great success, as I think we would agree. I am thinking of a number of people on both sides.

The other thing is that when we speak of the possibilities of limiting the timing in which ex-Ministers can take on private employment, at issue is not that such ex-Ministers should be generally banned from taking on private employment for any period of time, but rather that they should be limited in taking jobs in the particular areas of industry or commerce for which they have had direct ministerial responsibility. Do you not accept that important distinction?

JOHN MacGREGOR: Dealing with those points in reverse order, I have not taken up a post with a transport firm, which would have been directly related. Secondly, on the question of people from industry or the trade unions not being greatly successful in Parliament, I can think of two in my past experience. In both cases, the problem was that they rose to ministerial office extremely quickly and did not get the feel of the House. One does need parliamentary experience as well.

As to outside advisers, we employ them of course, but we do not have to take their advice. Sometimes the advice we receive depends on the adviser we have chosen. I would wish to be able to have my own view about the advice I received; frequently I did so.

421. PETER SHORE: I could pursue this at some length, but there are one or two other matters that I want to go on to without monopolising too much time. I think you accepted that access to Ministers is extremely important, not least because of the enormous workload and the number of engagements that Ministers have. Therefore, if MPs have some priority, as they undoubtedly do in reaching Ministers, surely it does matter that a PR firm has MPs on its books and is able to make the case for them. Does that not normally weigh with a Minister when deciding whether to receive a deputation?

JOHN MacGREGOR: I have very few cases of this sort. The two MPs involved in Ebbsfleet were the local MPs in question. I cannot remember many cases; there may have been one or two when I was at Agriculture, although I cannot remember them, where I agreed to see a body such as the NFU at the request of an MP. There may have been an MP or two in the delegation sometimes, but we were very careful about giving preferential access to a lobbying group just because an MP had asked. This question is very difficult. When you said that we were subjected to all sorts of lobbying, I was reflecting that frequently when I attend a lunch or dinner at which I am speaking or outside engagements throughout the country, I come away with a list of five points about which someone has talked to me after the dinner—someone who happens to know what they are talking about and is concerned about it. They spend five minutes talking to me. That is a frequent occurrence in a Minister's life. One has to constantly to judge which points to take up. It is the same when I go to my constituency at the weekend: I usually come back with quite a number of points. One has to judge which are material. It is inevitable.

422. PETER SHORE: It is, but may I bring you back to the more precise point about the Ebbsfleet decision. In that hyped marketing document that Decision Makers put out they said that you had been personally briefed by their team and had both written and oral submissions on behalf of Ebbsfleet. I should like to know whether the Stratford people had access to you personally and were able to brief you verbally and in written evidence and whether the same thing applied to your special adviser, Eleonor Laing, whom they also claimed had been briefed orally and in writing.

JOHN MacGREGOR: Let me tell you exactly what happened; it may help to illuminate the process. I saw the two MPs for Ebbsfleet. It is a question of dividing one's time. Roger Freeman also saw the two MPs for Ebbsfleet and, from my recollection, had two other meetings with Ebbsfleet and three with Stratford. I saw the minutes of the meetings, of course. He and I talked on a day-to-day basis about these sorts of issues. He was telling me what had resulted from the meetings that he had had. Then it was all put into the pot. The points that were made in the representations were all made to Union Railways and covered eventually in the report that we received from Union Railways and in the drawn-up reports by the civil servants. All the points were in the official submissions at the end of the day. There was no question of anyone getting preferential access.

Secondly, it is the case that Decision Makers left some documents on the Ebbsfleet issue with my special adviser. She looked at them and did not pass them on to me, because she said they contained nothing that was not already in the official representations that she had seen coming in. I did not see them and never used them.

There is a point about special advisers. I know that some special advisers get sick to death of being rung up and lobbied by people who think they get preferential access that way; they do not.

423. PETER SHORE: Thank you for that reply. I wish to switch to one last area. You made an important distinction about MPs on the payrolls of PR firms or other outside bodies. You made it very clear that in your view MPs should not be advocates—that is to say, they should not be seeking to get access to Ministers or to put down questions or other things if they were acting as a paid agent for an outside body. You then drew the distinction and said, "It's a very different matter just giving advice". Can you really practically draw the line between them? If I wanted to advise somebody outside about Parliament, my advice might be heavily influenced by the reply to a letter to a Minister that I had obtained or a question that I had put down, yet a letter to a Minister and a question can also be obviously part of advocacy rather than advice. Is this a possible distinction? Can it be maintained?

JOHN MacGREGOR: I am not sure that I have any greater contribution to make than both of you, as distinguished colleagues. I have been thinking quite a bit about this issue since you wrote inviting me to give evidence on it. I hope that I made clear in my opening comments that I had difficulty knowing exactly where to draw the line. I find difficulty in drawing the line between those working for a lobby firm and those working for a trade association; but I did feel that specific actions in Parliament on behalf of those organisations were moving a bit far. I take your point that sometimes it will be difficult to draw the line between advisory and advocacy—of course that is right—but my main point is that one needs to find some logic and principle in the distinctions one draws. That is what I hope the Committee will do. I am sorry to throw it back at you.

424. CLIFFORD BOULTON: I am sorry, but I want to pursue that point a little, if I may. May I leave on one side the Member who has a relationship with a general agency and talk about those who are advisers to specific groups, trade unions or whatever? You said that that relationship can be mutually beneficial and does not harm the public interest. You then said, "Nevertheless, once it exists, the Member to some extent has got to act with one hand behind his back as a Parliamentarian". We also agree that the Member should not take instructions from the group about how he should conduct himself in Parliament; he should never be briefed by them in the form of an obligation to speak or to vote in a particular way. That is common ground. But on the assumption that he has retained his own discretion and independence and, if you like, has something written into his agreement that there is no obligation or expectation to speak or vote in a particular way, I am a little concerned that he should be then limited in the full range of his parliamentary activities, because it seems to me that that is his first duty, if he is chosen to go into Parliament. I was worried about not putting your name in the top six of an Early Day Motion and one other thing you mentioned that was going to be banned—amendments. What about speaking in debate, explaining the position of farmers or Post Office workers, the cause of this mutually beneficial arrangement you have? Why should the House not have the benefit of that? What about voting? If you are an adviser to someone connected with the motor industry, you are going to say, "I can't vote in the Budget if it adversely affects them, because I shouldn't". I should like something that permits Members to be full-blown, fully active Members of Parliament as well".

JOHN MacGREGOR: You have illustrated some of the difficulties. It is very important that MPs should speak and contribute in debates, including those with outside connections which they declare. That does happen, and there is a great benefit in hearing someone speak who has real knowledge of an issue. That is very important, for all the reasons I gave earlier. Voting must be done on the basis of the merits of the case. I excluded voting from what I said, because that is right. It would be ridiculous if a Member could not vote on a matter concerning the motor industry, for instance, because he was an adviser to a motor association and therefore could not vote on any issue affecting the motor industry. Clearly, that would be wrong, but, as always, he must make his own judgment. Perhaps it is the case that one cannot even draw a line about what he can do in Parliament. I have been slightly concerned sometimes when people who are known to have a direct interest put down amendments to Bills. That led me to wonder about questions and Early Day motions.

But you may conclude that one cannot draw a line there, either.

425. CLIFFORD BOULTON: If a Member can speak and advocate something in the course of a debate, I cannot see why they should not be able to initiate the debate by tabling an amendment in, say, a Standing Committee, so long as everyone knows the Member's interests and it is declared.

JOHN MacGREGOR: I agree that there is a problem there.

ANNE WARBURTON: I will not take you into new territory. Given the time, you may prefer to move on.

426. LORD NOLAN: We are very grateful to you, Mr MacGregor. You have been so interesting that we have gone more than 15 minutes over the appropriate time. Is there a final word that you want to say?

JOHN MacGREGOR: It is a different issue, but I thought it would come up. I apologise for raising it, given the time, but I thought that you would ask me, because it was in the letter you sent, about the sanctions and procedures in the House for people who transgress. May I offer two thoughts on that? First, I think that the sanctions are sufficient, because at the end of the day the ultimate sanction is very powerful. As occurred in one case in the previous Parliament, suspension sometimes leads to a Member losing his seat. He would have been expelled, had he not decided to leave the House voluntarily. The ultimate sanction is expulsion and is very severe. That is sufficient, and the House must judge.

Following on from that, in relation to the procedures of the House, I have become concerned about the extent to which the Select Committee on Members' Interests is asked to be judge and jury, working out the evidence and so on. The procedures of that Select Committee—I am not criticising anyone on it—may not be appropriate where there are serious issues affecting a Member's total career. I am trying to see in my own mind whether there is an analogy with a court of law, because some of these issues are getting quite close to a court of law, or more with bodies such as the General Medical Council or the Law Society. Members of Parliament know how the procedures of Select Committees can vary. Our procedures in a situation like this do not abide by the original Salmon Rules of 1967. For example, a Member is not entitled to question witnesses who are putting the case against him. I therefore feel that there is a case for having outside involvement in a Select Committee when it is dealing with such matters and a case for applying some of the Salmon Rules.

427. LORD NOLAN: We are grateful to you for adding that. It is most important and germane. Would you be kind enough to consider doing a further service for us and put that in a note and send it to us?[2]

JOHN MacGREGOR: Yes.

LORD NOLAN: Thank you very much, Mr MacGregor.

[2]See Evidence, pp. 505–506.

JOHN MacGREGOR: Thank you very much.

428. LORD NOLAN: Good morning. Is it Jifford or Gifford?

ANDREW GIFFORD AND CHARLES MILLER

ANDREW GIFFORD (Association of Professional Political Consultants): Gifford.

429. LORD NOLAN: And Mr Charles Miller. Mr Gifford, you are the Chairman and you, Mr Miller, are the Secretary of the Association of Professional Political Consultants. You have been kind enough to supply us with written evidence, which we have all read. Do you have it in mind to make a short statement summarising that evidence or would you prefer to go straight into the questions which Sir Martin Jacomb is going to ask you?

ANDREW GIFFORD: I should like to make a brief opening statement to clarify where lobbyists fit into the overall picture that some of the witnesses are also looking at and to try and differentiate the lobbying groups that we represent, PR companies, law firms and accountants, all of whom are also involved in lobbying along with trade unions and other representative bodies of special interest.

Clearly, over the past 10 or 15 years in which I have been involved in lobbying there has been considerable growth in the complexity of legislation and in competition between different groups to influence policy making. One has also seen considerable growth in the amount of regulation coming in from Europe. Amongst that and within it, there has been not a lessening of the mystifications of how government works, but a greatening of that feeling among many companies and outside bodies. It was into that context that our company grew, as did other companies that are members of our association. It grew quite naturally over that period of time.

It is important to differentiate lobbying companies from the other groupings and be quite clear where we fit, because all the work that we do is in advising companies, pressure groups and other outside bodies on the workings of government, both in the UK and, increasingly, in other countries—obviously, noticeably within the European Union.

Also in looking at where the growth has come from, we have seen increasing competition to our own companies coming from law firms in Brussels and in the UK, from a number of merchant banks—if one was looking at privatisation, quite a few of them would have their own in-house capability and would recruit quite busily from the civil service and from Parliament. One has seen exactly the same happening from the accountancy firms, where on an average finance Bill one would see a number of representatives from professional accounting firms on the benches in the public arena.

It is important to look at how this market has grown and the scale of it. We estimate that the overall market, if one is looking at those people who are directly involved in lobbying amongst all the different groups, is probably well in excess of £1 million a year—that is, the law firms and these broader people who wish to make representations into the policy making arena. Clearly, with that scale of market there is pressure among the different groupings to gain access. This is where the problem has arisen, because there is competition between different groupings looking to have their voice heard. Within that context, because of the experience that we have had over the years, we had no problem as a grouping in saying that we did not wish to have any special access or privilege to the House of Commons or to meetings with Ministers. If one looks back at examples of lobbying activity, the case that one's client, or of the person one is working to, is putting forward should have enough merit in its own right to gain that access. As a lobbying outfit, one should not need any privilege other than is already available to the public. The strength of the argument and of the debate that is being put forward should be quite sufficient to get the access that one needs.

That is why, as a grouping, we had no problem in deciding recently, when we first set up, that one of the first rules should be that we would not pay MPs in any way whatsoever. That is where we are coming from; that is where we feel that we are different from other groupings, and that is why we felt that we did not require any special privilege.

LORD NOLAN: Thank you very much.

430. MARTIN JACOMB: So your association is exclusively firms connected with lobbying and lobbying only?

ANDREW GIFFORD: Yes.

431. MARTIN JACOMB: Your Members do not include, for instance, Decision Makers, but do include Ian Greer Associates?

ANDREW GIFFORD: Yes. That is correct.

432. MARTIN JACOMB: You have felt that because the standards of all firms engaged in this work were not as high as they should be it was desirable to form your association, set down rules and try to raise standards?

ANDREW GIFFORD: Yes. Over the years we have made representations to a number of bodies that have been interested in the conduct of lobbying, most noticeably, I suppose, the Select Committee of Members' Interests. It has been over a period of 10 years that that has emerged as a significant anxiety, that there should be a code of conduct. It was in response to the Select Committee that we set up this association and put in place the code of conduct that we felt was relevant at that time. Quite a lot of the points that were made in the press about the activities of lobbyists were made before the formation of the association and the construction of the code of conduct.

433. MARTIN JACOMB: I should like to come back to the conduct in a minute. You heard Mr MacGregor give his evidence, and I should like you to feel free to comment on it as we go through some of the points that I wish to make, or indeed later.

Could I first ask what sounds like a question directed to a conclusion rather than an opening question? Do you and your association think that lobbyists should be registered so that people can identify them absolutely clearly?

ANDREW GIFFORD: We do now. That has grown over the years, the feeling that we should respond to public pressure and come up with a register that would be

combined with a code of conduct. Initially, many members of this group were against a register, because they felt that it would give some unique importance to lobbying companies which might not be applicable, because of the wide variety of lobbying groups.

434. MARTIN JACOMB: Would that registration include registration as and when they came on board clients and the interests of clients?

ANDREW GIFFORD: That is what we have proposed to the Select Committee and indeed set up in our code of conduct.

435. MARTIN JACOMB: Correct me if I am wrong, but is it right that the theory is that when you register—I am taking you as a firm now rather than an association—you register the firm, you register the client, why the client wants the lobbying process? That is then on the record so that the opposing point of view can see it and mount its own lobby if it wishes.

ANDREW GIFFORD: No. The purpose of the register is more so that MPs, Members of the House of Lords and officials within government can look at the register, and, if they have had a telephone call or inquiry from a lobbying company, can check it against the register to see if that company has properly put forward the client on behalf of whom it is lobbying. Typically, in putting a question to an official, one would say, "I'm phoning up on behalf of", and one would state quite clearly the company or pressure group on whose behalf one was phoning to seek information, maybe on a timetable or on a particular point. One would not be trying to hide behind a grouping of other companies.

436. MARTIN JACOMB: Could I come to your views about the borderline between what is legitimate advocacy to MPs or Ministers and what is illegitimate inducement to them to do something on behalf of your client? How do you draw that borderline?

ANDREW GIFFORD: We began by drawing it in our own code of conduct. Typically, we would say that one would expect in the ordinary manner of lobbying that one would be working with a client, company or pressure group and that one would be lunching or meeting with a Minister or officials in the ordinary course of their business, therefore there should be no need for any greater inducement other than potentially to wine or dine or, more typically, meet in an ordinary way in a room or meeting place of that nature. I would not expect any payment beyond the normal course of entertainment.

437. MARTIN JACOMB: I will come back to the lunch in a minute; clearly it is of great interest to everyone. It certainly attracts a lot of headlines. What I was really after is this. When you are advocating something to a Minister, clearly you want to get your client's point of view across. That is right, is it not?

ANDREW GIFFORD: I do not think that it would normally happen in that way. Normally we would be advising our client how to put their own arguments across to Ministers. Typically, we would not make the point to Ministers; it would be our client, as advised by us in the light of the conversation and after debating an issue with the client. Most of our time is spent with the client debating how best to put their arguments across.

438. MARTIN JACOMB: That method is absolutely acceptable, but the point I am making is that that is a legitimate process, getting a point of view across to a Minister. Where do you draw the dividing line between that and going one stage further and asking an MP to use his position in order to promote that cause?

ANDREW GIFFORD: Again, in that situation it would not be us necessarily going direct to the MP. It would be more likely that we would say to the client, "These are the MPs who are likely to take an interest in your case". They would then adopt that case and pursue it with Ministers if they felt it was relevant and of interest for them to do so. One is selecting quite carefully MPs who might have a constituency interest or a particular interest in the subject that the client was interested in pursuing.

439. MARTIN JACOMB: In advising all the Members of your association, do you say to them categorically, "Advocacy to MPs and Ministers is okay, but inducing MPs to be an advocate on your behalf is not"?

ANDREW GIFFORD: No. We would say that pushing forward an argument through the client with MPs and thereby through to Ministers is clearly okay; it is part of the process of lobbying.

440. MARTIN JACOMB: Quite. What guidance do you give them about entertainment, for example, which can give rise, certainly in the public eye, to the feeling that through that MPs are being illegitimately induced to act as advocates in the way that you have just described?

ANDREW GIFFORD: We actually say in our code of conduct:

"Save for entertainment and token business mementoes, not to offer, give or cause a client to give any financial incentive or other incentives to a representative or employee of Parliament or to any public servant or person acting on their account or to receive any incentive, whether from a client's supplier or would-be supplier to the company or elsewhere that could be construed in any way as a bribe or solicitation of favour."

It is not so much the quantum one is talking about.

441. MARTIN JACOMB: I was quite interested in the way in which you express that. It is not directed to MPs, is it? It does not say "Members of Parliament'; it says "a representative or employee of Parliament".

ANDREW GIFFORD: A "representative" would be a Member of Parliament or a Member of the House of Lords.

CHARLES MILLER (Association of Professional Political Consultants): It was designed to refer to Members of Parliament. The point we make about this is that if a Member of Parliament is going to have his or her opinion swayed by a drink or some food, they are not the sort of people that any lobbyist or people making representations would wish to spend much time with. The fundamental purpose is not whether we are making representations to MPs or through MPs or to civil servants or whatever; the guiding principle of our code of conduct is that those representations must be made honestly, that

all the facts of the issue must be accurately deployed and there must be no attempt to mislead.

442. MARTIN JACOMB: It is a strange use of words, is it not, "a representative of Parliament" rather than "a Member of Parliament"? Maybe you will consider whether the words are appropriate. When Members ring you up and ask whether it is legitimate to take MPs out to lunch, to the opera or on a day's shooting, what advice do you give them?

ANDREW GIFFORD: I do not think that we have any problem with that. We would take the view that that is part of the ongoing process of lobbying. We feel that MPs should be sufficiently grown up in their way of looking at arguments to be able to say, "That's a good argument" or "That's a bad argument", and not be swayed by entertainment.

CHARLES MILLER: The important thing is to take this in perspective. It could be suggested that there is a welter of entertainment and freeloading going on that is entirely instigated by professional lobbyists. The role of professional lobbyists within the context of all the submissions and approaches being made to MPs and civil servants is relatively small.

443. MARTIN JACOMB: No. I was merely interested in what guidance you give, because everybody knows it is an incredibly difficult borderline to draw. If a day's shooting is okay, is the air fare to get to the shooting okay? Everybody knows that this is a very difficult line to draw, so presumably, as with every other professional organisation, you have to be in a position to respond to questions asked of you by your members.

ANDREW GIFFORD: One would have to look at the subsequent effect of such entertainment. If an MP then suddenly tabled lots of parliamentary questions, one could examine the link. On the whole, however, it is fairly obvious where the situation is being abused, because other people come to one and say, "There seems to be an ongoing relationship of some sort, which seems to be more than purely one of listening to a particular point of view being put across".

444. MARTIN JACOMB: Basically, your response would be that it is not up to you as a firm, but up to the MPs.

ANDREW GIFFORD: Yes. At the end of the day it has to be the MP's judgment of what is correct.

CHARLES MILLER: But we are under the circumscription that we are not allowed to seek to induce a Member of Parliament through any form of payment or any other form of inducement.

445. MARTIN JACOMB: That is the generalised rule. What I was asking had to do with what response you would give when questions of doubt arose in your Members' minds.

I do not want to take up all the time, because there are masses of other questions that people would like to ask you, but you say in the stuff you have helpfully put before us that you think that no MP should be paid anything by a lobbying firm, whether as a director of the firm or in any other way. That is absolutely clear. At some point in your submissions you say that it is the fact of payment rather than the quantum that is really important.

ANDREW GIFFORD: With MPs, yes. I do not think that any of us had any problem in saying that we would not have MPs on our payroll. The problem that we came across is that it was increasingly difficult from the public's point of view not to see potential or actual conflict of interests. That is why it became very clear to us that we wanted to make that severance.

446. MARTIN JACOMB: So it is absolutely categoric that your Members do not pay MPs?

ANDREW GIFFORD: Absolutely categoric.

447. MARTIN JACOMB: You do draw a distinction between Members of the House of Commons and Members of the House of Lords. Could you explain how that arises and why it should be so?

ANDREW GIFFORD: It was something that we discussed in some detail at the time. We decided not to include Members of the House of Lords, simply because Members of the House of Lords are not elected and some of them do not necessarily choose to be Members of that House; they may be there by accident of birth. Therefore we felt at that time that it might be unfair for someone who might not be a very active Member of the House of Lords not to be allowed to work for a lobbying company. The same would also apply to councillors. We looked at that at the same time.

448. MARTIN JACOMB: Are you considering changing the rule in relation to active Members of the House of Lords?

ANDREW GIFFORD: Yes. Some of our Members have had Members of the House of Lords, but no longer have them; some continue to have Members of the House of Lords on their boards or as consultants. That is under consideration and we shall be giving evidence to the House of Lords on it.

449. MARTIN JACOMB: May I go to a different question? It arose during Mr MacGregor's evidence, but it is of interest to people anyway. It relates to privileged access to Ministers. Sometimes your Members have direct access, do they not? I want to ask about privilege. Mr MacGregor was saying that there was no privileged access, but would it not be a natural consequence of ordinary human reaction that people listen more readily to a skilful and professional advocate who can lead to the point and be precise than to someone who is not such an advocate and does not have the expertise that comes from experience? Does that not automatically bring with it what you describe as privileged access?

ANDREW GIFFORD: It will from time to time. Against that, Ministers are going to be heavily advised by officials. That is all part of the legitimate debate. It is one of the reasons that companies such as ours get hired by outside interests, because they expect a degree of intelligent advice on how to proceed in putting arguments to government departments. Having said that, government and Ministers are robust enough in looking at the arguments on their own merits.

MARTIN JACOMB: That is a fair answer, because it is one of the things that firms that are members of your association offer.

ANDREW GIFFORD: We certainly offer advice and guidance on how to put arguments forward. We tend to recruit, obviously, from a political or civil service background. A lot of people who work for organisations such as our own come from those backgrounds, quite naturally.

450. MARTIN JACOMB: That would be your answer to the question "Why do clients come to you rather than to their solicitors or an ordinary PR firm?

ANDREW GIFFORD: Yes, because we have the type of expertise that can help and guide them through this labyrinth that they do not specialise in on their own.

451. MARTIN JACOMB: Yes, right. That was the last specific question I wanted to ask, but do you want to comment on anything that Mr MacGregor said during his evidence?

ANDREW GIFFORD: I do not think so.

CHARLES MILLER: No, I think it was very clear. What he was suggesting, if I may add to the answer my colleague gave to your last question, is that Ministers entertain representations for two reasons; either they have to, because the organisation making the representations is of a sufficient size or importance to be unavoidable, or because the individual or the organisation knows what it is talking about, understands the system, is "user-friendly" and can contribute real expertise.

Obviously no professional lobbyists are of a size to be able to compete with ICI in terms of being representative, but they do have considerable experience of working inside the system and therefore, arguably, they are able to waste less time than those who have not been trained inside that system.

LORD NOLAN: Thank you very much. Since we are running short of time, I wonder if I could now go round the table. Dame Anne, I think you have a question you wish to ask?

452. ANNE WARBURTON: Yes, Chairman, I have. May I say, Mr Gifford, that I thought your submission was very comprehensive and I imagine there will not be many questions. May I begin by asking how many firms belong to the Association?

ANDREW GIFFORD: Eight are in the process of applying at the moment.

453. ANNE WARBURTON: Out of a field of 17?

ANDREW GIFFORD: About that; at the moment we have five of the largest companies and would represent 60-70 per cent of the turnover.

454. ANNE WARBURTON: Is Ian Greer the largest of the five?

ANDREW GIFFORD: One of the largest.

455. ANNE WARBURTON: The reason I am asking is that I have been shown an extract from the day before yesterday's *Observer* (I do not know whether you have seen it), and it does not seem to tally altogether with the

passage in heavy print which I think has been quoted before, that it is a fundamental requirement on your Members (of all regulated lobbyists) that no payments may be made to any MP or official. According to the *Observer*:

"a researcher for a Member of Parliament is listed in their Register of Interests as having relevant gainful occupation with a lobbyist firm, namely Ian Greer."

ANDREW GIFFORD: Yes. I have had a letter today from Ian Greer's Managing Director which I can give you. Basically it says that this particular researcher was not working for Ian Greer at that time.

456. ANNE WARBURTON: At which time?

ANDREW GIFFORD: The time to which the Register applied.

457. ANNE WARBURTON: But then why did he record it?

ANDREW GIFFORD: I will read the letter to you: it says:

"As you know, at no time have you been a full or part-time employee of Ian Greer Associates, although you did work for us as a consultant in late '91 early '92, which was, I believe registerable. Whilst I accept the entry in the House of Commons register of secretaries and research assistants was the result of an error on your part, it was nevertheless the cause of considerable embarrassment ...".

According to this letter and to the Register, it has now been corrected.

458. ANNE WARBURTON: But he was in the past working both for the Member of Parliament and for the lobbying firm?

ANDREW GIFFORD: In late '91/early '92, which was before our organisation was formed.

459. ANNE WARBURTON: You are saying that the Register is out of date on this?

ANDREW GIFFORD: That is what the letter says.

460. ANNE WARBURTON: Yes. Does that tie in at all, because in your submission you said that one or two firms seem still themselves to have financial links with MPs. Have you any updating on that?

CHARLES MILLER: When we were encouraged to form our body by the Members' Interests Select Committee, we calculated that there were something like 17 recognised lobbying firms—in other words, firms who earned their living by doing nothing but dealing with the institutions of government. Of those 17, according to the Register of Members' Interests, three at the time had some form of financial connection with Members of Parliament. One firm immediately severed its connections, with, I think, four Members of Parliament in order to join our body, another gave notice that it would do so with its single Member of Parliament (and I think has now done so). The final one decided that it wished to

retain its link with a Member of Parliament and therefore could not be eligible for membership, so of 17 recognised lobbying companies, only one now has any form of financial link with an MP.

461. ANNE WARBURTON: Thank you very much. If I knew the names of your other members, would I find any of them in this list that the *Observer* printed?

CHARLES MILLER: I do not know because the public does not have access to that list.

462. ANNE WARBURTON: It is that list [showing Mr Miller]. Have you seen it?

CHARLES MILLER: I have not.

ANDREW GIFFORD: I have. There are one or two Members on it and this is an area where we feel we do need to look again at the Register of Research Assistants.

463. ANNE WARBURTON: You are going to try to get practice into line with your own precepts?

ANDREW GIFFORD: Yes.

ANNE WARBURTON: Good. Thank you, Chairman.

LORD NOLAN: Thank you very much. Peter Shore?

464. PETER SHORE: When did you introduce this rule of prohibiting payment of MPs?

ANDREW GIFFORD: May this year.

PETER SHORE: May of this year?

ANDREW GIFFORD: Yes.

CHARLES MILLER: May of last year.

ANDREW GIFFORD: Sorry, last year.

PETER SHORE: May last year?

ANDREW GIFFORD: May 1994.

465. PETER SHORE: Yes and you have, of course, had a considerable influx of members since that time?

ANDREW GIFFORD: Yes, definitely. One of the reasons we put the grouping together at that time was to coincide with the Select Committee which we addressed in February last year. A natural follow-on was to set up the Association and clearly the press and media interest in the whole area has pushed many other people towards joining.

466. PETER SHORE: What triggered your decision to prohibit payment of MPs?

ANDREW GIFFORD: I do not think anything really triggered it. It was just a natural feeling around the table at that first meeting, that this was probably the most positive thing we could do on day one—to make quite clear that we did not wish to have that overlap and that was something we wished to clarify straight away.

PETER SHORE: Thank you.

467. WILLIAM UTTING: You say in your very helpful written evidence that you would prefer political consultants to be regulated by institutions of government. I wondered what you meant exactly by that. Are you looking for formal regulation by statute and the establishment of a council and a code?

ANDREW GIFFORD: Initially we wanted some statutory code and the reason for broadening beyond Parliament is that so much of our work is not within Parliament, but other parts of government, whether with officials or local authorities. It is a far broader spectrum than purely Parliament and that is why, in a sense, we have always tried to remove ourselves from being described as "parliamentary" lobbyists, because that is potentially quite a small part of our work. There are specialist areas in which most of us work that do not involve Members of Parliament at all.

CHARLES MILLER: What also concerned us at the time was that a self-regulatory body like ours has no ultimate sanction. We cannot require people to be regulated; we are a voluntary body and we felt that despite the circumstances that led to the establishment of this Committee, government is still held in far higher esteem than we are as individual companies and therefore official regulation would command far greater respect.

468. WILLIAM UTTING: Yes. One could foresee considerable technical difficulties about getting legislation passed that would achieve all the objectives you have in mind. One might have to fall back upon a self-denying ordinance by Members of Parliament in relation to parliamentary activities and perhaps leave the rest.

CHARLES MILLER: If I could draw a parallel here, parliamentary agents are regulated by statute and, as I understand it, the parliamentary agent must give up any connection with his profession on becoming a Member of Parliament.

WILLIAM UTTING: Thank you, Chairman.

469. DIANA WARWICK: Just two brief questions: first I would like to pick up on one point that Sir Martin made about your statement on not paying MPs. You go on to say, in the other evidence you gave us, that it is not the amount, but the very fact of it being paid (and you repeat that). I do not understand the relationship between those two. Does that mean that you do pay MPs for certain things?

ANDREW GIFFORD: No, I think it is clear that we do not pay MPs. The point that we have made all along is that the reason for that is that we felt that as far as the public (and, indeed, our clients) were concerned, any payment of any size of that sort would lead to a potential conflict of interest. Many of our clients would take the view that they would not want to be involved in seeming to be paying MPs.

470. DIANA WARWICK: But you go on to say, "We don't believe that MPs or others should be required to declare sums paid.". It is the oddity of why you should be referring to sums paid to MPs that I am trying to get at. Am I misunderstanding something here?

CHARLES MILLER: We are not referring to sums paid by professional lobbying companies, but to sums paid for any of their outside interests. We are suggesting it is the fact that they have outside interests that is the declarable trigger point, as it were, not how much they are paid.

471. DIANA WARWICK: That at least explains it; but can I then ask you a simple question. Do you really not believe that there is a difference between receiving £5 or £10 and £500 or £5,000? Because you say the sums should not be relevant, do you not think in terms of human nature that there is a difference?

ANDREW GIFFORD: Clearly there is a difference. We just wanted to be absolutely clear what our own situation was, not least because working for a number of clients one would wish to make that abundantly plain, both from their point of view and from that of the public.

DIANA WARWICK: Yes. It just seemed a little ingenuous.

LORD NOLAN: Is that all?

DIANA WARWICK: Yes, thank you.

472. LORD NOLAN: Thank you both very much. You have covered the ground very thoroughly and we are grateful to you for coming along.

Now, Mr Witherow and Mr Jones, I am sorry that you have had such a long wait. I hope that it has not inconvenienced you too much. This is of course Mr John Witherow, Editor of the *Sunday Times* and Mr Michael Jones, the Political Editor. We have the advantage, together with your other readers, of seeing pretty often in your paper what you think generally about the subjects in front of us and I am sure we have all read the constructive and helpful leader which appeared last Sunday.

Mr Witherow, I am now going to ask Mr Tom King to go through with you a number of particular questions we wanted to raise.

473. TOM KING: This is an inquiry into standards of conduct in public life. We are focusing initially on the issues of Members of Parliament, Ministers and their activities on leaving office and the business about appointments to quangos. I wondered if you would like to start by telling us what you think on those issues.

JOHN WITHEROW AND MICHAEL JONES

JOHN WITHEROW (Editor, *Sunday Times*): In broad terms?

TOM KING: And whether you feel competent to talk about them.

JOHN WITHEROW: We have a particular interest in this because when we did the story last year about MPs accepting cash for putting down questions, we uncovered a very grey area about what MPs thought was acceptable and what was not. As you recall, we went to 20 MPs, posing as businessmen, using subterfuge, and discovered when those questions were put that some MPs thought it was acceptable to take the money (because it was within the rules of the House as they interpreted them) and others thought it was completely unacceptable and unethical.

It seemed to us that there were no clear guidelines about what MPs could and could not do in such situations. Even from those MPs who did accept the money, one sent it back saying that he had had second thoughts, so even they had no clear idea how they should behave in these circumstances. This seemed a legitimate area for the public to debate and, indeed, our defence before the Press Complaints Commission was that it was in the public interest to bring this out. This seems to be a key area to ask what MPs can do in such situations. They seem to have no clear guidelines.

Our questions drove us across a variety of phases. Sir John Gorst encapsulated it best I think when he said, in response to whether a question should be put down for money,

"It's legal, but it doesn't look very nice if you simply ask questions because you have been paid to do so."

I think that goes to the heart of the matter.

474. TOM KING: Do you have views on this, or do you just see your role as opening it up for public debate?

JOHN WITHEROW: As a newspaper we do have views; we do not have views in the story—we reported what we found—but we have views in our editorials. We have advocated that there should be much more openness over this; there should be a code of practice for MPs, in the same way that we are regulated by a body which has a code of practice that we abide by. The same should apply for MPs and there should be a form of censure if they transgress that.

475. TOM KING: What about outside interests? Do you think MPs should have outside interests?

JOHN WITHEROW: As we have said, to cut MPs off entirely and make them a professional paid class is not a good idea. It would be very expensive and would arguably remove them from aspects of public life.

At the same time, what exists at the moment is unacceptable, in that it seems that MPs are prepared to take money for putting down questions, in effect abusing their power in the House. There should be some system that prevents this happening.

476. TOM KING: But is that not actually an interesting illustration of what you decided to highlight? One of the issues that arose out of that is whether you identified a situation that was already happening or, by entrapment, actually made something happen to make your story.

JOHN WITHEROW: No. We clearly identified something that was happening. We only undertook this investigation because we had been told by a businessman that this was a practice that was going on. He would not go on the record, so our only means of establishing whether it was true or not and to what extent it went on, was to undertake this exercise—which was limited to 20 MPs. We could have gone to more or fewer, but it was essentially a straw poll of the scale of this. The fact that two MPs were willing to take the money and that others flirted with it gives us an impression (and that is all it is) of how widespread this is.

477. TOM KING: Do you think that there is any evidence that the ones who were deceived into believing this (and I think the story was constructed in different ways, though I do not want to go into the background of it, of your reporters seeking to establish this) have ever done it before?

JOHN WITHEROW: Do I think—?

TOM KING: You said it was a practice that you wanted to expose. You said that a businessman told you about this. I am not personally aware that this had ever happened before (although I do not claim to know everything that happens in Parliament)—people simply walking up and saying to an MP "Here's £1,000; will you put a question down for me?". I am not aware that the people who were induced, by whatever means, by your agents in this matter to actually do it on this occasion had ever done it before.

JOHN WITHEROW: I do not know that. All we know is what we were told by the businessman—that he had paid MPs for this service—and then we did this exercise. You will have to draw your own conclusions about how widespread it is. We do not know if those MPs have done it before—that was not the purpose of the exercise. It was to show whether MPs were prepared to take one-off payments for putting down questions, which a small minority clearly was.

478. TOM KING: But, with respect, you have just told the Committee that it was because it was a practice that you understood was widespread that you conducted this particular exercise. Whatever the merits and comments one may have about the conduct of your newspaper and others, that had the effect of inducing people to act in this way. The interesting thing was that you presented it to your readers as you doing a valuable public service in exposing something that was a prevalent practice. You are now saying that you do not know whether it is a prevalent practice, but you were told by a businessman that it was.

JOHN WITHEROW: We can only state the facts, that the businessman told us that he had done it and that when we tested it, they were prepared to take the money. You must draw your own conclusions. Is 10 per cent of a poll of 20 MPs widespread or not? Is 15 per cent?

479. TOM KING: Is there not a much bigger issue here? You focused on a particular point—whether you could somehow induce people to believe that they were providing a service, or the friend of friends (whatever it was) and could they just on this occasion help and "by the way I believe there will be a cheque", whether some of them knew it was coming or not—but the much bigger issue is whether MPs have outside interests, whether there should be a limit on what those are and the sums that might be involved. That is a far bigger issue than the odd question being put down. That is the real issue is it not?

JOHN WITHEROW: Yes.

480. TOM KING: And on that issue, you do not think there should be any restraint?

JOHN WITHEROW: On what?

481. TOM KING: On occupations that they can take up?

JOHN WITHEROW: I think there should be restraints. I believe that MPs should be allowed to have outside interests, but that there should be restraints on what those are. For example, should they work for lobbyists, accept money, be directors or consultants to these firms? I do not think so, because they are essentially being employed to do a service in the House.

482. TOM KING: For a lobbying firm?

JOHN WITHEROW: For a lobbying firm—doing a service using their authority in the House to achieve that.

483. TOM KING: Right. But they can be a journalist?

JOHN WITHEROW: I would say that there is not a huge conflict of interest being a journalist, or a lawyer or farmer.

484. TOM KING: And advocate any causes they like in their columns?

JOHN WITHEROW: Yes, but then they declare that they are an MP in the course of that.

485. TOM KING: Lawyer?

JOHN WITHEROW: Yes.

486. TOM KING: Represent the Police Federation and be an advocate for it in the House of Commons?

JOHN WITHEROW: That is openly stated, though I personally have some discomfort over it. What we are really worried about is that MPs might be representing certain interests and that that is not known about. That was clearly the case we investigated. Transparency will remove some of the areas about which the public have serious doubts. Do you want to add to that, Michael?

MICHAEL JONES (Political Correspondent *Sunday Times*): There is a distinction between lobbying firms and lobbying interests. If a Highland Member of Parliament advances the interests of the Scotch Whisky industry, one would not be entirely surprised. One of the great events of the year that we go to is the annual Spectator lunch, where a Scottish Whisky company kindly picks up the bill (as we understand it) and uses it quite openly to harangue Cabinet Ministers, Ministers, ex-Ministers and journalists there about their need for fiscal protection. But that is within the spirit of lobbying, which I do not think arouses any cause for public anxiety. It is the professional lobbying firms, where money changes hands and the Member of Parliament, either openly or in some cases surreptitiously, advances interests that the public knows not of.

487. TOM KING: The very first witness we had was Professor Ivor Crewe, who quoted a poll that said, I think, that 68 per cent of the British people believe that Members of Parliament were there to further their own financial interests. He then went on immediately to say that he did not actually believe that was true. He was followed by Simon Jenkins, the next witness, who also said he did not believe it. Do you believe it is true?

JOHN WITHEROW: I do not know about the scale of it. I think that the attitudes of many people have changed, particularly in the past year.

488. TOM KING: I am sorry. The point I am making is not whether 68 per cent of the British people believe it.

We accept that poll and I think the Committee accepted that as a fair poll, but those two witnesses did not believe that the public perception was correct. Do you believe that the public perception is correct?

JOHN WITHEROW: I think that MPs, together with journalists, are held in pretty low esteem and there is a perception that a number of MPs, not all—

489. TOM KING: I am sorry but I was asking whether you think it is actually true that 68 per cent (the vast majority) of Members of Parliament are only there to further their own financial benefit?

JOHN WITHEROW: No, I do not believe that.

490. TOM KING: If that is not true, who do you think is responsible for the fact that the public have what, now, three distinguished Members of the media and observers have said that they think is a totally false impression?

JOHN WITHEROW: The MPs are responsible for that impression.

491. TOM KING: And the media have no responsibility for that?

JOHN WITHEROW: Of course, we have highlighted it.

492. TOM KING: In looking at standards of conduct in public life, I gave you the first three topics and we shall be turning later no doubt to the role of the media and I believe you will have certain appearances to make in connection with your activities in these matters.

On the question of the conduct of the press, do you pay Members of Parliament for information about private parliamentary meetings?

JOHN WITHEROW: Not that I am aware of.

MICHAEL JONES: No, certainly not. We do not.

493. TOM KING: Do you make any payments to Members of Parliament?

MICHAEL JONES: No.

JOHN WITHEROW: No.

494. TOM KING: And never have?

JOHN WITHEROW: No. We have in the past. Gerry Malone, I think, was our Scottish editor when he was an MP and acted as a journalist.

495. TOM KING: No, I am not talking about people in an activity; I mean specific payments made by the press to individual Members of Parliament for information that they provide.

MICHAEL JONES: For a retainer for information?

496. TOM KING: Any payment at all, either in the form of a retainer or specific payments for specific pieces of information.

MICHAEL JONES: Not in all the years that I have been on the *Sunday Times*, which is since 1971.

497. TOM KING: Can I ask Michael Jones, who obviously has unrivalled knowledge of the House of Commons. Do you think it is done?

MICHAEL JONES: Yes.

498. TOM KING: How many Members of Parliament would you guess are in receipt of such payments?

MICHAEL JONES: A tiny handful.

499. LORD NOLAN: Are we talking about payments from newspapers or the media?

MICHAEL JONES: Yes.

LORD NOLAN: Or more generally?

MICHAEL JONES: Yes. I do not know that it is done now. I would hazard a guess that it has been done in the period I am talking about.

500. TOM KING: Yes, thank you. On this question though about presentation, you say it is all the fault of MPs. I come back and say it is all the fault of the media and we all know that, whatever its origins, is very corrosive to public confidence, respect and, in the end, to good government and administration, whichever party is in government. If there is this continual undermining (and we all know that we are down with estate agents and others at rock bottom—I am not sure where newspaper editors rank—in public esteem, not as individual Members of Parliament, but as a collective institution), what steps do you think would most help to correct that situation?

JOHN WITHEROW: What became evident to us was this immense grey area where MPs did not know where they stood. Therefore I believe that MPs need a detailed code of practice that handles situations with which they might be confronted and even hypothetical, ethical questions should be put into it with suggestions of how they should deal with them. This would an enormous advance because clearly they disagree on many things and somebody needs to establish what is acceptable and what is not.

501. TOM KING: The code of practice, with outside scrutiny or outside regulation?

JOHN WITHEROW: Yes. It is important for confidence that the public feels that somebody outside, other than MPs, the Committee of Privileges or whatever, is examining this and making sure it is implemented.

502. TOM KING: Do you think there ought to be a wider presentation? We are talking about codes of conduct and this would obviously include greater transparency, declaration and accuracy of declaration. Do you think that affects the media as well, in their covering of politics?

JOHN WITHEROW: Yes. If there are shortcomings in the media's covering that could be taken in to that. We have our own code of practice which should cover how we behave in these matters. Is that what you are asking?

503. TOM KING: This is slightly at a tangent, but I was very struck by the embarrassment that appeared to have been caused to Mr Newt Gingrich on his arrival in a very powerful position in the United States to find that he was about to receive a very large payment from your proprietor, wearing another hat I think, with his stake in Harper Collins. That seems to me to be a mirror example of overlap of interests of which the reader may not be aware.

MICHAEL JONES: The way that situation resolved itself was a tribute both to the American political system and the way that the media picked the story up. It was public knowledge that he had been offered several millions of dollars. Enormous embarrassment, as you say, was the result and he ended up by agreeing to take one dollar and a share of the royalties.

504. TOM KING: Right. Can you think of comparable situations over here?

MICHAEL JONES: Former Prime Ministers take large amounts of money from newspapers for memoirs.

505. TOM KING: Do you think that they should not?

MICHAEL JONES: It is probably now regarded as part of their constitutional perks.

506. TOM KING: What about other people's constitutional perks? I do not know whether you heard the exchanges with John MacGregor expressing his concern about the decline in the standards or in the range of experience of Members of Parliament (and Michael Jones has seen Parliament over a considerable period of time). I asked him whether he thought that there had been a deterioration in that respect in Parliament in the past 10 to 15 years.

MICHAEL JONES: I think there probably has been, but that is because of the nature of the political control during that period by one party with large majorities. I would just like to say—

507. TOM KING: Let me make his point. I illustrated that by a point that came out of the last European Elections when there was a big swing and a lot of new MEPs came in. It is interesting to see that the vast majority of the new Labour Members come from further education. I see that as a risk of the narrowing of the channels through which people can see the opportunity of a political career and playing their part in Parliament and I wonder whether it is healthy.

MICHAEL JONES: That is the result of the selection processes within the parties themselves. It is many years since the National Union of Mineworkers was a force inside the Labour Party. I would have thought that this is part of the bourgeoisification of British society as a whole.

508. TOM KING: And of the range of people able to offer themselves? I drew on the background which I remember originally; there is a continuing complaint in Parliament, as you know, that few people have any experience about industry. To try to overcome the terrible lack of people who are prepared to come out of industry with any practical experience to serve in Parliament, we started, as the least worse alternative, to try to give

Members of Parliament short courses and secondment in industry. That is part of the rationale of the Industry and Parliament Trust.

What I am on about is the obstacles to people being Members of Parliament and Ministers. It is not just the salary (the salary may be a lot lower than that of a doctor, deputy head teacher, solicitor, dentist and a range of other professional activities) but the much greater aggression of the press, which Chris Moncrieff described in his evidence to us. He said that in his judgement the press were now vastly more aggressive and intrusive than they used to be. You have given a classic illustration of that in your activities, whatever view one takes of them. (One thinks of a few editors in the past who would certainly not have countenanced that sort of behaviour.) That may be acceptable in a modern society, but do you feel that you have any responsibility towards trying to ensure that there is not such a climate created that you discourage worthwhile people coming into public life?

JOHN WITHEROW: I think that turns it on its head completely. The purpose of our doing that was to show the kind of contradictions that existed. If those are eradicated you will not have these problems because people will know exactly what they can and cannot do and what is acceptable.

One reason for going into Parliament is not just to make money, but for public service, for a variety of reasons, for preferment, for getting into government, for changing things. Those are many of the incentives to people, not to make money. Money is a minor factor in this and if as a result of your inquiry or any changes that are made the issue of what MPs can and cannot do is clarified, that seems to me to be a public service.

509. TOM KING: That is exactly the point I am making. It is not actually about money. A lot of people, in spite of the money, are willing to serve, but a lot of them are less willing to serve (and I have personal experience from people who I have tried to encourage to come in) because of what they see as the exposure of themselves and their families and the much greater intrusion of the press. I think this is a genuine worry. You may just brush it aside.

JOHN WITHEROW: I am not brushing it aside.

510. TOM KING: May I just turn it from the point you may have thought you were going to give evidence about, to asking you whether you think you have a contribution to make, quite apart from the investigative side (which is obviously important) to getting a better balance of understanding, a more accurate picture of the truth that you could in your powerful position communicate to the British people that may help enhance and improve the quality of Parliament?

JOHN WITHEROW: I would say that is exactly what we have done through this process because there are clearly things wrong with the way Parliament is run at the moment. Any system that comes up with reforms of that and improves it is for the benefit of the country as a whole. Our process of investigation leading to this is a positive aspect in improvement.

LORD NOLAN: Thank you very much. I wonder if Members of the Committee could be even more than usually succinct in any further questions they have. We have two more witnesses to come. Sir Martin?

511. MARTIN JACOMB: I shall try to be very brief. Is what lies behind your approach to this, not just the cash for questions issue, but the belief that there is either a deterioration in the behaviour of MPs or, on the other hand, that higher standards are today required than in the past?

JOHN WITHEROW: I would not know about a deterioration. What has happened is that some areas have become more confused and certain practices have grown up in the House that have become acceptable. Whether they are right or wrong, we need to look at that. Some MPs clearly think, when they behave in a certain way, that what they are doing is quite acceptable. We need to look at that again. I certainly think that what happened in our case showed this up and that it would be very much in the public interest that these areas are clarified completely so they know exactly what they can and cannot do.

512. MARTIN JACOMB: Do you think one of the things that is wrong is the sanctions which are imposed by Parliament itself? Do you think they are too uncertain?

JOHN WITHEROW: Sanctions they can take in any form of censure?

MARTIN JACOMB: Yes.

JOHN WITHEROW: Yes, I do. For there to be public confidence in Parliament requires an outside body to be seen openly ensuring that any code of conduct is effectively practised and that there should be a form of public censorship if it is broken.

MARTIN JACOMB: Thank you very much.

513. LORD THOMSON: Apart from the Press Complaints Commission, does the *Sunday Times* have a code of conduct for its own journalists? I am thinking in terms of freebies, hospitality and all that sort of thing.

JOHN WITHEROW: Yes, we do.

514. LORD THOMSON: Can you tell us about it?

JOHN WITHEROW: Every employee of the newspaper has a contract which has strict guidelines. For example, we are not allowed to accept any gifts of over £50. Below that—such things as a bottle of whisky for Christmas or a lunch—is not forbidden, but anything above that (any free trips) either is refused or has to be sanctioned by the Editor. For example, we take trips from travel companies, but that is always stated in the article.

515. DIANA WARWICK: Simon Jenkins told us that he had ceased to report a great deal on Parliament because he was rather more interested in the real locus of power—which is the civil service. (I may be paraphrasing him, but I think that is pretty much what he said.)

I want to link that in with something that John MacGregor said in response to questioning; that was that there was a difference between senior civil servants and Ministers. He referred to them not getting pensions and so on, but I think he was really meaning that there was a difference in the influence that they could bring to bear. Given the contrast between those two statements, do you feel that Ministers should continue to be treated differently from civil servants when it comes to taking on outside appointment which links in with the work they did as Ministers?

JOHN WITHEROW: The sort of work they can do once they have ceased to be Ministers?

DIANA WARWICK: Yes.

JOHN WITHEROW: I think there should be very tight guidelines on what areas they can go into and a timescale on that as well.

DIANA WARWICK: There are none at the moment.

JOHN WITHEROW: We have seen some cases in the past and it does lead to an erosion of public confidence if people feel a Minister can go straight out of office and into some sort of firm where he clearly benefits himself and the firm because of the post he held.

516. DIANA WARWICK: Briefly, you said that the main concern was MPs representing an interest that people are not aware of. Do you think that the current Register of Members' Interests is adequate and, if I can ask a supplementary, do you have access to what I believe are two other registers—the register for staff interests and the one where I believe special advisers have also to register their interests?

JOHN WITHEROW: On your first question, no. I think it is completely inadequate. It is rarely updated, as far as we can find out. I think it should be updated almost weekly. When they register an interest we do not know how much they are being paid for it. That should clearly be part of this.

As for the other two—Mike I do not know. Do you?

MICHAEL JONES: There is another register of Lobby journalists' interests, which the House insisted on at the time when they had their own.

517. DIANA WARWICK: Is that public?

MICHAEL JONES: I presume so—I have never looked myself up because I have nothing to declare.

518. DIANA WARWICK: Do you have access to the other registers?

MICHAEL JONES: I would imagine so.

DIANA WARWICK: Thank you.

519. ANNE WARBURTON: If we were to ask you which subjects we have not touched on today you think really cause public concern, what would you say?

JOHN WITHEROW: As part of this code of practice there should be rigorous rules of disclosure which would have to be enforced. Any questions relating to a private interest should be signalled in some form. You could argue there could be full tax returns. Generally we would say that any kind of transparency is good because it increases public confidence and, far from undermining Parliament, quite the reverse, that people will have

greater confidence in MPs if they feel they can see what is happening. At the moment we are in a kind of uncomfortable halfway house where we know a little about what goes on, which in some ways increases distrust because it seems it is hiding something. If MPs have nothing to hide, why not let them publish all these details—how much they receive from outside interests. That should be freely available and regularly updated.

LORD NOLAN: Thank you both very much. It has been a very interesting morning.

520. LORD NOLAN: Let me thank you for coming and apologise for the fact that we are running almost half an hour late in starting your evidence to us. Colin Thompson and Leigh Mendelsohn representing the Public Relations Consultants Association. I am going to ask Dame Anne Warburton to take you through your evidence. Had you a preliminary statement you wanted to make?

COLIN THOMPSON AND LEIGH MENDELSOHN

LEIGH MENDELSOHN (President, Public Relations Consultants Association): Yes, I think we would. The PRCA is twenty-five years old and has approximately 150 Members throughout the country earning about eighty per cent of the PR fee income in Britain. About 40 per cent of our membership offers either what they term Parliamentary or Public Affairs service to clients. We know that the amount that our members say that is spent by clients through them on public affairs is about eleven million pounds.

The PRCA, like many trade associations, has an overriding concern about standards within the industry and in addition to our professional charter, which is a code for all members, we do produce specialist codes and registers for particular areas, such as health care, financial and political affairs. We did produce our own code and register for Parliamentary advisers. This was actually started two years ago this month and took about ten months to put together. We spent a lot of time on this—we had, as you can probably well imagine, quite a lot of research carried out amongst MPs, amongst businessmen, amongst the client section, amongst our own members and amongst non-members who actually worked in this field—and we came to the conclusion that it was very difficult to draw a line, and I think it is something we have heard this morning "Where do you draw the line?" and so we took the route that you couldn't draw a line and you had to go for complete disclosure and openness.

At the back of the document there is a register which I can assure you has caused a few problems amongst members and clients but we have insisted it went ahead and one of the things I think that everybody knows who works within this field, people know where the grey, the murky areas are, and what we tried to do with this was to cover it. So, for example, we have things like not only naming the MPs that are actually working directly for you as a consultant or director, but naming any MPs through the clients that you actually will be working with and we are also all the way through talking about "and the MPs' staff and staff of the House", so we are aware of the murky areas and we have definitely tried to cover it in both the written words and in the declarations.

We have also, within the details of the clients at the back, said if the client is not the beneficiary we want the names of the beneficiaries. So, for example, if you have got a grouping and it may have a special title we want to know who is behind that. We have also said we want to know what the principal activity of the client is and we want to know the nature of the work that is being carried out, the assignment or the lobby—whatever you want to call it. We want to know the period of assignment.

One of the things that we also said was this really was not much good if it was retrospective. If we are going to be open we need to know now what is going on. So all our members—the register will actually be open on a rolling basis through our head office—and all our members have got four weeks to actually register either a new client or a new assignment, and this will be open to the press—and, priced, to the public—I think it is £50.

I think, when we went before the Select Committee in November 1993, when we put the final draft before them, they asked us to look to the rest of the lobby industry and get us all to work together, which is something we did, and we did get the IPR, which is the Institute of Public Relations, we did get the IPR in agreement to work with us and, in fact, they have their own code but it mirrors this one and ours mirrors theirs. We did also speak to the APPC which had very recently formed—in fact, I think when I first spoke to them they were about to form—and they decided that they didn't want to work with us. One of the statements made to me was that they didn't want to be involved with public relations people.

So I think that we have taken the route that we have put together a code and register, long before the sleaze allegations, we have tried to work on the basis of full disclosure and openness on a rolling basis and our plea really—which was the same as what we said to the Select Committee—we do need the other side of the coin, which is the MPs, to also have a code and register.[3]

LORD NOLAN: Thank you very much.

521. ANNE WARBURTON: Miss Mendelsohn, thank you very much for that. I wanted to clarify in my own mind your relationship to the IPR the Institute of Public Relations, which numerically seems to be far the largest organisation, is that correct, in this field?

LEIGH MENDELSOHN: The IPR represents individual members working in consultancy, with charities, in local government—anybody who actually works in the field of public relations in any sector of business or ——

522. ANNE WARBURTON: So it is not the firm, it is the person?

LEIGH MENDELSOHN: It is the person.

ANNE WARBURTON: Yes, I see. But you are working with them on ——

LEIGH MENDELSOHN: We work closely, yes, on all sorts of issues.

COLIN THOMPSON (Director, Public Relations Consultants Association): And our members are corporate bodies.

523. ANNE WARBURTON: Yes. I was interested in your reference to the APPC because they were here earlier this morning—were you present?

LEIGH MENDELSOHN: Yes.

---

[3]See Evidence, pp. 506–509.

524. ANNE WARBURTON: Well then I do not need to tell you that they gave a little boost, I thought, to your activities—they were making it clear that they were not covering themselves. What proportion of the political lobbying sector do you have Members in?

COLIN THOMPSON: I did some analysis just out of interest and we have as members 160 consultancies and I have figures working in anything from local government to political lobbying, environment, local government, medicine, pharmaceuticals, and the figures vary of consultancies working in that area between 35 at the bottom end to 92 at the top end. So you have got quite a big coverage of areas which would lead, in my opinion, to some form of lobbying.

525. ANNE WARBURTON: But these are not specifically in political lobbying?

COLIN THOMPSON: No. Within the consultancies you get divisions, so you would have a political lobbying division within one that would also do crisis management and financial PR as well.

526. ANNE WARBURTON: What would lead your clients, as opposed to your members—or the clients of your members—why would they choose to do any political lobbying through those firms?

LEIGH MENDELSOHN: I think the situation is that we obviously have clients within the PR umbrella and some of us—40 per cent we reckon, approximately, of our members—offer some form of public affairs service, and within the normal communications structure there are obviously specialisations and some of our members offer the specialisation of political affairs. That could be local, it could be national, it could be Brussels, America. There are specialisations within our membership, not only in political affairs but in financial—we have financial PR specialists, we have health care specialists, we have travel specialists—and I think clients come to you because you have a knowledge of their industry or you have a specialist knowledge of communications, and I think one really has to understand that from our point of view we believe that political communications is just a specialisation of our normal work. So clients will come to us, probably some of them in the first place because they already work with us on other areas, perhaps on marketing or corporate affairs, and the second thing is they would come—because you have built a reputation with this area they would come to you directly for that particular service.

527. ANNE WARBURTON: Thank you. Your code of conduct makes it quite clear that your members are not to pay MPs or their employees, but it is a new code of conduct. Do you have problems getting it applied throughout your membership—is it taking some time?

LEIGH MENDELSOHN: The code itself we are not having a problem with because obviously it has been going round our membership really for a year, certainly in draft form and then in its formal form.

528. ANNE WARBURTON: Nobody has left—they won't sign?

LEIGH MENDELSOHN: No, we haven't seen anybody leave. We have had some arguments but we haven't had anybody leave. Why it is a little bit slow is actually because of the amount of work involved in getting all the details onto computer and what we had hoped was to have it up and running by the beginning of January this year and it looks like it is going to be the middle to end of February, but that is because there is an enormous amount of data to put into the computer.

529. ANNE WARBURTON: But in this conversation we can rest on the premise that you are not concerned with paying people in Parliament for performing services?

LEIGH MENDELSOHN: No. Well, we haven't banned or barred from employing an MP as a board director or a consultant—we haven't done that. What we have said is "if you do it then it must be all written down what they are working on and what they are doing".

530. ANNE WARBURTON: Or a consultant, you said?

LEIGH MENDELSOHN: We haven't banned our members from employing an MP as a director or a consultant.

531. ANNE WARBURTON: And your code doesn't ask that any value should be put on the services?

LEIGH MENDELSOHN: No, we didn't believe that it was our role to actually say — I think it would cause problems amongst other members of staff. If you are going to start to say "Well, if we have an MP as a consultant and we have an MP as an employee we are going to put out how much he or she earns", then I think that has a problem of confidence. It is a completely different matter if the MP chooses to disclose his or her salary.

532. ANNE WARBURTON: I am not altogether clear how you can say in the code say that nothing should be paid, "neither offer, nor give, nor cause a client to give any inducement to any Member of Parliament with intent to further their interests of any client", if they are paying them as a consultant or, indeed, as a director.

LEIGH MENDELSOHN: There is in a particular part——

DIANA WARWICK: You couldn't refer to the section, could you?

ANNE WARBURTON: Section 5J was what I was recalling.

MARTIN JACOMB: 5J—it is the bracketed words which are the relevant ones.

ANNE WARBURTON: Ah. "Except that a director, executive or retained consultant of any firm in question shall be entitled to receive proper remuneration." I didn't read to the end of the paragraph—I beg your pardon. But I don't altogether instantly see the difference between that and what we call the lobby firm retaining the services of an MP.

LEIGH MENDELSOHN: The line we took was that — we have only got seven members who actually employ MPs and there is one each and they are all as a consultant, there are no board directors. But I think that we took the stance that we couldn't tell our members to ban something

that wasn't illegal, that wasn't against any rules. Also there was the problem that even if we ban it for our members, and that is accepted, then we may work through MPs who are employed by our clients. So we decided it was far better, rather than to start putting bans anywhere, that we would just try to have the sort of code and document registration that at least showed everything, who worked for whom and doing what.

533. ANNE WARBURTON: Yes. I would be wrong, wouldn't I if I said what would you expect an MP who was a consultant to do, but perhaps I can say what would you think your clients would expect an MP who was a consultant to them, to do?

LEIGH MENDELSOHN: With our members who actually employ MPs as consultants—some of whom I have talked to, the majority—all say that they employ them to give advice on Parliamentary procedures, that none of their consultants actually work for any individual client, do not lobby on their behalf, but do advise the consultancy, which presumably would be the same situation where the client has an MP employed. I mean, each client would be different—some will use them to make the letter-heading look good, some will use them for advice and some will use them, perhaps, for some form of lobbying.

534. ANNE WARBURTON: For some sort of lobbying where?

LEIGH MENDELSOHN: Well, you would have to ask the client sector. One of the points I feel strongly about is that there has been a focus on the link between lobby firms and MPs. I mean I personally feel the whole lobby industry—there are thousands of in-house Parliamentary Affairs directors and managers and officers. Every walk of life has got these people in-house as well as employing their own independent consultants as well as going to lobby firms and I think that one has to look at the whole lobby area and it is the feeling of the PLCA that really the MPs have had many years, they know — we know because for twelve years we have been called in by the Select Committee to ask "what are we going to do about this, and what are we going to do about that?", so the MPs themselves know where the grey areas are, they know what the problems are and we've done, we feel—and I won't speak for the IPR but I am sure they feel the same way because we have put a lot of work and effort into this—we feel with our code and registers that we have gone as far as we can on self-regulation and we are tough with our own Members in other areas and we will be tough with them with this.

But the MPs—really in a sense, as I think I said in the written thing—have to stop passing the buck and actually look at themselves. They know what they can and cannot do within an ethical relationship. They need to set it down in writing, not only for themselves, but so we can all see. Not just the lobbyist firms but also the people working in-house.

535. ANNE WARBURTON: You would like Parliament to do a bit of regulating. What are your proposals?

LEIGH MENDELSOHN: I think real self-regulation is what is needed as a first step and I think they have to sit down and go through the agony, if necessary, of actually putting down in writing a code of conduct for both their behaviour within the house and with external pressures, whether they are lobbyists or constituents, pressure groups, whatever, and I think there needs to be a general code. We know they know the sort of things they need, because they told us what they wanted.

Then we also think that this should be open—I mean you have got to go down the route of disclosure and openness and we need a proper register. Most of our members feel it should be compulsory and it should go for complete disclosure. It is, I believe—it has to be that the guiding light, if you like, is disclosure and openness.

536. ANNE WARBURTON: Complete disclosure, including money?

LEIGH MENDELSOHN: Yes, I think there has to be. I think in the past it wasn't an issue but I think it is now. There are two lines of thought. One is that some people do believe that the problem is if you get £500 for representing a company or a lobby firm or whatever and you get 10, 20, 30, 50 thousand, there is a huge difference and that people ought to know. And the other viewpoint is this could become extremely cumbersome and that really the best approach is to put an overall figure in. I think that is something the MPs have to look at themselves and decide what they feel is right And I think we should always remember that—particularly now it is all in the public limelight—that peer group pressure and public opinion will constantly keep the MPs on their toes. I do also think that the code and register should be open to review every now and again because things change over the years.

537. ANNE WARBURTON: Thank you very much. What about a register of lobbyists, either individually or by their firms?

LEIGH MENDELSOHN: I think from when we spoke to the Select Committee there was concern at the cost of actually operating it. We have done one for our members and I have to say that we have actually opened it—the wording will be slightly different because the opening sentence is "this refers to the PRCA"—but the code we actually have officially opened since this month in response to a number of private companies who wish to actually be able to register, and a number of small, say two to three man-bands who are pure lobbyists, if you like, but are not of the size that can join the APPC. So ours will be open—but to be honest, apart from announcing it will be open, we haven't promoted it because of the problems of getting everything on the computer. But it is open if people want to register.

538. ANNE WARBURTON: I was thinking, when I asked the question of course, of a comprehensive one, which went beyond your own range. Could I just ask one last question? I am sorry to report that it has been suggested to us that the actions of lobbyists themselves have helped to reduce the reputation of Parliament, if not to do more real damage than that. What would you say to that?

LEIGH MENDELSOHN: I think in all walks of life you get a certain fringe element that overstep the mark—they may not be absolutely illegal but they certainly overstep the mark—and I think probably over the years the lobby industry has had the same problems as we find in other areas of the PR industry that we find with some of the MPs. It does take two to tango and you need the MPs to actually agree to what you are doing. You are

bound to get this problem. What one needs is a mechanism that can sort out the problem.

ANNE WARBURTON: Openness.

COLIN THOMPSON: If I can take that one stage further, we have had no complaints about any of our members and if we had we have an arbitration disciplinary procedure that would assess what the problem is, and that facility for complaint is open to the public at large.

ANNE WARBURTON: Thank you, Mr. Thompson and Miss Mendelsohn. Thank you.

LORD NOLAN: Yes, Clifford?

539. CLIFFORD BOULTON: Just a quick question on a matter of detail, really. In the code under "Conduct towards Members of Parliament" paragraph 8 says "Any person to whom this code applies and who is in possession of a Palace of Westminster access pass (other than if he is a Member of Parliament) shall not use any facility of either House to which that person has access in order to make any representations, or otherwise to assist clients". Was that put in to meet a perceived problem that there had been some abuses and could you tell us a little bit about what was in your minds when you put that paragraph in?

LEIGH MENDELSOHN: Yes, because we know that some MPs' researchers were employed as lobbyists and this goes back certainly to the early eighties to my knowledge. In fact I think I was interviewed by the now defunct TVS on the very subject in about '84, or something. So we knew there was this area which has caused a problem—the Select Committee, I think, investigated it a few years ago—and so we put that in as part of the code. As I said at the beginning we try to look at the grey areas and incorporate them in here and that is why within the actual written declaration it does say "And staff". I would make the point, though, as well, that I do feel that it is wrong, that the register of interests of researchers is secret.

540. CLIFFORD BOULTON: Available to members but not generally?

LEIGH MENDELSOHN: Yes, I gather it is only available to members.

ANNE WARBURTON: It is not as secret as it was before ——

LEIGH MENDELSOHN: Well, I know the journalists ask MPs to go in and copy it.

541. CLIFFORD BOULTON: But this was effectively also something that Members could control because it is what use is being made by people for whom they have obtained passes, was that really one of the problems?

LEIGH MENDELSOHN: There are, I have heard—I have no proof but I have heard in the past—that some lobbyists have actually got research passes without the MP even knowing how. How they do that I don't know, but apparently I have heard on two or three occasions that has happened.

CLIFFORD BOULTON: Thank you.

542. PETER SHORE: You have criticised the Select Committee on Members' Interests as being inadequate and you have in reply to a question said that they should declare amounts received in the register. What other deficiencies do you detect in the Register of Members' Interests and what other items would you like to see in?

LEIGH MENDELSOHN: I think if they are working for a consultancy of any description, whether it is a lobby firm or managing consultants, accountants, that they ought to also declare the clients of that company.

PETER SHORE: A number do already, I gather.

LEIGH MENDELSOHN: Yes, I know some do, but it is not compulsory as far as I know. And I would like to see that if, presumably links are in some way allowed to continue with lobby firms, that certainly if should state if they are actually involved in anything other than advising that the "company" rather than the "clients"—and I think if they are going to start to work on the clients this has got to be put down. What we are hoping is that we have got a sort of mirror image of this, that people can cross-reference. I think also you have to look at the MPs who are working directly for private companies and whether or not they are being used as a funnel for lobby work. I think one of the areas that the public is concerned about, the perception of politicians, is on the lobby side—where are they actually working for money to favour a particular issue, or a company, I suppose.

543. PETER SHORE: You heard the APPC evidence earlier this morning and you know that their policy is to ban the payment of Members of Parliament by public relations firms. Can you say again—because you have touched on this—why you, yourselves, don't adopt that same policy?

LEIGH MENDELSOHN: When we looked at it we decided on two levels; one, we felt we couldn't tell a member firm not to do something that wasn't illegal, or against any rules. Secondly, we felt there was a danger of driving things underground and going back to the original premise that everything should be disclosed and open we said "Don't ban it, let's make it open and written down". One of the dangers we do know happens—I mean, I know it happens—that you can drop a case of best claret at somebody's back door. Some people have had holidays. So you start to drive it in a different way which I think becomes very difficult then to control. And then, of course, it actually causes all sorts of problems. And bearing in mind you will always have the fringe people who will sail close to the wind. We decided not to ban things, keep it above board, but put it down—what's going on.

PETER SHORE: Thank you.

LORD NOLAN: Now, we are running very short of time indeed. May I ask the other Members of the committee, remembering that we have still got to hear from Emma Nicholson, to confine any questions they have got to the burning one. Have you got anything else, Bill?

WILLIAM UTTING: I will pass, Chairman.

LORD NOLAN: Well, thank you very much indeed. I think with your written evidence and your statement this

morning supplementing it you have given us a clear picture of your views. I am much obliged.

LEIGH MENDELSOHN: Could I make one final point? The PRCA feels that lobby firms need no special treatment, no special access to the House and I do feel that there should be no privilege of any description for lobby firms.

544. LORD NOLAN: Thank you very much. Emma Nicholson, Conservative Member of Parliament for Torridge and West Devon. The time I am afraid is twenty-five minutes after we were hoping that you would start your evidence. We have no difficulty in going on a little after one, but it may be very inconvenient for you and I am so sorry for the delay.

EMMA NICHOLSON MP

EMMA NICHOLSON MP: No, please don't worry. It is not a problem for me at all.

545. LORD NOLAN: Thank you very much. Did you by any chance prepare any kind of opening statements you wanted to make or are you content to go straight into questions?

EMMA NICHOLSON: If you would be kind enough to allow me to I would like to spend five minutes just outlining my general philosophy on this?

LORD NOLAN: This would be very helpful. Please do.

EMMA NICHOLSON: Thank you very much indeed. First of all, may I say how much I welcome the work of the committee. I am particularly anxious that Parliament—the House of Commons in particular, where I work—is respected in the fullness of our society. Many questions have been asked lately of Members of Parliament to do with how we operate, how we discharge our responsibilities, and I want to discuss the question of the perception by the public of our role and what I see as the actuality.

To me there is a firm central question that we need to answer. Are we on a continuing road from having Members of Parliament serve the public with no pay and outside employment? To having Members of Parliament with full pay and no outside employment at all? In other words are we moving from being self-employed, which we are at the present time, to becoming wholly-owned servants of the State, or is there a possibility of a combined role, a stepping-stone on this road, or not a stepping-stone? In other words, may we find a mid point at which it is comfortable for all of us to rest or not? I believe that we should explore this quite aggressively because it will avoid the sacrifice of what I see as a unique independence of the Member of Parliament in our society, versus the degenerative effect of the role in the public perception, partly because of the impact it has on my fellow Members of Parliament. A small story, perhaps; late at night a Labour Member of Parliament and I were in the tearoom—it was about one in the morning—and he said to me "What is the point of all of this? We are not even respected any longer". And I am unhappy about that. If we are going to become the whipping boy or the Aunt Sally of society then we have got to take a long hard look because of the degeneration of our view of the public on Members of Parliament. It means that the quality of our work is inevitably suffering already.

I also wish to keep our unique independence because with it comes the key element of personal service. So many of the things we do for our constituents we do well over and above the normal perception of work and our independence is the trigger, I think, for that personal service. But I also feel that we need to examine our role because I think there is a lack of respect for the work of Members of Parliament just now.

Looking for a moment at the strengths of our Parliamentary inheritance, which I think we should preserve in any change at all, first is our antiquity in international parliamentary terms and the role model that offers for newly emerging democracies, such as in Eastern Europe. I think we have a heavy obligation here—we are the mother of Parliaments, we should offer the best examples. And, secondly, in society at large the British people have a very healthy independence of spirit but I still believe that they request of us in Parliament examples of good governance and from that examples of best practice and best personal behaviour. Maybe this is unfair, particularly when it is the written media who seem to haul us up in front of the public tribunal when their own personal standards may not be those that they require of us. But the fact is that the public require these standards of us, in my view, and I think that we have to respond to that demand. Indeed, I think that only if we respond with the appropriate political probity can we continually re-earn the public underlying respect that in my view the House of Commons ought, by virtue of merit of its omnipotence and omnicompetence position in our written constitution, to deserve.

I am not suggesting for one moment that either individually or collectively we Members of Parliament should be immune from criticism. I would like to make the point immediately that our political adversarial system is, in fact, built on criticism, on searching and pungent criticism of each other's views. I happen to be particularly unhappy on an allied point to this, which is raised by the very strength and power of modern journalism which is when questions of personal morality of individual Members of Parliament, through media investigations, cause lasting harm and damage to children particularly. But I think that has to be addressed separately from this committee if only because it can't be viewed objectively until the current belief that Members of Parliament are misbehaving financially is cleared up, and that maybe is the most important piece of work that this committee can undertake.

I would like to suggest that in a very few years recently the work of a Member of Parliament has changed quite dramatically because the immense growth of the State intervention into citizens' lives, which has taken place at the citizen's continuing request, to my mind means that we now take executive responsibilities in the political process which we never used to do. Actions are agreed by us in Parliament, in the House of Commons, which directly affect virtually all aspects of a citizen's life. I think this is a new dimension and that our very heavy workload reflects this new dimension which has resulted in steps to recompense us financially, to give us time to carry out the work. But I think there is still a perception in the public eye, internationally as well as in the United Kingdom, that the old institutions don't properly align themselves with modern issues. I would suggest that it is in an attempt to meet these concerns that a mix of new and older outside sponsorships of Members of Parliament, such as companies, pressure groups, trade unions, has led to an alteration of the political process in the House of Commons itself. That is the point at issue, maybe, between the public and ourselves.

In that the public believe that they now don't know whether or not a Member of Parliament is paid additional sums of money to carry out standard political tasks for masters other than the electorate, I think there has been a sequence of excellent attempts to solve this problem which have not achieved a solution. The Register of Members' Interests is one. I personally see the Register of Members' Interests as a snare and a delusion. I think it misleads both us, as Members of Parliament, and the public and it also provides a very rich harvest for the media, because declarations are seen as an absolution as well as an information offering. In my view it would be better to have a few generally enforceable rules than the current mish-mash and maybe we would be better off without the Register entirely—I think it misleads.

Incidentally my own views on how we should proceed do not offer any criticism of my colleagues on either side of the House. The reason for that is that the current rules allow one to "free range" for extra pay. It is unfair in my view to criticism Members of Parliament who, of their own initiative, have taken advantage of this situation. But I do think that the present situation leaves the electorate to believe that Members of Parliament are no longer addressing the real issues, the ones that come out in their daily life because our energies are taken up by the demands of other paymasters. I believe that the Register of Members' Interests feeds the public mania for insularity whereby crossing the Channel is such a crime that hefty declarations are mandatory—and this is in a world where Britain's interests as a trading nation are international. And I believe the most important point to me is that the present situation leads to confusion in the lobby, the Chamber and the tearooms because you are no longer clear as to whether or not a colleague approaches you because they have a real interest in a topic or because they have undertaken to do so or an outside paymaster. I think that this muddies the clarity of our political debate and our political debate is very important.

I have touched critically a moment ago on the written media. I would like to suggest that by virtue of the explosion of new forms of communication in the last ten years particularly, individual parliamentary actions are or can be broadcast internationally and can even affect judgments of the United Kingdom globally, for good or ill. In this sense I believe that we are all ambassadors of the United Kingdom now—particularly in the House of Commons, the crucible of democracy, now that we have let in the television cameras.

In summary, therefore, I think that our world is more and more compact, that British interests are affected by actions reported all around the globe and we have to take account of that. I think that good governance issues may be the central issues of today in the world's democracies, and rightly so—we need to think of that. It is five years since the fall of the Berlin wall and Eastern Europe are looking to us for example. The voters expect us to have the highest standards and we have to respect that requirement. And finally, I think while it is important to have guidelines it is just as important not to over-prescribe.

LORD NOLAN: Thank you very much for that clear and helpful opening. Now, we have been taking it in turns as Members to lead particular witnesses and I am going to ask Sir William Utting to carry on the questioning with you, please.

546. WILLIAM UTTING: Thank you, Chairman. One or two general points, if I may, on what you have just said, Miss Nicholson, and then I would like to pick up one or two points about yourself as a Member of Parliament and your own experience there. You referred at the beginning to the slightly depressed conversation you had had with a Labour colleague about "what good we were doing in this place." That actually seems to me to be a symptom of a general decline in deference towards the institutions of the establishment from the monarchy through to the professions and that decline is not something that Parliament is automatically excepted from. Other bodies in dealing with that are reviewing their purposes and the ways in which they conduct their business. I wondered if you saw any relationship between this decline in esteem for Parliament and scepticism about its effectiveness and efficiency as an institution. You referred warmly to the traditions of antiquity but you also spoke about old institutions not aligning with modern issues and I wondered if you thought that that was a problem that Parliament itself had now got?

EMMA NICHOLSON: First of all, could I suggest that there has been no golden age—if indeed it would have been golden—when the British people were subservient and dripping with respect for institutions. As we look back we see, if only from the cartoonists, how disrespectful—how healthily disrespectful in my view—the British public have always been of those who try to serve them, whether it is the Monarchy, whether it is Parliament, or whether it is other institutions. I believe that there is an underlying unhappiness in many Members of Parliament just now, however, in that we believe, irrespective of party, that we give a great deal, not just of our personalities, but of our family lives, of our time, but much more than just the hours in a day, that our concern for our constituents and for the nation is real and continuing. I can hardly find a Member of Parliament in the House of Commons who, if a human rights or humanitarian issue or something affecting someone in need arises, would not immediately give time to assist and would take vast trouble to help.

Of course, when Members of Parliament were unpaid that was more readily noticeable. I think we are at a very difficult balance at the moment in that we receive pay for our activities and yet we give insuperable abundance of energy and effort over and above what that pay level—or any pay in a sense—would demand. I think the sadness is that Members of Parliament feel that these great efforts that they make to help other people are no longer recognised and respected as such. It is not that we are asking, I would suggest, to be respected just because we are Members of Parliament but to have the worth of our work recognised and respected. So I suggest there was no golden age and I wouldn't have enjoyed it if there had been—I think it would have been extremely boring—but I believe there has to be a closer match between what the Members of Parliament are giving in the broadest sense of the word to the nation and to their constituents and what the nation is demanding. Somehow at the moment I don't find the two fitting—the institution of Parliament is very very old indeed and I don't feel that we have managed to progress the way in which we work to fit the way in which the outside world behave sufficiently well for the outside world to understand what we are doing on their behalf or to welcome it.

547. WILLIAM UTTING: You spoke about a continuum between a low paid group of people with lots of outside interests, possibly moving along to a salaried professional class of legislators. Where do you think we are on that continuum at the moment in the House?

EMMA NICHOLSON: I recall my father's surprise and shock when he learned that he was to be paid £600 a year for the first time as a Member of Parliament—that was after he had been in Parliament for many years indeed. When he went into Parliament in 1931 the Trades Union Movement sponsored Labour Members of Parliament, so that they also had an equal chance of getting into Parliament, alongside those who had, maybe, managerial or legal or professional responsibilities and were able to marry the two tasks. We have moved to paying Members of Parliament about ten or eleven thousand pounds less than a general practitioner, twelve thousand pounds less than a dentist, and at the same time we have accepted in Parliament the explosion of pressure groups, of advertising agencies—in other words, modern methods of communication with companies clients—and we have responded to the desire of those clients to be close to the political process or—and I think this is the important point—to be seen to be close to the political process. So we now take in funds individually from companies from pressure groups, as well as accepting sponsorship from Trade Unions. I make no party political point here—I believe that it is the entirety of the House of Commons that needs to be looked at in this frame—and we have given ourselves, therefore, the opportunity of earning outside funds.

The example of full-time professional politicians that I know best is the one in the USA where, of course, recently rules were brought in which forbade outside earnings, other than I think in the Upper House, journalism and speaking. I would guess that we are two-thirds along the way towards that—as much as that. From £600 to £32,000 plus £42,000 for staff over a relatively short period of years is a very big leap indeed. I think we are two-thirds or three-quarters of the way towards having full-time professional State-owned Members of Parliament.

548. WILLIAM UTTING: Good, thank you. You offered a pretty caustic view of the value of the Register of Members' Interests and said you would prefer to see this replaced by a set of general principles. Do you believe that such a set of general principles could be established as a binding code of conduct on Members of Parliament?

EMMA NICHOLSON: I am absolutely confident that if a sane and sensible code of conduct were outlined and accepted by Parliament then we would have no difficulty in honouring it. I have a high regard for the personal conduct of my fellow Members of Parliament on all sides of the House.

549. WILLIAM UTTING: Good, thank you. And in spite of your views about the Register you are obviously most conscientious in filling it in yourself because I am told that yours is the longest single entry of any Member of Parliament. But having said that I had better add that your remunerated employment is down simply as "Author and occasional public speaker with all fees going to charity" and that the long list of your other interests are all of a charitable and voluntary nature. Is this a matter of personal preference on your part, that your activities outside Parliament are spent in voluntary and charitable activities, or is this a principled choice?

EMMA NICHOLSON: Perhaps the two come together. I have always felt that "he who pays the piper calls the tune" and that if the electorate were paying me then I would prefer only to be answerable to the electorate. There may be many political misjudgments I may make or may have made—I would prefer them to be a matter between myself and the electorate, rather than to have my thinking muddled by another organisation also paying me. That is both maybe a personal choice and a personal principle.

550. WILLIAM UTTING: Thank you very much. In the activities that you undertake on behalf of charities—I mean, these presumably would include giving them advice about how to go about getting Parliamentary business done, facilitating their access to Parliament?

EMMA NICHOLSON: No.

551. WILLIAM UTTING: It doesn't? It doesn't approach anything that resembles a paid consultancy that another MP might take on?

EMMA NICHOLSON: No.

WILLIAM UTTING: Good.

EMMA NICHOLSON: Why did I put them down then? Which is why I think the Register of Members' Interests is such a nonsense. Because I wanted to make it absolutely clear that if I wished to I could claim a rail fare from a charity, if they asked me to go to speak in the North of Scotland or in Iceland or in Timbuktu—I wanted to make that absolutely clear. It got me nowhere, merely a heavy criticism for being greedy of space. The Register of Members' Interests, I promise you, is just plain silly.

WILLIAM UTTING: Yes. Well, yours is totally transparent anyway.

EMMA NICHOLSON: Then again—have a dozen sane rules, my colleagues, generally speaking, are people of the highest standards and they will honour them.

WILLIAM UTTING: Good. Thank you very much, Miss Nicholson. Thank you, Chairman.

552. LORD NOLAN: Just one question, Miss Nicholson. Do you think the present system of self-regulation in the House by the Committee of Privileges is adequate?

EMMA NICHOLSON: I suggest that the principle of self-regulation ought to be adequate in Parliament. If it is muddled at the moment my suggestion is because the rules they are trying to monitor are a muddle.

LORD NOLAN: Yes, thank you very much. Now, Sir Martin?

553. MARTIN JACOMB: Just one generalised question and one detailed one. I have found everything you have said incredibly interesting and very persuasive, so I will try and be brief. Given your own experience and by hearsay your father's experience, leaving aside the public regard for Parliament and for Members of Parliament, do you think the actual standard of conduct on average has got worse?

EMMA NICHOLSON: It is not for me to judge other Members of Parliament. All of us have different pressures

on us. I come again to the present rules. I think it is massively unfair to judge people critically or negatively if they are inside the present rules. That is just not fair. I mean my personal view is that the present rules—if you leave those aside as rules per se, as judgment criteria—they do lead to muddle and confusion simply by virtue of some of the types of extra occupation that they allow. But that is the question you haven't asked me.

554. MARTIN JACOMB: Is there a deterioration of adherence to basic principles, that is really what I was asking.

EMMA NICHOLSON: Sir Martin, could you say that again?

555. MARTIN JACOMB: Do you think there has been a deterioration of adherence to basic principles—on the basic principles which are required of Members of Parliament?

EMMA NICHOLSON: It is not for me to ask the questions of you but I would need the identification of what those basic principles were meant to be before I answered.

MARTIN JACOMB: Well, perhaps it is too difficult—perhaps it is too generalised a question.

EMMA NICHOLSON: Our basic principles, as Parliamentarians, surely are to serve our constituents and the nation by struggling to make the most effective political judgments in the light of all the circumstances around the debate. That is our job.

MARTIN JACOMB: I meant a basic principle would be not to hold out one's position as a MP for hire—that kind of thing.

EMMA NICHOLSON: In our society, right up to the present day, Members of Parliament have always held outside jobs or had that ability to do so. I think your question has to relate implicitly to should that activity be confined to assisting the companies or organisations or Trades Unions outside the House of Commons or inside. My belief, as I think I indicated, is that exerting influence from companies through Members of Parliament into the House of Commons arena has muddied the debate in a way that I do not feel is to the best interests of good legislation.

556. MARTIN JACOMB: Could I just ask you one detailed question because you referred to it and it is one which interests me, which is the unvouched expense allowance for secretarial services? In the private sector most responsible companies abandoned the unvouched expense allowance many years ago and only allow expenses on the basis of actual expenditure incurred, properly vouched. Do you think it would improve the public regard for Parliament if Members of Parliament were paid proper taxable salaries with expenses only claimable on the basis of vouched expenditure?

EMMA NICHOLSON: I think this is a difficult question. I understood our salaries were taxed at the moment.

557. TOM KING: You have the right to claim expenses—they may have an expenses allowance. I don't want to interrupt but that is the point.

EMMA NICHOLSON: Yes. The Parliamentary allowance for Members' secretaries and research assistants is a highly contentious item.

MARTIN JACOMB: That is what I am talking about.

EMMA NICHOLSON: I think because it comes in one single block. I would myself very much welcome a permanent outside body with which Parliament couldn't tamper which would determine our pay and expenses. I believe that should be an outside body. I think I have already indicated that I believe on other matters Parliament should continue to judge its own affairs, but I think that that outside body would best be tasked to look at all these difficulties. It is a bone of great contention at the moment which leads to both misunderstandings, to too high payment for poor quality service sometimes, to a belief that Members' wives are used illegally. Of course if they are doing the job they should be paid but you then have to question whether or not they should do the job. Surely these questions should be given to an outside body. It is very uncomfortable year upon year to vote on our own pay. I dislike it intensely. We should place this outside the Parliamentary area entirely. But not the other matters pertaining to our work. Pay is a complex and technical subject on which constant comparisons have to be made with other institutions and other organisations. I don't think we are knowledgeable enough about that either to be able to do that scrutiny effectively. So it is both embarrassing and I think imperfect as it is at the moment.

558. DIANE WARWICK: You said in your very interesting presentation that you were going to address the difference between appearance and reality and one of the things that we have learned is of an opinion poll which says that 64 per cent of the population believe that most MPs make a lot of money by using their public office improperly, and yet almost everybody who has given evidence to us has said that they don't believe that is true of most MPs. Do MPs share that perception? You said that it is no longer clear when a colleague approaches you whether they are doing it out of genuine interest or whether they are doing it because they are paid to do it. Do MPs themselves believe that lots of their colleagues are up to this—do they talk about that in the tearooms?

EMMA NICHOLSON: Two points, if I may. First of all, the declaration in the Register of Members' Interests gives the proper justification for accepting payment from an outside organisation, therefore it would be curious if a Member of Parliament felt that they were behaving improperly when having made that declaration they are clearly behaving properly. My suggestion is twofold; first of all, that it is impossible to keep the Register of Members' Interests in one's head and on the other side of the House—I am a Conservative—how can I remember which Trade Union a Member belongs to? It just isn't a possibility any longer, because the explosion of activities is so large. Improperly, no, because once it is declared it is proper. Confusing—to me, yes. And on a question of judgment I have the personal view that accepting a sponsorship from advertising agencies, pressure groups, lobbying companies, leads to a complete inability from the Member who hasn't accepted that sponsorship to be able to judge accurately precisely where the nudge is coming from to change a political view. Because you can't possibly tell who the clients are—it is not meant to be a smoke screen but that is how it actually works. Even if you could remember the name of the lobbying company you couldn't possibly remember all the clients whom they may

be representing at a given time. I think that is very muddling in the debate, if it very muddling in the lobby, it is very muddling at supper when somebody presses you hard to take an interest in something and you subsequently discover that that is, in fact, one of their outside registered interests. There is nothing improper about it—I am just saying that it is exceptionally muddling.

Then I would suggest that if we have Trades Union sponsorships my belief is that that has exactly the same effect because Trade Unions are so enormous that naturally they represent a huge range of interests. I see no difference. Since we are now paid salaries the initial justification, the original reason for having Trades Union sponsorship has gone, which was to give people a level footing on entering Parliament. I think it leads to the same confusion as lobbying companies.

Where single interests are taken up and declared, whether they are a personal farm or a company, then I believe we should respond to public concern now, even though we are in a different position, say from local councillors, because we don't have planning decisions, for examples, on which huge sums of money revolve these days. Even though we are in a different position, as I have indicated I think we do now inevitably take some executive-type decisions, therefore I think that if a Member does take out that responsibility they should not speak in the Chamber, nor use their political influence to put questions, to get introductions to Ministers and so on. I think that that influence should be used to keep the company abreast of what is going on in Parliament. Although even there I believe that perhaps because our Parliament has always been, in line with many of our institutions, somewhat secretive, I think that serving a company in this way can lead a company quite wrongly to believe that there is a great deal more to be gained from having a Member of Parliament as a consultant than can be gained. The truth of the matter is that any Minister worth his or her salt will always listen to a genuine problem brought by a colleague, whether it is to do with a company, a constituent or anybody else. We have a very fine Parliamentary system, it works extremely well, and I often think that by accepting these additional paid posts we merely defer the day when all of our Parliamentary procedure will be on Internet, including Hansard. Even now people write in and ask for a copy of Hansard as if it was some enormous gift. It should be open to the world through Internet. We are moving towards that, thank goodness, but it is terribly slow and part of the problem with these company assignments is that they tend to think they get much more out of it than anybody else would do if they didn't pay and, of course, they don't. One of the best examples of this is one of our big PLCs, which is in computers, IBM, nobody paid and they are right alongside the Parliamentary process all the time.

LORD NOLAN: Thank you very much. I know there are three or four others who may want to ask you questions. Tom, have you any?

TOM KING: No, thank you very much.

LORD NOLAN: Peter?

559. PETER SHORE: You have made your position, I think, very clear on a number of things. Would I be right in saying that you would welcome among your few short

principles or guidelines the banning of payments to MPs by public relation firms?

EMMA NICHOLSON: Yes.

560. PETER SHORE: Yes. And following that would you also be prepared to ban consultancy arrangements between firms, professional associations and other bodies, with MPs for pay?

EMMA NICHOLSON: Individual companies, no, provided the guideline was that that position was not used in Parliament but was used to advise the company outside Parliament, or to work with the company outside Parliament.

561. PETER SHORE: Yes, it is very difficult, though, isn't it, to draw precisely that line between working inside Parliament for a firm and helping it outside?

EMMA NICHOLSON: It is difficult. I suggest it is not impossible and it used to happen. It is historically the system we used to run. I would also, however, go a little bit further than public relations companies and add advertising companies, any company with a web of different and moving clients and also, I am afraid, trades union sponsorship, because I believe the reason for that has also gone and it merely adds to the fog and confusion. I am after clarity between ourselves and the electorate.

PETER SHORE: Thank you.

562. CLIFFORD BOULTON: I was a little anxious that one answer you gave might have been a little misleading as it came over and that was the business of Members' office cost allowance—the £42,000. Perhaps one ought to make it clear that any individual employed by a Member has to have a contract of employment and now virtually every person employed is paid through the mechanism of the House of Commons by the Finance Department. So it is not a question of a Member taking home a bag of £42,000 and giving it out like that. I just wanted an opportunity to correct the impression that might have been given.

EMMA NICHOLSON: Well, Sir Clifford, thank you for making the point. You saw at once that in fact I was trying to duck Sir Martin's question because it is so tactical and didn't seem to me to be something that was very easy to address without proper background in front of a whole committee. But, of course, it is possible to employ—with respect to yourself—somebody who is paid through the Fees Office mechanism without a contract—point one. Point two, it is worth pointing out also that the Fees Office is only acting for the Member of Parliament. The Member of Parliament is self-employed and the amount allotted by Parliament for the sustenance of that political work is, in fact, identified with that particular Member of Parliament.

563. CLIFFORD BOULTON: Yes. The reason I raised the issue—I think that all Members virtually now have complied with the rule about contracts of employment—there may be one or two who haven't yet completed them—but the point I was making is that I thought you attached importance to the fact that the Members was self-employed, it enabled him to do the job in his or her own ways, and there are very many ways of being a good Member of Parliament. Are there not advantages in the concept of the Member being able to employ staff at his or her own discretion to do the job as that Member wishes it to be done?

EMMA NICHOLSON: Well, the staff of Members of Parliament generally speaking work the most astonishing hours, most of them, and have a great loyalty to a particular constituency, to a particular political party—which may be the most important point—and generally speaking some loyalty at least to a particular Member of Parliament. So if you can forge a good team with your staff then your constituents really get first class service. So, yes, if a Member of Parliament is self-employed then I believe the Parliamentary allowance properly is associated with that individual Member of Parliament. After all, the Fees Office, as a paymaster system only came in because some Members of Parliament didn't pay their secretaries at all.

LORD NOLAN: Well, that seems to have completed the questions. Thank you very much indeed for your help—you have been a most interesting helpful witness and we are most grateful to you.

WEDNESDAY 25 JANUARY 1995

Members Present:

The Rt. Hon. The Lord Nolan (Chairman)

Sir Clifford Boulton GCB   The Rt. Hon. Peter Shore MP
Sir Martin Jacomb   The Rt. Hon. The Lord Thomson of Monifieth KT DL
Professor Anthony King   Dame Anne Warburton DCVO CMG

Witnesses:
Mr Peter Preston, Editor in Chief, *Guardian* and *Observer*
Ann Taylor MP, Shadow Leader of the House
Roger King, Director of Public Affairs, Society of Motor Manufacturers and Traders
Sir Geoffrey Johnson-Smith MP, Chairman, Select Committee on Members' Interests,
and Roger Willoughby, Clerk to the Committee and Registrar of Members' Interests
Stuart Bell MP

564. LORD NOLAN: We have another very full morning. Yesterday and last week we heard from organisations in the lobbying business. Today we will be hearing from a trade association about their relations with Members of Parliament. We will have the benefit of the views of three Members of Parliament: Stuart Bell; Anne Taylor, who is shadow Leader of the House; and Sir Geoffrey Johnson-Smith, who will be able to tell us more from his perspective as Chairman of the Select Committee on Members Interests. I should mention that we will be hearing from Tony Newton, Leader of the House, next Tuesday morning as we complete our sessions specifically directed to Members of Parliament.

To start, in welcoming Peter Preston, I should like to congratulate him on his elevation to the post of Editor in Chief of the *Guardian* and the *Observer*. Mr. Preston, am I right in thinking that, like many of our other witnesses, you prefer to begin by making a short opening statement?

PETER PRESTON

PETER PRESTON (Editor in Chief, *Guardian* and *Observer*): Just very briefly, if I may, Lord Nolan.

LORD NOLAN: By all means.

PETER PRESTON: Simply to say, and I put in some rather long-winded notes which I do not propose to refer to, but if there is one thing very much on my mind in terms of this committee it is the question of how the best regulatory framework in the world actually appends to the delivery of that framework in practice.

I have talked in my notes about, for example, my experience with Questions of Procedure for Ministers, blessedly now printed, greatly to the credit of the present Prime Minister, but looking at the delivery of that when somebody wishes to make a complaint, to find out who is responsible, who is not, what is an adviser, what is an arbiter and detailing that in just the same way across other things which one has recently become involved in. You are looking at the Privileges Committee or the Select Committee on Members Interests. When controversies break out does one, if one is involved in the process, or perhaps do the public if they are observing the process, feel confident that the regulations and the codes are being delivered in practice.

I touch briefly at the end on my brief experience on the Press Complaints Commission which is self-regulatory

and continues to strive to be self-regulatory but, nevertheless, has always had a substantial lay presence on the Commission and now a clear lay majority. That again is something that one would want to look at in the context of the delivery in a Westminster context of self-regulation, because if that is designed to reassure the public about the PCC, whether for good or ill on the outside, how is the public to be reassured about anything that your committee may recommend in terms of new codes, new practices, new codes of ethics, or whatever. That is my central point.[4]

LORD NOLAN: Thank you very much. I have no doubt each of those areas will be explored a little more fully in the course of the questions which the Members of the committee will want to put to you. As I mentioned, I am asking Lord Thomson to begin by taking you through your evidence.

565. LORD THOMSON: Mr. Preston, in view of the pressure on time thank you very much for making such a succinct opening statement and the fuller written version which you submitted to us in advance will be made available to everybody so it will be properly on the record.

We are, of course, examining standards in public life, the public perception of them, the reality behind the public perception and what changes in the rules and regulations it may be appropriate to recommend. There are really, I suppose, three major actors in the drama that we are investigating. One, the people in public life and, at the moment, we are concentrating on Members of Parliament. A second major actor, of course, are the lobbyists, that new and burgeoning industry. A third major actor, of course, is the media. We are not investigating the media but we are bound to want to examine closely the role the media plays in creating the public perception about standards in public life and whether the rules of behaviour for the media are a help or a hindrance in all this.

Against that rather long preamble of mine, could I ask you to comment on the evidence that we had earlier from Chris Moncreiff, the doyen of the Press Association in the House of Commons and can I just quote the evidence he gave us. He said:

"In recent years the Press, including television, has become far more aggressive in its approach to MPs, to

---

[4]See Evidence, pp. 509–510.

seek out what they consider wrongdoing. Indeed, in some cases, as we know, the Press has resorted to acting as an agent provocateur, perhaps even as an impostor ..."

these are his words not mine——

"to find out what they consider to be the truth. They say that the ends justify the means."

He then went on to say:

"It is simply something that 30 years ago would never have happened—a move by a newspaper or any part of the media to try to entrap an MP into doing something which he should not do."

This is strong stuff but it is a legitimate point of view in the argument we are engaged in. Would you like to comment on these comments?

PETER PRESTON: Just in two ways, I think, if I may. One would be to agree that times do change and if we are talking about, for example, lobbyists and the growth of the lobbying industry one has to read that into the record. Westminster is not an unchanging sort of goldfish bowl over the centuries; it is part of the world we live in; and the world we live in, for good or ill, has new factors operating in it. In terms of the ends justifying the means, I would never, as an editor, say that any ends justify any means. Chris, I assume, was talking about the *Sunday Times* case. What I would say though is that to attempt to look at standards in British public life and to look at the conduct of Members of Parliament, not I hope in a hostile sense but for the purpose of actually telling people what we would consider people ought to be told about what goes on and the practices that grow up, that that needs to be done with a good degree of rigour. I am not going to describe this very well but to have, in a sense, the old rules of a gentlemens' club of 25 years ago tossed back at one as though one was a sort of unwelcome guest at a party which had been going on in a goldfish bowl for a very long time, there is a sort of dislocation in perception and standards. It is difficult for the Press to conduct these kinds of enquiries. I hope most of them are conducted in a reasonable spirit but they are involving very difficult areas.

It is hard to get away from the fact that in a club atmosphere—which is what Westminster is—there will be a lot of joint anger and feeling that the club rules have somehow been transgressed by people, and Chris Moncreiff was very much a part of that club atmosphere for a long time. I am not part of the club. I think that, from the outside, we have to have ways of asking the questions and have ways of the interrogation which people understand as part of a democratic process.

566. LORD THOMSON: One of our tasks which we are finding increasingly delicate is how to draw the line in terms of behaviour of one kind and another. Would you draw a line in terms of media behaviour between serious, rigorous, investigative journalism and some of the forms of what are sometimes called tabloid journalism though they sometimes spill over into the old, so-called, quality papers.

Let me take a casual example. I happened to see yesterday Mr. Jack Straw in a speech apparently made some light remarks about his role in bullying at school. He wrote an article yesterday in the *London Times* describing how a posse of reporters had descended on the local library and spent some time trying to find out a great deal about what had actually happened and intruding a great deal on elderly relatives, and so on, and his former school friends. How do you draw a line between what is fair investigative journalism and what is unfair investigative journalism?

PETER PRESTON: It is an almost impossible line to draw in that context. As I understand it, what Jack was complaining about in what we used to call one of the "expensive" papers, which we do not any longer, was behaviour which, on what he said, I would not condone at all for a moment. In a Press Complaints Commission sense, he clearly, if he wishes, has the ability to take that to the PCC and see what they say about it. I do not know the details sufficiently closely.

LORD THOMSON: No, I was not asking ...

PETER PRESTON: It is very difficult and I would counsel the committee to beware of the argument that because the Press does a variety of things—the Royal Family or whatever—that somehow they do not have a role in the monitoring and the processes of our democracy too. We are an imperfect lot in a very imperfect world and when it is said, for example, that the Press is too powerful I have always felt that the moment the Press says it is too powerful actually it will fall apart because one half of the Press will start attacking the other and this is self-evidently not power. What it is, in a fairly miasmic way occasionally, is the duty to monitor the workings of government and the workings of the legislature on behalf of the people. It is not a profession, it is a trade but that is what we are there for.

567. LORD THOMSON: Could I ask one final question about the role of the Press in terms of standards in public life because the Press itself is, in its own way in public life and then I will move on briefly to get your views on the more general questions we are wrestling with.

You will know the famous old quote from the Civil Service poet, Humbert Wolfe:

"You cannot hope to bribe or twist, thank God, the British journalist but when you see what he will do unbribed there is no occasion to."

What is the code of conduct of the *Guardian* itself internally in terms of the standards of its reporters and writers and how do you apply it? Is there a contract? Do you lay down conditions? What are the rules?

PETER PRESTON: Very simply, on the paper we have, I hope, a tradition and a clearly understood core of behaviour which operates from day to day. But, apart from that, just to remind you, we are subject to a number of codes including, I think, primarily the Press Complaints Commission; the editor's code of practice, which I am sure you are familiar with which I, in some ways, helped draw up and which seems to me constantly there to be amended, to be a very useful working framework for the way we should proceed.

568. LORD THOMSON: I was thinking more particularly of an internal code in relation to writing about

things where reporters have enjoyed free hospitality or free travel, that sort of thing, rules with regard to gifts and hospitality.

PETER PRESTON: I could provide the latest statement of that, if that would be helpful to the committee. In a sense, that formulation hails, if you like, from what we call the Bottomley rules after Peter Bottomley who, I think, intrinsically, in talking about how Members of Parliament should behave, said that they should do nothing which they would find embarrassing to have on the front page of their local paper. I have always been reluctant internally to draw up a completely rigorous code of practice in a sort of mechanistic sense because, for example, if I had a problem with the registering of interests in Parliament it would be that the moment you have a line, you do not have to register a directorship or an interest which lasts for under four weeks, that produces a situation where three weeks and six days is one thing and four weeks and one day is another. You have to apply more to peoples' common sense in those terms.

In terms of trips, "freebies" or whatever they are called, we have something now on the "*Guardian*" which is called actually "TRIPWIRE" where everybody invited to go on a trip has to register it, clear it with their Head of Department and the Head of Department will refer it upwards if he feels there is any danger of being compromised. That is the way we operate. I am sorry not to have understood you clearly.

569. LORD THOMSON: That is very helpful. Now, two general questions. Behind your recent investigations, of course, lies a view about the behaviour of people in public life and, in particular, Members of Parliament. I just wondered what your general views were about what the rules for Members of Parliament should be. One of the distinctions we have been wrestling with, for example, and there will be others, is whether it might be legitimate for a Member of Parliament to receive pay for representing some particular interest in Parliament, let us say the Police Federation which has come up under discussion, a trade association, a trade union, whatever, but it might not be acceptable for a Member of Parliament to be part of a multi-client public relations firm where the clients come and go but they represent their interests when they are concerned with any immediate piece of legislation.

Do you have any views about what would be proper and improper in terms of the payment of Members of Parliament for outside interests?

PETER PRESTON: I am not of the view that Members of Parliament should be cut off entirely from the outside world but I am of the view that it is difficult for anybody to see quite where a Member of Parliament as part of, for example, a lobbying company operating on behalf of a number of ever-changing clients, without being at all condemnatory, is coming from or who he is serving at that particular time. I sometimes sucked my thumb, long ago and far away, about whether Jim Callaghan should be the Police Federation spokesman on earth but basically at least you knew clearly what Mr. Callaghan, at that time, was saying and there was no confusion about speaking for many interests. The difficulty over the past few years has been the growth of lobbying companies with a huge range of potential clients. That has made the whole situation, certainly in terms of the Members of Parliament register, extremely complicated to police or to keep a fix on. I think something needs to be done there.

570. LORD THOMSON: One final question about dealing with complaints about the behaviour of Members of Parliament. You mentioned the Press Commission dealing with complaints about Press behaviour. Clearly, from the evidence you submitted to us you are very far from satisfied with your experience of dealing with complaints about Members of Parliament. I just wondered if you had any views about that.

There is the role of the Cabinet Secretary, Sir Robin Butler, whether he is an arbiter or whether he is a confidential adviser to Ministers. Members of Parliament at the moment police themselves totally and that has very ancient and important roots back to the 1688 revolution. Is there now in changed circumstances some role for some outside element in deciding the behaviour of Members of Parliament. What are your views?

PETER PRESTON: My view is that I very much welcome this committee and I think that is a testament to the degree of concern inside and outside, in crude terms, the system about the way it is working and the way it is regarded. I strongly doubt, though willing to be persuaded, that when this committee produces its prescriptions in this, or other, related areas that the public, which is very important if we are talking about respect for a democracy, will be easily convinced that things are moving dramatically in what it would perceive as a better situation. The first test will come with the first case, or the second case, and if it feels that the systems are being self-regulated by Members of Parliament, perhaps in a heated pre-election atmosphere, with too much party influence operating—I am not saying whether it does or does not, I am talking about perceptions—if that is the perception then a lot of good work which, I hope, will come from this committee will go to waste. There must be some way of assuring the public, in a regulatory or self-regulatory framework, that what is actually being prescribed here can be delivered by the systems working within the Palace of Westminster. I think that is absolutely crucial.

LORD THOMSON: Thank you.

LORD NOLAN: I am now going to go round the table, Mr. Preston, if I may. Professor King?

571. PROFESSOR ANTHONY KING: Could I ask you to elaborate a little bit more than you did in your opening statement on the document that you put before us. We are dealing mainly at this stage with Members of Parliament and their interests but, obviously, we are concerned about Ministers and the Questions of Procedure for Ministers. Could you quickly answer three closely related questions. First, what was your experience that you described in that document, very briefly. Secondly, what did you think was wrong with it and, thirdly, and this is really trying to draw you out on what Lord Thomson asked you a moment ago, what kind of mechanism do you think would be appropriate for dealing with that kind of situation?

PETER PRESTON: In simple terms, Questions of Procedure published a very comprehensive set of rules and guidance for Ministers and that is obviously related to Members of Parliament anyway because if you are lobbying Members of Parliament you are lobbying them, in a sense, to influence Ministers in their decisions.

In the matter of Mr. Jonathan Aitken, I am not seeking to rake over the particular details of that at this meeting. I had 15 months ago worried about a hotel bill but I was reluctant to publish anything about it because I thought I should go to Sir Robin Butler, the Cabinet Secretary. Mr. Aitken agreed that the matter was not for publication, it was for Sir Robin to look at. Then a Minister said that Sir Robin was the arbiter. The process was gone through. Sir Robin wrote back and said that he was not an arbiter but an adviser and that the reasons for his decision could not be vouchsafed to me who had, if you like, raised the complaint. They were advice to Ministers.

I was, at this stage, looking for who was the arbiter of these published rules. I wrote to the Prime Minister and said, rather more politely than this, that if it was not Sir Robin it must be him. The Prime Minister wrote back and said that it was not for him to arbitrate in these matters and so, at the end of the process, raising, I thought, a serious matter which I did not want to put in the papers I just wanted to have it looked at in the public interest, I was left totally baffled as to whose responsibility it was actually to decide. I draw from that a more general lesson that in all the delivery of codes of conduct and ethical codes,—and I, myself, have no great problem with Questions of Procedures for Ministers which are pretty commodious,—there must be a delivery system where, if the member of the public feels that something has gone agley, even if nothing has gone agley, it must know who has investigated it, on what terms, and be told something about the process and the reasons for the decision, otherwise it is obviously unsatisfactory. I raised that because I think it is very germane to a range of issues that the committee will be considering.

572. PROFESSOR ANTHONY KING: But what form do you think such a delivery system, as you put it, might take?

PETER PRESTON: In terms of Members of Parliament and, say, the Privileges Committee or the Select Committee, I would myself be thinking slightly along PCC lines of saying can there be some outside element impregnated into that process which would still be essentially self-regulatory.

573. PROFESSOR ANTHONY KING: But what about Ministers?

PETER PRESTON: Ministers Questions of Procedure, I think that needs to be cleared up. In a curious sense, I do not mind, out of the Questions of Procedure controversy which I raise, who is responsible as long as it is clear that somebody is responsible. I do not, as a matter of fact, think it ought to be the Cabinet Secretary I think there is a tremendous confusion of roles there, and I do not think it ought to be the Chief Whip or the Prime Minister. It should be somebody else. It is a detailed prescription but that is unsatisfactory in just the same way that Select Committees pronouncing are a little unsatisfactory unless there is an outside feeling attached to this continuing committee.

574. PROFESSOR ANTHONY KING: There is just one more question of a completely different character. You must occasionally feel like a policeman when the thief complains about having been caught, but it is a striking fact that if you go back through the broadsheet newspapers over the past five years or so, looking for examples of the kind of behaviour that has led to this committee being created you find more examples in the *Guardian* than any other newspaper. Could I just ask you,

partly for the record, why it is that the *Guardian* seems to have been, if I can use this crass phrase, on "sleaze patrol" more than any other broadsheet paper?

PETER PRESTON: There is some attempt, at the moment I understand, to portray us as slightly berserk Ayatollahs. I can only say for myself that I have always, over 20 years and before, thought that the monitoring of public life was an essential part of what a newspaper was there for and we have always, under my editorship, instituted and then developed, if you like, a Whitehall correspondent, somebody looking at the way the system works. Over the past five or six years we have had a particularly distinguished journalist with a keen nose for the point and the story. It has not been part of some holy crusade. The probity of government, of course, is one of my interests and has been over 25 years.

It is an area we have developed because we think it is important and we would think it important under any government in any situation.

575. LORD THOMSON: Could I just ask you very quickly, to make sure I have the drift of what you are saying correct. What you are going towards is, effectively, an independent tribunal of some kind. It may be that it is part of the House of Commons with a majority of lay members, as you have on the Press Commission, or something like that, but whatever the form the substance you are aiming at is an independent tribunal to investigate and impose sanctions. Is that right?

PETER PRESTON: Or an independent element to the present self-regulatory committee system. For example, it might be just one out of a panel of people perhaps nominated by a committee like this committee on a continuing basis.

LORD THOMSON: But the independence ...

PETER PRESTON: There would be somebody sitting there who was not part, if you like, of the party political atmosphere.

576. LORD THOMSON: And that is more important to you than investigating whether the current standards are up to the right level or not?

PETER PRESTON: I am asked in half an hour to prioritise so I am not saying one thing is more important than the other. The thing most on my mind at the moment, because I so much want things to get better, is the delivery of whatever is prescribed.

577. LORD THOMSON: Yes, I understand. This is the last thing I want to ask you. If that applied to Members of Parliament and there was an independent element adjudicating on their behaviour and imposing sanctions, how would you begin to reconcile that with the supremacy of Parliament?

PETER PRESTON: That is a very difficult question and one which is there for Members of Parliament to worry about. I, myself, would have no great feeling that if Parliament itself had decided that such a step was necessary then Parliament has taken that decision itself and I would say Parliament ought to take that decision itself.

LORD THOMSON: Thank you very much.

578. LORD NOLAN: Mr. Preston, I wonder if I could ask you this. We were told that a poll showed a substantial proportion of the population, something like 64 per cent, say that they thought Members of Parliament were in it for the money, to put it crudely. Do you share that view?

PETER PRESTON: I think such polls are valuable in showing public perception of Members of Parliament at the moment. For myself, I know a great many Members of Parliament and I think that 64 per cent would not be my judgment at all. I think most Members of Parliament are there, normal human beings, from a variety of motives and it would be quite wrong to characterise them as sleaze merchants, or whatever; one could be wildly out of kilter on this. But I think there is a real problem and I do not think that my kind of generalisation as a response to the poll's generalisation actually does not mean that something does not need to be done. It needs to be done on behalf of everybody including, in my view, Members of Parliament.

579. LORD NOLAN: I sometimes wonder whether they, like perhaps the judges, need a public relations organisation themselves because if so many of the public have this, as you say, exaggerated perception of the problem in the House they must get it, must they not, from the media because that is their only source of information?

PETER PRESTON: The public pick up their perceptions from all over the shop. Of course, the media, in its various forms, is part of that. Cynicism about politicians is not purely there from the media. I am not doing a dissertation on French public opinion at this moment in time but there is a great deal of cynicism about politics in France which is not appended to the way the media behaves there, which is rather different.

580. LORD NOLAN: Do you think that the media might present a more balanced view, reflecting perhaps your own view, of the true state as you see it of things that perhaps need looking at in Parliament?

PETER PRESTON: I hope there should be, in the argument, balance all the time but the media, in the broad, is not presenting an unbalanced picture. The media has in recent months and years been looking at a number of issues which have clearly caught the imagination of the public and which the public feel are wrong. When those problems remain unaddressed it is not surprising that cynicism spreads. I am not saying the public is wrong to have a 64 per cent view of a fairly corrosive nature, not at all. I am saying that something needs to be done as a result of it and it is not going to be helpful for the media if it were possible, suddenly to grind to a halt and say, "Hang on, chaps, we haven't put the positive side of all of this", because that is not the way, obviously, that things work.

581. PETER SHORE: Can I take you back, Mr. Preston, to what your note had to say about cases where allegations are made against Ministers. I am sure you are right when you say that the Cabinet Secretary cannot be a satisfactory arbiter. He does not have the investigative powers nor has he authority in dealing with Cabinet Ministers. Having said that, who do you think is best equipped to carry out what must be preliminary investigations when allegations are made?

PETER PRESTON: We have been talking about independent tribunals, or whatever, and remembering, if you like, that this is away from the Palace of Westminster, this is talking purely about Ministers, then I see some strong outside role for somebody taking, if you like, the Questions of Procedures for Ministers with a little time and in no sense being defensive one way or the other about the system, and investigating. I am not asking for a sort of running policeman to run checks on Ministers but in that case there clearly needs to be somebody outside the political orbit and outside the Civil Service orbit—perhaps a judge—who can be relied on to look at the case and form a view whether there is something to be investigated or not.

582. PETER SHORT: Yes. The difficulty, surely, amongst others, is to judge at what stage of an allegation such a tribunal ought to be triggered. Many things are said about individual Ministers; some of them, frankly, are not very serious, others could be very serious indeed. How about distinguishing between the two? Has not somebody else got to do a kind of preliminary job?

PETER PRESTON: Absolutely. Tribunal is much too heavy a word. This could be just one person, an Ombudsman type. If you are looking at the way self-regulation works then, for example, many of the complaints coming to the Press Complaints Commission are looked at initially in terms of the code and investigated by a small directorate and the complainant is told that there is a case, in the directorate's view, to answer or not and reasons are given. I would not think of this person, or series of persons, as being deluged with zillions of complaints. It is just a question of getting something serious and serious reasons given and a structure which allows a complainant to feel that the complaint has been seriously considered by somebody outside the system.

583. PETER SHORE: And if that person who was given this charge of looking into a particular case came to the conclusion that there was, indeed, a prima facie case it could then, presumably, go on to be investigated by a tribunal or enquiry?

PETER PRESTON: That is right.

PETER SHORE: Thank you very much.

584. CLIFFORD BOULTON: Have you ever heard of newspapers paying Members for information about what is going on in Parliament?

PETER PRESTON: Not to my knowledge and certainly not on the *Guardian*.

585. CLIFFORD BOULTON: Certainly nothing that you would feel should happen?

PETER PRESTON: No, I agree.

586. ANNE WARBURTON: The question you put, Chairman, was the one that I was most concerned to put but if I may end on a slightly downbeat note, I would just like to ask a little more on the fiddling expenses side which, from time to time, some of the material put to us has referred to. I would like to know whether you think that is an important element of the reputation for sleaze or not?

PETER PRESTON: Members of Parliament fiddling their expenses?

ANNE WARBURTON: Yes.

PETER PRESTON: I do not think anybody should fiddle their expenses. I do not think it is the most overriding and crucial part of the process but it is an important part because, again, from the public perception point of view and also in terms of the way I think people ought to behave, if there is a feeling that people are creaming around, or bobbing and weaving around, that again goes to make the public cynical. I am not for the public being cynical about Members of Parliament at all. That is one of the things that is a bit of a rot for democracy. People have to be as clearly accountable as possible and also, in the framework of the regulation, for the public to feel that self-regulation is not a sort of misty corridor where the club rules operate in terms of everybody being nice to everybody at the end of the day. The public want to feel that Members of Parliament are behaving to reasonably high standards of what the public expects of them and the fact that they do not at the moment is one of the reasons for worrying about democracy and hoping that something could be made better.

587. ANNE WARBURTON: But you do not have an enormous dossier on the subject?

PETER PRESTON: I do not have an amazing dossier on expenses, although I am sure I could have a rake round if you wanted one.

588. LORD NOLAN: As I understand the law, if a Member of Parliament, or anybody, fiddles his expenses in the sense of dishonestly reclaiming money has he not spent that is a criminal offence for which he can be prosecuted in the courts, but you need evidence. Thank you very much, Mr. Preston.

Good morning, Ms Taylor. You are here, like all our witnesses, as a volunteer. We are very grateful to you for coming. You are, I understand it, going to speak to us in your capacity as Shadow Leader of the House and a very experienced Member of the House, but not—is this right?—as a representative of the Labour Party.

ANN TAYLOR MP

ANN TAYLOR MP (Shadow Leader of the House): That's right, though I think perhaps that just drawing that distinction at the beginning explains the dilemma that often faces MPs in terms of their responsibilities. You invite me to give evidence in my capacity as Shadow Leader of the House, but, like all of my colleagues, I fulfil a multiplicity of roles. I am Shadow Leader, I do have a view on the rights and responsibilities of Members of Parliament, but I am also a Member of the Shadow Cabinet and responsible for part of that collective responsibility, and I am also a Member of Parliament with my own individual experience in terms of what that job entails. I think that it is a very useful starting point if the committee, and indeed the public, were to understand that the job of a Member of Parliament is in fact a unique job; it is one for which there is no job description, it is one which is interpreted in different ways by every single Member of Parliament and I think that the combination of how we fulfil our role is interpreted differently by every individual.

In fact I would identify four main roles that I think we have as Members of Parliament. First of all, we are

Parliamentarians, and that in itself involves several roles. We are Members of the legislature, we are also responsible for scrutinising the Executive and the administration of government, we are sometimes Members of the Executive itself, or Members of the Shadow Executive in my case, and we are also responsible for representing the interests of our constituents in the House of Commons. Secondly, we are politicians. The fact that we represent a political party and speak in a partisan way is perhaps the first identification of us that many Members of the public may have, though that is not our primary constitutional role. Thirdly, we are public figures in the widest sense of the word. Some Members of Parliament are expected to perform public responsibilities and roles such as sitting on bodies like this or the War Crimes Commission or many others, and that can impinge on the time that a Member of Parliament has for other activities. But, fourthly, the role that we have which I think has expanded most in recent years is the role which involves giving advice and information to constituents and indeed acting as their advocates. I think that this applies both to constituents and indeed to a wide range of individuals and groups on a national basis who, when facing a problem, seek the help and support of their own MP or indeed of a wide range of MPs. As I say, I think it is obvious that each individual Member balances these in a different way.

From the point of view of this inquiry, Chairman, if I may suggest so, the most important question that I think we have to ask is to whom a Member of Parliament owes his or her first duty. The answer to that must very clearly be to his or her constituents, and I think that ought to be the starting point that underpins all discussion about how we ensure that Members of Parliament are performing their responsibilities in a proper way. Members of Parliament are, first of all, elected to represent their constituents and, because of that, we enjoy very significant privileges. We are able to speak in the House of Commons without risk of action for defamation, we are able to ask questions of Ministers, we are able to gain information, we have access to Ministers, all for the purpose of performing that primary duty, that primary responsibility, to our constituents. It is, therefore, important to realise that that is the basis of the trust between Member of Parliament and electorate. If that trust is broken, I think that public confidence in the whole system will be damaged and that that is, to a certain extent, what has been happening in the recent past. Therefore, it follows from that that no activity of a Member of Parliament should conflict with that primary duty of working for their own and the wider electorate. I think that is a very useful first principle.

That brings me to the questions that you asked in the letter of invitation, and perhaps I could suggest some of the ways in which I think those questions could be answered, before you ask me further questions.

LORD NOLAN: Thank you.

ANN TAYLOR: You asked where on the spectrum the line should be drawn between what is acceptable and what is not. My view is that the majority of Members of Parliament would agree that the "anything goes" approach is totally unacceptable, and I believe that that should be obvious to everyone. There is a minority view that no outside interest at all should be allowed. I disagree with that, but I think it depends on how we define outside interests and also on what ground rules are established. This is a particularly important point, because the ground rules that some Members—indeed, I believe the majority of Members—believe existed have certainly not been followed by some Members in individual cases. It is clear, and "Erskine May" has made this clear over the years, that certain actions are just not acceptable, such as Members of Parliament accepting payment or inducements for any kind of Parliamentary activity. Most of us have taken that for granted as the situation that operated. One or two cases have cast doubt on whether that was always the case for everyone.

It may be that we can divide the types of interest that Members have into three different categories—first of all, the outside work which is not directly related to a Member's position in the House. That might be a profession, a family business or some interest which they had before they came into the House and which they may wish to continue later. I think we have to be realistic and acknowledge that Members of Parliament do not have a great deal of security and that many Members of Parliament have very wide family and domestic responsibilities and are bound to consider their longer-term career. Secondly, there may be work that Members undertake which is complementary to their work as a Member of Parliament, such as journalism or broadcasting, which is a spin-off activity but which is part of promoting their political ideas, representing constituents or talking about the issues which arise. But, thirdly, there is outside work where a conflict of interest could arise, and into this category falls any activity which exists solely or mainly because the person is a Member of Parliament and which would fall away if the Member left the House. I think it is impossible to prohibit such activities, and indeed many may be perfectly benign. The Member concerned may draw little or no additional income, or that income might be used for genuine office expenses. However, I think that questions of conflict may arise where a Member receives a significant personal income for acting as a consultant or adviser, in some cases more than the Member's salary, and a conflict certainly arises if the Member uses the facilities of the House to advance a commercial interest. I think that those three categories are different types of activity and perhaps have to be seen in different lights.

I would like to make some specific suggestions about what could be done to improve the situation. First of all, I think we need an absolutely comprehensive system of registration of all the interests of each Member of Parliament, with full information about the relevant details. I think that the present Register has some failings. For example, if a Member receives any income which is paid from public funds, that does not have to go on the Register. There is no description on the Register of the nature of the Members' interests. There is a very minor but strange point that if an inducement or benefit is offered to all Members, it doesn't have to appear on the Register, which seems to imply that collective bribery is all right. Other things that are difficult are areas where Members are not quite sure how to interpret what they should put into the Register. I know that you are seeing the chairman of the relevant Committee. It is fine to have some doubt if Members always consult the Registrar, but sometimes people don't consult because they think they know, and that could also lead to difficulties. So I think the first thing that has to happen is that there needs to be a more complete Register, that there should be greater transparency by establishing in the Register a description of each interest that a Member has, with any contract or agreement being deposited with the Registrar, and that that should be open to public inspection.

The amounts which Members receive from outside interests should be disclosed, even if only in a banded form. My personal view is that disclosure of exact amounts would be preferable. I believe that all foreign visits not paid for by the Members themselves should be entered into the Register and also that we need a new approach in certain areas. For example, I think we need a new and clear code of conduct for Members of Parliament which should codify the relevant sections of "Erskine May" and the rules as we understand them at the moment with regard to payment for Parliamentary activities and declarations of interest and should clarify any area of doubt.

Another suggestion that I would make is that at each general election, and indeed at each by-election, each candidate should be required to sign a declaration to be presented with nomination papers as a condition of nomination, to the effect that they would, if elected, comply with the requirements of the Register of Members' Interests and the code of conduct, and that failure to do so should invalidate a nomination.

There has been some discussion, I know, in the committee with regard to the question of an independent body or an independent element in any investigation. I think that there should be an independent element in any inquiry into an alleged breach of the requirements of the Register or indeed of the code of conduct that I am proposing. This could probably best take the form of an ethics advisory office, which could have a role in respect of the Privileges Committee similar to the role of the National Audit Office in respect of the Public Accounts Committee. That body could then assess any evidence and report to the House of Commons. That would be an improvement in our present situation and would guarantee the degree of independence that is necessary without undermining the sovereignty of Parliament. I think that that is extremely important and something that we must bear in mind.

I think that those issues are important and would be helpful, but the committee must also be aware that, even with a better system of registration, even with a code of conduct, even with better mechanisms for investigation, we will still depend to a significant extent on the individual integrity of Members of Parliament. I think it is important, and that is why I suggest the code of conduct and the signing at election time, that Members should be made aware of their obligations on all occasions. If we had a system which incorporated the aspects that I have suggested, perhaps your committee would have a sound basis to help to create a new climate of transparency and hopefully also a new form of trust in public affairs, which I hope can be the outcome following your deliberations.

589. LORD NOLAN: That is extremely comprehensive and clear, and I am most grateful to you. In fact you have covered all the areas which my questions raised. I wonder if I could take you back to two of them in a little more detail. You said that you regarded the first duty of the Member as being to his constituents.

ANN TAYLOR: Yes.

590. LORD NOLAN: And you said a little later that there should be no payment for Parliamentary activities. Is that because, if you have an outside paymaster, your independence as the representative of your constituents may be endangered?

ANN TAYLOR: I am not saying that there should not be any outside interests at all.

LORD NOLAN: No, no.

ANN TAYLOR: I am saying there should be no payment for the way you vote, the way you speak, the way you ask Questions or table Early Day Motions, or are actually using the privileges which you get as a Member of Parliament. Those privileges are there because we have that direct responsibility to our constituents, to our electorate, and I think it is important that the trust which comes with those privileges is maintained. If you like, that element of our work is ring-fenced and outside payments for using the procedures of the House should not be possible.

591. LORD NOLAN: Would that rule out a Member being a paid director or employee of a lobbying organisation?

ANN TAYLOR: No, I would not actually draw a distinction between a lobbying organisation and any individual company, because many of those have lobbying departments themselves. The real question is what actions the Member is undertaking. That is where the breach occurs.

592. LORD NOLAN: Perhaps I put it badly by tying it to a lobbying organisation. If we look at it in terms of function, I think perhaps you put it as clearly as you could, that you should not be paid for carrying out your Parliamentary functions.

ANN TAYLOR: I think that is the bottom line and that is the key, and that has to underpin every other decision that follows.

LORD NOLAN: It doesn't matter whether you are paid by a lobbying organisation or by a particular company with a particular controversial interest: you shouldn't be paid to get up and speak in the House in that interest.

ANN TAYLOR: That's what I believe.

593. LORD NOLAN: Would it be all right to do it voluntarily—for example, for Oxfam—if you felt there was some charitable cause that needed a spokesman?

ANN TAYLOR: I think there is a very clear distinction between different types of activity. If you have a field of interest where you, as a Member of Parliament, are seeking advice from outside or where somebody is providing briefing material or research material which goes with the grain of your work and which facilitates your operation as a Member of Parliament, that is absolutely different from you saying "I will only do this because I am receiving payment from somebody outside".

Indeed, there are probably three questions that Members of Parliament could usefully ask themselves when they are considering any outside interest. The first has to be "Does this conflict with the interests of my constituents?"; the second has to be "Am I doing anything which I would not consider doing if I was not being paid for it?"; and the third has to be the very simple test of "If my local newspaper found out that I was doing this, would I be pleased or rather concerned?" If Members of Parliament asked themselves those three questions whenever they were considering an outside interest, that might give them a very good sense of direction in terms of what they should and should not be doing. If you are someone who has campaigned on overseas aid issues and you want to work with an outside organisation, then they are facilitating you doing something that you would have been prepared to do and wanted to do anyway.

594. LORD NOLAN: And, for example, if you are a farmer and everyone knows you are a farmer, you should be allowed to speak on farming matters.

ANN TAYLOR: You should be allowed to speak on farming. I think the difficulty in terms of declarations of interests is that there are grey areas. We are all affected by general taxation, but we are all allowed to speak and vote on that. We have situations, however, where a very small group of Members could be affected by one particular change. I am thinking of the Lloyd's example, where Members stood back from voting because their direct interests were so significant. It is that kind of grey area where definition is needed.

595. LORD NOLAN: Yes. What about sponsorship either by commercial organisations or by trade unions?

ANN TAYLOR: I think there is a very clear distinction. Sponsorship by commercial organisations, as I understand it, is payment to individual Members. Sponsorship by trade unions is of no benefit to an individual Member: there is no financial gain there. It is almost, I think, better considered as part of the funding of political parties rather than of individual Members of Parliament.

596. LORD NOLAN: Am I right in thinking that it can take a number of forms? I am talking about trade unions. The trade union might say "We think it right for our Members to support the Labour Party and so we are going to donate £X to the Labour Party", and under present systems and conventions that is absolutely accepted by, I think, all parties.

ANN TAYLOR: It is accepted, and we have pressed both for the registration of political parties and for complete openness in terms of donations to political parties. I think that that would greatly assist the process, if all political parties were not only registered but made full disclosure of the amounts that they received, whether from donations in this country or from external donations. I think that that whole area is something that you may have to go on to at the end of the day.

597. LORD NOLAN: If I may bring it closer to sponsorship, does it sometimes take the form of payment by the union of a local candidate's expenses, or contributions towards them?

ANN TAYLOR: There will be a contribution to election expenses at election time. There may be an ongoing contribution on the basis of what is called the

Hastings Agreement, which I have a copy of, so I can leave it with the committee. That details the very strict limit—I think it is £600 a year—which can be made to a constituency party. As I say, that is not directly to the Member.

598. LORD NOLAN: And does that tend to create a feeling of loyalty, of dependence, of good will on the part of the Member to the union concerned? Is there any danger there, do you think, or not?

ANN TAYLOR: No. I think you have to remember that many of the Members of Parliament who get sponsorship have been long-term members of the union which sponsors them, so it is not asking them to do anything that they were not already interested in. It is again going with the grain of their activity and helping to facilitate their activity, rather than trying to divert them into new fields of interest or dictate new things that they should be doing or how they should act within the House setting.

LORD NOLAN: Thank you. I am going now to go round the table, if I may. Dame Anne, would you like to ask any questions?

599. ANNE WARBURTON: I thought I would like to put the 64 per cent question. That is really why we are here, I suppose, in part, that public perception of the standard of integrity and probity amongst Parliamentarians is so poor. First of all, I would like to hear your comment on that as a perception and, secondly, I would like to ask whether you see the ideas which you have put forward as a way in which actuality might be improved as sufficient to reassure public opinion.

ANN TAYLOR: First of all, on the 64 per cent, MPs are always frustrated by the global perceptions that people have. I think that your questions to the previous witness were very pertinent and important, because I don't think it is good enough for the press to say "We don't think that all MPs are desperately awful, we just happen to have papers which push this idea forward." It is extremely frustrating, and we often find, as Members of Parliament, that when our constituents meet us or when a group which is lobbying on a particular issue, be it the Disabled Persons Bill or anything else, comes to the House of Commons or comes to our constituency surgeries or we go to meetings, the public are quite surprised that we are quite human really. I think the fact that we haven't got horns coming out of our heads is something that Members of the public sometimes don't accept until they see you for real. The televising of Parliament and the way Parliament is reported in the papers hasn't done our image a great deal of good. I am in favour of televising, but I think that the concentration on just the exciting, "yah-boo" aspects hasn't always been helpful to our image. I hope, therefore, that people will take an interest in what is going on here, not just in your recommendations but in much of the evidence, so that they can understand exactly what the role of a Member of Parliament is. I have always been saddened that there is not sufficient awareness in schools or any arena about what our civic responsibilities are and what the individual's civic responsibilities are, and I think there is a great deal more that could be done there.

600. ANNE WARBURTON: Is there a role for MPs in the country at large, perhaps in the light of our recommendations but anyway to put themselves across better?

ANN TAYLOR: That is always something that I think we are trying to do, by visiting schools, by going to voluntary groups, by talking to people generally. As I say, when we do go to talk to people, they are often surprised how human and normal we are. But obviously we can't talk in each year to 65,000 electors, and that is why we are to a certain extent dependent on the media, but the boring day-by-day work of a Member of Parliament is not going to make front-page headlines, even in the local paper.

ANNE WARBURTON: Good news is no news.

ANN TAYLOR: Good news is no news.

ANNE WARBURTON: Thank you, Ms Taylor.

LORD NOLAN: I am going to ask Sir Martin Jacomb to come in next, because unfortunately he has to leave us at 11.15.

601. MARTIN JACOMB: First of all I would like to apologise to you and to my fellow committee Members and everybody else for having to leave. I just wanted to ask you one question. It is very, very clear what you said just now and in your press release about how you would like to see the independent element introduced, but what you propose is that that should be merely advisory and that the jurisdiction over MPs should be left with the House, both as regards the finding of guilt or otherwise—or misfeasance, or however you describe it—and as regards the sanction. Does that mean that you think that so far, given your experience, the House has dealt with these questions satisfactorily?

ANN TAYLOR: No. I think that many of us in the House were very complacent when we thought that the rules were actually being followed. Because instances of breaches had not come to light until very recently, most of us thought that the Register was working reasonably well and that all MPs were actually acknowledging the rules that, as I said earlier, all of us thought were in operation—rules about not taking payment for specific activities such as asking parliamentary Questions. When there is a blatant disregard of that, I think the whole structure that we have comes into question. That is why I think we need to change the registration requirements. That is why I think we need a code of conduct to clarify in Members' minds and to remind Members exactly what their responsibilities are. I think that the independent element along the lines that I have suggested, parallel to the Public Accounts Committee's support system, could be very strong and very important indeed, but I believe that at the end of the day MPs are answerable to their electorate. It is only Parliament that can make any decision about taking disciplinary action, outside the legal sense, against a Member of Parliament, because otherwise you would have an independent body, another group, that was overriding the sovereignty of Parliament, and I think that that would have very widespread implications.

MARTIN JACOMB: That is a clear answer. Thank you very much indeed.

602. CLIFFORD BOULTON: Can I pursue what in your system would be acceptable behaviour, because, as you say, there is a great need for clarity and help to

Members? Because it is obviously a Member's duty to protect and preserve the privilege of freedom of speech which his Membership gives him, you are saying that no Member should enter into an agreement or arrangement with an outside body which puts him under their direction or control as to what he should say or do in Parliament.

ANN TAYLOR: Yes.

603. CLIFFORD BOULTON: At the same time you are saying that Members may enter into legitimate arrangements, to which there is a financial side, with outside bodies. So you must be envisaging that so long as they decide when they speak and what they say and what they vote on, it can be OK.

ANN TAYLOR: Yes. I think that that comes back to what I said right at the end, that what we need is a system which is as clear and comprehensive as possible, but at the end of the day the integrity of individual Members will be very significant. If we had an ethics advisory office, then just in the way that Members could, if they wished, ask the Registrar of Members' Interests whether they needed to make a declaration and what form that should take, so a Member who was in any doubt at all, especially after what has been happening recently, would be able to consult the ethics office with regard to advice on what was appropriate and what was not. In the kind of example that you are thinking of, of perhaps an outside organisation like the Police Federation, which has Members on all sides, what happens is that when an issue arises which is of particular interest to a Member on one side, they will go to that Member, but when it is something that that Member would not want to pursue, they go to the Member on the other side. I don't think that the Police Federation or any similar type of body actually tries to go against the grain and influence individual Members as to how they should behave: they provide briefing and they let Members decide whether it is appropriate for them to follow that. I think that "going with the grain" is the best description I can give.

604. CLIFFORD BOULTON: All I am seeking to ascertain, and I think that really you have established it, is that you can envisage relationships that Members have with outside bodies, which they have only got because they are Parliamentarians, which involve money but which don't stop the Member being able to speak and vote on that subject in the House, the great test being whether the Member has actually signed away his ultimate freedom of action in how to behave in the House.

ANN TAYLOR: That's exactly right.

605. CLIFFORD BOULTON: Thank you. That's terrible helpful, if I may say so, to some of the areas that we have been pursuing as to what is acceptable and what isn't.

Can I just ask you about your proposal for what has to be registered by way of interests? You say: "The Register should in future contain a description of the interests of each Member, with contracts and agreements being deposited with the Registrar and open to inspection. The amount that Members receive from outside interests should be disclosed." Can I just establish that what you are talking about there is the kind of arrangements and interests that a Member has that bears some relation to parliamentary activity? I assume that you are not asking for all his private arrangements in these firms or interests

that he is keeping ticking over against the black day when he loses his seat. You don't want all that to be published?

ANN TAYLOR: I think there is an absolute requirement that the amount should be disclosed of any of the responsibilities or interests that a Member has which arise from being a Member of Parliament, and I think that that is clear. But I think that if a Member also has a family business in which he is a sleeping partner, all of that detail need not be tabled in the Register, because that is something that pre-dates his membership, is not even tangential. It might be parallel to his membership of the House of Commons, but it isn't actually relevant.

606. CLIFFORD BOULTON: But what about this journalism you said he was getting because he was in the House? What are you going to do about his fees?

ANN TAYLOR: I think there could be an indication, which is one of the reasons why I said possibly not the absolute figures but banding, because I know that income from journalism varies year on year, and perhaps an indication rather than specifics might be more useful.

607. CLIFFORD BOULTON: But if he was a lawyer keeping his hand in, you wouldn't want to know the fees he was getting as a lawyer?

ANN TAYLOR: I think that someone who is keeping their hand in has really to explain their commitment to their constituents. I have thought about whether it would be possible to get a time limit or an income limit or a source limitation. I think all of those are extremely difficult, not least because some people can earn significant amounts in a very short time, through writing or indeed at the law. So I think that those kinds of restriction are probably blind alleys, and we are not going to make progress. That is why I come back to the principles, and I think it is the principles that have to underpin what is suggested rather than looking for amounts or time involved.

608. CLIFFORD BOULTON: Just a quick one about candidates. Almost certainly it would involve a change in the law, but you want candidates to be under an obligation to indicate that all will be revealed, so to speak, but you don't go so far as to say that candidates should actually register their interests so that the electorate can take a decision at perhaps a rather more effective time as to whether they want a part-timer or not.

ANN TAYLOR: I have thought about that and I have discussed that with some of my colleagues, but we feel that, whilst there are elements in that suggestion that are very attractive, we are not sure how it might be open to abuse. There is also the fact that some of the interests that cause concern are interests that Members have taken on after they have been elected and therefore would not be present at the moment of election. It might be that they would be there for re-election, but then their constituents would know, because the Register would have been published anyway.

CLIFFORD BOULTON: I think there is also a relevant argument about candidates who know they are not going to have a chance of winning are going to have to talk all about their private affairs when it will not be relevant because they will not get in. I know it is a very complex subject. Thank you very much.

609. PETER SHORE: Can I go back over the ground about what is legitimate and acceptable and what is not? I thought you made it very plain that there should be no payment by outside bodies for the Parliamentary activities of a Member. That would seem to rule out a very great range of things, including arranging to see Ministers and, I would have thought, possibly—indeed, probably—including speaking on behalf of that interest in the House. That being so, what remaining activities, as it were, would be sanctioned? If a person had, for example, an arrangement with the Police Federation or a firm to act as a consultant to them, what useful things could such a person still be able to do to justify any outside payment at all?

ANN TAYLOR: If I may say so, Peter, you are assuming that once a person makes an arrangement, for example with the Police Federation, they only speak or ask questions because of that arrangement. If they are already interested in law and order issues and then the Police Federation comes along and says "We would like to provide you with briefing", but they are not obliged to ask any questions or reflect the views of that federation exclusively, they are still allowed to take that briefing and speak on those issues. The question is: are they saying anything different from what they would have said, had that arrangement not been in place? Is the Police Federation actually facilitating a better contribution, more wholesome contribution, more complete contribution from that Member or is it redirecting that Member's interest? That is why I think that there is a very difficult dividing line there which at the end of the day will depend on the integrity of the Member, because we cannot have a situation where somebody only says something because they are paid, but nor can we have a situation where somebody doesn't say something because they know more about it than anybody else, but they know more about it because they have that type of connection with an outside organisation.

610. PETER SHORE: And, in addition to that, obviously there would be no obligation at all upon the Member who was representing the Police Federation, arising out of his arrangement with them, to do anything, including speaking in Parliament.

ANN TAYLOR: I think there would have to be that agreement that it was not an obligation; it was providing the platform, providing the information, but not insisting that that Member followed a certain course of action.

611. PETER SHORE: Thank you for that. Just one further question, on this possibility of establishing something like the role that the National Audit Office plays with the Public Accounts Committee. Presumably the advantage of this is that the National Audit Office is run by the Comptroller and Auditor General, who is responsible to Parliament as a whole. It isn't a ministerial appointment, as I understand it.

ANN TAYLOR: Yes.

612. PETER SHORE: And therefore your ethics officer would be responsible to Parliament and would have the kind of powers, as it were, of the Comptroller and Auditor General, but would be under no obligation to the government of the day.

ANN TAYLOR: The person I have in mind would be under no obligation at all to the government of the day. As I understand it, and I haven't had time to work out all the details of how this might operate, the Comptroller and Auditor General is actually appointed by letters patent, which means that nobody can sack him except the monarch. Whether it would have to be that direct parallel I am not sure, but he would certainly have to have a very high degree of independence, as do officers of the House of Commons at the present time. That is why I thought that that parallel and the relationship with the committee might be a useful indication of a way forward.

613. PETER SHORE: Yes, and he could investigate allegations made about misconduct on his own volition. It wouldn't have to be, as it were, triggered by a prior decision of the House of Commons or the Privileges Committee.

ANN TAYLOR: That is what I would envisage. I think it would mean that he could look at a wider range of allegations, because, as you know more than most people, a reference to the House of Commons Privileges Committee at the present time is considered to be a very remarkable step. It is not something that is done with regard to a minor quibble about whether something is in order or not. The kind of ethics advisory officer that I am talking about could investigate anything, be they small allegations or very significant ones, and obviously the consequent action would depend upon the scale of the misdemeanour.

PETER SHORE: Thank you.

614. PROF ANTHONY KING: Could I ask you two questions. The first is this. You say in your evidence that there should be a new and clear code of conduct for Members of Parliament. I have to say that I have a continuing difficulty with codes of conduct, because people keep telling us there need to be codes of conduct without telling us what should be in them. But you actually go and say "This should codify the relevant sections of "Erskine May" with regard to Parliamentary activities and declarations of interest and clarify areas of doubt". Am I entitled to infer from the way you put it that you think there is an adequate code of conduct implicit in "Erskine May" that doesn't need to be modified or expanded; it just needs to be pulled out and written down in one place so that we can all read it?

ANN TAYLOR: Sir Clifford, of course, is the expert on "Erskine May" and I am concerned about answering questions on "Erskine May" in his presence. However, I did look at the relevant sections of "Erskine May" last week and again yesterday, and they have to be, because of the way that document is written, in different places. There is not one consolidated guide to Members of Parliament. I think that there is a sufficient basis in "Erskine May" for clarifying many of these issues. One of the problems is that these days Members of Parliament take less interest in procedure generally than used to be the case, and I think, therefore, they are less aware of the conventions of the House and less aware of the statements in "Erskine May". To consolidate together those provisions so that each Member had a copy would at least make people think twice before overstepping the mark and would get people to ask the right kind of questions before they undertook any particular interest. It really is remarkable how, when Members of Parliament are first elected, they don't actually get a guide to the House of Commons that tells them the rules: just as there is no job description of a Member of Parliament, there is no set of rules which you are given once you arrive by which you must abide. If we had a code of conduct and a more specific Members' interests register, it would create a different framework, perhaps a different climate, and would certainly help MPs to establish exactly what was acceptable and what was not.

615. PROF. ANTHONY KING: Could I then ask you about the Register, because you say that in future: one, it should contain a description of the interests of each Member; two, contracts and agreements should be deposited with the Registrar; three, it should be open to inspection; and four, the amounts that Members receive from outside interests should be disclosed. There are a lot of questions that I can ask about that, but could I ask you specifically about your own entry in the Register, which said simply "Westminster Communications Group (Non-executive)". That of course is perfectly in accord with the rules as they now exist. What would you feel you would have to go on to say if the Ann Taylor rules were in force?

ANN TAYLOR: Right. There is a section underneath that which talks about clients that you have any contact with, and I think it is important that the new rules which were updated recently have had to specify, so that that explains that the only clients with whom I had contact were the Foundation for Sport and the Arts and the Commission for Racial Equality. I think that, even if you are only doing it for a year, as I did, there needs to be either any contract that exists between a company and an individual Member and any specification of what that relationship should be, whether you are acting on behalf of clients, whether you are advising in a general sense—what the role that you are fulfilling is going to be.

616. PROF. ANTHONY KING: We asked Dame Angela Rumbold about the circumstances of her departure from the firm for which she had been working. Why did you feel constrained to leave Westminster Communications?

ANN TAYLOR: Well it was not feeling being constrained, it was something that I took on, almost from the beginning, on a temporary basis to see what it would be like and for the experience of doing it. It was something for which I had very little time; being on the Front Bench is quite an onerous responsibility. I saw how they were working, got a feel of it but really had not got much time to be doing anything as the lack of information in client contact shows; I had very little contact and time for that kind of activity.

617. PROF. ANTHONY KING: In that short time, what did you actually do for them?

ANN TAYLOR: I met the Foundation for Sport and the Arts and talked about how they could impress on MPs the fact that they were there as a charitable body funding sports and arts activities, so that MPs, who are frequently asked for advice by sporting groups or local theatre companies or whatever, would have an awareness. So it was to improve the awareness among MPs that these grants were available. I met some representatives of the Commission for Racial Equality, who were actually appearing before a Select Committee, and were somewhat in need of reassurance that they would not be eaten for breakfast and that MPs were human and would be interested in relevant questions, not trying to trip people but trying to get genuine information. So there was that kind of advice.

618. PROF. ANTHONY KING: Did you at the time have any doubts, hesitations, worries about whether that was an appropriate role for a Member of Parliament to be playing?

ANN TAYLOR: No because they were things that I would have been very happy to do anyway, which is why I did not charge those organisations as you could through that lobbying system.

PROF. ANTHONY KING: Thank you.

619. LORD THOMSON: Could I just ask on this last point, were you a Member of the Select Committee before which the Commission for Racial Equality was appearing?

ANN TAYLOR: No.

620. LORD THOMSON: And would you, in drawing up general rules, draw a distinction there?

ANN TAYLOR: Oh yes, I think if you are on a specific Committee then obviously that is another constraint on what you should be doing. I think that almost goes without saying, but it is another of those areas which because it almost goes without saying, perhaps does need saying.

LORD THOMSON: Yes. Thank you.

621. LORD NOLAN: Thank you very much. You have been extremely helpful. I am most grateful to you.

I am afraid we have to remind ourselves that, not for the first time, we are running about 12 minutes late. We do not keep to strict punctuality but I do ask both Members and witness to please bear the time in mind.

Now Mr Roger King, you are Director, Public Affairs of the Society of Motor Manufacturers and Traders. You helpfully sent us a paper telling us how the Society goes about making its case to Members of Parliament and we have studied that. I am now going to ask Sir Clifford Boulton to take up the questioning but before he does that, is there any preliminary statement you would like to make?

ROGER KING

ROGER KING (Director of Public Affairs, Society of Motor Manufacturers and Traders): Thank you very much Chairman. Can I just say that the Society of Motor Manufacturers and Traders has some 1,000 members and as such—because we obviously are interested in the development and the prospects for the motor industry—those members cover importers as well as UK car manufacturers, components people and indeed some areas of the retail trade. We tend to focus our lobbying, if I can use that expression, directly concerning the motor industry. We do not tend to make comment on the state of the economy generally. We leave that to the CBI, the Institute of Directors and others. Ours is a much more targeted approach to problems of the industry.

We think the industry has, and is, showing tremendous potential but, of course, because of the changing environment that we live in and people's perception of the motor vehicle, it is under a great deal of challenge and we are always faced with a number of very, very difficult and challenging issues. Hence our need to keep Members of Parliament, both here and in Brussels, well informed of our views on these changes.

622. CLIFFORD BOULTON: Good morning Mr King. You are a valuable witness to us because you have seen the activities of the Society from two different angles, during your Membership of the House and of course now. As you say you operate largely in approaching Members, at least in the first instance, through the Motor Industry All Party Group do you not, and indeed while you were a Member you were actually Vice Chairman of the Group, I believe. So you have seen this thing from both sides.

In order to fill in your own personal history of involvement, while you were a Member did you also have registerable interests from other groups?

ROGER KING: Yes I did. I was an adviser for some while to the Retread Tyre Manufacturers' Association. I was also an adviser to a small electrical professional association and a Non-executive Director for a few years of National Express, the privatised coach company.

623. CLIFFORD BOULTON: So would you say all those interests were also related more or less to the motor industry or perhaps the last one was not very directly related?

ROGER KING: It was indirectly, in that the company concerned was very much engaged in buying British-built vehicles and in terms obviously of the tyre side, that was very closely related to my previous work before becoming a Member of Parliament, when I was actually a manufacturer of wheel-related products. The relationship with an electrical association really was not directly connected in any way with the motor industry.

624. CLIFFORD BOULTON: If we can perhaps talk first about Members and what is inadmissible and admissible and desirable in their conduct and then perhaps move on to what the Society does. Are there some limits that you would like to see put on Members' involvement in commercial activities which then rub off on to their parliamentary activities? Are you happy with the arrangements, the acceptability of fees and those sorts of things or do they give you some anxieties?

ROGER KING: I think they do tend to give rise to some anxiety, although my own personal experience was that arrangements were quite satisfactory. I did not feel that one was operating in any excess or disadvantage to one's constituents. In fact in the case of the Retread Manufacturers' Association, the debate at the time concentrated around safety-related issues and the desire by the tyre manufacturers and the keen enthusiasm of many Parliamentarians, that the minimum tread depth at the time was ludicrously sub-standard in that it was inherently dangerous, and it was an exercise at lobbying Government in order to change the view and bring us more into line with what was happening in the rest of Europe. But I think in terms of what is happening at the moment and the pressures that Parliamentarians have placed upon them, some controls certainly need to be considered.

625. CLIFFORD BOULTON: I mean your interests were related to matters with which you were personally conversant, and as Member for Birmingham Northfield you also had a constituency area interest in that sort of thing. Do you see some distinction between that and the Members who sign up with general agencies, who cover a wide range of subjects and there is no obvious connection between the Member and what is going on?

ROGER KING: Yes, I definitely do. I mentioned I was an adviser to an electrical professional managerial association. I always had difficulty in understanding what I could bring to the party, as it were. It was only a tiny financial consideration and I attended conferences and was able to present a few thoughts from the Government side on how we viewed current issues. But in terms of actually lobbying or campaigning for the motor manufacturers, the motor industry, clearly in my parliamentary time I had the country's largest car plant bang in the middle of constituency and their future was very much related to mine. Therefore I had no qualms about campaigning as actively as I possibly could in order to create an economic environment which was supportive of the motor manufacturers, and incidentally helping my constituents maintain their jobs and indeed increase employment opportunities. I would add that this was not in any way remunerated, it was simply, if you like, good politics.

626. CLIFFORD BOULTON: So you felt you could have "shrugged off", or explained perfectly well, the MPs for hire jibe but that there are some things that go on which you think we ought to look at because they can give rise to legitimate anxiety?

ROGER KING: I think where a Member of Parliament does not have a direct constituency interest, or a direct practical knowledge—I think one would extend it to that area—then there are areas which might give cause for concern. Where a Member of Parliament might be actively engaged in promoting something, for instance if he was a City Member of Parliament and he was campaigning for an agro-chemical firm, then I think one would have to raise one or two eyebrows and wonder for what reason he or she was actively pursuing that remit.

627. CLIFFORD BOULTON: You think a Member would not be doing this at all if it were not for the financial incentives that he is getting from some other group?

ROGER KING: I would be inclined to think that way, yes, certainly.

628. CLIFFORD BOULTON: Can I just move on to the Society now? You say that you have got so much natural interest and support for the industry in the House, that you do not feel any need yourselves directly, as a Society, to have Members on a kind of fee-paying basis; you deal with the All Party Group and they are all available for the services and things that you give and the information you provide. You do not actually feel any need to have any Members with interests with you?

ROGER KING: No, yes, that is right. I have no doubt in the past the Society has looked very carefully at this and I suppose it will continue to look in the way in which it is successfully carrying out its presentation of its thoughts and policies to Members of Parliament. But I think we see that with the expansion of the industry over the last 10 years or so, where we are opening up plants in the North-east and expanding in South Wales and North Wales, areas like that, it becomes very important for Members of Parliament representing those areas that the overall health of the industry continues in an upward way and that therefore it is in their own and their constituents interests that at least they understand the problems that we have and indicate their support or otherwise and join in the debate with us as to how best to tackle those problems.

629. CLIFFORD BOULTON: Quite a lot of the Members of the All Party Group could have a direct relationship with an actual firm or association, whether a tyre manufacturers' association or whatever; they could have a relationship with them could they not? Do you know how many firms or associations within your broad area actually have individual Members with a financial relationship with them?

ROGER KING: I cannot be specific on that Sir Clifford, I have not checked that out. I do know of some that do have consultancy arrangements.

630. CLIFFORD BOULTON: There is at least a handful who do?

ROGER KING: Yes.

631. CLIFFORD BOULTON: Can I just ask a little bit about the financing of the assistance you give to the All Party Group because you do provide their Secretariat do you not?

ROGER KING: That is right.

632. CLIFFORD BOULTON: And as part of your operation, legitimate operation, you provide them with opportunities to visit sites and hear presentations and so forth. Is it possible for you to give us any kind of broad brush indication as to how much it costs the Society to have this relationship with the Group in a year?

ROGER KING: It is a very small sum. I do not think in the budget that I have for my department's work that I actually have a specific figure in there, in that the person who oversees our direct contact with the All Party Motor Industry Group Government Affairs Officer is also responsible for other aspects of our Society's work; presentation of reports and research programmes and so on. So he is not devoting his entire time to liaising with the All Party Motor Industry Group. I suppose if one really wanted to try and put a time or a price on that it would probably be no more than about two to three days a month, that he would be directly involved in working for that Group. As far as the funding of visits goes, that is done in conjunction with our manufacturers who will provide the hospitality and the cost of a parliamentary visit, and that is made aware to the Joint Chairman of the All Party Motor Industry Group in the compilation of the programme of activities that they wish to follow.

633. CLIFFORD BOULTON: Oversees visits always attract attention. I was thinking of Members who do have an opportunity to go to Ford in Germany and Fiat in Italy and the people who draw the "poor card" in "Blind Date" can go to Wolverhampton—and Milan I think was another one. There is real money involved in this is there not? Are there any limits to the kind of entertainment and visits? Visits are a sort of bogeyman in people's minds. I prefer to stay at home and have an ear-bashing than be taken on a six-hour flight for an ear-bashing followed by a compulsive folklore evening, I do not think it is a great catch. But it attracts attention and costs money. Are there limits, things that you do not reckon to do?

ROGER KING: Well there are not limits, no, in that I do not think we have ever reached the extremities of what we might wish to offer because I do not think the question has ever arisen. By and large our programme does tend to

centre on the United Kingdom but we do ask our members if they are able to extend hospitality to select members of the Group; by and large those that have trawled round a truck factory in Slough and one or two other places, who have obviously shown some great interest in the industry, if there is a specific purpose and they would like to visit. As I visited Togliatta (LADA) plant in Russia, then on another occasion the Saturn car factory in Tennessee, which is part of General Motors. There you could witness two extremes of manufacturing expertise and study the relationship, as we did, between the shop floor management team working and make comparisons. And in both cases we were the host of the company that we went to visit and I suppose in view of the fact that we were visiting Tennessee we were shown some old-fashioned Tennessee hospitality whilst we were there. But the message that we came back with was that we had seen a car plant of the future, with a lot of very interesting and innovative ideas which I think our Members then were beginning to talk about with our own manufacturers in the UK.

634. CLIFFORD BOULTON: And any Member who went on that would have to register it of course?

ROGER KING: Oh indeed, yes.

635. CLIFFORD BOULTON: So that is open. Just a final question, is there anything that you want to say to us about limitations on Members' activity that you feel the need for; is there anything that has occurred to you that ought to be done to improve the situation?

ROGER KING: I think in terms of looking at the numbers of consultancies that Members can gather together there may well be a cause or a case for limiting the number that are available, or that they were allowed to register or allowed to take on. When you look at some that have got six or eight you wonder how much time one has ever got to actually go about the parliamentary work, which can be very demanding. Or I think one would exclude regular journalists and presenters from that because that is something that one might be invited to do at very short notice and it would be very difficult to eliminate a consultancy or some other part of your work, or outside work that you have got at the drop of a hat, in order to take on a regular column in a newspaper.

There may well be scope for looking at the existing Register and perhaps whilst the existing Register of Member's Interests could remain more or less as it is, there ought to be a master register which would detail in a greater degree of clarity exactly what the consultancy or extra parliamentary work in which the person was engaged. I would look at things like approximately hours of commitment; it is not too difficult to work that out because you would have negotiated it with the consultancy in the first place. May be a salary band—not a specific salary but a band. More elaborate description of the nature of the consultancy perhaps, together with details on the business concerned. None of these are adequately covered in the present Register of Members' Interests, so I think this element of transparency would probably be very useful. But I think the danger of moving towards something that is over-bureaucratic could really make life more difficult than it is presently, so one needs to develop a system halfway between the present one and one that would require separate ethics boards or consultants to present your ideas before you took on any consultancy.

CLIFFORD BOULTON: Yes that chimes in with the direction a lot of the evidence there has been. Thank you very much.

636. LORD THOMSON: You say Mr King that the parliamentary group is the largest All Party Group—112 MPs. It is a large number, quite a proportion of the House. How many of these would have a direct constituency interest in terms of industrial provision, the kind of interests that you were very properly describing when you were a Member of Parliament?

ROGER KING: I think the vast majority of them. I do not think from my own personal experience we would necessarily, at the meetings held in the House, attract people from the south-western tip of Cornwall. We do attract people from the main conurbations where motor manufacturing exists and really throughout the country there does tend to be a component plant in most constituencies that are represented by the 112 Members. Now we do not get meetings of the 112; we would probably find at one of our meetings, at any one time, 12 or 15 Members in the room but during the course of that meeting there may be as many as 20 to 25 who will come in and walk out during the course of the meeting. Our calculation of 112 is based on an annual return of who we would actually have coming through the door at one of our meetings, who might go on a visit, or who may have expressed an interest to something that we have written to them about and they have written back saying, please keep me informed about what steps you are taking to overcome the particular matter you have indicated in your letter.

637. LORD THOMSON: How many, roughly, go on these various visits?

ROGER KING: About six Labour Members, six Conservatives and two Members from the Lords. Overseas, the numbers would probably be less than that and higher for the UK, but around that area.

638. LORD THOMSON: I think one of the interesting questions that we have been exploring about the lobbying operations of one kind and another amongst MPs, is whether there is value for money from the point of view, in this case, of the motor manufacturers, since at the end of the day decisions in Parliament are taken by the Government enjoying a majority in Parliament and then carrying its legislation through on that basis. Suggestions have been made to us that a lot of that kind of lobbying activity is rather wasted money because it does not in fact go to the point of decision.

ROGER KING: I think you have to look at what you are lobbying for. Most of what we do is to establish a "feel good" factor between the industry and Members of Parliament, in that the industry is developing well and we acquaint them with a general range of problems but also a number of areas that we have addressed, in terms of competitiveness, that the industry is making progress and we want them to feel good about the work that is being done. After many, many years of decline the reverse is now true.

Where we found items that we are particularly concerned about, for instance the reform of company car taxation, then we can issue briefing papers to Members of Parliament and explain to them that the present system, as

it then operated, was disrupting industry, disrupting manufacturing and also causing all kinds of disruption in the marketplace. Members of Parliament were clearly persuaded with that and joined in our approach to the Treasury to get the whole system reformed, which we quite successfully were able to achieve. There are other areas which we are looking at. The year identifier, which is an anomaly which has been around for a very long time, that is now accounting for something like 25 per cent of annual car sales in August. When it was introduced in 1963 or 1964 it was only about 7 per cent and in times of lean manufacture and lean distribution, manufacturers cannot just stock cars on airfields waiting for August. Now that is seriously disadvantaging the industry and we want to make the strongest representations to Government that this is something that is making us uncompetitive and could well cost jobs as a result of us being uncompetitive. I think that is where we would tend to focus on many of the 112 MPs and the Members of the House of Lords, to see if they could help us in getting Government to review this very difficult matter.

LORD THOMSON: Thank you.

PROF. ANTHONY KING: If I could just intervene to say that it sounded rather as though you were lobbying us.

ROGER KING: If I am doing that and you are supporting us then I am delighted about that Professor.

639. LORD NOLAN: Now you mentioned the overseas trips and relatively small numbers taking them up. Are spouses invited?

ROGER KING: No. Quite definitely not.

640. LORD NOLAN: Well thank you very much. You have been extremely clear and helpful.

Sir Geoffrey, thanks to model timing by Sir Clifford and Mr King, we are almost back on schedule. I hope you will not feel in any way restricted in giving us the benefit of your views. We are, as you know, particularly glad and interested to see you because of your position as Chairman of the Select Committee and as a very experienced Member of the House. Would you wish to make a preliminary statement before answering questions?

SIR GEOFFREY JOHNSON-SMITH MP AND ROGER WILLOUGHBY

SIR GEOFFREY JOHNSON-SMITH MP (Chairman Select Committee on Members' Interests) : Well, thank you very much, Lord Nolan, I would very much like, if that is of convenience to the committee, to do so. May I introduce Roger Willoughby, who is the Clerk to the Committee but also wears another hat as Registrar of Members' Interests and he is, of course, the person to whom Members can go if they wish to seek advice and that advice is of a confidential nature, and I often refer Members to him who ask for my opinion because I think it is better to go to a senior official of the House.

The Committee, I might say, Lord Nolan, is very happy that I should give my evidence to your committee in a personal capacity in the light of my experience as Chairman. I believe that you already have in your possession certain key documents, in particular the current register, the Rules and Registration of Declaration and the Committee's first report of the session '91/92. As you will gather, the Committee has been in existence for almost twenty years and I think it is now accepted by all Members as a permanent and necessary feature of parliamentary life. While the essential principles of registration have remained unchanged from the beginning, the form and the detail of the Register have developed over the years in an attempt to try to reflect changing circumstances.

The first report of the session '91/92 which you have, carried out a comprehensive review of the registration form and its proposals were approved by the House in July '93 and are incorporated in the '94 Register. We widened the scope of the Register and, of course, the amount of detail required by Members in their registration of interests and in the cause of, I might say, that well-coined word "transparency", which is an important one.

Perhaps the most important of the Committee's recommendations was to introduce for the first time an objective criterion for the primary purpose of the Register, which now refers to "the financial or material benefits which may reasonably be seen by others to influence a Member's actions" and, of course, with it we responded to the request of Members that we should issue a separate guide on how to complete the rules of registration, to avoid any confusion or any doubt about what the purpose of that Register is.

One of the objectives of the Committee in its review of the rules was to create a climate in which Members regarded the rules as sensible and fair and positively wished to comply with them. I feel sure that the rules are now better understood by Members and more widely accepted by them than was the case some five or ten years ago. Certainly we have very little evidence of deliberate non-compliance. Of the seven complaints which the Committee has dealt with in the last five years, all but one have been of a technical nature which required no further action from the House and I believe that those reports on individual cases have had a positive effect in clarifying the rules and encouraging compliance. One such complaint led to the issue of a further report establishing the guidelines which are now followed for the declaration of interests by Chairmen and Members of the Departmental Select Committees.

I should make it clear, however, that the House has given the Committee a very specific and limited function and that it has power only to consider complaints relating to the actual registration and declaration of interests. It is not an ethics committee and it cannot, therefore, concern itself with the propriety of the activities for which payment is received by Members. If your Committee were to conclude that certain activities—for example, paid advocacy on behalf of outside bodies—are incompatible with a Membership of the House I would regard this as thoroughly helpful both to the Members and to those, such as the Registrar, who have to advise them. I do not think that this need pose any problems for the procedures of the House or that it would create any difficulties which the existing machinery could not deal with. We would certainly willingly incorporate into our handbook of guidance for Members any necessary advice about activities which were held to be contrary to the rules of the House. I think that any complaints which were then made about breaches of such rules would in any case almost certainly be raised as contempts of the House and would go to the Privileges Committee and that the question of registration would be unlikely to arise.

Finally, if I may, Lord Nolan, I would just like to make a point which arose really, I think, in the Times, arising out of the hearings which you have been holding. Two days ago in the Times their distinguished political correspondent, Mr. Peter Riddell, wrote that the Select Committee on Members' Interests had failed to maintain public confidence over Members of Parliament's own rules. This is an important point. If that is so, that may be because most people have little understanding of what we do and how we work, particularly with regard to enquiries into the conduct of Members. They may think that we are more concerned, with the more personal interests and activities which give rise to the more lurid headlines in the tabloid Press and even, if I may say so, occupy space on the front page of the Times itself. It is these scandals which reinforce, I believe, the public belief that we in the House of Commons are failing in our duty to maintain standards. There is also the suspicion that because some of our work is done in private we are seeking to conceal the truth and are mainly concerned with protecting our fellow Members who are sometimes the subject of a complaint.

Perhaps I think it is worth explaining, if I may, very briefly, why some of our meetings are held in public and some in private. Our proceedings are open to the Press and public when we are taking evidence concerning changes in the Register, for example, our hearings on lobbying. But when our proceedings are concerned with the investigation of a complaint against a Member for not complying with the rules of registration and declaration of interests, our meetings are held in private. However, when we have completed our work, enquiring into a complaint concerning a Member, we send our report, which is available to the public, to the House. It contains all the evidence, the questions the Members have put and the answers that were given, the reasons for our recommendations, the votes that were taken when there is disagreement and even minority reports. There are two principal reasons, however, for the privacy prior to publication. First, we have to recognise that we are not a court of law. Our proceedings are not conducted along strict judicial lines. A Member facing interrogation has not got an adviser to whom he can turn to protect him from answering questions which may lead to self-incrimination. The media coverage, were we to go public, would not be subjected to the restrictions which a court imposes. Thus the media would have the freedom to cover our enquiries in the way they cover a news event, with all the selectivity and sound-bite reporting that that entails. The Member against whom the complaint is made would be exposed, therefore, to speculation which, as the enquiry proceeded, could turn out to be totally untrue. I think that would be an intolerable situation, contrary to natural justice. That is all I would like to say at this stage.

LORD NOLAN: Thank you very much indeed. I am going to ask Professor King to take up the questioning.

641. PROF. ANTHONY KING: Thank you very much for that. You covered a good deal of the ground I was actually going to ask you about, but could I very quickly put to you a number of straightforward factual questions? How—you alluded to this but you didn't actually describe it—how is the Register policed?

GEOFFREY JOHNSON-SMITH: It is policed in one important way, Professor King. It is open to scrutiny by the public and, of course, by Members of Parliament. So that if, for example, as a result of some investigation a journalist had come to discover certain facts about a Member's commercial life or outside interests in this way, he could check that story with what has been registered and declared and, in fact, this had led on occasions for Members of the public and for the Press to lodge a complaint. That goes to the Registrar and he must consider whether or not it has any validity—he must test it.

642. PROF. ANTHONY KING: Anyone can complain?

GEOFFREY JOHNSON-SMITH: Yes.

ROGER WILLOUGHBY (Clerk to the Committee on Members' Interests and Registrar of Members' Interests): Either a Member may complain or a Member of the public may complain. If a Member complains we would automatically have to refer it to the Committee on Members' Interests. If a Member of the public were to complain I would be given some discretion to write to him and say "Can you back up your complaint with some supporting evidence?"—and that I would certainly do and the Committee would then have to consider whether he had enough to make that consideration.

643. PROF. ANTHONY KING: If it comes from a Member of the public?

ROGER WILLOUGHBY: My description just now referred to coming from a Member of the public. What I was saying was that a Member of Parliament—if you got a complaint from a Member of Parliament that would go automatically to the Committee.

644. PROF. ANTHONY KING: That is why I was a little puzzled. The Member of Parliament does not have to produce any evidence?

ROGER WILLOUGHBY: No, not a Member of Parliament, no.

645. PROF. ANTHONY KING: That does sound a little odd on the face of it, but let that pass. Can we, by the way, have a copy of the Handbook of Guidance to Members that you referred to earlier on? We have had various documents but so far as I know not that particular one. Can I ask you more generally, Sir Geoffrey, with regard to the purpose of the Register, is it your impression that the fact that Members of Parliament have to register their interests has the effect—intended or otherwise—of deterring Members from taking on outside interests of a kind that they would prefer not to have to register? Does this alter their behaviour?

GEOFFREY JOHNSON-SMITH: Yes, I think it could have that effect and I think it does have that effect but the Register itself is not, of course, the sole—it concentrates the Member's mind but, of course, it is not the only way his mind should be concentrated on whether or not that activity which he is contemplating taking is appropriate.

646. PROF. ANTHONY KING: You said in the course of your introductory remarks that as far as you could make out the incidence of non-compliance with the requirement to register was low, but we did read in the papers—and as far as I could tell the reports were pretty accurate—a few months ago that in the light of certain

allegations about people not having registered there was a sudden upsurge of interest, shall I say, in registering. That suggests that at least there is a certain amount of non-compliance about the place. Do you have any sense of the scale of it?

GEOFFREY JOHNSON-SMITH: Perhaps the Registrar might make comment on the upsurge. I can only comment to this extent: I said that we had little, if no evidence. I mean, if I begin to hear people talking about X,Y and Z not registering, then I could get worried. All I would say is that I have noticed that certainly since we were seen to be taking action for non-compliance on dealing with complaints against Members, that there seemed at that time to develop an increase in the numbers of Members who were registering. I think that was the first time one began to have sufficient confidence that the Register was doing the job it was set out to do. Now, it cannot be perfect, of course, and I do not know if the Registrar could comment further.

ROGER WILLOUGHBY: I think it is also fair to say, sir, that that upsurge which came right at the moment when I took over the job, I have to say, partly consisted of a number of Members raising with me matters, asking if they were registerable, and having to be reassured that, in fact, they were not. I think a lot of Members approached me at that time out of abundance of caution and in connection with matters that they never really considered to be registerable and in many cases I assured them that there was not in fact a problem.

647. PROF. ANTHONY KING: Could you say a little bit more about the history of your Committee in dealing with complaints? I think you said in your opening remarks that there had been seven complaints only in the last five years, which is certainly not very many, only one of which led to any kind of action being taken. Could you go into just a little bit more detail about what the nature of the complaints were and what was done in the particular case?

GEOFFREY JOHNSON-SMITH: Yes, they were not of the category of I would say the case against Mr. John Browne which led to a debate in the House of Commons. The complaint against one colleague in 1990 was that he had failed to declare a pecuniary interest in firms with defence connections as Chairman of the Select Committee on Defence, and the Committee ruled that he should have declared his interest when asking questions in the course of evidence about flight simulators. There seemed to be some relationship between the company and its interest in this area. I recall that he said at the time that the position he was holding was a position he expected to hold, but I think we have in recent years advised Members that if they expect in the foreseeable future to take up a position with a company and hold a financial interest which may be thought by others to influence them, then they should register that, and they should declare it certainly in the Committee. This led us, of course, to tighten up the rules about declaration and registration for Members of select committees.

There was one complaint about a Member who failed to declare an interest as a COHSE sponsored Member, both in the House and during evidence before a Public Accounts Committee. He argued that there was no need to declare it, he had received no direct financial benefit, but we considered that was a technical breach of the rule.

A case involving a Minister, Mr. John Gummer, about the refurbishment of a garden pond by an international food company for the purposes of a local show in the grounds of his home, etc. etc. They were, I don't think, issues which caused a great stir at the time, though there was a degree of publicity which I don't think the Members welcomed.

648. PROF. ANTHONY KING: May I ask you a couple of questions about the way in which your Committee does or should function? John MacGregor appeared before us yesterday and said in the course of some remarks that the Committee on the Register of Members' Interests acted in investigating particular cases as "detective, investigator, judge and jury all in one" and he seemed rather unhappy about this. Can you see why somebody might be unhappy about the Committee's role in this connection?

GEOFFREY JOHNSON-SMITH: Yes. I think we first detected that we were in danger of fulfilling all these roles in the case of the John Browne case, which I will not go into detail, if you don't mind at this moment, but it was a complicated case—it wasn't like the ones I have just described. We are at present called upon to investigate a case against a Member, a former Minister who has resigned, and has issued a writ for libel against the people who have criticised him. And I am bound to say we feel uneasy in this role, we lack both the powers and the expertise to act as an investigative tribunal.

649. PROF. ANTHONY KING: Are you saying implicitly that you and perhaps the other Members of your Committee might actually welcome some kind of outside independent element that would participate in your work?

GEOFFREY JOHNSON-SMITH: In that sort of case I think we would, because we know that if a civil action is contemplated, although the matter is not sub judice, even when the case is set down we can still go on with our enquiries. It is almost impossible for the Committee to do justice to the complaint without prejudicing the Member's action.

650. PROF. ANTHONY KING: But even if a case were not before the courts your colleagues on the Committee might still feel that they would handle a delicate situation better if there were people from outside involved and the whole operation was conducted in a rather more "judicial" kind of way?

GEOFFREY JOHNSON-SMITH: Well, certainly I take your point because our procedure is criticised. When a complaint is made against a Member, the complainant inevitably has the initiative. He may be selective in the range of documents he brings to our attention and the burden of proof can be placed to an unfair extent on the Member concerned, who has no legal representation or power of cross-examination of his accuser. And there are moments of doubt as to whether one is fulfilling the best principles of justice and fairness. I am not suggesting that anyone should become a permanent Member of the Committee but certainly it might be helpful on these occasions to call in some outside advice. Or if it is a more serious case I am bound to say then one begins to look away from my Committee and towards the Select Committee on Privileges.

651. PROF. ANTHONY KING: I was about to ask you precisely about that point because it does seem on the face of it to an outsider a little bit strange to have your Committee dealing with a range of cases, some of which, on the face of it, would appear to amount to a contempt of the House (as that term is normally understood) and the Committee of Privileges dealing with others. I mean, might there not be a case, for example—and I just put this up as a cockshy—for having a committee on standards of the House which would deal with both these kinds of matters?

GEOFFREY JOHNSON-SMITH: Well, that depends on what the nature of the complaint is, Prof. King. If it is a complaint against the Member for non-compliance of the Register by registration or declaration, then it is our duty to consider it as a complaint in that context. If a complaint, however, is made on the grounds that it is a contempt of the House then that is not for us to consider. It may be that the House, in its wisdom of various processes it has from time to time, can throw the thing back to us, or certain aspects of the complaint to us.

PROF. ANTHONY KING: But you can see that an outsider might find that a rather strange division.

GEOFFREY JOHNSON-SMITH: Yes, I do.

652. PROF. ANTHONY KING: Can we turn briefly to the Register itself? At the moment, I think it is fair to say, that even under the new rules the entries in the Register are fairly sparse. Do you think that Members should be required to reveal more about the nature of the business or organisation with which they are associated, because many of the organisations that are set down in the Register have really quite opaque names and some Members append to those a brief description of what the organisation does, but some don't seem to?

GEOFFREY JOHNSON-SMITH: Well, they should do. In fact we did make very strong recommendations to Members as part of the rules with which they now comply in '94, whereby they give the nature of the business. At one time you just had a Member saying "Non-executive of Joe Bloggs PLC", and we didn't know who Joe Bloggs was.

653. PROF. ANTHONY KING: If I can give you an example—and I will not name the Member in any sense—but here is one that I noticed yesterday. "Occasional consultancy, Gulf Centre for Strategic Studies". Well, now, I would not have thought that most people would have much notion of what that was just from reading those few words.

GEOFFREY JOHNSON-SMITH: No, it might be economic strategic studies or defence.

PROF. ANTHONY KING: It could be all kinds of different things.

GEOFFREY JOHNSON-SMITH: Yes.

654. PROF. ANTHONY KING: And I wonder whether you feel that even given that the rules have been tightened up already they perhaps ought to be tightened up a bit further.

GEOFFREY JOHNSON-SMITH: (To Roger Willoughby): Would you like to comment?

ROGER WILLOUGHBY: May I just say, sir, that we were conscious of deficiencies in that respect in that Register. We were rather having a drive on that particular point, to try and get Members to explain the nature of their consultancy. We have a reminder exercise in December of each year and one of the things I put into my letter to Members was "Could you give us more information about the nature of your consultancies?". It has not been a one hundred per cent success but I think we have got a lot more information in this one than we had in the previous one.

655. PROF. ANTHONY KING: When you say "nature of the consultancies", that could mean one or other of two things, or both. One is the nature of the organisation being consulted to and the other was the nature of the work being done for that organisation. Which did you have in mind?

ROGER WILLOUGHBY: Principally to distinguish whether they were parliamentary adviser or adviser on legal affairs and so on, but also if the nature of the firm is not apparent from its name we do try and encourage Members to give a brief description. So both of those, in a sense.

656. PROF. ANTHONY KING: Where the relationship with an outside interest is clearly related to the work of the Member of Parliament, do you think there is a case—and this has been put to us by several people by now—for there being required to lodge with your Committee, or its successor body, a pretty full account in writing of what the nature of the relationship with that organisation is—what exactly they are required to do and on what basis?

GEOFFREY JOHNSON-SMITH: In only very general terms is that done. If a person puts down that he is a consultant, the nature of it is in only very broad terms. I recognise that people have asked for greater detail along the lines you have suggested.

657. PROF. ANTHONY KING: And what would be your response to the suggestion?

GEOFFREY JOHNSON-SMITH: I think we would have to consider that. At the same time I think one ought to bear in mind that we ought not to get into such a state that we are going to actually compile something which is so massive when it comes to describing in detail what a Member may do. Some of it is pretty obvious and in some cases, if someone is a non-executive director, the company itself, the very nature of the company, should give a pretty good indication of the field in which he is working, without going into the details of the work he did as a non-executive director. If I may say so at one time I was a non-executive director of a well-known television company. I don't know how I would quite describe the day-to-day work—which wasn't day-to-day—but on the occasions when I visited the company there were different questions that came up. There was one thing that was perfectly clear in these matters—that I was not acting as a lobbyist and I think that is the thing that has concerned many people—that whatever the interest is, the nature of it, there is a lobbying connection here.

658. PROF. ANTHONY KING: And if there is a lobbying connection, or if some reasonable person might think there was a lobbying connection, would there not be then a case for having, if not in the printed Register, at any

rate on file, documentation setting out what the nature of that relationship was?

GEOFFREY JOHNSON-SMITH: That is something —yes—I don't know if it has been put to you, but it certainly could be——

ROGER WILLOUGHBY: Even if it weren't, in fact, made public, sir, were you thinking? If we had it on file it would be basically a confidential matter between ourselves and the Member?

659. PROF. ANTHONY KING: The suggestion that has been put to us—and I am not making this up as I go along, it has been put to us—is that it ought to be part of the registration mechanism that documentation relating to the nature of the relationships—and we have had many examples of these documents submitted to us—should be part of the public file, even if the whole lot wasn't actually published at——

ROGER WILLOUGHBY: The public file. I see. Well, sir, I mean the only comment I would like to make on that is that one of the virtues of this register is that it is a very easy and accessibly quick work reference and not all that expensive and it is quite valuable, I think, from the point of view of the member of the public who wants to look briefly at what his constituency member's interests are. One would have to consider, you know, how much detail would vitiate from its ease of reference.

660. PROF. ANTHONY KING: Sure. But I think I may have been misunderstood. Suppose this document still existed and I turn to a Member of Parliament and it says adviser to a particular company, I might think "Goodness the advice that he gives that company might have to do with his parliamentary duties", I might then want to be able to go, in effect, to a filing cabinet in the Palace of Westminster to see what the connection was. Do you think that would be a reasonable line for the Committee at least to think about—that is all we are doing at this stage?

GEOFFREY JOHNSON-SMITH: Yes, we certainly could think of that and I don't say "Yes, we could" and then toss it in the waste-paper basket as an idle thought. After it was put to the Committee we would have the grounds—the reasons which have led people to suggest this to you—and it is something we should take seriously. The amount of disclosure is important, obviously it is. We have to bear in mind that behind all this—if I follow the line of questioning—is the uneasy feeling that many people have that there is too close a relationship between Members and professional lobbying companies. Now, I don't think there is anything wrong in having professional lobbying companies, but one of the reasons why we looked into the question of a registration of lobbyists was a result of this unease and that is why we went to Canada to see their system. They have a register which does look very carefully at the activities of lobbyists, mainly in connection with Ministers but also with the Parliamentarians, and therefore a lot can be discovered about not only the activities of lobbyists but the relation between them and Members of Parliament. One of the consequences of our enquiries into lobbying in this country—and we have had two goes at this—as the House rejected our proposal that we should look at a register of professional lobbyists, was to re-open discussions with the lobbying companies to see if they would set up a register, a register which would include not only their own staff who liaise with Government and the sorts of clients they have, but also indicate to us which Members of Parliament had a relationship with them. It may be that one of the consequences of our talks has led a group which—I don't know what the technical name of this group is, but anyway they call themselves the Professional Lobbyists—a group of about five companies—to decide that in the register and the code of conduct they are drawing up that there should be no Members of Parliament who have any pecuniary involvement with them, either as non-executive directors or as consultants. So these sorts of enquiries can lead us along the path which you have suggested but it comes in other ways. It need not necessarily be a register that we have, but it is a register that private industry has set up.

661. PROF. ANTHONY KING: Two more questions only, though there are many more that one could ask and which probably will be asked. One is simply the details of the relationship between a Member of Parliament and an outside body paying him or her to provide Parliament-related services. Those details might well include remuneration, might they not?

GEOFFREY JOHNSON-SMITH: Yes, they could. As you know, Prof. King, the House has been for many years very concerned that registration is the important factor. It is the knowledge that the public gain of any outside activity, but they are entitled to a degree of privacy. This has been well-rehearsed, I know, before this committee and I don't think I can add to the argument. It is for the House in the end to decide. I don't think it is for me, as Chairman of the Select Committee of Members' Interests, to tell the House that I firmly am convinced the only way in which we can guarantee more transparency is to ask Members to disclose the precise sums they receive. I think there are arguments both sides of this question.

662. PROF. ANTHONY KING: But you will appreciate that it is for Parliament to decide but it is for us to recommend and we have to come to some conclusion on this kind of point.

GEOFFREY JOHNSON-SMITH: Of course.

663. PROF. ANTHONY KING: Finally, could you tell us about a document that I confess in my ignorance I had not known existed until a few days ago, the Register of the Interests of Members' Secretaries and Research Assistants. Could you tell us briefly how that works and how it happens not to be public when the Register of MPs' interests is public?

GEOFFREY JOHNSON-SMITH: Yes, please go ahead.

ROGER WILLOUGHBY: Well, how it works—it is in my office, I am ultimately responsible for it. When a staff Member signs on and gets a pass from the pass office that is passed on to us and so that is how we know of their existence. We then send a letter to them asking about their outside interests. Why is it not public? When the Committee set it up in 1985 there was really no discussion of that, particularly, was there, sir?

GEOFFREY JOHNSON-SMITH: No——

ROGER WILLOUGHBY: It simply assumes in the report—it said that this should be kept privately by the Registrar. I am not sure that that has ever been——

GEOFFREY JOHNSON-SMITH: I agree—my memory is such that there was no real discussion as to whether it should be public. It was——

664. PROF. ANTHONY KING: Should it be public and available?

GEOFFREY JOHNSON-SMITH: Oh, yes, I certainly have no objection—I can speak very freely on this matter. But I think it really arose because a lot of Members, including Members of the Services Committee, got fed up with the extra number of people who used to be wandering round the House of Commons wearing labels round their neck and saying they were research assistant to a colleague, or had somehow gained admittance by having this ticket. They thought that the place was over-crowded, the library was filled with people, and that something ought to be done about it. So "let's cut down on the number of research assistants"—I think one Member was thought to have ten. I don't think any Member, however busy he is, could have ten. So they were probably up to something else. So, in order for Members to keep a check on one another, we thought it was a good idea if we had a register—we took this up and said "Okay, in future secretaries and research assistants should be registered".

665. CLIFFORD BOULTON: Can I just mention a factor which portented this consideration, and that is that many of the people who work for Members and have these passes may be only part-time and have many other interests and haven't entered into public life in the same way that a Member has, and it was felt that although the information was interesting and relevant to other Members, because they saw these people all around having facilities and access, it was not necessarily something which should fall into the public domain without much more thought as to what effect one was having on the private affairs when asking about the other interests of these people. It wasn't a case made that it manifestly should be in the public interest. I think that was one of the arguments.

GEOFFREY JOHNSON-SMITH: That is a very fair point, I am grateful to you, Sir Clifford, because some of these people do come in willingly to help a Member of Parliament—true for remuneration, but by doing that why should they be exposed to the sort of questions or declarations which Members have?

666. LORD NOLAN: Sir Geoffrey, may I take you back to an earlier point? In 1947 the House passed a resolution to the effect that it was inconsistent with the dignity of the House for Members to enter into contracts which, to put it shortly, covered their role as Members of Parliament and what they could do as MPs. Now, the later resolution setting up the Register of Members' Interests in effect amends that, does it not, by recognising that such contracts may indeed be made, as long as they are registered? You have said this morning, as have a number of our witnesses, that you can see objections to Members acting as paid advocates, of being employed to be paid advocates. Is there anything that a Member can properly be employed to do by an outside body which does not interfere with his independence as a Member of Parliament?

GEOFFREY JOHNSON-SMITH: Yes, I do, and I think in the end it has to come to a Member's respect for his duty as a Member of Parliament. That involves him in exercising self-discipline. It also involves him—and I am indebted to an American lobbyist for reminding me of this——

"In the end the electorate must depend upon the basic honour and integrity and compliance with the fundamental principles that are part of human nature as the shield against undue influence of lobbyists."

Or, shall we say, undue influence brought to bear on him as a result of some outside activity. I don't know how you can deal with that problem unless you decide to forbid any form of paid outside activity. I think there are two points one can make and one that has been familiar to you and I will not rehearse it in any detail—and that is I would say, looking back over the years I have been in the House, which is getting on for some thirty odd years, there are many Members I know who have been extremely busy and highly respected both when they carried out their duties as Ministers and as backbenchers, who also had outside interests. It did not at any time seem to undermine their integrity nor, indeed, their commitment to their duties. There are some very distinguished Members who came to the House before I did—Sir Winston Churchill was one of them—who spent a great deal of his time on outside activities.

667. LORD NOLAN: I may not have made myself clear. I was not suggesting that the objection was to Members being farmers, journalists, teachers, directors of brewing companies, perhaps, with some sectional interest, and openly appearing and speaking in the House, everyone knowing that that was their personal interest. The question was directed to a contract regulating in some way what the Member would do in return for payment as a Member, whether by way of lobbying or advocacy or, for that matter, advice and consultancy.

GEOFFREY JOHNSON-SMITH: Well, I think advocacy, lobbying, is that area which increasingly has met with disfavour and no doubt your committee will have something to say on that specific point. I think also the payment for a specific service which benefits the Member—or not receiving a payment unless he put down a question or did whatever was asked of him; that, again, is something which I think people would find difficult if they were to exercise self-discipline and to think, indeed, about their responsibilities as Members. But if as a part of an outside interest there is no specific action he is asked to take in the House but he has more of an advisory role—or as a result of his advice that there are things to do with the running of the company that his experience is particularly fitted to give—I do not see any conflict there or anything dishonourable.

LORD NOLAN: You think that is an area in which one relies on the good sense of the Member and his colleagues who will know what he is doing?

668. GEOFFREY JOHNSON-SMITH: Lord Nolan, in the end—we went to Canada, I think they are the nearest to us of the countries we visited—I go to America a great deal. That nation has got all kinds of bits of legislation and rules and regulations about what Members of the Senate, Congress, should not do. With no disrespect to that great nation I don't think that the consequences of that have led to higher standards in the country. Some might argue it is more ... but I make no further comment—I have great admiration for many of the

legislators that I meet. But in the end there is the danger, if we go too far down the road—I don't know where we stop—of piling on Members of Parliament that they can't do this, can't do that, must declare this, and go into all greater details—it gives rise to two things: one, that a Member thinks he has discharged his obligations when he has filled in all these forms and then begins to find ways of getting round the rules. That inevitably seems to happen when you get over-complicated methods of registration either backed up by statute or resolution, and therefore excuses him from the responsibility which I believe above all he must have and that is he must primarily be responsible for his or her own conduct and not just rely on the rules.

LORD NOLAN: Thank you.

669. LORD THOMSON: I wonder if I could be reminded about the role of the Registrar, Mr. Willoughby's role? Is Mr. Willoughby an officer of the House?

ROGER WILLOUGHBY: Yes, I am a Member of the Clerks' Department.

670. LORD THOMSON: And was your previous experience as a Clerk in the House or did you come in from outside?

ROGER WILLOUGHBY: No, I've been a Member of the Clerks' Department since 1962, sir.

671. LORD THOMSON: And has there been a Registrar from the beginning of the Register? I should know the history.

ROGER WILLOUGHBY: There has always been a Registrar, yes. He has always been a senior Member of the Clerks' Department.

672. LORD THOMSON: And could you remind me—I should really know from my reading of the documents we have had—but could you remind me exactly under what authority you operate? Mr. Willoughby used a revealing phrase "that we try to encourage Members to do this, that and the other". Do you operate under a resolution of the House? Is the detail of Membership—the information—something where you have discretion to determine how much detail there should be, or is it laid down in some provision of the House of Commons?

GEOFFREY JOHNSON-SMITH: Basically, sir, I am subject to the Committee on Members' Interests. They, in a sense, set the detailed rules and they were set up for that purpose, and the detailed rules which they recommend are approved by resolution of the House. And I have to the best of my ability to deal with the Members who are in the business of making entries in the Register and I have to advise them as to how to interpret the rules in many cases.

673. LORD THOMSON: The Register is a voluntary register, it is not a statutory register—that is the underlying reality of it, is it not?

ROGER WILLOUGHBY: It is in accordance with a resolution of the House.

674. LORD THOMSON: A Member is not in contempt of the House by refusing to register. We have had distinguished examples of that, have we not?

GEOFFREY JOHNSON-SMITH: One.

LORD THOMSON: Oh.

GEOFFREY JOHNSON-SMITH: Mr. Enoch Powell came to our Committee to argue his case and we suspected he hadn't any interest to declare but he stood on principle here——

675. LORD THOMSON: What I am anxious to get at—do you have the right as the Registrar, acting on behalf of the Committee, to insist on certain basic requirements in the Register? I am thinking—if I may just ask you about them specifically—the period during which you must register I think I understand is once a year. I mean, could it not be once a month?

ROGER WILLOUGHBY: Actually, sir, it is. May I just make that clear, that Members are required by the rules which have been approved by the Members' Interests' Committee to register their interests within a month of that interest occurring. When I referred to our annual reminder, this was simply the preliminaries to the annual publication of the Register when we make an effort to write to all Members concerned to say "If you haven't updated your entries, then may we remind you to do so in time for the publication of the next register?"

676. LORD THOMSON: It is this phraseology, "trying to encourage Members", "may we remind you"—if they do not fulfil their obligations what do you do about it?

ROGER WILLOUGHBY: If they do not fulfil their obligations at all——

LORD THOMSON: Well, fulfil them inadequately in your judgment of the amount of information——

ROGER WILLOUGHBY: If I had a problem of that kind I would go to Sir Geoffrey as Chairman of the Committee and I think ultimately I would require the authority of the Committee to pursue the matter further.

677. LORD THOMSON: And is everybody obliged to make an entry? I mean, do you have to make a nil entry if necessary?

ROGER WILLOUGHBY: Yes.

LORD THOMSON: So everybody is there?

ROGER WILLOUGHBY: Yes everybody is there.

678. LORD THOMSON: And going back to the point that Prof. King mentioned in terms of getting adequate information to identify the interest, should one not at least have a name and address of an organisation with which you are involved, a registered office, something like that, that an interested person could follow up?

ROGER WILLOUGHBY: I am sure that would be possible, sir, and quite a lot of it would probably be contained in the letter that we would originally get from the Member of Parliament describing his entry. I mean, there would be a certain amount of background information very likely in that, though that, of course, as far as we are concerned, if he didn't appear in the Register and was simply a communication to us, we would have to regard it as confidential between us and the Member.

679. LORD THOMSON: And finally on Prof. King's point about more adequate information but still keeping the basic register down to a manageable size, could there not be annexes that are available for public access?

ROGER WILLOUGHBY: Certainly.

GEOFFREY JOHNSON-SMITH: There is, of course—it is difficult to go into this in any detail because one has really to look at the document we send to Members as a guide which would become quite clear—if a Member was deliberately avoiding the guidance we have given this would come to the Committee. We didn't have this document written just for the fun of it, for some window dressing. Some Members, when it was introduced, did not quite understand the force of it, as just at one time when I took over as Chairman of this Committee I used to spend some part of my time at the beginning of a session going round and reminding Members, who had already been reminded by a Registrar, that he had not yet signed the Register, and there were one or two who said "Well, I don't have to", taking your point, Lord Thomson, and I said "A resolution of the House is a resolution and if you do not get in there"—and I had to speak this sort of way—"if you don't get in there in the next 24 hours your name is going to be reported to the House. I will report it to the Committee and they will report it to the House and what is more your Constituency Chairman will be one of the first to hear about it. So what is the point of trying to come here and trying to break a resolution of the House? It doesn't make sense, does it?" And it is that way. Now I am finding that you don't need to go round sort of twisting people's arms. Things have changed.

680. LORD THOMSON: Following up the useful point you made a moment or two ago, Sir Geoffrey, does the fact that you have registered in any way absolve a Member of Parliament from what used to be the normal declarations of interest?

GEOFFREY JOHNSON-SMITH: No, you still have to declare.

LORD THOMSON: Do you?

GEOFFREY JOHNSON-SMITH: Yes, it is very important indeed.

681. PETER SHORE: Just going back to what you were saying right at the beginning about the number of complaints, did I understand seven complaints have been received? Over what period of time?

GEOFFREY JOHNSON-SMITH: That was 1990——

ROGER WILLOUGHBY: Over the last five years.

682. PETER SHORE: Five years—over the previous five years. I am correct, am I not, in saying that those seven complaints came from Members of Parliament?

ROGER WILLOUGHBY: Two from members of the public.

GEOFFREY JOHNSON-SMITH: Two were from members of the public. One of the more serious ones—I think the John Browne case—came from a member of the public. A journalist.

683. PETER SHORE: I see. And how many complaints, if you have a record, have come from the public during the same five year period? Only, what, the two or three you have just mentioned?

GEOFFREY JOHNSON-SMITH: No, there have been others which have come to the Registrar and he has told me about them, and if they haven't been proceeded with he has explained why he thinks they were frivolous or ill-founded, there was no evidence. The person concerned, ignorant of our procedures, just saw something in a newspaper and thought we might be interested.

684. PETER SHORE: Well, I am sure that a number of frivolous complaints are received, but if one is dealing with a complaint which is not, as it were, entirely frivolous, what capacity has the Registrar and the Committee got for making a satisfactory preliminary investigation of the complaint that is made?

GEOFFREY JOHNSON-SMITH: It would come to me and if I felt that it was borderline I would take the initiative by getting a letter either from the Registrar or from myself seeking more information and if that person could not give it who could? That is the only proper way to proceed. And if on the basis of that there was still some dubiety then, of course, I would have to report that to the Committee.

685. PETER SHORE: Yes. Most complaints, though, are accusatory, are they not—somebody else is involved? So writing directly back to the accuser does not necessarily provide any more information. It is really how you deal with a charge involving someone, presumably a Member of Parliament. Do you contact the Member of Parliament who is——

GEOFFREY JOHNSON-SMITH: Yes, we do. Not only out of fairness but in fact he may have made a mistake. I mean, he may not have registered what he should have. There are occasions when, you might say, he should have done it in the particular period of time. You know we update every month and he is given so much grace—he or she is given so much grace—and it is possible, especially if he had been abroad, that he had gone out of the period of grace and said "I am very sorry". But, I mean, there is a limit as to how far one can accept as apology is a sufficient reply.

686. PETER SHORE: Right at the end of your opening statement I think you dealt with the possibility that the declaration of interest in the Register might have led some people to believe that that is all that is involved, and that good behaviour is, as it were, simply assumed from what you have declared. Do you not think, in fact, that that is a very serious point about what has happened in Parliament since the introduction of a Registry of Members' Interests? Is not a fact of the case that a number of Members, perhaps new Members, perhaps others, have been, as it were, misled or have misled themselves into the belief that having declared an interest that is all that needs to be done?

GEOFFREY JOHNSON-SMITH: You are asking me to make a moral judgment about Members, especially new Members. I am not so sure that it is right for me to do so because I might say that when the Register was first introduced in 1975 although I was a new Member of that Committee, it seemed to me that many of the objections to actually having a Register came from very senior Members of the House who—I don't mean to be disrespectful about them, all huffed and puffed—"we are honourable Members, what is going on around here?" And certainly when I first became Chairman there was still a residue of such Members. New Members coming in understand what the rules are—that is the current situation—and I don't think that they are less likely to pay regard to the fact that they have got to exercise self-discipline. I have no evidence to support that view. It may be a general view that is felt as a consequence of some of the stories in the Press which may have something to do with other activities of Members which do not come within the purview of this Register.

687. PETER SHORE: Is not really though the problem almost implicit in what you said at an earlier stage about the Committee—it is not an ethics committee. It is therefore simply a register of interests. The judgment about whether those interests are acceptable or not is not for the register, it is for, presumably, other people and the lack, presumably, of guidance as to what it is acceptable or not acceptable is something that inevitably by-passes your committee and has to be referred to, if it is sufficiently adequate for the purpose, the Privileges Committee?

GEOFFREY JOHNSON-SMITH: That is quite correct. In fact, however, the fact that it is now part of the job as a Member of Parliament when they consider what to register to take into account the change we made in the rules. It is not what they think—whether it would influence their position or their duties in the House of Commons, their outside interest—it is what might be thought by others. And this was one step that we thought important to take in order to correct any ambiguity in their minds. I think this is also why you are asking this question. Why, in the guidance we have given, we add in the introduction these words:

"Correct observation of the rules of registration and declaration does not exempt a Member from the overriding obligation to have regard to the long-standing rules and resolutions of the House concerning financial inducements and bribes...."

—and then we go on to quote Erskine May. I think one has to keep on emphasising that particular point, otherwise we will find a situation developing, as I believe happens in other countries, where they have all the rules and regulations all by statute and people are spending a great deal of time with the advice of lawyers trying to get round them.

688. CLIFFORD BOULTON: I am afraid we are running over time, so I will confine myself to one point, and that is the clarity that there appears to be a need for and whether, having to have a written contract would help enforcement of the existing rules. It has been suggested to us that any Member who came into a financial arrangement with an outside body which involved in any way parliamentary activity should, as part of that agreement, have it put in writing, so that it was clear what his function was in regard to that Trade Association and one could have some rules, for instance, which said "no one should agree to limit his own freedom of action in Parliament and be under any direction to speak or vote in a particular way". If that were one of the rules of the House and then as part of registering one had to submit

one's agreement and that agreement then would be available for examination, do you think that might help the Registrar to advise Members about what their obligations were and what the limitations were?

ROGER WILLOUGHBY: Yes, I am sure it would be helpful. Yes.

CLIFFORD BOULTON: Thank you.

LORD NOLAN: Do you have any questions, Anne?

689. ANNE WARBURTON: I am afraid I do, yes. Could I first of all say that I would very much hope at some later stage to benefit from the enquiries that you made in Canada and the United States about lobbying—it would be very helpful. Could I then clear up one or two questions on which I am a little uncertain: the Register includes both paid and unpaid interests and I am not clear what guidance Members get on the unpaid interests and how useful they are to the Committee.

ROGER WILLOUGHBY: The unpaid interests are very much at the option of the Member. There is no obligation on them to register unpaid interests but some of them prefer to have on the record the kind of connections that they have even though they don't receive any remuneration. So we have a sort of section at the end of the Register for them to put in anything which is unpaid, but that is entirely at their wish and not at our request.

GEOFFREY JOHNSON-SMITH: It can lead to problems, I think. I just thought the other day if we are getting into discussions on the environment I am Chairman of a Trust connected with my favourite hobby, which is fly fishing—perhaps I had better get it down because if there is something to do with the enforcement of pollution laws—the Trust has an interest as we are bringing salmon up the Thames. But generally we don't want to clutter up the list with people declaring lots of harmless unremunerated interests which have no possible bearing on their activities in the House. Actually I think Members, if it comes to anything, tend to load it up with unremunerated interests just to make quite sure that they are protected.

690. ANNE WARBURTON: Thank you very much. And another short one. When you have to report to the whole House you do this without a recommendation— you just put the facts before the House?

GEOFFREY JOHNSON-SMITH: We could do either. We have recommended—and one instance I referred to we wanted the powers to get on with a register of professional lobbyists and the House did not approve. Sometimes we don't make a recommendation—we leave it to the House—and see where that takes us.

ROGER WILLOUGHBY: Dame Anne, in certain cases where we are reporting on individual complaints we very often say "This is a very technical matter and we don't think that further action by the House is required".

ANNE WARBURTON: Yes, thank you very much.

691. PROF. ANTHONY KING: Could I just pursue that for a moment? My understanding, which may be

wrong, but from something I read, was that in the case of individual cases you did not recommend to the House what should be done.

ROGER WILLOUGHBY: Not what should be done, no.

GEOFFREY JOHNSON-SMITH: That is quite correct. Sometimes we perhaps might be remiss in this respect—sometimes it may be because we couldn't agree. There is often a consensus "Well, we just don't know, let's see how the House reacts". But there is always the fact that we have to bear in mind—our report is to be judged by the House as being a good report if it takes into account the evidence. If they think we have "funked it" in some way or the other, or have been over-burdened by differences of personality or even party political differences, then that can be quite easily shown to be the case by anyone who carefully looks at the evidence and sees to what extent we have taken note of it. I am bound to say, so far as party politics are concerned, Members on the whole I found have been very co-operative under my Chairmanship.

ROGER WILLOUGHBY: Were you referring to individual complaints, Prof. King?

PROF. ANTHONY KING: Well, Dame Anne's question could have been thought to refer either to general recommendations about the future of the Register or to individual complaints.

ROGER WILLOUGHBY: With individual complaints we would either say "We don't think further action by the House is necessary" or we would say in the rare case "We think that the House should consider what further action to take".

PROF. ANTHONY KING: Without, in fact, recommending——

ROGER WILLOUGHBY: Oh, without recommending——

PROF. ANTHONY KING: That is what I was trying to say.

ROGER WILLOUGHBY: I thought you were, yes.

692. ANNE WARBURTON: I have one other, if I might, Chairman, and perhaps Mr. Stuart Bell will forgive us because it actually foreshadows a recommendation which is in his paper to come. In his submission Mr. Bell suggests that perhaps the Interests' Committee and the Privileges' Committee should be combined into a Scrutiny Committee and I just wondered whether the Chairman of the Interests' Committee would like to comment on that proposal?

GEOFFREY JOHNSON-SMITH: I find it very interesting!

ANNE WARBURTON: (Laughter) Off the cuff that is all you would like to say?

GEOFFREY JOHNSON-SMITH: I would not take a negative view of that at all.

ANNE WARBURTON: Thank you.

693. LORD NOLAN: We have found everything you have told us very interesting. We have taken up a lot of your time—thank you both very much for coming along.

Mr Bell, may I begin with an apology that we are running so late and I fear will take you over one o'clock. I hope that will not put you to any great inconvenience.

STUART BELL MP

STUART BELL MP: I anticipated it my Lord, and arranged my lunch for half past one.

LORD NOLAN: May I follow it with a word of warm thanks from all the Members of the Committee for the great care you have taken to give not only the analysis of what you see as the problems before us, but also a number of very helpful, carefully thought out and constructive possible solutions. It has been extremely helpful. Would you, like many of our witnesses, like to begin by making a short introductory statement or would you rather go straight into specific questions?

STUART BELL: Since you already have my submission, I would be happy to go straight into the questions.[5]

LORD NOLAN: That is straightforward then and I shall ask Dame Anne Warburton if she will be kind enough to take up the questioning.

694. ANNE WARBURTON: Mr Bell, I second the thanks the Chairman has expressed for the care you have taken over your submission and also thank you for the originality of some of the ideas you have put forward. We have seen and heard a lot and it is nice to have some new thoughts to work on.

I would like to come back a little later to the code of conduct and the code of ethics. In view of the time I shall omit some questions which might be obvious from your various extra-curricula activities, though they may come up. First I want to take up the idea you have about the scrutiny committee. Is there anything more you would like to say about that before I ask a question or two?

STUART BELL: Not really, Dame Anne. It may seem that the scrutiny committee I suggest in my submission should be made up of Members of Parliament or those who had been Members of Parliament. That may be slightly limiting; it was certainly not designed to exclude Professor Anthony King or yourselves and those who have deep experience. My worry with the outside element is that we might get people who did not understand the House and its current. I was not seeking to limit it to former Members or Privy Councillors, but to those who have a deep knowledge of how the House works.

695. ANNE WARBURTON: Yes, I wanted to ask you about your idea of the composition of the committee. You would be prepared to envisage it beyond Parliamentarians, but you would like them to be people who have been connected with Parliament. What is your thinking in wanting to extend it beyond? Is it simply taking up things you think we might be interested in, or do you have some ideas yourself as to why it might be a good thing to have a wider membership?

STUART BELL: The essence of my submission is that we represent the public and the public interest and that

therefore we have to be sure as MPs that we do not diminish our own authority. If we did that, we would then diminish our authority to act on behalf of our constituents.

It is clear, sadly, that over the past year or two our standing has diminished in the public eye and therefore simply to leave ourselves in a self-regulating situation might not necessarily be the best way forward in relation to the public. We are moving as a party towards statutory regulation in other areas and it would seem wrong to exclude that in terms of the House of Commons.

Having said that, I think that the majority of the scrutiny committee ought to be drawn from the House and that those who are coming from outside the House, who might bring a breath of fresh air to our somewhat cloistered proceedings, ought to have a knowledge of our business. Clearly the House of Commons is unique in terms of the work we do, the hours we sit and the variety of roles we play in the national interest, our constituency interest and in the breadth of press and therefore it would not be helpful to have others involved who are not aware of these different roles and do not understand the nature and history of the House.

I was interested by Lord Nolan's comments on the Privileges Committee in 1947, which shows a river flowing through. I think it was Lord Wade in 1910 who put forward a view that contracts made by Members of Parliament with outside interests were not enforceable, so there is a current running through our affairs and unless someone had knowledge of that, the scrutiny committee could turn into a bit of a witch-hunting body.

696. ANNE WARBURTON: Would you see this committee having investigative powers beyond those which exist at present?

STUART BELL: Yes. I see the committee as having powers over paper and people, in the same way as a select committee might have. Obviously I would wish its hearings to be in private because I would not wish it to turn into a witch-hunting experience where the finger was simply pointed and a whole series of episodes was started on television, with the rest to follow. Therefore it should have the dignity of hearing in private, with its findings in public. That might answer your question.

697. ANNE WARBURTON: Then there is the question of sanctions. One of the issues that comes up from time to time in our discussions is whether it should be arranged that a Parliamentarian who breaks the law is subject to the law.

STUART BELL: Yes. We have again to distinguish between the proceedings in Parliament over which we have authority and for which we are responsible ourselves and actually breaking the criminal law of the land. The criminal law of the land is a matter for the courts. How MPs conduct themselves in their ethics, morality, integrity and the work they do is a matter for the House. Therefore I would think that by having first of all a code of conduct and then the etiquette, we would set a framework for Members which they would know and it would be up to them to live within that. If the scrutiny committee were to find and reveal that there had been transgressions, it would be a matter for the House in its entirety to decide what action should be taken.

698. ANNE WARBURTON: Perish the thought, but if a Member were to receive a bribe, would he have to be in the precincts of the Palace for it to be within Parliament?

---

[5]See Evidence, pp. 510–513.

STUART BELL: Since we have jurisdiction for our own affairs, if an MP received a bribe within the framework of the House of Commons it would be an interesting question as to how the law would handle that. Essentially, criminal activity is a matter for the criminal courts and if a situation such as that was brought to our attention, it would be for the House to waive its authority over regulation of its own Palace.

Certainly I believe there should be a clear distinction between breaching the criminal law of the land, a matter for the criminal courts, and a matter for our own misbehaviour, of which we have had many examples over the past few years. I am not talking of the present examples which are being subjected to investigation or scrutiny by the House, but affairs going back into the seventies where clear breaches of our codes and the dignity of Parliament led to Members resigning from the House.

699. ANNE WARBURTON: Thank you, Mr Bell. Can we now turn to the subject of Members' interests. You say in your paper that outside interests should be acceptable, except in the case of a paid position in parliamentary lobbying, if I have summarised it adequately.

STUART BELL: The Committee has obviously heard great evidence on this by now, but it is clear to me in my 11 years as a Member of Parliament that the worst aspect of lobbying has developed over the past few years, where Members of Parliament who are paid for the job then lobby their colleagues. This puts the colleague in a difficult situation; because a friend or colleague may be doing it, one may feel the need to respond and then the Member turns out to be being paid for it. That is very poor in terms of parliamentary reputation.

700. ANNE WARBURTON: I was interested to see that you had suffered from being lobbied because to some extent we have been hearing that it is possible to distinguish between the role of a lobby retainer, advising the client and advocating in Parliament. Clearly you have found people advocating in Parliament?

STUART BELL: Yes.

701. ANNE WARBURTON: Can you tell us how this is distinguished from a consultancy (and I think you hold one), or indeed from a union sponsorship, which I believe is also your case.

STUART BELL: To answer your questions in reverse order, I think it is accepted by the Committee and others that an MP does not receive any financial remuneration for sponsorship by a trade union. He receives financial help at general election times and with his constituency party and I would feel that the actual financial aid is a matter of how we fund our political parties, which I understand is not the remit of the Nolan Committee. I would make a distinction on that.

Secondly, the other work we do for trade unions is essentially on an entirely unpaid basis in terms of furthering the interests of the working people as we see it, and is therefore a very legitimate interest.

I have forgotten what your first point was.

ANNE WARBURTON: The consultancy.

STUART BELL: My view of a consultancy is that it should arise out of an interest which the Member may have in a specific subject or area. It should be part of the national interest and it should be strictly limited to advice. In my own case with Merck Sharp and Dohme, they were interested in patent restoration at a particular time—what should be the length of the life of a patent, 10 or 15 years—which was a very legitimate interest. There was a big debate within the European Community and our own Parliament and my role was simply to say to them "Here are six or seven MPs who I am aware have an interest in health matters. Take it up with them.".

If we were to narrow the framework of the advice for a Member's paid outside interests, that would make Parliament a much more wholesome place.

702. ANNE WARBURTON: You say there should be only three such roles outside; is this simply on grounds of time?

STUART BELL: No. I was interested in Sir Geoffrey Johnson-Smith's comments about fly fishing and the rest of it, which you could say was a legitimate national interest because there are people who have an interest in such subjects. But if we are talking about an outside interest linked to the furtherance of the national interest, to have 10 consultancies seems to me to be completely outside any parliamentary framework and can hardly be said to be furthering that. I make no criticism of any individual, but I do not feel that those MPs who have an excessive number of interests can be said to be furthering the national interest or their work in Parliament. When I keep the category down to three, it is because I am aware of the great variety and versatility of Members of Parliament. We have writers, barristers, as you have seen in my own case, and it may be that they can do that and have an outside interest, but to have more than three interests in a variety of areas seems to me to be pushing the boat out too far in terms of Parliament.

703. ANNE WARBURTON: You have an idea on the parliamentary question side—that interests' parliamentary questions should go to a special department?

STUART BELL: Yes. It seems to me that many of the questions that are put on the order paper are legitimate questions to elicit information on matters of public interest. I myself have put questions down on cholesterol levels in relation to the incidence of heart disease, which is clearly an important matter of national interest, and the Standing Medical Advisory Committee then took it up and made a report on that. But those bodies on the outside who wish to receive general information which can be helpful to them (and there is no reason why that should not be in the public domain) ought to be able to place that question on a Treasury order paper for a Treasury division to handle and then pay for that. In my view it could be paid for at cost, but others think a bit of profit could be added—it depends on your political motivation. The information would then find itself in the public domain and be of help to outside bodies; it would be paid for, and thereby reduce the cost to the civil service of questions on the order paper (which is now very burdensome). It then also makes it very clear that a Member of Parliament who has an outside interest is not required to put questions on the order paper, and part of that should be putting down early day motions, or other matters of that nature,.

704. ANNE WARBURTON: Would the result be published?

STUART BELL: The information would be published. The Treasury division agency that handled the questions could publish the documents as it publishes others—the DTI publish lots of documents. First, it would reduce costs, secondly, it would obviate the need for a Member to put questions on the order paper and thirdly, it would ensure that suitable information would be available in the public domain. We would hope that the civil service would respond with proper answers to questions, which is not always what they do with Members of Parliament.

705. ANNE WARBURTON: I am going to skip the code of conduct, because Sir Clifford will have a better chance of putting the right questions there. On the ethical code, I was not clear from your suggestions who would draw it up. Was it the interested firm, Parliament, the committee or who?

STUART BELL: It was two-sided. I have a code here from Merck Sharp and Dohme on ethical business practice. I did not put this in as evidence because I did not have their permission at the time, but they have since given me permission to give it to you. The firm itself, as part of its corporate policy, has an ethical business practice which you are requested to stand by as you would if you were working for them on a full-time basis.[6]

I would think that any Member of Parliament who wanted to have a paid outside interest ought to ask the firm who puts this question to him, what is their own code of ethics and whether they have a code of ethical business practice. If they do not, they should get one and draw it up properly. Then I would suggest that the House itself should draw up its own ethical code as to what should and should not be possible for a Member who has an outside interest and that code would exclude the placing of questions on the order paper, the placing or organisation of early day motions and, as Mr Wakeham said yesterday, the moving of amendments in legislation for payment. The Member of Parliament would then have not only his code of conduct, which covers the generality of his conduct as a Member, but also a specific Parliamentary etiquette covering his paid outside interest.

706. ANNE WARBURTON: You would see it as negotiable between the Member of Parliament who would want to include the right things from Parliament's point of view and the employer?

STUART BELL: Parliament would lay down a Parliamentary etiquette for all Members that would exclude the things I have mentioned, but obviously situations might differ. If you are covering fly fishing you may need a different set of criteria than if you are covering pharmaceuticals, steel or whatever. The essence of the code should be for all Members and that would say very clearly what they could not do. It would be a great help to them as they decide on a paid outside interest and would certainly help the firm, so that everyone would know where they stood, what was proper and what was not.

ANNE WARBURTON: Thank you, Mr Bell.

707. CLIFFORD BOULTON: Can I ask a supplementary based on your advisorship on patent law. While that was in operation (and perhaps it still is), if a Bill

came along that was relevant to the subject, would you feel inhibited about taking part in the debate? You would not have so bound yourself into an interest that you were not free to speak your mind, would you?

STUART BELL: The best examples I can give are of my sponsorship by the General, Municipal and Boilermakers Union on two specific issues over the past two years. The union were in favour of Sunday trading and I was opposed to it; I spoke and voted accordingly. Lately, the union was opposed to the abolition of Cleveland County Council, which I felt very strongly about and I spoke in favour of abolition. On neither occasion did my union ever suggest to me that this was improper conduct. They understood perfectly well my position; I certainly felt no inhibition about the action I would take, nor would I, under any circumstances.

708. CLIFFORD BOULTON: But these arrangements can exist side by side with full Parliamentary activities so long as there is nothing in the arrangement which, in itself, inhibits that freedom because that would itself be intrinsically something that should not have been entered into.

STUART BELL: Yes, so that could be stipulated very clearly in the etiquette code.

709. CLIFFORD BOULTON: Can I talk a little bit about the codes of conduct because there are two opinions about them based on the fact that either they are so general and pious that they do not really help very much, or they are so specific and detailed that they are open to the criticism that anything which is not banned by them must be all right. I take it that your proposal for a code of conduct is intended as part of the help, for new Members particularly, but in reminding all Members, of the standard of public service that is expected of them. What you are perhaps asking us to do is to make some suggestions for how Members can have in the forefront of their minds what that function is. Is that right?

STUART BELL: Yes, that is very true. I noticed with interest Mr Willoughby and Sir Geoffrey Johnson-Smith reading through the booklet that we have. I would have studied that with great care when I became an MP, but I would not have looked at it since. There is a tendency, as the years pass, that one becomes one's own man and then forgets why we are here and who sent us in the first place.

The code should be a general code of conduct reminding the Member, as I said in my submission, that he must maintain certain appropriate standards, and that if he falls below those, he brings himself but also the House into disrepute. One of the things we have seen of late (and I have met this point on a number of occasions) is that if one Member falls, all of us fall into disrepute. That is the old principle that no man is an island, entire unto himself. We are all part of the whole and what we have seen is that if one or two Members fall into disrepute we are all tarred with the same brush. That is how the public sees us.

Therefore to have a code of conduct which clearly sets out that the interest of the Member is to serve his country and his constituents, abide by his conscience when he needs to and in the end remember that he is elected to serve rather than rule, and puts those principles in the forefront of his mind so that they do not slip as the years go by.

---

[6]See Evidence, p. 514.

710. CLIFFORD BOULTON: But you made the point that Members become their own man, conduct their Membership in their own way and are responsible to their constituents. That is quite an important constitutional fact is it not? Consistent with ethical considerations of course, it is up to the Member to decide how he best pursues his Membership and looks after the interests of his constituents.

That is where I get into some trouble about an arbitrary rule on the number of consultancies you can have. For instance, we know that there are two Members now (and that is the lowest number for a long time) whose electorate are aware that they are also going to serve in the European Parliament. They are content with that and they send them back here knowing that they are going to be in two places at once. Is it for the House to say what is a reasonable volume of other activity or should we simply aim to make public what is happening? Is that the key issue?

STUART BELL: I think it is a little bit more than that, Sir Clifford. I have a constituency which regularly gives me 65 per cent of the vote and if I was not there, it would no doubt give the next Member of Parliament 65 per cent of the vote. If I was a Member of the European Parliament, if I had other outside interests, that might impinge upon the vote, but it certainly would not prevent me from coming here. Therefore the obligation is upon Parliament to set aside these external criteria and say "We, as a Parliament, think that you cannot be involved in too many other things." In the case of the European Parliament, the Labour Party said in the end, "You cannot be a Member both of that and of the House of Commons.".

We ought to say that we understand those electoral considerations, but some people can regularly behave as scoundrels (and I will not mention any names) and still regularly get voted back into the House of Commons. Therefore we ought to be in charge of our proceedings, as we are, and lay down clear rules that a Member of Parliament cannot serve more than three masters, if that is the way we are putting it. Certainly no one nowadays would say that you could be a Member of the European Parliament and of the House of Commons and serve both masters well.

711. CLIFFORD BOULTON: But the code of conduct is really part and parcel of your wish to improve the quality and amount of help that Members get to understand their role and to be reminded of it?

STUART BELL: Yes. We all see this when by-elections take place—it gets a bit disguised when there are general elections—and a new Member comes into the House. He frankly is a forlorn figure. He does not know his way about or how he should conduct himself. He does not know the proceedings of the House—I have known new Members come in at by-elections who make a maiden speech and then disappear and never come back for the wind-up, where they are supposed to be sitting. Therefore my code of conduct would cover the matters before this Committee, but it would also be an opportunity for the House to sharpen up itself in terms of its presentation and of what Members should or ought not to be doing. That is why I separate out the code of conduct from the etiquette code in a specific outside interest.

CLIFFORD BOULTON: Thank you very much.

712. PETER SHORE: Just one question. I am very interested in your ethical Parliamentary practice code because it specifically lists actions that may not be undertaken by a Member of Parliament who might be otherwise receiving money for various things. You exclude direct lobbying—ie "Ministers of the Crown will not be approached, nor civil servants nor other Members of the House in furtherance of a paid interest"—and you will not have questions on the order paper or EDMs. I want to be quite clear where you stand on amendments to Bills and the right to speak.

STUART BELL: Amendments to Bills—certainly not. I did not say that, because I know Mr Wakeham had actually said it. If he wishes to speak, a Member should declare the interest.

713. PETER SHORE: If you speak, you simply declare the interest?

STUART BELL: Yes.

PETER SHORE: Thank you very much.

714. LORD NOLAN: Following up the same point, your code says that if a matter comes up in which the company for which you act as a consultant is in any way interested, you would not think it right to lobby your fellow Members about this. You would, however, think that you could inform the company of the names of Members who might be interested?

STUART BELL: Yes.

715. LORD NOLAN: This is one of the areas which a number of our witnesses have found difficult. Many of them thought that paid advocacy was on the wrong side of the line, but some thought a paid consultancy was on the right side of the line, given that certain strict limits were imposed. Is that your position?

STUART BELL: Yes. We talk of consultancy; I talk of advisorship, but it does not make a lot of difference. We should so constrain the Member of Parliament that he is extremely limited in the advice he can give. That assists the outside interest firm as well because from the inside we have seen lately that the outside interest thinks the Member has much more influence than he really has. The Member can play on that for his own personal gain and if the outside interest knows quite clearly what is not available to them through the Member, that would be very helpful all round. It would clarify the situation; probably it would reduce the number of advisorships, but nevertheless it would mean they would be on a limited basis and that might be in the public interest.

We have talked about paid interests, but on the unpaid interests to which Dame Anne referred, I remember a very specific case on my first Finance Bill in 1983 where there was an anomaly in the Bill that would have liquidated the Co-operative Insurance Company for example. The Co-operative Society came to Members who were co-operators and said "Have you noticed this anomaly? It will put us out of business." Of course the case was taken to the Chancellor of the Exchequer who then saw the anomaly and the Finance Bill was changed, so there is a role for outsiders coming in, but not on the basis of payment.

716. LORD NOLAN: Yes. Do you think it is going too far to say that a Member must not be paid at all for his knowledge or actions as an MP?

STUART BELL: It is unfair in relation to those who are writers, broadcasters, barristers, accountants, farmers and property men; they can say "I'm all right, Jack.", but the Member of Parliament who has no access to any of those, yet has an interest in steel or engineering would find it very unfair and unjust if he was not allowed to receive any remuneration for that.

717. LORD NOLAN: I can see that it could have important practical consequences that one should look at, but is the difference not that the farmer or writer is not working for one particular paymaster?

STUART BELL: I made a note in my submission that I have a great regard for those who write and broadcast, but nevertheless their constituents are obviously very patient and generous with them. It would be wrong, therefore, to tell a Member who is not a writer or broadcaster and who has no great accomplishments by being a barrister or accountant, "You have a strong interest in engineering; we would like to retain you, but we cannot and you cannot take the fee." He could say "The other fellow across the House of Commons is getting £150,000 a year for broadcasting and writing." That would create a sense of unfairness in Parliament.

LORD NOLAN: Thank you very much.

718. PROF. ANTHONY KING: I have one quick question. I apologise for protracting the proceedings, but it is concerning me. We have been told repeatedly that it must be left to the whole House to take action. At one level under our constitutional system that must be true, in the sense that we cannot deprive the House of the ability to do that, but experience over the past 100 years suggests that when the House is invited to take action, it will sometimes, for example, divide strictly on party lines.

Would you be prepared to contemplate a system in which there was a committee, possibly like the scrutiny committee you are proposing, which had the capacity to make a decision on behalf of the House, provided the House did not decide by a majority to overturn the decision taken by that committee. Legally it would remain for the whole House, but in practice, the decision would be taken, more often than not, by a much smaller group.

STUART BELL: Making it a negative decision of the House, rather than a positive one?

PROF. ANTHONY KING: Yes.

STUART BELL: The reason I am always reluctant to take powers away from the House is that I do not want to diminish its authority and thereby the prospect of Members of Parliament being able to properly represent their constituents. Any action we take that diminishes our responsibility and authority weakens us in relation, first of all to the executive whom we are supposed to hold accountable, and secondly, to the constituents whom we seek to represent. Therefore in my view anything that weakens us, weakens our nation and our people. We, after all, are the only people they can turn to because we are the only ones who are elected to represent them. My reluctance to take powers away from the floor of the House is a feeling that we might be diluting its authority. That has been done before and I indicated in my paper that we have given away the power to decide disputed elections; we have also given the power to set our own wages to an outside body, so it is not unknown. I do think it diminishes us.

LORD NOLAN: Renewed thanks, Mr Bell, for all your help and time. We are most grateful to you.

THURSDAY 26 JANUARY 1995

Members Present:

The Rt. Hon. The Lord Nolan (Chairman)

Sir Clifford Boulton GCB
Sir Martin Jacomb
Professor Anthony King
The Rt. Hon. Tom King CH MP

The Rt. Hon. Peter Shore MP
The Rt. Hon. The Lord Thomson of Monifieth KT DL
Sir William Utting
Dame Anne Warburton DCVO CMG
Diana Warwick

Witnesses:

Angela Eagle MP, Alan Jinkinson, General Secretary and Rodney Bickerstaffe
Associate General Secretary (UNISON)
Keith Henshall, Mike Beard and Michael Ward, Institute of Public Relations
Rt. Hon. Tony Benn MP
Peter Luff MP

719. LORD NOLAN: Today we hear from the third of what we might loosely call the lobbyists' organisations, that is the Institute of Public Relations, and from two very different Members of Parliament. Tony Benn is an MP of great seniority, who entered the House thirty years ago, while Peter Luff entered the House only at the last election.

But first we welcome representatives of a type of organisation with which MPs have had external financial links I think for more than a century—the Trade Unions. From UNISON we have Alan Jinkinson and Rodney Bickerstaffe, together with Angela Eagle, the Member of Parliament for Wallasey, who is sponsored by UNISON and who is a Member of the Select Committee on Members' Interests.

Now, Mr Jinkinson, you, I think, are ex-NALGO, are you not?—and thus connected more with the non-affiliated group, whereas Mr Bickerstaffe, of course, is connected with the affiliated group. Am I right in thinking that you have prepared an opening statement, like many of our witnesses, which you would like to start with?

ANGELA EAGLE MP, ALAN JINKINSON AND RODNEY BICKERSTAFFE

ALAN JINKINSON (General Secretary, UNISON): I have a brief one, my Lord.

LORD NOLAN: If you please. Thank you.

ALAN JINKINSON: May I thank the Committee for inviting UNISON to give oral evidence. I understand that you are particularly interested in the question of trade union sponsorship of Labour MPs. So, as you say Lord Nolan, I am accompanied by Rodney Bickerstaffe, Associate General Secretary of UNISON, who was previously NUPE's General Secretary, and by Angela Eagle MP, who was, until her election to the House of Commons, COHSE's Parliamentary Liaison Officer. Angela is a UNISON sponsored Labour Member of the House.

We have given you a written note which sets out UNISON's relationship with Members of Parliament and which I hope you find helpful. I will not therefore go into detail at this stage.

I should point out however that UNISON, as well as being Britain's largest union, has some unique political arrangements. We were formed on 1 July 1993 as a result of an amalgamation between COHSE and NUPE which were affiliated to the Labour Party, and NALGO, which was independent of any political party. Those two traditions have been incorporated into UNISON's Political Fund rules and, as our memorandum explains, we have continued the traditional political relationships we had as three former unions.

We also point out in our memorandum that the TUC will be submitting evidence with which we will be associated. However, neither we nor the TUC have previously had cause to develop detailed policies on the questions you put to us as part of this stage of your inquiry. We will have a lot more to say when you come to the issue of quangos.

Nonetheless, bearing in mind that we were asked to come before you at comparatively short notice, we would like to make some recommendations on how you might pursue the issue of Members' interests.

We believe in full disclosure. All MPs' outside remuneration of whatever kind should be declared in detail in a register of interests.

We do not think it practicable to bar MPs from having any other sources of income, although that is not a particular concern of ours. We are however deeply concerned that the "sleaze" factor may be devaluing the importance of politics and politicians in the public mind. We therefore welcome, as we understand it, your initial thoughts than an element of independent scrutiny may help to determine where to draw the line.

On the question of sponsorship, you will be aware that the current rules require disclosure, although the money goes to the MPs' Constituency Labour Parties. We are in favour of full disclosure but we think that that should apply to all financial contributions to all local political parties of whatever colour. We see merit in extending the register to cover MPs' local interests of this kind.

This, I suppose, takes us on to the question of the funding of political parties. Unfortunately, our understanding is that this is not part of your remit and, for ourselves, we wish that it were because much of our parliamentary involvement is motivated by the perceived need to establish a "level playing field". All political parties should be required to publish their accounts and reveal donations above a minimum level.

We would also support the TUC's established policy that there should be state aid to political parties.

May I remind the Committee that the political involvement of trade unions is more highly regulated by law than that of any other institutions in British society. In four weeks time UNISON will be balloting its members on the continuation of our Political Fund, at a cost to us of several hundred thousand pounds. Apart from trade unions, no other organisations have to do that.

We are confident of a resounding "Yes" vote in that ballot because one of the reasons we will get that resounding vote is because our members, from whatever background or walk of life, expect their union to pursue their interests in Parliament, as well as at the workplace. I do not need to give this Committee a history lesson but the tradition of trade union political involvement goes back to universal suffrage itself. It is a tradition based on giving ordinary people, in our case 1.3 million members and their families, a voice. It is not based on financial gain to MPs or on commercial advantage. It is an honourable tradition and one that we will be very proud to continue. Thank you my Lord.

720. LORD NOLAN: Thank you very much. You have made it clear, as anyone who knows anything of the history of UNISON will appreciate, that your system, if that is the right word, has many variations, largely inherited from the component unions. Indeed, in your note to us, you say that you would suppose that your arrangements cover the whole spectrum of possible types of sponsorship. I do not think it is going to be helpful to enter into great detail at this stage in listing all the various types, but I wonder if you could tell us first of all how many MPs are in the affiliated group?

ALAN JINKINSON: Nineteen.

721. LORD NOLAN: Nineteen. And those are all Labour members?

ALAN JINKINSON: Indeed, yes.

722. LORD NOLAN: And the non-affiliated group?

ALAN JINKINSON: Eleven.

723. LORD NOLAN: Do you only sponsor or engage the help of Labour Members of Parliament?

ALAN JINKINSON: We have two Members of Parliament whom NALGO traditionally described as consultants. I do not know when that arrangement precisely started. I have traced it back certainly to the early 60's. But the tradition was that there was one Labour MP, at present Mr Norman Hogg, and one Conservative Member of the House, at present Mr Stephen Day.

724. LORD NOLAN: A number of witnesses have given evidence to this effect, that there is in principle an objection to a Member of Parliament acting as the paid advocate for any individual outside group. But some have said, however, the same objection does not apply to mere consultancy. Then, of course, one gets into the difficult area of distinguishing consultancy activities from advocacy and how you switch from one to the other. At least in the case of your Conservative member, I imagine

that difficulty cannot arise. He is in no sense your paid advocate?

ALAN JINKINSON: I do not think either we or Stephen Day would assert that that was the position. Mr Day, like Conservative predecessors who have assisted us, have been broadly sympathetic to the aims and values of the former NALGO and now the aims and values of the present UNISON. But certainly Mr Day would not go along with all the policies of either the former union or the present union.

725. LORD NOLAN: I wonder if you could tell us, in a little more detail, what you, as UNISON, get for your money. What do you expect to receive in the way of benefits to your members for the support you give?

ALAN JINKINSON: You mean through Mr Day and Mr Hogg?

726. LORD NOLAN: Through the whole of the body of Members of Parliament whom you sponsor.

ALAN JINKINSON: Well, as far as Mr Day and Mr Hogg are concerned, what we get from them is that they facilitate wider contacts within the House. They do assist us from time to time in approaches to Ministers. They do introduce us to groups of members, whether they be Labour Members or Conservative Members, Back Bench Members, who have a general interest in the kind of interests that our Members have. We then have another category of people whom we assist and they tend to be Members of the Labour Front Bench. We assist them by way of payments for research workers. Can I say that we do not tout around a bag of money and look for people to award it to. In every instance, the approach has come to the union—whether it was NALGO or whether it was UNISON—from the Front Bench Member concerned, normally by way of a research proposal. Certainly one of the basic rubrics that the General Political Fund Committee will apply in looking at the proposal is: Is this of general interest to UNISON members at large; is it a subject of interest to a particular discreet group or groups of UNISON members? So that is of value directly to UNISON members.

But also, we feel very strongly that there is and has been for a very considerable period of time in our parliamentary system a considerable imbalance as between the resources that are provided for the Executive, through the Civil Service and so on, and Opposition parties. In some countries I understand that the Civil Service gives assistance to Opposition parties. I understand that there is, in other countries, substantially more money available for Opposition party activities than there is in our country. So we certainly regard that research money as, if you like, part of the process that I referred to earlier of trying to create some more assisting towards creating something of a level playing field.

727. LORD NOLAN: Can you give an approximate idea of the level of financial support that would be given to, let us say, a member of the affiliated parliamentary group over a year? What sort of figures are we talking about?

ALAN JINKINSON: Well, it works out at £600 that goes to the constituency each year and you will know that also, at election times, the sponsored Members of Parliament make a contribution to the elections. That is usually in the region of £1,500. In two instances, the figure was as high as £4,500—£5,000 because it is all under the Hastings Agreement which, as you know, has been in operation since the early 1930s. There is a maximum level and that is the position.

728. LORD NOLAN: Yes. Do you have any problem over this: the Member whom you have supported, perhaps for a long time, strongly disagrees with you over a particular matter. What happens?

ALAN JINKINSON: It has occurred. From time to time there are issues and when that happens they can be talked about. It has occurred, for instance, over abortion: that was one particular issue. There have been other issues and there is no pressure—if that is the point that is being made. Obviously our membership like to see that all MPs vote the way that they themselves would like them to vote, but that is not always the case. Our sponsored MPs may grumble, but at the end of the day it is not down to the union to tell people how they should vote and our membership well understands that.

ANGELA EAGLE MP: Could I say that the most recent example of that was actually the vote on the age of consent, which was a free vote in the House of Commons as you all know. The union has specific policy on that, a very active policy on equality issues. There were members of the UNISON affiliated group of sponsored MPs who did not vote to equalise the age of consent at 16. The union provided briefings on the issue. It let it be known what union policy was. There were also, after the vote, some opportunities for MPs who had not supported the equalisation of the age of consent to talk to some members of the union on the Equal Rights Committee who did. There were constructive dialogues, but there was actually no threat or any indication that there would be any kind of penalty. It was understood from the beginning that the MPs had to make up their own minds, particularly on a free vote, but also that their first responsibility is to represent their constituents.

729. LORD NOLAN: Yes. Well that is a very important point. I think it is clear from what you have told us and from what we have heard from others that you operate with complete openness. You expect all the Members who support to declare their interest, of course, and to register it. I believe in some cases the Members actually disclose the amounts of support they receive.

ALAN JINKINSON: Yes, that is so.

730. LORD NOLAN: What is said is that, taking up Angela Eagle's point that of course a Member of Parliament's prime duty is to his constituents, that he should not be affected by obligations of loyalty or financial dependence on anyone other than his constituency party. One appreciates the historical development and the reasons for it, but do you subscribe to that view, that in principle it is undesirable for Members to have individual organisations supporting them?

ALAN JINKINSON: Well I think that a Member has a number of duties and plainly has a duty to her or his constituents. Certainly in some matters a Member will have a duty to his or her conscience and, given our political system, there is of course loyalty to the political party. I do not think that it is proper for any outside interest to lean on a Member of Parliament and say: You must pursue this particular line otherwise we will sever our connection with you.—I think that would be wrong and we do not do it and we would not do it.

ANGELA EAGLE: Could I make it clear that there is not a financial obligation. I receive not a penny of payment from UNISON in this. I think it is a misnomer to call it sponsorship, actually. I think many people misunderstand the nature of it because of the language used. £600 a year goes to my constituency party. No money exchanges hands between myself or any of the UNISON funds. Therefore I would never regard myself as under any kind of financial obligation to behave in a certain way. It just does not arise.

731. LORD NOLAN: I follow that entirely in your case, but I understand that the arrangements vary a good deal and that in some cases it is a payment of the candidate's election expenses, and that sometimes grants are made to Members to help with secretarial or research expenses. Am I right?

ALAN JINKINSON: Well certainly as far as the General Political Fund is concerned there are direct payments to Mr Hogg and to Mr Day. I think it would be impolite of me to say precisely how much that sum of money to each is without consulting them. But can I say it is small; it is under £4,000 p.a. As far as researchers are concerned, and it is stipulated very very clearly to the MPs concerned, this is not a payment to them. This is a payment specifically for research, to pay to employ a researcher, to pay the on-costs of the research work. That, in a sort of ballpark figure, if that is full-time assistance, that could be a sum of money of up to £25,000 p.a.

RODNEY BICKERSTAFFE (Associate General Secretary, UNISON): Can I just say that on the affiliated fund side, apart from the election expenses in the Hastings Agreement and the £600 p.a. to the constituency, there is a payment currently, a one-off, of £15,000 to the Shadow Health team. That is public too. That is for the effort to help with administrative research and support in the area of Health Care and the National Health Service, all of which of course are very dear to UNISON.

ANGELA EAGLE: I think we also ought to remember the "Short monies" as they are—I speak as someone who is not on the Front Bench but of colleagues who have gone from being on the Back Bench on to the Front Bench and suddenly been hit with not only the extra administrative burden—especially in an area like Health where you do get a great number of letters that have to be dealt with. The "Short money"—it is about £18,000 per Department—which was voted by Parliament to support the Opposition. It is around a million pounds at the moment. The way that it divides down, in my understanding, is that each Front Bench team, which can consist of 4, 5 or 6 Members, gets about £18,000—enough to employ one researcher. The person who always employs that researcher is the Shadow Secretary of State. Therefore if you are on a Front Bench team, and you are not the Shadow Secretary of State, in essence not leading that team, you often have to take on these extra burdens with no financial help except your office costs allowance, which of course is stretched to the limit with the increase in constituency mail that we have all had, I suspect, with the televising of Parliament! So there is a real resources issue there that perhaps the Committee could look at.

732. LORD NOLAN: I follow. If, to reduce the apparent link between a particular constituency or

member and your union, if you made instead a global contribution to the Labour Party for them to distribute, would that raise entirely different principles as far as you are concerned?

RODNEY BICKERSTAFFE: Much of it is tradition, custom and practice. You yourselves know that this has been going on for nearly a hundred years now. There have been discussions with the Labour Party certainly by affiliated unions about the best way of spending money and it has been argued—I think we actually put it in our written note to you—that my old union NUPE from time to time suggested that there be a way of ensuring that monies go to those constituencies where they are marginal, but that debate is going on and on and on and may take many, many years before it gets to any other sort of conclusion.

733. LORD NOLAN: Yes. If one of your members wants to know the total amount being spent by way of political funding, can he find out?

RODNEY BICKERSTAFFE: Yes indeed. I think that is the point that Alan Jinkinson made. We try to be as open as possible. We have to be in many respects because of the law. But our general feeling is that the more open that we make it, the better it is for everybody. Our members do ask how much do individual Members get—constituencies. All the stuff is published. Any questions that are asked today, if we have not got the immediate answers, we will endeavour to get them to you as quickly as possible. We would like to say that we have got nothing to hide. We hope that we have got nothing to hide. We generally feel that that should be the case right across the political spectrum. Until you know who gets what from whom, then it is very very difficult to start drawing lines about what is proper and what is improper. So openness is the first thing and we would like to be as open as possible. When it gets to questions about 'What benefit? Is it of benefit to an individual MP or a prospective MP that part of the monies for the election campaign is going to the constituency, is that personal as against Party?'—That is obviously something that can be discussed and debated but in general terms the national affiliations to the Labour Party are in a much higher order than any payments to individual MPs' constituencies.

ALAN JINKINSON: Could I make it absolutely clear, because I think it is important, that under present statute any individual trade union member has a legal entitlement to delve into whatever aspect of his or her union's affairs she or he cares to. So, in law, nothing can be kept secret.

ANGELA EAGLE: I mean, on that matter of sponsorship being registered nationally, could I just draw the attention of the Committee to what I think is an inconsistency in the way that the Register is currently written. That is that it is required—and I do not particularly object to this—that the £600 sponsorship monies, which do not go to individual Members, are registered. As I say, I make no particular objection. But it is not required that if a payment were made to a local constituency party, a Conservative Association for example, that would not be required to be registered.

The Register makes the distinction—and I think it is false and increasingly false—that Labour Party sponsorship, trade union sponsorship, must be registered because it might be seen to affect a chance of selection or re-selection in the internal mechanisms of the Labour Party. Whereas a payment to a Conservative Association, perhaps by a local business, need not be registered because it does not have that effect. I think the Committee should look at this, particularly in the light of the move to 'one member one vote' which happened in the Labour Party's internal arrangements for selecting its candidates.

But also it should perhaps consider the fact that it was very rarely the case that trade unions could have that much of an effect in a local constituency to ensure the selection or re-selection of a particular Member anyway. It is now impossible with the move to one member one vote in our election procedures.

734. LORD NOLAN: Thank you very much. I have just got one final question before I ask other Members of the Committee to speak. Do the affiliated unions have a written contract with a constituency or Member of Parliament whom they are supporting?

RODNEY BICKERSTAFFE: Well there is the Hastings Agreement in that sense.

735. LORD NOLAN: It is all covered by the Hastings Agreement?

RODNEY BICKERSTAFFE: Absolutely, yes.

LORD NOLAN: Thank you very much. Now we will go round the table. Dame Anne, would you like to ask any questions?

736. ANNE WARBURTON: I think it probably is answered by those who know what the Hastings Agreement is, but I do not and I did wonder earlier whether it would not be possible for the contract actually to set things out in a way which is very helpful to the Member who must be a little uncomfortable sometimes.

RODNEY BICKERSTAFFE: We have got a copy of the Hastings Agreement which we can leave with the Secretariat afterwards if that helps?

LORD NOLAN: If you would be so kind. Thank you very much.

737. CLIFFORD BOULTON: Could the Agreement be said to explain to the individual Member what his sponsorship involves as far as what is expected of him in Parliament? I say that because it has been suggested to us that any Member at all who has an arrangement with an outside body could with advantage be made to have such an agreement in writing and then deposit it as part of the system of registration. Could there be parallel individual understandings for the sponsored Members which they could also register?

RODNEY BICKERSTAFFE: It may well be in different unions that there is something that is written down. I do not know of a particular one so far as the affiliated membership of UNISON is concerned, but in principle I would not be opposed to that. I think that it is fair that people know what they are into, as it were. But I have to say that most of the people that are made sponsored candidates have a history themselves of support for the sorts of ideas, beliefs, principles that the union has. Very many of them worked in local government or worked in the National Health

Service—just for an instance. So in a sense it is understood that what we are saying is that we support you in the line that you take.

738. CLIFFORD BOULTON: Oh yes. I am only talking about this, or we are only thinking about it, in the interest of transparency so that people who have got an arrangement with a commercial body might have to have a bit of paper which makes it absolutely clear that commercial body is not asking for a pound of flesh in return for it. A similar parallel thing could be done for union-sponsored Members. I think it could be practical if it arose.

ANGELA EAGLE: I mean are we referring to bodies that have an arrangement that is not paid, because we have to remember that this arrangement is not paid. There is no direct financial interest to a Member to be sponsored or not. I do think it is important when you are considering these two types of arrangement that have grown up to remember that not a penny changes hands between a sponsored Member using the affiliated fund and the trade union.

739. CLIFFORD BOULTON: Yes. I think we are aware of that. But the sponsorship is personal. It is to the Member and, again, talking about public reassurance, it would be possible to argue that the end of the sponsorship would be an embarrassment to that Member and might affect that Member's chances of re-selection personally. I see that in the note you kindly gave us you say:

"Sponsorship of APF MPs is reviewed after each General Election. This allows the union to consider whether it continues to sponsor all those APF MPs who have been returned to Parliament."

So what I was asking about was, although we all know that it would be a parliamentary offence to threaten a Member that if he did not do a certain thing his sponsorship would be withdrawn—that has been clearly demonstrated in the past—but it would not be an offence to drop per se, to cease to sponsor a Member for the next election. But I was talking about the possibility of giving more reassurance that it was not going to be done as a punishment for voting the wrong way in a division or something of that sort.

RODNEY BICKERSTAFFE: Can I say that I think it is well understood in any event. Because over the years the differences between Members of Parliament and in UNISON, the spread of opinion—although it is within the Labour Party obviously—the spread of opinion is very wide and it is impossible to expect that on each and every occasion they will all agree amongst themselves, let alone agree with the union. It is cut and thrust certainly but at the end of the day I think nobody believes that sponsorship would be stopped on the grounds that on x occasion they did not vote a particular way.

ANGELA EAGLE: The NUM has just decided to drastically cut its levels of sponsored Members because it has lost its membership. It does not have the money to pay it. That is the simple reason for that. And it is well understood if you look at their finances.

740. CLIFFORD BOULTON: I think that over the long history of all this presumably there are examples of Members whose sponsorship has not been continued?

RODNEY BICKERSTAFFE: Yes, I think there will be shortly. I think we have said in our written evidence that we will have to decide on the size and composition of the parliamentary group in the light of a whole number of factors. One is our hope that there will be more women Members of Parliament and that we would hope to encourage that. But this is not a question of—'You didn't vote this way or you did vote that way.'

CLIFFORD BOULTON: Thank you very much.

741. PROF. ANTHONY KING: Could I ask not about sponsored Members but about Mr Stephen Day and Mr Norman Hogg? And it is against this background: one of the questions we have to ask ourselves as a Committee is: What—if anything—is it appropriate for a Member of Parliament to do on behalf of an outside body which is paying him or her?

Now I think we are beginning to distinguish amongst three possibilities. One is simply providing advice: going along to the outside body which is contributing financially to the Member of Parliament and finding out what is going on in Parliament—legislation that might affect the organisation or whatever. Another kind of activity is advocacy: actually getting up in the House of Commons and making a speech on behalf of the organisation, tabling a question, or whatever—the kind of thing that Jim Callaghan used to do openly on behalf of the Police Federation. But there is a third category which one might loosely label 'facilitation'. That is to say, acting on behalf of the outside organisation by—and here I am quoting Alan Jinkinson—facilitating contacts with other MPs and assisting in approaches to Ministers.

Can I just put it to you straightforwardly that it does seem strange on the face of it that Members of Parliament should be paid by outside organisations either to advocate causes for money or, alternatively, to engage in this case of facilitating activity on behalf of an outside organisation for money. Now I am not saying for a moment that under the present rules either Stephen Day or Norman Hogg is doing anything improper, but it might be thought that this kind of relationship is intrinsically unhealthy or, even it is not that, certainly looks like it.

Could you just comment on that as a general problem from your point of view?

ALAN JINKINSON: Well, I think it is, in financial terms, very small beer. I personally would find it improper if, for example, Mr Day or Mr Hogg or indeed any MP were to provide lunches, dinners, facilities for any organisation with whom they had contact, on a very regular basis, on a weekly basis. I would find that personally improper.

742. PROF. ANTHONY KING: So it is not the principle, it is the amount?

ALAN JINKINSON: Well I think—I forget the phrase he used, but I think that when Alex Carlisle appeared before you, I think he expressed a view that there should be some proportionality, if you like, between any money received and, if you like, services rendered. I am bound to say that I personally have some sympathy with that particular point of view.

743. PROF. ANTHONY KING: Could I ask another question again about this particular relationship? If one

looks at the Register of Members' Interests, it says—and again I am not suggesting there is anything remotely improper about this—it says next to Stephen Day's name:

"Remunerated employment of his profession . . . parliamentary consultancy UNISON trade union NALGO section."

Following up something that Sir Clifford Boulton said, do you not think it would be appropriate for there to be contained in the Register not simply that bald statement, but also—or at least on file if not actually printed in the Register—a spelled-out contract or arrangement between your two MPs and the union, including the amount of remuneration?

ALAN JINKINSON: Absolutely. Yes, I have absolutely no problem with that. Certainly I think it would be entirely proper and indeed I would personally advocate that the amount of money was stipulated. As far as those two Members are concerned, initially there were exchanges of correspondence and I would be entirely happy if that correspondence were to be lodged wherever it is appropriate to lodge it—either with the Registrar or in the House of Commons Library or wherever.

744. PROF. ANTHONY KING: One quick final question that arises out of something that Rodney Bickerstaffe said. We are concerned not merely with actuality but with perception. One of the problems about sponsorship—and I have noticed the rather defensive tone of your replies—is not that anyone is suggesting that UNISON-sponsored MPs are obeying UNISON orders, but that it has to do with the look of the thing. It would look rather strange, I think, if a Conservative MP simply put down in the Register that his election expenses were contributed to up to a certain sum by a private company. Would it not in fact be better, as Rodney Bickerstaffe suggested the union had been discussing for some time, for the same amount of money that now goes to individual constituencies and might be thought to raise the kinds of issues we have been talking about, to go directly and centrally to the Labour Party? Would not that look better?

RODNEY BICKERSTAFFE: It may well look better, but I think I said earlier that custom and practice and tradition and, if you want, reaffirming the fact that what we stand for is also what the candidates actually stand for, is important. The trade unionists, as constituents, like to think that they have got a link in some way into Parliament and this has gone on for so long now that whatever people think, I believe that most people understand that it is not improper. It does not mean that there is a clash with constituency views and wherever the individual MP chooses to take a line that is different from the sponsoring union, then he or she takes that decision and no harm comes from it. So I honestly do not think it is anywhere near as big a problem as perhaps other perceptions.

ANGELA EAGLE: Could I just make a comment that because of the rules of registration of the Register, these quite minor payments to local parties are all in the national Register and available for everybody to see. The way that the rules work at the moment—other payments to local constituency parties, be they Labour or Conservative, do not feature.

PROF. ANTHONY KING: Yes. I think you said that before.

ANGELA EAGLE: I think that perhaps a local register, a register which allowed lists of such contributions to local parties to be public, would be a very much better way of proceeding. Again, it would be the level playing field and it would be open and transparent.

745. PETER SHORE: Yes. Custom and practice and of course history strongly determine the relationship between trade unions and the Labour Party. But you presented us a picture which, I suppose, almost uniquely as a union, is more complex than that of any other union assisting Labour Members or affiliated to the Labour Party. Because, really, there are two traditions embodied in your merged union. There is the NALGO tradition and there is the COHSE NUPE tradition. Now, am I right—as I believe I am—in saying that it is the COHSE NUPE tradition which is the most typical of the Labour Party?

RODNEY BICKERSTAFFE: Yes.

746. PETER SHORE: And Members who are sponsored normally by trade unions constituencies, they are receiving that limited amount of money for their constituency upkeep, and no payment is made to them individually?

ALAN JINKINSON: That is so.

747. PETER SHORE: Yes. It is only because this separate tradition of NALGO, which was not affiliated to the Labour Party, that NALGO like, for example, the Police Federation, which also is not affiliated to the Labour Party, enters into this almost bipartisan arrangement of looking for an adviser from both Parties in the House of Commons. And it is only in that very limited circumstance, and in the NALGO tradition, that payments are made to individual Members of Parliament?

ALAN JINKINSON: That is so. I mean I do not know the precise arrangements, but that former NALGO now UNISON arrangement is not untypical of what other non-Labour Party affiliated unions do. And certainly as far as being, you know, even-handed, one from each side of the House and I think some have Liberals as well, to a certain extent public service unions—Civil Service unions, NALGO is principally a local government union—sort of reflects the nature of the membership, reflects the nature of people who in their individual jobs, if you like, serve different political masters and mistresses.

748. PETER SHORE: Right. And to come now to the actual relationship. Quite clearly, the only possible pressure that could be put upon a Member whose constituency party is being financed at £600 a year is the loss of money to the constituency, if in fact an attempt was made to be coercive. But I am right in saying, and I think we are all agreed, Members are wholly protected against coercion because it is a breach of privilege and no union, I think, other than a Civil Service union some 50 years ago, has every attempted to coerce a Member of Parliament from the outside.

ALAN JINKINSON: Yes.

749. PETER SHORE: Good. Now let me just turn to what was another unusual feature of your union, but not unique. The payment of research money to particular teams, as it were, in the Shadow Front Bench. Do not you think on that there is really a strong case for individual

unions who are prepared to do this, to supply the money collectively as it were to the parliamentary party secretariat, so that it can then be left to the parliamentary leadership to decide which teams really need the greatest amount of financial reinforcement?

ALAN JINKINSON: Rodney may wish to say something, but there are two systems. There is an organisation—Trade Unions for Labour—which is studying that work.

RODNEY BICKERSTAFFE: There was an organisation called Trade Unions for Labour, through which an attempt was made to ensure that support, in a way, for the shortage of "Short money" could be found by the trade unions. That did happen for a number of years. I understand that that has broken down now and that, for one reason or another, from time to time individual unions' make one-off payments to support research, for instance as we do in the health area to the tune of the £15,000 that I told you about, but that is now and it is open. I think you are probably right. In the best of all worlds if there is insufficient money to run our parliamentary democracy properly through state funding or whatever, it would be better, I would have thought, for the money to go directly to a central organisation rather than to have alliances with particular areas, though again—custom and practice—it would seem better under those circumstances for a health union, for instance, to see their political fund money going into the health area than perhaps anywhere else.

750. PETER SHORE: Yes. I suppose really that, inevitably, the unions' contribution to the Labour Party in different ways is absolutely central to this whole question of the finance of political parties. It began, presumably, with the obvious imbalance of finance adversely affecting the Labour Party and the unions' attempt to right that balance. That seems to be part of the tradition of both unions, but more strongly in the case of COHSE and NUPE.

RODNEY BICKERSTAFFE: Yes, and it goes back of course to the turn of the century, as the Chair has said. Without that, there would not have been worker representative MPs in the Houses of Parliament, because there were no salaries paid, as you know. That has changed, but none the less there is still this view that there is an imbalance, and until somebody ensures that there is a better balance, perhaps this is the only way that an attempt can be made.

751. PETER SHORE: And it really is in that context of the finance of political parties, and the unequal finance, that the role of unions should be judged.

RODNEY BICKERSTAFFE: We would hope so, yes.

PETER SHORE: Thank you.

752. LORD THOMSON: I much agree with what Peter Shore has just said, but could I follow up from that? Part of the thrust of the case that you have been putting to us, rooted as it is in the history, which some of us are very well aware of, is to create this better balance. I have two questions that arise from that. I agreed with what Mr Bickerstaffe said about the problem that exists for Opposition parties under our political system, where the government has the resources of the Civil Service behind it to brief people for the debate in Parliament and an

Opposition party doesn't have that. Now that we have moved away from the far-off days when trade unions created the Labour Party and MPs were not paid, what change would there be, if any, in the unions' position when the next Labour government comes back into office and Shadow Ministers become real Ministers with a Civil Service behind them? Will you want to carry on the funding of research assistants and so on in those circumstances?

RODNEY BICKERSTAFFE: If you mean, would we want to carry on funding the then Shadow Cabinet——

LORD THOMSON: I wasn't going as far as that.

RODNEY BICKERSTAFFE: —I think that's highly unlikely. If I thought, and I don't for a moment, that the payment of those small amounts would turn the head of a then Opposition Shadow spokesperson in the direction of my sort of policy, I would be very pleased to try it, I think. No, my assumption is, and it is only an assumption, that an incoming Labour administration would perhaps want to open more fully, if you don't open it yourselves, the debate about the funding of political parties. I may be wrong, but if that were the case, perhaps the whole political world would turn.

ALAN JINKINSON: Can I say from the non-affiliated side that in the event of a change of government, I am quite sure that what we call the General Political Fund Committee would be more than happy to consider any research proposals that came from whatever Opposition Front Bench. However, I would like to think that the system will change and that, if it were a Labour government, they would ensure that there was a more level playing-field. In those circumstances the General Political Fund Committee would be more than delighted to cease to pursue that particular part of its activities and spend its money elsewhere.

753. LORD THOMSON: Thank you. That clarifies it very much for me, because you were making a very important case about, in a sense, substituting for the lack of state funding of the democratic, political process, and if that changed, your position no doubt would change on that. But that would leave the legitimate interest, as you are arguing it, for a union to have a relationship with Members of Parliament where there is a general common interest, without having a detailed interest on particular issues, and no doubt you would want to sustain that. Does that mean, in terms of a level playing-field, that you would equally accept that the other commercial and business interests would have the same right to pursue their interests through Members of Parliament, provided there was an equal degree of transparency and openness about it?

RODNEY BICKERSTAFFE: I suppose at the end of the day it would. We are talking about commercial interests. I don't see the union interest as commercial.

754. LORD THOMSON: We are talking about the historic Labour interest against the historic interest of capital in its wider sense.

RODNEY BICKERSTAFFE: Yes. I don't know exactly all the business and commercial interest pressures that are brought to bear on other Members of Parliament. All I say is that, from the outset, if everything is open, then we can see. It is a question of whether Members of Parliament's position—their constituency position, if you want—is turned by rewards of one sort or another. What we say so far as the unions are concerned is that that does not happen. Whether that happens with business and commercial interests people must judge, but until we know the amounts involved and why they are being given, then it is difficult to gauge. On a future occasion, if there were state funding of all political parties in a bigger way, so that there would not have to be exchange of moneys either to constituencies or to individuals, Parliament would have to draw up—somebody would have to draw up—a way of showing the arrangements between commercial and union links perhaps with specific Members of Parliament or with political parties.

755. LORD THOMSON: So you are not against paid advocacy in Parliament, provided the whole thing is open and transparent and you know how much money is involved in it.

RODNEY BICKERSTAFFE: I don't say I am coloured politically, but I am not anxious. The union hasn't had a debate about this, that's the first point, so I speak for myself on this occasion. It would depend, I suppose, on the amounts involved. This is something that somebody has already mentioned: it's a matter of levels. If it is sufficient to turn somebody's head, as it were, then obviously I don't think that should occur.

ANGELA EAGLE: Could I say, and it's a purely personal view again, that I am worried by paid advocacy? I think transparency is absolutely essential and I don't think that we've got it now, and I think that your committee needs to think very carefully about any parameters that you may think are acceptable for this. I personally don't like it.

756. LORD NOLAN: You would prefer paid advocacy to be reflected in the written contract that is registered, showing what was required and what was paid for.

ANGELA EAGLE: As a minimum.

757. LORD THOMSON: With respect, isn't the whole trade union case, the open and argued case, for remunerated advocacy of the general Labour interest, provided it is done under proper rules with proper openness?

ANGELA EAGLE: But I would like to see changes in the system—as we have said, state funding of political parties—and that would transform the situation. I think we are talking about a situation now where there isn't a level playing-field. I personally, and I stress it is personal, would want to take a completely different look if the parameters changed.

LORD THOMSON: That is very interesting, thank you.

758. TOM KING: I must say we seem to have a very bipartisan approach here this morning. I am glad to hear pledges of support for any future Opposition. I must say, having listened to Rodney Bickerstaffe's clarion call for custom, value, tradition and history, that there may be a Conservative lurking in there after all.

Can I start on a slightly fringe note, if I may, Mr Jinkinson? I should just like to ask Angela Eagle a question. She may not know this, but what she said at the start is very germane. One of the things this committee is concerned about is that we need to see an improvement in the standards of conduct in public life, but not in such a way that it prevents the widest range of people being able to offer themselves as Members of Parliament. We think that would enhance Parliament. I don't want to speak for all my colleagues, but I think there are one or two who share that view. I wonder if you could comment, because I believe I am right in saying that you were the parliamentary liaison officer for COHSE before you were elected to Parliament.

ANGELA EAGLE: Yes.

759. TOM KING: And you actually worked for the union in various research capacities for, I think, eight years before you were elected.

ANGELA EAGLE: Seven, I think, yes.

760. TOM KING: And you did that, effectively, when you had come down from university.

ANGELA EAGLE: Well, no. If we want to go into my entire employment history, I spent some time on the dole and then a period at the CBI.

761. TOM KING: According to your "Who's Who" entry, that was just a few months, wasn't it?

ANGELA EAGLE: Yes.

762. TOM KING: A few months in the CBI. The question I actually want to ask you is this. Your activity since leaving university, apart from a few months in the CBI—your working life—has been in the union and political process, which is a perfectly respectable career, and there are a number of people in both parties who find themselves in that situation.

ANGELA EAGLE: Yes, that's a fact.

763. TOM KING: What I am interested in is how many people do you think that would be true of? Would it be true to say that, in the Labour Party—and there are too narrow routes in the Conservative Party—the trade unions have played an important part in making it possible for people to work in careers which give them some training, give them some background experience, before they come into Parliament? We talked, avoiding Diana Warwick's critical look, also of people who have come through the route of higher education, but would you say that quite a significant number of Labour MPs come through the route that you have come?

ANGELA EAGLE: I don't know the figures, but it is certainly true that the trade union movement over the history of the Labour Party has supplied a place where people sometimes are politicised by the work they do, the injustices they might see at the workplace. Originally sponsorship was invented to provide a salary for people of low incomes, working-class people, to go in and represent their own interest in Parliament, the social interest of people of the working class, and it is certainly the case—I don't know what the percentages are off the top of my head—that there are other Labour Members of Parliament who have a similar background to me.

TOM KING: Thank you very much.

ALAN JINKINSON: I am not quite sure what the thrust of the question is. I sometimes get the impression that there are those who think that to have a business background is somehow respectable and a good thing, that to have spent your life in a trade union or in the public sector is not such a good thing.

764. TOM KING: No, no. I am sorry if I didn't make that clear. The point is not that any background is in any way more creditable than another, but there is a feeling that Parliament would be more effective, would be perhaps more informed and the standard of debate and discussion would be improved if it could draw very widely across a whole range of different occupations, and I think there is a concern, and it is partly financial, which affects this, that it is very difficult to move from many occupations into a parliamentary political career and offer yourself for public service.

ANGELA EAGLE: I think one example of that is women, with their historic under-representation in Parliament. The trade union movement are actively encouraging their own members who are women to consider taking up the route to Parliament, so that is——

765. TOM KING: I understand the importance of that. May I move on, because I just wanted to say that, as you have kindly come here as a witness and it is a point that does concern some of my colleagues.

RODNEY BICKERSTAFFE: May I just add there, if I can, Chair, to Mr King, that when you are talking about the wider spread—the low paid, the unemployed—it is not just gender balance; it is right across the board. Opportunities are needed, and there ought to be a system which shows that there can be true representation. That is why in fact the unions in the first place said that it didn't just have to be landed interests, it didn't just have to be legal beagles, it didn't just have to be medical people. That was our whole point at the time, and it is now. Obviously miners come through and shop workers come through——

766. TOM KING: Thank you very much. I'm sorry, I don't want to cut you off, but I know others want to ask questions.

Can I now turn to what is perhaps a more central point? Of course you have been keen to defend the position of trade unions and the sponsorship that you give, and I have been very impressed by the frankness with which you have talked to us this morning. As I understand it, you have said that there are some 30 Members of Parliament whose election expenses you contribute to, in a certain extent, whether it is £600 or £1,000—even £5,000 was mentioned; that there are two Members of Parliament whom you pay very directly; a sum was mentioned of £1,500, which you give to, I think, the Shadow health team; that you are paying for researchers in perhaps other fields as well. You also employ a consultancy firm, Connect Public Affairs, who you use to support your interest. This quite clearly, I must say, is a much bigger web of interest than I actually realised. This business of sponsorship of MPs has been a party political football on the trade union side. I must say it is much more extensive than I had appreciated, and I see you even employ a consultant and pay him in the House of Lords. I think that is correct, and that was in your written

evidence. Professor King took you through the points: you do actually do a number of things. You say that you "promote the interests of our members" in the House of Commons and "facilitate approaches to Ministers and other decision makers at Westminster". Do you get Questions put down? Do you get Early Day Motions sponsored? You do, I think.

RODNEY BICKERSTAFFE: Yes. At least you know about that. Yes, we're——

767. TOM KING: Your people that you contribute financially to, do you get them to put down Questions?

RODNEY BICKERSTAFFE: I say it again, as far as the affiliated fund is concerned, we don't finance individuals; it is the constituency. But all sorts of people that we approach might put Questions down. They may be sponsored, they may not be sponsored. That is the truth of it, but it is certainly not a matter, if that is your suggestion of—you use this term—"a web of interest". There is no intrigue here. It is all above board. Yes, we expect from time to time to be able to approach Members of Parliament, some sponsored, some not.

ALAN JINKINSON: Can I say that there is no way in which any of the Members with whom the General Political Fund has any contact at all receive a single penny from that fund towards their election expenses.

768. TOM KING: No, but your position of course isn't just the funds you give to their election campaign. Many of them you originally nominated: you were the nominator for them to be the candidate for that constituency. Is that correct?

ANGELA EAGLE: Could I explain——

TOM KING: Could I have an answer to that?

RODNEY BICKERSTAFFE: Some, yes. I mean, the fact——

TOM KING: Your power is not merely the money, but it is also that you have the nominating power. Obviously the issue of reselection comes up. Your members will have views in that as well.

ANGELA EAGLE: Perhaps I could explain how that works in the party at a local level.

TOM KING: I'm sorry. You see, I'm really talking—Do you mind if I——

ANGELA EAGLE: There is not only one nomination. I wouldn't want the committee to go away and think that a trade union making a nomination for a candidate is——

769. TOM KING: No, no, but it's not right to say that your interest in a Member of Parliament——

ANGELA EAGLE: You can be nominated and not selected or short-listed.

TOM KING: —or the impact you can have on him is purely a financial impact. You took an illustration on this point about how much influence, how much pressure, can be brought to bear, and the illustration that Angela took was one which I would have thought was not actually a typical illustration, because she took the illustration of the age of consent. I was quite interested to hear this and I must admit I didn't know this. On the age of consent, which I thought was a free vote, which I thought was a matter of conscience for individual Members, I would have been extremely surprised if any union had sought to discipline its members over that. But if I look at something like Clause 4, it is not a matter of the same category. Rodney Bickerstaffe, I ask you straight, because I know you well and I know you have strongly held political convictions and your union that you lead has pretty strong views on this. You are actually not going to look very happily at people who you fund and support if they turned out to be totally contrary and took a totally contrary view to Clause 4.

RODNEY BICKERSTAFFE: I think, if I may say so, it actually is happening already. The spread of opinion is very, very wide, almost as wide as on Europe. I don't know what is going to come out of the consultation process and I don't know what individual——

TOM KING: Right. Fair enough.

RODNEY BICKERSTAFFE: —Labour Party-sponsored MPs——

TOM KING: Fair enough.

RODNEY BICKERSTAFFE: Chair, sorry. The question has been asked. I would just like to finish it.

770. TOM KING: Well, you said there are many other issues than that and there is a wide spread of opinion. I take that view. Some of your members will vote against that and won't be disciplined for it. That's what you are saying.

RODNEY BICKERSTAFFE: I am sure that will happen, yes.

TOM KING: Right, but if that happened——

RODNEY BICKERSTAFFE: Unless of course, if I can say, a position is arrived at where everybody is totally at one and happy, and that is possible.

771. TOM KING: And if that happened on frequent occasions, you would have reason, if not to express your displeasure in whatever ways you do, but, if reselection comes up, not to be keen to support them for being reselected.

RODNEY BICKERSTAFFE: I don't think that's true. I was General Secretary from 1982 until 1993. So far as I recall, nobody was deselected for any reason at all. I think I see not the line of questioning but the line that you are pushing. I don't think that that is the truth.

LORD NOLAN: Now we must move back to the more general. We have already overrun our time.

TOM KING: I'm sorry, I must ask one more question. I'm so sorry.

LORD NOLAN: Very well.

772. TOM KING: Because I think this is the largest union in the country—is that right?—in number of members.

ALAN JINKINSON: Correct.

TOM KING: In terms it is a very important point, obviously one of the big arguments that exists over this matter. I just want to ask you this question. You used the word "sleaze", Mr Jinkinson, in your introduction, which is applied often to people who pay money to people in Parliament to represent their interests, and that has been caught up in the issue of sleaze. Professor King politely used the word "unhealthy". Having listened to all you have to say, I would not use the pejorative; I would say that it can invite questions of unhealthiness in the way in which you have presented the case and the situation that we find. Can I ask this question as well? I notice that you employ Connect Public Affairs. I had actually never heard of that consultancy before until I read The *Observer* article, which was printed here, about a number of lobbying groups who appear to be employing or paying for researchers in the House of Commons, and I find that Connect Public Affairs is actually supposed to have a researcher working in the House of Commons for John Prescott. I don't know if this is true or false. Most of the information I have about these particular illustrations that I have tried to investigate appears to be pretty incorrect. But you pay a fee, presumably, to Connect Public Affairs also to represent your interests in the House of Commons. Is that correct?

ALAN JINKINSON: We pay a fee to Connect Public Affairs to provide us with a monitoring and information service, but there are no MPs' interests whatsoever involved in that relationship between UNISON and Connect Public Affairs.

TOM KING: And the person who is working for John Prescott——

LORD NOLAN: I think we shall have to leave this, because we are getting too much into the detail of individual members.

773. TOM KING: I just wanted to ask this last question. Apparently John Prescott isn't funded by a union for that, through Connect Public Affairs.

ALAN JINKINSON: I did read that article. As far as I know, the person named in that—I think it is a table you are looking at, Mr King—at a point in time did work for Connect. I believe that she no longer works for Connect.

TOM KING: Thank you very much.

774. DIANA WARWICK: Could I just ask this, because we seem to have strayed into a rather different area from the one that we had thought to ask you questions about, and that is the area of the funding of political parties? I think that is a big question, but it is not the question that we asked you to come and talk to us about. I wonder if you can say something about the nature of the relationship with MPs, because it seems to me that the information that you have given us throughout your evidence is that, first of all, individual MPs are not funded by the union: the money that is given is either to the constituency or for general assistance to the party in certain areas. Am I correct in that?

ALAN JINKINSON: Yes. I mean, there are the small sums to Mr Day and to Mr Hogg.

775. DIANA WARWICK: But, other than that, the money is given for the work of the party, as you say, to level the playing-field.

ALAN JINKINSON: Yes, indeed.

776. DIANA WARWICK: Could I then ask, because it seems to me that our general interest is in the way in which MPs are influenced by payment or by pressure from those who seek to lobby or to advocate, whether or not you feel that there is a difference in the kind of advocacy or influence or facilitation that you seek from MPs than the other kinds of pressure or advocacy that is paid for? I ask the question because it was put to us by Emma Nicholson, and I think it was this point that came up in relation to a web of inferences. Emma Nicholson said to us "I would ... go a little bit further than public relations companies and add advertising companies, any company with a web of different and moving clients", which would include trade union sponsorship. Would you associate the activities of the unions, both affiliated and non-affiliated unions, in their so-called sponsorship with the kind of advocacy that public relations companies normally exercise? Do you see a difference?

ALAN JINKINSON: Yes, I do. I don't know an awful lot about that side of the business. I read about it. I don't have any personal links or any personal knowledge of it. But certainly I think our written evidence, I think that what we have said to the committee this morning, is that, as far as we are concerned, our relationships with Members of Parliament are respectable, transparent, above board. If we can do anything to make them more transparent, we will gladly do that.

DIANA WARWICK: Thank you.

LORD NOLAN: Thank you all very much. We have kept you longer than the allotted time. You have been very interesting indeed and we are very grateful to you for coming.

Now we have with us Mr Keith Henshall, Mr Mike Beard and Mr Michael Ward from the Institute of Public Relations. Have you prepared an opening statement that you would like to make before the questions are put to you?

KEITH HENSHALL, MIKE BEARD AND MICHAEL WARD (INSTITUTE OF PUBLIC RELATIONS)

KEITH HENSHALL: I have, Chairman, yes.

LORD NOLAN: Is it long?

KEITH HENSHALL: Very short.

LORD NOLAN: Very helpful, I am sure. Please make it.

KEITH HENSHALL: Thank you. If I could introduce my colleagues and myself, Mike Beard is the immediate past president of the institute. He is a director of corporate communications for the Taylor Woodrow group and has worked as a political organiser. Michael Ward is a fellow of the institute. He has just completed two years as our chairman of Professional Practices Committee, and he was MP for Peterborough from 1974 to 1979. I am chairman of a training consultancy group and a former managing director of one of the large consultancies in public relations, and I am this year's president.

The Institute of Public Relations is the recognised professional body for individuals practising public relations in the United Kingdom. We have 5,300 members; we represent two-thirds of this country's senior practitioners and our members are drawn from every aspect of public relations, including government relations, of which lobbying is a part. We have four MPs, two MEPs and three Lords in membership of the institute. For many years we have been working towards the requirements for chartered status and we are getting close to the situation where we could apply for that status. Our intent is to professionalise the practice of public relations.

We have existed since 1948 and we have operated a system of self-regulation for the last 45 of those 47 years. Our code of professional conduct places a positive duty on our members to declare in a national register the names of any public officeholder employed or retained by them, or their employers. In September 1994 we added a second register. This records those members who are professionally engaged for all or part of their time in lobbying. It also records the interests on which they lobby.

We wish to highlight the difference between lobbying and general political consultancy, because we believe this difference to be of central importance to the work of this committee. In our guidance notes to members as to whether they register as lobbyists or not we define lobbying as "pressing for change in policy or seeking to prevent such change". That is a shortened definition.

We live in a representative democracy, and every citizen and organisation has a right, and some would say a duty, to lobby for their point of view. Lobbyists exist to help them exercise that right effectively in a complex democracy. It is necessary and good to have lobbyists, but if representative democracy is to work, that lobbying must be on the basis of reasoned argument. It must not be by means of bribery or coercion.

In that representative democracy the representatives themselves must be exactly that. It is their duty to represent diverse opinion. They should not be paid to lobby for narrow interest. But lobbying must be distinguished from general political consultancy. Members of Parliament have specialist experience and knowledge about the process of government. It is right that they should be allowed to share it through openly declared political consultancy. Banning such work would cause a valuable resource to be lost to the UK economy.

In all evidence given on these matters on previous occasions this institute has always favoured working towards comprehensive statutory control. However, we appreciate that this is a large, complex task which takes in, for example, the role of the press and media. Our register of lobbyists was one more piece of self-regulation designed to help us towards this eventual goal. We believe that it is now time for independent regulation of the activities of the legislators themselves—that is, Members of both Houses and their staff. These general principles guide our answers to the specific questions on MPs' outside interests that the committee is considering at this point in its deliberations and we turn to those now.

We believe that on the spectrum from total freedom to total ban MPs should be banned from entering into contracts to lobby—that is, to seek to alter their own legislative behaviour or that of their fellow MPs. They should, however, be free to give strategic advice through directorships or consultancies and to pursue such other outside interests as allow them to function as MPs.

All contracts of outside employment by MPs should therefore be evidenced in writing and lodged for open inspection with an independent body. The nature and extent of the services provided by an MP and the size of the consideration received must be made public. When the reward is out of proportion to the work, bribery can be suspected. Such a rule would require detailed guidance on the borderlines, on the grey areas. It would, for example, be needed on the point at which gifts, hospitality or employment of close family or researchers become consideration for services. Such guidance is already given to Ministers. It should be extended to MPs. An independent commission could provide guidance on the borderline and rule on when it has been crossed. Its rulings should provide guidance by precedent. It would need to be completely open in both its rulings and its guidance. Rules alone don't prevent malpractice; public scrutiny does. For this reason all registers should be open, including the current register of researchers.

Any incident throwing doubt on the integrity of MPs undermines our democratic system if it seems to be beyond society's control. An independent element is needed, but the new net should not have so fine a mesh that important democratic rights are excluded along with malpractice.

Our institute exists to promote high standards in public debate. All lobbying seeks to influence public debate. Lobbying is part of public relations and we have long experience of regulating public relations. We stand ready to assist the monitoring and regulating process in any way that we can.

These are our view on MPs' interests. We have views on the wider concerns, to which the committee returns, I know, at a later date, and we would appreciate the opportunity to speak to those at the appropriate time.

LORD NOLAN: Thank you very much. That is very clear and comprehensive. I am going to ask Mr Tom King to carry on with the questions.

777. TOM KING: Thank you for your opening statement. It was very helpful. We had your sister body, as you might say, who represent, I think, the member firms. You represent all the individual members?

KEITH HENSHALL: Correct.

778. TOM KING: I didn't know how comprehensive you were. What percentage of people in the field of public relations do you represent?

KEITH HENSHALL: At the senior level—that is those who qualify for full membership—we represent the majority, about two-thirds. At the junior levels we have quite a low penetration.

779. TOM KING: Right. You are talking about public relations and you then go on to the field of lobbying. One of the points that have been made to us is that a lot of people are coming into lobbying from quite different directions. I mean, quite a lot of law firms are now setting up lobbying departments in Brussels and London, and accountants and others. Do they recognise that they are in the world of public relations or do they tend to stay right outside your membership?

KEITH HENSHALL: I wouldn't think they recognise they are in the world of public relations at all. Public relations is concerned with the management of an organisation's reputation. Everybody is concerned with the management of an organisation's reputation. Public relations people do it for a living. So somebody can lobby as part of being a lawyer without being a public relations practitioner.

780. TOM KING: You are a body that has suddenly changed its rules. That may be a bit unkind, but you introduced a second register system in September 1994. Why did you do that?

KEITH HENSHALL: It actually wasn't terribly sudden. It took quite a long time. It was done because we had been pressing for some time, in our evidence to the Select Committee, for there to be statutory control. The understanding we had——

781. TOM KING: Which Select Committee was that?

KEITH HENSHALL: The Select Committee on Members' Interests.

TOM KING: Right.

KEITH HENSHALL: The evidence on that was left by my colleague. There came a point where we decided that we were running counter to the prevailing mood, and the prevailing mood was that it would be appreciated if we made a start now with self-regulation rather than wait till we developed some experience, and we were happy to go along with that. We have made the point all along that we would prefer any such regulation to be statutory, but we were prepared to take any steps that were felt helpful. The register of lobbyists' interests was considered helpful and we introduced it.

MICHAEL WARD: May I add something to that as president of the day, if you will forgive me, Mr King? We didn't change any of our rules at all in fact. Our code of conduct was not changed by one iota as a result of this change. All we simply said was that we will give more detailed guidance as to how our code should be interpreted in the lobbying area and we will ask our members who lobby to sign an additional register to make their activity more transparent, but the controls and the practices which they were meant to carry out did not change one iota.

782. TOM KING: Thank you. You talked about what MPs should do: there should be standards set and there should be a code as to what was acceptable to receive in terms of hospitality, gifts, whatever it may be. Does your code incorporate that requirement on your members?

KEITH HENSHALL: Yes, it does. Because this is obviously a difficult area, the way we have always expressed it is that there should be no rewards given to holders of public office that would tend to exercise undue influence, and then you have to interpret the particular cases. If you are very clear on the rule, common practice will always come to the worst allowable, human nature being what it is.

783. TOM KING: Have you ever enforced that code? Have you ever taken any disciplinary action against any of your members?

KEITH HENSHALL: Yes, we have enforced the code—not very often. We have enforced the code. I don't know of any occasion on which we have enforced it on that matter. To be honest, the largest single category of breaches of the code have tended to be public spats between members that have got out of hand. It hasn't tended to be a breach of their duties not to coerce—corrupt. That largely tends to be because you don't have to join our institute. People can earn a perfectly good living outside of our institute. The ones who join our institute are the ones who seek voluntarily to take on this code of conduct. It is not necessary. So it tends to be rarely breached. If it is breached, it is often in the spirit that the person didn't think they were breaching it and there's a ruling on whether they were or they weren't, which I think is germane to what you are talking about in this committee. There will be occasions when people are saying "I am behaving perfectly properly" and a dispassionate ruling is "We don't think you were", and presumably the reprimand would be commensurate with that. But that has tended to be the tenor of our disciplinary hearings in the past.

MIKE BEARD: If I may, Chairman, I think also it depends on the complaints we receive. We receive something like a dozen complaints every year, which we process. Some go to our disciplinary committee for action. The majority are dealt with informally or resolved in some other way. I don't recall in the last three or four years any case of this kind touching upon relationships with Members of Parliament or other public bodies.

784. TOM KING: But when you look around there is no question that there are some organisations that do make pretty lavish offers to people of trips, fairly tangentially connected with overseas visits, connected with some political issue or whatever it may be, but you don't believe any of your members are doing it.

KEITH HENSHALL: That's correct.

785. TOM KING: You haven't had a single complaint of one of your members being involved in such a thing, which would be in breach of your code?

KEITH HENSHALL: That's right. I am also a member, and if I saw evidence of such a thing, I would complain myself. So I have neither seen the evidence nor had complaints from my fellow members.

786. TOM KING: Would it be a bit unkind to say that actually it's quite difficult for you to discipline your code? Your belief is that it would be better done at the other end, controlling the recipient; it is not very easy to control the donor, as it were.

KEITH HENSHALL: I think it would be unkind, yes. Clearly we are a voluntary organisation, so our sanctions are limited to those of any ultimate disbarring from our institute and, as I say, plenty of people have earned a perfectly good living outside of it, but we are in a business where reputation is important. The public relations

industry does not have a good reputation. We are attempting to do something about that from within. For most public relations practitioners, a good personal reputation is extremely valuable to their future. To become known as a sharp practitioner entirely alters the nature of the clients, because some clients want sharp practitioners, and that's why they exist. For most people, to be labelled a sharp practitioner is a very difficult thing to happen indeed. That's the only power. We don't have the power to compel people to belong to our institute. If we did, I think we would have more cases before disciplinary committees.

TOM KING: Thank you very much. That's very helpful.

787. MARTIN JACOMB: Can I just ask you a couple of question? In the remarks which you made at the outset, which you kindly gave us a copy of, you say at the bottom of page 1 that "if representative democracy is to work, the lobbying must be by means of reasoned argument. It must not be by means of bribery or coercion", which is absolutely fine. What guidance do you give to your members who ask you about levels of hospitality and levels of foreign travel, or indeed any travel? Do you get asked questions by your members and what guidance do you give them?

KEITH HENSHALL: We do, and Mike Ward has a very good answer that he usually gives them, which is a nice clear definition.

MICHAEL WARD: My own personal advice to members, which goes beyond the code, but my personal interpretation of our code would be to say "What is the size of what is offered and what is the response of the person who receives it?" If you are offered an invitation to come to one of our companies for a very exciting lunch for an hour and listen to what the company is about and disturb your very busy parliamentary day, you are not going to get too excited, but if the organisation says "Come and listen to a presentation from a company and, by the way, it's in the south of France during the Monaco Grand Prix" and the recipient says "Wow, that's great, thank you very much", the recipient's reaction is some clue sometimes as to whether the invitation was over-couched. But I think it is such a grey area that it is very difficult to say. If you look at corporate hospitality outside Parliament in the business area, the chairman of a company would not expect to be entertained to lunch to discuss business in a fish and chip shop, but on the other hand there are plenty of people I have to talk to who would be delighted to come to a local fish and chip shop for a debate. So I think you have to look at the recipient and their response, and that's the general advice I give.

MARTIN JACOMB: I am not sure you are right about the fish and chip shop, actually.

MICHAEL WARD: I know several very good ones.

788. MARTIN JACOMB: Leave that aside. Why I asked you that question particularly was because this is a grey area, as you said, that it is to you that people will look for guidance because there are very few places they can get guidance from, and what guides most people most effectively is peer group behaviour and they look to you to get that.

MICHAEL WARD: I know one leading company which I have some connections with that considers a box of chocolates at Christmas to people who generally advises and are helpful to us is perfectly OK, but several bottles would not be OK. One can only give individuals individual advice based on individual experience and behaviour.

KEITH HENSHALL: Our advice tends to err towards the side of caution. We say if you feel there could be any suggestion of undue influence, do not do it.

789. MARTIN JACOMB: Could I then go to just one other area. At the bottom of page 2 you say quite clearly that

"MPs should be banned from entering into contracts to lobby: that is, to seek to alter their own legislative behaviour or that of their fellow MPs. They should, however, be free to give strategic advice through directorships..."

that is quite clear. There you have identified the clear borderline between information and advice coming from the MP to the client, but never transgressing into an undertaking to change the behaviour that they otherwise would have had as MPs. Can you just tell me how you think, human nature being what it is, people deal with the situation where they are in receipt of significant material benefit for giving advice, but they know their conduct as an MP will conflict with the interests of the person who they are advising and therefore their retainer will, in all probability, come to an end? I have put that rather bluntly, but that is a real life situation which must come up. How do you think that fits in to your clear borderline?

KEITH HENSHALL: It is not a clear borderline, this is the point. This is a difficult borderline, that is why there are two needs; there is a need to actually come to the correct decision and there is a need to be publicly seen to come to that correct decision. The suggestion of an independent body with whom the terms of any undertaking would be lodged, the amount that you are going to get paid for and what you are expected to do for it, would give a body that that MP could turn to to say "This is the situation that I am in, do you think I should be giving up this retainer or am I perfectly OK to continue with it? What is your view?" I would imagine if he or she feels they should continue with that retainer they will argue vigorously, that is their profession. If the ultimate decision is—"We advise you, we guide you that this would be falling the wrong side of the borderline and you should err on the side of caution", which tends to be the conversation we have with our members, then somebody who flew in the face of that would be doing it in the full knowledge and the full public glare that they have opened the suspicion of undue influence.

790. MARTIN JACOMB: That is one of the reasons that you are in favour of disclosing the amounts of remuneration, and probably the main reason, is it?

KEITH HENSHALL: It is the main reason, yes. A thousand pounds a year for a day a month is very different to a million pounds a month for a day a year.

MARTIN JACOMB: Quite, thanks very much.

MICHAEL WARD: May I just add a point to what our President has said. Personally I have been involved with talking to Members of Parliament for 30 years on behalf of organisations and I think one should keep this issue in perspective in that in those 30 years I have never witnessed, or seen, or had any indication of any malpractice by any Member. Whereas I fully support my Institute's position that paying for general information and counsel is fine, I personally have never needed to make such payments so I believe that companies that develop their public relations programmes in an appropriate way do not need to because in my experience Members of Parliament are anxious to see that both sides of an issue are aired. There are always Members of Parliament available and willing to listen and be supportive and interested in company and other organisations' cases.

791. DIANA WARWICK: Could I just ask two brief questions? One follows on from Sir Martin's question because you indicate in your evidence to us that you have consulted with the Association of Professional Political Consultants. In their evidence to us, and we had a discussion with them about this, they said—it is the fact of the payment not the quantum that is relevant. You seem to be saying the opposite. Is that correct?

KEITH HENSHALL: I am saying the opposite; that we have a different position. They are saying, as I understand it, that no Member of Parliament should be paid for anything outside of Parliament. That is not our position because we believe that it leads into the illogical situation that somebody who has been a Member of Parliament and has ceased to be can give political advice, somebody who has never been but has watched can give political advice, but somebody who is cannot. That seems to me to be a waste of a great deal of skill and knowledge and experience that could be of value. It could be given freely, it could be given occasionally, it could be given on the basis of a retainer in private or in public.

DIANA WARWICK: Your position then is that he who pays the piper well probably calls the tune.

KEITH HENSHALL: In which case everybody has to be clear who is paying what to whom, and what is expected in return, and there needs to be a mechanism for saying to people "You have gone beyond the pail".

792. DIANA WARWICK: Fine, thank you. My second question is, you have talked about a register for lobbyists; I think you also have implied that professional lobbyists have no privileged access to the system and should not have. Am I right in that? Would you agree with that?

KEITH HENSHALL: Do you mean in fact have no lobbyists? I have only seen what I have read in the papers as well and it appears some of them do have. Whether they should or not is another matter entirely.

793. DIANA WARWICK: I go on from that then to ask, if there is a register do you think that the price for being on that register should be, for example, a pass to get access to the House of Commons, a room available for lobbyists and so on, as has been argued to us?

KEITH HENSHALL: I am now expressing a personal view on this based on the representations I heard from senior members of our Institute who are engaged in this area. What people have said to me and what I tend to agree with is that there should not be any special access for somebody who is a professional lobbyist, and nor should they have any special restriction. As long as it is declared that they are professional lobbyists then they go on the lobby like any other citizen, just as a soldier carrying arms can only use those arms in peacetime when they are acting as a soldier. That is the same principle; they are still citizens, so are we.

DIANA WARWICK: Thank you.

MIKE BEARD: If I may, the authority for that access lies between the authorities of the House, Serjeant at Arms and the individual Members, and we would expect the control to be exercised from that point. It could well be that members of our Institute will be employed, as I am, in the public sector for some common cause, in my case criminal justice, and it could well be that one of our number would be given access in order to assist a parliamentary or party group, or something of that kind. Again, similarly with commercial interests, those things should be regulated by the House authorities and Members.

KEITH HENSHALL: Chairman, could I make just one last point on that subject very briefly? On access, there are two reasons that you give access, one is out of conviction and one is as part of a contract of employment, and we are talking about giving access as part of a contract of employment. This would certainly fall within the interpretation of borderlines that any independent body was looking at. Giving access for conviction is a different matter entirely.

794. CLIFFORD BOULTON: Some witnesses have suggested that if a Member has a relationship with a fair commercial interest for the purpose of giving advice and information about what is going on in Parliament, for the sake of avoiding any misunderstanding that Member should impose a self-denying ordinance upon himself and not speak on that particular subject in the Chamber, or table amendments, or advance arguments by way of early day motions and so forth. From what I understand you to be saying, so long as the agreement is open and fully understood that he is not under any expectation or obligation to speak or act in a particular way, you would say that he ought therefore to be free to do what he would have done anyway and speak on those matters as the whim takes him.

KEITH HENSHALL: I think as the duty takes him, yes. That is the point of having the declaration of independence made at a separate considered moment rather than at the point of debate. The interest is declared for open inspection well in advance of the debate. I would hope it to be extremely rare that MPs were prepared to represent conflicting views for money. Mostly, I would have thought, it was something on which they had a conviction anyway, and then there is a contribution made towards costs to make it easier for them to follow that through. The point that everybody has to be concerned with is at what point that assistance starts to exercise an undue influence on their behaviour, or their behaviour with other people.

795. CLIFFORD BOULTON: But if an industry or an interest group discerns some problem that will arise in a bit of legislation that will adversely affect them, and they think that this could best be clarified by an amendment to a Bill, and they take tactical advice and get information from a particular Member, if they took along that little draft amendment to the Member and said—"We've got

this problem, would you care to advance this argument by way of an amendment?" and it appealed to the Member, you are saying he should be free to do it. He should not say "Take it away because it will muddle people, they will think I am doing what you are telling me to do".

KEITH HENSHALL: I think, again, we are into this grey area where his instinct should be to turn to the Commission and say, "Look, this is what is being suggested, these are my motives. This seems perfectly straightforward. What is your view because if you say, 'Take it away' then I'll send it away, but I think you will be wrong."

CLIFFORD BOULTON: Thank you.

MIKE BEARD: The greater openness and transparency about the publication of monies received by the Member will make this process much more acceptable, I would have thought.

796. ANNE WARBURTON: May I ask a practical question? The two registers, the National Register of Public Officeholders employed by professionals, and the Register of Members professionally engaged in lobbying, what access is there for other Members of your Institute?

MICHAEL WARD: One has more recently looked at that issue. The register of those who are employed as holders of public office by our Members is available for public inspection at the Institute's headquarters. The register of our Members who are lobbyists was launched in co-operation with the PRCA, so we are together running two halves of a joint register which will be published annually and made available to the library at the House and to any other place of importance and significance for reference such as the Press Association, but can be inspected daily by members of the public with an interest at our Institute headquarters.

797. ANNE WARBURTON: Could I ask, do a lot of people come and consult the one which is already open, the National Register?

MICHAEL WARD: The last inquiry we had was a few months ago and it was as a result of the recent debate and controversy about these matters, and that was the first time for some time that the Register had been accessed, I believe.

MIKE BEARD: It might help the committee to know, sir, that there are about 40 entries on the Register of whom 27 are Members of Parliament, 7 are Members of the House of Peers, 4 are Counsellors from local authorities, one works for the Equal Opportunities Commission, and one is a Member of the European Parliament.

ANNE WARBURTON: Thank you for that information.

798. LORD NOLAN: Thank you all very much. You have made your points very clearly, if I may say so, and we are most grateful to you for your help.

Mr Benn, thank you very much for coming along. You are well-known to us and need no introduction, but I say for the record that you are a very senior Member of the

House of Commons having been a Member I think for over 30 years, and that amongst your responsibilities has been membership of the Committee of Privileges for a period of some 10 years until recently. Have you, in addition to the very helpful memoranda, which you have supplied to the Committee and which we have read, any short opening statement that you would care to make at the start of your evidence?

RT. HON. TONY BENN MP

RT. HON. TONY BENN MP: Yes if I may, Lord Nolan. First of all may I register my interests: I am a writer and a broadcaster and shareholder, and that is published in the Register of Members' Interests. I am not a Member of the Committee of Privileges because I was removed before Christmas. Although leaks of it are now appearing in the papers, so that is the normal process, you do not publish a leak.

I think my general argument, if I may summarise it very briefly, is that this is not a problem of individual scandal and corruption; it is a systemic problem. The way British government works is inherently contrary to the interests of the electors. Members of Parliament have a very marketable product at their disposal, influence. Ministers have even more to sell; they know how Government works. This is not a party matter; I am not interested either in muck-raking, nor am I interested in political advantage. That is why I do not think that the media or the Opposition are the right people to make much of this, but Ministers have a lot of dealings with industry. It is not unknown for Ministers or even senior civil servants to arrange the Honours List to promote the interests of a particular company and then when they retire they are taken on board. That is applied across the board and it is a problem which, I think, undermines the rights of the electors to look to the ballot box to countervail the historic power of the wealthy to run the country. If they thought that when they elected a Member of Parliament that Member of Parliament was not representing them but had been catapulted into a position where they could actually make money for themselves, that would be destructive of the parliamentary process.

I think I have summarised the argument. I have suggested a number of things—the extension of the Code of Conduct, the extension of the principal of disqualification, the role of the Election Courts. Perhaps I may say I have myself been expelled from Parliament by the Committee of Privileges; in 1960 I appeared before an Election Court, I was unseated by two of your brother judges who put into Parliament the man I had defeated; and so I have had some experience of the system that I am describing. I believe that this whole thing needs to be looked at much more fundamentally and much less in terms of the headlines that may flow from what individuals may have done. I also think the whole thing should be in public. I did suggest modestly that perhaps your own Committee might meet in public. I think the Committee of Privileges should meet in public, and I paid the price for pressing that view. Thank you very much.[7]

LORD NOLAN: You have already touched on a number of points which are of great interest to us and which we shall want to raise in a little more detail. I have asked Professor King to lead with the questions.

799. PROF. ANTHONY KING: Mr Benn, can I refer fairly frequently to the memoranda, but I will try to make it clear to everybody in the room what exactly I am referring to. On page 6 in paragraph 1 you say——

---

[7]See Evidence, pp. 514–519.

"Another change that needs to be made is to legislate to make it an offence, in law, for any person to offer to pay, or for any Member of Parliament to accept payment, for the use of influence to obtain a commercial or financial advantage for either party to such a transaction."

Could you just spell out in a little more detail what you mean by that? What would be ruled in, what would be ruled out?

TONY BENN: I think the detailed registration would need to be worked out very, very carefully, but it is already a criminal offence. If I offer a constituent money to vote for me, I am guilty of a corrupt offence, I am taken to an Election Court on a petition and I am unseated. If it is a practice that will go to the normal procedure and I may also be punished. I cannot see the difference between both sides of that equation, and I think you have to draw a very clear distinction—I listened to some of the evidence of UNISON today—between an organisation that has a legitimate interest on behalf of its members, and a private arrangement where somebody says "Give me money and I'll give you some advantage that is a pecuniary advantage to yourself". I know it is a difficult line to draw, but I have argued as best I can that this should be individual transactions that benefit people individually and are conducted in secret, as many of them would normally be.

800. PROF. ANTHONY KING: Just for the purpose of clarity, for example I am a Member of Parliament and I am approached by (to take a totally notional example) the Welsh Whisky Trade Association and am invited to be, in a sense, their parliamentary representative, though I am not entirely happy with that word. Is that the kind of thing that you would wish to have banned?

TONY BENN: Let me be clear; I am a consultant, I have been a consultant for 45 years, a consultant on behalf of my constituents. I have never been offered a bribe so I cannot claim that I have rejected it, but I take up cases that I believe to be right. But it does not always happen. I give one example that went contrary to a constituency interest. As Postmaster General I banned cigarette advertising on television. Now, Bristol was the home of Imperial Tobacco and a lot of my constituents were employed in the tobacco industry and I gave a view, and, indeed, I reached a decision as a Minister, that that was to be banned. On the other hand, I have taken up a great many cases, individual companies in my constituency have approached me with problems, of course, if employment is involved. I represented a mining area till every pit was closed, and I am a strong supporter of the National Union of Mineworkers, but I have not received money for it. I think, if you are talking about an organisation that has an interest and does it openly, for example ballots by trade unions, there is no ballot by shareholders if they give money to a company. Where you have an open agreement that there is to be support for a policy then that money should go to the organisation and not to the individual. That is the distinction I have tried to draw.

801. PROF. ANTHONY KING: Again, if I can press you, I am genuinely puzzled. Clearly you have behaved properly, not only according to your rights but according to everybody else rights. I am just keen to be clear about what you want to be ruled out. Are you saying that Members of Parliament should not be paid by any organised interest or company or charity for work in connection with their parliamentary duties?

TONY BENN: I am trying to draw a distinction—perhaps I have not made it clear but I have tried to in the paper that I have submitted to the Committee—between a personal payment and payment for a campaign. For example, there would be nothing wrong, and there is not anything wrong, in the National Union of Mineworkers of which I am an honourary member, 001, though I am not a sponsored member of the NUM—with the National Union of Mineworkers trying to win public support for the campaign to keep the pits open, and I work very hard with them for that. That is open; there is a ballot among NUM members as to whether they wish to have a political fund, people can opt out if they do not wish to do so, the fund is available and that fund is for the campaign. But I do think there is a danger if people have a personal pecuniary advantage in secret which is paid in a way that benefits others individually. I listened to the cross-examination by Tom King of Rodney Bickerstaffe, there is no benefit to a General Secretary of a trade union if the Health Service is preserved, and I think this is a distinction that needs to be drawn. It is very important to draw it otherwise it would appear that there is really no difference; unions fund people privately and business funds do, and I think this is a different thing. For example, a great many charities have parliamentary officers and those parliamentary officers promote the interest of the charities quite openly. Information they get is available to everybody, not confined simply to the company that pays them, and similarly a trade union sponsored Member will make information available. I put down a great deal of early day motions, I table a great many questions, nobody has ever offered me money for it and I would not accept it if they did. I think it is a distinction that needs to be drawn. All I have been able to do is to indicate the general principles upon which the rules should apply.

802. PROF. ANTHONY KING: Still on the question of the general principle, at several points in your memorandum you say things like this——

"....it is hard to resist the conclusion that the same disqualification should apply to any Member who receives money to perform a political act on behalf of some commercial organisation".

At several points in the memorandum, to repeat, you lay emphasis on the fact, or appear to, that it is commercial organisations you are worried about, the implication being that you are not as concerned about non-commercial organisations.

TONY BENN: I think that is a proper distinction to draw. If in a free society people band themselves together, as they are entitled to do, on animal welfare, for example, to take the recent example of the export of live animals for slaughter, they raise money, they write—I have a great many letters from people about it, I am sympathetic to their view, I have tabled a parliamentary motion about it. I think it is a total distinction between that and somebody coming to me and saying "You being a Minister, we would you like to join our board because you know a lot about what goes on in Government". That is really a very dangerous situation.

As a Minister I had responsibility for 11 years for determining whether permanent officials would be allowed to join commercial companies. They used to come to me, there was a Two-year Rule, I do not know if it still applies, and I had to give very careful consideration not only to whether it was desirable in the future, but whether the principle of employment in the future might influence people in the present. You do not have to be very clever to realise that if a person who has a public function knows that if he advantages one group or another they may return to him that benefit when he or she retires, then you are moving into very dangerous territory. I think the real danger is the knowledge that a Minister or a civil servant might have that in certain circumstances, if they play it correctly, they might benefit when they retire. That is the danger. It is a systemic problem, not about individuals, because this has gone on for a very long time.

803. PROF. ANTHONY KING: I still find this a little puzzling because, on the face of it, if you are going to home in on commercial organisations you raise a question such as the following—it would be improper for a British Member of Parliament to be paid to act on behalf of the Society of Motoring Manufacturers and Traders, but it would be proper for him to act on behalf of Pinochet's Chile which is clearly not a commercial organisation.

TONY BENN: I have not dealt with payment from abroad, but, of course, there are offshore funds in this country to which people are invited to contribute. I am not making a political point, but I believe it is a fact that people who are members of a political party abroad are asked to put their money into—is it Barclays Bank offshore, I forget who it is—and that money is then fed in. I mean, you might want to tighten the rules in that respect, but where somebody goes abroad that is already required to be reported in the Register of Interests. Where I have been abroad, sometimes to give lectures, I will report that I went to a university in America, they paid my fare, they paid my hotel, and I gave a lecture and so on. That will apply to people who travel abroad on visits to governments, but I think it would be wholly improper for a foreign government to pay somebody of course, and if I did not specify that I should have done.

804. PROF. ANTHONY KING: Can I raise a completely different question? On page 5 of your memorandum you say, and you repeated it in your introductory remarks——

"If public confidence in democracy is to be maintained, the rights of the electors must be safeguarded and these rights may be summarised as follows:-

a. The right to elect whomsoever they wish, and for whatever reason, to represent them."

You repeat the point a little bit below——

"If these rights are accepted as fundamental it must follow that the only body of persons who have a moral and democratic right to elect, or remove, an MP are his or her constituents."

But you then go on to say in the same sentence, and repeat at several other points in the memorandum, the following general consideration——

"It should be considered whether this list of disqualifications should be extended to include those who have received money for political services, regardless of whether such transactions have been declared in the Register of Interests."

Again, I am puzzled. On the one hand you seem to want to make an MP's electors the sole arbiters of whether he or she should continue to be a Member of the House. On the other hand you seem to want the House of Commons to lay down additional disqualifications thereby restricting the range of choice available to the electors. I am genuinely not clear how you square this.

TONY BENN: If I may refer you to what I said. I said that——

"...the only body of persons who have a moral and democratic right to elect, or remove, an MP are his or her constituents, unless and until an MP is convicted of a breach of the law"

For example, if you become a bankrupt, or if you are in prison, you are disqualified. I can think of a number of occasions when Members of Parliament have come before the courts, the judges have made a report to the Speaker, the Speaker has announced the matter and then a motion is passed that an election take place in the room of Mr So and So who has been disqualified. I am saying that the rules of disqualification should be tightened because a government contractor under old legislation is excluded, and I am really saying, I think, that the words "government contractor" should begin to move into areas that have caused concern now. It is a difficult argument to make, but I am trying to concentrate on the principles rather than the actual draft legislation.

805. PROF. ANTHONY KING: But on your own first principle, that the electors should decide, should not the rules of disqualification be loosened so that if voters in a constituency want to elect to the House of Commons a bankrupt or somebody who is in prison, should they not, on your over-arching principle, have the right to do that?

TONY BENN: I have said, of course, that the Returning Officer should issue to every elector a Register of Interests of all the candidates because, you will know, candidates put forward election addresses, I have done it myself very often, setting out your political opinion. But the electors have no knowledge whether you are also a director of 22 companies, or you have some interests or other, so I think disclosure is the main ingredient. The law does have to make some provision. For example, I put it in a strange relationship, convicted felons and judges—I put them side by side in my paper—are both excluded from the House of Commons, and I do not think it would be right for the House of Commons to be able to elect somebody who is disqualified by law. I am arguing for the tightening of the law of disqualification. There is a danger, this is the principle that lies behind it, that you elect somebody thinking that they are going to work for you or the faith they hold, and actually they are going to be selling their influence. That is, in my opinion, what has caused such terrible disillusionment among the general public which is really damaging to the democratic power. It restores you to where you were before 1832 when you may all have the vote, but the power still rests with those who have got the power to buy it.

806. PROF. ANTHONY KING: Could we talk about judges just for a moment, since you mentioned them? The thrust of most of the argument in your memorandum is that the kinds of matters we have been talking about, notably disqualification, should not be left in the hands of the House of Commons but should be transferred to the courts, and Members of Parliament should be treated by the ordinary courts. Could you explain in a little more detail why you think going down a judicial road, especially in view of your own experience that you referred to earlier, should be thought to be better than the House of Commons itself continuing to decide these matters?

TONY BENN: The House of Commons is Parliament, it is the High Court of Parliament, it is a court of law, it is protected by privileges. They always leave a big no-man's land between the powers of the House of Commons and the powers of the courts, and neither the courts nor the Commons want to move into that no-man's land. Parliament would, of course, be legislating the disqualification, and so this is simply a question, and not so very different from Parliament saying it is illegal to drive dangerously, and then the courts deal with whether you have or not. If you look back on the history of this, which I had to go into in great detail when I was expelled from the House of Commons, in the old days the election courts did not exist, the House of Commons itself voted on disqualification. That was then tackled on a party basis, it went then to a tribunal and then subsequently in 1868, as I point out, it went to an Election Court. As I understand it, when the Election Court has reached a judgment, and I think I am right about this, Sir Clifford Boulton will correct me, the judges report to the Speaker. Whether it is open at that stage for the House to reach a contrary view I am not sure—Sir Clifford shakes his head. So in effect what the judges are doing in reaching their judgment on the law is to make a mandatory report on the House and the House is then obliged to follow it because it is the law of the land and nobody is exempt from the law of the land. I am not suggesting that the Code of Conduct of Members should be administered outside, I have some doubts about that. I do say that the idea of an independent watchdog who would come along and say "You misbehaved. You cannot be a Member," I do not agree with that at all, and I have always voted against the expulsion of any Member unless they have been convicted of an offence, as, for example, John Stonehouse. I recall pressure to have him thrown out of the House of Commons because he was before the courts on some offence, and having been thrown out myself by the House I took the view that the only people entitled to throw you out, unless you were already in breach of the law, were your electors. That is why I want the electors to be informed before they vote for you exactly what your interests are, and I think that is a distinction that can reasonably be drawn.

807. PROF. ANTHONY KING: Would you not have outsiders in any way shape or form involved in interpreting and enforcing the Code of Conduct that you refer to in the memorandum?

TONY BENN: There are a lot of outsiders and they are known as the electors, and rightly or wrongly, believing very strongly in democracy, I think the electors are the best judge. I could imagine circumstances, although it would be difficult to visualise in detail, where the House condemned a Member who had not broken the law for a breach of the Code of Conduct and then instructed the Returning Officer to notify all the electors in that constituency that that Member had themselves been guilty of a breach of the Code of Conduct. That is going a bit further than the Returning Officer doing it in advance, but clearly, if a Member is censured by the House for his own conduct, and that is reported, then it will take the matter back to the only independent watchdogs I really trust, and that is the electors themselves and they have to determine whether or not they wish to re-elect that Member when the next election comes.

808. PROF. ANTHONY KING: Could I just ask two final questions about the Committee of Privileges? You refer in passing in your memorandum to the possibility of a "strengthened" Committee of Privileges. How would you like to see the Committee strengthened?

TONY BENN: The Committee of Privileges has changed its composition a bit. When I was summoned before it in 1960 the Leader of the Opposition, Mr Gaitskell, sat on the Committee of Privileges, Mr Clement Davies, who was the then Leader of the Liberal Party, sat. The Leader of the House still presides and the Attorney General is always present, but I think that the trouble with the Committee of Privileges, and I have argued this in many memoranda to them, is that it is understood by the public quite wrongly to be about the privilege of Members of Parliament, when it is really there to protect Members of Parliament from improper pressure brought upon them. I did secure one success on the Committee of Privileges where Birmingham City Council threatened somebody who had given evidence to a Select Committee about the Birmingham Road Race Bill, and I persuaded the Committee that they should rule that the Birmingham City Council, which was Labour controlled, was guilty of a breach of privilege. People think privilege is about the privilege of Member. It is not, it is about the rights of the Members to have free access to Parliament so Parliament is not improperly influenced by pressures that should not exist. I think that maybe it would be better to call it the Committee of Electors or something of that kind, because the word "privilege" is totally misunderstood although I think many Members think it is to protect them, and, if so, they are totally wrong in line with parliamentary history.

809. PROF. ANTHONY KING: My other question about the Committee concerns a matter that you have raised and been associated with for some time, and that is whether the Committee should meet in public or in private. You yourself have rehearsed the arguments that other people advanced for its meeting in private in your speech in the House of Commons in December. Could you spell out for the Committee your positive case for the Committee both hearing evidence in public and deliberating in public?

TONY BENN: May I just emphasise, first of all, I am not interested in the muck-raking aspect of it. It has never been my interest that if the result of the Committee of Privileges or this Committee, and I am sure it will not happen, were to point a finger at a few people and say, "you are the cause of the trouble", either that committee or this committee would really be failing in its function. My own opinion of the matter is that if this Committee wants public understanding for its recommendations, you would want to hear what the Committee said in the debate. I am very interested in the debates, the conclusions are less interesting than the arguments that flow into them, and I think that knowing what people were saying about Parliament is as important. For example, Mr Hansard was imprisoned on one occasion and the publication of the Parliamentary Reports was a very serious offence, and yet if we look at the House of Commons, if all we saw was the legislation but we never heard the debates, the public education about the argument would be minimal. It is that arguments, and they are very interesting arguments. I am a diarist, as you know, but I find the debates in the Committee of Privileges absolutely fascinating because they do bear on people's perception of the function of Parliament, the function of Members and so on, and similarly it would be terrible if the debates of the House were kept quiet. There

is the problem that has been raised that if individual Members are hauled up are you prejudicing their rights in law, and that matter would have to be dealt with. I am strongly in favour of open government, I always have been, and nothing has ever happened to me to persuade me that secrecy is other than a bar to the operations of the democratic system.

810. LORD NOLAN: I wonder if I can take you up again on the method of self-regulation as it is presently practised. Leave aside, of course, any idea of an outside body telling the House, or telling a Member of the House, that he has disobeyed this or that rule and must be punished accordingly, does that not leave scope for the House itself to bring in an independent element into the investigation, and perhaps the adjudication, of offenses so that it is not left simply to the possibility of personal or party considerations coming into the reckoning?

TONY BENN: Party considerations are quite legitimate, and there is nothing wrong with that, and the media are entitled to pursue their interests though I think their interests in integrity of government is more related to the circulation boost you can get from exposing scandal. I think that if the House is aware, and it is now as a result of what has recently happened, of the very wide public concern on this matter, that in the question of standards the House will have to respond as it has to to other matters. If you take a whole range of issues public concern expresses itself. I mentioned the export of live animals, I think of motorway building, I think of the future of the Post Office, Parliament is sensitive to public opinion, Poll Tax and so on. I think it better that all this comes out and Members then pick up, as they are now doing without any doubt, great anxiety about what is happening and set up the Code of Conduct, but I am not in favour of somebody coming in who is not elected, is not accountable to anybody, cannot be removed on Polling Day, saying you can and cannot do that. I am not implying you do say that, but I think it is either legal or illegal. If it is legal it is reasonable to lay down certain rules. After all in Erskine May—Sir Clifford Boulton, is a great expert on this—there is a huge volume of what you can and cannot do, and nobody says that you should bring in some outsider to decide how the House should so organise itself. This is, in a way, a development of the Erskine May view that Parliament must determine, and if you break a rule and the Speaker could name you, you can be suspended, there are all sorts of punishments the House can apply. Probably the most severe is that the Speaker does not notice you when you rise to speak. As a matter of fact I do not think much of the idea of an independent watchdog coming into Parliament. Parliament must respond, as it does on everything else, to public opinion, set out its Code of Conduct, lay down the law, and if the law is breached the courts should deal with it in the ordinary way.

811. LORD NOLAN: Leaving aside its obstinate insistence on sitting and on deliberating in private, do you think that the Committee of Privileges is a satisfactory machinery as it stands?

TONY BENN: I regarded it always as a junior Member as the most important committee in the House, and when I was put on it in 1984 I was immensely proud of the fact that I was a Member of the Committee of Privileges. I have devoted myself very fully to it, submitted memoranda on every issue that has come up, I have been in a minority of one sometimes, sometimes I have persuaded the Committee, and I find it an extremely interesting committee because it is, to some extent, free from ordinary party dispute. It is a committee that considers Parliament and its relationship with the outside world, but I must admit that in recent times when I put forward the idea that we should publish, and I did publish, and I broke the parliamentary rule in so doing and was punished as a result, I think that the publication of what happened was thoroughly healthy. Now we are back to the old business of leaks. The *Guardian* two days ago described what happened. I have written to Tony Newton, I have asked him whether he has reported that to the Committee of Privileges, what action are they going to take, because the House of Commons is lubricated by leaks and there is wild hostility, passionate hostility, to open this and that is a view that is widely shared, I believe even by one Member of your own Committee.

LORD NOLAN: I am not sure whether your answer to my question was "yes" or "no".

TONY BENN: It is a human organisation. I think it should be strengthened. I think its terms of reference should be clear, that is a point I made. It is not about privileges of Members of Parliament, it is about the protection of the parliamentary process for the benefit of the electors, and I would therefore hope that when the Committee finally reaches its decision the House will have some consideration about its future function because it would not be satisfactory to leave it on the present cosy basis—have them in quietly, have a chat, then pump out something that quietens it all down. That is no basis for dealing with matters as important as this.

LORD NOLAN: Thank you very much. I will now go round the table quickly, if I may, and ask other Members of the Committee to give their questions.

812. MARTIN JACOMB: You must forgive me if I am not so well acquainted with the procedures, but I think what you are suggesting is in paragraph 8, for instance, as has already been quoted to you by Professor King—consideration of

"disqualification... to any Member who receives money to perform a political act"

That is a political act other than one which he would pursue according to his own conscience presumably, that is what you are talking about?

TONY BENN: His conscience, his political commitment, and the interests of his constituents. I mean, there are occasions when I raise matters that I may not be entirely happy about.

813. MARTIN JACOMB: Supposing such a disqualification did apply and somebody was found to have infringed that, your view is then that that would be a case for discipline by the House of Commons, or a committee thereof, and that would presumably include the risk of expulsion?

TONY BENN: May I say two things. My argument really is is it should either be legal or illegal. If it is illegal the matter goes to the courts. If it is legal the House would handle the matter in the way in which it handles breaches of its own Rules of Order which are clearly set out in Erskine May. I must add as an addition to that that the expulsion of a Member for something that is not illegal is,

in my view, very dangerous because I am not a Member of Parliament myself, nor is any other Member, because other Members like us. If that were the case there would be no Opposition as they would be expelled by the majority. I am there because the electors currently at Chesterfield have put me there and I think it is important to protect that right because I am accountable to them. When I go to Chesterfield everyone I meet is my employer; the street sweeper, the bus driver, the ticket collector and so on, they all employ me. I am not employed by the House of Commons and that is why I have never attached my loyalty to the institution. I am there simply because I have been sent there and they can take me away and nobody else should be able to do so unless I am in breach of the law.

814. MARTIN JACOMB: Of course it would be possible to have a system under which expulsion was on the cards and that would be the best way with no bar on them standing again, and that would be the very best way of getting an immediate response from the electors before they had forgotten about it as to how serious they thought the breach was.

TONY BENN: Well, I suggested that if there was a breach it might be possible to consider—I have not gone into it in detail—the House notifying an electorate that such-and-such has happened. But once you start expulsion as an instrument then you enter into new dangers because then I think party influence might come in. Imagine circumstances where a Government had a very small majority—and I have served in some—and it was thought advantageous to expel a few Members in order to reduce the majority, or something of that kind. No, I don't think that is right. I think people have to take responsibility for what they do, answer for what they do to the House and the electorate but if it is not illegal you should continue to represent the people who sent you there. But they should know before they elect you exactly the nature of your commercial and financial interests.

MARTIN JACOMB: Yes. Thank you very much.

815. DIANA WARWICK: I wonder if I could refer you to Section D of your evidence where you indicate that the declaration of interests should include all sources from which an MP receives money. Forgive me if I have missed it in your evidence, but do you say that the amounts of money that are earned should be declared, or simply the sources from which the amounts come?

TONY BENN: Well, I have put the "sources". Of course, in some legislatures—and evidence of this kind has been submitted to the Committee of Privileges, which I had before I was removed—I think I am right in saying that in some countries candidates are required to publish their income tax returns. I have not gone as far as that—I have simply said the sources should be there—but it would be open to do whatever was thought right and candidates would then have to decide whether, given those rules, they were ready to stand or not. But sources seem to me to be the key of the matter. I am a writer and a broadcaster, for example, and it is reasonable that people should know that—I mention my other interests. And I think that it is all a question of disclosure, that is the key to the whole matter, so at least you have got some idea of what are the forces that might influence a Member in the course of their parliamentary duties.

816. DIANA WARWICK: It has been argued to us that he who pays the piper most calls the tune. You would not

accept the view, then, that for somebody who earns a large amount of money from one part of their activities would necessarily be more influenced by that and therefore if that amount were known it would make a difference?

TONY BENN: Well, it is difficult for me to say. I mean, I have tried to assert in one passage, which you may find rather political, the principle of public service—that is what I passionately believe in—and I think we live in a time where money is supposed to be the right answer to every problem and unless we challenge that idea—I mean I can imagine some very poor people who were corrupted and some very rich people who weren't, or some rich people who were and some poor people who weren't, but the important thing is that we should re-assert this principle that when you are elected to Parliament you are elected as a public servant and you should not do anything there other than out of your convictions or your duties of representation. I know it is a difficult point to put forward after many years where Mammon has been put into Canterbury Cathedral, but I think that is really what needs to be done. Even the Chaplin says we should set aside—I quoted the parliamentary prayers, I doubt if they have ever appeared before, but it says:

".. all private interests, prejudices and partial affections...."

—we pray about that every day and I am not sure that is not the proper recommendation for your committee to come out with.

817. DIANA WARWICK: Could I ask you one very specific question because you are talking later in your paper about contributions of money or people by trade unions, charities, other organisations, businesses etc. One of the points that has been made to us is if you declare an interest you should not vote or put down an EDM in Parliament. If, for example, you were a sponsored MP—as we have heard earlier there are sponsored MPs, MPs who directly are given fees—do you think such an MP, even having declared that interest, should be prevented from putting down, for example, an Early Day Motion or voting?

TONY BENN: I think you have to be careful here about the conflict between the rights of the electors. If you elect a Member of Parliament who is then hobbled and prevented from participating, it could actually have an effect on the outcome of the vote. I have never served on a local authority but I believe it has been true in the past—someone will correct me if I am wrong—that if you are a council house tenant you couldn't vote on council house rents. Now you could imagine circumstances where a majority party in a local authority were council house tenants and couldn't vote, so that they became the minority party on that question. And you see every Member has an interest in everything and we are all income tax payers, we are all defended by the armed forces, we are all dependent upon education and health, so to say that would, I think, raise difficult questions. When you elect a Member you must elect that Member with a full capacity to act, provided everybody knows and provided that the law that is laid down is absolutely clear in its exclusion of the possibility that corruption has occurred. I perhaps have not spelled it out—I would have had to write a book, I think, to answer that question in detail—but that is the principle behind my argument.

DIANA WARWICK: Thank you.

LORD NOLAN: Tom?

TOM KING: No, thank you.

LORD NOLAN: Lord Thomson?

818. LORD THOMSON: I simply have one question, Mr. Benn: in your original note to us where you gave a copy of your evidence in 1992 to the Privileges Committee, you defined the new list of disqualifications for being an MP in paragraph 13 pretty widely, directorships of companies, contracts in the Government, of course, or the public sector, or those companies created by or receiving money from the Government. In your later memorandum your phrase is "receive money for political services". I just wondered if you would define more exactly what you had in mind of the range of disqualifications you want to add to for being an MP.

TONY BENN: Well, I think it is a matter that would need—if the general principle was accepted that disqualification should be extended you have got the precedent, I think probably the best precedent is Government contractors. I am not entirely sure how that is applied—Sir Clifford would tell you how it is applied—but clearly if you are a Government contractor you are excluded. The question is if you have other relationships that might corrupt you—for example, as you all know, the absurd question of steward or bailiff of the Chiltern Hundreds excludes you from Parliament, it is the only known method of resignation and the Chancellor normally gives it to you, although I read in Erskine May that in fact that has been refused in the past.

LORD THOMSON: I have myself held that office.

TONY BENN: You have. Well, then, you will know how unsuitable you were for public service as a result. (Laughter) But I think that is the principle which needs to be explored and I am only anxious to explore an area because I listened to what Lord Nolan said earlier and have thought about it for a long time—this question of independence, what is meant by an independent watchdog, and I draw this distinction between the courts and the House and one is a matter of legality, the other is a matter of practice, and the court should be able to disqualify within the law, the House should be able to discipline within their rules but not expel. I don't know whether that makes sense but how you define it——Remember when I was speaking in the House the circumstances were not quite the same as speaking before committee and if I use slightly different words than the measured words I have used in this paper, that is the explanation for it.

LORD THOMSON: Thank you.

819. PETER SHORE: Thank you, yes. You made it quite clear that disclosure is very important but not enough and I think you tried to encapsulate your feelings about what is improper by identifying that the sale of influence, the selling of influence by MPs to outside bodies is really almost the heart of the matter. Accepting that I am still wanting to get a little bit clearer where you think the line should be drawn between the illegitimate, as it were, selling of influence and to some extent being paid by legitimate bodies to pursue legitimate causes. I know partly this comes up with the trade union question, partly with charities, as you have mentioned already. Can you

give a little clarity in your thinking about just where this frontier should lie?

TONY BENN: Well, you see, the funding of public activity seems to me to be totally legitimate and essential. I mean there is a proposal in the Labour Party, for example, at the moment, that the Government party should be funded like the opposition parties are—Mr. Short brought out his report which led to opposition parties being funded. Now, it has been the policy of the Labour Party, which at one stage I favoured and now I am opposed to, that Government party should be funded. So from the point of view of some Labour leaders you would not be dependent on the trade unions because you would have public money even when you were in Government. Now, once you do that you turn Parliament into the Civil Service and I think once you start turning Parliament into the Civil Service where it is all funded by the machine, then all sorts of dangers occur. First of all it is so much money in the public exchequer that people outside who want to raise money because they are vegetarians or because they are against motorway building, or whatever it is, they would never have a chance of putting forward a point of view because all the real work would be done from the public exchequer and I think that is a consideration you have to have in mind, and I do believe that it is quite reasonable—I have done it myself for forty-five years—to go round and say "I am a candidate, I hope you will support me, I am trying to do this for the pensioners, this is my view of comprehensive education, this is my view of the National Health Service" and if people either collectively or individually give money that doesn't seem to me to be improper. But, as I say, there were occasions when, you all know very well, my view differed from that of a Cabinet of which I was a Member and my view differed from the alleged interests of a constituent—I have cited the banning of cigarette advertising. I think the essence of it really is that in the end you have to be accountable for what you did and the motives that led you to do what you did have to be open. I have made a lot of mistakes in my life but I hope I haven't made mistakes because I have been improperly influenced—I have just been wrong—and being wrong is one of the privileges of public life and, indeed, is widely practised! (Laughter)

820. CLIFFORD BOULTON: I just want to explore a little this distinction between the sponsored Member and others in that he is going to be sponsored by a union which represents a good cause or a cause which is on a public matter and brings with him a dowry—this sponsored Member—of finance for the local party. Because those are the situations, no money goes into his own pocket and with the nature of the interest you are inviting us, as other witnesses have done, to take a different view of that to other forms of financial sponsorship. I simply wanted to say, what if a candidate seeking to be adopted by some other party went along and said "You may care to know I am sponsored by a large trade association or the Tobacco Manufacturers' Association (if there is such a thing), and you might care to know that they are going to be willing to contribute 80 per cent of my election expenses and give you £750 a year thereafter". Now, that is his dowry as a potential candidate. Is that all right or is there some difference between——

TONY BENN: Well, at my first election conference in 1950 I was asked "If you are selected as the candidate what money will you give to the constituency?" and I said "None, and if I had any I wouldn't tell you now"—and I added, if Tom King will forgive me, "this is not a Conservative Selection Conference" But I think there is a distinction between an organisation and a company. For example, as Minister of Technology I worked very closely with the Society of Motor Manufacturers. For example, one of the things—maybe Peter Shore will remember this—they wanted the code on a car changed to a slightly different date because it helped them to get their flush of autumn sales. Nobody suggested to me that I should be paid for that and I was trying to represent the British Motor Industry which I have tried to represent because it is a national interest. But I think there is a distinction between a trade association on the one hand and a trade union and a commercial company where people actually make money out of it. Therefore I would see no particular difficulty if there is disclosure and somebody coming along and saying "I represent..."—I don't know what it might be, "the British Medical Association", or "I represent things that are not trade union"—don't think I am simply talking about trade unions. But I must also say this, and this is where the first part of my paper is relevant, the country was run for so long by rich people that it was only by collective action by people who were not rich that you ever got any shift in the balance of power, and that is why I am a supporter of the trade union movement, why I am a supporter of the Labour Party and why I am a Socialist; because I believe collective action was the only way that poor people could have any influence over the country which had been run by the rich for years. And if the rich could now get back and buy influence through Ministers or Members of Parliament of any party, then you have actually by-passed the struggle for the franchise by the chartists and the suffragettes. But I would draw a very clear distinction between a collective—even on the side of industry, if you know what I mean—I think the CBI is perfectly entitled, if it so wishes (I don't think it does any more than the TUC, of course it is not affiliated to the Labour Party) but I think so long as it is open and everybody knows "Well, he is being supported by the Motor Manufacturers". If he is a Member for Coventry that might seem quite a sensible thing to do.

CLIFFORD BOULTON: That is very helpful, thank you.

821. ANNE WARBURTON: Mr. Benn, as you well know, we are here quite largely because of the public view—the perception the public have—of what happens in Parliament. I was a little surprised in your paper that this did not seem to be a major consideration that you took into account and particularly about the code of conduct, the code of conduct which you would like to be statutory, that you thought it would be suitable entirely that any breach of the code should be investigated and dealt with by the House itself, perhaps in the Committee of Privileges. It is something which I think the Chairman has already talked to you about, but I would just like to come back to the question of whether a purely "in House" (with a capital H) enquiry and action in your view would actually meet the public perception point. I think at present the public perhaps has some questions in its mind about how effective "in House" committees are proving themselves.

TONY BENN: Well, may I say this about the public perception—you see my whole argument is that this is a problem with the system. Nobody has known about it, nobody has commented on it, but it is the system that is wrong and the so-called scandal (if that is the way to describe it) of recent cases has drawn attention to the system. What we should be looking at is the system. So far from taking a light view of this I take, in my first and second pages, a very very serious view of this. I think this is a real weakness of a system and the House has had some responsibility for setting such low standards, and therefore the House should raise the standard. But I did differentiate—and I hope I carry you with me in differentiating—between what Parliament, which is responsible to the public, rules to be illegal and what they regard to be improper. There are many things done in the House which may be held to be improper and the House has its own mechanism for dealing with interrupting, shouting from a seated position, and so on and so on. Indeed, two Members in my lifetime have tried to help to carry the Mace and that is not considered a proper thing to do, but I wouldn't expel them from the House for that. So I hope my paper doesn't imply that I don't take this seriously—I take it extremely seriously. I think the whole democratic process is being undermined and public attention to it is being drawn because some individual publicised incidents that have occurred. What is really wrong is much much deeper. Even in the Civil Service, which you all know very well, it is not unknown for a civil servant to recommend an industrialist for a knighthood and then for that civil servant to end up on the Board of the company. Even I have been a beneficiary, quite by accident, of a thing not involving money—I got an Hon. Doctorate from a university and then I discovered that the Vice-Chancellor had got a knighthood. Now, whether there was a relationship between my Hon. Doctorate and his knighthood I never knew, but it gave me an insight at the time into the inter-relationship between quite innocent influence and what could flow from it. If a civil servant thought "If I am rather helpful to that person then I might be a beneficiary"—if they think that then that is something that goes right into the period, while they are Ministers——

LORD NOLAN: Mr. Benn, it is fascinating, but I can't help feeling that you are straying from Dame Anne's question.

TONY BENN: I am sorry if I am—that is not uncommon, I am afraid, in my case! (Laughter)

LORD NOLAN: Would you like to put it again, Dame Anne?

ANNE WARBURTON: No, I think I will leave it there.

LORD NOLAN: We are very grateful to you for, if I may say so, not only a very interesting but an enjoyable period with you. Thank you very much for coming along.

TONY BENN: I have permission, I believe, to make available the paper I have written. I rang on Monday.

LORD NOLAN: We would be very glad if you would.

TONY BENN: Yes. I didn't want to get into trouble with this committee as well. (Laughter)

822. LORD NOLAN: Good afternoon, Mr. Luff. Please sit down. I must apologise for the fact that, as I fear has happened in each of the last four days, the last witness has come to his chair some time later than he was warned and I don't know whether it would greatly inconvenience you if we went on a little beyond 1 o'clock as we have had to do?

PETER LUFF MP

PETER LUFF MP: Absolutely not.

823. LORD NOLAN: It is very good of you to come and be with us. Have you an opening statement which you would like to make?

PETER LUFF: If I may, sir, yes. I can short-cut it in part because I am a Member of the Institute of Public Relations and have been for many years. I would like to associate myself with almost all their evidence except the questions of remuneration and independent regulation where strangely I find myself in agreement with Tony Benn. I believe that Members of Parliament should have links with the outside world and that is what my evidence is predicated upon and I believe those links are equally valid whether they are commercial or with trade unions. I believe that both these relationships bring benefits both to the House and for the individual Member. Public relations—a much misunderstood trade, as I think the Institute itself suggested during their evidence—I believe is a valid way of doing that—and I think the fact that the Institute is now seeking chartered status shows the growing maturity of that trade.

I do think the distinction between advocacy and advice is important. There are practical problems, though, in drawing the line between these two points and I think they may be particularly acute for trade union sponsored Members of Parliament. The consultancy of a commercial nature, of which I myself am a practitioner, as my evidence to you makes clear, is largely about taking advice outwards from the House of Commons to commercial interests, seeking to bridge the gulf of misunderstanding that exists between business and Government. It is not about influence. I feel that any rules that this committee seeks to recommend on this question about the distinction between advice and advocacy must apply with equal force to trade union sponsored Members of Parliament. this is because I do believe that trade union sponsorship confers personal benefit just in the same way as remuneration from a commercial interest does. The knowledge that your election expenses are going to be paid is a huge relief. I go into an election campaign completely uncertain as to whether or not I will be able to raise the money to pay for that campaign. A bad campaign in a marginal seat certainly would result in the loss of the seat. So, in fact a trade union sponsored Member of Parliament has an enormous advantage and an enormous debt to the trade union. I think the support that is given on a continuing basis to local parties is also an important personal benefit to the Member of Parliament—an effectively-run local party machine is of great value—and the provision of researches to Members of Parliament is also of enormous personal value to the MP.

I also believe that trade union sponsorship does influence behaviour. I have cited evidence on that in my written memorandum to you concerning the National Union of Railwaymen's evidence to the Select Committee in 1988. I have quoted from the current document from UNISON which seeks to persuade the trade union Members to vote for the political fund—a voice in Parliament—both political sections support MPs in Parliament who take up issues on behalf of UNISON members and campaign for changes to legislation. So it is clear that Members are expected to behave in a certain way as a result of that sponsorship.

I have also got here an academic study on the influences on Members of Parliament published by David Judge from the University of Strathclyde in which he makes clear that non-sponsored Labour MPs are more likely to involve themselves with the wider connections between industrial policy and economic and trading policies whereas sponsored Members from industrial unions concern themselves more with specific aspects of Government assistance for particular industrial sectors, industrial safety and health matters and, not surprisingly, trade union matters. He also describes the passage of the 1984 Trade Union Bill, a debate from which on the Labour side was dominated almost exclusively by sponsored Members of Parliament.

It is also clear that the trade unions do expect their Members of Parliament to earn that sponsorship. In evidence to the Select Committee on Members' Interests in 1991 the TGWU said if they did not respond to that influence and I quote Mr. Reagan Scott——

"If they are not then there are procedures for that relationship to be terminated by either party or mutually".

But having said that I do believe the public concerns that exist about commercial relations between Members of Parliament and the outside world are entirely proper and need to be addressed. I believe they can be addressed by a series of important and overdue changes to the Register of Members' Interests, not by necessarily bans and constraints on what a Member of Parliament himself or herself does, nor by independent regulation which I believe would be a major innovation of a constitutional nature which I think would be regrettable. But we do need more clarity, more openness and more accountability for Members of Parliament's actions in the House. That would make us better subjects, I believe, to the only important independent regulator that exists, our constituents.

LORD NOLAN: Thank you very much. I am going to ask Dame Anne Warburton to take up the questions.

824. ANNE WARBURTON: If we can move, Mr. Luff, from the question of trade unions to the question of lobbying and so forth, I wonder whether I might first of all put to you—you are, I think, unique in the witnesses we have had in yourself being a consultant.

PETER LUFF: I think in terms of the witnesses—there are a number of my other colleagues in the House who have been public relations practitioners before coming to the House but I think I am the only one who is giving evidence to you, yes.

825. ANNE WARBURTON: Right. You were that before the election and, indeed, your background is very much in that, and I really wanted to ask your views on how far that role has been in any way constricting or confining to you in the House?

PETER LUFF: I am very fastidious about not acting as an advocate for my clients—I do believe that is an important point. I think it is perfectly proper to give advice but I am very nervous indeed about actually standing up and advocating their calls robustly or improperly. I don't think it really has been a constraint. The clients I represent actually don't have a constituency base—it is one of the values which is addressed, I think, implicitly in your own document, Issues and Questions,

that you have produced before this committee, that those organisations which lack a constituency base can often not have an effective voice in Parliament. So I would actually argue it has not been a constraint on my action but actually has helped me in my Parliamentary duties by understanding issues I might not otherwise have been exposed to.

826. ANNE WARBURTON: Do you think it has had any reaction, not perhaps you as an MP but perhaps before when you were working with Ministers, other Ministers, would it have had any effect on your acceptability as a confidant, perhaps, from other business people—people representing other interests?

PETER LUFF: You are talking as a Member of Parliament?

ANNE WARBURTON: I was really talking about previous to your Membership of Parliament, but it could, I think, also apply in Parliament itself.

PETER LUFF: I don't think so. I am certainly not aware of any circumstances in which that has been the case. I am not aware of it, no.

827. ANNE WARBURTON: You are not aware of any reserve in your position—your stated position—it may have introduced?

PETER LUFF: No, I am not aware of it.

828. ANNE WARBURTON: Your distinction between advice and advocacy is one which has come to us from many sides. I am left wondering at this stage how monitorable this is. Self-regulation is a bit out of favour at present. How do you see that?

PETER LUFF: It is very difficult to draw the line. I think, as Tony Benn was suggesting in his evidence just now, one issue on which I advise I am also under some constituency pressure on from one or two individuals who take a close interest. I wouldn't want to be prevented from taking up their concerns because I also have a commercial relationship with a large organisation that is interested in the same set of issues. I faced this in the House of Commons last week and actually chose to raise the issue because I knew it was a matter of concern to somebody who had written to me only the previous week. I raised the issue, not because I was retained by the interest that was concerned about this particular matter, but because I had constituents who were concerned about it. So there is a very difficult line to draw between advice and advocacy which in practice is quite tricky.

829. ANNE WARBURTON: Yes, it may not be enough just to leave it as being tricky. When I used the word "monitoring" I was actually not thinking of one's own dilemma so much as how can the world at large know?

PETER LUFF: Yes. I think there are a number of important changes we do need to make. I think the whole question of Parliamentary questions, for example, is unsatisfactory at present. It is not clear when you ask a question at present in the House of Commons, whether it is written or oral, whether you have an interest to declare. I believe I am right in saying that the Commons Procedure Committee in the past has ruled out the declaration of interest during oral questions. I think it would be perfectly easy to find a form of words that would meet that objection and so when a Member of Parliament had an interest or whatever kind, whether it was commercial or sponsorship or personal he or she could just say "The House will be aware I have in interest to declare", the Members interested could then consult the register. It is that increased openness and accountability which I think is possible by a series of useful practical changes which the House could and should make.

830. ANNE WARBURTON: But when it comes to the Register of Members' Interests you are perhaps a little more restrictive than some witnesses have been in your view of what changes should be introduced. I think you say that you don't think that time spent should be listed and I must say there I wholly agree with you because I think it is terribly difficult to estimate the time spent, apart from anything else, and also you don't think that the amount paid should be listable?

PETER LUFF: This is a difficult issue. I have reached the view it is not proper to declare it. I think what Tony Benn was saying about sources of income being absolutely crucial. I think whether you are paid £5, £50, £500 or £5,000, the fact is money has changed hands and that is what your constituents need to know about. I think also there are a series of practical difficulties, which I go into in my paper, about Members of Parliament who are involved in commercial activities for which a straight contractual relationship does not apply—businesses from which dividends may be received at the end of the year. I think also there are important points about the general privacy that Members of Parliament enjoy—we don't enjoy protection from privacy law. I think a lot of this would interest the public a great deal but I am not clear that it is in the public interest to declare any more than the fact that there is cash or other remuneration changing hands. I think it is crucial that is in the public domain. I am not certain what benefit is obtained from making it more detailed than that.

831. ANNE WARBURTON: There are some people, of course, who think that it does tell you things. Would you be particularly opposed if something along the lines of banding income were used?

PETER LUFF: No, I wouldn't. I think that is one possibility that the committee might well wish to look at. That may be a route through. Though I do repeat I think it is a bit strange that those of us who have to rely on earned income to finance our lives would have to declare everything but those who have the great fortune to have large sources of unearned income would not have to make such a declaration, and I think that might be an unfortunate consequence of declaring remuneration.

832. ANNE WARBURTON: Looking particularly at your paper which you very kindly prepared for us, one comment that you made was that

"MPs should not be allowed to hold consultancies which arise entirely out of their Parliamentary position."

I was struck by that phraseology because on the whole people have been saying to us things which rather contradict that. It is entirely out of Parliamentary position.

PETER LUFF: It is this wretched word "consultancy". It is a much abused word. In the new Register of Members' Interests I will be changing that word to "adviser" in my own entry because I think it clarifies what I actually do. Consultancy has become a word which I think is seen now, wrongly probably, to imply other activity. So let me change that "should not be allowed to hold advisory positions which arise out of the Parliamentary position". In other words it is perfectly proper, I think, for an organisation which—and we must not forget the degree of ignorance that still exists in many commercial organisations about Government and Parliament. I mean, I remember as a Parliamentary Consultant before going to the House a number of occasions on which a major organisation could be panicked by Early Day Motion. I had to explain to them that Early Day Motions were, in effect, little more than parliamentary graffiti these days which had very little practical impact on the workings of Parliament. They were excuses for Press releases more than anything else. That degree of incomprehension is real and I think Members of Parliament are in a very good position with authority to explain to companies that they need not over-react to that kind of Parliamentary development.

833. ANNE WARBURTON: There is another statement in your paper, page 5 which I think needs perhaps a little bit of clarification. You say that you yourself have tabled questions, made speeches etc. "though never at the request of a client, but only because I believed in the argument." That may be a distinction you can make in your heart but the auditors cannot be so clear and yet you go on to say "this activity may need to be more carefully controlled".

PETER LUFF: Well, this is a question of judgment. I mean, my personal judgment is that a full declaration of the interest you hold is sufficient for people to judge the merits of the argument they are putting forward. If it is clear that you believe in the argument that is intellectually rigorous and supportable I think the House listens with interest and respect. If it would seem to be a case of a special pleading coming simply out of your own commercial involvement it would not listen with respect and I think one must be wary—for the reasons your previous witness was setting out—about placing too many restraints on Members of Parliament. If that was felt necessary it would pose no great personal problem for me and certainly I do seek to avoid putting myself in that position. But I would be very reluctant to see constraints in that. I think greater openness in the Register, more ability to declare, particularly questions, where I think there is the possibility of real concern about the relationship of the Member with the question asked, would actually address the concern and I would like to see that form of declaration for interests when questions are asked.

834. ANNE WARBURTON: I think that again others have suggested to us. As a last question I would rather like to put something which is perhaps a little personal and it also depends on how accurately the *Independent* is as a source of information. I know that you are a consultant to Lowe Bell and I believe that they are currently advising Northern Electric—if it is not to be taken over by Trafalgar House. If that is correct—and as I believe you are also PPS to the Minister of Energy, is there any question of——

PETER LUFF: I have written to Jeremy Warner, the Business Editor of the *Independent* to make clear that the only client I advise of Lowe Bell is the Chamber of

Shipping—and that is the only client I advise—I have clarified that to him. I have also clarified the position with the Department as well and they are aware of that. There was an exchange of correspondence which I will very happily let the committee see.

ANNE WARBURTON: That has clarified that. Thank you very much.

LORD NOLAN: Sir Clifford?

835. CLIFFORD BOULTON: Can I just ask you of the personal impression you formed when you came into Parliament? We have no idea, of course, of the amount of money that is available for consultancies and advisorships and other similar forms of arrangement, but we can get an idea of the number of them that are available from the Register. Were you surprised at all by the amount of it you found around and the amount of advisorships on offer to Members when you came into the House?

PETER LUFF: I can say to you, Sir Clifford, first of all that I have been offered no new consultancy since coming into the House. All my arrangements pre-date my membership of the House. That is one point I wish to clarify. Obviously I was involved in the world for ten years before I joined the House so, no, it came as no surprise to me. I also know, of course, that whenever a Member of Parliament is made a Minister and has to resign his consultancy arrangements outside consultants like to make pitches to the businesses that used to retain the Member of Parliament because effectively they are in competition with the Members of Parliament. But, no, I was not surprised at the level of it—I was well aware of it.

836. CLIFFORD BOULTON: They seem to be very readily taken up by Members—a lot of Members do it. Have you ever felt any anxiety that some of them do it because the fee is really helpful to them?

PETER LUFF: Yes, I do. Most—I think a very large number, I must not be too ambitious in my claim—a very large number of Members of Parliament, probably particularly in the Conservative side—take significant pay cuts to become Members of Parliament. It was certainly true in my case, it is true in a large number of my colleagues' cases and I think it is a material consideration, that there is that——I think public service should involve an element of sacrifice. I think the public concern that Members of Parliament are in it for what they can get is misplaced but it is a legitimate concern for the public to hold—there should be sacrifice involved. But those consultancies often do play an important part but they also bring other benefits to the House as well, a more detailed understanding of an industry or organisation that the House wouldn't necessarily have access to.

837. CLIFFORD BOULTON: So if somebody says to his spouse "I am thinking of going into Parliament, it is only £32,000 a year, but don't worry, there are consultancies available"—we have got to a situation where in the back of somebody's mind there is this knowledge that there are these things available.

PETER LUFF: I think the important point is not so much the consultancies as the ability to continue your previous trade or profession, although I would also defend consultancies robustly. In my case I am continuing my previous trade or profession. The people I advise I have advised for five or six years—for longer than I have been a Member of Parliament—but I would defend the existence of consultancies certainly. I think they do bring real benefits to the House as well as to the Member concerned.

838. CLIFFORD BOULTON: Yes, but you would perhaps agree that it would be unfortunate if they became part of almost the understood way that Parliament is run, that there is always some money on the side?

PETER LUFF: Oh, there isn't. I mean for many people they are never offered any of these arrangements. As I have made clear already in the three years I have been a Member of Parliament I have been offered none—my arrangements all pre-date my membership of the House. I don't think there are quite as many available as people might like to believe. I would also make the point that many people who—and this is perhaps arguing against my own interests—many people who seek to employ a Member of Parliament to advise them on Government work are often misplaced and misguided because Members of Parliament can have an excessive focus on parliamentary activity, which is an important, but only one part, of the constitutional process by which legislation is changed, by which contracts are awarded, by which the public is influenced. And quite often those Members of Parliament who are retained by outside interests may actually be giving unhelpful advice to the organisation because it has centred too much on Parliament.

839. CLIFFORD BOULTON: The reason I was asking you the questions was that I am wondering whether it would not be a reassurance to the public if we did think along the lines of registering the amount that was being obtained so that there could be some comprehension of how much of it there is about.

PETER LUFF: Yes. And I think you would also probably need to declare the Member's previous income before he joined the House and what he expects to earn when he leaves the House—that would put it in the right context. In my own constituency—I mean it is quite clear my salary is regarded as being large—it is well above the average male wage in my constituency, well above it—but the fact is I have moved from a much higher salary to take a lower salary to go to the House and that kind of issue, I think, does need to be taken into account in the way the committee considers the declaration of remuneration.

840. CLIFFORD BOULTON: It was more being able to get a view of whether the fee was in proportion to the service that was expected.

PETER LUFF: Yes.

841. PROF. ANTHONY KING: I must say that I am very taken with the idea of registering pre-entry into the House income and comparing it with post because we would then be able to trade off—the trade-off that MPs make between power and money. It would be nice to be able to do that. Can I just press you a little bit on the question of remuneration? What you said initially in response to Dame Anne reminded me of a story of the unusually honest American federal land agent who, in the nineteenth century, cabled the then President of the United States "Relieve me of my post, they are getting near my price" and I do find the notion that it does not make any difference whether you are receiving £5, £500 or

£5,000 intrinsically implausible. I don't know what my price is but I would have thought that an awful lot of Members of Parliament could not possibly be influenced for £5 but might well be hugely influenced by some multiple of that. You do not really believe that the amount is totally irrelevant, do you?

PETER LUFF: I accept that there is a level at which it becomes inconsequential—I don't accept a Member of Parliament can be bought for a lunch or a dinner, for example, I think that is clear. In fact I would give a lot not to have to have so many lunches and dinners as I currently have to go through. So I accept that there is a level at which it is totally inconsequential. But I think that if a cheque is written out, if money is transferred to a bank account, then that is the important question. I think that is really how I would see this. If a Member of the House of Commons has received money for doing something he or she would not otherwise have done, I think that is the important question. Not so much how many noughts are on the cheque.

842. PROF. ANTHONY KING: You object in your paper, and I can see why, to revealing all sources of income. Could one—and this has been suggested already—make a reasonably clear distinction between those sources of income that relate directly to the Member's performance of his parliamentary functions and those that do not, with a requirement that remuneration be listed in connection with the former but not the latter?

PETER LUFF: I am not sure—it is an interesting question. I was thinking about the problem of the gentleman with large land and estates who had an income from farming or other activities on those estates. Would that be declarable or not?

PROF. ANTHONY KING: On my hypothesis, not.

PETER LUFF: Not. Well, you see, I would argue that it may well be because the way the Common Agricultural Policy develops and the way agriculture policy develops would have a very direct impact on the level of income from those estates. I think it is not quite as straightforward and clear where you draw the line, if that were to be the line you wish to draw.

PROF. ANTHONY KING: It might be a difficult line to draw but one might still be able to draw it. I mean, one spends one's entire life drawing lines and——

PETER LUFF: Yes.

843. PROF. ANTHONY KING: Could I just ask you, again following something Dame Anne asked you about—and let us take the specific case and I do not want to press you further than you are prepared to be pressed—your relationship with the Chamber of Shipping, just as an example. What do you do for the Chamber of Shipping?

PETER LUFF: I advise them. I go to meetings about once a fortnight, lasting about an hour and a half, and I tell them what I think the mood is in the House and I tell them who I think it is important that they make sure their case is made to. That is the essence of the relationship.

844. PROF. ANTHONY KING: Do you ever facilitate connections between the Chamber of Shipping and, say, the Minister of Transport or whoever?

PETER LUFF: No, I do not. If a case has intrinsic merit an organisation will be able to get that kind of access. If it does not have intrinsic merit it probably won't, whatever a Member of Parliament seeks to do. And there are lobbying organisations around who claim to be able to gain access that wouldn't otherwise be gained. I am very sceptical of those claims. In my ten years in the private sector before I went to the House I took the same policy—we advised the clients on how to present their case, to whom they should be speaking and we made sure their case was presented effectively, as it needs to be. Businessmen are often very bad about being sensitive to what politicians are actually interested in. We might rehearse them before a meeting with a Minister to make sure they put the case well with the Minister. But as a private sector lobbyist I would never have gone into a meeting with a Minister, or sought to arrange a meeting with a Minister—there should be no need to do that. The case should have its own merit.

845. PROF. ANTHONY KING: But as a Member of Parliament who is also a consultant might you do that?

PETER LUFF: No, I wouldn't. I actually don't think it would be proper. I would be very uncomfortable about doing it and I have never been asked to do it. I note—actually I was talking to a number of colleagues. I believe some organisations now do put in their contracts the kind of things that were being talked about before about not asking questions, not arranging meetings, not using influence. I think that is a very sensible arrangement and it is not one I had been aware of before this week. I think the idea of actually stipulating that a Member of Parliament may not use his or her influence. But I actually think it is very difficult in practice to use——I think a Member of Parliament who claims that is largely claiming—if he did, I am not aware of it—but certainly lobbyists claim it and I think they are behaving largely fraudulently when they do because Ministers are busy people. Issues actually generally speak, I believe, for themselves.

846. PROF. ANTHONY KING: Going on from what you have just said, do you think this committee should recommend that Members of Parliament who are paid by outside organisations should be barred compulsorily from doing what you say you do voluntarily, namely using their positions to facilitate access to Ministers and so on?

PETER LUFF: I have a great deal of sympathy with that argument. There is another argument on the contrary side I put, which is I do understand that a number of Ministers find that businessmen are so bad at putting their cases to them they find it helpful if a colleague comes along and helps the discussion, to make sure the businessmen actually keep on the right line of argument. But I think there is a strong case for the remedy that you are suggesting.

847. PETER SHORE: Yes. Well you have made a great play of the distinction between advocacy and advice in paid relationships with outside firms. You have acknowledged, too, the very considerable practical difficulties in applying or drawing the line between one activity which is okay and the other which is not. Now let me put a point to you which arises out of your own position: is not this dilemma, the difference between drawing a line between advocacy and advice, at its most acute in the case of a PPS? A PPS by definition has a

relationship with a Minister of a virtually unique kind. Apart from the Private Office the PPS is the person with whom the Minister will have the most frequent contact, and as a Minister's diary is generally a very busy one indeed, the PPS has a very considerable opportunity to influence the Minister. Now, if you were—I am not pursuing your personal thing, by the by—but if you were an adviser to an outside firm and you were also the PPS to a Minister, would you not find it very difficult in your dealings with the Minister to draw a line between not advocating things and just simply acting as previously, as an adviser? Would it not overlap in your relationship with the Minister?

PETER LUFF: No, in practice I don't think that is the case. Parliamentary Private Secretaries are not Members of the Government, they don't generally see confidential documents, policy papers and so on. I see the role of the PPS in the classic old-fashioned style which is actually acting as the bridge between the Minister and the House of Commons, as the problem solver for Ministers leading busy lives in the Departments, out of touch with what is going on at the Commons—the practical thing is organised and then he would feed back from the House. That is how I interpret my roles—there is no practical difficulty as far as I am concerned.

848. PETER SHORE: Well, if you were made PPS to the Minister who is responsible for shipping and you still had your consultancy with the Chamber of Shipping, would you not find that an intolerable——would it not be thought to be in terms of public perception——

PETER LUFF: It would be a perceived difficulty and for that reason I think I would suggest that it was not appropriate. I do not think in practice it would be a difficulty. I think the perception might be there and therefore I think I would suggest that it was not an appropriate appointment to make. But we are talking about perception rather than reality there.

849. PETER SHORE: I think we might be talking about both and, of course, the access that PPSs do have to Ministers' information varies from Minister to Minister and PPSs are normally regarded as part of the payroll vote.

PETER LUFF: They are part of the payroll vote but they get paid nothing for it and they are not Members of the Government.

PETER SHORE: Thank you.

850. TOM KING: You said you did four hours a week on this consultancy. How many hours do you reckon you actually work a week?

PETER LUFF: It is a very interesting question as to what constitutes work for a Member of Parliament. But, I mean, certainly I regard myself as on duty between the hours of eight o'clock in the morning and midnight, so multiply that by four, plus Fridays, Saturdays and Sundays with variable hours, it is probably seventy or eighty hours, something like that.

851. TOM KING: And actually on the point about PPS—this is to draw you on, because I agreed actually very much with the point that Peter Shore made—actually you would not be offered that job, nor could you take it

—I mean a transport job which involved shipping. My own experience—and you may like to comment on this—is that actually no sensible Minister would invite you if you continued to have that connection because it is quite true that Ministers have different relationships with PPSs and its the perception that counts. Are you aware of any PPS at the present time who holds any manifestly conflicting or unsuitable. In other words, am I wrong, am I out of date——

PETER LUFF: I am aware of no such conflict and I have made it perfectly clear, also, to the consultancy I am involved with that it would be inappropriate for me to seek to advise any client where there was even a suggestion of an overlap.

852. TOM KING: And if by some frightful mischance you were not successful in being re-elected as MP for Worcester you would want to go on or back to the profession in which you have earned your living?

PETER LUFF: This is the only trade I have got. Again I think it is a terribly important point. I do not want a political world in which politicians are all full-time professionals desperately clinging to their power, I want a world in which politicians can come more easily in and out of other professions and trades from the trade union movement, from the shop floor, from board rooms, and if we seek to inhibit or frustrate the professions that Members of Parliament can follow, then I think that will make it much more difficult to attract the pool of talent of able and qualified people that we need in political life in this country.

853. TOM KING: So the situation would be that unless you took on Ministerial office, in which case obviously you would have to discontinue those activities, if you were a backbencher you would see it as a major handicap from your own family point of view—your family and everybody—if the condition had been that if you stand for Parliament not only have you got to say "I am going to take a cut in salary but I am going to actually agree that I may not any longer pursue the profession which is the only profession I know and in which I have earned my living"? Is that right?

PETER LUFF: That is absolutely right. It would jeopardise my long-term career as well.

TOM KING: Right, thank you.

854. DIANA WARWICK: I wonder if I could take you back to one of the first points you made about the influence——we were talking about trade union sponsorship and you talked of the relief that was given to an MP knowing that election expenses were being paid. I wonder, given the point that was made by the MP who accompanied the trade union representatives when she said that all financial contributions to local political parties and particularly for election expenses should be recorded, whether you feel that, for example, donations from a local company to your election expenses should be registered?

PETER LUFF: Very interesting question. You see, I am totally ignorant about who gave what to my election campaign last time around and I actually prefer it that way—I prefer not to know. I understand it was a majority of donations of £5 and £10 from ordinary members, but it may not have been, there may be a cheque there from a local employer which I am not aware of. I would actually rather not know about that but if this committee took the view that those things should be declared well then that is an interesting question. But I would actually prefer to live in ignorance of the source of that income because I think that removes a potential influence from me.

855. DIANA WARWICK: This may be true in your particular case but if there is a donation by a company would you regard it in the same way as a donation by a trade union?

PETER LUFF: Well of course any donation by a company does need to be recorded in its report and accounts—at least a reasonably large company would need to record that donation—but I don't really feel qualified to talk about the issue of party funding. I am afraid, that is an issue on which I don't claim any expertise and I think we are getting to waters which I am less familiar with.

856. DIANA WARWICK: It is only that you inferred in your comments that there was likely to be undue pressure, that was the impression I got.

PETER LUFF: Well, I think I said in my evidence to this committee—I can't remember the final version—that if I was aware of a large donation from any entity there would be some kind of responsibility resting on my shoulders, some kind of a sense of gratitude which would be bound to influence my thinking. I agree with that.

857. DIANA WARWICK: That seems to sit rather uneasily with your comment or your response that you do not think the size of a donation or the size of a contribution or the size of a payment would affect an MP's views.

PETER LUFF: Yes. I think it would be a source of pressure from the constituency association, or the constituency Labour Party on top of one's own personal views, that is the issue. Most political organisations in this country live from hand to mouth and I think there would be a certain pressure from the Constituency Labour Party, or the Conservative Association, in those circumstances.

858. MARTIN JACOMB: Could I ask you just one thing to clarify the point has actually come up in several

of your answers, or several of the questions and your answers, and it is the connection between the dividing line between advocacy and advice on the one hand and not declaring the amount paid for parliamentary work on the other. You say that dividing line is very difficult to draw between advocacy and advice, but it is a key dividing line. How do you square that with the question which Diana Warwick was really leading up to, I think? Supposing the market price—I have no idea what it is—but supposing the market price for advice is £10,000 a year, but you find an MP who is in receipt of £50,000 a year, which is then a substantial part of his income, and the loss of that would be a blow. How do you square that, the non-declaration of that amount, with the difficulty of drawing the dividing line between what is proper and what is not?

PETER LUFF: Well, if the Member of Parliament is not acting as an advocate in practice, not asking questions and is declaring his interest whenever it is appropriate to do so, I don't think there is a great difficulty there. I would be very surprised if you did find anyone with that level of income, I have to say. I think £50,000 would be a very large figure.

859. MARTIN JACOMB: Well, the figure is quite hypothetical—my figures are quite hypothetical—but you see the point?

PETER LUFF: Yes, I accept there is a point there but I think equally well—we were hearing from Prof. King about the man with the large estates. I mean, the incomes could be much much larger and his concern of Agricultural policy could be much much greater. I refer you to my evidence on remuneration. I have set out the concerns I have. I think it is practically difficult because for some natures of business activity by Members of Parliament there won't be the level of the earnings until the accounts have been finalised. It would be some time after the end of the year. It is very difficult to put like with like. I make the point about privacy, but I can accept that the question of banding may be a solution to this—maybe some level of declaration would reassure people. I think people would actually be surprised about the relatively low levels for most people in practice.

MARTIN JACOMB: Thank you very much.

LORD NOLAN: Well, Mr. Luff, I think as a result of your written and spoken evidence today you have given us a very clear picture of your views. We are extremely grateful to you for coming along. Thank you.

TUESDAY 31 JANUARY 1995

Members Present:

The Rt. Hon. The Lord Nolan (Chairman)

Sir Clifford Boulton GCB
Sir Martin Jacomb
The Rt. Hon. Tom King CH MP
The Rt. Hon. Peter Shore MP

The Rt. Hon. The Lord Thomson of Monifieth KT DL
Sir William Utting CB
Dame Anne Warburton DCVO CMG
Diana Warwick

Witnesses:

Rt. Hon. Tony Newton MP, Leader of the House and Lord President of the Council
Rt. Hon. Sir Terence Higgins MP
Adam Raphael, *The Economist*
Sir Peter Kemp, former Second Permanent Secretary, Cabinet Office

860. LORD NOLAN: Today we begin our third week of oral evidence.

Our first witnesses today will be dealing with MPs' financial interests. Later, however, we shall broaden our questioning to cover the rules for the conduct of Ministers and civil servants.

That will be the main subject of our questioning for much of the next two weeks, but there will be some overlap as we have always anticipated. Some witnesses will be able to comment both on that issue and on Quangos. There will still be a few witnesses commenting principally on MP's interests, and, no doubt some will want to comment on all three of these issues.

Today we shall be hearing from Sir Terence Higgins MP, a senior backbencher with wide experience; from Adam Raphael of *The Economist*, and from Sir Peter Kemp, formerly the senior civil servant responsible for managing organisational change in the civil service, and now a member of the Audit Commission.

But first, can I welcome the Rt. Hon. Tony Newton MP, Lord President of the Council, and Leader of the House of Commons. I need to make two points clear. First, Mr Newton appears in his capacity as Leader of the House, and we shall be questioning him about MPs' interests. We shall be talking next week to David Hunt about Ministers and Quangos. Second, we recognise that, as Leader of the House, Mr Newton cannot in any way commit himself to particular positions at this stage. We shall understand that any views that he gives will be his personal views and do not commit either the Government or the House to any particular course of action.

Mr Newton, I hope that is the right statement of your position?

RT HON TONY NEWTON MP

RT HON TONY NEWTON MP, Leader of the House and Lord President of the Council: Indeed I am grateful to you, Lord Nolan. The only thing I would add which complements what you have said is that although I am a Minister I am not speaking on behalf of the Government in the normal sense of stating a position which has been collectively discussed with and agreed by my colleagues.

861. LORD NOLAN: Thank you very much. Of course, as you know, last week we had the Shadow Leader, Ann Taylor, and she similarly was not speaking for her party but really for herself as a very experienced and senior Member of the House.

Now Mr Newton, as Leader, having the experience which that office reflects and gives, do you detect particular worries amongst Members of the House about what appears to be a public view of them which is not favourable?

TONY NEWTON: Yes, of course. Whatever people think about politicians, and they do sometimes suggest that they do not listen, politicians do actually listen quite hard and I think some members of your group would probably agree, do pick up public perceptions quite rapidly. So I think people are very aware of the fact that there is a public perception that they would prefer did not exist, and are very concerned that that should be addressed.

862. LORD NOLAN: To what do they attribute it?

TONY NEWTON: That is a much more complicated question, I am afraid. I notice that one of your early witnesses, I think it was Professor Crewe, referred to something from the past that suggested that the public had always had a pretty low view of its politicians, though he went on to say he thought that that was worse at present. I suppose one factor in this is the fact that in most democratic countries people are cautious about their politicians from time to time. It is part and parcel of the systems under which our countries are governed.

I think the other two factors that come to my mind are the fact that there manifestly have been problems that have caused public concern. They are the problems that underlie the establishment of this committee, they are problems which have lead to the current work of the Privileges Committee of which I am Chairman, and also to a number of other things as well.

Lastly, I suspect that there is at least some contribution—and again I think you would find this in most western countries—from the fact that all of us as countries and many individuals have been through a very difficult time as a result of economic circumstances. If you look at what has been happening in France, America, lots of places, that does have an effect on people's view of their politicians I think if they feel that things are not going well.

863. LORD NOLAN: One particular area which has been spoken about in a number of pieces of evidence we have had both in writing and across the table has been the growth of the lobbying industry, and the degree of pressure which it is said is put on particularly new Members of Parliament by lobbying organisations. Also the question of the extent of the links that are in existence between Members of Parliament and lobbyists. How do you see the lobby as a problem?

TONY NEWTON: May I make one or two preliminary points before coming directly to the thrust of that? I am sometimes a bit concerned that the word "lobbying" has acquired a pejorative flavour in almost all circumstances, whereas, of course, what we are in fact talking about is the making of representations towards democratic decisions which is actually part and parcel of our political process. Any Member of Parliament, for example, to use the word in the sense I am now using it, is lobbied all the time in his own constituency about road schemes, about school, about political problems, about a whole variety of things. One of the things I recall most clearly from my early years as a Member of Parliament, my years as an Opposition backbencher from 1974—1979 when I served on a large number of Finance Bill Standing Committees and was subject to a great deal of lobbying/representation connected with those Bills, was the fact that a great many people who had perfectly legitimate reason to make sure that their views were properly heard within the decision-making process, were actually not very good at doing it. You would find that the brief on an amendment that you had discussed two days earlier arrived two days later. Quite frankly, it might just as well have been simply consigned straight to the waste paper basket at that stage. In general I am in favour of the development of arrangements which mean that those who, as I say, have a legitimate interest in ensuring that their point of view is taken into account in decision making, whether of policy or of legislation, know how to get their point across, not in any improper way but so that it is, as I say, taken into account.

The reason I make these preliminary remarks is, as I say, the assumption that anything that can be described as "lobbying" is improper seems to me to ignore the basic nature of a democratically based political system. There is a role, a need, for effective representation of views in the course of making decisions and passing laws.

That said, I do, of course, understand that a great deal of the concern has been directed at the activities of lobbyists used in a more limited sense, and I certainly have to take note of that. I think that it has created some concern in the public. It appears to have done in this Committee. I do not think Members of Parliament would wish just to wave a hand over those concerns, though it is quite difficult to determine precisely how those concerns should be reflected in action—for example changes in rules—in circumstances (and I apologise if I am now going back to where I started) where the effective making of representations is a necessary and important part of the political process.

864. LORD NOLAN: Well, Members are there to represent their constituents, certainly, and one understands, of course, their constituents quite properly expect them to put forward, and thus to lobby, legitimate interests. I think the most difficult area that has come across in the evidence is the extent to which Members can properly act as paid advocates for concerns which are not representative of their own constituents.

TONY NEWTON: May I just add one further point to my earlier reply. I think in your first question on this subject you referred to pressures on MPs and asked whether they had increased. In one sense they certainly have because in my judgment the representation of views is more effective than it was 20 years ago, and that does lead to some very effective campaigning directed at MPs generally over big public issues from time to time. It has certainly increased the mailbag, for example as a result of more organised activity to communicate views to Members of Parliament. But that is not pressure in the sense in which you mean it. As I understand it, you are referring to the pressure of perhaps being offered employment with a firm of "lobbyists".

Now, I am not in a very good position, despite being Leader of the House as you said at the outset, to make as good a judgment about that as I would like because it is, after all, very nearly 16 years since I was in the position of anybody being in a position to think it worth approaching me in that way because, of course, as a Minister the question would not arise. I certainly do not sense in the House people complaining endlessly about people making what they regard as improper or unfair approaches to them, but, since there has been an increase in the number of firms specialising in this field, no doubt there may have been an increase in the number of people approaching MPs to see if they would wish to help.

865. LORD NOLAN: Do you think that the Register of Members' Interests as it stands is adequate in all respects to contain the problem and bring it out into the open so that people can see what is going on?

TONY NEWTON: The frame of mind in which I approach this Enquiry, and I think it is very much the frame of mind in which Members of Parliament, the House of Commons generally is approaching your work and will approach your conclusions, is certainly not to stand on the status quo and suggest that there is no possible room for further improvement. Indeed, one of the points I would have made, had I made a longer opening statement, is that even in the 20-plus years since I became a Member of Parliament you can see the House responding to changed circumstances and new concerns. I cannot now remember whether the Register was established immediately before or immediately after I became a Member of Parliament, but basically it scarcely existed when I became a Member of Parliament in 1974, it was only just being created. Since then it has been developed in various ways, and most notably in a debate in which I myself took part, and indeed the resolution would have been in my name, has been very considerably clarified and strengthened by the changes made just under two years ago. So, just as I would want to indicate that I would be very keen to examine what recommendations you make, I think that is the frame of mind of the House; not to say "We've got it all right, no room for further improvement". They will be very interested indeed to see what this Committee suggests.

866. LORD NOLAN: The Register, correct me if I am wrong, seems to represent a reflection of what had become a reality, namely that although in earlier years, and I am thinking back to a resolution of 1947, the House had resolved in fairly clear terms that there should be virtually no paid involvement of Members which resulted in their being paid for being Members. By the 1980s when the Register was set up the House seems to have taken a broader view and accepted that Members could properly

take consultancies, take, indeed, any job that any other free individual may take within reason as long as it was declared and put on the Register. That is the position that we are in at the moment really, is it not?

TONY NEWTON: To judge from my study of your earlier evidence, the resolution of 1947 has probably been more quoted in these proceedings than almost any other text. But, yes, the point has come up on a number of occasions. I think there clearly has been a development which implies that activities like advising people on how to get their political point across, as well as a range of other activities, are acceptable provided they are transparent and the interest is declared on the relevant occasions and the like. I am sure it is in that area that you will be looking to see if you can make suggestions about further clarifying the position, and, indeed, maybe it is not for me to attempt to indicate what might have been in Madam Speaker's mind when the current Privileges Committee was set up, but you will be aware that effectively the terms of reference in the Speaker's statement went on from the investigation of particular points about two Members of Parliament and one newspaper to suggest that they need to ask the Committee really to clarify the law and practice of Parliament in these matters. I think it is the sort of area on which you have now touched which would arise in that respect.

That leads me incidentally just to make one other point I should perhaps have made at the beginning. Since I am currently Chairman of the Privileges Committee, and you have a Member of the Privileges Committee on your own group, he, I think, would be quick to stop me if I showed any sign of pre-empting or prejudging the Committee's conclusions.

867. LORD NOLAN: We very much hope that at any rate our first report will come out, as we were asked to bring it out, at the beginning of May and that it will be of value, we hope, to the Committee of Privileges. That is, at any rate, our ambition if nothing higher.

TONY NEWTON: I am sure that it will be and that would tie in very much with what I am absolutely certain is the general desire in the House to approach your recommendations, whatever they may be, very constructively.

868. LORD NOLAN: This brings me to the question which in one form or another we ask all our witnesses. What steps do you think should be taken to restore the public confidence which, according to the media and the polls in the probity of Members of Parliament, should be taken?

TONY NEWTON: I think I would make two points. One, of course, is that the very establishment of this Committee, and the support it is receiving and the numbers of people who are giving evidence and the way in which, on my reading, they are approaching that evidence, I think is an important step in bringing about what you seek to bring about and what we all seek to bring about. I think the other thing, before we know what your recommendations are, is that we should carry forward effectively the work of the Privileges Committee and that is obviously something that I am very much concerned to do.

869. LORD NOLAN: May I raise one other subject which has been put forward by a number of very senior

Members of the House. It is a fundamental and sensitive point, and it is this. That public confidence in the enforcement of the rules that govern the behaviour of Members of Parliament would be enhanced if the House were to bring in some independent element into the investigation of alleged breaches. A number of different ways in which it might be done have been suggested. One might be the appointment of some individual, he or she comparable in status to the Ombudsman, the Parliamentary Commissioner, who would have a standing remit to hear complaints, decide if there was anything in them and, if there was, look into them and have the appropriate powers to ask questions and then report back to the Committee of Privileges. Others have suggested that there might even be a role for outside assessors on the Committee of Privileges.

Taking those questions in turn, first of all do you think that there is a case for considering an outside involvement in that limited sense?

TONY NEWTON: I hope the whole spirit in which I have approached this has been, as it were, not to start by ruling things out. I do think that there is some potential sensitivity given that we are talking about people whose responsibility is to the electorate, who are accountable to the electorate and whose position rests on the votes of those people in their constituencies, in introducing either into committees of the House or into disciplinary procedures some person or body that is appointed rather than elected and could, in some sense therefore, be seen as superior to Parliament. I do not want to over emphasise this point. I do not think it is necessarily impossible to devise something that would be acceptable, but at the moment I must say I find it really quite difficult to see what it might be.

870. LORD NOLAN: Thank you very much. Well, Mr Newton, I think that concludes the questions I wanted to raise with you except perhaps for one. We are well aware that the House can impose very severe penalties upon Members of Parliament who, for one reason or another, are found to have broken the rules in a major way, including suspension and expulsion, and, indeed, I think imprisonment. There does not seem to be anything that is really suitable for relatively minor lapses, let us say careless failure to register an interest which by common accord should have been registered. There is a rebuke but that, too, I imagine is seen as a very major punishment for the Member concerned. Do you think that there are other minor penalties of a more familiar nature that might be introduced usefully?

TONY NEWTON; Again, my approach would be to look at any suggestions for such mechanisms with care. Unless these powers are to be deputed to an individual, which I have already indicated I think would raise sensitivities if it were an appointed individual and might be felt to be a responsibility which an individual Member of Parliament, however senior, would not wish to exercise on his own without some reference to a group of colleagues of some kind as represented on the Privileges Committee or the Select Committee on Members' Interests, I see some difficulty in devising a mechanism for what you are suggesting which would actually be acceptable for one reason or another. I do not think I would want to exaggerate the extent to which there is not a mechanism for dealing with these things in not too heavy-handed a way unless you regard the mere investigation of a complaint by, shall we say, the Select Committee's on Members' Interests as very heavy-handed. In practice it does serve as a reminder that there are rules and that there has been a breach of them without, I think, doing undue damage to the Member. I would be inclined to think that that remains the appropriate way.

871. LORD NOLAN: Simply the recording of a view do you mean of a particular lapse to register an interest, or whatever it might be?

TONY NEWTON: I do not simply mean the reporting of the lapse to the Committee, but an examination of some kind by the Committee and the making of an observation on it is a significant and proper reflection of the fact that something that should not have happened has happened, and I would have thought is actually quite close to the sort of arrangement you seem to have in mind for what you describe as a minor lapse. It would be quite different from, for example, a recommendation to the House that somebody should be suspended from the service of the House for a period of time, let alone the even harsher punishments that you suggest. So I think there is more of a grading than you perhaps allow for.

872. LORD NOLAN: I think it is plain that it must be the House that imposes any discipline because the House is, so to speak, the top, there is nothing above it, no right of appeal, but within that one wonders whether that in itself does not create a problem. If the whole House or, indeed, a committee of the House is to act as prosecutor, judge, jury, and executioner, the role is one, is it not, that is almost impossible to perform speedily and with obvious justice?

TONY NEWTON: I noted with particular interest that point made to a degree in my predecessor John MacGregor's evidence to you some week or so ago, and also in the evidence that Geoffrey Johnson-Smith gave to you as the current Chairman of the Select Committee on Members' Interests. It did seem to me that both of them, I hope I may say without upsetting either of them, made the point without really going on to suggest how they felt it might be addressed. Indeed it seems to me that part of the problem is that the cases that might give rise to a perceived need for some extra or independent assessor element, or however it is to be described, are actually in practice very rare. More normally the fact is there is no court of law kind of problem in establishing the facts. I am not saying always, but for the most part the facts are often clear, and what is at issue is the Committee's judgment about the degree of blame to be attached and any recommendation which is to be made. I am not quite sure what independent assessors could bring to that kind of judgment which it seems to me inherently is for Members of Parliament as Members of Parliament sitting, if you like, in judgment on one of their peers.

LORD NOLAN: Thank you very much. I will now take the questioning round the table, if I may. May I start with Sir Martin Jacomb.

873. MARTIN JACOMB: Could I just ask you one question. Many people have drawn a distinction between advice and advocacy, if I can put it that way, and have said that it is all right for Members of Parliament to be paid for giving advice as to how a case should be put and so forth, but absolutely not all right for Members of Parliament to be paid to advocate particular points of view which they otherwise would not. Do you think that is a distinction which is in practice possible to draw and, if so, how, or do you think that the borderline between those two is so blurred that that would be a will o' the wisp to try and identify such a distinction?

TONY NEWTON: I suspect, Sir Martin, that you and, indeed, I am pretty sure that other Members of the Committee, are wrestling with exactly the same problem that I and no doubt many other witnesses have had in thinking about the evidence we should give because we are in a position in which, as soon as you start to think about it, it is very difficult to draw some of these distinctions. The distinction between advice and advocacy as general propositions is really quite clear, but on the other hand if you take this too far it would seem to me that you would get into a position in which somebody who happened to be an adviser, shall we say to a trade federation, in a perfectly proper way, going back to something I said earlier, explaining to them how best to put their point of view across, who would then in the course of all that no doubt learn a good deal about that particular trade or industry, would then I suppose at the extreme be barred from speaking or voting in any proceedings that appeared to involve the interests of that industry. I think that would be very difficult indeed.

874. DIANA WARWICK: I know you said at the beginning that you are speaking as Leader of the House, and I wanted to ask you something that you have not touched on in your evidence and I hope you will agree because there has been enormous public concern about the role of Ministers when they leave office, and it has been raised with a previous Minister, John MacGregor. It has also been raised in various broadcasts and so on. One of your colleagues, Norman Fowler, made a very clear statement about his view. I wondered if I could ask you a personal view about the rules that should apply to Ministers when they leave office. Should they be the same as those that apply to senior civil servants?

TONY NEWTON; As you said, Lord Nolan, at the outset this is an area which I believe you are going into with my colleague, David Hunt, in a week or so's time. Nevertheless, Miss Warwick has asked me my personal views and I think I would want to say that I do not believe that as direct a parallel as is implied in the question and has, I think, been drawn by some of your other witnesses, can be drawn between the position of Ministers and civil servants. The main reason I say that is the most obvious thing in the world to anyone who is actually a politician, there are both practising ones and former ones around the table. Politics is inherently an insecure operation. That is not to say that there should not be guidance and the need (you have explored this a bit with John MacGregor) for judgment about what is or is not appropriate. Let us take the position of somebody offered a junior ministerial post, or a middle ranking ministerial post, shall we say in his thirties or forties, in a department with wide ranging economic or industrial responsibilities of which there are several. On some of the suggestions put to you by early witnesses certainly, it would appear to me that the very act of becoming a Minister would put him in a position where, if he ceased to be a Minister or for that matter lost his seat, a whole range of possible ways of obtaining alternative employment in those circumstances would actually be ruled out for him for some considerable period of time. Again, I do not want to overstate any of these points; that is not in general the position that civil servants find themselves in. It may be that the position of civil servants is not quite as secure as it was at one time, but essentially we are talking about a secure occupation leading naturally to a good well protected pension at retirement age. That is not the position in which many Ministers find themselves. They find themselves in the position where they may at very short notice for a variety of reasons find themselves not being Ministers and perhaps not even being MPs and needing to be able to support their families. If you shut off too much, what will happen is that they will not take the Ministerial post in the first place because they will think the risk has become too great.

875. DIANA WARWICK: The rules are not quite as draconian as that, are they? Civil servants have a moratorium for three months and then an independent committee decides whether or not an offer of employment should be accepted whether it is appropriate. Since we are dealing with this issue of the public perception and public concern, would it be, if you like in your terms, a gesture that Ministers will accept the same sort of rubric?

TONY NEWTON: I am sure that Ministers would be prepared to consider any recommendations you put forward in this field. I am really doing no more than to ask, and I suspect that it is something that the Committee will have in their mind anyway, the importance of recognising the nature of politics as an operation, and some of the additional pressures and problems to which that can give rise. If I may say so, my remarks were not so much directed at your very reasonable question, but at some of the suggestions that were made by witnesses in your early evidence that ranged at the extreme to people being banned from taking occupation of certain kinds for anything up to ten years. I think what you have just sketched is a good deal short of that.

876. CLIFFORD BOULTON: May I raise two subjects please. One is the nature of the permitted interest that a Member can take up, and the other is the power to impose sanctions on Members. In the first case you have been using the expression "paid advocacy" being permitted in many circumstances, but of course it is common ground that a Member must not for payment take instructions from anybody. He must not speak to order or do parliamentary business to order, and Parliamentary Agents, for instance, are disqualified and a Member would almost be turning himself into somebody's agent. We are not talking about paid advocacy in that sense, we are talking about the freedom to speak up for an interest in which one has a permitted interest as a consultant, adviser, or whatever it may be. That kind of speaking up for applies, of course, equally to Members who have relationships with trade associations or firms, or those sponsored Members by trade unions who also speak up for what they regard as a perfectly proper public interest. If we are trying to define more closely what are the permitted and not permitted, in the cases I have been talking about the Member chooses his client if you like. He can form a view that it would be in the public interest for him to have this relationship and further those arguments and give advice. Could you see a sustainable distinction between permitting that and not permitting a Member to sign up with a general PR agency where the clients are sort of served up to him almost on a "cab rank" principle and you take the one they tell you to work for, or you have lost control as a Member of whom you are actually in relationship. Do you think we could limit Members' relationships with these PR agencies that exist and have mushroomed lately?

TONY NEWTON: I think if there is a sustainable distinction to be drawn, it is probably in this area though I think you would again run into difficulties of definition which litter this whole subject. If in the case, shall we say, of someone who was not a paid employee in the sense that I think Sir Clifford has in mind a public relations or lobbying firm, or for that matter a wide range of other organisations, but an adviser to them, again you get into an area where the distinction is getting blurred again and again will reveal the difficulties. But, as I say, if there is a sustainable distinction to be drawn I think it is probably in the area on which Sir Clifford has just touched.

877. CLIFFORD BOULTON: On this business of sanctions, the House has been very jealous of requiring a decision by the whole House if a punishment is going to be inflicted on a Member. That applies, for instance, when the Speaker "names" a Member; it is not the Speaker who then suspends the Member, it is the House on a motion. You might leave by yourself according to your duty. There are certain things, of course, that Members can do which bring down an automatic penalty but those are the disqualification kind. You can get sent to prison for more than a year, or you can sit in the Chamber without taking the oath and things like that, but everything else I can think of at the moment has to be approved by the whole House first. One of the areas that we have got some comment on is that after a serious-minded quasi judicial inquiry by the Privileges Committee, Select Committee on Conduct of Members, Members' Interests Committee, has come out the subsequent debate which precedes the imposition of any penalty, this quasi judicial atmosphere tends to fall apart and we get a day's debate which is not always pretty to watch or listen to. Therefore I suppose this body is groping for some way of thinking, could there be some system whereby the fixing of the penalty could be devolved, let us say, to a small group who, if they made a unanimous report there would be a Standing Order of the House which said that that should take effect unless the House turned it down because the House must always keep that alternative. Is that not a starter at all? Would you say the House would not be interested in any such solution?

TONY NEWTON: Sir Clifford, your view on this might be at least as good as mine, but I think that the House would be extremely sensitive, as indeed it is in matters of legislation in general, to the delegating of the ultimate decision to somebody other than the House as a whole, and particularly when you are talking about what could be really very serious punishments indeed for a Member of Parliament. I think there would be a very strong sense that this is not the kind of decision that ought finally to be delegated to a small group of Members of Parliament, however senior and distinguished, but is one that the House itself should properly take in the same way, as you well know, on the legislative front. Even with the great amount of material that does go to Standing Committee there normally has to be a resolution on the floor of the House even if it is put forthwith to validate the decision.

CLIFFORD BOULTON: Thank you. I was not pressing a point of view; I was simply asking you for your opinion about a particular proposal. Thank you very much.

878. LORD THOMSON: Mr Newton, you give us a very clear definition of what you regard as proper lobbying, a definition I personally agree with. Would you like to try a definition of what you regard as Leader of the House is improper lobbying?

TONY NEWTON: I think we come back to the sort of area that Clifford Boulton was in. If there is a distinction I think it is in that area of being paid solely for advocating a particular cause as distinct from offering general advice. The more I think about it the more I am not sure that that distinction can actually be carried into rules, but I think there is a pretty clear conceptual distinction which has actually come through in a number of the questions that I have been asked. But it is not as clear as it has been suggested by some of your witnesses, for example. I notice that in the list of advocacy, so to speak, it is usually Parliament Questions, Early Day Motions, and either making speeches or moving amendments. I think Early Day Motions and moving amendments are clearly a form of advocacy, but a Parliamentary Question I am not sure is necessarily a form of advocacy. The great majority of Parliamentary Questions, or certainly a very large number, are designed to illicit information. I do not see how the eliciting of information can be regarded as advocacy, so, again, you get into another of these difficult definitional areas. I am sorry to keep emphasising that, but I suspect that any of you who have been thinking about these problems as hard as you have, and as hard as I have tried to both generally and in advance of giving this evidence, will keep coming up against exactly that problem.

LORD THOMSON: I am bound to say, Mr Newton, I think most of the Parliamentary Questions I have ever asked I have had the information already and was asking the question in order to advocate the point of view.

TONY NEWTON: That shows what an active advocate you were, Lord Thomson.

879. LORD THOMSON: Could I ask you, just following up your interesting reply, in almost an aside you said that it was a very long time since you had been a backbencher and therefore the subject of lobbying, and as a Minister you were not the subject of lobbying. I may have misunderstood you.

TONY NEWTON: No, no, I think I had better make myself clear. As a Minister—Health, Social Security, for a brief time at Industry—and now with my responsibilities to the legislative programme, I have to say I am subject to endless lobbying, I do not say people making representations about pieces of legislation they would like to see in the programme, about changes in Social Security policy, health policy, whatever it may have been at particular points in time. My answer earlier, I had hoped was clear, was directed at the question of pressure arising from approaches to me, for example, to take a position with a lobbying firm or, indeed, any other firm because everybody knows that Ministers cannot do that, so for 16 years the question has not arisen in my case.

880. LORD THOMSON: The reason I am asking this question is that we had evidence from one lobbyist that one of the advantages of a good lobbying firm, one of its selling points to a potential client, was access to Ministers. I just wondered whether you would comment on whether that was your view of the situation or not.

TONY NEWTON: I think this is an issue you explored a bit with John MacGregor as well and he was fairly vigorous on the particular case that underlay things in relation to his evidence. I frankly do not recall an occasion on which I felt I was being subject to improper pressures, and frankly anybody who has reached the position of being a Minister, and certainly who has been a Minister for any length of time, is quite capable of resisting pressures, in my view, to hear people that he does not think it appropriate to hear and, indeed, to weigh and if necessary dismiss arguments that he does not think stand up. If you are not able to cope with that kind of thing, then frankly you should not be a Minister. I think my colleagues are quite able to cope with it.

LORD THOMSON: Thank you.

881. PETER SHORE: You referred to those far off days when you were a backbencher, or a Member of the Opposition when you served on Finance Bill Committees. There is always a great deal of lobbying on Finance Bills, but do you not really distinguish in your mind amendments which are put down as a result of, if you like, disinterested lobbying, and amendments that are put down by a Member of the Standing Committee who is retained by an outside interest?

TONY NEWTON: This is the distinction I think that both Sir Clifford and Lord Thomson were feeling for as well, and as I have already said to them, Peter, and I will say to you, I think if there is a distinction to be drawn it is in that kind of area. Whether it is objectionable provided it is clear, that is to say that the interest is not only declared in the Register but is made clear at the time the amendment is moved, possibly even at the time that it is tabled, I would be less certain. As I say, if there is a distinction it is in that area.

882. PETER SHORE: Well, yes. Obviously if a distinction is to be drawn it has to be very carefully researched and a very clear dividing line has to be drawn. On the matter of Parliamentary Questions, some questions obviously have no purpose other than to put on the record certain things which might not otherwise be apparent to constituents, but questioning clearly can have a financial motive and I would have thought that was again something which you would not wish to support?

TONY NEWTON: That is true. I made my earlier point only to illustrate what I have now called several times the definitional problems. A Parliamentary question may or may not be a form of advocacy, but undoubtedly many are put down—and even more are asked as supplementaries—with a view to advancing a particular cause.

883. PETER SHORE: Yes. If I can now switch to your role as Chairman of the Privileges Committee and your experience there, we had evidence from Lord Callaghan earlier and he was critical of what he saw as changes in the composition of the Privileges Committee over time. He recalled the days when a Prime Minister, a Leader of the Opposition, or Leaders of the Opposition Parties served almost automatically on the Privileges Committee along with very senior people. Do you think there is a change here? Is he right in detecting this change and should we make a greater effort to make sure that people of real authority serve on the Privileges Committee?

TONY NEWTON: First, it would be true if you went back far enough—50 or more years I suppose, but possibly a little less than that—that the Prime Minister might more frequently have been involved in these matters, but then, until about that time, the Prime Minister was also the

Leader of the House. It is relatively recent that the job as Leader of the House was separated out and made a job on its own. That partly reflects the increased pressures on Ministers of all kinds, including, not least, the Prime Minister, so that if the suggestion is that he should take the leading role in the Privileges Committee, it would be difficult for him to combine that with all the other pressures on him.

I suspect that the main thrust of your question was on the membership of the Committee, leaving aside the question of whether, historically, the Prime Minister might have been involved, and it is important that those concerned with making the nominations to the Committee of Privileges should bear in mind the need for it to be a body of considerable authority within the House.

884. PETER SHORE: And the people who make those recommendations are presumably the usual channels—the Whips on both sides?

TONY NEWTON: Effectively, yes, but as you will know, that is usually done on the basis of substantial soundings in the Parliamentary Party on either side.

885. PETER SHORE: What do you think of another point, also made by Lord Callaghan I believe, about the size of the Privileges Committee. The present Committee is something like 17, which, in my experience, is larger than it has ever been before. What is your view of that?

TONY NEWTON: I am not sure that the latter point is right. I was provided before coming here with a note of the composition of the Committee of Privileges since 1979 and although I did not count them all up, I am pretty sure that they are all 17. Certainly the first one, which I have noted here, was 17 because I counted it. They all look about the same length, so I think there is some long-standing convention on that.

I too feel that 17 is a large number for the sort of proceedings that you and I are involved in (again, this evening if I remember rightly) and if you were to ask me whether that is something that might be looked at I would agree.

886. PETER SHORE: A point we have heard in previous evidence is that there is an area of overlap between the Committee on Members' Interests and the Privileges Committee. Is there a case for combining the two into a Scrutiny Committee, which was the proposal that was put to us.

TONY NEWTON: I noted that evidence and the best thing I can say is that it is interesting. There is at times a potential overlap and at this very moment the Select Committee on Members' Interests is looking at matters that could be said to link with another inquiry that the Privileges Committee has been asked to carry out, so again I would not rule out considering a single body.

887. PETER SHORE: In terms of "an independent element" that might assist the work of the Privileges Committee, one of the analogies that was put to us as being worthy of further study was the Comptroller and Auditor General, who is an officer appointed by Parliament and responsible only to Parliament and who makes his report with all the resources available to him. He is able to investigate in a very thorough way and then

report to the Committee—in that case, the Public Accounts Committee, in this analogous case, perhaps to the Privileges Committee. Might that be a way of increasing the investigatory effectiveness of the Privileges Committee, while at the same time keeping the final decision within the House of Commons?

TONY NEWTON: I am aware that this is a point similar to one that has been raised on a few occasions and I took the precaution of checking exactly how the Comptroller and Auditor General is appointed. As I understand it, he is appointed by the Crown on an address from the House of Commons on a motion made by the Prime Minister, with the agreement of the Chairman of the Public Accounts Committee.

I am not sure how sensitive Parliament would be these days, though I can certainly think of times many hundreds of years ago when it might have been extremely sensitive, to the notion of such an appointment being made by the Crown and on the recommendation of a member of the Executive. There might still be some sensitivity in that area.

PETER SHORE: Thank you.

888. LORD NOLAN: What if he was appointed by a resolution of the House?

TONY NEWTON: That would undoubtedly ease any sensitivity that there might be. We are getting into constitutionally quite deep water here. I shall end up looking to Sir Clifford Boulton for assistance and advice. We are ultimately talking about an appointment by the Crown, however the recommendation is made. As I say, that might raise in some minds questions about the position of Parliament.

889. ANNE WARBURTON: Mr Newton, I should like to anticipate some testimony that we shall be hearing later this morning from one of our witnesses, who has given us some written material. This prompts me to ask you a question about the constitution of committees of the House.

His suggestion is that it is fairly frequent (I think he says that it is true of the Committee on Members' Interests and also instances particularly aircraft investigations and broadcasting) that the membership of committees have included many people with interests in these areas. That put a question into my mind. The Register of Members' Interests is fairly recent; has the House and those who constitute Committees thought through that if you have a Register of Interests you could use it to make sure that your Committees are balanced, or indeed, squeaky clean in these respects?

TONY NEWTON: There is a balance of considerations in the appointment of Select Committees, one of which is the willingness of Members of Parliament to serve on them. Something that is occasionally overlooked by commentators on Parliamentary affairs, who have a tendency to advocate the setting up of more and more committees, is that the demands on Members of Parliament in this respect as in many others, have risen sharply over the years.

Membership of a Select Committee is itself quite a demanding role if it is to be done properly so that something does depend on harnessing people's interest (in another sense to the one in which you use it) and their willingness to give up the necessary time and work to it. It is inherently likely that those most willing to do that will be those who have an interest, however proper, in the sense in which you use the word, because they will feel they have most to contribute and the House as a whole may feel so too, as long as it is not an improper use of influence.

In practice it would be difficult to use the Register in the way you suggest, together with the other point, which is that the practice is to appoint Select Committees in accordance with the balance of forces in the House at any particular time. There is an understanding between the main parties about who shall have the Chairmanship of which committees. Therefore, the range of factors do not lend themselves to the kind of application of the Register that you suggest.

890. ANNE WARBURTON: I can see the problems, but on the other hand, I am sure that you can see the problem of public perception, faced with this kind of statement. Perhaps I can then anticipate another witness, who will be coming tomorrow, and a paper which has been put before us, which includes the following sentence:

"In our view it is the climate of secrecy and unnecessary confidentiality which persists in Westminster and Whitehall which does so much to engender public suspicion that what goes on behind the closed doors of government is not necessarily consistent with the public interest. Freedom of information legislation would dispel such doubts and misgivings and lay the foundations of a more open system of government and public confidence."

Please comment!

TONY NEWTON: While there remain differences of opinion about how far this should be pressed and in precisely what detailed information should be made more freely available, the direction of the point has been acknowledged by a variety of steps that the present Government has taken—you drive me into speaking as a Minister, and not simply as Leader of the House—to improve access to information and the openness of the proceedings of Government. The two most notable examples, I suppose, are the publication of Questions of Procedure for Ministers, which was undertaken for the first time under this administration and the publication of the membership and terms of reference of Cabinet committees. Those are only examples and I accept that they are examples of a genuine thrust in seeking to increase the openness and availability of information of the working of government.

ANNE WARBURTON: I am sorry that I drove you into speaking as a Minister because I was thinking of it as a question in the House.

TONY NEWTON: There would be different views in the House, as on many other issues. We have had several Private Member's Bills over the past few years in the area of freedom of information that have raised controversy. There are certainly those in the House of Commons who would go further down the path, perhaps along the lines that the evidence to which you referred is sketching.

In general there is support for greater openness and people acknowledge that many important moves in that direction have been made.

ANNE WARBURTON: Thank you, Mr Newton.

891. WILLIAM UTTING: If I could start with a general point, Mr Newton, we have had eloquently represented to us, in the course of evidence, the benefits that arise because of MPs' participation in outside interests vis à vis their capacity to conduct parliamentary business. We have not heard so strongly expressed a contrary view which may be that parliamentary business is now so demanding that it requires the wholehearted application of individuals and one should look to them to be full participators in the legislative process and experts in managing the parliamentary process. If one is going to have people like that in the House, they do need a good salary and good working conditions. Would you have any views on the sort of balance of people who ought to be in the House of Commons and on these difficult issues of how salaries, expenses and conditions of service are fixed?

TONY NEWTON: Taking the two points separately, so far as the question of what sort of people should be in the House of Commons is concerned, I am perhaps in a reasonable position to reiterate what I know some of my colleagues, including John MacGregor, have said before about what I see to be the importance of a wide range of people with outside interests—or certainly with previous experience—being represented in the Commons and the contribution that they can make. I say that as somebody who is rather closer to the definition of professional politician which some would like to see. I hope that there is a place for me in the House of Commons; on the other hand, I am not sure I would want the House of Commons to be made up of people who all had my particular experience, which is almost wholly in and around politics since I left university. You need both; the House gains from people having outside interests and previous experience and whatever the salary that would remain the case.

None of us would gain from a House of Commons made up of 651 people who were completely cut off from the rest of life, except on the basis of representations they received, rather than of experience of contacts they continued to have in various walks of life.

As to the question of salaries and related matters, the practice (certainly as long as I can remember) has been to act only on the recommendations of an outside body—in this case, the former Top Salaries Review Body, now the Senior Salaries Review Body—on the main issues, other than when, once a new real level has been established, to determine the indexing mechanism, which we have had to change recently in line with civil service pay structures. Apart from that, big changes, of the kind that you appear to have in mind, have normally been made on the recommendations of an independent outside body.

The problem over the years has been that the independent outside body has almost invariably come forward with proposals much higher than the government of the day felt able to recommend to the House. In the controversies that occurred earlier this year about Members of Parliament pay, I eventually ventured the view in the House (wisely or not) that those who were urging that it should all be settled independently and not by the House would almost certainly have ended up with a much larger increase than the one that was then being criticised.

892. WILLIAM UTTING: Yes, I am sure that is so. Could I turn to a specific point in what you said this

morning. You spoke about the sensitivity that MPs would feel about the introduction of an outside element into their regulatory and disciplinary processes. I am moving to the position where it seems to me to be in the interests of Parliament to do that, for the sake of its public reputation. I will not go into an argument along those lines now, but, say, one arrived at that view and thought about the best way of managing the issue, and said that Parliamentarians would find it difficult to put up with people who had been appointed to do jobs like this when they were elected, if one could find a satisfactory means of MPs actually appointing the outside element, that did not look as though it was too much of an inside job, would that meet the kind of sensitivity you have mentioned, which from a constitutional point of view is important?

TONY NEWTON: Yes. I am sure the House would be sensitive in this area and ultimately it is the point about Members of Parliament being elected and, at the extreme, penalties which might lead to them not being Members of Parliament at all.

It would be strongly felt (and this goes back on one or two earlier exchanges I had with other Members of the committee) that these are decisions that should be taken by the House as a whole if it reaches that point. I hope that my whole demeanour during the course of this session has not been to come here to say "This, that or the other is impossible and ruled out from the beginning." I would not say it is impossible that this Committee should come forward with a proposal that Members might find acceptable in this respect, but I would draw attention to one other possible sensitivity, if you got into a position in which pressure could be put on Members of Parliament for whatever reason by people threatening to refer them to some person distinct from Parliament.

I take it from what is being said that the area we are talking about is MPs financial interests and the like. If that were to spread, for example, into other aspects of what MPs do (like, for example, whether they vote in a particular way, pursue a particular cause or adopt a particular view). There would certainly be considerable sensitivity, if the word "conduct" was spread to take in all the activities of Members of Parliament, about the scope for putting pressure on them in relation to their political duties by threatening to have them investigated.

893. WILLIAM UTTING: Yes, that is very helpful. Finally, we have had some discussion about the difficulty of drawing lines between what is acceptable and what is not and one can see that there are problems in practice here. A practical approach to this would be to draw a line somewhere—in the best we can find for the moment—but to create a system that allows that to be redrawn in the light of experience and possibly to have difficult cases referred for advice to some sort of panel of wise people in the meantime. Do you think there might be merit in that sort of approach?

TONY NEWTON: Whatever system we have, it needs to be flexible to respond to changes both in circumstances (as some people would see the growth in lobbying in recent years), other changes that one can imagine happening in attitudes or external events of various kinds and to be capable of being adapted. I always much valued your advice, Sir William, at the Department of Health. If you can achieve the advice that gets us to the delicate balance that you have described, I shall be even more grateful.

WILLIAM UTTING: I could not conceivably ask any more questions after that.

894. TOM KING: It appears that the Lord President has just declared an interest, rather late in the evidence. Anyway, can I make his point. You have said something very frankly and we had Angela Eagle here last week, who also said that she had effectively come through the political route.

I think I am right in saying that you were one of the first to come all the way through, to Member of Parliament and then to the Cabinet. You have emphasised (and I certainly support it) that that is a perfectly respectable route to come to Parliament, but that one needs variety and not an overdose of any particular background. The reason that this is obviously important to us, is that if we are concerned and charged with issues about standards of conduct in public life, and we are looking at Members of Parliament, their quality, experience and background are key elements.

The Committee has not yet gone into deep discussions about these issues, but my concern has always been about how we ensure we do nothing as a Committee to limit the range of opportunities. You have talked about potential Ministers turning down jobs because they could not afford, in their family's situation, to take them. I sense that it is getting more difficult and that there is considerable narrowing of the backgrounds from which people come. I sensed, when I first came to the House of Commons, that there were far more people to whom you would want to listen when they were speaking because you knew they had not simply read the brief, but had genuine background experience of what they were talking about.

I sense it has got more difficult and that it is very important that we do all we can to try to prevent that progress merely continuing until we simply have full-time professional readers of briefs and parroters of other people's opinions. Do you agree with that?

TONY NEWTON: Yes. Can I clarify one thing that I do not think you meant. I did not seek to say to Miss Warwick that it was a question of people not being able to afford to become Ministers. That would sound like a ministerial pay claim—which is not what I am here to make. I was making the point that if you get the rules wrong in terms of what you might do after being a Minister, you will inhibit people from becoming a Minister, whatever the pay, because of the risk that they might find themselves in a sort of black hole on ceasing to be a Minister or a Member of Parliament. It is important that that should be clear, rather than the level of salary.

895. TOM KING: There are some well-known examples of the first category, particularly in the House of Lords.

TONY NEWTON: That may well be, but I was making a point about the uncertainty of the occupation and the difficulties that people would face if whole swathes of activity were cut off from them for a long period.

On the principal point you were making, I have heard this and there may be something about the quality of Members. I would be the last to deny that there may be something in it. On the other hand, on my observations, I would judge, from listening to them quite a lot, the quality of the intake in 1992 (on both sides of the House) to be of a high calibre—and obviously in my role I am often in the chamber.

Nevertheless there is a risk: it is a variant of the point about Ministers and I had at one stage thought I might say something about this in my opening remarks. There is a risk that if we, collectively, get the balance wrong in any restrictions and new rules you impose, it will further increase the reluctance of people to become Members of Parliament at all when taken in conjunction with various other things, such as exposure to publicity and all the other things we see happening, quite apart from the nature of the job. Manifestly if we got the balance wrong to an extent that it had that effect, the net result would not be an increase in the standards of public life, but a reduction in the number and quality of those willing to go into it at all.

896. TOM KING: Dame Anne talked to you about the membership of committees and you replied exclusively on the issue of select committees. The point we have not perhaps discussed very much in this Committee—although people talk about Members standing up in the Chamber and making speeches or asking questions—is that it is the power to move amendments in a standing committee that alters legislation. There have been comments about some—I think it was the Legal Aid Bill—which was staffed entirely by barristers (lawyers who are Members).

It is the issue about perception that Dame Anne raised as well. I entirely understand your point about there not being a rush of people longing to serve on every standing committee, because it is an extra commitment. However, what about that point on the overlap of interests on standing committees?

TONY NEWTON: I think Dame Anne asked me specifically about select committees.

ANNE WARBURTON: I said "committees".

TONY NEWTON: I apologise if I misinterpreted the question. Yes, you manifestly raise a point I would not want to dismiss in relation to standing committees. It takes us back into the advocacy area. On the other hand, your reference to barristers and legal aid illustrates another difficulty. I say this with some hesitation in front of a senior judge, but if all the lawyers in the House of Commons were banned from voting on anything that might be seen as affecting the legal profession, the effects on legislation would be to make it rather unpredictable by comparison with the overall balance in the House.

LORD NOLAN: On that thought provoking note——

TONY NEWTON: It was not meant to be an attack on lawyers.

LORD NOLAN: You have given your evidence with great clarity. We are extremely grateful to you for coming along. Like so many of our most interesting witnesses, we have taken up much more of your time than we said we would. Thank you very much.

TONY NEWTON: Thank you very much indeed.

897. LORD NOLAN: Sir Terence, good morning to you, Conservative Member of Parliament for Worthing

and a very senior Member of the House. We are extremely grateful to you for volunteering to come along. I see you have just handed to us an aide memoire. Would you like to begin by reading that out or taking us through it?

RT HON SIR TERENCE HIGGINS MP

RT HON SIR TERENCE HIGGINS, MP: My Lord Chairman, may I first thank you very much for inviting me to appear this morning. I should like to make some opening remarks, but I fear they are not the ones to which you have just referred. That is someone else's aide memoire.

Many of the remarks I should like to make on opening follow on immediately from the discussion that has just taken place. Perhaps when we turn to questions, you might wish to pursue particularly the points about select committees since, as Chairman of the Liaison Committee, which has the role of co-ordinating the select committees and acting as an interface between the Government and Opposition on the select committee system, my experience would be particularly relevant. Then perhaps we might pick up some additional points at the end, if there are some loose ends.

LORD NOLAN: By all means. I shall ask Miss Warwick to take up the questioning, when you have finished your statement.

TERENCE HIGGINS: Thank you. I should like to continue the earlier discussion. I noted that when your inquiry began, there were widespread press reports saying that you had had a great many representations that we should have full-time Members of Parliament. I very much hope that you will make it clear that we already have full-time Members of Parliament, or, more accurately, that we have Members of Parliament who work vastly in excess of the hours a week which anyone outside would regard as full-time.

I believe that the vast majority of Members work much in excess of what would normally be regarded as a full-time job. We only have out-of-date official evidence on that, because we have not had a survey of Member of Parliament pay since 1983. At that time the committee pointed out that over the year as a whole, Members spent on average just over 62 hours a week on all forms of parliamentary work. There is no doubt that since then, while the number of all night sittings (going right through until eight o'clock the next morning) have diminished, the amount of work otherwise has vastly increased.

When I first became Member of Parliament, I shared a secretary with two other Members. The situation now is almost reversed. I have almost three secretaries working for me at times and I checked with my secretary yesterday, who told me that it takes her on average an hour or more to open the post, with which I then have to deal, quite apart from the vastly increased work that now goes on, particularly of course in select committees. The idea that we do not have full-time Members of Parliament is completely wrong, whether or not they have outside interests.

If you look through the Register, many of those with outside interests are among the hardest working in terms of being Members of Standing or Select Committees. I feel bound to say also that those in the House most strongly advocating that we should have full-time Members with no outside interests, are often conspicuously absent, both from select committees and from standing committees. The two very often go together and I hope you will take on board what I think is a very important point in terms of public perception of standards of life in politics.

My second point is one that arose earlier with regard to Members' interests. I believe there is a strong case for Members having outside interests, but what worries me particularly now (and I go a little further than Mr Newton did on this) is that I believe we have a serious recruitment problem, both in terms of Members of Parliament and of Ministers. It is undoubtedly the case that the public perception of Members of Parliament, or indeed Ministers, is much less high than it was when I first came to the House.

That is something which I hope you will be able to improve, but nonetheless, it is not regarded as a respectable occupation in the same way that it was, perhaps 30 years ago. It is therefore something which those considering coming into the House or becoming Ministers need to take into account. In that context, while Mr Newton said he was not putting in a pay claim, we have to look at all of this against the background of Members' and Ministers' pay because this is clearly a relevant consideration, not least as to whether Members should have, as many have in the past, outside interests.

The figures are startling. I got the Library to dig out some statistics that I can let you have afterwards, which show what has happened to Members' and Ministers' pay over the 30 years I have been in the House. In that time, average real income, per head, in this country has gone up 80 per cent or perhaps a little more. Meanwhile, between 1964 and 1994 the real income of Prime Ministers has gone down 59 per cent, of Cabinet Ministers, 50 per cent and of Ministers of State, 60 per cent. As far as Members of Parliament are concerned we are just back to where the level was in real terms when I came into the House and throughout that intervening period it has been significantly below that level. Those are startling statistics: average real incomes have gone up 80 per cent, the real incomes of Cabinet Ministers have gone down 50 per cent.

Against that background, it is important to say whether there is a recruitment problem and I believe there is.

898. LORD NOLAN: Was the figure for the Prime Minister 59 per cent?

TERENCE HIGGINS: Yes, I shall let you have the figures. There are some qualifications, but in broad terms this is correct: Prime Minister, 59 per cent; Cabinet Ministers, 50 per cent; Ministers of State, 60 per cent; Under Secretaries, minus 39 per cent and Members of Parliament will, this coming year, just about get back to where they were, having been below the level throughout that period.

There is a serious problem here and while I am not necessarily saying that one should double Members of Parliament's pay, or perhaps treble the Prime Minister's (which would take him roughly to where one might get a reasonable chief executive for a middle sized plc), there are two important points that need to be considered.

First, if Members are not allowed to have outside interests, that has a significant effect for those who would otherwise (if they are reasonable high flyers) be in a

position of earning vastly more in an outside occupation. As far as Ministers are concerned, the point that Mr Newton was making about the risks involved in being a Minister and the possibility of a black hole if they were precluded from taking outside occupations afterwards, is a very real and important one.

Secondly, I come to a point on which I think you have had evidence already and which is quite apart from the one I have just made. It is also important to note that the fact that Members have outside interests enables them to act in a way, with expertise, which would not be the case otherwise. That is something which makes work in the House of Commons and Members of Parliament with a variety of interests, more effective than they would otherwise be if they were purely inward looking and full-time in the sense that they were precluded from having any outside interests. Again that is a traditional point.

One hears the remark made, "They could get experience outside without being paid for it.", and there are some facilities for doing that—the Industry and Parliament Trust does extremely valuable work in this respect—but I feel bound to say that sitting alongside someone and doing a job, usually at something below Board level, is not the same as being on the Board of a company and experiencing and learning from the impact of economic, social and other affairs on its operations in real life. However, there is a problem, which Mr Newton referred to. If one has such an outside interest, which may well have absolutely nothing to do with one's role as a Member of Parliament at all (it may be that the company concerned believes you have something to offer quite apart from your Parliamentary experiences), what should happen when one appears in the House of Commons? Should one then speak on something on which one has perhaps far greater expertise than anyone else in the House and if so, should one in turn vote?

That brings me to the next point on the issue of greater supervision and on which the question of the sovereignty of Parliament has been raised. I am inclined to agree with those who have implied that the present situation which divides somewhat between the Privileges Committee on the one hand and the Members' Interests Committee on the other is not a very satisfactory arrangement. It may well be that we should reconsider what the right structure is as far as that is concerned, perhaps also with some back-up from a body such as your own on broad issues.

Having said that, I am also inclined to agree (and I have served on it on various occasions) that the Privileges Committee is probably too large. It may well be that a sub-committee of the Privileges Committee, perhaps consisting of five Members, would be a more effective operational body, which could deal with matters far more speedily than is otherwise the case. That is something which perhaps the Committee should consider. However, I do not take the view that it would be appropriate for outsiders to participate in that process. It is a matter where there are real sensitivities as far as the sovereignty of Parliament is concerned.

A more difficult set of issues arises as far as supervision of Ministers taking outside jobs is concerned. Miss Warwick referred earlier to the situation with regard to civil servants. That was somewhat tightened as a result of the Treasury Select Committee report on this issue when I was Chairman. I am not at all sure that the regulation with regard to civil servants (particularly those involved in military matters) is as tight as it should be, but there may well be a case for a similar body as far as Ministers are concerned and it does not seem to me that that would raise the same problems on the sovereignty of Parliament. Ministers are different from Members of Parliament in this respect. Again, this is perhaps something that one might reasonably consider.

Having said that, my Lord Chairman, there are obviously a number of extremely difficult line-drawing problems that we have to consider and it may be that in some of these instances it is not possible to draw a clear line—where it can only be decided by a particular body considering whether a particular case is one side of the line or the other, even though that line has not been clearly drawn. Transparency is all important; wherever one draws the line on the issues you are considering, it is vital that there should be proper registration and it should be apparent both to the public, the House and Members themselves whether a person has an interest or not.

It seems to me that there is one principle that could be dealt with. There is a big difference between a situation where an individual, retained as a consultant, or indeed a director, is transferring information from the House to the outside body with whom he has a relationship. It seems to me that it would be very unusual for that to be particularly objectionable. It is when the flow is in the other direction, from the outside body, through a Member who has a consultancy or directorship to the House, that most of the line-drawing problems arise. Perhaps at least that is one distinction that might reasonably be drawn and which might stand up.

There are a number of specific issues to which you may wish to turn and perhaps I could just run down the list. On the issue of research assistants who are employed part-time and who have other outside interests, there was an article in the *Observer* the Sunday before last. Although it mistakenly thought I had a research assistant, it was in fact someone who had a pass in my name and who was the Director of the Industry and Parliament trust, they may have a fair point. Members may need to employ part-time secretaries or research assistants, but the secretary or research assistant need not have another outside interest at the same time. It also revealed a gap in the present arrangement: that the registration of those interests by the secretary or research assistant is done by them and the Member may well be totally unaware that it has taken place. I understand that is likely to be corrected. That is one area.

The second area perhaps includes people with consultancies arranging for entertainment in the House of Commons, the question already referred to, the question of EDMs, of Parliamentary Questions, of amendments, of votes and of deputations to Ministers. All of these are difficult issues where there are problems in drawing a line, but perhaps you might wish to pursue those in the course of questioning. Thank you very much.

LORD NOLAN: Thank you very much. Can I ask Diana Warwick please, to carry on.

899. DIANA WARWICK: Indeed. I think that you answered several of the questions I had scribbled down. You have had experience in Opposition, Ministerial experience, you have sat on Select Committees and you are on the Public Accounts Committee. You have been an MP, as you said, for 30 years. You have talked about the dangers of limiting new MPs coming into the House, but I wondered whether, over that time, you have seen any key changes in the standards expected of MPs?

TERENCE HIGGINS: No, I do not think there has been a great difference but undoubtedly, of course, the advent of outside lobbyists has changed the general atmosphere in a number of respects. I should incidentally say I am a Member of the Public Accounts Commission and I suspect—I may be wrong—Mr. Newton, when he spoke earlier, referred to the Public Accounts Committee when he should have said "Commission". They are, of course, two different bodies. I am not on the PAC, I am on the Public Accounts Commission. No, I do not detect a great deal of difference but undoubtedly, particularly with the advent of television and so on, the general atmosphere in the House has changed quite significantly. And I think to some extent that has reflected differences in pay levels and an earlier precursor of my fear that we do have a recruitment problem. Not, of course, in terms of numbers of applicants for any given seat—we are unlikely to have any uncontested general elections—but in terms of the quality. And reference was made to lawyers—a huge difference in the House now as far as lawyers are concerned. When I first came in there were a number of really quite distinguished lawyers. It would be a very benevolent lawyer of the top rank who now decided that he would give it all up and come into the House of Commons and concentrate on that. I hate to think by what fraction his income would decline.

900. DIANA WARWICK: If standards have not got worse, or they do not appear to have got worse, what do you think accounts for what appears to be a very considerable change in public perception about MPs? You have probably heard the statistic that we have used quite a lot, that 64 per cent (I think I have got it right) 64 per cent of the population think most MPs make a lot of money out of their parliamentary position. That is a rather extraordinary statistic—can you account for that?

TERENCE HIGGINS: Yes, I think it is a very understandable view because the remarks which I made earlier have to be put against the background of what the public's perception is of these kinds of amounts. And certainly pensioners living on a National Insurance pension with a top-up of income support will view these figures as something beyond belief and will therefore be under the impression that Members of Parliament are making a large sum of money. But as far as your own enquiry is concerned I do not think it is the relevant consideration. The relevant consideration is whether those levels and the fact that people are also earning money outside are appropriate in circumstances where we have to get the right people into Parliament, and if you are concerned with standards in public life then the fundamental of that must be—what quality of person is going into public life, what quality of person is becoming a Member of Parliament, what quality of person is becoming a Minister?—and that is not inconsistent at all with the public perception which you have just mentioned. What I think is important is that you should not look at it from that point of view.

901. DIANA WARWICK: How do you think that can be conveyed because you placed a lot of emphasis on the number of hours that are worked, for example, by MPs and the huge drop in the salary of Ministers and the virtual

level-pegging only of MPs' pay. How could the public be convinced that the quality of the work done is as high as you and, indeed, many of our witnesses have said?

TERENCE HIGGINS: I think it is a difficult task for you but I think it is a task that you have to face and I think you will be helpful in this respect and I hope will help to persuade the public. It is unlikely that one will get the same response, I feel bound to say, from the Press. The misrepresentation of the increase which took place recently—Members are paid many times the rate of inflation, double the rate of inflation—if you took the period from the last increase that was totally untrue—I do not think that one is likely to get a very supportive view, looking at the broader issues, as far as Press presentation is concerned. This is a problem, it is a hazard of political life, it is an occupational hazard. I recognise that that is so. But I do think you have a role to play in this.

902. DIANA WARWICK: Do you think that has anything to do with outside interests of MPs, that they are perceived not only to earn an income but also earn a lot of money outside?

TERENCE HIGGINS: Yes, no doubt that is part of it. But, as I say, I think nonetheless there are arguments in favour of outside interests which I have already deployed.

903. DIANA WARWICK: Yes. You gave us, I think, some very convincing arguments about the need to maintain the ability of MPs to earn money outside. You yourself have some outside interests. I wonder—could you say in general terms whether there are outside interests which give you cause for concern and perhaps more specifically where you yourself would draw the line?

TERENCE HIGGINS: I think it is very much a question of the relationship with the individual organisations concerned and I think one must bear in mind very much the normal rules of the House and in particular Madam Speaker's statement which was made, I think, on a particular day—I do not have the exact reference in front of me—but, yes, I think on 12th July, and I think it is not inappropriate one should, if one has an outside interest, make it clear that that is the standard which one ought to operate. Though I feel bound to say it may well be that one's outside interests have absolutely nothing whatsoever to do with the House of Commons. One may have been asked to go on a particular board quite regardless of that. And, indeed, that is certainly the case in the directorships which I hold. There is then a problem, as I say, which is nonetheless if you then find that you have a particular expertise, what should one do about it? Generally, I must say, I have not felt it appropriate to do so. But that is a matter for individual Members' judgment, I think.

904. DIANA WARWICK: Have you yourself ever been presented with a problem of conflict of interest?

TERENCE HIGGINS: Not that I can recall.

905. DIANA WARWICK: Could I go on to raise a point that has come up in this whole question of both outside interests and in particular in relation to lobbying and lobbying firms? The distinction has been drawn between advising an outside body and acting for it in the House and you drew a quite interesting distinction, I think, between outflow of advice about the House and its nature and inflow into the House. Do you draw that distinction then between advice and advocacy on behalf of an interest—do you see that as a real distinction?

TERENCE HIGGINS: Yes, I think there is clearly a real distinction. The point I was seeking to make was this: that I think as far as the flow in one direction is concerned, that is to say from the House to outside, generally speaking I think it would be true to say that is probably not objectionable. As far as the flow in the other direction is concerned you then have much more difficult problems as far as drawing the line is concerned and some of those came up in the earlier discussion.

906. DIANA WARWICK: Do you have any particular views about professional lobbying firms? We have had several witnesses from those firms and a lot of questions about the role of lobbying firms, vis-a-vis MPs. Do you have any views about whether they should be distinguished as inappropriate?

TERENCE HIGGINS: I think it is important to bear in mind the point which Mr. Newton was making. I think that Ministers generally are well able to cope with the situation. You, of course, you do have a question as to whether Members of Parliament should be employed by lobbying firms. That is something which you will have to decide. I personally do not think it appropriate to become associated with such a firm which may then have a variety of interests which are not distinguished. I think the professional lobbying firm is a recent innovation and it does create real problems on which you will need to take a view.

907. DIANA WARWICK: You said that transparency is all important and that proper registration was a part of that transparency and it ought to be apparent whether an MP has outside interests. Do you think the current Register adequately reflects that concern, that need for transparency?

TERENCE HIGGINS: I think so but it is a question of it being properly enforced and as far as I am aware that is the case. But, of course, if there is a situation where it is discovered that someone has not registered properly then that is obviously completely wrong and it seems to me incompatible with the view which the House would take on the matter.

908. DIANA WARWICK: The entries are very varied. Do you think there is an argument for giving guidelines about the way in which the entries should be clarified—there should be more information given about the nature of the contacts and so on?

TERENCE HIGGINS: Well there is, of course, the stipulation with regard to lobbying firms, that any particular client of that firm should be disposed. That seems to me appropriate. But generally speaking I think the Register is working reasonably well.

909. DIANA WARWICK: One of the points that has been put to us is that the financial gain made by Members of Parliament from their outside interests should be declared as well as the source of the income. I wonder if you could comment on that and whether you think that would be an aid to transparency?

TERENCE HIGGINS: This has been discussed on a number of occasions, of course. I do not myself take the view that that would be appropriate simply because one either has an interest or one does not, and the amount I do not think is actually relevant. I think you either do or do not have an interest.

910. DIANA WARWICK: Could I just ask you about the possibility of introducing a code of conduct for MPs? When we saw the *Sunday Times* to ask them amongst other things about the issue of "Cash for Questions", one of the issues that emerged was in approaching MPs they had identified the fact that MPs were not really very clear about what the ethics of that situation were. Do you think that could be helped by a proper code of conduct for MPs?

TERENCE HIGGINS: It might well be appropriate to clarify that. I would not myself think it appropriate to put down a question on behalf of an outside interest but this is a personal view and, of course, colleagues may well take a different view on that as, indeed, you may do.

911. DIANA WARWICK: I was quite interested in a note that I saw in the House Magazine about the possibility—I think it came up from a report last year—about the possibility of there being, as there is a Citizen's Charter, an MPs' Charter or a Constituent's Charter, possibly a Voter's Charter. Do you think if members of the public or constituents understood better the relationship with their MPs, were able to ask MPs how they spent their time, what they could expect of them, whether, if they had a mechanism for complaint about an MP that that would increase the understanding by constituents of the role of MPs that you talked about earlier?

TERENCE HIGGINS: Yes, I do not think the public at large really understands to any great extent the way in which a Member of Parliament works—I think that is true—either in terms of constituency mail, in terms of "interview nights" on a Friday, which may well go on for many hours, and so on, or, indeed, their role in the House. I think there is a lack of understanding of what the work of an MP really involves. That has, however been improved to some extent by television, I think. They get a clearer idea, but I feel bound to say in that context the concentration on Prime Minister's Question Time presents a distorted view of what life is normally like and certainly in that respect I think the televising of Select Committees, which I think has been an enormous advance in increasing Ministerial accountability to the House of Commons, is something which, generally speaking, the public now are beginning to understand and I believe it does have very considerable value.

912. DIANA WARWICK: Could I ask then one final question? Several of our witnesses have criticised the adequacy of the House regulating itself—I think it came up also in the discussion with Tony Newton. How effectively is misbehaviour identified and punished, in your view?

TERENCE HIGGINS: Well, as Mr. Newton was pointing out, this is a matter for the Privileges Committee or the Members' Interests Committee. I have already indicated that I think there may be a case for looking at the structure of the House of Commons as far as dealing with these matters is concerned and I would hope that that might improve the situation. I am inclined to the view, as I said, that it is not satisfactory at the moment. I would be somewhat doubtful about the analogy drawn earlier with the Comptroller and Auditor General; looking into those

matters is vastly different from looking into the kind of matter which we were just considering, and I am not at all clear how such a body would in fact operate or whether it would, in fact, be appropriate.

913. DIANA WARWICK: Do you think then that when there has been serious misdemeanours that the punishment metered out by the House in your recollection has been adequate or do you think that being inadequate it has added to the public's concern?

TERENCE HIGGINS: I think those decisions of the House it would not be appropriate for me to comment on. I think the House has taken a view in any individual case. I think it is true that it is difficult to think at times of appropriate punishments, but this is a matter for the House. I do not think it would be appropriate for an outside body, on the kind of issues we are discussing here, to make decisions on that kind of thing.

LORD NOLAN: Going round the other way this time, Tom King, have you got any questions?

914. TOM KING: This issue about where you draw the line—and certainly we have had some very interesting evidence here—we have this issue at the moment in Parliament about what is called "Cash for Questions" and yet we had some very clear evidence from a trade union which, and you will know from your time in Parliament, sponsors and pays a number of MPs—in fact pays them on both sides of the House—and I asked them whether part of their duties, having been paid, was to table questions, and they said "Yes". Does that surprise you?

TERENCE HIGGINS: Well, I think there is a great variety of opinion on these issues. I have made my own position clear on this. I think it is also important to recognise that there may well be outside interests which, as I say, do not arise at all from one's position in the House, where it would be perfectly clear to both the person with the outside interest and that interest that there was no question of taking any action in the House—if you like, as I was saying, a flow in the other direction—and that is, I think, often the case.

915. TOM KING: I think you were here when I asked Tony Newton a question about Standing Committees. Do you have any more thoughts on that? Did you hear the question—maybe you do not remember.

TERENCE HIGGINS: Perhaps you would repeat it for me, yes.

916. TOM KING: Well, it is the point really about—we are tending to focus on declaration of Members' interests, particularly in relation to the Chamber, speeches, questions, Early Day Motions, and I raised the issue—and Dame Anne—talking about Select Committees and also Standing Committees with the power to amend Bills and whether it is possible to screen the Standing Committees more carefully in that respect. Whether it is necessary.

TERENCE HIGGINS: Well, I would certainly agree that, if you like, the most serious error where problems may arise would be with regard to actually amending the law and I think it is absolutely vital, in those circumstances, that interest should be declared. And if that is so then I think, as Mr. Newton was pointing out, Ministers are likely to understand what the pressures are, would still consider the matter on its merits. But transparency is vitally important there. As to screening Standing Committees that is a very interesting point which I think deserves consideration. It is related to the situation on Select Committees and there is a distinction there between Standing and Select Committees and perhaps I might turn to that if you want to pursue the Select Committee issue. But it is true that there is a distinction, I think, between membership of Standing Committees and membership of Select Committees. I think there is not generally speaking as much attention paid to interest as far as Standing Committees are concerned as is the case with Select Committees.

LORD NOLAN: I hate to interrupt but I must mention to other members of the committee that we are running short of time. Have you finished, Tom?

TOM KING: Yes, thank you.

917. WILLIAM UTTING: One question, Chairman. What you were saying about transparency, Sir Terence, seems to lead on to the formulation of a general principle along the lines that any paid interest that may influence an MP's conduct on parliamentary business ought to be both clearly identifiable and clearly identified. Would that be an acceptable formulation of a general principle, as far as you are concerned?

TERENCE HIGGINS: Yes, but it is very general and I am not sure it greatly helps in drawing lines.

WILLIAM UTTING: Okay. Thank you very much.

918. ANNE WARBURTON: Could I just raise a marker—not, perhaps, so much to be discussed now—we do not talk very often about constituencies. We were told that every constituency thinks that their MP is an exception to the generally low standard so that that, perhaps, is encouraging, but I just wondered whether Sir Terence had reflected at all on whether relationships between Parliamentarians and their constituencies could in some way be developed in a way which would reassure public opinion. As I said—no notice—this is perhaps just a question to throw out.

TERENCE HIGGINS: I think it is a matter for the individual Member of Parliament and I would hope my relationship with my constituency is entirely satisfactory. It is something which one develops over a long period of time and certainly as far as both mail and interview sessions and so on are concerned I think that is something which is extremely important. But it is then a question of making oneself available and publicising one's interview nights and so on. But you may be right—I think every Member of Parliament thinks his is all right but there may be others who do not have the same relationship.

919. PETER SHORE: Yes. Sir Terence, you drew the line in a rather interesting way, where you said there was a big difference between information flowing out of the House to an outside interest and actions, as it were, and advocacy flowing in from an outside interest. Can you apply that principle, or that distinction, to two, I think, very important areas of possible influence being used by a paid Member of Parliament? One is in access to Ministers—would you accept that it would be not acceptable for a Member of Parliament, who was tied to an outside interest in a financial sense, to seek to influence Ministers directly by access to them or in other ways?

TERENCE HIGGINS: I think I take the same position which I understood Mr. Newton to take—I think it is a question of transparency—and if it is entirely transparent then I think that the Minister concerned will discount accordingly.

920. PETER SHORE: You would say the same, I gather, from an earlier reply, about what you yourself accepted as very important, moving amendments to a Bill, something that was going to become a law. You think that there again all that is required is transparency and declaration of interest, not some actual prohibition of advocacy?

TERENCE HIGGINS: I find that one extremely difficult. I think that is where drawing the line is particularly difficult and I think you will find that opinion in the House probably varies quite a bit on that. But, as I say, I think if it is transparent then it is certainly the case that those listening to the arguments will discount it accordingly. It may indeed be the case that they take the view that they ought to look at this particular set of arguments even more carefully than they otherwise would.

PETER SHORE: Thank you.

921. CLIFFORD BOULTON: Could I just take the opportunity of your presence here to ask you about the working of Select Committees, because you are Chairman of the liaison committee which consists of the Chairmen effectively of all the other Select Committees. In a really desperate attempt to get a little good news on the record, it is a fact, is it not, that your committee does have regard to standards of conduct in the Select Committees. For instance, you have developed rules for the behaviour of Members who find they have got interests in a particular inquiry, which works to such an extent that the Chairman could be of a very sensitive and important inquiry—and I happen to have Pergau Dam in mind—but can, in fact because of some previous industrial or commercial experience stand down, with the consequence that the Chairman of the inquiry would actually be a Member of the other side of the House? This is a very striking example which one would find very very difficult to find in any other Parliament anywhere, of Members behaving in that kind of sensitive way. But I am afraid it does not get very much attention when that kind of thing happens.

TERENCE HIGGINS: Well, I am glad to have an opportunity of dealing with this particular point which I think also arose in an earlier discussion with Mr. Newton and I want to pursue that in a moment. Yes, I think the rules with regard to Select Committees have been tightened very significantly, partly, I think, because Select Committees and particularly Departmental Select Committees are such an important part of our parliamentary procedures which have developed over the last decade. But the situation is as you have described it, in fact there are even more points to be considered, that is to say if a Member on a Select Committee has an interest in the particular matter on which the Committee is taking evidence, deliberating, he has to declare that interest whenever he is examining a witness. He has to say to the witness "I have to declare an interest". It is also the case that now, as a result of the report of the Select Committee's first reporting session 1991 and a subsequent debate on the floor of the House, that the system has been in practice very much tightened. Largely, if I may say so, Sir Clifford, through the operation of the Clerks who monitor these things very carefully indeed. And it is therefore the case that Members have to declare to their colleagues on the Committee whether they have interests and I was particularly concerned—and perhaps I might let you have my evidence to the Select Committee on Members' Interests who, in the event, together with the debate on the floor of the House, largely adopted what I suggested—that the role of Chairman is particularly important. Chairmen obviously have a leading role in the committee, they are responsible for drafting the report which, while it may get amended by the committee, is probably going to form the basic framework of the recommendation, so it is very important indeed that the position of Chairman should be absolutely clear. And I therefore suggested—and this is now general practice—that before a committee elects a chairman all the possible candidates make absolutely clear to their colleagues whether they have any relevant interests and they are taken into account and I imagine that generally speaking a committee would not elect a chairman who clearly had such an interest which was broad and covering the same range as the committee itself. That seems to me to be very important protection.

I feel bound to say, also, that a committee is a comparatively small group and the crucial question is what is the relevance of the interest to the committee's work and I do think the best group to decide whether it is relevant or not is, in fact, the members of the committee. So I believe we have made a very considerable improvement as far as that is concerned.

There are, however, problems if a particular matter comes up which was not foreseen, if you like. It may be a Treasury Committee or the Trade Committee which has very broad remit and the chairman then discovers, or a Member discovers, that he has an interest which was not previously relevant, and in those circumstances I think it is appropriate for the committee to consider the matter and if need be the chairman will stand down. Mr. Shore will know that that happened in the case of the Pergau Dam affair and it seems to me entirely appropriate. It may be, however, that the interest is relatively remote and there was a case recently where the committee decided that it was not appropriate for the chairman to stand down. But I think select committees generally are very conscious of the importance of this because the committee may make a recommendation which the Government then subsequently implements. And vitally important, therefore, that any interests which are relevant should be declared and witnesses appearing should be clear what they are, whether the committee is meeting in public or in private. I think myself that the protections which we now have in that respect, largely working by custom rather than resolution of the House (though some of the matters are dealt with in that way) on the whole is working pretty well. I was therefore rather surprised by the remark which Dame Anne made about evidence which I gather you are about to hear and about which I was unaware.

LORD NOLAN: Well, Dame Anne was putting down a marker rather than asking a question, but I hope you may be able to stay and listen perhaps.

TERENCE HIGGINS: Was it in relation to Select Committees?

ANNE WARBURTON: I do not know if I can answer that—Mr. Raphael will no doubt be revealing shortly.

TERENCE HIGGINS: If it is in relation to Standing Committees as I say I think there is a distinction between the two. But generally speaking I think the Committee of Selection and Members themselves would be doubtful—and it would raise questions—of going on a committee where clearly their interests are specifically relevant to the work of that committee. But I am not myself aware of a case where that is so. Maybe people have expertise in the area but not as far as I am aware otherwise. At all events they would certainly have to declare them and if it were the question of the chairman then he would certainly have to declare them before he was elected chairman and the committee would have to take a view on whether the matter was relevant to his election or not.

LORD NOLAN: Well, I think you have helped very much to prepare us for that evidence when we hear it.

922. MARTIN JACOMB: Could I go right back to the beginning? You put tremendous emphasis on the level of pay and its effect on the quality of people and that I can understand. I hope that does not mean that public service freely given—the days of that are numbered. But could I just ask you, do you think the pay of MPs is directly connected with the number of MPs who are reaching outside the House of Commons for income from sources which give rise to the problems we are investigating?

TERENCE HIGGINS: I should make it clear I do not think the answer is simply to change the pay structure and then to say "no outside interests". I think that the House would be a poorer place anyway if that were so, not least because Members would tend to be very much dependent on their parliamentary situation and very much in the clutches of the Whips. So I think that is another point which needs to be borne in mind. No, clearly, as the successive reports of the pay review bodies have pointed out, pay is only one of the considerations which lead to someone determining whether he wants to become a Member of Parliament or, indeed, to become a Minister. But naturally having family responsibilities, a Member of Parliament is likely to take into account a whole complex of issues and whether he is able to have outside interests I think is likely to be something which is relevant. And also as far as when one takes on the job of a Minister is concerned—particularly the problem which Mr. Newton rightly drew attention to—as far as Ministers finding themselves barred after they have become a Minister from taking some other outside occupation. But, as I have said, I think there is a case in that context for considering whether some outside body similar to that which exists—or indeed the same—which exists with regard to Civil Servants is a relevant consideration.

923. LORD NOLAN: Thank you very much, Sir Terence. We have taken up a lot of your time and we are very grateful to you for the views you have put forward. You have been most helpful and interesting. Thank you.

I wonder if Mr. Adam Raphael could join us? Mr. Raphael, you are the former Political Editor of the *Observer* and now, of course, a writer on Home Affairs for the Economist. Have you prepared an opening statement which you wish to make before we ask you questions?

ADAM RAPHAEL

ADAM RAPHAEL: I have just got one very brief thing, if I could, Mr. Chairman, which is that I very much welcome the establishment of this committee. My own view is that the House of Commons has proved incapable of reforming itself and that the need for reform is very urgent. In particular I believe there needs to be much fuller disclosure of interests by MPs, including monetary amounts they receive from consultancies or outside employment, which they are speaking to on behalf in the House. I also believe that the record of the disciplinary bodies within the House of Commons, the Privileges Committee and the Select Committee on Members' Interests, do not inspire public confidence and therefore those are some of the reasons why I think the establishment of this committee is very necessary and very welcome.

LORD NOLAN: Thank you very much. Now, as you know, we take it in turns to take the lead, so to speak, in asking questions of the witnesses who have been kind enough to volunteer and jump into the public arena over these matters and it is Mr. Tom King's turn to ask you questions, please, from now on.

924. TOM KING: Do you, looking at Parliament—we had a little discussion, I think you were here, a little earlier and I asked Tony Newton a question—about the question of a range of backgrounds for MPs and trying to ensure that one kept open the widest possible recruiting field for MPs so that it genuinely was a form in which people came with experience of wide aspects of all our national life. Do you think that is right?

ADAM RAPHAEL: Yes, I do, I share that view. I think it would be wrong to have a solely professional body of professional politicians.

925. TOM KING: But you did suggest in one of your articles the point that you could—I am not sure if it was an earlier kite that you were flying, in other words to invite comments—but you suggested there might be a situation where we had "full-time" MPs who were paid a higher salary and "part-time" MPs who were paid a lower salary and that could be offered to constituencies to decide which they liked. I think you wrote that in the *Economist*.

ADAM RAPHAEL: Well, it was printed in the *Economist*. It is not a view I personally share but I can see some people might see some merit in it and some of my colleagues saw some merit in it. The rest of the piece is written by me. That particular bit of the article I must say did not appear under my name, may I say, and therefore I would not wholly subscribe to it. I can see it is an interesting idea but I think it would be impracticable and I also think it would be undesirable to have two classes of MPs, a professional MP and a sort of lay MP who would be allowed to have outside interests. So the *Economist* is often stimulating—but not views I always share.

926. TOM KING: Thank you very much. That is fair enough because it makes it consistent with your view about a wider interest. Do you hold a view that it is acceptable—even you may say desirable—that people have a range of different backgrounds, a range of outside interests, that there are some that should be prohibited?

ADAM RAPHAEL: When you say there are some aspects that should be prohibited, I am very uneasy. The practice that has grown up over many years in Parliament—certainly over the past twenty years—of people speaking to paid interests in Parliament and

putting down Early Day Motions, putting down questions, a whole range of activities, actual lobbying of fellow MPs, and there is obviously a wide range of views in Parliament which I suppose is one of the reasons why Parliament has been unable to act against what I saw—and MPs have seen—is a clear abuse.

927. TOM KING: But what has come out of our investigation so far—very clear evidence that people have given us—is that there is a lot of lobbying going on, that it is desirable that it should—as Tony Newton said—arguments that are to be made should be properly and clearly made, and efficiently made, to Members of Parliament and there seem to be some that are acceptable and some that are not. One of the ones that has come up as "acceptable" is the Police Federation which I think under the Police Act, because they do not have the opportunity to strike, Parliament agreed that they should be able to have a representative in Parliament who could put forward their position. Do you think that is acceptable—it is a two-part question really? The other evidence we have had which is very interesting, was the evidence from the UNISON union, which includes NALGO, but also includes NUPE and COHSE, and one bit of evidence which came out is that COHSE is funding to the extent, I think, of £15,000, the whole of what the Labour Party hope will be the future Government health team. Now, no lobbyist, I think, would go that far. Is that acceptable lobbying, or not?

ADAM RAPHAEL: Perhaps I could deal with the Police Federation point first? Obviously that is a practice that has been in existence for many years, but I must say that I am attracted by the distinction that I believe some members of this committee are drawing, between lobbying which consists of advice which appears to be permissible and which I would agree is permissible—you are giving advice on parliamentary procedure, you are giving advice on how to approach Ministers—and paid advocacy in the House of Commons which is not. And even though there have been eminent spokesmen of the Police Federation, including a former Prime Minister, I believe that is a practice that should cease and that it should no longer be permissible to be a paid advocate in the House for a fee. Of course, that is by far the most respectable element of it, widely understood and widely considered. But clearly if one is going to make a distinction between paid advocacy and pure advice I think the line has to be drawn there. I think it is very interesting that the former Prime Minister I was referring to once got into considerable trouble with the House himself because when on a finance committee he said "When I look at Member X and I look at Member Y I think of the coal industry. When I look at so-and-so I look at—I do not know—the Securities Industry" and what have you, and he was made to apologise for that remark. There was another Labour MP who again, talking about MPs for hire, was forced to apologise to the House. Both these remarks in my view were perfectly justifiable and permissible and shows in a sense, I suspect, how Parliament has been very slow to get hold of this for very good reason. So I am rather tough on it, I believe there has to be a sharp distinction drawn.

On the question of COHSE and its members—this is a point often raised about Labour MPs and their sponsorship of one kind or another, and I think it would be much better if any money that was paid was paid directly to constituency parties to avoid misunderstandings. But the influence that trade unions exert on MPs to the extent that they do is not really a question of money, £500 to £600 here or there that is really irrelevant. What is relevant, arguably, is not a question of money, but a question of whether the MP is going to be selected or de-selected and that really is obviously a considerable influence. So I think to try and draw parallels, as so often is done I know in the House of Commons between paid sponsorship of MPs and paid consultancies and advocacies which are going on, I think that the comparison doesn't really stand up.

928. TOM KING: And yet there is a Register of Members' Interests, everybody declares those. If one achieves that measure of transparency is that acceptable? Would you like to comment your views on the Register?

ADAM RAPHAEL: Well, I must say I regard the Register as an extremely flawed instrument and I believe, contrary to what the Select Committee on Members' Interests has always maintained, that it is absolutely essential to register the precise monetary amount which the MP is receiving. I would also like to know what he is getting the money for. There is a world of difference, and I am sure you would agree, between an MP who receives, shall we say, a consultancy of £1,000 to advise some company on parliamentary procedure, and a company which is paying an MP £20,000 or £30,000 for quite different activities which might involve lobbying, which might involve letters to Ministers, which might involve speaking in the House, which might involve a whole range of activities which I think many MPs would disapprove of. Terence Higgins was a very good example: he wouldn't touch certain activities with a barge-pole—he didn't say it in quite those words. That is just a journalistic approximation of what he was doing, but he showed his distaste for certain things, and this is widespread through the House. A lot of MPs dislike very much what is going on but don't feel that they can actually rule it out because the view of the House generally is incapable of reaching agreement on these areas and I am afraid will always be unable to reach agreement, in my view, given the composition of the House.

929. TOM KING: Have you watched, in your long career, the efforts of the House to discipline—in other words, the operations of the Privileges Committee? Do you have any comments on that?

ADAM RAPHAEL: Yes, I do. When I first arrived at the House one of the earliest stories I did was involving the MPs who were linked to Poulson. As far as the MPs were concerned, it was obviously traumatic; it was quite traumatic for me as well, as I was being sued for libel by all the MPs who I named in the article. So I took a considerable degree of interest in how their cases were handled by the House and I suppose my attitude to some extent dates from that time.

I was appalled, actually, by the way these cases were handled by the Select Committee on Members' Interests. For a start, they were totally incapable of conducting the sort of detailed investigation that was necessary. That is not a criticism of the individuals who were on that committee at the time. They lacked the facilities, they lacked the abilities and they lacked the research staff to be able to do a fair job, quite apart from any question of impartiality and fairness in relation to the MPs and the fact that they should have a fair hearing; after all, their professional careers were at stake.

But what worried me even more was that the committee eventually came to a unanimous view, with some

difficulty, I suspect, because of the range of interests around the committee, but when it came to the House they fell apart. The committee voted in different ways. Even those members of the committee who had signed the report then voted against their own report, and, if anyone goes back to it now, I think the debate in the House on the Poulson MPs was a disgrace. I suppose that from that point onwards my attitude has been rather sour in relation to these committees. MPs have many qualities, but a judicial quality is not one of them, and particularly when they are divided by party and by interest, it is impossible for them to be a properly functioning judicial body, quite apart from an investigative body.

Therefore, I believe there has to be an outside element. In fact, I am very wary of the idea of just having two assessors sitting on a body dominated by MPs. I think that would be a great mistake. I do not believe those assessors would be able to help a great deal. I think there has to be a separate body, possibly, as the Chairman mentioned, a form of ombudsman of some kind, which would be separate and it could then make recommendations which the House would be free to accept or reject.

930. TOM KING: I think you have been very clear on that, and others may want to explore that a bit further. Can I just ask you one last question? Ministers leaving office—have you any comments on that?

ADAM RAPHAEL: Yes. There is clearly public concern, and I think there has got to be a tightening up of what Ministers are or are not allowed to do on leaving office. I take the point that there is obviously some distinction and insecurity in relation to Ministers' lives compared to civil servants', but I don't see why there shouldn't be a code of conduct and I don't see why there shouldn't be an independent body which might look at whether a Minister should indeed go straight to an industry which he privatised perhaps 12 months or two years previously. I think that would be very wise. I think it would be a protection for the Minister as well. I cannot think that these ex-Ministers who are being criticised can enjoy the sort of public criticism they have been subjected to, and I think it would be very sensible to regularise this area.

931. WILLIAM UTTING: On these questions of restoring public confidence in the way the House regulates the conduct of MPs, you are advocating in the first place a much fuller Register of Interests, with much more detailed information and, in the second place, the introduction of an independent element into the disciplinary processes. On the latter point, the example of some of the professional colleges has been trailed before us as quite a good one, in which they have brigaded in, so to speak, up to about a third of lay people in considering disciplinary charges against members of the professions. Do you think that something based on that model is a possibility?

ADAM RAPHAEL: I am slightly worried about mix and match. I think MPs are such a peculiar group. When I say "peculiar" I don't use the word in a pejorative sense, but they are a very, very distinct group of people and they have their own imperatives and their own forces working on them, and I think the idea of matching lay people in with a group of MPs would be very, very difficult indeed. I think it would be bitterly resented by the MPs, apart from anything else. MPs have a knack of nosing out political sympathies—within 30 seconds as well—and though they may originally be regarded as lay people, I think they would be quickly identified with particular interests by those MPs. Therefore, I don't believe it would work.

932. WILLIAM UTTING: On the other hand, if you take this out of the hands of MPs altogether, or at least propose doing that, in view of the sensitivities that have already been exposed to us and the importance of the constitutional principle about MPs controlling everything that relates to Parliament, it would seem to be quite difficult to come up with something that is going to be acceptable.

ADAM RAPHAEL: I don't think necessarily that is so, though this really gets quite outside the area of my competence, but what I would have said is that an outside body would make recommendations to the House. It would be open to the House to reject them, if they wanted to, as has happened with recommendations of the Privileges Committee and indeed of the Select Committee on Members' Interests. I think it would be difficult for the House to reject a well-considered finding, but nevertheless it would be open to it to do so. Parliament would still be sovereign, but there would be an outside body with proper investigative powers who would be able to make a recommendation to the House.

933. WILLIAM UTTING: Thank you very much. Could I just go back to the point you made about trade union-sponsored MPs, which seems to me to be a kind of a special case in the situation that we're looking at. In effect, what you are suggesting here is that one simply does away with the problem by getting the money taken away from specific MPs and put into specific constituencies, or even as a political donation to a political party.

ADAM RAPHAEL: Yes. As I say, I regard it as a very minor problem. The real problem, as I think I suggested, was not the money but the question that these people's jobs—selection and deselection—may or may not depend in certain circumstances on a trade union's influence, and that will remain. I don't think the money is really a very important thing. In fact I frankly think it's one of those hares, a very useful political hare, which has run for many years and no doubt will continue to run.

934. WILLIAM UTTING: There's a general question about how important the money is, in any case, because there may be other kinds of links between people that are actually more influential than the passage of money, but I think we're focusing on money at the moment.

ADAM RAPHAEL: We're talking about very, very small sums on the whole. Certainly in all my time in Parliament I was not aware that it ever played a major part. That is not to say that MPs may not be influenced by their sponsorship. You wouldn't find, for instance, an USDAW-sponsored MP speaking very loudly in favour of Sunday trading. I wouldn't have expected him to do so.

935. ANNE WARBURTON: I am not sure, first of all, whether to apologise to you or thank you for having introduced into our discussions the subject of membership of committees in the House. I was drawing particularly on a sentence in one of your articles, which reads: "MPs with direct commercial interests are allowed to serve on committees that draft legislation which might affect those interests", and I got slightly into trouble because I wasn't able to answer the question as to which committees you had in mind.

ADAM RAPHAEL: I am thinking of Standing Bill Committees, and what worries me is that membership of those committee, as I understand it and I am subject to correction by people who know a great deal more around this table, is a result of the Committee on Selection. The Committee on Selection, as I understand it, usually appoints to Standing Bill Committees on the basis of Second Readings in the House of Commons. What happens, and has happened in the past, certainly on some of the Standing Bill Committees that I have monitored, where there are considerable commercial interests involved, is that those MPs with commercial interests will speak on Second Reading and will declare those interests quite properly as the House demands, and will then be selected to serve on the Standing Bill Committee. There have been times, certainly in the 1980s, on crucial committees such as the Cable Bill Committee and the Aviation Bill Committee where there have been very considerable commercial interests and where, frankly, a clause which was of no interest whatsoever to the press as a whole, or indeed the general public, and will be unreported will go through as a result of the membership of that Standing Bill Committee and it may be worth millions to the industry concerned.

There was this extraordinary example on the Cable Bill Committee where Member after Member got up to declare, when the Committee began, a commercial interest linked to the cable industry. They knew a great deal about it. They had huge great briefs, the lobbyists were buzzing round this Committee and, as one neutral observer said, it gave that Committee a very unusual "flavour". In fact the Committee knew a great deal more than the poor Minister who was trying to take the Bill through, because these people were briefed to the nines, they all had commercial interests, they knew what they were talking about. These were very technical, difficult areas. The press were totally uninterested in it. It is just not self-correcting. My own view is that membership of the Standing Committees must be very much more carefully selected than the Committee on Selection does, and I would be very wary of putting a majority of MPs with commercial interests on a Standing Bill Committee.

I have given you one, I think flagrant, example and I am not trying to suggest that this happens every day of the year. It clearly doesn't. After all, there aren't all that many Bills with huge commercial interests involved. But this happened at least twice in my experience and it has probably happened a great deal more. There is an idea that the press are a very effective monitor of what goes on in Parliament—not so. The times I got on to things was purely by random. Someone may have spoken to me, a friendly MP might have said something to me, or maybe even a lobbyist. It was pure fluke. Then when I did get on to things, it was always quite worrying, because the libel risks were very, very considerable as soon as you started writing about this area. As I say, I've been sued quite a lot of times for libel by MPs at varying times.

So these are not areas that newspapers want to go into. Very few journalists ever, ever want to go into these areas, and they don't. Of course they are great stories if they can be proven and they are established, but most of the time they are time consuming, they are difficult and they probably command very little enthusiasm amongst your editors. So the idea of leaving it to the random, haphazard inquiries of the press I think is a great mistake.

I'm sorry, I have rambled on a bit, but I just wanted to illustrate what I think is a very, very worrying area.

ANNE WARBURTON: I was much interested in the last part of what Mr Raphael said, Chairman, but I wonder if on the first part, the committee part, others around the table who are more expert than I might want to take it on. I rest.

LORD NOLAN: Thank you very much.

936. PETER SHORE: I was also very interested in what you had to say about the aircraft, shipbuilding and other particular interests, where you had Bills affecting them. Obviously there is a great area of influence by Members who are on the Standing Committee, but when pressed on this, Mr Raphael, you said that there ought to be more careful selection for these Standing Committees. Are you not really saying that people with paid outside interests should not be able to put down amendments or serve on Standing Committees?

ADAM RAPHAEL: Yes, I'm glad you correct me. That must be the right view. If I could just reinforce that point, I don't want to make an attack on any individual, but when the chairman of a Committee on Selection quite recently was a paid director of a lobbying company, with considerable lobbying interests, you can see how difficult it is, I believe, and how negligent by default Parliament had become. This particular individual was, I have no doubt about it, a man of honour, but it is absolutely wrong that a crucial job like that, the Chairman of the Committee on Selection, the key guy—I suppose there is some sort of to-ing and fro-ing with the Whips, which you will know about, which I don't—should be a director of a lobbying company. It shows in a sense why Parliament was incapable of making sure that these Standing Committees did not have paid interests on them. But I absolutely accept your correction of what I was saying. You are absolutely right: there should not be paid interests on these committees.

937. PETER SHORE: What other activities in Parliament do you think that Members paid by outside interests should be debarred from pursuing? If I may run over them, putting down EDMs is No. 1.

ADAM RAPHAEL: Certainly. For instance, just to give another example on that, in hostile takeovers Early Day Motions have sometimes been used by firms to attack the bidders. There have been cases on IC Gas and others where the Early Day Motions have been subjected to that type of lobbying, where the merchant bank, the PR consultant and others have all got down Early Day Motions attacking the bidder, or the non-bidder, in these situations. The Barclay brothers once said they would have sued if—The Early Day Motion obviously was protected by parliamentary privilege, but they felt they had been grossly unfairly attacked by paid interests in the House.

938. PETER SHORE: Do you think also that people who have paid interests on behalf of outside interests should be prohibited from, as it were, using their influence to get at Ministers, being given the opportunity of special meetings with Ministers?

ADAM RAPHAEL: Again I must say I think the distinction the committee appears to be drawing between advice and paid advocacy is a good one. For instance, for an MP actually to sign the letter to the Minister "Will you see Bloggs and So-and-so?" I don't think is really proper conduct, even if he says "I am also a consultant to So-and-so". On the other hand, for the MP to draft a letter for some chairman who may or may not know quite the form to address a Minister strikes me as perfectly proper. That would be the line I would draw. I do not believe the MP should lend his name on a paid basis for making representations to Ministers. You then get into the difficult area of whether he is allowed to accompany the person. I leave that to better minds than my own.

939. PETER SHORE: To come to another really very difficult area, what about the freedom to speak, as it were—to advocate in speech in the House of Commons, whether on a committee or on the Floor of the House, when you are being paid by an interest to do so?

ADAM RAPHAEL: I think you should not do so, for the very reasons you stated in relation to Standing Bill Committees. I do not believe in the House, or indeed Parliamentary Questions—anything you are paid for directly—you should be allowed to do so. I think the line can be drawn. I'm sure it's difficult, but I'm sure that there can be a line drawn between giving advice and paid advocacy, and within that paid advocacy definition I certainly would include Parliamentary Questions, I certainly would include Early Day Motions, I certainly would include speeches in the House and I certainly would include representations to Ministers.

940. PETER SHORE: What would you say in respect of a prohibition on speaking in the House to those who say "Oh well, you will be ruling out from making a contribution people who have a very special knowledge of the subject in hand"?

ADAM RAPHAEL: Well, they don't have to have a paid interest. If they feel that they are being disbarred by taking a consultancy of £4,000 or £5,000, they can say "Look, I'd much prefer not to have my hands tied and to be able to speak on your behalf, because I think this is such an interesting and valuable area". I have no doubt, for instance—the police have been raised as a good example—that the police could find a representative in Parliament who would be keen and anxious to speak and who had a knowledge of police activities who would do it for no money at all. The idea that there has to be some form of payment I don't think is necessary. In fact I believe that any body such as the police or anyone else can always find an MP who is sufficiently interested in their affairs to do it on a voluntary basis. I do not believe it's necessary that they have to pay. I don't think it's essential and probably some of this money has been wasted in the past.

941. MARTIN JACOMB: Can I just ask you one question? I am so sorry to delay things, but you emphasised very understandably payment and the fact of payment ruling people out. How would you put a landlord of residential property speaking on, say, the leasehold enfranchisement Bill? Where would he stand?

ADAM RAPHAEL: He certainly would have to declare an interest.

942. MARTIN JACOMB: Obviously, but would he be in the same category as the Cable Bill Committee Members?

ADAM RAPHAEL: No, I don't believe he would be.

MARTIN JACOMB: Why.

ADAM RAPHAEL: Because he is not a paid advocate. He has a financial interest to declare. If he was paid by a landlords' association to represent them, then he would have a paid interest. If he has a financial interest, because he is himself a landlord, he would have to declare this interest, but he would not be disbarred in the same way. But I do believe that, if he is putting down Questions or putting down Early Day Motions, the nature of his interest should be disclosed. At the moment there is no disclosure of interest in relation to Parliamentary Questions or Early Day Motions.

TOM KING: That's not right.

ADAM RAPHAEL: Am I wrong? In Parliamentary Questions there is not.

TOM KING: And Early Day Motions, because I put one down recently about the live export of animals and I suddenly found that somebody had automatically put "R" against my name because I have interests in a small farm, and that I think comes out of a sort of automatic transfer from the Register of Members' Interests.

ADAM RAPHAEL: It must be fairly recent then. I'm sorry, I am subject to correction there. Certainly on Questions there is no declaration of interest.

943. TOM KING: You were just making the point about not contributing if you are a lobbyist but not if it's own background, your own interest, your own knowledge? That was the point, I think, that Sir Martin was asking about.

ADAM RAPHAEL: That is right.

944. MARTIN JACOMB: No, I understand the point you are making. I was just on the difficulty of drawing the line. I didn't follow the cable debate, but I gathered roughly what you were saying. You were saying that if you were a director or employed by a cable company, you would be debarred, but if you were a shareholder in it, you wouldn't be.

ADAM RAPHAEL: On the Standing Bill Committee, where the selection depends on the Committee of Selection, I would have thought all interests were relevant. You were asking me about speaking in the House of Commons. I do believe there could be a stricter test on Standing Bill Committees, where it is very sensitive. I don't know how many are on Standing Bill Committees, maybe a dozen, maybe a few more. Speaking in the House of Commons as a whole, where you declare an interest, I think there could be a laxer provision. I think there are difficult areas where the precise distinction needs to be drawn, but the idea that it can't be drawn in a way that would be understandable and followable by MPs, I don't believe that that is the case.

945. LORD NOLAN: Mr Raphael, you have been very clear and you have covered all the points I would have wished to put to you in answer to my fellow members of the committee. Thank you very much indeed for coming along.

Now we have Sir Peter Kemp. Sir Peter, thank you very much for coming to join us. We had of course an earlier letter from you which, speaking for myself, I read with

care. I can't say that I have had a chance to do more than glance quickly at another paper that you put before us this morning. Would you be able to cover them both in an opening statement? Would that be a good way of going ahead?

SIR PETER KEMP

PETER KEMP (Former Second Permanent Secretary, Cabinet Office): Yes, certainly, Chairman. I gather this is the first time the committee is coming near the Civil Service. I feel a bit awed by that, because I am an ex-civil servant of some two or three years ago and I worry a little bit.

I wrote to the secretary on 14th December in response, to your advertisement, from the point of view of somebody who has spent a good deal of my recent life involved in the reforms and, I like to think, modernisation of the British Civil Service and trying to bring it into the 21st century. I won't repeat in full what I said in my letter, but I touched on points such as thinking that the Civil Service on the whole, from my own personal observation, was, as it were, pretty clean, that there were perhaps some problems related to 15 years of one government, which maybe need to be thought about, that quangos weren't such a bad thing as they are made out to be, provided that the audit end and the appointment end are looked at a bit more, and of course trying to distinguish between the Next Steps agencies, which I helped to create, and quangos and so on, which are totally different animals but are often confused in the public mind.

946. LORD NOLAN: I wonder if, before you say any more, I could remind those here of what I said, which you perhaps hadn't heard when we started this morning. You are, I understand, someone who was formerly the senior civil servant responsible for managing organisational change in the Civil Service and you are now a member of the Audit Commission.

PETER KEMP: That's right, yes.

947. LORD NOLAN: You asked whether this was the first time we'd come really close to the position of civil servants. Well, people have touched on it, but we haven't come close to anyone with the same amount of experience and authority as you. Did you want to add to what you have said?

PETER KEMP: Just a couple of things. The secretary indicated a couple of specific questions which you want to ask me, and of course I am very pleased to try to answer them, but I would just like to say a couple of words about how I would approach these questions. These questions relate to codes of conduct and threats to ethics and so on.

The position I take on this is that, while the Civil Service is often described as a great national asset, which of course it is, it is also, and perhaps more importantly, a severely practical instrument. It is there to serve the public in the best possible way it can, doing what governments want done in the most effective and up-to-date way that it possibly can, and it really affects every aspect of our lives—personal, social, economic and so on. It's a very practical business, and of course it is not a cheap business. I did spend many years in the Treasury, but I hope I am forgiven for pointing out that it costs about £20 billion a year, which I believe is around 10p on the income tax.

Of course there have to be proper standards in the way the service behaves, but I think it is important not to lose sight of what the machine is actually there for and what it costs. Standards of conduct are, in my view, not actually the job of work to be done; they are an important part of the environment in which the job of work has to be carried out. That's the background to which I would answer your detailed questions.

LORD NOLAN: That's very helpful. I'm going to ask Lord Thomson if he will please take up the questions on behalf of the committee.

948. LORD THOMSON: Sir Peter, you are, if I may say so, a very appropriate and valuable witness from our point of view, as we start this section of our inquiry dealing with the Civil Service and ministerial aspects of standards in public life. Could I begin with my own favourite story about the Civil Service's role in our political system? It comes from an article that was written many years ago by Clement Attlee, as he then was, in "The Political Quarterly", where he described the Potsdam conference at the end of the second world war and how the conference took place in two parts. First there was Winston Churchill as Prime Minister and then there was Mr Attlee as Prime Minister, and both the Americans and the Russians were equally astonished when, after the British general election and a total change of government, exactly the same team of civil servants came back to serve the new government and new Prime Minister. I would regard that as one of the qualities—I was a working politician during most of my life—that I value in the Civil Service. Do you feel that it is being put at risk by 15 years of government of one particular party and do you think it's at risk in the future in terms of the new model Civil Service, of which you are one of the architects?

PETER KEMP: I think there are two separate things there. Yes, I think there may be a little bit of risk, after 15 years of one particular government. One has to remember—I am nearly old enough to remember—that in the Potsdam affair the Civil Service had been serving an all-party coalition government devoted to one special, unique aim, which was winning the war. Therefore, there was no notion of anybody having separate ideas. The civil servants were there: they were serving Mr Churchill, as he was, and then they served Mr Attlee. They were serving their country because they had got accustomed to doing that over the years and no doubt, if Mr Attlee had had different views about the Potsdam policy and so on, he would have said so, a good Minister will always say so, and the civil servants would no doubt have adjusted, if you like, what they were doing accordingly: they are servants.

I think that things are a little bit different now. We have now had 15 years of rather adversarial matters. There have also been very substantial changes happening in the outside world—information technology, Europe, globalisation, the way the Civil Service is run and all the rest of it. Very substantial changes have been going on. We've got a Civil Service where the power house of the Civil Service, as it were, that very narrow range where knowledge meets power, which is about 35 to 40—people like that—will never have served under any government except for the present government and without being in any way overtly politicised. I am not suggesting for a moment anyone was ever appointed to a post because of his political views. They take it in through their finger-tips, they take it in through their pores, they take in the way in which that particular government thinks and behaves and expects, and they go accordingly. So I think there has to be some kind of risk in that one.

On the other question you ask, I don't like the distinction between "policy" and "execution", I think it's a non-distinction, but if I may use policy and execution for the moment, I think on the policy side that could be so. On the execution side I think different problems arise and I don't think they're nearly so acute. We've got 100 or so agencies; we've got 75 per cent or so of Civil Service coming up that way. They are being led by new and different sorts of people recruited from outside, devoted to the job to be done, they are focused on doing the job and also, in my view, they are acutely aware of the special considerations that go with the delivery of public service the ethical considerations, the problem that if you're delivering service to somebody who has no choice where to go and often doesn't pay, you actually have a higher standard than otherwise. I think these are very much in all their minds. That isn't to say that I don't disagree with the Treasury and Civil Service Committee. The TCSC said they thought that the new way of doing things was not incompatible with ethics, etc., but went on to say you had to keep an eye on it. I would agree with that. I think you do have to keep an eye on it, but I think it can be kept an eye on and I think it will work.

949. LORD THOMSON: Our Civil Service tradition is really based on the Northcote-Trevelyan report of 1854. I notice you make the interesting comment in your article in *The Independent*, which you circulated to us, that the White Paper that came out recently is first major White Paper on the future of the Civil Service since that report. I want to probe whether there are any risks to the standards in the Civil Service arising out of the new structures that are proposed. I have in mind the new arrangements for the appointment of the heads of executive agencies. I think there are now around 90 of these.

PETER KEMP: A hundred, I think, yes.

LORD THOMSON: A hundred now, is it?

PETER KEMP: Yes.

950. LORD THOMSON: What I am really probing and trying to get the facts about is what is the role of Ministers in these appointments? As I understand it, Ministers receive a recommendation from an interviewing panel, but are not necessarily bound to accept that recommendation. Could you tell me what the situation is and comment on it?

PETER KEMP: I may be sounding a bit feeble on this one. To tell you the truth, I think that one isn't always terribly sure on this. I think that all the appointments to these agencies either are internal appointments or they will have been handled by the Civil Service Commission, possibly following outside appointment. The Civil Service Commissioners have very strict rules about fair and open competition, appointment based on merit and so on, going right back, as you say, to 1854 and Northcote-Trevelyan, and the Commissioners—you may be hearing from them—are a powerful, independent set of people and will choose properly and will make a proper selection of what they want. Thereafter, of course, I believe it's right to say that the Minister doesn't necessarily have to accept the individual who might be put in front of them, but that is not to say that the individual the Minister does accept must not have been also appointed through fair and open competition and on an ability to do the job properly. That's the way it is, and in my experience very many times, most times as far as I know, Ministers did accept the job that came up through the Civil Service Commissioner apparatus.

951. LORD THOMSON: I don't in any way wish to comment on an individual case, but there was of course a notable case recently in the prison service, where it was said that the appointment made by the Minister was not the recommendation of the interviewing panel. I make no comment at all on the quality of the appointment, but is a basic fundamental tenet of the Northcote-Trevelyan proposition of total politician neutrality not put at some risk if there is that degree of Ministerial intervention in a very sensitive top appointment?

PETER KEMP: I think it depends what the job is to do. I don't know about the detail of the prison service appointment, I only know what I read in the newspaper, but I think it's what the job is to do. Perhaps in the past, and for the great majority of Civil Service jobs, it is relatively uncontentious: the job is there, you can write a job description, and the job is to do a thing in a certain way. I don't know what Ministers felt about the relative candidates for the prison service, but it could just be that one of the candidates was going to do the job in a particular way, in a particular manner, which the Minister felt, although he would do it extremely well, was not what he wanted; he wanted the job done a different way. These are servants to deliver the public services the Ministers want. If the Minister felt that, no matter how worthy and admirable candidate No. 1 was, he wasn't actually going to deliver what the Minister wanted, then I think as a citizen, and as a former civil servant, that the Minister is right to choose the second person, provided he too is adequate to do the job and has been appointed fairly and openly.

952. LORD THOMSON: Thank you. Another foundation of the way the Civil Service has been run up until now has been the role of the Civil Service Commissioners. The White Paper, as I read it, seems to mark something of a reversal in the decline of the powers of the Civil Service Commissioners. Would you like to comment on that?

PETER KEMP: I don't know that there has been much of a reversal over time. I think that the White Paper does propose a strengthening of the Commissioners. For instance, the first Commissioner is now to be a man or woman who comes from the outside. I think that probably is a strengthening; certainly it brings a different view to the thing and I believe the job is being currently advertised. The First Commissioner will in future sit on Robin Butler's Senior Appointments Selection Committee, which makes recommendations to the Prime Minister for the appointing of senior civil servants. That is certainly a strengthening of the Commissioners. I think one could argue, as indeed the Treasury and Civil Service Committee did, that government might have gone further and actually strengthened it even more. The thing about the Civil Service Commissioners is that they are excellent people for getting, as it were, under the wire. Appointing you into the machine is fine. Once you are under the wire though, you are in the hands of the machine, and the Commissioners don't have much say about whether you get promoted or posted or, come to that, fired.

953. LORD THOMSON: One final question, really to draw on your own personal experience. One of your relevancies to us as a first witness in this area is that I think I am right in saying that, first of all, you served for a long time in the Civil Service—25 years—but you did come in from elsewhere, you didn't start your career in the Civil Service, and you left before the normal retirement age. I just wondered what sort of conclusions you would draw from that as to how we should recruit our civil servants for the future.

PETER KEMP: I think there are two answers to that. Yes, indeed. I started doing some naval time and then I went forward to be a chartered accountant and then joined the Civil Service as what was then called a direct entry principal. I spent 25 years as a civil servant and I enjoyed it very much. I like to think that my experience as an accountant and so on was actually valuable in the jobs that I was given to do, so I am all for late entry, with men or women with appropriate skills to come in afterwards. I did leave before time, for reasons which have been much discussed in public and, perhaps curiously, I rather approve of that particular method of doing things. I'm not sure I was pleased that they started with me, but I approve of that method of doing things, because I think that people should not have tenure, people shouldn't be just there right to the end. If a Minister can't get on with his Permanent Secretary, there are no prizes for guessing who wins: the Minister has to win.

954. LORD THOMSON: Thank you for a very disinterested reply. Just one final matter that comes out of the paper that has just been circulated to us. You are commenting on the new proposals in relation to the code and the appeal machinery, and you comment on the fact that the government propose that there should now be an ability to report to Parliament if there is a dispute over the substance of the appeal, and you wonder how wise this is. I wondered why you wondered how wise that was.

PETER KEMP: I think it is an interesting thing, and perhaps the committee will want to consider this in itself. You see, if you have an appeal machinery and you have a civil servant who is asked to do or not do something which he thinks is wrong against the code or some other standard, and he goes through the ordinary department or agency internal procedures and he turns up in front of these Commissioners, obviously if the Commissioners say "This instruction is a perfectly legal, proper instruction. Go away and do it", at that stage he's got no choice: either he goes and does it or he resigns. There's no argument.

But if then the Commission, who are, as I say, so to speak unelected—this new First Commissioner, however strong, is going to be appointed—if then they can take a view on that when we must assume the Minister has given what the Minister thought was a perfectly reasonable instruction, it seems to me to open up a double-guessing of, almost to put it pompously, the democratic process which I think a government might come to regret. It's not really for the civil servant perhaps to judge. If a Minister wants something done, he should do it. It ought to be an internal affair. The TCSC draws analogies with the judicial process and the law, but the fact is that the judicial process has been with us a long time. We know the rules of the game, we have experienced practitioners in law and so on, and even though there's more judicial review than there's been before, it's all against the rules of the game. Here we have a new sort of ball going on to the deck and I'm not quite sure that it's actually right that this new First Commissioner should have almost a nuclear power to go to Parliament with what some individual civil servant, who may be grumpy, may be aggrieved, he may well be very wrong, has done and unleash it in that way.

955. LORD THOMSON: But I think you do mention somewhere in your papers how intimidating the present process is, where if you have some crisis of conscience about the orders you have been given, you finally have to go to the head of the Civil Service and the Secretary of the Cabinet. What would you do if you disliked this process? What would your alternative be?

PETER KEMP: I think, Lord Thomson, there are two separate things here. I agree entirely that the present machinery of appeal to the head of the home Civil Service, personally charming and all that, is a most unuser-friendly piece of machinery for your average civil servant, so I think it has to be somebody independent, or somebody different anyway, such as this First Commissioner. My argument is what happens when it gets to the First Commissioner. What I am saying is that I am not sure that we should give the First Commissioner power to take cases through to Parliament, as opposed to the First Commissioner finding some other way of doing it, like, for instance, quietly persuading the civil servant to do it or shifting him to another post or something. You can imagine, I suppose, instructions given by Ministers that are so unethical, so appalling, so illegal that you need that machinery, but I trust Ministers; I don't actually think you get many like that.

956. DIANA WARWICK: You referred to the issue of tenure for civil servants and you said you didn't agree with it. We have had evidence from the Civil Service unions, where they talk about the new contract for senior civil servants, and they make two statements about that contract, where they say they believe that the proposed draft, as currently framed, suggests there is a grave danger that it could politicise the Civil Service, and you referred earlier to the role of government over a long term. They then go on to say that they object to any civil servant being asked to sign a contract which reiterates the government's belief that civil servants must, for all practical purposes, give loyal service to the government of the day. Is there a conflict there between loyalty to the government of the day and the public perception of the neutral role of the Civil Service?

PETER KEMP: I personally don't think so. I know that the Civil Service unions and others spend a great deal of time debating this issue about whether their loyalty is to the government of the day or to some concept of "the state", and I know that the Civil Service, and I think the present government, has always taken the view that, and I think I quote, "for all practical purposes they are the same". I agree with that. I think that for all practical purposes they are the same, so that point doesn't really worry me very much.

The other point that the unions I think are making is that they seem to be suggesting that because the new contract will have in it explicitly the power to ask people to go early, which is implicit at the moment—implicit but can be effective, as I know—somehow it might be used more often. I think that's what worries them. Again, with great respect to my friends in the unions, I don't have too much sympathy with that point, I'm afraid.

957. DIANA WARWICK: Could I ask you a question about the way in which appointments to quangos are made? Is it your view, because it has certainly been alleged in many articles, that undue political weight has been given to certain appointments? Is it your view that, over the years, that has been the case?

PETER KEMP: I'm sorry, I don't know enough about it. I'm a member of one quango myself, in the shape of the Audit Commission. I'm not quite sure how I got there, but I'm sure it wasn't any political pressure. But I think there is a perception of that. One could probably write a history about these things, starting with the Victorian institutions—what we would now call quangos—the Philanthropists and so on, who set to work to do public work and were largely self-appointed, and moved through into organisations like the older quangos such as the Arts Council and so on, where Ministers would appoint people, perhaps because they knew them but also because perhaps they knew something about the arts and so on, onwards to now, when we are told that health trusts, it is alleged, have Ministers' wives on them and that sort of thing. I don't know whether that's true or not, lots of facts are produced, but there's a very simple way of dealing with it. That is to advertise all those posts and to have, if you like, a public service commission of some kind, let the Select Committee interview the proposed chairman of such-and-such a health trust and quiz him or her as to their beliefs and all the rest of it, and perhaps, incidentally, whether they know anything about health too. There would be an answer to these things. The Civil Service has a Civil Service Commission and it works very well, and I think a public service commission would help with that one.

958. DIANA WARWICK: What is relevant to that in relation to what you said earlier about the question of Ministers intervening to appoint somebody other than the name put forward by the Civil Service Commissioner seems to me your point about their being appointed fairly and openly. Are choices made by, say, a Secretary of State which don't reflect the name put forward by the Commissioners made openly and fairly?

PETER KEMP: I would hope they were made fairly. Openness is another question. There might well be something to be said for machinery where, if the Civil Service Commissioners have worked their independent approach and have said that, according to their views, Mr or Mrs X is the right person for the job and the Minister says "No, I have nothing against Mr or Mrs X, but I just don't think they are going to do the job in the way which I, the Minister want it to be done. I just don't believe it, I'm sorry. You've got the wrong spec. Right person, wrong spec. And therefore I wish to have somebody else. You've also produced as your second candidate this person. He or she too has been selected fairly. He or she too, in your own judgment, can do the job perfectly well. I would wish to have this particular person." There may be something to be said for some statement to be made as to the first and second one publicly, to allay any fear on that front. I'm not sure how good an idea it would be. Appointing people to public posts, once they've got past the fairness net and so on, I'm not sure, but it would be possible to do it that way. All I want to do is to hang on to the notion that Ministers must be allowed, provided the person is suitable in other respects, the person they need to get the job done, because it is, after all, Ministers who, as it were, govern us.

959. CLIFFORD BOULTON: Can I just get clear in my own mind the future status that is planned for the First Commissioner? On appointment, the Commissioner will be on the outside, so to speak, but not necessarily found from the outside. At the moment, once appointed, the First Commissioner is a civil servant, I understand, who might have come from anywhere, but in future the First Commissioner won't be a civil servant: he will be standing outside that Civil Service system. Isn't that the change?

PETER KEMP: As far as I know, in recent times all First Commissioners have been serving civil servants who have come in from existing jobs, so are some of the other Commissioners serving civil servants. But there are also people who are not serving civil servants who are Civil Service Commissioners, and I imagine the juridical status of the new First Commissioner coming from outside will be rather like one of the present part-timers, who also comes from the outside.

960. CLIFFORD BOULTON: I see, but I had thought the idea would be that the person wouldn't be a civil servant any more.

PETER KEMP: I'm afraid I don't know. We've got the White Paper here, and I don't want to dig into it right now. Again you have put an interesting question which we can't spend time on today, because people spend so long on it, but what is a civil servant? Perhaps this person who comes in will be a civil servant for many purposes.

961. CLIFFORD BOULTON: It's an area which we can obviously clear up as we go along. Can I just follow up very quickly the reason you agreed with Lord Thomson that there were perhaps additional strains on the impartiality of the civil servant resulting from 15 years or whatever it is going to be of one party in power? By agreeing, were you saying that this was really a reflection of human nature, that somehow the chameleons had got stuck in one colour, or were you saying there had been some quite significant change in the way government was done, which made it more likely that an incoming government would be looking around for new servants very close to the policy-making area level?

PETER KEMP: I think I mean the first. I think it's more that these are chameleons; they've been stuck on one part of the tartan rug for an awful long time.

CLIFFORD BOULTON: There's no cause for alarm on the other side.

PETER KEMP: I don't think there is much cause for alarm. It certainly is not political cause for alarm. It may be cause for alarm from another point of view, namely the tradition and, so to speak, breeding of civil servants. After all, a civil servant has 40 years. People now joined in 1955. That's an awful long time ago for one person to have been in one job. When we think of all the changes in 40 years, whether the people will be, so to speak, capable of running a Civil Service in the 21st century is a different question, but I think it's a political question. I think that's simply a question of the process and the pace of change, and the need for the people doing the work to keep up with the pace of change.

962. LORD NOLAN: You suggest on the subject of appointments to quangos that all should be openly advertised and reported to the appropriate Select Committee. The Select Committee could then, if it wishes, examine the individual proposed to be chosen. I am thinking of a problem of scale. There are how many—is it 40,000 posts?

PETER KEMP: Something like that, yes.

LORD NOLAN: —which over a period have to be filled by Ministers. Would it be possible to do more than have a sort of random selection, certainly to have an appropriate supervising body, but they couldn't look at all appointments.

PETER KEMP: You are absolutely right, sir. They couldn't possibly look at all of them. But then not all of them raise these sort of excitements. If you had a public service commission of some kind who did the first sift, and maybe the commission could indicate to the appropriate Select Committee that this particular, rather sensitive quango—let's say the Director General of the BBC or the head of British Railways, if it still exists, people like that—might be the sort of people to look at. If I may mildly criticise the Select Committee system, I think the St. John Stevas reforms of 1980 were absolutely brilliant, but my own personal experience, and I've been on the receiving end of this for quite a long time, is that Parliament hasn't always used that weapon to its best advantage.

963. LORD NOLAN: Yes. Could I just follow it up with this? With a view to allaying public anxiety if possible, it should be prepared to receive complaints from members of the public—why was So-and-so appointed? I know that might seem to open up an endless vista of mischievous and totally unfounded complaints, but, speaking with some experience as a judge, this is what we get in the courts sometimes and you just have to distinguish, first of all, whether it's worth going into it. It shouldn't be impossible, I would suggest, to build in a sieve that could sort out genuine public complaints and allow them to come to the Select Committee, quite apart from the Select Committee itself taking the initiative. Do you think that would be a helpful idea?

PETER KEMP: I think it might well be a combination of both. A Select Committee would have within its sights—I put it that way—its important quangos and it says "Those are people who we will always examine". But also, if we get allegations in the press or privately, I'm sure it's not beyond a good chairman to sort out the worthless and the malicious from the genuine.

LORD NOLAN: Thank you very much.

964. PETER SHORE: Just one question. What was your own view of the Business Appointment Panel that looks at the retirement of civil servants and jobs they may wish to take up?

PETER KEMP: Again, I only know it from two angles. One is what one reads in the papers about jobs that are taken up and the other is when I myself, after being out for about six months, wanted to get a job, which apparently, I was told, was referred to the Business Appointments Committee, I just got a letter in due course saying it was all right. So I'm afraid I know little about its deliberations. I think it's sensible. I think it is absolutely right and proper and sensible, as indeed Mr Adam Raphael was saying in respect of Ministers. I think it allays concern, as long as it doesn't give too much comfort. We don't want to find a way in which, simply because it's been through, it must be all right. Perhaps that is the rule, but I don't know. I feel I don't even know who the Members are, but that such a machinery exists seems to me right.

965. PETER SHORE: Do you think the same model might usefully be applied to ex-Ministers?

PETER KEMP: I don't see why not. In some ways it is really very odd that a relatively junior civil servant, say a deputy secretary, might have to work out a long time before he is allowed to take a job with somebody he might have done business with, whereas we see some Ministers who seem to go very fast into other jobs which they have been concerned with. I don't see why it shouldn't. The trouble with all this business is that you are piling grand person on grand person, and you end up with who's selected the selectors, and who's appointed the committee of appointment? But I don't see why it shouldn't work with Ministers, provided the members of the commission or committee or whatever it was were the sort of men and women who command the fullest possible respect.

966. ANNE WARBURTON: Sir Peter, as it happens, like yourself, I entered the Civil Service—the Diplomatic Service—late and left early, although in my case it was perhaps less felicitously called "over-age entry". I had no problem in those days far away with assimilating public service values, but looking at the service today and looking at the service as it is likely to become after the new White Paper and so forth, do you feel that it's going to be easy or possible, with people coming in and out on relatively short-term service sometimes and in much larger numbers than in those days when very few arrived late and we had very few visitors from industry for two or three-year periods, to preserve the same sense of public service? Do members of the service need to be reminded in some way more positively than previously what their duties and responsibilities are?

PETER KEMP: I don't think so. I think that people who join the public service join it because they want to join the public service as such. They don't usually join it for the money or anything like that. They join it because they want to serve. That's my experience of it. They have some consciousness of what it means in serving the public—a job to be done. I think that the continuation of that desire to serve, that almost ethical view of the thing, will continue. It may be, as the Treasury and Civil Service Committee said, that certain steps have to be taken. For instance, some of the chief executives we are getting in are actually relatively lonely people. They are at the top of their own organisation; it may be very big or very small. They don't have the sort of collegiate "mess"—I mean in the sense of dining—approach of a traditional Department. They may find themselves lonely out there. There may be steps that might have to be taken to keep them in the line there. Against that, I am sure if you asked any of the chief executives, they would tell you instantly that the pressures on them from the media, from the press, from Parliament and so on are vastly greater than anything that is on no matter how grand a captain of private industry. It reminds them of what they are on about and keeps them with it.

I think there may be something. For instance, the White Paper suggests there should be a handbook for chief executives. I am rather surprised to find there isn't one already, being the Civil Service. I think that, in appointments, the Civil Service Commissioners might do more to prise out what this man or woman actually feels about the Civil Service and, without calling for a psychiatrist, to ask why they are joining it and so on. I think there could be steps found that way, but I think at the end of the day public service will always attract, hopefully, the right sort of people, who believe in public service, even if, as in any walk of life, occasionally we get people who let us down.

967. WILLIAM UTTING: I too have to declare an interest on the subject of open appointments and open advertisements, because I came into the Civil Service by that route in middle age as well, so I am not likely to

disagree with the principle of that, but, having got in, I found myself working with people who were not only extraordinarily able but also did possess what I thought was this distinctive sense of selfless public service that Dame Anne has referred to. But, in addition to that, it also seemed to me that the management of government business in relation to Parliament and legislation might almost amount to a peculiar profession in itself. I wondered if you saw any merit in that kind of view, that, simply because of that, because of the peculiar nature of the business, it was a good idea to maintain not only the traditions but also the actuality of an old-fashioned Civil Service alongside the new-fashioned Civil Service that is being created.

PETER KEMP: I think it is absolutely essential that you have to do that. I am very glad to hear you use the word "profession". I think it is a profession and it is more of the nature of a profession than a single employer. I see the Civil Service as a profession, but it does have its specialities. Things like preparing legislation, helping Ministers with speeches, answering PQs, dealing with the finer points of estimates and the public expenditure system and all that are highly specialised, highly skilful, unique arts and skills which have to be done if the country is to be properly run. I think that you may end up with two sorts of skills. If, for instance, you were appointing somebody to run, let's say, agency X, which might have, say 10,000 people in it, I'm not sure that I would choose anybody to run agency X other than the chap who could actually run it best. I wouldn't much care whether he could draft elegant PQs. I would say I keep other people to draft the elegant PQs. Equally, I'm not sure that the elegant PQ-drafter is going to end up as the sort of person to run agency X. Now it may be that this ultimately points to two sorts of Civil Service, and perhaps that's where we're going.

968. WILLIAM UTTING: If I could move from the past to the future, I was struck by what you said earlier about the difficulty of distinguishing always between policy and execution, and yet in a sense it was that separation upon which the creation of Next Steps agencies was predicated. Is it possible that we shall see Next Steps agencies taking on greater responsibilities for policy advice and policy formation in future? It seems that already some of them are operating in areas that might be regarded as highly political, and this would be a natural development for them.

PETER KEMP: I think one might see some of that. One might see the merging in on that one, and I'm not sure that it would be necessarily a bad thing. Some of us can remember times in the past when policies were produced by Ministers—elegant policies, beautiful policies—which then failed when they were put into practice, and that may have been because the people who thought through the policies weren't aware of the practical requirements of actually getting that particular policy working—what I think some people call the production engineering function, the translation of the policy into something which actually works on the ground. If you consult with the agency and the agency comes back and the chief executive or their operational people say "Yes, Minister, it's a good idea, it's a nice idea, I understand you want it and all the rest of it, but I'm afraid it just isn't going to work", then the Minister has perhaps to start thinking again. I think one could impinge across that, but I think that at the end of the day a Minister must be in charge of what he wants and the job of the Civil Service is to give him the right sort of policy advice and then, having taken a decision, to translate that policy, one way or another, and the agency can help, into a deliverable, which the citizen on the ground can use, and then to run it in the way that the agencies are run. I think there is a spectrum down that way, but the reason why I don't like policy and execution is that on the whole one man's policy tends to be another man's execution, and it can get very complicated.

Just on a point, I don't think, when we were setting up Next Steps, we ever sorted things out on the basis of policy and execution. We sorted things out on the basis that if somebody wants something to be done, somebody else has to do it: can you write it down in a way which makes sense and is, as it were, deliverable? I think that's a more practical approach.

LORD NOLAN: We are all very grateful to you, Sir Peter. You have given us a very interesting close to the morning's business and I'm afraid we've kept you late for lunch. Please forgive us.

WEDNESDAY 1 FEBRUARY 1995

Members Present:

The Rt. Hon. The Lord Nolan (Chairman)

Sir Clifford Boulton GCB
Professor Anthony King
The Rt. Hon. Peter Shore MP

The Rt. Hon. The Lord Thomson of Monifieth KT DL
Sir William Utting CB
Dame Anne Warburton DCVO CMG
Diana Warwick

Witnesses:

Elizabeth Symons, Chair, Major Policy Committee, Council of the Civil Service Unions and General Secretary of the Association of First Division Civil Servants, and John Ellis, Secretary, Council of the Civil Service Unions

Ann Bowtell, First Civil Service Commissioner and Geoffrey Maddrell, Part-Time Civil Service Commissioner

Michael Bichard, Chief Executive, Benefits Agency

Rt. Hon Robert Sheldon MP, Chairman, Public Accounts Committee and Sir John Bourn, Comptroller and Auditor General

Vernon Bogdanor, Reader in Government and Fellow of Brasenose College, Oxford

969. LORD NOLAN: I am very conscious that as our hearings have progressed we have tended to over-run our time slightly. With five groups of witnesses this morning we will need to move at a fair pace but, at the same time, I want to make sure that all witnesses and committee members have an opportunity to explore the issues fully.

Our witnesses this morning have a wide range of experience to offer. Later on we will have the benefit of hearing from Mr. Robert Sheldon, Member of Parliament, Chairman of the Public Accounts Committee, together with Sir John Bourn who is the Comptroller and Auditor General. They will be followed by Vernon Bogdanor, the distinguished academic, who has been following changes in the Civil Service for many years. Before then we will hear from Michael Bichard, who is Chief Executive of the Benefits Agency and could be described as one of the "new style" civil servants and, before him, Ann Bowtell, the First Civil Service Commissioner. The Commission, amongst other things, is responsible for senior appointments to the Civil Service. I note that the Government's White Paper, published last week, envisages a widening of the role of the Commission to act as an independent appellant authority under their proposed Civil Service Code of Practice.

To start with, I would like to welcome Elizabeth Symons, who is here with Mr. John Ellis. Elizabeth Symons is, of course, General Secretary of the Association of First Division Civil Servants and Chair of the Policy Committee of the Council of Civil Service Unions. We had the benefit of a long and clear letter from you in December and you point out in your covering letter that it was prepared before you received our issues and questions paper. Have you prepared an opening statement to make this morning?

ELIZABETH SYMONS AND JOHN ELLIS

ELIZABETH SYMONS (Chair, Major Policy Committee, Council of the Civil Service Unions and General Secretary of the Association of First Division Civil Servants): A brief one. It was received, as you say, before we received that paper from your Committee and, of course, we also sent it in before we had the further White Paper, which was published last week on January 26th. I think it is important to say one or two things about

that command paper because, quite clearly, this is the Government response to the Select Committee report which was published last November and, also, it is its response to what people said about the earlier White Paper.

As far as we are concerned, obviously, we would welcome very warmly the Government's decision to introduce a code of conduct for the Civil Service. We make the point in the letter we wrote to you on December 16th that this was a very important issue, particularly for the FDA, but supported by the other Civil Service unions, and we believe that whilst there are things not covered in that code which we covered in the code which we sent you, that nonetheless the difference between not having a code and having a code is the important difference. We hope to be able to persuade the Government that the code should be a little more robust in certain areas but we are very pleased that it is there in principle.

We also welcome the fact that the Government is now persuaded of the importance of having an independent appeals body. They have said that it will be under a newly independent First Civil Service Commissioner. In our evidence we suggested that it would be most proper for this to be a cross-party committee of Privy Councillors. We are interested, obviously, in the Government's decision to go for the Select Committee's recommendation for the First Civil Service Commissioner and much will depend on that appointment and much will depend as well on the powers that the First Civil Service Commissioner has. The White Paper makes it clear that there will not be any powers of enforcement. On the other hand, the White Paper states that there is recourse to a Select Committee and maybe recourse to the Select Committee is very often one of the most potent powers of enforcement as far as Ministers are concerned. We are very interested in that.

There are one or two other issues in the White Paper which we touched upon: such as, the question of running costs, the Senior Civil Service, and other matters but we particularly wanted to draw your attention to the fact that we believe that the Government has met us, in part at least, on some of the areas where we have been arguing—at times an uphill and at times a rather lonely argument—in favour of a code and an appeal body.

LORD NOLAN: Thank you very much indeed. I am going to ask Professor Anthony King, whom I think you know, to take up the questions to begin with.

970. PROF. ANTHONY KING: Could I ask you in a little more detail about the Government White Paper. One reads the code in there and one reads your proposed code and, while they are clearly country cousins, while they clearly overlap, there is an awful lot in your code that is not in the Government's proposed code. Could you elaborate on what you said a few moments ago. At what points do you think the Government's code should be more—to use your word—robust?

ELIZABETH SYMONS: The Government makes it clear in the White Paper that what it is seeking to do in publishing the code is to publish the status quo as they see it at the moment about the function of the Civil Service. Our code deals much more with the relationship of Ministers and the Civil Service and says rather more about ministerial obligations as well. We believe that *Questions of Procedure for Ministers* now also needs looking at. If we are to see a code in the way that the Government has suggested in its White Paper, the other side of the coin must be also to look at questions of procedure and the obligations Ministers have on some really quite difficult and vexed areas that have been the subject of a lot of comment recently on questions of Ministerial responsibility and ministerial accountability, for example, on how that should work.

971. PROF. ANTHONY KING: Can you be a bit more specific. You are quite right, the Government's White Paper lays great stress on the duty of civil servants to Ministers and says virtually nothing about any duties that Ministers may have.

ELIZABETH SYMONS: It says a little but not enough.

972. PROF. ANTHONY KING: It says a little but not nearly as much as in your document. What specific duties would you like to see put on Ministers in the context of a code like this?

ELIZABETH SYMONS: There are general duties about the importance that Ministers must attach to political neutrality. These are covered but they are not covered in the detail that we have covered them. There are also questions about what Ministers should ask civil servants to do. We have produced much more by way of examples which are practical, working examples of things that happen. For example, Ministers should never ask a civil servant to produce a speech for a constituency meeting. Ministers should never ask civil servants to produce speeches for party conferences. We have examples of those sorts of instances arising. Ministers should not ask civil servants to produce briefings for their own back benchers on Private Members' Bills. Again, we refer to that sort of problem which has arisen. We are more specific because in our experience when civil servants find themselves confronted with a request, or indeed an instruction, from Ministers to undertake work that may be on the margins they need quite a lot of help and guidance about what is and is not proper.

The Civil Service relies very heavily on what Sir Robin Butler rightly describes as the Civil Service culture but a culture does not get transmitted by some curious process of osmosis; people have to be told what the culture is and we would have preferred a more detailed exposition. We also think that there is difficulty about the understanding of any relationship between the Civil Service and Parliament and the Civil Service and the public.

973. PROF. ANTHONY KING: Could I interrupt and press you a little bit on that. Suppose that I am a reasonably senior civil servant—although that does not matter—and I believe that my Minister is lying to the House of Commons, or being excessively economical with the truth. What should I do?

ELIZABETH SYMONS: In our code we actually deal with this "misleading information". We feel it is wrong in those circumstances. What one should not do is go straight to the newspapers. The basis of the relationship between civil servants and Government Ministers has to be one of confidentiality otherwise everything breaks down and the process of discussion between Ministers and civil servants at very senior levels, the giving and taking of advice or the giving and refusing of advice, must be a matter of confidence. But, on occasions, civil servants may, for example, hear their Minister misleading Parliament. Whether that is done knowingly or unknowingly, a civil servant has very little recourse at the moment. We would hope that the civil servant's recourse now would be to the Civil Service Commission. That is what we suggested, that it would be to the independent tribunal of Privy Councillors, but we would hope that the path of recourse now would be to the Commission and the First Commissioner would be in a position to go to the Minister and say that he had put the Civil Service into a very difficult position.

It is quite obvious from what we see in the Press at the moment that there is a view that when civil servants are in that position—it may not be misleading over matters of fact; it may be misleading over, for example, the public espousal of one policy and the private practice of a rather different policy, which is also a very difficult area for civil servants.

PROF. ANTHONY KING: It is another committee that is dealing with that.

ELIZABETH SYMONS: It is another topical area of difficulty. But many people would say, "Why did the civil servant not say so? Why did the civil servant not rush off to the Press?" and we must be clear that that is not proper. It will lead to a breakdown of confidence and will not tend to good government, but there should be some recourse and a Minister ought to be brought up against the fact that the Civil Service has been in difficulty over that sort of issue.

974. PROF. ANTHONY KING: You give the impression that although the procedure adopted by the Government is not the one you recommended, nevertheless that may be satisfactory. Is that right?

ELIZABETH SYMONS: I think that we are fairly open-minded. Believe me, after five years of arguing for this in principle and at times arguing alone for this in principle, it is extremely pleasing that the Government has at least conceded that, first, there should be a code and that it should be publicly available and it is still a matter of consultation and, secondly, that there should be an independent appeals procedure. We must ask some questions about how really independent the First Civil

Service Commissioner is when it is obviously going to be a prime Ministerial appointment but there are many prime Ministerial appointments which are, to all intents and purposes, independent. We felt that the use of Privy Councillors would be even more independent but, after all, the Prime Minister has a good deal to do with the appointment of Privy Councillors as well so, all in all, we are prepared now to use this as a basis to go forward.

975. PROF. ANTHONY KING: Can we go on to more general background questions. This is a committee on standards in public life and, looking first at any problems that may arise under that heading in connection specifically with civil servants, is there any reason to think that standards of civil service behaviour have fallen over the past few years?

ELIZABETH SYMONS: I do not think that I could say that civil servants' behaviour has been seen to have fallen in its standards. I think that, rightly, there is much more concern and interest about the way in which civil servants operate. That, we think, stems from two main sources. There is much more scope for civil servants to act independently because of the delegation of powers from the centre than there used to be. I think we touch on this in our evidence to you, that where there are powers delegated from the Treasury and from central government departments to individual departments then the scope for individual Ministers—and, thus, those who are advising them on the way in which the civil service machine operates—is that much greater.

Secondly, there is the question of the fact that there is a much closer relationship between public servants and the private sector than there used to be. I make no comment about whether that is desirable or not in political terms, that is a matter for the government, but, quite clearly, if there is going to be further privatisation, market testing, contracting out, the relationship between the civil service and the private sector must get that much closer and in those circumstances I think people are bound to ask questions about whether the civil service, sometimes individual civil servants, may not be a bit too close to the private sector. That is quite apart from the issues which we have just dealt with about politicisation.

There are arguments, as I am sure you know, that after 15 years of single party rule—and I am sure the arguments would be as potent if this had been single party rule of any other party—that senior civil servants get too much alongside government Ministers and lose their impartiality. Those are three main headings of concern.

976. PROF. ANTHONY KING: If we would just probe a little bit under those headings. After all, the Public Accounts Committee gave the impression that it was really pretty profoundly worried under, I think, the first of your headings about the cumulative consequences for the public service ethic of contracting out, of bringing people into the civil service, of delegation to civil servants of decisions they would not previously have taken. Can I repeat my question. Is there any reason to think that in this new environment and, perhaps, subject to new temptations, there have been in your experience problems of the kinds that the PAC talked about? You were very guarded in what you said.

ELIZABETH SYMONS: I have not received, as General Secretary of the FDA, any substantial evidence

that indicates that there has been the sort of possibility of corruption that is alluded to. That notwithstanding, I think, the KPMG report on the "fraud" barometer which we quoted in our evidence to you which pointed out that the closeness of relationship may put temptation in the way where temptation was never there before.

One of the important points which we would make about this is that this should be more clearly addressed in a civil service code. We have seen a lot of managerial change in the Civil Service and that has not been matched by giving civil servants more guidelines on how to deal with the consequences of that managerial change in their relationships with the private sector. We have covered this more in our code, of which we sent you a copy, but we do not believe that is really covered in sufficient detail in the Treasury and Civil Service Select Committee code, nor indeed in the White Paper one.

977. PROF. ANTHONY KING: You referred to politicisation and you referred in your opening statement, or at some stage, to the making of illegitimate requests of civil servants by Ministers. Is this just the occasional Minister asking for help with the occasional party speech or do you have reason to think that this is now a pattern of behaviour with Ministers across the board, being likely to ask civil servants to do more and more things of a partisan or personal character?

ELIZABETH SYMONS: I have been General Secretary of the FDA for six years and in those six years I have seen a steady flow and on this there is evidence, although we are always in difficulty, to be brutally frank, over saying exactly what the evidence is because people come to us in confidence and they ask for our advice in confidence. Therefore, to say that a particular civil servant in a particular Government department has raised an issue is rather invidious.

978. PROF. ANTHONY KING: If there were an independent person monitoring these things that person would, in fact, be getting a pretty steady flow of complaints?

ELIZABETH SYMONS: If they saw anything of the nature that I see doing my job. Somebody within the union hears that there has been a problem and very often there are three or four more problems because people say that that has just happened to them too. Some departments are freer of this problem than others. If problems tend to cluster in departments quite often they emanate from the same Ministers and one can identify the source of some difficulties in that way.

979. PROF. ANTHONY KING: It is rumoured—I put it no higher than that—that some civil servants either have been damaged or believe they have been damaged in their careers by giving their Ministers unwelcome advice, by advising against a course of action, perhaps rather vehemently, that the Minister wants to undertake. Is it your impression that that does happen?

ELIZABETH SYMONS: I have certainly talked to very senior civil servants—and by that I mean in the senior open structure, in the top three grades—who do believe that they have been damaged by giving advice to Ministers which was contrary to a Minister's political decision and they felt very unhappy about that happening to them, yes.

980. PROF. ANTHONY KING: As I recall, and I may simply be wrong about this, you do not say anything explicitly about that even in your proposed code?

ELIZABETH SYMONS: Again, what we say in our proposed code is that a Minister must listen to Civil Service advice and give it due weight. That is extremely important. We have had examples, and I have given the evidence to the Treasury and Civil Service Committee about this, where some Ministers have simply refused to take Civil Service advice because it was Civil Service advice and, therefore, was public sector advice and of no weight to them whatsoever. Whilst, of course, it has always been the case that Ministers can have civil servants give them advice and then say to the civil servant, "Thank you very much, we would like you to leave the room now", and the Ministers will have a private discussion, all administrations do that, but to refuse even to listen to the advice in the first place is a pretty peculiar development that we have seen in the past few years.

981. PROF. ANTHONY KING: But that is not what I was asking you about. I was just intrigued, reading your code, that you did not explicitly touch on a different point which is civil servants not being disadvantaged by giving unwelcome advice.

ELIZABETH SYMONS: I hope that it was covered implicitly in the point about the Minister giving due weight to the civil servant's advice and I think also we say elsewhere in the code that it is very important for the Minister to remember the civil servant's impartiality and treat the civil servant with courtesy. That seems to me to tend to say in that case retribution for unwelcome advice is clearly beyond the pale.

982. PROF. ANTHONY KING: Can I just ask you one final question under the general heading of redress of grievances because that is, on the whole, the way both your code and the Government's code tends. I am a civil servant, something has happened to me that I think is improper or I see something happening that is improper and I am to take a certain course of action. One of the charges levelled against some senior civil servants at the moment is that they have become much too closely identified in public with the specific policies being pursued by their Minister or by the government, they have become politicised in that sense.

Suppose I am in, say, a next steps agency and I see the head of that agency, in effect, going around the country saying, "What we're doing is wonderful and the government's policy is marvellous", and so on; what, under your proposed procedure—or, indeed, the Government's—should such a civil servant do?

ELIZABETH SYMONS: The fact is that the head of the agency should not be doing it and, in those circumstances, I suppose, the civil servant could, under the Government's proposals, go to the Civil Service Commission but, you are right, I do not think that is explicitly drawn out anywhere. If I may say so, it is very hard to produce actual evidence about the senior Civil Service having got too far alongside the Government. There are one or two instances and they have tended to be amongst agency chief executives—I think we draw your attention to a couple of specific examples—but amongst the policy areas of the Civil Service it is very hard to find any evidence at all that the Civil Service has become politicised. It may be the sort of thing that people like to talk about in newspapers but there is very little actual hard evidence.

PROF. ANTHONY KING: As usual, I have a lot of other things I would like to ask, but I am not going to monopolise you.

LORD NOLAN: We will start on the left-hand side. Dame Anne, do you have any questions you would like to ask?

983. ANNE WARBURTON: I have a lot I would like to ask too, but I shall try to select. You spoke earlier of the closer relationship between civil servants and, I think you said, the government and also the private sector. I was left wondering whether you had any specific suggestions for ways to handle that. I imagine you are not saying that, for example, appearances before Select Committees should now be stopped, but have you thoughts about how the Civil Service can maintain its parameters?

ELIZABETH SYMONS: I am sorry. I think maybe I have confused two points there. The point I was making was that the Civil Service now has a closer relationship with the private sector as a function of contracting out. I do not think the Civil Service relationship with Government Ministers is any closer than it was. There are, of course, questions about responsibility and accountability as between the Civil Service and Government Ministers.

ANNE WARBURTON: That was going to be my next question.

ELIZABETH SYMONS: I do not believe that it is sensible that civil servants are directly answerable, in the way the Select Committee suggested they should be, to Select Committees for the running of the agencies. This is not to say that civil servants do not have responsibilities; of course, they do, and they are clearly laid out not only in the contracts of the chief executives but also in the plans put forward for the agencies each year, but I think it would tend to detract from ministerial responsibility if it was the civil servant who was responsible to answer for the running of an agency. It should be a ministerial responsibility. That would have to be one of the cornerstones we rest on in a democracy, otherwise you put non-elected officials into the position of having a lot of power which, I think, would be inappropriate.

984. ANNE WARBURTON: Good. Thank you very much. May I just choose one other question, or perhaps two, the question of morale in the Civil Service. You have told us that you receive a lot of confidential information. The opening up of appointments in the Civil Service, up to and including Permanent Secretary level, to outside competition seems to be one obvious place where you start asking what that does to morale and I would like to couple that with a question as to whether in your view training in public service values, or reminding of public service values, becomes rather important?

ELIZABETH SYMONS: On the second point, I think training is extremely important. I think the Civil Service College tries to address that but, of course, when there is great pressure on numbers, as there is in the Civil Service at the moment, training, as always, takes a bit of a back seat. It is not peculiar to the Civil Service, it happens in all large organisations but it is enormously important that civil servants are reminded about their duties in that respect.

On the question of morale in general. I am sure my colleagues representing civil servants right the way across the Civil Service would say that the problems of morale are worse than they have ever been amongst junior civil servants as well as the more senior civil servants I represent. You asked me specifically about the opening up of appointments. The problem here is that we have two things happening at the same time. There are senior management reviews going on as a result of the White Paper published in July last year. Those are delaying exercises. In effect, they are stripping out a lot of the senior management in government departments. The Treasury has just completed its review and is due to lose nearly 30 per cent of the senior posts between Grades 1 and 5. Coupled with that, if you are also opening up appointments to the outside and inviting people who are not currently civil servants to compete with civil servants for jobs, inevitably you are diminishing a career prospect that was there.

The past couple of weeks has been quite extraordinary. The number of civil servants at grade 5 and grade 3, and even at grade 2, who have approached me and said that this is having an appalling effect on morale because jobs are being stripped out and such jobs as are left are now being opened up for competition. They are very afraid of the "glass ceiling" effect, beyond which civil servants cannot go.

Last week's White Paper tried to reassure civil servants on this but, frankly, it is very hard to see what assurance can be given against that sort of background. In practical terms there must be a great diminution of career prospects. People join the Civil Service not because they think they are going to be very rich in doing so; they join it, yes, because they want to have a career and because of public service but if the career is taken away it is very hard to see what incentives there are for good civil servants to stay in their jobs.

985. DIANA WARWICK: Could I ask two completely unrelated questions. The first one is linked to the point you have just made about appointments. Yesterday when we were talking to Sir Peter Kemp about the way in which Ministers had intervened in certain appointments after a fair and open selection had been made he was quite robust in his view that this was a prerogative that Ministers might actually need to exercise in the interests of the particular job. Could you give us your perception—this is now very much an FDA question—and your members' perception of the role of Ministers in this process and its impact on perceptions about open and fair procedures?

ELIZABETH SYMONS: We raised this point with the Treasury and Civil Service Committee. There was a particular appointment and it may have reflected others, where the Minister had intervened at the point where the Civil Service Commission had decided there were three candidates, what they described as, above the line; that is to say, three candidates who would have been able to do the job. The Minister intervened, asked who interviewed the civil servants and chose for the job an individual who, we understand, was not the one that the Commissioners had put at the top of the list. We said that this raised questions about fair and open competition. The Minister in question said it was open because it had been openly advertised and fair because he said so. That, of course, was very difficult to challenge. It is terribly important, in the circumstances I have just described to Dame Anne where you have a lot of people possibly coming in from outside, to ensure that we are getting the best person for the job and that that is independent of party political considerations.

To take Sir Peter Kemp's point. Of course, ultimately, the Minister may be able to say, "I don't want X, I want Y", but the Minister must do so for reasons of public interest not because of personal chemistry or because of political bias. The Civil Service Commissioners report which was published in July last year made that very clear. They said in that report that it is always possible for a Minister, using the procedures of the Order in Council, to set the Commissioners' first choice on one side and pick his own individual and that, I think, must always be there if we really believe that Ministers are accountable and responsible for what goes on. In saying that, a Minister must produce a reason and, according to what the Commission said last year, the reason must be communicated in writing to the Commission and the Government has accepted that now and the Commission would expect a report on that in its annual report. We also believe that it should be reported to the appropriate Select Committee and the Select Committee should have the opportunity to ask the Minister why the Minister chose an individual who was not thought by the independent Commissioners to be the best person for the job.

986. DIANA WARWICK: And my unrelated question links in with discussions that we had last week. It is about the role of Members of Parliament as advisers to trades unions. Does your union have advisers? Do they come from different parties? What is their role and do you see any problem of having Members of Parliament advising the union?

ELIZABETH SYMONS: My union does have advisers. We are obviously not affiliated to the Labour party; we are affiliated, of course, to the TUC. We do not have political funds. We took legal advice about the position of our union in having what we term consultants, advisers. We have one Conservative and one Labour, which, we hope, reflects the fact that we are not politically aligned. We are talking to the Liberal Democrats about having a Liberal Democrat adviser as well.

987. DIANA WARWICK: Is there anything about the things you ask your Member of Parliament advisers to do that gives you cause for concern?

ELIZABETH SYMONS: No. I would not do that. I cannot stress strongly enough the importance that my union attaches to political neutrality. Our members advise government Ministers every day of the week. It would be putting my members in an impossible position if we adopted a party political stance ever in any relationship. We are extremely careful about our relationships. We might ask people advice about what was happening in Parliament, about the position of parties, for example their views on contracting out; equally, we might say, "Look, we have a real problem at the moment". For example, we talked to our Members of Parliament about the code of ethics that we sent. We have been talking to our Members of Parliament about the future of the Crown Prosecution Service and, indeed, have written to all Members of Parliament on both subjects.

988. DIANA WARWICK: The distinction we have been drawing has been between advice and advocacy and it seems to have honed in on the question of whether Members of Parliament put down questions in the House on behalf of special interests. When we talked to representatives of Unison they were quite happy with the thought that Members of Parliament sponsored by the unions could put down questions which were in the interests of the union. Does that specific issue give you any cause for concern? Has it ever arisen?

ELIZABETH SYMONS: We have asked Members of Parliament to put down questions but we have asked Members of Parliament of all political parties to put down questions. I have asked Conservative Members of Parliament to intervene with Government Ministers over a particular problem that has arisen with a Member. The very difficult issue of military service counting for pensions in the Civil Service comes to mind. I have asked Conservative Members of Parliament to intervene with Ministers over that sort of issue. Frankly, we have taken a lot of legal advice over this. I have no reason to believe that we have done anything improper legally and, as far as the union is concerned, my executive committee would take an extremely dim view of activity which could be described as party political.

JOHN ELLIS: Across the unions as a whole, speaking from the Council position, I think the difference is that no Member of Parliament or Member of the House of Lords would ever feel under pressure from the relationship with ourselves to do anything that we asked them to do. There are many other sources asking Members of Parliament to do things which would be quite legitimate and quite proper and they would be exactly the same as ourselves. The relationship with our Members of Parliament, because we are not party political, because we are not affiliated, is purely on a two-way advisory basis. They will often come for advice from the unions on particular developments and we will freely give it. They will use it as they feel fit. There is no financial exchange taking place or no feeling of being bound to that organisation that puts pressure on them to do anything that they do not want to do against their own interests or against the interests of the State.

LORD NOLAN: Thank you. That is important and you have made it very clear.

989. CLIFFORD BOULTON: But some unions might be having a relationship involving a fee with a member, an annual fee?

ELIZABETH SYMONS: Yes.

JOHN ELLIS: Yes, indeed. I should add that that fee is a very nominal fee—I shall speak as an ex-General Secretary of the biggest Civil Service union that paid no more than £500 and it was, in fact, a token gesture for the additional work that may be involved in things that we may be discussing with a Member of Parliament coming to see us. That, in our case, was always given to a charity by that Member of Parliament. They always made it clear they were doing that.

CLIFFORD BOULTON: I asked the question simply because we are concentrating on financial services and that is why I asked the question. I have no other questions. Thank you.

990. LORD THOMSON: Could you just briefly give us your views about the question of Civil Service appointments when people retire from the Civil Service and whether there ought to be comparable arrangements for Ministers?

ELIZABETH SYMONS: Our view is that there should be comparable arrangements for Ministers. Questions of Procedures for Ministers goes into quite a lot of detail about Ministers' financial interests during the period they hold office. That does not say anything about the sort of interests that they may go to on quitting office and that is obviously a matter of some interest at the moment. Similarly, civil servants, as I am sure you know, above a certain level when quitting the Civil Service go through a two-year period when they must ask the Business Appointments Committee about the propriety, or otherwise, of their accepting employment outside the Civil Service.

There is a lot of interest in this at the moment. We touch upon it in our evidence to you. It is very important to say a couple of things about it. The Business Appointments rules must operate to protect the public interest. What the test is, and should be, is whether a civil servant—or, indeed, a Minister—on going to take up an appointment in the private sector is either getting some sort of pay-off, if you like, for decisions taken when they held public office, which would be quite improper and wrong, or whether that civil servant or Government Minister is taking with them knowledge to a private sector employer which would damage the interests of that employer's competitors.

It is not wrong for a civil servant, or indeed a Government Minister, to sell in the employment market place their expertise, their skills or their contacts. That is not wrong and we have to be quite clear what the Business Appointments Committee is actually there for. It is a pity that it does not operate in a more transparent way because, quite obviously, there is enormous public anxiety, possibly some of it whipped up by the Press but, nonetheless, it is there, about the way in which public servants, whether they are elected or appointed, move into the private sector. There ought to be a more transparent system operating and something that can be demonstrated as protecting the public interest.

991. LORD NOLAN: And, of course, protecting the individual civil servant if the appointment is cleared?

ELIZABETH SYMONS: Indeed because, of course, the implication that people have behaved improperly is very damaging to an individual who has very little opportunity of clearing their name in those circumstances and if there were something more transparent it would be of enormous help.

992. LORD NOLAN: You have made it clear that in order to maintain the highest standards in the Civil Service you attach great importance to a code setting out principles, a right of appeal or complaint to an independent body or individual. Actual training of young civil servants in everyday behaviour or a proper ethical character, does that come from leadership from the community spirit in the department, must it not be learned from individuals?

ELIZABETH SYMONS: I think, obviously, to a certain extent it must be. We have to say, however, because young civil servants are put under a great deal of pressure, they are producing briefs for Ministers, they are the end of the line that produces the brief. I have been a junior civil servant myself and I am sure that the pressure is very much greater now than it was when I was a civil servant. In all that, it is terribly important to stop that process and make sure that people are properly trained, that they actually leave their office environment and go and have training periods—the Civil Service College does this. I, myself, have spoken on a number of courses to young civil servants, and not so young civil servants come to that, about ethics and about the way in which the Civil Service operates. Concentrating on that and actually getting people to think about their role as public servants is terribly important.

993. PETER SHORE: You have given us a very clear statement of your view about the necessary checks on ex-civil servants or civil servants who leave to take up jobs in the private sector. You have not mentioned the fact that a number of redundancies are now being imposed on the Civil Service. Is it still acceptable and fair to impose the kind of rules that have operated in the past on middle rank civil servants who are made redundant, who have been working in particular areas with the private sector and, therefore, have some obvious qualifications for being employed there?

ELIZABETH SYMONS: I think that the test of this has to be the public interest. It has certainly been put to me that civil servants who are forced out through redundancy—and you are quite right, there are many more of them than there used to be, sadly—they should somehow be in a different position to civil servants who opt to go or who take up appointments on retirement. I do not think that is a logical position to adopt, much as emotionally I might like to think that these poor people are in a terrible position and they could be let off some of the rules. But if you really believe that the test is the damage to the public interest, then the public interest is not affected by the reasons the individual left the Civil Service, the public interest damage is the same whatever the reason. The function the civil servant carried out and the function the civil servant will carry out must be the test.

It is invidious to say that one can have hard and fast rules, that there must always be a certain length of "purdah", as we call it, or that you can lay down a rule that says that a civil servant who has actually been very close to giving advice over the giving of a contract can never follow that contract into the private sector. It is very tempting to want to have those nice, clear cut rules but the moment you start you are then in the position of, "Well, I was the lead adviser but somebody else actually got much more alongside the private sector on this or that issue". Every case must be looked at on its merits.

994. PETER SHORE: That again is very clear. The public interest, obviously, would be affected if a civil servant carried with him into the private sector some special knowledge, as it were, of what was going on in government. Would the same rules apply to a civil servant moving into another part of what might be called the quasi public sector—in other words, moving into a Quango? Would it be right for a civil servant to move without impediment straight from a civil service job into an important post in a Quango, even if the Quango is in not a real market, but a bogus market economy?

ELIZABETH SYMONS: I think that very often the same rules would have to apply. I do not think that one could say that all Quangos would stand outside those rules, because the nature of Quangos, as we know, varies enormously. There is quite often a lot of power in the marketplace, even if it is not a real marketplace in the same sense as commercial life; there is quite often a lot of power there. Obviously there will be some cut-off point—in our evidence to you we have said grade 5 upwards, simply because grade 5 is the identity now of

senior civil servants and the point at which many crucial management and policy decisions are taken.

995. PETER SHORE: We had a very interesting example of movement from the civil service direct to a Quango only yesterday and it is bound to be in all our minds. A movement at that level of civil servant would not come before the Business Advisory Committee which looks into the movement of top civil servants. Who would it come before of an independent character?

ELIZABETH SYMONS: The Permanent Secretary. It seems to me that in any case the business appointment rules will have to change. At the moment the Business Appointments Committee looks automatically at grades 1 and 2; grade 3, as I am sure you know, goes before Sir Robin Butler. But the definition of the senior civil service, as a result of the two White Papers we have seen, one in July and the other last week, is going to be extended to include not the top 650 jobs, but the top 3,500 jobs. In those circumstances, the logic of the position determines that the Business Appointments Committee's remit should extend down to grade 5.

996. PETER SHORE: Thank you very much. May I ask just one more question? Obviously the independent advice of senior civil servants to Ministers is crucial and a highly valuable commodity. Do you think, though, that with the new system, which has yet to be introduced, with contracts for senior civil servants limited in time, as it were, civil servants will feel that they will retain the same degree of independence in relation to Ministers that they had previously, when they were in permanent employment?

ELIZABETH SYMONS: I think that there may be a misunderstanding here. There are time-limited contracts for the chief executives of the agencies. It is not proposed to extend time-limited contracts to all the senior civil service. The model contract that we have received from the Cabinet Office is a permanent contract or, on occasions, a rolling contract. I do not think that we would argue that the very existence of a contract would itself tend to politicise the civil service, but we have very grave concerns that the contract as currently written would tend to politicise the civil service. We have written at length to the Government about this. We did a paper on it which was part of our response to the White Paper of July last year. We have serious worries about the contract as currently drafted, but the most recent White Paper from last week gave us some comfort, because it indicated that the period of consultation over the contract would extend well into this year and that the Government were proposing to issue a further draft contract some months into this year. We hope that we shall be able to persuade the Government to drop what we see as the most damaging elements.

997. PETER SHORE: The terms of the contract are clearly very important. Does the Civil Service Commission have a watching brief over those terms?

ELIZABETH SYMONS: Not as yet. I do not know whether that will change, given the new role of the Civil Service Commission, as detailed in last week's White Paper. We shall want to examine the new role of the Commission in some detail, because clearly it will be quite different. The First Civil Service Commissioner will no longer be a civil servant. At the moment, however, the contract is being dealt with by the Treasury, the Cabinet

Office and the law officers. We have raised a lot of questions, including the use of the royal prerogative in the contract. There are tricky issues ahead of us over this, for instance, who the employer is—all sorts of issues like that. No doubt we shall be saying more about it in due course.

WILLIAM UTTING: I have no questions, Chairman.

998. LORD NOLAN: We are very grateful to you both for volunteering to come along. Your evidence has been extremely clear, succinct and helpful. Thank you.

Now we have Mrs Ann Bowtell. Good morning. You kindly sent us a short paper which we have read. Would you like to start by summarising that or would you prefer to go straight into questions? Is there anything else you would like to say?

ANN BOWTELL AND GEOFFREY MADDRELL

ANN BOWTELL (First Civil Service Commissioner): I should like to say a word in development of the paper, partly in the light of something that Elizabeth Symons said in the course of her evidence. I should like to stress that the authority of the Order in Council, as far as it concerns recruitment and the Commissioners' powers, stretches to all appointments within the civil service. All appointments must be made either by fair and open competition on merit or under one of the quite specific exceptions that are listed in the Order in Council. That applies to all appointments at whatever level. It is not the case that Ministers can overthrow that in any way. Any appointment at any level must have the approval of the Commissioners.

The point to which Elizabeth Symons was referring is that if a Minister does not want to appoint the lead candidate, either the competition must be rerun or he can approach the Commissioners under one of the sections of the Order in Council to ask that some other candidate, who had been placed above the line, could be taken instead. That procedure has never been used: no Minister has ever done that; but it is not possible for him simply to say that he wants his candidate. He cannot do that without the approval of the Commissioners. The only way in which anyone other than the lead candidate can be appointed is by using this power of exception, which, as I say, has not yet been used.

In the particular case to which she was referring, what happened was that a procedure was being followed—which I discontinued last summer—which existed before that case. It was not a case of the Minister intervening in that way. Under that procedure he was allowed to see the candidates who were above the line and then to report back to the selection board, which had adjourned. They made the decision after hearing what he had to say. The candidate who was eventually appointed did have the Commissioners' approval, but there was a great deal of controversy about that case and considerable disbelief about the way in which it might have happened. It seemed to us better not to use that kind of procedure any more and we have discontinued it.

LORD NOLAN: Thank you very much. I am going to ask Sir Clifford Boulton to take up the questioning.

999. CLIFFORD BOULTON: Good morning. We understand that in your position you are a civil servant at the moment, although that may change for successors. For that reason we are not going to ask questions about your private opinions about government policy, but your presence is a very valuable chance for us to get on to the record the way in which the Commissioners work and for you to describe to us some of the changes that are being planned.

Could you state briefly for the record what the role of the Commissioners—and your own role—presently is?

ANN BOWTELL: The Commissioners are central to one of the key civil service values, that is, recruitment by fair and open competition on merit. I will say briefly what that means. It means that all vacancies must be advertised, the selection must be made equally on merit at every stage, the selection must be made against clear criteria, which are applied uniformly to all candidates, and the selection must be made by valid techniques.

Those criteria must be applied to all appointments in the civil service, unless they fall under a number of specific exceptions in the Order in Council. For example, the Order permits secondments: it would allow you to make a secondment from another organisation without carrying through fair and open competition on merit, since the civil service is anxious to have cross-fertilisation between the civil service and other organisations.

The Commissioners' role in all that is to advise the Minister for the Civil Service on the rules which the civil service, under the Order in Council, has to apply in relation to recruitment. Secondly, the Commissioners have to monitor those rules in departments and report back to the Minister for the Civil Service. Thirdly, the Commissioners must approve every appointment to the civil service at grade 7 or above. Changes are proposed to those roles, but that is the Commissioners' current role.

As to my role as First Commissioner, I am the only Commissioner who is occupied full-time on Commissioners' business, and therefore I do carry out most of the boarding business of the Commissioners. I also supervise the office that undertakes the work of monitoring and auditing and so on.

1000. CLIFFORD BOULTON: I imagine that, although you see your role as being at arm's length, as a civil servant you are answerable to someone. Who is that?

ANN BOWTELL: As a Commissioner, I am independent and not answerable to anyone within the civil service. Commissioners' decisions are absolute. If we decide that a particular appointment could not be approved, that would be the end of the matter. As a civil servant, I am answerable in the normal way to Sir Robin Butler, but not for my decisions as an independent civil service Commissioner.

Commissioners are appointed under the Order in Council, so in a sense they are accountable to the Queen. We make our annual report to the Queen.

1001. CLIFFORD BOULTON: Is the Order in Council made under the prerogative or under a statute?

ANN BOWTELL: It is made under the prerogative, and it is the Order in Council that governs the management of the civil service.

1002. CLIFFORD BOULTON: There is no parliamentary consequence of the making of the Order in Council?

ANN BOWTELL: No. Parliament would normally be notified that the process was in train, but there is no parliamentary procedure connected with it.

1003. CLIFFORD BOULTON: Nor an obligation to lay the Order in Council before Parliament?

ANN BOWTELL: No. It is published in the London Gazette, I believe, in the normal way.

1004. CLIFFORD BOULTON: Who actually makes the appointments of Commissioners?

ANN BOWTELL: Appointments are made by the Queen in Council. The process would be that the Prime Minister would need to approve the names being put forward; then they would be approved by the Queen and formally made by the Privy Council.

1005. CLIFFORD BOULTON: It is on the advice of the Prime Minister?

ANN BOWTELL: It is, yes.

1006. CLIFFORD BOULTON: It has been a heady time of change, has it not, for the Commissioners over the past decade? How would you describe the way in which the role has changed? Has it developed in the light of the changing scene around you?

ANN BOWTELL: Yes. The principles for which the Commissioners stand have not changed—in other words, selection on merit by fair and open competition—but the way in which they carry out those principles has changed dramatically. Originally, the Commissioners were set up to conduct competitive examinations for all posts in the civil service, so every single post, however lowly, had to have the individual approval of the Commissioners and normally had to be competed for by an open examination. That has gradually changed over the years as public examinations came to be acceptable.

The big change in the way in which the Commissioners operated came in 1983, when clerical recruitment was delegated to departments. In 1991, executive recruitment was delegated to departments. This came about because, with increasing managerial responsibility being given to departments and to individual units within departments, the idea that some other body out there was actually recruiting their staff and they were not having a say in the staff that were doing their work became increasingly untenable. One could not manage an organisation in that way. The switch has been to the Commissioners becoming regulators rather than doing the recruitment. Under the 1991 Order they have power to advise the Minister on the rules and to monitor the application of the rules in departments. The new arrangements will take that one step further. The Commissioners now are regulators of recruitment for the vast majority of civil service appointments, but they still retain the direct power of approval for the senior appointments, where there is the greatest likelihood that one might get into the business of patronage, which is why the system was set up in the first place.

1007. CLIFFORD BOULTON: There is now a Recruitment and Assessment Services Agency, is there not? Departments and agencies are not required to use it.

ANN BOWTELL: No. The agency operates on a repayment basis. Departments can use it if they like. It deals with about 10 per cent of civil service recruitment, but a much higher percentage of senior recruitment. It is quite independent of the Commissioners and merely provides a service for departments. They can use the private sector to carry out recruitment, if they like, but all of it is subject to the recruitment rules, wherever it is done.

1008. CLIFFORD BOULTON: Obviously, what one would be anxious about is whether the same general standards are operated throughout and whether people who are not using the agency, but are doing things their own way, are matching certain criteria and are able to ensure that, broadly speaking, civil servants will be of the same calibre and kind, according to what they are needed for. Would you like to describe what is done to make sure that that is happening?

ANN BOWTELL: There are two approaches. Firstly, the Minister's rules, to which I refer in my paper, set out the basic processes that departments should follow in carrying out recruitment. The monitors who work for the Commissioners go to individual recruitment units and look to see under what instructions they are working and how they have carried out individual competitions. They then report back to the Commissioners, who report to the Minister. We publish an account of that monitoring in our annual report.

We have found that in general the standard is pretty good. The difficulties that we have encountered have mostly arisen under the pressure of the enormous number of applications that are received nowadays. Sheer numbers make it very difficult to cope with those applications fairly. The monitors have had to give advice to departments about how to deal with them and still carry out a fair competition.

1009. CLIFFORD BOULTON: I see that the "fast stream" entries are going to be delegated to departments. At present, I understand, graduates coming into the fast stream on competition are given an opportunity to specify which department they would like to serve in, how they see their role and what things they are most interested in. Are we saying goodbye to the concept of "fast stream" civil servants, almost regarding themselves as a unified cadre to be moved around from one department to another? Are we waving goodbye to all that?

ANN BOWTELL: No. The delegation is from the Commissioners to a "consortium" of departments that will continue to run a competition that will allow people to apply for the civil service rather than for individual departments. Since, under the new arrangements, the Commissioners will approve only appointments from grade 5 upwards, it seemed sensible that they should no longer approve appointments that are at a considerably lower initial level; but there will still be a competition, which is a high-flying, graduate competition. The management of it, however, will be with the departments that recruit people, but with OPSS in the chair, as it were, since a consortium of 20 departments is not a good means of managing anything directly.

1010. CLIFFORD BOULTON: You spoke of the enormous number of entries. Is that true for fast-stream candidates? Do you get an enormous number of those?

ANN BOWTELL: Yes, we do.

CLIFFORD BOULTON: For quite a small number of vacancies.

ANN BOWTELL: In recent years we have been getting over 10,000 applications for 100 or so vacancies.

1011. CLIFFORD BOULTON: Are you satisfied, as far as is humanly possible, that your weeding out is fair? Have you done any tests to see what you have lost by the weeding out process and been worried about it?

ANN BOWTELL: We have taken a lot of trouble with the initial weeding out process, which, as you say, is a very difficult stage, when you are getting down from such very large numbers. We use cognitive tests and a variety of other questions about people's experience, attitudes and personality. Those combined are totally objectively marked. We do not do any initial interviewing in the way that other employers do. We are as satisfied as we reasonably can be that that is a fair system. Currently, though, we are having an audit of the system carried out by someone from outside to make absolutely certain that we are right. One can never be sure that one has not missed someone. There is always an enormous band between the people who are just in and those who are just out.

1012. CLIFFORD BOULTON: But you have been asking yourself the question? You have been testing it?

ANN BOWTELL: Yes. Recently we have had some very extensive tests with the CRE, because they were somewhat concerned on the racial equality side. We have been right through the competition with them and they are satisfied with what we have been doing.

1013. CLIFFORD BOULTON: You gave us in your opening statement an account of the change that you decided to make in the intervention that Ministers could make, seeing people above the line and sending you back their recommendation. You said that no breach of the then rules had taken place. Had there been much experience of it before, do you know? Did the records reveal that Ministers had been taking the opportunity to see the candidates above the line?

ANN BOWTELL: I think this procedure had been very rarely used. That was one of the troubles in using it in this case. There was no breach of the rules. The appointment was perfectly properly made. It was simply that in retrospect it did not seem a terribly sensible procedure to have, since people did not believe that it had been properly carried out.

1014. CLIFFORD BOULTON: There was nothing secret about it. It was canvassed in the Select Committee's report, was it not, the Civil Service Committee's report?

ANN BOWTELL: Yes, indeed.

1015. CLIFFORD BOULTON: Have the Commissioners a role in ensuring that no conflict of interest arises when senior staff are recruited from outside the civil service, for example, by imposing restrictions for a time on people working in areas of previous employment? An employer might have an interest.

ANN BOWTELL: It is not really the Commissioners' responsibility; it would be departments' responsibility.

But obviously it is an issue that could arise in the course of the selection process. If it became apparent early on that the conflict of interests was really too great, one would not take that person's candidature any further. But more often one might reach a stage where one wanted to make the appointment and someone would then become subject to normal civil service rules in cases where they might have a conflict of interests. I have known one or two cases where some restrictions have been imposed, but the issue has arisen very rarely, in my experience.

1016. CLIFFORD BOULTON: There is an awareness that it could be relevant?

ANN BOWTELL: Oh yes. There are rules in the civil service management code to cover it.

1017. CLIFFORD BOULTON: Do you have any role in respect of departmental public bodies or health service appointments?

ANN BOWTELL: No. Our role at the moment is strictly confined to the civil service. There are a couple of non-departmental public bodies that employ civil servants—ACAS and the HSE. They come within our remit, but we have no remit in relation to the health service. There used to be a number of non-departmental public bodies whose staff were on civil service terms and conditions. Some years ago we had some responsibility for them, but once they were no longer on civil service terms and conditions and were given increased authority, they fell outside the Commissioners' purview. The numbers would not be great. On the whole it has always been civil servants.

1018. CLIFFORD BOULTON: Has the proportion of appointments nowadays to the public service overseen by the Commissioners risen or fallen?

ANN BOWTELL: All appointments to the civil service have generally been within the Commissioners' remit, although there was a time when that was restricted to permanent appointments only. That restriction has gone. We oversee all appointments, even if they are temporary and short term. In terms of the civil service, we probably oversee a higher proportion of them now. In terms of our total remit, we would have lost some bits—for instance, the Post Office went outside our remit—so in terms of things that are within the public service, we probably have a slightly smaller coverage.

1019. CLIFFORD BOULTON: You told us in a note that the proposed changes will strengthen the Commissioners' role. Would you like to highlight the areas you have in mind?

ANN BOWTELL: There are three main areas. Firstly, the Commissioners will in future themselves interpret the provisions of the Order in Council for departments, whereas now they advise the Minister. The Minister will have no role in future; it will be directly between the Commissioners and departments. We shall issue to departments a short and simple recruitment code, to try to bring the principles to life for them. What they have at present is some rules; there is a tendency to apply them mechanistically. There are so many different situations in recruitment that we want people to understand the principles on which they operate. That is what our guidance will seek to do.

Secondly, we shall have a new power to require departments to provide information about their recruitment. One of the things that the delegation of recruitment to departments means is that departments themselves have to take responsibility for seeing that their recruitment is done by fair and open competition on merit. They should not assume that somehow that is the Commissioners' business. The publication by departments of information about their recruitment will help to bring home that accountability.

Thirdly, the Commissioners' monitoring system will be changed into an "audit" system to audit departmental systems of recruitment rather than individual competitions, again pushing the responsibility on to departments to see that their recruitment is in order. We shall be required to publish the results of that audit in our annual report, whereas at the moment we simply make a report to the Minister.

In those respects the Commissioners will be standing much more on their own feet and there will be less of a role for a Minister in future.

1020. CLIFFORD BOULTON: You are accompanied by Mr Maddrell, who is a part-time Commissioner. You have been a Commissioner since 1992. Is that correct?

GEOFFREY MADDRELL (Part-time Civil Service Commissioner): That is right.

1021. CLIFFORD BOULTON: Were you alarmed by what you found when you took up this job, or were you broadly reassured?

GEOFFREY MADDRELL: Over the past two years I have become more reassured. As Mrs Bowtell has described, the role had some executive as well as regulatory functions. Now it is clearly defined as regulatory. Certainly for people who are part-time it is easier to understand and to know exactly what their role is.

1022. CLIFFORD BOULTON: You are broadly satisfied with what you have found and feel that you can take responsibility for what you are expected to take responsibility for, the information you need and that sort of thing?

GEOFFREY MADDRELL: There is no doubt about that.

CLIFFORD BOULTON: Thank you very much.

1023. WILLIAM UTTING: If I could push the Quango point a bit further with you, Mrs Bowtell, it has been represented to us by some people who have criticised methods of appointment to Quangos that an independent monitoring system of the kind that you apply to certain grades in the civil service would be appropriate. I do not know what proposals the Government may have for improving methods of appointment to public bodies—and I would not ask you to anticipate what they are going to say, even if you know. The kind of monitoring system that you apply must apply to large numbers of staff in the civil service. Do you have a rough idea of how many staff?

ANN BOWTELL: We are monitoring 3,000 separate recruitment units. I have no up-to-date recruitment figures, but the last one I had was of some 20,000 appointments a year. It may be less than that now. We shall monitor a sample of those appointments and recruitment units. Over the past few years we have monitored about 500 recruitment units right across the civil service.

The difference between the civil service and Quangos is that civil servants are all operating on one system. The civil service is an organisation which until recently had all its recruitment done for it centrally. It was accustomed to a tight recruitment system. The people in it are all working broadly in the same system, and always have done. The difficulty of translating that into the Quango area is that there is a greater variety of bodies and appointments, some of which are unpaid. One could not apply the same rules. There would have to be much more flexible and open rules. That would make the auditing process a good deal more complex and much more judgmental. I suspect that, technically, it could be done, but it would be a much bigger, more complicated job than the one we do. One might get into a much more extensive executive operation. We do ours with only 25 part-time monitors. It is a very light-handed operation, but it works because everybody is pointing in the same direction.

1024. WILLIAM UTTING: If we were to target attention on a certain number of Quango appointments and eliminate some of the complexity that you properly referred to, the methods that Commissioners use might be appropriate.

ANN BOWTELL: Yes. The more one limits the field, the more clearly one defines it, the more the field is like the kind of full-time, paid appointments we deal with, the easier it would be. You would still have to deal with the different situations in which different bodies find themselves and the statutory basis upon which some of them were set up. You probably would not be able to have the same formal powers as you have in relation to the civil service, but you probably could apply the systems.

1025. WILLIAM UTTING: Thank you. One clarifying point. Your responsibilities extend to staff in Next Steps Agencies as well as to the "proper" civil service?

ANN BOWTELL: Staff in Next Steps Agencies are proper civil servants.

WILLIAM UTTING: That is what I wanted you to emphasise.

ANN BOWTELL: They are absolutely on all fours with the rest of the civil servants.

1026. WILLIAM UTTING: You are responsible for the appointment of staff in Next Steps Agencies?

ANN BOWTELL: Yes.

WILLIAM UTTING: At grade 7 and above.

ANN BOWTELL: Yes.

WILLIAM UTTING: The Agencies appoint staff below that level.

ANN BOWTELL: Yes.

WILLIAM UTTING: Their methods are monitored by you.

ANN BOWTELL: Absolutely.

WILLIAM UTTING: In the same way that you monitor the central ———

ANN BOWTELL: If anything, we probably do more appointments in agencies, because their chief executives are generally appointed by open competition. They come our way more often than other civil servants do.

1027. WILLIAM UTTING: We can underline the fact that the staff of these agencies are civil servants in the full sense of the word?

ANN BOWTELL: Absolutely.

1028. WILLIAM UTTING: They too will be subject to any civil service code that is introduced by the Government?

ANN BOWTELL: Yes, indeed.

WILLIAM UTTING: Thank you very much.

1029. ANTHONY KING: I had two questions. One has already been asked; the other is very simple and straightforward. There is a thing called the Civil Service Commission, there are people called Civil Service Commissioners. Does the Commission ever meet?

ANN BOWTELL: There is no Civil Service Commission. It was abolished in 1991. There are Civil Service Commissioners who meet on a monthly basis.

1030. ANTHONY KING: Would you gloss that a little further? Here we have a body that was formally abolished, apparently. Someone took the trouble to abolish it four years ago, yet it meets on a monthly basis.

ANN BOWTELL: No. The Commissioners meet. What exists is the Commissioners. The Order in Service talks about the Civil Service Commissioners. The point was that the old Civil Service Commission was an executive body which dealt with civil service recruitment. The executive role was taken by the Recruitment & Assessment Services Agency. Although I was not around at the time, my guess is that to have kept the term "Commission" for the very different kind of body that the Commissioners were going to turn into was thought to have been confusing, hence the Commission itself disappeared.

LORD NOLAN: If you will forgive the comparison, we have Commissioners of Inland Revenue, but no Commission.

ANN BOWTELL: Thank you very much. That is helpful.

1031. LORD NOLAN: I wonder if I can ask you about your monitoring sample, because there seems to be a particular interest when one needs some outside agency to oversee a vast range of appointments. How do you choose your sample?

ANN BOWTELL: We have first to identify the recruitment units on the method we use now. It is quite difficult, because they keep changing in departments and I

have to say that we are finding it increasingly difficult to keep track of where the delegation exists, hence the fact that we are going to change our system so that we deal with departments themselves rather than recruitment units. Part of that is because of the difficulty we have found in keeping track of where the delegated responsibility is. Some departments will have a lot of units that are all the same, so we tend to sample them relatively lightly, because they are working on the same systems.

1032. LORD NOLAN: On a random basis?

ANN BOWTELL: We start off on a random basis, but if we find that we are getting particular difficulties in a particular area, we target the monitoring in that direction. If you take it on a totally random basis, you find that you are monitoring very junior appointments all the time, because that is where most of the recruitment is. Last year we targeted the more senior appointments on an out-of-order basis, because we were not getting enough of them in the ordinary sample.

1033. LORD NOLAN: If there is a complaint about a particular appointment that is made, can that be referred to you?

ANN BOWTELL: An appointment which is not one that is subject to our approval?

LORD NOLAN: Yes.

ANN BOWTELL: It has not been, in my experience since I have been there. That appointment would be the responsibility of the department, strictly. We would want to have a jolly good look at how that department was operating its systems, if that happened.

LORD NOLAN: Thank you very much.

1034. DIANA WARWICK: I have just one question, because everything you have said in response has answered various questions that I had. It has to do with perception rather than anything else. You made it clear in the one example where we had asked Elizabeth Symons about ministerial interference with an appointment that in fact no rules were broken. There was a particular aspect of the process that you have to change. Given her additional evidence that in many areas where Ministers might influence civil servants, it was very difficult to gain anything other than anecdotal evidence. In your experience, is there any cause for concern that there is an underlying problem here that cannot be proven by evidence, but which you have come across, that might have given you cause for concern? Or is it a system that works well and fairly in all aspects?

ANN BOWTELL: I have never had any cause for concern. I find that both the civil service and Ministers accept this as a system which is the best way to keep a politically impartial civil service. Because of the procedures that we put in place to allow Ministers to see the job specification, the person specification, they do not have the feeling that somebody is suddenly going to be wished upon them who is not capable of doing the job they want done, and I think that goes a long way to diffuse those worries. The process keeps the Minister in the picture all the way through and gives him the opportunity, if he wants to, to say, "You've got the specification wrong. These are not the sort of people I thought you were going to get on the long list", without him ever getting involved in the individual process. I have found that respected, despite what I am sure must be great temptations, when people are very keen to get a particular job done. I have found that it does work, as long as you are careful to see that everybody is kept informed as you go along, so that there is no feeling that one is going away and producing a rabbit out of a hat. I have had no concerns on that front.

1035. ANNE WARBURTON: May I ask you, Mrs Bowtell, if you can cast any more light on the new role that Commissioners will have in respect of problems of civil servants who are not happy and have no satisfaction. The paper you have given us refers to further consultations and the proposed code simply says that people may report the matter in writing to the Civil Service Commissioners, but can you forecast whether you will take action yourself or see yourselves taking it to a Select Committee? Has that thinking come to you yet?

ANN BOWTELL: The role was only announced last week at the Command Paper. It is a completely new area for the Commissioners. We have been solely into recruitment regulations so far. The Command Paper says that in the first instance this would be something between the Commissioners and the Minister of the Department, but if the matter could not be resolved to the Commissioners' satisfaction, they would have the right to report to a Select Committee or to Parliament. There would be that route. The Commissioners will now be joining in this consultation process and will need to look closely at the procedures to satisfy themselves that they are going to work. It is early days yet.

ANNE WARBURTON: A premature question.

ANN BOWTELL: For my successor.

1036. LORD NOLAN: Thank you both very much, Mrs Bowtell and Mr Maddrell. You have been very helpful and we are very grateful to you.

Good morning Michael Bichard. You are the Chief Executive of the Benefits Agency. Mr Bichard I do not know whether you propose to make a short opening statement or whether you would like to leave it to us to ask you questions?

MICHAEL BICHARD

MICHAEL BICHARD (Chief Executive, Benefits Agency): Well maybe sir I could just develop slightly the evidence that I submitted. I think the most important thing I would want to emphasise is that in my view the long overdue emphasis on management within the Civil Service should not, and need not, lead to a reduction in the standards in the traditional values of integrity, impartiality, objectivity and confidentiality. That I think is very, very important.

I do not see any reason why it should, and I see no convincing evidence yet that it has led to a reduction in standards. But I would want us not just to be thinking about how we protect and retain existing standards, but how we strengthen those standards and if we are to do that I think we need to take account of changing circumstances and environment. There are two particular ways that I try and bring out in the evidence where I think we can strengthen standards.

The first is by taking advantage of the greater openness and accountability that Next Steps Agencies in particular give us. The fact that targets, objectives, business plans, annual reports, framework documents, are all now available. The fact that people like myself, I hope, are a touch more visible than perhaps traditional civil servants have been, and the fact that we retain the panoply of accountability represented by the Public Accounts Committee, the Parliamentary Commissioner, the Chief Adjudication Officer, and I could go on. We need to take advantage of the greater openness and not be so concerned with an alleged loss of accountability and openness.

The second way in which we can strengthen standards is by injecting greater clarity into some key areas. What we have tried to do is to inject greater clarity into issues such as the values of the Agency, what is it that we stand for and want to achieve. Greater clarity particularly around the extensive devolution which is happening in so many organisations and I think is necessary but nonetheless is a cause for some concern about changing and different standards of behaviour.

We need to inject greater clarity into the key areas of personnel recruitment that you have just been discussing, to finance gifts, hospitality, taking account of this changing relationship between the private and the public sector and the key area of purchasing too.

Now I have tried to outline some of the things we have done to inject that greater clarity. I think it is very important that we do not take for granted that everyone is aware of what is required in those areas.

LORD NOLAN: Thank you very much. It is a very helpful opening. I am going to ask Diana Warwick please to take up the questions we wanted to put to you.

1037. DIANA WARWICK: I wonder, you come from outside the Civil Service, so in a way you are in a very useful position for us to ask you to look at, perhaps objectively, the way in which the Civil Service or the Next Steps Agencies, as part of the Civil Service, operate. We have just been dealing with recruitment, could you explain how you were recruited?

MICHAEL BICHARD: I was recruited by open competition. The First Civil Service Commissioner was involved in my appointment and in my interview, but there was external competition on a fixed term contract.

1038. DIANA WARWICK: I have no idea whether this was the case, but we were referring earlier to a case where Ministers had appeared in some way to be involved in the appointment. Was there any indication in the approach to your appointment that there was a specific interest by Ministers?

MICHAEL BICHARD: There was no indication and to the best of my knowledge it did not occur.

1039. DIANA WARWICK: I wonder if I can go on then to the general question that you have raised and I think is absolutely crucial to our questioning and to the report that we will produce, and that is the whole point about "ethos". I believe you were in, is it Brent and Gloucester?

MICHAEL BICHARD: I was in Brent and Gloucestershire, yes.

1040. DIANA WARWICK: Have you been able to perceive any difference between the ethos of public service in local government, from which you come, and the ethos of public service in the national Civil Service? I mean have there been any differences and were they unexpected?

MICHAEL BICHARD: I think when you work in local government, to get used to the diversity of local government and when you work for two authorities so different as Brent and Gloucestershire, it is difficult to generalise. I think the ethos was different in different authorities, some stronger than others, and I would perhaps restrict my comments to my impressions of the Civil Service, where I have been impressed by the commitment to impartiality, integrity and objectivity. In our case, of course, also equally important, confidentiality. I have been impressed by the way in which that has been maintained, despite the fact that one political party has been in power for so long. I am impressed by the emphasis that is placed upon that and if you look at the guidance that we have been offering to our staff, which of course I did before today, it is quite interesting to note that right at the beginning of the Conditions of Service manual that our staff receive, is a clear statement that the "Civil Service expects you to maintain a high standard of integrity and conduct. You must be beyond any suspicion of dishonesty". So I am impressed by that and I speak as someone who has actually worked—unusually I suppose for a current civil servant—for all three political parties at different times and different places.

1041. DIANA WARWICK: Do you think somebody who came from a totally different background, say came from industry or from commerce, would find a greater degree of difference? Do you feel they would be just as impressed?

MICHAEL BICHARD: I would hope they would be just as impressed. I think they would note a greater difference of course because managing in a political environment is always different to managing in a private sector environment. I would not want to get drawn into debates about which is more difficult, but it is different. How individuals adapt to that obviously depends upon the individual but I am sure they would find it more different than I did, coming from a local authority background.

1042. DIANA WARWICK: Can I just pursue a point that you made earlier, that I think perhaps I should pick up. You said there were differences in ethos between Brent and Gloucestershire and I think there was a sotto voce comment from the other side of the table that your reply was a typical Civil Service reply. But since one of the things that we are looking at is whether, in devolving authority within the Civil Service structure, being created is a different set of ethos's, if I can put it that way, and that that might be a cause for concern, did it matter that when you went from Brent to Gloucestershire things were different? Did you have to do something about the differences?

MICHAEL BICHARD: Well yes, I have always tried to emphasise the importance of the values that I have referred to; I have always tried to establish those, whether it was in a local authority or in central government, as the bedrock on which we should build. I happen to believe that those values alone are not sufficient any longer and that one should try and build upon those more relevant, if

you like, business sense of values, such as customer service and value for money, to name but two. That was my approach in both authorities; it received a ready ear in some places more than in others. But if I may say, the most critical point in your question is around this question of devolution and the extent to which we are able to protect standards of behaviour in a devolved environment.

I think devolution is absolutely critical in an organisation of my size, if we are going to deliver a responsive service, if we are going to free up some of the initiative and some of the innovative ideas that exist there, if we are going to be efficient. But we do need to ensure that is done within a framework and I think too often people try to devolve without establishing the framework within which the people must work, within which their new power must be exercised. Now we have taken great steps to try and deliver that framework, so that our people are clear about the new extent of their power, but also the limitations on their power. We have tried to set minimum standards and as I say we have tried to give very clear guidance on how they should go about, for example, recruitment, what they should do about finance, budget management, how they should deal with offers of hospitality. That has been made very clear to them and I think is extremely important.

1043. DIANA WARWICK: You describe these very clearly in the evidence that you have given to us. Are there any areas that still seem to you to remain rather intractable?

MICHAEL BICHARD: I do not think there are any to which I would point particularly. One should never be complacent. One has always got to be aware, of course, that we are experiencing a reasonable turnover of staff, not as great as it was, so you are always dealing, in our case with 3,000 or 4,000 new staff each year, and you must make sure that they are as clear as their predecessors about these fundamentals.

1044. DIANA WARWICK: And is that done through training?

MICHAEL BICHARD: That is done through guidance, some written guidance. Everyone, for example, receives what we hope is a reasonably readable Conditions of Service handbook when they come through the door.

1045. DIANA WARWICK: It is like a computer manual?

MICHAEL BICHARD: Maybe, yes. We try and support that with different sorts of training. It is very difficult to get every single member of staff and every member of staff has an induction programme which should ensure that they understand what is in there. We have also laid on training in areas of ministerial/civil servant relationships, so that people understand that better. We are about to launch a discipline and misconduct handbook, so that people are absolutely clear, even clearer, about what we regard as misconduct and how it is going to be dealt with and we shall be running workshops around that. We have tried, on occasions, to set up helplines, where purchasing and supply is concerned, which is an important area, the boundaries of the public/private sector relationship. We actually have a helpline where people can ring up and get advice if they have concerns. So we try to approach it in a range of different ways.

1046. DIANA WARWICK: Could I raise another issue that I think has been covered in a couple of, certainly radio, reports recently, and that is the whole question of compulsory competitive tendering, which I believe in fact has long been enforced in local government. The allegation has been that it has not only reduced standards, and there were various examples of that, but more particularly and I think this is the relevance for our Committee, that it has led to increased charges of corruption and it is certainly a fear that has been expressed to us in the evidence from the Civil Service Unions in relation to this whole general area of delegation and of power.

You are obviously in rather a good position to comment on this, from both your past experience and now your experience with the Agency. Do you see the Civil Service and Agencies going in this direction? You crossed over, do you see there were problems of this kind in local government?

MICHAEL BICHARD: I have seen no convincing evidence of that having occurred, either in the local authorities for which I worked, you may be surprised, and certainly since I joined the Benefits Agency. But again I think that does depend upon establishing very clear ground rules, giving staff advice and guidance and I think particularly where you are talking about purchasing services, which is what you are, getting clear divisions between the specification of the service, the purchasing of that service and the payment for that service. If you do not do that, then there is real potential for improper influence and outright fraud.

1047. DIANA WARWICK: Could I move on to another issue that has come up in several of the discussions that we have had and that is the boundaries of responsibility. There has been quite a lot of debate about Ministerial accountability as opposed to delivery of a service and so on. Is it difficult for you to know where the boundaries lie as far as you as the Chief Executive is concerned. Does the buck stop with you?

MICHAEL BICHARD: The accountability for the service that we provide rests and remains with the Secretary of State to whom I report directly. There is no doubt about that. What I think we have seen is a sharpening of the operational accountability—an additional level, if you like, of accountability—and to that extent, accountability for the operational service is, in the first instance at least, now mine. I think that is a healthy development but it must be seen as an additional layer, an additional level, and not a substitution.

1048. DIANA WARWICK: Do you see there are clear differences because Sir Peter Kemp, when he was giving evidence to us yesterday, said, I think rather sotto voce, but nonetheless said, that he did not really see there was a great deal of distinction and that the debate was a bit sterile, I think he was suggesting.

MICHAEL BICHARD: The distinction between accountability and responsibility?

DIANA WARWICK: Yes.

MICHAEL BICHARD: I think that is an interesting debate to indulge in, both with regard to the Secretary of State and also myself. If you are a Chief Executive of an organisation that employs 70,000 people, to what extent can you be accountable for everything that happens in a local district office to what is the difference between accountability and responsibility, I think the same issues apply. My own view is that there is a distinction to be drawn between accountability and responsibility but it is as difficult to draw that where I am concerned, as it is to draw where the Secretary of State is concerned.

1049. DIANA WARWICK: Could I go on to another issue, which is about the way in which decisions are reviewed? Companies and indeed, non-departmental public bodies, usually have a board of independent members. Do you have anything like that, a group of people who would be overseeing the decisions that you take?

MICHAEL BICHARD: No, we do not have an independent board, either advisory or executive, but I do have non-executive directors on my own board, one of whom is the Chief Executive of a national building society, so there is that, if you like, independent involvement, which I want to encourage and extend. I encourage him if he feels it necessary to seek direct access to the Secretary of State or to the Department, if he feels that something is not to his liking or something is seriously wrong with the management of the organisation.

1050. DIANA WARWICK: He does not have any authority? It is a question of advice and your discretion and encouragement, rather than any interventionist rights?

MICHAEL BICHARD: That is right because I think the use of non-executive directors in that kind of situation is quite new and I would have to say that we are still learning as we go along.

1051. DIANA WARWICK: Could I ask you two questions about your contract? We have raised the issue of short-term contracts and again the evidence from the Civil Service Unions casts doubt on some of the relationships that might be affected by the introduction of short-term contracts. Do you think that the knowledge that your contract might not be renewed if you gave a Minister advice that he did not really want, would affect your judgment?

MICHAEL BICHARD: Well, of course, I can only speak as an individual and again, not being a traditional civil servant, I have been used to having fixed term contract. I actually felt, when I was in Brent, I was probably on a weekly contract but more seriously when I went to Gloucestershire I was on a fixed term contract and when I came to the Benefits Agency I was on a fixed term contract. The point I am making is that I have become used to living in that world and frankly, no, it does not affect me and I think the reason why it does not is because I understand that I can probably compete in the marketplace for another post if that became necessary. I am in the last year I think now of this fixed term contract and I can honestly say that it is not affecting my advice at all. But I understand the concerns which people who have only worked in the Civil Service do have and I think there is the greater danger, perhaps, that they could be influenced, simply because they are not used to competing in a marketplace and many of them, frankly, are not confident about their ability to compete in the marketplace. So I think the conclusion that I have reached is that I am more sceptical about the kind of rather crude fixed term contract that I have and that perhaps we ought to be looking, and of course the Government is now looking, not so much at fixed term contracts but at sharper arrangements with staff, so that their positions are reviewed and they are genuinely appraised on a regular basis. I do not think there has been enough of that in the Civil Service frankly and I welcome that development.

1052. DIANA WARWICK: The other point I was going to raise came up in relation to one other witness, the question of conflict of interest and it is obviously relevant, not just to Next Steps but to the issues that we are going to raise in relation to Quangos generally and appointments to Quangos. Were you aware that there was investigation of any special interests you might have before you were appointed? In other words, is this a process that is normally gone through?

MICHAEL BICHARD: Well I was aware that there was some clearance because of the seniority of my post but I was not aware of any further investigation of potential conflict of interests.

1053. DIANA WARWICK: You were not ever asked to declare anything or to identify anything that might be relevant.

MICHAEL BICHARD: Well I recall being asked a series of questions which is part of the normal clearance procedure. I cannot recall actually what they were because I do not think I would have any which I would need to declare.

1054. DIANA WARWICK: Perhaps I could ask you one final question. We have talked quite a lot about Ministerial appointments and the move by Ministers to outside appointments which might be said to be of advantage because of their experience. We raised a similar question with the Civil Service Unions about civil servants. Do you think that, as somebody on a series of short-term contracts, who has come in from outside to do a job likely, as you say, to be very marketable, that these rules should apply to you when you—I have no idea if you are going to move—but if and when you move, do you think those rules should apply to you?

MICHAEL BICHARD: I think they should and the answer which Elizabeth Symons gave earlier, that the reason for one's departure from Government is not the relevant point; the points I think she raised are the relevant points. I hope that would not dissuade people from coming in from outside and perhaps there is a point I could just make on the back of your question. I think it is desperately important that we do attract people from outside the Civil Service, not so many as to undermine the morale of civil servants and convince them that there is no career path—frankly I do not think we have got anywhere near that happening yet—we should not do that, but enough to inject maybe a greater emphasis upon achievement, end product and output. In my Agency we have tried to bring in people, at critical points within the organisation, to ensure that happens, but I think if they were to leave the Agency then the same issues of conflicts of interest should apply to them as to a permanent civil servant.

1055. DIANA WARWICK: But in general terms is your view that, particularly as the organisation management and morale in your Agency is concerned and

perhaps by analogy in others, that things are in pretty good nick, that everything is all right?

MICHAEL BICHARD: Oh I do not think I could say that. Again because of the size of the organisation, it would differ from place to place and often depends upon the quality of the management and most important, in my view, the extent to which the people have been involved in what is going on in their particular business unit. So it does differ substantially and one does need to understand, and it is important, that the Civil Service is going through an enormous change process. One hears a lot about market testing and competitive tendering but the cultural change which we are trying to achieve and which others too are trying to achieve is enormous.

Now there is no way, I think, in which you can go through a change of that significance, without people feeling uncertain, threatened, to some extent without their morale suffering, so I am by no means complacent about morale when, in my own organisation, you can have on top of all of that the problems of workload. I think we need to deal with problems of morale, be very concerned about them, but I do not think we should assume that they are solely the cause of one or even two particular developments. I think that is a mistake.

LORD NOLAN: Mr Bichard's evidence and indeed the position he holds, is one of exceptional interest and I do not want to hold up any Member of the Committee from asking questions, but we are running short of time. I wonder if I might suggest this, may we keep our questions for him to answer to those which can be answered shortly. If there are questions which may require substantial thought and longer answers, could we please state them and perhaps ask Mr Bichard if he would be kind enough to reflect on them and let us have his answers in writing. Would that be an acceptable way to deal with it? Yes.

1056. CLIFFORD BOULTON: Do you feel you have got enough flexibility in what you can offer by way of pay, to get people of the right quality into your Agency?

MICHAEL BICHARD: I think that is a difficult one. Clearly I understand that there does need to be some control and regulation. I think on occasions I have found it a constraint. Normally, I have to say that I have been able to negotiate my way through that constraint, either with the centre of Government or with the individual concerned and, in that case, persuade them that it is such a good organisation they should want to join us anyway and that it will stand them in good stead in their future career development. But there have been one or two other occasions where I have not been able to do that and attract, therefore, the person that I was keen to get.

CLIFFORD BOULTON: Thank you.

1057. LORD THOMSON: Can I go back to the question of policy and operational responsibility. Policy lies with the Minister, operational responsibility lies with you and that is a simplistic way of looking at it. But are you one of the Minister's advisers on policy?

MICHAEL BICHARD: I am his primary adviser on operations. The Permanent Secretary remains his primary adviser on policy. We must each consult, one with the other, on policy matters which have operational implications or operational matters which have policy implications. My role and our role as an Agency, is to ensure also that we are involved in the development of new policy because we have a contribution to make and that we are also feeding back to Ministers and to the Department, problems which may be arising with existing policy. So we have a policy role but it is not our primary role.

1058. PETER SHORE: One question you claimed in your opening statement, that one of the advantages was greater accountability. When you use the word accountability, is it accountability to Ministers, accountability to Parliament, or accountability to the people whom your Agency serves?

MICHAEL BICHARD: Well I regard myself as having accountability to all three and certainly in all three respects the accountability has sharpened as a result of Agency being set up. If you take the people who come through our door, our clients or customers, whatever term you want to use—claimants used to be the term—and I think the focus that we have placed upon the service we deliver has increased tremendously and I think there are all sorts of statistics I could produce to show that, which I will not.

In terms of Parliament, as I said, what we have done, or what is happening, is that we are retaining, or we have retained, the traditional methods of accountability, the PAC, the PCA and the rest of it. The only difference in that respect is, of course, that I now answer parliamentary questions which affect the operations of the Agency, or at least most of those, although the answer to those too are now published, as you know, sir, in Hansard, and I deal with most Members' questions. But at the end of the day, if Members are not satisfied or if Parliament is not satisfied, with the reply that I have given, then of course they have the right to go to Ministers, or the Secretary of State, and there is no circumstance in which that would then be referred to me. They would receive a reply from the Secretary of State or from Ministers and they clearly would want my account of the difficulty.

I think so far as Secretary of State and Ministers are concerned, what we have seen within the Department is a sharpening of the focus on operations, a greater identity for operations and policy, and one of the concerns when Agencies were set up, was that the two would drift apart. I believe that, within the Department of Social Security at least, exactly the opposite has happened, because they have each been able to establish their identity, because they each, I think, have greater respect one for the other now, they are each involved, as they should be, in each other's activities. We need, as I have said, to have an involvement in policy; they need to understand operations and to get a feel for what is happening in our local office and I think that is happening. So I think accountability across all those three fronts has improved.

1059. PROF. ANTHONY KING: Can I ask one question about your public role? Clearly the Benefits Agency is responsible for administering a system of benefits, a benefits regime. When you took up your post, were you told, both that you should not publicly criticise that benefits system and that you should not publicly declare yourself as being in support of the currently established benefits system?

MICHAEL BICHARD: Well, I think, first of all you have to define what you mean by benefits system. I mean

there is an operational system and there is a benefits policy system?

PROF. ANTHONY KING: The latter.

MICHAEL BICHARD: You mean the latter. Well I do not think, as someone who has worked in a political environment for all of my life, I needed to be giving guidance on how I should react to, or how I should publicly comment. As far as I am concerned, policy issues are ultimately a matter for the Secretary of State and for Ministers. I give my advice; hopefully, on more occasions than not, that advice is listened to. On some occasions it is listened to but disagreed with. Ministers then remain responsible for the policy that ensues and I do not publicly criticise that policy. Now as far as operations are concerned, then I will take a higher profile, in terms of commenting upon the Agency and actually celebrating its success and I think that is important because I lead a large organisation.

1060. PROF. ANTHONY KING: You say you would not publicly criticise the policy. Would you publicly defend it or support it?

MICHAEL BICHARD: I think there is a limit to how far I would go in defending a particular policy. I will explain Ministers' and Secretary of State's reasons because I think it is important that my staff understand that. I mean if they have to deliver it in a difficult inner city office, they need to understand that there is reasoning behind it. But they are professionals as well as I am and once they understand the reasoning behind it, then they will explain it too, they will not defend it, they will not attack it, but they will explain it.

1061. WILLIAM UTTING: It is one thing to defend and explain it to staff in the privacy of one's own organisation, but you said at the beginning that Chief Executives of Agencies had a bigger public profile than civil servants who had been in the decent anonymity of a central Government department. Are you put into a position, publicly, in which you appear to be taking political sides, in fact, about policy—is that unavoidable for the Chief Executive of a Next Steps Agency?

MICHAEL BICHARD: I think it is one of the things that you must always be conscious of and you must desperately seek to avoid. You must be aware of people's perception of what you are doing and what you are saying because I think, if you fall foul of that, then your credibility will suffer. The one thing that I hold very dear is that I am perceived, I hope, and always have been, as an apolitical official, then I have lost that and I hold that probably more dear than anything else. So I am very conscious of the need to avoid that happening. It is not a difficult line to draw, I do not find it difficult, but I think you must not allow that to detract from the increased visibility because one of the ways in which we increase the accountability is by greater openness, greater transparency and greater visibility on the part of individuals. I think too often in the past people have allowed themselves, because of their fears of being drawn into and criticised in that area, to become defensive and invisible and I think that is a mistake.

1062. WILLIAM UTTING: And to the public you must appear to be enthusiastic about the work that you are doing and the work that your Agency is doing?

MICHAEL BICHARD: I hope I am enthusiastic, both for public and for staff and as I say, I think it is important that my staff know that I believe in what they are doing and I think it is important that I am seen to celebrate their success. I do not see that as running counter to my need to remain apolitical because I am celebrating success.

WILLIAM UTTING: Thank you.

1063. LORD NOLAN: You have given us a lot of help. You have given us a lot of food for thought. Thank you very much for coming Mr Bichard, we are very grateful.

Now we have the Rt. Hon. Robert Sheldon MP, amongst other things Chairman of the Public Accounts Committee, and Sir John Bourn, the Comptroller and Auditor General. Thank you very much for coming along to see us. Did you want to make an opening statement before we start on the questions?

RT HON SIR ROBERT SHELDON MP AND SIR JOHN BOURN

SIR ROBERT SHELDON, MP: I would, if you have no objection because the background to all of this is really quite interesting. It is really the eighth report of the Committee of Public Accounts that really established a number of areas and I drew attention to this in the annual debate. We have an annual debate in Parliament on the Public Accounts Committee where we review the forty-five to fifty reports each year. In the 1992 debate, in the autumn, I drew attention to the number of areas which were causing a certain amount of disquiet, particularly in the non-departmental public bodies, and I said something would have to be done. In the debate the following year, 1993, I saw nothing much had happened and there were a number of further disquieting reports which we had issued and I said we would be producing a special report dealing with some of these areas that did cause us some great concern, and that led to the eighth report of the Public Accounts Committee where we showed a number of things that had gone seriously wrong in a way that we had not had in previous years. The most important aspect of all this was the standards of public conduct and the "Proper Conduct of Public Business" was the title of that report. Part of our job is, of course, to look after value for money but another part of it, of course, is to make sure that the standards of probity which we have come to accept are there as well. Fraud and corruption have not taken up a great deal of our time, but when these matters arise they take priority over everything else. We are extraordinary fortunate—there are, what, 184 countries in the United Nations, the number of them which have standards somewhere approaching ours are just a handful. We are a rare exception and it is up to us to make sure that we retain those standards. So many of these countries come and ask my advice as to how they can acquire those standards but once you lose them I am afraid it is extraordinarily difficult to return to them.

1064. LORD NOLAN: The first paragraph of your report is very strikingly worded in this connection. You have really summarised it—if you had not done so I was proposing to read it out—but you have made your message very clear, both in that passage and in what you have just said. I interrupted you, Mr. Sheldon—were you going on to other matters or was this your first point?

ROBERT SHELDON: Well, that is the most important point. There is a lot of change in the Civil Service, of course, and when there is change there is room for inefficiencies and there is room for corruption and that is one of the matters that concerned us greatly. We have seen in the past, of course, some of these very big ones—I mean, the Welsh Development Agency was a striking example of something that we had not come across. I mean, the idea that there could be somebody recruited who has been in prison three times for fraud, recruited through a Government agency and entertains models in his hotel room on a Sunday afternoon paid for by the public purse—I mean it is something that was quite alien to anything we had come across before.

There are a number of examples, not perhaps quite as striking as that, but very serious ones—the Wessex Regional Health Authority and the Development Board for Rural Wales and those sorts of things. But one feature that we saw which, again, we had not seen before, are the "silence clauses". There have been a number of cases where people coming in from outside—and, of course, they have not got the ethos of the public service and they feel that they are running their own show, and without those standards they have been buying off people that they disagreed with, but inserted into their dismissal have been "silence clauses"—they are not allowed to say anything. We have seen a number of those cases. That cannot be the case when you have got public money—public money must never be allowed to have silence clauses. Whether the standards were higher in the past I am not in a position to say. All I know is that the penalties in the past seem to have been clearer, that if you were found that you had not obeyed the standards—and they were very loosely defined but in the Civil Service, in the public service generally, one knew what they were—then you were banished from public life. That does not seem to be quite the case today. Perhaps that is all I should say at this stage.

1065. LORD NOLAN: But it does, of course, go right to the heart of the subject matter of our enquiry. You say in the report that you are not calling for any more detailed rules. The trouble is really that the existing rules have been broken. What is to be done about that?

ROBERT SHELDON: Well, as it stood, people did know broadly what they could do and what they could not do. Once you get people looking at the details then, of course, they can start bending those rules and it worked very well up to now. I think perhaps now we really have to perhaps codify it but I am not sure that that in itself is going to be enough—it is the standards that everybody knows and they are the results of 130 years. Gladstone, of course, who had started all of this, was seven years as Chancellor of the Exchequer before be became Prime Minister. He had immense authority. I mean, he had the authority to create as the Chairman of the Public Accounts Committee a Member from the Opposition. I cannot think of any other time when that could have been accepted, but it was, and I think it is valuable, too. There were standards arising from that from which we have benefited. All right, things have changed now—a pity we cannot retain them—but the ones that we saw there were clear defiance of the rules. Whether you need to have fresh rules I think is probably right but they are not going to be enough in themselves—it is the ethos we have got to protect.

1066. LORD NOLAN: I am not, I am afraid, as clear as I should be about the extent of your jurisdiction over non-departmental public bodies. It is not complete, is it?

ROBERT SHELDON: Not at all, and that is one thing I would like to say because one-third of them are not audited by the Comptroller and Auditor General.

LORD NOLAN: One-third?

ROBERT SHELDON: One-third of them are not. We do have oversight of some of them—perhaps the C and A G would like to come in just on that—but I am concerned about both having these accounts audited by the National Audit Office because arising from that—this is where we get the information—the raw information comes from the audit and based upon that audit certain matters come to light which we subsequently examine. But even in those, where they are not subject to the National Audit Office, then I would certainly wish a greater change of auditors in the non-departmental public bodies. I think there is a real danger of auditors and the public bodies getting a little too close together. I would suggest three to five years so that they do not get too closely interwoven. You see, so many auditors now make very much of their income from consultancy aspects of their work and these are much more profitable than the auditing work so there is pressure upon them. And I think that we in the Public Accounts Commission—the Commission oversees the pay requirements of the National Audit Office—we change our auditors. And I think this is a valuable exercise, too.

1067. LORD NOLAN: You have said that your worries have mainly arisen—I think this is right—in the area of the non-departmental public bodies. Sticking strictly to the Civil Service, do you find that standards of behaviour in the Civil Service are unsatisfactory?

ROBERT SHELDON: Well, there is a greater danger because you are dealing with more money. Twenty years ago I was in charge of the Civil Service of this country because there was nobody else that knew anything much about it and the Prime Minister at that time was Minister for the Civil Service—he had other things on his mind between February '74 and October '74, the two elections. So I was in charge of it. I went to his room one evening and we had a drink and he asked me about what problems I saw and I said "Well, there are two problems that I see concerning senior Civil Servants coming up for retirement". Two problems—one that after retirement they might make contact with the people who were under them and, of course, had a rather easy route to make representations. That was one problem. The other one was those who were coming up to retirement, in the last two or three years, facing people who were able to offer them employment. And these were serious problems because the age of sixty nowadays—or then even—did not mark the end of one's earning opportunities. There were plenty of other jobs available and they must, naturally, as they come up to the age of sixty, be thinking about what they are going to do. And when they are in charge of public money there was a danger there. I won't say it was anything more than a danger. To my surprise Harold Wilson sent a note round to all forty-two Permanent Secretaries asking them if they thought this was a problem and he got forty-two answers saying "No"—but things have moved on since then!

1068. LORD NOLAN: They have moved on for Civil Servants—not for Ministers—and, of course, that is part of our area of enquiry. Would you care to express a view on the possibility of a similar regime for Ministers?

ROBERT SHELDON: Ministers are a bit of a problem because they may only be Ministers for a very short time. They may be only Members of Parliament for a

very short time and there have been a number of cases where somebody has been promoted early, lost their seat, left Parliament. You cannot deny them the opportunity of earning a living as perhaps you might operate in a slightly different way somebody reaching retirement age, or what is thought to be retirement age. So there are greater problems there. If you want me to go further I can. I would draw the distinction between three types of people. There are those who had a business before coming into the House and it just carries on and can return to it. There are those who have a business following entry into the House and, of course, that may not have any direct bearing on what they do in the House, and there are those who get some employment as a result of them being in the House. It is the third one that is the more serious one to which I think we should pay particular attention.

1069. LORD NOLAN: Would it be right that it is very hard indeed to deal with the matter in terms simply of time limits or by general rules and that really one might have to look at each particular case to see what the involvement of the Minister or ex-Minister had been with the company, if any, in the course of his Ministerial service, and what bad influence might be suspected, even if the suspicion was totally unfounded, if he went to a particular organisation? In other words, some system of outside scrutiny or some umpire who was acting rather in the role of the Permanent Secretaries with Civil Servants and advising whether a particular appointment would be proper or not.

ROBERT SHELDON: I find it very difficult, this one. There was a time when Attlee just dismissed a Minister—just because he had done something which the Minister would never resign for today, but he had standards and as long as you did not adhere to these very strict standards that was it. Now, who is going to decide these standards? I find this very difficult. Fundamentally, if you are talking about Ministers, it is the Prime Minister really. All right, he can get advice from all sorts of people, but it is the Prime Minister who would have to make the decision, as indeed Attlee did and others did. I don't think you can delegate that kind of responsibility to the Ministers. As far as Members of the House are concerned—just ordinary Members—then I think the Privileges Committee is the right body to deal with it but I would have somebody from outside sitting on that Privileges Committee. It is like a board of directors, it is very helpful to have a non-executive director, as long as he is not appointed by the Chairman, which they usually are, when their ability to apply outside standards is rather more difficult. But I do believe that if you had somebody—and there are plenty of people one can think of—just sitting in with the Privileges Committee, I think it can transform some of the ways in which they operate, could make it more readily accountable. That is what I would like to see. He or she may not speak very much but their very presence there I think would be useful.

1070. LORD NOLAN: Am I right in thinking that the Comptroller and Auditor General does assist the Public Accounts Committee in its work?

ROBERT SHELDON: Enormously! Fundamentally part of it—and the success of the Public Accounts Committee in the eleven years that I have been Chairman has been that we have a superb relationship. I mean, it is very important and we must not take this for granted. I have a number of countries (I won't specify the countries) that come where they are at loggerheads with each other, the Public Accounts Committee and their equivalent of the National Audit Office. We have respect, affection and a close working relationship which is enormously valuable to us and, of course, you can say "Well, he does all the work, what do you need us for?" Well we provide the impetus and we do the questioning and this is what gets things done. But perhaps I should ask the C and A.G—or perhaps you might ask him.

1071. LORD NOLAN: I wanted to go on to this—that in the same way some have suggested that another officer of the status of the Ombudsman might be brought in, rather in the manner you suggest, to provide an independent element—independent, that is, of Members, but under the control of the House ultimately—to assist in matters affecting the conduct of Members of Parliament. Would that be a possible way to proceed?

ROBERT SHELDON: I am not much in favour of that.

1072. LORD NOLAN: You would prefer to have someone on the Committee itself?

ROBERT SHELDON: I think the Privileges Committee is a body consisting of people who know Members very very well—we know each other, we live with each other, so we know each other—but it is useful just to have somebody from outside whose presence there can be quite valuable.

1073. LORD NOLAN: Thank you. I have not so far brought Sir John Bourn into the discussion. I wonder, Sir John, if you would like to add to anything that Mr. Sheldon has already said?

SIR JOHN BOURN: I don't think so, Chairman. I am very happy to endorse what he has said and to underline in particular his final point. I am an Officer of the House of Commons, I have the particular responsibility, as convention has developed, to serve the Committee of Public Accounts but, of course, I have a responsibility and a concern to serve Members generally.

LORD NOLAN: Yes. Well, thank you very much. I think with the remaining time I am sure the others would like to ask questions as well. Bill, would you like to start?

1074. WILLIAM UTTING: Yes, thank you, Chairman. The serious failures that are reported are associated in your report with changes in the way in which Government conducts its business. I just wanted to make clear that these failures in your view arise from the process of change rather than from any serious flaws in the nature of the changes that have been made. Is that so—they are the product of the process of change?

ROBERT SHELDON: They have been both, but the outstanding examples that I could give have been in the non-departmental public bodies where people have been brought in from outside without the culture of the public service, and that really has to be made quite clear, that they have those kinds of responsibilities. In the Civil Service generally there have been failures but failures with a few exceptions, not wholly different from those of the past but they have deteriorated.

1075. WILLIAM UTTING: These people brought in from the outside were, you say, subject to the same rules

that applied before they were brought in. I mean, this was simply a case of people not catching up with what they were supposed to do or disregarding what they were supposed to do. Is that not one of the inevitable penalties of large-scale changes that have been carried through pretty quickly—one has to get up and go with the changes, cannot wait five years to get everything perfect before we set off?

ROBERT SHELDON: Clearly there is a risk but also there was not in my view sufficient attention given to the need to explain the kind of obligations that such people were entering into when they entered the public service. It has to be quite clear that there are certain things you cannot do in the public service, which they might well have done with their own money or with their company's money.

1076. WILLIAM UTTING: Yes, I just wanted to eliminate these as problems that would have corrected themselves over the course of time as people woke up to them and started putting in correcting mechanisms. You are saying there were serious problems from the outset that would probably have continued unchecked without the kind of scrutiny that they received from you and from the Comptroller and Auditor General?

ROBERT SHELDON: There are great risks, of course. I mean, we are talking about the standards in public life and once they start to deteriorate then I am afraid there are very serious failings ahead of us. We have been extraordinarily fortunate and because of that the Public Accounts Committee regards the committee as being in the forefront of trying to retain those standards which are absolutely essential.

1077. WILLIAM UTTING: If I could ask one other quick question; I was surprised that the National Audit Office did not, in fact, audit one-third of non-departmental public bodies. Could you say briefly what they were? C and A.G. perhaps.

JOHN BOURN: Well, an enormous range of them. You can see the ones that have been mentioned where we do have the audit, but if you look across the whole range of public bodies engaged in economic activities for promoting economic development, some we have, some we do not have, you have a range of bodies concerned with environmental matters, you have a range of bodies concerned with aspects of social matters, you have a range of bodies concerned with the Arts and the interesting thing is that these have evolved over time and it is very difficult to see the logic that has led some of them, as it were, to be given to me and some of them not—perhaps one can trace fashions in this over time. But as the Chairman has said and which I do certainly endorse, it would be an extension of the service that I was able to provide for the legislature if I were to have the responsibility of the audit of these bodies, to be able to report to Parliament on them—and to the extent that was decided not to be right by the Government, at least to be able to look at their books, records and papers and pick up some of the cases in the Report on the Proper Conduct of Public Business. From the inspection rights that we have, there have come points of importance. So it is interesting to see in British Government this great range of difference and, as I say and endorse what the Chairman has said, this is a contribution that the office I think could make to accountability to Parliament and to the transparency of public administration in this country.

WILLIAM UTTING: Thank you.

LORD NOLAN: Professor King?

1078. PROF. ANTHONY KING: Could I take you back to the famous PAC Committee report? Part of the report consists of a column of failures and a check-list of things that ought to be done. The report attracted a good deal of attention when it was first published but if people had read it in detail I think they would have found it even more remarkable than the Press reports suggest, because the catalogue of failures is long and pretty devastating, ex gratia payments made without authority on termination of employment, sometimes in circumstances where disciplinary action might have been more appropriate, provision of official cars to see your executives without requiring to pay for private motoring and the list goes on and on and is quite staggering—at least I found it so. Could I ask, really both of you or either of you in very general terms, how widespread do you think this kind of problem is?

ROBERT SHELDON: Well, since that report we could put one or two more in, of course, if we were to produce a revised edition, as it were. But, I mean, we would have had the Pergau one, for example, where we had the note of dissent from the Permanent Secretary there. Very interesting, this one, because there have been one or two achievements arising from the report, that now—only in the last few days—we have the agreement that when a Permanent Secretary writes a note of dissent the Public Accounts Committee is going to be notified. This is saying that he disagreed with the Minister about the expenditure of money but the Minister has the power to order him to make the payment, but then he writes that note of dissent. Now, we have that power where a case of fraud comes before, or where these matters are being examined by, the Comptroller and Auditor General, but now we will have all those notes of dissent. Now, I am not saying there is going to be a large number of notes of dissent—I think the very fact that there is this sanction might have some useful effect—and we have seen another consequence, of course, and that is that the National Health Service has undertaken to ensure that where there is a conflict of interest this is announced and understood by the various management boards, whatever they may be. We would like to see this extended, of course, to all the non-departmental public bodies at the very least. But that is progress—that is considerable progress—and there are other things that have happened as well.

1079. PROF. ANTHONY KING: In general terms—I will not ask you to do this—but were you to go through the check-list of things that you say in the report you think ought to be done, would you say that you were satisfied with the kind of progress that has been made across the board?

ROBERT SHELDON: The progress is going and I think that this committee, Chairman, of course will obviously help it along very much as well.

1080. PROF. ANTHONY KING: Could I ask you just one other question which intrigues me—and, again, in very general terms—that concerns "whistle blowers"? Presumably doing the kind of work that both of you in your different ways do, whistle blowers are actually rather important people. Now, you referred to "silence clauses" and you used that term very precisely to refer to people who promise to shut up after they have left employment, but, of course, we do hear about silence clauses of a more general character, making it clear to people that they will get into trouble if they do blow the whistle. What is your reaction to that kind of development?

ROBERT SHELDON: Well, we have had a number of these and some of them are anonymous, but we do make enquiries and, of course, the Comptroller and Auditor General follows these things up and a number of useful leads have come as a result of that. But perhaps the source of this ought to say something about that.

JOHN BOURN: Yes, that is certainly the case. We do get, either in letters to myself or to the Chairman for us to look at, cases drawn to our attention and some of these, of course, are, when you look into them, the result of envy and jealousy of superiors. Others of them, of course, are very much to the point. An important question is the extent to which a person, having raised the point, he or she is willing to stand up and be counted. If they are you can usually do a great deal more with it. But very often, of course, they are not willing because they feel that their employment and their position in life would be menaced if they were seen as providing information. If somebody wishes to provide it in confidence we respect that but taking the lead that comes from that information we look at it with the department or agency concerned. So it has been, I think, an important development over the last two years when I think perhaps greater public attention has focused on the work of the committee and of the National Audit Office, that we are getting a larger number of people in all walks of life drawing our attention to areas and that has been very useful and very helpful.

If I can just add a point to the earlier question you asked about people coming into a public appointment, one of the things that struck me in a number of cases where we had had to report on the activities of a chairman or a chief executive, who came in, not usually from a large company which has a developed system for managing its financial and other affairs, but very often from smaller scale industry and commerce where the necessity for well-ordered standards perhaps do not immediately arise, and the point was very often that people were recruited and asked to do these jobs but they were not really given any proper briefing or explanation as to this side of what was expected of them. They were brought in, you know, to encourage the Japanese to invest, but it was not really said to them "But as well as encouraging the Japanese to invest you need to remember you are handling public money and there are standards" and I think, as the Chairman has said, the introduction of codes of conduct—but I think more especially important a responsibility, perhaps on the Minister who appoints the man or woman, but certainly on the Permanent Secretary, on the Principal Finance Officer, to take the time out with the person appointed and explain why all this is important. It is not any good sending a memorandum six weeks after they are in office sort of listing all these things—that must, of course, be done—but the personal discussion of what is involved, why it is important, what some of the dangers are. Because I have had people say to me "You are writing this report on me, why are you doing it to me?"—because, in a sense, they had not, I feel, been properly briefed, had it properly explained to them why this was so important in British public life.

LORD NOLAN: Individuals must set an example. Nothing better. Yes. Peter?

1081. PETER SHORE: I could follow really from that. I am sure that discussion with Permanent Secretaries and Permanent Secretaries pointing out what the responsibilities are would be a useful adjunct, as it were, to recruitment procedures, but surely the problem is in the actual recruitment? We had evidence earlier and we know that throughout the Civil Service and, indeed, the Next Steps Agencies, the Civil Service Commission lays down the rules and supervises the rules for recruitment. We also got from them the news that they did not play any part in the recruitment of people to Quangos, including National Health Service Trusts. Does this not point really to the need to change the methods of recruitment rather more radically than frankly asking a newly appointed person to have a chat with the Permanent Secretary?

ROBERT SHELDON: Yes, I am very disturbed about that one. I feel that the Opposition ought to be consulted much more widely on these matters—after all they were more widely consulted in the past than they seem to be now. Now this is not just a question of trading this person against that person but it does provide a different viewpoint. I used to be in charge of the list—in that brief period when I ran the Civil Service effectively—of "The Great and the Good"—and I ran through a few things about them and it was a very poor list in those days. It may be much better now, I don't know, but that is not enough. Nor is it enough to choose by the Minister the actual people as a result of people he knows, because there are so many of these appointments. He cannot even appoint enough people he knows, he has to appoint the people that somebody he knows suggests should be appointed. Now, this is really not the way to go about it and so I would want to see something a little objective—perhaps the relevant Select Committee might have investigations but that could probably take too long except for the very top appointments. But there needs to be some other body, whether it is just discussions with the Leader of the Opposition's office, or whatever it may be, to bring about some different viewpoint as to the way these people are being appointed.

1082. PETER SHORE: Can I press you a bit further on that? I am sure for some particularly prominent appointments there might well be some advantage in discussions with Opposition people before Ministers make their move, but the range of appointments is so large, as you know, and would swamp, of course, even Select Committee examination. So what kind of change can one envisage to supervise the appointment of people, making sure we get the right people, the right standards, in Quangos?

ROBERT SHELDON: Well, there is one obvious way—I am not saying it is necessarily the best—and that would be to appoint a body that had that supervisory right, that would make the recommendations. Like you do for the appointments to the House of Lords, for example. Peers—there is a body that examines those. I will not say that is very effective—there are one or two disagreements that I had with them—but nevertheless something of that kind, suitably adapted, might allay some people's suspicions about the way these things are handled, but it has to be something that is outside the political appointments that we have at the present time. They can make those but somebody must oversee it and say "yes, that meets the kind of requirements that we have".

1083. PETER SHORE: Thank you for that. Could I just ask one further question? There are two ways of approaching this problem, obviously; one is through

better recruitment and different standards of recruitment and the second way is through audit. The National Audit Office, I understood, is excluded from doing an Audit of one-third of Quangos. Does that exclude National Health Service bodies as well—are they brought within your Audit or not?

JOHN BOURN: Yes, I do have access to the National Health Service. I am the Auditor of their Consolidated Accounts, the Audit Commission are the Auditors of the Trusts and the subordinate formations, if you can call them that, but I have the right to look at the books, records and papers, so I do have full access to the work of the National Health Service.

PETER SHORE: Thank you.

1084. CLIFFORD BOULTON: Sir John, could you let us have a list of all the bodies to whom you would like to have access, please?

JOHN BOURN: Yes, I should be glad to do that.[8]

CLIFFORD BOULTON: Thank you. And if you are able to give us an indication of what would be necessary in your view to open them to you that would be very helpful. I mean, in many cases you get it——If a body has an obligation to lay its accounts before the House you are let in by that, as I recall, but if you could let us have some more information about the gaps as you see them and any suggestions you can make about remedying that—the mechanics—I would be very grateful.

JOHN BOURN: I would be pleased to do that and I would also take advantage of your invitation to cover the point that arises through market testing and contracting out where activities previously conducted by directly employed public servants are then conducted on contract to a company. A perfectly reasonable manner to do this, of course, but it can mean that where we had access to the activity in the past we do not have access to the activity in the present and therefore the opportunity to look at it, to draw Parliament's attention to the scope for improvement in it, is denied to us. Arrangements have been made to give us access to the contracts relating to the provision of financial services—questions arise about what that means—but there are a whole range of other activities to which we do not have access and it would be very valuable to be able to look at the books and records of the companies in relation to those matters. Not, of course, the company accounts generally, but in a sense to restore the position to what it was and to give the National Audit Office of the United Kingdom the same powers as the General Accounting Office of the United States has, the same powers as the European Court of Audit has in relation to the United Kingdom and the same powers that the Audit Commission has in relation to local government in this country. So if I may cover that in what I bring to your attention I would be glad to do so.

CLIFFORD BOULTON: Thank you very much.

ROBERT SHELDON: May I just add one thing to it because that is very important? We did meet the Chancellor of the Exchequer who was going to examine these areas where the European Court of Auditors has access but the National Audit Office does not and although the Public Accounts Committee is on record very frequently of wanting to pursue public money, most of the places where it goes to—and there is a large number

---

[8] See Evidence pp. 519–530.

of places it goes to where we do not have access—nevertheless to see some other body having that kind of access which we do not, we feel is particularly unfortunate.

CLIFFORD BOULTON: Thank you.

1085. DIANA WARWICK: In your opening remarks you placed a lot of emphasis on dangers inherent in change and the need for structures and framework in response to those changes. Does the recent Government White Paper on the Civil Service in your view, in looking at it, respond to your concerns adequately?

ROBERT SHELDON: Well, you see, change has to come but, of course, with change there are risks. But, of course, one wants to see the better use of public money and the better administration that we hope will come from that change. What we don't want to lose are the standards that we have had the privilege of enjoying for so long and that is one of the aspects of it. The code that has been suggested—I think that is a very interesting one—and I think we will end up with something of that kind. But I don't think that is going to be enough in itself. It is the background to it and the way people react which is still going to be a very dominant factor here.

1086. DIANA WARWICK: My other question is that in their evidence to us the Civil Service Unions emphasise the difficulty in obtaining information in certain circumstances when authority was devolved and they instance commercial "in confidence" restrictions that were sometimes placed on information. Have you come across that problem—is that something that has been a difficulty?

ROBERT SHELDON: One always has that problem, of course. Before I became Chairman—well, sometime before I became Chairman—all the meetings of the Public Accounts Committee were held in private and now we have practically nothing in private because I am not of the view that the stuff that we have is so confidential. So we have been engaged in a reduction of the classification very considerable and virtually everything that we do now is open to the public and is printed for the public to see.

DIANA WARWICK: Thank you.

1087. ANNE WARBURTON: Mr. Sheldon, could I ask you—the check-list in the Committee of Public Accounts' eighth report seems to me to have the makings of a very good code for all those responsible. Do they already get something like this?

ROBERT SHELDON: Moving some way towards it, as I said earlier. There are a number of areas where we wanted to go further but they have made, as I said—and one or two things that we did not ask for but we have been making private representations since, where we have got some success. I mean, the Pergau one was the origin of the note of dissent being made available to the Public Accounts Committee which we had not asked openly before but we now have. So there is improvement.

1088. ANNE WARBURTON: Is there a way in which you can get that accepted for all departments—how do you do that?

ROBERT SHELDON: Well, we were hoping that all departments would be coming to us. The National Health

Service, for example, did, and they told us exactly how they were meeting our requirements. I think it is now time to have a further bit of pressure—perhaps from your Committees Chairman, of course, but elsewhere as well—to bring about perhaps a move further in that direction.

1089. ANNE WARBURTON: Thank you very much. And could I ask Sir John: who is it who audits the one-third that you do not audit of the NDPBs?

JOHN BOURN: They are private sector firms who have the audit appointment and of course these are professional people who do it well but their duty is to the auditee and does not encompass a duty to Parliament that I have.

1090. ANNE WARBURTON: So this is where what Mr. Sheldon said earlier about changing auditors becomes relevant, yes. Could I ask you another question—we have looked from time to time at arrangements, for example, for Members' Interests, do you at present have any role with regard to Members of the House? Neither of you?

JOHN BOURN: No.

ANNE WARBURTON: No. Good, thank you.

1091. LORD NOLAN: Well, you have given us striking evidence on matters crucial to our enquiry. We are very grateful to you for that and also for your telling us about the steps you are proposing to take to improve matters. Thank you both very much indeed for coming along.

Now we have our last witness for this session—running, I am afraid, a little late, Mr. Bogdanor. It is Mr. Vernon Bogdanor, who is the Reader in Government at Oxford University and a Fellow of Brasenose College. You helpfully supplied us with an opening statement. It is certainly no part of my wishes to constrain your remarks in any way. Would you like to read it as it stands or is there any scope for summary?

VERNON BOGDANOR

VERNON BOGDANOR: Would you wish me to read it, Chairman, or would you like to take it as read?

LORD NOLAN: Well, I think, if I may suggest it, for the benefit of those who are listening but have not read it, it would be very helpful if you could either read it or summarise it.

VERNON BOGDANOR: Since submitting my written evidence to the Committee in November, the Government has produced a White Paper on the Civil Service "Taking Forward Continuity and Change". This proposes two reforms designed to maintain standards in the civil service. The first is a new Civil Service Code. The second is a new independent line of appeal to the Civil Service Commissioners where civil servants believe that this code has been breached.

While these reforms are welcome they do not meet the concerns which were in my mind when I submitted my evidence. This is so for a number of reasons. First, the proposed code is in general terms and insufficiently specific. It concentrates upon the duties of civil servants and has too little to say on the duties of Ministers. Second, the code does not draw a precise line between what is a matter for government and what is party political. Is it appropriate, for example, to ask a civil servant to draft a party conference speech? Is it appropriate to ask him or her to assist with back-bench amendments to bills? The code gives no answer.

Third, the code fails to clarify the convention of Ministerial responsibility which has come under pressure through the devolution of power within the Civil Service to agencies. This has enabled Ministers to pass the buck by publicly blaming known officials for what are called "operational" failures. But what is an "operational" failure? One official has cynically suggested that if a problem is difficult then it is operational! In his recent report on Whitemore Prison Sir John Woodcock has noted a considerable confusion of responsibility and this shows the danger to the public service in lack of clarification. Nothing can be more demoralising for any organisation than to find itself blamed for failures while Ministers continue to take the credit for success.

Fourth, the independent appeal mechanism, while welcome, may lack sufficient leverage to be effective. Admittedly, the Civil Service Commissioners will, under the government's proposals, have the right to report to Parliament, but a more powerful mechanism would be the creation of a Civil Service Ombudsman, with the right to report to the Treasury and Civil Service Select Committee where the government ignores his or her recommendations. The experience of the Parliamentary Commissioner for Administration and the Select Committee on the Parliamentary Commissioner has shown what a powerful mechanism this can be.

I would hope, therefore, that the Nolan Committee can propose a much tighter code than the Government has done, laying particular stress upon the precise duties which Ministers owe to their civil servants. For it is from Ministers that standards in public life must flow.

I hope also that the Nolan Committee will clarify the concept of Ministerial responsibility, the central constitutional convention regulating standards in public life.

LORD NOLAN: Thank you very much, that is very clear. I would ask Dame Anne Warburton to take up the questions, please.

1092. ANNE WARBURTON: Mr. Bogdanor, I know you have been here all morning, I think. I feel really I should begin by saying would you like to continue the discussion from things you have been hearing. Perhaps we don't start quite there but I hope before we finish that it will be interesting to hear comments that you may have on that score. It was very good of you to prepare a second paper and opening statement in the light of the new draft Civil Service Code in particular and I am struck that you find it inadequate—in fact I think you are more forthright about that than the representative of the First Division was. Would you like to say a little more than you just have about the ways in which you find it inadequate?

VERNON BOGDANOR: The Government's central position, I think, is in paragraph 2.8 of the code, where it says that the code should "reflect the existing constitutional position rather than seek to change it" and I think the question is whether the existing remedies for things that go wrong are sufficient. I fear that they are

probably are not for two reasons. I think the new management methods adopted in the Civil Service give rise to two particular dangers; first the danger of civil servants appointed from outside, possibly on short-term contracts, who do not share the traditional public ethos of the Service; and, second—and I regard more important—the danger of buck-passing by Ministers to blame civil servants, named officials, for their failures. And because civil servants are more publicly known, because they are widely known not only through Select Committees but through the media, it is easier for Ministers to shuffle off responsibility to them.

1093. ANNE WARBURTON: Do you take the view that has been mentioned this morning that the current process of decentralisation or devolution is a large part of the problem?

VERNON BOGDANOR: I think the process of delegation has caused problems, not just because it is a change, because they are new methods, but because there are more outsiders being brought into the public service, many on short-term contracts. There is a danger, I think, of the Civil Service seeming to people working in agencies as merely a heterogenous collection of agencies and departments, not one unified Civil Service with a public service ethos. People will see themselves as belonging to this agency or that agency, not to the organisation as a whole, but most fundamentally, I think, because the managerial changes have not, I think, yet fully taken account of the fact that there is no equivalent in the world outside the public service to the particular principles that regulate our own public service—in particular the central principles of Ministerial responsibility and Civil Service impartiality to which there is no parallel in the business world. And I think that is the particular difficulty.

1094. ANNE WARBURTON: We are obviously in a state of transition at present in these matters. How would we achieve the goals that you would have in mind, particularly as concerns standards?

VERNON BOGDANOR: I think first we do have to clarify Ministerial responsibility. Do we wish to say that chief executives should themselves be responsible for what is delegated to them, and that would mean, if we did that, that they would speak to Select Committees in their own names rather than in the name of the Minister concerned and the Minister would then be responsible simply for the terms of the delegation. If we want to take that line that is one direction. If we do not want to take that line then we must accept that Ministers are responsible for anything that happens in their department, whether you call it operational or whether you call it policy—indeed, I think that distinction itself is in some difficulty because I don't think matters come labelled as operational or policy. I think it is a very difficult distinction indeed. I think we have to do that.

Then I think we have to find a way of filling what I think is the gap in the convention of Ministerial responsibility by which Ministers can shuffle off the blame for what goes wrong to civil servants who have no means of redress or answering. And I think that this has been a gap since the Crichel Down case in the 1950s when, I think, in the Maxwell Fyfe guidelines they do not take account of what I think actually happened in that case, where the Ministers concerned were able to blame civil servants for what had gone wrong and what was really, I believe, a matter of policy. But that danger has become much greater now because civil servants are so much more in the public eye, they can easily be blamed by name and therefore the danger is that they are blamed and Ministers take the credit for successes and that is deeply demoralising to the public Service.

1095. ANNE WARBURTON: It is perhaps the obverse rather but this morning we have heard that the complaints from the Civil Service about Ministers seem to come largely to the unions and I think in one of your papers you have foreshadowed that that is how you thought it was happening. Keeping that in mind do you see the proposed new access to the Civil Service Commissioners as meeting the needs?

VERNON BOGDANOR: I think the important thing is there should be a remedy and what I wonder is suppose the Civil Service Commissioners say that a Minister has acted unethically and they report back in that light, what then follows? It seems to me that the machinery of the Parliamentary Commissioner has worked so well because he has leverage through the Select Committee of Parliament and therefore if the Parliamentary Commissioner is not satisfied with what he believes to be a response to maladministration he can report that to the Select Committee which may make the issue public. And I would like to see that well-tried mechanism used in this particular case. After all the use of the first Commissioner—the first Commissioner in particular—is a new status this person will have, it is untried, it is unknown, but the mechanism of the Ombudsman is well-known and well tested and well proved and found to be very effective, and I think that would do more than anything else to ensure that Ministers behaved appropriately towards officials.

1096. ANNE WARBURTON: What sort of matters would he report on "politicisation"?

VERNON BOGDANOR: Suppose a civil servant went to the Commissioner and said "My Minister has asked me to help draft a speech for the Party Conference and frankly I think that goes go beyond my remit, it is political", or suppose a civil servant were to go and say "My Minister has asked me to help draft a back-bench amendment, I am not sure whether that is in within the remit of what I am meant to do, could you advise me?"—those sorts of issues.

1097. ANNE WARBURTON: Yes. Would you want a code of conduct to be statutory?

VERNON BOGDANOR: No, I don't think so. I think passed by resolutions of both Houses would be sufficient, because I think these issues probably are not justiciable and I think to make it statutory would involve time and expense and difficulty in getting legal redress and also perhaps make it more difficult to change when defects in it were discovered. So on the whole I would not make it statutory, no.

1098. ANNE WARBURTON: But you would hope that codes of conduct or similar documents would be fairly much standardised or comparable for all different parts of Government?

VERNON BOGDANOR: Oh, yes, indeed and particularly, of course, it would include those working in agencies as much as those working in Whitehall.

1099. ANNE WARBURTON: Well, I think if I may I would just like really to come back to what I said at the beginning. It would be interesting to have your reaction to some of the witnesses we have heard before, before you took the "black chair".

VERNON BOGDANOR: Yes. I am very sympathetic to the proposal that chief executives of agencies might be examined by the relevant departmental Select Committee before appointment to ensure that they have imbibed the public service ethos that is needed. I think this would be one way of doing it. The Government propose in the White Paper that a handbook be given to agency chief executives—obviously that is helpful—but perhaps more is needed and of course what I am suggesting would be, perhaps, analogous in some way, they are not completely similar to the American advise and consent procedure, but I believe parliamentary involvement in that to satisfy itself would be needed.

I am also very sympathetic to the idea that Robert Sheldon suggested that the Opposition should on occasions be involved in senior appointments at the policy level. If I can take one example which is in question there—we have an advertisement (the first time, I think)—a Permanent Secretary's position has been advertised in the Department of Employment, and obviously the Minister, as is right, should have a certain input in that because the successful candidate will have to work with Mr. Portillo who has his own individual style. Now, the question is whether if we had a Labour Government within the next year or two—it is perfectly possible—whether that same person would be able to work equally well with the Shadow Secretary for Employment. We are not, I think, talking here about a question of political views but the style of the person concerned. And, therefore, I think there is a case for an Opposition input into that procedure when a position of Permanent Secretary is publicly advertised, to ensure that the person who wins the post is acceptable to the Opposition which, after all, could be the Government in the near future.

ANNE WARBURTON: Good, thank you very much.

LORD NOLAN: Diana?

1100. DIANA WARWICK: Could I just ask, you have placed a lot of emphasis on the problems of developing a shared ethos—I think a lot of your criticism stems from that. Were you convinced by the arguments that were put by Michael Bichard—he gave a very robust defence of his ability in his agency to be able to recreate that ethos?

VERNON BOGDANOR: I think this remains an open question and in two particular agencies we have seen evidence that this ethos has not yet been created. I am referring to the prison service and Sir John Woodcock's report on that, and the report last week by the Ombudsman on the Child Support Agency and the methods used there which were not wholly in accordance with what we think of as the public service ethos. So I am not wholly convinced and, of course, it is very difficult to manage that cultural change successfully.

1101. DIANA WARWICK: And could I ask one more question? When you were talking about the responsibility of Ministers to civil servants and placing the emphasis squarely on Ministers, Elizabeth Symons earlier—and I think you also—listed one or two area where civil servants should be given advice. Do you think Ministers would share that list, the general list that was produced both by you and by Elizabeth Symons?

VERNON BOGDANOR: Well, I hope they would. I believe it would have been quite acceptable without question during the 1950s and 1960s—I hope it would be acceptable. If I can just return for a brief moment to the question of the public service ethos, there is further evidence about it from the Government's Committee on Career Management and Succession Planning which carried out a survey. There was a very strong feeling in the Civil Service that its ethos was being eroded and that Committee said it was significantly stronger than any other of their findings and something that should be of concern to those responsible for the management of the Service. So I think there is a great deal of evidence of worry about that ethos.

1102. CLIFFORD BOULTON: I am a little bit concerned about inviting a departmental Select Committee to share responsibility in some way for the appointment of a Chief Executive. I think that there is some anxiety already about whether Ministers are feeling less personally responsible for what these Chief Executives do than they should. If the candidates at the stage when they were only candidates were shown to a select committee and they approved somebody, doesn't the Minister get away there—if the chief executive turns out to be a dud is he not able to say "Well, this was a decision shared with the committee"?

VERNON BOGDANOR: The establishment of the agencies is, I believe, altering the constitutional relationship of civil servants to Parliament and partly that is shown by the fact that the written answers of the chief executives are now published in Hansard which seems to be a very striking constitutional innovation and Parliament is very deeply involved in the management of the agencies. The select committee cannot, as you put it, share responsibility with the Minister. All the select committee could do would be to investigate whether the candidate proposed is sufficiently aware of the public service ethos and if it thought not it could issue a negative report and then it would be up to the Minister to take what action he or she chose.

CLIFFORD BOULTON: Thank you.

1103. LORD THOMSON: I wonder if I could ask about a different aspect of responsibilities—you have been producing some very interesting views to do with the rights of civil servants in relation to Ministers. What about the situation in which Ministers are accused in the Press, for example, as has happened recently, of improper behaviour and at present the Secretary of the Cabinet has been involved to make some enquiries and then give advice to the Prime Minister. Have you any ideas as to how there might be a better system than that?

VERNON BOGDANOR: I think this does put the Secretary of the Cabinet in an embarrassing position and partly because there is no code, so it seems, or precise public code, to which he can refer. But further, you may argue, he is not the sort of person who ought to be dealing with this because he is at the same time, as it were, an adviser to Government, the nearest perhaps we have to being Permanent Secretary to the Prime Minister, so it puts him in a very difficult and embarrassing position.

And, again, perhaps that might be something that could be referred to an Ombudsman, to an independent figure.

1104. PROF. ANTHONY KING: Could I just ask you to say a little bit more about your conception of the Civil Service Ombudsman because, as I understand it, one of the features of the Ombudsman, the Parliamentary Commissioner at the moment, is that he is very much a long-stop, you have to have gone through a lot of hoops before you get to him, whereas you were actually, as I heard you, suggesting that civil servants who had problems, perhaps even before they arose, should be approaching this person for advice and guidance. Could you just say a little bit more than you have about——

VERNON BOGDANOR: Yes, I did intend the Civil Service Ombudsman to be a long-stop and I apologise if I gave the impression that a civil servant should immediately go to the Ombudsman. The first step would be, as today, within the department and then to the Permanent Secretary, and the Ombudsman would be a long-stop. I think he or she should remain that and one should not perhaps exaggerate the number of complaints that this person would receive. I don't suspect that it would be a full-time job. Indeed, I believe the very existence of such an official would have an inhibiting effect on Ministers who thought to persuade civil servants to do things they ought not to do, but it would be a long-stop and I hope I didn't give the other impression. I did not mean to.

1105. PROF. ANTHONY KING: But this person would issue, on the model of the Parliamentary Commissioner, even though we are talking about (to use American language) the executive branch, would actually produce an annual report for the Treasury and——

VERNON BOGDANOR: There would be an annual report and where he or she was not satisfied with the response of a Minister he or she would take that to the select committee which could make its own recommendations.

1106. WILLIAM UTTING: You have commented on certain things amounting to constitutional changes—you are not, perhaps, objecting to any necessary constitutional changes but to their, so to speak, occurring by stealth. Is that your position?

VERNON BOGDANOR: Yes, I think the "Next Steps" proposals, the setting up of the agencies and so on, and the other reforms, are very radical, managerial changes and whether they are right or wrong is a political question. But it seems to me you cannot make radical managerial changes of that kind without the constitution being affected and the Government's view was that no change in the constitutional relationship was necessary with the agencies and we are now seeing the consequences of that in the confusion of responsibilities, in particular in the Prison Service, and also I believe in the Child Support Agency. And these problems, I believe, will get worse in the politically sensitive agencies unless some clarification occurs.

1107. WILLIAM UTTING: Yes. I can see that this is in part an administrative reaction to, so to speak, excessive burdens of work. I mean the amount of correspondence that departments and agencies have to deal with has increased enormously in recent years and it seems to get to a point at which it is unreasonable for every reply to a letter to a Minister to be signed by the Minister and there seems to be some sort of case for some of this being delegated, say, to chief executives of agencies. That is okay if it is explicit, is it, so far as you are concerned?

VERNON BOGDANOR: Yes. Well, how the Minister chooses to run his or her department is a matter for the Minister but in the last resort under our arrangements, as I understand it, the Minister takes responsibility and takes responsibility even for what we may choose to call an operational failure. That does not mean the Minister is necessarily personally at fault, responsibility does not mean that, and it does not mean that he or she necessarily has to resign and perhaps we have been over-playing the coinage, as it were, of calling for Ministerial resignations. What it does mean is the Minister is responsible for putting things right, the Minister who has to account to Parliament for what has happened and the Minister cannot shuffle the blame onto anyone else by saying it was an operational matter or a matter of detail, or something else, for which he or she is not to blame. That is the issue, as I understand it, and how the Minister organises his department and how the Minister obtains information from the agency and how letters are dealt with is a matter for that Minister it seems to me.

1108. WILLIAM UTTING: Fine. We have got this interesting booklet *Questions of Procedure for Ministers* which does refer in one paragraph to Ministerial accountability and it has got a few odd paragraphs later on about the kinds of things that Ministers should not ask civil servants to do. Do you think that this is the place actually to develop and state more explicitly ideas about Ministerial accountability and about the kind of duties that Ministers have got to civil servants?

VERNON BOGDANOR: Yes, it might be developed there. At present it is inadequate in regard to the duties of Ministers, it simply says, if I remember rightly, that Ministers should not ask civil servants to do what they ought not to do, but that is not perhaps terribly helpful. But it does, as you say, re-state the convention of Ministerial responsibility, but in recent weeks we have been seen to depart from that on the part of Ministers who have said that they are not in fact responsible for operational matters and other Ministers have said that the convention is a fiction—the convention of Ministerial responsibility is a fiction. Now, Ministerial responsibility seems an arcane matter but it is one of the defences we have, in my judgment, for standards in public life and when Ministers start disclaiming that we wonder who is accountable for the redress of the citizens' grievances, and this does seem to me a very central question.

WILLIAM UTTING: Well, the statement about accountability in Questions of Procedure for Ministers seems fairly clear to me at any rate. It may be that it does not go quite as far as some other people's expectations of accountability.

VERNON BOGDANOR: I think people have departed from it because we have had a distinction, drawn between accountability and responsibility which I think is a bogus distinction I must confess and as I have said in my previous answer Ministers have sought to disclaim responsibility for operational matters within the working of the agencies. If they are to do that then the corollary would be that the chief executives were themselves directly responsible to Parliament for matters that were delegated to them and then, of course, the corollary would be that while they can be blamed for failures they also get the public credit for successes, but Ministers are less keen on the second part of that proposition, I think.

1109. WILLIAM UTTING: The QPM says "that each Minister is responsible to Parliament for the conduct of his or her department and for the actions carried out by the department in pursuit of Government policies or in the discharge of responsibilities laid upon him or her as a Minister." I mean, is that a satisfactory formulation as far as you are concerned?

VERNON BOGDANOR: Yes, it is, if one sticks to that and ensures that Ministers do not disclaim responsibility. But it seems to me the committee will have to make a judgment on recent comments, that there is a distinction between responsibility and accountability and statements by Ministers in Parliament that they are not in fact responsible for operational matters. Is that a corollary of the agency concept?

WILLIAM UTTING: Thank you very much.

1110. LORD NOLAN: I wonder if I could take you back to the last passage in your opening statement, which reads as follows:

"I argued in my written evidence that 'there is a need within the British system of government for some moral reference point that can help determine when the conventions have been broken'. I hope that the Nolan Committee can propose a set of precise rules which bind Ministers as well as officials, and which can provide that 'moral reference point', a constitutional framework for the preservation of standards in public life."

As you know the area of public life which we have been asked to deal with is simply enormous. Is this in your mind—that one has to start somewhere and one had better start at the top?

VERNON BOGDANOR: Yes, I do believe that standards flow essentially from Ministers.

1111. LORD NOLAN: Get that right and with any luck the rest will follow?

VERNON BOGDANOR: I believe so.

LORD NOLAN: Thank you very much indeed for coming. You have been very helpful and very interesting.

THURSDAY 2 FEBRUARY 1995

Members Present:

The Rt. Hon. The Lord Nolan (Chairman)

Sir Martin Jacomb
Professor Anthony King
The Rt. Hon. Tom King CH MP
The Rt. Hon. Peter Shore MP

The Rt. Hon. The Lord Thomson of Monifieth KT DL
Sir William Utting CB
Dame Anne Warburton DCVO CMG
Diana Warwick

Witnesses:

Lord Younger of Prestwick
Rt. Hon. Norman Fowler MP, former Chairman of the Conservative Party
Sir Michael Quinlan, former Permanent Secretary at the Ministry of Defence
Lord Armstrong of Ilminster, former Cabinet Secretary and Head of the Home Civil Service

1112. LORD NOLAN: Today we have four witnesses who have all held very high public office in recent years. All are now free from the constraints of office and will, I have no doubt, express clear, personal views.

During the morning we shall be talking to Sir Norman Fowler, who has already spoken publicly about former Ministers taking up employment, to Sir Michael Quinlan, former Permanent Secretary, first at the Department of Employment and then at the Ministry of Defence, and to Lord Armstrong, the former Cabinet Secretary.

First, however, we welcome Lord Younger of Prestwick, Chairman of the Royal Bank of Scotland, and former Secretary of State for Scotland and then for Defence. Lord Younger first came to public notice when, in an act of true self-sacrifice, he stood down as candidate for the Kinross and West Perthshire by-election to allow Sir Alec Douglas Home to stand for election after disclaiming his peerage on becoming Prime Minister. Lord Callaghan said, and I am sure Lord Younger would agree, that the traditional priorities in politics were country first then party then self. No doubt Lord Younger will tell us whether he thinks those principles are still being satisfactorily observed today.

Lord Younger, the way we have been proceeding is for Members of the Committee to take it in turn to go first in asking questions and I have asked Professor King, on our right here, to begin in your case. I gather that you are happy to go straight into questions and that you do not wish to make any particular opening statement.

LORD YOUNGER OF PRESTWICK

LORD YOUNGER OF PRESTWICK: Yes. Thank you very much, Lord Nolan.

1113. PROF. ANTHONY KING: Could we start by talking for a few minutes about Ministers and their business interests rather than Members of Parliament in general, focusing on Ministers. You had very extensive business interests before becoming a Minister, how did you set about disengaging from those?

LORD YOUNGER: Yes, that is right. It was 1970 when I first became a Minister and it was quite simple because I held, I think, two directorships at that time and I just resigned those directorships. There were no other commitments that I had in business. The only other slight side effect of it was that at the time, I remember, I held quite a number of brewery shares and I was requested by No. 10 to get rid of them when the then government was denationalizing the brewery at Carlisle. I did that at a slightly, for me, unfortunate moment but that was the only other effect.

1114. PROF. ANTHONY KING: And you ceased to be a Minister on two separate occasions in the mid-70s and in the 80s. How did you set about recreating your business career after you ceased to be a Minister?

LORD YOUNGER: It was entirely related, in my case, to the firm that I had previously worked for which, by that time, was called Bass—it had been called various other things en route. I had a small and modest directorship in a subsidiary until 1970 which I then gave up. After 1974, when I went into opposition again here, they gave me actually a slightly different subsidiary directorship which kept me going until 1979. These were pretty modest but extremely useful—indeed essential—for me personally at the time and the objective of the firm in doing so was to try to bridge the gap between the pay one received as a back bench Member of Parliament and what roughly I had been earning before 1964.

1115. PROF. ANTHONY KING: And what happened when you left the Government the second time around?

LORD YOUNGER: 1989 that was, and I had already been asked to join the Royal Bank of Scotland and so I then did that.

1116. PROF. ANTHONY KING: Could I ask you—this is not ad hominem but it does raise a general question—could I ask you about the kinds of questions that arise in people's minds as they look at Ministers going directly into business. Two questions arise particularly. One is, is it possible that the Minister, while still a Minister, has in some way favoured a company in the private sector in the belief or hope that he may go and work for that company when he ceases to be a Minister or that, in moving into the private sector after being a Minister the Minister may take with him inside knowledge and contacts that are going to be of enormous and unfair use to the company that he goes to work for. Do you think those worries are at all well founded?

LORD YOUNGER: I think it is very important to have those very much in mind, to address those points.

There are two angles to it. The first is the question of whether Ministers can really favour particular companies and while, in general, I think that is pretty unusual and pretty difficult to do, in some particular specific cases it could be and in that case, therefore, I would think that if I was leaving government I would expect to be very much questioned if I was going into some commercial post which had some very close linkage to my ministerial concern. For instance, I think I would have been reluctant to go from the Ministry of Defence as Secretary of State straight into a major defence contractor, had one asked me to do so. That is very important.

The second thing is, of course, that if there is such a conflict, or a potential conflict, it must be seen to be right, as well as being right and, in that context, I think that the rule which normally is carried out at the moment of a two-year fallow period during which time permission can be refused to a senior civil servant, or indeed a Minister, to do this—or should be—I think that is about right actually. I think beyond two years you are getting a bit old hat anyway, as far as any knowledge you have as a Minister. Provided that is implemented I think it is probably quite good.

1117. PROF. ANTHONY KING: A number of follow up questions. You said that there could be particular cases in which Ministers might be in a position to favour firms. Could you give some examples of such cases?

LORD YOUNGER: I think the best one I can give from my experience would be that I suppose it would have been possible for me, as Secretary of State for Defence, to have had before me some big contract from a big company and I suppose it would have been possible for me to favour that company in some way or another—it is not just as easy as it seems but supposing one could—and it would then be most unfortunate,I would have thought, to leave the Ministry and then go into a paid position in that company. I would expect that to be criticised and I would avoid it.

1118. PROF. ANTHONY KING: You said a moment ago that you would expect to be questioned about that kind of move. Who would you expect to question you?

LORD YOUNGER: I suppose it would first emerge in the public domain in the Press probably. One never quite knows who starts these particular hares going but I think the case I have outlined would be pretty obvious and it would be pretty foolish to do it and I think if one was questioned one would expect to be criticised.

1119. PROF. ANTHONY KING: You gave the impression a moment ago that you thought there was a two year rule which applied to Ministers and civil servants equally. Is that right?

LORD YOUNGER: I think I was wrong in that. I thought, as I was saying it, that it certainly applies to civil servants, because I had to help to implement it myself, together with No. 10 Downing Street, as far as civil servants were concerned in my ministries, but as far as Ministers are concerned there is no such formality. I think what I have said indicates that there is a necessity for Ministers to be conscious of that.

1120. PROF. ANTHONY KING: Should there be such a formality, because the view is certainly held that the kinds

of rules that apply to civil servants ought also to apply to Ministers on much the same grounds?

LORD YOUNGER: I see no reason why it should not.

1121. PROF. ANTHONY KING: How would you respond to the argument that, after all, civil servants have their pensions and, possibly, their redundancy pay, if that is what has happened to them; they can, therefore, afford to wait. Whereas Ministers, by and large, simply find themselves tipped out on to the job market—they may lose their job overnight—and ought not to be as constrained as civil servants are?

LORD YOUNGER: I think there are different considerations. Ministers are in an even more prominent position than civil servants and that makes it a bit more difficult. I believe that since my time Ministers do get some terminal pay of some kind when they lose office. I do not think it covers two years but it certainly is notable. I am afraid that I think Ministers have to take the rough with the smooth in this. The prominence of Ministers means that they simply cannot afford to have any public suspicion that something untoward has happened and, therefore, I think that discipline and the disadvantages thereafter have to be accepted.

1122. PROF. ANTHONY KING: So, without necessarily having thought about it in detail, your inclination would be to take the Civil Service rule and simply apply it to Ministers?

LORD YOUNGER: Yes, I would.

1123. PROF. ANTHONY KING: Would you want to have any special kind of consideration applied to Ministers who might go and work in privatised industries, either the ones they privatised themselves or ones they were involved in privatising as a member of the Cabinet, or whatever? Should there be, perhaps, a more than two year rule under such circumstances?

LORD YOUNGER: As I say, I think that two years is quite a long time in this context. It may not sound it but two years after you have left office you are quite extraordinarily "ex" or out of date, if you like to put it that way, and one should recognise that. I think that there is discretion and the two year rule, as operated at present for civil servants, allows for discretion in the committee which considers these matters and I think it is perfectly right that an ex-Minister should be perfectly free to get employment outside but it should be in something that is not overtly and directly connected immediately to what he has been doing and there is, of course, a huge field for that.

1124. PROF. ANTHONY KING: What about civil servants in fact because an argument could be made that civil servants should indeed wait quite a long time before going to work in the private sector, especially in companies that they may have done business with. On the other hand, you can argue that it is highly desirable that they should do precisely that, that the more civil servants with their experience who can take something out and offer it to the private sector, and do so, the better. How would you personally want to reconcile those two?

LORD YOUNGER: That is where I would say that the two years is probably about right. I would not die in a ditch for it but I think two years is about right. Beyond two years the civil servant in question still has a great deal of background information. What he lacks by then is intimate, immediate information which could be directly converted into gain, if you like. I think it is probably about right.

1125. PROF. ANTHONY KING: You said when you were Defence Secretary that you had to monitor these procedures as regards civil servants. What was your experience?

LORD YOUNGER: My experience was not a great number of cases but a certain number of cases where a retired civil servant or senior Civil Service person would be hoping to get employment with a certain firm and they go to the Appointments Committee people who monitor this in No. 10 and say, "Look, can't I take this now?", and they say, "No, not yet" and sometimes it comes back two or three times when they are requesting and it comes eventually to a Minister. In my case, I remember one or two occasions—only one or two—where this happened and, in most cases, we had to say, "I'm very sorry but you will have to wait the two years".

1126. PROF. ANTHONY KING: You imply that the rules as regards civil servants are working reasonably satisfactory?

LORD YOUNGER: I found it reasonably satisfactory, I must say, in my experience at the Ministry of Defence, yes.

1127. PROF. ANTHONY KING: Could we talk about appointments to quangos for a few minutes. Ever since the middle of the 19th century one of the great principles of public service in Britain was that people should be appointed to the public service solely on the basis of merit and, by and large, by people who were independent of the government of the day. Clearly, that principle was being breached in a very large way as regards quangos. Do you think, in fact, it is justifiable that such a large number of public appointments are in the gift of Ministers?

LORD YOUNGER: I, of course, had a very large number of such appointments in the Scottish Office which, because of its nature, had a tremendous number of such appointments to make. My overwhelming memory of making those, over the very long period of six and a half years which I had there, is of enormous difficulty in finding the best and right sort of people to do these jobs. Any idea that it is an easy question of just putting a lot of people you want in is very wrong. It is quite difficult to find people. I found that it was not a problem as far as political agencies were concerned because people rapidly take on the interest of the job they are doing and some of the best chairmen or senior members of quangos who served me were definitely not of my political persuasion. I found that not a problem.

To answer the other part of your question, I do think, however, that the government of the day has the right to ensure that the people in prominent positions in these quangos are prepared to support its general policy. It is absurd to think that a government could have somebody deeply hostile to its political philosophy leading an important quango; that is not realistic.

1128. PROF. ANTHONY KING: But suppose appointments to senior quango positions were put in the hands of some kind of independent commission on the general model of the Civil Service Commission, would not that commission be very unlikely to put in a senior position somebody it knew was about to set about sabotaging the policy? It seems improbable.

LORD YOUNGER: Yes. I, personally, would have found such a commission extraordinarily helpful because it would have helped my main problem which was how do I find good people to fill these positions but I would expect, as a Minister, to have a right of veto if the commission produced somebody that I thought was totally unsuitable because one must have confidence in the people who are serving one.

1129. PROF. ANTHONY KING: To repeat the point: you yourself would not mind if some kind of independent element were introduced into the making of these appointments?

LORD YOUNGER: I would have found it extremely helpful, provided I could veto in particular cases if I thought they were unsuitable.

1130. PROF. ANTHONY KING: You have heard this said frequently, but what do you say to people who report that at the moment, as regards senior quango appointments, the distribution as between Conservative and Labour or Liberal Democrat, or whatever political allegiance, is pretty skewed towards the party that happens to be in government. How would you defend that or would you try?

LORD YOUNGER: I do not know if that is the case or not but I certainly accept it if you say that it is the case. I can only say that it certainly was the case, when I inherited in 1979 a whole pile of quangos, the skew was very much the other way and I think that is perfectly proper. Mr. Callaghan's government had every right to have people in there in whom it had confidence.

1131. PROF. ANTHONY KING: That seems slightly to contradict what you were saying a moment ago about having an independent body largely involved in making quango appointments. There seems to be a tension here between the Minister having the right to decide and somebody else having a large say.

LORD YOUNGER: I do not think, with respect, it is a conflict at all really because I am saying that I think this body would actually be very helpful because the biggest problem I faced was finding enough of the right good people and this commission would undoubtedly suggest a lot of good people. The only qualification I have to make is that I really would not be happy to have somebody, shall we say, appointed to head a major health board who was deeply hostile to everything that my government was trying to do. I think that is understandable.

1132. PROF. ANTHONY KING: We may flatter ourselves but I imagine you have been following, at least in a casual kind of way, what this committee has been up to so far. As you have been reading about it in the newspapers or watching it on television, or whatever, have you had the sense that we might be leaving out a peculiarly Scottish dimension that if, for example, we were to have a hearing in Edinburgh or Glasgow things would be said that would be different from what is being said south of the border?

LORD YOUNGER: I do not really think so, no. My experience of hearings of such semi-parliamentary things in Scotland is not very encouraging in that I find that people do not actually turn up very much. In theory they do, in practice they do not. There is a Scottish aspect to all these matters which is that the combining of political life mainly at Westminster with some commercial activity, which is part of what you have been considering, is quite possible to do if you are London-based and with an English, or London, constituency. It is enormously difficult to do if you have a Scottish constituency because you are simply never there on the ground in Scotland during business times because you are either in Westminster or in your constituency. There is a Scottish dimension to the point of the pressures on the personal lives of Members of Parliament that I am sure you will have been aware of.

PROF. ANTHONY KING: Thank you.

LORD NOLAN: Now, if I may go round the table. Sir William, do you have questions that you would like to put?

1133. WILLIAM UTTING: I would like to pursue the quango point a little further, if I could, with Lord Younger. When you were Secretary of State for Scotland the quangos that we are talking about were actually undertaking government business and the appointments for most of them must, by statute, have been your responsibility but any intermediate body that is created to assist in the appointment of members of quangos must surely be only in an advisory capacity to the Secretary of State and the responsibility ultimately rests quite properly with the Secretary of State?

LORD YOUNGER: Yes, I tried to cover that in my remark about the Minister having a veto on people.

1134. WILLIAM UTTING: Yes. You would not, as Secretary of State, though have been involved personally in very many of these appointments. That would have been, I would have thought, humanly impossible given the number that have to be made. You would have been concerned with chairs of quangos and probably not below that level and not every quango in that case.

LORD YOUNGER: Yes, that is nearly right, but I had a team of Ministers and any important quango would be dealt with by the junior Minister. He would recommend to me what was done and normally I would leave it to him. In the case of certain, very prominent quangos—shall we say, like membership of the Scottish Development Agency, for instance, which was a very major one—that would always come to me but with a recommendation from the junior Minister. It is a team effort and the civil service, of course, also make their recommendations.

1135. WILLIAM UTTING: Good. Thank you very much. If I could just switch to "Questions of Procedure for Ministers". I wanted to ask you how this was drawn to your attention when you became a Minister and whether you were reminded of its contents periodically during your period of service as a Minister?

LORD YOUNGER: It was certainly very formally and definitely drawn to my attention when I was appointed as a Minister—first of all, a junior Minister in 1970 and, secondly, as Secretary of State in 1979. I do not recall it being re-drawn to my attention in the various re-appointments that I had.

1136. WILLIAM UTTING: Yes. You obviously followed, in the answer you gave Professor King, the process for dealing with your private interests when you were appointed as a Minister. It sounded to me, from the conversation you were having with Professor King, as though it would be quite appropriate, as far as you were concerned, for that section to be extended to cover the question of the appointments of Ministers to private businesses after they have stopped being Ministers?

LORD YOUNGER: I think it is perfectly appropriate, yes.

WILLIAM UTTING: Thank you. Thank you, Chairman.

1137. LORD NOLAN: I wonder, if I am in order, if I could exercise the Chairman's privilege and go next because there is one matter on which I believe you may particularly be able to help us. You have spoken about Ministers and their involvement before or after their period in office with business. You yourself, in this as in every respect if I may say so, have an exemplary record of probity. I wanted to ask you if, as a Member of Parliament, you have anything to say to us about the position of Members of Parliament and outside financial interests. Do you have any views on that, whether there should be limits on what a Member of Parliament should do in the way of outside, financial activity?

LORD YOUNGER: Thank you, Lord Nolan. I am quite sure that the pressures on ordinary Members of Parliament dictate that they should be free to take some forms of outside remuneration and unless and until we come to the stage, which I personally hope we never will, that Members of Parliament are paid a full salary for 100 per cent time then that is inevitable.

If you ask about the degree of such outside activity and remuneration, it is extremely difficult to draw lines because people's lives and practices and skills and professional backgrounds are so completely different. I know that in my case, which may or may not be a good one, I was twenty-eight and a half years in Parliament during that period. It was a marvellous period. I enjoyed every second of it and I am very glad I did it but it would not be an exaggeration to say that it was not financially a very successful period for my personal finances. I was fortunate in having some modest private income to help me through that time and also, as I indicated, some also pretty modest outside employment whilst I was in opposition. That is essential.

The other reason why I am in favour of outside interests is that I would consider Parliament to be enormously poorer if it did not have people with some outside interests in it. Their contributions are different and valuable to debate and it is the case that when one disappears into Westminster on Monday morning and emerges, in my case on Friday morning off the sleeper in Scotland, you have lost quite a lot of touch with real life which it is very refreshing to have replaced Friday, Saturday and Sunday.

LORD NOLAN: Thank you very much. Dame Anne?

1138. ANNE WARBURTON: Could I follow on that theme, Lord Younger. I think you may know that we have been somewhat concerned at the possibility of drawing a distinction between advice and advocacy by a Member who has outside interests. I wonder if you could help us to find the right line, in particular between those who are either advising or advocating as representatives of a lobbying firm with many interests and those who simply have a single interest, perhaps with a company or even a trade association?

LORD YOUNGER: I hope this answers your question, Dame Anne, and if it does not you will tell me. Firstly, the simple rules I would put as follows. There are no circumstances in which any Member of Parliament should accept any payment for anything from his constituency, whether from a firm or an individual or anything. A Member of Parliament is paid to serve his constituency and that should be done.

Secondly, I do not think there are any circumstances in which a Member of Parliament should accept payment or be offered payment for taking any Parliamentary action directly, like putting down Questions, like making a speech, like putting down an Early Day Motion. Those are things that a Member of Parliament is expected to do and should receive no remuneration for.

Thirdly, if a Member of Parliament is a consultant or in some other form of employment with an outside concern, a firm or whatever it is, I think it is perfectly proper for general advice to be given by that Member of Parliament to the firm, or whatever, in any normal question about public affairs, parliamentary affairs, the progress of Parliamentary Bills and that sort of thing. Finally, all this should be superseded by the fact that any such interest must be declared in the Register of Members' Interests—you know all about that—and should pretty well always be verbally covered if the Member in question is making a speech or taking part in a debate on the precise subject which is in question here. It should be stated in a speech so that the people listening will know that what the Member says may be coloured by a personal interest.

1139. ANNE WARBURTON: Thank you. So, you would draw no distinction between what I think we have been calling a secondary and principle representation of interests?

LORD YOUNGER: No. I think once you have an interest it is an interest or a potential interest and the House is entitled to know about it in writing in the Register of Members' Interests and verbally in speeches and once the House knows about it there is no further problem. It is perfectly in order for a Member, shall we say, who is paid by a trade union to make a speech strongly advocating whatever the policies of that union are provided the House knows.

ANNE WARBURTON: Thank you very much.

1140. PETER SHORE: Could I just follow that same line of thought. You are very clear, Lord Younger, about not accepting payments for taking actions in Parliament. Equally, you are clear that it is useful for Members of Parliament to have outside employment and you yourself described your period when you were a director of a subsidiary of a brewing company in 1970–74. Do you think one can in practice draw a sharp line between people in the latter category as to the actions they may be not able to take in Parliament, the same sort of actions which presumably would be prohibited by people who were employed by a PR company or a lobbying firm?

LORD YOUNGER: Just one point for the record, if I may, a slip of the tongue. It was not 1970–74 because that was when I was in Government.

PETER SHORE: I am sorry, 1974–79.

LORD YOUNGER: I think this is quite an interesting case. If I had been asked by those for whom I worked in those opposition periods—the brewery company—to put down a Question or to make a speech about beer duty, or something like that, I would certainly have refused point blank to be paid for doing any such thing and if I had made such a speech—which, incidentally, I would have thought it most unwise to do—I would have made it clear at the beginning of the speech that I held a directorship with this company. If that was so the House would know what weight to put on my remarks. I have to add in parenthesis that if I did that and if I did it properly I think it might be quite valuable to the House and the debate to have somebody with some knowledge of that subject actually contributing, but only if they knew from whence I came.

1141. PETER SHORE: Would you accept a similar constraint on, say, making private approaches to a Minister in favour of the firm in whose employment you were?

LORD YOUNGER: I think there is no objection to that, provided the Minister and his department know what your private interest is.

1142. PETER SHORE: Can I switch you to the question of quangos. I thought there was some contradiction between what you said when you said that political allegiance was not a problem because people naturally got involved in the interests of the job itself and your second statement that a government was right to expect people to share their own philosophy. Are those not contradictory statements?

LORD YOUNGER: They are indeed and, if I may suggest it, they are rather encouraging contradictions because I can think of quite a number of distinguished people whose political views are very different from mine who served me extremely well and most loyally during my time as Secretary of State for Scotland and I value those relationships very much and it is a tribute to the system that it can happen. Perhaps it does not happen often enough.

1143. PETER SHORE: I think that may well be the case and, of course, a lot of the evidence, such as there is, about appointments point to a very clear bias in favour of people whose philosophies are thought to be the same as those of Conservative Ministers. Your acceptance of the idea that the Minister in making appointments should have the right of veto but that an outside body should actually produce the shortlist and the nominations would go some way to correcting that, would it not?

LORD YOUNGER: I think it would.

1144. PETER SHORE: Yes, thank you. One last question. We talked about the rules about senior civil servants retiring and Ministers retiring. Do you think there is a special problem with officers in the armed services who tend to retire considerably earlier—at least I think they do, about the age of 55—and who really are full of vigour and looking for outside employment?

LORD YOUNGER: I think there is a special problem there and it is certainly partly that they are perhaps younger in age but also that the nature of armed services officers' involvement in the Ministry of Defence involves quite direct and particular knowledge of companies and negotiations with companies. They are in a very delicate position. It also happens that they are a pretty high minded lot who are strong on principle in these matters and while some of them do chafe a bit at having this up to two years blank period after they retire I think they accept the principle and I have not found anyone who has argued strongly against the principle.

PETER SHORE: Thank you.

LORD NOLAN: I have to say, I am afraid, the usual thing, that we are tending to over-run. Please, Lord Thomson, carry on with any questions you have.

1145. LORD THOMSON: Could I just put one point to Lord Younger. By coincidence at a Scottish occasion yesterday evening I heard that in terms of quango appointments in Scotland the current Secretary of State has, in fact, appointed a body under the chairmanship of the Lord Provost of Edinburgh, who is of a different political persuasion from the present Government, which does put forward nominations in the Health Service field but with the Secretary of State appointing the chairman of these Health Service bodies. I just wondered what you thought about that as a formula and whether this might not be the first time in which the way they do it in Scotland might, with advantage, be looked at south of the border?

LORD YOUNGER: Yes, indeed. It seems to me that my successor, the present Secretary of State, is finding the same problem as me, that he could do with some help in getting advice for such appointments. Having said that, I would just like to reiterate that I think it is perfectly proper for a government to have people that will speak and conduct themselves in these quangos in a way which is consistent with government policy. I think it would be quite intolerable for any government to have to put up, as sometimes they do by accident, with a chairman of a leading quango campaigning against the government which appointed him. That would be quite unacceptable and we should be quite grown up and adult and face that.

1146. DIANA WARWICK: You have agreed that Civil Service rules should apply on outside appointments and this is all part of the general public perception that we have certainly received in our evidence and opinion polls that Members of Parliament are feathering their nests. The Rules for Ministers also deal with another area on which public concern has been expressed and that is in relation to gifts and hospitality. The Rules for Ministers place enormous emphasis on the discretion of Ministers. Given public concern, do you think in this area as well the Rules for Ministers should be tightened up and do you think there are any areas which ought to be excluded entirely, gifts and hospitality which should never be accepted?

LORD YOUNGER: I think as far as gifts are concerned the Rules are fairly effective if somewhat strange at times. There is, as you know, a fairly low figure below which a Minister can accept a gift. I am not quite sure what it is at this moment but it used to be about £80 in my time.

TOM KING: It has gone up to £125.

LORD YOUNGER: £125, right. This seems to me to work all right. It is a fairly modest sum and it enables a Minister to accept a small gift and probably to give a small gift in return when this is appropriate, particularly visiting overseas. I see nothing wrong with that. It is open to Ministers to buy the gifts from the government afterwards if they wish. I do not know if many ever do that.

As far as hospitality is concerned, there is a clear line on hospitality, whether it is Ministers or not, it seems to me, and there is quite a bit of distortion comes about this. I think it is perfectly proper that a Minister, or a Member of Parliament for that matter, should be given hospitality when they are involved in some activity which is requested by an outside body. If one is asked to go and help a company in doing something to pay the hotel bill when you go to do it seems to me to be perfectly proper. However, I think a fortnight on the Riviera at the payment of the company afterwards is not acceptable and there is a fairly clear, commonsense line one can draw.

As far as Ministers are concerned, Ministers basically should never accept hospitality except when it is connected with, say, an invitation to a factory or something. Nobody minds that.

1147. DIANA WARWICK: Do you think these Rules are very clear and everybody understands and accepts them?

LORD YOUNGER: I believe so.

1148. DIANA WARWICK: Could I ask you one other brief question. This is to do with the relationship between Ministers and civil servants. We were told yesterday about various things which were regarded as improper which senior civil servants, or even more junior civil servants, were occasionally asked to do by Ministers. They included things like speeches for constituency meetings or for party conferences or briefing for back-benchers on Private Members' Bills. Do you accept that those things are improper and do you think that this should be spelled out quite specifically for both Ministers and civil servants?

LORD YOUNGER: I think if there is any need to spell it out it should be but in my experience it is perfectly clear. My civil servants never knowingly did anything which was a party political content, like writing a speech for a party conference or for a constituency meeting. We had a political adviser, which is a relatively new development but a helpful one, because what my private office always said was that they would get the political adviser to do something and he did it. I think the line is clear and I think the line should always be stuck to. It is extremely important; indeed, I found that the chief value of my civil servants, particularly in the private office, was that they definitely did not have any political views—they probably did but they never told them to me—but their advice was a thousand times more valuable to me because they were not political.

DIANA WARWICK: Thank you.

1149. MARTIN JACOMB: Just one question. I am sorry to detain you but you are in a good position to answer it. Going back to the Ministry of Defence, do you not think there is something to be said for a high degree of cohesion between the Ministry of Defence and British manufacturers of defence equipment? In France the transition of individuals from government to industry is very, very easily done in each direction and you drew such a clear prohibition on Ministers and civil servants going from government on the one hand to industry on the other, would you just like to comment on the comparative position?

LORD YOUNGER: Yes, certainly. I agree with you entirely that this is extremely desirable and I think the way this should be done, and very often is done, is that the cross fertilisation of ideas between industry and government should be done, carefully avoiding departmental clashes. For instance, in my current position as Chairman of the Royal Bank of Scotland, we greatly welcome civil servants coming on secondment to us, and we have some doing that right now, because they are not directly connection with banking in any way but we learn about each other that way. I would not be in favour, in the Ministry of Defence case for instance, of too close a linkage between contractors and the Ministry because these people see contracts all the time and there can appear to be too cosy a relationship. I think the relations between industry and government can be achieved quite easily by cross postings between other ministries that are not intimately involved with each other in contracting.

MARTIN JACOMB: Thank you very much.

LORD NOLAN: Lord Younger, I wish we could keep you for longer but the time you have given us has been extremely valuable and your views have been most clearly expressed. We are all very grateful to you.

LORD YOUNGER: Thank you very much, Lord Nolan.

LORD NOLAN: Sir Norman, good morning to you.

RT. HON. SIR NORMAN FOWLER

RT. HON SIR NORMAN FOWLER, MP: Good morning.

1150. LORD NOLAN: I see that—is this right—you have helpfully prepared an opening statement which you would like to make before we go into questions?

NORMAN FOWLER: Yes, if I might just say something in introduction to show what my beliefs are. Basically it is that I believe very strongly that MPs should be permitted to have outside interests and I also believe that those interests should be governed by sensible rules. In summary my views are that, first, I would not favour a House of Commons made up of MPs who were financially entirely dependent upon Parliament; I don't think that makes sense when, by the very nature of the workings of democracy, many MPs lose their seats and serve only one or two terms in Westminster. They are then forced to resume their outside careers. But perhaps even more fundamentally I think that banning outside interests would make the MP entirely dependent upon his party for his very livelihood and it would help destroy the element of independence which I think is extremely important in an MP's life.

Second, I think a ban on outside interests would be a deterrent for many people coming to Westminster. It would not deter the rich, either those who had inherited wealth or those who had acquired wealth in their outside careers. Doubtless it would not deter the professional politician who could not conceive of any other job. It will, however, I think undoubtedly deter the middle-income

man or woman with a family to bring up or, perhaps just as important, an elderly relative to care for. As far as the Conservative Party is concerned I think it would turn the clock backwards. The rules over the last half century have been intended to ensure that there is a spread of candidates from all income groups but that no advantage is given to the rich.

Thirdly, I do not accept that outside interests should be confined to journalism (although I was once a journalist) writing and television presenting. They have no special merit or inherent virtue. Much paid for writing is based on Parliamentary and Ministerial experience. The writers of fictional sagas, like Roy Hattersley (who I think has given evidence to you) I think are not by definition more meritorious than those who work in industry or in business. Indeed, for as long as I have been in the House of Commons the call has been for there to be better links between industry and Parliament. That was why the Industry and Parliament Trust was set up in the first place. I think it would be perverse if temporary attachments to industry—which by their very nature are superficial—were encouraged while more permanent working arrangements were banned.

Fourth, I think that much of the criticism of Members of Parliament who are company directors is actually misplaced and the role of the non-executive director is often misunderstood. I think that role is now set out fully by the committee under the chairmanship of Sir Adrian Cadbury that reported at the end of 1992 on the financial aspects of corporate governance. The committee set out a code of best practice—that code, as everyone working in industry, I think, would recognise, is now followed generally in industry—and among the provisions are that about the board of directors that they should include non-executive directors of sufficient calibre and number for their views to carry weight in the board's decisions; that non-executive directors should bring an independent judgment to bear in issues of strategy, performance, resources, including key appointments (which often takes a very long time) and standards of conduct. And if I may say in parenthesis I think MPs meet that criteria very well. That the majority of non-executive directors should be independent of management, free from any business or other relationship which would materially interfere with the exercise of their independent judgment. Again I would believe that MPs fit into that category extremely well. That non-executive directors should be selected through a formal process and both this process and their appointment should be a matter for the board as a whole. If I could just give my example, when I was appointed to the board of NFC I was interviewed by the non-executives and the executives in separate and formal meetings and that is now part of the code of practice.

It should actually also be added that directors, executive and non-executive, do carry legal responsibilities for the good governance of the company. The idea that they are simply "names on the notepaper", I think, is years and years and years out of date.

I think that adviserships do raise different questions. They are not governed by the same rules as directors of companies. I would have thought that there was a distinction to be made between advisers who are employed to be advocates in Parliament and advisers who simply employ their skill and judgment to tell outside companies of the position as they see it. The division is perhaps a difficult division to define exactly. What I think is reasonably clear is the position of the Parliamentary lobbyist. Legitimately enough lobbying organisations take up the cases which they are employed to pursue. They do not have to be politically consistent and a lobbying organisation can be employed to put the case, for example, in favour of privatisation or against privatisation. Indeed, there is a recent case of that kind. Commercially that might be acceptable and justifiable for a lobbying organisation. I think it is difficult to see how the role of a Member of Parliament is compatible with that kind of occupation.

As far as ex-Ministers taking up outside jobs are concerned I actually believe there should be some form of checking process similar but not identical to that governing civil servants. Evidence before you has made the point that Ministers and civil servants are not the same and of course I accept that. Ministers can rapidly—sometimes very rapidly—move from one department to another department. When they leave they often don't retire, they continue with their political career and their career generally. Only recently has there been any "redundancy" payment. When I resigned at the beginning of 1990 the immediate effect was that my income was halved overnight. Nevertheless, having made every allowance for the difference, I think the aims of the Civil Service Code seem to me at any rate equally applicable to Ministers. The aims of the Civil Service rules are first to avoid any suspicion that the advice and decisions of a civil servant may be influenced by the hope of future employment; and second to avoid the risk that a company might gain an improper advantage. There is no difficulty, it seems to me, in making that statement of aim applicable to former Ministers as well.

So one way I put forward—and there may be others—but one way I put forward is this. That an ex-Minister who wants to take up employment in a company with which he has just had departmental dealings (say in the preceding two years) would need the approval of an independent committee on the lines of the Civil Service's Advisory Committee on Business Appointments. I would suggest that he would be asked to seek approval in the two years following his departure from the department. I think the date which is relevant is the date at which the Minister leaves the particular department, not the date that he leaves the Government. I don't think such a check would apply if an ex-Minister was going to a job which self-evidently has nothing whatsoever to do with his last department. It also, I think, should be emphasised, in case there is any misunderstanding, that the committee could quite well give approval to the ex-Minister taking up an outside appointment, even if it was departmentally connected, provided that it did not offend the spirit of the aims of the rules. It, in other words, would be a check, it would not be a ban.

Lastly I would just make this observation: I actually believe that both the public and former Ministers would benefit from a clearly stated set of rules. So that is all really that I would like to say in introduction.

LORD NOLAN: Thank you very much indeed and very clear it is. I am going to ask Lord Thomson please to carry on with the questions.

1151. LORD THOMSON: Sir Norman, we are covering at the moment really three areas, MPs' financial interests,

the problems relating to Civil Servants and Ministers taking jobs in the private sector and finally Quangos, and you are in a uniquely valuable position for us as having experience in all these three areas. Could I begin by asking you about the comment you have just made about Ministers on leaving Government and taking up posts in the private sector? We have just been listening to evidence from your former Cabinet colleague, Lord Younger, and we had evidence the other day from your former Cabinet colleague, John MacGregor. They were not exactly of the same view in terms of the way of dealing with this problem. I think they were of the same view that you have just expressed that there is a need for some kind of process of dealing with the Ministerial problem. But Lord Younger has just said that there should be a similar arrangement to the one that you have for Civil Servants and that Ministers by and large must take the rough with the smooth and if there are difficulties about something associated with Ministerial responsibilities there are a lot of other jobs in the world that Ministers might be quite attractive candidates for. I think John MacGregor was inclined to emphasise the differences—and there are real differences between the position of civil servants with their pensions and all that side of thing—and the uncertainties of political life for a Minister. I just wondered where you stood between these two points of view—are you for taking the rough with the smooth or do you think that there ought to be a great deal of emphasis on the special circumstances of Ministers?

NORMAN FOWLER: Well, I don't see personally why the Civil Service Code, which I think has worked quite well, should not be adapted so far as Ministers are concerned. I am not, as I said, making the argument that Ministers and civil servants are the same—they self-evidently are not the same—they switch departments much much more regularly, for example, than civil servants. But it seems to me that the Civil Service Code, which is basically to prevent civil servants taking actions which will give them favours in the future, or civil servants should take business secrets (or things of that kind) into their next job, it seems to me that those aims apply to Ministers as well. So I see no particular reason why the code cannot be adapted so far as ex-Ministers are concerned. I think it is important to say this: it is not all jobs, it is the jobs which are connected with the ex-Minister's last department or, in my view, over his last two years if he has done two departments. I, for example, became non-executive chairman of a newspaper and I mean, I don't think anyone is going to claim that that had anything whatsoever to do with my Ministerial career. It had quite a lot to do with the fact that for ten years I worked on the *Times* earlier in my career. It does not seem to me that that kind of job goes to the committee. But I think a job—my last department was Employment—if I was taking up a job with one of the, I don't know, big recruiting agencies, or something of that sort, that would be an appropriate thing to go.

1152. LORD THOMSON: Do you think that the present Business Appointments Committee would be an appropriate and adequate body for dealing with this? I have in mind the particular situation at the moment when there is the maximum redundancy, and unemployed Cabinet Ministers are looking for alternative means of earning their living, that is at the point of losing a General Election. Under the civil service arrangements the final decision lies with the Prime Minister. Is there a political problem about the final decision for ex-Ministers lying with the new Prime Minister of a different party?

NORMAN FOWLER: I think that is for debate. I am not trying to actually set down a kind of completely concrete proposal but just to put the suggestion that it should go this particular way. You either have the Prime Minister, I suppose, as the kind of final arbiter, or you have somebody else. I wouldn't actually mind either way. I think that what is important—and I think it is important from the ex-Minister's point of view as well as from the public's point of view—is that there is a checking process that he can go to. I think it actually makes his position better as well as assures the public, because otherwise at the moment I mean any ex-Minister who goes virtually anywhere is subject to criticism on any kind of basis. I think that from his point of view it is useful to have a checking process. But I am entirely neutral where the final buck stops as far as that decision is concerned.

1153. LORD THOMSON: Thank you. Could I now come to your responsibilities as Chairman of the Conservative Party—former Chairman of the Conservative Party—and to the area of Quangos? The allegations that have been made that are part of the climate on which we are operating our enquiry, as you very well know, is that there has been a vast extension of the role of Quangos in our Governmental system and, therefore, a vast extension in the political patronage that is involved. I think they say, what, 40,000 appointments now to Quangos of one kind or another and a lot of very serious allegations that in fact there is a very strong political bias in these appointments and that particular allegation that some of the appointments are associated with companies or individuals who make substantial donations to the Conservative Party. What are your answers to these comments?

NORMAN FOWLER: You mention the fact that I was Chairman of the Conservative Party. I actually had next to nothing, in fact, of experience in this area when I was Chairman of the Conservative Party because the appointments of this kind are not made by the Conservative Party, they are made by departments. I had much more experience when I was, say, at the Employment Department or at the Department of Health. When I was at the Employment Department we set up, for example, Training and Enterprise Councils. These were councils—and I notice that the Labour Party says that these come into the Quango area, broadly defined—they certainly were separate as far as Government Departments were concerned. What we tried to do was to set up a series of, if you like, non-executive boards around the country. Our criteria was to get, basically, chief executives locally to sit on them. Politics did not come into it—we didn't actually know what the politics were—but they were the people in the area who had most to contribute as far as training was concerned and who, above all, made the decisions as far as that was concerned.

As far as health was concerned the same kind of criteria I think would apply. What one wanted—and it is perhaps easier now than it was in my day when we had Health Authorities and a rather different kind of structure, but as you perhaps have detected I am a great believer in the non-executive director and the board—what one needs are people of independent judgment to check on the running of the Health Authority, or the hospital, or whatever it is, but obviously they need to help to make the organisation better. If someone is against the whole idea then I don't think he should be on the board. But that is self-denying ordinance for the person himself. I wouldn't

expect to be appointed in the old days to the National Enterprise Board because I wouldn't have actually believed in it. But, I mean, my experience has been very much that it has been quite difficult to find people of background and independent skill to actually sit on these kinds of boards.

1154. LORD THOMSON: You were at one point Health Minister, were you not?

NORMAN FOWLER: Yes.

1155. LORD THOMSON: I am told that at that time when you were Health Minister, Area Health Authorities included a number of members who were appointed, not by the Secretary of State but by local authorities. That situation has apparently gone now though I notice also that in terms of the police quite recently—last year—that the practice of appointments to police authority not being made by the Home Secretary as a balancing element was inserted in the legislation. Do you not think it would be a good idea for an element of that to be part of the appointment to the Health Boards for instance?

NORMAN FOWLER: Yes, I think the Health Authorities—I think they pre-dated me, in fact—I think that the Area Health Authorities had been created and abolished by the time I got to the Health Service. I think I had the District Health Authorities and the Regional Health Authorities. And it is true that, I mean, I remember making some changes in the Regional Health Authority Chairmen and one was criticised for that. But in the main—well not in the main—actually what one was trying to do was to get the best possible people to do these jobs. I am a little reluctant to have a situation where people, whether it is local authorities or anybody else for that matter, have the right of nomination. I think really what one should do—I mean, certainly I think it is entirely fair that the local authority might have the right of suggestion. I don't mind that in the least. But the right of nomination begins to make it a sort of representative body, not necessarily what I would regard as a board of directors who are seeking to take the organisation forward.

1156. LORD THOMSON: We had evidence—I think it was from Sir Peter Kemp who was in many ways one of the architects of the new model of the Civil Service——

NORMAN FOWLER: Next Steps Agencies.

LORD THOMSON: —— and all that. Who said he thought there ought to be some kind of public appointments commission. Would you think there was something to be said for that?

NORMAN FOWLER: I would not be averse to that in any way. As I say, my experience was that the most difficult thing to do was to find people who actually wanted to do the job and who were good and experienced people to do it. I don't think people with political backgrounds locally should be excluded from that because obviously you have a lot of people who—on either side—a lot of people who have got a public service belief. I don't think they should be excluded but nor do I think they should be given an inside track. So as far as I am concerned I think that in a way what one wants to do is to kind of—and it is a very difficult thing to do—what one wants to do is to get a register, if you like, of people who are prepared to do these jobs from as wide a background as you conceivably can do. That actually again would, certainly from my Ministerial experience, have been a great great help.

1157. LORD THOMSON: Do you accept that from the political point of view there is a real problem of perception for the Government in terms of some balance of the composition of these Quangos?

NORMAN FOWLER: Well, it has always been thus, has it not? I remember when I was in opposition in 1974-79 we made exactly the same points as far as the Labour Party was concerned at that stage, and I remember it was George Woodcock, the former TUC General Secretary, who said in '77 that "seniority, the muscle-power of your union and competence, these are what you need to get a public job and in that order"—competence being at the end. And in 1977 the thirty-nine members of the TUC Council held 180 public appointments and the Prices Secretary, who was Roy Hattersley at the time, said "Having set up the National Enterprise Board, or the Price Commission, or the Monopolies Commission, or the General Medical Council, I would want to believe that I had so equipped it in terms of the membership that they took the right decisions". (Laughter) I think it would be wrong, therefore, to believe that this was something that was entirely a unique issue. I remember it was a great debate between 1974 and 1979. As far as I personally am concerned, as I say, I think that—and I think most Ministers would take the same view—as far as I am concerned what one wants are good people to run whatever they are, Health Authorities, Training Enterprise Councils, and the rest. Incidentally when we set up the Training and Enterprise Councils we thought that——and a great feather in our cap was when Bill Jordan of the Engineering Union joined the national body. That was extremely good news because he was a prominent trade unionist but above all he was extremely good.

1158. LORD THOMSON: I did not realise I was asking such a leading question—I almost regret it now. (Laughter) But that is very useful and very helpful. Can I now just finally turn to MPs and can you help us to wrestle with the problem of what is a legitimate outside paid interest for an MP and what is an illegitimate interest? Have you any views about this?

NORMAN FOWLER: Well, as I indicated in what I said initially, I think that it is extremely difficult to justify the position of the political—if you like, someone who is an employee of a political lobbying organisation when, by its very nature, the political lobbying organisation can take on any case. In a sense it is a taxi for hire, it is standing there and whoever pays is the case it will put. Now, you can argue about that and commercially I imagine that the organisations would say that that is entirely legitimate and I suppose that that is the case. What I think is very difficult to see is how that is good and sensible as far as a Member of Parliament, or right as far as a Member of Parliament is concerned. So that is on one side. On the other side—and I heard the last bit of what George Younger was saying—I think that you have to actually exercise a certain amount of common sense in these things. When I came out of Government I was offered a number of outside posts—I, in fact, declined to go onto the board of a public relations company for many of the same reasons that I have just actually stated. But I think that if you go into industry, into business, into areas which are away from politics, then it

seems to me that that is capable of bringing to the House of Commons some experience which they don't otherwise have. If we just have MPs who have none of this outside experience our debates on industry or aspects of industry—let us say the media, for example—are going to be pretty barren affairs because no one is going to have any kind of experience in the up-to-date industry in which they are working. So I think that it is advantageous for the MP obviously in the outside interest it has, but I think it also has advantages for Parliament as well. But as I say I think sensible checks of the kind that I mentioned in terms of ex-Ministers—I think that I would entirely support.

LORD THOMSON: Thank you.

1159. LORD NOLAN: Sir Norman, I wonder if I could take you back to the question of Ministers moving into private industry when they have left office? The rules for civil servants, which most of our witnesses have accepted as being apparently pretty good rules, are based on the proposition that an individual while still serving must not take up a job if he has been influenced in his work as a civil servant by the hope of taking employment with that company; and equally, once leaving the Civil Service it would be a strong red light if he carries with him information or influence which would be useful to the company he is going to. Those principles, I think, you are saying are equally applicable to Ministers?

NORMAN FOWLER: Yes.

1160. LORD NOLAN: Yes. The difficulty put to us very clearly and forcibly is the very great financial adverse consequence for a Minister generally speaking, compared with that of the civil servant. One sees that as a real problem—you do not want to discourage people from taking up office because of the fear that they will be out in three months or three years—and unduly restricted from taking up employment. But whatever changes are made or required for Ministers they must not, must they, conflict with those two principles?

NORMAN FOWLER: That is very strongly my view. It is the principles—and I think you can construct any checking mechanism round those principles—but I think that the principles seem to me to be very strong. And I think that what I would suggest is that the period in a Minister's departmental career is the last two years of that departmental career, thus—it has always seemed to me fairly absurd that, for example, I became a director of NFC nine years after ceasing to be Secretary of State for Transport. It is very difficult to think that I took any inside knowledge of transport at that particular stage to the NFC, and it is quite difficult to think that back in the 1970s I was actually thinking "Ho, ho, in 1990 that will be where I am going to go to".

LORD NOLAN: Please do not think that I was suggesting that for one minute.

NORMAN FOWLER: No, no, I was just simply volunteering that as one of the criticisms that one has as a politician to face. You know, it is fair enough. And I think that that is why I say in a sense that it is useful from the point of view of the politician, as well as from the point of view of the public, that there are set out rules and firm rules that one can rely on and say "Well, look, those are the rules".

1161. LORD NOLAN: And how is one to cope with the financial disadvantage to the Minister? There is now,

Lord Younger was saying, some sort of redundancy payment. If the difference between the two cases is the difference in financial consequences, could it be remedied by money?

NORMAN FOWLER: Well, there is now, I think, a three-month redundancy. I think that Ministers who go are paid three months' salary and, I mean, I suppose that helps a bit. But I think that Members of Parliament—in the main Ministers—have got slightly to take the rough with the smooth in this position. There are jobs that they can go to, if they have been Cabinet Members, probably. People will want to use their experience which are way from their last department and I think it is not unreasonable for the public to say "Well, in that two year period after leaving that is actually where they should be going."

LORD NOLAN: Thank you very much. I am going to ask Sir Martin to go on next, please.

MARTIN JACOMB: I have no questions.

LORD NOLAN: Diana?

1162. DIANA WARWICK: Could I just ask two questions. The first is to try and see whether we can take a little bit further the relationship between an MP and a public affairs company or a lobbying company, which we have had quite a lot of evidence on and we have been wrestling with in terms of how to react to that as a committee, and an MP who sits on a board, either in a non-executive or, indeed, executive capacity. Is there a distinction in your view between the activities which such an MP, say in a non-executive capacity, could undertake and an MP who is paid by a lobbying company?

NORMAN FOWLER: Yes. I think whether he was a non-executive director of the lobbying company or whether he was the employee of the lobbying company I am not sure that I would make too many distinctions there.

DIANA WARWICK: I am sorry, I meant a non-executive director of any company.

NORMAN FOWLER: Generally, yes. No, I think a non-executive director of any company takes on responsibilities, has a code of conduct, which goes far beyond anything, you know, laid down by the Register of Interests, or anything of that kind. The Cadbury Code is very clear about what is expected. Apart from anything else you also have legal responsibilities. A board of directors, whether they are non-executive or executive, as you know, carry exactly the same responsibilities for the good governance of the company and if things go wrong then they are liable just as much as their executive colleagues are liable. So I think that in a sense, with the right background, a non-executive director is exactly the sort of thing that a Member of Parliament should be doing because what he is being asked to do is to employ his experience and his independent judgment, going out into the industry. He is not a sort of lobbyist inside the House of Commons. Non-executive directors don't get up and ask questions on their own particular company. They might, I suppose, speak in a general industrial debate and bring that experience, but it is basically taking their experience out into industry rather than the other way round. The difficulty with the lobbying organisation, it

seems to me, is that you are being asked to—and being paid for—putting a case and it often could be a case which is not entirely compatible with what you have actually been elected to do. So I think when you get into that region there are very real difficulties and I think it is very difficult to see how that role can be compatible.

1163. DIANA WARWICK: Thank you. My next question relates to your role as Chairman of the Conservative Party. When the representatives of the trade unions were here we pressed them very hard on both the nature and size of the donations that they made to individual MPs and to constituencies and, indeed to parts of the Labour Party's work. One of the issues that arose was the question of transparency and certainly I think when you were Chairman of the Party the question of funds to the Party and transparency about them did arise. But in particular do you think that just as the trade unions confirmed that donations to constituency parties were declared, in the interests of transparency it is appropriate for donations at local level to constituencies from, say, a local company, should also be declared, bearing in mind what Lord Younger said about MPs not taking any kind of payment for constituency work?

NORMAN FOWLER: Well, it would not be the MP taking it, would it, that would be for the Association as opposed to the Member of Parliament? I am against that. We have had a select committee which has looked at the financing of political parties only last year and I gave evidence over two or three hours to the select committee at the time. My view in precis on this is basically that we have a voluntary form of fund-raising in this country, we don't have the state-controlled and state-financed political parties, and if people want to give money to political parties that is up to them and if they wish that to be anonymous that is also up to them. Obviously the Tory Party will abide by any rules and regulations that are made in this area, but I think that the rules at the moment are rules which actually have served the public quite well, but I don't see any reason why someone who wishes to make a donation anonymously to a party of any kind, in the same way as he can do it to a charity or voluntary organisation, should not be allowed to do so.

1164. DIANA WARWICK: The point was that donations of that kind could well exercise influence—that was the point that was made, I think, to the trade unions.

NORMAN FOWLER: Well, the difference there is that we make it absolutely clear to any people, anyone, any organisation, any company, any individual, who donates to the Conservative Party that it in no way buys influence, it in no way directs our policy whatsoever. So if people wish to give money to the Tory Party that is a matter for them—they give it because they believe and support the kind of general stance that the Tory Party takes, but they receive certainly nothing in terms of assurances that they are going to have a particular policy taken forward. That is simply not the case and we make that clear and it is set out—and I have set it out on numerous occasions.

DIANA WARWICK: Thank you.

1165. TOM KING: The first witness we had talked about the public perception—Diana Warwick mentioned it—that 68 per cent of the public think that MPs are there for what they can make out of Parliament financially for themselves, and a succession of witnesses, including senior editors, have confirmed their view that while that may be the public perception it is not a fair perception, nor true. Yet there is a big public perception of sleaze. You are actually part of it because the public has been told in so many words that you walked straight out of the Department of Transport into the board position on NFC, the National Freight Corporation, carrying a large suitcase full of the most secret and up-to-date information from the Department of Transport, and is this not absolutely outrageous? Everybody who leaves Government and takes any job, the cutting service then sort of check from the files and out comes the list and you appear and Lord Wakeham and Lord Young and everybody else, and yet you have told us, you as a former journalist have admitted that what the papers have been printing is absolute rubbish and that you actually left nine years ago and much later in the day you actually joined the board. I don't think transport policies have been totally static in the last nine years and I should think you could not be more out of date in that respect. So I am really asking you this as a journalist, because my concern is that it is important for the democratic process that there is respect for the institutions of democracy and there is not at the moment, and part of that is because they have been grossly misrepresented and there seems to be no effective way to correct it. What do you think about that?

NORMAN FOWLER: I could go on for a very long time on this because I have slightly suffered as a result of it. When the issue was first raised a Labour front-bencher came to me and said "I am awfully sorry, we have actually made a mistake. You are outside the two-year limit that we are putting forward". But then I became Chairman of the Conservative Party and the fact that I was Chairman of the Conservative Party meant that any links of this kind were just incorporated in. So I fear that I have kind of come into it mainly as a result of my Chairmanship of the Tory Party. But what I would argue—and I think one of the great things about these debates is that Jack Straw has now accepted my position on radio publicly to millions of listeners—what I would argue is that if you actually leave a Government department nine years previously it is very difficult to think that you are actually taking any secrets of the transport kind into that department, and of course you are not. The whole ball game had changed in many ways. We had gone from the kind of traditional transport to logistics. You were taking more experience of the world and of running organisations but you were not taking the——

LORD NOLAN: Sir Norman, I must——

NORMAN FOWLER: Yes, all I was going to say on this is that all it does is underline my point, which I have been trying to make throughout, which is that rules set down are not only in the interests of the public but they are in the interests of the ex-Minister as well.

LORD NOLAN: Yes, I think Mr. King's point—he will correct me if I am wrong—was rather more generally based. If an unfair impression is being created of the behaviour of politicians what can be done to correct it? Was that it?

1166. TOM KING: That is right. One thing I was a little surprised you said was "I've gone off and I am on the board of a chain of newspapers or a newspaper and that is obviously all right, so nobody needs to advise me on that,

but then if there is the NFC or something, that might be misunderstood, so that would be a good idea if that one was put through something like the Civil Service Committee or whatever." Now is that not actually, on reflection——I mean you were most recently Secretary of State for Employment and is it not possible that a newspaper group might have some relation? You have classified ads or, I don't know how you get into it but, you know, the vacancies—some of them are connected with employment areas of activity. So I am just stretching it—the Press are going to look for every wrinkle. Would it not actually be more satisfactory for Ministers—that you did not make that judgment and that somebody else actually—everything, whatever you were thinking of doing—was put through that committee?

NORMAN FOWLER: Yes. I mean I think again——I don't mind if that is what you want to do, as long as there is a time limit on it. I think that what I was proposing was the last two years of one's departmental career—last two years in a department. If you wished to say in the two years after leaving then any job that you are going to do you send to the committee then I would not object to that because I think it is self-evident that being the Chairman of a——it is a fairly tenuous relationship, if you don't mind me saying so, between that and the Employment Department, tenuous to stretching it, I think, beyond any kind of reasonable point. But I don't mind in the least if a committee look at that and say yes or no. That is why I say it is not a banning process, it is a checking process. But as far as your point about correcting it is concerned, correcting allegations that are made, the answer is that it is extremely difficult to do that at the moment. It is all political debate, that is why a checking process—again I repeat the point—actually helps in that respect because any ex-Minister can say "Well, look, this has gone to the checking process."

1167. LORD NOLAN: And you said that would help both the Minister and the public?

NORMAN FOWLER: Exactly.

LORD NOLAN: Thank you very much. Peter?

1168. PETER SHORE: Yes, if I could just follow on from there. You made the point that correcting allegations is difficult—allegations that have been made of sleaze or improper conduct—and I think that is true and it is certainly true that allegations that have been made have been damaging to the institutions of democracy. But when you say correcting these things is difficult, is there not one very simple way of dealing with such allegations? That is, of course, to publish and to make it absolutely plain that the Conservative Party is not in receipt of large sums of money from unnamed people, so far unnamed, so that the record can be put right? The record can be put right and the instruments for doing so lie in your own hands.

NORMAN FOWLER: We are talking now about party funding?

PETER SHORE: Yes.

LORD NOLAN: Not as a general issue—the buying of favour by party contributions.

NORMAN FOWLER: Well, if the law is changed then clearly the Tory Party will have to do that, but at the moment the position is not that and therefore I think to have a situation where people who have given under one set of rules actually have it changed on them I think would be completely wrong. I don't see how that could conceivably be justified. But I go back to the point—and I think it is simply a basic point and a basic point that the select committee looked at and although it was divided the majority found this way—is that it is the right of an individual or, indeed, an organisation, to make contributions to a political party, or a voluntary organisation, or a charity and not actually have their identify published so far as it is concerned. Of course, if it is a company, if it is a British company, then it has to set it out in its annual report.

1169. PETER SHORE: Well, turning to companies, you are quite right that companies do have to declare, not the exact amount but bands of contribution which they make to political parties, but here some analysis has been made of those companies that do make a contribution as compared with companies that do not make a contribution. One of the things that I think appeared in a recent BBC broadcast, having done this analysis they found that companies that had made a contribution to Conservative Party funds did significantly better in obtaining positions on public boards, Quangos, than those companies which did not make contributions. Now what really do you say to that?

NORMAN FOWLER: Well I would like to look at the evidence on that very, very carefully indeed. It sounds to me highly suspect. Because in the main, you see, the Boards that we are talking about—whether you are talking about Health, or Training and Enterprise Councils and things of that sort—I wish it was the case that people are jumping over each other to try to get to these Boards from industry. But that actually is not the case. The case is that we actually have to try and persuade very good people from industry to come onto the Boards. Because, obviously, there is a great deal of work; they are pursuing their own industrial careers. It is not some sort of sinecure that we are giving them. I have not seen the evidence that you talk about. It sounds to me highly suspect.

1170. PETER SHORE: I will see that you get a copy of that because it will be interesting to have your comment. But, leaving aside then that particular worry about there being a possible connection between money paid into the Conservative Party and quango appointments, what about the more frequently made allegation that political preference and sharing of political beliefs has played a very important part in the selection of people to serve as chairmen and members of quango boards?

NORMAN FOWLER: Well, again, I have not the experience in that to actually know whether that is the case or not, but certainly I tried to explain the principles that I followed when I was in charge of those sort of things. I mean the Chairman of the Conservative Party is not remotely in charge of that. We do not have that kind of power. It is the Departmental Secretary of State that often has power to make it, and I think that the general principle that I followed and I am sure other Secretaries of State have followed—and it has not always been the easiest thing to do simply because of lack of supply—is to find the best possible people. If I am running a Health Trust or running a Training and Enterprise Council, what I want to do is run the most effective Health Trust and the most effective Training and Enterprise Council. I do not want passengers on it from any political party if they are not good.

1171. PETER SHORE: Yes, I am sure that certainly must be the most important factor. But the point was made earlier today and I think in the earlier part of your own evidence, that you are worried about appointing people who you think would criticise or oppose Government policy. Is that really a serious worry?

NORMAN FOWLER: Well, what I said actually there was that if it was me, I would not accept an appointment to a body that I did not believe in. Because, again it goes back to the Board of Directors concept. A non-executive member of a Board of Directors is there to use his independent judgment. He is not there to blindly follow. On the other hand he has got to have some kind of commitment to the Board itself. If he does not have any kind of commitment to the Board itself, it seems to me that it is a particularly valueless thing for him to do, let alone anyone else. So I think it is up to the individual. But, speaking personally, if you wanted to put me on the National Enterprise Board—which I doubt if you would but if you had have done—I would not have wanted to serve on it because I would not have believed in it. It seems to me that way round that the protest goes.

1172. PETER SHORE: I think that is simple and, in a sense, quite an extreme case and I would accept what you say there. But when you come to bodies like National Health Service Trust where you get a lot of people who are quite devoted to the Health Service and to serving their community, but who nevertheless are critical of what are I think generally accepted as very radical changes, are they to be automatically excluded from appointments?

NORMAN FOWLER: No, I do not think they should be automatically excluded. I think it would be up to them. If they are devoted and dedicated to the Health Service and they want to work in the confines of the organisation that is there, while at the same time believing that there is a better way of doing things but they will make the contribution—that is the organisation, I think that that is entirely fine. I think, certainly from my own experience, when I was Secretary of State for Health, we had obviously Health Authority Chairmen who were quite openly political opponents of ours and some of them were extremely good. So I think that it is not in any remote way a bar.

PETER SHORE: Thank you.

LORD NOLAN: We are running over time, but if you have any questions to ask?

1173. ANNE WARBURTON: I am afraid I will not help us to catch up either because I would like to change subject. Sir Norman, I suppose that for all of us that one of the main points of our being here is to try to help rehabilitate politics and politicians in this country. We have spoken already about ways in which perhaps we might be able to help Ministers as such. I would like to talk about Parliament and in particular the House of Commons, which I imagine to be exercised by the low esteem of the public. Perhaps transparency, openness, is the key that we keep coming to in various ways and I suppose that that will include, perhaps, making rules clear. Another aspect of it which comes up from time to time is the possible need, as in professions, of an outside element when it comes to the application of rules—including of course scrutiny when Members' Interests are at question. That is what I would now like to hear your views on.

NORMAN FOWLER: Yes. I have not given a great deal of thought to it. Speaking personally, I would not be opposed to that but I think it would depend very much upon the model that you put forward. There are difficulties obviously in it and I think that the Leader of the House, Tony Newton, is in a much stronger position to speak than I would be on that. The whole tradition of the House of Commons—and it is quite difficult to see how else it is done—is that the discipline of the House of Commons is done by the House of Commons itself, and one does have at times these occasions when literally we have debates on the expulsion of Members of Parliament itself. But I think if you can find a method by which an independent element is inserted, I for one would not be in any way opposed to that. I would like to see what it was but I am certainly not opposed to it and I take very much your point that what we do need to do is to demonstrate to the public that the system that we have is a good one. I am totally and strongly opposed to having full-time professional and entirely no-outside-interest Members of Parliament. I am totally opposed to that. I actually think that the public is probably opposed to that as well. But I think that, therefore, if that is my belief, it is incumbent on me to say also that if there were checks that can be introduced which will ensure that the public is convinced that what is taking place is totally open and above board, then fine.

ANNE WARBURTON: Thank you.

1174. PROF. ANTHONY KING: I like the way you linked donations to the Conservative Party to charitable donations and I am sure that in the present state of the Conservative Party finances it came naturally to your mind! But I do not want pursue that.

Could I just ask you one question about your opening statement where you referred to adviserships. You say:

"I would have thought that a distinction should be made between advisers who are employed to be advocates in Parliament and advisers who simply employ their skill and judgment to tell outside companies of the position as they see it."

You draw a clear line between advocacy on the one hand and merely advising on the other. Suppose this Committee were to suggest that that distinction be taken very seriously and that paid advocacy on behalf of outside interests should not be allowed but that the giving of advice for pay should be allowed. Do you think that distinction could actually be drawn and enforced in practice?

NORMAN FOWLER: Well it could be, yes. I think the lobbying organisation is the strongest example in fact of, if you like, paid advocacy or possible paid advocacy. But it does bring you into more difficult areas like, for example, the Police Federation. For a long time Jim Callaghan, for example, was the adviser to the Police Federation. Every time he stood up he was speaking on behalf of the Police Federation. Everyone knew that that was the case but he was, if you like, a paid advocate as far as that was concerned. I think it is a matter for decision whether that is right. I think Home Secretaries would actually take the view that it was useful to have that. I do not disagree. It is an extremely difficult line to draw. But the people that I was also thinking about were the people who advise in the most general terms. Rather than being a director of a company, they advise that particular company on the world scene, on the political scene. They

never stand up in the House of Commons and put forward the views of that particular company. It does not seem to me that that actually raises any particular problems.

1175. PROF. ANTHONY KING: But you sound, despite what you have just said, as though you are at least tempted by the idea of continuing to permit the giving of advice but you do sound doubtful about whether it is desirable for people to be paid to advocate.

NORMAN FOWLER: I think that it is quite a difficult line to draw there and I have not actually tried to do it any more than actually talking about the lobbying organisation itself. I think it would require a great deal of study and a great deal of care and a great deal of evidence, which I obviously have not the ability to take. But I think there is a distinction between the advocates and the general advisers. But I think of the advocates, the lobbyist is by far the strongest and clearest example.

1176. WILLIAM UTTING: I think, Sir Norman, that that takes us inevitably into the area of something like a Code of Conduct for Members of Parliament. We are being presented with a draft code for civil servants and I think that *Questions of Procedure for Ministers* might be classified as a code for Ministers. Do you think that it is reasonable to move on to a Code of Conduct for Members of Parliament that covered matters like this: their financial interests and issues like the kind of responsibilities that they have got to their constituents? Do you think that is likely to be runner?

NORMAN FOWLER: Well it is a runner—but I think what actually helps, and I think John MacGregor made this point, that whatever rules there are, they are firm rules. It depends how the Code of Conduct is put. If it is put in the most general terms, I am not sure that it helps very much. It in fact probably worsens the problem rather than helps it. I think it is better to have firm rules in a sense. If you like, that you can have the Code of Conduct as long as there is a kind of stipulation about what is not allowed, what is not permitted. Or circumstances under which if you do it you have to do it, as with ex-Ministers, under particular requirements. But I think that just a general code—well, I would want to see it. It is true that the Cadbury Code has worked well in industry. I think it has worked well. Not necessarily everyone would agree with that but I think most people would agree with that. But it does mean that you do need specific rules as well and the difficulty with this area is that it keeps on moving all the time. I think it would be nice if we had a bit of certainty in it.

1177. WILLIAM UTTING: If we have the specific rules, that does then lead back I think to the issues that Dame Anne raised about the monitoring and enforcement of the rules.

NORMAN FOWLER: Yes, of course.

1178. WILLIAM UTTING: I think, to an outsider, it does look as though the processes that are used for disciplining Members of the House might be inherently flawed and that sometimes their operation is not as effective as an outsider might think that it ought to be. These are matters that I think probably have to be addressed and have to be addressed seriously by the House. The question is how it can be persuaded to accept outside advice on the best way of doing it.

NORMAN FOWLER: Yes. I do not disagree with that. Where I would slightly disagree is that I think that the procedure whereby it is considered whether a Member of Parliament should be expelled from the House, that is a fairly terrifying procedure. I have actually seen it in process. One sees the debate taking place and the person almost waiting outside for the vote of the House of Commons. I think that that is a fairly strong deterrent. I do not think anyone should regard that as being a kind of soft option as far as discipline is concerned. I cannot think of any more public or ferocious way, in a way, of actually exercising discipline in the House.

1179. WILLIAM UTTING: No, and I do not doubt the gravity of the execution in that particular case. It was simply the processes that had gone through before one gets to that stage.

NORMAN FOWLER: Yes, well I accept that, yes.

WILLIAM UTTING: Thank you.

1180. LORD NOLAN: Sir Norman, we have taken up a lot of your time but it has been very valuable from our point of view. Thank you very much indeed for coming along.

Sir Michael, good morning. You have kindly sent us two letters and also a copy of an article you wrote, all of which we have read with great interest. I wonder if you would prefer to make a short opening statement, or to go straight into questions? It is a matter for you.

SIR MICHAEL QUINLAN

SIR MICHAEL QUINLAN (former Permanent Secretary at the Ministry of Defence): Could I just introduce myself for a couple of moments? You know that I retired from the Civil Service nearly three years ago. I represent now nobody but myself and I have to say that I do not have professional reasons to keep up with all the detail of developments now. But your Secretary notified to me three issues for discussion and I offered some commentary. Perhaps I could just recapitulate very briefly the position I took on each of those?

LORD NOLAN: Please do.

MICHAEL QUINLAN: On the acceptance of business appointments by officials after retirement, I do think that it is entirely right that there ought to be certain constraints. But, given that those would be constraints upon what is otherwise within a free society a general freedom within the law, I do think they need to be quite solidly grounded upon specific concerns and not upon some vague general sentiment. I do think also that the system may need to consider further how to deal with particular situations where there is serious disadvantage to the individuals. That is not the norm but I think it does occasionally happen. I should say I am certainly not an aggrieved party myself in any sense.

Now, on a code of Civil Service ethics, I did write without knowing that the Government was in fact on the point of making a major statement. As to that, I am entirely content. I think the Select Committee's draft was a very good one. I think the Government amendments make it better still and I think that comes out well. On the question as to whether it ought to be statutory, I am not sure I fully understand what that would imply but my instinct is to be pretty leery of it.

The third issue was the possible effect of management changes in the Civil Service upon standards. I think there are potential risks: I would not describe them as threats,

quite. But the fact of those risks is one of the reasons why I have come round to favouring, as I do, the idea of an explicit code and I am glad, therefore, that there is to be one.

LORD NOLAN: Thank you very much. Our habit is to take it in turns to ask the questions first and it is Mr Shore's turn. So if he will take up the questioning now?

1181. PETER SHORE: Sir Michael, let me start by asking you why you believe that a new Code of Ethics for Civil Servants was necessary, such as has been published in the recent White Paper?

MICHAEL QUINLAN: For two main reasons. I began, as I think I said in my notes, by being rather sceptical of this. I thought the Service understood perfectly well what was and what was not OK. But there does come a point, as I think I said, where if enough people think that there is a problem, then there is a problem. I think that had begun to be the case at least in terms of external perceptions. I am less sure that it was so within the Service. That was one reason, and the other reason is the one I have already touched upon. It is that with a lot of changes in the Service which are bringing to bear, often in positions of management authority, people who have come in from outside and who bring many strengths but who have not absorbed the ethics with their mother's milk, I think there is a case for having it all written down and set out so that there cannot be any misunderstanding.

1182. PETER SHORE: Thank you. Take the various speeches of the response that the Government has made: the Taking it Forward—Continuity and Change White Paper. What are your comments upon, and why do you think it was necessary for the Government to accept that there should be an appeal for civil servants to the Civil Service Commissioner?

MICHAEL QUINLAN: I think that goes again to the question of "if enough people think there is a problem, there is one". It is, I think, fairly widely known that in the several years since the current appeal system to Robin Butler has been in place there has been only one appeal. Well you can argue that that is because there is not a problem, or you can argue that it is because somehow people do not trust the system and think that that will not do. Well, enough people have commented that it is more likely to be the latter than the former that, without taking a view on which it is, I would accept that, well, I had better have something which more obviously commands confidence. Provided one sets up the right kind of appeal—in particular an appeal which does not operate until people have given the proper channels a fair run, and also that the appeal is to somebody who has at least some sense of how business actually works—I am quite content.

1183. PETER SHORE: Right. Well now, turning to a point which I know you attach much importance to, the decentralisation of the Civil Service and the changed methods of recruiting people and the various bodies that are set up. In your view this does present a problem of maintaining the traditional standards, ethos, of the Civil Service?

MICHAEL QUINLAN: I think it could present a problem and I would sooner move to guard against it before it might become a serious one. Some of what is done, quite apart from the recruitment of more and more people from outside, almost deliberately to bring in a different ethos—a different ethos in management, quite aside from that, the fact that the Next Steps programme deliberately puts sharper boundaries around operations and may have the effect of putting distance between operations and, let us say, a central department. That could, over time, pose some risk to the sense of being part of the Civil Service powerful, self-confident profession. I think, therefore, it is wise to pre-empt dangers that might come from that source. I cannot pretend that, in the time during which I saw Next Steps operate, I had seen any actual problems materialise, but I think there is some ground for thinking it is wise to take precautions.

1184. PETER SHORE: Right. Can I turn now to what you have to say about the Business Appointment rules? I am rather taken by your point that there is no compensation for former civil servants who are obliged to wait before they can take on an outside appointment. Is it really realistic to expect that compensation would be paid when a civil servant—all right, has been retired but has been retired on a fairly reasonable pension?

MICHAEL QUINLAN: Well I think it will depend from case to case. I can well see the difficulty of suggesting compensation if somebody has retired after a full career and has a substantial pension which will look to many people, especially if we are talking of a senior civil servant, as considerable comfort. It may nevertheless be a halving of income. I would not want to go into cases but I have to say that the instances which were in my mind particularly were not so much civil servants as the occasional military officer, required to retire at a rather early age—in one sense with a less obviously wide field of opportunity: a rather narrower direction in which they would naturally look. The occasional cases which I came across, which made me a little uncomfortable, were in fact rather of those than of my own class. And I do think that if you tell someone at 55, when commitments may still be high and one is clearly moving people out of their career at a time when they must look for something else, that they cannot go, or cannot go for a year or two years, in what is, for a variety of reasons, the most natural direction, I think you ought at least to think about what the compensation might be. The point could apply even more sharply where you have brought in, say, a high-powered businessman on contract for five years—that you operate, say, across the whole of the defence industry—then to say: But you cannot go back into that for a year or two years!—that is quite a restriction.

1185. PETER SHORE: They certainly are the most difficult cases, the ones you have mentioned. But then with an advisory committee, the advisory committee can act very flexibly within its parameters.

MICHAEL QUINLAN: It can but the advisory committees, as I understand, exist mainly to guard against the risks of perceived misbehaviour. I do not think it was within their remit, because there is not a system, to balance that against some sense of compensation. It does seem to me, at least for consideration, not as a general rule but in particularly hard cases, that there ought to be some ability to give compensation as it were, to pay waiting time. I can well see the difficulty. It could very easily be tabloid headlines! You know—So-and-so on the dole at a thousand a week! How very nice! I think there is a problem or potential problem.

1186. PETER SHORE: Employment in the Civil Service used to be a permanent career, uninterrupted,

with lots of expectations which were normally fulfilled. But we are living in a time when a number of redundancies are affecting the Civil Service and affecting people at very different levels. Do you think that this in itself requires some more flexible approach to rules affecting civil servants when they seek employment outside?

MICHAEL QUINLAN: In the sense of taking more risks about the two specific heads of concern which I noted, I rather doubt it. But I do think it may point to taking a rather different view about the question of some sort of compensation. If you are pitching people out involuntarily, at an age well short of the expectation at which they joined, I think that strengthens the case for at least having an option of easing the passage.

1187. PETER SHORE: Indeed, and that would be the normal expectation anyway when redundant people are made redundant in other occupations?

MICHAEL QUINLAN: Yes.

1188. PETER SHORE: Thank you. My last question to you is whether you think that the rules that presently apply to retired civil servants in taking appointments outside should also apply to former Ministers?

MICHAEL QUINLAN: In principle it seems to me the same considerations can arise and there probably ought, I would have thought, to be some process of scrutiny for dealing with that. Whether it is of precisely the same character as applies to officials, I have no particular opinion. But in principle I think there is the same sort of case. But I do think, despite the generosity with which I heard Sir Norman Fowler just now dismiss the notion of compensation, that the considerations which may point to something of that kind are, if anything, rather stronger than they would be in the Civil Service case and, again, I think the provision of some option at least deserves more thought than I have managed to give it.

PETER SHORE: Thank you.

1189. LORD NOLAN: One thing that—is this right?—one must rule out, is letting the hard cases justify the relaxation of the basic principles: that the company should not be able to buy the services of the Minister or the civil servant, both when he is in office or make use his contacts after he has left office.

MICHAEL QUINLAN: Yes. I accept that entirely. I would not be, as it were, letting the hard cases change the rules. I would deal with the hard cases by, perhaps, some sort of compensation route. Rather by saying: Well, it looks a bit rough; you can go off to firm x with which you have been dealing after only three months rather than wait two years.

1190. LORD NOLAN: Yes. That is precisely how I understood it. It is very clear. Thank you very much. We were told yesterday, and I think this surprised some of us, that the ordinary Civil Service rules do not apparently apply to a civil servant who goes to a quango, perhaps at a much higher rate of remuneration.

MICHAEL QUINLAN: I was not aware of that. It is not a type of case that I think I have come across in the defence world, which is what I know best.

LORD NOLAN: I will not pursue it with you. We are as usual, I am afraid, running short of time but I will if I may go round the table. Sir William, have you any questions to put to Sir Michael?

1191. WILLIAM UTTING: Well if I could just follow up the Business Appointments issue for one moment. The Business Appointments Committee deals with civil servants of Grade 3 and above and Permanent Secretaries deal with requests from civil servants below that level, so you will have had experience of operating this sort of system yourself as a Permanent Secretary?

MICHAEL QUINLAN: In practice as it happens, Sir William, I did not. The Ministry of Defence is a very big department and, for that reason, has two Permanent Secretaries. There was myself and a second Permanent Secretary. And just as a matter of load-splitting, the operation of the system in the Ministry of Defence was looked after by what we called the Second Permanent Secretary So I did not see what I sure was quite a large flood of cases that came up through the system. So my own detailed familiarity with that would be pretty low.

1192. WILLIAM UTTING: But you might have become aware if any particular problems had arisen in that area? I would have assumed that there might be more demand for people at Grade 5, say, than for people like me when I left the Civil Service?

MICHAEL QUINLAN: I can see a number of arguments why one might have supposed the use would be higher, by implication, at the earlier age, but no particular problem surfaced to me. I am not aware that there was a general unease about how the system operated—unease either on the business side or on the individual side.

1193. WILLIAM UTTING: It was suggested to us yesterday that in view of the changes that are taking place in the Civil Service, the definition of a senior civil servant might be re-drawn and that therefore officials at, say, Grade 5 and above might come within the provenance of the Business Appointments Committee in future. Would you see that as desirable or necessary?

MICHAEL QUINLAN: I do not have a very strong opinion. The only hesitation I have is simply one about what the volume would be. The Business Appointments Committee is an august body with lots of busy people like yourselves, Chairman. I just wonder whether they would welcome, or whether their business would be aided, by a further load resulting from an extension of the ambit.

1194. WILLIAM UTTING: If I could move on just for one question about appointments to non-departmental public bodies and quangos. An impression is sometimes created that Secretaries of State and Ministers are personally involved in all appointments to all of these bodies. I doubt very much, from my own personal experience, that that view can possibly be sustained by the evidence. I wondered what that looked like from your perspective as a Permanent Secretary? How far were you involved in advising Secretaries of State and Ministers on appointments to NDPBs and quangos?

MICHAEL QUINLAN: Only to a limited degree. Though I had five years as Permanent Secretary under Mr King and others in the Department of Employment, most of my time was in Defence and Defence is not a great spawner of quangos—if quangos are spawned! Therefore this did not come my way a lot. I certainly do not recall

having had any particular unease that there was a kind of bias which was inappropriate to the role creeping into the selections which Ministers made.

WILLIAM UTTING: Thank you. Thank you Chairman.

1195. ANNE WARBURTON: Could I ask you a quick question, Sir Michael? You make a point in your papers that you kindly supplied to us of the question of what sanction there is if advice is given to a retiring civil servant, and if we would follow some of the ideas put forward here, it would also be for a Minister who actually did not want to take advice that that appointment was not appropriate: what could then happen. To save time, I wonder what your reaction would be if I were to put the proposition that perhaps no detailed sanctions are required because the media are always with us and perhaps because the firm itself might withdraw?

MICHAEL QUINLAN: I think that is probably right. I do not have a proposal for a sanction. Indeed I do not see one. But I think the fact that there is not a sanction—this is my main point—put an especial onus upon operating the system in a way which is fair to everyone. I would not want to see the system strained so that people exploit the absence of formal sanction.

ANNE WARBURTON: Thank you.

1196. TOM KING: It is a great pleasure to be advised once again by a Rolls-Royce mind that I recognise very well. Can I ask you this question Sir Michael? The issue that you raised particularly about serving officers. If we start introducing some automatic cooling-off period or whatever, and paid for it, it is expensive for the country and it is expensive in two ways. Not only in the financial consequences, but in many cases because of the loss of very real personal contribution, very often in the export field which many of these people can discharge. If I remember rightly, on the serving officers in some of these areas, did we not under the system consult with competitors in this country to make sure that there was not perceived to be domestic advantage and that we were not favouring one company as against another in that recruitment field? Is that right?

MICHAEL QUINLAN: Yes we did, and I think it was also done occasionally for a senior civilian. I think that is entirely proper. I think that is part of what ought to go into the Advisory Committee's consideration, or the Government's—or a Department's submission to the Advisory Committee—on what the balance of factors was.

1197. TOM KING: And without necessarily going into individual details, you used to consult me on the number and one tried to recognise what was in the national interest and the personal interests: not to unduly prejudice because of public perception or political embarrassment or anything the position of individuals and to give them a fair position. I do not remember any criticisms when we did actually waive some of the normal cooling-off periods or reduced them. Is that correct?

MICHAEL QUINLAN: That is right.

1198. TOM KING: Because of the safeguards that were operating?

MICHAEL QUINLAN: Yes. I certainly cannot recall a case, other than by hearsay many years ago in one case, I cannot recall a direct case where there was grumble from that side. I can recall three or four cases in which I think the individual felt that the Advisory Committee had been a bit heavier than the real consideration warranted.

1199. TOM KING: But do you happen to remember—and it may be an unfair question—whether any of them then were not able to take up the position, even though it meant a slightly greater delay? Did it lose them opportunities?

MICHAEL QUINLAN: Not that I recall. No, not that I recall. But then I would not have been sure of all the details.

1200. TOM KING: Just a quick last question on something rather different. We have looked at the question of Members of Parliament and attention was drawn to the fact that Members of Parliament receive no training. They arrive having been elected, in a by-election or an election, and suddenly turn up in the House of Commons and suddenly find themselves thrown into this completely new environment. The same is true of Ministers. And Departments are very good at loading Ministers with tremendous piles of policy briefs on what all the policies of the Department are. Do you think it is a bit thin on some help and advice to a new junior Minister who suddenly finds that, because of his political position or prominence in the Party or whatever, he is suddenly made a Minister? Ought there to be more help in the business of being a Minister?

MICHAEL QUINLAN: I think it would be quite salutary to offer—I won't say a sort of formal course which you have to pass before you become a Minister——

TOM KING: That would be really a—!

MICHAEL QUINLAN: Yes—I might reflect further upon that, Chairman! But I do think it would be useful if the prospective or new Ministers wish to receive it. But I would not guarantee that all of them would. To offer some further grounding in just the mechanics, if you like, of the job.

1201. TOM KING: But not seriously that the Prime Minister should say: "I am offering this appointment subject to receiving the requisite grades in your exam!"

MICHAEL QUINLAN: I think that would be pushing it a little far out!

TOM KING: Thank you very much.

1202. DIANA WARWICK: You said, Sir Michael, that if enough people think there is a problem, then there is a problem?

MICHAEL QUINLAN: In this kind of thing, where one is talking about public confidence.

1203. DIANA WARWICK: We have been told that two-thirds of the public think that MPs and Ministers are using their parliamentary position for personal gain, and that has been very much linked in a lot of the evidence that we have had with MPs lobbying on behalf of particular interests. I wondered if I could ask you, from your experience of advising Ministers and watching the process, whether first of all you think there were methods of lobbying that were frankly unacceptable in your experience, and whether there were ever meetings with MPs with Ministers on issues that were outside their constituencies and where it was clear that they were pursuing a particular interest—and it was known to everybody that they were?

MICHAEL QUINLAN: I cannot remember such a case. MPs often came in to see Ministers and put arguments which I might not think much of, but I do not recall attempts to adduce arguments which I thought improper or to use the MP position in ways that I thought did not fit the role.

1204. DIANA WARWICK: And would it have been known if they were representing a particular interest—a company that was bidding, for example, for a particular contract? I am thinking obviously particularly of MoD with its huge procurement responsibilities. I mean, would it be known, I think, is the point I am getting at?

MICHAEL QUINLAN: I would have thought most of the time, yes. One cannot exclude the possibility that there was some obscure relationship which was concealed. But, one way and another, one would become aware most of the time obviously whether there was a constituency interest or if there was some other kind of business link. I should be rather surprised if it were possible for an MP to rely on concealing a link.

1205. DIANA WARWICK: I am really trying to pursue the issue of whether or not it would be well-known by the civil servants who were advising Ministers as well as by Ministers that there was a link. I am not suggesting the link is improper, only that it would be well-known.

MICHAEL QUINLAN: In general I would think yes. It would depend of course upon what the exact character of the link was—whether it had a formal character, whether as it were it had to be recorded somewhere. But for the most part I think people who worked, not in the procurement business, would have a pretty clear sense of where people were coming from and why.

DIANA WARWICK: Thank you.

MARTIN JACOMB: I have no questions.

1206. LORD NOLAN: Well, Sir Michael, we are very grateful for your advice and for the great care you have taken to present it in a full and clear form. Thank you very much.

Lord Armstrong, good afternoon.

LORD ARMSTRONG OF ILMINSTER
LORD ARMSTRONG OF ILMINSTER: Good afternoon, my Lord.

1207. LORD NOLAN: You have helpfully written to us on more than one occasion, so we of the committee, having read what you have written, have a good idea of what your views are. Would you like to start by giving us a short summary of what you have said or would you rather go straight into particular questions?

LORD ARMSTRONG: I am very happy to go straight into questions, my Lord Chairman, though when it comes to the second of the subjects which you said you would wish to discuss I have a bit of written paper which is, I think, being made available to members of the committee, which perhaps might save time in the oral discussion.[9]

1208. LORD NOLAN: That is on Ministers taking up appointments?

LORD ARMSTRONG: Yes.

LORD NOLAN: Yes, quite. We have a, I hope, democratic system of taking it in turns to ask the questions, and this time it is Sir Martin Jacomb's turn, so I will ask him, please, to take you through your evidence.

1209. MARTIN JACOMB: Lord Armstrong, I think actually you refer to it as the second subject, and it is, but we might start with that, because it is obviously very important. Just to get it on the record, I think I am right in saying that, amongst your other jobs, you are a director of N.M. Rothschild.

LORD ARMSTRONG: I am—a non-executive director.

MARTIN JACOMB: A non-executive director. I thought it was sensible to get that on the record——

LORD ARMSTRONG: I agree.

1210. MARTIN JACOMB: —because it comes up later, and later on we can deal with the question of Lord Wakeham. Could you summarise for us very shortly where you stand on the question of Ministers taking up appointments in the private sector after they leave ministerial office?

LORD ARMSTRONG: Yes, Sir Martin. It's clearly very important that Ministers, like former civil servants, should not, certainly in the period immediately following their ceasing to be Ministers, take on industrial or commercial appointments which are, in some sense, improper because of a connection which existed during their recent time as Ministers or for other reasons. But I think that it would be undesirable and sad if the rules about this were so strict that a Minister was almost prevented from being able to take on any such appointment when he ceased to be a Minister. It may be that there should be an interval, as with the senior civil servants, of a minimum of three months, and longer if somebody thinks that's appropriate.

I think there are two points. A point that was being made by Sir Michael was that Ministers, like former civil servants, have talents and general experience which can be used to the benefit of the industrial and commercial life of the country after they cease to be in ministerial office and are leaving the public service, and if the rules were too draconian, we should not only lose the benefit of that experience, but, given the chances and changes of ministerial office and the unpredictability of departure from it, I think that if potential ministerial candidates felt that, once they had become a Minister they would bar themselves from taking on appointments after they ceased to be Ministers, it might affect their willingness to accept ministerial office in the first place.

MARTIN JACOMB: Yes, but there is a problem of perception right now.

[9]See Evidence, p. 531.

LORD ARMSTRONG: Yes, there is, I agree.

1211. MARTIN JACOMB: And, given that problem of perception, do you think there is still really a case for a marked difference between the fairly strict rules which apply to civil servants, such as you yourself were, on the one hand and Ministers on the other? In your memorandum I think you come down rather against strict rules, but, on reflection, could you help us there?

LORD ARMSTRONG: If one were talking about the reality, I should like to believe that anybody who had been sufficiently responsible to hold ministerial office could be expected to behave responsibly and sensibly, consulting whoever was appropriate, when he ceased to be in such office. But I readily accept that we are dealing with appearances as well as with the reality, and I actually think that it could well be useful to have a similar arrangement for Ministers, as we now have for civil servants—that is to say, a business appointments committee like the Carlisle Committee, which would consider proposals for Ministers to take up employment outside and would make recommendations on those proposals to the Prime Minister, on the basis of clearly understood criteria. I think that at the end of the day the decision has to rest with the Minister concerned and the Prime Minister. They must take responsibility for their decisions, but I believe that the existence of such a committee and the knowledge that it had been consulted and, in the appropriate cases, had approved what was proposed would be a valuable reassurance both for the Ministers concerned and to the public at large.

1212. MARTIN JACOMB: Thank you very much. Just going further with that, one can see why it would be impossible to have such a procedure entirely open at the time, because the prospective employer might well not want to reveal the thing publicly until the employment arrangement was actually concluded. But would there be any argument against publishing in retrospect, ex post facto, the minutes of the meetings of the committee which considered such a possible employment?

LORD ARMSTRONG: I should have thought that the only objection would be the possibility of arguments about commercial confidence. There might in many cases, I think, be elements of information or items in the discussion which were commercially sensitive and might preclude publication of minutes.

1213. MARTIN JACOMB: You said in your opening remarks that, unless Ministers were free to take employment in the private sector after a reasonable interval, there might be difficulty in recruiting them. Do you have personal experience of that?

LORD ARMSTRONG: I don't, because of course they have been freer than civil servants to take up appointments after leaving ministerial office, so I have no personal experience of that possibility being a deterrent, but I think that in some cases it could be a real deterrent.

I think it is fair to say that the situation is different for a Minister, because in most cases the civil servant is going on retirement or after a period, as a result of a considered decision to leave the public service. It is, therefore, as it were, foreseen, and of course he is in receipt, if it is on retirement, of a pension. In the case of a Minister, his employment in that office can cease overnight as a result of a general election or a decision by the Prime Minister that it's time for him to move out. It seems to me that it might be necessary to consider whether any rules to which such a committee operated should take account of those differences. It can obviously be a traumatic event to lose office in those circumstances. It can also have financial consequences which create embarrassment.

1214. MARTIN JACOMB: Yes. Thank you very much. Could I just go to another area, about the behaviour of Ministers while they hold office—gifts and hospitality—which you deal with in your memorandum, and the question of the openness of such gifts and hospitality. Would you like to give us in summary your observations about those areas?

LORD ARMSTRONG: Openness is clearly an important protection against improper acceptance of gifts. I think that the general rules that are set out in questions of procedure for Ministers as general rules are reasonable and I wouldn't want to propose any general change in them or addition to them. I think rules in this area are extremely difficult to police and I think you have to consider case by case, and the judgment has to be made according to the general rules set out in the questions of procedure for Ministers, but in my experience it is very difficult to provide in such a document of general rules for every circumstance that may arise, and therefore something has to be left for individual discretion in individual cases to suit circumstances.

I think that Ministers should, if they are in any doubt whatever, consult. I think they should consult the Prime Minister. They can consult their Permanent Secretary in the first instance. If, after that, they are still in doubt, they should consult the Prime Minister, and the Prime Minister may want to take advice on precedent from the Secretary of the Cabinet, who keeps a precedent book on these matters, or of course he may want to take advice from political colleagues—for instance, the Chief Whip. If there is to be any policing of the activities of Ministers in this area, it should be done by other Ministers, or by politicians, and not by civil servants. Clearly the Cabinet Secretary will advise on precedent and so on.

1215. MARTIN JACOMB: So your role there was really confined to advice and not to investigation or quasi-judicial——

LORD ARMSTRONG: I never undertook any investigation. I was consulted by the Prime Minister on a number of cases, which then of course took their place in the precedent book. I was consulted on one or two cases by Ministers direct, where I tried to tell them what would be the advice that I should give to the Prime Minister if I was consulted by him. But I didn't consider that I was or should be asked to, as it were, give approval or clearance, and I don't think that's an appropriate role for the Cabinet Secretary in relation to Ministers.

1216. MARTIN JACOMB: Yes. Openness in relation to hospitality is very difficult, you feel? I think what you say is that Ministers might be unduly reluctant to accept hospitality if they had to——

LORD ARMSTRONG: There is such an enormous range of possibilities in the hospitality field, isn't there, from a casual drink or a lunch to attendance at Wimbledon or somewhere or some kind of overseas visit?

1217. MARTIN JACOMB: Perhaps I could interrupt you by asking you this. Perhaps that was too general a question. During your time as Cabinet Secretary, and indeed both before and afterwards for that matter, have you detected any deterioration in the standards that Ministers of the Crown have followed in relation to gifts and hospitality generally?

LORD ARMSTRONG: I have seen what seemed to me, looking from outside, to be unwise decisions, but as to whether they were symptomatic of a general decline in standards I don't think I do think that.

1218. MARTIN JACOMB: Thank you very much. Could I just come on to this? During your long central experience have you come across cases of the misuse of powers by Ministers in such areas as appointments to quangos or trying to generate contributions to party funds or even obtaining employment for themselves?

LORD ARMSTRONG: I have not come across cases in that area. I think it has to be said that the Ministers whom I served outside the Cabinet Office took an interest in appointments to quangos in their areas: they expected to be consulted about proposals for appointments, and I would not myself have expected to approve such appointments without consulting the Secretary of State or the Minister in charge of the Department. Those matters were taken an interest in. But I don't think I ever met a case where I felt that the Minister's interest was being improperly exercised to promote a particular political interest or a particular personal interest. I suppose it does sometimes happen in these fields that in non-governmental bodies which are close to the activities of a Department Ministers like to feel that they know something about the people who are appointed to quangos, either to know them directly or to have a chance of meeting them, or to have a full account of their qualifications and their experience. I have known of cases where the Minister said that, before he agreed an appointment, he would like to meet the person concerned, and then I would ask the person concerned to come in and he or she and I would have half an hour with the Minister. That seemed to me to be a perfectly reasonable exercise of the Minister's right to know whom he was appointing.

MARTIN JACOMB: Yes, but nowhere near improper.

LORD ARMSTRONG: Nowhere near improper.

1219. MARTIN JACOMB: Thank you very much. I was going to switch very, very briefly to a final question about the position of civil servants. Would you like to say something about Lord Wakeham's appointment now? I know you have given us a document about it.

LORD ARMSTRONG: I don't want to spend the time of the committee setting it out in full. I thought that in the public comment on it there was insufficient recognition of the relative remoteness of any connection which Lord Wakeham had with Rothschild's during his time as Secretary of State for Energy. In relation to electricity privatisation, Rothschild's were not advising the Secretary of State or the Department; they were advising those who were on the other side of the fence, if that's the right way to describe it, the regional electricity boards and Hanson Plc about their bid for PowerGen, so the connection was extraordinarily remote. Rothschild's were asked during Lord Wakeham's time as Secretary of State for Energy in 1991, now four years ago, to make a study of the options for the future of the coal industry, but that request was made after it had already been announced that the government were not going to proceed with coal privatisation during the currency of that Parliament, not until after a succeeding general election, if they were returned; and of course when Lord Wakeham was appointed a director of Rothschild's he had been away from the Department of Energy for three years and out of the government for over six months. I tried to look at it obviously, as I think a Carlisle Committee might have looked at it, and it didn't seem to me that the appointment was one which they would have wished to oppose or would have wished to delay.

1220. MARTIN JACOMB: Thank you very much. Just switching to the position of civil servants, there are very clear rules there about the acceptance of appointments after they leave office. Those work well in your opinion, do they, or how would you like to see them amended, tightened up or varied?

LORD ARMSTRONG: I wouldn't want to see them amended. We reviewed them a number of times while I was still Cabinet Secretary, and there were those who felt that the periods should be longer. As you know, the present arrangement is that you are required during the first two years after retirement to seek approval, and not thereafter, and the committee can recommend deferring the taking up of an appointment for up to two years. There were those who suggested that that was too short a period and that it should be three years or even five years. That seemed to the government to be too great an interference with the right of the individual. The fact is that events move very fast in most of these fields: after six months you are pretty out of date about what is going on and after two years you are very out of date, and I think two years, therefore, is quite long enough. I of course have been the subject of this process when I left the public service at the end of 1987 and I can only say that I thought that the decisions that were taken in my case were very fair and reasonable. They were for extended periods, but I thought that in the circumstances those decisions were reasonable and I had no problem with them.

1221. MARTIN JACOMB: Of course the perception difficulty may come from the fact that there could be a perception that there is a nod and a wink while the civil servant is in office dealing with the industrial company which is a contractor to that Department, for example. Nothing is said, but there's a nod and a wink, and the favour is done then, and therefore the length of time between leaving the Civil Service and gaining the private sector employment is not particularly material. The harm would have been done whether it was one, two or three years.

LORD ARMSTRONG: Yes. You are expected to declare if you have had relationships with a company that you are joining, which would enable the committee to probe to see whether there might have been any such nod and a wink. I can't actually remember any case where there were nods and winks, but you may know more than I do.

1222. MARTIN JACOMB: No, I certainly don't, no. I was just asking for your views and your experience. There again, would you think there was anything to be said for more openness in the process by which the approval was given to the private sector employment, albeit on an ex post facto basis?

LORD ARMSTRONG: I think it would have to be ex post facto. I would see myself no difficulty in the Prime Minister making some statement about why he had given his permission. It is a Prime Ministerial decision, and to that extent I think that the responsibility must rest with him, to decide both what action to take on any recommendation he receives from an advisory committee and what he is going to say about it. That is why, on the whole, I think that is when the openness should occur rather than in the previous process, but I would be in favour of it being a matter for openness—that the matter had been considered by the Prime Minister on the basis of a recommendation from the advisory committee and that for the following reasons he had decided so-and-so.

MARTIN JACOMB: Thank you very much. I mustn't take up all the time, so that will be my last question.

LORD ARMSTRONG: Very good, Sir Martin.

LORD NOLAN: Lord Armstrong, I know it is absolutely essential for you to be away by 1 o'clock, because you've got to catch an aeroplane.

LORD ARMSTRONG: A flexible 1 o'clock.

1223. LORD NOLAN: We'll try to keep it exactly. I hope I won't exceed my ration as chairman if I ask you just two questions. The first is this. Staying with the Minister taking up a post or wanting to take up a post in industry after he leaves office, a ban on his doing so is likely to have greater financial consequences in his case than in the case of a civil servant, or may well do so. How does one recognise that and attempt to ameliorate any injustice caused? You can't relax the rules, can you?

LORD ARMSTRONG: No, you can't. You can't relax the rules. I think you might say, if you were in doubt about whether the period ought to be three months of delay or longer, that there would be a bias in favour of making the period shorter rather than longer if you were considering just the interests of the Minister concerned, but the rules and the propriety must take priority.

1224. LORD NOLAN: Yes. Sir Michael Quinlan was floating the idea that there might be a case for compensation if, by reason of his period in office, a Minister was placed at an unfair disadvantage in the labour market.

LORD ARMSTRONG: There are some quite difficult questions about how long that should last, what it should consist of. I can't remember whether there is any such arrangement.

LORD NOLAN: I believe that there's a redundancy payment now.

LORD ARMSTRONG: I believe there's some kind of redundancy payment for a short period.

TOM KING: Three months, I think.

LORD ARMSTRONG: Yes, and one would obviously take that into account. But I wouldn't go to compensate beyond that.

1225. LORD NOLAN: I wonder if I may go to a quite different subject, back to the time when you were secretary to the Cabinet. You mentioned occasions when the Prime Minister of the day had consulted you because there were some worrying allegations about a particular Minister, and you told us that you yourself never investigated or adjudicated on such cases. Without going into any particular case, can you tell us how the investigation was carried out? Was it with the Law Officers or the Lord Chancellor or how?

LORD ARMSTRONG: I don't remember a case where there was a necessity for investigation of that kind. It was sometimes the case that a Minister, or sometimes his Permanent Secretary on his behalf, would say "We have this problem. My Minister has been given a gift or has been offered a gift. What should we do about it?" In that case I might ask, if I needed to know more about it, but usually the way in which the case was stated would give one the background one needed, and then one would say, looking back at the precedents, "I think such-and-such in this case", but it was very much on the basis of advice, not on any prescriptive or mandatory basis.

1226. LORD NOLAN: But if it was a case in which facts had to be established, was there a machinery——

LORD ARMSTRONG: No. I think I would have said to the Prime Minister, if he had asked, "I think you should ask" or "you should get your Parliamentary Private Secretary to ask" or "I think you should get the Chief Whip to find out"—or possibly the Lord Chancellor, though I am not so sure about that—for this additional information. I don't think it's a very satisfactory arrangement for the Secretary of the Cabinet to be put in the position of conducting an investigation into that sort of matter. The only exception to that would be if there were security considerations. Clearly there is a proper official role for the Secretary of the Cabinet in relation to such matters.

LORD NOLAN: Thank you very much. Now, if I may, I'll go round the table. Diana.

1227. DIANA WARWICK: Lord Armstrong, if I can bring you back to Ministerial conduct, you said that anyone who has held Ministerial office in this country could be expected to behave responsibly and sensibly, and I'm sure that's absolutely right.

LORD ARMSTRONG: I said I should like to believe that.

1228. DIANA WARWICK: You would like to believe it, yes. Well, I concur. And I think that is based on the fact that Ministers know what the rules are and adhere to them, but it is precisely because the rules were allegedly broken or at least, as I think you put it, "unwise decisions were taken", among other things, that this committee was set up. Sorry, Tom?

TOM KING: No—sorry.

DIANA WARWICK: Therefore, it was for precisely these sorts of issues, among others, that this committee was set up, to advise to see whether we could help to put things right in terms of public perception of what Ministers and MPs did. We've been looking at Civil Service rules in relation to gifts and hospitality and in relation to Ministerial appointments, and we have dealt with Ministerial appointments, but in most government Departments gift and hospitality are registered, or recorded in some way. That isn't the case in relation to gifts and hospitality to Ministers. Do you think that the time has come for them to be registered in that way? Do you think that would be a useful protection in these circumstances?

LORD ARMSTRONG: I would be reluctant to go that far, because I think there is a considerable element of self-policing about this. For instance, if you accept hospitality, you will be seen to accept it—other people will be aware; the act itself is open—and the penalties for acting improperly for a Minister can be very severe. They can be not just loss of office but destruction of a career, perhaps even loss of a seat in Parliament, and all the penalties that go with it. I would expect a Minister to be conscious of those sanctions, if that is the right word—those penalties—that he could incur if he took the wrong decision and that was discovered. As I heard one member of the committee say, the media are always with us. I think one has to assume that, if you are a Minister, anything you do of this kind may well become a matter of public knowledge. You should, therefore, decide what you are going to do in the light of that. If you feel comfortable that you have a good justification for doing what is proposed or accepting the hospitality that is proposed, that's fine. Then if it does become a matter of public knowledge, you've got a good defence: you can show that you have thought about it and have taken a reasoned view. There may be some people who think you have taken the wrong view, but at least it's a reasoned view. I would prefer to keep policing arrangements in this area to a minimum and to rely, as it were, on those sanctions, which I think in this day and age are pretty devastating.

1229. DIANA WARWICK: So you would rely really on the press in what would be rare circumstances?

LORD ARMSTRONG: I would rely upon the Minister's consciousness that he might be required to defend what he had done not just to his colleagues or to the Prime Minister but more widely.

1230. DIANA WARWICK: Thank you. Could I ask a totally different question? That is in relation to the ethos of the Civil Service. I can't think of another word for it.

LORD ARMSTRONG: No, it's a perfectly good word.

1231. DIANA WARWICK: It's been said in relation to the delegation of responsibility and powers that there are those coming into the Civil Service who, because they are new to the Civil Service, might not be accustomed to its ethos, and therefore a code of ethics and a code of conduct is useful. I wondered if you could tell us something, from your experience of business and commerce since you have left the Civil Service, whether you perceive any difference in the ethics that apply in those circumstances from the ethics that you defended in the Civil Service.

LORD ARMSTRONG: I think that most of the basic principles are probably very similar. I think that their application in the private sector may be different from in the public sector, because the nature of the business that one is talking about is different. Perhaps I don't need to run over ground which I covered in a speech that I made in the House of Lords yesterday in the Civil Service debate. I haven't on the whole felt that there was need for a more detailed code of conduct, because it's very difficult, again, to define every circumstance that arises and I think the important thing is to get the principles clearly defined and then to make sure that people relate what they are proposing to do to those principles, so that the question with which they face themselves is "Is what I am proposing to do consistent with the principles?" and not "Is this within the rules?" and "If it's not covered by the rules, it's OK" To treat this sort of code as if it were almost a legal code—you were in trouble if you broke the code, but you weren't in trouble if you didn't break the code, even if what you did might be in principle undesirable—I don't think is the nature of the thing we're talking about. On the whole I would prefer to leave it at the kind of guidance that exists in the memorandum which I issued when I was in government and in the Civil Service "Code of Management Practice". I don't actually feel very strongly about the code of conduct which is now being proposed by the Select Committee and by the government and I wouldn't wish to object to its use in the form now suggested to be amended by the government.

I am a little doubtful about external appeal, on two grounds really. First of all, I think that the grounds of appeal as set out in the code as at present drafted are rather too wide. Secondly, I still believe that it would be preferable to keep the process of appeal within the system rather than introduce even a semi-external character like the First Civil Service Commissioner. The reason why I feel that is that I think that the knowledge that this process of appeal exists and has been had recourse to will not do any good to the relationship of confidence between Ministers and civil servants. That confidence will probably be less eroded if the appeal is within the system, through the Permanent Secretary and then to the Head of the Home Civil Service, rather than if it is to some external body.

The objection that has been made to that is that some civil servant who felt the necessity to appeal would be deterred from doing so by being intimidated by the process or by a fear that an appeal to the Head of the Home Civil Service would not do his career prospects any good. I don't know that an appeal to the First Civil Service Commissioner is any less intimidating than an appeal to the Head of the Home Civil Service and I don't think that, in terms of its effect on career prospects, whether the appeal is to the Head of the Home Civil Service or to the First Commissioner is particularly relevant. What if anything is going to affect his career prospects is the fact that he has decided to appeal. I don't actually think it will necessarily affect his career prospects, but I don't think it makes much difference which way the appeal goes from that point of view.

DIANA WARWICK: Thank you.

1232. TOM KING: The point I was muttering about just now, and I apologise to Diana Warwick, was not that we are here because Ministers have misbehaved, but because there are allegations that Ministers have misbehaved.

DIANA WARWICK: I said that.

1233. TOM KING: If you did, I certainly apologise. We have dealt with one aspect of that, and the allegations about Norman Fowler were the illustration of it, with

people rushing off to take advantage of their immediate past appointments and activities, and that, in Norman Fowler's case, was clearly and manifestly not true. There was another case, in which the Cabinet Secretary is very much involved, more recently. What I took from the answer here was this. How is a Prime Minister protected? He's got something like 100 members in the government. They've all got their own lives to lead and their own responsibilities to discharge. Allegations have been made against Ministers in various ways, and it's part of the political process that people will try and make allegations against Ministers. There are many people in journalism whose whole business it is to try and uncover something that shall be to the disadvantage and disrespect of Ministers. You have said that really it is very difficult for the Cabinet Secretary to be an adjudicator, and I understand that, or much of an investigator. So in that case, what protection have Ministers themselves and the Prime Minister got so that it can be seen that such allegations can be dealt with in a way that commands public confidence?

LORD ARMSTRONG: You're quite right, Mr King. I do think that it's difficult and perhaps inappropriate for the Cabinet Secretary to be saddled with that, for obvious reasons. I think that there's a great deal of politics in allegations of this kind, as you have just said, and I think that the remedy ought to lie in the political network. In other words, if the Prime Minister needs advice or needs somebody to look into something, it had better be done by the government Chief Whip or by some other Minister rather than by a civil servant.

1234. TOM KING: But if the government Chief Whip says "Mr Jones is a splendid Minister", do you think that commands public confidence and would be adequate for all occasions, or would it be seen as "He would, wouldn't he"?

LORD ARMSTRONG: I don't know that a certificate of good conduct from the Cabinet Secretary is going to be any better in that regard. I think that is to put too heavy a weight on the civil servant and his relationship to Ministers. I don't think that he can be a certificate of good conduct or a white sheet, as it were, for Ministers. I remain of the view that those matters have to be dealt with at the political level.

TOM KING: Thank you. I see the difficulties. I think you see the difficulties of that solution as well, which I think is a real problem.

LORD ARMSTRONG: Of course I do. Again the sanction is the fact that the media are always with us and that the Chief Whip will be expected not just to pour a bottle of whitewash over the thing but to look into it and to report to the Prime Minister.[10]

1235. TOM KING: One of the things that command public confidence we have talked about—should Ministers be subject to the same rules as the civil servants on this—and you suggest perhaps some parallel committee, another committee. I'm not quite clear why, even if there was some recognition of slightly different circumstances, the same committee couldn't do both jobs.

LORD ARMSTRONG: I think it could. I am only concerned about the burden of work, and I think the criteria might well be slightly different. It might be,

---

[10]This should be read with the second paragraph of Lord Armstrong's letter to Lord Nolan of 7 February, see Evidence p. 531.

therefore, for the convenience of everybody concerned that you had one body which had its own criteria for dealing with Ministers and another body for dealing with civil servants. But I haven't any objection in principle to having the one committee do both.

1236. TOM KING: Thank you very much. One very quick further point. Sir Michael Quinlan drew attention to the fact that, although you both use the phrase that civil servants "are required" to behave in a certain way after they go, there is absolutely no sanction on them if they decide to ignore such requirements. Do you think there should be?

LORD ARMSTRONG: In my experience no company was very willing to take on somebody on conditions which did not coincide with the decision taken by the Prime Minister on the advice of the advisory committee. I can't remember any case where a civil servant has gone ahead and I would indeed be reluctant to introduce further sanctions, unless there was a clear need for them.

TOM KING: Thank you very much.

1237. LORD THOMSON: Can I quickly go back to the point that Tom King raised about the committee to deal with the special situation of Cabinet Ministers? I should declare an interest as a Member of the Carlisle Committee, and it's a very excellent committee. I am a little doubtful about whether the burden of the special position of Cabinet Ministers is wholly appropriate to our committee as at present constituted, for the rather special reason that the occasion on which there is the problem on a big scale is the occasion of a general election, where there are a number of unemployed, ex-Cabinet Ministers and where, under our system, it is the Prime Minister who has the ultimate responsibility, and then it would lie with the incoming Prime Minister. I just wonder against that background whether one might not need a rather special kind of advisory committee that would carry even greater authority and weight than our committee carries.

LORD ARMSTRONG: Any committee which has Lord Carlisle and Lord Thomson on it has pretty good weight.

LORD THOMSON: And Mr Shore.

LORD ARMSTRONG: And Mr Shore. So in terms of weight I don't think it's a problem. I think in terms of workload it might be, because you are all busy men in other spheres and you could be, as you say, faced with a spate of these things. That would be true, no doubt, for a special Ministerial committee. I think it is workload as much as anything, and possibly the slight difference in criteria, if there was one, which leads me to wonder.

LORD THOMSON: Perhaps we need Lord Nolan.

LORD ARMSTRONG: I fear the Lord Chancellor will be asking for more Law Lords if we do that. The Treasury wouldn't like that.

1238. PETER SHORE: On the standards of conduct of the Civil Service during your period as Cabinet Secretary, that period coincided with the arrival in Downing Street of an unusually powerful, very forceful and very clear-headed Prime Minister. Did that particular combination of qualities in the Prime Minister lead to pressures on the standards of neutrality of the Civil Service? Was there pressure to, as it were, shift the traditional neutrality into a position more favourable to government policy, government thinking, than had previously been the case?

LORD ARMSTRONG: No, there was never that sort of pressure. Certainly in the process of appointments, where I perhaps saw it most closely, Mrs Thatcher was anxious that the appointments that were made of the senior civil servants—the grade 1s and grade 2s—should take account not only of their skill as advisers to Ministers on matters of policy but also of their qualifications for managing large Departments. She liked to see people who were doers, who would be effective in managing Departments and who would go along with the need to manage the Department efficiently and effectively. I never detected any signs of political bias behind that at all. I was never asked by Mrs Thatcher, and I never asked myself, about the political leanings of particular civil servants who were recommended for appointment. If I had been asked, I should have refused to say. That, I don't think, did become an issue. I should think she made quite a lot of appointments of people who would not be natural Conservatives.

1239. PETER SHORE: Did the same pressures affect, in your judgment, appointments to outside bodies—public bodies?

LORD ARMSTRONG: I saw much less of that, because most of those are done at departmental level and they don't cross the Cabinet Secretary's desk. No, I don't think I detected anything in the Prime Minister's approach to those public bodies to which she had to make appointments. This is of course relevant to the museum world, of which I am part now. It was suggested that I had been appointed to be chairman of the trustees of the Victoria and Albert Museum as an emissary of Mrs Thatcher in order to put into effect her desires, whatever they might have been, to influence the activities in the museum. Nothing, I assure you, could be further from the truth.

PETER SHORE: Thank you.

1240. ANNE WARBURTON: If I might put a question about the Civil Service and the code, some concern has been expressed to us about the growing change in the composition of the Civil Service in terms of more people coming in from outside and for short terms and so forth. I wondered whether perhaps, in considering the code, you thought that that would be a way of helping to absorb the management reform effect on the Civil Service or whether that is something which you are concerned about.

LORD ARMSTRONG: This has all happened since I retired, so I speak rather unadvisedly, in that sense, on it. I think that there could be a problem on the ethos side with somebody coming in from outside, and from that point of view, if the code of conduct helps in that regard, that would be a good thing. I think that, even without the code of conduct, somebody coming in absorbs that ethos pretty quickly, because the ethos is all around you, as it were, when you come into a thing like that. But if the code of conduct helps to articulate it and to make it clear to somebody coming in like that at an early stage, well and good, that's fine.

I have worried a little bit about the effect of putting some of these people on five-year contracts, and I think this is where there is a difference between the public service and the private sector. The issue is not just one of effectiveness and efficiency in performance. In those terms clearly a fixed-term contract which you review after four years and decide whether to renew it or let it lapse has a lot to commend it. It would not, in my view, have so much to commend it if the effect was that, in the time when the contract was coming up for renewal, the civil servant concerned trimmed the advice he was giving to his Minister with a view to increasing the prospect of his contract being renewed, rather than giving the advice which he felt was the best honest, dispassionate, impartial advice he could give. I haven't any evidence that that is happening or has happened. There is a bit of anecdotage around, but I wouldn't put it higher than that. For that reason, I welcome the fact that in the later papers on the whole the emphasis has been on indefinite contracts with a review, rather than on fixed five-year contracts which then have to be renewed.

ANNE WARBURTON: Thank you, Lord Armstrong.

1241. PROF. ANTHONY KING: Could I come back to the question of politicisation, and I don't here mean party politicisation but something else, which will become clear? I have been struck over the last few years, in going to what I'll call semi-public gatherings—say, small conferences on Chatham House rules—by the fact that senior civil servants have, in my presence, advocated government policy, expressed enthusiasm for government policy in a very striking, committed kind of way, and that surprised me just as much as it would have surprised me if they had distanced themselves from government policy to the same kind of degree. There have of course been cases in the past where civil servants have become publicly or semi-publicly identified with government policy. The close relationship between Edward Heath and Sir William Armstrong is well attested to. But is it your impression that over the last decade or two decades there has been a tendency for civil servants to feel that they had to identify themselves with the policy of the government of the day in a way they wouldn't have in an earlier generation?

LORD ARMSTRONG: I don't think I am conscious of a feeling that that has changed. I am certainly aware that on such occasions civil servants may well identify themselves with the policy which their Department is committed to, but in a way that is part of the formation of a civil servant, that he should be able, as it were, to defend and justify the Minister's policy, whatever he himself might privately think about it and say about it in his innermost counsels.

I think there can come a kind of personal commitment, because it is what the Department or the Minister is trying to do, even if the person concerned might in other circumstances take a different view. We all want what we are doing to be successful, and there is this kind of general identification that people want what is being done by the Department to be successful. They certainly don't want to go in there and say "This is the Minister's policy, but I don't think much of it". That's not a good position to be in.

1242. PROF. ANTHONY KING: Might particular problems arise in the case of, specially, the visible heads of some of the Next Steps agencies? Might there not be a real problem that, although they are civil servants, as they are

executing a very large chunk of government policy, they might come to be publicly identified with it in a way that wouldn't be the norm for a civil servant?

LORD ARMSTRONG: You might be referring to the Child Support Agency, I suppose, in that. I think two things about that. First of all, I think it's unwise to make a Next Steps agency of something where the process as well as the result is very much a matter of high political interest and high political controversy. I don't think the system is robust enough, at any rate yet, to stand that and I think it puts the civil servant in charge of it in a position which civil servants shouldn't be put into. So I would hesitate to create agencies like that. The other thing is that if you do create an agency like that and something goes wrong, especially if it goes badly wrong, and Murphy's law is that if something can go wrong, one day it will, when it does go wrong not only the agency itself but the whole agency principle is put into disrepute. I think it would be better not to put that kind of strain on it. One that comes to mind is the Driver and Vehicle Licensing Centre in Swansea. The controversial matter is what the licence fee should be. That is dictated and laid down by Ministers and Parliament. The process of collecting it is a matter which excites much less political interest and controversy and can more readily be left to the head of the agency to deal with.

1243. PROF. ANTHONY KING: I have only one other question, and it is under the same broad heading. If you look at the new draft code that is proposed for civil servants by the government, the emphasis is very much, not surprisingly, on the duties of civil servants. I think nothing is said about any duties that Ministers may have vis-à-vis civil servants, and presumably Ministers do have a duty not, for example, to ask civil servants to write party political speeches; perhaps they have a duty not to ask them to draft amendments for Bills being proposed by Back-Benchers. Do you think in fact the incidence of pressures of that kind on civil servants is sufficiently high, or is thought within the Civil Service to be sufficiently high, that that kind of case should also be covered by the code?

LORD ARMSTRONG: The duties of Ministers in relation to civil servants were defined by the government in their response to the Treasury and Civil Service Select Committee in, I think, 1986. They are not defined in anything like the detail that they are defined for civil servants, but the general principles are clearly laid down there, and I think that that particular section of that response to the Committee stands today. I'm afraid I haven't got it in front of me, but it has been defined—the duty of Ministers not to deceive or knowingly mislead Parliament and their duty not to put civil servants in positions which they ought not to be put into. I am not using the right words, but the words were carefully chosen at the time.

LORD NOLAN: Lord Armstrong, you have given us a great deal of time and work, both this morning and in the preparations you made for it. I can't tell you how grateful we are to you and to all our witnesses for volunteering and for doing so much to help us. Thank you.

LORD ARMSTRONG: I've enjoyed it. Thank you, my Lord Chairman.

TUESDAY 7 FEBRUARY 1995

Members Present:

The Rt. Hon. The Lord Nolan (Chairman)

Sir Clifford Boulton GCB

The Rt. Hon. The Lord Thomson of Monifieth KT DL

The Rt. Hon. Tom King CH MP

Sir William Utting CB

The Rt. Hon. Peter Shore MP

Dame Anne Warburton DCVO CMG

Witnesses:

Jeff Rooker MP

Rt. Hon. David Hunt MP, Chancellor of the Duchy of Lancaster, and Sir Robin Butler, Secretary of the Cabinet and Head of the Home Civil Service

Giles Radice MP, Chairman Treasury and Civil Service Select Committee, Sub-Committee on the Civil Service, and Professor Sue Richards, Office of Public Management

1244. LORD NOLAN: Today we pass the half-way mark in our oral evidence, as we begin our fourth week. We are still receiving, in addition, a considerable amount of documentary evidence.

Later today we shall be talking to Mr. David Hunt, the Chancellor of the Duchy of Lancaster, and to Sir Robin Butler, the Cabinet Secretary. Mr. Hunt, of course, published the Government's evidence to us yesterday and we shall be exploring that with him, though we have not yet had the opportunity as a Committee to examine it in detail.

Our other witnesses today come from the other side of the political divide but we shall see Giles Radice MP later in his non-partisan role as Secretary of the Civil Service sub-committee of the Treasury and Civil Service Select Committee. Mr. Radice will be accompanied by Ms Sue Richards, who acted as professional adviser to that sub-committee.

First, however, can I welcome back Mr. Jeff Rooker, MP, the deputy shadow Leader of the House who I know attended our proceedings as an observer when Ann Taylor gave evidence. We now look forward to hearing from him as well as seeing him! Mr. Rooker, have you prepared an opening statement which you would like to make before we go into questions?

JEFF ROOKER MP

JEFF ROOKER, MP: Yes, I have, which I can dispose of within ten minutes. Thank you very much. It is in two parts, the first part deals with ex-Ministers and the second part deals with Members' Interests—Members of the Commons that is.

In the past when a Member of Parliament, usually a Minister or ex-Minister, left the House of Commons to head up a nationalised industry or other public body the only blip was a by-election. The charge of lining one's pockets or abuse of public office was never made. It was still seen as public service. Today it is different, therefore different considerations must apply. There are no nationalised industries, only privatised companies and utilities, which are mainly monopolies and mainly unregulated. Furthermore, the process of contractorisation and government by quangos where billions of pounds of public money is involved has widened this interface. Of course, Parliament itself has created these bodies as a consequence of Government policy and therefore the interface between civil servants, Ministers and these bodies is a legitimate area of public interest.

Ex-Ministers who had no professional interest or experience in these industries prior to becoming Ministers are clearly trading on their Ministerial experience by obtaining directorships. Such transfers to companies or industries which the Minister had detailed involvement with as a departmental Minister should be made more difficult by a specific delay, as is the case with senior civil servants. I considered suggesting to this committee a delay until the following Parliament—i.e. after a general election—but for many reasons I do not believe this to be practicable. But the delay should be one or two years without exception.

Of course, the position of an ex-Minister is not straightforward. They could be remaining in the House of Commons, in the House of Lords, a private citizen in neither House or in the Euro-Parliament or Euro-Commission. In the main, ex-Members of Parliament are not very employable. There would be, in my view, considerable difficulty in preventing private citizens seeking employment. This is especially so when they have not, as MP's or Ministers, been working to a detailed employment contract such as is available to civil servants. I see no reason, however, to draw any distinction between the seniority of ex-Ministers—they should all be treated the same. If they were dealing with a company or industry then the limitations of crossing over should apply.

Of course, the ex-Minister may not be a voluntary "ex". They could have fallen out with the Prime Minister or not suit a new Prime Minister and they could, indeed, be "ex" as a result of a policy clash which had nothing whatsoever to do with their departmental duties or performance as a Minister. I believe this committee has to indicate in clear terms to the public that "some things are right" and "some things are wrong" and ex-Ministers remaining in public life and being seen to use inside information for commercial purposes without a vetting is wrong. I choose my words carefully because I would not see anything wrong in, for example, an ex-Education Secretary or Minister of Higher Eduction becoming a University Vice-Chancellor, in the same way that recently the former distinguished Permanent Secretary at the Department of Education retired and became Vice-Chancellor of one of our prominent universities. It is non-commercial. Any reasonable person would declare it to be public service.

251

On the other hand a former head of the National Health Service (or Minister for that matter) leaving for an academic post is acceptable, but for the same person to join the board of a private health company within a short time, is not.

There will be grey areas which is why an independent body is required to adjudicate, in my view. The nature of the exact duties of the ex-Minister regarding the interest or company has to be considered along with the period that they were a relevant Departmental Minister and how long ago this was. These points are relevant but must not be used as an excuse for doing nothing. I believe that a Parliamentary Ethics Advisory Office, suggested to this committee by Ann Taylor on 25th January, would be suitable for ex-Ministers to seek a ruling as to whether their new proposed interest was acceptable. If the ex-Minister did not accept the view of the Ethics Advisory Office then I believe a final decision should be made by a committee of three people, none of whom can be influenced or dismissed by any Political Party or Government, namely the Speaker of the House of Commons, the Clerk of the House of Commons and the Comptroller and Auditor General. They each hold a unique position and bring experience and judgment from different sources. Their decision should be final and if necessary should be sanctioned by suitable amendments to the House of Commons Disqualification Act which, of course, for Members of Parliament, would be the ultimate sanction as to whether they chose to follow the interest or not.

So far as Members' interests are concerned, Mr. Chairman, I just want to make it clear that—this is my own view obviously—when I was seeking election first in February 1974 I committed myself to the electorate to being a full-time Member of Parliament. No one asked me that when I was being selected as a candidate two and a half years previously—it was a personal decision that I made. At that time I was in the manufacturing industry for sixteen years prior to entering the House. I had been an apprentice toolmaker and a production manager. I was not in a field of activity where I could keep my hand in while being an MP even if I chose to do so. It is a very narrow range of occupations where other jobs are compatible with life in the House of Commons. There are some people who say they don't want a House of Commons full of professional politicians. Well, I don't want a House of Commons full of part-time London lawyers, London journalists, London heart surgeons, City financiers or West End shop managers. I think I've made my point on that.

It is, however, true and regrettable that there are now Members of the Commons on all sides who have never had what I, or I suspect, this committee, would consider a proper job. Attendance at university followed by political research, political lecturing, or special adviser to senior politicians, followed then by membership of the House of Commons, is a very disturbing state of affairs. God forbid we ever inflict upon the public such people in large numbers. My view has been always, I think, a minority view and I suspect it will continue to be so. Since 1979 in particular I have held seven different junior front bench positions and no one, either in the House or outside, has ever said I did not know my brief. And I have not had to accept full-time lobbying help in order to carry out those briefs either.

I want to remind this committee of something that is in your own statement "Issues and Questions" and that is regarding the Royal Commission on the Standards of Conduct in Public Life report, the Salmon Report, published in July 1976. It may be a surprise to this committee but that report as such has never ever been debated by the House of Commons—never. I complained to my own Party Leadership about this between 1976 and 1979. After the 1979 election I asked the new Government what proposals were to be made to improve the standards of conduct in public life and the answer I received from the then Home Secretary, now Lord Whitelaw was "To set a good example to others". I think we should take heed of Lord Whitelaw's views.

I believe, as is the view of the Salmon Report, that the law should be changed to include bribery or attempted bribery of a Member of Parliament acting in their Parliamentary capacity within the criminal law as recommended in paragraph 311. In your own discussion paper you mention that this might prejudice the sovereignty of Parliament. Well, I don't want to be misunderstood by this committee or anybody else at all. I am honoured to be a Member of the House of Commons and, indeed, to represent the area where I was born and raised, but I do not accept that Parliament should be sovereign. I am for a written constitution and reform. I think in a unitary state political power should be divided up and not reside within one institution however old, however democratic. There should be written codes and laws, agreed and enforced by the Courts. And to this extent I think the rules set out in Erskine May are a classic example of the failure of self-regulation.

No MP should be paid for being an advocate in Parliament or in connection with any Parliamentary activity. The Register of Members' Interests should be more detailed and include spouses, partners and children of the Member as well as the Member's staff. This should prevent laundering. I would also ask—should Members' tax returns be published? There is a caveat on that because it could not be done as it is today; you may find this remarkable but our tax returns contain the personal details of our staff's salary payments, so it would require some changes in that respect. But should the details of the finance received from outside sources be published? One of those is probably an alternative to the other.

I would also say that sometimes these issues have been discussed privately amongst Members in the House of Commons but there sometimes is an unspoken assumption that if we on our side raise aspects of reform that we want to probe the other side might raise quite different matters. Hence the vital need for the work of this independent committee, which I think the House of Commons will ignore at its peril. Parliament does not draw up the constituency boundaries and neither should it be the sole arbiter of the public interest boundaries, in my view.

I have already aired my views on the access to Parliament by lobbyists by using the passes as a member of an MP's staff. I think it should be banned outright. No MP's staff pass should be available to anyone not paid from the MP's allowance by the Fees Office. It should also be mandatory that employment contracts of staff should be lodged at the Fees Office rather than only being required by a Resolution of the House as is the case at present. That resolution has been there for several years and is not fully followed. Your committee might also wish to consider, of course, the position of a Member's spouse holding a spouse's pass who happens to be a journalist or lobbyist. I haven't got an answer round that one.

Obviously part-time employment working for a Member has to be allowed, but if any other employment is related to any kind of involvement of Parliamentary activity or lobbying I don't think the pass—that is the House of Commons pass—should be available to that person. I also believe that the Register of Journalists' Interests should be published instead of being kept with the present Register of Staff Interests in a cupboard in the House of Commons Library.

My final point concerns a proposal floated before this committee last week—and, indeed, has been floated in the media in the past as, indeed, during debates in the House—and that is that we should pay Members of Parliament better and improve the allowances and then put a complete ban on outside earnings. I don't propose that—I wouldn't object to it—but I would say leaving aside the problems associated with people who have got individual wealth, whether it is a farmer or a writer of non-political fiction, there would be a public expenditure implication of any such recommendation made by this committee. Although it is outside this committee's remit I think the answer is simple but it does open up a new area of debate and that is to cut the Members of Parliament to between 500 and 550.

LORD NOLAN: Thank you very much, Mr. Rooker. Now I am going to ask Lord Thomson to take up the questions.

1245. LORD THOMSON: Well, thank you, too, for an extremely interesting, stimulating and thoughtful introduction to some of the problems with which we are wrestling. Your first remarks related to Ministers, or ex-Ministers, going into employment outside the House and in the private sector and could I therefore follow up and ask you about some of the detailed problems and what your answer is to that. First of all, the argument has been put to us by others that if you discourage ex-Ministers too much and put too narrow restrictions on them—you and I know the uncertainties of being a Minister and you have referred to them in your opening statement—do you think this would then discourage people from accepting a junior office and, in fact, limit the capacity of Parliament to get the best people as Ministers?

JEFF ROOKER: No, it depends where your starting point is from. If, for example, you look on being a Minister as a long-term professional career then there are major problems if you lose that position. Now, that can't normally happen, (a) unless you have got single party Government, therefore you enter the party that is permanently in Government in the hope that you can remain a Minister for ten, fifteen or maybe twenty years. Well, I don't accept that provision to start with. There are those who would argue that you should not accept that even for the House of Commons—there should be a greater turnover. Nevertheless I don't look on it as a career. I have been fortunate to be continuously serving for over twenty years. But the problem for Ministers is if they decide that they are going to be a Minister at any cost, then that begs the question about the kind of decisions they take as a Minister, that they are not going to want to fall out with the Prime Minister over an area of policy; they are not going to operate, if you like, as independent Ministers looking and making a judgment in respect of their department if their only business is to cling on to office as a Minister at all cost because it is more difficult for them when they leave in terms of loss of salary. And if you start from the point, therefore, that people should be allowed to consider that their life's career is to be a

Minister then you might say "Well, of course, we mustn't make it difficult for them if they lose the job, we must give them lots of severance when they lose the job". Well, I don't start from that proviso and I don't think many of my colleagues do.

1246. LORD THOMSON: In the case of civil servants there is a committee that advises the Prime Minister of the day on senior civil servants going into the private sector and a time-limit—up to two years' delay—on taking a job can be imposed and other conditions can be imposed. Would you see that same kind of committee examining the applications for former Ministers to take up private employment?

JEFF ROOKER: Yes, I do, but I also draw the distinction between Ministers and civil servants. Civil servants are there as professional career civil servants. I don't accept the concept of a professional career Minister, therefore it is different. So far as the civil servants are concerned—I have said two or three years for Ministers—I think that would be acceptable so far as the public is concerned. It isn't so much what the views are of, if you like, even the House of Commons. Your committee is only sitting because of basically a failure in public confidence and I believe there ought to be a vetting process. If ex-Ministers leave office in whatever circumstances—they leave office and wish to go into the private sector—they should be free to do so. I don't object to that. However, if the sector they are going into is an area they dealt with as a departmental Minister then there should be a vetting procedure. It is only in that respect where the vetting is required. So there can be transparency so far as the public interest is concerned.

1247. LORD THOMSON: Did I understand from your opening statement that that vetting in your view should be done not by the same committee that vets civil servants but should be done by this committee of three independent people associated with the House of Commons?

JEFF ROOKER: No, that would be the final appeal. What I've suggested is exactly what Ann Taylor proposed on 25th January—that Parliament is requested by this committee, or recommended and I think that will be followed—to set up a Parliamentary Ethics Advisory Office to look at aspects of complaints about even Members' interest, so that if the public have a complaint there is a vetting process before, if you like, the Committee of Members' Interests or Committee of Privileges starts work. I think that office would be a suitable operation for an ex-Minister to submit a proposal if they have had an invitation to join the board of a company and they are in doubt whether or not they had a major interest as a departmental Minister—to submit that to the Parliamentary Ethics Advisory Office to get clearance. If they are given clearance, fine, they can go ahead. If they don't get clearance and the ex-Minister remains unhappy then the appeal by that Minister should be to that committee of three people that I have just mentioned. Their decision should be final.

1248. LORD THOMSON: Can I ask you on a narrow but practical and I think quite important point about how the procedure for ex-Ministers would operate? You have talked about a two year or three year gap. I mean, let us assume for the sake of argument that the same up to a two year delay that is imposed on civil servants might be imposed on former Ministers, when would you have the clock start ticking? From the time they left the Government or from the time that they left the department that might be related to the employment that they were going into?

JEFF ROOKER: I have given some thought to this in the statement that I have made where I've bolded and indeed underlined one part—I want to be realistic about this. I want this committee to propose new measures that the House of Commons would feel able to accept, in fact would be in a position to dare not to accept, if you like, and therefore I think the realistic time to set the clock ticking is when the Minister has left the department when they were involved. That means they may have only just left the Government because they could have been in another department, but if the department that they left was more than, say, two years ago, then that would be okay. It has to be when they have just left the departmental interest. I mean, I do not subscribe to the view that just because someone is in the Government they therefore know everything that is happening in every other department while they are a Minister. Frankly to make that kind of claim actually makes the call for restrictions unbelievable and impracticable.

1249. LORD THOMSON: Could I ask you also about the final decision in the matter of Ministers, as you see it, with this committee of the Clerk of the House, the Auditor General and the Speaker? They would be the absolute final Court of Appeal under your proposition—it would not be left to the Prime Minister of the day to take the final decision?

JEFF ROOKER: No, no. This issue—the ex-Ministers in public life—if they weren't in public life I don't think this thing should apply. If they remain in public life I don't think the Prime Minister should have anything to do with it. Why should the Prime Minister have anything to do with it? This is a matter of public life. The Prime Minister—whoever he or she may be—is not the guardian of public life. Like I have said in my statement I don't think Parliament should be the sole arbiter of the public interest. You have to find some mechanism that is acceptable, however—acceptable to Parliament and can be trusted by the public—and to have the thing removed, whether it is to the courts or completely from Parliament, I don't think would be practicable. But to have a committee of three, which I think really would have to be brought into being, whose sanction would be final, because I think if their decision was added to the list of bodies, if you like, under the House of Commons Disqualification Act, therefore you are out of the House of Commons, it is a simple as that, and therefore those three people—it is a burden on them but I think it is a burden that they could carry from the kind of experience they bring to it.

1250. LORD THOMSON: I think we appreciate that you have been searching for a practical alternative to the Prime Minister of the day because one of the objections that has been put to us is that the moment when there is the maximum number of ex-Ministers seeking suitable employment is at a time of a general election and a change of Government, so it would be left to a Prime Minister from another party to take the final judgment under the Civil Service type of arrangements?

JEFF ROOKER: That is absolutely right and, of course, one has to also imagine the position in that situation that a lot of ex-Ministers may also be all of a sudden ex-MPs, but the same Prime Minister may still be in office. Now, that position is even worse than a change of Government because left with, say, losing let us say half your cabinet in a general election but you remain Prime Minister and if you are seen, therefore, to be, if you like, looking after the people who have just lost—quite a shock to them I would imagine—that would raise a lot of questions about your decisions and I don't think any sensible Prime Minister would want to be placed in that position.

1251. LORD THOMSON: Could I ask you about one other—again narrow but, I think, quite important point in the procedures that one would apply—you mentioned very interestingly in your opening statement that if a former Permanent Secretary—and I suppose this would apply to a former Minister—went into a public service post you would take a different view from going into a private sector post?

JEFF ROOKER: Yes indeed I would. I would. I used the universities—I mean some people might argue that the universities these days are more like private companies, that is not strictly true. I think that is one example I used, simply because I could use the analogy of the former Permanent Secretary at Eduction. I could also use analogy, if you like, as I did with health in some ways. Yes, if it is in the public service then I don't think that calls into question the public interest, to be honest. It doesn't leave you open to charges of abuse of, if you like, playing the Stock Market, with share options, and things like that.

1252. LORD THOMSON: I was interested that you referred to the Health Service in this respect. Our purpose in our enquiry, as you well know, is not to comment on individual cases or to investigate individual cases but to look at the overall situation and make recommendations arising from our judgment about it, but there is a topical case at the moment, as you will know, of a senior official moving—a very senior official close to a Minister—moving out of the Health Service Department to a job in the Health Service, in a hospital, and that has raised controversy. Do you think that sort of situation, that sort of problem arising, needs special rules?

JEFF ROOKER: No, I don't. On that particular case—that is not the case that I allude to in my statement because the case I allude to in my statement is two years ago -the case you are alluding to is the one that was announced last week. Whatever people might say with the Party argument across the House of Commons the Health Service is still the public service and, therefore, I don't see a problem. This individual has not gone into the private sector, has not gone to Chair a private health company, will not be involved in stock options and therefore, if you try and include that as a part of the rules then I think it would be so byzantine that you wouldn't catch the real problems. Such as, for example, the one I do allude to in my statement, of a former senior official of the Health Service who went into academia, in which I see no problem, but in a very very short time then joined the board of a private health company. That, I do think, ought to have been prevented under the two-year rule.

1253. LORD THOMSON: Yes, thank you. That is very clear. Can I just move on before I finish to the second part of your statement on Members' interests and really just two points: you say that no MP should be paid for being an advocate in Parliament or in connection with any Parliamentary activity. On the second point of any

Parliamentary activity, how would you deal with the MP who came into the House of Commons with an outside business interest that he carries on in a perfectly proper way—would that be considered being paid for Parliamentary activity? How would you distinguish—would a declaration of interest whenever he spoke on the aspects of the industry in which he was involved be sufficient?

JEFF ROOKER: I don't know what kind of example of interest you would be talking about——

1254. LORD THOMSON: I am thinking of someone who is, let us say, a director of an engineering company who comes into Parliament, goes on being a director of the company, a non-executive director of the company—perhaps it has been a family company. When the problems of the engineering industry come up in Parliament in one way or another, he is a paid non-executive director, should he be banned from speaking, voting?

JEFF ROOKER: Yes, but he is not being paid because he or she is a Member of Parliament—he is being paid because he was a director of the company to start with. I mean, that is the distinction. I mean the Parliamentary activity, whether it is leading delegations to Ministers, organising lobbying, speaking in the House—that is the Parliamentary activity and that is what I don't think he should be paid for. If you had this interest before you came into the House, as a director of an engineering company, for example, and you retained that directorship and you are speaking on engineering in the House of Commons which I think would be quite valuable—because I have to declare an interest that there are too few engineers in the House of Commons—I don't see that being paid for Parliamentary activity. The company hasn't taken him on because he has become an MP to speak on engineering—that is the distinction.

1255. LORD THOMSON: Thank you, that is very clear. And then an associated question with which we are wrestling all the time—is there a sustainable distinction to be made between an MP being a paid advocate on behalf of a private interest (which you would ban absolutely) and being an adviser to an outside industry, a trade association, the Police Federation—keeps coming up in our discussions. Do you see a valid distinction there and one that would be sustainable in terms of the rules of the Ethics Advisory Office, if one was set up?

JEFF ROOKER: I have thought about this because I have attended the hearings of the committee. I understand the position of the Police Federation—indeed I understand the position of sort of the, if you like, public service organisations which are not "political" with a capital "P" and are not affiliated to political organisations, who feel as though they want to make sure their case is actually heard in the interest of the nation in Parliament. It is difficult—I don't deny that—but I don't think a Member of Parliament should be paid for being an advocate. You can be an advocate if you have an interest and you are sufficiently committed to it for a body, like the Police Federation, without being paid for it.

1256. LORD THOMSON: But would that then apply to Members of Parliament who receive either directly or indirectly entirely under the present rules proper payments, or historic payments, from a trade union of which they had been a member?

JEFF ROOKER: Yes. I think at the end of the day—and I allude to it partly at the end of my statement—there is going to be, let us say, some collateral damage over your enquiry and I think we have to accept that. We have a once and for all chance, in my view, to try and clean up public life. Parliament, in my view, has failed to take sufficient action over the years and if there is some collateral damage to the charities and the voluntary sector in the interim—because I think that can be corrected where it is a legitimate, non-commercial interest at a later date—then so be it. But it is important to get a nub of the argument which is not about trade union sponsorship, most people don't understand the issue, but if to get to the nub of the argument of the commercial interests and the grotesque lobbying that has gone on over the years, that we have to clean out completely and start again, then I for one would accept that and I think then we could take on board the provisions that are required for, if you like, the Police Federation, the Committee of Vice-Chancellors, the charities. I mean, I can tell the difference between a charity and a company. Charity law doesn't tell that difference, though, unfortunately.

LORD THOMSON: Mr. Rooker, thank you for answering my questions so thoughtfully and so frankly.

LORD NOLAN: We will now go round the table, Mr. Rooker. May I ask Sir Clifford Boulton to speak?

1257. CLIFFORD BOULTON: Can I just explore this business of the sanctions that the House imposes on its own Members for breaches of the House's own rules, because I gather really that you feel that the House has been remiss in imposing sanctions on those Members who have been in conflict with the House's own resolutions and what you are saying is that the real answer to that, which would give confidence, would be effectively to bring the law into this so that Members would be committing some sort of an offence which would be justiciable in the courts? That is what you are saying would be your preferred solution to this problem, is that right?

JEFF ROOKER: Yes, it is, Sir Clifford and, indeed—I do not want to quote back at yourself but you are the only person that I can quote back to here—but pages 119, 120, 121 and 128, 128, 386, 382 and 388 of Erskine May embody a set of rules, some of them going back 300 years, designed in a bygone era which basically only romantics will stand up and quote as to order our affairs today are not sufficient, and I really do think the Salmon Report of 1976 did raise an important issue and I think Parliament was neglectful at not debating the report and we were neglectful at not changing the criminal law.

1258. CLIFFORD BOULTON: I think you will agree that a bill which was introduced into the House which would, for instance, bring the police into enquiring whether a Member appeared to have taken money to table an amendment in a bill in the Public Bill Office—a bill that was going to do that would not have an easy passage through the House—might have a difficult time?

JEFF ROOKER: Well, with respect, neither do complaints about Members taking money to do that today have an easy passage through the House because by and large the House does not attend to these issues.

1259. CLIFFORD BOULTON: Yes. What I am trying to work towards is if we had to look for more and more bite in the House's own regulations at least to fill in the gap before we got your law, what you felt might be an improvement there, and I am just gathering from what you are saying that you would approve of some appointment under the authority of the House of someone, or some body which could, on their own initiative, present to the House a situation and say "We find (or I find) that such-and-such Members have not tabled their staff's contracts of employment" or "We find that a Member has got an admissible arrangement with an outside body" and those people would have the authority to publish that and draw it to the attention of the House and really put the ball in the House's court, whereas at the moment if nobody does anything nothing happens and nobody knows about these things. Would you think that that, at least, would be an improvement on the present position?

JEFF ROOKER: Absolutely and very practical. I mean, you could embody all the sanctions if you like set out on those pages of Erskine May, and there are probably others, in a resolution or as a guide and checks, coupled with what is the spirit of the Salmon Report and say to a Parliamentary Ethics Officer, appointed by the House, who can't be dismissed, appointed in the proper manner with a set of rules, with complete freedom to publish, with an instruction to publish, so the House cannot ignore this issue as an interim measure and I mean—far be it for me to withdraw recommendations I am making whilst I am giving evidence—but I suspect that if that was done properly and seen to work then Parliament might not find the time to pass the legislation that I am advocating that Parliament should pass. If it was done properly and seen to work. That would be a major step from the present position because it is simply not seen to work. You know yourself from your own experience, even in the latest case—the money for questions case—the Committee of Privileges was not in being, it was not set up, it didn't start to take evidence and the public think it is a joke that Parliament is not taking the issue seriously. It doesn't sit during the recess because it has no power to sit during the recess. It is the only select committee, I understand, that can't sit during a recess. It is absolutely crazy. Now, these issues have to be attended to. Parliament has proved itself not capable of doing so, in my view. Now, an Ethics Office that can take complaints from the public, take complaints from Members, with instructions to public, with the power to investigate and to lay its results before the House, I think is the very beginning—it is the minimal position really that is required.

CLIFFORD BOULTON: Thank you very much.

LORD NOLAN: Sir William?

1260. WILLIAM UTTING: Mr. Rooker, you said in your evidence that no MP should be paid for being an advocate in Parliament or in connection with any Parliamentary activity and later on, talking to Lord Thomson, indicated that it would be okay for somebody who was the non-executive director of an engineering company to continue in that position after he got into the House of Commons. What is your view of the position of a non-executive director of a public relations firm or a general lobbying firm, or a firm of solicitors that undertakes lobbying work in Parliament—should that person continue in office as a non-executive director after becoming a Member of Parliament?

JEFF ROOKER: Not with payment if it relates to any Parliamentary activity. I mean, that has got to be the distinction. I am not putting forward a proposal banning outside interests. My own personal view is I don't have any and I don't wish to do that, but I know that is a minority view. In the grey areas—there will always be grey areas—that is why an independent body like an Ethics Office is required to make a judgment. Now, if a Member of Parliament arrives either as a solicitor or as being a journalist or work professionally full-time for a lobbying company, who may have been lobbying on non-Governmental work as well, then it might be argued they would stick to the non-Governmental work and don't do anything relating to anything to do with Parliament or Government—fine. If there is a cross-over that has got to be registered and the Ethics Office would have to report on it. And I think it ought to be possible because the climate would be different. If Parliament did have this kind of mechanism the climate would be totally different about the kind of interest to be registered, the sanctions that can be brought upon a Member of Parliament, but I think the grey areas over a period of time would be narrowed and there would be very few and you wouldn't get these difficulties. There will be these difficulties if you try and apply a new set of rules to the current variety of interests of Members, and I think if you add the new set of rules the interests of Members would radically change.

1261. WILLIAM UTTING: So the system could be managed if there is an Ethics Office that would provide this interest and advice to the Member and if this were based on comprehensive disclosure of interests?

JEFF ROOKER: Oh, absolutely.

1262. WILLIAM UTTING: You go on to say that the existing register should include the interests of spouses, partners and children of MPs as well as Members' staffs?

JEFF ROOKER: Yes, I do.

1263. WILLIAM UTTING: One is talking then about a monumental piece of work. Coming onto this committee caused me to reflect upon my interests and I thought I led a fairly simple life, but I am not actually sure that I have identified all of them that are relevant to this committee's work yet. I mean, it is actually a very difficult thing to do, to identify from day to day all the interests that one has that might bear upon the issues that you are raising.

JEFF ROOKER: Yes, it is. And it amounts, of course, to, if you like, a monumental invasion of public privacy but that is part of the price of being in public life, I think. If there is scope for laundering, if there is scope for the MP's spouse, let us say having the free car, as an example, or having the retainers or the free holidays without it being declared, then it is that kind of thing that I referred to in our private conversations in the House over the years, where it is alleged things go on but other people say "don't start raising that because they will rake over things that we would rather not have raked over". Well this committee has the chance to air that. You have got to be able to stop a laundering operation and the only way you can do that in my view is to include the Member's spouse and/or partner and children and to include them on the register so that if there is a registerable interest——That is only a consequence of the MP being an MP, by the way. I am not interested in interests that are not related to being in Parliament—there will be interests that are nothing to do with that and therefore it is not a massive invasion of publishing everything about a family's life and existence. That would not be involved at all.

WILLIAM UTTING: Thank you, Mr. Rooker.

1264. PETER SHORE: Just following that one up a little bit further—so really what you are saying is that your extended register would be broadly those relatives of a Member who were employment-related to the Member of Parliament?

JEFF ROOKER: Yes. Well, employment-related—I wouldn't call the spouse and children employment-related but——

PETER SHORE: If the spouse, for example, was working as a——

JEFF ROOKER: Oh, no, no, no. If the spouse wasn't working they would have to be included. I mean, it is the only way to stop laundering—of someone giving the Member a gift that the Member does not need to disclose because it wasn't given to the Member but it was given because the Member did something for someone and it was given to the Member's spouse. Now, presently you are not required to register that and that is the way to get round the present register—it is one of the ways to get round the present register—and I think you have to block off that laundering operation if you are going to, if you like, tighten up the register completely.

1265. PETER SHORE: Yes. Can I press a bit further on this area of Members again—Members' interests? You did draw a distinction being questioned by Lord Thomson between Members of Parliament who are paid for advocacy and a Member of Parliament who might be a director of a company. Now, the situation you envisaged was the director of a company who had been a director of that company, as it were, at the time of his election to Parliament. What about a Member of Parliament who subsequently has a directorship in a company, either because it follows from Ministerial experience outside whatever limitations you propose? What would be your view on that?

JEFF ROOKER: Well, it if was perceived and the record showed that the only function that Member performed as a director for that company was to speak in Parliament, ask Parliamentary questions, lead delegations to Ministers, then you don't get paid for it. If the Member was, if you like, a fully-participating non-executive director—some of them may be executive directors, if they are London based, that is the distinction I draw—then there is a grey area and I accept that, but that Member under a regime that I envisage would be very wary before they started asking questions, leading delegations to Ministers and making major detailed speeches about that company in the House of Commons, because they would be subject to a complaint to the Ethics Advisory Office. So there is going to be a grey area—I don't want to rule out and I don't think this committee would indeed suggest ruling out outside interests. I don't take that view, although my personal decision is something different. But you can draw a distinction if you become a director later, having been a Member of Parliament, but as I say if the only thing you do as a director is Parliamentary activity and Parliamentary advocacy then as far as I am concerned you should not be paid for it.

1266. PETER SHORE: You are drawing, in a sense, a familiar distinction now between advocacy and other forms of advice. A number of Members, I think, do register consultancies and some of them they maintain are nothing to do with advocacy in Parliament but only with advice to the company that is employing them. Do you think it is a practical distinction between advocacy and advice and if a Member of Parliament had a consultancy which he maintained was a consultancy simply to give advice, how would you make sure that that did not step over the bounds into advocacy as well?

JEFF ROOKER: I said both "advocacy in Parliament" and "any Parliamentary activity". This may be taking too hard a line, but going outside as a Member of Parliament to make yourself a one-off consultant to sell advice about Parliament, its rules, how to use them, get round them and operate them, to a company should not be done for payment. You may say that that is taking advocacy and advice too far. If one is elected a Member of Parliament, one operates as a Member of Parliament; because of that one should not sell one's knowledge, experience and expertise in the House, but use it in the House of Commons. Anyone can raise any issue in the House under any regime envisaged under my recommendations. There is no issue that could not be raised. If outside companies want professional and legal advice on the way Parliament works, there is a whole body of qualified Parliamentary agents outside who are more than happy to sell that advice. I do not think that Members of Parliament should sell it.

1267. PETER SHORE: That is a very clear answer. Can I move on to the business of ex-Ministers and their jobs? Your views on that are very clearly expressed. What is special to your way of treating this problem—and was first put to us by Ann Taylor—is that there should be an Ethics Office to look at particular cases. What kind of office is this Ethics Office to be? Is the Ethics Officer to be appointed by Parliament or is it something outside Parliament?

JEFF ROOKER: No. I think it is to be appointed by Parliament. I had discussions with Ann about this, when she was drafting her own statement. I served for two years as a member of the Public Accounts Committee when I was on the Back Benches. I learned more about the machinery of government in those two years than during eight years on the Front Bench. I was conscious of the work of the National Audit Office, both in looking for value for money and in effectiveness and efficiency and the ethics of looking after taxpayers' pounds.

One of my original views was to have a team of Ethics Officers, pulled out from the audit side, and to make them accountable to Parliament through a separate officer of the House, similar to the Clerk and the Comptroller and Auditor General. An Ethics Officer of the House cannot, in my view, be a rolling Clerk of Committees. That is no good at all. I am not envisaging a super Clerk, but an officer of the House with the same status and appointment as the Clerk of the House and the Comptroller and Auditor General, so that he cannot be dismissed. It is crucial to secure his independence. The Ethics Advisory Office could be manned by people who are external to the House as well as by people from inside it. They could be rolling; they need not be career civil servants or officers of the House. A set of rules and guidelines would be laid down either by the Committee or by a resolution of the House. It has to be that powerful so that the public can see that Parliament is taking the issue seriously. With no disrespect, if it is left to a junior officer of the House, who wants promotion to other areas, there will always be the nagging doubt that decisions and exposure have not been made where they should have been.

1268. PETER SHORE: The appeal from that Ethics Officer would be to the troika of senior officers of the House?

JEFF ROOKER: For ex-Ministers. Ann Taylor's original proposal, which I think is still there, was that Members' complaints—I am talking about ordinary Members—would go via the Ethics Office once they had ruled—they would decide whether to report to the House, whether it was suitable for investigation by the Privileges Committee on Members' Interests. This is the separate issue of whether a Minister should take up a job within two years in an area where he or she had an interest. The final appeal, if the Minister or ex-Minister does not accept the view of the Ethics Advisory Officer, would be to that troika and its decision should be final.

1269. PETER SHORE: The ultimate sanction would be disqualification?

JEFF ROOKER: The ultimate sanction would be disqualification, yes.

PETER SHORE: Thank you very much.

1270. ANNE WARBURTON: A very quick question, Chairman. In your statement, Mr Rooker, you said that you thought that it should be mandatory that employment contracts of staff should be lodged with the Fees Office rather than being required only by resolution. You may wish to say something about that.

JEFF ROOKER: I would respectfully recommend that you take some evidence from representatives of employees in the House on this. It is a matter that has been brought to my attention more than once. We do not pay members of staff individually; we do not hand over money or pay cheques, but payment is made by the Fees Office on our instruction. I cannot remember the exact date, but it was probably in 1986—Sir Clifford will correct me—that the Fees Office was told by a resolution of the House that the only people to whom Members could sanction payment were persons for whom the Member had lodged an employment contract with the Fees Office. There is no model employment contract, although there are model employment contracts by staff representatives—the trade unions have got model employment contracts, which have been suggested to Members. These are for full-time staff. I have asked parliamentary questions two or three times over the years—the latest occasion was in October of last year. I asked how many individuals for whom payments are made by the Fees Office are being paid, although the Member has not lodged an employment contract with the Fees Office. I was told that the figure was in excess of 300. Some of those will be part-time casual. My own position is simple: I have two staff, one of whom is full-time—more than full-time, I might add—more than 80 hours a week, for which I cannot pay properly. I have lodged an employment contract with the Fees Office. The other member of my staff works on an hourly basis—as casual as one can be. This person is also paid by the Fees Office on my instructions, but no employment contract is required, because it is a casual relationship.

That conforms to the resolution of the House, but other MPs have full-time staff and, because it is not mandatory

and the resolution is not policed, nothing is done about it. The individual staff are frightened to complain, because they will be up the road—the Member will dismiss them. That area needs toughening up.

ANNE WARBURTON: Thank you.

1271. TOM KING: Just very quickly, in relation to a point that Sir William Utting raised. You mention including children as well. Some Members enter the House quite young. Should their parents not be listed as well, and sisters and brothers? I make this point because in the end one is thrown back on the problem that the integrity of the Member is the only real and lasting defence.

JEFF ROOKER: That is right; it does come down to that. The whole system has relied on every Member being honourable, following the rules of the House, being a person of integrity, understanding what public service means and what it is like to be in public life. Unfortunately, the fact that this Committee is sitting today shows that there has been a failure in the system. Finding some new way to police the system that will stand the test of time is not easy, I accept. I fully understand the dilemma that you face, but you cannot leave the situation as it is.

1272. TOM KING: Just a quickie on this Ethics Officer. It would have to be somebody who was not looking for promotion or further advancement, because that would expose him to influences that might be open to criticism. Is this a single person? I took it from the way you answered one question that he would adjudicate—Members could bring issues to him and say, "Is it all right if I do this or that? I have been invited to take on this responsibility. Would it be all right?". If he said, "All right", would that be sufficient authority?

JEFF ROOKER: An Ethics Advisory Office has to be headed by someone, therefore there has to be a person at the top. He would be someone who was not looking for promotion. With due respect, persons reaching the pinnacle of their career, such as the Clerk of the House and the Head of the National Audit Office, may or may not go on to other things, but they are at the pinnacle of their career, perhaps with a lifetime of public service behind them. The head of the National Audit Office may have been in the private sector. The Speaker would be the other Member of the troika; no Speaker is going to look for promotion in any other role. You are absolutely right to say that it must be someone who is not looking for promotion, but I also believe that if Members of the public or other MPs want to make complaints about MPs, at the moment the sanction does not work, because all they can do is complain to the Registrar of Interests or the Privileges Committee. It is like using an atom bomb instead of a grenade: one does not do it. If there is something small that one can do to open it up and get it looked at, people are more likely to raise the issue. If later on it is seen to be a frivolous, invalid complaint, the Ethics Office will throw it out and one does not have to bother the Privileges Committee or the Committee on Members' Interests; but at least the issue has been raised. That is important. For ex-Ministers, the issue has to be looked at with a slightly different set of rules.

1273. LORD NOLAN: Could I take you up briefly on that last point? I think we shall hear a lot more about it later this morning. As I understand it, you said that in considering whether rules similar to those governing civil servants should apply to Ministers taking up employment in industry, Ministers should not regard themselves as being in a long term or secure job as Ministers. Is that right?

JEFF ROOKER: Yes.

1274. LORD NOLAN: They have to allow for the possibility that they find themselves out of a job and looking for something in industry or commerce and must simply avoid taking up jobs that raise a conflict of interest or a conflict of duty with the office they have held.

JEFF ROOKER: If they remain in public life. If they are still in the House of Commons, they are not on the street or penniless. If they are in the House of Lords, I accept that Members of the House of Lords are not paid a salary. The issue is whether they are in public life. If they are private citizens, one cannot impose any censure or restriction. I understand the implication of that, namely, that one can leave the Cabinet and the House of Commons on the same day and, as a private citizen, chair the board of a company one was dealing with as a Minister. I have to accept that, because those cases are extremely rare. If one uses the excuse that it is "so difficult", one ends up not tackling the other issues. One has to be realistic about it, in my view, and accept it so that one can put a ban on all the others.

1275. LORD NOLAN: The evidence given to us by Sir Terence Higgins showed that Ministers' pay has fallen in real terms by about 50 per cent over the past 30 years. Mr MacGregor told us that Ministers who had served in a number of Departments might find that large areas of employment were barred to them if there was a restriction similar to that affecting civil servants. Sir Michael Quinlan, recognising that there could be a severe disadvantage for a former Minister in the labour market if he could not have free choice of jobs, wondered if the problem, being a financial one, could be solved by money. Although Ministers' salaries are not in any way a matter for us, is there a case for saying that Ministers would be more ready to come from industry and take up the office of Ministers if the conditions were better?

JEFF ROOKER: This goes back to the issue. I have not been in this position, although I hope one day to be so. I declare my interest in that respect. Any MP who becomes a Minister and then relies on the ministerial salary to adjust their lifestyle and financial commitments is so stupid that they should not be a Minister in the first place. The Prime Minister has appointed the wrong person.

1276. LORD NOLAN: They have got to take the rough with the smooth, do you say?

JEFF ROOKER: Exactly, yes.

1277. LORD NOLAN: Thank you very much. I am most grateful to you. We have taken up a lot of your time on two occasions now and you have been very helpful to us. Thank you.

Now we have Mr David Hunt, Chancellor of the Duchy of Lancaster, and Sir Robin Butler. Mr Hunt, am I right in thinking that you have prepared an opening statement which you would like to make at the beginning?

RT HON. DAVID HUNT MP AND SIR ROBIN BUTLER

RT HON DAVID HUNT MP (Chancellor of the Duchy of Lancaster): If I may, my Lord. Before getting into the detail of my opening statement, I want to voice a few personal reflections.

Since I came into politics in the 1960s, and in my student days, I have been involved often in close contact with leading public figures in this country and abroad. I have always believed, and still strongly believe, that the standards of conduct in our public life are amongst the highest in the world.

For most of my lifetime in politics, there has been a consensus about that, and rightly so. The events of the past 18 months or so, however, with the public breakdown of that consensus, have been traumatic for many of us, particularly with colleagues and revered institutions being defamed and attacked with slurs, innuendoes and, often, downright lies. It seems almost as if nothing is sacred any more, and even that nothing can ever be the same again. That is why I was so pleased to be involved with the conception and establishment of you and your colleagues and this Committee, my Lord.

Public figures have always been subject to temptations and to the attentions of those who would seek to manipulate them or subvert them, for personal or political purposes. In this age of rather rapid and invasive communications, when the ends are too often lightly assumed to justify almost any means, the need for integrity in public life remains absolute. What has changed, however, is the greatly increased need for durable and above all demonstrable safeguards, in order that our public life should once again be seen to be beyond reproach.

My Lord, you and your colleagues on this Committee therefore have an enormous but essential task—to show that public servants, public figures and public institutions have nothing at all to fear from the greatest possible openness and the most effective public scrutiny. On a personal level, I set great store by your success so that we can all put this unnecessary and unhappy chapter well behind us.

For all the reasons I have given, the Government is for their part determined to ensure that standards of conduct in public service are maintained and seen to be maintained. The existence of this Committee is one mark of that determination, and we welcome the debate that the Committee's inquiry has already generated.

But our commitment, I hope, can also be demonstrated by the action we are taking across a broad front to clarify and codify standards and to increase openness, accessibility and accountability in our public service.

The evidence I submitted to the Committee last week, and which we published yesterday, sets out what I believe to be an impressive record of progressive improvements in this area.

Looking back, it was a decision of our Prime Minister to publish for the first time ever *Questions of Procedure for Ministers.* So far as civil servants are concerned, detailed rules of conduct are already set out in the *Civil Service Management Code,* issued during the period of this Administration, and we have now accepted the report of the Treasury and Civil Service Select Committee's recommendation for a new, concise and more accessible code, summarising the constitutional position of civil servants and the values they are expected to uphold, and incorporating new safeguards against impropriety and politicisation.

On public bodies more generally, our aim has been to improve accountability to users of those services by, for example, decentralising the management of schools, hospitals and other public bodies to bring them out of the shadows of the large bureaucracies where responsibilities were to some extent rather confused and accountability was unclear, and by setting sharper standards and targets for those bodies and clearer responsibility for performance for those who deliver them.

We have also seen the introduction of specific initiatives such as the *NHS Code of Conduct,* the *NHS Code of Accountability* and the new *Treasury Code of Best Practice for Board Members of Public Bodies.*

On public appointments, we have just published the report of the review carried out by the Cabinet Office's Public Appointments Unit, which was commissioned by the Prime Minister last May. This builds on the improvements in procedures made in recent years, particularly in terms of greater openness. For example, full-time appointments have normally been filled through advertisement or executive search. Where a single job advertisement is not used, advertisements seeking interest in a range of posts are not uncommon. I instituted such a programme when I was Secretary of State for Wales, and new advisory committees have been established in Scotland, dealing with health appointments, and broadly similar arrangements are being introduced in England.

The process of compiling databases of names to use as sources for appointments has also been amended. Now the lists held by departments, including that held by the Public Appointments Unit, are increasingly filled by self-nomination. The 5,000 names on the PAU's list are not just "the great and the good"—which was always an inaccurate description of the wide range of people willing to put themselves forward for public service—but people from all walks of life, including, I am pleased to say, an increasing number of women and also an increasing number from the black and Asian communities—a very good list of the public spirited and the well qualified.

The aim of the report is to sustain and increase these more open procedures. But the report also recognises that the approach used should be the most open possible consistent with value for money. An important test of "proportionality" is recommended, because it would be wrong to apply the same approach in very different circumstances. What is right and value for money for the less than 170 posts paying £50,000 or more a year may well be quite inappropriate for the unpaid specialist part-time post which only demands one day a month.

In all these areas there is room for further debate, and of course there are always improvements to be made. In seeking to take forward action on these issues, the Government wish to take full account of the views and recommendations of you and your colleagues on this Committee. On the Review of Public Appointments, in particular, I would highlight the following points, where we are looking for the guidance of this Committee.

First, my Lord, do you and your colleagues consider that the changes recommended will ensure that selection procedures in this area meet the highest standards so that they command public confidence?

Secondly, does the Committee endorse the approach outlined to explore a range of ways for making more information readily available?

Thirdly, does the Committee accept that the test of proportionality set out in the report is an appropriate one and that it is important to treat different types of appointment in different ways?

Fourthly, what is the Committee's view on the sensitive question of the declaration of political affiliation or political officeholding? How can we take action in a way which does not seem McCarthyite and does not deter or debar good candidates who may already be active in their local communities? Does the Committee believe that any change in current practice is either necessary or feasible in the light of the sensitivities set out in the report? If so, where would it be relevant and what should be done?

I believe that if we can get the answers to these questions right, the steps set out in the report will do much to restore faith in the work of public bodies and the public-spirited individuals who give up so much of their time to serve on them. But, of course, the Government will consider whether any further action is necessary in the light of your observations and any recommendations you want to make in this area.

But that is the case in all the areas under consideration by this Committee, and the Government will look carefully at any recommendations made, for example, on the question of the business appointments of former Ministers. But I have to say that I believe—and the Government believe—that it is still right to leave decisions about these matters to the judgement of the individuals concerned. There are enormous advantages in the interchange between business and industry. Businesses employ people for their abilities. If there is anything that former Ministers bring, it is wider vision, and surely it is a good thing for the country to give them opportunities to exercise this.

Ministers are given guidance, of course. I referred earlier to the publication for the first time ever of *Questions on Procedure for Ministers.* Paragraph 103 makes it clear that

"Ministers will want to order their affairs so that no conflict arises or is thought to arise between their private interests and their public duties."

Paragraph 105 states that, on leaving office, ex-Ministers

"should naturally avoid any course which would reflect adversely on their or the Government's reputation for integrity or the confidentiality of its proceedings."

That is clear: Ministers must not do anything which would call into question their integrity or that of the Government that they served.

I agree with a number of previous witnesses that Ministers are in a very different position from civil servants. It is not just a matter of tenure or the severance arrangements. Ministers, unlike civil servants, are public figures and they have a public reputation to protect and defend.

The call for new procedures suggests that somehow there is a new mischief to be prevented. Most examples of former Ministers' appointments that have been attracting recent notice were in fact taken up after an interval longer than that normally applied to civil servants. The Prime Minister has said that he was aware of no occasion where the question of abuse of previous Ministerial interests has arisen. He did in fact invite evidence to the contrary—and I understand that he has received none.

In conclusion, my Lord, I would say this. Surely we want to attract into Parliament people from all walks of life, and, as far as I can recall, it has always been accepted that we have too few people coming from the wealth-creating industrial, business and commercial sectors. If we turn that route into a one way street, then the traffic will stop and public life will be the poorer.

1278. LORD NOLAN: Thank you very much, Mr Hunt. The way I propose to proceed, if it is agreeable to you, is that I should ask some questions of a general nature of you and of Sir Robin and that Sir William Utting will then take up in more detail the papers on Quangos, to put it broadly, he being one of our working party on that subject. The other Members will naturally want to raise their own questions after that.

I wonder if I could begin with the statement that you have made this morning about the Government's attitude on the question of Ministers and the possibility or otherwise of some similar rules being applied to them as apply now to civil servants when they take up outside employment. I happened to notice a broadcast report of an interview last night with you by Justin Webb, when you mentioned the rules of guidance for Ministers which cover these matters at present. You were asked:

"You don't want a change in those rules?",

and you are reported as replying:

"Well it's now for the Nolan Committee. We set up the Nolan Committee to look at these issues. We now look forward to hearing their recommendations."

In this morning's statement you say:

"In all the areas under consideration by this Committee the government will look carefully at any recommendations made"

—that is, by us——

"but on the business appointments of former Ministers, I have to say that I believe, and the Government believes, that it is still right to leave decisions about these matters to the judgement of individuals."

Is the Government's mind made up on this?

DAVID HUNT: We set up you and your colleagues on this Committee to advise us, my Lord. Nothing has changed. You are completely free to tender whatever advice you think. What I am trying to put across is that I do

not think it is widely known that the rule is as wide and over-arching as it is. I cannot think of a rule that could be wider that no ex-Minister must ever do anything that would call into question his or her integrity.

I have just heard Mr Rooker giving evidence. He said that we should have some sort of delay, without exception, for two or three years. Without exception? What about lecturers in government or politics who come into Parliament, then lose their seats—were Ministers—and then wish to return to lecturing? Are they to wait two or three years before they are able to stand up in front of their students? Industrialists, who move from business into politics, are they to wait for two or three years?

My Lord, you will know that the judiciary has long had a very clear view about this. Any such restriction would clearly be in breach of the law. It would be in restraint of trade.

1279. LORD NOLAN: If it was not justifiable in the circumstances.

DAVID HUNT: Therefore it has to be left to the individuals at the end of the day to guard their integrity. The same is true of lawyers, doctors, teachers. The world of journalism would be so much the poorer if Members of Parliament and ex-Ministers who had lost their seats were unable to sit down and write articles afterwards relating to their experience as Ministers and receive payment for them. The world of journalism would be so much the poorer if that was to be prevented. I am not too sure that people who have been advocating these bans have really thought through the consequences. What I am trying to do is to explain some of the background, but then, of course, I leave the advice to you and your colleagues.

1280. LORD NOLAN: Thank you very much. The evidence that we had last week from Lord Younger and Sir Norman Fowler, as you know, was to the opposite effect. One of the things that came through from both of them, but particularly from Sir Norman Fowler, was this. He felt that where the Minister had behaved impeccably, where there could have been no criticism of him, even if the civil service rules had been applied, there was still at the moment a grave danger of unfair, uninformed criticism which in itself was doing great harm to confidence in public behaviour. Certainly one of the points made to us very clearly on Thursday by those two witnesses was that in fairness to the individual and in the interests of reassuring the public it was now time to consider introducing an outside arbiter of some sort. Would that really interfere with the freedom of Ministers to take up employment in cases where there was no conflict of interest?

DAVID HUNT: I do not think I am really talking about the need to avoid interference. It is really whether there is a need to set up a new structure. Sir Norman Fowler did get in touch with me to make it clear that he was not proposing in his evidence last week—I have the transcript here—that there should be a moratorium or a quarantine for ex-Ministers. What he was arguing for was a check to be made against a set of rules to ensure that after a Minister leaves a Department he does not take up a post that might give a company an improper advantage. He firmly believes that that should be in both the public's and the Minister's best interests. What I suppose I am saying is that at the end of the day, whatever rules or guidance is given, it has to be left to the individual. The individual has a public reputation to maintain, which lasts after he or she has left office. It is that protection which is so crucial and fundamental to confidence by the public in the whole system.

1281. LORD NOLAN: Is the present system maintaining that confidence? We all know the number of ex-Ministers who have been attacked in the press. We have heard from Sir John MacGregor, who gave us a very full account of his service with the bank before he became a Minister, of his return to the bank after he had left office and of his total refusal to have anything to do with banking matters while he held office. If the public had known about that or, even better, if some outside figure had been able to vouch for all those facts, then not only would Mr MacGregor have been proved, as now he has, to have done nothing whatever wrong, but the public would have been satisfied. Do you think that is too high a price to pay, putting restrictions on Ministers, as distinct from leaving them to behave honourably?

DAVID HUNT: I am arguing that there is a very severe restriction on Ministers at the present time. I think what my former colleagues are seeking to do is to find some way of protecting themselves against the slur, the innuendo and the downright lie. Therefore they are proposing a whole range of measures. I am saying that at the end of the day the restriction is very clearly set out in the rules of procedure. The Prime Minister recently said "If anyone has any evidence that there has been a breach, then I want to hear about it", and no one has come forward with any evidence. We still have the innuendo, we still have the slur. A lot of my colleagues want to find some way through all this.

But there are enormous dangers, because in a way one is singling out specific areas for protection. I do not think anyone has seriously said that a barrister leaving office should then be prevented from standing up in court and arguing the case for a particular client, even though in arguing a case he might be able to draw on the wider public experience that he or she has had. What we are in danger of doing is trying to find areas of occupation where we can say, "In these areas there should be tougher rules"—for instance, we have had the notion that if there has been any connection with a privatised industry. There is no demarcation line to be easily drawn if someone has been in an energy industry and then goes to work for an oil company that has never been subject to privatisation in the past. This wide-ranging rule catches everyone. I think that any attempt to dilute what is a very clear principle will lead into a large number of anomalies.

1282. LORD NOLAN: May I turn now to the part of your paper which suggests that the rules on civil servants are being reviewed in the light of civil service and military cuts. Can you give us any indication of the thinking on that?

DAVID HUNT: So far as these rules are concerned, they are under review. If the Committee has any particular points to raise on the rules, we should be very happy to consider them. They are indeed under review at the present time. I do not know if Sir Robin has anything to add.

SIR ROBIN BUTLER (Secretary of the Cabinet and Head of the Home Civil Service): Yes. Just to make clear that I do not think there are any specific grounds for dissatisfaction that are causing the rules to be reviewed. An increasing number of people are leaving the civil service earlier in their careers. Similarly, a number of military officers are leaving under *Options for Change* at an earlier stage. We did think that we should look to see if there was any area in those circumstances where the rules risked operating unfairly. That is the purpose of the review. It is an open review. I have not heard of any conclusions from it; I think no conclusions have been reached. It is simply just to see how the rules are applying in the changing circumstances.

1283. LORD NOLAN: Thank you. If I could turn to Ministers for a moment, the suggestion was made by two of our other witnesses last Thursday, that is to say, Sir Michael Quinlan and Lord Younger, I think, that the disadvantage to Ministers of finding themselves inhibited in the range of employments they could take up if there were some rule of the kind that they were advocating resulted from the way that Ministers are remunerated at the moment. They have no security of tenure, of course; they have a relatively small redundancy payment to expect. It was Sir Michael who particularly said that there is a disadvantage here that can be cured by money without infringing on the principle that there should be no real or apparent conflict of interest. But, as I understand you, you think still—and Lord Young, I see, in this morning's *Times* has written a column to the same effect—that the present position does retain the ability to attract good people from industry into government, and that is something that must be preserved without altering the rules.

DAVID HUNT: Yes. Of course, the remuneration of Members of Parliament was a topic on which the Lord President addressed you. Ministers have always been a difficult area. I do not think that anyone is drawn into politics by the high salaries—far from it. Many people come into politics and into Parliament and make financial sacrifices, because they believe that there is a wider aspect to the contribution they can make, the service side—"service before self" has been echoed in many senior Parliamentarians over the years. Clearly there is a need always to look at the level of salaries. We do gain advice from time to time from the review body on top salaries, but at the end of the day I do not think that that is a route that provides a helpful course of action to overcome the difficulties we were talking about earlier. It is necessary to find some way to make sure that ex-Ministers do not face difficult financial circumstances. I do not think we shall ever see a situation—I have never seen one in my lifetime—where a Cabinet Minister's or Minister's salary can have a direct "read across" either to the same salaries paid in other countries to similar people or indeed to occupations occupying a similar responsibility outside politics.

1284. LORD NOLAN: I wonder if I could put the point more clearly if I go to a situation which I am sure both you and I have considered over the years, that is, an employment contract that places a restriction on the employee after he leaves the employer's service. As you indicated earlier, the courts have put strict limits on what can properly be imposed in a free country without putting an improper restraint on trade. But there are such contracts, and very important they are, and as a term of the deal no doubt the employee is better paid to compensate him for the restrictions that he accepts. It was in that context really that it seemed to me that if there could be some way of reducing the damage to the Minister put on him by restricting his activities to those which, quite plainly, could involve no conflict of interest, that might be one way of looking at it. But I think it is not the way you are looking at it at the moment.

DAVID HUNT: Well my Lord, I do not want to go down this route because I am merely a solicitor and you are a judge and you have also adjudicated in many wide-ranging cases on this topic. All I would say is, that generally my experience has been that these clauses are in to protect the confidentiality of the company's business and I would merely repeat again that, in the Rules of Guidance for Ministers, there is a clear prevention on confidentiality.

I do recall that a Cabinet Minister once left office and almost immediately wrote a book on how to be a Minister. I think it was very carefully checked through but there was no feeling at the time that he should be prevented from writing that book, or indeed that he should keep the profits from having done so. But there is that issue of confidentiality.

Equally, I think the rules have been evolved in order to stop the individual working for a competitor. I am not quite sure how you would define what is a competitor to Government. So I do come back and say that ex-Ministers have a reputation to protect, and the integrity of the Government that they served in to protect, and I think that is a very wide-ranging restriction and I cannot think of an area in which one could even begin to think of having something more restricted.

1285. LORD NOLAN: Now I am going to turn please to Sir Robin because there were some questions particularly concerning him that we wanted to raise. Then, if I may, I will come back to you Mr Hunt, before we start on Quangos.

Sir Robin, we heard evidence last week, from your predecessor's Cabinet Secretary, the effect of which was that he had never investigated cases in which allegations of impropriety or whatever had been made against Ministers and that he did not, as I understood him, think that this was a proper function of the Cabinet Secretary. I have hesitated to raise this with you for, of course, you are still in office and if you had felt in any way inhibited from speaking on it while you were still serving, that I could understand, but I believe you have got a view that you have expressed on this. Is that so?

ROBIN BUTLER: Yes and indeed I have discussed it with Lord Armstrong since he gave evidence and I think he would agree with what I have to say. I do not think that he intended to give the Committee quite such an absolute view as you describe. He did, in his evidence, say that there might be circumstances where the Cabinet Secretary was asked to investigate because, for example, security issues were in mind.

An all too common example is leak enquiries. Both he and I have had a long series of those and, of course, he carried out the investigation into the way in the which the Law Officers' advice in the Westland case, in which Ministers were involved, reached the public. So he would not want to suggest, and I would not want to suggest, that one can always advise without some degree of investigation. I think then it is a question of what matters

are suitable for a civil servant, an official, to advise and to some extent investigate on, and what not. But there are certainly some areas in which both he and I would say that advice needs to be preceded by a degree of investigation.

1286. LORD NOLAN: And in the areas where it is not appropriate for the Cabinet Secretary to carry out the investigation in the more serious cases, obviously the Prime Minister is in a difficulty, he has got to try and find out whether there is anything in it, how serious it is and it may be an allegation involving the commission of offences. Now is there any other machinery, within the Government or the Cabinet Office, for carrying out those inquiries?

ROBIN BUTLER: There is a very wide range of possible circumstances and similarly I think the Prime Minister needs a wide range of people that he or she can turn to in that situation. As you have said, if it was a question or suggestion of a criminal offence, the Prime Minister ought, like we all ought, to look to the police to investigate it. If it was a largely parliamentary or party political matter, the Prime Minister would undoubtedly, I would have thought, go to the Chief Whip in the first instance. If it is an official matter, then the Prime Minister might well go to the official machine and go to the Cabinet Secretary as the official closest to him, to ask him to advise on what are the facts. So, I think there is a wide area and there needs to be a wide area. I do not think one solution would meet all cases.

1287. LORD NOLAN: Has the Chief Whip sometimes been called in?

ROBIN BUTLER: Yes, the Prime Minister asks the Chief Whip for advice in a very large number of cases; not all of them, or indeed many of them, that I am privy to.

1288. LORD NOLAN: And the Law Officers? I can remember one case certainly, in many years past, where the Law Officers were asked to conduct an inquiry.

ROBIN BUTLER: Yes, I do not know that I can recollect the Law Officers being asked to advise on the facts; their main job is to advise on the law. I was racking my brains to think of the case that you might have in mind and the case I think that comes closest to it that I recall was the Profumo case, where the Lord Chancellor advised the Cabinet on whether security had been breached. I imagine, although I have not gone back through all the papers to check this, of course there had been a considerable police investigation. A lot of the information that was available was available through the police and I suspect that is why it came up the legal channel in that case.

1289. LORD NOLAN: Turning to business appointments. Are you satisfied that the rules and procedures for civil servants strike the right balance as they stand?

ROBIN BUTLER: Well I think that balance is the right word. Yes, I think I can say that they have been working reasonably well. We have, indeed, two distinguished Members of the Prime Minister's Advisory Committee who are on your Committee. I think the test of it is that I am not aware of any recent case of a civil servant or a military officer where there has been sustained public criticism. On the other side of it, the individuals sometimes grumble, they sometimes think they have had rough justice but they have acquiesced and we would be in trouble if they did not because, of course, it has to be a voluntary arrangement, there is no statutory backing. So from that point of view you could say yes, it does strike a reasonable balance, though people are never going to be completely satisfied in individual cases.

1290. LORD NOLAN: Can you tell us whether those rules apply if a civil servant moves to, let us say, much better paid employment in a National Health Service Authority? Is that covered by the Carlisle Committee?

ROBIN BUTLER: Not by the Carlisle Committee, formally, because the Carlisle Committee automatically looks at cases at Grades 1 and 2. For cases below that there is an arrangement whereby the Chairman does an audit on them. He does a sample check once a year and sees whether procedures are being rigorously followed. But that individual would come within the Business Appointment Rules. The Business Appointment Rules apply in all cases where the appointment is not actually made by a Minister; if it is made by a Minister it must imply that the Government is content with it. So, yes, that would apply and in the particular case I expect you have in mind which had some publicity recently, an application was made to the Department because the individual, not in the job as Private Secretary but in the previous job, had had some dealings with the body that he was joining.

1291. LORD NOLAN: Yes. I think the rules apply to companies but they were taken as applying in this case?

ROBIN BUTLER: Yes.

1292. LORD NOLAN: Thank you very much. Now Mr Hunt if I may please come back to you, just with one or two general points about that much misused word Quango. Lord Armstrong expressed some doubts about the use of Next Steps Agencies in areas which were politically sensitive, and he referred to the distinction, which is often made in such cases, between the Minister's responsibility for accountability and the Chief Executive's responsibility for operational matters. Do you have any concerns over that question?

DAVID HUNT: As long as it is made clear, my Lord, that at the end of the day the Minister remains accountable for Agencies, just as the Minister remains accountable for the rest of his Department, and that I believe should reassure any concerns that there are. I do not think, for a moment, that Agencies are inappropriate for any area which is politically sensitive—I have to say that political sensitivity seems to be much more extensive now than when I came into politics—but Agencies do provide a very valuable approach and I think the Treasury and Civil Service Select Committee acknowledge that in their report. As long as it is understood the Minister, at the end of the day, is accountable.

1293. LORD NOLAN: And as long as the lines are clear, and this is really something that you stress throughout your paper, as long as the methods of appointment are open. The Americans say that they have a Government in the Sunshine Act do they not, going back about 20 years. I think one of the Supreme Court Judges spoke of the healing effect of sunshine on corrupt places. That is at the heart, is it not, of your approach to the appointments of individuals to Quangos, that the public should be able to see much better than at present how it has been done?

May I just, before handing over to Sir William, ask you this, I think many members of the public will find in the papers helpful information which, no doubt, has been published but which is not always remembered, namely, that only one-third of such appointments carry any pay, the other two-thirds are done for nothing. So there still is a great tradition of public service going on in this country, without reward, and that is reassuring.

The problem of explaining though these numerous different types of bodies to the public and how they run, in terms that will satisfy their thirst for information, is surely a very great one. I see, in paragraph 9 of the Public Appointments Unit's paper, that a Non Departmental Public Body can be defined as a body which has a role in the processes of national government. It is not a Government department or part of one, operates to a greater or lesser extent at arms length from Ministers, and then they are divided into three main categories, Executive NDPBs, Advisory NDPBs and Tribunals. Well we, as you know, at this stage are just looking at Executive NDPBs so defined. But three paragraphs later, five other different types of body have to be distinguished from NDPBs, each with their own characters and rules. We have Next Steps Agencies, Utility Regulators, National Health Service bodies, governing bodies of Grant Maintained schools and Further Education colleges, Training and Enterprise Councils in England; can the public really ever quite understand what is going on in this myriad community of different types of bodies?

DAVID HUNT: Yes, my Lord, as long as the information is there, available, particularly to those who wish to seek it. In Public Bodies 1994, which we have now published and in fact has been published every year for a number of years but has not really received the attention that it deserves, there is a wide range of explanations. Each body is, of course, required to publish and to make public, its membership and, indeed, always to test itself against accountability to the public. That is clearly laid down. So I do not have any misgivings about the system, as long as there is openness.

I agree with you, my Lord, that we have a rich tapestry of public service in this country, of which we have every right to be proud, and you cannot sort, or categorise everybody in exactly the same way, which is why we always stress that the individual strategy has to be for individual departments, so far as the bodies under their control are concerned, and at the end of the day all the processes must ensure there is the maximum accountability and the maximum openness.

LORD NOLAN: Thank you very much. I am now going to pass you over to Sir William Utting. I know that Mr Tom King and I am sure others, will wish to take up the first part of your evidence but I think probably, in the interests of clarity, we should stick to the pattern we originally envisaged and deal with the Quangos first and then put it to the Committee generally for any matters to be raised. Sir William.

1294. WILLIAM UTTING: Thank you Chairman. I will be sticking largely to the Review of Guidance on Public Appointments that has just been published, Mr Hunt, and I would like to register appreciation of the value of the Review and particularly its emphasis on greater openness, probity, equal opportunities, accountability and responsiveness. But it is, of course, the product of an inter-departmental group, it is a Whitehall view of the world, an informed view, no doubt, but not a comprehensive one and we have received a substantial amount of written submissions and correspondence, with complaints about public appointments, about the exercise of political patronage, about a network of acquaintances being rewarded with paid jobs, about a lack of accountability to local communities on the part of public bodies that have local functions. We have had even some correspondence from people who have offered unpaid service and then appeared to be disregarded and other criticisms of appointments procedures from those operating them, as well as from those on the receiving end. So there is, I think from our perspective, a substantial amount of public disquiet on some of these matters, whether there is objective evidence to that or not.

Now Mr Sheldon told us last week that, in his Committee's view, things had gone wrong in the past because poor appointments had been made and existing rules had not been observed. It is quite clear that if the guidance in this review is followed, processes of appointment will be improved. I am not really clear about what guarantee though comes with the document, that this guidance will be better observed, in future, than existing guidance has been observed in the past.

DAVID HUNT: Well first of all Sir William, may I thank you for your comments. In fact what we are doing, so far as this report is concerned, is opening up the process. Normally this guidance would come to Ministers and we would then make decisions on the basis of that guidance. I take your point that it is Whitehall guidance but Ministers would look at the guidance in the context of the much wider world and reach decisions. What we are now doing is sharing with you, and indeed with the public, the detail of the guidance, and then, once we have your recommendations, your views, will reach the decisions and then implement this new guidance. I think it is much more wide-ranging than ever before. I have no information that the previous guidance has not been observed. I greatly regret that some involved in politics have made this very much a party political football. In fact, the Labour Party instructed its Members not to sit on public bodies until they issued a new guidance note in, I think it was, 1993. So that ban has now been lifted. What I want to ensure is that appointments are made on merit and it is the best people who get appointed. That is what this guidance is intended to achieve and I share your resolve that it should do so.

1295. WILLIAM UTTING: I think we might be able to make some constructive suggestions about how a guide of this nature might be monitored. If I could pursue now the point that I think you raised about the best people being appointed to these jobs, I was particularly concerned about these complaints that local communities were not adequately represented on public bodies that were dealing with local issues. It seems to me that the guide is actually rather light on what might be the local accountability, or the accountability to local communities, of some of these bodies. I think I would put forward the case for consideration of the best person for the job, including reference to including on the Committee people who have some standing in the local community. Now I do not want to get into the issue of whether this should be local government or not. In a sense that is a distraction, I am simply concerned that there should be some consideration of the best person, including some representation of the local community.

DAVID HUNT: I agree with that. It is very important for a Local Hospital Trust not only to have close links with the local community, not only to ensure that the local people are aware of what is happening within the National Health Service Trust, but also to ensure that people of standing locally do sit on the Trusts.

Ministers do not appoint any more the members of the Training and Enterprise Councils, the private companies supplying training. If one looks through the membership one generally finds that the key local employer, key local people, are represented on the boards of Training and Enterprise Councils and I would agree with you, that it is very important that there is that identification of the local community interest, which always seemed to be satisfied but never was satisfied by the emergence of one or two councillors sitting on the body who, of course, have a tremendous amount of other duties. I remember, particularly, the establishment of the new governing bodies of Further Education colleges, who have now become independent, have got, in the main, no longer the statutory local authority representative but local people representing local interests and greatly value their independence and are moving forward in a very positive way. But at the end of the day it must be vitally important for that local identification to be there.

1296. WILLIAM UTTING. Good. Thank you. If I could move to the paid and unpaid question. I do not take quite such a sanguine view as the Chairman of the proportion of paid as against unpaid appointments. To be told that one-third of these appointments are, in fact, salaried seems to me to represent a pretty high figure. It would work out at something like 15,000 posts which are, in fact, remunerated in some way, although I of course quite take the point that only a very small number, I think he said 170, attract salaries as high as £50,000 a year.

I was genuinely surprised to find, for example, that 93 per cent of NHS appointments are now paid and I wondered who decides whether or not a post is paid, who sets the level of pay and whether there is any central control over this?

DAVID HUNT: Yes, well, quite often Parliament will decide whether a post should be paid or unpaid and Ministers, of course, deliberate on the level of pay. So there is a clear policy behind this.

Sir William, dealing with your first point, I think that the distinction between paid and unpaid is there really to put matters into perspective. Now you, from all your knowledge, were aware, already, of the number that were unpaid. I have to tell you, in my postbag, the general view from my constituents and other members of the public, seem to be that they were all paid. I think, therefore, it has been a valuable distinction. Criticisms have tended to concentrate on the paid appointments and in fact, many have suggested that all the paid appointments are handsomely paid; as we know that is far from the truth. Payment, I suppose, does sometimes indicate the importance and the scale of the post involved but it is only one guide, as you pointed out Sir William, and I quite accept that some unpaid posts can be very sensitive indeed and deal with politically controversial issues. I suppose all this emphasises the difficulty of producing simple classifications in what is a very complex area.

1297. WILLIAM UTTING: I agree with you about the importance of making clearer to the public the number of these posts that are unpaid and the unfortunate consequence that appears to be developing of the public assuming that all such posts are now remunerated. I think that has got unfortunate implications for people who actually wanted to carry out unpaid public service, if everybody now thinks that they are getting a good salary for what they are doing.

The report mentions one of the aims of the appointments system as being to allow the best tradition of voluntary public service in the UK to be sustained. That actually does not seem to be something that will occur of its own volition and that some further consideration may be needed by Government as a whole, about how voluntary effort in this country is to be sustained and developed and is something that I would simply offer you as a comment rather than a question.

DAVID HUNT: Well I would be very interested Sir William if you had any specific proposals on that because as his Lordship mentioned at the outset, voluntarism in the United Kingdom is very strong indeed. In my own constituency I think I am President of about 30 or 40 different charities and in those charities there are an enormous number of people who give all their time and effort absolutely free. Voluntarism has always been extraordinarily strong in the United Kingdom. What I want to do is to build on that and any suggestions which you and your colleagues have as to how we might better build on those strong foundations I would greatly welcome.

1298. WILLIAM UTTING: Good. I hope that we might be able to give that some further consideration in our deliberations on the Committee.

You have made a virtue of the principle of proportionality in your presentation and I quite take the point that it is self-defeating to expend massive resources on filling posts that are perhaps one day a week and unpaid, but the concept of proportionality has got an air of a sort of classic bureaucratic get-out, in that it appears to give latitude to each Department to decide for itself what the needs of the situation are and, of what cost-effectiveness actually consists. Is it possible for each Department to be clearer about what is required for each category of appointment and, in fact, to inform us what action it is proposing to take for each category of appointment? My point would be that there is a value in demonstrating that things are done openly and equitably and that the cost of that is one that ought to be regarded as a reasonable and proper cost.

DAVID HUNT: Yes, I am attracted by that approach Sir William. It demonstrates the need for clear, central guidance and for Departments to operate within that guidance. You are quite right that different posts call for different approaches. It is always necessary to have a job description, but it may not always be necessary for some of the other aspects which are recommended in the report. For paid jobs, full-time jobs, it is important to advertise and to do so widely, perhaps to use consultants. Therefore, I agree we need clear, central guidance and for Departments themselves to operate within that guidance and for everyone to know exactly what is happening within the appointments system.

1299. WILLIAM UTTING: You make very clear in the papers that these bodies are the responsibility of a parent

Department, though not a central responsibility in Government. There is a slightly tetchy sentence I think in one place in the papers, where they say that the Treasury and your Department should not have to do Departments' jobs for them. Even so, one does wonder if there is not actually too much latitude still left to Departments here; there is a degree of departmentalism in protecting Ministers' rights and responsibilities and not a strong enough central grip on the situation. It is slightly disconcerting to see that most departmental co-ordination is at the level of Higher Executive Officer and Executive Officer part-time, which must be two or three levels below Grade 7 in the Civil Service and that only three of them have a central appointments unit with full-time staff. I think I would actually be looking for some tighter control, or some stronger encouragement to Departments, to get their house in order on these matters.

DAVID HUNT: Yes, Sir William, but you always pay a price for that tighter central control and it must always be at the expense of the discretion of Departments. But I do not know whether Sir Robin wants to comment on the points you make about the different gradings of those involved in dealing with it.

ROBIN BUTLER: I think you must preserve Ministerial accountability and, of course, the accountability is with the departmental Minister and should not be shifted on to the centre. Of course, we are moving in a world where much more is being delegated to Departments and there is a good deal of resistance from Departments to the centre telling them how to do their jobs for them. So, I think we are moving to where one sets clear standards and the Departments then have to be judged against them and be accountable for their performance and that this approach is of a piece with that.

1300. WILLIAM UTTING: Yes, it is simply that the issues that are being raised about public bodies do seem to cause so much public interest and concern that there may be a case for a stronger grip by Government as a whole on some of these processes.

I was interested to see in one of the papers that there is going to be a continuation of increased financial flexibility for these Departments, which goes four square with what Sir Robin was just saying about these being responsibilities of individual Departments.

I would perhaps end by asking about some clarification of the Chief Whip's role in public appointments in future. The document starts off by saying this is going to be reduced or eliminated but later on clarifies that, it seems to indicate that some jobs will still go through the Whips' Office but others will not now. I wonder if you could just restate what is the difference.

DAVID HUNT: Thank you for giving me the opportunity Sir William, just to demonstrate that there is a distinction between the Chief Whip being involved at the outset, when names are being sought, and the Chief Whip being involved at the much later stage, when the intended appointee has been identified. In future the Chief Whip is not being invited, specifically, to suggest names for particular appointments. Names, of course, will be fed into the Public Appointments Unit from all parts and all sides of the House of Commons I am sure, as well as from everywhere else, but the Chief Whip's role is confined—let me make it clear—to those cases which fall within Questions of Procedure for Ministers and where political sensitivity might arise through the appointment of some particular individual, for example a current or former Member of the House of Commons. That is the distinction maintained and it is only at the latter stage that the Chief Whip would be involved.

1301. WILLIAM UTTING: Good. So the Chief Whip comes in at the end of the process and only on appointments of political importance or sensitivity?

DAVID HUNT: Yes and the ones that fall within *Questions of Procedure for Ministers,* that is correct.

WILLIAM UTTING: Thank you.

ROBIN BUTLER: Can I just correct one impression Sir William might have? The Chief Whip comments on anything that may be politically important. The appointments that he sees are appointments that are important enough to go to the Prime Minister but his interest in it will be if it raises any political aspects. So you would not pick out one and say, this is one that has got political connotations, therefore we refer it to the Chief Whip.

WILLIAM UTTING: Good. Thank you.

1302. LORD NOLAN: Mr Hunt, may I just add one question which I overlooked, before passing the questioning round? In your opening statement you number amongst the questions for us, what is the Committee's view on the question of the declaration of political affiliation and political office holding? May I take it that is a question you are putting squarely to us, it is not one on which the Government have taken a line at the moment?

DAVID HUNT: Well at the moment, my Lord, we have taken the view that with the vast bulk of these appointments it is not necessary for someone to have a political affiliation, it is not a requirement and, in fact, it is not recorded in the vast majority of names which are on the Public Appointments List. There has, however, been a call, particularly from politicians, that there should be some identification and I would very much like to hear the Committee's views on that.

LORD NOLAN: I will go round. Mr King.

1303. TOM KING: Can I deal, my Lord, firstly with these Ministerial Rules, so that we do not muddle it up. I do not really want to ask my question about Quangos, I would rather come back, is that agreeable?

So if I turn first to this question about Ministerial Rules and you say there is a very tough restriction, which there is because it is an absolute, as you say, prohibition on anything that will in any way reflect on the integrity and behaviour. But we are dealing here, of course, not actually with what happened but also with the perception. Part of the reason we are here, there have been some totally unfair allegations made and from the witnesses here we have heard enough of the actual story to know that they were totally untrue. Yet we have this problem of perception. What quite clearly some of your former colleagues were looking for, out of some embracing of similar rules to the ones that apply to civil servants, was the protection of their own name. That it was not just left

to them to say they have behaved with total integrity but that they were able to demonstrate that the issue had been addressed independently and was seen to apply. And, moreover, that these are not, of course, total prohibitions in the rules for civil servants, they are merely a form of vetting procedure and, in some cases, it may only be three months—I do not know whether any less than that—where it seemed to be perfectly reasonable and there is nothing objectionable.

Now, I just press you on this because you have been pretty clear, in the evidence to the Committee, that you do not think that is appropriate. Now I applaud, absolutely, the stand that the real defence is the integrity and proper reporting—accurate reporting and not unfair, malicious, vicious and mendacious reporting—which has occurred. But, having said that, do you not think, in the climate of the world in which we live, sadly, there does need to be some outside procedure which would actually be a proper protection and entitlement of people leaving office?

DAVID HUNT: Yes, this is one of the key questions, my Lord. May I just answer Tom King in this way? First of all, I do not believe it is widely enough known that there is Paragraph 105. Although we publish this Guidance, I do not think people are aware—indeed at some of the meetings I have had I have made people aware of it and they have said they had not realised the extent of the very clear message that is sent to all those leaving office. I do think there is a huge distinction between civil servants and Ministers leaving office, Ministers leaving office sometimes in their 30s or 40s, having lost their seat as well, having a substantial salary today and nothing tomorrow, apart from a small payment in comparative terms. I am not too sure that we are going to attract the right calibre of people if we suddenly start introducing a whole range of procedures which apply to those who have, in the main, completed their career and are retiring on a full pension and trying to read across into those who are leaving office.

Now, Tom King will know that during the '80s there were quite a large number of people leaving office—I think I counted 57 at one stage. Even more so in the early '70s, when in 1970 a whole Government left office; in 1974 another whole Government left office. So, within four years there were enormous numbers and I am not too sure, in that sort of situation, that it is easy to formulate rules.

It may be possible to have some procedure whereby those who think someone's integrity has been put in question could go to some body but that is really the Prime Minister at the end of the day, at the present time, and the Prime Minister has said allegations have been made, let me see the substance of the evidence and no-one has come forward.

We had the outrageous allegation on the floor of the House of Commons, my Lord, that one of my Cabinet colleagues had received a cheque for millions and millions of pounds in some shadowy circumstances, since proved to be a complete lie. I am not sure what procedure we could evoke for trying that sort of accusation being made.

I think the answer is, it is not the reporting as well, it is the making, by some of our parliamentary colleagues, of these outrageous allegations, often under the protection of parliamentary privilege that I strongly deplore. Those allegations should never have been made and therefore the integrity of the individuals concerned would never have been called into question. So I go right back to source and say, let us stop making unjustified allegations, rather than let us set up some new procedure to cover some new mischief which is not there.

1304. ANNE WARBURTON: Chairman, will it be in order to ask two questions? One is concerned with Public Appointments and other is with Civil Service?

LORD NOLAN: I am sure the witness is well able to deal with the questions.

DAVID HUNT: We do not yet know the questions.

1305. ANNE WARBURTON: The Public Appointments question is really a lot of mini-questions which I hope adds up to a question. I will start out on the basis which has already been laid that the principle applied is merit but that this is not always obvious to all observers. It leads me to ask these questions, is it possible now to say what sort of scale the Public Appointments will be running at in future? I take it that in the last few years that they have been rather intense because so many new bodies are being set up, but at what sort of regular rhythm is it expected that they will be running? Shall I go on?

DAVID HUNT: Yes please.

1306. ANNE WARBURTON: Secondly, I wondered whether there is any way of giving an idea where the one-third paid appointments actually are or, alternatively, where the two-thirds unpaid are to be found? Looking at the various moves which are being considered and implemented to improve recruitment—I suppose that is the right word—the lists for appointments, I would like to stop particularly on advertisement because if two-thirds of the appointments are not paid, presumably your rule of proportionality operates particularly on that sector, so does advertisement come out of the list for unpaid posts?

Advisory Committees. You mention, Minister, in your letter—in fact I think you mention it in your speech too—that there is a Scottish precedent for an advisory committee which seems to work happily there. I think in the paper it tells us that the NHS here is looking to possibly introducing it more widely and I wonder if there is any more to be said about its applicability, both within the NHS and perhaps in other areas?

In general it is quite remarkable that when one comes to this as a novice what a lot of different answers there are which are used for different purposes.

For example, you commented I think that Ministers no longer appoint the Members of TEC Boards. I happened to be talking to a TEC Chairman yesterday who told me that he had in fact chosen his board. That is probably a special circumstance but I wonder if there are other places where the Chairmen are left to choose their own boards.

Am I going on too long? Yes, probably, but I have got one or two more I would like to ask.

If all these appointments are made by Departments or departmental Ministers, I am left wondering who the people are who screen the nominations in the Departments, what standard of comparability there might

be, what sort of research and investigative powers they have. In other words, how much can they really find out before they put names forward to Ministers?

Have the limits of standardisation now been reached as between one organisation and another or is there still scope for exploring whether, as I think Sir William said, the thing could be made simpler by using rather more of a formula—not just guidance but actually setting out how these bodies should be appointed?

Then the last question on this one—auditing. We were told last week that one third of NDPBs are not subject to the National Audit Office and we had the impression that the Comptroller and Auditor General would be very glad to perform that service more widely. Would that be seen as being helpful?

If any of these questions are too detailed, please just ignore them.

LORD NOLAN: We are running a little short of time, so if you could please try and make whatever main points you have in reply to Dame Anne as briefly as possible, I should be grateful.

DAVID HUNT: Am I allowed to pick and choose? There are eight questions. My Lord, shall I just run through each of the eight?

LORD NOLAN: If you please.

DAVID HUNT: And then I could leave the committee to come back, and then Sir Robin may want to add something.

Can I just say that I understand that tomorrow the head of the Public Appointments Unit, Mr Fox, is coming to give evidence with Richard Mottram, so if I don't pick up some of the detail, they, I know, would be delighted to deal with that then.

First of all, what sort of scale of public appointments? There is no doubt here a political difference. We have made the political point that the number of non-departmental public bodies has declined over the last 16 years by, I think, something over a third, and other political parties have a whole range of new bodies that they would want to institute. Indeed, some of them are running into the thousands. So I can't predict what would happen if there was a change, but certainly this document, which we have now published, "Public Bodies 1994", demonstrates the regular decline which has occurred and can of course be compared to "Public Bodies 1993" and previously, which set out the position as at those dates.

The paid appointments are set out in "Public Bodies 1994", those appointments for which Ministers are responsible. It demonstrates which are the paid appointments and in fact sets out the salary figures. So it is all there very clearly. I am always willing to consider whether we should produce a huge tome which contains all the names of the individuals, but I am not persuaded that it would be worth the expense, because those names can be found out from the bodies concerned, so there is a wide degree of openness here. You can go along and find out who sits on your local body very clearly.

Lists of appointments—I want to see many more people coming forward, nominating themselves to serve and also nominating others. I think the Prime Minister's opening out of the honours system has been a great success. Many of my constituents are now coming forward, and we had some examples recently in the latest honours list, nominating individuals who they felt had contributed to a substantial degree, and there was great rejoicing when two of the individuals received an honour. There is then much more public participation in the process. I would like to see that applied to the public appointments system generally, with many more people feeling that they can nominate themselves and nominate others.

The advisory committee is the fourth question. The Secretary of State for Scotland has in fact brought in his own approach to appointments, and I think approaches are tailored by each of the countries, each of the Departments, meeting the needs of its types of bodies and of course its size and organisational and regional differences. Of course the Scottish Secretary has a number of quasi-judicial appointments which I think he felt had to be approached in that way. As we do with the appointment of justices of the peace: we are advised by local committees who put forward names of individuals. So I think that there are circumstances in which panels are helpful; there are circumstances in which panels certainly wouldn't be appropriate for one-off appointments, of which there are many. Given the variety, delegation is much more appropriate than a uniform and centralised approach in Scotland, and that is what the Scottish Secretary decided. In fact it runs through our reforms and runs through our civil service reforms as well.

The Training and Enterprise Council chairman you met. There are, I think, 75 Training and Enterprise Councils in England, and I think that you would find a variety of approaches, but certainly the boards themselves are responsible for appointing to the boards, but they are private sector companies: I think they are limited by guarantee, my Lord. They receive a contract to carry out the provision of training in a particular area, but it is a matter for the Secretary of State whether the contract is placed with that particular body or whether, and I suppose this is, at the end of the day, the ultimate guidance a Minister can give himself or herself, another body is asked to proceed, if it is felt that the body in question is not delivering the service in the way that is being looked for by the Department.

I don't know whether Sir Robin wants to add anything on screening, but I am satisfied that a considerable number of checks are carried out on the individuals who are put forward and recommended.

How can the limits of standardisation be explored between departments? How can the process be made simpler? I did say to Sir William before that central guidance is essential. Sir William was making the point that perhaps it needs to be wider and more comprehensive. That is something I await with interest, my Lord, the committee's views on.

So far as auditing is concerned, of course we rely on internal auditing, buttressed by the long-standing procedures of the National Audit Office and the Public Accounts Committee. We have laid down very clear auditing processes, ensuring that Departments check that the procedures laid down in the reports are being applied correctly. It could of course eventually involve an outside check from the National Audit Office, and that is a real

incentive for everybody involved to get things right before they get that far. The Public Appointments Unit will have a role in ensuring that the best practices are identified and then publicised to all those involved, and at the end of the day of course we and everyone attach the greatest importance to the maintenance of high standards, and long may that be the case.

1307. PETER SHORE: Mr Hunt, I am surprised and disappointed at your attitude towards the vetting of appointments for ex-Ministers. It seems to me that there is here a matter of genuine public concern, and I would have thought that rules that were thought to be applicable to senior civil servants, who are generally accepted, no less than Ministers, to be honourable people and to behave properly, should be felt to be inappropriate for Ministers.

Let me put the point to you very strongly in this sentence. The reason why ex-civil servants are, as it were, vetted and their appointments, if necessary, checked is because they may have acquired special knowledge during their post as senior civil servants which would be of competitive advantage to any firm that then employed them. In addition to that, there is of course the general knowledge which they have acquired of potentially forward thinking in government, which again may be of considerable influence. Finally, of course, there is a danger that if there is a simply a revolving door from senior government positions to private industry, people will suspect that Ministers are being influenced by the prospect of future lucrative employment. For all those reasons, surely there is a very strong case for applying the same kind of procedures to Ministers as now apply to senior civil servants.

DAVID HUNT: I don't agree, Mr Shore, and I have laid out the clear reasons. I think it is wrong to differentiate between a Cabinet Minister or a Minister who goes into business or returns to his profession and, say, a Cabinet Minister who decides, solely as a result of having been a Cabinet Minister, and several of your colleagues have followed this path, to sit down and write their memoirs, memoirs which quite often will influence government and government policy, particularly when the same party is still in office, and they only gain remuneration from writing their memoirs because of the office they held. That is why I believe at the end of the day, and I regret that many people have not focused on this sufficiently, in the requirement that Ministers who leave office should avoid any course of action that would reflect adversely on their or the government's reputation for integrity or the confidentiality of its proceedings. If that second aspect had been upheld with greater rigour, perhaps some of the concern about public life would not have been as great as followed the publication of some of the memoirs. But I don't think you can pick and choose and say "That profession is barred". I don't think you can say to a trade unionist that they can't return to their trade union employment or to a lecturer that they can't return to lecturing, and then to someone from business that they can't return to business. I think you have to rely on the integrity of the individual.

1308. PETER SHORE: But the point is that the vetting procedure does not bar ex-Ministers from a whole wide range of jobs, and, as we well know, there is a natural connection between Conservative Members of Parliament and the City and firms in industry. Nobody is suggesting that that would be interfered with. All we are suggesting is that in those particular areas where a

Minister has held responsibility and has had direct dealings with a firm, perhaps to their advantage—or with an industry to its advantage—it would be sensible and would be seen and welcomed in public if there was a vetting procedure, even, if I may say, on the somewhat strained analogy with a Minister writing his memoirs, as I understand it, he has to clear it with the Cabinet Office.

DAVID HUNT: Yes, solely because of paragraph 105, just as he or she has to make sure that they respect the integrity of the government that they serve. I just greatly regret, my Lord, that Mr Shore should have chosen to make a party political point, because I had hoped that we could look at this in a non-political atmosphere. I recall that when he and his colleagues left office in 1979 there were a number of Ministers who moved into positions in industry where it could have been said, if they didn't observe paragraph 105—I have no evidence that any of them failed to observe it—that they were able to move into positions where they could bring a wider vision. I have spoken before about people moving into industries that they had some connection with when they were in office. At the end of the day, provided people observe the importance of their own integrity being maintained, no committee of experts will assist the situation. I have just said what I believe personally and what the government believes, and I would certainly hope that we could focus on the differences with civil servants, who, in the main, have had a career and are retiring at the end of a substantial career on a substantial pension, and differentiate in the way that I described without throwing up the comment that Mr Shore has made.

1309. PETER SHORE: We are going to have to differ on that, but let me move on now to the general area of public appointments and quangos. I have no doubt you will think that this is also a party political point that I am going to make, but I start off by referring you to today's *Financial Times,* which is not a notoriously partisan paper, which described the evidence that you gave as being "breathtaking in its complacency", and I want to make this point to you. An awful lot of evidence has been accumulated, some of which has come to this committee already. I refer to Robert Sheldon's PAC report, with that long list of misdemeanours committed by quangos and quango Members which was attached to his general paper; also the evidence that undoubtedly exists, although it is only partial, of actual use of political patronage in appointments, or at least the perception that there has been a great deal of the use of political patronage. Those are serious matters which are not, in my view, addressed in these documents which you presented yesterday and are before us today, and I would like to ask you first this direct question.

Knowing that there is public accusation or public anxiety in this area, did the reviewing body of officials, in drawing up this new document presented to us yesterday, investigate any of the accusations that had been made? Did they take even a handful or a sample of quangos and look at them and see whether the criticisms made were justified, unjustified or only partially true? Did they do that?

DAVID HUNT: First of all, Mr Shore, I said that you were introducing a party political point because you mentioned Conservative ex-Ministers. I am dealing with all ex-Ministers and I felt it was wrong for you to single out Conservative ex-Ministers, so I defend what I said before. Secondly, on the point that you have made about the

Financial Times, I don't want to bandy editorials with you, but I do hope you will have time today just to gaze at *The Times.* Under the heading "Hunt for Principles, An agenda for Lord Nolan's committee today", is a very interesting editorial, which includes the comment "Mr Hunt's recommendations are a reasonable start". I hope you will then develop a more balanced view of what these proposals are. They have of course, in all the deliberations, taken into account the criticisms that are made, many of them unjustified, and I believe the report that you have before you is a genuine attempt to meet those criticisms head on. They have been taken into account. But I now await you and your colleagues, my Lord, on this committee before implementing those recommendations. I await your comments, and if you have any proposals to make which you believe would improve the system still further, I would be very keen to hear them, because we as a government are determined to ensure that the charge that some "quangocracy" is being set up will not stick, certainly with this government.

1310. PETER SHORE: Mr Hunt, you have made a number of comments, but you haven't actually replied to my question, which I gather was in the negative, whether the official study attempted to establish, by investigation, whether there was any truth in the criticisms that have been so widely made, and I understand from your reply that no such investigation was made. So let's move on——

DAVID HUNT: No, I haven't said that at all. I didn't realise that we were going to get into this sort of a mode. What I have said is that these proposals come against the background which we have been able to identify ourselves, in which we have seen various allegations thrown around about the way in which people are appointed. Tomorrow you have the Public Appointments Unit coming to give evidence, and you can address that question to Mr Fox, but certainly when the proposals were presented to me they were presented against the background of all the public comment which has been made.

PETER SHORE: But without investigation of them.

Let me turn now to the proposals that have been made in the White Paper. The only serious proposal that I can see there is that advertising of appointments should be the general rule, to which I suppose one is entitled to say that it's very surprising in many ways that advertising has not been the general rule. But is advertising in itself, do you think, sufficient? What distinguishes the appointments to quangos from appointments of central government and local government is of course not that appointments are advertised but that there is no competitive entry requirement, that nobody, apart from the Minister who appoints, sits, as it were, examines the relative merits of the candidates who have answered the advertisement. Isn't that really the distinctive feature and isn't that a very serious missing factor in the appointment to quangos?

DAVID HUNT: I don't accept that, Mr Shore. As you gaze through "Public Bodies 1994", I think everyone will realise the point that has been made earlier, that there is a complete range of appointments here and that there has been for a number of appointments, particularly the higher-paid appointments, a degree of competition. I just give the example of the research councils, for which I am responsible, where often a range of eminent scientists is put forward, and at the end of the day I have not sought to second-guess those who are advising me on the calibre of the individual scientists involved. A competition is held. For instance, for the latest research council created—Daresbury and Rutherford Appleton Laboratories (DRAL)—there was open competition for the individual to become chairman and chief executive. This is the latest appointment I have made, so far as research councils are concerned. In fact, after an open competition the existing holder of the office of running that particular council was confirmed in office. That was the recommendation I received. So there is a good degree of competition. I don't know whether, Sir Robin, you want to add to that aspect.

ROBIN BUTLER: The only thing I would say is that the purpose of both the Public Appointments Unit and the proposals for self-nomination is to get a choice, and a choice which can then be made on merit. I would just like to refer back to the point that Sir William Utting made: of course the vast majority of these appointments go nowhere near Ministers at all.

1311. PETER SHORE: I am glad to hear that open competition is sometimes used and I would certainly urge that much more extensive use be considered of open competition, because that really does meet all the requirements of fairness, merit and so on in making appointments.

My last question to you on this is a reference again, to make quite sure I understand, to the role of the Chief Whip. Would it be right to say that in the past at any rate, up till this, the Chief Whip had to "be consulted before Ministers make or recommend appointments to significant committees, Commissions and other public bodies in case there are any names the Chief Whip would wish to be considered with other candidates"? That is what happened in the past—am I right in saying?—and now it is proposed that the Chief Whip should have a lesser role, but nevertheless he should be consulted. At which end—at the nominating end, as it were, or before a final appointment is made?

DAVID HUNT: Before the final appointment is made.

PETER SHORE: Before the final appointment is made. So that is a time where clearly a decisive intervention could be made.

DAVID HUNT: Yes, but only in an advisory capacity and only in respect of those appointments that fall within the rules of guidance for Ministers. I can't speak for what happened under, say, a previous Labour administration, but I had always understood that under successive administrations the Chief Whip had been consulted at the outset to see if there were any particular names the Chief Whip wished to be considered and I had always understood that that had happened under the administration when Mr Shore served in the Cabinet.

PETER SHORE: Let me assure you, Mr Hunt, that the rules that are being considered here will apply to any government, once they are accepted, whatever its political colour is.

DAVID HUNT: I am grateful to Mr Shore to speaking for any future administration.

1312. LORD THOMSON: I wonder if I could raise just two brief points. The first is really a factual one, going back to the comparison that Mr Hunt drew between ex-Ministers going off to outside posts and ex-Ministers writing their memoirs. Is it not a fact that in the case of memoirs there is a detailed procedure for reviewing clearance, I think involving a formal committee, which sets out the rules and goes a good deal further than paragraph 105 in "Questions of Procedure for Ministers"?

DAVID HUNT: But, my Lord, at the end of the day that paragraph does override everyone in what they do. I understand that a former Cabinet colleague of some of those involved in previous administrations has now recorded and broadcast a number of tapes, including his comments following Cabinet meetings, and we have been hearing those on the BBC. I understand that he chose not to submit those for scrutiny through the procedures his Lordship has just outlined. At the end of the day it is for the individual—that is the point I am making—and the individual must always ensure that nothing calls into question his or her integrity.

1313. LORD THOMSON: I hope Mr Hunt won't feel it's a party political point if I tell him that, although he described paragraph 105 as "wide and over-arching", my reaction when I first read it, when we started our work some months ago, was to feel that, by itself, it was so general as to be rather banal and meaningless, and therefore that was the case for looking to whether there were not additional requirements for Ministers comparable, in changing circumstances, to those for very senior civil servants, whose integrity is as important as the integrity of Ministers, of course.

DAVID HUNT: To me, just the reference to the word "integrity" couldn't under any circumstances be banal or meaningless. But these rules are now published, they have been published for nearly three years, and it has always been open to any individual or organisation to come forward with what they consider to be improved wording, and it may well be that this committee will wish to do so.

1314. LORD THOMSON: Perhaps we will in due course. Could I turn to a quite separate matter relating to the very helpful evidence that Sir Robin gave us, but directing my question to you, Mr Hunt, because it relates to ministerial responsibilities generally? I think it was very helpful to hear from Sir Robin that there is a proper role for the Cabinet Secretary in certain circumstances: security matters are very specially a Cabinet Secretary's responsibility. Leaks are, more often than not, leaks relating to whether it came from civil servants and are very properly the Cabinet Secretary's responsibility as Head of the Home Civil Service. But when it comes to the behaviour of Ministers, is it not really a ministerial responsibility, and I put it very carefully in this way, for the Prime Minister and other Ministers to deal with the behaviour of a ministerial colleague in a way that preserves absolutely the political independence and political neutrality of the Secretary to the Cabinet, because is not that political independence and political neutrality of the Cabinet Secretary and Head of the Home Civil Service at the very heart of standards in public life in this country?

DAVID HUNT: Yes, and, my Lord, we have just published a White Paper, following the White Paper on continuity and change, called "Taking Forward Continuity and Change", stating quite clearly that perhaps one of the most important things about British public life has been the acceptance that the integrity, the honesty, the impartiality and objectivity of the British Civil Service is beyond doubt, so I would agree with that, and Sir Robin has given examples of the limited circumstances in which he may be involved. But at the end of the day it will always be for the Minister, or the ex-Minister, to reflect on his or her position, and the rules of guidance, the "Questions of Procedure for Ministers" lay down in several places that if anyone is in any doubt about any of this, they should consult the Prime Minister, but at the end of the day it must be for the individual concerned.

LORD THOMSON: Thank you.

CLIFFORD BOULTON: My questions can wait till tomorrow.

1315. LORD NOLAN: Well, Mr Hunt, end of examination. Thank you both very much indeed for your help and for giving us so much of your time. We are very grateful to you.

Mr Radice, I am so sorry you have had such a long wait, but I hope, with some confidence, that you weren't bored.

GILES RADICE MP AND PROFESSOR SUE RICHARDS

GILES RADICE MP: Not at all, no. It was very interesting indeed.

1316. LORD NOLAN: It is very good of you to give us the extra time which I am afraid we are going to ask of you now, you and Sue Richards. I must apologise also for having in my opening remarks referred to you as the Secretary of the Treasury and Civil Service Select Committee's Sub-Committee on the Civil Service, when you are in fact the chairman—that's right, isn't it?—and Miss Richards is from the Office of Public Management. Had you proposed to make an opening statement?

GILES RADICE: Very briefly, if I may, just to say that you are right, I am chairman of the Civil Service Sub-Committee, and it is obviously in that capacity that I shall be answering questions, though I assume that there may possibly be times when I will be speaking in a personal rather than chairman's capacity. That's the first point. Secondly, our major report from the Treasury and Civil Service Select Committee, which is presumably the reason why you have called us here, is a consensus report—it is unanimous—and has the support of a majority, who are Conservatives, on the committee. I think it is absolutely right, when we are talking about a non-partisan civil service, that you need to deal with it on a consensus basis. I am sure that is also true, if I may say so, of standards in public life.

I was very pleased to hear David Hunt say that of course the civil service is a great national asset, because it is in that spirit that we have looked at the whole problem facing the civil service, that it is a permanent and important instrument for all administrations and that it is committed to impartiality, integrity, selection and promotion on merit and accountability. Of course there have been a number of problems arising from the sweeping managerial change, the fact that one government has been in power for a long time and that you have had some quite controversial episodes leading to, for example, the PAC report, the Scott inquiry and of course your own committee looking at standards in public life.

What we have tried to do is to come up with a civil service code. Of course there hasn't been one, and we

have tried to make what we believe is a clear and simple exposition of the values underlying the civil service and indeed of the constitutional position of civil servants and Ministers. I should like you to note that in our code it does in fact have a special position, because the civil servants owe their loyalty to Ministers, for all practical purposes, subject to the code. That is a new departure, which hasn't even been accepted by the government. Secondly, we are arguing that there ought to be an independent element of appeal: there never has been one. At the moment, as you know, it's to the Head of the Civil Service. Thirdly, we are saying it should have statutory backing. I think that's important, because this code needs to be on a permanent basis and it needs to have the support of Parliament, which any code which just comes from the administration by definition does not have. And it should apply to all civil servants, though we do have a paragraph in which we say that we ought to consider whether it should apply to quangos, particularly where those quangos are taking over former government functions. We say also that, where private contractors are doing formerly civil service work, they should also be governed by this code.

We also argue for more openness in the civil service and we have a major proposal there, which is that the Civil Service Commission should take over the top appointments of civil servants. That has not been accepted by the government, but we believe that if we are going to have a more open civil service, with more advertising and more top civil service jobs coming from outside, you need to have all of that monitored by a Civil Service Commission which should be on a statutory basis. Thank you very much.

LORD NOLAN: Thank you very much. I am going to ask Dame Anne Warburton to take up the questioning.

1317. ANNE WARBURTON: Mr Radice, it must have given you and your colleagues on the committee some pleasure to be congratulated by the government on your report. I am thinking in particular of the code of conduct. You have just told us various points on the code which you would like to see taken further. Was that a complete review of the government's version of the code after they had worked on it?

GILES RADICE: We are obviously very pleased that the government have accepted our code, particularly as they argued against it for about 18 months in hearings, and also the independent appeal system, so we are quite delighted about that. But there are one or two areas where they have differed from us. They have basically accepted our code in its entirety, so we are very delighted about that. In one or two cases I have to say I think they have actually improved on our code.

1318. ANNE WARBURTON: Nothing but compliments on the code. The committee said in the report that you thought it should be put on a statutory basis.

GILES RADICE: Yes.

1319. ANNE WARBURTON: What would be the advantages that you see of that?

GILES RADICE: If it wasn't on a statutory basis, it wouldn't actually have the authority of Parliament behind it. It would basically be the code of the administration; it would have this superior or this special position which we are saying it ought to have. So I think it has to be on a statutory basis. I am glad that the government hasn't actually ruled it out. They have said that they are prepared to consider it and they think there are advantages and disadvantages. I very much hope that the Opposition will accept our code and would accept that it should be on a statutory basis.

1320. ANNE WARBURTON: Thank you very much. As to the independent appeal arrangements—the First Commissioner of the Civil Service—that has, I think, been largely accepted also. We heard last week, when we had the General Secretary of the First Division Association here, that the civil servants would like to go on negotiating about some of the details of that, and I wondered what you thought about this. I was struck by the fact that the independent approach through the Civil Service Commissioners would be envisaged only after departmental processes had been completed and I wondered whether that would achieve the anonymity which perhaps is necessary. Given that only one complaint has been raised in so many years, perhaps something rather more protective might be proposed.

GILES RADICE: We argued about this for some time, but I think we came down in favour of exhausting the existing procedures first—this is a good employee relations rule—because otherwise you might get a situation where, at a very low level, some aggrieved civil servant would go straight to the Civil Service Commissioner, and I think that would be a bit of a waste of time, frankly. I think it should only be where the existing procedures have not satisfied the civil servant concerned. I think the fact of having an independent element would in itself mean that the existing procedures are likely to work more effectively. As you probably know, in our proposals we have said that the Civil Service Commissioner should oversee the whole appeals procedure, and it may well be that he or she would want to make some proposals as to the improvement of that procedure.

1321. ANNE WARBURTON: We have had some evidence put to us suggesting that there is a great reluctance to take it through the departmental procedure.

GILES RADICE: In a sense, you've got Sir Robin Butler. He's the Head of the Civil Service. I think there's a feeling that it might affect your career chances. But what I am saying is that the very introduction of an independent element seems to me to alter the context in which the existing procedures work. That's the argument. We certainly had precisely this argument on the committee and we came down in favour of the proposal that I am suggesting.

1322. ANNE WARBURTON: When we talked about the code a little while ago, we were talking more about the Civil Service, but I think you would see that code as being applicable also in the non-departmental public bodies.

GILES RADICE: We certainly think that that ought to be considered, particularly, as I say, where they have taken over functions of the existing Civil Service. I think that would answer one of the problems about the quangos, in a sense: there is no overriding code of behaviour or of ethics which inspires or informs the way they work.

1323. ANNE WARBURTON: What about the contract question? More contracts are being issued now for what have been Civil Service appointments. Is that a——

GILES RADICE: Is that a thing that worries us?

ANNE WARBURTON: Yes.

GILES RADICE: I don't think so, no. We are supporters of the agency principle, that there should be a much more clearly defined contract, if you like, or a framework in which the responsibilities of civil servants should be laid down. I think one of the problems in the past has been that we haven't had this kind of thing, and I think that we have had enough experience of the framework of doing this to see that they may have some application when you are talking about the top civil service—the policy advisers. But we are not arguing for a New Zealand type of situation, where you have fixed-term contracts—or not yet, at any rate—because I think there is a danger of politicisation, and we were persuaded that we shouldn't go that far.

1324. ANNE WARBURTON: So you welcome the slight retreat on that point——

GILES RADICE: I think so.

ANNE WARBURTON: —shown in the White Paper.

GILES RADICE: I don't know if Professor Sue Richards would like to add anything there.

PROFESSOR SUE RICHARDS (Office of Public Management): You referred to the dangers of politicisation. Evidence you took last week from Mr Michael Bichard suggested that it is not a necessary concomitant of contractual appointments. Indeed, in local government, where he comes from, it is the norm that chief executives and others are employed on three-year contracts and expect to act independently and without being politicised in that role, and then to move on to their next job, or indeed be re-appointed if that is appropriate. But in the culture where that hasn't been the case, to introduce that raises natural fears that politicisation would accompany it.

ANNE WARBURTON: I haven't actually read that particular bit of your report, I'm afraid. Your report defeated me a little bit, I'm afraid, in its thoroughness

GILES RADICE: Sorry about that.

1325. ANNE WARBURTON: No, it was my lack of time, I'm afraid. There's so much to read. But I understand you have had some interesting ideas about the possible reform of the process of policy advice by civil servants when you are meeting?

GILES RADICE: I am going to ask Professor Richards to reply to that, if I may.

SUE RICHARDS: You referred Mr Radice to sweeping managerial changes that have taken place in the Civil Service over the last 15 years, and I think few people could argue that those were necessary, that in the operational services for which government is responsible the reforms have been worthwhile and have improved both value for money and quality in terms of their effect. But I think they have very interesting consequences for the policy process. If you are ICI or Shell, you manage your production divisions and your research and development divisions rather differently, and I suspect that that diversity has not really been respected in the way that reforms have run through government. So the kind of "can do" philosophy which is appropriate for production management if you are delivering a benefit service or whatever it might be has rather invaded the world of policy, where a more questioning, more reflective and a more "This isn't possible, we haven't got the answer, think it through again and find another way of doing it" mind set is appropriate. I think that is the fear that I have about politicisation. It is certainly not party politicisation that I see but the invasion of an R&D culture by another sort of culture which is not appropriate for it, and I think that the code offers the opportunity to recover some of that ground and to restore older values like integrity, use of information and so on. I don't think of itself it will do it, but with appropriate managerial leadership, I think it would be possible to regenerate what was very much a quality policy machine in the past and which I believe has deteriorated because of that.

GILES RADICE: Can I just add one point on politicisation? We don't believe that in general there has been a politicisation of the British civil service, certainly not in the appointments. It may be that one or two civil servants became too close to particular Ministers, particularly one Prime Minister I am thinking of. It was noticeable that Bernard Ingham and Charles Powell didn't continue as civil servants once Mrs Thatcher—now Lady Thatcher—had left. At the time I remember the Civil Service Committee was somewhat critical: we felt that the boundary lines in those two cases had been stepped over.

But, apart from those isolated cases, we do not believe that the Civil Service has been politicised. Of course the fact that you have one government in power for a long time does have an influence. Somebody described it as the creep factor. Maybe that is somewhat unfair. I find that younger civil servants who have never known any other government look on an Opposition Member in a slightly different way from the older civil servants. I just put it like that. If I could step outside my neutral chairmanship, I would say that it may well be that a change of government might have quite a good effect on that particular point.

1326. ANNE WARBURTON: I thought, Mr Radice, that I wouldn't ask you about business appointment rules—we had quite a lively debate on that just now—unless you wanted yourself to say something about it.

GILES RADICE: The only thing on the Civil Service rules is that I think we would like to have another look at that. We didn't look at that in detail. The Civil Service Sub-Committee looked at that in 1990-91 and we said there should be more openness, but there are rules and, if I could just speak on my own, there is a case for having rules for ministerial jobs as well. It is rather difficult to draw that sharp distinction between Ministers and civil servants that David Hunt was doing, when you have a civil service which is now becoming much more open and where those who enter it cannot be guaranteed a job for life in the way that people used to be: in fact some are leaving early. So it seems to me that there isn't the distinction there, and I don't see why there shouldn't be some rules.

1327. ANNE WARBURTON: That leads me perhaps to ask you one other question. You are in favour of some kind of independent element in regulating the conduct of civil servants. Does that extend also into Parliament?

GILES RADICE: Yes, I think so. I think we are not very good at investigating our own affairs and I think it is invidious to ask clerks to do it. It may well be that we could ask the National Audit Office when it's a question of business interest problems of one sort or another. So that is one possible outside element you could bring into the process. I know that procedural experts are very worried about the idea of having somebody from outside, a judge or somebody like yourself, Lord Nolan——

LORD NOLAN: Perish the thought.

GILES RADICE: —on the various key committees where public standards come up. But certainly we should look at that. Maybe there are procedural reasons why we can't have it, but I would certainly like to look at that.

1328. ANNE WARBURTON: Perhaps I should have asked this at the beginning. Does your committee decide each two years what its main subject will be? So would you expect, as developments take place, perhaps to be able to revisit the sort of comprehensive study that you've done this time?

GILES RADICE: Yes, I think we would, and obviously we are going to look very carefully at what you have to say. I should say that we will be having Sir Robin Butler in front of us in early March on the precise issue on which I think you were questioning him, which is whether it is appropriate for a Cabinet Secretary and the Head of the Civil Service to be involved in questioning Ministers about whether or not they have adhered to the "Questions of Procedure for Ministers", and we will be looking at that, because I think it is something that should be looked at.

ANNE WARBURTON: Thank you, Mr Radice.

1329. CLIFFORD BOULTON: We hear a lot of negative comment about the ability of the House of Commons to do an objective job on anything, so isn't it a matter for some satisfaction—nobody gets any credit for it really, because it is taken for granted—that your committee was able to come out with a unanimous report based on work by your sub-committee, chaired by a Member of the Opposition on a matter which is potentially so sensitive? I think this is the kind of good news about the working of the constitution that never seems to get any comment.

GILES RADICE: Don't make me blush, Sir Clifford.

CLIFFORD BOULTON: As I am now discharged from day-to-day responsibilities, I can say that I think that it's remarkable and I would find it difficult to find any other country in the world that could work in such a matter-of-fact way and produce a report which is then accepted by the government.

GILES RADICE: I think we are lucky in our timing. We have had an eye to timing all the way through on this, but the fact is that you are sitting and the Scott inquiry will be reporting, and the government does actually have to have something to say about these matters, as we have seen. It may be that the brilliance of our arguments and perhaps the experience of the hearings actually did influence the various players in this whole debate, and I hope very much that that is the case, but I think political considerations also came into it, so it wasn't entirely our own work. I mean, the credit is not 100 per cent ours—95 per cent perhaps.

1330. CLIFFORD BOULTON: Moving to an area where you have anxiety, and that is the self-discipline of Members over themselves and the need for, let us say, public reassurance and transparency about Members' own conduct and their interests, would you think that it would be practicable in your case for instance, where you are a sponsored Member, for the arrangement that you have with your sponsoring union actually to be put in writing so that that could be registered? If we had an understanding whereby Members who had any kind of outside relationship of that sort needed to have it reduced to writing and deposited, would you personally think that that would be practicable?

GILES RADICE: I think that would be a very sensible thing, to be honest. My situation is like that of most Members who are trade union sponsored. There is no direct financial gain, but the General and Municipal Workers Union gives £600 to my constituency annually and, at election time, pays 80 per cent of the constituency expenses. They also have to pay my own expenses at election time. That basically is the situation. I can't say that they've ever asked me to do something that I haven't wanted to do. They don't ask a great deal of me. Indeed, they are reviewing, I understand, the whole sponsorship system. I know that you are not meant to be looking at the financing of political parties. Speaking personally, I would be in favour of state financing of political parties, precisely to avoid some of the questions that arise, but I won't stray into that territory.

CLIFFORD BOULTON: It is just that, as it exists at the moment, sponsorship is personal, but as it is working at the moment, in your case, you don't find anything intrinsically objectionable to it, but you would welcome, or not oppose, more clarity.

GILES RADICE: Yes, I think I would be strongly in favour of more clarity. It could be objectionable if my union asked me to do something I didn't want to do, and these cases have arisen, as you know, Sir Clifford.

CLIFFORD BOULTON: Certainly. Oh yes. I am assuming that nothing improper is being asked of you and that you certainly wouldn't respond if it were. Thank you.

WILLIAM UTTING: I don't have any questions, Chairman.

1331. PETER SHORE: I only have one question. The conduct of civil servants is universally accepted as being of a very high standard indeed, and that is very important, particularly in their dealings with private industry and private interests. But what is your view of the possible effects on the Civil Service of, one, bringing in a lot of people for temporary appointment from the private sector—in other words, free two-way movement in and out—and, secondly, the danger of the quite considerable redundancies now in the Civil Service at levels where people have yet, as it were, to complete their careers?

GILES RADICE: In principle, having temporary people in should not undermine the values of the Civil Service. After all, during wartime, if you read Professor Hennessy's book on Whitehall, he sees this as the golden era of the British Civil Service. So in principle, it shouldn't. However, you have had the warnings of the PAC, and it is partly in response to those kind of warnings that we produced our code, so that there is something that

is there to protect civil servants and remind them of the duties which they owe and the values to which they subscribe. I think it is a priceless gift that we have an impartial, non-corrupt Civil Service—you only have to go to countries where that doesn't apply to see problems—and we've got to hold on to it. It may well be that over the last, say, 10 years in some managerial reforms, which I personally back on the whole, and my committee certainly does, we have occasionally forgotten about these underlying values. It is precisely for that reason that we have come forward with the code in the way we have.

1332. TOM KING: Just a couple of questions. I am sorry, I didn't hear the answer to Sir Clifford Boulton. Did you say 80 per cent of your election expenses?

GILES RADICE: My election expenses, not my personal expenses.

1333. TOM KING: I just couldn't hear the figure. Thank you very much. The second point: we have talked a bit about the idea of rules and committee oversight. You said that it had been looked at a bit before your time—is that right?—or were you on the committee then?

GILES RADICE: On the rules of civil servants?

TOM KING: Leaving the civil service, yes,, taking up other jobs and going through the procedure. Are you aware of any subsequent serious criticisms that people were allowed to do things——

GILES RADICE: No. I think on the whole this has worked well. There have been one or two isolated cases, and you probably know them better than I do, but on the whole this has worked well. It is only that I think we need to look again at it, because if you are getting civil servants leaving their jobs much earlier than before and getting much more openness, you have to see whether the rules as they stand are still applicable, or whether they need tightening or relaxing in any particular area. That is the reason why I think there is a case for us looking again at those rules. Am I right in saying that I think Sir Robin Butler said that they are looking again at the rules?

1334. TOM KING: What I found in a number of Departments I worked with was that there was quite an active programme of secondment, of positively encouraging civil servants—coming in from merchant banks, doing a couple of years and going straight back again.

GILES RADICE: We think this is a very good thing. We are strongly in favour of it.

1335. TOM KING: Terrible access to all sorts of information, isn't it? What about that?

GILES RADICE: On the whole it's done, as you would expect, with propriety, subtlety and finesse, so that the conflicts of interest do not arise in that way.

1336. TOM KING: So the view of your committee, having studied this closely, which I would certainly support, is that the more interchange there can be and the more we move towards almost a French model or others, the more welcome it is.

GILES RADICE: Yes. The answer is yes, but I think the professor would like to say a few words.

SUE RICHARDS: It occurs to me that we might like to look at where the secondments are going to. There is indeed much greater secondment between finance and business than there used to be, but civil servants working in social policy departments equally need to understand the world that they are dealing with, and rather more of that would help to improve their understanding of that world.

1337. LORD NOLAN: I only have one very broad question, which is this. We have tended, I think, as a committee to approach our enormous job by trying to find out the particular areas that are causing the greater part of the public concern and trying to see what has gone wrong. We haven't, in other words, started by trying to define some broad ethical principle and see whether we can apply it generally. One would have perhaps to work towards that from practical examples. In the civil service you have found very high ethical standards. This has been the evidence we have heard from many witnesses and I don't think it is disputed. How do they do it? What lessons have they for other departments of public life?

GILES RADICE: I think that they have had an ethos. That's what it's about. It's going back to Northcote-Trevelyan in the 19th century. It's esprit de corps, a pride in their job. It was precisely because we were concerned that that ethos could be under threat, with all the managerial changes and the problems of one party in power for a very long time, that we thought there therefore was a case for putting down on paper those

values which the Head of the Civil Service, for example, when he came before us, said "These are our values". We said "OK, we'll put them on paper". That is perhaps one reason why he found it difficult to resist our arguments.

LORD NOLAN: So any young person coming into the Civil Service knows what is expected of him because it is there in black and white.

GILES RADICE: Absolutely.

LORD NOLAN: And also, no doubt, because of the example set by his seniors and their supervision.

GILES RADICE: Yes.

SUE RICHARDS: Can I just add, in the light of the earlier discussion with the previous witness about employment law, that I think the committee would be quite interested in hearing your thoughts about whether the code might be part of the employment contract for new and indeed existing civil servants, whether that might help to entrench it more firmly than might otherwise be the case.

LORD NOLAN: If you have further thoughts or wish to expand that thought, Professor, I would be most grateful if you could let us have something in writing. But I think for now we'll thank you very much indeed for letting us trespass beyond the allotted time, and for all your help. We are very grateful.

WEDNESDAY 8 FEBRUARY 1995

Members Present:

The Rt. Hon. The Lord Nolan (Chairman)

Sir Clifford Boulton GCB
Professor Anthony King
The Rt. Hon. Peter Shore MP

The Rt. Hon. The Lord Thomson of Monifieth KT DL
Sir William Utting CB
Dame Anne Warburton DCVO CMG
Diana Warwick

Witnesses:

Richard Mottram CB, Second Permanent Secretary, Office of Public Service and Science, and Brian Fox, Under-Secretary Cabinet Office, responsible for the Public Appointments Unit

Philip Hunt, Director of the National Association of Health Authorities and Trusts, Dr Chris Robinson, Chairman of the Association and Northumberland FHSA, and Rosie Varley, Chair of Mid-Anglia Community Health NHS Trust

Andrew Foster, Controller, and Sir David Cooksey, Chairman of the Audit Commission

Noel Hepworth, Director, John Whiteoak, Chairman Corporate Governance Working Group, and Martin Evans, Head of Technical and Research Division, Chartered Institute of Public Finance and Accountancy (CIPFA)

1338. LORD NOLAN: Yesterday we heard a good deal from the politicians. Today is entirely devoted to the professionals.

Philip Hunt, Chris Robinson and Rosie Varley, from NAHAT—the National Association of Health Authorities and Trusts—might perhaps be called Quangocrats, but we must be careful of our terminology, for National Health Service bodies, although Quangos, are not NDPBs.

In contrast, the Audit Commission is an NDPB, and a very influential NDPB, because it is responsible for the audit of both National Health Service bodies—which are not NDPBs but are appointed bodies—and local authorities—which are also not NDPBs, but are elected bodies. Sir David Cooksey, the Chairman, and Andrew Foster, the Controller, will be with us later.

Finally this morning we shall hear from Noel Hepworth, John Whiteoak and Martin Evans of CIPFA—the Chartered Institute of Public Finance and Accountancy—whose members play a large role in the corporate governance of public bodies.

First, however, we are pleased to welcome Richard Mottram, Second Permanent Secretary of the Office of Public Service and Science in the Cabinet Office, and soon to be Permanent Secretary at the Ministry of Defence. Mr Mottram is responsible for advising Ministers on Civil Service matters, on Next Steps Agencies and on Public Bodies. He is accompanied by Brian Fox, the Under-Secretary at the Cabinet office responsible for, among other things, the Public Appointments Unit.

Mr Mottram, thank you both for coming along this morning. I understand, is this right, that you do not wish to make any opening statement; you are quite happy to go straight into the questions?

RICHARD MOTTRAM AND BRIAN FOX

RICHARD MOTTRAM: Yes.

LORD NOLAN: Very well. Thank you very much. I am going to ask Prof. King please to open the questions to you.

1339. PROF. ANTHONY KING: Can we talk first for a bit about appointments to Quangos, and let me offer you a definition of Quango, picked up from the Report of the Public Appointments Unit: "It can be defined as a body which has a role in the processes of National Government, is not a Government Department or part of one and operates to a greater or lesser extent at arms length from Ministers." Is that a fair definition?

RICHARD MOTTRAM: I think it is a fair definition of what we all recognise when we are talking about Ministerial responsibilities in relation to appointments to Public Bodies. They are not strictly speaking Quangos because of course they are not non-Governmental, many of these organisations.

1340. PROF. ANTHONY KING: Okay but on some such rough definition and indeed referring to the question of Ministerial appointments, what is the scale of the whole thing? How many appointments to Bodies of this general nature are Ministers in a position to take, or to have taken on their behalf?

RICHARD MOTTRAM: Can I ask Brian to answer on this Chairman?

BRIAN FOX: There are about 42,000 such appointments.

PROF. ANTHONY KING: 42,000.

BRIAN FOX: 42,606 at the last count, for which Ministers are responsible directly, or indirectly. An awful lot of them, of course, are decided upon in the machine, rather than at Ministerial level. Some indication of the spread of that is given in the Report.

1341. PROF. ANTHONY KING: But would you accept that on the face of it that seems a very large quantum of Ministerial patronage indeed? 42,000 appointments is an awful lot.

BRIAN FOX: Well yes, if you have a look at the numbers, for example, of people who are appointed to

Tribunals of one kind or another, of which there are some 20,000 I think, that halves that number but, yes, it is a lot of appointments.

RICHARD MOTTRAM: Perhaps I could just add a point that of course one reason why there are a significant number of these appointments is because the Government wants to actually bring in people with outside expertise to assist it in the process of Government. I mean a number of these people not only operate in what are essentially quasi-judicial capacities, but they are operating on Advisory Bodies and the reason why we have the Advisory Bodies is to make sure that Ministers have available to them advice from people other than people like me. It seems to me that it is absolutely in the public interest that there are this whole range of Bodies, drawing in people with different backgrounds.

1342. PROF. ANTHONY KING: Now some of the appointments, clearly, are to executive positions that make very considerable demands on the people who hold them. How many top jobs in the "quangocracy" are there approximately? That is to say people who are either earning substantial salaries, say £50,000 a year or more, or alternatively are working part-time. What sorts of numbers are we talking about?

BRIAN FOX: Most of the appointments are part-time and unpaid. If you are taking definition of top jobs by salary for example and that is often linked to full-time employment or substantial part-time employment, then about 15,000 or so of those appointments are paid, of which 10,000 of those are fee paid—paid on a daily basis—of which another 4,000 are paid under £10,000 and quite often, they are non-executive members of boards. Then in the bracket £10,000-£20,000 there are about 800 jobs and that leaves roughly 300 or so jobs earning £20,000 or more and a substantial number of those are, of course, going to be part-time. So on that kind of definition of what is a top job, those are the numbers.

RICHARD MOTTRAM: Just to be explicitly clear, these are the jobs to which Ministers appoint—whether Ministers actually appoint is something we can talk about—but they are the jobs listed in Public Bodies which are the responsibilities of Ministers. There are other posts in organisations, which you might loosely call Quangos, below the level of board members, not appointed by Ministers, which might be earning sums of money which are substantial. Chief Executives of various kinds, who are actually below board level and not appointed by Ministers.

1343. PROF. ANTHONY KING: But still, the kinds of numbers of people that Brian Fox was talking about are very large are they not? I mean we are talking about at least hundreds and depending on the definition, thousands of people, who are making a very substantial contribution to the Bodies on which they sit and are, in addition, earning fairly substantial sums of money.

RICHARD MOTTRAM: Yes.

1344. PROF. ANTHONY KING: In other words, I am just trying to establish the point that the scale of the thing is pretty big. Now, if we pick a number, the top 2-300 jobs how, in practice, are those appointments made, how is it done?

BRIAN FOX: Those top jobs which tend to be full-time and paid, are mostly advertised and go through open competition. It is not exclusively the case but I believe they are mostly made through that route and, as with any competition of that kind, often supported by other mechanisms for identifying people, either with Executive Search or a search of the lists which we hold, in the Public Appointments Unit, or which Departments themselves hold. So the range of normal recruitment methods, for the most part.

1345. PROF. ANTHONY KING: If there is a competition, who runs the competition and who decides who has won?

BRIAN FOX: The Department will run the competition, with a properly constituted board representing a number of interests, and will make a recommendation to the Minister. In the end the Minister decides who he wishes to appoint.

RICHARD MOTTRAM: Perhaps, Chairman, it may be helpful if I just give a little illustration about how this works in relation to our own Department because my own Department is responsible for the Research Councils, which are classified as Non Departmental Public Bodies, they are not Quangos but they are part of the total of which we have been talking about with Prof. King.

My Department makes appointments not only of the Chairman of these Research Councils but the members and they are all paid a very small sum of money, I think about £4,000 per year from memory, and also the Chief Executives. The practice we have followed is essentially, in the case of the Chairman, we are looking for extremely distinguished people, mainly from industry, for reasons we could explain, and they are identified, using a variety of sources, including the Public Appointments Unit, and frankly the problem we then have is in persuading the people to take the job, because the people we want are extremely distinguished people who have many demands on them.

For the members there are similar considerations but we essentially generate lists of very distinguished people. Prof. King, you may have been a member of one of these Research Councils in the past, I do not know. But for the Chief Executives, which are full-time paid appointments, with very substantial salaries, £60,000 plus, one of them I think on over £100,000, we essentially apply exactly the same procedures that we would have applied if these were Civil Service appointments. That is, we have advertising, we have used Executive Search, we have a constituted selection panel, which I have chaired, we have outsiders on the selection panel. Out of that whole process we produce a recommendation to the Chancellor of the Duchy of Lancaster, the whole process is entirely documented, it can be seen to be open, it could be audited as quite clearly having been fair and open competition, of a kind almost identical to the experience we would have had if these people had been civil servants.

I only go into this because I think it illustrates the point that we were trying to capture in the Review that we published, that we do need somewhat different approaches, according to the nature of the post. In every case we need openness and for those posts which are executive appointments, which are substantially paid, we quite clearly do need clear procedures which everyone can understand and can be publicly defended. That is the best practice that we are seeking to spread right across the system.

1346. PROF. ANTHONY KING: Mr Fox said a moment ago that a very large proportion of these appointments, including top jobs, were subject to an open competition and you have just given an illustration where that has happened. What kinds of posts are not open to public competition because one gets the impression that the Chairmen of some pretty important boards have been appointed without such a competition taking place.

BRIAN FOX: I believe that the situation will vary very considerably between the different kinds of functions of the board and the nature of the commitment in terms of time and the salary, if any. Quite a number of Chairmen of boards are part-time and unpaid and I believe in those circumstances it is likely to be less the case and quite often probably not the case that they would be advertised and go through competition. The presumption that is already in the system, that we are reconfirming in this Report, is that open competition should be therefore full-time and paid posts.

1347. PROF. ANTHONY KING: Under present circumstances, am I right that the role of the Minister is to appoint to these Bodies whomever he or she wishes on whatever grounds he or she chooses? It sounds, on the face of it, from what I have read, pretty arbitrary in that sense.

RICHARD MOTTRAM: Well, it is the Minister who is ultimately accountable for the appointment and to that extent the Minister can appoint how the Minister so wishes, but what we have tried to bring out in the Report and what we are trying to explain now, is that in a large number of these appointments, as I think you will go on to discover—and I know you talked, for example, I think to the Secretary of State for Scotland and so on—you find that there are processes to assist Ministers in taking these decisions.

In the case of full-time appointments, in my Department for example, as I just explained, we have very clearly laid out procedures against which the Minister takes the ultimate decision and certainly none of those processes, in relation to a very significant set of Non Departmental Public Bodies for which we are responsible, are arbitrary. They are all clearly worked out and are open to audit.

1348. PROF. ANTHONY KING: Could I just pause a moment. Taking the case of your own Department, would it have been open to the Chancellor of the Duchy of Lancaster, if he had wanted to, to refuse to accept the recommendations that resulted from this open competition and simply to appointment somebody else?

RICHARD MOTTRAM: It would have been, yes.

1349. PROF. ANTHONY KING: So the power to the Minister in this sphere, with a very large number of appointments, is essentially a political power and not one subject to the kinds of procedures that would be in place in the making of straightforward Civil Service appointments. There is a difference between these two zones of activity?

RICHARD MOTTRAM: I think there are two differences. One is that the appointments in the broad area of Quangos, that is the appointment in Public Bodies, which are made by Ministers, the 42,606, are a much more diverse collection of appointments than is the case in the

Civil Service, for very obvious reasons that we need not waste time on.

The second difference is that the process through which these appointments are made is not regulated in the same way that Civil Service appointments are regulated and there is not, for example therefore, in the case of a full-time appointment, the same procedures as Mrs Bowtell explained to your Committee, my Lord, I think in relation to Civil Service appointments, where a Minister decides not to accept the recommendation of the system. So quite clearly we are talking about two somewhat different systems, but we certainly, in the case of our appointments for full-time posts, apply effectively the Civil Service procedures by analogy.

1350. PROF. ANTHONY KING: Could we just pause a moment on the Public Appointments Unit, of which you Mr Fox are the head. What exactly is the Public Appointments Unit, of which I confess I had not heard before being asked to serve on this Committee? What does it do?

BRIAN FOX: Essentially we have an advisory role. We make no appointments ourselves, nor do we directly recommend appointments. Now the main functions: perhaps I could start first with the maintenance of the Central List, which covers the collective interests of Departments and for which we seek candidates to reflect the wider public interest, those of consumers, of women ethnic minorities and what have you. We construct that list through an open nominations system, a simple form which people can nominate themselves, or others, through a rolling programme of writing to trade associations, trade unions, businesses, special interest groups, academic institutions; seeking nominations from them; through maintaining especially close contacts in pursuit of the Prime Minister's initiative on equal opportunities with women's organisations.

1351. PROF. ANTHONY KING: And who makes use of the list?

BRIAN FOX: Largely Departments. Our main customers by far are Central Government Departments.

1352. PROF. ANTHONY KING: All of them?

BRIAN FOX: All of them from to time but a number of Departments maintain their own lists of their rather specialist interests and will tend to come to us when they are looking for someone with rather wider skills and experience.

1353. PROF. ANTHONY KING: It seems odd, on the face of it, that one might make use of a central list because given the kind of decentralisation of function and great variety of activity to which Mr Mottram was referring, a central list would seem somehow superfluous to requirements. That you would actually want a series of lists that were directly related to the kind of job to be done. Do people actually make use of that central list very often?

BRIAN FOX: Yes indeed. To answer your first point about the requirement, that is why I think that there are 10 Departments who have a substantial number of appointments in any one year, who maintain their owns list for their specialist interests. That is not to say that they do not, from time to time, require of any one of their Bodies someone with much wider experience to represent, for example, the consumer interest. Yes they do in terms of making use of it. Last year we had some 350 requests for formal searches from Departments. That figure can be a bit misleading because we count a single search as one, even though they may be looking for three or four names and in one case recently, for 40 names. So we have a regular flow of such requests.

1354. PROF. ANTHONY KING: Coming to this Report by the Public Appointments Unit, reading the Report one is left with the impression that the people who wrote it and the Public Appointments Unit takes responsibility for it, were really pretty deeply unhappy with the way in which the system has been working until now. The quantity of implicit criticism of the present system contained in this Report is really very substantial on all manner of grounds; it is a very long Report. When both of you were involved in drawing up this Report, did you have as vivid a sense as I have in reading it, that there was an awful lot that needed to be sorted out and cleaned out?

BRIAN FOX: I think that both in the working group which I chaired and in this Report, we were conscious that the basic systems were reasonable but that more needed to be done to ensure that the good progress that had been made in some Departments was reflected and that Departments were helped so that all could reach the standards of the best and that a number of firmer and clearer guidelines, and some mandatory guidelines, were necessary to ensure that all Departments followed all the procedures which make for a good and sound appointments system. That was the nature of concerns that we had and why the Report is in the form that it is.

RICHARD MOTTRAM: Perhaps if I could just add Chairman that, as somebody who gets a lot of these reports across my desk about all aspects of the way in which Government works, since that is mainly what we do in my Department, this one did not strike me as being unusual. All the time our big job is to find best practice and then to spread it around the system and this is an example I think of that in action.

PROF. ANTHONY KING: I look forward to reading some of the other reports.

RICHARD MOTTRAM: Yes we do publish some of the others, the work of our Efficiency Unit for example, with which you are familiar, where we look at the activities of all Government Departments and we identify those who are really doing well and those practices which really are up to date with the needs of Government and those which are perhaps doing less well, and suggest how things might be carried forward. So I do not regard this as being in a strikingly different category to a number of the reports that we have published over the last few years.

1355. PROF. ANTHONY KING: Could I ask you in all this about the role of the Chief Whip because I read with great interest in this Report the following sentences: "The Guidance provides that the Chief Whip's Office be notified in advance of any significant appointments. This includes any appointments of political importance, for example because of the circumstances surrounding the appointment, or the background of the candidate, and appointment of Deputy Chairmen when they are being appointed with a view to succession." And it goes on to

say: "The first of these provisions [and that is the one I have just read out] reminds Departments and Ministers of the political significance of some appointments and the need for the Chief Whip to be forewarned, both for general awareness [I like the phrase general awareness] and in case the Prime Minister seeks his advice on some aspect of the appointment, we recommend this reminder is retained in any new Guidance." Could you expand a little bit on that. What is the role of the Chief Whip, what do you envisage his role being in the future?

RICHARD MOTTRAM: Perhaps I will start on this. We touched on this a little bit yesterday, when the Chancellor of the Duchy of Lancaster and Sir Robin Butler were here, and I think that the point that was being made yesterday was that there might, for example, be a case where it was proposed to appoint a Member of Parliament, or an ex-Member of Parliament where there would be scope for political controversy in the House of Commons and it would be right, in those circumstances, that the Chief Whip was forewarned that there was potential for such controversy. That would be one example.

What was being said in this Report was that we needed to clarify the role of the Chief Whip and that role is laid down in *Questions of Procedure for Ministers*, the role we are talking about now, and I think goes back really quite a long time. We needed to distinguish that from the practice that is in present Public Appointments Guidance, which involves the Chief Whip in a much earlier stage in identifying names. What the Report says, subject to Brian correcting me, essentially is we should put the Chief Whip on exactly the same basis as everybody else, that is that everybody can suggest names to go on the list that we keep. The Chief Whip certainly is a useful source of such names, so would the opposition Chief Whip be a useful source of such names, but we should have only one aspect of the procedure which still involved the Chief Whip. That is, the aspect which is in *Questions of Procedure for Ministers* and I think there is nothing unusual, in areas which are potentially politically controversial, being drawn to the Chief Whip's attention in that way. I can think of whole areas of Government business where the Chief Whip has his attention drawn to things.

1356. PROF. ANTHONY KING: But the way the Chief Whip could, presumably, just jot down a note to the Prime Minister saying, I happen to know this fellow he really is not "one of us" and I would not appoint him if I were you. It could work that way, could it not? You have given a benign example.

RICHARD MOTTRAM: He could indeed.

1357. PROF. ANTHONY KING: One of the things that is often said about the people who are appointed to Quangos, is that they are, at the moment, disproportionately drawn from the ranks of the Conservative Party, from Conservative donors, from Conservative Office holders. Sir Norman Fowler told us last week that when the Labour Party was in power it was the same but different, if you follow me. How does this happen, how does it come about, given the kinds of procedures you have been describing, that it turns out, by accident, that a really quite disproportionate number of people happen to be drawn from the Party in power?

RICHARD MOTTRAM: Well I am not sure that we are in a good position to judge this Chairman. We do not ourselves keep the political affiliations of people who are appointed to these Public Bodies, other than in defined circumstances which we could explain, and I am not sure that as a Civil Servant I particularly want to get into the argument about whether the Quangos are or not disproportionately filled with Members of one Party or another.

1358. PROF. ANTHONY KING: But are you personally sympathetic, and I might ask Mr Fox the same question, with the suggestion that is contained in this Report, that details of actual political office-holding should be registered, made available, when appointments come forward?

RICHARD MOTTRAM: I would not like to offer an opinion on that because that is a specific issue on which we have asked for the advice of the Committee.

1359. PROF. ANTHONY KING: I will leave questions about the Next Steps Agencies to my colleagues if I may, but could I ask you an overarching question? You referred to this topic earlier on, is there not a case, in your view, for there being, and I will not suggest that anyone used this particular term, a Body of, if you like, Quango Commissioners, running in parallel with the existing Civil Service Commissioners and ensuring that appointments to Public Bodies, except of the most highly political character, are made on the kinds of criteria of merit and suitability on which appointments to the Civil Service are made?

RICHARD MOTTRAM: Well I think we would argue the key requirement is to establish that the system is being used for this great diversity of appointments, which certainly have to be different in different areas, are right. So we have set out, in this Report, a set of proposals for consideration by your Committee, and in the light of the views of your Committee would then be issued to Departments as guidance, which we think would ensure that the procedures meet the various requirements laid down, which are basically requirements about various values, to ensure that this is a system which is appropriate, given that they are public appointments. Whether, in the light of that, you then need a further regulator is something on which I do not have a strong view.

1360. DIANA WARWICK: I wonder if I can refer you back to the *Review of Guidance on Public Appointments* of which you very kindly gave us a copy. Throughout this and in the Government's evidence to us and in all the criticism that has come to us about public appointments, the words openness, accountability, demonstrable standards, all of these come out very, very clearly as absolutely necessary in the changes that are to be produced. Can you tell me, very simply, given that the Government, I believe, has accepted the general recommendations in your Report, what new public information will be available if your changes are introduced?

BRIAN FOX: I think that the information will be available, will be first a very clear guidance, our guidance, which will be revised in the light of this Report and this Committee's views will be published. I think that is important.

1361. DIANA WARWICK: Is it not published at the moment?

BRIAN FOX: Yes, we publish the existing Guidance and the new Guidance will be published too.

1362. DIANA WARWICK: That will be a change will it? It will be changed Guidance?

BRIAN FOX: It will be changed Guidance in the light of this Report and the Report of this Committee. There will be more information available about what Departmental lists exist and how people might apply to get on to them. We will, for our own central list, be looking at ways of improving the profile of that list, perhaps considering as we recommend for other Departments, advertising for names, getting our leaflets into public libraries perhaps. There will be more open competition, a mandatory requirement on Departments for easier access to information about which Bodies exist and who serves on them, and there will be a requirement on Departments to advertise the appropriate national, regional or local level, whenever a new appointment is made. That range of things, I think, improve the openness and the transparency of the system.

RICHARD MOTTRAM: The key thing we are looking for I think is absolute visibility about how many Bodies there are, who has been appointed to them and the basis on which they were appointed.

1363. DIANA WARWICK: And all that information will be public so that if, for example, the accusation is made, as it has been on occasions, that a relative of a Cabinet Minister has been appointed to a Public Body, it would be quite clear why that appointment has been made?

RICHARD MOTTRAM: Well I think that would be clear with the criteria used in making that selection, yes. For example, one of the recommendations in the Report, as I recall, is there should be clear job specifications, job descriptions, and visibility about the process through which the people were selected. I only hesitate about answering your questions because I do not think we would want to foster witch hunts of various kinds about why particular individuals were chosen in particular circumstances. What we want is clear visibility about the processes that were used.

BRIAN FOX: And clear recording of each of those processes, why each step was gone through and why decisions were taken. I do not envisage all of that being published but it will be there and available if it needs to be demonstrated.

1364. DIANA WARWICK: And to how many of the 42,606 appointments will these Guidelines and this new openness be applied?

RICHARD MOTTRAM: All of them but the process through which the appointment is made would differ in different cases. We must be quite clear that one of the doctrines that we have in this Report is the doctrine of proportionality, so we are not saying that all the 42,606 posts will be appointed on the same basis, that is through open advertising and so on and so forth. There would be an appropriate process in relation to each sort of post and, as we explain in the Report, there is already diversity and involvement of different sorts of people in those appointments, and the key thing would there would be visibility about the process used in each case.

1365. DIANA WARWICK: Yes, what I am trying to get at is what new information will be available because one of the other words in your Report, as well as openness and accountability, is discretion and a lot of these decisions are going to be left still, as I understand it, to the discretion of Departments. That is why I am trying to press you on just how much real new information will the public have to reassure them that their concerns about public appointments are no longer necessary.

RICHARD MOTTRAM: Well what they will have is who was appointed on what basis. Whether that satisfies them—I would hope that it would.

DIANA WARWICK: Thank you.

1366. CLIFFORD BOULTON: Can I ask you a bit about how the system of payments, remuneration, is working out? We do not seem to get a lot of criticism about the amounts of remuneration unless it is attached to perhaps a controversial appointment, or if there is a suggestion that someone has become a kind of "quangoholic" and is collecting these appointments. Then one finds that the sums are added up and we hear how much someone is getting in total. On the other side of the picture, we hear that it is sometimes difficult to get people to serve on Quangos. Could you answer me rather generally about how the amounts are decided. Are they graded according to function? Do you wish they were higher and that you had more flexibility? Would you just like to tell me how it is working?

RICHARD MOTTRAM: Well I think that in each case it is a matter for the Minister in the Department concerned and if I go back to my Research Council example, for instance, which may help us, we pay the Chairman for a given amount of work a year. We do not pay the rates of remuneration which are realistic to the people who we employ. We pay them really what is a token amount. For the full-time Chief Executives we try and derive a salary which we think is sufficient to attract a credible list of candidates who can do the job. So to that extent their salaries would be market-related. These are decisions which are for Departments, in consultation as necessary with the Treasury, where you are producing sums of money which might seem unusual or controversial or whatever, according to normal procedures. So they are decisions taken by individual Ministers. My impression would be that all the time the main focus is actually not really on remuneration, the main focus is on persuading people that they want to serve in the interests of making a contribution. We are not "scooping up" people who are doing it for the money.

1367. CLIFFORD BOULTON: So there is no prospect of Departments asking to spread the range of paid appointments, you think that is pretty static at the moment?

RICHARD MOTTRAM: No I think there would be a possibility and if they discovered that they just could not get people of the right quality for a function of a certain kind, then yes I think they would need to look at that and conclude that they needed to pay somewhat more.

1368. CLIFFORD BOULTON: But you are not aware of any general pressure?

RICHARD MOTTRAM: I am not but Brian may be.

BRIAN FOX: I am not aware of general pressure.

1369. CLIFFORD BOULTON: It is merely a question of persuading people to give the time rather than tempt them with money?

RICHARD MOTTRAM: Absolutely, certainly in the areas in which I deal. I would not be very interested in the people who were tempted by the money.

CLIFFORD BOULTON: Thank you.

1370. WILLIAM UTTING: There are two areas I would like to go into Chairman. One of them is complaints about appointments. I said yesterday that we have received a substantial volume of complaint and comment about appointments in this sector. They do not arise just because this Committee has been appointed. I wondered to what quarter are such complaints directed, who is responsible for dealing with them?

BRIAN FOX: The Departments and Ministers who make the appointments are the recipients of those complaints, whether they be from members of the public or in answering on the Floor of the House.

1371. WILLIAM UTTING: So these are Departments and Ministers that are being asked to re-examine their own decisions in fact?

RICHARD MOTTRAM: Yes. To justify their own decisions.

1372. WILLIAM UTTING: I see that in seven Departments, which is over one third of the total, Ministers either make or are directly consulted about every appointment. It is not my experience that Ministers, having taken a decision, are easily overturned. Is this really a satisfactory system of objectively examining complaints or should there be some system operated from the centre, say in your Department?

BRIAN FOX: I would think, as Mr Mottram said, it would be for the Minister to justify his decision. I think it would be quite difficult for the centre to gainsay that Ministerial judgment.

RICHARD MOTTRAM: But of course a number of these appointments, I suppose potentially for all of them, we operate within the framework of the law and there have been cases, for example, of judicial reviews of particular appointments by Ministers. It is absolutely for the individual Minister, exercising his personal responsibility, to defend the decisions that are taken inside his or her Department and to ensure that the procedures that are operated inside the Department conform with the law and should there be judicial review, that they can satisfy the Judges that the processes were proper. So people are not operating—I am going back perhaps to a point that Prof. King made that I should have brought out then—in a framework which is unregulated by the law.

WILLIAM UTTING: No I accept that.

RICHARD MOTTRAM: I think this Report brings that out rather clearly and I think that also is a helpful part of the process. Because speaking rather more generally, one of the big changes in the framework of the way in which the Government now operates, is that for all of us Civil Servants there is a much stronger sense of the legal framework in which we are operating and the likelihood if those processes are not in conformity with the law we will find ourselves having to defend them in judicial review.

WILLIAM UTTING: Your red-covered Report helpfully sets out that legal context in which Ministers have to operate.

RICHARD MOTTRAM: I think it is important.

WILLIAM UTTING: There is simply the question then of whether these requirements are being met in every case. The requirements are certainly there and they ought to be met.

RICHARD MOTTRAM: Yes and as we say in the Report we also believe that there should be clear processes of audit, internal audit, and the internal audit reports of Departments are available to the Comptroller and Auditor General. In cases where there was concern that clearly inappropriate people had been appointed, incapable of discharging the functions, who did not meet the stated job specification, then in those circumstances I would expect that we would end up in a position where these cases are being drawn to the attention of the Public Accounts Committee.

1373. WILLIAM UTTING: The second related area, Chairman, concerns how the recommendations in this Report, when your Guidance has been issued, are to be monitored and enforced. One of the criticisms that I think one would make of this document at this point is that those arrangements are not very clearly spelled out. They do appear to rely extensively on the processes of internal audit to which you have already referred. I quite understand the difficulties here because the appointments that are being made by Secretaries of State under statutory powers and they would, I think, be reluctant to impose too much control from the centre. But one does really need to be satisfied that these good recommendations are going to be implemented in practice, that they are going to work and a number of points have been made to us that might enable them to be better operated. For example, if your Public Appointments Unit had a monitoring as well as a facilitating role. Is that the sort of proposal that might not be unacceptable?

RICHARD MOTTRAM: Well this is an example of a generic issue that we face, particularly in my Department, which is to try and ensure that we are spreading best practice round the system and placing responsibility on individuals, individual Ministers, under them individual officials, to discharge that responsibility, not continually second-guessing people because it is very expensive and actually it is not very effective. The key to success is they all understand the requirements laid upon them, but I quite agree, there is an issue over monitoring that we would need to look at, yes.

WILLIAM UTTING: Thank you Chairman.

1374. LORD THOMSON: Could I ask just one question on the Public Appointments Unit's operation. You have talked about your desire for absolute visibility—you used that phrase. Is there a case for an annual "Who's Who" of all appointments, so that we know who the people are?

RICHARD MOTTRAM: We certainly looked at that, sir, and it is touched on in the report. We are just rather hesitant about the scale of what would be involved: 42,606 people listed is, I believe quite a big document.

LORD THOMSON: That's not every year.

RICHARD MOTTRAM: No, there aren't 42,606 new ones every year, or indeed it might not be needed every year, but we are looking at whether there is a case, for example, for getting departments to make the information available on the Internet or whatever. That would be one example. But the clear underlying requirement, which I would want to emphasise, is that in my view it is absolutely the public's right to know who these 42,606 people are, and if they are having difficulty in establishing who these 42,606 people are, we would certainly want to assist them in encouraging departments to make clear their contribution to the 42,606.

BRIAN FOX: We don't find it an issue of principle. We find it an issue of mechanics, in not only producing the document in the first place but making sure that, by the time it is published, one-fifth of its contents are not out of date. That is why we are establishing this second working party, to look at the Internet proposals, where we can make that information available but whereby it would be kept up to date and relevant. So it's a matter of mechanics rather than principle.

RICHARD MOTTRAM: And of course, if it is being made available on the Internet, we could pull down relevant bits of it for people or departments who asked for it.

1375. LORD NOLAN: I wonder if I can take a little further the idea of a possible outside monitor, with it very much in mind that public reassurance is what we are all aiming at. Under your proposals, as I understand it, the inquiring member of the public, if he looks, will find good systems, he will find criteria applied, he will find an internal audit machine going, he will find, in many cases, an area for ministerial discretion. No one, I think, can sensibly object to that: governments have to govern; Ministers must have a choice. And you have made the point, Mr Mottram, that if there is any suggestion of illegality, if, for example, it were proved that a Minister had chosen a particular appointee because she was his niece or whatever, there would be a remedy in law, but that's a bit of a sledgehammer and rather slow-moving, I'm afraid, as you know.

What I was wondering was whether, at the lower level of maladministration, which is not necessarily illegal—the Parliamentary Commissioner level, the Ombudsman—there might yet be scope for an official such as that who can, in the vernacular, exercise as a whistle-blower, if there is a public complaint, and look into it, and whether, without building up some huge new quango, one might build into the machinery what would almost be a public relations reassurance or, to put it more positively, a genuine check on cases that weren't demonstrably cases of improper appointments but cases where the procedure hadn't been fully followed, or carefully enough followed, and a bad impression might have resulted.

RICHARD MOTTRAM: Yes—I slightly hesitate, my Lord, because I have to own up to you that I don't entirely have at my fingertips the powers of the Ombudsman in this area now, which is something we could look at.

BRIAN FOX: I don't know either. I rather doubt that he has powers in this area.

RICHARD MOTTRAM: Yes. I think he doesn't, actually. Obviously I can check that, but I am not sure that he is perhaps the natural person to do this, in that personnel cases of this kind are rather kept away from that particular avenue, I think.

LORD NOLAN: I wasn't suggesting the present Ombudsman.

RICHARD MOTTRAM: No, you were suggesting an established Commissioner of some kind.

LORD NOLAN: Exactly.

RICHARD MOTTRAM: Yes. As I tried to say earlier, that is then another body—I am not calling it a quango—another regulator, another set of cost, and I think you have to judge whether, if the systems are really put on an absolutely top-quality basis on the lines that we are suggesting, such a further regulator is needed. It is just balancing those two things, I think.[11]

LORD NOLAN: Thank you very much.

1376. PETER SHORE: I asked the Minister yesterday whether, given the number and variety of criticisms about public appointments and, in particular, the use of political patronage, the government itself or his department had made any analysis of public appointments in order to rebut, moderate or whatever the criticisms that had been made, and I think I am right in recalling that he said that he hadn't done this, but he thought that you might be able to assist.

RICHARD MOTTRAM: Yes. We have not carried out an analysis of the basis on which public appointments have been made in relation to political affiliation because we do not have that information. We do not hold that information; as far as we know, departments do not hold that information. The basis on which the system, as is clearly set out in this report, is designed to operate is in relation to merit, so we have not done an audit of the system in relation to political affiliation, because we wouldn't have the means of doing it. As you know, there is a regular exchange in the House of Commons between the government and the opposition where names of various kinds are bandied around in both directions, but we have not done any work that is designed to underpin those charges or counter-charges.

PETER SHORE: Those research bodies—BBC, Birmingham University and others—have attempted to do this.

RICHARD MOTTRAM: They have, yes.

1377. PETER SHORE: You don't think it would be worth your while, as it were, to check what information they have put forward?

RICHARD MOTTRAM: I am very well aware, for example, of the work of the people at Birmingham University—John Stewart and his colleagues. I am well aware of their views on these matters, yes.

1378. PETER SHORE: And does any of this give you reason to be concerned or do you think that it would be valuable to have a study, given the enormous amount of information you have about people, of such charges as, for example, that appointments are overweighted in favour of

particular occupational groups, like businessmen, accountants or whatever, quite apart from political affiliation? Do you not think that would be valuable?

RICHARD MOTTRAM: We probably do have some data about the occupational backgrounds of people, and I will come to Brian in a second about what we hold. Whether one considers it is overweighted or not overweighted can partly be a political issue, but certainly we are interested, as Brian explained. For example, as a matter of public policy, the government is quite clearly interested in ensuring appropriate representation on merit from women and ethnic minorities. So that would be an area of public policy where we are quite clearly attempting to monitor, and we are reporting annually, the progress in improving the ratio between, say, men and women in all these public appointments and increasing the proportion of people from ethnic minorities more towards the proportion of the ethnic minorities, for example, in the population as a whole. So those are cases where there is clearly a public policy, which we are required to monitor and where we are all the time encouraging departments to do better, including through the process—and this comes back to Professor King's point—of generating high quality people on the public appointments list from these particular groups and saying to departments "You should be getting people of these categories. Here are a lot of names you could choose from on merit".

1379. PETER SHORE: One further question on appointments. When asked about appointments, you cited the appointment, I think, of the chairmen of the research councils and said that it was very analogous to that of the Civil Service appointments itself.

RICHARD MOTTRAM: Chief executives, I meant to say.

PETER SHORE: Chief executives—not the chairmen?

RICHARD MOTTRAM: Not the chairmen, no.

1380. PETER SHORE: Ah! I think that might have given us to some extent a misleading impression about how quango appointments are made in general, because the example you gave was indeed a very full—open competition, etc.—process. But when one thinks of bodies like urban development corporations—I have one in mind particularly in my own area in London, the LDDC—or when one thinks of hospital trusts and the chairmen there, there is no suggestion, is there, that anything like an open competition process is gone through before appointments are made?

RICHARD MOTTRAM: No. I'll come to Brian in a minute. The point that I was trying to make, just to be absolutely clear, is this. The reason why I gave the example of the research councils was to try to illustrate to the committee how different considerations might apply in relation to the chairmen, the members and the chief executive, and that you might use different procedures. I was really just trying to give you an illustration of the principle of proportionality—no more, no less really. I think the answer is that it would rather depend on the character of the post. If you were appointing what is essentially an executive chairman—a full-time appointment or a very nearly full-time appointment—to a post that had significant remuneration, we would expect

---

[11]This should be read with Mr Richard Mottram's letter to Lord Nolan of 13 February, see Evidence p. 532.

that there would be clear openness about the basis on which it was done. It might not necessarily be an open competition; it might be Search or whatever, but a clear sense that this post was going to be available and a clear set of criteria against which it had been filled. As you say, in relation to chairmen of NHS trusts, those are appointments made by the relevant Secretaries of State against the job specifications and they are not through open competition.

BRIAN FOX: I think there's a twist on that, in that of course those appointments and other categories where there are quite a number of appointments are often advertised generically. The health service has a system for generic advertising and in England, as in Scotland, is considering a system of advisory boards on top of that generic advertising. So that's a rather different form of open competition.

1381. PETER SHORE: I understand about openness and to some extent about generic advertising, but do you not think that public confidence would be greatly restored and strengthened if it was known that the chief people in quangos, particularly the chairmen, went through a process of open competition as well as general openness before they were appointed?

RICHARD MOTTRAM: I think it does slightly depend on the nature of the post, but I would myself agree that where they are full time or significantly towards full time and substantial sums of money are involved, there is a strong case for open competition.

BRIAN FOX: And this report recommends that there should be a presumption in favour of that route.

RICHARD MOTTRAM: And where it is not, what we are saying quite clearly, as we have tried to bring it out this morning, is that there needs to be a clear understanding of the basis on which the appointment was made.

PETER SHORE: Thank you.

1382. ANNE WARBURTON: Might I first make an observation as a footnote to the discussion with Sir William a while ago? The papers insist quite frequently that one of the advantages of appointments is that the person appointed can be removed—"summarily" perhaps is the right word—rapidly, if occasion demands, as compared with a person elected. But that's simply because I thought that had not come out in what you were saying.

I wanted to ask one or two questions about the PAU list. We get a lot of anecdotal evidence—it has been in the evidence which has been put to us as well as one's personal experience—to the effect that names put forward to the PAU are then just lost: that people don't actually ever hear any more. I wonder what explanation there might be for that, and perhaps I could couple that with a question about what powers of investigation, what resources, there are in compiling the list to scrutinise names which are put forward.

BRIAN FOX: Can I tackle the first point? Yes, I understand and have heard that accusation about names getting lost. One of the, I think, deficiencies that we have in the unit at the moment is that we are not as good as we should be about feeding back to individuals who join our list what has been happening to them over a couple of

years. It may be that somebody has been put forward for consideration by departments on a couple of occasions in that time; it may be that they have not been put forward at all. I think we ought to be developing systems where we can feed back to them, telling them, within a reasonable timescale, whether their name has been put forward, whether we have failed to find opportunities for the names put forward and whether, in those circumstances, they wish to remain on the list. I think this issue of feedback is obviously a very big job, but one we are very conscious of and want to make improvements on.

On the issue of, in a sense, screening those names for quality, we do of course seek referees and we approach those referees for information about the individual's qualities, their special areas of expertise, their skills as a chairperson or a mzember of a committee, and we look at that information along with all the other information that we have. The ultimate screening about that, of course, is when and if somebody is put forward for an appointment and the department has then the main screening positions about their relevance and suitability for the post they are considering.

RICHARD MOTTRAM: If I could add one very small point, having myself used the Public Appointments Unit list recently for a particular task I had, I found the references for the individuals who were sent over, which were provided on a confidential basis, really rather illuminating. People do offer really quite clear opinions which give you a clue as to the suitability or not of people, and a number of the referees we use do quite well understand the system and give very good advice about the level at which people might make a particular contribution and the nature of that contribution. So I think that part of the system works quite well. The screening part, as we discussed yesterday, certainly needs to be rigorous.

1383. ANNE WARBURTON: Could I also ask a question about the benchmark guideline side of your work? I think you have said this morning that you are in favour of standardisation across the whole field. Is that a real problem or is it a matter of time?

RICHARD MOTTRAM: Persuading people to adopt best practice?

ANNE WARBURTON: Well, persuading people to adopt the same best practice, subject of course to local variations.

RICHARD MOTTRAM: I don't think we're in favour of standardisation. I think what we are in favour of is people adopting best practice principles in relation to the particular nature of the post, not uniformity. We are not an organisation that really likes nowadays to tell people precisely how to do things, because we have discovered that actually doesn't guarantee they do them that well.

1384. LORD NOLAN: Thank you both very much indeed. As has so often happened, your evidence has been so interesting that we have taken you well over the time we had set aside for it, but we are very grateful to you for coming and for all the help you have both given us. Thank you.

PHILIP HUNT, DR CHRIS ROBINSON AND ROSIE VARLEY (NAHAT)

This is Mr Philip Hunt, Dr Chris Robinson and Mrs Rosie Varley. Good morning. Thank you very much for coming along. Have you an opening statement you wish to make?

CHRIS ROBINSON: Your Lordship, I have, with your permission.

LORD NOLAN: If you please.

CHRIS ROBINSON: NAHAT is the leading organisation of NHS management bodies within the UK and it covers NHS authorities, health boards and NHS trusts. It also has close links with GP fundholders who are affiliated to our organisation. We have in our membership virtually all the commissioning agencies within the United Kingdom and also the great majority of the NHS trusts, and I apologise for a slight printing error on your script.

The association welcomes the setting up of the committee to inquire into standards of public life and, in particular, the inclusion of the NHS within its remit. The NHS is not only a vital public service which we all use; it spends, as you are aware, over £40 billion per annum. As we said in our written submission to you:

"Public service values are an essential element of the national health service—its organisation, management and operation. We believe that throughout its life the health service has, with very few exceptions, operated in accordance with those values."

There are, however, two areas we would like to address—the appointment arrangements for the boards of NHS authorities and trusts and how best to ensure high standards of conduct within the NHS.

Let us look at the appointments arrangements. As local agents for the Secretary of State, the boards of NHS authorities and trusts need to have the confidence of both the Secretary of State, to whom they are accountable, and the public, whom they serve. Without both, they cannot do their job properly.

The present boards and their predecessor committees have always been composed of appointees. However, concerns about appointments to quangos, coupled with the growing number of management bodies arising from the devolution of management to individual hospital and community trusts and the reduced size of the management boards, have led to some unease about how the membership of the NHS boards is selected.

The vast majority of board chairmen and members are of very high calibre and serve the NHS, Ministers, patients and the local population well. Nevertheless, we believe that changes in the appointments arrangements are desirable to make them more robust, open and transparent, and this includes an independent element. They will thus have the confidence of local communities. But this must be done in a way which enables each Secretary of State to carry out their statutory responsibilities for providing the health service.

If we look at the standards of accountability and conduct, despite one or two notable lapses, which are very much the exception, we believe that standards in the health service are extremely high. We also believe that measures taken over the last year or so in terms of codes of conduct and accountability, guidance on business conduct

for staff, the drafting of a code of openness and improved training for board members will enhance those standards and ensure compliance with them.

However, there are a number of additional measures that we would like to see put in place. These are: more explicit arrangements about declarations of interests and also the implications of board membership, so that prospective board members are fully aware of what is involved; specific training and familiarisation for board members and senior staff in the standards of conduct and accountability inherent in the NHS; strengthening those monitoring arrangements to ensure compliance; and a common standard of financial accountability and responsibility throughout the public service. We would be very happy to discuss these issues with you in more detail.

Your Lordship, if I could perhaps introduce my team, on my right-hand side I have Mrs Rosie Varley, who is chairman of the Mid-Anglia Community Trust. Mrs Varley in her previous life was an academic at the Health Service Management Unit. She has also had leading roles in two important charities concerned with health, the NSPCC and Mind. On my left is Philip Hunt, who is the director of NAHAT. Philip has had experience on a CHC and was also a member of Oxfordshire Health Authority. I am a pre-clinical lecturer in the medical school at Newcastle, I am chairman of Northumberland Family Health Services Authority and for some 10 years I was a member of my local parish council and for two years its chairman.[12]

LORD NOLAN: Thank you very much indeed. Now I am going to ask Peter Shore to take up the questions.

1385. PETER SHORE: Thank you, and thank you for that opening statement. That satisfies my curiosity as to the nature of the organisation, which presumably has been formed fairly recently?

CHRIS ROBINSON: It was formed some four years ago from a coming together of the Society of Family Practitioner Committees, which were the predecessors of the FHSAs, with NAHA, which was the association for the district health authorities and regional health authorities.

1386. PETER SHORE: Thank you. Before turning to appointments, which are to be the main thrust of my questions, I want to ask you about one or two things in your paper. You said that there was no case for giving local authorities a role in the NHS. It is not part of our remit to argue that local government should extend its role into the NHS, but is there not a case for saying that representatives of local authorities have a firmer and closer contact with the users of the NHS more than almost any other group of people you could think of?

CHRIS ROBINSON: I will ask my director, Philip Hunt, to make the main statement. Could I say two things? The board appointees are only five in number of the new health authorities and trusts, and moreover they will cover a large area, so inevitably they must be in contact with them, and obviously local representatives have a place in that scenario. The second thing is that it is implicit in the appointments process, as we say in our paper, that those considered for appointments must have strong links with the community, preferably through residence or, if not, certainly through their place of work,

---

[12]This should be read with Dr Robinson's letter to the Secretary of the Committee of 27 February, see Evidence pp. 532–533.

so that they actually not distant from the communities which they are serving.

PHILIP HUNT: Chairman, I think we have to be clear that the accountability arrangements for local government and the health service are very different. The accountability arrangements existing in the health service have been with us since 1948—namely, of a Minister responsible to Parliament for a national service, with uniform provision and equity in the service that it provides. I think that, because of that, Ministers have worked through a system of delegated responsibility to local boards, using appointed members. That has worked well and I think is appropriate in relation to the accountability arrangements. We have experience of local authority nominees appointed to the boards of NHS authorities between 1974 and 1989, and I think it is general experience that that didn't work, because the local authority councillors' sense of accountability did not fit with the sense of accountability of the appointed members, and many of those authorities found it very difficult to achieve some sort of corporate ethos and working together. I think the advantage of the new boards is that there is a corporate ethos, the members are quite clear where their accountability lies, but they also understand that, to be successful, they have to be sensitive to local views and opinions. I think overall the boards do work well: we have a high calibre of membership, people give a lot of time. So I think that, overall, the system is working well, but we would suggest some improvements, namely more openness in the appointments system and, as the chairman has said, an independent element to make sure that the public feel the system is credible.

1387. PETER SHORE: Are you not really saying that local authority representatives in the previous period—1974-89—articulated rather strongly the views and the criticisms felt by the local community, and the health service managers found that to be really rather difficult and embarrassing?

PHILIP HUNT: I think not. My experience as a local authority nominee on a health authority would suggest that, whilst all members would certainly articulate concerns about the health service in the locality, the real problem was that the local authority nominees felt accountable to their own local authority, whereas the other appointed board members felt a different sense of accountability. With a board of around 20 on average, it was actually very difficult to get a sense of a business-like approach to policy development. I think that appointed boards need to be close to the community, they need to be sensitive to the community, but ultimately they are there to help the national health service, and ultimately the Secretary of State sets the policy parameters in which they operate.

1388. PETER SHORE: Mr Hunt, let me move on to another question. You say in your written evidence that NHS board members are in the same legal position as local councillors, and I think you are referring to section 125 of the National Health Service Act 1977, if I have it right. But is that really the case? Two of the signal distinctions about being a local authority councillor is that you can't take part in business without declaring an interest if you have one, and, secondly, that you are liable to surcharge. These are very strong, as it were, accountability disciplines on local authorities. Neither of those disciplines operates on national health service bodies. Is that correct?

CHRIS ROBINSON: Perhaps I could ask my director and then Mrs Varley to speak to that.

PHILIP HUNT: If I could just take the question of surcharge, our view is that the same standards should operate across the public sector and we would not oppose the imposition of the possibility of surcharge in the case of NHS boards. We have seen the evidence that you have received from CIPFA on that count and we would support that.

CHRIS ROBINSON: Mrs Varley, do you want to talk about the accounting officer?

ROSIE VARLEY: First, I would like to echo what my colleague said about the possibility of surcharge. I think that the chairmen and directors of NHS trusts should be subject to exactly the same obligations as their local authority colleagues, and I think that most people serving on these boards now would agree with that. As regards the declaration of pecuniary interests, it is my understanding that we are now, through the codes of conduct and accountability, under exactly the same obligations as members of local authorities. We all must declare any pecuniary or other interest that we might have that has a relevance to our NHS trust or authority activities, and I would go so far as to say that I think that any active political interest should come under that requirement as well.

1389. PETER SHORE: Mrs Varley, did I understand you to say in the first part of your answer that you were in favour of bringing NHS bodies into line with local authorities, in respect of surcharging for offences?

ROSIE VARLEY: Absolutely.

PETER SHORE: You are?

ROSIE VARLEY: I would support that absolutely.

1390. PETER SHORE: Thank you very much, yes. That is a very interesting statement. I want to move on to the general questions of accountability, and I see again in the evidence that you are in favour of accounting officer responsibility being decentralised. If that takes place, I suppose the right question is: to whom will the accounting officers then be accountable and is it really expected that the Parliamentary body in the lead in this area, the PAC, should examine each and every NHS chief executive?

CHRIS ROBINSON: Perhaps I will ask Mrs Varley to lead on that one.

ROSIE VARLEY: I think it flows naturally from the present arrangements in the NHS that the accounting officer function should be delegated to the chief executive of the NHS trust or authority concerned and that that individual should have a clear obligation to advise his chairman and board members of their conduct in respect to regulations and as to whether he thinks that they are properly administering the funds allocated to their body. I don't see why there should be an any more onerous responsibility on the Public Accounts Committee than there is at the moment. The Public Accounts Committee already has the power to call before it any NHS trust chief executive, or indeed chairman, who it believes has a case to answer.

PETER SHORE: I think it widens its remit—that's the only point made—very considerably.

ROSIE VARLEY: Yes.

CHRIS ROBINSON: As a supplementary to what Mrs Varley said, of course the chief executive of the trust or the authority, as we understand it, will be directly accountable for the exercising of the accounting function to the chief executive of the NHS, so that is the management line.

1391. PETER SHORE: Now let's turn to appointments, because I think this is very crucial. One of the people who submitted written evidence to this committee, herself a member of an NHS trust, described her feelings as follows:

"As I see it, the main danger of the present NHS appointments system, if such it can be called, is that it is based on highly idiosyncratic selection processes in which subjective judgment, personal whim and political patronage all play a part."

What is your reaction to that as a statement?

CHRIS ROBINSON: As an academic, a qualified degree of sympathy and recognition. Could I say that in fact we will be providing you afterwards with a paper on our suggestion for the process of the appointments. We do believe that it has to be open, that it has to be against explicit criteria, that there has to be a degree of independence within the process and that we have to exclude the potential for what has been termed "croneyism" in that appointment process. We believe that all those essentials are dealt with in the paper which you may already have, or, if not, we are providing you with at the end of the sessions.

PHILIP HUNT: I think, Chairman, it is worth making the point that there is a variable pattern of appointments within the national health service, certainly in England, and that a number of regions have adopted what I would regard as good practice in the sense of public advertisement, the interviewing of people who put their names forward and the establishment of a list of people who are then considered to be appropriate for appointment. We would argue that we should be building on best practice that is currently in the system and then should introduce an element of independence to provide some reassurance to the public. However quirky people may feel the system has been, at the end of the day I think most boards have arrived with some very good people who have been appointed non-execs.

1392. PETER SHORE: I thank you for that very frank and non-complacent reply. On the details, as it were, of appointment, I think you mention in section 4 of your evidence—probably paragraph 33 again—that you propose appointment panels and I think you had in mind the Scottish model.

CHRIS ROBINSON: On mature reflection we wish to develop that slightly. What we are looking at is open nominations, and this will be either from chairmen of the existing authorities, from self-nomination, from applications in response to a wide set of advertisements across the whole spectrum, and that will then be sifted by this panel. The panel will have independent people upon it, but not totally independent: they will be people who have NHS experience, in order to reflect the specific requirements for an NHS board. But it is open and transparent. That panel will then determine whether the candidates are perceived to be above or below the line in respect of the specific criteria for the boards, and that again gives a degree of uniformity. When that has happened, that pool of names will then be available to the chairmen of the individual health authorities and trusts, who will select from that the people who they believe best provide the mix of people with the specific complementary skills to comprise the board which will deliver the agenda with which that board is charged—i.e. an NHS trust, or a commissioning authority in my case.

ROSIE VARLEY: And this is the system that is currently operating in the best places.

CHRIS ROBINSON: Yes. That set of names will then go back to the panel, in which the regional policy board member has a crucial role for vetting, in terms of ensuring that croneyism has not been exercised and that there is a balance and, arising out of that the regional policy board member will then submit a list of names, obviously with additional choices, to the Secretary of State, who will then make those appointments.[13]

1393. PETER SHORE: I think that would be a helpful step forward. What about one or two alternative approaches? What about the appointment of an outside, as it were, referee to look at and study various appointments or to give an independent report on whether the thing is working as well as you would wish?

CHRIS ROBINSON: Could I ask you to expand that? I am just wondering—would this be an outside referee to look at the person with finance background? I think we need to be quite clear about what the role is.

PETER SHORE: I would suggest for the appointed members of the board, not the full-timers, as it were.

CHRIS ROBINSON: Those are the two out of five independent people who we would see on the sifting panel. They would exercise that specific function.

1394. PETER SHORE: Oh, I see, yes. Let me ask you one other question then. You probably heard the evidence we took earlier this morning, and reference was made to open competition in appointments as well as openness in the whole procedure. Do you think there is a case, particularly given the number of national health service appointments, but given the fact that it is within a discreet area—one health service trust is rather like another—for appointing a special appointment commission to operate procedures for appointment, rather like the Civil Service Commission does for the Civil Service itself?

CHRIS ROBINSON: With respect, I think that what we are looking at within England, if I take England—there are eight regions now, instead of 14—the advisory appointments panel that we have identified as the first step is precisely that group of people.

PETER SHORE: Thank you.

1395. PROF. ANTHONY KING: When Mr Shore read out that eloquent passage from the anonymous person who wrote in expressing doubts about the way in which appointments were made, you gave that quotation your qualified assent. Could you say a little bit more about

---

[13]This should be read with the second and third paragraphs of Derek Day's letter to the Secretary of the Committee of 23 March see Evidence p. 533.

your sources of unhappiness, from where you sit, about the way in which the appointments system currently operates?

CHRIS ROBINSON: Yes. Again, it is the concerns which Mr Shore identified—the question of whether in fact the appointments process is actually seen to be open, transparent and balanced, and those are our main concerns.

1396. PROF. ANTHONY KING: But is it just a question of what the appointments system is seen to be as distinct from what it is? I am more concerned about what it is and I got the impression from what you said that you weren't entirely happy with the system in actuality at some points. You referred to best practice. Best practice rather implies worst practice. What are you actually worried about, even if we didn't know about it?

CHRIS ROBINSON: The worry we have is that there has been anecdotal evidence of, I wouldn't necessarily use the term "patronage", but that in fact the selection process was perhaps not as wide as one would expect in something which was associated with public bodies.

1397. PROF. ANTHONY KING: Do you speak for all three of you?

ROSIE VARLEY: Yes. I mean, for instance in the past there was no requirement, and indeed no general practice, of advertising posts. There were no clear criteria issued to nominees as to the judgment and selection that was going to be made. Indeed, it was not uncommon for the interview to consist merely of a conversation between the regional chairman and the proposed candidate. I think that is quite clearly unsatisfactory, we would all agree, but I have to say that enormous strides have been made in the past year and I think that if we could adopt the best practice that is currently operating, we would have a satisfactory and rigorous system.

PHILIP HUNT: I think that if you had been inquiring three years ago, we would have had some difficulty in defending the current procedures in operation. There is no doubt that most regions have really pulled their socks up—the best really have good systems—and I think that by next April all the regions will be required to pull themselves up level with the best process.

We have one other concern about the current system. That is that I think that many non-executives who have been appointed and are doing good work see and hear the criticism that is made about the appointment process, and there is a danger that they themselves can become undermined by that. That is why we think an independent element is so important, because it is in all our interests that the non-execs who sit round the board tables feel that they got there by a robust mechanism, that they are seen by the public, by the professionals, to be people who are certainly suitable to be there, and I think they will have much more confidence about what they are doing.

ROSIE VARLEY: We all have to take decisions at times which we know will not be universally popular and we have to be able to justify the basis on which those decisions are taken. I think that it will be much easier for us to do that if we have been seen to have been properly appointed.

1398. PROF. ANTHONY KING: I am a little puzzled and I may have missed something, but Mr Hunt rather implied that by next April everything will be perfect, but yet you submitted a paper to us with some suggestions

about the kinds of improvements that ought to be made. If everything is going to be perfect in April, what is it that you want us to recommend?

PHILIP HUNT: Can I explain that we only became aware of the changes that the Department of Health were proposing to the appointments system after we submitted our written evidence. We think that they haven't gone quite far enough. What they have not done is introduced an independent element. As the chairman has reflected, we think that the appointment of five people from outside the health service to oversee the process in each region is the missing ingredient in ensuring that the system works effectively and the public think it is a credible system.

1399. ANNE WARBURTON: Could I ask first who appoints the panels who do the appointing? I can't say it in Latin, but you know what I mean.

PHILIP HUNT: That is an interesting question, and we have no ready answer to that. Clearly it could be the Department of Health. Equally, if there were to be bodies set up to monitor more generally the whole process of appointment to public bodies in the UK, it could be that that body could take that responsibility.

ANNE WARBURTON: Thank you.

CHRIS ROBINSON: I should say that we have suggested that at the end of our submission to you.

1400. ANNE WARBURTON: Sorry, but I am glad to have it on the record here anyway. Could I go to another area? It is not the question of appointments that I want to ask about but rather the question of what happens if staff members feel that there is something going on which they are not happy with: if they have perceived something which they would like to report? I know from another piece of evidence that has been submitted that the Audit Commission did a study on probity in the National Health Service and concluded that a third of the staff interviewed indicated that they would take no action in the face of impropriety because of fears of losing their jobs. Is this a thing which has become the problem?

CHRIS ROBINSON: We are obviously not aware of the statistical nature of that problem. There is only anecdotal evidence which appears in newspapers. We obviously support the principle of openness, which we think is crucial—particularly in terms of a public service. I do not know if Philip would want to add to that?

PHILIP HUNT: Well there is guidance to the Health Service, issued in 1993, about the procedures to be adopted by staff who wish to draw concerns about the operation of the particular organisation to senior management. Our view is that those guidelines, if carried out, ought to be effective. They should ensure that senior management takes such concerns seriously and establishes an enquiry as to whether what is alleged is true or not. I think that one would have to say that at the moment there is some evidence that staff do not have confidence that those guidelines will be operated correctly and I think that one of the key challenges for the Health Service is actually to reinforce some confidence in procedures.

I think that, particularly in relation to patient care issues, it clearly must be in the public interest that staff, if they are concerned about problems with the treatment of patients, must be enabled to feel able to raise those concerns and that the management will consider those seriously. Equally, I think we would say to staff that we would expect you to use those procedures rather than simply, say, go out to the media to make unfounded allegations. So I think the key thing is making sure the procedures are operated in a way in which everyone has confidence in them.

CHRIS ROBINSON: I think, if I could add to that, that obviously the majority of those will occur within Trusts for obvious reasons and I do not know if Mrs Varley would like to—?

ROSIE VARLEY: I would agree with all that has been said, but I would just add that I think that the Chairman and non-executive or independent directors have a very important role in this respect and they should be visible and accessible to the people that work for their Trust.

LORD NOLAN: Informally accessible?

ROSIE VARLEY: Informally accessible, yes. I think their home telephone numbers and where they can be contacted should be available and they should be seen to respond. In the same way that they have a role to play in the complaints procedure.

CHRIS ROBINSON: With respect to your Lordship, in a paper I wrote for the NHSTD on the new Boards, I made the point that in fact being a member of an NHS Trust or Health Authority is not just simply another directorship. It is much more an interactive role and that is crucial to delivering this sort of service.

1401. ANNE WARBURTON: It is possible for staff members to bring their concerns forward without necessarily the people they are working with or they are accusing knowing who it is?

ROSIE VARLEY: Again, I think that comes down to the Chairman and the way he or she operates their trust. But certainly within my Trust I have made it known that this option is available to them.

PHILIP HUNT: If I could just add to that. The Association produced guidance eight years ago for staff wishing to raise concerns about patient care, which I can certainly submit to the Committee. But there is the clear understanding whereby these complaints will be treated in confidence—although at some stage with such a complaint you may have to confront the staff against whom that complaint is made. But I think there are well-tried and trusted procedures. It is a question of people having confidence to use them.

1402. LORD THOMSON: Could I follow up Dame Anne's point? We are about to receive evidence from the Audit Commission and can I ask you about another aspect of best practice? I ought perhaps to preface my remarks by putting on the record what you already know, that the Audit Commission's assessment of the Health Services is that the instances of detected fraud and corruption are very low and that by and large there is a good record of performance. But when it comes to best practice in terms of running the new kinds of businesses of the Health Service, the Audit Commission in the evidence that they have put before us say, for example, that in a recent survey

they made of 2,600 directors, it showed that half felt it would be permissible to sign contracts and get approval afterwards. Or break the rules if it was in the NHS's interest: 46 per cent of them said that. More than half of Board members would prefer to agree to severance terms discreetly rather than pursue a dismissal or involve the police. Do you dissent from that analysis?

CHRIS ROBINSON: I dissent from the principle. I do not dissent from the analysis which presumably was a reaction to a survey carried out two years ago. I think, again with respect, that would be anticipated and dealt with by the principles we were talking about, about the briefing and the obligations of the members of the new Board. Certainly as far as we would be concerned, such behaviour is inadmissible.

1403. LORD THOMSON: Yes. I found this evidence a little disturbing. If I may just follow up one other aspect of it. There are also tables of good practice: the conduct of non-executive directors. There are also various percentages relating to some of the basic rules for non-executive directors and the percentages are really very, very low. When you have a similar table on the conduct of staff on such matters as Register of Hospitality and Gifts, and Register of Private or Pecuniary Interests, again the percentages seem to be extraordinarily low.

ROSIE VARLEY: But since that document was produced, we have had the Codes of Conduct and Accountability within the NHS that has required us to operate in a different way.

1404. LORD THOMSON: But are the Codes of Conduct being followed up? Do they bite, do you think?

ROSIE VARLEY: Yes.

CHRIS ROBINSON: Each of us at our Board meeting has done that and, for instance, my company secretary has an explicit register of Members' interests. Perhaps Mr Hunt would like to——

PHILIP HUNT: Yes. I think that some of the problems have arisen because of the inevitable tension between public service ethos and the adoption of more of a market-orientated health service. Now clearly the Codes of Conduct and Accountability have been brought in to try and resolve some of those tensions. What I think it also shows is two things. One is that the Health Service must continue to have a vigorous approach to openness so that openness in relation to quality indicators or prices charged for procedures should be available and in the public domain. Secondly, when we go back to the question of trawling for potential non-exec's, we think that there ought to be some briefing systems and seminars available to people who put their names forward where we can start right from the beginning to inculcate a sense of the public service values that we would expect them to adopt within the Health Service. At that stage I think they can then decide—Well, maybe this is not for us!—or, Yes, we can sign up to that and we would like to be considered to be a non-executive.

I think that in the past we have tended to appoint people and then we tried to give them some education about what it involved. I would like a system where we actually tell people right from the start what it involves and then say to them, on the basis of that, will you sign up to the public service values that we expect from you.

LORD THOMSON: Thank you.

1405. WILLIAM UTTING: We have received many complaints and criticisms about the way appointments are made in the NHS. In fact, the NHS and Executive public bodies are the main targets of the people who have written to us and for that reason I am very encouraged to hear your proposals for improving the appointments system. But it does mean that the reality is that thousands of these appointments have been made in the past according to systems that are not wholly objective or satisfactory. What we are getting now is a stable door being slammed shut. That was a comment really that does not require an answer. If I may add another comment to it, I hope that you will, in your more detailed guidance, firm up the advice that is given about the representation of people from local communities. Because again, in the complaints that have been made to us, among the most strident, is the fact that people in a local community now feel more separated from the people running the NHS than they did before. Now I do not think this is a simple question of whether it is local government or the NHS that is in charge here. There is coming through to us this strong sense that local people are no longer as strongly considered in relation to running the NHS as they were. I do not know whether that is true or not, but——

CHRIS ROBINSON: Could I make two comments? Of my own Board, all the people are local people. They reside within Northumberland, with the exception of one of the professional members. The second thing is that in fact we recognise the inevitability that as the Boards become smaller, the greater the distance between them. I made the point that for 300,000 people in Northumberland there will be five non-executive members. However, the important point, which I think the Director referred to, is the visibility. Most of us are now producing newsletters which are delivered to every household within the patch for which we have the responsibility, that identify the people. I certainly get stopped in a number of areas and get contacted, as do my fellow non-executives. We also have very strong links. I actually chair the Joint Consultative Committee for Northumberland, which has both the County Council and the District Councils on it, and we have strong links with those local communities and I believe that way one begins to command the respect. But it is very much getting away from the distant grey-suited men, to people who are visible and accessible to the population and sensitive to their views.

1406. WILLIAM UTTING: Well from my knowledge of Northumberland, I would expect nothing less from that particular part of the world! If I could quickly raise one other point that concerns me. I was genuinely surprised in this red document from the OPSS to see that 93 per cent of appointments in the NHS were now salaried appointments. That seems to me to spell the end of unpaid voluntary service in the management of the NHS and if it does, is this a good thing or a bad thing?

CHRIS ROBINSON: Could I make two comments. I am not sure whether the word 'salaried' is appropriate. I think you actually received an honorarium and certainly from some of the comments that have been made about the level of remuneration for non-executives, it has been argued, as I think was indicated in some earlier evidence to you, that the level of remuneration may not be adequate. I think, and again I look at my ex-AUT colleague and Professor King, public service values are

the most important thing in terms of the commitment to the NHS and the financial considerations are very much secondary. Perhaps Mr Hunt would want to add to that?

PHILIP HUNT: Well I think that there is no doubt that non-exec's are expected to take on much more responsibility in the new circumstances of the Health Service than in the previous Authorities. The smaller Boards has meant that the discussions are much more businesslike and focused and, in a sense, without being unkind to the old-style Health Authorities, I think they tended to rather be rubber-stamps for decisions that had already gone through a system of management tiers. Whereas in the current Boards there is much more of a sense that that is where the key decisions are made. I think when you then take account of the other things that non-exec's have to do, like chairing Mental Health Tribunal appeals and some of the public activities, I think there is a strong argument that says we need to compensate people for that. We should never, I think, lose sight of the public service ethos and we should never want people who are coming onto those Boards because they are attracted by the remuneration. Equally, I think we should not disbar people who could not give service to the NHS unless there was some form of remuneration.

WILLIAM UTTING: I will not prolong the discussion, although I am tempted to Chairman. Thank you very much.

1407. DIANA WARWICK: Could I just ask, because it is to pursue a point that Sir William made in response to a question about the Audit Commission's criticisms of appointments. I think you said you felt that the changes that had taken place since that report two or three years ago meant that there had been very considerable improvements and you expected further improvements.

CHRIS ROBINSON: Indeed.

DIANA WARWICK: And yet I refer not to something three years ago but to a debate in the House on the 25th January 1995, i.e. two weeks ago, when in a debate on the Health Authorities and Trusts the MP for North Cornwall said:

"A glance down the list of West Country health quangos shows distinct bias towards Conservative Chairmen and Board members."

My question is: when will the National Health Service be able to declare a clean bill of health on appointments? What is the timescale, given the number of appointments that have been made and about which there may be criticism?

CHRIS ROBINSON: You made the point that the debate was in 1995. Many of the appointments to which you refer may well have taken place some three years ago and so they could have pre-dated the process that we are talking about. Clearly there will be the new Health Authorities, subject to Parliamentary legislation passing of course. The establishment of new commissioning agencies will actually take place in April 1996 and so the whole of the commissioning side will be subject to the new process. At the same time, as you are aware, the re-appointment process to Trusts is either on a two-year or a four-yearly basis, and my understanding is that the suggestion is that it will then be two-yearly and so hopefully within the next two years that process will have worked itself right through the system.

1408. DIANA WARWICK: Could I just ask a final question. It must be immensely frustrating and galling for those people who have been appointed on a proper basis, who are doing a proper job, to hear all these criticisms of appointments. Do you think there is any case for evaluating what has happened so far? We heard from both the Secretary of State and the Public Appointments Unit that they have no evidence and no information that would enlighten us about those appointments. Do you think there is at the moment a case for that investigation?

CHRIS ROBINSON: I think that there is a seductive attractiveness in it. The difficulty is that you are actually against a moving baseline. As an academic I would find it very difficult and I would look perhaps to those who are better qualified than me to give advice as to whether you could make a useful and informative evaluation given the changing status that we are under. But certainly I think it is important that it is looked at in order to perhaps reinforce the confidence. That may be more appropriate when the due process has taken place post-April 1996.

LORD NOLAN: You have given us a lot of frank and very interesting and helpful information. We are extremely grateful to all of you. Thank you very much for coming.

CHRIS ROBINSON: Thank you my Lord.

1409. LORD NOLAN: Now we have Sir David Cooksey and Mr Andrew Foster. Sir David, you are the Chairman of the Audit Commission and Mr Foster is the Controller. I believe you have a short opening statement which you would like to make before we go into questions?

SIR DAVID COOKSEY AND ANDREW FOSTER (AUDIT COMMISSION)

SIR DAVID COOKSEY (Chairman of the Audit Commission): Yes. I would very much welcome, if I may Chairman, the opportunity to quickly explain what the Commission does and how we operate. You have heard from the previous witness that we undertook two studies last year into probity and fraud and corruption in both local government and the Health Service and, indeed, increased the amount of audit effort that we applied in this particular sector last year because of the public concern that we were hearing.

One of the reassurances that we got from those studies was that in fact the standards of probity and conduct in local government and the National Health Service was reassuringly high. This came as an acceptable outcome as far as we were concerned. But what we do feel very strongly is that this reflects a degree of openness and accountability, particularly in local government, which is not necessarily prevalent right across the public sector in the same way. We believe that our part in this, in terms of the delivery of independent public audit, is an extremely important part of that. If I may, what I would like to do is to just explain the principles that we mean by independent public audit and then just ask Andrew Foster very quickly to explain how we deliver that.

LORD NOLAN: That would be very helpful.

DAVID COOKSEY: What we believe is that, whenever public money is spent in any significant quantity, then the principles of public audit ought to apply.

By the principles of public audit we mean:

That external auditors should be independently appointed and be independent of the body under audit.

That the audit should comprise not only a probity audit which ensures that money is honestly and properly spent, but that there should be a value-for-money element where one is looking at the way in which the funds are spent and that they do deliver both efficient and effective use of those funds.

Then, finally, that auditors should be entitled to publish reports in the public interest wherever they feel that it is important that the public understands where misappropriation or misuse of funds has taken place. Those reports in the public interest are a very important check and balance to ensure that high standards of public life are maintained.

Perhaps, if I may, Andrew will just explain how we do this.

ANDREW FOSTER: If I could just give the briefest pen-picture of what we actually do, because I think it will make our evidence more helpful. We actually appoint auditors across the whole of local government and the Health Service. We specify what they have to do. We regulate the quality of their work and have a substantial quality control programme as well. We identify good practice and hope to see it disseminated. 70 per cent of our work is around the probity of public service accounts, something that people will readily understand. Something that is different about our operation is, however, that 30 per cent of our work is in doing value-for-money studies every year. In the last year we have done ten major studies. As it happens, yesterday we published a major study on the Fire Service which you may well have read about. We have also published, during the last year, a major study on GP prescribing and its efficiency. We have looked at 16-19 year old education—and I could go on.

A key part of our approach is that we then follow those through at a local level, in either local government or the Health Service. In summary, we actually audit £93 billion of public expenditure, which is 15 per cent of the Gross Domestic Product, which is of course a substantial operation. Without going into minute detail, just to remind you that that means we appoint auditors for some 450 local authorities, 240 health authorities, up to 600 Trusts. I could go on but will not.

If I could just say the four key tasks that our auditors carry out. One, that you will readily understand, is to audit the account in a proper stewardship of public funds. A second, different in public sector audit, is to put in place measures to detect or prevent fraud and corruption. An important aspect—why we have done this study that Sir David mentioned earlier. A third, again different from other parts of auditing, our auditors look at the legality of expenditure, which takes us into different areas. Finally, and I have already referred to this, we carry through value-for-money work on the basis that the shareholder of public service is the citizen and that they have a right to see that their money is being well-spent as well as being properly stewarded.

That is the work we do and it is the bringing together of those different functions of regulating, specifying quality control that I think allows us to make sure that our auditors are independent. Frankly, it is the independence from the body under audit, I think, along with our comparative information, that makes us an influential and potentially positive force in public service life.

Just the mechanics—and I have almost finished. 30 per cent of our work at a local level is done by the big eight private accountancy firms. I could tell you the detail. 70 per cent of the work is done by our own arm's length agency of public sector accountants called the District Audit Service, and we have them at arm's length from us. They do that work. There is another thing that I really want to emphasise here and that is that we do a national study. We then make it into a product for our auditors to follow up, be it in a health authority or in a council. They might be spending 20 or 30 days examining against the national good practice we have seen, or comparative data, and then feeding back to the council, or feeding back to the management of the trust hospital or to their board, what they found and how it compares against good practice. This is done independently. If well-used, it is a very powerful tool for the corporate governments of the body because they do not have an influence over this work being done. So that is followed through at a local level.

Then, what we do at the end of the year—we will do this with the study we brought out yesterday on the Fire Service—we collect a picture of what has happened across the country and we will play it back to health authorities, Fire Service, and to government. So we like to see it, but then I suppose we would, as a virtuous circle of good practice follow-through national report, independently done. I think, to be brief, I would stop there Chairman.

LORD NOLAN: Thank you very much indeed. I will ask Diana Warwick to take up the questions, please.

1410. DIANA WARWICK: Could I just ask you, following that process through, is all of it in the public domain?

ANDREW FOSTER: A very large part of it is in the public domain. There will be some aspects of the auditors' work which legally does not come into the public domain unless there is challenge or objection. In the local government side there is a long history of the elector having a right to inspect a local authority's accounts and to object. It is only at a later stage in that process that it becomes fully in the public domain. There is a general principle. The Commission signs up to wanting as much as possible to be in the public domain but there are some areas where it does not come into the public domain until a later stage in the process.

1411. DIANA WARWICK: Right. Could you tell me: you have raised 16-19 year olds and the Fire Service. What do you actually cover? What are the criteria which determine the bodies that you cover?

ANDREW FOSTER: We cover the whole of the Health Service, the whole of local government. So the Fire Service, for instance, is run by county councils and metropolitan authorities. It is all of those functions that we have described. We choose the studies we do by consulting widely with the Councils concerned but then our own Board makes a choice because they feel that that should be done independently. We also would consult the Government.

1412. DIANA WARWICK: But are there any other public bodies besides those which come under the ambit of local government and the National Health Service that you audit?

ANDREW FOSTER: Sir David?

DAVID COOKSEY: The only other bodies are the non-metropolitan police authorities in this country which, again, are partly Home Office and partly local authorities. But, essentially, its function is of local government and the National Health Service only.

DIANA WARWICK: Thank you.

ANDREW FOSTER: And we have recently been invited to do some work by the Government in the housing corporation. I think that our specialty, frankly, is to look at local public bodies that are similar but geographically separate, which we can compare their performance. We also have auditors all around the country and we can follow up. So that is the unique contribution we have to make, I think.

1413. DIANA WARWICK: Thank you. You sent us a very helpful submission which I think goes into considerable detail, expanding on the points that you made in your presentation. Would it be accurate to say that your view is that the key to preventing misconduct is good corporate governance? And what do you think is the most important element in all of that?

DAVID COOKSEY: I agree that good corporate governance is an essential and it is this element with which I opened—which is openness and accountability. In local government there has been a long history of access and accountability and that is a very important aspect of corporate government's process. Getting back to what I was saying, having the independent audit there so that all of this comes out for inspection, is I think an extremely important part of that process. The auditor's ability, if he does not like what he sees, to report publicly. You asked the question about whether this is an open process. The answer is that there is a relationship between the auditor and the Authority whereby the normal secrecy is there until such time as something which is unacceptable is found. Normally this will be disclosed through the management letter which has to be taken at full council meeting and discussed and a response given to the auditor about the issues that he finds unacceptable and are disclosed in the management letter. If the process is more serious than that—and we have auditors issuing probably 15 to 20 times a year reports in the public interest—then this becomes a much more serious affair and the council concerned would have to answer publicly to that report and will normally be required to rectify the situation.

1414. DIANA WARWICK: Could you tell me: you make a statement here in your evidence to us that:

"As in the corporate sector, individuals should be required to confirm annually that they have complied with the Code."

The Code of good rules and procedure. Could you expand on that a little bit? What do you actually have in mind there?

DAVID COOKSEY: If you look at the private sector, at what directors are required to do today: in signing off their accounts on an annual basis, the directors of a company are required to sign off that they have complied with everything that is required of a director. More specifically in the financial services area, one has to normally sign off on a quarterly basis in compliance with the regulatory authority that you are involved with. Now we believe that there is a lot to be said for senior officers and senior elected members of an authority who take responsibility for the actions of that authority to sign off that they have complied with a code of practice and a code of conduct which is very similar to the private sector requirements.

1415. DIANA WARWICK: And are there aspects of local government practice and procedure, or alternatively National Health Service practice and procedure, which you would like to see transferred between the two? Good practices which you feel should become universal?

ANDREW FOSTER: We think that, certainly in local government, the obligation to declare interests—which is a longstanding one—is very positive indeed and I think we would commend it to you for your consideration for extension to other parts of public life. That would be the first thing I would say. The second thing I would say is that, if you go through the gamut of local government powers—Sir David has explained the public interest report which is a very strong deterrent: people do not like the oxygen of publicity to bring forward negative things—declaration of interest helps. But then the two extreme powers in local government are surcharge and disqualification. We think that the principle of surcharge, or of an individual fiduciary responsibility for executives and non-executives, is a very powerful one and we would again commend to you the consideration for that. I think that I heard NAHAT saying something similar. We certainly think that nothing quickens people's minds so much as the thought that they may carry some personal financial responsibility. So, declaration of interest we think is helpful; surcharge we think is helpful. And, frankly, as our evidence says, we actually believe that some of the corporate governance improvements which the National Health Service is now putting in place, such as audit committees—we actually think that local government, which comes out of these considerations quite well, could learn from the Health Service about the extension of audit committees. So, some suggestions going both ways.

1416. DIANA WARWICK: Do you think that, having said that, that the current management practices in the National Health Service are working well?

ANDREW FOSTER: That is a broad, sweeping question. If one looks over the Health Service reforms, there has clearly been massive change to 600 trusts being established, a lot of purchasing organisations, and I think the time of our survey was a period of great volatility in the Health Service. A lot of people are being introduced from the private sector, both at non-exec level and at exec level. It did demonstrate some worrying things. Our own response, I think, to put that in context is that people did listen to and hear what we said. I think it troubled the Department of Health and we think that the corporate code that has now been brought out is an appropriate and positive response to what we discovered. Candidly, the job for us is now to monitor and see whether it works. So I think that my answer is: there were some things that clearly were not desirable in the earliest times; there has been some exposure of them; there is some proposal to put it right. I think it is too early to say whether it has been put right and I think we should police it. We in fact intend to publish something in the next few months on the role of non-executive directors in the Health Service, because we do not yet think that is as clear as it should be.

DAVID COOKSEY: Perhaps I could just add one point to this and that is that there is an interesting difference between the Health Service and local government in that the auditor can issue reports in the public interest in local government, but reports solely to the Secretary of State in the Health Service. Now may I just say that the Secretary of State has been very open about then publishing those reports so there is nothing hidden there at all. But it is a different regime and perhaps one which might be more useful if it was a proper public interest report.

1417. DIANA WARWICK: Yes, and monitoring of course does depend on openness. The draft NHS code of openness specifically says that there is no public right of access to documents. In other words, one interpretation of that would be, I think, that it is possible to have release of material that is actually packaged for release. It is managed. It also preserves a right to refuse to release information on the basis that it is considered either incomplete or unreliable. How do you view those limitations on openness?

ANDREW FOSTER: I think that my response to that is that the key driving imperative should be an obligation to be honest to the citizen, the user, the patient, and that should be what drives things. I think that the balance struck in the Code is not an unreasonable one. If you actually look at the complexity of some medical information and some other complicated situations, that full disclosure of documents is not necessarily obligatory to make sure that an honest and clear understanding is struck. That is my response. The final point I would make is that if you were to look at the Wessex and West Midlands troubling situations—it is of interest to us, we have been involved as an organisation since the reforms—it has been since audit has been externalised with the independent powers that some of these things have been pushed into the public domain. Whilst Sir David rightly says that the system is slightly different, candidly when our auditors push and we are very troubled about things, things do end up in the public domain in a way that historically they did not always.

1418. DIANA WARWICK: Perhaps I could just make one final point. You say in your evidence to us that a visible commitment to integrity will help to raise the standing of public bodies and encourage good people to come into public life. We have had debates at each level that we have been investigating about just how much disclosure and how much there ought to be a visible commitment to integrity. You will be aware that we have been talking to Ministers about their moves from ministerial office to private interests. Do you think that is a general principle, that a visible commitment to integrity, irrespective of the probity of the decision, is a general principle that should apply throughout public life?

DAVID COOKSEY: It has to. I do not think there is any question about that at all. Certainly we see the need to assess people for appointment right through the process of appointing to public life and then for them to adopt the appropriate codes of practice and so on, and be seen to be publicly adherent to those, is an extremely important part of this stewardship of public finance.

DIANA WARWICK: Thank you.

1419. CLIFFORD BOULTON: Can I just ask about relations with the National Audit Office? We asked the Comptroller and Auditor-General if he would like to send us a list of all those bodies that he would like to audit that he does not now, or have access to their papers. Do you have a regular relationship with the National Audit Office and are there any problems of, let us say, overlap in the National Health Service where there are some parallel functions and are you comfortable with the present division between the work of the two bodies?

DAVID COOKSEY: Could I just start by explaining where we have come from, because I think this is very important, and then I will ask Andrew Foster to just deal with the detail. You have to recognise that the Audit Commission was brought about to deal with local government in the first place and the separate democratic process of local government and, therefore, it was inappropriate to have a body which reported directly to Parliament as obviously the National Audit Office does with its forum of the Public Accounts Committee. So this is where matters started. But, because our technique of developing knowledge of best practice and being able to promulgate that through rather comparable bodies across local government than the National Health Service etc., we have in fact developed to the situation where our remit has been broadened by government and therefore there is a difference between the two. But the main principle of what you can see happening is that we are involved with the delivery of public services at a local level, some £93 billion a year of them, and the National Audit Office is much more concerned with the spending of central government departments and agencies. Now in terms of the actual interface, Andrew, if you could pick this up?

ANDREW FOSTER: Just for the record, the easiest and clearest distinction to make between the role of the National Audit Office and ourselves is of them auditing main departmental government votes and us auditing at a local level or appointing auditors for the Health Service and local government. For the largest part, those are clear and separate and distinct roles with the point that Sir David makes of one being accountable to Parliament and the other having a different set reporting arrangements. There are, however, as you rightly draw attention to, territories on which we are close in the Health Service, where Sir John will do some value-for-money work and follow it down an audit line into the Health Service to satisfy himself the way that the Department of Health is exercising its responsibilities. That does take us into similar territory. It was our work, for instance, on Wessex and West Midlands that serviced the P.A.C. when they discussed that. I think, in the spirit of directness, that sometimes that is not as satisfactory as it should be and people in the Health Service complain about it. Now, Sir John's and my response to that is to see that we should coordinate and collaborate our programmes as much as we can and we do. Over the last couple of years we have done a lot of staff secondment so we understand each other's working methods. We also are doing some joint studies and work. So, collaboration between us is important and we are working on that. But I still think it does leave a fuzzy edge which is not always as good as it might be. Its cause is the different accounting: accountability, constitutional arrangements and their history.

1420. CLIFFORD BOULTON: Would you have any practical suggestions you would like to make to us—I do not mean necessarily in answer to my question immediately—about how a system might be tidied up? Because I can imagine it is very irksome to people at the receiving end if they are not clear about these two bodies.

ANDREW FOSTER: I think we need to educate people as to what our different responsibilities are. I think it is irksome to people. I think that the types of approach that I have described—of collaboration, cooperation, joint studies and all—redresses it. But I think that we are open to other ways that we make sure that we do not ever run the risk of duplicating each other, which is not helpful.

1421. WILLIAM UTTING: A couple of points from your conclusions and recommendations; one of them is there is a fascinating couple of sentences, the first of which is "Bureaucracy is not the answer to problems of corporate governance or failed ventures". One cheers when that sort of sentiment is expressed but one is then confronted by requests from people for ever more and ever more detailed regulation of what they are doing. Could you just expand on your views on that interesting point?

ANDREW FOSTER: Yes. The Commission's view is definitely that the spelling out of clear principles, which is what we have attempted to do, and see them exercised across the services is what needs to be done, the mechanisms that deliver them may need to vary according to the type of arrangement. Our worst fear of people's stereotype of auditors is that the public clamour—we have more and more rules and regulations—and that frankly the worst end of the old public service was sometimes it was rather constipated, very bureaucratic, hierarchical and actually against the public interest. I personally believe—and I think the Commission does—that some of the entrepreneurialism and innovation that the changes have brought forward are positive and useful. It is about whether there are intelligent checks and balances. So we would favour principles, consistent mechanisms across the public service, but not a return to massive check lists which frankly lead to things against the public interest because they lead to inertia in the status quo. And the worst end of local Government—local Government is good, we believe—the worst end of local Government was that at times it could be inert because it was so heavily regulated.

DAVID COOKSEY: Perhaps I could just add something to that. One of the issues that has come up to the Commission time and again in my eight and a half years as Chairman is that within local Government in particular—and we have seen it again in the Health Service—very often accountability and responsibility did not reside in the same person and a lot of this excess bureaucracy was actually bridging that gap. One of the areas that we have pushed very hard is to get the management processes in local Government and now in the Health Service into much better order, so that accountability and responsibility did reside in the same place and the right checks and balances for that process. This has led very often to a simplification of the bureaucratic processes, which I think is all to the good.

1422. WILLIAM UTTING: You conclude by saying that the most rigorous and best practice ought to apply in whatever sector, local Government, NHS, central Government and you say in brackets "(and other public bodies)". Are you there intending that these should be applied across this big swathe of non-departmental public bodies and Quangos about which we have been having evidence today and yesterday?

DAVID COOKSEY: The answer is definitely yes. We believe that the checks and balances that are processed as part of the accountability checks in local Government and the Health Service has produced a situation where there is openness, and we are getting improved delivery of public services out of that process. And we believe that that same accountability process should apply right across the public sector.

ANDREW FOSTER: If I could just add two points to that; one is that the principles of public audit, which Sir David spelt out at the beginning, we think are a very helpful mechanism lever tool towards accountability in the public services generally. That would be the first point I would make—and we think that there is no reason why they should not be considered across other Quangos. The second point I would like to make is—I mean, as you clearly will be aware, we are a Quango and obviously the most often asked question in life is "Who audits the auditors?" And I guess to pre-empt, perhaps, somebody asking us that, and to say we actually think external scrutiny and accountability improves performance and is in the public interest and it is for that reason our Commission has agreed, as an NDPB that we will, despite the other—we are audited by the NAO and another regime—that our Commission should be subject to external scrutiny and that there should be full publication of whatever that throws up and we bluntly expect to, you know, have to swallow some of our own medicine and we are not desperately looking forward to it!

WILLIAM UTTING: Well, I have had to swallow some in the past so I won't volunteer to join that! Thank you.

1423. LORD THOMSON: Just following up for one moment the question of Quangos. We were told when the Chairman of the PAC and Sir John Bourn, came before us, that one-third of the Quangos are not in fact under public audit. If you were to take some of that on, does that require legislation, does it require a statutory authority?

DAVID COOKSEY: If it is the Commission we are talking about here, the answer is that we have specific powers to audit certain bodies and some of those are mandatory, particularly local Government and the National Health Service bodies, other bodies, such as colleges of education, grant maintained schools, etc. can ask us to audit them. But that regime does not normally include a value for money element—it is much more of a probity element only. So whilst we are not bidding to expand the size of the Commission at this moment in time, I think the areas where bodies that are consumers of considerable amounts of public money but have the right to appoint their own auditors and, secondly, are not necessarily subject to value for money scrutiny, are bodies such as grant-maintained schools, colleges, universities, housing associations, the TECs. And then the other area to which I am sure Sir John Bourn referred is that a lot of local authorities have set up companies to manage former assets that they had and very often you cannot see through the use of those public funds through the company because it is subject to a separate audit regime. We believe that that should be rectified and I know that Sir John feels equally about that.

1424. LORD THOMSON: Your public interest reports are obviously very important. You mentioned, I think, that there were fifteen to twenty of them last year. Were they all published and was there a delay between you submitting the report to the Secretary of State and the publication?

ANDREW FOSTER: There were fifteen published in local Government last year and there were three in the Health Service and there will always be a level of discussion. Well, with local Government they would be published after a certain amount of pre-consultation with the Council concerned, but the auditor has the right to publish and it would only be proper professional practice to make sure that the facts were correct. Exactly the same would happen in the Health Service and whilst the framework is different the net result is the same, the three in the Health Service all ended up being published but there would be some consultation with the Department of Health along the way. The difference here, of course, being that one is ultimately a managed system and the Secretary of State answers for the performance of the Health Service at the despatch box whereas clearly in local Government it is different. But the net result is that they do get into the public domain. I think that if the Health Service sees something coming it gets very very worried indeed and jumps around a lot.

1425. PETER SHORE: Just one question further to what you have just said. You say that reports on the Health Service are published ultimately, after being submitted to the Secretary of State. Is there any requirement—and do you think if there is not there should be—on the Secretary of State to report those reports to Parliament?

ANDREW FOSTER: Yes, I probably need to make the system exactly clear. There are two different steps in the process. There is something called Section 23, which is a confidential report to the Secretary of State of something that concerns the auditor but which is not of massive moment. And the Secretary of State by law is not obliged to make those public. They would be troubling but not major. Then there is Section 15.3 which is exactly the same and they are Public Interest Reports and the nuance of difference is that there is not the same obligation to publish by the Health Service but the net result candidly of the way our auditors deal with it is that it is shared with the health authority concerned, and by being taken in public session the Press either know about it or are there, and it comes into the public domain. I mean, clearly you could—although the Commission has never suggested it—require more bringing together of those and a requirement for some discussion in Parliament. I guess our role here is about the oversight of local bodies—the accountability at a national level is not ours, it is clearly the Secretary of State's.

1426. ANNE WARBURTON: Can I raise with you the study which you commissioned on probity in the National Health Service? I understand that it was a bit disappointing that your study took place after the Secretary of State had taken measures to try to tell staff that matters of concern to them could be raised with proper safeguards and so forth, and that you found that actually most of the staff—what was the proportion, I have forgotten—were of the view that they would not dare risk their job by raising concerns. What I wanted to ask you is what more do you feel should be done and how applicable are any findings in the Health Service to other public bodies?

ANDREW FOSTER: Yes. I mean, if I could just respond. I mean, clearly our report says generally that we found honesty and integrity positive. The most worrying thing we found was actually about a small proportion of general practitioners and pharmacists where there had been self-regulation and we actually discovered some "collusion" between them and actually quite a lot of misrepresentation about things to do with prescriptions and people inflating practice lists. That was the most worrying thing that we found on approvable nature and the Department of Health is responding to that. On the issues that you raise I think that the most troubling thing we did discover is shown in, I think, the executive summary you have got, which demonstrates a more "closed culture" and I think it is very interesting to observe the gap of what staff thought they could do and what directors and senor people thought—and there was clearly a gap of perception there. I think it is difficult to give a conclusive answer. I suspect that during the period of great change in the Health Service people were even more frightened and worried than they may be as things stabilise. But that is speculation rather than proof on my part. I think that the management culture has got to make it plain—and I think the code of corporate governance does do that—the preparedness to encourage what are called whistleblowers or responsible sharing of information is important. We in our study, as you may have observed, did some joint work with an organisation called Concern at Work to spell out what a responsible employer should do to let staff come forward and what are the responsibilities of staff. We also set up in that study a call line whereby staff could phone in and anonymously tell us what was happening. In one of the sites we did that in we actually discovered things it was quite clear would never have come through in other ways. So I think it has changed. I think we don't know how well it has changed, but I think that the approach the Department of Health is taking is broadly in the right direction, but we must monitor it.

1427. LORD NOLAN: Well, thank you both very much indeed. You have been extremely helpful to us—you have given us a lot of your time and we are all very grateful to you.

Now we have got Mr. Noel Hepworth, Mr. John Whiteoak and Mr. Martin Evans from CIPFA. I think you have an opening statement, is that right, that you wish to make before questions?

NOEL HEPWORTH, JOHN WHITEOAK AND MARTIN EVANS (CIPFA)

JOHN WHITEOAK: That would be very helpful, Chairman.

LORD NOLAN: If you please. It would be helpful to us.

JOHN WHITEOAK: In terms of just precisely which of us is which, I am John Whiteoak, the Chairman of our working party—it is a team of eight people—that spans public service at officer level and at also very senior level. Noel Hepworth is the director of our institute and Martin Evans heads the technical division and also supports the working party. In fact the working party has been in existence about eighteen months which reflects the concerns of the institute at about that time about the very issues that have brought about your committee—public perceptions, public concerns. We in that time have spent quite a bit of time working into this very topic. Initially we actually had aspirations of doing sector specific codes of practice. I think having attempted that we recognise the complexity of public service and then recognise the need to actually try and establish a core framework of general

principles, and we believe that is a very appropriate way forward.

We actually have seen corporate governance as being how a policy-making body comes together, how it operates and manages, how it accounts for itself both in the public interest and to a higher authority in terms of a boss figure who is, in effect, the person or the body involved in making appointments and being responsible for appraisal. The framework we have worked on is pitching for clear processes, clear roles, clear emphasis on performance and clear reporting.

As we set out in our submission to the committee and in the list of key points which I understand have been circulated to you, we believe it is crucial that the committee should address the processes and systems of corporate governance and accountability of public service bodies, in order to rebuild public confidence in them. We actually believe that the three principles of corporate governance defined by the Cadbury Committee should also apply to public service, emphasis on openness, integrity and accountability. In structuring our own work we have had in mind three levels. The organisational structure and process—this is the question of the top policy-making body and how it comes together—internal controls and, thirdly, standards of personal behaviour. A lot of the latter area—standards of personal behaviour—is about the work that is needed to establish a good style and culture throughout the organisation and in many respects the business of declaration of interests and so on is about setting an example at the highest level. So that is basically how our submission has been constructed.

Recognising the limited time we have we aim to concentrate on organisational structure and processes and standards of personal behaviour, although I think we also recognise that forty minutes before your committee can feel a very long time as well.

Our work on corporate governance reflects the firmly held belief that the principles of corporate governance are "politically neutral", that is they can apply equally well to an elected authority on the one hand and appointed "quango" or NHS trust board on the other. We have tried to devise a framework that should help any public service body to operate in a more efficient, effective and publicly acceptable way. We have not sought to prescribe a framework of corporate governance or to comment on the validity of current structures or policies. The public sector is extremely complex and does not have a standard legislative framework or organisational shape. We have therefore sought to devise a framework of general principles, which captures the spirit of corporate governance. This can then be used as a basis for establishing codes of practice within each sector by those who best understand the challenges and "nuances" of their industry. So we recognise the diversity of the public services, each part with unique features which require special attention, and each of which is governed by different statutory and managerial frameworks. These inevitably impose different sets of accountabilities.

We also recognise the changing environment in which public services now operate. However, we remain of the view that a presumption of openness and accountability is in the interests of good public services. The last fifteen years has seen wide-ranging structural and managerial changes in public services. These have included compulsory competitive tendering, the creation of internal markets and the "purchaser provider splits". This has led generally to a more commercial style of management and a competitive environment which has inevitably resulted in a stronger desire for secrecy.

However, public service bodies cannot be run as if they are private companies; they must operate within a clearly defined framework of accountability for the actions and performance of the corporate body itself, board members and employees. This framework should comprise the following elements: full disclosure of information about the body and its activities, including information about the body's role, how it meets, how members are appointed and especially by what criteria, and members' and senior executives' remuneration. Rigorous standards of financial and performance reporting are crucial and external audit and performance review. These are set out in our formal paper work.

Wherever public money is spent it should be clear who appoints those who spend it, why and to whom they report. Proper reporting procedures must be in place; financial and annual reporting must be of the highest standard and the body's activities must be subject to rigorous and independent audit. What is needed is a robust system of corporate governance which apart from restoring public confidence in the conduct of public business would enable everyone in the public services—board members and employees alike—to know where they stand. And that is the opening statement, Chairman.

LORD NOLAN: Thank you very much indeed. I am going to ask Sir Clifford Boulton to take up the questions.

1428. CLIFFORD BOULTON: Thank you very much for your statement and also for the material you sent us in advance. It is obvious that you have given a lot of thought to this subject and we shall find the material very useful and to that extent many of my questions will be on the fringe of the substance inevitably. Could I ask before we start really—have you had a chance to see the Government's paper on a review of *Guidance on Public Appointments* that has been issued this week and do you have any comments to make about that aspect because appointments is one of the areas that you have been covering?

JOHN WHITEOAK: Obviously there has been very little time for that in the sense that the paperwork was only issued yesterday and in my case the opportunity to glance at it on the way down in the train. I think many of the points that are made are very appropriate but we are keen to put emphasis on the question of having a very very clear process and criteria in the sense of a person specification and in the sense of job description. If either of my colleagues would like to come in on that particular point, that might be helpful.

NOEL HEPWORTH: I think we would say that it does move in the direction that we would like to see it move. I think for our part we would prefer it to go further and that is implicit, I think, in the evidence that we have submitted to you. So we would say it is a move in the right direction.

1429. CLIFFORD BOULTON: Could you highlight any individual areas where you would like to see more progress—as you see it?

NOEL HEPWORTH: Yes, for example, in 1, where the Government talks about making appointments, I think it is, to all quangos being wholly the responsibility of the Secretary of State. I think we would feel that there is scope for devolution of that power further down and that is one of the points that we would like to address. To some extent it may be dealt with later—but the NAHAT evidence you heard this morning I think suggested much the same. That there is scope in the local trust for devolving power further down and responsibility—I don't think that is allowed for in quite the way that, for example, NAHAT envisaged in the document that the Government have produced.

1430. CLIFFORD BOULTON: But you accept, do you, this point about proportionality, that one should not get out of proportion—the nature and scale and operation of these non-departmental public bodies is so enormous, is it not, and there are small advisory bodies that you couldn't really give a full set of precisely the same requirements that would be necessary for some very large executive authority?

NOEL HEPWORTH: I think in reading this I found it a bit difficult to understand what proportionality actually meant; and an awful lot, I think, does depend on what it is the body is supposed to do. I think we would accept that the bodies need to be drawn from various constituencies but how far the body should reflect the areas of interest in which it is involved does depend upon what type of body we are actually talking about. To some extent if you said that the body, for example, should be a wholly representative body of the different interests and constituencies, that would not necessarily make it a very good operational body, so there are other issues at stake which need to be taken into account in our view. You must make sure, for example, that there is the right range of skills within the body to perform the task in hand and that may not come about through just drawing groups from the appropriate constituencies.

1431. CLIFFORD BOULTON: But once you have drawn up your public service Cadbury Code, you accept then that to apply that in each individual circumstance will need further rules and thoughts to make it more directly applicable to the particular body, that this would be a kind of 10 Commandments of the thing and then after that each group will need to have its own particular rules?

NOEL HEPWORTH: That is correct.

CLIFFORD BOULTON: I understand.

JOHN WHITEOAK: It is a robust framework which we think has then to be interpreted in relation to each sector, regardless of the size or the environment in which it operates. We think to counter that that one of the dangers is that without a robust framework no matter how small the body you could end up with that body trying to invent corporate governance—reinventing wheels—when many of the features are rather standard.

1432. CLIFFORD BOULTON: So they draw from the framework what is appropriate, do they?

JOHN WHITEOAK: Yes.

1433. CLIFFORD BOULTON: When one is talking about the fact that not all of them can be treated in the same way there are some bodies where, for instance, ministerial appointments are almost inevitable, are there not, and others where political considerations might well be held to be—or it would be argued that they are—irrelevant because of the nature of the work and you cannot have people who manifestly oppose the policy, and that sort of thing. You recognise that there are those situations as well?

NOEL HEPWORTH: Yes, we do. I think to some extent one needs to understand what one means by political. I think we would say that the Secretary of State inevitably will want to appoint—and should appoint— somebody who is going to run that quango (or whatever it is) in accordance with the policy that they have laid down. That seems to us to be a reality of the practical side of life. So, for example, the Chairman of, say, the Funding Agency for Schools ought to be a person who is sympathetic to the idea of the Funding Agency for Schools. So, yes, we do see that there has to be that relationship between the Minister and the Chairman—a certain empathy about the policies that are being pursued by the quango, yes.

1434. CLIFFORD BOULTON: But you would want the terms and conditions and the kind of competition, if appropriate, that was being undertaken to be transparent, so that people could see what the reasoning was behind the appointment?

NOEL HEPWORTH: That is absolutely essential, yes.

MARTIN EVANS: And on that point we have made one suggestion, that public bodies should be specifically required to report in their annual report and accounts how the board has constituted, how the members are appointed.

1435. CLIFFORD BOULTON: I asked a few minutes ago of a previous witness about the role of the Comptroller and Auditor General and some evidence that he had given about certain areas where his powers were currently limited and you have got some examples in your material, I think, in Attachment B, where there is an interface between the CAG and the Audit Commission, for instance. But do you think that the NAO should be the sole auditor of public bodies or is that a degree of uniformity which is not necessary?

MARTIN EVANS: I think as you have indicated there are currently four statutory audit bodies with responsibility for auditing public bodies, they are the NAO, the Audit Commission, who you have just had as witnesses, the Accounts Commission which perform a similar function in Scotland, and the Northern Ireland Audit Office. Generally we believe those arrangements work well. We certainly believe—and we have made it clear in our submission—that all public bodies should be subject to public audit. An increasing number now fall outwith that framework and we think that is a matter for public concern. I think when Sir John Bourn came before you last week he was talking about specifically the non-departmental public bodies to which he does not have access and certainly we would agree that he should be the appointed auditor for all NDPBs. But I would draw a distinction between the Comptroller and Auditor General and the National Audit Office—there is a distinction. It would be a matter for him who to appoint as auditors to those bodies. He could, if he so chose, appoint private firms of accountants, provided they had the

necessary expertise and skills, and he would obviously have to establish appropriate quality control and assurance mechanisms. But the critical thing is that the audit would be being carried out within this Public Audit framework which Andrew Foster described—the three basic elements, independence of the auditor, a wider scope to the work and more informative reporting. He also described how they used private sector firms to actually carry out much of their work.

1436. CLIFFORD BOULTON: Could I ask you again about this code which contained principles of public service? Is it possible, do you think, to apply the same code that we were talking about—the basic rules—to all areas of public life? Would you think it would be practicable to include Members of Parliament and Ministers and everybody who is in public life in the same code or is it really then getting so remote from the practical application that it would lose its value in that way?

NOEL HEPWORTH: I think we would say that it is possible to apply the same code but obviously with different people it would have different emphases. So you would have a general code which would deal with all the relevant issues but, for example, those bits about, say, the delivery of a service would not obviously apply to Members of Parliament, but there would be other features of it which would. So the appropriate person who was effective would pick out the points that were most relevant to them and, of course, you can never be precise about the definition of the boundary, so in large measure you would get a degree of overlap between the different parties. But if you are all talking about the same basic document then it would seem to us to be sensible. And, in fact, if you look at the documents that are around, like the *Best Practice Code for Board Members of Public Bodies*—that is the Treasury document published in June 1994, if you look at the *Code of Conduct and Code of Accountability in the NHS*, if you look at the *Citizens Charter*, then indeed the paper which you discussed, I think, with Sir Giles Radice (was it yesterday) they have in a sense four sets of values or principles and they are not all that different, but they actually are different and they don't need to be different. They could actually be using the same terminology and they could be addressing the same things. Some examples we have looked at is that, for example, only the Citizens Charter statement expressly states that "Standards, choice and consultation, courtesy and helpfulness in putting things right should be key principles"—those are not addressed in the others. The NHS Public Service Values and the Civil Service Values do not themselves refer to value for money in the use of public money, although the actual introduction to the NHS code does, but the actual code itself does not. So there are things like that, but there is absolutely no reason why they should not actually be encompassed within any particular document. They all should be there.

I think we would go a bit further, though, than some of those because those codes are basically addressed at the Boards and they do not mention a number of other things that we think are important in corporate governance, things like the importance of internal audit, risk management and internal controls and then proper financial reporting. Those are not in. So we would feel that there needs to be consistency and there needs to be an extension.

1437. CLIFFORD BOULTON: It sounds as though you have gone through these and made that kind of analysis yourself. Would you like to submit another bit of paper to us pointing out how you think the thing could be co-ordinated?

NOEL HEPWORTH: Yes, we could do that. As John Whiteoak indicated in his opening statement we are looking at the development of our work and one of the questions we would like to ask you is that if you were interested in it when would you want it from us by to be helpful to you?

CLIFFORD BOULTON: That is something to pursue with the secretariat.

NOEL HEPWORTH: Right, if they could let us know, please.

JOHN WHITEOAK: We are actually in the stages of actually trying to put this work together and so we would welcome as much time as possible, but be in a position to do it relatively quickly.

CLIFFORD BOULTON: We have not been given much time!

LORD NOLAN: We are hoping to get in our first report as requested by the beginning of May, so we are under great pressure of time, as you know. But, of course, I realise your problems and other commitments.

JOHN WHITEOAK: That leaves us adequate time. It depends how much of the period between now and May you will give us.

NOEL HEPWORTH: But we will give it to you as quickly as we can.

LORD NOLAN: As quickly as possible, yes.

1438. CLIFFORD BOULTON: Could I just ask you about internal controls? You drew attention in your submission—not surprisingly—to the PAC report, the Proper Conduct of Public Business, and you say "Although the media reported these breakdowns of failures as being caused by introducing managers who had no traditional grounding in public sector management and the norms of behaviour expected of public service managers, others have interpreted them as being caused by a misunderstanding by traditional public sector managers of what is acceptable in the so-called freer environment of the private sector." That is nicely hedged reporting of what other people are saying. Do you have a view yourself about which of these areas have proved wrong, or any comment to make yourself about the situation that was revealed by the PAC bringing together all those cases?

NOEL HEPWORTH: Well, the PAC did some very useful work in bringing together all of those points and identifying what seemed to us to be quite serious problems which needed to be addressed—getting accustomed to the new environment in which these services were being delivered—and we were getting people in from outside who in a way might be familiar with the new environment, the actual operational environment, but were not familiar with the public service ethos. We then saw some analysis which raised an alternative question which said, in effect, that there were people who were conventional public

servants who actually were having to deal with a wholly new operational environment and they had made presumptions about the way the private sector operated and they were not necessarily justifiable presumptions. So there was an educational process on both sides and that seemed to us to be quite a balanced position to take. It is too easy to say it is all people coming from the outside who are wrong—there actually is a new operational environment and those who have been used to the alternative need to understand that, too. And it is very easy indeed to make assumptions about how the private sector operates without actually knowing how the private sector operates because you have never been there.

1439. CLIFFORD BOULTON: Is the situation settling down now—is there an improved general environment, do you think, discernible?

NOEL HEPWORTH: It is hard for us to say.

MARTIN EVANS: I think also in including that piece in our submission we wanted to sort of flag up an alternative view about that report, the way it was presented as a critique of the new public management which had occurred primarily in quangos and agencies. If you actually look through the detail of the report you will find some of these things occurred in the traditional Departments of State and a lot of the points highlighted related to the sort of basic controls—nothing to do with new public management, they are to do with traditional public administration. And so I think that is why we are saying that as part of a general statement on corporate governance you do need to reaffirm the basics of good internal control.

1440. CLIFFORD BOULTON: Can I just ask you about this rather worrying reference you make to possible collusion to circumvent controls? Do you have anything on that subject of whistleblowing and reporting of worries and developing systems to allow that kind of internal control to take place?

MARTIN EVANS: I think most accountants and auditors would accept that any system is capable of being evaded by collusion but clearly you need to build in appropriate controls into any management information or financial system to minimise the chance of that happening and, of course, have an effective internal control procedure to highlight any weaknesses that do emerge and any misconduct that does arise.

JOHN WHITEOAK: In a way a fundamental objective of the whole of this is probably to aim for a style and culture within the organisation which individuals can trust and feel involved in and have an opportunity to diffuse legitimate concerns. The whole phrase "whistleblower" itself has lots of connotations and angles to it. I think one of the concerns that seems to be around is this issue of at what point does somebody within the organisation—an employee—have an opportunity to properly air concerns, and that really is capturing hearts and minds and probably, through example, the board should have this openness, declaration of interests, and gradually work on hearts and minds within the organisation. One of the difficulties is that if you don't have the openness within the organisation it ends up being a situation where individuals have concerns and tensions that kind of burst in an unmeasured, perhaps ill-motivated and perhaps not even material way. So that it is important to try and develop a system of openness within the organisation that is unthreatening.

Again, thinking about this whistleblowing issue, a further angle is whether or not there should be some role on the management board which is quite explicit in terms of having responsibility to monitor and keep an eye on whether things are being handled in a proper, legal way within the powers of that body and to make it quite clear that if an officer—for example it could be a finance officer or a company secretary equivalent—has a very very specific responsibility to report out to the external monitoring organisations which could include the external auditor, an ombudsman if one exists, a regulator and even others that we know exist, such as the police, etc. Now, those things exist but what seems to be best is to have a system that actually does diffuse things that are not momentous, that can be talked through, to get the balance that every organisation wants to have between loyalty and commitment and also ownership of these public service values and feeling that they are able to talk over those things that do not seem to be compatible with perhaps these values.

1441. CLIFFORD BOULTON: A system of safety valves rather than waiting till the whistle blows?

JOHN WHITEOAK: Absolutely. Most of the things in our structure is again about having frameworks and processes that are very healthy rather than having over-investment in creating further bodies—further monitoring organisations. A lot of this, we think, is actually just commonsense, logic and philosophy/processes that most public sector bodies could operate within. The crucial area that seems to need a lot more development work is the issue of who appoints, how, on what criteria, is it explicit and is that well reported?

CLIFFORD BOULTON: Thank you very much.

1442. PROF. ANTHONY KING: In your earlier statement you referred to various changes that have taken place in Government in recent years and you say these have led generally to a more commercial style of management and a competitive environment which has inevitably resulted in a stronger desire for secrecy. You are too polite to go on to say "and greater temptation for malpractice". In the next paragraph you say "However, public service bodies cannot be run as if they are private companies"—and you expand on that thought. In fact, in your view can that circle be squared—is there not a tension between creating public sector bodies which are invited to act as though they were private sector companies and then tell them "Oh, no, you must not do that, you must in fact behave as though you were in effect part of the Civil Service"?

NOEL HEPWORTH: Well, there is a tension there but I think we have to recognise that a number of the features of what has been called the "new public management" are very good and it would be a shame to lose the benefits of those. So the problem really is how to maintain the benefits without, as it were, bringing the system into disrepute because of some of the points that we are well aware of. I think there is a concern about secrecy, competitiveness—one trust is competing with another trust, one housing association is competing with another housing association, the different business units. Another feature of that is that, of course, they tend to be very narrowly focused as well. So the traditional Civil Service perhaps had a broader view about the overlap between different activities, whereas the performance related pay tends to focus people into very narrow areas. I don't think there is an easy answer to that problem but I think that where the answer does lie is in ensuring that there are proper procedures, that people don't make hole-in-the-corner decisions, very importantly that there is proper reporting about what they have done and what they intend to do. If those things are there then, in fact, there is a degree of openness which would enable the analyst, the observer, the academic to actually get at those issues and make them more generally available to the interested parties. Without that then I think the risk is that the new public management will get into disrepute.

MARTIN EVANS: I would say that it is not possible to close the circle completely. There are going to be constraints and people going into public life have to recognise those. And I think one of the things that we have said in our submission is that people coming into the public service, as a board member, for example, should receive proper induction training, so that they understand not only the business that they are going into but the context, the environment in which they are going to have to work. We have talked about the public audit model. I think a member or a Chairman of a NHS trust board coming from the private sector would perhaps regard the sort of audit arrangements as intrusive and expensive. I think they have to understand why that model exists and why it has been set up.

1443. PROF. ANTHONY KING: Can I ask you a question on a completely different subject? We appear now in this country to have two national Civil Services—one is the Civil Service with a capital "C" and a capital "S" and the other is a kind of alternative or shadow Civil Service which consists of the people who have been appointed—especially if they have been paid—to quangos of one sort or another. Now, you said in your evidence—and the point has been repeated by a lot of people—that of course a Minister does not want to appoint to the chairmanship of a public body in the quango area someone who is unsympathetic to the policy the Minister is pursuing. But that principle on the face of it appears to apply equally to the conventional Civil Service and yet in the conventional Civil Service the view is taken that civil servants are expected to display politically neutral competence and to do their best job in whatever position they are put. Why should that principle not also apply in the quango part of the Civil Service? If it were it would have a lot of implications for the way in which appointments are made and for who makes those appointments.

MARTIN EVANS: I think it should at executive level. I think there is a difference between the Chairman of a quango and board members and the actual paid officers that are carrying out the policy of the board.

1444. PROF. ANTHONY KING: What is the difference between the chairman of a quango on the one hand and the Permanent Secretary of a big Government department on the other, for these purposes?

MARTIN EVANS: Is not the equivalent of the chairman of the quango the Minister him or herself?

1445. PROF. ANTHONY KING: Except the Minister appoints the chairman, does he not?

MARTIN EVANS: Yes, but the equivalent in terms of setting the policy framework and directing the business of the department.

JOHN WHITEOAK: Yes, we are seeing a distinction between the appointed non-executive and the executive but I can see that one of the points you are making is that they actually merge on one of these boards, where you have the non-executives and the executives. I think we have already acknowledged that the chairman of a body—probably an important criteria has to be one of whether or not the chairman who has roles in terms of leadership, shaping, strategy, team-building, is sympathetic to the whole objectives of the organisation and therefore there might well be around a chairman some kind of political element to it and that can be quite explicit. There then can be others that are being appointed for other criteria and there are then people, potentially on the board, that are official, executive and——there are issues about the composition of the board in terms of what the majority is. I think in our submission we are arguing that the non-executives should always be in the majority. Once we get into the executive area we are arguing for principles of impartiality politically, objectivity, declaring of interests which apply to all, but there are many of the similarities once you go into the executive part of the structure that apply to the civil servant. I think perhaps one area where there will remain a distinction is the degree of visibility.

1446. ANNE WARBURTON: I would like to put two questions together—I think they might make one question. The first is you are a charity—your institute is a charitable one. How do you go about exercising your influence in this field of work that we are considering? How much are you actually in touch with individual departments, with individual bodies concerned? Then the second question takes up the point of training which was just mentioned. You make quite a point about the need for induction training and training throughout the period of appointment. I wanted to ask you how would you see this training being put together—where do the different elements of it come together and do you see it as a centralised activity or done by the light of ideas in each separate body?

JOHN WHITEOAK: Would you allow us to answer the question in several parts? With great difficulty. I think probably one of the things in terms of how we as an organisation through this working party put these issues together, we have to be very aware on the one hand that we have a lot of expertise in the sense that there are people operating at senior levels. But on the other hand it is very easy to tread on other people's toes that feel they have authority, responsibility and a bigger right to say than we have. So it reflects in a way how we have actually embarked on this work. We have actually been through a stage of issuing a discussion paper asking for consultation, we have tried to build a working party that does reflect a good cross-section of public service, and it probably reflects a good deal of the rather tempered language that we are using and—well I hope it will be apparent that there is a fair degree of thoroughness to how the material is coming forward. Obviously the director can put more flesh on those bones and probably also in relation to some of the induction issues.

NOEL HEPWORTH: Although we are a charity we are a membership body—we have about twelve thousand members—and of course they are concerned to influence,

as it were, what we do and to help us set our agenda. We also carry out a considerable amount of research in one form or another which helps us think about the agenda. As John Whiteoak said in his introduction we have been thinking about these issues for some considerable period of time. So there are various pressures on us to intervene in various areas, of which this just happens to be one, and as John has indicated we draw on—as far as we can—the widest possible range of experiences.

On the training point then there could be some elements of national training, as it were, but I would have thought that by and large the training should be pushed as far away from the centre as possible. If you take, for example, groups of organisations like health trusts then clearly there will be a role for the National Health Service Management Executive in specifying what should be done. I have no doubt they would then encourage the various trusts to go about doing a lot themselves, but they would also feed on whatever the centre does. And that would be true in other organisations as well. So it would seem to me that there would be a combination of both and where the balance would lie would depend upon the judgments of individuals who were involved in the training process.

JOHN WHITEOAK: It is possible just to add to that, in a way induction and training and support really must follow the clarity of the role. One of the things that we are quite keen on is developing some quite specific description of, for example, what the roles are and especially the chairman. It seems that with all these bodies in existence quite often spelling out precisely what the role of a chairman might be, whether politically appointed or not, is quite an important thing in terms of actually being seen to lead, build a team, develop strategy, develop a style and culture within the organisation which is about openness, integrity and accountability, and so on. We feel that some of those roles ought to be spelt out more clearly. That also can help, not only in relation to induction and training, but also in terms of measuring performance. Whoever appoints I think ought also to have an obligation in relation to measuring performance and to actually describe the kind of objectives that the leader of the team and the team are expected to work on.

1447. PETER SHORE: Professor King's sort of "shadow" Civil Service which he described when he was questioning you, surely there is a distinction between those quangos were public service must be the obvious and dominant consideration and those quangos which do require an element of entrepreneurship—the difference, for example, between the Health Service and an urban development corporation. In the former category, the Health Service category, when you speak of "people should be appointed through a formal process", given their public service nature, is there any real reason why that formal process should not be just the same kind of open competition and open advertising as is today practised in appointments to the Civil Service by the Civil Service Commission?

NOEL HEPWORTH: I think we would say that in fact there should be that sort of openness, if you take National Health Service trusts. But I think we would also say that in appointing the chairman of the trust it would be sensible to appoint somebody who has got sympathy with the idea of the way in which the Health Service is delivered.

PROF. ANTHONY KING: Or is at least not unsympathetic.

NOEL HEPWORTH: Well, at the very least not unsympathetic. There needs to be that degree of commitment to it. I think where we maybe differ from some of the others who have given evidence to you is that I think we would argue that there probably needs to be a greater responsibility on the board itself to make sure that it is properly balanced and has all the skills that are there. That is a key role for the chairman. So whilst, for example, there might be those who would say that, say, the Secretary of State or some other outside group should appoint the whole of the board, I think we would think that there should be a pretty powerful influence from within the board itself to make sure that the board does have the skills that are necessary to deliver the service. So we would see, in a way moving towards your point, some sort of arrangement whereby it is not perceived as an external appointment, it is to do with the proper operation of the board and the activity itself. That is why I go back to the very opening remarks that we made, where we said that I didn't understand the proportionality point altogether because if you were just seen as drawing people from various constituencies it was not necessarily compatible with having a board which actually would run the organisation and well. At the end of the day in those areas then success depends upon running the organisation well and I do agree with you that there are differences and we didn't actually deal with that in our comments this morning. But in preparing for this meeting we understood that very well indeed.

1448. PETER SHORE: I make the point to you that I would have thought, frankly, that if a formal process of open competition was used in selecting the chairman and, indeed the other non-executive board members, the problem of political opposition or political favour for the particular policies of the Minister really would not emerge. It would be just the same as with appointed Civil Servants.

NOEL HEPWORTH: Yes, correct.

JOHN WHITEOAK: Although open advertising can be winning but not necessarily a solution because the crucial issue is how somebody uses the material when it emerges, what criteria and who judges. I think actually you drew out very helpfully the issue of the distinction between one sector and another. I think this business of capturing flair and initiative and also remembering public service values, there are—openness and so on matters but there might be different degrees of balance in different areas and different issues that might need to be captured. But the openness of the process and the declaration of it gives at least something to challenge.

1449. PETER SHORE: The question of a balance of skills and abilities and background on boards of Health Service Trusts and other Health Service bodies you raised yourself and you thought that that would be one of the roles of the chairman. At the moment you get some, as it were, non-Ministerial input via the regional health authorities, but regional health authorities are on their way out and as far as I can see that in future, say as from later this year when the Act comes into force, all the non-executive members of Health Service boards, together with the chairman, will be appointed by the Secretary of State. Do you think that is a satisfactory prospect?

NOEL HEPWORTH: Are you talking about the regional boards or are you talking about the trusts?

1450. PETER SHORE: The regional boards will disappear and the chairman of the regions which now have—the chairmen have the right to, as it were, nominate or to basically select two members of the National Health Service Trust—that power will lapse when the boards disappear and the non-executive members, or five of them is the normal number, all of which in future will be appointed by the Secretary of State. I was wondering whether you have given any thought to that as an emerging problem and how best to solve it?

NOEL HEPWORTH: I don't think we have thought about that particular problem specifically, but it would be unfortunate if in fact that then meant that all the appointments to the trust boards then moved up. That would seem to us to be a mistake.

JOHN WHITEOAK: Yes. If the objective is public confidence I doubt very many in the public would see that as being manageable by one or even a group of individuals.

PETER SHORE: Thank you.

1451. WILLIAM UTTING: I was interested particularly by your section on standards of behaviour because those are matters that have concerned us up to now greatly in relation to Members of Parliament and Ministers. I wondered whether you thought it feasible to apply your thinking about standards of behaviour to people in public bodies to Members of Parliament and Ministers. Can we establish similar sorts of codes for people working in those environments?

JOHN WHITEOAK: Just while my colleagues collect their thoughts I will gather a little bit of time. One of the things that we have actually been very careful of in addressing this work is to try and actually direct our attention very specifically to Government and the Civil Service. We have tended to try and address areas outside. However, I hope that you will find our submissions helpful in relation to the areas you are addressing. We felt that it was very inappropriate for us to be specific in terms of actual behaviour of Ministers or Members of Parliament or the Civil Service. Speaking personally I think there must be a lot in here that could be helpful.

NOEL HEPWORTH: I think that the argument that was put forward by the Audit Commission that there is a lot to be learned from the local Government approach is quite important actually, that the rules that apply there—but they don't, of course, go all the way on some of the matters that you have been discussing about, for example, people taking appointments after they have left Ministerial office or whatever—but there is quite a thorough code of disclosure of interest. As I say it does not deal with that other issue and some of that is publicly available, some of that is not publicly available, but is available to the auditor. One has to be careful about frightening people off in a sense. So I think that it is very important that information is available to one group or another, whether it is just generally publicly available or is available to the auditor. I am not sure we can be more helpful to you about MPs and Ministers in that.

WILLIAM UTTING: Stimulated thought, anyway, on our part. Thank you.

LORD NOLAN: Diana?

1452. DIANA WARWICK: Yes, just on that very point, where the Audit Commission acknowledged that not all rules and requirements would be the same across the whole of the public sector—and we have talked about forty-odd thousand appointments—they said where the standards were more rigorous the onus should be on those who opposed such measures to show why they are inappropriate. Do you concur?

NOEL HEPWORTH: Yes, we do.

1453. DIANA WARWICK: Could I then ask you that where the Public Appointments Unit in their very positive recommendations decide to exercise this test of proportionality, i.e. whether each step of the process should be tested against both need and cost-effectiveness—and they list the various steps that should be taken and then those where discretion might be exercised—they go on to say "Nonetheless when one of the steps is not followed it should be the result of a conscious decision and the reasons recorded." Would you add to that sentence "and open to public scrutiny"?

NOEL HEPWORTH: We would have said that there should be something in the annual report of the organisation to say what they have done or not done. In other words, where there are codes in force, whatever they are, then the organisation should be required to say in its annual report whether it has abided by those codes. If it has not, why?

1454. DIANA WARWICK: And you would apply that to Government departments?

NOEL HEPWORTH: I don't see why not.

DIANA WARWICK: Thank you.

LORD NOLAN: Well, gentlemen, the questions I had to raise have all been covered by my colleagues. We have kept you well over the agreed time. We are immensely grateful for the care and thoroughness with which you have prepared and presented your evidence. Thank you very much indeed.

THURSDAY 9 FEBRUARY 1995

Members Present:

The Rt. Hon. The Lord Nolan (Chairman)

Professor Anthony King
The Rt. Hon. Tom King CH MP
The Rt. Hon. Peter Shore MP

The Rt. Hon. The Lord Thomson of Monifieth KT DL
Sir William Utting CB
Dame Anne Warburton DCVO CMG
Diana Warwick

Witnesses:

Lord Carlisle of Bucklow, Chairman, and Jim Barron, Secretary, Prime Minister's Advisory Committee on Business Appointments
Roger Lyons, General Secretary, Hilary Benn, Head of Research and Roger Kline, National Officer for the Health Service, Manufacturing Science Finance Union (MSF)
Iain Duncan-Smith MP
Dale Campbell-Savours MP

1455. LORD NOLAN: Today we have witnesses from several different parts of the spectrum and on different parts of our work.

Roger Lyons, General Secretary of MSF, the Manufacturing Science and Finance Union, which represents a wide range of professional and technical staff in the health service and in NDPBs, will give evidence mainly on quangos. Mr Iain Duncan-Smith, a Conservative Member of Parliament, and Mr Dale Campbell-Savours, a Labour Member, are in effect a continuation of our earlier consideration of Members' interests and will, I hope, give evidence mainly on this subject.

First, however, and on our third topic, can I welcome Lord Carlisle? Lord Carlisle is of course a former member of the Cabinet and is chairman of the Business Appointments Committee. This is the committee which vets applications from senior civil servants and military officers to join private firms and other organisations. I am sure he will give us useful advice on the issues surrounding movement from the public to the private sector. Lord Carlisle, I believe you have helpfully prepared an opening statement to set us off.

LORD CARLISLE OF BUCKLOW AND JIM BARRON

LORD CARLISLE OF BUCKLOW (Chairman of the Prime Minister's Advisory Committee on Business Appointments): I have, my Lord. I thought it might be helpful if I prepared a statement setting out the present position, and with one or two thoughts of my own included in it.

LORD NOLAN: Good. Thank you very much. Would you be kind enough then to make it?

LORD CARLISLE: Certainly. My Lord, all Crown servants, which includes members of the armed forces, are subject to rules which affect and may restrict their right to take up outside employment on either retirement or resignation from Crown service. It has been said that the rules have two specific aims: firstly, to avoid any suspicion, no matter how unjustified, that the advice and decisions of a serving officer might be influenced by the hope or expectation of future employment with a particular firm or organisation; and, secondly, to avoid the risk that a particular firm might gain an improper advantage over its competitors by employing someone who, in the course of

their official duties, has had access to technical or other information which those competitors might legitimately regard as their own trade secrets or to information relating to proposed developments in government policy which may affect that firm or its competitors.

I would myself add two further purposes: thirdly, to ensure that those joining private companies do not use their position to obtain an improper advantage by exploiting their relationship with their previous colleagues; and, finally, and importantly in my mind, to provide a safeguard to protect individuals from unfair criticism and unwarranted innuendo of improper behaviour.

The rules apply to all civil servants, but only some have to apply under the rules. All those below grade 3 only have to apply if, in general terms, they have had official dealings with their prospective employer or its competitors. The rules require applications from all Crown servants of grade 3 and above. That, I think, is the old under-secretary level. The rules are administered by Cabinet Office unit, although the majority of decisions are taken by Ministers within individual departments.

All applications for staff of grade 3 level or above have to go to the Cabinet Office unit. Applications at grade 3 have their cases decided by individual Ministers, but on the advice of the Head of the Home Civil Service. Applicants of grades 1, 1A and 2 are decided by the Prime Minister on the advice of the Advisory Committee.

The rules apply equally to the equivalent ranks in the armed services. That is basically, my Lord, if I might say so, ranks in the Navy of Rear-Admiral and above, in the Army of Major-General and above and in the Royal Air Force of Air-Vice-Marshal and above. They apply to all applications within two years of leaving Crown service, including any change of employment during that two-year period.

The Advisory Committee was set up by the then Prime Minister, Mr Harold Wilson, in 1975 for the purpose of looking at all applications from people of grades 1, 1A and 2 or any other cases referred to them by the Head of the Civil Service. On top of that, there is a responsibility on the chairman and vice-chairman of the committee to check from time to time that the rules have been properly applied to other grades.

The membership of the committee consists of three leading parliamentarians, all of whom are Privy Counsellors and former Cabinet Ministers, three retired Crown servants, one of whom is from the armed forces, and two senior industrialists.

We are totally independent and are merely advisory to the Prime Minister of the day. We have the power to recommend that applications should be approved unconditionally or to impose waiting periods of up to two years, or to impose behavioural conditions for a similar period.

We deal with some 40 cases a year and if we are minded to impose any form of conditions, we always give the individual concerned the opportunity of making representations to us. All cases are looked at on their merits. There are no automatic limitations, save for a three-month waiting period for those of grades 1 and 1A—the Permanent Secretary level. This automatic waiting period does not apply to anyone who is on a fixed-term contract, but the rules do apply to anyone on secondment to the Civil Service unless he is returning directly to his previous employer. Subject to those limitations which I have set out, each case depends upon the committee's own assessment and judgment.

In general we have to ask ourselves three questions. Firstly, has the individual himself been in a position which could lay him open to the suggestion that the appointment was in some way a reward for past favours? Secondly, has he been in a position where he has in fact had access to trade secrets of competitors or knowledge of immediately impending government policy which would give his company an unfair advantage? Thirdly, and importantly, what do we assess will be the public perception, rightly or wrongly, of the particular individual taking up the particular appointment?

Our aim must be to ensure the continuance of public confidence in the integrity of the Crown service, and to that end we may from time to time impose conditions on someone who has not had any direct dealings with the firm which he wishes to join, but whose position in the Crown service has been such that the public might reasonably feel that he must have been in a position generally to influence policy in a way that could be of benefit to a particular company. It is not unusual, for example, for us to recommend the imposition of waiting periods on senior officers or senior officials of the Ministry of Defence wishing to join defence contractors, even if it cannot be suggested that they have had any direct connection with the firm involved.

Our task, as I see it, is to balance on the one hand the right of the individual to work for whomever he wants, and indeed the importance to industry generally to take advantage of the individual's expertise, against the vital and intangible asset of retaining public confidence in the Crown service. It is to that end that the imposition of waiting periods or behavioural conditions, particularly in relation to previous colleagues, is to my mind justified. It has been suggested that waiting periods should be automatic in all cases. I personally would certainly be against any such approach.

Whilst it is correct to say that the enforceability of the rules has never been put to the test, and not wishing, if I might say so, my Lord, to intervene in the discussion between a solicitor and a judge that took place two days ago, as a lawyer I myself consider that any blanket restriction other than of a minimal nature would be likely to be considered by the courts to be unenforceable as being in restraint of trade, whilst if cases are looked at on individual merit, any condition imposed would in my view be likely to be held to be reasonable and therefore enforceable. Likewise, I myself would not like to see the current rules extended. By that I mean that I do not believe there is a case for extending the two-year period. The fact is that two years is a long time for the person who is applying, whether it is someone wishing to make a change in mid-career or someone wishing to take up employment on retirement, particularly if he is taking reasonably early retirement from the armed services.

Finally, I would like to make four general points. Firstly, I believe there is very little criticism of the current situation, although clearly from time to time cases arise which do attract criticism, which I believe is usually unfounded. Secondly, the question of future redundancies within the Crown service could raise new and further questions. It seems to me that you cannot apply the rules in the same way to those whom you have required to leave as to those who have chosen to do so, and I believe that, at the least, more flexibility will be necessary. Thirdly, whilst respecting, as the committee always has done, the individual's right to privacy, I myself see no real objection to the eventual conditions imposed being made known, once the individual has taken up the post concerned. Finally, and I assume, my Lord, that this is a matter on which you may wish to ask me some questions, if the rules that apply to Crown servants are to be extended to cover other groups of people, it must realised that the conditions of employment of those people may be totally different from the conditions of employment of Crown servants and they may make the current rules, therefore, inappropriate.

LORD NOLAN: Thank you very much indeed. Lord Carlisle, as you know, we take it in turns on the committee to lead with the questions, and it is Mr Tom King's turn this morning, so I am going to ask him to continue.

1456. TOM KING: Thank you very much. Lord Carlisle, thank you very much for the very helpful opening statement. One understands that the purpose of your committee is to give public confidence outside that there is some check and control over senior officers moving into future employment. One point about public confidence: is the Membership of your committee secret?

LORD CARLISLE: No, the membership of our committee is not secret. It is published. It is announced, I think, through *Hansard*. It contains, as it happens, two Members of your own committee investigating standards in public life. But certainly I have, and will supply the committee with, if you wish, a list of the membership of the present committee. As I said, they are all published.

1457. TOM KING: And you have, in addition to the two distinguished Members on this panel, three industrialists?

LORD CARLISLE: The two industrialists at the moment are Sir Denys Henderson, former chairman of ICI, and Sir Robin Ibbs, who is now at Lloyds Bank, and the three ex-Crown servants are Lord Bridges, who is the deputy chairman, Sir John Blelloch, who was the Permanent Secretary, I think, of the Northern Ireland Office, and Sir Charles Huxtable, who is a retired general.

TOM KING: Right. Thank you very much. I don't know why, but it has a sort of aura of secrecy about it, and I have never quite understood why.

LORD CARLISLE: It does, but there is absolutely no reason why it should have. In fact certainly appointments are made by the Prime Minister and are publicised, as far as I know.

1458. TOM KING: Yes. You have set out how it is meant to work and the job you seek to do. Does it work? Does it work—perhaps I could ask you—against two criteria? One, does it work in terms of subsequent complaint that you have let people take up jobs that actually would not have been proper for them to take up?

LORD CARLISLE: I think it does work. As I say, there are from time to time complaints in the press, or comments, about people leaving the public service and going into commercial enterprises or other jobs. I often find it surprising that somebody hasn't done the arithmetic and asked why it was they didn't join the firm they were joining until 12 months, let us say, after the day when they left public service, or six months after their last day in office. In fact many of the times when criticisms are made are cases which have been before the committee—in fact all the cases I know where comments have been made have been before the committee—and in many of them conditions have been imposed. Indeed, in the case I was referring to just now, the individual decided himself to make known the conditions which had been imposed on him taking up the appointment. So I don't think, frankly, that the criticism is fair. We get some complaints from some of those who appear before us of course that, by imposing any condition, we are going to prevent them getting the opportunity of the job which they have been offered.

1459. TOM KING: That was my second question. Do you have any evidence of people not getting jobs that they have sought to achieve, because, while they have told you that this will mean that they won't be offered the job, you impose some condition and they still actually move on to the job?

LORD CARLISLE: I don't think we have any direct evidence of people—well, that is untrue. I can think of one case where I think it has been said that someone did not get a job that he was anxious to get. On the whole, in fairness, the attitude of people normally is that they feel the imposition of conditions may well affect their opportunity of getting the job. As far as I know, in practice they have normally persuaded the potential employer, if it is a waiting period, to wait for the necessary time. It is in the interests of the employer as well as the potential employee to co-operate with the rules, particularly as, by its very nature, the employer is likely to be someone who is doing business with the government, which is why the restrictions have been imposed. So they are aware, when they invite a person, that they have to get the permission of the Prime Minister and they are aware that the Prime Minister may, on advice, recommend conditions.

1460. TOM KING: Is there an appeal against your recommendations?

LORD CARLISLE: To the Prime Minister.

1461. TOM KING: And the final decision?

LORD CARLISLE: The final decision is the Prime Minister's.

1462. TOM KING: Right. How long on average does it take to consider a case? There is reference here to possible redundancies in certain areas and what this would represent in terms of extra workload and whether the committee could cope. Could you link those two together?

LORD CARLISLE: I might have to ask Mr Barron to answer this, but my own impression is that we act very quickly on cases we see. The uncontentious ones are cleared by correspondence and can be dealt with quickly. Again my experience is that where we wish to impose conditions, we invariably somehow manage to arrange a meeting within a week or two with the individual concerned, because usually he wants to know fairly soon. Do you want to add anything to that?

JIM BARRON (Secretary, Advisory Committee on Business Appointments): Surely. We certainly aim to turn the cases that come before the committee round within three weeks, so that is not a great period of time. Also, on the question of redundancies, of course a lot of the people who are going to be made redundant or leave early will be at the more junior ranks in the Civil Service and the armed forces, and their applications wouldn't come to the committee anyway: they would be dealt with by the department concerned.

1463. TOM KING: That leads me on to the next point I wanted to make. My impression from government is that usually the people with the most sensitive information and the people who are of most value aren't actually the grades 1 and 2 but are lower down the scale. You say in your submission:

"there is responsibility on the chairman and vice-chairman of the committee to check from time to time that the rules have been properly applied to other grades."

I see that as a very important area indeed. If I recall, one or two recent allegations of really major corruption involved people significantly further down the line placing very substantial contracts indeed and alleging to have made substantial money out of them. What about these grades further down?

LORD CARLISLE: Can I make three points? Firstly, if there is direct allegation of corruption, that is not really a matter for the committee; it is a matter for internal disciplinary procedures and maybe——

TOM KING: I am illustrating the point that further down the line there is often the greater——

LORD CARLISLE: I accept that. It is often said before the committee by senior officers that they have no direct say in the letting of contracts, that that is done at a level lower than them. Therefore, yes, I suppose it is right that there is potentially more direct involvement of the individual at that level with contracts. All I can say is that each department, I think, and I will ask Mr Barron to say a word in a moment—certainly the Ministry of Defence, which of course is important in this field—has its own vetting, its own committee, its own unit responsible for looking at these cases. We look at a random selection, and I have no reason to think that the rules are not carried out. Would you like to add anything to that?

JIM BARRON: Yes. That is true. Departments have their own units which look at applications. I ought to say that in fact all grade 3 cases come to the unit, and we look at those cases against the same criteria as the committee looks for grades 1 and 2, and put recommendations to Sir Robin. Further down the line departments deal with the applications themselves, but they do refer to us cases where there has been direct contact between the individual concerned and the organisation which they are joining. I think that throughout the Civil Service you have about 1,000 applications a year. We as a unit will probably see about 300 of those.

1464. TOM KING: Who actually is the vice-chairman?

LORD CARLISLE: Lord Bridges.

1465. TOM KING: Thank you. Can I then take you on to the point that you made at the end, which is this issue as to whether there ought to be, in your judgment as a former Minister—not wearing your chairman of committee hat at the moment, but as a former Minister—a similar procedure for Ministers leaving office and, if there was, do you think your committee would be an appropriate body to discharge it or do you feel that, because the background of Ministers and career civil servants is different, that ought to be recognised by having a different arrangement?

LORD CARLISLE: I obviously assumed that this question would be asked and I have given thought to what I ought to say, and perhaps you will allow me to make a few general comments.

Firstly, I fully accept of course that whether you consider it is necessary to introduce new rules applying to Ministers at all levels so as to restore and maintain confidence by the public in the standards of integrity in public life obviously is wholly a matter for the committee to decide, and I am aware, obviously, of some of the evidence that has been given to this committee of the loss in that public confidence. Speaking purely as an individual, I would be sorry if you came to the conclusion that it was necessary. I like to believe myself that we can rely on the judgment of the individuals concerned. It has been a view taken by successive governments in the past. Harold Wilson said in 1968 that these matters are best left to the discretion and good sense of the individual concerned, and I would like to think that that still applied.

I would only suggest to the committee that, when asking the question "Is that sufficient or does one now need rules?", if I may put it this way without being presumptuous, a sense of proportion is maintained. It seems to me that there is nothing new in Ministers of different political persuasions taking up employment on leaving office; that has always happened. What I think has changed is that the issue has suddenly come within the political arena and the result is that a good deal of innuendo is expressed, which often, I believe, may be totally unjustified. I think that part of the task of this committee, if I might humbly suggest, is to dispel that innuendo. Also it is important that nothing should be done which discourages people from becoming Ministers. Also I think one has to bear in mind that people leaving ministerial office and going into private jobs do so in the glare of publicity.

But, having said all that, I can see that there is a case for saying that these appointments are now subject to what is often unfair and uninformed criticism, which nevertheless has done great harm, as I think was put by one witness to your committee, to public confidence in the Ministers taking jobs of that kind. If the committee came to the view that some form of new control was required, and you ask me whether we could take on the task of advising Ministers, I think my answer must be yes. I can see no reason why we couldn't take on the task of advising in those circumstances, in that we could apply, presumably, the same tests as we apply to senior civil servants leaving the service and we could recommend to the Minister some restraint on the job that he chose to take.

But I do think that the comparison ends there. I do not think it would be possible for us to retain our role as being advisory to the Prime Minister of the day on matters of that kind. I do not see how it could possibly be acceptable that the Prime Minister of the day, particularly following a general election, should have control over the conditions he should be entitled to impose on Ministers. I think that the most one could do would be to have a situation where Ministers could feel free to seek the advice of the Advisory Committee. If they had any doubt of the wisdom of taking a particular job, they could receive our advice and then be in a position to make it clear that they had approached the committee for advice and say what the advice that they had received was. But I don't think you can impose restrictions.

That leads me on, if I might, to say one or two other things. I do think, as you yourself said, Mr King, that it is vital to recognise the totally different nature, and I think the fundamental difference is this. The rules which we operate at the moment were rules devised for Crown servants leaving their employment voluntarily, whether on resignation or on retirement. A Minister invariably, by the nature of his job, leaves office not voluntarily but against his will, either on the will of the electorate rather than himself or on the decision of the Prime Minister of the day that he or she no longer wishes that person to continue to serve in the Cabinet. But there is this total distinction between one where you leave voluntarily and one where you leave involuntarily. Secondly, the life of a Minister is totally transient, and he has no control over the time that he might be a Minister.

Then I think one has to ask oneself the question: if you are going to have rules, how are they to be applied? Presumably it would be accepted that the rules must be the same for all people. I understand that one suggestion has been put forward that there should be some form of blanket restriction. I frankly don't see how a blanket restriction could be either acceptable or workable. If rules are to apply to everyone, does it mean that I myself, as a lawyer, cannot return to being a lawyer, that an accountant cannot go back to being an accountant? I don't think you can say that one person can't go back to his previous job in industry or the City but another person can go back to his previous job as a lawyer, as an accountant or as a journalist. I think you have to apply the same rules. Therefore, you have to be extremely flexible in any rules that you have.

Then it is said that at least one could limit it to those areas where a Minister has had direct contact with the firm he may be wishing to join. I have never been in either of the departments concerned, but it seems to me that, if you are either a trade Minister or a Treasury Minister, the chances are that you have had contact with a great sector of industry, or the City or finance whilst you were there. I did wonder whether you could use the analogy we have with those who are seconded to the public service. There, as I say, the rules apply to a person who is seconded, subject to the fact that he is entitled, free of any control, to return to the firm from which he came. Therefore, the analogy would be to say that a Minister who has worked for a particular firm is free to go back to that firm, but that in itself raises problems, because we have found, even in the area of secondment, that sometimes the job that the person left isn't available to them when they want to go back. If you are an accountant and your accountancy firm has for some reason closed down in the meantime, or your partnership has been annulled, it has joined someone else, or for some reason you can't go back and you are offered instead a job by a merchant bank, are you to say that you're not free to go to the job with the merchant bank whereas you would be free to take the job with the accountant? I think that many difficulties arise in this area.

I repeat what I said earlier. It is not for me to be so presumptuous as to comment on whether you feel that the lack of public confidence requires rules of this nature to be imposed at this moment, but I do say that, if that is the view you come to, I feel, with respect, that you have to have flexibility and you have to have a situation that is looked at individually. I think Lord Nolan would agree that any blanket restriction, if it was likely to be held in restraint of trade so far as a civil servant with a full background is concerned, with a transient Minister is much more likely to be held in restraint of trade.

I think I have said all the various points I wanted to make, but I do think there are great differences. I know the situation has changed since I and those on this committee were Ministers. I know that now, I gather, there is some form of severance pay on ceasing to be a Minister, which there wasn't before. But one has to be realistic and accept that the remuneration, the pension rights, are not comparative to those in industry or the professions for people with jobs of comparative responsibility, and one must try to avoid doing anything which discourages a wide section of people from coming into Parliament and being willing to take Ministerial positions.

1466. LORD NOLAN: Thank you very much. I wonder if I could as briefly as possible, because I am sure other members of the committee will also want to ask you questions, say this. It is, I think, true that one of the most prolific sources of suspicion and concern that we find raised in the mail we have received, and of course one sees it in the media, is the fact that there are no rules at present, other than the appeal to the Minister's integrity, to govern Ministers in the same way as civil servants. The other ground upon which, as you know, the case for altering the situation has been placed is the one which must always appeal, and it is one you raised yourself: it is justice to the individual. One knows that the suspicion is engendered very often by totally inadequate information, and yet the individual can suffer very unjustly and for a long period.

Of course we are going to consider all these matters and the strong views which have been expressed in both directions to us, but when we look at the three questions that you mention in your opening statement, which you ask yourselves in relation to civil servants—has the individual himself been in a position which could lay him open to the suggestion that the appointment was in some way a reward for past favours, has he been in a position

where he has in fact had access to trade secrets of competitors or knowledge of immediately impending government policy which would give his company an unfair advantage and what do we assess will be the public perception, rightly or wrongly, of the particular individual taking up the particular appointment?—if there is to be a system applying to Ministers, can one avoid asking those same three questions?

LORD CARLISLE: In answer to your direct question, the last one, I think that, if there is to be a system, those other questions have to be asked. I think I accepted that in what I said, when I said I thought the committee could run it. It seems to me that the same questions have to be asked and they do apply.

Perhaps I ought to make two other points, in case it was felt that I haven't given a balanced picture. It is true of course that there are those in the Civil Service who feel it is unfair, and say so at times, that the rules are geared to be different in relation to themselves and Ministers. One knows that that is said. Equally, when I said that the committee may well feel that it is necessary to change the rules so as to restore public confidence, in that I included the fact that it may feel it is necessary, in the interests of the individual, to protect that individual to show that he has some form of outside committee to whom he goes. So for the reasons I gave, although I personally would hope that we could still believe in the integrity point, I do accept that there are other arguments.

1467. LORD NOLAN: Would those questions normally give rise to difficulty if, instead of going to an employment, the Minister was going back to his old profession? Would it be likely in that case that there would be difficulties over trade secrets?

LORD CARLISLE: Yes, and this, I think, is the real difficulty. Can you prevent a person going back to their previous employment? Sir Michael Quinlan, in his evidence to you, posed what seemed to me a very relevant point when he put it this way:

"I suggest there should be an initial presumption, given a free society with a free labour market, that the individual is entitled, within the law, to undertake whatever remunerated employment they wish to, and that business are entitled, within the law, to take on whatever employees they judge will help advance the commercial interests of that enterprise. The question is: what specific concerns justify the public in watering down their general right?"

As I say, on secondment of civil servants, they are entitled to go back to the firm from which they came, and they may carry with them, presumably, knowledge of future government policy or knowledge of the secrets of other companies.

LORD NOLAN: I was thinking of the professional men whom you mentioned. As you and I well know, it has been very common in the past for a former Attorney-General to come back to the Bar.

LORD CARLISLE: Exactly

1468. LORD NOLAN: And has that given rise to any difficulties?

LORD CARLISLE: I don't see that that has ever given rise to any objection. What I was saying was that I think that any rules would have to apply equally to everyone, even if it was merely only the rule that they had the opportunity to apply. But I can't see that it has done, nor can I see that it has, in the past, to either journalists or professional people generally. But, having said that, I would add, purely from my own point of view, that I think the areas which often are difficult for the committee are areas where people are going into consultancies, because there you may have clients with whom you have had dealings, although as a consultant you are not yourself directly employed by them.

LORD NOLAN: Thank you very much. I think I exceeded my ration. Diana.

1469. DIANA WARWICK: Lord Carlisle, you said that you hoped that we and others would adopt a sense of proportion. One of the problems, it seems to me, in this whole question of innuendo is knowing what weight to place on the information that is uncovered. You have given us the number of cases that you actually look at. Do you have statistics on how many cases are actually deferred and for how long?

LORD CARLISLE: Yes, we do and we would happily give you them. Looking just at the last five years, it is fair to say that on average 70 per cent are approved unconditionally at the level at which we look at them. It varies from 68 per cent to 74 per cent over those years, and I think that is pretty well a constant.

JIM BARRON: It is, yes.

LORD CARLISLE: I looked back at some earlier statistics and it seemed to me that that is fairly constant, because on the whole, and I am sure this would apply to Ministers, you are more likely than not to be going to a job which hasn't had any direct dealing with your department.

1470. DIANA WARWICK: Do you produce a report, which reflects these statistics?

LORD CARLISLE: We did produce an annual report of statistics, but I have a feeling that this is no longer so. Is that right?

JIM BARRON: The statistics have been produced in a variety of forms over the last few years. We used to produce an annual report, and we could easily do that again if that was required.

1471. DIANA WARWICK: It just seems such a simple point, that Mr King didn't know the membership of your committee, I didn't know you produced a report. If you do, that seems to me at one stroke rather to help.

LORD CARLISLE: We of course respond and have responded to various Select Committee examinations, both by the Treasury Select Committee and the Defence Select Committee, and we have taken on board, I think it is right to say or—it is really for the unit to say—the unit has taken on board the various suggestions that have been made. Certainly we would look at any suggestions for improving the openness of our committee, subject only to the one matter, where I trailed my coat a bit in saying that I believe there is no real objection to it being known what conditions we have imposed once the person has applied. I think, nevertheless, the application and our dealings and

our advice to the Prime Minister are matters which should be kept confidential—certainly applications, because people may apply to inquire what the reaction would be if they were offered a certain job and for some reason they may not come up, and they may not wish it to be known that they weren't offered the job in the end.

DIANA WARWICK: But the statistics rather than the individual cases would probably be helpful.

LORD CARLISLE: The statistics we happily would produce, and used to produce in fairly substantial detail.

1472. DIANA WARWICK: Could I take you back to your point about the difference between those who retire or leave voluntarily and those who leave unwillingly in whatever form? How do you balance the difficulties you see in relation to those differences with the quite fundamental questions that you do ask, which clearly reflect a need to respond to public interest and concern?

LORD CARLISLE: I think it is fair to say at the moment that we have never had to face the situation of someone who is being retired against their will. All our applications, I think, come either from people who are retiring and wishing to take employment or from people who are wishing to have a mid-career change, which of course is again within their conditions. I don't think, certainly in the time I have been on the committee, we have had any question of someone who has been forced against their will to retire. But it does seem to me that, of its nature, it must raise different questions. If you tell a person "We don't want you to work for us any longer, thank you very much", you can hardly in the same breath say "And incidentally you can't go and work for anybody else". It depends to some extent on what the redundancy package is, but people who choose to change jobs can inquire in advance and make the choice whether it's all right for them to make such a move.

1473. DIANA WARWICK: And could I just ask you one brief question? You said you were against any automatic rule applying. What is your view about the automatic three-month rule for top-grade civil servants—Permanent Secretaries and others? Do you have any feelings about that?

LORD CARLISLE: Not really. I must just add this, although it wasn't in my opening remarks. Of course that rule can be waived by the Prime Minister of the day if he considers it is in the national interest to do so, and to my knowledge has on one or two occasions, where he considers that the job that the person wishes to take up is of such overwhelming interest to the nation that he should take it up forthwith. It's been imposed on the basis that it applies only on retirement, it is a short period and, by its very nature, a Permanent Secretary—I suppose you might use the same argument about a Cabinet Minister—will be in a position where he has a much wider overall knowledge of government policy than someone of a lower rank. But we have always said that whether or not the three months applies is a matter for the Prime Minister and not for us.

DIANA WARWICK: Thank you.

1474. WILLIAM UTTING: Lord Carlisle, I would like to take advantage of your presence this morning to ask you about another area of this committee's interests, because we are also concerned with appointments to quangos, non-departmental public bodies, the national health service, and I suspect that the committee that you chair is a non-departmental public body and that somebody like you plays a role in other public bodies. I thought I would like to seek your views, if you have any, on the system of public appointments in this country.

LORD CARLISLE: I am grateful that you have asked that, if I might say so. I actually happen to be chairman of two quangos, so I think I am entitled to speak. One is the Advisory Committee, which is of course totally unpaid and is in a way, I suppose, looked on partly as a public duty. The other quango of which I am chairman, which is paid of course, is the Criminal Injuries Compensation Board. I think there is one very simple question that has to be asked, certainly on the appointment of chairmen of quangos, and that is: are they or are they not suitably qualified to do the job? I think that that is the issue. I think that their party political allegiance is really irrelevant as against their suitability to the appointment. It is, I think, inevitable to some extent that any government making appointments will make appointments to public bodies of those who, in general terms, are in sympathy with the views that that government is putting forward and that the public body is aimed to promote.

Again, if I might say so, there is absolutely nothing new in this. Without going into names or details, during the whole of the period I was Member of Parliament I had two classic quangos in my constituency, in that I had two new town development corporations, both of them with Labour chairmen who were publicly known, averred, active supporters of the Labour party, appointed by the then Labour Minister and it seemed perfectly sensible that he should do so and I do not think it was ever questioned. Therefore, to some extent it is inevitable that people will, when looking for people to appoint, tend to think first of those they know and have had dealings with.

Of course, you must try and make the appointments to quangos reflect entirely society as whole, the community as a whole particularly at a lower level, and one must try and get them to be balanced but I repeat it seems to me that certainly when you are looking at the level of chairmanship the real issue is, is the person qualified to do the job? And I hope, as far as I am concerned as a practising barrister, I was qualified to be asked to do the job. Can I also say that, again, in the nationwide quangos it is not surprising that Ministers of both parties tend, quite often, to look to ex-Ministers or ex-Members of Parliament because, in a way, they are jobs which are in the public eye and they are looking for people who are in the public eye and, equally, as was put to me personally when I was asked to take on the chairmanship of the C.I.C.B., they were looking for a member of the Bar who also had a knowledge of the workings of Whitehall. Again, it is a question of keeping a sense of balance.

WILLIAM UTTING: Thank you

1475. PETER SHORE: Just one line of thought. We have discussed the three criteria which today apply to civil servants applying for new posts after they have left the Civil Service. All three are, to some extent I would have thought, relevant to ex-Ministers but the one which has particular relevance is number two where the ex-Minister had access to trade secrets of competitors or knowledge of immediate impending government policy which would give to his company an unfair advantage. That is a fairly narrow criterion but it is a very important one particularly in terms of public perception. I think you would accept that.

If that is so, does not a vetting procedure help very much to avoid that particular problem because if an ex-Minister is being valued by an outside company for his general wisdom, knowledge and experience he will not be worried if he has to wait a year or so to take up an appointment because those qualities of wisdom, knowledge and experience will still be there at the end of that year, or two years even, as they were at the beginning, but what will have been lost during a vetting period is that intimate and immediate knowledge which could be of commercial advantage. Is that not a very strong case?

LORD CARLISLE: I think that your point is a very powerful one on the second half of that paragraph, namely the knowledge of immediate, impending government policy. I think it is probably less applicable to access to trade secrets of competitors. I doubt that the Minister ever gets involved at the level where, say, the financing arrangements of companies come to his knowledge. The only point I would make is, yes, if you are leaving the government of the day while it is still the government of the day; surely not if you are leaving the government at the will of the electorate when the government changes. It can hardly be said that you would then have a deep knowledge of the immediate, impending intentions of the government any more than anybody else who reads the papers would have.

PETER SHORE: That presupposes abrupt changes in policy at the moment of takeover.

TOM KING: That is quite a common experience.

LORD CARLISLE: I hope I have accepted that I can see nothing in principle, if that is what the committee decides, which says that those questions could not equally be asked. I have expressed my view as to whether it is right for the committee to come to that view but I have to say that I can see no objection to that being so.

1476. LORD NOLAN: So when you say in the very last line of your opening statement about extending the present rules to cover other people that the conditions of employment may be so different that the current rules are totally inappropriate...

LORD CARLISLE: "Totally" is, I think, a word I would withdraw. This morning looking at it I realised it was too late to get it reprinted. What I meant there was the way in which the current rules are implemented; being advisory to the Prime Minister of the day who then has the decision is totally inappropriate. The most one could expect of the committee is that they should be in a position to advise the individual concerned who can then, if criticised, say that he went through the normal things and he approached the Advisory Committee who said they could see nothing inappropriate in him taking up the appointment.

LORD NOLAN: Thank you very much. Dame Anne?

1477. ANNE WARBURTON: Lord Carlisle, you reminded us that the enforceability of the rules has never been put to the test and you suggested that blanket restrictions would not work legally but individual assessment might. I have been struck, I think we all have perhaps, at the absence of any obvious sanctions and I wondered what you might have to say on that.

LORD CARLISLE: There are no obvious sanctions. I think one comes back to the situation that one must start on the principle that, in a free society, people are free to take any job they can. When you say there are no sanctions, I question—I leave it to others to decide—I question why they are not enforceable. It seems to me that it has not been put to the test but, as far as I know, there is no reason why a department of the Crown cannot apply for an injunction to prevent something which appeared to be contrary to the contractual obligations of the individual. I know you do not sign a written contract but I would have thought by usage it had become a term of the contract of the Crown servant that on leaving office he had to seek permission to join a firm within the two years and if there was clear evidence of the breach of that requirement it would not be impossible to apply for an injunction to prevent the individual taking up the job but I do not know whether that gains favour with your Chairman.

1478. ANNE WARBURTON: You would look that way rather than to suspension of pension?

LORD CARLISLE: Yes. I think it has been shown that you cannot go down the route of suspension of pension and I think there is authority on that.

1479. TOM KING: Could I just interject on that because you answered this question to me. Is not the fact, as far as you know, that it has never been that a recommendation has never actually been abused or not honoured is that there is a very powerful implied sanction that by definition the company from whom they may have had the offer is in relations with the government—is seeking, perhaps, contracts from the government—and it would not be at all the most helpful way to proceed with such a relationship if, in fact, you take on somebody in defiance of the government's wishes?

LORD CARLISLE: I agree entirely. Let me say that whilst I know of no case where the advice has been ignored, we do know from time to time of cases where someone who should have applied has failed to apply but we believe, following on from what you have said, Mr. King, that those cases are likely to come to the knowledge of the department concerned because they are likely to have gone to a firm which is still in relationship with the government and, therefore, people would learn that that individual had gone there. I cannot say that has not happened, that there have not been people who have taken employment without going to the committee. Indeed, I think there is one where we learned of someone who should have but it was beyond the two years after he had gone that we were aware of it. I agree entirely with your general point. If you are dealing a lot with the government the last thing you want to do is sully your own reputation by taking on people who are acting contrary to what the government expects of them.

LORD NOLAN: That must be the last question otherwise we shall exceed our time limit but, Professor King, of course you must have your turn.

1480. PROF. A. KING: My questions will be very short. Could you remind us, Lord Carlisle, how long have you been the Chairman of the Advisory Committee?

LORD CARLISLE: I have been Chairman since 1988. Lord Diamond was Chairman since 1975. I might add that the life of a normal member of the committee is now accepted as six years and I should have gone this Christmas but was asked to stay on for a year because the Nolan Committee was sitting and I might be required to give evidence.

1481. PROF. A. KING: You have been there for six or seven years and, roughly, how many cases a year does your committee deal with?

LORD CARLISLE: There are about 40 applications a year.

1482. PROF. A. KING: So you have dealt with about 250 cases?

LORD CARLISLE: Yes.

1483. PROF. A. KING: And in how many of those cases has the recommendation of your committee not been accepted by the Prime Minister of the day?

LORD CARLISLE: I know of one.

1484. PROF. A. KING: You know of one. Does that suggest to us, in practice, that the committee actually takes the decisions in the vast majority of cases?

LORD CARLISLE: I suppose it could be put that way, yes, although, I think, we would wish to reserve our position as being advisory. I am right, am I not?

JIM BARRON: That is right.

LORD CARLISLE: I know of one and, in fact, it was made public knowledge.

1485. PROF. A. KING: Does that, to any degree, alleviate your concern about the possibility that an incoming Prime Minister of a new administration might overturn your recommendations on such a scale as to make it inappropriate to extend your remit to include Ministers?

LORD CARLISLE: Not entirely, no. Let us forget an incoming government for a moment, let us take the position that happens to many of us when we cease to be members of a current government because the Prime Minister of the day may decide that he no long wishes one's services. It seems to me fairly ironic that he should then have the say as to what job that individual can go back to. It does not seem to me to be fair for two reasons.

One, the Prime Minister of the day would fall over backwards to be seen to be fair and, therefore, anything goes completely or the individual would say, "What do you expect? They got rid of me; of course they are not going to let me take the job I want." Whichever way it went, it would be open to comment. If I may make one final point on that, although I accept the importance of the Advisory Committee and rules about retaining public confidence, I think one would be deluding oneself if one necessarily believed that the fact that people did have to apply to the Advisory Committee would immediately, in effect, stop comments and innuendo being made. It cannot be said that the existence of the Advisory Committee has succeeded in all cases so far as senior civil servants are concerned.

1486. LORD NOLAN: One of the matters we heard this morning on which we can take particular satisfaction is that the appointment of this committee has had the happy by-product of retaining you as Chairman of the Advisory Committee. Thank you very much for all your help; we are very grateful to you.

My Lyons, good morning to you. I wonder if you would be kind enough to introduce your team before we start.

ROGER LYONS, ROGER KLINE AND HILARY BENN (MSF)

ROGER LYONS (General Secretary of the Manufacturing Science and Finance Union): Good morning, Lord Nolan. On my left is Roger Kline, National Officer for the Health Service of MSF; on my right is Hilary Benn, Head of Research of MSF.

1487. LORD NOLAN: We received from you this morning, and were very grateful for it, the submission in this folder which certainly I, for my part, have not had a chance to do more than skim through. Had you prepared an opening statement apart from that or is there some summary of this that you would like to make before we go on to questions?

ROGER LYONS: Yes, if I could just briefly refer to the summary which summarises our main points and I was intending just to draw attention to the summary. The rest of the submission goes into the detail and clarifies the points.

Firstly, we wish to put on record our welcome of the establishment of the committee as we share the widespread concern there is about standards in public life and we would like to thank you for inviting us to give oral evidence. We believe that the concern can best be addressed by applying the following three principles to the work of public bodies—public accountability, transparency and openness.

With particular reference to the NHS, we believe that the appointment process has become politically unbalanced as a result of centralised control and there is far too much secrecy. We propose that appointments to NHS quangos be devolved as far as possible and a system of politically balanced appointments be introduced; alternative methods be considered for the appointment of chairs of NHS quangos; all quangos in the NHS be obliged to meet in public; a charter of staff values—a draft of which we attach to this submission—should be introduced in the NHS and all NHS staff should have the right of access to the Health Service Ombudsman.

In relation to non-departmental public bodies, we favour a representative appointments system and, in very brief summary—although we spell it out in more detail—we suggest that appointments be politically balanced with parliamentary oversight and that all such bodies be obliged to meet in public. In relation to parliamentary lobbying—we are a lobbying organisation ourselves—we support an open process and we propose that all dealings between Members of Parliament and lobbyists should be transparent with full declaration of all financial arrangements and we propose that a register of lobbyists and a code of conduct be drawn up and that companies like us should have to establish separate political funds following a shareholder ballot with the right to opt out and also that State funding of political parties be introduced.

Can I say in conclusion before I invite your questions that I, personally, have been purged by a local authority in the London Borough of Barnet where I was a school governor appointed as an LEA governor. A few years ago the then Conservative majority removed all Labour appointed governors, or Labour nominated governors, from every school in the borough at the same time regardless of their position—chair or otherwise, including wards represented by Labour councillors. I am pleased to say that the new Labour administration in Barnet has restored political balance of the LEA governors and my own experience gives me a personal commitment to support in every way possible the submissions that we are pleased you are hearing this morning.

LORD NOLAN: Thank you very much. I am going to ask Mr. Peter Shore to take up the questioning.

1488. PETER SHORE: Mr. Lyons, you have made it quite clear what your objections are to the present appointments to the National Health Service quangos. I would like to ask you about your alternative proposal. You propose more devolved responsibilities for appointments and more local involvement in appointments to NHS bodies. How really do you see this working?

HILARY BENN (Head of Research of the Manufacturing Science and Finance Union): If I may answer that question. The principle we are trying to establish is that if you devolve the appointments as much as possible you broaden the base from which those appointments are made and we are arguing in our evidence in particular that to re-establish a link with elected local government would be probably the most obvious way of doing it. There used to be that link with local authority representation on health authorities. That has now, as we know, disappeared completely. We think it would help widen the process. We think it would provide a greater political balance and it would provide an element of local accountability which is currently completely absent from the arrangements.

In particular, as the structure and management of the NHS has moved from the old system to Trust Boards, there have been a number of very significant changes. If one takes the example of access to meetings. The Regional Health Authorities are shortly to disappear, the District Health Authorities and the Family Health Services Authorities are covered by the Public Bodies Admission to Meetings Act and the public have a right to attend those meetings and see what is going on. As soon as organisations acquire Trust status that requirement to meet in public disappears completely and although the Trusts are obliged to hold one public meeting a year in our view that is not a satisfactory substitute for public oversight of the ongoing work of the bodies.

If I may give another example. Community Health Councils under the old arrangements had a right to be consulted on closures or changes of use. As soon as bodies acquire Trust status that obligation to consult the Community Health Council as an independent representative of the local community disappears. Those, I think, are two very good examples of the commercial ethos which now applies in the National Health Service, which tends to operate more like a private company rather than a public body that has responsibility for taking decisions and very large amounts of public money.

1489. PETER SHORE: I will come to openness a bit later. It was your first reply which was important to me.

You would like to re-establish links with local authorities. You are not actually saying that you can see local authorities playing the major part in appointments to Health Service bodies?

HILARY BENN: We are arguing that a part of the appointments to Health Service bodies should come from local authorities who are locally accountable.

1490. PETER SHORE: Yes. Can I ask you this question. Leaving aside for the moment the composition of boards, do you think there is anything to be said in favour of the smaller boards which now exist. In the old system the boards were pretty large and many people felt that they were cumbersome. These are meant to be somewhat smaller boards. Do you think that there is merit in this from the point of view of the Health Service and its delivery of services?

HILARY BENN: There is clearly a size above which it becomes difficult to function effectively as a group of people taking corporate decisions. Whether 11, in the case of the Trust Boards, is the maximum that you can operate effectively with, I am not entirely sure. I think one might be able to go a bit larger than that. In that sense I do not think the size matters as much as the question of the accountability and the means by which the appointments are made.

1491. PETER SHORE: Yes. Let me move you on then to your, in a sense, very interesting proposal about explicit political balance. Would you make it clear, however, that if that proposal is to be contemplated seriously nevertheless the greater number of appointments to health authority bodies should be on the basis of merit and nothing to do with political allegiance as far as that can be achieved?

HILARY BENN: I think that is certainly the case. What we are arguing very strongly is—and you have received evidence on this subject, I understand, previously—is that it is quite clear that there is a political element to the current appointment process and we are arguing that it would be much better if that was brought out into the open.

If I may give one example. When I was drafting our evidence and I looked at the part of London where I live there are four Health Service quangos. They are chaired respectively by a former Conservative council candidate, a Conservative life peer, the wife of the former Conservative deputy leader of the council and the wife of a Conservative Member of Parliament. I have no doubt that they are all highly competent. Three of them are women, and that is excellent for gender balance, but nobody could argue that that is politically balanced representation with a Labour local authority and two Conservative and one Labour Member of Parliament in that area.

1492. PETER SHORE: Those were the chairmen?

HILARY BENN: Indeed, yes.

1493. PETER SHORE: Very, very interesting. Thank you very much for that. Let me turn to the question of public meetings which you touched on a bit earlier. We are all in favour of public meetings but we all know that in local government a lot of matters, because of the formal public meeting, are decided in caucus or in sub-committees to avoid too much exposure when serious matters are being considered. Do you think that would not be the case if all meetings of health authority bodies were public?

HILARY BENN: I think in whatever forum publicly you take decisions, be it Parliament, local government or NHS Trusts, the possibility that people will meet outside those public forums to take the decisions is ever present. All I would say is that there would be a lot to be said for Trusts having to meet the same obligations of openness and accountability that, for example, local government has where there is public access to the meetings, the sub-committees and public access to the reports. I think the reports are particularly important because they provide the information on the basis of which the members then take the decision and, subsequently, they have to justify that decision.

1494. PETER SHORE: Can you help us on this? The health authorities vary somewhat, do they not, in their practices. The purchasing authorities—what used to be the District Health Authorities—are, I believe, open, are they not, and also they are somewhat larger than the Health Service Trusts which are not open; indeed, I think they have only requirement to meet once a year on an annual report. Do you think that the experience of the District Health Authorities really indicates that they are much more responsive to local opinion and, therefore, that that pattern of having local representatives should be transferred to the Health Service Trusts?

HILARY BENN: I think it is unquestionably a better system because it is open and because there was that element of local representation previously.

1495. PETER SHORE: Can I move on now to a bit of your evidence which I thought was rather striking. You talked about "gagging clauses". Can you tell us what those really are?

ROGER KLINE (National Officer for the Health Service of the Manufacturing Science Finance Union): They take a variety of forms; I do not think there is a pro forma arrangement of words. In effect, and if you like I will give you an example of one—this is one from the Burnley NHS Trust, this was a draft proposal which states:

"as some of the information which may be made available it could be of a sensitive, confidential and even of a commercial nature, recognised organisations"——

by which they mean recognised trades unions——

"shall not disclose such information to outside bodies such as the Community Health Council"

and there is a range of lots and lots that we have on file, sometimes referring to trades unions more often suggesting that there is an implied duty of employees of fidelity and confidentiality to the employer that ought to restrict, in some cases very greatly, the ability to disclose information even when in their view as professional staff there may be an overriding duty either of care or of the public interest.

1496. PETER SHORE: Yes. You come to that particular matter in your proposed charter, do you not, when you say that complaints should be made to a competent person where particular matters of concern arise. I understand that complaint to a competent person but you also envisage, do you not, going beyond that, if the competent person does not give satisfaction, to an independent person?

ROGER KLINE: Can I answer that in two halves. The first half is that we have come to understand over the past five years since the introduction of the NHS Act in 1990 that there is, in our view, an agenda which has led many, perhaps not all, but many Trusts to operate in a way that inhibits the ability of staff to speak out. With your permission, may I quote from a document that was circulated from the Trent Regional Health Authority in 1990 at the start of the process. They were talking here about managers and said:

"Suppose people in key positions manifest a lack of commitment to organisational goals, ideals and values of self governing trusts, what then? What about renegades, subversives and opposers of what is being attempted? Tolerance of difference is not the same as tolerance of destructiveness. There will be a nettle to be grasped in terms of recruiting, keeping and getting rid of people in key leadership positions right throughout a self-governing trust."

That was in 1990. I will be happy to provide you with a copy if you wish. Since then, we have both monitored what has been going on and the gagging clauses and what our members perceive as restrictions on their ability to speak out have become, for us, a very important issue. Our concerns are shared by bodies such as the UKCC, the nursing regulatory body, and as a result we have consistently given evidence on a variety of issues to the draft guidance on freedom of speech in the NHS. Our advice had some effect on the guidance but I have to say we carried out a comprehensive survey one year after the introduction of the guidance of our representatives in the Health Service, representing 65,000 professional staff, 70 per cent of our representatives who one would have expected to see this had not seen a copy; 40 per cent had not heard of it and in 72 per cent. our representatives were unaware of such policies that were supposed to be introduced locally to ensure that there would be some right to balance the duty of care in the public interest against the duty of fidelity.

We then come across and we monitor and we sometimes have to talk to very distressed people who feel that there is information that they are in possession of that they feel uneasy about disclosing.

1497. PETER SHORE: What do you propose to rectify that situation?

ROGER KLINE: The key for us is that because there clearly is a climate in our view—and I will say in a moment why it is not just our view—of secrecy and sometimes of fear that the only way of making a start in correcting that is to have some independent element which, where necessary—not necessarily as a first resort, we are not suggesting that everybody should immediately ring up their local radio—but either as a matter or urgency or where all other means have failed there ought to be some means of going outside their employer to draw to the attention of other responsible persons the matters about which they are concerned. We made one suggestion,

which is that it should be the Parliamentary Ombudsman, a suggestion that was endorsed by the Parliamentary Health Select Committee but rejected by the Minister. We have actually met with the Ombudsman to discuss the practicalities of that.

If that is not appropriate, it might be that the Community Health Councils could have some independent vetting role in that. Unfortunately, we have had very little success at local level in bringing about those sorts of arrangements.

1498. PETER SHORE: Would you not be satisfied by complaining to your local Member of Parliament?

ROGER KLINE: An interesting question. We have had to draw attention to the fact that in more than one case there have been suggestions that it is improper for staff within trusts to communicate directly with their Member of Parliament and, indeed, the Secretary of State obviously shares that concern because she sent out a reminder to trusts to draw their attention to the fact that any trust's chief executive so acting might find himself in front of the Privileges Committee. That matter is now established, but clearly it sometimes takes courage to contact one's local Member of Parliament these days.

1499. PETER SHORE: Let me move you at this point away from the Health Service to other NDPBs. I do not know whether you had a chance to study the Government's proposals to us published at the end of last week. If you have, we would like to know what you think about them, whether they have proposed changes which satisfy your worries about quangos?

HILARY BENN: I think we would make two comments really. First, we think that the notion of political balance ought to be accepted publicly and, as far as I understand it, that is not a view that the Government have taken. Secondly, I am not aware that the Government have supported the notion that non-departmental public bodies should have to meet in public and that the same standards of openness and accountability which we are arguing for in relation to NHS quangos, should also like apply to non-departmental public bodies. We think that would go a long way because then people could judge for themselves as to the decisions that those bodies are taking and how they are spending public money and have a better opportunity to call them to account than they have at the moment.

1500. PETER SHORE: Yes. But you would presumably welcome a more open system of appointment to quangos?

HILARY BENN: We certainly would welcome a more open system than applies at the moment, yes.

1501. PETER SHORE: All right. I will move you on to my last subject of interrogation, which is your views on lobbying and paid lobbying. I notice that in your evidence here you do not seek to prohibit or inhibit lobbying by Members of Parliament for payment; you only seek disclosure. Is that correct?

ROGER LYONS: We seek maximum transparency.

1502. PETER SHORE: Only disclosure, thank you. That brings me on to your own views about sponsoring of trades unions. Would you take the view, as a union that sponsors Members of Parliament but pays nothing to Members of Parliament only to their constituency parties for their expenses, would you take the view that the system of sponsoring Members of Parliament is, to some extent now, out of date and that it would be perfectly reasonable for you to sponsor a constituency party direct without going through the Member of Parliament at all?

ROGER LYONS: The system we have is the best system we have at the moment. Alternatives could easily be examined. We ourselves, of course, only pay to the constituency party in the case of sponsorship. We are bound by a system that has been in existence for a number of years and originated, to some extent, in the days when Members of Parliament did not get any salary at all. The distant origins meant that people who did not have alternative sources of income could not realistically stand as a Member of Parliament. As to the future arrangements, we are prepared to debate these. We refer to public funding of political parties as another factor here but we are certainly prepared to take part in the debate. I think the arrangements, to some extent, have developed a bit like Topsy.

1503. PETER SHORE: Yes. Would you not agree that the sensible way to approach this subject would be in the context of a proper enquiry into the financing of political parties, both at local and national level?

ROGER LYONS: Clearly some of our evidence could well be seen as asking for that.

PETER SHORE: Thank you.

1504. PROFESSOR ANTHONY KING: In your oral evidence and also in this document you used the phrase "politically balanced" quite frequently. To what kinds of bodies, quangos and so on, do you want the principle of political balance to apply?

HILARY BENN: That is a slightly difficult question to answer because the degree of political appointment currently is something which you as a Committee are currently looking into. We are not aware of the full extent of it, but I think you have received considerable evidence to suggest that it goes on currently. Where that is the case it would be preferable for a system of balance to apply. For example, Mr Lyons referred in his opening remarks to local authority appointments to school governing bodies. That is a good model. To pick up Mr Shore's point, a minority of the representation on school governing bodies are expressly political appointments, but in the vast majority of local education authorities those appointments are made on a politically balanced model reflecting the relative strengths of the parties in that authority at a particular moment in time.

It seems to us that that is a clear system which is well understood. It provides accountability and brings the process into the open. The rest of the appointments—in the case of governing bodies, parents, staff representatives and others co-opted for their expertise or the contribution they can bring—provide a balance overall and within the expressly political appointments it is balanced between the parties and everyone can see what is going on.

1505. PROFESSOR ANTHONY KING: Given that there are going to be political appointments, it may obviously be desirable that those appointments be balanced. Should one not, however, be pushing in the direction of trying to reduce or indeed eliminate political appointments of that kind, especially given the small memberships that our political parties have and the declining public esteem in which the parties are held?

HILARY BENN: It is not political in that sense; it is political in that it is reflecting the elected political representation. I think that is the way we see it; it provides an element of accountability. In the end, if people do not like the decisions that a body is reaching, then at least through that route they have a reasonably clear idea of who it is they should go to and lobby and say "We don't like what you've done and we want you to do something different.". Ultimately, if they are that dissatisfied, they have an opportunity at the next election, locally or nationally, to throw people out and put others in their place.

I do not think that we should throw away completely that very important line of democratic accountability because it is the only one we have.

ROGER LYONS: Our experience also, as we said in paragraph 10, is that it is very difficult to find a neutral situation. Political neutrality is a very strange animal to construct.

1506. PROFESSOR ANTHONY KING: Do you think the civil service is not politically neutral?

ROGER LYONS: We are talking about, for example, school governors or NHS trust membership and there we have found that it is very difficult to find people who are neutral. I am not experienced to comment on the civil service as a whole, although I have my views about some parts of it.

1507. PROFESSOR ANTHONY KING: If I can just press the point, there is an obvious problem about political appointments to these kinds of bodies, given the fact that the politically affiliated in this country now probably constitute a smaller proportion of the total population for the last century.

HILARY BENN: I think it is more a case of the government of the day. That was the point that Lord Carlisle made in his evidence a moment ago. It is reasonable that the government of the day should expect to have some influence through those appointments which it directly makes over the direction of policy. We are saying, let's accept that, but also let's accept that the government of the day does not have a monopoly on political support. Obviously there is support for the different parties in different proportions at different times. Let us make that explicit.

1508. PROFESSOR ANTHONY KING: Quite a number of witnesses have seemed to take the point that, "It is all right for our lot to pack quangos now because the other lot packed quangos when they were in power" and you could reasonably take the view that neither side should pack quangos at all and that this is a bad precedent.

HILARY BENN: That is just what we are arguing—that it should be balanced.

ROGER LYONS: We have also argued, apart from balance, that stakeholders and other interest groups should be well represented. We argued that in our submission.

1509. PROFESSOR ANTHONY KING: This may seem a matter of detail, but it raises political questions as well. There is, you say, also evidence here that the appointment of individuals to NHS authorities and trust boards is politically unbalanced and is weighted in favour of business people. Is that a bad thing? The thought of NHS trusts being run by professors or judges frankly frightens me!

ROGER LYONS: I do not want to comment on professors. Our view is that there is a place for people with business experience—that is important on trust boards. The problem we have found is that instead of that being one place, it has often been that of the five places available, three, four or five places will be taken by such appointees. There is a balance to be drawn, in terms of representing a particular interest, or understanding of some of the issues, between those with business expertise and those either with other expertise in terms of clinical and professional expertise or, indeed, those who specifically see themselves as representing the local community. In many cases our concern is that that does not always seem to have happened.

1510. ANNE WARBURTON: Might I ask a question about comments on parliamentary lobbying in your submission. You say:

"Our parliamentary committee currently comprises 47 Members of Parliament and eight Members of the House of Lords and that includes sponsored MPs."

I was not at all clear about what this parliamentary committee is and what it does.

ROGER LYONS: We have many more MPs in our Parliamentary Committee than we actually have arrangements to sponsor, so we have two tiers in terms of assistance to their constituency parties. The ones who are not sponsored may well get some measure of support at election time through their constituency party.

In our parliamentary committee structure, the MPs and Peers meet monthly with us to discuss those areas of joint interest and concern. They advise us and we advise them. It is an advisory relationship and up to 47 MPs come to that, which includes anything up to 16 sponsored.

1511. ANNE WARBURTON: Is this a committee which especially has the name "MSF Committee"?

ROGER LYONS: It is the MSF Parliamentary Committee and it is organised by those MPs and Peers in the two Houses of Parliament.

1512. ANNE WARBURTON: Do they all tend to be from one party?

ROGER LYONS: Because our union is affiliated to the Labour Party, this particular committee is made up of those taking the Labour whip. There are other Members of Parliament with whom we work who are in other political parties.

1513. ANNE WARBURTON: When they meet to discuss, it is about things in which your union is directly interested?

ROGER LYONS: Our National Executive refers matters to them for their consideration. For example, we may be seeking amendments to legislation, have points to raise in inquiries or have questions to raise about industrial or employment matters. They then decide whether they wish to take them on board and if so in what form and through which mechanism.

1514. ANNE WARBURTON: Are you unique in having this sort of arrangement?

ROGER LYONS: It is probably the largest and most structured one and has been going for longest, but I do not think we are unique, although I would like to believe we are in most things!

1515. TOM KING: I should like to follow up what Professor Anthony King was talking about. My observation—certainly in my own area, which I know best—is that there has been a vast improvement in the management of the hospitals because they have a smaller Trust board and hardly any politicians. I do not know the politics of most of the people who are on it, but there is certainly a consultant on it for the first time and people who work in the hospital. I notice from this that although it has disappointed Conservative councillors and others who have traditionally looked to appointments to such boards (and some Labour representatives and union members looking for representation), there has been a significant improvement in the management.

If I may, I will give you one illustration. For the first time ever, while we had wonderfully politically balanced boards before, nobody ever talked to the GPs about what they looked for from their local hospital. The first thing the consultant Director of the Trust did was to get hold of all the GPs in the area whose patients came to the hospital. Do you not think that merit comes before political correctness?

ROGER LYONS: We do not have time to debate whether the Trusts are better managed, but (because it is reported in this week's Health Service Journal) I can say with some authority that in respect of the issues about which you are concerned, secrecy and openness, that more than half of Trust managers believe the NHS has become more secretive over the past five years—the period since the document I referred to at the beginning—and 56 per cent of them thought that the NHS code of openness, that was introduced to codify the suggestion that openness was a good thing, that this code would make no difference. That is not a survey of us, but of Trust chief executives and senior managers within the Health Service. Therefore it seems that in terms of the management of Trusts in respect of the issues you are interested in, things have got worse.

1516. TOM KING: That is certainly not my experience, but I am interested in the research and the figures you claim have come from some journal.

I was a bit worried about Mr Benn's comment about gender balance. I am not sure if you insist on gender balance as well. In my area I have noticed that women seem to be taking over the key jobs and I see nothing wrong with that—they are doing them extremely well.

HILARY BENN: I hope that you did not misinterpret my remarks, Mr King. I am all in favour of gender balance and I was not criticising those particular appointments on that basis. My remarks were to do with their party political nature.

The only other thing I would say is that you can good management under the old or the new arrangements. As far as we are concerned, the issue is the extent to which the public can decide for themselves whether the management is good or not. It seems to us that if you allow access, information and openness, the public can make that judgement. In relation to the Trust boards in particular the public do not currently have those rights.

1517. TOM KING: You referred also to the concern about employees who felt aggrieved or that things were not satisfactory and said that they should have an independent, outside appeal process. You represent members not only in the Health Service but throughout industry and many other activities. Would you propose that whatever company your members work in, there should be an independent ombudsman to whom they can complain about the management?

ROGER LYONS: Normally our position as the representative organisation in the company or service concerned enables them to have an adequate channel to raise issues. The Health Service though has been somewhat different and we have had to set up a special whistle-blowing hotline to deal particularly with Health Service issues. My colleague will pick up the detailed points, but as far as the general MSF membership is concerned, we have had much more ability to raise issues that have come up occasionally where information has needed to be checked out and possible causes of concern allayed or dealt with.

ROGER KLINE: I will briefly supplement that. As well as that being a general principle, there are particular issues in respect of the Health Service because the areas about which we are most concerned and about which people ought to responsibly have the right as a last resort or in cases of emergency to refer to outside, are those where there is tension and potential conflict between their duty of care and the public interest and a duty of fidelity and confidentiality. It is our belief that unless there is an independent element, the tendency will be for the duty of confidentiality and fidelity, accompanied by the threat of discipline, to prevent some people under some circumstances exercising their duty of care or the public interest. We have had members who have been in such a situation—some of you will have heard about one of them, Mr Chris Chapman.

1518. TOM KING: Can I turn now to your very helpful paper and the interesting information you have given us about parliamentary lobbying. You make clear your belief in the need for total transparency in this area. You mention that you have 47 Members of Parliament under your heading of parliamentary lobbying who are available to you on your committee, of whom you say 16 are separately sponsored.

Dame Anne Warburton asked you about the distinction there. What is the financial arrangement for the 16 who are separately sponsored?

ROGER LYONS: We have sponsorship agreements with the constituency parties of the 16 Members which involve a total of £9,600 per annum shared between them. That is approximately £600 per annum.

TOM KING: £600 a year each, plus £9,600?

ROGER LYONS: No, the total is £9,600.

1519. TOM KING: I am sorry. What about the others? Do they get nothing?

ROGER LYONS: They get nothing on an annual basis, but when an election comes—and obviously we do not control the timing—we would be prepared to consider making available limited assistance to their constituency party. If you take all the 47 and dozens of other candidates who were not elected, because we make the same arrangement there, we spent a total of £34,000 during the last election year and that includes the sponsorship for that year.

1520. TOM KING: I take it that the 16 key Members who are separately sponsored tend to get most support from you? I do not quite understand how it has been set up, but is that right?

ROGER LYONS: We have a policy on the Executive of only having 16 sponsored Members.

1521. TOM KING: What percentage of their election expenses do you pay?

HILARY BENN: The maximum we gave to the constituency party of any one of them at the last election was £2,000.

ROGER LYONS: Six of the sponsored ones received the highest maximum award.

1522. TOM KING: That was the most you did—because other unions pay much more than that? I think we were given a figure of 80 per cent of election expenses, which presumably could be £6,000 or £7,000 in a constituency. You say here that no MP derives any personal financial benefit from sponsorship.

ROGER LYONS: Correct.

1523. TOM KING: Does the selection committee at the time of selection know whether a candidate before them will bring with him the benefit of a "dowry" for election costs from the union to which he belongs?

ROGER LYONS: No, because we do not have a panel of potential sponsored candidates or MPs. It is only after selection and then election that such a person could apply to become sponsored.

1524. TOM KING: Therefore your members are at a disadvantage against other unions where it is known that they would pay 80 per cent of that person's election expenses if he was chosen?

ROGER LYONS: The point has been raised on occasion, but it has not been mentioned about us having 47 MPs and 16 sponsored ones.

TOM KING: Thank you very much.

1525. LORD NOLAN: I wonder if I could ask just one question concerning the need to have an effective complaints procedure. Would it be possible for the National Health Service ombudsman to be brought in to this area?

ROGER KLINE: In our view it would. We made a formal submission at that time of the draft code on freedom of speech in the Health Service which was later issued. Our proposal was indeed in the report of the House of Commons Select Committee, but it was not one that was adopted by the Minister. That is something we would like to return to because it is hard to see who else would be better qualified. This is someone who already takes a look at the Health Service and certainly in terms of issues of maladministration and some of the difficult areas we have highlighted we think that would be most appropriate.

LORD NOLAN: Thank you very much.

1526. LORD THOMSON: One of the questions with which we have been wrestling over a week or two now is that of what payments can be properly received and what actions properly be taken for payment by MPs. Do I take it from your evidence, both about your sponsorship of MPs and the general principles you have applied, that in your view, provided the financial arrangements are open and transparent, it is just as legitimate for an MP, whatever his party, to be paid by some trade association or public relations firm to pursue certain interests in Parliament as it is for your MPs to have general support for matters that are of interest to your union?

ROGER LYONS: As we have confirmed in our evidence, we do not make any financial payment to MPs, but we do not have a firm view against MPs receiving payment, provided it is open and transparent.

HILARY BENN: Obviously, the difficulty the Committee faces is trying to draw a distinction between what some people might see as a legitimate payment for a relationship and an illegitimate one. The choice is whether to say that an MP will receive no outside payment at all, which is clear cut; but it seemed to us that it is very hard to draw a line between the different types of relationships. If you find that difficult to do, at the very minimum full disclosure of those relationships then allows other people to judge.

LORD THOMSON: Yes, thank you.

1527. WILLIAM UTTING: If I might comment on a couple of points, there seems to me to be a stronger case for restoring local authority representation to health authorities than to health Trusts. It seems to me that a health authority with the job of assessing health needs in an area and planning to meet them, would have that process substantially informed by the authority and knowledge of the local authority as a whole, but that local authority members as individuals may not necessarily have a great deal to contribute to the management of the services that are providing health care to the population. There was criticism of local authority performance in that sector in the NHS before they were turned off health authorities in the 1980s. I offer that as a comment rather than wanting to engage you in a lengthy discussion of its merits.

I feel some scepticism about the practicality of achieving political balance in the NHS and in other non-

departmental public bodies because this would be done on the basis of nominations by political parties in the end. That might not necessarily be in the interests of the effectiveness of the organisation to which appointments were being made. Will you clarify that point for me?

HILARY BENN: You are right in assessing how the process would begin. If you were to combine it with some scrutiny of those appointments, to then check on the suitability of the particular persons to the posts to which they were being appointed, that might cover your reservation. In other words, the parties would be allowed to make those nominations. If you then combine it with scrutiny, by, for example, an all-party committee looking at questions of competence, qualifications and what they had to offer, that might overcome that difficulty.

1528. WILLIAM UTTING: I see. So the scrutiny of suitability for the post would over-ride the political choice?

HILARY BENN: In the end, it might. Then obviously if the whips, locally or nationally, knew that that was going to be the case, they would wish to take it into account in making the nominations in the first place.

ROGER LYONS: We have actually put forward a suggestion of an all-party parliamentary committee to deal with this.

WILLIAM UTTING: Thank you.

1529. DIANA WARWICK: In relation to lobbying and your suggestion that there should be declaration of all financial arrangements, do you draw a distinction between payment for lobbying activity, which you have described in some detail, and other financial income of Members of Parliament, other than their payment as MPs? Would you, for example, wish to see disclosure of income from an occupation which has continued during time as an MP?

ROGER LYONS: My colleague explained that we feel it is difficult to draw the line on income. We believe that the main thing that will give the public confidence is transparency. If people choose to be public representatives, they have to expect greater transparency of their financial dealings. I would have thought that all income should be declared because otherwise there is a possibility that you could have, for example, laundering. You could have income coming from undeclared sources on the grounds that it does not come under the precise definition of what should be declared. Public representatives in all organisations with public accountability should be prepared to disclose all their financial dealings.

1530. LORD NOLAN: Thank you all very much. That has been very clear and helpful and we shall take this away and study it in greater depth.

IAIN DUNCAN-SMITH MP

Good morning, Mr Duncan-Smith. Thank you very much for volunteering to come along and give us your time. Have you prepared an opening statement, or would you like to go straight into questions?

IAIN DUNCAN-SMITH, MP: I have a few points which I should like to make. I have hand-written them, which will perhaps convey some idea of my thought process, but I did not really want to make a big issue of it—I would just like to make a few opening remarks really.

LORD NOLAN: That would be very helpful to us. Please do.

IAIN DUNCAN-SMITH: Perhaps I can start, Mr Chairman, by raising a concern at the outset. I was under the impression that this Committee was to listen to evidence, investigate and come with recommendations. I must say at the outset that I was deeply concerned to find that in January there were quotes from yourself about what you were likely to come to in terms of your considerations and recommendations. I have in front of me a Daily Express (and I know there were other papers) that made comments which they alleged came directly from you, which I might quote here. It said:

"It seems plain from the evidence so far that rules on MPs connections with lobbyists need to be tightened up, that MPs need better guidance on what is and is not acceptable . . ."

I make no other point except I was concerned—as others were—that it was as though you had already reached some conclusions and people had not had an opportunity to make their points.

LORD NOLAN: I very much regret that that impression was gained; it was meant to be no more than a summary for the benefit of future witnesses of some of what had appeared from the evidence we had heard so far.

IAIN DUNCAN-SMITH: If I could start by saying a bit about myself. I came into politics (I suspect much the same as many other people) simply because I wanted to do something for my countrymen and women and for my country. From all those I have talked to, by and large that is the impression I get from most others who come into this job as a Member of Parliament. It certainly is not for financial gain. I took a cut in income to come here and I think the same is true for many people. Frankly, I had some commitments previously, which were declared; I have none now on Members' Interests, because I find myself too busy at the moment with what I am doing. The complaints about financial gain sometimes have to be put in perspective.

With regard to the concept of advancement, my record over the past two and a half years may lead people to expect that I have also dismissed that to some degree, but that is important because others think it is simply a treadmill for financial gain, for political advancement and then subsequent financial gain. That has been put out of all proportion.

I believe that being a Member of Parliament is a privilege, not a career. It is something you do for motives that are not wholly or utterly for personal advancement and it is so different from any other job that I have done or known of that it is impossible to draw comparisons with it and therefore whatever this Committee comes to, I hope they accept the fact that this is utterly unique and that comparisons with business and other occupations do not run at all.

For example, if you are in dispute with your party, you cannot leave it easily and find advancement elsewhere, as you could in a business. You cannot jump into another company that is competing, because there is no such competition. Very rarely do people leave one party for another simply because they join that party because their views coincide so directly with it. The disputes and the end of career can often be complete for people who find that problem and therefore there is absolutely no comparison.

I am very concerned, Mr Chairman, that your investigation should not therefore be driven by limited political considerations that may take place on the Floor of the House or elsewhere, most of them on a party political basis and short-term advancement. We have to achieve a balance on this issue because there is a grave danger of throwing the baby out with the bath water here.

There seems to be a gap in public perception of what Members of Parliament do and how they rate them—and Professor King made this point. As politicians generally we are rated fairly low in people's regard. But I would also put it to the Committee that if one looks at individual politicians in terms of their constituencies, (and often there have been limited surveys I accept) where people have been asked what they think about their individuals constituency Member of Parliament, there is a complete reversing of that process. Often you find that regard for an individual MP puts them high in the list of public perception within that limited area. That needs to be borne in mind because on both sides we have different facets of being a Member of Parliament; one is the general public perception, but the other is the more limited and very effective local perception, which has to be taken into consideration.

This Committee has been set up because of the frenzy of allegations of sleaze and what has been going on more recently—perhaps over the past two years—and yet when we look at all this noise and fury, I wonder what we really find. We find essentially at the moment that there is still no Minister who has been charged with impropriety while acting as a Minister. We find that there are a couple of MPs accused of not registering interests currently—one of whom is taking legal action to clear his name. We also find a couple of MPs who, it is alleged, took money to table questions—and that in itself is being investigated. And, of course, we find the ever present number of those who have fallen foul of that tabloid demon, sex, which, I have to say, has been interwoven through this concept of impropriety in such a way as to blur the edges of what the concept is about and sex and people's problems with it has anything to do with their ability to carry out their jobs may of course not be relevant. I could perhaps ask therefore after all this sound and fury, how much it actually signifies.

In concluding, I previously worked in industry and ended up on the board of a publishing company. I travelled the world and carried out contracts in various countries; I came into contact with politicians in pretty well every country in the world and I have to say that the system and the policies we have in Britain stand head and shoulders above almost any other that I have come across, both in Europe and the Far East, as well as amongst what I might call the English-speaking Anglo-Saxon community where we perhaps have the greatest synergy in terms of our concept of propriety.

To my knowledge, all the MPs I have ever come across work diligently and hard in pursuit of their constituency's interests and in their job as political parliamentary MPs.

When I look at places such as France and Italy, I find serious allegations against Ministers, which will be substantiated by the sound of things, with Ministers actually being put in prison, in Italy the collapse of a whole political system and in Germany down in Bavaria we see the CSU collapsing under serious allegations of financial impropriety.

I have to say also that in Europe we have to be careful because their press are of course nothing like as diligent or powerful as ours—perhaps some observations can be made about that. When we look across the Anglo-Saxon English-speaking world, we see a greater, closer synergy to our position, but certainly nothing that we can identify as being better. The only thing you could say is that perhaps we have some lessons to learn about freedom of information, which is the key.

This is not a statement of complacency, but makes the point that when Roy Hattersley for example made his earlier statements he said that MPs should not be allowed to vote for personal financial advantage, although that sounds a fantastic and wonderful statement of principle, the reality is that every year MPs vote on their salaries and parliamentary allowances. They vote for financial benefit because it is part of their job. You cannot say simply that they will not and should not—they do. The question is therefore in what areas they should do so and how they should declare them.

It is important that Members of Parliament continue to be allowed to have outside interests. Personally I believe it helps the debate. I take absolutely no issue with those who have union sponsorship, and as long as it is open and declared and above board and that when they get up to make statements on particular subjects, like everything else, they declare it, I think it helps the debate. I wish that unions sought to look to other sides of the House to help them and also to engage in some of the argument. I would say the same for businesses—that it is very important that businesses have access to Members of Parliament to air their views, particularly in the case of small businesses whose views are often hidden behind a plethora of nonsense produced by people who pretend they know something about it and do not. The truth is that my experience in business has stood me in good stead in the House and I wish that others had some of that experience as well. We have tended in the past, I believe, to draw too much from a more and more limited base of industrial experience. Perhaps it therefore becomes more necessary that people should have outside interests.

The key must surely be to make certain that we have greater visibility and that we tighten up the rules necessarily on declarations—I would run with that. But I would oppose any outside organisation being set up to investigate what Members of Parliament did, either on an ad hoc or a regular basis because I still believe that Parliament ultimately must be sovereign. If you start leeching away activities from Parliament you end up questioning its role. That leads one to ask whether this Committee should not be looking at some of the leeching away of the powers of Parliament anyway because that is very much at the root of the issue. The less MPs feel they can influence events, the more they turn to other things to fill their time perhaps.

I am aware that there is often a confusion with government. As Nick Budgen said, government perhaps thinks it is responsible for Parliament too much, rather than responsible to Parliament. Therefore the job is to drive as much responsibility back to Parliament and get them to fulfil those obligations in an honest and open way with some clear criteria. If that were the case, we might end up with a better discussion about this matter.

Lastly, at the root of all this also is the press. They carry a heavy stigma for the way they have reported things that go on in the House and in Whitehall. They have too often allowed themselves to fall into the category of reporting what I call the minor events, the more trivial and sensational and never reporting what Parliament actually does or how government works. In support of some of Professor King's findings, it is not surprising that the public know less and less about what goes on in Parliament because it is now less reported than ever before. Since the television cameras came in, the public now have less access. The visual media no longer put debates on in prime time (as they promised they would); the newspapers, because of the television cameras, do not report it any more and so the public think nothing happens. I put to you that visibility is a two-edged sword and it is time that the media stood up to their responsibilities just as we are supposed to.

Thank you, Mr Chairman.

LORD NOLAN: Thank you very much. I think we will go straight into questions. Ms Warwick, will you start please.

1531. DIANA WARWICK: Mr Duncan-Smith, you have given us a ringing defence of the probity of MPs. Do you just blame the press for the fact that 64 per cent of the population believe that most MPs are making money out of their parliamentary work?

IAIN DUNCAN-SMITH: No. I hope I was not confusing the issue by pretending that I did think that. The press are not wholly to blame. It is simply a fact of life that Members of Parliament now are responsible for far less in many senses and have far less real power than perhaps they ever had. In some cases that has led them to get involved in much more trivial affairs. I notice that we now see Members of Parliament appearing on chat shows, game shows and so on, which I think is to be abhorred, because I do not believe that is why we were elected.

I believe the public perception is often guided by what they read in the press. I am not criticising the press, because they would not be able to make reports if things did not exist. But there are other things happening in Parliament too.

1532. DIANA WARWICK: If things do exist, how should we try to get at them?

IAIN DUNCAN-SMITH: As I said previously, the key lies in utter openness. I was always a great supporter of freedom of information. I still believe that we shall benefit from that eventually when we get that clear and laid down in law. The key factor is that for Parliament we should follow the rule that all interests should be declared and, as far as possible, the details of those interests so that the public are aware of them. I would then hope that the press would not talk only about people for hire, but about what those interests really were and whether they were representing outside interests properly.

1533. DIANA WARWICK: You said in your presentation that you were too busy as an MP to do other things and yet you are arguing that MPs should be able to do other things. Do you think that part of the public perception is that MPs do too many things and that they are not as conscientious as MPs like you who can only concentrate on their parliamentary work?

IAIN DUNCAN-SMITH: No. I might be in a slightly different category. Over the past three years I have found myself in dispute with my own Government on the issue of Europe and therefore I have pursued a particular exercise over that, which has absorbed a great deal of my time. That notwithstanding, I have also tried to be diligent on constituency activities. I do not think I am any different from the vast majority of MPs. You will find that when Members of Parliament have causes or issues they wish to pursue, those absorb a great deal of their time. That is a critical point. For those who do not have such issues, they may find they have a little more time—but I cannot comment on that.

1534. DIANA WARWICK: In your declaration of interests, you say that you are a consultant to Jane's Information Group.

IAIN DUNCAN-SMITH: No, I am not. That ceased in May last year.

DIANA WARWICK: So you have no other outside interests at all?

IAIN DUNCAN-SMITH: No, not now.

1535. DIANA WARWICK: Could you then tell us, in your plea for greater transparency, whether, were you to have such an interest, or indeed for those interests declared by other MPs, you think that great degree of transparency should be accompanied by the amount of income that is attributed to that outside interest?

IAIN DUNCAN-SMITH: I would have no objection to that.

1536. DIANA WARWICK: This is only asking for your opinion, but do you feel that that is something which would be strongly resisted by other MPs?

IAIN DUNCAN-SMITH: I find it difficult to comment on that because I have not talked to the vast majority of MPs about it. I simply give my opinion that most MPs would be happy for openness.

1537. DIANA WARWICK: Of whatever kind, including income?

IAIN DUNCAN-SMITH: I think so, but as I said, that is my opinion.

1538. DIANA WARWICK: When you were a consultant, what did that activity involve?

IAIN DUNCAN-SMITH: It is slightly peculiar because I was on the board of the same company before I became a Member of Parliament and so I had a direct interest in what you might call a gradual handover of some of my responsibilities. I was involved in issues to do with technology and changes in the company. There was a

genuine interest involved in gradually seeing the company through to a different position, along with the other board members. I also acted, in a genuine parliamentary sense. I still use the company, though I am not a consultant to them; they are one of the great British success stories and they have a huge pool of information about defence and related activities around the world. I find it very useful to be able to bring them in to brief Back Bench Members of Parliament about actions and activities of the Government and give them facts and figures that perhaps were not always available in the public domain, or which, at least, they were not able to get hold of. I certainly believed that has helped and improved the debate and a number of my colleagues have said that the information given to them has pointed them in directions where they have questioned the Government over certain aspects of policy. They have also briefed the Labour Party quite extensively as well.

1539. DIANA WARWICK: I wonder if I could ask you to help us with a distinction that we have been struggling with. You touched on it in your presentation. It is the question of whether there is any distinction between an MP advising an outside body and acting for it and being seen to act for it in the House. You seemed to be suggesting that such activity was perfectly proper, as long as it was declared. Would you include in that, for example, acting for an outside company by seeking meetings with Ministers and accompanying such representatives in Meetings with Ministers?

IAIN DUNCAN-SMITH: I do not quite understand what the problem is here. The key factor is that Ministers, as MPs, we assume are not stupid. They are not therefore going to accept the first bit of information that is given to them. They are able to take views and make judgements. It is important, however, that Ministers are pulled out of Whitehall's embrace every so often and told categorically that they are getting something wrong.

Often a particular interest would be very useful in saying to a Minister "The information you've been given on this issue is not correct. These are the facts. You may go back and verify them (which you surely will), but these are the facts and there is a better balance.". The key factor is that we certainly want to retain that aspect. Therefore briefing of Ministers, as much as Members of Parliament is a reasonable activity. Again, it is important that the individual concerned makes it clear from the outset if they represent a particular company and take financial gain from them. Therefore the evidence or information given is weighted accordingly.

It is important, however, to make sure that companies and trade unions as well get access to Ministers because, after all, if we live too much in an ivory tower, we shall ignore the people we are supposed to be serving.

1540. DIANA WARWICK: Do you think that transparency in those circumstances would be assisted by the number of lobbyists being made readily available who have seen a Minister if a relevant question is asked in the House?

IAIN DUNCAN-SMITH: If it is relevant to a particular area, a Minister should always be able to say that he has had representations from whatever companies.

1541. DIANA WARWICK: Thank you. Could I ask you to expand on the point that you were making when you said that the Register of Members' Interests should be expanded. Could I ask you to say in what way, because reading it, it is enormously variable as a document. How would you see that improved?

IAIN DUNCAN-SMITH: I think that within the strictures of the House it is quite possible to have the Register of Interests put on a more statutory basis—that is to say that it is not at the whim or wish of the Member, but that Parliament requires them to register their interests and that it is Parliament that will carry out any action should they not do so. There are plenty of powers that lie with the Speaker to take whatever action is required if somebody clearly refuses to register interests if Parliament has said that they must do so.

1542. DIANA WARWICK: One final question: you were quite vehement in your comment about an independent arbiter of impropriety in Parliament. Part of the evidence we have been given is that other committees like ours have made recommendations to improve standards of conduct in Parliament, and there was at least one occasion when the recommendations were not even debated by Parliament. There does not seem to be much evidence that Parliament has taken conscious decisions to introduce those changes that have been recommended. It is difficult to see on the face of the evidence so far that Parliament is very good at regulating itself.

IAIN DUNCAN-SMITH: There are two points that have been made about this. Parliament is the elected body. Whatever anyone's personal views about Parliament, it has to be said that we remain the only body that is ultimately elected by the population of the United Kingdom. Therefore it must be for Parliament ultimately to take those decisions and put them to the public at the next election.

Personally I think it would have been helped had the Executive not just gone ahead and set this Committee up. I think that we should have debated it on the floor of the House and then set the Committee up because that involves Parliament. It comes back to my earlier point. You could argue that the more you cut Parliament out, the more irresponsible Parliament may get. It is important that Parliament recognises that it has certain powers and with those come responsibility. If you cut out those powers, you cut out some of the responsibility.

I think that Parliament should certainly debate whatever findings are made. I certainly would not want to accept anything imposed upon me by the wish either of the Executive or of some other body. To my mind it remains absolutely the case that Parliament is sovereign; the problem is that it has become less sovereign, not more. It is time to restore that and with that will come a vast measure of responsibility as people understand that they have to debate in the open in clear public view and make certain that their recommendations are followed.

DIANA WARWICK: Thank you.

1543. WILLIAM UTTING: We have had one or two people mention the importance of freedom of information to us and you have joined that group. Could you tell us briefly what improvements greater freedom of information would make in relation to the terms of reference of this Committee and our concern for MPs' interests, Ministers and civil servants and appointments to non-departmental public bodies?

IAIN DUNCAN-SMITH: Yes. There are a whole range of facts about freedom of information. There was a Private Member's Bill about two years ago which encompassed a vast range of those. They stretch right the way through from Whitehall to Parliament and further afield. The only point I would make is that I have always believed simply that the power of people to do anything is very much restricted by their ability to get access to information in the first place to inform the debate. Therefore the public perception of the way that parliamentarians engage in various aspects of their lives would be greatly enhanced were they able to understand that instead of this frenzy that takes place on the front pages of newspapers, they were able legitimately to check what their Members of Parliament were actually up to.

That is something which none of us should shy away from. I fully believe that our system is likely to be able to produce that effect much more easily. Without a shadow of a doubt, the present Government has moved a vast degree towards freeing up access to information, but there is still quite a long way to go in my opinion. There needs to be a greater culture of access to information which would not go amiss.

WILLIAM UTTING: If you have any specific recommendations to make in that area and wish to give us a written note, that might be most helpful.

IAIN DUNCAN-SMITH: I should certainly like to do that.

1544. LORD THOMSON: You put forward a strong case a few minutes ago for Parliament reasserting its sovereignty as against the Executive. What is your judgement about the way Parliament has behaved recently over the events that finally led to this Committee being appointed?

Are you satisfied about the two Members of Parliament, for example, whose problems are being investigated by the Privileges Committee? This matter has now gone on for months. Is this satisfactory as a method of Parliament dealing with that sort of matter with sufficient urgency? Are you satisfied about the rigour with which the Committee on the Register of Members' Interests deals with the problems of public perception on the way Members register and make visible their interests? What would your comments be on the adequacy of Parliament dealing with these matters which are essentially something for Parliament?

IAIN DUNCAN-SMITH: There are really two points to be made on this. The first thing is that I abhor what has been going on with the Privileges Committee and I have to say that I think there are individual Members who take a share of the blame for this. It was allowed to sink into a sort of party political slanging match which, as ever in these issues, doesn't necessarily help. I have to say, however, that any Parliamentary Committee always has one major limitation. If an individual Member disputes allegations made outside of the House about his actions and activities and wishes to take that through the courts, which is his only recourse in this particular case, I think at that stage the courts become the better judge of his position in this matter ultimately, because the problem with a Privileges Committee, or a committee generally, is that it can ask general questions, it can investigate matters specifically or generally, but the fact is that there does not exist the same possibility for advocacy on either side of the argument that will exist in a court of law and therefore as soon as somebody wishes to dispute something and wishes to take somebody to court over it, I think at that stage we have to bow in favour of the court then sorting that matter out for that individual and not try and interfere in that process, because I think it would be unfair on the individual. But I do think that it would have been possible to have got on with this a lot faster and to have done so reasonably comprehensively had they not got into this absurd slanging match which existed at the beginning.

1545. LORD THOMSON: Thank you. I appreciate that comment. But is not, with respect, what you have just said about the importance of being able to go to a court to deal with matters that arise from Parliamentary behaviour, somewhat inconsistent with what you have been saying—that you did not wish to have outside interference in the sovereignty of Parliament?

IAIN DUNCAN-SMITH: No, no, we have got to remember what the definition and guidelines that exist for law and for Parliament are. The fact is that I was talking about Parliament's ability to set guidelines and to rule on behalf of itself, but it has never attempted to interfere in disputes between individuals which is also the sovereign right of an individual—to defend themselves against unjust allegations made and that is why we have law courts. And that is why under English common law quite clearly there is such a separation between Parliament and those courts of law. I put to you simply this: that an individual must always have the right to defend themselves and to do so must be able to get full advocacy on their part and in so doing obviously the person that they accuse of maligning them must have the same benefits. You can't get that in front of a committee because then you start setting up another court of law and you are dealing with an individual and an individual's disputing the charge. If he wishes to take that to court that has to be their right. That doesn't cut across Parliament's sovereign right to declare for itself and to work out guidelines for itself and to judge those general guidelines.

LORD THOMSON: Thank you.

1546. LORD NOLAN: I am afraid I am not entirely clear. Suppose a Member of Parliament is accused of taking cash for asking a question. That is not a crime, is it?

IAIN DUNCAN-SMITH: Not if Parliament has not said that it was wrong then clearly it is not.

1547. LORD NOLAN: So how do you see it resolved?

IAIN DUNCAN-SMITH: Well, in this particular case it may well be that the individual concerned thinks it is a defamation and therefore takes it to a court of law on the basis of defamation in the usual way. That is the distinction I am making. But if, however, Parliament says that it is wrong to take money for any activity, shall we say, and the individual has taken money for that activity then he is in breach of Parliament's guidelines, but Parliament has made no such guidelines.

1548. LORD NOLAN: Yes. On a slightly different aspect of the same question: you said that you would deplore the idea of an outside body regulating the affairs of Parliament. I think what has been suggested to us by a number of people is not so much that but the setting up of something of the order of an individual with the status of

the Parliamentary Commissioner or the Comptroller and Auditor General or possibly an Ethics Committee with a registrar set up by Parliament, answerable to Parliament for the, at any rate, preliminary investigation of complaints. Now, was that what you meant by an outside body or would you regard that as not an outside body?

IAIN DUNCAN-SMITH: I think the key factor is that it depends on how far Parliament retains complete control over the final decisions with regard to that matter. My personal view is simply that I think Members of Parliament are capable of investigating this. I know there are those who say "No they are not because they will always come with some whipped interest and so therefore they will block things off". I think that providing it is made clear to them that they have responsibilities in this matter it is possible for them to do so. And I think one of the great saving graces of the system anyway is its party political nature, that is to say one side will always be seeking to investigate the other side and therefore that has a certain healthy aspect. The only thing I would say finally is that I don't think there is ever such a person who has no particular interest. I mean everybody that you pick from the public—hence the discussion about quangos—somewhere has an interest that somebody doesn't like, so I wonder if such a person can be found who then would not bring those same prejudices to such a committee.

LORD NOLAN: Mr. Shore?

1549. PETER SHORE: The Comptroller and Auditor General is, of course, responsible to Parliament and is not appointed except with the consent of Parliament, yet he has investigatory powers which really could be very helpful—certainly very helpful to the Public Accounts Committee and I would have thought an analogous post could be very helpful to a Parliamentary Committee investigating breaches or alleged breaches of conduct of Members. Would you agree with that—does that not breach your view of maintaining, as it were, the sovereignty of Parliament?

IAIN DUNCAN-SMITH: I think the key factor is that Parliament must retain the ultimate right to decide on these matters and I think I make that my final point. It is simply that I do not wish to see that power leeched out somewhere else for some other body which in itself may well be yet another quango. And I am making simply the point that Parliament should be sovereign in this matter and make the decision, much as I would like to make the decision on what this committee comes to on the floor of the House and not be told to accept it.

1550. PETER SHORE: I think your point is entirely clear—it is that an investigatory official responsible to the House is one thing but the final decisions on any report that he produces, or any other process, must be left to Parliament itself—to committees?

IAIN DUNCAN-SMITH: Yes, I would like to see if there ever was such an individual or body that first of all their findings would never ever be public until after Parliament had seen them and decided what they thought of them. And the second point must surely be that they would work alongside elected Members of Parliament. It would not be a separate committee as such but it would actually be part and parcel of Parliament's own investigations.

PETER SHORE: Yes, but probably in the first place could work to a particular committee.

IAIN DUNCAN-SMITH: Yes.

1551. PETER SHORE: Can I just go back over an answer you gave previously? When you were being asked about Members of Parliament receiving pay for consultancies and things of that kind I think you rather dismissed the importance of it by saying "Well, Ministers are not stupid—they know when they are being got at. They know when, as it were, a public relations effort is being pushed at them via a Member of Parliament". I accept that but do you not think there is something in a sense derogatory to the position of Members of Parliament themselves if they are seen to be, as it were, available for receiving payments from public relations firms with the express purpose of using their influence as Parliamentarians to gain advantage for their clients?

IAIN DUNCAN-SMITH: Yes, I personally would never want to be involved in that exercise, or such an exercise, or be retained by anybody who was in a general sense a lobbying company, which I think is what you are referring to. But I have to say that the way round that has got to be complete and utter disclosure. For example, if a company was a lobbying company and retained the services of a Member of Parliament then in the Member's interests the disclosure should be that it is a lobbying company and I think that they should disclose who their clients are in that disclosure and on that basis I think that many of them would hesitate perhaps before wishing to retain the services of a Member of Parliament. And also when that Member of Parliament was engaged in anything they would have to declare the interest wherever those companies touched, which may cover quite a wide area. So I think the point would be made quite clearly that people would recognise when they were finding themselves caught on a hook and I would think most Members of Parliament would not wish to go down that road and therefore disclosure would actually work to the benefit rather than putting some outright ban which I think would not necessarily work. But lobbying companies do act and do offer a service—some companies cannot afford to retain a scrutiny of Parliament on a regular basis and so they pay a lobbying company to do it for them. So it is not as though they are some sort of evil—they do actually offer a service to both companies and, I think, to trade unions too. So I think there is a necessity. So again it is a case of the baby and the bath water.

1552. PETER SHORE: There are plenty of lobbying companies available to give advice on payment. The question is whether a Member of Parliament should be associated with that particular operation?

IAIN DUNCAN-SMITH: Yes, I agree, but I have to say that—I said earlier on that an involvement with industry and trade unions probably helps and promotes the debate in Parliament. I don't see that as a problem. What I do see as a problem is where they are simply there perhaps to just gain access and I think one of the ways of dealing with that is simply to declare and make it absolutely clear. And I think if all the companies involved with that lobbying company were declared I suspect you would find quite a lot of reticence.

PETER SHORE: Thank you.

1553. TOM KING: Can I just ask a quick question, because I think you were here when MSF were giving their evidence and had given us a paper calling for strict political balance and gender balance in the appointments to—I think health boards they were talking about, possibly health Trusts as well. As a Member of Parliament and your own particular area, is your experience that the new system which actually has tended rather to exclude politicians, whatever party—locally elected politicians—and go rather more for people with real experience and merit in the Health Service, has it led to a significant improvement in, for instance, hospital Trust performance?

IAIN DUNCAN-SMITH: I think undoubtedly that it has. I know that this will be a party political point and will be seen as such but my general view is that the dilemma lies in the fact that they are essentially now producing much more information, much more in the public domain, it is possible to get to annual reports and the way that they perform in a much easier way than it was previously, and I remember the old elected bodies, for all their great up-front seeming accountability actually probably were far less accountable in many senses than the present bodies. There is bound to be a dispute about that. My point is that rather than try and row back from that and make, you know, the old system the norm, I would say why not build on what we have already got and if it is a concern that there are too many people that are appointed to these bodies, why not eventually go down the road of making one of these people eventually elected, of some sorts. I think you can build on that by perhaps even making the chairman elected—just one person who then is accountable to their local electorate. But there are ways of building, is what I would say, rather than destroying it and I think by and large there is a great deal more information available—you have got to find ways actually of making certain it is accessed.

TOM KING: Thank you.

1554. LORD NOLAN: Thank you very much indeed. You have been very interesting.

Mr. Campbell-Savours, may I first of all thank you not only for coming along this morning but for the enormous diligence and thoroughness with which you have prepared the submission that you are going to put before us. Its only fault, I think, so far as the members of the committee are concerned, is that we have got about forty-five minutes, we hope, with you and there is material here to keep us hard at work for very much longer than that. But we will, I assure you, go through it all with the care it deserves. I think in the time that we have before us we will hope to concentrate on the questions that the committee is immediately addressing for the purposes of its first report. Was there anything you wished to add to the material by way of a brief opening statement, or would you like to go straight into questions?

DALE CAMPBELL-SAVOURS MP

DALE CAMPBELL-SAVOURS, MP: Well, I would like to spend perhaps three or four minutes reading a statement because I think that I should place on the record essentially the recommendations that I am making—perhaps not in the detail that I make them but certainly a few words.

Can I say that I have been in Parliament for fifteen years, I have been a member of the Select Committee on Members' Interests for nine years, I was a Member of the

Public Accounts Committee for twelve years, a member of the Procedure Committee for six years and a member of the Agricultural Select Committee for one year and I spent two years on the Labour front bench. I had to resign for reasons of ill-health.

Can I then perhaps just set out basically what my recommendations are? The come up in the form of five different reports *Members' Private Interests: Code of Conduct; Ministers' Private Interests; Ministerial Accountability to Parliament in the Context of Lobbying; Lords' Pecuniary Interest* and *The Registration and Declaration of Trade Union Sponsorship by members of Parliament and the Local Register.* I am recommending:

1. That an Ethics Registrar be established to head up an ethics secretariat to advise and to investigate complaints into breaches of a code of conduct for MPs and to report to Parliament.

2. That the Ethics Registrar would carry out enquiries into the conduct of Ministers where appropriate and report to the Prime Minister and the Chairman of the Privileges Committee.

3. That this committee, the Nolan Committee, should consider the broad principles governing penalties for breach of the code of conduct.

4. That the pre-election declaration be considered, which has been already discussed at earlier meetings.

5. That consultancy advocacy by Members of Parliament be prohibited whether it be for a lobbying company or through direct employment by the client.

6. That Members be prohibited from being shareholders, directors or non-executive directors of lobbying companies.

7. That Members with other forms of consultancies be required to register their contract.

8. That amounts of money only be registered where Members are acting as consultants in an advisory capacity or where substantial contributions are made towards general election campaigns.

9. That the committee should recommend shareholding thresholds, both for

   a. registration in the Register of Members' Interests; and

   b. in the determination of what restrictions should be placed on MPs in their use of Parliamentary proceedings and their rights of access to Ministers in the context of lobbying.

On the question of trade unions and sponsorship by Members of Parliament and the local register of local political contributions I propose:

10. That there should be a separate local register of donations from trade unions, trade associations, industrial councils, industry and commerce, professional bodies, special fund-raising organisations and perhaps even individuals—I have an open mind about that—to local associations of political parties and constituency parties or local associations.

11. Substantial contributions towards general election funds of particular candidates should be registered nationally in the Register of Members' Interests.

12. I am recommending that the Lords should establish a Register of Members' Interests and adopt a code of conduct governing the use of proceedings.

13. The Nolan Committee, I recommend, should consider the remuneration of working peers.

On the question of accountability to Parliament:

14. That the committee should consider the operations of the Canadian Lobbyist Registration Act.

15. That Ministers should not be allowed to use disproportionate costs in answers to questions, thereby avoiding answering questions on sensitive issues.

16. Ministers should not be allowed to hide behind the distinction between formal and informal engagements for reason of avoiding embarrassment, particularly where lobbying issues are involved.

This is all part of this approach that I have tried to adopt in my documents of developing some accountability on the activities of lobbyists I am recommending:

17. That the Secretary & Research Assistant's Register be published.

18. That more information should be disclosed in the Register of Members' Interests on the location of and activities of Member-related companies.

19. That registration of spouse interests should be introduced.

20. That neither the Privileges nor the Members' Interests Select Committee should have a Government majority because its proceedings are essentially quasi-judicial.

21. That neither Government nor Opposition front bench Members of Parliament should be appointed to either the Privileges Committee or the Members' Interests Select Committee.

Thank you.

LORD NOLAN: Thank you very much.

DALE CAMPBELL-SAVOURS: I am sorry if it went on for a long time, but there is quite a lot of material.

LORD NOLAN: It has covered a great deal of ground. I think if I may now I will ask Professor King to lead us straight into the questions he wanted to put to you.

1555. PROF. ANTHONY KING: Can I just echo what the Chairman said about the comprehensiveness and thoughtfulness of your evidence. I wish we had an afternoon to go through it, rather than only about three-quarters of an hour. Can I begin on a relatively modest point? In your written evidence you gently chide this committee for not addressing the question of the interests of MPs' spouses and I suppose by implication close Members of their family—children and so on. Why do you think we should address that question?

DALE CAMPBELL-SAVOURS: Because there is without doubt evidence based on conversations that some of us have had with individual Members, that some Members' spouses have substantial interests which impinge upon the responsibilities of their spouse Member husbands or wives.

1556. PROF. ANTHONY KING: Without naming names, could you give some examples of the sort of thing that you say goes on?

DALE CAMPBELL-SAVOURS: Some Members have spouses who are directly involved in public relations and organising the lobbying of Ministers and other Members of Parliament. In my brief I think I refer to the fact that only a matter of a couple of weeks ago I was approached by a prominent, well-regarded, well-respected Conservative Member of the House who told me that he had been approached by the spouse of a colleague of his who was involved in one of these companies and that she was asking him to take action in Parliament on a particular matter and he felt embarrassed.

1557. PROF. ANTHONY KING: And what do you think we should try to do about that?

DALE CAMPBELL-SAVOURS: I think that the committee might well recommend the kind of arrangement that I was trying to introduce when I moved the amendment in the Members' Interests Select Committee in 1991, when we were reviewing the rules on registration.

PROF. ANTHONY KING: Which was?

DALE CAMPBELL-SAVOURS: Essentially that there should be a register of spouses' interests where those interests have implications for the conduct of a Member and any actions that the Member might take. So if a Member's wife was involved in public relations or was a consultant to a major company and it was quite clear that it had implications for the conduct of the Member, then it would be registerable. It would not be declarable but it would be registerable.

1558. PROF. ANTHONY KING: Other Members of the MP's family?

DALE CAMPBELL-SAVOURS: One has to draw lines. I think there is a principle involved here. I mean, one could go further, which is what I was arguing in 1983 during the course of the Thatcher Cementation row in Westminster when I sought appointment to the Select Committee on Members' Interests. I was put on it by the Labour whips and having been put on the committee I was able then to argue that there was a need for an enquiry into family registration. However, over the years I have mellowed and I have ended up with a compromise position, which is essentially that spouses interests should

be registered where they are relevant and only where they are relevant.

1559. PROF. ANTHONY KING: On a larger question, in your written evidence you draw an analogy that we have talked about this morning in this room between the Comptroller and Auditor General and the Public Accounts Committee on the one hand and a possible ethics procedure of a similar sort on the other. Could you just say briefly how you describe that kind of apparatus working?

DALE CAMPBELL-SAVOURS: Well, I think what we need is an Ethics Secretariat, headed up by the Ethics Registrar. The Ethics Registrar would, as far as the evidence that I am giving here is concerned, deal with complaints made against Members of Parliament and complaints made against Ministers. In the case of complaints made against Ministers the Ethics Registrar, having carried out an enquiry, would report to the Prime Minister and the Prime Minister would then make what I describe in my report as an unambiguous statement. The problem at the moment is that I do not believe that Prime Ministerial answers when the PM is pressed, in letters or in the House on these matters, are unambiguous, and I quote the example in my evidence which has been submitted to you in the case of the Landy family and Michael Howard. I must make it absolutely clear I am in no way questioning the integrity of Mr. Michael Howard but I do believe that I was entitled to a clear answer from the Prime Minister and I was not given that answer. If there were an Ethics Secretariat headed up by the Ethics Registrar the Registrar would complete his report, he or she would submit it to the Prime Minister, the Prime Minister then would authoritatively be able to make a statement and to deal with concerns in Parliament—a copy of that report—which would never be published—would be passed to the Chairman of the Privileges Committee (or the appropriate committee) and the Chairman of the Privileges Committee would, at his or her discretion, decide upon whether it was to be referred onto the Members of that Committee, dependent on whether it was thought necessary to do so. By that means I think it avoids a lot of public debate, it means that Parliament is reassured, it means that the Prime Minister can give very clear statements—but that of course is only the system as it relates to Ministers for the Crown.

1560. PROF. ANTHONY KING: Can we just pause on that? You have said rather forcibly that the report in question in the case of a Minister would never be published. Why should it never be published—it might raise very important questions of public interest?

DALE CAMPBELL-SAVOURS: Because if the Prime Minister believed, or if the Chairman of the Privileges Committee believed, that there were issues of public interest which had been raised in that report, then he or she, as Chairman of the Privileges Committee, would be able to raise the issue, as I said, at his or her discretion in the committee, and if there were issues of public interest which should be aired, then that committee—as indeed is the case with any parliamentary committee—would be free to publish and report its evidence to the House of Commons. We talk in terms of reporting evidence because that is parliamentary terminology. So the committee would effectively be able to make a statement. One is not closing down debate but what one is doing is avoiding the very adverse publicity that might arise where a Minister inaccurately and unfairly is accused of something which they did not do.

At the end of the day what do the public want? The public want to be assured that standards of propriety are being maintained—that is all. And as long as the mechanisms are in place to secure that, then I think it is quite satisfactory ie the arrangement that I am promoting. But that is only in the case of Ministers.

1561. PROF. ANTHONY KING: Well, exactly. Could you go on and describe how this procedure would operate in the case of Members?

DALE CAMPBELL-SAVOURS: Now, in the case of Members the Ethics Registrar would receive a complaint, as against the present position at the moment where the Clerk to the Select Committee on Members' Interests would receive the complaint. Or the Clerk to the Privileges Committee might receive a complaint, it having been referred by the Speaker of the House of Commons. The Registrar would receive the complaint, the Registrar would carry out the enquiry, the Registrar would then, having produced a report, provide the appropriate committee with a copy of his or her report. Now the appropriate committee would obviously be either the Members' Interests Select Committee or the Privileges Committee, depended on the nature of the complaint that had been made. If the complaint had been made about registration or declaration then obviously it would go to the Members' Interests Select Committee. If it was about wider issues of conduct it might well go to the Privileges Committee. However, I have also in my proposals that I submitted to the committee suggested that they might wish to combine these two committees—it is not necessarily my view, by the way—and have a sub-committee to deal with Members' interests to the Privileges Committee.

The appropriate committee, having received this report which at that stage would not have been published, would then consider the report and if it found the report satisfactory it would effectively make its own statement to the Commons in the form of a very brief report, saying it had received the report, considered the report, regarded the findings of the report acceptable, and it would report to the House of Commons making recommendations for penalty. However, in the event that the Privileges, or the appropriate committee, decided that, in receiving this report, it was dissatisfied with the examination or the enquiries carried out by the Ethics Registrar, they themselves could take evidence—which is their right, as any Parliamentary Committee can—take evidence and if, having taken evidence, they decided that they wanted to publish an alternative report, then they could do so and they could recommend whatever penalty, that they thought might be appropriate or no penalty at all. But when the appropriate committee had published its report it would then be required—critically important—to publish the original Ethics Registrar's report and I did not set out in my document why that is important. It is important for two reasons: firstly, it is important for the public to know that the Registrar (if I can put it crudely) can't be "fixed" and that Parliament is in a position to double-check the reports this particular person might have produced, even though that Registrar would be an officer of the House of Commons in the same way as the Comptroller and Auditor General.

Secondly, it is important for the appropriate Committee to recognise in deliberating on this report that if they try and meddle with the report for political reasons then the public and the media outside would naturally focus on the distinction between the original report and the report that had been produced by the appropriate committee. I think that it is the dynamics in the relationship between these committees and the Registrar which will ensure that we get as near to the truth as is possible in the circumstances. But at the end of the day under my proposals I have safeguarded the right of Parliament to decide on penalty and the right of Parliament to decide on what is finally reported and what——

1562. PROF. ANTHONY KING: A detail—who would be allowed to make a complaint to the Ethics Registrar under your proposed system?

DALE CAMPBELL-SAVOURS: Any person, as is the case at the moment. Under present arrangements any member of the public can approach the Members' Interests Select Committee clerk and make a complaint. Under that procedure the clerk is not required to report it to the committee. He simply has to deal with it as he thinks fit. However, in the case of a Member making a complaint the matter is automatically referred to the Select Committee on Members' Interests. Under this procedure the Ethics Registrar would take on the a responsibility.

1563. PROF. ANTHONY KING: In your papers you make various proposals about things that Members of Parliament ought to be prohibited from doing and one of them touches on the question of consultancy or advice versus advocacy which you have heard us talking about for a considerable period of time. In your written evidence you say "Where Members are directly employed by companies as consultants they should be prohibited from using Parliamentary procedures and exercising their right of access to Ministers where this is in furtherance of their client's interests." Can I ask you what you have in mind when you refer specifically to "Members who are employed by companies as consultants"?

DALE CAMPBELL-SAVOURS: Let me give you a very good example. I have no links at all with British Nuclear Fuels, but I use it as an example. If I were a consultant to British Nuclear Fuels I would not be allowed to advocate on their behalf in the House of Commons, nor would I be allowed to advocate on their behalf with civil servants or Ministers. I would be prohibited from using any Parliamentary proceedings, I would not be allowed to lobby Ministers, facilitate meetings with Ministers, correspond with Ministers, correspond with civil servants, lobby civil servants, or facilitate meetings with civil servants—it would effectively be prohibited activity. I am drawing a distinction there between the consultant who advocates on behalf of his client direct—British Nuclear Fuels in that case—as against the Member of Parliament who advises British Nuclear Fuels. Yes, that would be a permitted activity. However, there would be restrictions placed on what they could do in terms of using Parliament, Parliamentary proceedings and access to Ministers.

1564. PROF. ANTHONY KING: Can I interrupt, I probably did not make my question quite clear. I understand that part of it—it is the emphasis on directly employed by companies as consultants. Suppose that you were a director of British Nuclear Fuels—would, under your proposals, you be prohibited from using Parliament in this way? If the answer to that question is "no" how do you make the distinction?

DALE CAMPBELL-SAVOURS: How? Because the person employed as a consultant is employed to use

Parliamentary proceedings. The person employed as a director of a company is employed in a director function—their function is to operate as a director—and in the case of the director of British Nuclear Fuels even there I would be introducing a restriction because if you look under Category 4 and 5—non-executive directors and directors of companies—I am arguing again there that they would be denied access to Ministers, to lobby Ministers, to facilitate meetings with Ministers, to write to Ministers, and the same with civil servants.

1565. PROF. ANTHONY KING: Leaving British Nuclear Fuels aside, what about Age Concern?

DALE CAMPBELL-SAVOURS: That comes under charities. In the case of charities if a person was a director of a charity and they were a remunerated director of a charity, I see no distinction between that and being director of a company. The case for the charity, Age Concern, can just as well be put by a Member of Parliament who has no connection at all with Age Concern, because we all receive their briefs, we all speak to their briefs, and we all go on committees and speak to their briefs and ask questions in Parliament on the basis of their briefs. We don't need to be paid to perform that function.

1566. PROF. ANTHONY KING: Could I ask you in a similar vein about your proposed prohibitions in the case of specifically lobbying companies? What is a lobbying company for your purposes?

DALE CAMPBELL-SAVOURS: Well, I heard some of the early exchanges when you were taking evidence from Nigel Forman and also Peter Luff in this particular area. I remain—I must confess—as confused as perhaps you are about the distinction between a lobbying company and a public relations company where the public relations company is actually operating within Westminster. However, it is an area of activity which based on "cab-rank" principles would require a Member to represent a client with whom they had no direct contract. Direct contract in the sense that they were not employed directly by that client. So we are talking really about professional lobbyists, people who in Canada would be referred to as "Tier 2"—I think you perhaps know the distinction already.

1567. PROF. ANTHONY KING: Could I ask you about the specific case of Peter Luff? He was very forthcoming—I think you were present on that occasion—very forthcoming about what his situation was and he actually runs a company and ran a company before he became a Member of Parliament that might be described as a lobbying company. What in your view should be done about him?

DALE CAMPBELL-SAVOURS: Well, I listened very closely to the questions asked by Tom King of Mr. Luff on that particular issue and I did so because the recommendations that I am making have implications for his relationship with that company and I can see no way round the difficulty. The reality is that Mr. Luff, under the proposals that I am making to this committee, would no longer be able to have a direct relationship with his lobbying company. I answer it directly because Tom King's question to Peter Luff on that matter was very pertinent to my case.

1568. PROF. ANTHONY KING: Would you be prepared to phase in changes of this kind?

DALE CAMPBELL-SAVOURS: As I have said in the reports that I have submitted, this document here, is a first step in reality actually setting—I mean, I have been working on this obviously for quite a long time, long before (if I might modestly say) the Nolan Committee was set up—this has been an area of historic interest to me. I can actually see contradictions in my own document. If we were to sit here and discuss this for several hours I am sure we would actually begin to focus on the areas where I can see other problems, because they are there—if I can just give you one of them—the advisory consultant of British Nuclear Fuels. It might be argued that there are certain proceedings in Parliament which could be used by that Member but you know it is all part of the debate that is taking place. So what I am really saying is that there is room for flexibility in what I am proposing here and that might be an area where there is flexibility, because there are implications for someone's income.

1569. PROF. ANTHONY KING: Could I just choose one final question from the 200 other ones that I have and it relates to your deep concern, clearly, about Ministers meeting with lobbyists and a lot of your written evidence deals with that. Can you explain to members of the committee why you think the question of Ministers meeting with lobbyists is so especially important?

DALE CAMPBELL-SAVOURS: This is one of the reasons why I originally got involved in this whole area, because whilst I recognise that Parliament is a good forum in which to advocate a case, the real forum is in the Minister's private office, or at a private function, or wherever a Minister may meet a Member of Parliament or a lobbyist. I think that it is quite obvious that some people—Members who act as consultants—are deliberately avoiding using proceedings in Parliament in favour of direct contacts with Ministers. It interestingly came out during the course of the evidence being given the other day by George Younger, because he was asked—I think by Mr. Shore—I think he was asked, you'll know, "What are your views? What are your feelings about, if you have a pecuniary interest, actually getting up and talking about it on the floor of the house, advocating it?" There was a sort of hesitancy in his response, he was sort of saying "Well, you know, it is not really the way one should do these things". There was a sort of reticence in being prepared to use proceedings in Parliament. However, when he was directly asked whether he would go and actually talk to a Minister about it, there was a slight pause and then the answer came "yes". So in other words, what we have, are Members of Parliament who do not really want to be seen to be advocating in Parliament openly and publicly in front of the television cameras where 52 million people could watch them doing it, where the Minister is sitting on the bench listening to what they are having to say, because the process of advocacy obviously requires someone to listen and to absorb information that is being provided by the advocate, but they are perfectly prepared to go into a government department and advocate the case. I think that is going on extensively.

Secondly, there was a very interesting excerpt in the tape that was taken by the *Sunday Times* on the Terrace of the House of Commons when the *Sunday Times* journalist interviewed Mr. Bill Walker. This is what he said.

"I can certainly find out what the reported incidences are. I can either table Parliamentary questions .. but the most effective way is probably . . ."

tape stops.

LORD NOLAN: Mr. Campbell-Savours, I hesitate to interrupt you, but is this the subject of any other enquiry elsewhere?

DALE CAMPBELL-SAVOURS: It is being referred to in the Privileges Committee.

LORD NOLAN: I do not think it would be right for us to discuss something here that is before the Committee of Privileges.

DALE CAMPBELL-SAVOURS: All right then. Could I put it to you, Lord Nolan, that I am not necessarily seeking to elicit a response from you, I am simply drawing attention to the fact that a Member of Parliament has stated, according to this tape, that he would be reluctant to put down a PQ—it is better if I write a letter to Ministers. What I am arguing here is that Members of Parliament very often will not put down PQs, they will not ask a question in Parliament, they will actually write a letter to a Minister to get a response, if it is that they are representing their own private interests.

1570. PROF. ANTHONY KING: What I am not clear about is what could be done about that—what recommendations we could make that would deal with that.

DALE CAMPBELL-SAVOURS: Well, as far as directors, non-executive directors, directors of charities, major shareholders in companies where the threshold is to be set and in other certain conditions, that would be prohibited activity. One would not be able to do it. In other words, if I was a director of some company or a major shareholder in that company, I would not be able to write to a Minister. It would be in breach of the code. I would not be able to further my private interest in that particular way.

I think this is quite a modest reform because, of course, it allows the Member to actually still use proceedings in Parliament to advocate their case but in the conditions whereby we can all see them doing it. We know he is a director, or she is a director, of company Y, we can see them advocating, we can see the whole process, but what we cannot see is where the letters are sent to Ministers and the replies that are being given. I have to say, and I use my words very carefully, I would suggest to your Committee, Lord Nolan, that they may care to ask the Privileges Committee and the Members' Interests Select Committee whether they might be prepared to let your members have sight of letters that they may have at the moment that were passed between Members and Ministers, because I think that any such correspondence would have a major bearing on your enquiry in this particular area. It would prove my case.

1571. ANNE WARBURTON: Might I ask one or two questions about the mechanics of your concept of an Ethics Registrar. First, I think it is perhaps relevant, what is your own view about in the future whether there should be both a Privileges Committee and a Members' Interests Committee? You indicate there might be a change there. What do say yourself?

DALE CAMPBELL-SAVOURS: I was not on the Privileges Committee but on the Members' Interests Committee, as I have said in my report, for a long period,

and it operated without rancour and without trouble. There was a great deal of cross-voting that went on in that committee, and I think I produced for you somewhere in the evidence a division where the Labour Member Robert Adley voted with me on a very, very sensitive amendment on spouse registration. I actually think that the Members' Interests Select Committee can function properly in certain conditions. The problem is that it has now become discredited. First because of the way that the reforms on Lloyds were bulldozed through to reverse the Committee's decisions that were taken in 1992 because we changed the rules in 1992 on the registration of Lloyds interests, reversed despite the fact that a large number of Members of Parliament had registered their interest in Lloyds. It was bulldozed through the Committee, it created tremendous resentment, and then, of course, the Government, if I might use the term, like fools went and put a Government Whip on the Committee. It was the most stupid thing they could ever have done because what they did was to completely undermine the workings of the committee and now the committee is effectively discredited, certainly its reports are, as far as many of us are concerned. But it does not mean that it cannot work. I believe that the Members' Interests Committee can function under the new regime that I am promoting.

Secondly, I think that the Privileges Committee—I have no experience of it apart from once giving evidence to it in 1981—clearly can work although, again as I point out in my evidence, it was discredited when it was set up laden down with pecuniary interests to adjudicate on a matter which you now have taken over responsibility for. If you remember, I was one of those Members of Parliament in August who made a point of repeatedly surfacing on national television to discredit the work of the Committee because we were worried that they could not do what you are now doing in this Committee because it was riddled with pecuniary interests.

So as long as we can get over those problems then I think the present structure can be maintained, but if it is that the Committee is guided towards combining the two then obviously there will have to be a sort of Members' Interests sub-committee to the Privileges Committee. My personal preference is to retain the two within the regime of an Ethics Registrar. I think it will work perfectly well as it has over the years before these latest difficulties.

1572. ANNE WARBURTON: Thank you very much. You mention in your paper on Ministers' Interests that if there is any problem there it should go to the Ethics Registrar, but what if a Minister is in the Lords?

DALE CAMPBELL-SAVOURS: Under the recommendations I make for reforming this area in the House of Lords, I also propose a code of conduct. That code of conduct would equally apply. I see no distinction; they are both Houses of Parliament.

ANNE WARBURTON: Yes, "An Ethics Registrar shall be a servant of Parliament and not of one House or the other".

DALE CAMPBELL-SAVOURS: Yes, servant of Parliament.

1573. ANNE WARBURTON: Finally, could I just ask this. Your pre-election declaration concept. I was just asking myself with the questions that you envisage, why pre-election?

DALE CAMPBELL-SAVOURS: I have thought long and hard about this and I will tell you what was behind it. It is that proceedings in Westminster are very often so divorced from the electorate, and I was trying to establish some kind of principle which the electorate in one's constituency would understand, would comprehend, with which they could identify and by which they could measure the conduct of their own Member of Parliament. What we do in Westminster is very often obscure to our electorate, and of course the way that the declaration is worded, it is that a constituent of mine would be able to say "You have breached your own pre-election declaration. You said you would not do these things and you have done them". It is my way of devising a local mechanism for measurement by the electorate in a constituency. It is a slight variation on what has been proposed by others, but I see it in a way far more in terms of local accountability.

ANNE WARBURTON: Thank you.

1574. TOM KING: I am not quite clear on that last point. The Pre-Election Declaration is one of what Members' interests are, is that the idea?

DALE CAMPBELL-SAVOURS: The Pre-Election Declaration would not require the detailing of interests.

TOM KING: What does it involve?

DALE CAMPBELL-SAVOURS: It is a broad statement on principles that you accept that you will not conduct yourself in a way whereby you allowed your private interests to conflict with your——

TOM KING: I have it here, this is complying with the code of conduct.

DALE CAMPBELL-SAVOURS: There are three points to it. It is a general statement, it does not invade people's privacy, but it is a measure by which the local electorate could determine whether they believe that their Member has acted properly or improperly without leaving it to Parliament to determine. It presumes people at local level will make their own judgments.

1575. TOM KING: How would that be pursued by the local electorate if it was maintained locally?

DALE CAMPBELL-SAVOURS: In its simplest form in the letter to the editor—My MP has breached

A. He has not complied with the code of conduct in relation to registration and declaration.

B. He has not complied with his undertaking to conduct himself in such a way as to avoid his private interests conflicting with his public duties.

1576. TOM KING: Those letters, if I may say so, are quite frequently written by our opponents in the local press, it is part of the system, but there is no more sanction behind it than that.

DALE CAMPBELL-SAVOURS: Yes, but it is very hard. I do not want to go into a particular incident that happened with an MP in the period before I came in in the 1970s where he was re-elected by his own constituents despite the fact that he was in difficulties. It might well be that it was hard for members of the public at that time to actually measure to what extent he had erred from the straight and narrow, and I just think that constituents need a way of measuring conduct so that they can make an estimate as whether they are satisfied that their Member has acted properly or improperly. There is suspicion that in Parliament when we do these things that perhaps we are making a political judgment.

1577. TOM KING: You would need to have some way of adjudicating it, would you not? There would have to be some declaration and there would be a sanction behind it. I mean, there would have to be somebody determining whether it was a valid charge.

DALE CAMPBELL-SAVOURS: As far as local assessment of breach is concerned I cannot say more than I have. I think it is a very subjective view that the individual would take as to whether these rules had been breached. However, nationally the Ethics Registrar might actually use it as the anvil almost on which to actually make his or her final adjudication. They may say that you are in breach of your pre-election declaration. They may not choose to use it in that context, but I suppose it is possible, it could be used in that context.

1578. PETER SHORE: Can I bring you back, Mr Campbell-Savours, to the most helpful and certainly most mind-clearing part of your evidence, which is the financial connections that Members of Parliament may have and the regulations of their conduct which would then follow from their financial connections. You have, in my view, very correctly identified the particular advantage that a Member of Parliament has and may offer to, as it were, a possible employer in his very position as a Member of Parliament. That is to say, he has access to Ministers. Access to Ministers certainly is the leading, I think, asset that a Member of Parliament has.

What worries me is not that you have identified this, which you have done extremely well, but that of all the activities of a Member of Parliament perhaps the most difficult to control and to make visible is a Member's access to a Minister because he may call on him in his private room, he may write him a letter which is private in any event, and so on, he may invite him to a dinner party in a closed group. How do you face this really very practical problem?

DALE CAMPBELL-SAVOURS: You cannot police it in detail, but what you can do is if you were to establish a code of conduct based on these principles the Minister would be aware of them. I think it would simply make Ministers more diligent about the conditions in which they were prepared to listen to people lobbying or pressing their pecuniary interests. It must be difficult at the moment for a Minister who sits down at the dinner table, someone raises a subject and it is going through the Minister's mind—this is a friend of mine, I cannot stop my friend in mid-track, I am a little embarrassed about what he is talking about. I think Ministers probably often do get embarrassed when they are approached by colleagues. If it is realised that it is a breach of the code of conduct I think both parties to what would have been that conversation will simply not get involved and I think it avoids a great deal of embarrassment, and, of course, it avoids abuse where it may have lead to an abuse. It is almost a self-regulatory arrangement over and above a code of conduct. We can demand compliance but we cannot police compliance without invading people's privacy, and I think that is wrong.

PETER SHORE: I am sure it would have a considerable effect if it was a Parliamentary code upon Ministers as well as backbenchers.

DALE CAMPBELL-SAVOURS: If I may just say one word. What would happen if it ever came out that a conversation had taken place between a Member of Parliament and a Minister?

1579. PETER SHORE: How would you deal with accusations that such contacts had taken place? Who would, as it were, investigate to see whether in fact it was a smear or a truthful allegation?

DALE CAMPBELL-SAVOURS: I think it would depend on the circumstances what arose as a result of the conversation, but you would never be able to bring it down to a fine science whereby you would know absolutely what had happened in any particular relationship. It is impossible to do so. To some extent I have tried to draw on these issues in all these parliamentary questions that I have been tabling and I understand that some members of your Committee may have been receiving them, I think there was a hundred or so of them. I have to tell you that there was a very interesting series which came in yesterday afternoon as well. I have been trying to draw out to what extent Ministers are prepared to talk freely about the lobbying of a department and of civil servants, and it seems to me that there is not much information currently made available. It is a sort of secret world that we know very little about, and of course I have come up with some rather weak recommendations in that particular area but I only ask that you consider them.

1580. PETER SHORE: Can I now take you to the Ethics Register and the Committee of Privileges or Members' Interests Select Committee. Am I right in thinking that you feel that the composition of a Privileges Committee should be changed so that there is never a majority for the governing party?

DALE CAMPBELL-SAVOURS: I understood, based on a conversation that I had with a colleague last week, that there was no government majority on the Privileges Committee which is why I qualified it in the document. There is certainly a government majority on the Members' Interests Select Committee, but I think that there should be no government majority on either of these committees because they are quasi judicial, and the chairman should have the casting vote.

1581. PETER SHORE: Did you also say that in your view no member of the Government and no member of the Shadow Cabinet should sit upon the Privileges Committee?

DALE CAMPBELL-SAVOURS: I believe that no member of the Government, no one from the Whips Office, and no member from the Opposition front bench should sit on either committee, yes.

1582. PETER SHORE: You mention the Whips Office, is that a problem?

DALE CAMPBELL-SAVOURS: It is certainly a problem in the Members' Interests Select Committee at

the moment. If I may say in a more responsible mode, I did sort of protest the other day in the Members' Interests Select Committee to what was going on. I really take quite strong exception to what is going on in the Members' Interests Select Committee. I was on it for all those years. It was excellently chaired by Sir Geoffrey Johnson-Smith who gave evidence the other week. He ran a very, very good committee that, in my view, was objective. It has now lost that objectivity because the Whip is basically there representing the interests of those who would not, in my view, be particularly objective on the inquiries that are currently under way.

1583. PETER SHORE: But that is the normal thing to happen with either the Privileges Committee or the Select Committee of Members' Interests.

DALE CAMPBELL-SAVOURS: It is unprecedented on the Members' Interests Select Committee. I do not think it has ever happened on the Privileges Committee. I have not checked that but I would be very surprised if it ever had.

PETER SHORE: Thank you.

DALE CAMPBELL-SAVOURS: Could I ask that I be pressed on Labour sponsorship because I am very concerned that some of the questions that Tom King has been asking have not been answered properly and I think there are a number of issues in that regard that have to be placed on the public record.

1584. LORD NOLAN: If you wish to add to your previous answers, please do so. We are running over time but if that does not embarrass you it does not, within reason, embarrass us either.

DALE CAMPBELL-SAVOURS: On the question of the nomination of Members of Parliament, can I say that I have just been through my reselection procedure where every member of the Workington Constituency Labour Party had the right to vote. Every vote in the whole constituency was cast in my favour. There was no nomination from a UNISON branch, and I am UNISON sponsored, none at all in the whole constituency. Indeed, not only did they not nominate, they did not even have delegates to nominate, yet this is the organisation that I am being told repeatedly over recent weeks is actually manipulating selections. They were not even involved in my selection at all. They were not involved in my original selection for Parliament. That is the first critically important issue.

Secondly, I have never ever in all my years in Parliament ever known any candidate ever have any figure anywhere near £6, £7, £8,000 which was quoted by Tom King in terms of election campaign support.

TOM KING: No, it was quoted to us.

DALE CAMPBELL-SAVOURS: It may well have been but the information that you were given was incorrect. The reality is that the most I have ever known is £3,500. It very rarely would be that amount of money. In the great majority of cases it would be £1,500, and sometimes even less, in fact very often even less.

LORD NOLAN: If it helps we did have a lot of evidence from UNISON, I do not know if you have seen it.

DALE CAMPBELL-SAVOURS: Yes I did, I was here when they gave it. It is just that I feel that there is a sort of slant being put on trade union sponsorship which is quite unrealistic in the sense that unions are being presented as organisations that are able to manipulate Members of Parliament.

Can I say in answer to the questions that you asked them the other week on Clause 4, there is no way that my union would ever tell me which way to vote on Clause 4. There is no way that they would interfere with me. I took a contrary position to the union on abortion legislation, on embryo legislation, on the age of consent, on a number of issues, and there has never been any question at all of my judgment being in any way interfered with. I think that what is happening over the sponsorship debate is that Conservative Members of Parliament, to put it bluntly, have realised that if they want to justify commercial payments, receipts through consultancy and directorships, they have to do it in the context of a debate about Labour sponsorship. I know that is happening. That is why this debate takes place. It surfaced yesterday, interestingly enough when I left here at 11.30 to go to my Agriculture Select Committee where we were in the ludicrous position in the Agriculture Select Committee where two members of the committee, sponsored by the Transport and General Workers Union, actually declared their sponsorship by the Transport and General Workers Union. During an inquiry into agricultural workers' pay, they declared that they were sponsored they receive £600 a year in their constituency parties. Meanwhile the chairman of the committee who is in farming did not have to say anything at all. I am not criticising the chairman in any way at all. I do not think he should have to declare it because everyone knows it. He also registers it. Fundamental if we are looking at these rules is the distinction between registration and declaration, but I do not expect the chairman of the committee to walk in every day and declare that he is a farmer. Nor does he and nor should he have to do so. The point is that those two Members who are receiving £600 for their constituency parties found themselves in a position where they were declaring £600 to their constituencies and meanwhile the farmer, who was in the chair, did not have to say anything at all. I think it is ludicrous and it is going on all the time in Parliament.

LORD NOLAN: Thank you very much, Mr Campbell-Savours, I think we have got your point on that. If we could please now move on because there are two or three other Members who have not had a chance to ask you questions.

1585. TOM KING: Can I just step in seeking to ask a question I have not asked, I would like to put a supplementary. The UNISON evidence that was given I thought was very honest. They made a completely open statement of what they were doing, and the figures that I have quoted since were the figures they gave in evidence. The union officials, who came here to give evidence to this committee in good faith, I think were seeking to address the issues, because there are real issues, and I did hear about the incident yesterday and I admire the Members for declaring their interests. I do not quite see what the problem is. I think it was about rates of agricultural pay. Two union members for the National Union of Agricultural Workers, part of the Transport and General Workers Union. I think it is absolutely proper, and I thought under the evidence you have given to us that you would say there must be greater transparency and that they should give it and I applaud them for it. I do not see it as a matter for resentment.

DALE CAMPBELL-SAVOURS: Well, I am not objecting to them . . .

LORD NOLAN: Can we have one answer please otherwise I will leave you and Mr King to debate this elsewhere.

DALE CAMPBELL-SAVOURS: I am not in any way suggesting that that information should be hidden from the public record. What I am arguing is that it should be logged in a local register available in my constituency whereby monies of an equal nature paid to the local Conservative Association are equally registered along with that payment from the union to my party. I do not believe it is a matter for Parliament because I am unaffected by this arrangement to pay monies to my constituency. I am utterly unaffected. Indeed, I use my union because I ring them and ask them if they can provide me with briefings in areas where I might want to speak and where I want more information to substantiate the case that I already would wish to advocate.

LORD NOLAN: Thank you very much indeed and thank you for all the other information you have given us. We have kept you a long time but we are grateful for all your hard work.

TUESDAY 14 FEBRUARY 1995

Members Present:

The Rt. Hon. The Lord Nolan (Chairman)

Sir Clifford Boulton GCB
Sir Martin Jacomb
The Rt. Hon. Tom King CH MP
The Rt. Hon. Peter Shore MP

The Rt. Hon. The Lord Thomson of Monifieth KT DL
Sir William Utting CB
Dame Anne Warburton DCVO CMG
Diana Warwick

Witnesses:

Sir Jeremy Beecham, Chairman, Association of Metropolitan Authorities, Elgar Jenkins OBE, Leader, Conservative Group, Association of District Councils, David Heath CBE, Leader, Liberal Democrat Group, Association of County Councils and Geoffrey Filkin, Secretary, Association of District Councils

Alan Langlands, Chief Executive NHS, John Shaw, Director, and Isabel Nisbet, Deputy Director, Corporate Affairs NHS Executive

Archie Kirkwood MP

1586. LORD NOLAN: Today we continue looking at quangos and we shall be hearing from Mr Alan Langlands, the Chief Executive of the National Health Service. The NHS has been at the eye of the storm as far as board appointments are concerned, and we look forward with interest to Mr Langlands' evidence, particularly in the light of the announcement about improvements to National Health Service appointments procedures which was made this morning. We shall also be hearing from Mr Archie Kirkwood, Member of Parliament, who has been prominent in calling for greater openness in the National Health Service.

First, however, we are pleased to welcome representatives from the local authority associations. It has sometimes been said that the differences between the three main local authority associations make it easier to follow a policy of "divide and rule" towards local authorities. It is particularly impressive, therefore, not only that today's team will give joint evidence on behalf of the three associations, but also that they have achieved scrupulous political balance. The Association of Metropolitan Authorities is represented by Sir Jeremy Beecham, their chairman, who is a Labour supporter, the Association of District Councils is represented by Mr Elgar Jenkins OBE, leader of their Conservative Group, and the Association of County Councils is represented by Mr David Heath, leader of their Liberal Democrat Group; and they are supported by Mr Geoffrey Filkin, Secretary of the Association of District Councils, of whose politics we know nothing.

Sir Jeremy, am I right in thinking that you propose to make an opening statement?

SIR JEREMY BEECHAM, ELGAR JENKINS, DAVID HEATH AND GEOFFREY FILKIN

SIR JEREMY BEECHAM (Chairman, Association of Metropolitan Authorities): Yes, Mr Chairman, a very brief opening statement, if I may.

LORD NOLAN: If you please.

JEREMY BEECHAM: As you rightly say, this is an ecumenical presentation on behalf of local government, although there might be a few independents and the odd Plaid Cymru or Monster Raving Loony Party councillor who feel that they are under-represented this morning. But generally of course the local authority associations do represent local government in its contact with government and also, in terms of representing its members, is in a position to offer advice and guidance, and we seek to do that on some of the issues with which this committee is dealing.

Our approach is to regard three principles as fundamental to our concern with the committee's agenda: they are propriety, transparency and accountability, and we think those three themes must run through consideration of the diverse aspects with which the committee is concerned. We are far from the view that everything in the local government world is perfect, and there are one or two matters which we may identify this morning where we think perhaps our current practice could be improved upon. Nevertheless, we do feel that we have an extensive system of scrutiny which ensures that, for the most part, those three principles are respected in local government practice, and it may be that some of the procedures which are applied in local government could with advantage be applied elsewhere in our system of governance, in terms both of national government and of quangos and other bodies. Indeed, one outcome of the committee's deliberations that we would like to see is something approaching a degree of uniformity of practice, so far as that can be attained, in respect of those three principles. I don't, Mr Chairman, intend to elaborate on the submission that we have made, which is fairly concise, but we would of course be happy to answer questions.

1587. LORD NOLAN: Thank you very much. You have been kind enough to prepare very carefully two separate documents, of which the first sets out concisely and comprehensively the statutory and regulatory provisions which govern the conduct of local authorities' councillors and staff. Are there any particular points on that part of your evidence which you wish to develop at this point? I have one small one which I wish to raise, but, subject to that and subject to any points you have to make on Part I, I was proposing to go on to the particular topics which you discuss in Part 2.

JEREMY BEECHAM: No, I think in general we are content to rest on the document that we have put forward and to deal with questions as they arise.

1588. LORD NOLAN: The one point which I would like to clarify with you occurs at paragraph 1.1. I am afraid this may be very heavy-going for those who haven't got copies of the documents in front of them, but I will try to keep it as general as I can. That is the paragraph in which you say:

> "Responsibility for the discharge of the function remains that of the authority, however, and it cannot avoid liability for e.g. negligence or failure to perform statutory duties because the work is being carried out by someone else on their behalf."

So far, so clear. And you go on:

> "Indeed, the Commission for Local Administration (Ombudsman) has recently confirmed its intention to hold local authorities liable for compensation awarded as a result of maladministration, regardless of whether the complaint relates to work which has been contracted out and the fault is that of the contractor."

Am I right in thinking that the Ombudsman can't, so to speak, order compensation to be paid—that he can only recommend?

JEREMY BEECHAM: That's right, but the experience of most local authorities is that, with whatever reservations we may have about particular findings, almost universally they are accepted and implemented. It is fair to say that that is not absolutely the rule, but in most cases it is the rule.

1589. LORD NOLAN: Yes. Thank you very much. Coming on, if I may, to the second part of your written evidence, you deal first with Members of Parliament and their financial interests and compare the position in Parliament with the position in local government. In your first volume you have set out the rules under the Local Government and Housing Act 1989, which provide for

> "a compulsory register of pecuniary interests of [council] members, to be specified in regulations; non-compliance in disclosure to be a criminal offence; the register to be open for public inspection".

Can you tell us this? Is there a requirement for councillors to spell out the remuneration which they receive under registered employments?

JEREMY BEECHAM: No, there is not. The registration requirement is simply to identify the nature of the interest, but that in itself then precludes the member from participating in a decision-making process and indeed from informal activities which would be prohibited by the code which we all have to subscribe to on taking office.

LORD NOLAN: He is prohibited from voting or taking part. The amount he is paid, therefore, is of no real significance.

JEREMY BEECHAM: That's right.

1590. LORD NOLAN: Yes. How wide does the disqualification from voting go? For example, over matters like the setting of the rate of council tax, everybody?

JEREMY BEECHAM: Everybody, providing they are not more than two months in arrears with their council tax, may participate in that determination.

ELGAR JENKINS (Leader, Conservative Group, Association of District Councils): There is also the question of people who occupy a council house, which can, in some authorities, cause a problem, if you have a large number of members, in terms of having adequate discussion of matters appertaining to council housing. You can actually apply for a dispensation in order to be able to take part in that sort of debate.

DAVID HEATH (Leader, Liberal Democrat Group, Association of County Councils): If I might just expand a little further, there are broad dispensations of other kinds, such as those for the many councillors who have children at schools within their authority area and serve on an education area and clearly it would be inappropriate for them to be disbarred from any consideration of educational matters, although many councillors do make it a practice to declare interest when it is a school at which they have children.

1591. LORD NOLAN: Thank you very much. I now come on to lobbying, which, as you know, has engaged a great deal of our attention, as it has yours. You say in paragraph 1.5 of your second volume:

> "So far as lobbying is concerned, it should be noted that any councillor who had any form of relationship with any lobbying firm would automatically be barred from promoting the interests of the firm or its clients within the authority."

Is there a definition of what is meant here by a lobbying firm, or does the prohibition just follow from the general rules about registration of interests and the exclusion from voting which follows them?

JEREMY BEECHAM: It is the latter position which is effective, and that applies both to formal and informal discussions, and I think it is the case that all the political parties require interests to be declared in political group meetings, which occur in local authorities as well, so that it goes right back to meetings which are not open to the public, too.

1592. LORD NOLAN: And how far does the disqualification extend—of course to voting and I think more generally you said "taking part"? What about informal lobbying of colleagues? Would that be included?

JEREMY BEECHAM: That would be in breach, as well—most emphatically.

1593. LORD NOLAN: Yes. Next I wanted, please, to turn to the monitoring officer, which you refer to in the first part of your paper. This is something which the 1989 Act requires, and his function, as I understand it, is this.

> "He is under a personal duty, if it appears to him that any proposals, decisions or omission by the authority, any of its committees or officers, would give rise either to a contravention of any enactment or rule of law or any code of practice, or to any maladministration or injustice within the Ombudsman's jurisdiction."

He has to prepare a report on such issue and send it to all members of the authority. How he is selected? What sort of people are monitoring officers?

JEREMY BEECHAM: They tend to be, but this is not uniformly the practice, the chief legal adviser to an authority. It can be the chief executive, or indeed it could be another senior officer appointed for the purpose.

LORD NOLAN: So he is an appointee of the council and reports to the council internally.

JEREMY BEECHAM: Yes.

1594. LORD NOLAN: He is not an external regulator. He is something like the compliance officer which nowadays you find in many business organisations.

JEREMY BEECHAM: That's right, yes.

LORD NOLAN: To make sure that, in its own interests if for no better reason, the organisation is keeping within the rules.

JEREMY BEECHAM: Yes.

LORD NOLAN: I see.

ELGAR JENKINS: I don't know, my Lord, whether it is worth saying at this stage, and I expect the experience of my colleagues is the same as mine, that members have become extremely careful to declare interests, sometimes in cases where you think their interests are tangential, you might say, to the matter in hand. I certainly notice that, as local government has grown over the years, and I have been in local government for 24 years or so, therefore the need for the whistle-blower to be there, if you like, is obviously something which is transparent and right, and that the system should have someone like the monitoring officer, but actually the need to call upon that person, I would say, in local government is very rare, and I think that's a point that it might be worth us registering with you. That is not to say that we are all saints or holier than thou, but that is the real scene in which we find all of us work in councils up and down this country.

JEREMY BEECHAM: It can be taken to almost extreme levels. In my own authority, the chairman of the development control sub-committee was a council nominee on the local health authority, and an application for some planning permission came before the development control sub-committee from the health authority and he sat in it, and of course he said he was a council representative on the health authority. The decision was made and the local government ombudsman found maladministration, despite the fact that he was on the health authority and representing the local authority and not the other way round. But that's an indication of the care with which we are all, perfectly properly, having to act these days.

DAVID HEATH (Leader, Liberal Democrat Group, Association of County Councils): I think the strength of the monitoring officer lies in the fact that the relationship between the monitoring officer and the council is based on the statutory duties of the monitoring officer once appointed, and no one could rest on an employer/employee basis. The monitoring officer has not only the ability but the duty to advise the authority on any potential grievance by their codes of conduct, or indeed the law, and cannot be prevented from doing so or advised not to do so by a majority group within the council. It is a robust defence against any manipulation of legal advice—or should be. It's a little early to say how robust

that will prove in practice, but nevertheless clearly the mechanism is there.

1595. LORD NOLAN: Yes. Is there any fear that employees would none the less be reluctant to complain to the monitoring officer about breaches or suspected breaches of which they were aware, for fear of jeopardising their own employment? Is that a fear of which you are aware in the local government service to any great extent?

DAVID HEATH: I am not aware of it. I think quite the reverse. If anything, there would be more of a readiness to do so than in many other services, especially since, although the authority as a whole is the employer, there is no direct management link between the employee and the councillor, and therefore the proper officer—the monitoring officer—can give advice to the authority in a wholly dispassionate way.

LORD NOLAN: Thank you very much.

GEOFFREY FILKIN (Secretary, Association of District Councils): I would add one point, I think. The point has been touched on about implicit self-policing. Because there is a clear national code which members are aware of and have to sign up to, you develop traditions in most authorities of members being vigilant upon each other, and officers as well are aware of their duty actually to try to maintain propriety. I think that is reinforced by the fact that there is external monitoring as well, because, given that we are human beings, the internal monitoring will never be perfect.

1596. LORD NOLAN: Now I wonder if I could turn to the heading "Ministers and Civil Servants". In relation to that topic you say:

"Much emphasis in local government is laid on the need for the proper recording of hospitality"——

you are talking here about gifts and hospitality——

"in whatever form, and the associations would suggest that openness is both the best safeguard so far as the individual is concerned and the most certain way of reassuring the public. It is felt that too great a reliance is put on ministerial discretion, and it is not easy to see why all gifts should not be recorded."

We do have, don't we, in the "Questions of Procedure for Ministers"—I think it is paragraph 81—a requirement that they should at least be reported to the Permanent Secretary? Are you envisaging something more formal and open to inspection than that?

ELGAR JENKINS: Not really, my Lord.

1597. LORD NOLAN: I see. I don't know quite how it works under your rules, but where do you draw the line at hospitality? Is a lunch at the Guildhall attended in an official capacity? Is an invitation by a constituent to go to drinks at his house? Is all that recorded if it is associated in the mind of the recipient with his official position?

ELGAR JENKINS: I think the question here, which brings us back to some of the points we were making earlier, is that it's important that openness should be the fundamental principle. Therefore, we would expect that a member would be open in declaring whatever one of those opportunities that you have laid before us. In fact I was in a council only last week, and the register showed that the chief executive had been given a corkscrew, which you might say is not likely to corrupt anybody, but he dutifully recorded it, and apparently the leader of that council had had a turkey given to him for Christmas, presumably by the local butcher, and he duly recorded it, so perhaps you might say that some of our members in councils take that to an nth degree, but I think the critical thing is that we should be open in recording what we receive, whatever that hospitality may be. Indeed, I think there may well be a case for saying that, if there is any doubt, a member of the public should have an opportunity to consult such a register. I think the most times in life that you are ever confronted with more generous hospitality are if you are in one of these roles. Certainly I have been all these roles at one time or another, first as leader of a council, and I happen to come from Bath, where we have a very large corporate estate of private property, so we do a considerable amount of work involving buying and selling property; secondly, as chairman of a housing committee, where obviously a lot of contractors are interested in housing and housing business; and thirdly, probably, in education, where, if you are building schools, supplying schools, again there is a great interest by outside contractors. Certainly in all of those roles perhaps you get more approaches in major hospitality terms than you would in some other roles of council life, and my experience is that that was true.

DAVID HEATH: There is, Chairman, a clear test laid out in the Code of Local Government Conduct, which is whether the impression of impropriety is given to an ordinary member of the public by the acceptance of any gift, and I think that that is the key test; and there is implicit in that a sense of scale, so that a weak cup of tea in a village hall probably would not be held by any reasonable member of the public to be an inducement, whereas a Caribbean holiday from a building contractor might. So there is clearly, as I say, some sort of relevance of the gift to the inducement, or the perception that an inducement might be being offered, and I think that a sensible arrangement could be come to, but clarity is the most important thing.

JEREMY BEECHAM: I think also that in most authorities it is well-established practice that a member, particularly a member with a position of responsibility, should not see, whether it be on council premises or outside, somebody with whom the council might have contractual or other relationship alone, but should always be accompanied by an officer, so that a built-in chaperon is available in such cases.

1598. LORD NOLAN: You are painting a picture of strict limits guarded by the criminal law and, within those limits, a code of conduct, the whole illuminated by what the Americans call "government in the sunshine"—complete openness about what is going on. This is what you recommend and, if I understand you rightly, you are saying that this is reflected in the attitude of local government officials and employees: they know what is expected of them without being complacent.

ELGAR JENKINS: And let's be frank: we have examples of things going wrong like in any other aspect of public life. We are not seeking today to lay down any prescriptive rules. We are really suggesting that the rule of openness and the answer to the question "What will the

public think if we take this hospitality?" are sensible principles that can be applied throughout public life.

DAVID HEATH: And if Parliament in its wisdom feels that they are appropriate for local government, I think it is difficult to argue that they should not apply to other areas of public life on the same basis, amended as required to local circumstances, but as a principle the same sort of rules, or at least the same principles, should apply to all those engaged in public life and certainly in the spending of public funds.

LORD NOLAN: As best practised.

DAVID HEATH: As best practised, yes.

LORD NOLAN: To be aimed at everywhere, though not, of course, always going to be achieved.

DAVID HEATH: Precisely so.

GEOFFREY FILKIN: There is the guidance which members should take into account when they are deciding what they do, knowing that, if they get their decision wrong, they could be found at fault by the Commissioner for Local Administration, which, both for a member and for a council, is properly treated as a serious black mark.

1599. LORD NOLAN: Now may I turn, please, to the subject of taking up employment after a period in office? You describe the rules for civil servants as "proper and appropriate" and you contrast in that respect, in your view, the position as regards Ministers. I am not sure what the position is as regards officers or members of local authorities in taking up employment.

JEREMY BEECHAM: I don't think it's satisfactory at the moment in respect of officers and I would like to see us move to a system more akin to the Civil Service. I think this is true of all the associations, that we feel there ought to be a system under which officers cannot depart from an authority and then, without permission and perhaps after a reasonable period, take up employment with those with whom they have had dealings on behalf of the authority. That is something I think we do need to improve in our present situation.

So far as members are concerned, the only restriction is that of employment by the authority on which they have themselves served: they cannot be employed for a period of 12 months. That is probably all right, but it doesn't cover the point of a leader of a council or chairman of a major committee possibly also following the route of an officer of the authority or a Minister in taking up employment with or an association with organisations with which they have had dealings in their elected capacity, and I think we should be looking to extend the code in respect of such positions.

ELGAR JENKINS: But I think we might be thought, on the principle of anti-corruption legislation, that you could have an offence if it was shown that the employment was in consequence of favours extended while you were a committee chairman or holding some other senior office of the council, so I am not sure quite how much it needs to be strengthened in that regard. And the people probably mostly in the position to benefit, as is suggested by Sir

Jeremy, would of course be those who chaired major committees, of the three I have listed particularly, who would be most likely to be handling major contracts within the council. The individual councillor of course has no power to make decisions. Even chairmen have no power to make decisions. They are just in a better place to influence in that position which they hold, as it has to be decided by the whole committee, or the whole council in some cases, to confirm such a contract.

1600. LORD NOLAN: Would it be fair to say that some chairmen are stronger than other chairmen?

ELGAR JENKINS: I think, Chairman, that might be so, without any doubt.

LORD NOLAN: I take your point.

JEREMY BEECHAM: It is an area that, I think, raises concerns and should be further investigated.

TOM KING: Just to indicate that sometimes you have arrangements when authority is delegated to a chairman.

ELGAR JENKINS: We delegate to an officer in consultation with the members. There can be no delegation to an individual member.

TOM KING: With respect, I think you will find in some authorities, for what are considered more minor matters, it may be delegated to a much smaller group, and that might include the chairman perhaps and one other, and an officer.

ELGAR JENKINS: To a sub-committee, definitely that is so, but there is no situation in local government when you can actually delegate to a member. It has to be, if there is a delegation, not to a committee or a sub-committee; it has to be to an appropriate officer in consultation with, usually, the two members of the majority party.

JEREMY BEECHAM: There used to be a system which is called chairman's action, but that was subsequently deemed unlawful and it is no longer available.

DAVID HEATH: Any executive action that is taken can only be taken by an officer of the council. It cannot be taken by elected members. Elected members can advise and can propose, but the officer actually executes the action.

ELGAR JENKINS: It is possible, my Lord, that Mr King might be thinking of situations where, if the small group does take a decision, that small group could be in a very powerful position. I think the protection there of course is that small groups are composed of more than one party, there are opportunities to refer matters back to a committee or back to council, and of course the monitoring officer, if he had any doubt, or the legal officers, would step in to comment upon it, so I think we have adequate protections in local government to guard against that situation.

GEOFFREY FILKIN: Just to emphasise the point, members only have authority when they are acting in committee.

DAVID HEATH: Just to re-emphasise the point, Chairman, that Sir Jeremy made, I think there is a hole in our arrangements at the moment in terms of officers receiving employment with contractors after finishing council service. It is complicated, I have to say, by the provisions of compulsory competitive tendering, which I won't bore the committee with, but nevertheless there is a flow of officers between councils and private contractors or companies which are formed from internal working organisations. We do need to look in detail at how any proposition might be framed in order to cope with that, but it is something that all three associations recognise.

1601. LORD NOLAN: Thank you very much. You envisage then, as you make plain in your paper, the possibility of some such regulation, and I think you envisage something for Ministers, if we may go back to them, which in your view should be at least as strong as if not stronger than in the case of councillors. Why stronger?

JEREMY BEECHAM: If stronger, because Ministers have executive powers and councillors, as we have just heard, don't, individually.

ELGAR JENKINS: Maybe what lay behind us mentioning that was that sometimes the scale of operation of Ministerial decisions in terms of contracts is much larger than perhaps the scale that councillors might be involved in. We are putting this forward as a suggestion for consideration. It is obviously a matter for your committee to decide whether that is appropriate or not and in what way it should be carried out.

JEREMY BEECHAM: It is also a question of public perception.

1602. LORD NOLAN: Thank you. Now may I turn, and I shan't be much longer before I invite the other members of the committee to put their questions, to quangos? In the second volume of your evidence you speak of the difference between the level of remuneration for elected councillors and that of appointees to quangos. What had you in mind in saying that? Is there an overall discrepancy or are there individual cases that bother you?

DAVID HEATH: You can't generalise about quangos, Chairman, and I think we also ought to say that this is not a local government whinge about councillors' payments, because I think that would start us on the wrong footing, but there are very substantial discrepancies between what is felt to be appropriate for members of local authorities and what is thought to be appropriate for members of quangos. Just to give you some idea of that, there is a very complicated system within local government as to how we work out individual members' allowances, but on a broad basis in county councils and metropolitan authorities the amount of money that is distributable amounts to about £3,065 per annum, I think I am right in saying, per councillor. On all but the largest districts that falls to £1,500. If you compare that with various quangos—I am not sure that I have up-to-date figures—but certainly on health authorities it is £5,000-odd per member and health service trusts £5,000 per member. The chairs of those various authorities, who may be held to have similar responsibilities to the leader of a major local authority, will be paid, I don't know, £15,000 to £18,000, that sort of area. Local authorities are in a different league.

Just to give you an anecdotal example of the lack, to use the cliché, of a level playing field, I, for my sins, am a county councillor. I am also chairman of a police authority. If I leave my house in the morning and drive towards County Hall, Taunton, I am paid a reimbursement for my mileage of just over 20p a mile. If I choose, on the other hand, to drive towards police headquarters in my role as chairman of the police authority, I am paid 35p a mile. The car doesn't know where it's going, but nevertheless it apparently uses a different amount of petrol. Were I to be a Member of the House of Commons or the House of Lords, I understand it's nearer 70p a mile. That sort of discrepancy is hard to justify. I think our suggestion is simply that of course we don't expect there to be absolutely level remuneration across the board, but there might be some comparable sums involved and there might be some general guidelines which are applicable to public life in all its aspects and which could be agreed at national level, which would remove the suspicion that some areas are favoured above others in public life.

ELGAR JENKINS: I have declared to you, and I will declare now to the other board members, that I have been a chairman of a health authority and am currently chairman of an NHS trust, but what I am going to say now I don't think is related to that, but as we are all being transparent and honest here, I think it is fair to say it at this stage. We also ought to add one thing to you, that all the comments made by my colleague are quite right, but that the government has just recently allowed local authorities to decide the level of payments which they make, which is a step forward, we think, and something the local authority associations has been asking for for some time, to allow us, as it were, to compensate in some way for the immense workloads that fall upon, particularly, senior members. Thus the new arrangements will allow local authorities to make adjustments, having regard to the special allowances payments made to members, although we are still bound on the car side, I think, under other regulations which are still in place.

JEREMY BEECHAM: But the important point is that the same rules as to disclosure and propriety should apply to these organisations as to local government, and at the moment they don't.

1603. LORD NOLAN: You suggest the creation of a Public Appointments Commission, a development, as I understand it, of the Public Appointments Unit, as one by which key appointments could be scrutinised. You say that there might be merit in an appointment code which would guide the process towards plurality. I wasn't quite sure in what sense you used the word "plurality". Was that a plurality of appointees of different political shades?

JEREMY BEECHAM: Political, gender, ethnic—the mix—and indeed geography.

DAVID HEATH: There is a strong perception, Chairman—I will put it no stronger than "perception"—of which I think members are aware, that that is not the case at the moment, that there is a bias in the appointments system. I think that that needs to be addressed as a perception, if not a reality, and that is what we are urging.

LORD NOLAN: Yes.

ELGAR JENKINS: I think particularly what we were thinking of is numbers of men and women of race and backgrounds of employment—in other words, a more reasonable reflection of society itself in terms of the background of people who serve on various public bodies.

1604. LORD NOLAN: Yes, and you see the Public Appointments Commission as a possible vehicle for the exercise of an independent influence on the making of appointments, recognising the vast number that have to be made, recognising also that some of them are bound to have a political content: governments have to govern, and there are some areas in which government policy must be pursued by those presumably who at any rate are not totally out of sympathy with it.

DAVID HEATH: I think that is accepted, Chairman. Certainly we don't envisage a Public Appointments Commission that would make every appointment to every non-governmental body. That is not what we are saying. What we are saying is that there may be a case for what is perceived to be a commission with independence to make—or to vet: there are two possibilities there—particularly prominent appointments in the public service at large. One could envisage an American Senate system of post-appointment but pre-taking up a position investigation of that kind, or alternatively direct appointment. Certainly we would envisage a Public Appointments Commission perhaps producing codes which could be applied elsewhere, which would give a clarity to the process at the moment and, where there is a political involvement, to make it clear that that is the case. At the moment there is a danger that political bias is perceived where there is none. There is also, certainly where the appointment of members of quangos serving on a geographical basis does not accord with the political geography of that area, a sense that these are in some way provincial governors, which I don't think helps the quango in its local operation, and I think that anything that can be done to dispel that impression would be of benefit.

1605. LORD NOLAN: I speak only for myself and in a very tentative way, but it seemed to me that in a number of areas the introduction of an independent reference point—the ombudsman and the local ombudsman—does seem to have served a useful purpose as a lightning conductor, as a body, or individual or group of individuals, whom the country has found, who have commanded confidence: they've been straight and it's a good system. You are really envisaging a development along those lines—am I right?

DAVID HEATH: I think so.

LORD NOLAN: This is as flexible and informal, one would hope, as possible, because we don't want more quangos on top of existing quangos.

ELGAR JENKINS: There is a slight irony, yes.

DAVID HEATH: Yes, we recognise that paradox in what we are saying, but it is a truism that politicians are not widely accorded a great deal of trust. We fall into that category as much as central government and Parliament, and it is sometimes helpful to have an outside body as a stamp of approval, if nothing else, which the public can have a degree of confidence in.

ELGAR JENKINS: I think it is going to be important, my Lord, that that body, if it made any appointments, would make only a very few, but the main thing is that it would act as a reference point and would ensure that the procedures for selection were open. I think it is perhaps fair for me to say to you, and you know my background, I having been chairman of a health authority, now a trust, the people outside do think that these organisations are stuffed with people who are all of one political party or another. In fact, I didn't know the politics of anybody on my health authority; my health authority chairmen, and I only know—I know this by accident—the politics of one of my non-executive directors on my current trust. The perception is that somehow they all got there, including the chairman because they were actually identifiable public supporters of one particular party. This would certainly help and protect in that regard too to those people who often serve despite the fact that they get paid more than in local government and they often work far beyond the hours that one would as a non-executive director of a private company for an equivalent amount of money.

1606. LORD NOLAN: I do not know whether you have had a chance even to see the new proposals that have been brought out this morning giving guidelines for appointments in the National Health Service which, I think, are intended certainly to make the procedure there a good deal more open and free from political bias. Perhaps Mr. Langlands would be better able to deal with it but the suggestions that independent members should be brought on to sifting panels for appointees is recognised but the examples of independent members do not seem to include members of local authorities. Would you think that that was wise or unwise?

ELGAR JENKINS: In answer to the first question, I managed, in my position, to get faxed from my region of the South and West the pages which Alan Langlands was speaking to. Far be it from me as chairman of a health authority to step in front of Alan Langlands and steal his thunder from presenting himself to this committee. I think the proposals are very strongly down the line of openness we have all been recommending and it is a pity that sifting panels do not allow some councillors to be present. There is no reason why they could not have a councillor on one of these sifting panels alongside other people from other walks of life. That is a personal comment which is only made in the capacity of only being able to have the documents in front of me for a very short period of time.

LORD NOLAN: Quite so.

ELGAR JENKINS: I must say that the procedures here are very much like the ones to which I am accustomed both in Wessex previously and in the South-West now in the way that we go about our appointments. I think most people would see them as a major step forward in transparency and meeting some of the criticisms that have been put forward.

LORD NOLAN: So far as what you have carefully considered and put before us under the heading of common threads, you would ask us to try and draw up a code of common principles of conduct which can be applied with necessary variations across the board and, in effect, say that it should be based on the principles of openness and independent scrutiny which the local authority associations have endeavoured to adopt in their arrangements.

Thank you very much. I am now going to go round the table and invite members of the committee to put questions to you. Diana, may I start with you.

1607. DIANA WARWICK: Could I just ask two brief questions and take you back to the point you made about pecuniary interests of councillors and their relationship to Members of Parliament. You said that Members of Parliament should similarly be barred from taking part in decisions on an issue related to their particular pecuniary interest. You have linked that to whether payment should be declared, and it is an issue we have been looking at, but if they are not barred from voting would you consider that the only way to demonstrate transparency would be to declare the amount earned as well as the interest itself?

ELGAR JENKINS: I do not think that overcomes the fundamental difficulty in public perception. There is a choice to be made; they either participate or they do not. The terms, the exact amounts they receive, and the rest of it, as with councillors at the moment, I do not think are material. It is a question of whether they are representing their constituency, or some other wider public interest, or, to some degree, a private interest. They can only be dealt with on the basis that they do not take part in a decision or discussion if they have a private interest.

1608. DIANA WARWICK: So, in no circumstances do you think the actual amount of the payment is relevant; it is the nature of the interest that is relevant in all circumstances?

JEREMY BEECHAM: Yes.

DAVID HEATH: It is possible that de minimus conditions might apply that there might be something that was of such a minimal involvement as to be a non-debarring factor. I also have to say I think it is possible to carry this argument ad absurdum. There are elements of the duties of a parliamentarian which are different in many respects to those of a councillor. For instance, I do not think we would be arguing that Members of Parliament should be disbarred from voting on the Finance Bill simply because they would be affected by it. That would be absurd. It would not provide for good government.

I think the arguments apply rather more cogently if, for instance, we were talking about the Committee stage of a Bill dealing with a particular industry where a member of that committee were to have a strong interest, or even not such a strong interest, in a company engaged in that industry or a lobbying group representing that industry and they were seeking to put forward amendments which would affect the legislative framework within which that industry worked. That seems to me to be an appropriate level at which, perhaps, Parliament might like to consider an appropriate code of conduct which would prevent that happening because I think that is the sort of thing which does bring the House into disrepute. That is easy for us to say from outside but I think it is a more complicated matter once you actually look at it in terms of parliamentary procedure.

1609. DIANA WARWICK: And my second point relating to lobbying. You emphasise the point that lobbying is a legitimate activity but it must be regarded as improper for parliamentarians to accept money. Are there any aspects of lobbying which themselves are improper? I think you said informal lobbying in the corridors you would regard as improper from a councillor's point of view. Are there elements of the relationship with Ministers, for example, that you would regard as improper?

DAVID HEATH: I have to declare an interest here. I have worked as what is loosely called a parliamentary consultant before now. I hasten to add that I have never attempted to provide any money for any Member of Parliament or Member of the House of Lords in order to persuade them that my argument was a satisfactory one but, nevertheless, I have walked the corridors of Westminster attempting to argue cases on behalf of organisations and charities so I have some insight into that. It is clear that simple persuasion is a democratic right of any citizen in this country to persuade a parliamentarian of the rightness of a cause or a course of action.

There is a substantial difference between that and actually retaining the services of a Member of Parliament of either House for the purposes of advancing that cause so that that individual has a split loyalty between their constituents and a commercial undertaking. I think it is that which would concern us and would concern most members of the public because there is clearly a division of loyalty there which cannot be in the interests of the constituents who that person was elected to represent.

ELGAR JENKINS: I think the best of the lobbyists themselves are asking, are they not, for a code which they would wish to subscribe to and as part of that code the giving of money in order to further their ends has been something that the best lobbyists, to my knowledge, have never actually engaged in themselves. The fact that they might give a lunch or a dinner or a drinks do would in itself seem not unreasonable to bring people together. It is part of a democracy that we should all be able to ensure that the case is put on any matter and put clearly. Certainly, provided they are registered and there is an accepted code which is accepted as being reasonable, the key thing we are concentrating on is the concern about the actual direct payment to a Member of Parliament or, indeed, a Member of the House of Lords in order to further a lobbying interest.

JEREMY BEECHAM: As a personal point, I am not entirely happy about the use of parliamentary facilities and premises for some of the lobbying activity that appears to go on of the kind that Elgar has just referred to. I do not think that is perhaps so hugely significant but it is slightly distasteful to some people.

ELGAR JENKINS: I think the only point I would put on the other side—we are all independent people around here—is that it is often easier to be able to talk to Members of Parliament if it actually takes place somewhere within the curtilage of the Houses of Parliament than it is if you have it at some distant part in London. I think that more often dictates the use of parliamentary premises than perhaps any other factor. Some of us do it, may I say, in throwing receptions for Members of Parliament in order to be able to put across a point of view that we might hold.

1610. DIANA WARWICK: Do your associations retain Members of Parliament to advise you on parliamentary process?

ELGAR JENKINS: We have vice-presidents, as we call them, and we do not retain them in the sense that we pay them. They are Members of Parliament, Members of the House of Lords and members of the European Parliament who have generally expressed an interest in the broad aims of our respective organisations and often some of them have experience of having been county councillors, metropolitan councillors or district councillors. We would regularly supply them with briefing. From time to time, perhaps, at least once a year we would have a reception and there might be an occasion when one or more of them is actually lunched but they are not paid by us to be our voices. Sometimes, in fact, they do not always go down the line, depending if that line differs from their own party's point of view or their own personal view, in the House of Commons or the House of Lords or, indeed, in the European Parliament.

DIANA WARWICK: Putting aside the question of payment—my final question on this—do you think there is an advantage in having a contract or an agreement with a Member of Parliament who works with you so that the relationship is set out quite plainly?

DAVID HEATH: No.

ELGAR JENKINS: No.

JEREMY BEECHAM: Do you mean for ourselves or more generally?

DAVID HEATH: You are talking about us presumably, as associations?

DIANA WARWICK: Yes, I meant in terms of a complete understanding of the nature of the relationship and again putting aside the question of payment of any kind of fee at all.

JEREMY BEECHAM: I think it needs to be less formal than that. It is a reciprocal process. We look to our vice-presidents to advise us as well as receiving advice from us but it is informal and we have as vice-presidents of all three associations members of all parties so that there is a diversity of view. I do not think we would want it any more formal than that.

GEOFFREY FILKIN: We do, as an association, have a "light touch" agreement which is no more than basically explaining that we will send them regular briefings and understanding that they are at liberty to take whatever position they like on those briefings. We know that we cannot in any way expect them to follow our line unless we have been able to persuade them of it.

ELGAR JENKINS: May I say that, in fact, I can remember in the recent debate on the Cleveland Order in the House of Commons that one Conservative Member did get up and declare that he was a vice-president of the Association of District Councils when he put a case for a unitary authority. There was no obligation to do so but our vice-presidents would probably declare their position in the House if they were particularly going down a specific direction or another if that might cause people to wonder whether they were speaking objectively.

DIANA WARWICK: Thank you.

1611. CLIFFORD BOULTON: Can I just ask you a question about your own rules for declaration. The House of Commons rule is that in any debate or proceedings of the House or its committees or transactions or communications which a Member may have with other Members or with Ministers or servants of the Crown he shall disclose any relevant pecuniary interest or benefit of whatever nature whether direct or indirect that he may have had, may have or may be expecting to have. The parliamentary rule for declaration goes beyond the proceedings of Parliament but into communications outside. Do you have rules or guidance about the kind of declaration that councillors should make when they are approaching people outside or coming to see Ministers. Are there rules for that form of declaration?

ELGAR JENKINS: Only that they should follow the code of conduct which applies really to all their relationships as councillors that Jeremy was spelling out earlier on. Therefore, you should be applying the same principles whether you are in the council chamber or a committee, meeting an officer or acting in any way in your position as a councillor on that authority.

1612. CLIFFORD BOULTON: So it does happen that if a delegation comes to see a Minister if any of the members of the delegation have an interest then the Minister will be made aware of that?

JEREMY BEECHAM: They would not be on the delegation.

ELGAR JENKINS: Let me just say one thing. Of course, often delegations come in order to put a particular position to that authority so they will have the interests of that authority. Ministers have been besieged on rate support grant recently—"Let us have some easing of our capping" or this, that or the other, "in order to make our financial life easier" and, indeed, on reorganisation of local government. One day you received a delegation from the county of members all committed in saying, "Please, we think the county should be retained"; another day you might get all the district councillors coming in. In that sense, on delegations, often they are specific and members have an identification with particular interests for their area.

JEREMY BEECHAM: I can give an example. In my own authority we have had considerable difficulty with Swan Hunter's shipyard and we have had delegations to Ministers about Swan Hunter shipyard. The vice-chairman of our Development Committee is, or was, an employee of Swan Hunter shipyard and, therefore, he did not join any delegation to the Minister.

1613. CLIFFORD BOULTON: I see, so you tried to avoid the situation where a declaration would be relevant?

DAVID HEATH: It is more than trying. Because of the force of the local government regulations if there is an interest then that member may not participate in that activity. Therefore, it is more than a question of having to make the declaration. In the instance Sir Jeremy suggested where a member has a direct pecuniary interest, he simply would not be in a position to be appointed to that delegation because he would have been excluded from the word "go" from consideration of that matter by the declaration of interest.

Just to expand further on your question. As was mentioned earlier, it is normal practice for the provisions of the code of local government conduct to be extended to private meetings of political groupings as well by virtue of the Standing Orders. It is the clear advice of the various political party councillors' associations that that should be the case and, therefore, even in private and between members of a single political grouping the same rules would apply.

GEOFFREY FILKIN: And that is part of the commission to local administrations explicit advice to councillors which the associations and most local authorities endorse.

1614. CLIFFORD BOULTON: Can I just ask you to put on the record what you mean by non-pecuniary interest. You say the important concept of declaration of non-pecuniary interests but you also say that the Widdecombe Committee recommended that non-pecuniary interests should also be registered. That is not in the statute. Just for the sake of the record, could you give examples of non-pecuniary interest and why you yourselves appear to think that they should be registered.

JEREMY BEECHAM: Membership of a club or association, for example, would not give you a pecuniary interest in a matter but it might be sufficiently proximate in the public view to disentitle you to participate in a decision-making process. Again, it is really a matter of making sure that propriety is seen to be achieved and that there should be no taint on the decision of the authority.

1615. CLIFFORD BOULTON: And you would welcome an obligation to register interests of that kind?

JEREMY BEECHAM: Yes.

ELGAR JENKINS: I think so if they are likely to reflect on why you were supporting a particular matter. If I may give you an example of my council. I constantly have to declare on matters of planning, etcetera, affecting the university because I am on the university council. If my church wanted to extend its car park on a planning application—I have a non-pecuniary interest in my parish church but, on the other hand, I would expect to declare it. Similarly, I have known all political parties on my council at one time or another have to declare an interest when some planning application came in for their political headquarters. They do not have a pecuniary interest but they certainly have a strong non-pecuniary interest. I remember half the council, on one occasion, were unable to vote because, in fact, that particular political party had a large number of members on the council.

1616. CLIFFORD BOULTON: But declaration is one thing which comes up and it is relevant, as you say, but thinking of how to fill in a register . . .

DAVID HEATH: There is a very large discretionary element inevitably. It is for the individual to decide what might be appropriate and certainly the register is just part of that. You would incorporate in that anything that you think might come up on a fairly regular basis or might be held to be a disbarring interest in terms of a debate.

For instance, I am not required to but I make it my personal practice to declare, when considering planning applications, if they are in the vicinity of a relative of mine because the public might perceive that that was an interest which was affecting my judgment. That is my personal decision. I also make it my practice to declare in the Register of Interests that I am a member of Somerset County Cricket Club. If the redevelopment of the county ground Taunton were to come up I would have a very strong interest and it would be right that members should know that my views would be coloured by that.

There is a wide range of things that might be thought appropriate and really the test comes back again to what the public might feel was the test of propriety or otherwise.

ELGAR JENKINS: We would not want to put in place a system, Sir Clifford, that discouraged anybody in public life actually being involved in a variety of organisations. That is the richness of their contribution to their council, the House of Commons, the House of Lords, their organisation, but we do think that people are going to have to keep coming back to answering this question, "What will the public say if I do not declare that I have a non-pecuniary interest and it is X, Y, Z in this organisation" when they get up and contribute to some discussion.

CLIFFORD BOULTON: Thank you.

1617. WILLIAM UTTING: I thought that your reply to the Chairman about appointments to the NHS was a miracle of restraint in the circumstances and I think I must take advantage of the fact that we do have a Trust Chairman with us to ask a further question about those appointments. What do you make of the proposition that local authorities should have the right of appointment, say, to commissioning health authorities? Is that the kind of proposition that appeals to the local government world?

ELGAR JENKINS: I would probably have to split myself in two and say what would my colleagues feel in local government. As you know, one of the arguments that is raging around in local government circles is whether local authorities might put a case for being commissioning agents for health—i.e. to take over the powers of what were the district health authorities and are now the health commissions. That is one argument that is going round in local government circles.

Another argument going round in local government circles is the question of how really can they improve their relationship, monitoring or otherwise, with the health authorities and trusts which lie within their area. I do not think I am ducking the issue when I point out that these are matters of genuine discussion and debate.

For my own part, I think that people should be chosen because they have an all-round contribution to make to that health commission or to that health trust rather than just on the basis that they hold an elected office but some of my colleagues might well take a different point of view; indeed, I would say probably the majority of my colleagues would, including numbers in the Conservative party. That is why I tried to split myself delicately down the middle.

1618. WILLIAM UTTING: Yes. I really do not want to get into the question of whether local government should be running the NHS. I do not think that is our business. The question of appointments to the NHS, however, is.

DAVID HEATH: It is a key area of public policy; it is a key area of the use of public resources and many of us, I think, would argue that it should have a proper democratic accountability and I think it is questionable whether that is there at the moment and most members of local authorities would feel that there were ways in which it could be improved. That does not necessarily imply the taking over of the responsibility by local authorities. Local authorities have a wide range of functions at the moment and that is one that might, or might not, fit into the panoply of local government. I think what we would clearly state is that there is a lack of local democratic accountability which we should like to see rectified.

JEREMY BEECHAM: It goes a bit beyond that because local authorities are involved—at any rate, metropolitan authorities and county councils are involved directly in the provision of community care and it is inconceivable that community care can be split off from the Health Service provision. They need to be planned together and worked together and there is a very strong case for local authority representation at least on Health Service bodies without necessarily going as far as the revolutionary London Borough of Wandsworth in proposing the complete transfer of the role although personally I have a good deal of sympathy with that. You do not have to go that far to recognise that there is a legitimate role for local authority representation on health authorities.

ELGAR JENKINS: Could I make one last comment. In the same way that local authorities are exploring how best to establish a relationship, whether it is by asking for members to serve on health commissions or health authorities or in some other way, so health authorities and trusts are exploring ways in which they can improve their contact and working with the local, democratically elected councils. I think there is a dialogue going on here at this moment in time from both sides and one in which I do not think anyone has come to a final conclusion although you have heard some of the matters outlined here.

Going back in history, of course, councils did put members on to the health authorities, as you will remember Sir William, but still that health authority was answerable in democratic terms to the Secretary of State via the House of Commons and not answerable directly as such to the local councils. Things have changed in some ways since we established the ideas of budgets of provider and commissioning authorities and trusts.

DAVID HEATH: There is a good deal of "ad hocery" at present in the co-ordinating bodies—Jeremy is absolutely right—it is split entirely; the procurement of care in the community from the more general health provision does not make a great deal of strategic sense and, therefore, joint bodies have developed in which you have very little legitimacy and, in some instances, do not work terribly well. It would be as well to look at how that could be properly co-ordinated within a proper framework.

WILLIAM UTTING: That is a very helpful range of views. Thank you.

1619. LORD THOMSON: We have been asked to undertake our present enquiry because of a public perception about slipping standards mainly in Whitehall and Westminster. The last enquiry of this kind arose out of a perception of slipping standards primarily in the local government field. You have given us a rather impressive account of the arrangements that are made to maintain standards in local government. To what degree have these arisen out of recent changes in legislation and changes that arose out of that previous enquiry and are there lessons for us out of your experience?

JEREMY BEECHAM: I think it is fair to say that some of the provisions that we have now embodied in codes, statutory or otherwise, stemmed from disquiet felt within local government and outside local government from some of the events that perfectly properly caused public concern 20 years ago and perhaps more recently. Having said that, it was only ever a minority of authorities and an even smaller minority of individuals who were involved in practices which were thought to be reprehensible by the vast majority of people involved in local government.

Nevertheless, there has been some response to pressure that those events generated perhaps from other concerns as well. The monitoring officer, for example, was established partly to avoid not so much individual misconduct as local authorities trespassing dangerously near the territory of unlawful action in terms of finance and budgeting. It is fair to say that some of our procedures follow from parliamentary or governmental concern.

The general record of local government has been impressive and certainly we have not been slow, as associations for example, to recommend good practice and, as you have heard today, we are considering those areas which still need improvement even now.

DAVID HEATH: I think that is the key. What we have seen is a process of reduction to statute and codification of what already was good practice in good authorities to elevate all to the practice of the best. Our argument today is that that same process is now required in other areas of public life to establish what is best practice and then ensure that it is followed in conduct elsewhere. Certainly, that is the burden of our evidence today.

GEOFFREY FILKIN: Just to touch on your second point re our reflections. We are not, I think, able to give detailed advice or guidance on how the principle should be applied but our experience makes us believe that certain principles are important across the broad sweep of public life, the need for a clear code. Secondly, a clear understanding that if there is a pecuniary interest non-involvement has to follow and if people are aware of that, of course, they have the freedom at the beginning to decide whether they pick up the pecuniary interest.

Thirdly, as part of that, the duty to try to avoid the impression of impropriety because we all have a concern about the impression as to how the government is run and that requires a particular duty on us in local government to try to set ourselves firm standards. Finally, we would be dishonest if we did not also mark that we recognise, despite monitoring officers, despite the codes that we have, external scrutiny is necessary as well. None of us is so perfect that we can rely on ourselves to put our own houses in order at all times and in all events. As a club we tend to take a view of things from within the club.

ELGAR JENKINS: I think, my Lord, that we support these. Three of us here see a lot of Members of Parliament and we see a lot of people in councils and in public bodies and I must say all of us can positively say that 95 per cent, 99 per cent, of people who are engaged in public life are honest and hard working. In a sense, your commission has come into being, and we are doing what we can, to ensure that the good name of the overwhelming mass of people is protected. That is why we are putting forward the ideas that we are.

It is useful to put on the record that I do not think standards have actually slipped seriously right across the whole range but the few, whether they be in local government or national government or wherever they may be, undermine the high level of excellence of people in public life in this country and that we should seek to stop.

1620. PETER SHORE: I want to take you back to appointments to quangos. As I understand it, when local authorities are appointing their chief executives and other senior officers they rely upon a process of advertisement and then, I suppose, open competition among the candidates who have put themselves forward. This being so, why is it that you do not recommend a similar process of appointment to the paid executive quangos of which there are now so many?

JEREMY BEECHAM: I think there may be instances where that is appropriate but we take the view that in some respects quangos ought to be representative bodies. We made the point about Health Service organisations, that local authorities feel in general that we ought to be represented on those bodies. With development corporations, for example, local authorities informally can nominate; the appointment is still the Secretary of State's, nevertheless an effort is made to see that some members come from local authorities. There is a representational role and it is right that those who are being represented in that way should have a nominating right.

There would be other organisations where, as you say, it may well be more appropriate to have a much more open process in which people would be invited to throw their hat in the ring to be Chairman of the BBC, or whatever.

1621. PETER SHORE: Let me just put this to you. Let us assume that the representational desires of local government are met in that some bodies are, as it were, returned to local democracy and on others there is local government representation. Assuming that, what about the residual members of appointed boards by Ministers. Do you think that that whole procedure needs to be radically changed in the way that I was suggesting?

JEREMY BEECHAM: Yes. Certainly, it could embrace the proposal that you are making and we would have thought that the independent commission which we are suggesting would establish a code of practice to be followed in making such appointments and which would, amongst other things hopefully, secure the kind of balance that we refer to in our reference to plurality, by which I think we meant pluralism, in terms of appointments. That might be the process of advertisement and appointment by some independent organisation.

On the other hand, at the moment there are 40,000 appointments to make—hopefully, there will be fewer in future—but still 40,000 is an inordinate number of appointments to be made by a single commission. It is difficult to see quite how you would do that on a national basis.

1622. PETER SHORE: Do you think, therefore, that you could have an independent public appointments commission with panels of itself, or replicas of itself, at a local or regional level?

JEREMY BEECHAM: That would be possible. Again, I think you would need to look carefully at the workload that is involved and who then sits on the regional bodies but it is a possible way forward certainly.

ELGAR JENKINS: I was only going to say, Mr. Shore, to take the Health Service which I know best, and certainly in my own area, both in the Wessex authority when it existed and now in the South and West, regular advertisements have been placed in papers asking for people who might wish to be considered as non-executive directors and every effort has been made to contact organisations which might wish to put forward names. Panels now exist for interviewing people, to set before them what the nature of the work is and, secondly, as a sifting body, as it were, so that a whole range of names are available to draw upon. So, much goes on now in that regard.

I thought you said at the beginning about executives. I take it you are not talking about the paid employees which jobs are invariably advertised and go through the same procedures as if you are appointing to any private company or, indeed, to a council senior appointment.

DAVID HEATH: There is a distinction to be made between the executive and the non-executive boards of these bodies. I think we have argued consistently for transparency in appointments and any of the structures that we are proposing would move in that direction. There are instances of bodies which have a sort of hybrid membership between elected members either by primary or secondary election, and appointed members which can work perfectly well. I think, for instance, of the National Park Committees which form constituent parts of local authorities and yet have Secretary of State appointments on them.

I think the chair of these bodies is something that the committee might like to focus upon because there is certainly an argument that chairmen have the confidence of the membership of a committee to a much greater extent if they are appointed within that committee and by its membership. This is an argument that was addressed very much in the Police and Magistrates Courts Act last year where, you will recall, the original proposal was that the Home Secretary should appoint chairmen of police authorities. I say this with some feeling as being one who would almost certainly not have been appointed on that basis. In the end the House of Lords suggested that a better route would be for the chair to be elected by the body itself.

I think in a lot of instances we perhaps have appointment of chairs where it is not necessary to appoint chairs, that the body itself could quite properly elect its own chairman.

JEREMY BEECHAM: But there needs to be a reporting back mechanism. Magistrates are appointed usually after public advertisement. Often the forms invite nominees to say what their political position is and what religious background they have, and so on, in an effort, no doubt, to allow some balance to be made, but in practice it is somewhat difficult to tell how people have been appointed.

1623. TOM KING: Can I just turn, Sir Jeremy, to the interesting point you made about the delegation to Swan Hunter. Do you think it was actually appreciated by the Minister that you were able to say that you had come from Newcastle, representing the people of Newcastle, to put the case for Swan Hunter, that you guaranteed that nobody in your delegation had any practical working experience in Swan Hunter?

JEREMY BEECHAM: I think it was right that we should say that there was nobody on that delegation whose personal position was going to be affected by the outcome of the council's involvement. After all, none of the rest of the delegation had worked in Swan Hunter but all the members involved had very close contacts with the company and had been briefed about the company's concerns.

1624. TOM KING: I do not want to interrupt you but I want to ask a few questions and we can be fairly concise in the answers. I want to ask you this. It seems to me that that downgraded the value of that delegation to a Minister. I make this point. I used to see delegations about Swan Hunter when I was Secretary of State for Defence, it was obviously a matter of great concern. For instance, the trades unions would come, the Confederation would come unashamedly with members, I appreciated that. It made their contributions more valuable.

I am not undermining in any way the quality and sincerity of elected representatives and others coming but there is nothing that can equal practical, direct experience, the feeling in the yard, what the attitude was, and it seems to me that if you have reached such a state that that cannot be accommodated by an open declaration that seems to be very unfortunate.

JEREMY BEECHAM: But you are going to receive, as a Minister, that kind of representation anyway. What you are getting from the local authority is a view of the community as a whole without a particular vested interest being there represented. I think it is right that the two should be kept separate.

1625. TOM KING: May I just interrupt you because Swan Hunter is very important to Newcastle, we know that, and it is a very important part of the community. It seems to me that provided that interest is declared—I just say this sitting from a ministerial side—it is very much more valuable if the person comes. After all, it is not as though you have to declare an interest, the whole delegation is interested in Swan Hunter, it is the purpose of the delegation to argue a particular case.

In that case, is it not arguable that provided there is full transparency your rules have reached a state in which you so sanitise them that the value has really gone out of the delegation.

I take you on to the next point because your Press release, modestly entitled "*Local Government Leads the Way in Public Standards*", which was written by somebody in your delegation, goes a little further than your paper. It asserts that Ministers should be legally forbidden for taking up jobs. Your paper is actually rather more tentative on how far you go down this route.

One of the issues that we are looking at in this area is this business about Ministers leaving their posts. If you get a General Election and if, for example, you have a young Treasury Minister who has come into Parliament having worked in the City then, because of his expertise and knowledge of the City is an obvious person to put as a

Treasury Minister—and there are one or two at the moment I can think of who are much better Treasury Ministers because they actually know something about the City and understand it than people who have no knowledge at all. He comes in but at the next election he loses his seat and his ministerial position and salary and he is then told that not only has he lost his seat, his income and his Ministerial salary but he is not allowed now to go back to the firm that he was with who gave him leave of absence or whatever it was, when he went into Parliament and four years later he finds he is out of a job. How is he supposed to live, in what areas is he supposed to earn his living if you put an absolute embargo of one year as you propose here before they can resume their employment?

JEREMY BEECHAM: The question is what is the public perception of Ministers who having had dealings with organisations or industries in their official capacities who return to or take employment with such an organisation within a very short time of leaving office for whatever reason. The public perception is one of understandable concern and I think people who enter public life, all of us, whether Members of Parliament or councillors, do undertake certain responsibilities and recognise that we have certain sacrifices to make and some of them are financial sacrifices. I do not think it is asking too much for there to be a relatively limited period—it might be argued that a year is too short a period—between leaving office and taking up an appointment that might be related to the discharge of responsibilities in government.

1626. TOM KING: Excuse me. I do not want to interrupt you but you put that point and that is obviously the response you can make. You then compare that, as you said, "all of us in public life", and you compare it to councillors. What councillors are required to give up their employment to serve on a council?

JEREMY BEECHAM: No councillors are required to give up their employment to go on to local authority. Many, in practice, do or suffer substantial financial hardship in so doing, relating to a variety of matters including their pensions. They are also, with respect, considerably less well remunerated than Members of Parliament or Ministers but, having said that, I identified that I would like to see similar rules applying to leading members of local authorities as we are advocating for Ministers. I am not suggesting for a moment different rules in that respect.

TOM KING: But you take my point that Ministers are required to give up all outside employment; they have to cease whatever is there activity. What you are saying is, moreover, they would have the bar.

JEREMY BEECHAM: It is a partial bar.

1627. TOM KING: May I just make this point. The analogy you give is you say such restriction—like the Ministerial restriction—already applies to councillors who cannot become employees of the same council for at least one year after giving up their seat. That is not actually the analogy is it because Ministers are not seeking to return to the Civil Service in the same department in which they were employed?

JEREMY BEECHAM: I concede that and I conceded it in replying to questions earlier and identified a lacuna

with which I think we need to deal. But after all, to come back to your analogy of the Treasury Minister who might be unable to return to his merchant bank, if he has been a successful Junior Minister, presumably his knowledge, experience and services may well be sought in other parts of industry, with which he has not had dealings as a Minister. He is not, I would imagine, going to find it terribly difficult to find employment.

TOM KING: Just to be quite clear, you personally and it is on your joint evidence.

JEREMY BEECHAM: Yes.

TOM KING: And just to save time, if the others agree with it, you would support—your position is—that Ministers should be barred for at least a year, and you suggested possibly more, from returning to their previous employment.

JEREMY BEECHAM: No, no, not necessarily. From returning to, or obtaining, employment with firms or industries with which they have had dealings in office.

1628. TOM KING: And the question, should there be some committee, because you talk about an absolute bar, some system that vets the degree of that relationship?

JEREMY BEECHAM: I think that would be very sensible and only fair to those concerned, yes.

1629. TOM KING: Could I just ask this. You talked about earnings levels and one of my chores in early days as Minister of Local Government, you will recall, was trying to agree the issue about what the allowances level should be for special responsibilities. Just as a matter of interest and I ask this question out of interest, what do you think people are earning now at the top levels in local government, as councillors, I do not mean as officers. Officers we know would be very much higher than MPs and at the sort of current salary levels in their office.

JEREMY BEECHAM: The maximum for a leader of a large authority, allowing for daily attendance allowances and special responsibility allowance, would be in the order of £12,000. As leader of my authority I was entitled to, though I did not claim personally, £7,500 special responsibility allowance and I could, I suppose, have earned as much as £11,000 being leader of my authority, which is somewhat less than my secretary was paid.

DAVID HEATH: The Chairman of the Police Authority is £6,000 by statute.

1630. TOM KING: Is that declared?

JEREMY BEECHAM: Not only is it declared but in certain parts of the country it is regularly published in the newspaper.

TOM KING: But not declared—I do not know, that is a question of ignorance—not declared anyway.

JEREMY BEECHAM: There is a register and members of the public are entitled to inspect it.

ELGAR JENKINS: Any local taxpayer can ask for accounts, they can have the list published. The same thing applies, may I say, in the health world. I mean I was headline news, it was a slow Newsnight, you know "Chairman of the health authority gets X."

1631. TOM KING: But that is published is it not, in the health authority?

ELGAR JENKINS: They are all public information. There is no way in which we have to put a notice out that says, but it is publicly available information.

DAVID HEATH: Although many councils do actually publish it, Chairman. Indeed, councils in our own part of the world actually.

ELGAR JENKINS: You have to relate, of course, the fact that somebody that we are talking about getting £12,000, probably has a budget running to hundreds of millions. Now I think the Government have corrected that by saying, well, the local authority can take a more reasonable attitude, having regard to the burdens upon people.

Can I say, I think that whilst some of us were careful in what we said as to exactly how we applied the principles about jobs, the point that we are really trying to make is that a Member of Parliament or ex-Minister rather, has to be very careful as to what is the public impression. That is the problem. How that is best dealt with from advice from this Committee and indeed by concerned Members of the House of Commons, is the important point, although we do understand, of course, the pressures that you rightly outlined upon people who take up Government office and then find themselves out of Government office and need desperately to keep their families etc. So I hope that is helpful in saying that.

I must say, the delegation point, I think, can be met by saying that the elected representatives do not include perhaps someone from a particular industry. In my town it is the Admiralty which is a big employer in Bath, but that you do take with the delegation representatives of the trade unions and of that particular organisation. That is the way of balancing out things, so that the council is clearly seen, that the elected members have no logs to roll but they do make sure that that industry or their business is properly represented by other people who come along with them, who represent, who work, and I am sure that is what they do in Newcastle.

DAVID HEATH: Chairman, I understand the point we make about quarantine has been supported by those much better qualified than ourselves to judge, in the form of former Ministers, many of whom I would not normally agree with on such matters but who have made the point, I think, very forcibly.

LORD NOLAN: There are two more members of the Committee—we are very short of time but they must have a go.

ANNE WARBURTON: In view of the time, Chairman, I will forego putting a question. I would just like to say how much I appreciated the quality of the material put before us.

1632. MARTIN JACOMB: Could I just ask you two very quick questions? You dealt with the declaration of

non-pecuniary interests and if I may say so, I think the church and the cricket club are a very easy thing, but there is no suggestion of declaring friendships and friendships can very often be the root of the problem. Do you recognise that?

ELGAR JENKINS: I think we would expect that somebody would declare if it was their brother, or some relative of theirs who happened to own that particularly valuable site on which the planning application was made.

MARTIN JACOMB: That point was made.

DAVID HEATH: I think it goes further than that. I have to say—I have not experienced other authorities—but certainly in my own authority it is very often the case that somebody will say to a committee before a decision on a particular thing, you should know that this person is known to me and we are friends or whatever. On the question of an appointment that would disbar that member from taking part.

1633. MARTIN JACOMB: That would be required, would it?

ELGAR JENKINS: Yes. Do you know, are you known to a member of the council? words like that are usually on the actual form.

JEREMY BEECHAM: I would certainly expect—and I have done it myself- an interest to be declared, a non-pecuniary interest should be declared when I knew the person involved in an application for a grant for example.

MARTIN JACOMB: I appreciate that is the best standard but what we are talking about here is not the best standard, we are talking about requirements to cover people who are not naturally disposed.

JEREMY BEECHAM: That is why we have the code.

1634. MARTIN JACOMB: The other point I just wanted to make was you were referred to the press announcement which you put out today, but I think, if you were doing it again today, you would not phrase the second paragraph the way you have, is this right? Because you say Ministers should be legally forbidden as Mr King referred you to, and then you go on to say, such a restriction already applies to councillors.

ELGAR JENKINS: Mea culpa mea maxima culpa.

MARTIN JACOMB: That is wrong.

JEREMY BEECHAM: We would, I think, prefer to say that we are looking at the comparable position with a view to improving our own procedures.

MARTIN JACOMB: Because there is not a procedural restriction is there?

JEREMY BEECHAM: No.

MARTIN JACOMB: Thank you.

1635. LORD NOLAN: Thank you very much. You have clarified a number of points for us and helped, in doing so, to clear our minds. We are very grateful to all four of you very busy people for the time you have taken in presenting this united and harmonious front and for all the help you have given us today.

Mr Langlands, I am afraid we have kept you a little late in starting. I hope you do not mind. But when we have as many as four speakers it is hard keep to the strict letter of the timing. We are, of course, very grateful to you for coming along with your companions. I have just had handed to me an opening statement which I believe you would like to make.

ALAN LANGLANDS, JOHN SHAW AND ISABEL NISBET (NHS EXECUTIVE)

ALAN LANGLANDS (Chief Executive NHS): Yes, thank you and I will try and be as brief as possible.

I am the Chief Executive of the NHS in England. That is a Civil Service post and I am directly accountable to the Secretary of State for Health. I lead the NHS Executive, which is an integral part of the Department of Health, and I have overall responsibility for the implementation of policy in the NHS and for the management and performance of the NHS. I am also the Accounting Officer for NHS Expenditure.

The responsibilities in the Department of Health split, so that the responsibility for public health, social care and a range of other functions rests with the Permanent Secretary in the Department, and of course, separate management arrangements apply to the NHS in Scotland, Wales and Northern Ireland.

I am accompanied today by John Shaw, on my right, who is the Director of Corporate Affairs in the NHS Executive, and Isabel Nisbet, his deputy, and they have both been leading our work on NHS appointments and codes of conduct, accountability and openness in the NHS.

I worked in the Health Service for more than 20 years and my colleagues in the Civil Service are both for more than 20 years, and we are committed to high standards of public service and we are pleased to have this opportunity to give evidence to the Committee.

I have submitted a letter to you, which responds in detail to the issues that you raised prior to the hearing.

Let me make one or two points, just by way of background, before addressing the question of accountability, which I think is central to the discussion we have this morning.

Firstly, just to acknowledge that there has been a huge structural change in the NHS over the past four years but the fundamental purpose of the NHS is unchanged. It is enshrined in legislation, and has been since 1948, and it is to "secure through the resources available the greatest possible improvement in the physical and mental health of the people of England", and we do that by tackling four things. We promote health, we attempt to prevent ill health, we diagnose and treat injury and disease and we care for people with long term illness and disability.

I believe that everyone working in the NHS, including chairmen and non-executive directors of health authorities and trusts, is committed to that purpose.

Coming to the question of accountability, I would like to separate issues of local accountability from those of national accountability.

NHS Trusts are accountable to health authorities and to GP fundholders who purchase their services through contracts. Trusts also publish an annual report and they will soon be required to comply with the Code of Practice on Openness in the NHS, which is currently the subject of consultation. This will require them to meet all requests for information, save in the case of certain carefully defined exempt categories, the most important of which, of course, is patient confidentiality.

Health authorities have a clear and distinct role, a new role, in recent years. They are responsible for assessing local health needs and securing services to meet these needs. They are expected to engage the public in dialogue about how best services should be arranged and about setting priorities, and Ministers have been underlining that point in recent months. Health authorities hold their meetings in public and they too will be required to adopt the Code of Openness.

Running in parallel with health authorities, the Government is expanding the role of GPs, some of whom purchase health care, GP fundholders.

As well as being accountable locally, health authorities, fundholders and Trusts are accountable nationally, ultimately to the Secretary of State and to Parliament. The lines of accountability are clear and Ministers are able to pursue national health policies via the management relationship with purchasers, and trusts, of course, are monitored across a whole range of indicators by my staff, working in Regional Offices.

Whilst the Government's policy has been to strengthen local accountability by clarifying these roles and lines of accountability at a local level, they have also taken steps to strengthen national accountability and I think, perhaps, the single most important step in the 1990 Act was to extend the remit of the Audit Commission to the NHS.

I move on, just very briefly, to Codes of Conduct and Accountability. All members of health authorities and Trusts are now required, from 1st April last year, to work to high standards of conduct, both in the affairs of their organisation and in their own personal affairs as they affect the NHS. A commitment to these Codes is now a non-negotiable condition of appointment.

These codes are based on the Cadbury principles. I do not think I will run through them in detail—they are listed there—but the Health Service was quick to take up the challenge set by Cadbury and these Codes have been widely welcomed, including by the Public Accounts Committee.

Touching briefly on appointments, topical today. If the current Health Authorities Bill becomes law and the structure of the Health Service changes in 1996, the number of non-executive appointments in the NHS will have reduced from about 6,500 in 1990 to 3,500 by 1996. But that means that almost 900 appointments or re-appointments to health authorities take place every year. All such appointments will be the responsibility of the Secretary of State and those appointed will be accountable to her.

As members of the Committee will know, earlier this morning, the Secretary of State announced new guidance on the appointments procedures and this has been made available to the Committee. Again, I will not run through the principles that underlie that.

These arrangements, I think I should say, are not new, they have not come out of the blue, they build on current practice and they will apply in all regions from 1st April 1995, and of course Ministers will wish to take full account and further account of the view of this Committee on these procedures.

Let me make one final point, which is specifically raised with me and that was on the question of Whistleblowing. I believe firmly that the "Guidance for staff on relations with the public and the media", which were issued by my predecessor, are comprehensive and that they do set the right tone. I accept however and I think it has been clear in earlier evidence to this Committee, that sustained effort is required to ensure that these guidelines are properly carried through, both in spirit and in detail at local level.

A great deal has been done in recent years to make more explicit the standards required of those who work in the NHS. Today's announcement on appointments is a determined step to strengthen the procedures further. The NHS, we believe, is a valued public service. It is our intention to do everything possible to build public confidence in these arrangements to ensure that they are pursued consistently and fairly in every part of the service.

Thank you, Chairman.

LORD NOLAN: Thank you very much. That was very helpful and clear. Now I am going to ask Sir William Utting to take up the questions please.

1636. WILLIAM UTTING: I think the Committee is grateful to the Secretary of State for bringing forward the announcement of this new Guidance, so that we could discuss it with you in your giving oral evidence Mr Langlands.

Perhaps I could begin, however, just by asking you to knock some very obvious nails on the head once more. You referred to them in your opening statement but we have been bombarded with information about different kinds of Bodies, Non Department Public Bodies, Quangos, Next Steps Agencies. I just want you to repeat that when we are dealing with the NHS we are talking about a unique organisation that is accountable directly to the Secretary of State, from bottom to top, and that you and your Executive are an integral part of the Department of Health and you are a senior civil servant in your own right.

ALAN LANGLANDS: That is correct.

1637. WILLIAM UTTING: Good. Thanks very much. Well that is a very obvious nail knocked on the head but I think a useful one for us, in considering questions about appointments to the NHS.

You will probably know that we have had a fair amount of correspondence and submissions that are critical of present systems of appointment to the NHS. It is only fair to say that we have also had evidence that, although the procedures may be faulty, the results have actually on the whole been quite good and that they have produced lots of people who are genuinely motivated and successful in running the NHS.

Could I now, in the light of the new arrangements for the NHS, ask you a general question about the characteristics that you would look for in appointing members of commissioning or purchasing authorities and members of Trusts. I believe that these are now two quite distinct functions in the NHS and would require different sorts of people to carry them out. Is that so and could you say what those characteristics ought to be?

ALAN LANGLANDS: I think that is so and may I just endorse your view in suggesting that it is certainly my experience of the recent past that the standard of non-executive directors in the NHS has improved very considerably in recent years.

I think in our Guidance we have not tried to distinguish too much between those responsible for running health services in NHS Trusts and those responsible for purchasing health service. Rather we have defined a set of generic characteristics which are based on the fact that we expect people to have a genuine interest in health care. We expect people to have a commitment to public service. Health authorities are often complex organisations with budgets in excess of £100 million and therefore we often look to people who understand the business of managing in a large commercial or public sector organisation. We often draw on specialist skills or knowledge. We often draw members from groups of people who have experience and a track record in voluntary organisations, especially if these are associated with the NHS. So I think these generic characteristics are, to some extent, applicable in both parts of the NHS.

Clearly, the specialist skills that are required at both levels, are provided mainly by the executive directors, so that in health authorities one would expect a Public Health Director with good epidemiological skills in an NHS trust. It is a requirement to appoint a nursing director and a medical director who can provide leadership to these important groups of staff and advise Trusts on the development of health services and clinical practice, and often the interface between the provision of health services and the scientific research and academic communities.

So these are all ingredients of a good board and I think I would want to underline the importance of achieving complementary skills between the executive and the non-executive parts of that unitary board.

1638. WILLIAM UTTING: Thank you. If I could turn to some of the specific points that come out from the new Guidance. We had an opinion from the National Association of Health Authorities and Trusts last week, that the boards need to have the confidence of the communities they serve and that there needs to be an independent element in the recruitment and appointment systems so as to ensure public confidence. As I read the Guidance the only place for independent advice is optional. We were, I think, impressed by information that in Scotland there was an Advisory Committee to the Secretary of State apparently composed of independent people devised on appointments to the NHS.

Do you not think, if this is the only independent element and it is optional, that this actually ought to be strengthened in the English Guidance?

ALAN LANGLANDS: Let me make two points about the Guidance as it has been set out today. First of all, the members of the panels you referred to will be independent of the board concerned. In other words, they will be chairmen and non-executive directors from other Trusts or other health authorities and you are right, the Secretary of State has decided that Regional Policy Board Members, Regional Chairmen as they are currently known, may include an independent member on these sifting or selection panels.

I think the view of Ministers is clearly that the Guidance set out today is a very significant step forward. They want to see this develop. I do not think they preclude the possibility of changing in future. I think they also believe that the situation in Scotland is rather different. There is only one other health region, Trent Region, which is smaller than Scotland. Scotland do not, of course, have the post of Regional Chairman nor will they, in future, have the equivalent post of Policy Board Member who acts for the Secretary of State, or is the agent of the Secretary of State, at a local level.

1639. WILLIAM UTTING: Yes, I agree that these arrangements do represent a significant part of what has gone before, but we do need, I think, to press at certain points and I have to say that overall these arrangements do appear to be somewhat inbred as far as the NHS is concerned, and perhaps do not go far enough to meet people's wishes to see stronger representation from the local community and a bigger independent element in the selection process.

ALAN LANGLANDS: That, of course, is optional and I have no doubt that some Regional Chairmen will pursue that course and just as we have built the present guidelines on the experience of the existing arrangements, so we would want to build any future arrangements on the experience of the new arrangements announced today, and, of course, on the findings and recommendations of this Committee. Ministers will clearly take account of your views on this matter.

. 1640. WILLIAM UTTING: Thank you. Could I ask you to what extent this Guidance was influenced by the review of Guidance on public appointments that was published last week. I see a certain similarity on a number of points of principle.

ALAN LANGLANDS: The work was well advanced before we saw the detail of the other Guidance that you refer to, but of course we were in tune with that work, in fact, Isabel Nisbet, on my left, was part of the working group representing our Department in working through the wider guidance. So there has been a flow of ideas between the two. I think if I were to trace the origins of our Guidance I would look more to the experience of the Regional Health Authorities and the Regional Chairmen in particular and I think the Guidance that you see today was at least at the level of principle, agreed by Regional Chairmen and Ministers as far back as 30 November 1994. So it has been in the making for some considerable time and of course, as I have stressed, it is evolutionary in nature.

1641. WILLIAM UTTING: So this Guidance is a response to both constructive and negative criticism within and without the NHS over the years?

ALAN LANGLANDS: I think that is fair, yes.

1642. WILLIAM UTTING: Could I ask you a specific question about equal opportunities, where there does

seem to me to be a slight discrepancy between the red book guidance on public appointments in general and what is contained in the new NHS Guidance. There is a statement in your Guidance that appointing bodies will be expected to follow equal opportunities principles and certainly in the NHS you have done much better than in many other public bodies over the appointment of women to managerial posts. There is, however, quite a detailed and explicit commitment in the red book to equal opportunities, especially in relation to disabled people. Is this an area in your own Guidance that you would wish to see developed and strengthened?

ALAN LANGLANDS: It is certainly, I agree, not an area that is spelled out in any detail. It is a matter about which Ministers feel very strongly and you are right that considerable effort has been made to appoint women, to appoint people from different ethnic backgrounds and to appoint people who suffer from disability.

I agree that that could perhaps be spelled out in more detail in the Guidance, but I think that feeling is so ingrained in the NHS and in the process of selection and in Ministerial decision-making, that it would merely be confirming good practice that currently exists.

1643. WILLIAM UTTING: Yes, it has already been commented to us that equal opportunities here does not to appear to extend to local authorities and one reads this document, I think, having difficulty in finding any reference to local authorities at all and certainly local government councillors are not included in the list of examples of people who might become independent members in the selection process. Why is this?

ALAN LANGLANDS: Well, I think that list is not exclusive and it is certainly the case that many local councillors are members of health authorities in their own rights, selected on merit rather than in a representational capacity.

WILLIAM UTTING: Yes. There is a slightly disquieting sense of the NHS actually wanting to keep local government at arms length.

ALAN LANGLANDS: Well I think far from it in terms of the work of health authorities. I heard previous witnesses refer to the importance of co-operation between health authorities and local authorities at the boundaries of health and social care and whilst these relationships vary enormously around the country, I would venture that in the run up to 1992 and subsequently since the implementation of the new community care arrangements, relationships between health authorities and local authorities in this country, certainly in my experience, have been better and more productive at a workaday level than they have ever been. I think one can see all sorts of examples of good co-operation between the two bodies in different parts of the country, and that is not always an easy relationship, particularly in questions of the responsibility for health and social care which, of course, is a quite separate but topical issue at the present time.

1644. WILLIAM UTTING: It is fortifying to hear that Mr Langlands. Could I ask you to clarify the role of the RHA Chairs. The mythology about appointments in the past, both within and without the NHS, was that appointments by and large were in the gift of RHA

Chairman, that what they said went as far as the Secretary of State was concerned. I mean, they are going to continue to play an important but by no means a sole role now in filling appointments and their status is also going to change if Parliament agrees to the abolition of RHAs. Could you say something both about their role in appointments in future and about their changed status?

ALAN LANGLANDS: Let me take that in reverse order. Their changed status depends on the passage of the Health Authorities Bill which will essentially abolish Regional Health Authorities. That is not to say that there will not remain in the Health Service a regional tier of management and that will exist in eight places in the country matching the boundaries of eight Regional Health Authorities. But there will be no statutory authority at that level and therefore the current roles and responsibilities of Regional Chairmen will change substantially.

Regional Chairmen will remain but in a very different guise. They are currently, and will continue to be, members of the Policy Board which advises the Secretary of State on the management of the NHS and like many supervisory boards, some members of the board will have geographical interests and others will have specialist interests.

The Regional Chairmen, Policy Board Members as they will be in 1996, will no longer derive their status from being head of a Regional Health Authority but will derive their status as an agent of the Secretary of State directly accountable to her.

I do not think that their responsibilities in relation to appointments will change dramatically. I think that many Regional Chairmen have put a great deal of effort in recent times into improving the appointments process. I just heard a previous witness refer to the position in the South West and the Regional Chairman there has been blazing the trail on advertising, sifting panels, ensuring that a good database is kept of members and potential members, and we have learned a great deal from that process.

Other Regional Chairmen have been required to go through the discipline of offering the Secretary of State not just recommendations but choices in the appointment of members and she and Ministers have been able to pursue their policies in relation to the equal opportunities that you referred to earlier through that process.

So I would not like to leave the Committee with the impression that the previous process was somehow dormant. It has been developing quite substantially in recent times.

1645. WILLIAM UTTING: One more question, if I may, and that is about political affiliation. I have thought about whether I should ask you this or not and I think it is probably better that I should because I am an old civil servant and non-political and you are a current civil servant.

ALAN LANGLANDS: You probably know what my answer is going to be.

1646. WILLIAM UTTING: Even more non-political than I am, but much comment has been made to us about the political affiliations of appointees to the NHS in the last few years. One piece of analysis that we got, looking at the known political backgrounds of NHS Trust members in one part of the country, it seems to show that a third of them were known to be members of one political party.

Your new nomination form does not call for a party political membership to be disclosed and from what you said earlier it did not seem that party political membership was particularly relevant. Could you say something about that?

ALAN LANGLANDS: I think you referred earlier to the wider guidelines from the Public Appointments Unit and the working group which you referred to, as you know, considered that issue and concluded that it is never likely to be right to publish details of any political affiliation unless the individual wishes this to be so. We have taken our lead from that and we have excluded that question from our application form as a result.

WILLIAM UTTING: Well that was a jolly good civil servant's answer. Thank you Mr Langlands. Thank you Chairman.

LORD NOLAN: Sir Martin would you like to say something?

1647. MARTIN JACOMB: I would just like to ask one question and I think it is page 4 of the document attached to the letter of the 13th of February but it also comes up in your own evidence today.

The new process will be, as I understand it, sifting by this body of three local chairmen or non-executives and possibly including an independent person. As a result of that arriving at least two, what are rather depressingly called, credible candidates, which are then served up to the Secretary of State or the Minister—I have got that right, have I not?

ALAN LANGLANDS: Yes.

1648. MARTIN JACOMB: What I wanted to ask you is this simply, what public scrutiny, if any, will be present during that process of sifting?

ALAN LANGLANDS: Well, apart from the fact that members of the sifting panel, will come from other health authority bodies and the possibility of an independent presence, there will be no obvious public scrutiny. The question as to whether these decisions and these recommendations and indeed detailed information from the database that has built up from this process, can readily come into public view, is quite a difficult one I think given the personal nature of the information that is collected and I think that is not an issue that we have a very firm or clear line on at the present time, and one that we have identified as requiring further checking and discussion.

In the spirit of open government and of course of the code of openness in the NHS, I think we would want as much information as possible to come into public view. But in some senses we are dealing here with the equivalent of personnel issues and I certainly would not feel competent today to answer the question about data protection around any computerised database of people who have come through this process. So I think that is an issue that we will have to explore in more detail. I am sorry I cannot be clearer.

1649. ANNE WARBURTON: Can I pursue the sifting point Mr Langlands please? I was a little surprised in reading your new guidelines only to find the word merit lurking under equal opportunities. I was glad to find it there but it just struck me that it is under-emphasised in the papers, though it is actually highlighted in your press release, so may be somebody had noticed that it was not fully spelt out in the paper.

I would like to hear a little bit more if I might about how the sifting process is going to assure merit, and perhaps I will link with that the question of whether all short-listed candidates—I mean, I know how sifting goes when you get rid of the bottom, as it were—but will all short-listed candidates be interviewed by this panel—is that the intention?

ALAN LANGLANDS: That is the intention. There are clearly—and that is certainly the case at specific points in the year—often very significant numbers of these appointments to deal with and the new regions—currently the Regional Health Authorities—soon and, subject to Parliament's consent, the new Regional Offices, cover huge geographical areas with often seventy or eighty NHS trusts and fifteen or twenty Health Authorities to deal with. But the intention would be to interview short-listed candidates in the way that has been suggested, to apply the criteria that I have set out here as basic principles and which, of course, might be developed and improved at local level—to apply these criteria to assess people on merit for their individual contribution or likely contribution to the Health Authority and to make recommendations on that basis.

1650. ANNE WARBURTON: Thank you. One person in the set-up who seems not to be covered by the sifting procedure is the RPBM—how will these generally be chosen?

ALAN LANGLANDS: Your question is how will regional policy board members be appointed in future?

ANNE WARBURTON: Yes.

ALAN LANGLANDS: I think the best answer I can give to that at the moment is that they will be appointed by the Secretary of State. That function does not exist at the moment. I would imagine in the run-up to 1996—and, of course, there will be some turnover in appointments at that time and beyond that time—the Secretary of State will want to give careful consideration to how these very senior appointments are made.

1651. ANNE WARBURTON: Two other questions, really, about coverage. The independent member referred to—is this envisaged for all Health Service bodies, or is it at only a certain level? I could not be quite sure.

ALAN LANGLANDS: It is envisaged to be an option that could be pursued in relation to all Health Service bodies.

1652. ANNE WARBURTON: Yes, thank you very much. And similarly meetings—we are told they are public. All meetings?

ALAN LANGLANDS: All meetings of Health Authorities?

ANNE WARBURTON: Yes.

ALAN LANGLANDS: All meetings of Health Authorities are held in public and agendas are circulated in advance. NHS Trust Boards have a requirement to meet in public only once per year—they have other requirements by producing annual reports and all the rest—and, of course, many of them as a matter of good practice do not conduct their meetings in public but do create opportunities in which they hear from members about services in that particular area where they consult and take the mind of members of the public, voluntary organisations, local authorities and others about proposed developments—sometimes about difficulties or problems. So we have been encouraging—and the Secretary of State in particular in her direct contact with Trust Chairmen has been encouraging an open stance and, indeed, the criteria in the guidance that you have seen today include inter-personal skills and good communication skills as a requirement for these jobs, because I think she feels strongly that Health Authority Chairmen in particular should be in regular touch with members of the public and public bodies in their locality.

1653. ANNE WARBURTON: Then my last question on that point is how do the members of the public constitute themselves into attendees at the meetings? Who are the public who present themselves?

ALAN LANGLANDS: Well, that varies enormously and it often varies with the issues that are being discussed at the meeting. If there is a particularly controversial local issue being discussed it is often the case that substantial numbers of the public from all walks of life can turn up and often these discussions have been trailed by some public process of consultation, by a lot of interest and scrutiny in the local press. At, if you like, more routine meetings of Health Authorities where the issues are, perhaps, not so controversial, it is not uncommon to have some quite substantial numbers of staff attending meetings, it is not uncommon to have representatives of voluntary groups attending meetings and in many Health Authorities, of course, the chairman or the secretary and chairman of the Community Health Council attend as observers as a matter of course. So a rich mix of people attend meetings but attendance is patchy and often to do with the nature of the issues being discussed.

JOHN SHAW (Director Corporate Affairs, NHS Executive): Could I just add a word on the point about openness, and that is that Alan Langlands mentioned earlier I, with help from Isabel Nisbet, have been chairing I think what is called a "trust force" on greater openness which was a successor body to the one that produced the Secretary of State's code on conduct and accountability and I think the committee has an early consultation draft on the code of openness that is going to be published by the Secretary of State later in the year, in April in fact. But the whole thrust of the *Code on Greater Openness* is to make it quite explicit to members of the public what information they are entitled to demand as a matter of right and gives guidance to Health Authorities and Trusts and Family Health Service Authorities and also, indeed, guidance to the Independent Health Contractors, the GPs, the High Street pharmacists, and so on, as to the sort of information they are expected—or required, in many cases, actually—to provide to the members of the public. The aims of the code are basically to ensure that people have access to available information about NHS services, secondly that people are provided with explanations about service changes that are in train and have an opportunity to influence those decisions before those decisions are actually taken, rather than being sort of rubber stamped. Thirdly, that people are aware of the reasons for decisions and actions affecting their own individual healthcare treatment and, fourthly and finally, that people know what information is available and where they can get hold of it. The draft that the committee has seen has been subjected to a generally welcome, but quite significant, criticism particularly of the areas—the lack of clarity around the exemptions—and we are tightening those all up. We do have a much improved draft on the way and I think it will be a significant contribution to achieving what I know the Secretary of State wants, namely that the NHS should be more accessible, more open with members of the public whom we and they are there to serve.

ANNE WARBURTON: We shall look forward to seeing it. Thank you.

LORD NOLAN: Mr. King?

1654. TOM KING: Your opening comments made the point that the number of appointments are going to be reduced under the new Bill from 6,500 to 3,500 and I imagine deriving from that you get your 900 appointments a year falling to the Secretary of State?

ALAN LANGLANDS: Yes, that is right.

1655. TOM KING: How many people are involved in that?

ALAN LANGLANDS: In the process of supporting the Secretary of State——

TOM KING: The Secretary of State cannot do 900 on her own—she would do nothing else.

ALAN LANGLANDS: Well, clearly the eight regional chairmen play a critical role in the way that is being described today and there is a small group of staff—one of them is here and I would ask her to comment—within the Executive who support Ministers on these issues.

ISABEL NISBET (Deputy Director Corporate Affairs, NHS Executive): Yes, I have a team of six staff who at the centre put together the work on putting up information on candidates for appointments and the recent appointments to Trusts—there was a big batch of them in the autumn which, in fact, itself involved 900 appointments—and the groundwork is done in the regions and information from the six staff that work for me will make sure that in each case Ministers know something about who the recommended candidates are—and there is always an alternative—and also about the ethic and gender balance in the community and how that compares to the record of the individual organisation. So that is a standard bit of information which my people have in a proforma——

1656. TOM KING: What are their sources of information?

ISABEL NISBET: Their main source is the Regional Health Authority.

1657. TOM KING: Yes, I said what was their source?

ISABEL NISBET: Their source. It is a mixture of the bodies that the appointments are to and their knowledge of the local community. So, for example, in finding out what the ethnic mix of the local community is they would use local reference books, and things like that.

1658. TOM KING: And you would also draw on central sources, like the Public Appointments Unit?

ISABEL NISBET: Yes. And also each year we encourage Regional Health Authorities to go directly to the Public Appointments Unit and they put forty applications a year, I think, to the PAU for information.

1659. TOM KING: And the point about the Secretary of State appointing is a critical link in giving accountability to Parliament, because it is by virtue of her appointments of those posts that Parliament can raise issues affecting the appointment by the Secretary of State to particular trusts and authorities, is that correct?

ALAN LANGLANDS: That is so, and I think that is an essential element in the National Health Service.

1660. TOM KING: Because if it was done by some outside body the Secretary of State would not have any accountability in the same sense?

ALAN LANGLANDS: That is true.

1661. TOM KING: And what about Chief Executives, because Chief Executives of Health Authorities and the accounting officer—how does it work, the accounting officer can be called before the PAC, correct?

ALAN LANGLANDS: No, at the moment I am the accounting officer for the whole of the NHS and therefore I appear before the PAC and I am held to account for the stewardship of £32 billion worth of expenditure. There have been occasions in the recent past where the PAC have called to accompany the Chief Executive Regional General Managers and Regional Chairmen and, of course, there were two much-publicised cases about eighteen months ago where that process was used. We are considering and we are in discussion with ———

1662. TOM KING: I am sorry to interrupt you—just be clear; the Chief Executives of the Regional Health Authorities at the moment are appointed by the Secretary of State?

ALAN LANGLANDS: No, the Chief Executives of Regional Health Authorities are appointed at present by the Regional Health Authority, who are the employing Authority at the present time. In 1996, subject to parliamentary consent on the Health Services Bill, people working at regional level in the NHS will become civil servants and in preparation for that day, as we moved as we recently did last April from fourteen Regional Health Authorities to eight, the appointments were made by a panel which included myself as Chief Executive, to which in future the Regional Directors will account, the current Regional Chairmen and outside assessors who had been cleared by the Civil Service Commission—so the appointments were all made in a way that was consistent with the requirements of the Civil Service Commission.

1663. TOM KING: I really want to pursue this point about accountability. Will that increase the accountability, either to the Public Accounts Committee or the Secretary of State to Parliament, in that sense?

ALAN LANGLANDS: It is not the intention to delegate accounting officer responsibilities to the Regional Directors, but we are at present exploring with the Treasury and the National Audit Office the possibility of delegating some responsibilities to a more local level, to the level of Chief Executives operating in Trusts and Health Authorities, so that they would become accountable officers. In other words in instances where there was a particular issue of local concern to the PAC it could become a natural process for that Chief Executive to accompany me to the Public Accounts Committee. That work is currently under way.

TOM KING: Thank you.

1664. PETER SHORE: We received evidence from the British Medical Association in January and amongst other observations they made this one: "one of the major concerns about Trust Boards has been that the appointment system is open to political interference and the Association would like to see responsibility for appointments to be at a remove from the Secretary of State for Health and a broadening of the base from which Board members are drawn". Two criticisms there: political influence—and the other one is the broadening of the base, too narrow a base from which people have been drawn. I think they are referring particularly to people with business background. You have published today this interesting new document. What would you say to people like the BMA who have made these two criticisms—in what way are practices going to be changed under the new procedures which would allay anxieties about the two criticisms that I have put to you?

ALAN LANGLANDS: I would say on the point of opening the appointments process to a wider group of people that the process of advertising, of search, of widening the group of people who can nominate potential members, that we might meet that criticism. On the other point I would return to my earlier answer in relation to political affiliation and say that we intend to take our lead in the NHS from the work that has been carried out on this issue by the working group supporting the Public Appointments Unit and I honestly don't think I can go further than that.

I think I would make two other points if the BMA were sitting in this room. One is to challenge their assumption that the current membership is from a narrow base—I think that may be a perception, but one sees all over the country examples of Health Authorities and Trust Boards that are drawn from a wide base, including local councillors, business men, teachers, lawyers and others. The second thing I would say to the British Medical Association is that one of the significant steps forward—one of the significant achievements of the Health Service reforms and the creation of unitary boards has been the appointment to every trust in the country of a medical director and a nursing director, ensuring that high calibre professional advice is available to members of Trust Boards.

1665. PETER SHORE: That is very important. Well, we will see what the BMA has to say later. But I can turn to two of the most significant, I think, parts of the new proposals, one is the role to be played by the Regional

Policy Board Members, previously our Regional Health Chairman, I assume?

ALAN LANGLANDS: Yes.

1666. PETER SHORE: Yes. And as the paper says they are going to be responsible for the integrity and effectiveness of the arrangements in their region, so there is no doubt at all about the importance of the role they will be playing. Can I turn to the question—push it a little bit harder—that you were asked a short time ago; how are these very important people—there are only going to be eight of them—how are they appointed and will there be any change in the way they are appointed in the future?

ALAN LANGLANDS: Well, I think I said earlier—and you have clearly detected that I was slightly unsure of my ground because these people have not been appointed in their new form and cannot be appointed until 1996, but Regional Chairmen have traditionally been appointed by the Secretary of State. They are people who often have had a track record in other parts of the health system—I am thinking of two of the most recent appointments to the post of Regional Chairmen who were people who had been very successful, leading edge NHS Trust Chairmen. But these appointments are in the gift of the Secretary of State. I think I acknowledged the point earlier that the Secretary of State, in the run-up to 1996, may well wish to give thought as to how she handles these important appointments.

1667. PETER SHORE: That would be very important, I think, in terms of public confidence because these are the crucial men, as it were—or women—in the structure and their appointments clearly must be seen to be based on the highest possible standards.

ALAN LANGLANDS: I understand that and accept that. I think maybe I just take the opportunity to underline the point that Mr. King made, that they are an important link in the accountability chain and ultimately the decision on these appointments must rest with the Secretary of State if that accountability chain is to remain intact. That is not to say that there cannot be some mechanism to support that process.

1668. PETER SHORE: Is that essential—that responsibility depends upon the personal appointment by the Secretary of State? Surely the Permanent Secretary of the Department of Health is responsible to the Secretary of State and the Secretary of State responsible to Parliament and the appointment of that Permanent Secretary is done by an entirely different procedure?

ALAN LANGLANDS: That is so. I think there is probably a distinction to be made between a permanent member of staff, an executive in the Health Service jargon, and a non-executive director.

1669. PETER SHORE: Well, perhaps so. Now, the last question I want to ask is about the panel, because that is the second most important, I think, innovation we have got here. I just want to repeat the point made earlier—the panel is to be composed of, say, two or three Health Service existing chairmen and there is the possibility that it could include an independent member. Would it not really be much more satisfactory and give rise to greater confidence in the system if there really was an independent member appointed there and that could be part of the new structure?

ALAN LANGLANDS: Well, the Secretary of State's decision, as set out in the guidance that we have today, I think that, as I have said earlier, we do not regard these changes in a static way, we want to see this system evolve, we want to learn from experience and undoubtedly Ministers will take account of the findings of this committee. But that is the position at the present time.

PETER SHORE: Thank you.

1670. LORD NOLAN: On that same point we hope, do we not, if possible to dispel the impression that an undue proportion of these appointments are made in favour of Conservative supporters or relatives? How far that perception is accurate we cannot obviously say at the moment, but it is a widely held perception. Now, the independent member will, of course, be a help. The passage says "the agreed candidates might then go on to a Regional database for appointment". Would they know they were on the database, do you envisage?

ALAN LANGLANDS: Yes, and the intention would be to keep in regular touch with people who had been assessed to be suitable for these appointments. I think one of the criticisms of the existing system—and no doubt a criticism that has been drawn to the attention of this committee—is that often contact with the system from potential members is followed by long silence and signs of a rather laissez-faire approach. I think the whole emphasis in the new guidelines is to tighten that up, to recognise that people don't put themselves forward lightly for these jobs and if they are assessed to be suitable for these jobs, that we keep them informed about the prospect of vacancies arising. I think that is particularly so in relation to chairmen and we make a point of stressing the importance of the Regional Policy Board member keeping in touch with potential chairmen and signalling clearly if and when their nomination is forwarded to Ministers.

1671. LORD NOLAN: And the individual candidates will be assessed against the agreed criteria which I have no doubt will be published as criteria?

ALAN LANGLANDS: They will be. I make the point earlier that the guidance that we have dispatched today sets out basic principles. I have no doubt that that, if you like, is the minimum required of Regional Health Authorities but equally I have no doubt that they will develop these principles, develop the criteria to suit local needs.

1672. LORD NOLAN: I speak without complete knowledge but my impression is that when the Lord Chancellor's various committees are considering appointments to the local benches they do take positive account of political sympathy so that there does not turn out to be a preponderance of supporters of one party rather than another. That, I think, you effectively rule out here—you are not going to regard that as a relevant factor?

ALAN LANGLANDS: We rule out that on the basis of submissions already made by Government. I think on another day I would venture that selection has been made for two very different jobs.

1673. LORD NOLAN: Yes, I would accept that for my part. And the remaining problem then is if there is any question—if it persists—of a wrong balance one way or another, be it political or ethnic or gender—that the openness of the system and the, one hopes, transparent suitability of the candidate chosen by reference to the criteria, will satisfy the critics. That is the aim, I take it—is that right?

ALAN LANGLANDS: That is our aim and we will carefully watch the progress of these new arrangements with these questions of balance very much in mind.

LORD NOLAN: Thank you very much.

1674. LORD THOMSON: You mentioned in your introductory paper that perhaps the single most important step to strengthen national accountability was to extend the remit of the Audit Commission to the NHS. But the Audit Commission, in their evidence to us, told us that although they decide themselves when to publish public interest reports on local Government, that in the case of the NHS the report goes solely to the Secretary of State who has discretion as to whether to publish it in whole or in part. Is that not rather an unsatisfactory arrangement, especially compared to the experience you have with the Public Accounts Committee where there is the Auditor General and Comptroller General and a Chairman who comes from the Opposition side in Parliament, which is a much more rigorous requirement?

ALAN LANGLANDS: It is always dangerous for me to consider contradicting the Audit Commission, but it is certainly the case that Section 20(3) reports are made solely to the Secretary of State and do not always come into public view, although very often at a lower level in the Health Service, in the Health Authorities concerned, or in the Audit Committees increasingly of the Health Authorities concerned, these issues do come into public view as part of the annual audit letter, although they might not be referred to as such. It is the case, I believe, that Section 15.3 reports, which are very rare, are reports in the public interest and that the Audit Commission do have the capacity to issue these in relation to Health Service business and they would be public, as the term suggests.

ISABEL NISBET: Just to add one thing, that technically the person to whom they are delivered is different in the case of the Health Service because of the different accountability arrangements with the Secretary of State at the pyramid, but I think I recall the Audit Commission saying here that in fact the Secretary of State's record in publishing such reports was a very good one and there is no interest whatsoever in not publishing such reports except when there is some legal problem and there is hardly ever any such.

LORD THOMSON: Thank you.

1675. CLIFFORD BOULTON: Can I just ask about the submission of a choice of candidates to the Minister for appointments? Is there preference indicated—is there a first choice of the people who have been doing the sifting indicated to the Minister normally?

ISABEL NISBET: In most cases if the Regional Chairman had a preference that would be reported to the Minister. My staff would not then sit in judgment on the Regional Chairman's judgment but they would pass that onto the Minister. So they would know that there were two people and that the Regional Chairman preferred Mr. Y.

1676. CLIFFORD BOULTON: From amongst the 900 appointments I think that were made recently worked on through your office, did most of those go forward to the Minister with a recommendation as to which would be the most preferred candidate?

ISABEL NISBET: In most cases they did, yes.

1677. CLIFFORD BOULTON: Are you able to give us an indication of the percentage of first choices that were actually appointed?

JOHN SHAW: Yes, I think I asked the same question yesterday of my staff. I think the figure I was given was an estimate of five to ten per cent of preferred candidates are actually turned down by Ministers for one reason or another.

1678. CLIFFORD BOULTON: So more than 90 per cent really are appointed? I suppose there is no possibility of getting more transparency into that final stage? I know, for instance, in the appointment of Bishops—I think the Prime Minister gets the choice at the last moment—it does not stop all kinds of mutterings going on about the final appointment. I don't know if there is any possibility of what must essentially be rather a personal decision for the Minister, getting more openness about that very last stage?

ALAN LANGLANDS: I think that is extremely difficult because of the personal interests of the people involved. To have failed in one of these appointments may be regarded by some people as something they didn't want to be in public view. They may be pursuing other public appointments, they may have other interests that lead them to the view that they would prefer that information not to be open.

CLIFFORD BOULTON: I am very sympathetic about that—I accept it—but I just wanted to press—this really does look like the end of the road. But I think that statistic of over ninety per cent would be a reassuring one if there were a practice of perhaps letting it be known over a reasonably lengthy period of time how these recommendations were being dealt with by Ministers, on a statistical basis.

1679. DIANA WARWICK: I think that point about trends is really quite an important one because we may well be dealing with perceptions rather than reality but we don't know that. I wanted to ask you—it is very much on a similar point—you very kindly sent us specifications, person specifications and outline job descriptions, for non-executive directors. Could you tell me, are these new, are they part of the new procedures, or are these the criteria that have applied—the generic characteristics that you were talking about?

ALAN LANGLANDS: In many cases they have applied. I think I would mislead the committee if I were to say that these had always been explicit. The point of the new guidance is to make these criteria explicit. As I said earlier these guidelines which we are dispatching to regions are a starting point, they may be improved at local level, although many people currently working in the field have contributed to this work. I think the point is that these will now be applied consistently and hopefully fairly and I don't think we would have been able to stand up and say that with such conviction before the implementation of this process, although I must emphasise that many Regional Chairmen, many senior people working in the

Health Service, have put a great deal into the appointments process over the years, a great deal into ensuring fairness and a great deal into ensuring that decisions are made in a systematic way. This makes the process more explicit and I think provides a clear framework that everyone can work to and that, of course, will be open to the public.

1680. DIANA WARWICK: Yes. I raise the point because you have talked about generic characteristics, particularly things like commitment to public service as well as understanding management, and the non-executive director has to have a keen interest in healthcare, a commitment to the public service values of accountability, probity and openness and yet when David Hunt was talking to us about the procedures for quangos he placed a lot of stress—and others have as well—on the importance of not impairing Ministers' ability to appoint people to public bodies who are prepared to work within the policy and resources framework they lay down. Do you see—because he appears to see—some sort of contradiction in the requirements on which choices are made and his ability to be able to make a different choice—that there is something in the appointing people who are prepared to work within the policy and resources framework that is not covered in the job specification. Do you think there is such a contradiction?

ALAN LANGLANDS: I am not sure that that has ever surfaced as a significant issue in the NHS. I think that in providing information to potential candidates for these posts we will be very clear about the structure of the NHS. People undoubtedly, with this level of interest in these appointments, would be aware of the Government's approach to the NHS, they probably will be broadly aware of policy in relation to the NHS. That seems at a practical level to suffice. I don't think it is an issue which really has emerged as a major issue in the recent past.

DIANA WARWICK: It just seems to add to the concern that there might be a hidden political agenda here—that is really my point—and yet the criteria set out do seem to be very clear and very sound.

ALAN LANGLANDS: Well, I hope that I have been able to impart a feeling that there is not a hidden political agenda, that we want to continue to appoint people of high calibre to these posts and that we want to appoint people who are absolutely committed to the purpose of the NHS, which I deliberately today, in my introduction, outlined, because I think if you are not committed to that you should not be working in the Health Service, either as an executive or as a non-executive.

DIANA WARWICK: Thank you.

JOHN SHAW: Could I just make the additional point, because it has not come up really this morning—this which I regard as a splendid document, the *Code of Conduct/Code of Accountability*—I will not trouble you with the details of it because I think committee members already have copies of it—but I just wanted to make the point in support of what Alan Langlands has just been saying, namely that adherence and signing up to these two codes are a condition of appointment by a Minister to become a Chairman or non-executive members. First of all, Health Authority Boards, Trust Boards, have had to adopt them formally as soon after their promulgation on 1st April last year as possible and, secondly, the point I really wanted to emphasise was that nobody becomes a Chairman or a non-executive in the NHS since 1st April appointed by Ministers without actually having to sign on the dotted line that they accept that they will adhere to the basic rules, principles, set out in what I regard as an admirable document.

1681. LORD NOLAN: Thank you very much indeed. We are grateful to you and to the Department for getting your thoughts and your proposals down on paper so quickly and coming along here to explain them more fully to us. Thank you very much indeed.

Mr. Kirkwood, I do apologise, I am afraid that not by any means for the first time we found our witnesses so interesting that we have gone well over the allotted time. Are you all right to go beyond 1 o'clock?

ARCHIE KIRKWOOD MP

ARCHIE KIRKWOOD MP: Yes, sir.

1682. LORD NOLAN: I am very grateful to you. We have just been handed a summary prepared by you kindly of the evidence that you are going to give. Did you wish to make an opening statement?

ARCHIE KIRKWOOD: Could I just for a moment or two, Chairman? I am grateful. I should start by saying that I am flattered that I have been invited to give evidence and I had better start by making it clear that I will have a much more superficial knowledge and depth as to the actual situation compared to the other witnesses that you have had before you this morning.

A word by way of introduction—I am officer bearer of the Freedom of Information Campaign and in that regard have had the opportunity of piloting two Private Members Bills, both relating to freedom of information onto the statute book and I bring that experience and interest to the questions raised by the committee. I guess I had better just declare an interest before I start because I am a Member of the Royal College of Nursing (RCN) Parliamentary Panel—not that that gives me any financial reward but they do assist with expenses when I attend meetings on their behalf. Perhaps on a more personal note I should confess to the committee that when I was an undergraduate, having recently qualified as a pharmacist, I applied for a job with the Health Service and the trick question at the end of the interview when I was asked "Are there any people that you particularly admire?" in a weak moment I confessed that I was reading Vincent Gronin's excellent biography of Napoleon, whereupon the Chairman of the panel said "We have got too many people in the Health Service like you already"!

So seared by that experience I am interested and would just like to say a word or two about my own perspective on the questions that your excellent document raised. Firstly I would like to confirm the degree of priority attached by the committee to looking at the National Health Service Trusts in particular. It certainly reflects the concern that we in the Liberal Democrats have detected in the general public and I think it reflects the concerns that we politically expressed at the time when the legislation was going through, to the extent, at least—leaving the other political arguments aside—that the reforms were being undertaken too fast because it appeared to us to be impossible to establish the framework and get the people to operate it in the timetable that the Government set out at the time, and I think that we are paying a price for that

and that your committee is being asked to consider some of the difficulties that have been thrown up because of that precipitate haste in which the reforms were introduced.

I think that there is real evidence that the Trusts and Boards have not yet won the confidence of the staff or the public. I think that the whole argument about the new commercial ethic within the Health Service has not yet won favour in the public minds, if it ever will, and it is a matter of great concern to me in a party political context that the political consensus seems to have broken down in terms of the framework in which the National Health Service is delivered. But I am particularly concerned about the fear that I detect within the staff and this reflects the information in the briefing that the Royal College of Nursing have provided me with—indeed I have been moved to write articles as evidence. I think I submitted one earlier to the committee about the gagging clauses and the concerns that have been expressed by staff who believe that they are raising public interest matters in a way that conflicts with their contracts of employment and that is leading to some concern amongst the professional bodies, the BMA and the RCN, about the freedom of manoeuvre for staff in this new commercial background in which the National Health Service is being operated when they believe that professional standards are being compromised and it leads them into conflict with their employers in a way that is new and a way that I think is of concern, not just to your committee, Mr. Chairman, but to the public at large.

I also think that there have been—and partly for the reasons that I have explained earlier—I don't believe in conspiracy theories, I believe in cock-up theories and I think that the Government are the victims of their own haste in terms of the allegations of political interference. I think that there have been of necessity, because of the shortage of time, recourse to political appointments, simply because I think the Government of the day—and it would have happened whichever Government was in power at the time—were forced and obliged to look to the people who were closest to them in order to get the work done in time. And I think that that needs to be addressed. I think party political warfare should be kept well out of trusts and boards—I think that there is enough trouble trying to deal with party political warfare in the National Health Service on the political stage, without introducing it into trusts and boards and in that regard I certainly would not, myself, be interested in soliciting people's party political affiliations, although some of the evidence that your committee has received from other bodies relating to the fact and background of people who make big political donations to party political organisations might be something that might have to be at least considered by the appointment process.

I note with interest the Government's statement this morning that they have made about the appointment system. I think that I can short-circuit my evidence to the committee to this extent, that I am very happy to concur with the totality of the evidence given by the National Association of Health Authorities and Trusts—I have studied that evidence carefully, I think it is thorough, well thought out and I am very happy to subscribe to it, almost in its entirety. I therefore do not believe that the Government's proposals go anything like far enough, particularly in relation to the absence of the independent element that was pointed to by the National Association and I think that my own experiences—the people in my own local area have actually been put off simply because of the murky nature of the previous system as they saw it of selection and I think an independent element and a more open process would encourage people to come forward.

In addition to the actual selection and appointment procedure I think I would want to advert to the need for improving the way that the trusts and health boards go about their business. I have had experience in my own constituency and it is mirrored throughout the rest of the country, about the difficulties that flow from the fact that there is an atmosphere of secrecy and clandestine consideration of some of the key points and discussions going on in health boards and trusts and recently in my own constituency we had, in my view, a preposterous situation of the existing health board in the Borders area actually considering the discussion about whether to apply for trust status and taking that discussion substantially in private. That seems to me to be a complete contradiction of the public service ethic that the NHS aspires to and in addition to that I do believe that non-executive board members do require the level of training that was again adverted to by the evidence submitted by the National Association.

And so I think basically—and my own party political evidence will come later on in detail and I don't want to prejudice anything that may come in the detailed party political submission—but I think from my perspective if I had anything to do with the reorganisation of the National Health Service I would start by implementing a Freedom of Information Act, based on the American, Canadian or Australian models, which I think would put the onus on those running the National Health Service to determine what was kept secret, rather than the other way round. I think that I would go for a statutory framework, governing creating, appointment and operation and, indeed, if the political will was there I think the current bill going through the House of Commons dealing with Health Authorities and the proposed changes to them could actually be used as a vehicle for so doing.

Finally I think that the system of democratic scrutiny of appointments made has to be attended to as a matter of urgency; and just as a postscript I think that the committee will know, Chairman, that the Scottish situation is slightly different in two perhaps specific respects, the Irons Committee has been set up last August by the Secretary of State for Scotland and that is beginning to work. I think it is too early to say whether it has been successful yet but I certainly think it is a help. And I also believe that the addition of a Declaration of Interests in terms of the financial circumstances applying to trust and health boards in Scotland is a welcome development which I think could be emulated in other parts of the United Kingdom. I think that the whole process of accountability and the code of conduct which I think has been produced and made available throughout the length and breadth of the United Kingdom should also perhaps be considered for the situation which applies in GP fund holders as it relates to their fund-holding capacities. But I think, again, that may be argued in more detail by the evidence submitted in the National Association. So with these very few introductory remarks—as a Liberal Democrat, my Lord, you get used to becoming an "hors d'oeuvre" in the course of the debates—and I am concerned that I am keeping your committee back from its lunch! (Laughter)

LORD NOLAN: You are our savoury today and I am going to ask Miss Warwick, please, to take up the questions.

1683. DIANA WARWICK: I think I can be quite brief because you have actually answered many of the questions that I wanted to raise, particularly in relation to your main concerns and you have divided them really into two elements, it seems to me. One is the element of the staff within the service and their perception of the way the service is operating, and those people who are effectively running the service and the way in which they are appointed. You have said that with the new rules that we have all just received this morning you would still be critical that that second element is not necessarily going to be properly rectified because there would not be an independent element necessarily in the choice. Are there any other aspects of the new guidance that you feel are inadequate?

ARCHIE KIRKWOOD: Well, having only seen them an hour and a half ago——

DIANA WARWICK: I know, we are all in the same boat.

ARCHIE KIRKWOOD: It is an important question. But I don't think that I would—I think that that would be the one thing, were I given a choice, that I would introduce and I think given that I think that I would be satisfied. But without it I think I am dissatisfied—and I will remain dissatisfied—but I would in all honesty like a bit of time to consult some of my colleagues and some of the interested parties before I would actually go firm on that.

1684. DIANA WARWICK: Could I ask you then whether part of your concern is that all these appointments—this very large number of appointments—remain finally in the gift of the Secretary of State. Do you feel that that is part of the system that should be changed?

ARCHIE KIRKWOOD: Well, I am old-fashioned enough to believe that the Government of the day has to retain control over the senior and major essential appointments, otherwise you would get chaos which could lead to anarchy. I think that I would devolve the decision-making process and I would try and reserve those senior and major appointments—now, if you press me on what my definition of senior and major is I would be toiling somewhat without notice—but I do believe that a combination of retaining the principal upper tiers in the hands of the relevant Secretaries of State is an essential part of Government which I would not like to see lost. But everything else, I think, should be pushed down to a local level and decentralised as far as is consistent with sensible administration.

1685. DIANA WARWICK: Do you then concur with the statement made by David Hunt which I referred to earlier, which is that in tightening up procedures in the appointments to quangos generally he was making a comment, but it obviously applies to the National Health Service as well, it impairs Ministers' ability to appoint people to public bodies who are prepared to work within the Policy and Resources framework they lay down. Do you think that is a legitimate concern?

ARCHIE KIRKWOOD: Yes, I do, I concede that. I mean, it would be very easy to say that we must have people appointed exclusively on the basis of merit, but if you then found that you were putting people in charge of extremely important decision-making bodies which require a degree of leadership that are actually prepared openly to confront the political direction of the Government of the day, I think that that makes the process of Government almost impossible to sustain.

1686. DIANA WARWICK: I wonder if you could elaborate a little bit more on the arrangements that seem to operate in Scotland because there do seem to be long-established procedures that go a good deal towards maintaining public confidence in a way that you are suggesting public confidence has not yet been obtained by the National Health Service. Could you tell us something about the procedures in Scotland and how you would like to see them operating?

ARCHIE KIRKWOOD: Well, Scotland is a smaller community by definition and I therefore think it makes it easier for a pool of expertise to be acquired, maintained and used by the Secretary of State. The Government of the day, however, in Scotland, are labouring under some difficulties in terms of the shortage of people they have from within their own ranks to fulfil some of these roles and I think that that was part of the reason why the Secretary of State for Scotland rightly bowed to political pressure and set up a system which gives some degree of potential independent scrutiny of the nominations that were being brought forward under the old system. And I think that that will help and I think that we recognise that that is a concession to a genuine expression of public concern that was particularly evident in Scotland. But as I say the Scottish situation is more easily managed and it certainly is in areas like my own in South-East Scotland which have got a community of 100,000 odd souls, where people get to know one another very well and generally work very closely together and therefore can come together and agree that the people who are being suggested for public appointments are suitable or not, because they are all well-enough known——

1687. DIANA WARWICK: So there is not the same concern about political appointees in Scotland as there is here?

ARCHIE KIRKWOOD: Well, I think I would be deluding you if I went as far as that. I think what I am rather seeking to say is that there was such concern about political appointees that it drove the Secretary of State last August to set up this independent mechanism that gave him, some would argue, a fig-leaf behind which he could hide. I wouldn't go as far as that myself and I think I recognise that it was a genuine and legitimate attempt to respond to public concern. But I would be deluding you if I was to suggest that there was no public concern before August 1994 and that there isn't still a scintilla of concern still in some people's minds north of the border, even yet.

1688. DIANA WARWICK: This is my final question—do you think that the introduction and refining of codes of conduct of the kind that we have been hearing will help to allay public concerns, however real those public concerns are?

ARCHIE KIRKWOOD: Yes, I do. It may not, of itself, solve the problem—I think problems will continue—because I think there is a deep-rooted question and it is a question that can only be decided in the party political process, which is the move from the old medically driven health service of the years up to and including 1990 and the changes that took place in the recent legislation which were much more fundamental and far-reaching in a cultural sense than I think people imagined. And, indeed,

I confess that I fully appreciated, as someone who is intimately involved in the passage of legislation, through the legislative process and I think it is going to take years before people can understand—whether they will ever understand or approve—the need to get the managerial drive into the Health Service that this Government seems to think is essential to the further prosecution, in an efficient way, of the Health Service in the future.

LORD NOLAN: Sir Clifford? No?

1689. WILLIAM UTTING: You said that the appointment system has been open to political interference. Is there a case for arguing that this was merely a temporary phenomenon? I mean, you referred, yourself, to possible causes for this, that having got a new structure and a new direction to the NHS these party political things will actually die away and with the new system for making appointments it will revert to being something that is of interest to people in the NHS and not to people outside?

ARCHIE KIRKWOOD: That may be so. I think I am suggesting that if I had been the Secretary of State who had introduced these reforms and had been foolish enough to undertake them in the timescale set out by the Government I would have been looking for my granny and my aunty and my next door neighbour to fill the roles as well, because the prospectus was just an impossible one to fulfil in the timescale set. And so, therefore, I am not one of those who believe that this is all a contrived Conservative conspiracy in order to take over the commanding heights of the National Health Service—I think they had no option, because they couldn't do it any other way, they didn't have the time. And therefore it may bed down but it will lead you into a bigger and more far-reaching and fundamental political question about whether there is now an inter-party consensus about the management and administration of the Health Service and if I understand the official Opposition's position I think they may throw the whole thing up in the air and catch the pieces as it falls. For myself I don't believe that that would be helpful and anybody who suggested it to a Health Service professional these days might need treatment themselves if they actually meant that they were going to submit the system to a new set of reforms, because I think that is the last thing that they need. But if this current system continues to exist and if there are the kind of checks and balances that your committee are considering put into place, I think that the dust may well settle in a way that would make it manageable in future.

1690. WILLIAM UTTING: There seems to me to be some advantage in maintaining the strict and direct accountability to the Secretary of State in the system. I mean, we get complaints about other organisations and you cannot find out who is responsible and accountable—at least with the NHS you know that it is the Secretary of State.

ARCHIE KIRKWOOD: Indeed. I can perhaps be a bit more objective, since it is unlikely to happen to me, but—well, maybe that is not true in my political lifetime—but if I was the Secretary of State responsible for the Health Services in any of the constituent parts of the UK I would want to retain that direct control link and authority.

WILLIAM UTTING: Thank you.

1691. LORD NOLAN: Our previous witnesses from the National Health Service were speaking to the new announcement that they made this morning, which none of us has had a chance to study in great detail, but they were pressed on the fact that neither in terms of the independent member of the new sifting panel nor, indeed, in the criteria for appointments to the Health Service Boards, was any specific mention made of the advantage of someone with local authority experience. Do you think there is an odd degree of positive prejudice on the part of the Government against local authority people being associated with the Health——

ARCHIE KIRKWOOD: I regret that I do and I think that is a matter of real regret. I think that the former system, certainly in Scotland, derived a very great deal of benefit from the input from local authority members who were conscientious and did provide at least an indirect level of accountability which I think the system benefited from. But under the old system, pre-1990, I think that there was much less concern in the public's mind about what was being done on their behalf because it was medically driven. I think there is now a much greater concern that because the system seems to be commercially driven more than medically driven. I think it would benefit from the return of local authority members carefully chosen for experience, not just because they are local authority members. But I think the fact that they were elected to local authorities—I mean, now in Scotland, you may know, Chairman, we are about to elect new unitary authorities which will have a very great impact on an important aspect of healthcare—namely the introduction of community care, where community health trusts will be working very closely with local authorities. And so for that reason, if for no other, I think that the inclusion of local authority members in the new trusts and health boards in Scotland would be a very great advantage and would go a long way to allaying some fears about the unaccountability of the current structure.

1692. LORD NOLAN: A different point—you have expressed considerable anxiety about the dangers that unsatisfactory practices will continue because staff are afraid to complain, to put it shortly. You have spoken about gagging clauses and the work done by Public Concern at Work and so forth to give, I think, its confidential legal advice. How could that be carried forward? If you give people the legal right to be protected if they complain, it is a very blunt weapon, is it not? People are not going to be anxious to put their heads above the parapet?

ARCHIE KIRKWOOD: I absolutely agree with that. I think what I am calling for, more.than statutory blunt instruments, would really be an appreciation of the fact that there is a role for healthcare professionals who in a bona fide way believe that their professional standards are being compromised by the managerial systems they are being asked to implement; that there should be an explicit machinery—or there may even be a non-executive member designated with the sole purpose of providing an avenue for those concerns to be expressed and dealt with. Of course that is a much more constructive way of approaching these things, rather than reaching for your local radio station which I think people would be ill-advised to do. But I think there is no machinery—indeed, the reverse seems to be the case—that the system that is being set up seems to repress and refuse to contemplate that professional standards can be compromised in this new commercial ethic. I think that there is a clash in the interface between the old medical ethic and the current commercial ethic. But that needs to be addressed and I am sure it can be addressed and it would be a great shame if we had to take it all the way to get statutory protection because I think that that would really be the last resort.

1693. LORD NOLAN: It was suggested, I think by NAHAT—certainly by some—that the National Health Ombudsman might have a part to play in this.

ARCHIE KIRKWOOD: Indeed, as a backstop that might be a more satisfactory remedy.

LORD NOLAN: Yes, thank you very much. Sir Martin?

MARTIN JACOMB: No, thank you.

LORD NOLAN: We are very grateful to you for coming along and for staying so late. We wish we had more time with you but what you have said you have said very clearly and succinctly and it has been a great help to us. Thank you very much.

WEDNESDAY 15 FEBRUARY 1995

Members Present:

The Rt. Hon. The Lord Nolan (Chairman)

Sir Clifford Boulton GCB

Professor Anthony King

The Rt. Hon. Peter Shore MP

The Rt. Hon. The Lord Thomson of Monifieth KT DL

Sir William Utting CB

Dame Anne Warburton DCVO CMG

Diana Warwick

Witnesses:

Dr Peter Hennessy, Professor of Contemporary History, Queen Mary and Westfield College, University of London

Sir Ronald Hampel, Deputy Chairman and Chief Executive, Anthony Weale, Government Relations Manager, Imperial Chemical Industries plc

Colin Darracott, Co-ordinator, Charter 88

David Veness, Assistant Commissioner (Specialist Operations) and David Hamilton, Solicitor's Department, Metropolitan Police

1694. LORD NOLAN: Today we continue to consider matters relating both to Quangos, and to relations between government and industry, including the question of private sector appointments after leaving public office.

We shall be hearing from Sir Ronald Hampel, Chief Executive and Chairman-Designate of ICI, whose photograph I was happy to see in *The Times* this morning as he left Buckingham Palace, after receiving his Knighthood. He will be discussing with us how one of Britain's major industrial companies views its relationship with Westminster and Whitehall.

Mr Colin Darracott, Co-ordinator of Charter 88, which campaigns for constitutional and democratic reform, will be setting out their views of the current problems and their solutions.

Mr David Veness, the Assistant Commissioner Specialist Operations at the Metropolitan Police will talk to us about the incidence of actual crime in public life, and the police view of the legislation and available penalties.

First, however, I should like to welcome Professor Peter Hennessy, Professor of Contemporary History at Queen Mary and Westfield College. Professor Hennessy is a former journalist and experienced Whitehall watcher, who had such success in his former role that civil servants are said to have been specially warned against succumbing too easily to his honeyed questioning! I hope he will not have any difficulty in succumbing to us.

Professor Peter Hennessy, were you proposing to make an opening statement before we start?

DR PETER HENNESSY

DR PETER HENNESSY (Professor of Contemporary History, Queen Mary and Westfield College, University of London): A brief one, Chairman, please if that is all right.

Can I say, first of all, how much pleasure and relief I felt when you were established and when I saw your brief. I am convinced of the necessity, not just high utility, of your work for three or four reasons.

First of all because of the cases and episodes in recent years that have produced a climate of queasiness across

pretty well the whole spectrum, embracing otherwise sober and undemonstrative people. It is not a case of rounding up the usual suspects.

Secondly because I believe the public service ethic, widely defined, must be the bonding element of public life, in all its manifestations in this country, and that this has become even more important in an era when the state and its apparatus is fragmenting into Agencies—contracting out and so on.

Also because it complements and extends the work of the House of Commons Treasury and Civil Service Select Committee and it links very firmly, I think, with the Government's acceptance of a code for civil servants and an enhanced Civil Service Commission to oversee that code.

Also because your remit is very much part of the need, I have long thought, to unearth the hidden wiring of our Constitution—not entirely hidden, the area you are looking at, but a fair amount of it is—to examine it and to see whether it needs repair or replacement.

Also because we need more clarity and transparency generally in these matters, because to reprise Professor Sammy Finer's last sentence in his wonderful book "The Anonymous Empire" 1958, which is the first scholarly work really to look at a lot of this—which Tony will remember as well as I do—when he called for "light more light". I think that call has never quite been met in the intervening years but I think it is very necessary now.

I hope that you and your Committee will be able to set a series of what one might call gold standards for public and political behaviour of roughly comparable lustre across the whole range of activities, even though each one will have to be designed specifically for the area concerned.

I would like this morning as well, if your questioning will allow me, to talk a little bit about the document *Questions of Procedure for Ministers* because I have become very concerned about status. I actually thought, having read A V Dicey and others, that it was a constitutional convention in the normal accepted sense. Dicey saying "conventions express the constitutional morality of our system" and also dealing with the discretionary powers of the Crown prerogative and so on.

But Sir Robin Butler, in an occasion that he has now allowed me to make public, changed all that when asked by one of my undergraduates, from Queen Mary and Westfield College, if it was indeed a constitutional convention, he said it was not. It is entirely discretionary but could be changed at the behest of the next Prime Minister on day one. Though a year later, when I asked him if I could put this in the public domain, he told me he had just been getting ready for the Scott Inquiry and had decided that it was not entirely discretionary, only 90 per cent of it was. So I asked him which bit was not and he said it was paragraph 27, which deals with not deceiving or misleading Parliament.

I have got a very high regard for Sir Robin Butler—I do not want any impression to the contrary to be given—but it did worry me that the British Constitution could be changed by an undergraduate's question, by roughly 90 degrees and could be then tilted back on the basis of one telephone conversation between myself and a Cabinet Secretary. And I say this with no element of facetiousness, I think it is a very, very shaky basis for such a fundamental document to rest on and I have done a little bit of research in the Public Record Office, hence this great pile here, on *Questions of Procedure for Ministers* because that very first let-out clause, which you mention in your Issues and Questions document, that it will be for individual Ministers to judge how best to act in order to uphold the highest standards, is very recent. It has emerged at some point between Mrs Thatcher's 1983 version of *Questions of Procedure for Ministers*, which I acquired by, if I can put it delicately, private means and the version published by the Prime Minister in May 1992.

It is such an important let-out. I think it would be very helpful if you could find out at whose behest and why that opt-out clause, to use the modern jargon of Euromania, slipped in to this very important constitutional document. Because I think it is a very important constitutional document, if you accept Pickthorn's argument that "procedure is all the Constitution that poor Britain has", it is these fragments in Erskine May upon which we rest. And Burke Trend, Sir Robin Butler's predecessor but three or four, said *Questions of Procedure for Ministers* is not a surrogate Constitution, it is tips of etiquette for beginners. Well I never thought it was that.

I have a clue to offer how you might find out how the changes of QPM have taken place. I will leave this for the Committee if you want—I have got the early version of how they update it. Mr Attlee's first updating, this rather great chunk of bits here, but usually somebody at principal rank, grade seven, does it and re-tweeks it on the basis of the Prime Minister's directives that have gone out since the last issue. It is done at that level normally, with a Cabinet Secretary as a sort of quality controller. But I will leave this with you because I have good reason to believe the updating of it is done that way still.

The letter which I have given to you, which is an open document entirely from the Cabinet Secretary to myself, which the press are very welcome to have as well if they want, I think gives you a clue to how you might find out how it is done. Because in the Public Record Office, every time for whatever reason, the role of the Prime Minister's relationship with the Monarch or whatever is looked at, the kind of business that Cabinet does not normally discuss, there is a little scribble which says please place in Precedent Book.

Now this was started by William Armstrong just after the War, when Churchill was going to write his memoirs and he had taken home sacks full of classified material and they did not know quite how to handle this, so they looked up how Lloyd George had been handled in the '30s, when he had done the same. William Armstrong, the Cabinet Secretary's Private Secretary, thought this might be useful for future occasions and opened up a thing called the Precedent Book, and the Precedent Book has developed mightily since then.

So I wrote to Robin Butler, asking him if he could de-classify this on a rolling basis when 30 years ate into the Precedent Book—I know he means to keep it because he uses it, it is his equivalent of case law, on all the things that you are looking at—and release it to me and others in the Public Record Office after 30 years, keeping the whole thing intact in his office and the letter you have here from him tells me why I cannot have it. He says, it is like asking for my Filofax but of course I asked for both, in my reply, but he says it is not a public record and I have to say that he is plum wrong, every piece of paper that is an official piece of paper is a public record—I am not sure if he accepts that yet but that is the case—and he does not want me to start a campaign, as you can see from the last paragraph of his letter.

How one is misunderstood Mr Chairman, but I think that you could quite legitimately ask to see it, albeit in private, to see how it happens because that is his case law, that is these messy cases with which his predecessors had to deal, interviewing Ministers privately and so on. And I would think that you should ask for it, if I can make so bold and I also think it would very hard for him to refuse to let you see that, even if you cannot make it public.

Now, I have some serious doubts, as I said a moment ago, about the sustainability of *Questions of Procedure for Ministers*, as now used and interpreted, as the chief, almost the sole, constitutional-cum-procedural safeguard we have against Ministerial impropriety. But I do not want to go on too long or pre-empt your questions.

LORD NOLAN: That has been very interesting and helpful. Our first questioner this morning will be Sir Clifford Boulton.

1695. CLIFFORD BOULTON: Thank you very much for giving us that lead into *Questions of Procedure for Ministers* because I would like to start with that and then perhaps move on to civil servants and other matters later on.

Of course, when we have an unwritten Constitution, when we do find something that is in writing, we have a temptation to grab it and say, this must be a bit of the Constitution and give it a status which an unwritten Constitution does not really expect to exist. I wonder if it is not really more correct that this document is called Notes of Guidance, and having stated a high-minded principle that Ministers must conduct themselves protecting the integrity of public life, why then should not be placed in the Notes for Guidance a personal responsibility to judge in every circumstance how best to act in order to uphold the highest standard. You seem to have a complaint about that.

PETER HENNESSY: I do.

CLIFFORD BOULTON: Can I ask whom they should be consulting all the time, apparently, as to whether or not something is protecting the highest standards?

PETER HENNESSY: The first thing about this document is it has had much more bite since it has been made public; Ministers have had to re-read it and they by and large only used to read it when they took office. So already it has got a higher status in practical terms, which is how you test constitutional validity Sir Clifford, as you know, in an unwritten sense.

I do not quite accept that one should be so casual about it because precedent is all we have and as Philip Zeigler has put it so unforgettably, the way the system works, as indeed it did in your world, is on a basis of "instantly invented precedent". And if you are in the business of instantly inventing precedent, as Sir Robin Butler is before a General Election, if there is a hung Parliament threatening and so on, the first thing they do, in Sir Robin's own phrase, is they go to the cupboards, and if the cupboards is their only guide, the only collective memory, we have to give it a very, very high status indeed. In the absence of anything else. So I am not entirely sure I accept the drift of your argument or your contention but I tested out QPM on a Cabinet Minister recently, one of the most thoughtful Cabinet Ministers, a very experienced one, as to what they think it means to them and there was a bit of a pause because they do not normally think in these terms, as you know, and he said, what it really means to a Secretary of State: "The situations in which you won't get protected if you breach one of these things."—As always you have to count the negatives when Ministers talk and see if it is a positive or a negative statement—"However, I don't believe you can codify how people behave in a whole series of situations."—Your point—"In the end you have to go down to the House of Commons and justify yourself."

Now I understand that, it is very much what you have been saying but I think, at the very least, QPM should be made an Order in Council, like at the very least the new Civil Service Code of Ethics is going to be made an Order in Council. Because the prerogative is a very useful way of giving something a considerable status without the pain and time taken in formulating legislation. And I think, if you are going for gold standards, you do not have to write down whatever carat the gold is, it is the content and the spirit that matters, and the degree to which it is accepted generally by successive generations and buttressed by all the ancient usages of the Constitution you can find. So, in that sense, I think you need—toughening it up is another matter and no doubt we will talk about that in a minute -but in terms of status it has got to glow more profoundly and more consistently than it does now. I think that is, at the very least, a first step.

1696. CLIFFORD BOULTON: You will be aware that in Erskine May, which is Notes of Guidance for Parliamentarians, the attempts to list all the unparliamentary words and therefore codify, if you like, a list of unparliamentary expressions, was dropped because although these were interesting examples of what had been unparliamentary words when they were spoken, ceased to be helpful and we fell back on a general proposition, much like this one, about moderation and good temper are the hallmarks of parliamentary language and so forth. So is it not a fact that if you tried to give status to this ragbag of interesting precedents that Sir Robin apparently collects, they could be more misleading than helpful because what is proper and acceptable conduct in any decade is going to vary with the next one.

PETER HENNESSY: That is true in terms of the Precedent Book itself but it is not true in terms of

Questions of Procedure for Ministers which, to my reading of it, in all the successive versions since the first modern one in August 1945, have got one might call a mix of immutable principles with housekeeping practicalities; a very British pragmatic document. But the immutable principles I think should govern public life, whatever jargon, whatever acronymia, whatever the social origins of MPs, whatever the current obsession of the Cabinet; I think there are some immutable factors.

Therefore I do not accept that the first opening paragraph of this, human though it may be, it is up to Ministers to know for themselves. There is a lot in that. Last week a very senior retired Permanent Secretary said to me of the new Code of Ethics that is going to be for the Civil Service, that he accepts the need for it, as all the old Permanent Secretaries did in the House of Lords Debate the other day—it was very interesting. He said, of course, we did not need it in my generation because "we had it inside us", and he does not think the present generation always has and not because he is a buffer; he is far from being a buffer. So I think these let-outs are most unfortunate because, let me risk now going into the stratosphere of pomposity, if we had a Prime Minister like Major Attlee around and a Minister transgressed, one iota of this, their feet would not touch the ground. The understanding should be, not in the words of my anonymous current Cabinet Minister, that you just do not get protected by that, you are left to the mercies of the 1922 Committee and the tabloids and Mr James Naughtie.

It means that the moment you are known to have transgressed and come clean, as most people did with Mr Attlee because they were terrified of him, you were out, with two minutes by way of a thank you and dismissal. I actually think that should be the gold standard for Prime Ministers and that any serious transgression of the immutable bits of this should result in somebody having to leave public life at least for a decent period, a decent interval.

I am very old-fashioned about that and yet we cannot rely on the current morality of each new political class which mutates in many ways according to social factors. They have got to have their own gold standard to which they have got to aspire and we have must know that there has got to be some predictability about its usage.

There has been nothing more undignified than Ministers behaving like the worst kind of Test cricketer and waiting for the umpire's finger to go up after several action replays instead of walking off.

1697. CLIFFORD BOULTON: Now if we say that we go along with your idea of codification and putting into the form of an Order in Council, as things stand that would be made under the prerogative and would have no parliamentary side to it. I noticed that in general terms you have complained about the House of Commons' poverty of aspirations when you gave evidence to the Civil Service Committee. So come on, you should be more consciously in charge of these Ministers. Would you contemplate the possibility of, in fact, the Questions for Ministers being put into the form of an Order in Council which had to be laid before the House and was subject to some parliamentary control?

PETER HENNESSY: Absolutely. I think it should start with Privy Councillor discussions, on that wonderful ancient network, the Privy Councillors' net, agreed by all parties, placed as an Order in Council before the House of Commons and when necessary renewed. It is put together again after each election as you know. For example it is going up to 135 paragraphs after the next Election because what one might crudely call the "Miss Whiplash" paragraph will be in there, covering Mr Norman Lamont's expenses and the Public Accounts Committee's objections to the way Sir Peter Middleton and one or two others—I do not want to mention names and perhaps should take that back. But it is all public. So the "Miss Whiplash" paragraph will be in there.

So you need to update it, so it will need to be relayed occasionally before the House of Commons but I think you have to bind in on constitutional documents like this. The Executive in the form of Ministers and the Prime Minister above all, the would-be Executive in terms of the Party Leaders on the Privy Councillor basis and the House of Commons certainly, in fact the House of Lords too because there are Ministers in the House of Lords, and have it laid before both Houses in the form of an Order in Council. It gives it a bite and a status which will matter and it is very, very easily done. In fact, much of this has to do with the inconvenience caused to busy people if they do not do the right thing.

I see this document, as so many of the things we are looking at, in terms of Archbishop Temple, who was the nearest thing the Anglican Church has produced to a saint this century probably, who did admit, if I remember rightly, that when he was in a rush getting from Lambeth Palace to somewhere else—they went on the tube in those days—he sometimes wanted to get into the station and through without having to pay. But it was the knowledge in the end that there was a ticket collector—this is long before those machines—at the other end which always swung the issue for Archbishop Temple. I think that is the principle that one could fruitfully adopt in this country, of the penalties in human terms of time and effort and argument and looking rather "off" if you do not do the right thing in the first place. It is exactly the same as the Permanent Secretary's Accounting Officer's Note, very rarely used, but the merest whiff of it could terrify most Ministers who were even contemplating taking the odd short cut with public money. And this could be given not quite the same status because it would not be a question of Permanent Secretary's Notes, of course it would not. And also, if there was an overseer in the House of Commons, if there were outsiders—overseer is an unfortunate word—brought in to help in these areas, it could in fact help if they were made aware of this and complainants, if they wanted to, could perhaps report to them, but that is another issue. I think at the very least, you could very easily, using existing British Constitutional practices in other areas, give this the bite and the status that it needs.

1698. CLIFFORD BOULTON: I am getting a bit anxious—I have got one or two other things to say but may I just ask you about the sanctions then that you imagine would be appropriate for cases of alleged Ministerial conduct. Perhaps think particularly about paragraph 55 which talks about improper instructions to civil servants and things like that. We have obviously had in our minds the role of the Cabinet Secretary in a recent investigation of Ministerial conduct. Would you have any comments about how you see some sanction working when this document is part of our written Constitution?

PETER HENNESSY: I think Sir Robin Butler has been put in a very difficult position by the "Aitken-Ritz"

affair. Some of his predecessors have as well but we have tended not always to know about it. This is why I want you to look at the Precedent Book because I think you ought to know, it is all in there, and it is an impossible position because a Cabinet Secretary as a Crown servant cannot say I think you are lying Minister. Many people have made this point. So at the very least, if he is to be the Prime Minister's adviser on this, which is what he is, in difficult cases the Attorney General should be with him and if you look again in the Public Record Office at say the Profumo business, the Attorney General was the one who did the questioning.

If there is any area where somebody has got to take on a Minister and put them somewhat through "the wringer", not in judicial terms or not in any way comparable to a court case, but to go beyond the niceties that the Cabinet Secretary has to observe, at the very least the Attorney General should be there as well. But in the end it has to be the Prime Minister; the tone is always set from No. 10 and the Prime Minister is the one who has to ask them to, in Attlee's phrase, "put up their bat in the pavilion and end their innings" on the basis of this advice.

I think the Cabinet Secretary at the moment, if he has to do it on his own, is put in a very difficult position. It is exactly the same as Sir Robert Armstrong having to go to Australia in the Spycatcher case; it should have been the Minister and a Law Officer at that to go into the dock there. Because we all saw what happened to him in public gaze and there are dangers—of course it would be a restrained version of that because this is not an Australian court that we are talking about—it would be a restrained version of that but it puts him a very, very difficult position indeed. I think he should make it plain to this Prime Minister and future Prime Ministers he may serve, that it is not right for him to be put in this position, particularly if there is a good chance that his advice is going to be made public, which I think it has to be in difficult cases.

1699. CLIFFORD BOULTON: Of course one has to say that, sadly, the investigation of the Profumo case did not actually produce the right answer at the time, did it?

PETER HENNESSY: No. There were human factors involved which we do not have to go into but Jack Profumo, as we all know, in the end, was the kind of Test batsman of old, who just went.

CLIFFORD BOULTON: Yes but that was at a later stage. The investigation by Ministers did not succeed.

PETER HENNESSY: Not the first time.

CLIFFORD BOULTON: Nevertheless you say that they are the people who should carry the can and not a civil servant for the outcome of the investigation.

PETER HENNESSY: I think so if the investigation has got to get a bit rough.

1700. CLIFFORD BOULTON: Yes. Then only colleagues effectively can do it.

Can I move on now to the Government White Paper *Taking Forward Continuity and Change*, which of course is very much in response to the Treasury and Civil Service Select Committee Report. What do you think of the Government's version of the Code of Conduct?

PETER HENNESSY: I think it is absolutely fine. The refinements are, to use a very boring but common word, helpful and I suspect that Treasury and Civil Service Select Committee think the same. In no way does it weaken it, it taughtens it, which is fine. So I have no complaints at all about the re-jigging that is suggested.

1701. CLIFFORD BOULTON: Or about the substance of it as it stands?

PETER HENNESSY: No I think the substance of it is spot on and I actually think the Treasury and Civil Service Select Committee showed something approaching genius actually in terms of taking the existing constitutional understandings, the "tacit understandings" to use Sir Sidney Low's lovely phrase for these things and very often using the Cabinet Secretary's own words and stone-cladding it. Which is the way the Constitution works as you know. You take a quick fix or quite often a sensible fix, you put stone around it, let ivy grow up it, then you venerate it through successive generations, that is how we make our Constitution. I can see this one being exactly in that class. So the really brilliant bit of work of that Committee was to not try and take the Constitution on because if they had tried to take the Constitution on to different plateaus, they would have faced fierce resistance from this Cabinet in particular, who, when it comes to any kind of constitutional change of any substance, seem to be, in this sense if no other, deeply conservative.

1702. CLIFFORD BOULTON: I think we are all aware of the usefulness of encouraging natural growth rather than going in for transplants if one possibly can.

Now I think in front of the Civil Service Sub Committee you actually supported the idea of the code being defined in statute. That is still your position?

PETER HENNESSY: It is and I can understand why the Government did not want to do that in one go because it is rather frightened with its molten majority of, how can one put it tactfully, the fruit cake tendencies on the Back Benches, writing in clauses which would change the British Constitution, that is why they do not want to do it in one go. And if they get the Privy Councillors' discussions, which they have invited, in that reply to the Select Committee, so that it can be done on an all-party basis so the vote is secure before it goes into statute, so it is not changed. I think they will do it and put it in the form of a statute, which will be a very good thing indeed because as you know the Northcote-Trevelyan Report of 1853 wanted all this put in a statutory form so that successive Governments could not tamper with it without it being made very transparent. Because when they do change the Order in Council, which at the moment governs all that, you have to be like my friend Peter Riddell behind me here, to notice those changes because they are not the common reading of most journalists or even most Whitehall watchers. Whereas you know, if you have to change a statute it has to be a very public thing indeed. So that is one of the several reasons why I would prefer it to be a statute.

1703. CLIFFORD BOULTON: You are going to have to come back to the House with your new Code of Conduct for Ministers as well?

PETER HENNESSY: I do not think so. Always remember you have got to wean people in this country off old habits and you cannot do it in one go. It is like trying to get open Government. You have to go to a code first because you cannot leap to a statute in one go; their nervous systems will not take it. As you well know, Sir Clifford, because you have had to manage difficult people like that in the House of Commons for a very long time, you have to make it easy for them, step by step, to move from what was unthinkable to what in the end is desirable; that is the British way.

1704. CLIFFORD BOULTON: Actually I think you did say that you wanted your Ministerial Code to be in the form of a statutory instrument, so every time you wanted to amend your Ministerial Code it would have to come back would it not?

PETER HENNESSY: In Order in Council but it would be quite infrequent, only after each General Election, which is the practice now on *Questions of Procedure for Ministers.*

1705. CLIFFORD BOULTON: You mentioned in your introductory remarks the precious public service ethic. Do you feel that has been under threat through market testing and contracting-out as a development from the Next Steps?

PETER HENNESSY: Partly, because it is very hard to define it on a bit of paper and you cannot put it in the contracts. In fact there is no real attempt to do so. It is one of the things you learn by doing and you learn from previous generations, although I think you could attempt to define it if you wanted to but market testing of its very nature involves great risk to it because part of the public service ethic is equity of treatment. However difficult the Queen's subjects may be in need of State assistance, whatever they do in the Benefits Offices or whatever, you have to treat them equally.

I remember asking the head of a very good building society if he wanted to take over the Benefits System. He said, no thank you, I do not want the underclass coming in and vomiting on my carpet. Whereas if you are in State service, whatever the underclass does, wherever it is, it deserves and should get equity of treatment. And if you contract activities of the State out of that sort, the only way you are going to make the cost-savings that make it worthwhile for people to buy the licence to do this, is to strip out the time-consuming elements of it, the routine elements and that is the problem. Because very much of the public service ethic, which is why I think it does infuse all state activity, not just Ministers and Permanent Secretaries and Private Offices, is equity of treatment, due process and keeping your hands out of public tills.

There is much more to it than that of course but the rest of it gets a bit intangible and metaphysical and Pollyanna-ish but that is the basics of it. But most of it is learned by doing it and I think it can survive Agencies very easily but it is when the activities of the State, particularly if they involve compulsion over the Queen's subjects either in the form of tax gathering or penal policy, that is when it really does worry me in terms of public service ethic. Also because I am a great believer, being a complete throwback to the Victorian era, as you have already divined, in Crown service under discipline being the only proper way of doing certain things where compulsion is built into those activities. So market testing does worry me very much particularly for these reasons.

1706. CLIFFORD BOULTON: But you just think that it is a lost cause or have you got any specific ideas about how it might be protected?

PETER HENNESSY: It does concern me because Sir Peter Levine said this in giving evidence to the Treasury and Civil Service Select Committee, it is going to be very difficult to see market tested activity coming back in again because there is not going to be a team to make an in-house bid. But I am sure we could find ways, the ingenuity of the Office of Public Service and Science would not be too stretched by this, to try and build in something approaching a public service ethic into the contracting-out.

After all, in the bad old days of the Cold War—it still happens—if you contract-out military work, procurement and so on, weapons design and manufacture, you put the Official Secrets stuff in and how, very plain, it is Fortissimo in those contracts and I think a version of that should go out with the market tested work. Because it is one of the things that is indefinable about a nation that does have a clean and decent system of public administration and governance and one that does not. A lot of it has to do with these intangibles, how things are done in the margin as it were. We all know that and you only know it by having to live under a system that is not quite so fastidious.

1707. CLIFFORD BOULTON: So it might put up the cost but it is worth it to preserve the tradition.

PETER HENNESSY: It is not a tradition, it is an absolute necessity, Sir Clifford. These things are almost "pearls beyond price" because the moment you get corrosion here, other people think they can start cutting corners as well. You get a climate of decline, of short-cutting, short-termism and a distinct lack of due process and there are enough pressures in that direction already.

1708. CLIFFORD BOULTON: We shall have an opportunity to investigate whether the private sector ethics sees itself in quite the terms that perhaps you do.

PETER HENNESSY: I was not suggesting they put their hands in the till. I think some of them do practice very good ethics in their own way.

1709. CLIFFORD BOULTON: They have long term interests to protect as well I think. Can I just ask you briefly about the Business Appointment Rules for departing civil servants and Ministers? For instance, would you like to see the rules for Ministers brought closer to those for civil servants?

PETER HENNESSY: Yes, I would.

1710. CLIFFORD BOULTON: Are you satisfied with the way the Civil Service works at the moment and what about this glut of departures that has been planned for civil servants, do you think that might necessitate a modification of the system?

PETER HENNESSY: I think the existing rules for civil servants are very good, provided they are applied in a climate that mixes common sense with austerity. You do need to have the public reassured about these things and they must not get soft on the application of a two-year Rule. I think it should be applied to Ministers.

Ministers tend to take me on one side and have a kind of whinge about this, they say, we are not like civil servants at the top end, we do not get their pay and we do not get their pensions, all we have got to sell is ourselves when we go. I find that deeply depressing because one used to think, certainly when I was younger and slightly less bufferish than I am now, that there was an element of privilege about being a Minister of the Crown and had something to do with duty. You were thought to be very fortunate if you were put in a position ever to serve your country in that way. It is not a job creation scheme for the would-be upwardly mobile.

One of the problems has to do—again I keep bringing in my friend Peter Riddell but if you read his book on the making of, the modern political class *"Honest Opportunism"*, which I do recommend you to read, you will see how and why so many of the current political class, and I can mercifully except my friend Mr Shore from this because he is a different generation, have risen without trace. They start as would-be bag carriers to Ministers, they have never held what one might call a proper job, they have always been in politically-related jobs and they rise on the basis of the worst kind of patronage and again, at the risk of sounding absurdly pompous, the real divide in British political life I think is the one that Willie Whitelaw and Denis Healey have put their finger on, nothing to do with left or right, wet or dry, it is the generation that lifted the slump and fought in the War and that which did not. And the one that has come in recently, because its political formation is terribly narrow and also mainly in the era of, by British standards, intensely polarised politics, does not have the same experience or built-in restraints. If they say things to me like, I have to be able to sell myself when I go because I have got a family, what has happened to us? I have no sympathy at all with that kind of argument.

Also the business class say they will not come in because there is not enough money. If money is the main reason for them coming in, they can stay out. I also suspect the better end of the professional business class, those other professions, are put off by other things. The fact that the hours, even given the recent changes in procedure, are still absurd. You do not see your family. To get chosen by many of the constituencies these days you have to put on one side for the duration the selection process, all the things you have grown up to believe in, like evidence and truth and honesty. You have to mix with some of the worst charlatans in British public and political life for years to come, and crawl up what Nye Bevan called the ladder of preferment on your belly. That is why people do not come in Sir Clifford, it is nothing to do with the money, or the good people do not come in.

CLIFFORD BOULTON: On some occasion when we have got a day or two to spare, perhaps I could continue that very provocative comment with you but I think now is perhaps not the moment. I suggest my other colleagues may like to ask you some questions.

LORD NOLAN: Thank you very much. Dame Anne, may we start with you this morning:

1711. ANNE WARBURTON: It is a little difficult to find space between words after that, is it not? I would like to take you back if I might Dr Hennessy to your very eloquent testimony, also to the Treasury and Civil Service Committee in '93. I was struck by many things in it but let me mention particularly, you were asked, I think, where is the model Civil Service to be found? And you said, here. And then you went on later on to say that, we had one of the 20-25 clean and decent public services out of 190 in the world at large but you showed a lot of concern about how to keep it so and I would really rather like to ask, particularly politicisation, whether in the intervening two years you are more reassured or depressed?

PETER HENNESSY: I am more reassured, Dame Anne, because of the Treasury and Civil Service Select Committee Inquiry and the Government's acceptance of the crucial point about the Code of Ethics because that does reassure, I am sure, to some extent, the Opposition but Whitehall has not turned into Bluehall. And that was very necessary.

Politicisation does worry me but I think it is confined to two people, who I will name—Sir Bernard Ingham and Sir Charles Powell. You only have to read the memoirs, Sir Bernard's in his own case and Sir Charles's interview with *The Times* recently, to see that they did, very largely, go native on No. 10. Sir Charles explained why because it is very small, the Prime Minister has to feel you are entirely on her side and so on in this. I think that politicisation of the kind that too many people think is general in the Senior Civil Service was, in effect, confined to that pocket in No. 10.

The real problem, however, is the one that Lord Bancroft has identified—the former Head of the Home Civil Service—which is that after one Government being in office for so long, it is a very different Government this one—even though it has the same label—than some of it predecessors since '79. The problem of a predominant Party system, as Tony King and others have called it, not a single Party state, is that you lose familiarity with alternative ways of thinking and looking at problems.

Before the last Election, just over here in the QE2 Centre, certain very politically sensitive Departments, got the old sweats in to brief the young, on what Labour Ministers were like and how the vocabulary of the Private Office would have to change pretty quickly the moment they arrived.

So it is a lack of familiarity problem. If you are in the Department of the Environment for example and you are younger than me, you will not have worked closely with Ministers, in fact you may not have even been in the Department much since before '79, you certainly will not have worked closely with Ministers who do not see local government as part of the problem, rather than part of any solution. So it is this lack of familiarity with other ways of looking at things, certainly from the days when Mr Shore was Environment Secretary, that is the real problem, rather than politicisation. Because anybody who knows the Senior British Civil Service knows that it is very hard to get them to believe in anything, certainly not a Party Manifesto. They are not ones for "isms" and they would agree, I think, with the late Victor Rothschild about manifestos and talk about the "promises and panaceas that gleam like false teeth" in these documents. Rather than fall for the beauty of any particular ideology. So I do not think it is a problem in the crude and obvious sense but I think it is a much more subtle problem and I think that is a genuine one, but I am pretty sure it can be overcome very quickly, provided the incoming Government is not convinced that it is "Bluehall" and starts removing people

on the basis of they got too close to their Conservative predecessors. Once that happens, in one conspicuous and important case, the Northcote-Trevelyan principle on which all of this is based, which does keep us clean and decent, keeps us in the top 25 all the time—and higher—will crumble very fast.

1712. ANNE WARBURTON: Thank you very much. May I just follow that up with one other question? Do you think that the monitoring which is done by the Treasury and Civil Service Committee is first of all right and sufficient as a watch on this?

PETER HENNESSY: I think it is one of the very best of the post-'79 Select Committees in all sorts of ways and in this area, particularly now that it has moved into the constitutional patch, which used to be regarded as the great Secret Garden by Whitehall, you do not want Back Benchers getting in any of these areas, relationships between Ministers and civil servants. Norman Brook used to minute Edward Bridges about this quite frequently, 40 or 50 years ago.

That has now been changed by that Select Committee. In effect reasserting Parliament's, I would call it prerogative, to have a real say in the organic development of the British Constitution. It should never have lost it, but it has been a supine Parliament this century, it has been an executive-dominated century and they have let them get away with it but because that Select Committee has proved so pertinacious at looking at Next Steps, coming back to things time and again and watching it, not just doing a one-off, and then moving very carefully and sensibly into this constitutional patch, I would not say it is an ideal watchdog because in the end the Executive can treat Select Committees with cavalier contempt if they really want to, though they are not doing so at the moment for obvious reasons, but I actually think it is a very, very impressive record. And their own kind of case laws as it were in terms of their own aspirations and conduct, has developed marvellously since '79. It is not true in the case of some of the other Select Committees but the other Select Committees are only to a lesser extent involved in these matters of high seriousness that you are concerned with.

ANNE WARBURTON: Thank you.

LORD NOLAN: If we are going to even a reasonable distance into the next witness's time I must ask the Committee to confine themselves to their two best questions. Could you do that do you think?

1713. PROF ANTHONY KING: Let me ask you about relations between Ministers and their officials. Ministers have a right to confidentiality. The public has a right to know if Ministers are behaving improperly. Those two rights are on a collision course. How does the system deal with that at the moment?

PETER HENNESSY: Private Secretary has a very quiet word with the Permanent Secretary that he is on the bottle or seeing certain people he should not be seeing; I do not know what to do but perhaps you had better tackle it. If it then does not work at that level—it usually does, a quiet word—which is a sensible way of doing it, it goes to the Cabinet Secretary and the Prime Minister, does it not? It varies but the first line of defence is the Private Secretary. I remember Lord Redcliffe-Maud used to say it is in some ways "like a marriage", which is a very strange metaphor but there is something in it, the very first signs are seen there and it is always done extremely discreetly, as indeed it should be.

1714. PROF ANTHONY KING: Is the new Civil Service Code going to be make a difference do you think?

PETER HENNESSY: Only if Ministers ask them to do something that is verging on the illegal or absolutely improper. Then they can go federal on it if they have to. If they cannot get satisfaction by doing it with a line manager and going up the hierarchy then it goes to the Cabinet Secretary and then it will go to the Civil Service Commissioners. It has to be one of those areas that are specified in the new code, otherwise it will still be done on that very discreet basis I am sure.

1715. PROF ANTHONY KING: My second question relates precisely to that. In the famous paragraph 55 it says that "Ministers have a duty to refrain from asking or instructing civil servants to do things which they should not do." Is it your impression that Ministers nowadays are more likely than they were in the past to do that?

PETER HENNESSY: I am afraid so. Again we do not want to go into specific cases but I am sure the reason my good friend Clive Ponting went molten, was he found it quite offensive, given his experience of previous Ministers, to be asked to draft a range of Parliamentary answers, some of which set alarm bells ringing—I will not put it any higher than that. I think he was genuinely shocked. It is partly to do with the polarisation of British politics and the lack of the formation of the modern political task compared to some of its predecessors, that they do not know about the "code of the Woosters" actually because they have not grown up that way. Usually, I have to say in defence of the present political class, at the moment when they are told about what the informal "code of the Woosters" requires them to do and not to do they fall into line but not always. Some of them have a tendency to get very cross with public servants who do the impression of Sidney Carlton on the scaffold and assert Ministerial prerogatives where it is quite wrong for them so to do. We know the names of those and I am not going to give them to you.

1716. PROF ANTHONY KING: Could I just ask you, very quickly and for a very quick answer, do you think that in the new Civil Service Code there should be an explicit reference to paragraph 55 in *Questions of Procedure for Ministers*?

PETER HENNESSY: I think it is pretty well in there already actually. They use that as one of the bases for it but it may well be that it needs to be linked explicitly to this, particularly if it is going to form an Order in Council in itself. Cross reference.

1717. LORD NOLAN: I do not want to trivialise the nature of the debate but I thought the code of the Woosters was, you never let a pal down. Is that really what you had in mind?

PETER HENNESSY: The Secretary of State is not your pal, he is your boss, and a Crown appointee, which is very different.

1718. PETER SHORE: I just want one question, given the time constraint, to follow what Professor King has been asking you. In that White Paper *Taking Forward Continuity and Change* there is specific allowance for an independent line of appeal, is there not, to the new I think it is the First Commissioner of the Civil Service?

PETER HENNESSY: Yes.

1719. PETER SHORE: Do you think that line of appeal would, in fact, deal with the kind of problems that people have complained about in the past—you gave the example of Ponting.

PETER HENNESSY: It could well do, Mr Shore, in the sense that if Ministers are aware of how far it can go—and the civil servants will be able to report to Parliament their happiness or otherwise with this, although obviously they will not be able to go into the exact detail—it means that Ministers who want to dicker around with the niceties of the code of the Wooster will think it is not worth it, because it would cause too much trouble and they would have to explain themselves to the Permanent Secretary and perhaps even the Prime Minister and it may even reach Parliament, albeit in a muted form. It is enough to stop most people, is it not, even contemplating short cuts?

PETER SHORE: I would have thought so, being analgous with an accounting officer's note.

PETER HENNESSY: Exactly so.

PETER SHORE: We have seen recently how effective they can be.

PETER HENNESSY: Yes, exactly.

1720. LORD THOMSON: You mentioned Mr Attlee's standards as Prime Minister, which to someone of my age was music in my ears. Mr Attlee ran an empire and a post war country of controls with, I think, 33 junior Ministers.

PETER HENNESSY: Yes.

LORD THOMSON: The present Government requires 62, one of the biggest teams of Ministers in western Europe.

PETER HENNESSY: Yes.

1721. LORD THOMSON: Would not QPM be a good deal easier to manage and some of our problems with Ministers taking outside appointments be easier to manage if we were to go back to a more slimline Administration?

PETER HENNESSY: It would mean that the Prime Minister knew them all very well. The greatest problem was that when Mr Churchill came back in 1951, he could not remember the names of half the Cabinet at some meetings, let alone the junior Ministers. In that sense it would help, but that is a much wider question of overstretch and overload than the one we are dealing with. It sounds absurdly British in a way, but if it is quite a small platoon and everyone knows each other, everyone can watch each other. There is something in that.

1722. DIANA WARWICK: In your evidence to the Treasury and Civil Service Committee you seemed to place a lot of confidence in the structure of Parliament. In your presentation you talked about the "climate of queasiness", what I think the Americans call the "smell factor". Do you think that in the sorts of cases that we have been asked to look at in general terms Parliament is capable of regulating itself, given its past history on these cases?

PETER HENNESSY: No. I think it needs help to do the right thing, in the form of a very small number of people who would be servants of the House in the way that the Comptroller and Auditor General has been since 1983. They could report to the House, to the Privileges or Members' Interests Committee, depending on what it was, their findings and recommendations. They would not act on them, but make it plain to the Committee what the real problem was as outside consultants.

One of the problems with living night and day with each other in the House of Commons is that Members pick up each other's standards and can forget what it looks like to people outside. It would get round the problem of them not thinking that anyone should come into their sacred patch if these people were servants of the House, appointed by the House after consultations between the Prime Minister, the Leaders of the Opposition Parties and the Chairmen of the Committees of Privileges and Members' Interests. It could be an inclusive business, making them servants of the House and using them. I have the image of William Temple and the ticket collector in mind. That is the best way to proceed, because I do not think that public confidence exists; I do not think that the public thinks that Members can regulate themselves.

I do not want to bang on about the political class obsessively, but we all know that, compared to other professions, they are a group of chancers. One does not go into political life if one wants regularity, promotion and increments. Members are quite risky by temperament and are chancers—not all of them, of course. The climate in which the House of Commons operates sometimes is distinctly overheated. The House is prone to deluding itself that this is what matters and no one else understands. There is a professional de-formation about the way that Parliament often operates.

1723. WILLIAM UTTING: You referred at the outset to fragmentation in the way in which public business is now conducted. I am struggling with this great undifferentiated mass of Next Steps agencies, non-departmental public bodies—Quangos—the NHS, TECs and so on. There is an implication behind what you said that there is a need for greater central control across the board and greater consistency when these kinds of developments occur. Have you any views about how that might be achieved?

PETER HENNESSY: I would not use the word "control", Sir William. I would say that "consistency" was the key to it. One could draw up codes of conduct, or however one wanted to do it, for Quangoland, contracting out—agencies are all right, because they come under the civil service code, as they are still within the "inner ring"—that had the same values expressed, but slightly differently according to different circumstances. I think that if the best practices of public appointment and advertising, with a body such as the Civil Service Commission overseeing the probity of it, were extended to Quangoland, a lot of the problem would evaporate, especially if the National Audit Office was allowed to run through all that. It is a question of standardising best practice.

What really worries me is Quangoland. I think it was a Minister at the DTI who said that she had not knowingly over some years appointed a known Labour supporter to any public appointment. That is a nightmare. That is what I mean about the change in the political class. It would have been anathema to the generations of the 1940s and 1950s—and even the 1960s, where an element in the balance of the good and the great was much prized. When MacMillan looked at the burden on Ministers, he asked Lord Attlee to chair it. That would be inconceivable now, although it was built into that generation. It is no longer built in, so one has to help people to re-acquire the virtues of the past, because we are only here to help, are we not, Sir William?

1724. LORD NOLAN: I will forego my turn, because not only have you answered all the questions I had in mind, but quite a number that I did not have in mind. We are exceedingly grateful to you for such an invigorating and, if I may say so, carefully thought out and solid piece of research and advice. Thank you very much for coming along.

Now we have Sir Ronald Hampel, Deputy Chairman and Chief Executive of Imperial Chemical Industries and shortly to become Chairman, and Mr Anthony Weale, his Government Relations Manager. Sir Ronald, we were saying before you arrived that we were very happy to see your photograph in *The Times* this morning. It is a great pleasure to have you here so soon afterwards. Thank you very much for coming along, both of you. Is it right that you have prepared an introductory statement with which you would like to begin?

SIR RONALD HAMPEL AND ANTHONY WEALE

SIR RONALD HAMPEL (Deputy Chairman and Chief Executive, Imperial Chemical Industries plc): Just a few words, yes.

LORD NOLAN: If you please.

RONALD HAMPEL: Perhaps the first thing I should say is that ICI today does 20 per cent of its business in the UK. That is substantially less than 50 years ago and is a reflection not of the decreasing importance of our business in the UK, but rather of the increasing importance of activities outside the UK. The UK remains our heartland however, it is our technological base and our shareholding base. For the foreseeable future—by that I mean as far ahead as I can possibly see—ICI will have its fundamental base here; therefore in that context its relationships with government are critical to us.

A couple of words about myself. I joined the ICI Board in 1985, but I first came into the field of direct relationships with government in 1977, when I was appointed to a general manager post in head office which had overall responsibility for our relationships with government. One of Anthony Weale's predecessors reported to me at that time. From 1977 to 1980 and from 1985 onwards, I have been closely involved in our relationships with government.

Anthony Weale has been with ICI for 25 years. He is our Government Relations Manager. He has an executive with business experience. He spent three years on secondment to government and was Commercial Secretary in Mexico. He has been doing his present job for seven years. We have had Government Relations Managers in-house in ICI for as long as I can remember and only one, Alex Todd, was brought in from outside. He had political experience. All the rest have been insiders who have developed a relationship with government over time.

Our basic philosophy in dealing with the outside world in general is pretty simple. It is an ethos in which I have been brought up and which I understand. It is that we should establish with our customers, suppliers and competitors—and indeed with Parliament and the civil service in the areas of the world in which we deal—a relationship, that we should know people with whom we are likely to have dealings and that getting to know them is likely to be best done in non-confrontational circumstances and that the social element plays a part in that. This means that when one has an issue or a crisis—it applies on either side—there can be a debate against the background of the knowledge of the individuals one is dealing with and one can have a view of whether one trusts them. That seems to us to have worked extremely well over the years.

Our attitude has been non-political. We deal with both sides of Parliament even-handedly, and have done for as long as I can remember. We make no political contributions as a matter of policy. We do not pay MPs for advice, and have not done so.

Our fundamental relationship is, first, with constituency MPs. There are nearly 60 MPs who have ICI establishments in their constituencies. The basic contact with them is at the local level. We seek to keep them informed. For example, last week there was, sadly, an announcement of a reduction of a workforce at RDO in Scotland. The MPs involved were informed well in advance and there was a full debate about the implications. It was against the background that they knew us and we knew them.

We have a reception once a year, to which we invite all those MPs. This year over 50 came. It is normally held in November. I have to say that the attendance has more to do with business in the House than with the reception itself. It is an all-party affair that we value greatly.

We have relationships with Ministers and senior Members of the Opposition and seek to see them roughly once a year in a social atmosphere, where either side is free to raise issues; but we generally try to steer clear on those occasions of anything confrontational. It is entirely the Minister or the senior Member of the Opposition who decides whether to accept the invitation.

We have relationships also with the civil service and would expect to know on a regular basis the senior people in the Treasury, the Department of Trade and Industry, the Foreign Office, the Department of Employment, the Department of the Environment and the Office of Science and Technology. We provide briefing papers when we regard an issue as being significant. We are available at any time for consultation. Anthony Weale's full-time job is to be available to all arms of government and to provide that information and to arrange meetings, if necessary. members of the civil service and MPs visit our local sites on a regular basis.

In conclusion, the only thing I would say is that we believe that by and large industry needs to be better understood by government than it is. From our perspective, we regard the time spent in seeking to provide some background as absolutely vital. We would be concerned if that became less easy in future than it has been in the past.

LORD NOLAN: Thank you very much. I am going to ask Miss Diana Warwick to take up the questions, please, Sir Ronald.

1725. DIANA WARWICK: Sir Ronald, I wonder if I can ask both you and Anthony Weale this. You have given some indication of the elements of the government relations job. What would you say were the key elements?

ANTHONY WEALE (Government Relations Manager, ICI plc): Without a doubt, as Sir Ronald has made clear, being issue driven. The relationships that we have with parliamentarians or with civil servants are issue driven. To be quite honest, we begin with the civil service; it is very rare indeed that I would pick up an issue and start moving it with elected politicians before I had explored most aspects of it with civil servants. I really cannot think of an exception to that. The most important thing that I do is to deal with the civil service. After that, I do keep relationships going with all our constituency MPs, with MPs who are involved, let us say, in particular Select Committees or who have particular interests in a given issue. It all goes back to being issue driven.

1726. DIANA WARWICK: In terms of the amount of parliamentary activity, would you be judged on performance, according to what you achieve with MPs or Ministers?

ANTHONY WEALE: In a sense, I hope not, because success in this area is very difficult to measure. When I look back over the seven years since I have been doing the job and consider ways in which we might have successfully changed legislation, they are few and far between. All I can ever say in support of what I am doing is that I hope that things would have been a lot worse if I had not been here. That is the best I can say.

RONALD HAMPEL: There are perhaps two recent issues that we can give by way of example. One is the price of electricity, where we have been very vociferous, both as a company and through trade associations. Anthony and colleagues in the company have briefed everybody imaginable on what we regard as the problems associated with a very high industrial electricity price, which makes it non-competitive. That started as an issue and continues an issue.

Secondly, more recently the Goode Committee on Pensions has led to legislation coming before the House. We were anxious that there should be some balance put into that at an appropriate stage. We pursued that issue, first, with the civil service and then with the appropriate Secretary of State.

DIANA WARWICK: You have also got Government Relations Managers, you say, in Brussels and in the States.

RONALD HAMPEL: That is right.

1727. DIANA WARWICK: Are there key differences or similarities that you could draw to our attention between the three roles?

RONALD HAMPEL: There are key differences. The role is much closer here. First of all, this is a critical market for us and we live just down the road. The relationship in Brussels is one with a bureaucracy primarily rather than with an elected body, but we are very concerned about the development of regulation there, and again we may have issues.

In the United States, as you are no doubt aware, it is a much more regulated relationship. Indeed, our Government Relations Manager is, so to speak, "registered" with the government.

1728. DIANA WARWICK: As a lobbyist?

RONALD HAMPEL: As a lobbyist, yes. But it has nothing like the same closeness. We would not expect to be able to place in front of Ministers or civil servants at the most senior level the sort of general issues that we place here. It is natural that the American Government would listen first to the large companies that have their base there. We will be much more ICI issue driven there than we are on a general industrial basis here.

1729. DIANA WARWICK: You say in your evidence to us that you do not employ MPs and rarely employ lobbying companies to make your case to government, and that you have a policy, which you have repeated now, of being non-partisan in your dealings with government in Whitehall. There would be nothing to stop you retaining MPs of all political colours in office, if you wanted to.

RONALD HAMPEL: Nothing at all, no.

1730. DIANA WARWICK: Do you not regard MPs as good value for money?

RONALD HAMPEL: It is interesting, because some may recall that we had an unwelcome shareholder for a short period some years ago and were inundated with helpful suggestions as to who we might employ to assist us if it ever became a large issue. We actually discussed, mainly with our constituency MPs, whether in the event that we did need to get a larger campaign mounted, it would be helpful. The view that they expressed was that we had a good relationship and that that relationship, based on an effective Government Relations Manager, was perfectly satisfactory and was in a sense more trusted as a result. I have to say, however, that I think that it is something that only a large company can afford. One must be realistic about this. We have regarded the employment of someone like Anthony Weale as good value for money. In the event, the debates that we had with various Committees of the House during that period were handled directly by us and, from our point of view, very satisfactorily. But we do not specifically feel that it has any reflection on either MPs or lobbyists; it is more about what we think is good for ourselves.

1731. DIANA WARWICK: Let me take you back to something I should have asked you. You said that it was a matter of policy that you make no political contributions. Again in your evidence to us you say that you do not make political contributions in the UK. Do you make them anywhere else, or is it a matter of policy for the company?

RONALD HAMPEL: It is a matter of policy. I was slightly nervous about the statement, because there may occasionally have been something in the past in particular countries where we have large public companies with public shareholdings and one of them has done something

that I would be unaware of. But the company's general, stated policy is what I put in front of you.

1732. DIANA WARWICK: You say in your evidence that there are MPs and peers who at some stage in their career worked for ICI. If one of your employees stands for election and is elected, without naming any names, could you tell us whether you have agreed severance packages? If so, what have they included?

RONALD HAMPEL: I am not sure that I know the answer. Anthony, do you know?

ANTHONY WEALE: If somebody wants to stand as an MP, first of all he or she gets the period of the campaign as paid leave—that is, three weeks leading up to the election as paid leave. After that, they are allowed to stay on the books of ICI for the first five years that they are Members of the House. If, at the end of five years or during those five years they lose or resign their seat, they have a right to take up a job in ICI at the same level on which they left. If they come back to ICI, the period during which they have been absent is pensionable. Basically, those are the rules.

RONALD HAMPEL: But they are not paid by us.

ANTHONY WEALE: They are not paid by us, but the company takes on their contribution to the pension fund during the time that they are absent.

1733. DIANA WARWICK: So there is a continuing connection with ICI through the pension fund and you continue to make a payment individually to it?

ANTHONY WEALE: Yes, but we would only do that retrospectively, I think, if the erstwhile employee returned to us. If he does not come back to us, the gate is closed.

1734. DIANA WARWICK: What about an exit bonus or a company car? Would they keep those perks?

ANTHONY WEALE: No. They would not.

1735. DIANA WARWICK: Do you think this is common policy among large companies?

ANTHONY WEALE: I do not know very much about it. I know that the Industry and Parliament Trust, a group of which you will all be aware, I expect, has done quite a lot of work to discover what company practice is. I have to admit that I do not know what the result of that is; I have merely contributed ICI's system to the process.

1736. DIANA WARWICK: Thank you. One of the issues you have been dealing with is what I think has been called the "revolving door", where Ministers and others move into companies which have in some way been connected with their work in Parliament. Some Ministers, in their evidence to us, have urged tighter controls. Mr Hunt, speaking for the Government, did not want any restrictions at all. The CBI, in their evidence to us, say that, where the connection between the job in government and the new job is close, a delay would be in order. Do you think there is a danger under the present rules that someone might feather their nest in office in order to obtain future employment?

RONALD HAMPEL: I think this is very difficult. The public really demands a sensible gap, and the civil service rules seem to us to be the appropriate ones to apply. The idea that people of competence are disqualified from taking outside employment at a later stage seems to me totally wrong. To take it out of the UK environment, ICI has recently had Paul Volcker as an outside director, who was Chairman of the Federal Reserve in the United States. He made a significant contribution to our business as a director; he had absolutely no involvement with our business before he became a director. I would have regarded it as a considerable weakness if we had not been able to offer him that post.

1737. DIANA WARWICK: But in general terms, if the relationship is close, you believe the civil service rules would be appropriate?

RONALD HAMPEL: I do, yes. I think public concern demands it. It is a difficult arena, self-evidently, because any large company has a large interface with government and one could almost say that anybody who had been in the principal offices of state would have had some involvement indirectly or directly. Therefore I think that a gap of an appropriate period is sensible.

1738. DIANA WARWICK: One of the other issues we have been wrestling with is where to draw the line on the role of MPs acting as lobbyists. Do you think as a point of principle that there is anything wrong with MPs acting as consultants, either through lobbying firms or even to individual companies?

RONALD HAMPEL: No, I do not, so long as it is clearly declared. The fact that we have not adopted that process does not come out of a point of principle. It would be equally wrong of me to say that there are not people in the House who have a particular like or dislike of things that ICI might be about. Those who have historical relationships with ICI, particularly those who have been employed by us, often say, when they make a point in the House, that they were at one stage employed by ICI. That is perfectly proper and should be done.

1739. DIANA WARWICK: But the principle that has been put to us is that the idea of an "MP for hire", available to act on behalf of any company that a lobbying company is representing at the time, is really a bit off.

RONALD HAMPEL: I think the difficulty here is what is the role of a lobbying company. Originally, when I put this submission together, I was unaware—which you may find slightly strange—that we ever used a lobbying company in any way. We have used a lobbying company on a highly technical area, where it collected evidence. It having collected the evidence, we made the submission, so we did not in effect use the company for lobbying. From my perspective, the restriction that one places on people's involvement with lobbying companies is more about what the lobbying companies are there for and what particular aims they are pursuing. Speaking as an individual, I would not want as a general restriction to say that it is per se wrong. I am right down the track of believing that these things have to be right out in the open and publicly declared.

1740. DIANA WARWICK: If we were to move down the path of restricting that role, as we have been urged to do by many, how would you regard the role of your own in-house lobbying function or government affairs function? Would you object to any restriction that was applied to lobbying to be applied to your company?

RONALD HAMPEL: Again it depends on what the restriction might be. If we were inhibited from our day-to-day contact with MPs—if that falls under the umbrella of lobbying -I would find it a disadvantage both to ICI and, I believe, to MPs. All the evidence, and Anthony Weale's comments about his success rate, suggest that MPs are quite capable—as in a broader sense are Parliament and the civil service—of making up their minds independently. The issue that you are wrestling with is the degree to which an individual makes a particular case and a particularly slanted case. While I understand the particular difficulties of MPs with lobbyists, because of the type of name, I feel it would be a pity if the relationships between individual companies and government were in some way restricted because they fell within a case of lobbying. From my point of view, it is self-evident that we are peddling ICI's interests. We are bound to be: that is my job.

1741. DIANA WARWICK: So you really see a difference?

RONALD HAMPEL: I do see a difference, but in a sense it seems to me that lobbyists of themselves say that they are lobbyists, and therefore people know exactly what line they are taking. People have the ability therefore to disregard their advice if they so wish.

ANTHONY WEALE: If I may add to that, going back to your question about placing restrictions on lobbyists, as loosely a lobbyist myself, I should not particularly worry if I had to turn up at the House of Commons, float a paper about and say, "Here I am, I'm ICI's lobbyist". That would not worry me at all. What would worry me would be restrictions placed on what I might call "men from the coalface". When one is dealing with a fairly specific or technical issue in the House of Commons or in Parliament generally, it is necessary, I believe, to bring along people who really know what the effect of government's ideas might be on—in our case—ICI. They might turn up only once or twice while a given issue was running to make ICI's point to government. If they had to go through a performance of registration and limitation, effectively, it would in turn limit our ability to present our case to government, I think.

1742. DIANA WARWICK: Could I turn to one of the points that you made in your introductory statement about the social relationship that you have with MPs and Ministers? You also raised the point about declaration. You said that you offer hospitality to MPs, peers, officials and others, and that you are governed by what is acceptable "even to a stern critic". Could you tell us how that works and what is involved?

RONALD HAMPEL: The basis of our social relationship is lunch or dinner. The dinners frequently involve spouses, in the sense that the official or Minister is invited to bring the spouse is they so wish, and it depends on whether they wish to do so. In many senses, that is regarded as a welcome invitation, because the life that these people lead frequently keeps them away from their spouses. Beyond that, ICI has hospitality facilities at Wimbledon and the opera; from time to time senior people are invited to accompany us there. Again it is entirely up to them whether they wish to accept. In the nature of relationships, we get to know some people extremely well. Some of the people who were at university with me are now at the top of government or in senior positions in Parliament, and it would be ridiculous if I could not see them in the way I have in the past. Against that background, we do not regard that as unacceptable. As far as I am aware, we have never been criticised for it by either Government or Opposition.

It is important to say that throughout the 1980s we maintained assiduously our contacts with the Opposition as much as with the Government, because we regarded the Opposition as a critical part of the process. Self-evidently, as Anthony Weale has said, the civil service is where we start, basically because it produces the issue papers. We regard getting to know civil servants in the same light. That is the level of the hospitality.

1743. DIANA WARWICK: You have been organising in this way for 25 years, you say. Is any of this written down? Is there a code that you work to?

RONALD HAMPEL: No. We have never written it down. I do not know that anyone has ever turned round to us and said, "I think that's improper". In the way in which the company has built its traditional relationship, that has always been the case for as long as I can remember. We have not extended it.

1744. DIANA WARWICK: Finally, you were here during most of Professor Hennessy's evidence to us. He talked about the ethos of the civil service; you talked about "growing up" in ICI. You both gave the impression that ethics and codes can be imbued.

RONALD HAMPEL: Yes.

DIANA WARWICK: How did you feel about the way he described both the ethics and ethos of the civil service as opposed to what you would expect in business?

RONALD HAMPEL: To be honest, we were only here for the last 15 minutes, and I am not sure whether I heard the whole of what he was saying. My experience of civil servants at middle and senior levels is that in general terms they have exactly the same traditional view of relationships as we do. Basically, it is of value to them, as it is to us, to understand what we are about and why we are doing it. They are under no illusions that we are doing it because at the end of the day we are seeking to further ICI's business. There is no dubiety about the underlying background. They equally recognise—and we see that recognition in the way they ask us to provide people to sit on committees and investigations—that we have balance and experience which is valuable in developing their policy for industry generally. It is not an area that has troubled me in our relationships with the civil service. I broadly believe that the excesses that occur from time to time are single examples rather than a general lessening of standards, from our perspective.

DIANA WARWICK: Thank you.

1745. WILLIAM UTTING: A couple of issues arising from that last answer. It has been put to us that one of the problems with the public sector is the unwise importation of private business values. I have to say that the examples that have been given to us of things going wrong here would seem to be example of unethical or incompetent

behaviour, whatever context one was operating in. But you clearly do not see any fundamental incompatibility between the ethics of private business and those of public service. Does your organisation have a code of conduct for employees?

RONALD HAMPEL: We do. We have a published code of ethics which we publish worldwide and which is in the public domain. That is relatively recent. I am sure that it has been pointed out to you that standards vary in differing parts of the world—indeed, it was referred to by the earlier witness to some extent. From my perspective, like every organisation, from time to time we have an individual example of something that troubles us. We deal with it in an appropriate manner. From time to time that causes us to change slightly our general codes of conduct or our published statements. That is part of developing society. This is a similar area. But as a generality, the standards that I experienced when I joined ICI 40 years ago seem to be broadly the standards that apply today. We have become much more international and subject to much more short term pressure. We have to remind people probably a little more often. But I have always believed that it is the examples that are set at the top that set the standards through the organisation.

WILLIAM UTTING: That is very helpful. I should like to see a copy of the code.

RONALD HAMPEL: We will gladly send it to you.[14]

1746. WILLIAM UTTING: You also mentioned making staff available to do jobs for government. I want to ask you about your general policy in relation to members of staff taking up public appointments. You obviously have staff who are operating as local councillors or magistrates. Do you also enable staff to take up paid or unpaid public appointments as members of Quangos, NHS trusts and so on?

RONALD HAMPEL: We thought the question about Quangos might arise. We tried to test whether we had anybody on a Quango. Anthony could not find anyone in the literal sense. Denys Henderson, Chairman of ICI, is Chairman of the Quality Foundation, which was set up by the DTI, but he is unpaid. Rob Margetts, who is a colleague Executive Director, is on the Technology Foresight Committee and Chairman of Action on Engineering, which is a DTI initiative. Both those functions are voluntary and time-consuming. We regard them as a proper contribution to the development of those areas of activity in this country generally. That applies down the line: we enable people to do it.

We have downsized considerably over the past few years, as every company has, and have used that process to second people while we have continued to pay them as part of the process of transferring people out. There will be examples of people all over the country who have moved from our employment into other employment through that process. I cannot give you detailed examples, I am afraid, but we could give you more information if you want it.

WILLIAM UTTING: If you have a policy about employees taking up public appointments, I should be glad to know what it is.

RONALD HAMPEL: It is too strong to say that there is a policy, Sir William; it is more a matter of an individual

---

[14]See Evidence pp. 533–535.

case and the degree to which we can afford the release of time and the value we place on it.

WILLIAM UTTING: Good. Thank you.

CLIFFORD BOULTON: Sir William has covered my point.

LORD THOMSON: I have no questions, but, given the nature of our committee, I ought to declare an interest, as a former non-executive director of ICI who left the board some four years ago, but who still, in the language of Ronnie Hampel, feels some vestigual interest in the company. I can confirm that during my service on the board, when I was in the House of Lords, at no time did I ever do anything in the House of Lords for ICI, nor was I ever asked to do so, but I did of course give them advice about the public posture and the conduct of public affairs generally.

1747. LORD NOLAN: Sir Ronald, you spoke earlier, if I understood you rightly, of your wish that government was more familiar with the problems of industry and you told us a little about members of ICI staff being seconded into, amongst others, areas of government service. Is there movement in the opposite direction? Do you have civil servants seconded to you?

RONALD HAMPEL: We have done in the past. You could perhaps bring us right up to date, Anthony. I can recall that when I was Chairman of one of our divisions we had an Under-Secretary as a non-executive director of that operation. As I recall, it was someone who came, when I was Chairman of Paints, from the Department of Health and Social Security, a totally different area. His time commitment was roughly one day a month for a period of time. It was regarded as a piece of cross-education. If I am totally honest, I think they got more out of it than we did in the context of the development of the paint business. That is not to say that some very pertinent questions were not asked. That was 10 years ago and has not happened since about 1985. Anthony, you are more up-to-date.

ANTHONY WEALE: We have had one secondee from the DTI as a non-executive director for Chemicals and Polymers. Sir Ronald made it sound a bit as if it was always the case that they got more out of it than we did. There have been a number of cases where that would not be true. For instance, we did have a secondee in for a year or 18 months from Customs & Excise, who helped us radically to change our approach to the business of Customs & Excise. He was incredibly helpful to us.

RONALD HAMPEL: I was unaware of that.

1748. LORD NOLAN: If one of the principal aims is for government and the civil service to learn more about industry, one would expect them to benefit more than you. I should know this, but is the matter governed by similar rules to those governing civil servants taking up employment after they leave their jobs? Or is it left to the good sense and integrity of those involved at the time to ensure that there is no improper conflict of interests?

RONALD HAMPEL: I know that the people who became non-executive directors of the divisions were the then Head of the Civil Service. In the case of Anthony's secondment outwards, it was with the Head of the

Diplomatic Service. It was done within their rules rather than within ours, but I have to say that I do not know what those are.

LORD NOLAN: Thank you very much. That was my question.

1749. PETER SHORE: You do not use MPs as consultants; you were quite clear about that. You also in your evidence said that you do not contribute to political party funds. Is that decision part of your "corporate philosophy" or is it a calculation of ICI's best interests in the long term?

RONALD HAMPEL: It goes back in history. I do not know what started it during the first decisions of the foundation of the company not to make political contributions. We get requests from time to time, and in one sense it is the easy option to say that we clearly have interests even-handedly with all sides of Parliament and who knows who may be in power one day or the next. We have employees and shareholders who have widely-ranging political views; it is not therefore appropriate for us to make political contributions. When there is then a request, it is easy to deal with it.

PETER SHORE: I find that a very satisfactory reply. Thank you very much.

1750. PROF. ANTHONY KING: May I ask a pendant to that question? One hears stories from time to time of firms that think they have benefited because they have donated to political parties and equally of firms that think they have suffered through a failure to donate money to a political party. Do you come across in your life stories of that kind?

RONALD HAMPEL: I have heard it said and, more particularly, I have read it in the media. From my perspective ICI has been at no disadvantage at all through not making political contribution.

1751. ANNE WARBURTON: Might I just clarify one point I hope I did not miss when Diana Warwick was talking with you, Sir Ronald. You make a point of saying that you pay nothing to any Members of Parliament. You also said that lobbying was acceptable provided it was declared, but I was not quite clear whether you would be equally happy about lobbying which involves payments to Members of Parliament.

RONALD HAMPEL: I find this quite difficult so I really have not thought about it very deeply, to be honest. I find the principle of the relationships with Parliament being as direct as possible, one which lies really at the heart of our relationship, and therefore I am naturally wary of lobbyists who have their own particular axe to grind because they are in business over a length of time. Because we are large and can afford somebody like Anthony Weale, I think it would be wrong of me to make judgments about how others who cannot afford that should operate. So I believe there is a place for people to build cases with experience on presentation, and I can see no reason why they should not be helped in that so long as it is clearly declared, and if that involves some payment so be it. I fully understand, however, the public sensitivity of lobbyists and MPs, and I would not therefore find it a particular surprise if people found that exceptional.

1752. ANNE WARBURTON: Thank you very much. Might I just ask one other point of clarification. We have heard your views on the offering of hospitality to others. Do you also have a code or rules within ICI about the receiving of hospitality and, if so, is this something which we could be interested in in relation to the political world?

RONALD HAMPEL: Yes. I think the only area in which we are rigorous is in the purchasing area. People who are significantly involved in ICI's purchasing activities are cautioned, I think is the right word of putting it rather than there being a prescribed policy, about the acceptance of gifts I think rather than hospitality. There has been a propensity in some of the world for very large gifts to be offered to people who are significant purchasers, and ICI buys a great many goods around the world. In that area we are very circumspect. But general hospitality we operate in exactly the same way as we offer it. We behave in exactly the same way the other way round.

1753. ANNE WARBURTON: When you say you are very circumspect, you mean you forbid it or forbid to receive it?

RONALD HAMPEL: Yes, we basically forbid the acceptance of large gifts. I would not complain if I found out that somebody had been given a bottle of whisky at Christmas and fire him on the basis of that, and there is not an actual written down ICI rule which says he should not do that. If, on the other hand, there was a very significant gift given I would expect it to be refused or sent back.

ANNE WARBURTON: Thank you.

1754. LORD NOLAN: One more general question which, if I may, I would like to ask you before you leave us. You have enormous experience of the standards of behaviour of people in public life in this country, Ministers, Members of Parliament, and civil servants. What is your general impression of standards here? Are they as good as they ever were, are they satisfactory? Are there any areas that we as a committee should be particularly looking at?

RONALD HAMPEL: I think as a generality the standards are satisfactory. I think the increasing pressures, looked at if you like from the business man's point of view from short term performance, on Parliament, on the Civil Service for rapid action, the exposure to the media in every way, now produces reactions and counter reactions which are of a different nature to those 20 years ago. Somebody in my position 15 years ago basically had no dealings with the media and the relationships with government are on a very sotto voce level, if I can put it that way. We are conscious today that they might at any stage appear in the public domain, and therefore against that background I think there is a case for some more careful look at codes of conduct but not in an unrealistic way that restricts freedom of access. I think that if anybody approaches this issue on the basis that integrity has disappeared from public life they are doing a grave disservice both to Parliament and to the Civil Service.

LORD NOLAN: Thank you very much. Did you wish to add anything, Mr Weale, on that?

ANTHONY WEALE: No thank you very much.

1755. LORD NOLAN: We are extremely grateful to you both. You have been very clear and helpful and thank you very much for coming.

Good morning, Mr Darracott, thank you very much for coming to join us. Have you an opening statement that you would like to make before we go into putting questions to you?

COLIN DARRACOTT

COLIN DARRACOTT (Co-ordinator, Charter 88): Just very brief; I did send something over in writing on Monday. You have asked us since we made our main submission in December to address three main areas, one of which was the core principles that underlie our activity and our beliefs in the public service. Another was our proposals for regulating MPs and the Civil Service, and, lastly, our view on public appointments and quangos.

Our core principles are twofold. One is that we believe that all public officials, whether elected or unelected, are ultimately accountable to the people. Our second core principle is that good and efficient civic government requires positive encouragement for people to be involved and to participate actively. We believe our current constitutional arrangements and democratic processes and our basic laws at the moment fail seriously in both these areas.

There has been, we believe, a genuine tradition of integrity and probity in our nation's public service compared to most other nations, and it is still there. We believe it is also right to modernise the public service to make it cost effective and well managed, but we believe the good should be preserved and the best of innovation and new businesses' practices adopted at the same time.

We believe there is now widespread and deep distrust about what is happening and it arises because agents of public service appear even less democratically accountable than ever, and people cannot participate in their own government. We believe that democracy need not conflict with efficiency.

You will see that we have suggested a number of ways to regulate the conducts of MPs and Civil Service. These are mere suggestions for restoring trust, not because we particularly believe half the allegations or all the allegations of sleaze and wrong-doing. We have included as examples a beefing up of the Register of Interests, written rules and codes of conduct, an opening of the privileges procedures, better access to the Civil Service by opposition MPs, the register of lobbyists and an ongoing diary of their work, reform of MPs' working hours and conditions including some openness about the activities of the Whips' offices. Executives and other senior public appointees should be directly and ultimately accountable to Select Committees, not to Ministers. The Select Committees should be more democratically appointed than they are at the moment.

We suggest there should be common and consistent standards throughout the public service. We also think that MPs and Ministers should be paid more, but only paid pro rata if they are part-time MPs with other jobs. We think that Hansard and other parliamentary and governmental documents should be made available live on the Internet so people have better access to what is going on. For appointments and quangos we ask that the Committee be fairly imaginative. We believe that some bodies should revert to local authority control or accountability; we think others should have directly elected bodies such as health, police and education authorities because people care passionately about these.

Yet others should be answerable perhaps to a mix of local councillors and lay people, but all appointments should be made openly through advertising, at arms length from Ministers, and on an equal opportunities basis.

These are specific things related to the work of this Committee, but beyond these we believe that public trust requires substantial constitutional reforms, most especially in this context a Freedom of Information Act, a Bill of Rights, fairer voting systems, autonomy for local government, and the reform of Parliament.

LORD NOLAN: Thank you very much and we are very grateful to you for the clear way in which you elaborated those points in writing to us and summarised them this morning. I am going to ask Mr Peter Shore to take up the questions with you please.

1756. PETER SHORE: Mr Darracott, thank you for that very substantial agenda of reform. In both your papers to us you have, of course, dealt with the three main areas in which we are currently interested and I would like to take you through them one by one, if I may, beginning with MPs and their interests.

If I have understood it correctly, what you are proposing there first of all is that there should be complete disclosure, there should be a register of all MPs' income, interests. That is correct, isn't it?

COLIN DARRACOTT: That is right.

1757. PETER SHORE: Do you think that income other than related to work and employment is, in fact, a necessary item to be declared?

COLIN DARRACOTT: I think at the moment it is. I can see why it might be thought to be undesirable and a matter of privacy, but I think it is now necessary for people to know how much is changing hands for what.

1758. PETER SHORE: You think it is so bad that we need to adopt a kind of American habit of showing our Tax Returns to the electors in order to sustain our credibility with them?

COLIN DARRACOTT: I would stop short of Tax Returns because there are allowances that probably should be kept confidential, but I think in terms of income all sources and amounts should be declared.

1759. PETER SHORE: That links up with your proposal which you drew attention to just a short time ago, presumably in which you would like to see MPs who have outside employment related to Parliament or to any other of their affairs having those extra salaries deducted from their pay as MPs. Is that correct?

COLIN DARRACOTT: Not quite. This is a personal view rather than an official policy, as it were, of Charter 88, but I believe that MPs are currently underpaid. For the degree of responsibility and their lifestyles and the sacrifices they have to make, and I do believe most MPs anyway enter public service well-meaning, the current salary is inadequate therefore it should be substantially higher. But if they are part-time MPs and spend a considerable time as barristers or dentists or whatever, then they should claim only part of the full salary, the

higher salary that we would propose. I think then people would feel better if MPs are doing other jobs as well as the one they have been elected to do.

1760. PETER SHORE: You put this great emphasis on disclosure and, as it were, reduction of MPs' salaries for those who do take on outside employment, but do you accept that there are no restraints on the kind of activities that MPs can undertake for pay?. What do you think, for example, about public relations consultancies that MPs sometimes take up?

COLIN DARRACOTT: I do not think I am very comfortable being absolute in any of these circumstances, and we do believe that MPs should continue to do work as long as we know about it of a variety of kinds, and certainly a consultancy in public relations or even in lobbying is not necessarily something that we would say should stop. I think the only area we want to be a bit careful about is when there is a specific job to be done on behalf of a client and there is a fee associated with that specific job. I think we would like to draw the line and say, no, that is not really on. I think it is good for the life of Parliament and the democratic process that a variety of people are encouraged to participate and they should not have to sacrifice everything to take on those duties.

1761. PETER SHORE: Yes, thank you for that, that has cleared that one up.

Part of your submission is that MPs should be debarred from voting where they have indirect or direct pecuniary interests in the issue before Parliament.

COLIN DARRACOTT: That is right.

PETER SHORE: Do you see there some very considerable difficulties? Governments sometimes depend upon very narrow majorities. Do you not think that this might raise a very fundamental problem for the stability of the government itself?

COLIN DARRACOTT: Firstly I believe that the electoral system be different and therefore with a pluralistic way of electing Parliaments the problem would not necessarily arise so seriously. I think at the moment I would say that trust in our elected representatives and the system is more important than the kind of difficulty such disclosures and prohibitions would create. I do, I think, also say that there should be a let out if it is agreeable to some independent view such as the Speaker.

1762. PETER SHORE: I see. One of the great difficulties with that proposal is that pecuniary interests are very difficult to define, and pecuniary interests may involve, as it were, all Members of Parliament like when they are voting on matters of income tax or other public policy matters. Do you accept that as a real difficulty?

COLIN DARRACOTT: No, I think what we are saying is if there is a payment in terms of income from an entity which is directly related to the matter at hand, in normal circumstances that MP should not cast a vote.

1763. PETER SHORE: Perhaps we can turn now to the Civil Service and your views on that. You certainly put forward the idea that civil servants should in some way be accountable to the idea of the public interest rather than to their own Ministers. Have you spelt out your thoughts as to how that might be brought about?

COLIN DARRACOTT: Not in great detail. We are conducting an inquiry now around the country to get ideas from the public as to what they could suggest in the way of reforms of the Civil Service to make it more accountable to them. As a first step we believe that senior civil servants should report to Select Committees and be called in for interrogation, and those Select Committees should be more powerful than they are. That is one early step that we would propose.

We also believe that in terms of the agencies who deliver public services to people, whether that is social services or others, should have some form of annual general meeting or something like that where people who are directly affected by those services should have access and ask questions. We did think that the Citizens Charter kind of thing was innovative and could have helped improve the accountability of public servants to people, but we do not think they have worked very well for a number of reasons. We would like people to work on that kind of initiative and come up with ways in which people feel confident they could get at public servants to ask questions and feel comfortable that government agencies and departments are ultimately accountable to them. We accept that we have to be a bit sensible about this so that we do not have anarchy and the thing should be formalised.

1764. PETER SHORE: Since you submitted your two written papers to us in December and January, the Government has itself published a White Paper making a number of proposals. *Taking Forward Continuity and Change* is what it was called. What do you think of the proposals there? Do you think that what is new in any way meets the kind of criticisms that people have made about the position of the Civil Service in the past?

COLIN DARRACOTT: No not really. I think it is inadequate and I think it is actually a misnomer to call it *Continuity and Change* because we do not see a great deal of continuity in that particular paper, we just see more change and it is all more change in terms of becoming like a public limited company and trying to create a market circumstance behind public services which is too extreme, it is not tempered by the kind of codes and ethics that should also be addressed in the case of public service, so we do not think it is adequate.

1765. PETER SHORE: Not even the new code of ethics if it is given statutory force?

COLIN DARRACOTT: It is better than having none, but it is not robust enough in our view.

1766. PETER SHORE: What about the other proposal in that government White Paper to allow civil servants who feel very strongly about certain issues, about the conduct of their Ministers, to ultimately take the matter to an independent person, the First Commissioner of the Civil Service as he is to be? Do you think that that is a very helpful innovation?

COLIN DARRACOTT: Yes. I have not actually had a chance to study the Government's most recent proposals but we have always believed that there should be a way for a senior or any civil servant to express dissent if a Minister

chooses to ignore advice or take a course which that senior public service believes to be detrimental to the public good.

1767. PETER SHORE: Good. Yes. My third and last area is quangos and your proposals for them. I take it from your papers that you would like to see local government or local democracy in some form greatly extended so that many of the quangos would become responsible to elected bodies in the future.

COLIN DARRACOTT: Yes, I believe in true subsidiarity in that many decisions are best taken close to the people, and local authorities in most cases are the responsible body that many of the so-called quangos should be accountable through to the public. If things went wrong in local government it was local government that should be reformed rather than democracy removed, so we would like to strengthen the autonomy of local government and reform it.

1768. PETER SHORE: Yes, but however much reform does take place there is bound to be at the end of the day a substantial number of quangos who will remain, as it were, outside immediate direct democratic control, and it is how to make sure that the appointments to those quangos really do depend upon the merit and open competition of people who apply for the post rather than any kind of patronage or favouritism. That really is an extremely important matter. How do you see that being resolved?

COLIN DARRACOTT: We think it should be by open advert, and we believe that there should be appointment boards who are at arms length from Ministers, or whatever the appropriate authority is that that quango relates to. We are concerned about independence as well as decent open competition on merit, because I believe if you put an advert in and the Minister ultimately is still responsible it can just be a charade that there was an advert.

1769. PETER SHORE: Advertisement itself is not a great deal, I agree. So you would have, as it were, a sort of open competition procedure, or equal opportunities sort of recruiting procedure?

COLIN DARRACOTT: That is right, yes.

1770. PETER SHORE: I see. You say in that same context that you would like it to be arms length from the Minister. What does that really imply? That somebody else would actually do the appointing of quango chairmen and board members, or that the Minister would have the right to make a decision only from a list already sieved by this appointments board?

COLIN DARRACOTT: I think ultimately the appointment should be made by the board; that is, independent from the Minister. That is the ideal situation. I think one would have to look sometimes at the circumstances of the particular body. Particularly in some of the non-executive and advisory agencies a Minister or a departmental chief would probably have quite a large say in what kind of person ought to be recruited and appointed.

1771. PETER SHORE: Would there not have to be a very large number of boards taking account of the huge number of quangos that exist, and the fact that in many parts of the country—I have in mind the Health Service—the really local or regional sensitivities and closeness to the ground are very desirable. Would you see, therefore, a number of public appointments, commissions or boards being set up?

COLIN DARRACOTT: Yes I think so, but there is already a huge proliferation of these appointments which we are led to believe at the moment can be done by one person, i.e. the Minister ultimately, and maybe it is a slightly quicker procedure when the Minister has someone in mind for that particular job. There would have to be an element of proliferation of such bodies, but I do not think it needs to be as excessive as it might seem because the turnover is not necessarily one that would require as many boards to appoint people as there are actual boards.

PETER SHORE: Thank you.

1772. ANNE WARBURTON: Mr Darracott, did I understand you a moment ago to say that you were concerned as much about the independence as about the merit of appointees to quangos?

COLIN DARRACOTT: Yes.

ANNE WARBURTON: That seems to me to be putting political considerations above those of ability to carry out the functions well.

COLIN DARRACOTT: I am sorry if I misled you in that way. I do not believe that people who have a political interest should be prevented from being appointed to run quangos or any other public bodies. I think as long as the political flavour or work of somebody has been is in the open I have no particular problem. I would actually say that should be true of people who work in the Civil Service and local authorities. I think many people work in public life under political restrictions at the moment that are too severe. That should be relaxed as long as we all know what their interests are.

ANNE WARBURTON: So you are not really withdrawing merit as a criterion.

COLIN DARRACOTT: Good Lord, no.

1773. ANNE WARBURTON: I was very struck in your submission by the extent to which you say accountability should be to the public interest rather than to the executive. In some ways, if I may say so, some of the things you suggest seem a little unrealistic. For example, you seem to be saying that the Civil Service should be responsible to the great public rather than to Ministers. Could you develop that thinking a little bit more?

COLIN DARRACOTT: Yes, you have to have institutions which have people who are representative of the people to whom individuals in the public services seem to be accountable. We accept that. You cannot have it to the mass of people all over the place. In terms of being accountable to the public we are thinking of things along the lines of the Citizens Charters but slightly different whereby people who are responsible for delivering services to people can have meetings to which people can come along and ask questions. Also if there are members of the public who are unhappy they know who they can go to and express their unhappiness almost like an

information department within those areas of public service, whether that should be a health authority or whether it is a local DHSS. What we are concerned about is that there is some access for individual inquiry and redress.

1774. ANNE WARBURTON: Do you draw a distinction between departments and the "quangoland" as it was called recently this morning?

COLIN DARRACOTT: In the detail, yes. There are probably quite a lot of differences depending on the kind of department. Another example is how do people get true information about what is going on in the prison service which is not considered at the moment to be a quango, but it is an element in a way of a hived-off piece of Civil Service. We would like to know what the procedure should be in order for people to express their views and get answers to what is going on in all that kind of public service area.

ANNE WARBURTON: Thank you.

1775. PROF. ANTHONY KING: Just a detail arising out of Mr Shore's questions. One of our first witnesses was Roy Hattersley who, as is well known, writes novels and books on other subjects, he writes a column in The *Guardian*, does a great deal of other journalism, he appears frequently on radio or television. Can you describe what you think his entry in the Register of Interests should look like if your proposal was adopted?

COLIN DARRACOTT: I would think that on an annual basis he would say, "I earned the approximate amount of money from my activities as an author, pontificator on chat shows, whatever".

1776. PROF. ANTHONY KING: So you are not worried about the specific sources of the money, because I rather got the impression from something you said earlier on, or from something in your written evidence, that you wanted not merely the amounts but the sources to be identified.

COLIN DARRACOTT: I think when there is a huge number like that, and it could be hundreds, then one would look for the kind of source rather than the individual specifics. Then if there was a question to arise one would at least know what questions to ask.

1777. LORD NOLAN: You speak of the need for a statutory code of conduct for Members of Parliament. How would the code be enforced?

COLIN DARRACOTT: We believe that there should be sanctions if statutory codes of conduct are not met by individual Members ranging from temporary suspension or removal of certain privileges to in extremis expulsion from the House.

1778. LORD NOLAN: Do you envisage the machinery for enforcement being the Committee of Privileges or some similar body, or Select Committee, in the House?

COLIN DARRACOTT: Yes. We would prefer those committees to be open but we accept that that is not always desirable.

1779. LORD NOLAN: You suggest that the Privileges Committee should meet as a rule in public unless there are compelling and expressly stated reasons why not. Would that, do you think, meet the case? I have it in mind that there has been some suggestion (and of course all this is entirely a matter for the House) that there should be some independent element introduced into the examination of complaints against Members of breaching whatever the code or rules might be. Have you any views on that?

COLIN DARRACOTT: We have suggested that the Privileges Committee itself should have some lay people in the sense of non-MPs on it, not necessarily as a majority but as a sort of safeguard.

LORD NOLAN: Thank you very much.

1780. CLIFFORD BOULTON: Can I just press you a little further on this business about Members not voting on matters they have an interest in if only to see if I can get you to agree with me that it is not an easy one. First of all to distinguish in my own mind between what you think about Members who get fees, let us say, for consultancies and advice and Members who are actually in a job which they perform. I take it that if a Member has an interest in a matter which comes before the House which takes the shape of receiving money from an interest group, that would be an area where you felt he should not vote on that issue. That is one of the disqualifying areas presumably that you have in mind?

COLIN DARRACOTT: I think so if I have understood the example correctly. I agree, it is extremely difficult. I am very happy to agree, it is not easy.

1781. CLIFFORD BOULTON: He is a paid adviser to some industry or other and their affairs are being discussed in the House and you feel, because of that, because he has a financial interest, he should keep out of voting on that. That is the sort of thing you are saying?

COLIN DARRACOTT: Yes, that is right, because it is a paid interest.

1782. CLIFFORD BOULTON: Does that also apply to a farmer who is faced with a debate on a common agricultural policy?

COLIN DARRACOTT: No, I do not think it should apply in that case. Or a barrister if there is a legal question arising.

1783. CLIFFORD BOULTON: No, so it is really the people who are taking money for parliamentary services that you would want to say should keep out of voting.

COLIN DARRACOTT: Yes. I would not say necessarily in perpetuity. It is something that concerns people at the moment that somehow fees could make a difference to how somebody is operating in the way of a vote. It is a difficult area and we do not want to be too draconian, but we just want for the moment for that kind of thing to stop and see how it runs.

1784. CLIFFORD BOULTON: I look at it from the point of view of the electorate who have got this chap into Parliament and then is he not going to be able to vote on certain things. One might almost say that if it is going to have that drastic effect and the constituents are not to have somebody voting on certain issues perhaps it is the

job itself which he or she should be prevented from having.

COLIN DARRACOTT: We talk to MPs and try and persuade them to do things, but we do not pay them to try and get our point of view across and that should be the way of the relationship with constituents, and that is what we are asking to be considered. We have already said that MPs should not only be professional politicians in that it is their only source of income, and therefore we would not stop farmers from voting on agricultural questions or lawyers and so on. When there is a third party, like Charter 88, who is trying to get the services of an MP out with the constituency context we do not think the MP should vote if there is a fee.

CLIFFORD BOULTON: So what you are saying is you are agreeing with us that if we go down this path in our recommendation it has to be pretty carefully drawn.

COLIN DARRACOTT: Yes, it is very difficult territory. Many of the suggestions we have made require quite a lot of thinking and agreement.

CLIFFORD BOULTON: Thank you very much.

1785. DIANA WARWICK: You have said that you accept that it is good for Parliament that MPs should have outside interests, but I think many of the changes from the parliamentary point of view that you would like to see in relation to hours, for example, are really about getting MPs to do what they are supposed to do, that is be in Parliament and represent their constituents. It seems to me in that context that your recommendation for a hike in MPs' pay is an essential and integral part of all these changes. Do you think that is currently realistic?

COLIN DARRACOTT: You mean politically realistic?

DIANA WARWICK: Yes.

COLIN DARRACOTT: I think if a great many reforms were introduced, and particularly an opening up of the whole government institution and system, with a Freedom of Information Act for example, I believe that some of the less publicly palatable elements of what we suggest would be acceptable, but in isolation I think there would be outcry.

1786. DIANA WARWICK: You talked a great deal about a responsible citizenry and you referred positively to the Citizens Charter. Do you think there is scope for further development of that idea in terms of giving voters an understanding of what they can call on their MPs to do?

COLIN DARRACOTT: Yes, I think ultimately it may take a generation or two to improve the participation, if you like, by citizens in general in the governance of society, but part of our work is also to try and explain to the public how things work and how they can get access to democratic processes.

1787. DIANA WARWICK: Finally one of the things I noticed a lack of in your evidence was an indication of the role of the constituency and the constituency party. Given that you would like to see an increase in the pay of MPs, do you think there is a role for some sort of performance review of MPs, and do you think constituencies would play a part in that?

COLIN DARRACOTT: I think there is a role for that. I believe there is a pilot going on in the western counties under the auspices of the local newspaper as a sort of little audit of local MPs and how they have performed. I do not think at this stage we would recommend anything in particular because we believe the way that MPs are elected needs reform anyway—the role of the constituency party and the whole political system—the reforms that we suggest would to some extent determine how that relationship should be described. At this stage we are not suggesting there should be any statutory way of following what an MP is up to.

1788. WILLIAM UTTING: You are one of a number of witnesses who have mentioned to us the importance of having a Freedom of Information Act and they have then passed on before we have had an opportunity to ask them about the content of a Freedom of Information Act and its relevance to what we have to do as a committee. Looking at your evidence you say that the principle behind this is that everyone should enjoy the right to know what is being done in their name. Are you envisaging the kind of act that would consist of a number of general principles and put the onus upon the state to justify exceptions to that, or are you being prescriptive in a detailed way across the full range of government activities?

COLIN DARRACOTT: We do not tend to go into details but the kind of model we would look for is something like Sweden or the United States where you start off by saying everything is open except one or two things which are necessarily confidential. We would err probably for most people's tastes on everything being too open, that is the nature of our organisation in many ways. We believe that a lot of things that are so-called "commercially confidential" do not need to be. The Swedish model is very extreme in that all minutes and all messages and all correspondence of the Prime Minister are available for the public to read if they so choose. As I say, we have not prescribed this specific act because there are several already that have been drafted and attempts have been made to introduce them through private Member's bills. As a matter of principle we say, everything open until there is obviously a reason for something to be not open.

1789. WILLIAM UTTING: If that applied then this would automatically bring into the public arena all the requisite information in relation to MPs' interests, jobs for Ministers and civil servants, appointments to quangos and so on?

COLIN DARRACOTT: Yes, I believe that if there had been a robust Freedom of Information Act in this country we probably would not have the Nolan Committee.

1790. WILLIAM UTTING: That is a nice simple solution to the questions that we are dealing with. Could I just tackle you on one more point. Obviously what you wish to achieve would require some radical changes in the way public business is done in this country. I was thinking of the example of the National Health Service where we were re-establishing yesterday that there is a very direct line of accountability to the Secretary of State for everything that goes on in the NHS. The kind of changes

that you are talking about in the appointment of people to quangos might actually put intermediate bodies between the citizen and the Secretary of State that blur or deflect that straight line of accountability. Is this not a problem about, so to speak, bureaucratising the appointment system in some of the quangos?

COLIN DARRACOTT: I do not believe that in a modern nation with the speed now which information and technology is dealing with things with international money that all decisions and final authority and power should be at the level of the nation state. So we are arguing throughout all our agenda, not just that related to the work of this committee, that power has to be redistributed and authority has to be redistributed up, down, sideways. So the amount of work or the amount of bureaucracy need only be marginally higher if you disperse power, if at all, because so much less bureaucracy is in Whitehall and Westminster, and so much legislation coming out as well.

WILLIAM UTTING: Thank you, Mr Darracott.

1791. LORD NOLAN: Thank you very much indeed, Mr Darracott, you have been extremely helpful and clear and you have given us a lot of your time and a great deal of help. Thank you very much.

Now we have Assistant Commissioner David Veness. Your companion, Mr. Veness, is?

DAVID VENESS (Assistant Commissioner, Specialist Operations, Metropolitan Police): David Hamilton from our Solicitor's Department, Mr. Chairman.

1792. LORD NOLAN: We are very grateful to you for the paper which you sent us and the covering letter in which you brought out a number of the, amongst other things, core concepts to which you attach great importance. Did you wish to make a preliminary statement before we go into the detailed questions?

DAVID VENESS AND DAVID HAMILTON

DAVID VENESS: If it would be helpful—for about ten minutes, Mr. Chairman.

LORD NOLAN: Yes, please, we would like it.

DAVID VENESS: I am very grateful. I welcome the opportunity, Mr. Chairman, to present the view of the Metropolitan Police on these issues and it is my intention to briefly address four of those in opening. The first, the role of the Public Sector Corruption Index; secondly, the practical problems of combatting fraud and the response to these problems; thirdly, perceived deficiencies in the current law and possible new law; and, lastly, levels of corruption in London.

If I may start with the Public Sector Corruption Index. Following the Salmon report in July 1976 the Fraud Squad was tasked to set up a national fraud index including what has become known as the Central Public Sector Corruption Index and there is a duty on all Chief Police Officers to report allegations of corruption to this index. The index lists the searchable details of all allegations notified to us, with a view to minimising duplication of effort and identifying common features between cases. Following this in 1978 a squad was formed within the Fraud Squad specifically to deal with all allegations of corruption within the public sector within predominantly the London area, and the Public Sector Corruption Unit deals with all allegations of corruption in the public sector reported within the London area, excluding Ministry of Defence cases, and also deals with allegations of major public sector fraud. All allegations under Section 94 of the Local Government Act 1972 are also dealt with in this office.

In order to address the intention of the Salmon Report allegations of fraud or corruption in relation to privatised utilities are dealt with as though they were still within the public sector. Current cases include allegations against public servants and others in a wide variety of public bodies—the bulk of the work currently is in and around the London Boroughs.

If I may deal next, Mr. Chairman, with a summary of the practical problems which confront public sector employers and the police in combatting fraud. My comments are in no way intended to detract from the good work which is being carried out by public servants in all public sector organisations, not intended to suggest that public servants are anything other than predominantly honest and hard-working, my comments are drawn from experience in investigations carried out by my officers in totality. In many instances a criminal prosecution has not been possible. It is generally accepted that in fraud and corruption, prevention strategies are essential management issues at every level, but there is a general lack of awareness of the risks of fraud and corruption within and without public sector organisations. It is an almost invariable feature of investigations conducted in this field that managers—and sometimes to a very senior level—lack sufficient technical knowledge or the determination to effectively supervise the activities of their staff. I am told that there is a minimal amount of fraud, corruption, ethics awareness training in various universities and colleges dealing with business and public sector qualifications, for example, MBA courses. Inadequate financial controls are a common feature or, indeed, where controls are present, little or no meaningful supervision. This relates in particular to the type of control required to form the basis for a criminal investigation and subsequent prosecution of those involved in fraud and corruption. In other words, if the correct procedure in a given situation cannot be established it is often difficult to prove the criminal culpability of the suspect.

To sum up, controls must be clearly in place, they must be visible and completely accountable. A related issue is an absence of openness, despite statutory and regulatory requirements in this respect. There is a wealth of anecdotal evidence of important financial decisions being taken without appropriate supervision. Another problem is an absence of mechanism or limited means by which concerns of fraud or corruption can be brought to the attention by the work force without jeopardising the informant. From experience and in consultation with the charity Public Concern at Work there is a view that employees fear bringing malpractice to notice through concerns for their own position and this was particularly highlighted in the recent Audit Commission report on the National Health Service. In making these comments I bear in mind particularly the need also to protect individuals from malicious allegations.

If I may then address the progress which has been made to address these difficulties. The Fraud Squad Public Sector Corruption Unit has established a formal system of ongoing liaison with local authorities in which fraud and corruption prevention measures are a regular feature. Officers of the squad give detailed fraud prevention advice, assist with investigative strategies for local authorities for their investigators and internal auditors and, following our involvement in the Audit Commission Review of the National Health Service, a similar system is being considered in respect of National Health Service organisations. There is growing expertise within the public sector investigative units, both forensic audit and the investigation of crime, although there is a perceived lack of training. Following enquiries in one London Borough a Fraud Steering Group has been established with membership including the police.

Overall, a strong partnership drive has improved prevention strategies, led to the disruption of offences at an earlier stage, and to the arrest on the basis of effective evidence where appropriate. The need for early consultation with police where crime is suspected is a vital part of this process. I cannot stress the need for education enough and whilst there has been some achievement there is no room for complacency.

Turning to perceived deficiencies in the current law—and I refer to four groups; firstly, the Public Bodies Corrupt Practices Act of 1889; secondly, the Prevention of Corruption Act 1906; next, the Prevention of Corruption Act 1916; and, last, the Common Law offence of Bribery. Under the Police and Criminal Evidence Act of 1984 these corruption offences are not serious arrestable offences per se. This being so, evidence-gathering powers are limited. For example, the examination of special procedure material, bank accounts, can only be authorised by a Crown Court Judge in the investigation of serious arrestable offences. The definition of a serious arrestable offence would only extend to these corruption offences in the event of substantial financial loss or gain occurring or intended and this is difficult to establish, especially at the investigative stage. In order to increase the power to protect the public purse it is suggested that all these corruption offences should be included in the definition of serious arrestable offence. These three acts relate in various ways to most public servants, although there is some scope for rationalisation. In particular, proof that any public servant has accepted a gift or consideration from an interested party in any public service transaction, for example an application for planning permission, should perhaps be presumed corrupt in all cases, not being limited to those cases involving contracts only. It may be appropriate to deal with this by redefining the term "public body" to its widest possible meaning.

Next, if I may, Chairman, refer to the Local Government Act 1972, of which Section 94 deals with members of local authorities who fail to declare pecuniary interests at meetings, and Section 117, which deals with officers of local authorities who, in a similar fashion, fail to notify pecuniary interest with the added element of accepting a fee or award other than as proper remuneration. Both those offences are only triable summarily and are punishable by way of fine. There is thus a time limit of six months from the date of commission of these offences in respect of the investigation. It is suggested that the time limit be increased to facilitate investigation, perhaps by increasing the status of those offences.

In terms of possible new law there are circumstances reported as potential crimes, particularly where standing orders or codes of conduct have clearly been breached, which do not amount to crimes under current law. It is acknowledged that breaches of codes of conduct or internal regulations may in some ways corroborate criminal offences. For example, where members or officers of a public authority sell, by secret sale, property of the authority to a company under their control and then subsequently resell at a profit. In the absence of direct evidence of crime a criminal prosecution would fail, although there may be a clear abuse of information and power derived from that public office. It may be appropriate, therefore, that consideration be given to an offence of abuse of public office or information. There have been a number of cases in recent times of elected members of local government involved in crime other than corruption offences and they have remained in active office. It may be felt appropriate that a court should have the power to disqualify from public office in corruption cases and other offences of dishonesty. There is an existing parallel in the Crown Courts' power to disqualify persons for being a director or for being concerned in the affairs of a company. There may be a case additionally for saying that where such a person has been charged with an offence they should be suspended from office until their case has been determined by the courts, but it may be felt appropriate that a superior court should consider making such an order, perhaps on the application of the Crown Prosecution Service.

My Lord, I hesitate to mention the case of *Marcel & Others* v. *The Commissioner of Police & Others*. This case was concerned with the disclosure to a third party of information and evidence obtained in a criminal enquiry. Circumstances do arise where evidence of malpractice by public servant fall short of substantiating a criminal offence and may not be passed to a public authority to assist in the lawful removal of that individual. For example, this may apply to the evidence gleaned in an interview by police of a suspected public servant. It may be felt that it is in the public interest that such information and evidence should be disclosable with all appropriate safeguards. At present there are operational anxieties that the judgment in *Marcel* prevents the lawful disclosure in these specific circumstances.

On a related note, Section 28 of the Data Protection Act 1984 allows for the disclosure of data for the purpose of criminal investigation and crime prevention. However, the disclosure is likely to be limited in practice to what is regarded necessary for the investigation of individual cases, rather than extending to wider-ranging routine disclosure, designed to prevent crime generically. There is a case for allowing general disclosure of data held in the Public Sector Records for the purpose of crime investigation and crime prevention. This would allow for an accumulation of intelligence and analysis of data to combat fraud and corruption in and against public organisations.

Lastly, Mr. Chairman, levels of corruption in public life in London. I submit that it is not a realistic proposition to try and determine the levels of corruption in London purely on the basis of reported crime and I would not presume to improve on the words of Lord Salmon on this issue, who said:

"Corrupt dealings are secretive. Few, if any, crimes are harder to prove, there is no objective way of making a true assessment of the amount of public sector corruption that exists now or whether the amount has changed over recent decades."

However, to give a loose statistical measure, in London allegations of corruption average out at 31 new cases per year. It may be felt that the only realistic way of assessing the extent of corruption would be to carry out a survey in the style of the British crime surveys approaching the problem of crime from those who have direct or perceived direct experience.

In conclusion, Mr. Chairman, there have been a number of distinguished reports published on this subject. I have outlined areas of continuing concern. Looking forward, it is my professional judgment that the threat particularly of international and organised crime will increase the risk of the instances of corruption and therefore I would urge that the time is right to take this opportunity to enhance our defences against the crimes of corruption.

LORD NOLAN: Thank you very much. That was very interesting indeed. Now I am going to ask Lord Thomson to take up the questions on behalf of the committee in the first instance.

1793. LORD THOMSON: Thank you, too, Mr. Veness, and thank you for setting out the background of your current operations. Could I just seek clarification on the actual structures that you have been describing? As I understood it—and I may have got it wrong—the Public Sector Corruption Index which was set up following the Salmon report, is a United Kingdom index?

DAVID VENESS: That is correct.

1794. LORD THOMSON: And chiefs of police forces throughout the United Kingdom are expected to report into that index, is that right?

DAVID VENESS: Entirely correct. It operates under the aegis of a Home Office circular, therefore placing a responsibility on Chief Officers to bring these matters to notice nationally.

1795. LORD THOMSON: But the actual organisation—co-ordination of the index—is the responsibility of the Metropolitan Police, is that right?

DAVID VENESS: That is correct. That, of course, is a historical anachronism which derives from the origin of the case which led to that particular index coming into being.

1796. LORD THOMSON: I see. And then the Public Service Corruption Squad, on the other hand, is purely a Metropolitan Police squad?

DAVID VENESS: That is correct. Although it is, as such, the only squad of its size within United Kingdom policing and thus tends to take on matters outwith the M25, my Lord.

1797. LORD THOMSON: Yes. Now, fully accepting the difficulties about establishing the real level of corruption in the public sector, could I explore it just a little further? You said in the original note that you gave us that current cases contain allegations against civil servants in a wide variety of public bodies—local government offices in a large number of different London Boroughs and associated organisations, local councillors, contractors supplying goods and services—but when you put a figure on it as you have just done a moment or two ago—and you put it in your subsequent paper to us—your report reported corruption cases of around 31 each year. That is 31 reported cases in the Metropolitan Police area?

DAVID VENESS: That is correct.

LORD THOMSON: In the M25 area?

DAVID VENESS: That is correct, yes. If I was asked to expand that to figures that are applicable to the nation the figure would have been much closer to 100.

1798. LORD THOMSON: I see. That was a question I wanted to ask you. But are you arguing that by saying 31 reported corruption or 100 reported cases United Kingdom wide, are you arguing that that is the tip of a much bigger iceberg?

DAVID VENESS: The problem of the dark figure of unreported crime I think is particularly acute in relation to allegations of corruption. The dark figure multiplier in other areas of crime tends to be a factor of ten and our guesstimate on an anecdotal basis is that that would be at least appropriate in terms of corruption.

1799. LORD THOMSON: I see. Thank you. That is very helpful. Can I clear one area straight away? You mention in your original paper that Members of Parliament have not featured directly in recent years and, of course, quite a substantial part of our present enquiry is to look at the perception, because of the growth of lobbying and that sort of thing in the House of Commons, that there is a real problem. Is it the considered judgment of the Metropolitan Police and your squad in this respect; that in terms of the House of Commons, whatever the problems associated with Members of Parliament accepting payment for lobbying services, that they don't extend to corruption in the present legal sense of the term?

DAVID VENESS: As of now that is correct. If one looks at the totality of allegations of corruption dating back to the inception of the index it would be inaccurate to exclude Members of Parliament totally. But the bulk of work that is pursued by the squad relates to a broader problem and is not restricted or currently confined to Parliament.

1800. LORD THOMSON: So your current work, as you described it, is in those aspects of the public sector, particularly in the M25 area, that relate to local government people and to people in Civil Service operations?

DAVID VENESS: Entirely correct.

1801. LORD THOMSON: Now, on local government—we had evidence yesterday, I think (one forgets, we hear so much evidence) from the local government associations and they were describing with some pride, understandably, that one of the consequences of the Salmon Report had been to increase the regulatory element in terms of local government behaviour and as they described it it seemed that it could be described in some aspects as rather draconian, compared to what operates, for instance, in the House of Commons. Are you saying to us, really, that despite the draconian letter of the law on this the actual administration of the regulations within the local government field in London leaves a good deal to be desired?

DAVID VENESS: I think it is fair to give the local authorities credit, since the Salmon Report, for an enormous amount of energy on their part in order to ensure that proper mechanisms are in place, and we have been pleased to contribute very actively to that. So there is that basis on which to build. But in sheer numbers, it is true to say that the allegations of corruption lean towards the local authorities.

1802. LORD THOMSON: Yes. Now, on the local government front, one of the interesting bits of evidence yesterday from the Associations was the admission from them that one area in which they thought further action was required was the area where either councillors leaving the council become directors or employees of contractors to the council, or officers retiring from the council equally become involved with contractors to the council, and whereas in the civil service there are rules at the senior levels for that sort of situation there are presently none in the local government field. Do you feel it would help your work if there were such regulations, such arrangements that there should be a gap of time, there should be an examination as to whether there is anything improper in the move from the public service to the private sector contracting to the public service?

DAVID VENESS: The candid answer to that is unequivocally yes. I had some difficulty in framing evidence to your goodselves on that basis in order to identify the locus of police. To an extent there is a crime prevention element in there being a gap between public service and immediately related private activity. It is difficult to articulate that in terms of a time. But as you asked the question, undeniable that is correct.

1803. LORD THOMSON: On the civil service side in London. Have the new arrangements in the civil service—with a good deal of devolution of what was formerly traditional departmental civil service operations to operational agencies of one kind or another—in your view increased the risk of corruption?

DAVID VENESS: It is certainly the view of my officers that there are increased difficulties and, in purely operational terms, we have had to adjust the intentions of the Salmon Report with a public sector which, at that stage, was much larger in order to embrace the developments of the modern world. We have no underpinning in terms of law to take us in that direction. But our perception is that it is a difficulty.

1804. LORD THOMSON: Yes. Now you have put before us really two broad remedies for this situation that would improve the situation; one is a series of proposals in strengthening the corruption laws. I am bound to say as I listened to the list that you gave that I thought you were going to give us in Parliament a pretty heavy load of work in the immediate future! But I do not comment on that because I think it would be more appropriate for our Chairman to deal with these matters of changes in the law. But your second leg that interested me was to put a great deal of emphasis on the need for further training and education and, as an aspect of that, the application of the training and education in terms of procedures inside local government, inside the public service. Could you expand a little on the kind of training you have in mind and who would do it?

DAVID VENESS: I think the work is already beginning and as I have commented has shown very effective headway in relation to the partnership that has evolved through the local authority structure. That work is now progressing into the National Health Service systems, I think with very optimistic chances of success, and I would see the next logical development is in terms of education within the broader business structure, forensic audit and the basic qualifications leading to a business career. There is an element to which fraud, corruption and this form of behaviour is always going to be regarded as unsavoury and unpalatable, but it is necessary to bring attention to bear and to make it a formal part of training.

1805. LORD THOMSON: I was interested in what you mentioned about the possibility of formal education in this field in terms of MBA degrees, and that sort of thing. Perhaps my colleague, Diana Warwick, will ask you more expert questions on it, but did you have in mind something where real progress could be made in terms of the formal content of these courses?

DAVID VENESS: It may be a perception in which we are in error but our preliminary enquiries have suggested that there is scope for development in the whole area of where police, local authorities, and those engaged in business could interact more effectively on a partnership footing in order to ensure effective exchange of information, early identification of problems and working together to redress them.

1806. LORD THOMSON: Yes, that is very interesting. One final point and that is on the extremely difficult problem of whistleblowing. It has come up in a number of different ways in our enquiries and I wondered what you felt could be done in practice to deal with this. I just wondered whether your experience in a different field in London—the field of terrorism—whether any experience you had there in getting effective intelligence and private information was relevant to the more civil and less terrible field, really, of (serious though it is) corruption?

DAVID VENESS: There is an inevitable overlap from those other areas of criminal investigation and particularly one thinks of the measures that are necessary in the upper echelons of crime in order to protect the most vulnerable of witnesses. Necessarily the resources that are involved in those moves are so extensive that the number of cases in which that can be deployed are always going to be limited. But there are perhaps lesser remedies that can be applied of a lesser order in order to give people a greater degree of confidence in coming forward and a greater degree of reassurance of no imminent threat or otherwise. I think in the particular context of an employee or somebody working with others, there may be great advantage in exploring the notion of a nominated officer who is out with the line management structure, who has the clearly identified role within an organisation of being the recipient and having the duty of passing that on. So there is no question of it being lost within the line management structure. The ultimate malaise is where the difficulty rests with the line manager.

1807. LORD THOMSON: You mention Public Concern at Work. You have had some experience of their operations?

DAVID VENESS: Indeed.

LORD THOMSON: Do you commend them to us?

DAVID VENESS: Unequivocally.

1808. LORD THOMSON: I suppose the problem is the problem of confidentiality. One wants to have a system under which the employee who has a genuine feeling that something is not as it should be can report that and feel that action is taken on it without damaging their subsequent career prospects?

DAVID VENESS: Absolutely. It is the perception of what will happen to me that is the deterrent that we fear is preventing matters being brought to notice. So it is protecting the position of the individual but achieving a balance that does not open the door to malicious allegations.

1809. LORD THOMSON: Yes. That was to have been my final unanswerable question and you have partially answered it. How would you strike that balance yourself?

DAVID VENESS: Well, we are seeking witnesses of truth in order to place their evidence before the prosecuting authorities and ultimately the courts, so the evaluation of a witness of truth would be that which is broadly applicable in the broader world of criminal investigation.

LORD THOMSON: Thank you very much.

1810. LORD NOLAN: Thank you very much. You list in your written statement to us conditions which are repeatedly observed as leading to an environment in which fraud and malpractice can occur—and you have summarised them again by word of mouth this morning; inadequate financial controls and in particular little or no meaningful supervision, failure to follow systems and procedures laid down by statute or internal regulations, an absence of openness despite statutory requirements in this respect and, finally, no mechanism by which concerns over fraud/corruption can be brought to attention without jeopardising the informant. Time and again in the evidence that we have heard over various aspects of our enquiry, the first three have come up, that sloppy rules improperly enforced actually, if they don't encourage, permit misbehaviour of one sort and another. No mechanism by which concerns can be brought to attention without jeopardising the informant, you have touched upon in your answers for Lord Thomsom as well as in your opening statement, and you have touched on the idea of a kind of telephone line—an open line. I remember after the Cleveland enquiry and the opening of the Esther Rantzen Childline, the list of incest prosecutions on the Western Circuit trebled. It is a way of getting information. It does, as you said yourself, give rise to the need for great care to avoid mischievous allegations and to avoid, therefore, consequent injustice and unnecessary waste of public money and deep anxiety for innocent individuals. But do you see some further scope for that in this field?

DAVID VENESS: Certainly in the broader church of criminal investigation the role of "Crimestoppers", for example, Chairman, is a current example of this in practice, and that is supported by mechanisms which ensure that the matters which are brought to light by that process are subject to rigorous analysis before anybody's liberty is put in jeopardy. So it is always necessary to add safeguards to those mechanisms. But the experience both in terrorism, in organised crime and in lesser crime, is that it does take you into an area of information which you would otherwise deny yourself.

1811. LORD NOLAN: Yes. And you spoke of the work of Public Concern at Work on this area. We have heard also about measures that are being taken within the civil service to make it less unattractive for somebody to complain about what they perceive as wrongdoing by their superiors. Thank you, that deals with that. As Lord Thomson was saying, in the first part of our enquiry we are concerned with the standards of conduct of, amongst others, Members of Parliament. The Salmon Commission made a number of recommendations which were ignored, one of which was recommendation 36 that:

"Parliament should consider bringing corruption, bribery and attempted bribery of a Member of Parliament acting in his Parliamentary capacity within the ambit of the criminal law."

Now, you have told us that in fact in recent years there have been no allegations of which you are aware that have led to the need for any further clarification of the law in that respect. But am I right in thinking that the law is in an uncertain state? There was the case a year or two ago involving a Member of Parliament—he was ultimately acquitted and so I would rather not mention his name—but it gave rise to a judgment by Mr. Justice Buckley which was quoted by Sir Clifford Boulton in one of our papers, in which he took a different line from Lord Salmon and said that he did not think that it was necessary to infringe Article 9 of the Bill of Rights to do anything other than apply the common law in prosecuting someone who tried to bribe a Member of Parliament. Do you know if any further thought has been given to that?

DAVID VENESS: I am not aware on that specific point, Mr. Chairman. If I have omitted any of the recommendations in the Salmon Commission it is only due to the pressure of time. The tenor of that report is warmly welcomed by investigators.

1812. LORD NOLAN: Yes. Well, I am sure it is. You see, the first recommendation was to amend and consolidate the Prevention of Corruption Acts into a new act, to consider what changes are required in the application of existing legislation and going specifically to one point you mentioned about the 1972 Act and the six-months time limit, the recommendation that it should be increased to one year was not implemented. The answer that was given "The present limit of six months is considered reasonable and adequate" and you would like that to be looked at again?

DAVID VENESS: Indeed. The operational reason, Chairman, is that it may well be that a matter actually does not come to the notice of the prosecuting authorities until very close to the end of six month period, thereby rendering the process of investigation nugatory. I compare that adversely with provisions that are applicable to traffic law whereby if a matter is brought to the notice of the prosecuting authority then the six month period begins.

1813. LORD NOLAN: Yes. There may well be a strict limit to the extent to which we can usefully explore the criminal law, at any rate in our first report, because the subjects we are studying don't, for the reasons you have given, seem at the moment directly to impinge on it. But you have mentioned a number of respects in which you think the law could be improved other than those which I have spoken about. Are other avenues being explored: the Law Commission, or through the Home Office?

DAVID VENESS: There are and we have further research in train in-house in order to examine various issues which have not been brought forward this morning.

1814. LORD NOLAN: Yes. As you and I well know there has been a very great deal of amendment to the criminal law in the last couple of years. You have not managed to get these ones taken on board yet?

DAVID VENESS: No, that is correct.

1815. LORD NOLAN: You are asking for a bit of a help from us! Well, we will certainly carefully study what you say. We will look again at the Salmon Report in this connection but further than that I, for my part, would not like to go at the moment in making any promises. Clifford would you like to ask a question?

1816. CLIFFORD BOULTON: I only have, to start with, a very small detailed point. We sometimes talk rather loosely about the United Kingdom here in London. Does the Index contain both Scottish and Northern Ireland statistics?

DAVID VENESS: We have analogous indices and we operate on the basis of co-operation. For example, with Scotland we agreed jointly that the spirit of Salmon needed to be carried forward when privatisation affected both sides of the border, so there are broadly analogous arrangements in place for both the Province of Ulster and Scotland.

1817. LORD THOMSON: Your software is compatible, is it?

DAVID VENESS: Yes, it is.

1818. CLIFFORD BOULTON: Otherwise, because many of the points I had in mind have been discussed by Lord Nolan, you very properly confined your evidence to public life because that is what our terms of reference are about and you gave us your view of the scale of corruption. It is always more shocking in public life because of the breach of trust involved, but what is your general impression of setting the whole thing in its context? Do you feel that it is out of all scale, corruption in public life, with corruption generally in society, or do you think that you would give a relatively clean bill of health to those people who are involved in public life?

DAVID VENESS: As we are part of broader policing issues if I may start with the context of where we see it in terms of those officers we work with very closely in related countries—and I think we still enjoy a position which is envied by a great many close neighbours in relation to vulnerability, particularly to international organised crime and the increasing tentacles thereof—the view of my officers is that those vulnerabilities are greater and the risks greater, both in terms of the broad threat of corruption in our society and the particular dimensions of public life, than they have been in the recent past and thus the need for defences against that potential malaise is clear and present.

CLIFFORD BOULTON: So it is an increasing danger?

DAVID VENESS: That is a perception, yes.

CLIFFORD BOULTON: Thank you.

1819. DIANA WARWICK: Just briefly, you have raised three core concepts and I think you have particularly dealt with two of them on prevention being a matter for everyone and primary responsibility for management at every level. The one that comes first is that honesty cannot be taken on trust and you go on to say later that:

"It is apparent that the guidelines, where matters are left to the judgment of individuals, are not effective."

Would you apply that at every level, no matter how high in terms of position in an organisation, and do we have any lessons in the public service to draw from that?

DAVID VENESS: I think certainly applicable at all levels because the message is one of accountability and openness and therefore that cannot be restricted to particular tiers. The only work that I could point to that may assist is that which I have previously referred to, that has its origins within local authority arrangements and is developing elsewhere. Regrettably the absence of example is indicative of the fact that the work is at a relatively early stage in terms of those aspects of commercial and British public life that are on board with this concept.

1820. DIANA WARWICK: And would you, as an adjunct to that, given that guidelines usually do leave judgment to individuals, would you be very much more in favour of codes that were properly policed?

DAVID VENESS: Absolutely.

DIANA WARWICK: Thank you. [Sotto voce] Perhaps "policed" is the wrong word.

ANNE WARBURTON: Very naturally in a submission to a committee chaired by an eminent judge you never defined corruption. I wondered if you would like to end the proceedings by giving us a definition of corruption and perhaps indicating at what stage the police usually come in?

DAVID VENESS: Yes. In relation to public office I think it is abuse and misuse of that public office for personal gain, in a broad sense. That needs to be extended to the commercial sector, where it is abuse of position for personal gain.

1821. ANNE WARBURTON: And are you brought in only when somebody else has decided you should be brought in or are you watching all the time?

DAVID VENESS: It is broadly true to say that it is a reactive intervention rather than proactive. For very understandable reasons the number of cases in which we can be aware of activities within an organisation are necessarily limited. Again, to link to the point that I was making about building partnerships the benign effect of that is that we are involved at a much earlier stage so that is closer to being proactive, which is where we would wish to be, rather than being permanently reactive and on the back foot.

ANNE WARBURTON: Yes, thank you.

LORD NOLAN: Well, we are all extremely grateful to you for as clear and succinct a presentation of advice on a difficult question of the law in practice as we have come across. Thank you very much indeed.

DAVID VENESS: Thank you.

THURSDAY 16 FEBRUARY 1995

Members Present:

The Rt. Hon. The Lord Nolan (Chairman)

Sir Martin Jacomb	The Rt. Hon. Peter Shore MP
Professor Anthony King	Sir William Utting CB
The Rt. Hon. Tom King CH MP	Dame Anne Warburton DCVO CMG

Witnesses:

Stanley Kalms, Chairman, Dixons Group plc

Professor John Stewart, Howard Davies, and Chris Skelcher, Institute of Local Government Studies, University of Birmingham

Ms Santha Rasaiah, Secretariat, Parliamentary and Legal Committee, Guild of Editors

Sir Sigmund Sternberg, Member of the Advisory Council, Neville Cooper, Chairman, and Stanley Kiaer, Director, Institute of Business Ethics

1822. LORD NOLAN: Today we finish our second last week of oral evidence and once again we have witnesses from a broad spectrum of interests.

The School of Public Policy at Birmingham University is one of our leading academic centres for specialist research on public bodies and Professor John Stewart is himself a well-known commentator in this field. We look forward to hearing something of the results of his work.

The Guild of Editors represents the Regional and Local press. They have complained that access to information at local level has become more difficult in recent years as responsibility for more activities has passed to appointed bodies. The Guild was to have been represented by Mr. Geoff Elliott, Editor of the Portsmouth News, but unfortunately he is unwell. We send him our best wishes for a speedy recovery and welcome in his place Ms. Santha Rasaiah, Barrister at Law, of the Guild's Parliamentary and Legal Committee, who has stood in at very short notice.

The Institute of Business Ethics, represented today by its Chairman Mr. Neville Cooper, by Sir Sigmund Sternberg, and by its Director, Mr. Stanley Kiaer, is as its name suggests a body dedicated to clarifying ethical issues in business and to proposing positive solutions to problems. It has a Christian, inter-denominational background, but seeks to establish common ground with people of goodwill of all faiths.

Our first witness today also takes a keen interest in business ethics but is perhaps best-known as Chairman of the Dixons Group—Mr. Stanley Kalms. Mr. Kalms is the founder of a Chair of business ethics at the London Business School and also serves on a number of quango. He is Chairman of the Kings NHS Trust, and a Member of the Funding Agency for Schools. I think I am right in believing that his company is a benefactor in the educational field, having funded a City Technology College in Bradford. Dixons also contributes to the Conservative Party and has featured in a list of companies which are said to have more people on quango than similar companies which do not make such donations.

Mr. Kalms, thank you very much indeed for volunteering to come and talk to us this morning—we are very grateful to you as, indeed, to all our witnesses. Have you an opening statement which you would like to make before we go into asking you questions?

STANLEY KALMS

STANLEY KALMS (Chairman, Dixons Group plc): Yes, I would like, if I may, just to state my clear precise views on quangos and I believe that quangos do offer a unique opportunity for the skills and the commitment of the private sector, to be interfaced with the disciplines and the objectives of the public sector. I do find that there is a continuous attack on both the concepts of quangos and the individuals concerned and I think it is uniformly and wrongly motivated. I have not heard or seen any evidence that quangos, by definition, are either inefficient, uninformed, prejudiced or ineffective, although clearly their effectiveness is limited by the quality of the organisation for whom they are responsible. I further strongly believe that quangos would be less effective if their membership was subject to positive discrimination, either based on individuals' habitat, occupation, or ethnicity. I think the essence of a Quango should be based on personal qualities, skills and reputation and that means by necessity a strong element of head-hunting. I think there is no major corporation in this country which recruits its senior management other than by head-hunting. Senior management will not respond to any other enticements. No major corporation in this country positively discriminates in its choice of senior management except only in their skill range. But, however, if recruitment methodology can be improved, can be made more transparent and the net widened, I see no objection to pursuing this path, but only on the condition that the broad philosophy of non-positive discrimination is a fundamental. Thank you.

LORD NOLAN: Thank you very much. Now, if that completes what you would like to say in opening, please feel free at any time to expand on answers that you give to us, but I would like to begin, if I may, by asking Professor Anthony King to ask you some questions.

1823. PROF. ANTHONY KING: Since you talked about quangos can we talk about quangos? Which ones are you on at the moment?

STANLEY KALMS: I am on two. I am Chairman of the Kings National Health Trust, which is a large hospital in Camberwell, and I am on the Funding Agency for Schools and chair their finance committee.

1824. PROF. ANTHONY KING: Now, can we take just as an example the Funding Agency for Schools? How were you recruited to that job?

STANLEY KALMS: I have a long history of involvement in education—that is perhaps one of my major outside interests. I heard that the Funding Agency was being formed, I indicated to people who walked the corridors that it was an area that I ought to be involved in. As such I was asked to come along and be interviewed. So in a sense I hung out a shingle.

1825. PROF. ANTHONY KING: You say you indicated to people who walked the corridors. Who were they?

STANLEY KALMS: In this case I happened to mention it to a Minister at an earlier stage and I happened to mention it to the Chairman elect and said to him "I think this is an area where I can make a contribution because I have a knowledge and an interest in the subject".

1826. PROF. ANTHONY KING: So in this case you were not head-hunted—you hunted your own?

STANLEY KALMS: I hunted myself, yes.

PROF. ANTHONY KING: Yes.

STANLEY KALMS: But at a fairly senior level. I doubt if it would have been effective if I had just dropped a word somewhere else.

1827. PROF. ANTHONY KING: How was the appointment then made? Did you have some kind of formal interview?

STANLEY KALMS: Yes, I was interviewed by a small panel of a Minister, of the Chairman-elect and of a senior Civil Servant, and it was a thorough, normal interview. I have to say it was about as far as I would go to be interviewed—I would not have gone much further in that process. I was happy to have one interview. I was not prepared to expose myself to too many pressures in that area.

1828. PROF. ANTHONY KING: Would you have been happy if there had been in the room, as well as the people you have just mentioned, somebody who was independent of the process, who was not himself or herself going to be involved in the work of the Quango in some way?

STANLEY KALMS: No, I would not have been unhappy if it was that style of interview.

1829. PROF. ANTHONY KING: When the Funding Agency for Schools was set up last year you may well remember that John Patten, who was then the Secretary of State, was accused of packing the agency with Conservative supporters. Did you at that time think there was any evidence to support that view?

STANLEY KALMS: Well, I think in an agency such as the Funding Agency you clearly have to agree with the philosophy of Grant Maintained schools, otherwise this is not the place to be. If you don't agree with it you should be off the committee and attacking it. So clearly those who are on that particular Quango are supporters of the system. It doesn't necessarily imply they are Conservatives but it does imply that they are supporters of Grant Maintained. I suspect that they are not all Tories.

1830. PROF. ANTHONY KING: Are you conscious of anybody being a Labour voter or a Liberal Democrat voter?

STANLEY KALMS: Politics never come into it at all. We are very objective, we have precise rules of conduct and I have not heard a single word of politics except perhaps over coffee.

1831. PROF. ANTHONY KING: But at the time it was reported—and you will correct me if I have got this wrong—that at least three members of the Funding Agency were pretty heavily involved in Conservative politics in the sense that two were the Chairmen of companies that had in the previous year donated funds to the party and one was the leader of the Conservative group on a London Borough. Were you concerned at the time that the giving of publicity to these facts might itself call in question in some way the independence of the Quango?

STANLEY KALMS: Well, I would be more concerned if I was excluded because of my political opinions. So I think that is the greater good versus the smaller evil. I do insist that I have a part to play, notwithstanding that I am politically motivated.

1832. PROF. ANTHONY KING: Yes. How much money does the Funding Agency for Schools spend approximately a year?

STANLEY KALMS: About £2 billion.

PROF. ANTHONY KING: About £2 billion.

STANLEY KALMS: A lot of that is prescribed. The discretionary part of it, which is the capital part, is a couple of hundred million. Most of it otherwise is particular grants.

1833. PROF. ANTHONY KING: Yes. When you first joined that particular agency were you given any guidance as to how as a member of an agency dispersing that kind of money, you ought to comport yourself? In other words, were you inducted, indoctrinated, into the work of a public sector body of that kind?

STANLEY KALMS: Well, it was fairly primitive stuff. I mean, it was merely basic—telling us how to "suck eggs". Most of us are used to behaving in a certain style and don't need to be told that we have to conduct ourselves with integrity and discipline. But we did go through that process and a few other bureaucratic processes of the public sector.

1834. PROF. ANTHONY KING: Can you say a little bit more about the process because several people who have come to the committee have said they thought there was not enough in the way of pre-service training and that one of the reasons that some quangos have got into trouble was that whereas you do not need to be taught how to "suck eggs" it seems that some people do need to be.

STANLEY KALMS: Well, integrity is indivisible and so if you have integrity I don't see how you can actually discuss it as a subject. There are strict disciplines anyway as it is run by civil servants. Our ability to use any other outside discretion is very limited. I think the most important point that was made is that "if you have any conflict of interests—and there are several educationalists sitting round the table—you should not participate." But that only occasionally comes up. I think it is the only area where it is applicable. The rest I see no conflicts at all.

1835. PROF. ANTHONY KING: Can I ask you about the possibility of members of quangos being asked to register their interests, because it is quite a common feature in the public sector, with Members of Parliament, local councillors and so on. That is not a requirement at the moment—do you think it should be, precisely in the connection with the danger of conflict of interests that you referred to?

STANLEY KALMS: We are asked and there is now a form which is asking you to register your outside interests. I have deliberately not put anything on it because I feel that my interests don't overlap in the educational field, although I have interests in the educational field, but they are not funded by the F.A.S. You can fill out this form—it does not seem to me to be a——It's a mole hill.

1836. PROF. ANTHONY KING: You implied a moment ago that your experience in the private sector and your experience in the public sector were really not terribly different in terms of the ethics involved, that people behaved according to the same high standards in both sectors. Is that absolutely right?

STANLEY KALMS: I think there is a substantial difference between the ethics—I didn't say that—but in the integrity I think there could be discipline. There are entirely different ethics applying to the public sector than apply to the private sector. But in terms of integrity——

1837. PROF. ANTHONY KING: How do they differ in your experience?

STANLEY KALMS: The public service is very prescribed—all behaviourial patterns are written down—"this is how you behave", "this is what you do"—discretion is taken out of the situation. So you don't have any intellectual conflicts as in the private sector—it is all about behaviourial patterns, the right way of doing things, a better way of doing things and the discretion is yourself. It is not anywhere nearly so closely prescribed.

1838. PROF. ANTHONY KING: Do you think there is a case—because, again, this has been put to us—for some kind of code of conduct to govern the behaviour of the whole of what we are now taught to call the quangocracy? I take it there is not one as regards any of the bodies you are involved with at the moment—you don't have to sign up to some code of ethics. Do you think there is a case for doing that?

STANLEY KALMS: I think it is implied that you have a code of conduct to behave in the best interests of—you have a duty to care if you are on a committee or on a Quango. That seems to be quite sufficient. I mean obviously there are disciplines of expenses and conflicts of interest but I don't think you need to prescribe to the type of people you are asking to sit on boards a behaviourial pattern other than one of integrity.

1839. PROF. ANTHONY KING: But you might presumably feel differently if you were talking not about your own specific case and the quangos you know but ones which clearly have raised problems as the Public Accounts Committee showed in its report last year?

STANLEY KALMS: Well if exceptions prove the point then maybe you are right. I don't know. Mine—I don't find this a problem, nor an impending problem or a potential problem.

1840. PROF. ANTHONY KING: Can we turn briefly to Dixons in its different role as a contributor to the Conservative Party? Does Dixons still contribute a lot——

STANLEY KALMS: It is still hooked on that particular path, yes.

1841. PROF. ANTHONY KING: Thank you. I have seen a figure for the early nineties of something in the order over a period of about £100,000. Is that roughly right?

STANLEY KALMS: The company gives £25,000 a year. I give separately from that but the company give £25,000 a year to the Conservative Party.

1842. PROF. ANTHONY KING: Can you tell us what lies behind the decision of a company like yours to give money to the Conservative Party?

STANLEY KALMS: Yes. I think politics are the very fabric of our life, of our economic life, our social life and I think one has to be positive about one's views about contributing to that style. It is fundamental to us—politics. We can pretend it isn't and we can argue, as was argued, I think, recently here, that you can stand back from it. But I believe that it is fundamental to our life, that we are involved deeply and immersed in politics. Therefore it follows as a consequence that we should support the political views which we believe are economically, socially, right for the country, for the corporation. So it is a positive act rather than a negative act.

1843. PROF. ANTHONY KING: Do you see a contribution essentially as a charitable donation or a company investment?

STANLEY KALMS: No, it is an investment.

PROF. ANTHONY KING: An investment in what?

STANLEY KALMS: An investment in a political theory.

1844. PROF. ANTHONY KING: It is sometimes suggested that—and this is why this whole area comes within our remit, while the funding of political parties generally does not—that companies may invest in the Conservative Party, partly because they want a Conservative Government to be in power, but partly also because they hope to get something out of that Government.

STANLEY KALMS: Well, you know as well as I do that political pressures do not work like that and casting a small crumb on the waters is hardly likely to come back as all nicely toasted caviar. I don't think there is any possibility of that—I have never seen any opportunity. You can walk the corridors of power but it is quite often mostly a useless exercise. It is fallacious to think that one could influence directly. You can influence indirectly by being part of think-tanks, discussion groups. But I think that the immediate return on the investment to a political party can't be given as a statistic—it is a meaningless thing.

1845. PROF. ANTHONY KING: So that when Kingfishers was threatening to take over Dixons and you wanted that referred to the Monopolies and Mergers Commission and Nicholas Ridley did that, you don't think it ever crossed Nick Ridley's mind that, "Gosh, Stanley Kalms and Dixons give money to my party—I had really better ...."

STANLEY KALMS: Well, there are so many layers of bureaucracy beneath Nick Ridley that I doubt if speaking to him would have been any good. It went through, of course, the O.F.T., which is a very structured bureaucracy, it went through a great deal of public discussion. We had to make many submissions. I mean, I can't seriously answer whether he was influenced by the fact that we give a rather small amount to the Conservative Party—you could argue perhaps—but I would not have thought that there was a direct correlation.

1846. PROF. ANTHONY KING: Is it part of the gossip in the business world that there are businesses and people in business who think it worth their while to give money to the Conservative Party, if only as a kind of insurance policy, an umbrella against a rainy day, that they will be better off if they get into trouble and are thought to be on that side?

STANLEY KALMS: Well, you do know that every person has multi-motivations in every single action they do, so a smile in the right direction might have a motivation for long-term acceptability. But I seriously think that this is trivialising the subject—I do not think that there is a direct correlation—and you should consider the integrity of those who give rather than their worst motives. In other words there is a range of motives—you should look at their real motive which is, I think, a political motive, rather than a personal motive.

1847. PROF. ANTHONY KING: On the specific question of the connection that may exist between giving money to the Conservative Party and membership on quangos, quite apart from the fact that a lot of companies that give money to the Conservative Party have a lot of people on quangos there is some research that suggests that if two groups of companies, one of which gives and one of which does not, the group that does is more likely to be represented on quangos than others. Is it your impression that there is some truth in that?

STANLEY KALMS: Well, I don't think there is any real evidence. There was this BBC programme which flashed pictures of people on one or two Boards and I think they were meant to be derogatory. I think actually they were complimentary because what you are seeing is groups of people who think in a socially responsible way who tend to congregate together. I think it was a statistical quirk—for instance, it was shown that I, my wife and one of my non-executive directors and his wife were all active, but then we are active people. And I took it that if you really wanted to argue the case you would say this was a compliment. My wife has been involved in public service since we were married thirty-five years ago, she is totally committed to a hospital and inevitably she was invited to be a non-executive. I can only see that as a compliment. I have always been active in public service and my colleagues who joined the board have come with a long history of public service. So you put it together—it has to be seen as a compliment.

1848. PROF. ANTHONY KING: Are you at all worried or, alternatively, do you think we ought to be worried by simply "the look of the thing". You referred to that BBC programme—it was shown—and the kinds of rumours, allegations, investigations we are talking about

do attract a lot of attention and do appear to give an awful lot of people the idea that Quango-packing goes on, that one can buy one's way onto quangos and so on and so forth. The view is certainly widely held. This committee has had an awful lot of correspondence and a lot of submissions to that effect.

STANLEY KALMS: You are quite right, you cannot ignore public opinion or public perception, but we have to deal with facts only and the facts do not suggest that quangos are packed with lookalikes and people who share common boards. The facts are different but nevertheless—I mean, in a sense this is what this committee is about, to try and differentiate between perception and fact, and we would be very wrong if we took perception as the basis for our argument. We must deal only with the benefit and the fact.

1849. PROF. ANTHONY KING: Finally—and this may be unfair, to throw this at you at the end—but do you have any positive suggestions of things that you would like this committee to recommend in order at the very least to deal with those negative perceptions?

STANLEY KALMS: I think I would like this committee to come out strongly in favour of quangos and the ability of letting the public sector have an opportunity of interfacing with the private sector. I would like to make the point that I think my contribution from the private sector into the public sector has been very beneficial to every organisation I have been in. I bring a range of skills, objectivity, me being a personification of my type, senior business executives, and I bring fresh air, fresh thought, fresh challenge, to the Quango movement. I think it would be a sad loss to the public sector if I was eliminated. It would equally be a sad loss if the barriers of entry were too high for me to get over. I would not apply to an advert, I would only be a response to head-hunting. So there is a slight danger here—and I saw this yesterday in Virginia Bottomley's suggestion on non-executives and chairmen within the NHS. If we have to publicly apply I think you will lose us because it is not the process by which we are used to getting appointments—we have to be head-hunted. I think you have to leave that space open for us.

LORD NOLAN: Yes. Peter?

1850. PETER SHORE: Yes, thank you. A number of points arise, Mr. Kalms, from what you have already said. I take your emphasis upon people basically being recruited on grounds of merit and also to some extent having to be head-hunted, but do you not think in a number of quangos there is also an important representative role that has to be played on the board of a Quango? A board of a Quango which is directly associated with the local provision of health services and education services must take account of some of the strong local interests that are affected by the Quango's remit. Do you agree with that?

STANLEY KALMS: In theory one has sympathy with that view but if you are then limited to positive discrimination that, you know, you have to have an ethnic minority and there has to be a woman, there has to be this, that and the other, or a male, ethnic minority—I do not want to be specific—you do have problems in then getting the best quality and I think at the end of the day I would rather go for quality than for representation because we must not become too parochial in our outlook. Good quality people cross thresholds of areas and it doesn't matter if they are not an inhabitant of the local area as long as they are quality people. So I take the point—it is dangerous ground to make that a philosophy, it should just be a thought.

1851. PETER SHORE: Yes. I think the point in a sense becomes more serious when one considers the extent of public accountability that there is. Take, for example again, the National Health Service Trusts—their requirement of having, I think, one meeting in public a year is very different from the previous arrangements under which I think every meeting of a District Health Authority was a public one. Is there not a real danger of quangos which do have this rather restrictive public accountability of appearing to be remote and therefore unresponsive to local needs?

STANLEY KALMS: Well, there are other built-in mechanisms, community health service and other mechanisms, to adjust what you might call remoteness. In my particular hospital I have decided to have two public meetings a year. I might add that nobody—but nobody—turns up despite all the publicity. So, you know, you are really chasing a shadow here rather than a substance. We also have to produce very detailed accounts and I think gradually as the trust system becomes more mature and as you bring people—and this is a very interesting point—as people like myself come in we are much more used to accountability. One of the most interesting areas of conflict between myself and my professionals is that they, as professionals, tend to be rather more secretive, more defensive—the medical profession is known for this anyway—whereas I am much more enquiring and demanding. So there is a creative tension on my board—I want more exposure, I want more public involvement. So I think the system has got some built-in correctives.

1852. PETER SHORE: Have you looked at the recent publication by the Department—the Secretary of State for the Health Department—in which some modifications of the procedures for selection——

STANLEY KALMS: Yes, this came out yesterday.

PETER SHORE: Yes.

STANLEY KALMS: And I do have it here.

PETER SHORE: You have not had a chance to look at it?

STANLEY KALMS: Yes. I was a little bit uncomfortable with it. It seemed to me that there was a wind blowing and people bending to it without actually thinking about all the consequences and I think this is an example where we may be forced to have positive discrimination and to have to go to the processes of advertising rather than head-hunting and I passionately believe that head-hunting is the only way to get the qualities that I want round my board. But, you know, I accept the principles of this briefing from the NHS. I have studied it and clearly will observe it. But I do feel that it may not strengthen my board in the way I would want to strengthen it when there is a vacancy.

1853. PETER SHORE: What in particular do you think of the proposal that there should be panels consisting of, say, three local Health Service Chairmen to as it were vet applications for further Health Service ——

STANLEY KALMS: Well I would ask the question—would I get through that? That is the test I would give it—my own litmus test—"would I get through that process?" I think I have made a big contribution to this hospital in a variety of ways—I don't mean that to be immodest—but I just feel that the momentum and the results and the way we are running it is an improvement—I brought some good ideas in. Would I myself go through that process? I was head-hunted for the hospital as a non-executive by a member of the faculty who said "You would be a good guy to be a non-executive". Then the Chairman left and then I was interviewed by the Minister. I was recommended—it was a very informal, easy process, and you got me hooked on it. But I think if there had been strong barriers or committees or if I had had to go through a process of deep interrogation I would have thought it would have been difficult. So I am concerned that my type of person would not come on and I think my type of person is very useful in the concept of a hospital.

1854. PETER SHORE: Let me turn now to the problem of public perception. It is true that there is no totally comprehensive analysis of Quango appointments available to us, but there have been a lot of partial studies and a number of them—well, I have one in front of me here—a nationwide analysis of NHS trust shares found that of the 185 whose backgrounds could be examined from public sources, 62 had clear links with the Conservative Party, seven with the Labour Party trade unions, and one with the Liberal Democrats. Do you think that given the public role of quangos and the fact that they are administering public services, do you think that it really is an embarrassment to have what appears to be a rather heavily tilted representation of people who are connected with one political party rather than another?

STANLEY KALMS: It certainly is the problem of perception, yes. But presumably they are the best candidates, presumably they are the people who feel that the market economy type philosophy of the National Health Service—there is sympathy with that role. But I do accept that at the end of the day one has to have balance in everything. So I think it is an interesting area but I wouldn't like to comment excessively on it.

1855. PETER SHORE: You would accept that balance is an important objective in that?

STANLEY KALMS: Well, a balance in everything in life is important—it is part of ethics, isn't it—that you try and create some balance of perception of responsibility.

1856. PETER SHORE: I think you said to me a moment ago that it is really important that people who are appointed to these boards share the philosophy of those who are appointing them. I wonder really whether that is the case in terms of the kind of jobs that people are asked to do on quangos. For example, when a school opts out from the local authority system and goes for the Grant Maintained status, the headmaster of that particular school may, as it were, wish to remain in the previous local authority, but having been moved out of it into the other system, he is going to carry on doing his best for the school, isn't he?

STANLEY KALMS: Right.

PETER SHORE: So it is not really a problem there of personal, as it were, lack of conviction for the thrust of the policy.

STANLEY KALMS: Right. For the headmaster it isn't, except he is put under a great deal more strains and stresses and responsibilities. He is taken away from the cosy LEA relationship into the market economy. He has to produce budgets and be more responsible for his own decisions.

1857. PETER SHORE: But in the great majority of cases, as far as I can recall, there has been no change of headmaster, they have simply carried on?

STANLEY KALMS: It is usually headmaster-driven, quite frankly. It is the headmasters who want to get out of the LEAs into the GM system. I doubt if it works very well if a headmaster says implacably "no". So you have to capture his mind first, otherwise the system creaks from the beginning.

1858. PETER SHORE: Would you say the same of senior appointments of medical personnel to the boards of hospital trusts and so on? Do you think, for example, that an eminent surgeon who might also be a representative figure on a trust authority is likely in any way to be affected by the fact that once a decision having been taken to put his hospital under a trust, that he would not do his utmost to serve?

STANLEY KALMS: The medical directors on the board are usually semi-volunteers because not many of the medical profession actually want to serve on the board, but those who do serve on the board are committed to the system. I don't find any discomfort here—in fact in the hospital I represent generally speaking the medical faculty are in favour of the system. So I don't find any problem of intellectual differences between the system—I think they are committed to the present process of the NHS.

1859. PETER SHORE: Yes. Well, what I am really sort of trying to establish here is that the lack of a commitment to a particular new structure for a service is not a disqualification from people serving on a governing body?

STANLEY KALMS: Well, it would be if the lack of commitment was apparent. If it was overt I think it would be a disqualification. You can't have a board of anything that doesn't face—I know we have governments who don't face all the same direction and, indeed, oppositions—but basically a board ought to face and have a consensus of opinion and if you had a senior member of your board who didn't agree with your policy I think that creates a serious problem, particularly in the medical field, because the medical director has to take the faculty with him. So I do want consensus on my board, yes. Whether it is immediate or by long tortuous argument we need consensus, yes.

1860. PETER SHORE: Well, I am glad to hear that. Otherwise I do think there is some danger of, if you like, the Americanisation of British boards. When a new administration comes in in Washington you get a vast reshuffling of personnel reflecting the political interests of one party against another.

STANLEY KALMS: Yes.

1861. PETER SHORE: You would not like to see that adopted here as a practice, would you?

STANLEY KALMS: Not in the hospital system—it is too fragile at the moment. What it does need is

consistency and continuity. We are going through a difficult process of change. The last thing we need to do now is to challenge people. I mean, we are on a path—it needs improvement, of course—and in a sense——and an interesting point which I think I ought to make is that coming from the Quango and coming from the outside world and coming with a great deal of independence—and I think people like myself come with independence because we are not dependent on salaries or earnings (I don't draw a salary for it, but others do) but I come with independence and I am continually challenging and arguing. I am not a poodle. I think one of the things about quangos is that they are not poodles. It is sometimes seen as such but in my two quangos I think we are thorns and I think that should not be ignored. Not deep thorns and not offensive thorns—we are the little pea in the shoe or under the mattress—we are not accepting everything that comes down from head office. We have long arguments in education and we do with the Secretary of State in the hospital. We fight very hard for our corner on important issues. So we do bring something—We argue more than if we were purely bureaucrats. This is the advantage of bringing outside people in. We are not committed to the bureaucratic layered process.

PETER SHORE: Thank you.

1862. LORD NOLAN: I wonder if I could pick up something I think I just heard you saying? I believe that one of the cruder perceptions about quangos and National Health Service Trusts is that they are well-paid sinecures for the friends of those who appoint them. I think I am right in saying that of all Quango appointments only one-third carry any salary. I believe in the National Health Service Trusts, on the other hand, it is something like 93 per cent that do. Did I hear you say that you do not draw a salary for your Quango appointments?

STANLEY KALMS: I don't, no. That is purely a personal decision and of no significance except just as an attitude towards quangos.

1863. LORD NOLAN: Bearing in mind that many of them are paid and no doubt the pay is drawn, what is your impression of the level of pay for the work done and the quality of those doing it?

STANLEY KALMS: Well, it is very difficult here not to be subjective because the sums involved by my standards are very small. But if you take the non-executive directors getting £5,000 I get very good value for the buck from my non-executive directors—quite demanding—they have to play a real role in the hospital, they have to pick up responsibilities, I expect them to trudge round and be involved in the hospital. In terms of the market I couldn't get anyone for £5,000. My salary would be £20,000. You know, as a quantum sum it is reasonable but the demands are very onerous, very demanding, and you certainly wouldn't do it for £20,000. I think one of the dangers is that if you did it for £20,000 then there is a danger within the system. So bringing people from outside, from different salary structures, where the quantum sum isn't significant I think it an important aspect.

1864. LORD NOLAN: You also said—and now I am touching on a slightly different topic—when Professor King asked you about (I think the word "ethics" was used) whether business ethics were comparable to the ethics you found in the Civil Service and in the professions that you deal with in quango, and I think you said that the Civil Service was different, is that right, because it was all laid down in advance?

STANLEY KALMS: Yes, all prescribed, yes. I don't see ethics in the Civil Service, I see ethics outside. There is no room for ethics in the——I don't mean this in a sort of pejorative way but there is no real room for ethics in the system, it is totally prescribed "this is what you do in every situation". Ethics is about facing other challenges.

1865. LORD NOLAN: Ethics—and this, again, I think is a phrase you used—in the practical sense means avoiding conflicts of interest, conflicts of duty, and here you do, do you not, have the same problem in principle at any rate facing civil servants as well as business men?

STANLEY KALMS: Well, the conflicts of interest are very easily prescribed—it is not an issue of great discussion. You either can participate in a discussion or you can't. There are very simple rules. Ethics go far beyond that. Ethics go into a wider responsibility. In the Civil Service, in the hospital you have a duty to care—it is a very prescribed duty to care. It doesn't go beyond the discipline of what you have to provide. In the private sector one would look—or not always—but you could look at broader implications.

1866. LORD NOLAN: Yes. And would the same apply to Ministers because there again Ministers—and, indeed, senior Civil Servants—are often dealing with the private sector at arm's length, or nearly at arm's length. Should not the same approach in ethical terms apply on both sides?

STANLEY KALMS: Well, the Minister has a much wider range of responsibilities and ethics must be a major part of his thinking. His attitude to life, to politics, to society must cover ethical attitudes as a fundamental part of his make-up.

1867. LORD NOLAN: One of the ideas that has been put before the committee is that we should aim at suggesting, if not actually drawing up, codes of conduct, for, for example, Members of Parliament, or even an over-reaching code of conduct of general application. Business has gone quite a long way in drawing up codes of conduct in certain areas, has it not, and so of course has the Civil Service. Do you think there is—I think you may say no—do you think there is a helpful role for more general codes of conduct in public life?

STANLEY KALMS: Yes. Well, there is, clearly, but you have got to be very careful here that life isn't only by prescription. You then kill ethics off completely. So I think that as far as Ministers are concerned clearly there must be rules and guidelines, but if you make them too prescribed all of a sudden the guy no longer has to consider other applications of life and his role and responsibility. So this is where ethics and prescription have an interesting discussion between them.

1868. LORD NOLAN: Yes. Short and simple—would you rely more on example, leadership?

STANLEY KALMS: Example, of course, is——if it is a good example, not all example, no. You have to intellectualise and theorise and work it out yourself and if you can get a model of a thought pattern towards ethics then fine. But you have to have some prescription—there is no question about it.

LORD NOLAN: Thank you very much.

1869. ANNE WARBURTON: Mr. Kalms, as an erstwhile civil servant I must say I am slightly surprised to hear you say that ethics don't enter into the Civil Service—perhaps I do not paraphrase you exactly rightly. I have in front of me—because we are later receiving representations from the Institute of Business Ethics with which I think you have had connections yourself——

STANLEY KALMS: Yes.

ANNE WARBURTON: I see that the Dixons Group actually have a code of business ethics.

STANLEY KALMS: Yes.

ANNE WARBURTON: Why is that useful?

STANLEY KALMS: Well, I think there must be prescription in everything but it doesn't cover even remotely the role that we play in society and our attitudes towards issues. I mean that is just merely the simplicity of behaviourial pattern. That part which you can prescribe is very simple—you know—"thou shalt not do inside dealing". But ethics covers a much wider range—it is about creating a social fabric which can't always be specifically dealt with. It covers areas of behaviourial patterns to staff, to advertising, to a whole range of human behaviour patterns. I didn't mean to be presumptuous by saying that there are no ethics in the Civil Service. What I was really saying is most of their issues are very specifically dealt with in the routine of our meetings and one does not look at the wider implications of some of the decision-making process. For instance in a hospital you are dealing with the process of the patient as he comes in through an Accident and Emergency until he gets discharged at the other end. One doesn't necessarily think about the wider things. For instance, hospitals don't have any charity—they are a charity. Business is all about charity and about looking for ways of spreading your success or your profitability. Charity is a major function of the private sector. There is no charity within the public sector. So that is one area where ethics in the private sector exposes you to broader social responsibilities.

1870. ANNE WARBURTON: But do you see your own code of conduct—I think you call it Best Practice—as being helpful also to your employees and to your board members?

STANLEY KALMS: It is a start in the process. It is not by any means a total process. It doesn't work, it is merely a guideline. There are excesses all the time and, you know, it is helpful to set the standards by which you wish to operate and be seen to operate.

1871. ANNE WARBURTON: And would you accept that that might also apply in the world of politics and in the Civil Service?

STANLEY KALMS: Yes, there is a role for prescription but it is not the answer, it is not the end exercise and so I have cautions about it.

ANNE WARBURTON: I think I will leave it there, thank you.

1872. MARTIN JACOMB: Can I just ask you a couple of questions really by way of elucidation because I think what you have said has been incredibly clear and very helpful. There seems to be some suggestion lying behind Prof. King's question—not because he thinks it himself but because it has been reflected in the newspapers, and I think this is something the newspapers have got wrong—there seems to be some suggestion that because a company like yours gives to the Conservative Party that therefore Quango appointments are made available to people who you employ or who are on your board, and that that (the suggestion goes on) is in some way an advantage to the company. I would have thought—and I would just like your comments on this—that it was much more likely to be a sacrifice by the company, making people available for outside public service work rather than keeping their nose to the grindstone. Could you comment on that?

STANLEY KALMS: I don't think it is a sacrifice. It can be onerous. I think the work of a Quango is very onerous, it is time-consuming, very demanding, very challenging and in the case of a hospital it means walking round the wards at midnight to make sure it is working. I mean, it really does put a lot of personal strain. And as far as members of the company are concerned, yes, it can be inconvenient, but I wouldn't say that I would be unhappy with that responsibility. I would like to think in a company the corporate philosophy is to share the talents into the public sector. But there is no benefit to it, it is just a sense of playing your part in the community. I don't want to be pompous about it but that is what our theme is. We make our money out of the community—we have to return some of it back.

1873. MARTIN JACOMB: That is very clear. There is one other thing I would like you to help us with, if you possibly can. You made it absolutely clear how you were appointed and how somebody of your seniority would be unlikely to subject themselves to anything other than what you have described as the headhunting process. I can see that businessmen of your seniority would not want to go through an advise and consent procedure, but you are needed.

On the other hand, as you accepted, there is a public perception problem. How could we bridge that gap between the public perception of quangos being "packed" and the need to have people who are unlikely to subject themselves to a completely open and competitive process?

STANLEY KALMS: The process of the FAS was good enough for me, but you have to have headhunting—advertising is not sufficient—and as I said before, it is a fundamental part of the private sector. Providing that you headhunt and then have a reasonably senior group of people (who would have to be one's peers) interviewing, I would be happy. If one is interviewed by one's peers, one would be comfortable; but it would be uncomfortable and embarrassing if one was interviewed by others who were less than one's peers. I do not mean to be pompous about this either, but I hope you get the point I am trying to make.

MARTIN JACOMB: I do, indeed. My worry is whether that will really answer public perception.

STANLEY KALMS: Then that is the problem you face.

MARTIN JACOMB: I was hoping that you would help us to find the answer to it. Thank you very much.

1874. WILLIAM UTTING: Mr Kalms, I admire your personal contribution to the public good and I certainly value the qualities that you have advocated as being necessary in the public service, but I am rather concerned if you are generalising from your experience across the full number of non-departmental public bodies and quangos and suggesting that a system of headhunting is a suitable way of filling 40,000 appointments. Would this not lead to a wholly undesirable concentration of power in the hands of the national executive, particularly when one is dealing with bodies which are providing services or discharging responsibilities for local communities? I do not think you have really weighted the case for some sort of local interest representation on those sorts of bodies.

STANLEY KALMS: Yes. You are quite right; I can only speak from my experience of my particular quangos and I am sure that those who work on different types of quangos would have different points of view. I would just emphasise that there is a role for advertising and nominations, but at the top level if you ignore the headhunting aspect, all is lost—you will not get people like me. Of course I agree that the search must also be wider—I am only speaking for my own particular two quangos.

1875. WILLIAM UTTING: Thank you very much. That does indicate a degree of welcome flexibility. If I could just ask you two more very brief questions: first, is your firm has a policy of enabling employees to participate in public service and appointments on non-departmental public bodies?

STANLEY KALMS: Yes, it is encouraged.

WILLIAM UTTING: You enable and encourage employees?

STANLEY KALMS: Absolutely. It is fundamental that they have the right to participate. It starts with charity and then it goes on to personal commitment. For instance, in our City Technology College, we have a committee which interfaces and is totally involved all the time, but in other areas, anybody who wants to be part of a public sector committee, quango etc., would be encouraged to take time for it.

1876. WILLIAM UTTING: Good, thank you. The other question concerns the nomination forms that are increasingly coming into use in relation to people put forward for public service. Do you think that it would be right to include on that form a question about whether the person being nominated is a member of a political party and, if so, which one?

STANLEY KALMS: My first response, not considered or weighted, would be that it is irrelevant. But I understand the implications and then on the other hand, if it was a quango with a strongly political motivation, it may be a different question—though I think the answer would still be "no".

WILLIAM UTTING: Thank you.

LORD NOLAN: Mr Kalms, you have kindly run the gamut, but Professor King has thought of a supplementary he would like to put to you.

1877. PROF ANTHONY KING: This follows on from what a couple of other people have said. You referred—and you are the first living, human being I have heard refer to it—to the "quango movement". That is a new concept and it sounds rather like the Salvation Army! From the point of view of the quango movement—and I know that others have made this point—do you not think it has been rather unfortunate that the proportion of people appointed to top jobs in quangos who have been in some way publicly associated with the Conservative Party has been so large? Would it not be good idea, from the point of view of establishing the legitimacy of quangos, if more of those appointed to them were to be publicly identified as either being not Conservatives, or even as being associated with some other party?

STANLEY KALMS: You are suggesting that being a Conservative means being totally supportive of all Conservative policies and being an unquestioning devotee of the administration. It suggests that one has a totally unquestioning, unintellectual, unphilosophical approach to Conservatism. I do not think that people who call themselves Conservatives are unquestioning or undemanding. We also want change and positive action. I have to say that simply to call me a Conservative does not put me into a small box—in generally I support a market economy rather than a controlled economy, but I have almost as many disagreements with the Conservative Party as I am sure Mr Shore has.

We are not of one mould; I happen to be a Conservative because there are broad applications of Conservatism which appeal to me.

1878. PROF ANTHONY KING: I am sure that is true of you, but can you not see that an outsider might think "My goodness, a very large proportion of these people are capital "C" Conservatives. Almost none comes from any other political party. This just does not look right."?

STANLEY KALMS: We have had a Conservative Government for 15 years; we have a Conservative majority (or did have, if you exclude the polls). Therefore you might expect a majority of people to be of the Conservative inclination. These quangos are nearly all an extrapolation of Conservative policy, so they would naturally attract Conservative people. The best thing is not to pursue the political aspect of this.

1879. PROF ANTHONY KING: I will not pursue this, but one of the things that would worry me would be that an incoming administration would look at the fact that so many people on a quango were Conservatives, overlook the fact that they have so much to contribute, clear the lot of you out and replace you with some other lot.

STANLEY KALMS: That is a serious danger. I have considered that and my own view would be that, unless there was a total reversal of policy and someone said, for instance "We do not want GM schools." (in which case I would not have a job), or "We do not want the NHS to be in this area.", providing it was an evolution, I would be willing to continue to serve because in my role as Chairman of quangos, I see myself as apolitical.

PROF ANTHONY KING: Thank you.

LORD NOLAN: Thank you very much indeed for giving so much of the middle of a busy weekday morning. We are very glad to have had your help and advice.

STANLEY KALMS: Thank you.

1880. LORD NOLAN: Professor Stewart, we thank you and your colleagues very much for coming to join us this morning. Have you any opening statement that you would like to make before we go on to questions?

PROFESSOR JOHN STEWART, HOWARD DAVIES AND CHRIS SKELCHER

PROFESSOR JOHN STEWART (Institute of Local Government Studies, University of Birmingham): Not in any depth. I will just introduce Chris Skelcher and Howard Davies, who have both recently completed a research project on the membership of quangos at local level.

LORD NOLAN: And who we know of in writing, but have not yet had the pleasure of meeting in person.

JOHN STEWART: The only other thing I would say is that our main interest, as you are aware, has been in quangos operating at local level. We are less well informed about quangos operating nationally. Judging by the questions that have been asked of the previous witness, I think most of the issues we want to raise will be raised in questions.

LORD NOLAN: Good. I hope so. I shall ask Dame Anne Warburton to lead the questioning.

1881. ANNE WARBURTON: Professor Stewart, as a prelude I should like to get rather above the local appointed quangos and ask whether you (coming as you do from the most informed and, on these questions, concentrated academic school in the country) think that we, the Nolan Committee, are necessary?

JOHN STEWART: I definitely think that you are, for a variety of reasons. Obviously you are necessary because there has been public concern and quite rightly the Prime Minister has appointed a committee to investigate those. There are other reasons as well, particularly in the area of quangos. We have seen over the past 10 to 15 years a very large number of significant changes in this world, particularly at the local level, where a whole series of bodies has been created. In a sense, this has taken place step by step, without anybody actually having an overall look at the process.

Other important changes are taking place in the way government operates—the growth of contracting out, market forces, privatisation—which could raise issues of an ethical nature. That is not to oppose these changes, but to say that maybe we need new conventions in these areas.

The fourth reason is illustrated for me by the previous evidence and evidence that I have read in the press. We do not know much about this area—about how appointments are made, the extent of political affiliation, or even the rules governing these bodies. The press have been investigating it and parliamentary questions have been asked, but it is an unknown area and therefore, in a sense, it is important that the whole operation of the world of the quango movement is brought to light.

1882. ANNE WARBURTON: Good. Thank you very much and thank you for coming to help us to contribute to removing some of these problems. Would you like first to give us some idea of the work which is being done at the University of Birmingham? Perhaps I should say explicitly (it has been hinted at) that we know of some of your research work, because we have commissioned some from you, although I think that is not what we are discussing today particularly.

JOHN STEWART: I will ask Chris or Howard to come in on that, but just say that we have been interested in this area for a considerable time, partly because some of the functions have been removed from local government—which is my own field of academic interest—and we are interested in what is happening to those.

We began by doing work on the extent to which the rules about accountability that govern local authorities, govern these appointed boards, taking in a whole series of things such as surcharge and open meetings. We found that it was almost a research project in itself to find out what the rules were which govern these bodies.

At the moment we have just completed a research project, which I shall ask either Chris or Howard to speak about.

CHRIS SKELCHER (Institute of Local Government Studies, University of Birmingham): We have recently completed a project commissioned by the Joseph Rowntree Foundation which involved a major survey of members of local appointed bodies, including those in which the Committee is interested. We sought to identify the characteristics of members of those bodies, their perceptions about their role, operations, level of training and other relevant features. We hope that that work will be published within the next couple of months and it is beginning to show clearly that members of local appointed bodies tend to have certain common characteristics. In particular, they tend to be highly educated in formal systems, they tend to come from the business and senior public service areas, but also there is variety in the way in which they operate.

One of the main messages coming out of the work we are doing is that the growth of quangos has led to significant fragmentation in terms of the way those bodies operate, the way they are constituted and the way members are appointed. That fragmentation and those differences between bodies is an important area to investigate and I am sure that will be reflected in the evidence we shall be giving and that which you will be hearing from other colleagues.

Howard might like to say something about some of the other work we have been undertaking.

HOWARD DAVIES (Institute of Local Government Studies, University of Birmingham): Yes, thank you. The other significant area I should flag up is that we had a go at some local mapping—looking at the pattern of bodies in specific locations. In particular, we had a stab at this in the West Midlands Metropolitan County. Something which surprised us, even knowing something about the area concerned and essentially what sort of bodies we were looking for, was how difficult it was to get the basic information on them. We still ended up with a lot of question marks about some of the basic structural issues and rules under which bodies operate. Even in terms of

lists of members, where those can be obtained (which is not in itself always a straightforward operation) it does not necessarily tell you anything about them. It may not even tell you, for instance, whether they are male or female. You may simply get "A. Smith" and that does not tell you much.

It was certainly a surprise to us that even the basic information, never mind about the rights, wrongs and views of whether and the way things should be done, was not there. This, of course, contrasts markedly with elected bodies such as Parliament and local authorities where lists of members, electoral cycles and so on are all, in principle, available and take place in a known way.

CHRIS SKELCHER: If I could make a quick final comment; it is important to stress that in this process, we are not seeking to criticise or attack the individuals involved (and I would refer back to the previous witness's comments). We are aiming to investigate and understand how the system operates and certainly our research indicates clearly that people have a strong commitment to the roles they are performing. Our questions were addressed at the way in which the system operates, rather than challenging individuals and their commitment.

1883. ANNE WARBURTON: At the risk of making a break in the course of the conversation, I should like to ask two particular questions which stem from the letter you, Professor Stewart, and your colleagues sent to us in December. I should like to read two sentences from that.

"Public organisations have increasingly been adopting private sector management practices in pursuit of greater efficiency. While much of this has been valuable, there is a danger in not properly adapting these practices to the public sector and its need for accountability."

I would be most grateful if you could elaborate on the differences you see in the needs of the public and the private sectors.

JOHN STEWART: One of the biggest differences is openness. In a sense, the private sector is, to a degree, private; the public sector is subject to open government which is reflected in such requirements as public meetings, access to information and so on. That seems to me almost the most fundamental difference between the two and is one of the things on which some confusion has arisen in the operation of many quangos in that they have opted for a private rather than an open model.

It is a difficult and delicate area to know how a public body will behave in these circumstances, but we are asking them to compete for business in ways that may require them to be much more secretive about their information. They will not want to reveal their costs to their competitors in the way that, for example, local authorities have always done in the past. There is almost a tension between some of the requirements of public accountability and of operating in a competitive and market situation. I am not saying that those cannot be resolved, but they have to be faced and discussed.

1884. ANNE WARBURTON: Thank you. In that same letter, you make various recommendations and suggestions on things that this Committee might do. One of them is that we should draw attention to the need for new rules to meet the new circumstances and, in particular, the adoption of business practices in government, semi-government business and devolution. Who do you envisage might draw up these rules? I do not think that you see them coming out in May as a result of our report.

JOHN STEWART: No. I would see them normally in the first instance being drawn up by institutions within local government itself. For example, the local authority associations have recently commissioned work on a new code of practice for officers, aware that when they are operating in a competitive situation, there is a need for a review of the rules.

I would be in favour of there being some standing institution over-viewing the whole of the area in which you are actually operating. That would, over time, comment on the operation of different parts of the public sector. Obviously, if such an institution was in existence, it would look at the rules being adopted within institutions such as local government and comment on whether or not they were adequate.

ANNE WARBURTON: You see it evolving over the years?

JOHN STEWART: Yes.

1885. ANNE WARBURTON: More precisely, on local appointed bodies, what would you see as the main weaknesses in accountability and how can those problems be addressed? That is a very wide question.

JOHN STEWART: I would see the main weaknesses as being twofold on the whole. First is the fact that we know so little about them and that it is, as Howard was saying, an effort to get the basic information about many of these bodies, the rules that apply to them and the details of their membership. The first requirement of accountability is that one should know who is accountable and have basic information about them.

I would also argue, as I have done probably in some of the other papers you have before you, for investigating the extent to which some of these bodies should be made accountable to local people through an electoral process. I believe that those who exercise public power or spend public money should be accountable to those on whose behalf they do so. Where a body is making significant local choices on behalf of local people (not all quangos) there should be some system of accountability to them. I would want to investigate whether the local authority should be given some responsibility in relation to such bodies, or whether there should be separate elections for them. When I say that local authorities should be given responsibilities, I do not necessarily mean that we would merely set up a committee of the local authority in the normal way; our local authorities have learned to work in many different ways in recent years and there are a series of different models that could be pursued.

My two requirements are therefore, a form of accountability to local people, but also, where that is not done, much greater knowledge about the bodies, with registers held at national and local levels containing basic information about people on them.

1886. ANNE WARBURTON: You probably know that we had the Chief Executive of the NHS here earlier this week. He made the argument that a national body delivering services has to be accountable, through Ministers, to Parliament and the money it spends is under Parliament's responsibility. Perhaps I could ask you to go a little further into detail about how you can reconcile the local arrangements that concern you particularly with accountability upwards.

JOHN STEWART: In many of our institutions we combine local accountability with accountability upwards (in a sense). Local authorities have traditionally run national services; indeed the Education Service was called by many people "a national service, locally administered" and that was the phrase adopted by the Society of Education Officers. It is quite possible to have a national service in which legislation, orders and circulars lay down the national requirements and for there to be local accountability because the body at that level is making local choices.

Turning, as an example, to the district health authority; the job of the district health authority is to determine local needs and to allocate resources in relation to those. That is a local matter; it operates within a national framework, for which it is accountable, but for its local choices there seems to me to be a need for some form of accountability to local people.

HOWARD DAVIES: Can I just add something there? In relation to the point about a service with national standards that is locally accountable, a good current example would be the Fire Service which has clear central guidelines about standards of attendance, distribution of resources and so on. Yet, except for a brief period during the war years, it has always been a local government service and so far as I know there are no proposals to change that, nor, so far as I am aware, are there any suggestions that that arrangement does not work.

Building on John's point, the other more explicit issue, which comes up in relation to the health service particularly, is that of what these local appointed bodies are there to do—whether they are managing or governing. Mr Kalms, for instance, referred, in relation to quango membership, to recruiting senior management. That raises a question about the purpose of these boards. My colleagues can speak for themselves, but we tend to the view that many of them are making decisions about priorities, resource distributions, local needs and so on which are the essence of governmental (although maybe with a small "g") decisions, rather than simply managing or administering something which has come down from on high. The issue of the role of these bodies may be crucial in determining other factors about their behaviour and the standards expected.

JOHN STEWART: I would add just one point to Howard's comment. The distinction he is drawing between governing and managing is particularly appropriate to making the case of the district health authority which has ceased to be a providing body in charge of management, but has become a contracting or commissioning body which is, in a sense, making those governmental choices Howard spoke about.

1887. ANNE WARBURTON: The NHS itself makes a distinction, does it not, about policy making and executing? I take it that you have been able to see the new NHS suggestions and ideas this week?

JOHN STEWART: Only as reported in the press.

ANNE WARBURTON: When you see them, I wonder whether you will find that they move in the direction you would want in terms of the ways in which appointments are to be made.

JOHN STEWART: I think they move a little in that direction, but I would obviously want a representative health authority for the reasons I have given. If we are not pursuing that, I am interested in a greater independent element in the process which, I understand, they already have in Scotland and in the appointments to the police authorities.

There are two difficulties with that, from which I do not run away. First, who appoints the independent people? In a sense one has to appoint a quango to appoint a quango—but there are traditions in our country for independent appointments. Secondly, although you may think I might, I would not myself want the independent body to make the appointments because if the real problem is that of accountability and there is none to local people, then that to Parliament through Ministers is the only form of accountability and it is difficult to see how you could expect that of Ministers unless they themselves made the final appointment in the situation.

ANNE WARBURTON: That is how Ministers see it.

JOHN STEWART: I would want independence as part of the process scrutiny or vetting as one went along, but not that the Minister was presented with one name—which is, I believe, the practice in Scotland at the moment.

1888. ANNE WARBURTON: I was struck (and I think you heard it) by Mr Kalm's saying a moment ago that when he holds public meetings—which is part of the openness of course—nobody comes. What is the answer to that?

JOHN STEWART: There are two: first, if he made a certain sort of decision, I think the public would come. The public coming is a safeguard. Quite often council meetings are not well attended, but we can all go to a council meeting (those about the budget process in Shropshire at the moment are remarkably well attended) and that is a safeguard.

Secondly, we are concerned not merely about the public attending directly, but the press. It is much more likely that the press will get in the habit of attending if there is a regular process, rather than a special meeting called to be public and probably the press not really believing it is a normal meeting, but one set up for them. If you actually want to open meetings to the public, that should be the normal practice so that the public and the press can get accustomed to it—subject, of course, to the safeguards that certain business would have to be conducted in private, as for rules that apply in local authorities.

1889. ANNE WARBURTON: Professor Stewart, before I pass on the opportunity to ask you questions, is there anything that you would like to have been asked and have not and therefore want to say now?

JOHN STEWART: The only other subjects I would have mentioned (and they may well still come up) are the

issue of a code of practice governing these bodies and the extent to which the rules that govern local authorities should also apply to them. I believe there should be such codes.

I would also like to stress the issue of training and induction of appointed members. Many appointed people believe that they have been put there, and quite rightly, to bring in private sector experience. It is important that if there are distinctions about public sector accountability, they are made clear to people, particularly the ones about openness which I have stressed.

One of the things that is very important is that we have a new look at the information available on quangos. The restriction of the definition to non-departmental public bodies is misleading, since many of the bodies with which I am concerned do not fall within that definition. On all the subjects that have been explored in parliamentary questions—such as the number of posts that have been advertised, the numbers for which headhunters have actually been used, the rules governing them, whether or not there are public declarations of interests and the rules governing open meetings—there should be an annual or standing publication that sets out that information. Public information about these institutions is a very important requirement.

ANNE WARBURTON: Thank you.

1890. LORD NOLAN: I wonder if I might go out of turn to take up two of the last points you mentioned while they are fresh in mind. I for one was very much struck by the loose definition of NDPBs and by the Government paper which gave it to us, listing at least five other types of organisations, which all had slightly different functions, compositions and roles. I remember saying to the witness, "How are you going to explain them?" and you are asking the same question.

JOHN STEWART: I am. The NDPB is confusing in two ways. It excludes a large number of bodies, including a very interesting category, which is growing, of the self-appointing body exercising public powers, which raises issues. It also confuses in a different way: non-departmental public bodies differ very much within themselves. To me there seems to be a fundamental distinction between advisory bodies, executive bodies and semi-judicial bodies. I would want to apply different rules to those.

1891. LORD NOLAN: I remember once asking that question of a Member of the Bar about an absolutely impenetrable piece of statutory prose. I asked him how on earth he was going to explain it to us and he said that he proposed to rely on body language—but that did not really work!

The second, and more serious, matter was this: in paragraph 7 of your letter you touched on the need for training public officials and those who come into the public service from outside and your hope that we would endorse the need to give prominence to ethical issues and standards of conduct. Will the work that you and your colleagues are now doing include concrete proposals for some such training guidance?

CHRIS SKELCHER: Maybe I could respond to that. Certainly, as I mentioned earlier, the work that Howard and I have been doing for Joseph Rowntree has been looking at issues of training. It is clear there that in some appointed bodies there are high levels of training and training appears to occur early on in the process of appointment; in others there is a much lower level of training and it perhaps occurs later. That pattern varies across the appointed bodies.

One of the things we shall be doing is following that up with suggestions and proposals. We do not have any formulated currently, but it highlights the variety we were talking about earlier and the differences in practices that occur.

JOHN STEWART: Can I draw your attention to one other piece of work, not done by ourselves, but by Isaac Henry and Chris Painter at the University of Central England in Birmingham. They carried out an investigation, not of the formal requirements of accountability, but the actual practices about accountability pursued by the various appointed boards in the West Midlands Region. They drew up on that basis a code of good practice for accountability which, if you have not already seen it, can be made available. That, incidentally, was then adopted by the Joint Committee representing the seven leaders (two Conservative and five Labour) in the West Midlands, who have drawn it to the attention of all the quangos in their area and asked them if they will adopt this code of good practice. A lot of that is about open meetings and ways of consulting the public.

LORD NOLAN: I cannot say off hand whether we have it or not. May we approach you for it if we have not? Thank you very much indeed.

HOWARD DAVIES: Can I briefly refer back to the previous issue about the status of bodies. One of the things that may be relevant is that the precise legal status of the bodies may also be increasingly important. The Training and Enterprise Councils would be a classic example of that. At the moment these bodies are companies limited by guarantee and, as we are seeing in the unfortunate saga of the South Thames at the moment, a whole range of issues become potentially confused about precisely who is responsible for what and whether these are or are not public bodies. It may therefore be important in relation to the work of your Committee and future governmental considerations about the applicability of certain rules and standards as to whether these bodies are regarded as within the public sector or not.

LORD NOLAN: Yes, thank you very much. We touched on that point yesterday in connection with the criminal law, certain aspects of which may or may not apply to some of these bodies. It is an area that needs to be clarified. Mr Tom King, would you like to speak?

TOM KING: No, but I should like to say that I am delighted to see Professor John Stewart again, for whom I have great respect.

1892. WILLIAM UTTING: We have also had published recently the Government's review of guidance on public appointments and its desire to let more light into the process for public appointments generally. I do not know whether you have had a chance to examine that and have any general views on the document?

HOWARD DAVIES: It has been given to us this morning.

WILLIAM UTTING: Can I put one hypothetical point to you?

JOHN STEWART: I think, incidentally, it shows part of the answer to Dame Anne Warburton's question—the value of the Committee.

1893. WILLIAM UTTING: Quite right! One of the things that came out of this document for me is the tension that exists between the interests of different departments of state in looking after their own quangos and non-departmental bodies and also a more general desire to achieve more consistency in the system of appointments nationally. Do you think that bodies such as the Public Appointments Unit itself or the Civil Service Commissioners ought to have a monitoring and perhaps enforcement role in relation to appointments to bodies across the board?

JOHN STEWART: There were two different issues: whether you have a monitoring role and whether it is an internal governmental role or an external role. There may be a case for both. There is a need for some overview within government as to what is happening in these systems of appointments, as there should be in government generally concern about what is happening to the whole structure of government. Therefore I would favour a clearer role for somebody at the centre, whether it should be the Civil Service Commission or the Public Appointments Unit I do not know.

If you are talking about a particular category such as executive quangos, there should be normal rules of practice that should be kept to by all departments unless a specific reason is put forward. In other words, the onus should be upon people to justify exceptions from what is recommended as the code of practice for appointments.

To illustrate that point, there have been many requests coming from the centre in past guidance about the importance of advertising appointments. In practice of course that has happened very little, so there has to be some mechanism not merely for laying down practice but for overseeing what is actually happening.

1894. WILLIAM UTTING: Yes. I have become hooked on the importance of the NHS and of executive quangos because of the volume of public money that they are spending. I may have underestimated the importance of the advisory quangos. Is that right? How important are these advisory bodies in relation to the executives and the NHS?

JOHN STEWART: I tend to share your perspective. I see the issues about the advisory bodies as being less critical than those about executive bodies. In the case of the advisory bodies, you are not giving them executive powers or powers to spend substantial amounts of public money, so the issue of accountability is less significant. They are accountable to the people to whom they give advice and that seems to me to be less disturbing than the issues concerning some of the other bodies.

1895. WILLIAM UTTING: If we are dealing with the executive bodies and the NHS then, the Audit Commission advised us last week that we should really be looking for the most rigorous standards in any sector to be applied throughout the whole. Is that, in general terms, good advice?

JOHN STEWART: I see it as good advice; I tend to see the rules governing local authorities as being the most rigorous in existence at the moment. I would not say that they were necessarily a model because in many ways they are a haphazard collection of different bits of legislation, introduced at different times. I do not therefore say that the rules governing local authorities are correct, but they are the best we have at the moment.

WILLIAM UTTING: Thank you.

1896. MARTIN JACOMB: Could I go back to the first question that Dame Anne Warburton put to you because, to be frank, I find what you say in your letter rather surprising. You say:

"Public organisations are required to give an account of their actions and to be held to account for what they do. In this they are distinct from private organisations."

An ordinary private sector company has to publish an annual report with enumerable intricate details of all its financial affairs. Every year it has to have those accounts audited by independent auditors and go before its shareholders with some of its directors being subject to re-election. Are you really saying that you think the Ministry of Defence is more accountable than GEC for instance?

JOHN STEWART: I am saying they are accountable in different ways. You actually make a difficult one for me because, of course, I have laid great stress on openness and when security considerations come in that is obviously difficult to fulfil.

MARTIN JACOMB: Let us take a different Ministry. Actually, the Ministry of Defence is a bad example because Mr. King used to be responsible. Let us take a neutral one.

JOHN STEWART: Yes. My argument is not about the accounts because I accept the point you make, but that in the public sector policy decisions are publicly available, are debated and argued about between Opposition and Government. Those do not apply in the private sector in the same way where many of the policy decisions will be kept confidential for a while. I mean, you can trust a local authority, for example, which I know best—if I can go away from ministries—with a private sector firm. The local authority's day-to-day decisions will be made in public and be open to criticism by the Press as they make them, they will be open to criticism by the Opposition. Those things do not apply to the private sector, and quite rightly.

MARTIN JACOMB: But you are not actually talking about policy in this part of your letter, you are talking about the stewardship and expenditure of resources.

JOHN STEWART: I actually do not have the letter in front of me because I thought we were going to talk mainly about quangos.

1897. MARTIN JACOMB: I think it is important because what I am asking you is directly related to the absolutely central point you make, which is that quangos are behaving more and more like private sector companies and yet are not accountable.

JOHN STEWART: My point there is largely about the policy decisions they make, that they are not open and debated in the way that a local authority's policy decisions would be because they are, in fact, made in private.

1898. MARTIN JACOMB: You are not talking about accountability for resources?

JOHN STEWART: I am not talking about accountability for resources except insofar as I am talking about the resource allocation decision, the decision as to give priorities to this as opposed to that.

MARTIN JACOMB: I see that because I think actually that is quite different from what is said in your letter, to be frank, but just going on ...

JOHN STEWART: Can I just make one point about the letter. The letter was actually less meant to be about quangos than to be about the issues that the commission might wish to look at when it turned towards local government itself. Our evidence about quangos was really included in the various papers that we have written in other contexts. We were concerned that maybe local authorities, as they had moved into the area of CCT contracting-out, their own conventions required looking at. Maybe, in certain instances they might even be looking at some of the rules that govern the private sector to see whether they apply them. The letter was mainly written not as a criticism of quangos but as some of the agenda that you might want to look at when you look at local authorities.

1899. MARTIN JACOMB: Could I just go on, and it was referred to earlier, to drawing the distinction between executive action and matters of government with a small "g". All management has to do with the allocation of scarce resources, is it not, so how do you draw the line? You cannot say to somebody, "You're running a hospital but you don't have anything to do with the allocation of resources".

JOHN STEWART: No. Howard may want to come in on this, but I made those remarks primarily about the District Health Authority. I draw a distinction between allocating resources in order to attain a specific objective, like the profitability or long-term survival of the company, and the allocation of resources in the Health Service which is primarily concerned with the allocation of resources between competing needs and a value judgment has to be made by a governmental body as to whether it values, for example, the mentally ill as opposed to the acute care. It is a value judgment which seems to me to be a governmental or a political judgment which being made in those rather than a decision that can be judged purely by, for example, the financial viability of the firm or the desire to be efficient in the situation.

That is the distinction I am making, that the choice is the choice between different needs and, therefore, between the values that people place on one need as opposed to another. It is not a managerial decision, it is a governmental decision.

1900. MARTIN JACOMB: I see that is a distinction which you can make as a sort of matter of academic generalisation but in practice if you are running a hospital you are making those decisions all the time, are you not?

JOHN STEWART: I made the point actually about the District Health Authority which is not running the hospitals.

1901. MARTIN JACOMB: My question was about running a big hospital. You are making decisions about who gets the resources and who does not.

JOHN STEWART: Yes, and it is for that reason that I am interested in some form of public accountability locally for the Trusts as well because I recognise the point you make that they are also making that sort of decision. They are making that sort of decision on behalf of local people.

MARTIN JACOMB: Thank you very much.

1902. PETER SHORE: Yes. You have said on a number of occasions that we do not really know enough about quangos. It is rather surprising really, is it not, that we have not had a public register of quango members; indeed, one could exclude certain categories from this because it is the executive quangos which we have talked about earlier which appear to be of really the greatest interest, not only because of the powers they have but, presumably, because they are mainly the paid appointments?

JOHN STEWART: Yes.

1903. PETER SHORE: In addition to the publication of such a register annually, or a "Who's Who" of quango executive memberships, what would be the kind of headings of an annual report that you would find most useful in the furtherance of public accountability?

JOHN STEWART: You mean an annual report covering the whole world of quangos?

PETER SHORE: Yes, executive quangos.

JOHN STEWART: I think it would contain an analysis of the appointments according to certain categories. It would contain details of how the appointments were made, statistical details, some of the data that actually appears in the pamphlet published last week by Tony Wright, a Fabian Society pamphlet, which had been compiled from Parliamentary Questions showing the extent to which posts were advertised, the number of appointments made, the number in which the central unit was involved, and so on and so forth. It would contain all that sort of information.

It would contain details of the expenditures of these bodies. It would also—and this would necessarily need to be updated annually, the next bit of information—contain the rules governing those bodies as regards open meetings, as regards declaration of interests, as regards which auditors are involved, the application of the Ombudsman, all those sorts of issues would be on record about these bodies.

1904. PETER SHORE: I am sure that would be a very helpful addition to public knowledge. So far we well recognise that the analysis of existing quangos is inevitably fragmentary and only partial, far from complete, but we obtained from the School of Public Policy, the University of Birmingham, such material as was currently available. I want to put to you questions about two of the conclusions that you reached in that document, having said that the evidence is still only partial. The first conclusion is that the——

"likelihood of being appointed to public office is greater for those with Conservative party affiliations, including board members of companies donating to the party, than for those with other political links."

Against that background, and remembering the two White Papers we have had from the Chancellor of the Duchy of Lancaster and then the more recent one from the Secretary of State for Health, do you think in the changes that have been proposed in those White Papers that particular criticism would be met in the future?

JOHN STEWART: We have not had a full chance to study the recent documents. I think that in order to meet those criticisms we need two things. We need information, first of all, to know how valid these points are and, secondly, we need to increase the independent scrutiny of the process, some degree of independent involvement. That would go some way to meeting the criticisms.

1905. PETER SHORE: Yes. In one of the White Papers a point was made of reducing the opportunities of the Chief Whip, or "patronage secretary" as he is often called, to influence appointments. He has not been excluded from the process but his role has been reduced. Do you think that is a help?

JOHN STEWART: I think it is a help. It is always difficult in this area because there is informality in the situation. I would have thought that a reduction in the role of the Chief Whip would be seen as increasing public confidence in the system.

1906. PETER SHORE: Can I turn then to your second conclusion. You say properly——

"The issue is wider than just party politics. The occupational bias towards business and the professions combined with recruitment by personal contact can create bodies whose members collectively hold a set of values which may not adequately reflect those of the wider community. Even without direct party political affiliations, therefore, the composition of appointed bodies is politically unbalanced."

Again, the same question insofar as you can recall the contents of these two White Papers. Do you see there the prospect in future of the appointment process rectifying this perceived defect?

JOHN STEWART: It is really the same answer. I do not think it goes far enough in that direction to remove that. I think, if I am recalling rightly—and Chris or Howard may want to come into it—one of the interesting findings of our research has been that whilst a very sizeable number of people believe that they have actually been appointed to exercise business skills on these bodies, which is referred to here, one of the disappointments of many of them has been that they have not been able to exercise business skills upon these bodies, which is an interesting comment on the application of business skills in the public sector.

PETER SHORE: Yes.

CHRIS SKELCHER: If I could just add to that point. In terms of the statement you recently quoted with regard to occupational bias, the issue is that we do not know whether the recruitment process has resulted in the best people being appointed and that that group happens to come from a business and professional background that happens to be male, or whether that is a function of some kind of patronage. Certainly, one of the areas that would be interesting to explore is the whole process of public hearings for key appointments for the chairmen or chairwomen of particular appointed bodies. In that process we have a degree of openness which enables us to judge that that person is appropriately qualified and is a suitable and appropriate candidate for that position.

1907. PETER SHORE: Does it not also raise the question really of the shape and size, if I may put it like that, of the National Health Service Trusts. They have been set up with a strong emphasis on managerial efficiency and they are kept very small and the smallness of the bodies is, to some extent, one of the reasons it is said that you cannot get local representatives in the number that you might wish otherwise to have.

It is really, is it not, a question of getting the right balance between greater managerial efficiency than there has been in the past and a genuine representativeness for the community that is being affected by these bodies?

JOHN STEWART: I tend to see that the requirement to get the greater management ability should be primarily about the executives more than about the non-executives although, of course, it raises the question, if you are talking about the composition of Trusts and of Health Authorities, as to whether the executives should be members of the board. That is, of course, one of the factors in reducing the number of places available to other people.

There is some evidence from people who have been studying the behaviour of these boards, particularly at Warwick University, that many of these boards are relatively ineffective because if the executive members agree and have "squared the chair" they already have a majority on it and, of course, they have all the knowledge in the circumstances. I know it is probably not so much within your terms of reference but I think the whole structure of these bodies is something that requires to be looked at.

PETER SHORE: Thank you.

1908. PROF. A KING: Could I just pick up one point that Stanley Kalms made earlier and it is this. One of you referred a moment ago to the desirability of public hearings being introduced into the selection of people to serve on quangos and that thought is about, we hear it from a variety of quarters, but as I heard Stanley Kalms he was saying that if you really want to get top-class people who are very busy, who have lots of other things to do with their lives, if you put them through this kind of mill then the chances of their being willing to be recruited will be much reduced. Certainly, there are serious problems in the United States about Senate Confirmation Hearings causing a lot of people to say, "Forget it, I'll stay in California", or wherever. How do you respond to that suggestion that there is a problem there?

JOHN STEWART: We do not necessarily, being good academics, share views. I, myself, am a little reluctant to go as far as Chris on this because of that particular problem. I think, however, that some pre-private independent scrutiny is actually appropriate in the situation. I resisted carrying some of the evidence of the previous witness to its final point. I would expect people to submit to a degree of scrutiny and interviewing if they are going for these positions, even if it might discourage a few people. I would worry about the public scrutiny but Chris may have other views.

CHRIS SKELCHER: The other point, I think, is whether we are only interested in recruiting people from the senior echelons of business. There is perhaps a much wider willingness on the part of the community to become involved in these bodies and the local public life and the public hearing, or some form of endorsement by community or by government, may not put them off. Certainly, in our research we have identified a number of situations where the chairmen of quangos have, in some cases, said that people are willing to take a position but only on the agreement of the particular community that they are serving. That has come out in some of the work that Howard has been doing; a process where the Chair has said, "I want to meet representatives of the community first to discuss what they want from me, to explore whether I am the appropriate person and, on that basis, I will take the position". That is certainly one of the innovations which we are now beginning to see, which is to be supported.

JOHN STEWART: I was a little disturbed by one part of the previous witness's contribution, almost a suggestion that in many areas you would not be able to find enough able women, for example, to constitute the board. There is a danger, which was reflected in some of that evidence, of a little closed circle of people who know each other and I suspect that talent and ability is much more widely spread in our society than maybe the impression was given in that evidence.

1909. LORD NOLAN: Thank you all very much indeed. That was a very helpful and constructive piece of advice.

Ms. Rasaiah, we are overrunning, as is our wont, about quarter of an hour late. I hope it is not inconveniencing you. You are, I think, a member of the Bar and probably more used to asking questions of witnesses than having them asked of you?

SANTHA RASAIAH

MS. SANTHA RASAIAH (Secretariat, Parliamentary and Legal Committee, Guild of Editors): I am actually employed. I am not in private practice.

1910. LORD NOLAN: Have you prepared any opening statements you would like to make or would you prefer to go straight into questions?

SANTHA RASAIAH: If I could briefly make an opening statement. First of all, I must apologise for not being Geoff Elliott. Unfortunately, he is ill and unable to attend. I must also apologise for not being a newspaper editor. I hope I can accurately reflect the views of Geoff Elliott, the Editor of "The News" at Portsmouth, and of the local and regional newspaper editors who form the membership of the Guild. Obviously, I am very happy for the Guild to provide supplementary written evidence if you would find that helpful on anything that I cannot help you on.

The Guild's view is very firm. There should be greater statutory requirements of openness upon quangos, and I use that term in its widest sense. We are not actually arguing for anything particularly radical here. In many cases we are actually asking for the restoration of statutory rights of openness that have been lost or else for the extension of their equivalent to functions or to the bodies that provide the functions that public bodies previously performed.

At a local level quangos affect crucial areas of peoples' lives. Local editors have had no hesitation in using quite emotive and powerful words when describing the affect that has on their local communities. They say that there is a growing feeling that people are alienated and feel powerless to influence the decision-making of such bodies in crucial aspects such as health, education and planning matters.

One of the reasons for that is the secrecy with which quangos are shrouded. That is not just a lack of transparency about appointments procedures but it is the way that policy making and decision-making takes place behind closed doors and also a lack of ability to influence the implementation of those decisions.

The Guild has long campaigned on this issue and it feels that it is a growing problem. There are two reasons for that: first, because of the actual growth of quangos themselves as they take over functions from central and local governments and, secondly, the fact that as those functions, those powers and responsibilities, are devolved upon them they are not placed under the similar statutory obligations of openness that the bodies which previously performed those functions were subject to. Such statutory requirements as are placed upon them are inconsistent. They are often minimal and there is a vast difference between, for example, having to have every meeting open to the public and public access to the documentation and a requirement of, perhaps, at best one meeting open a year and one annual report published.

Those bodies, I am afraid, do not follow as best practice the statutory obligations of their predecessors. In the absence of statutory obligations they use their provision of information and their openness to the public is very restrictive. They actually impose further restrictions upon themselves by the type of guidance to which they work and their exploitation of developments—for example, of the law of confidence or even of data protection.

In contrast to that, I know the Government has brought forward new initiatives on openness which are welcome in themselves, such as the *Citizens' Charter, Open Government Codes*, the complementary measures that are in preparation, such as under the NHS and local government. But, unfortunately, they are insufficient. They are not of universal application. They do not provide equivalent rights to those that were lost. In many instances they are inconsistent between themselves and also, if you actually look at the detail of some of the codes including some of those that have been vaunted for the NHS, they actually introduce new restrictions. They are introducing guidance that is more restrictive than circulars that have been in existence for perhaps 40 years and they are also actually encouraging the bodies to be more restrictive by encouraging the use of the law of confidence, the incorporation of confidentiality terms, the balance between commercial interests and the public interest that we would not endorse.

Therefore, for that reason I would think there must be some increase in statutory access to information and we would say that that should include consideration of both central and local government, NHS, and other public bodies guaranteeing public access to documentation. There should be restoration and extension of statutory rights of public scrutiny over bodies which perform public and quasi-public functions and I would include within that Health Service Trusts, Urban Development Corporations and education bodies. That should include the sort of local government standards, if you like, of public access to meetings, the inspection of agenda and documents relating to them including background reports and also not forgetting the kind of technical details which Parliament in the past has given to improve public communication of information, such as statutory defences in defamation to newspaper reports.

Also, where there have been difficulties and people have been called in to investigate there should be provision for mandatory publication of reports investigating irregularities and their findings and the recommendations for those. In addition to that, we feel that there would be a need then for proper monitoring, guidance and enforcement procedures to prevent the avoidance of statutory openness requirements.

We are aware that there are difficulties even in local government which has, perhaps, some of the higher standards at the moment. We think there should also be, in addition to that, review of quangos' use of the law of confidence and that would include the incorporation of confidentiality clauses into terms of employment which are effectively "gagging clauses" which can stop communication of matters of public interest, the end of those types of clauses incorporated into terms of settlement in termination of employment which, once again, can be a means to cover up material which we feel is really of true public interest.

Also, of course, its implication in business dealings where it actually prevents public scrutiny of the expenditure of public money and the services which it received in return. We feel that in some places that balance has not been correct. Also, in respect of appointments, we would like access to information about the personnel on the public bodies and quasi-public bodies and that would include open advertisement, information about selection procedures, the terms of employment and detailed registers of interests that are open to public inspection. All that, we feel, would have to be backed up by effective enforcement measures to ensure a level of consistency.

I would add that probably at the grass roots level there must be effective training procedures to ensure that the staff, the officers, the people who actually implement these things, are aware of what they are and apply them consistently.

LORD NOLAN: That is very clear and comprehensive. I am going to ask Mr. Tom King to take up the questions he wants to put.

1911. TOM KING: Thank you very much. You are a barrister. Are you secretary for the Guild as well?

SANTHA RASAIAH: No, if I can clarify it. I am actually employed by the Newspaper Society. We provide the secretariat to the Parliamentary and Legal Committee of the Guild of Editors. I am qualified as a barrister but I am in employment.

1912. TOM KING: Right. You said in your evidence just now that, of course, no system is perfect. I am not quite sure what the situation is in local government. It used to be that the device used in some councils was to go into sub-committee and to discuss different issues where, I think, there was not access to the Press and there was not the same access as there would be, for example, for full council or full committees. Is that right?

SANTHA RASAIAH: Yes, only I think there are two issues. First, if you actually have statutory rights the public right is there and it is recognised and if there is abuse of that right it is ultimately enforceable.

1913. TOM KING: In full council?

SANTHA RASAIAH: In respect of local government legislation, yes, there are sometimes what we would see to be attempts to avoid the statutory openness requirements. I have heard of councils which have set up 58 or 59 panels which would not be subject to the statutory openness requirements. However, there are remedies if that council had actually been acting illegally, which I am not suggesting—there was a possibility of a threat of an action for judicial review, there was a possibility of a complaint to the Ombudsman about maladministration, there was a possibility of bringing in the Department of the Environment, but in that particular case the local newspapers campaigned against it with the effect that the local authority actually either opened up those meetings or made their documentation available in council meetings.

I am not saying that the local government system is perfect but at least there are the statutory rights there which is the first barrier against increasing secrecy. If there are difficulties there may be legal remedies but, once again, I think it is also helpful in local government from the fact that if there is central government guidance emphasising openness and expanding on the statutory rules and saying they should be applied in spirit as well as in the letter, that is helpful. Many local newspaper editors customarily have difficulties with local authorities in respect of private sittings or access to documents that they should be given.

1914. TOM KING: I think it is recognised there has to be a balance in these issues between people who see that the most efficient dispatch of the business and, therefore, the best service that can be given to the public is by meetings being conducted at some times with a measure of confidentiality and at other times in maintaining public confidence, that this is not some secret organisation operating behind closed doors.

In that connection, we have a different system here of smaller, in my judgment much more effective boards, for instance, in the health area. I think that hospital trusts I have seen operate much better. Previous ones were pretty good talking shops and left the professionals to get on with it. I think now they are much better managed and run. I only speak from what I know for myself and what I observe.

If that is the case, and so we do not lose the benefits that come from that, what do you think the Guild of Editors

can do in the new structure that exists to improve the situation in terms of getting more public confidence and public understanding for what is done. I say it from this point of view. There is no question but that the Government is keen, as has been made clear in the Citizens' Charter and the changes announced in the NHS document, to see greater openness and to build public confidence in that respect. Is there a role for the Guild of Editors in seeing how greater effort might be made, in a constructive and sensible way, in the work that is happening in, for instance, a Hospital Trust?

SANTHA RASAIAH: Yes, certainly. At the moment there is the lack of access. Take a hospital trust. If it is small and efficient it has nothing to hide by being open to the public. The functions that it is performing were previously those conducted under local government legislation and open to the public and open to public inspection of documents. If it is performing a public service or expending public money, making choices which are ultimately life and death choices for the community which they are serving it is important that it is accountable to that community, that there can be proper public scrutiny and there can be assurance that it is actually operating according to the highest standards.

At the moment it is extremely difficult to get access to NHS Trusts. Most of them do not open their doors to the public, apart from the one meeting that they are allowed to a year.

1915. TOM KING: You are talking particularly here about the role of the Press and I am very interested in what the role of the Press can be in this.

SANTHA RASAIAH: If the Press is actually allowed into the meetings and is given access to documentation that is relevant to those meetings it can then give the information to the community.

TOM KING: Could I ask you this question ...

SANTHA RASAIAH: It can provide information to the community. It can provide accurate information to the community, if you like from the NHS Trust, what a good job it is doing or explaining the reasons for the decision-making. It gives the opportunity for a better dialogue to take place between the National Health Trust and the community that it is serving because people are getting the information, they are understanding the basis on which perhaps very difficult decisions are taken and they can then play a role in it. It is ultimately, if you like—and to put it in an emotive term—their lives that are at stake.

TOM KING: I do not want to interrupt you but others will want to ask you questions.

SANTHA RASAIAH: Could I just add as well. The Guild of Editors as an institution is very happy, if there is statutory openness and if there are in addition to that codes of conduct, to help draw those up. It was an offer that was actually taken up at the time of the Water Authorities boards although, unfortunately, the decision was later gone back upon but we are more than happy to co-operate in those aspects.

1916. TOM KING: Thank you. What I wanted to ask you is that you talked about the legal situation that may exist at the moment but what I am interested in is are you aware of initiatives taken by editors and members of your Guild—you represent the regional Press in that area and so obviously these are matters of great local interest—where they have been refused by chairmen of boards, opportunities to discuss, full briefings.

I have seen very little Press reporting of, for instance, in-depth interviews with the chairmen, the chief executives of the health trusts. You are saying it all ought to go back to where it was. I do not want to summarise it unfairly but there is a bit of "Why don't we have the legislation like it used to be?" We have new bodies that bring benefits in certain respects, bring new difficulties, and I understand that in terms of the old reporting arrangements with the reporter sitting at the back of the hall while we sit here discussing every detail of how this hospital will be run.

Have the Guild given serious thought as to alternative ways in which those difficulties could be overcome and ways in which the public interest and your responsibilities can be met?

SANTHA RASAIAH: I think if you are actually concerned about the day-to-day scrutiny of matters that are going on, of course editors can have interviews with Trusts and those may be willingly granted and willingly entered into, but one wonders whether that same willingness is going to appear if that NHS Trust was in difficulties or if there are questions over it. I know that some editors have investigated matters. It is all very well when the person who wishes to grant the interview has something he wishes to communicate but it is going to be difficult for the editor to force an open discussion on those matters if it is basically at the grace and favour or whim of the chairman.

1917. TOM KING: I understand that but do you happen to know whether much effort has been made by the Guild of Editors in this respect?

SANTHA RASAIAH: The Guild of Editors has long campaigned for the opening of NHS Trusts.

TOM KING: That is not the point.

SANTHA RASAIAH: And greater openness at a local level obviously. Local newspapers try to keep in good and close contact with all organisations that are concerned, including the local hospitals.

1918. TOM KING: Can I ask you a question. Undoubtedly, one of the comments that would be made which, I think, in some respects might be less fairly made against the regional Press than against certain aspects of the national tabloid Press, would be that one of the benefits of not having the Press there for all time is the trivialisation of the Press and standards, which perhaps might have been observed in the past, are not necessarily accurately reporting or seeking to sensationalise issues which tend to discourage openness. Do you have any comments to make on behalf of the Guild about the question of standards of reporting?

SANTHA RASAIAH: Yes. I discussed this with Geoff Elliott beforehand. First of all, there is the feeling that the effect is the other way round. I think there is a feeling that local and regional editors try to cover such matters in their community in depth, the nuts and bolts if

you like of health planning, education, transport etcetera. However, as it becomes more difficult to get access to that information because of the changing functions of the bodies who manage it or who make the decisions in that, perhaps there has been a change. Because they cannot expend the time in gathering the information that they previously were able to perhaps there is a tendency to concentrate more on the human interest stories that skate over the surface of life.

It is not something that the local and regional Press can be accused of to a great extent but if you are concerned about accurate reporting, once again we are back to the provision of information and openness. You can have accurate reporting because you have access to all the relevant documents, the background reports, the reports on which decisions were made. You were there. The public was there and the Press was there as its representative to hear the debate and they had to give a fair and accurate report of that debate because if they did not they could be sued. Now, the channels of communication and the material on which that reporting can actually be based is closed to them; added to which, if you are involved with people where there may be difficulties, where they are bound by their contracts of employment to confidentiality it becomes even more difficult to get full information, to be able to publish full information, to be able to show the background of it.

1919. ANNE WARBURTON: I find the ground is covered well. You perhaps were here earlier when we were told that it really is the Press that is seen as the public at meetings, particularly with NHS meetings. That arose partly because our first witness this morning said that when his particular part of the Health Service has meetings only two people come. I put that as a background to asking, do you really have pressure from local Press to be allowed into meetings?

SANTHA RAIASAH: Yes. The Guild has campaigned on it for many years. Editors press to do so. We are not asking for special privileges for the Press. I think journalists have a tradition of wanting the same rights as citizens and no special treatment. Yes, meetings should be open to the public but the Press should be able to be there as the public's representative.

I do not think it is sufficient argument to say that if you open a meeting no one will turn up. One, please will you try it. Two, they did turn up to the meetings of the predecessors of these bodies to cover them and give the information to the community. The important thing is if there is a public right and if there is a right to be there, the Press will be expected to be there if there is something that is happening that should be reported or if there is some matter that the public needs to know. The public will expect the Press to be there to be able to communicate to them fairly and accurately what is going on because the public is not going to have time. If people feel effectively disenfranchised at the moment then you have to restore their participation in decision-making to them.

1920. MARTIN JACOMB: Could I just ask you one question. You have laid great stress understandably on the legislation governing the way local government is conducted as a basis from which you then draw inferences about what might apply elsewhere. But going back to local government, in many cases the council is controlled by a majority party and there are many examples of the key policy issues being decided by that party privately before the public meeting takes place. Is the Press concerned about that? It has been the case for many years.

SANTHA RASAIAH: Yes, the Press is concerned about that and the fact that there can be avoidance of local government legislation, as I explained earlier. Pressure should be brought to bear to get decision-making out into the open. At least where there are statutory requirements of openness something has to emerge in the public eye and there has to be public access to the documentation on which they are based.

Yes, we would argue for greater extensions of openness as a means to overcome that but, to a certain extent perhaps, that can only be done by training the people involved and inculcating them into a culture of openness rather than a culture of secrecy. That can only be done by the obvious means of legislation as in local government backed up by codes, backed up by guidance, backed up by any means that can be brought to bear to get those policy decision-makings into the open. Why should they have to hide it?

MARTIN JACOMB: But it requires a cultural change?

SANTHA RASAIAH: It is a cultural change but it is a cultural change that will come about by measures actually to impose it so far as possible.

MARTIN JACOMB: Thank you very much.

1921. WILLIAM UTTING: I just want to check that you think statutory authorization is absolutely necessary here because there is taking place a slow movement away from secrecy in the conduct of Government business and public affairs and my perception is that most sensible public organisations actually ought to be dealing constructively with the Press and taking the rough with the smooth, with certain safeguards for commercial law, patient confidentiality. In a sense, is not the tide with you and can you not depend upon the tide to carry you into harbour?

SANTHA RASAIAH: I think we are encouraging that tide to flow as quickly as possible. If these means were there before they should be restored, their equivalent should be extended. The codes that have come about at the moment are not enough. As I said, they are actually more restrictive. If you look at the NHS, the emphasis that is placed on confidence is highly restrictive.

1922. WILLIAM UTTING: Yes. I am aware that some of these documents promoting greater openness appear to have more pages devoted to exceptions than to the positive side of the policies. I am sympathetic towards your point there. Anyway, you have answered my point. You think that statutory authorization is necessary?

SANTHA RASAIAH: Yes, unfortunately, yes.

1923. LORD NOLAN: Thank you very much indeed. That was very clear and helpful and we are all the more grateful to you because you stood in at such short notice for Mr. Elliott, to whom we wish a speedy recovery.

Gentlemen, good morning to you. Thank you very much indeed for coming along. We're very glad to see you all. Dame Anne and myself are particularly glad to see Sir Sigmund again, whom we have come to know well over the last few weeks and with whom we have already had many interesting talks. Mr Cooper, I wonder if you have prepared an opening statement which you wish to make or whether you would like to go straight into questions from us.

SIR SIGMUND STERNBERG, NEVILLE COOPER AND STANLEY KIAER

NEVILLE COOPER (Chairman, Institute of Business Ethics): We have very brief opening remarks, if that's all right.

LORD NOLAN: Of course. We shall welcome it.

NEVILLE COOPER: You probably know our background. We were founded about eight and a half years ago and launched in the Mansion House by the then Lord Mayor, by perhaps happy coincidence the morning after the "Big Bang", which removed certain restrictions in the City and led, I think, to a greater awareness that standards had to be looked at. We are here not to pontificate on what we think is wrong with public life or even to suggest how it should be put right, but to share with you our experience of the last eight and a half years in industrial terms in order that those aspects which are relevant might be of some help in determining solutions. That is what we have been asked to do and that is what we are very happy to do.

We sent a written submission, which you have. You have kindly told us the sort of questions you would like to pursue on that. What we would like to do, if we may, is in a very few minutes, certainly less than 10 between the three of us, tell you our initial answers to those questions, and that will enable you to probe as you wish. I would like to take two to start with. One is, would we favour a code of conduct for MPs and the other one is the whole question of the general, prevailing moral climate and its effect on these issues.

I should incidentally, if you didn't know him already, introduce our director on my left, Stanley Kiaer. Sir Sigmund you already know.

The question of the code of conduct for MPs was answered by Sir Sigmund some one and a half years ago in a letter to the press. I know he would like to draw your attention to it again, although you do have it in the evidence. On the question of public standards of morality and indeed how we should basically tackle it, Sir Sigmund has again given you a paper. I know that he doesn't want to go through it all now, but I would like to invite him, if I might, to refer to what he refers to in this paper as the basic source of codes and principles in public life, the basic source which he feels we should take more seriously, and certainly the educational implications. So could I ask him just to outline his point?

LORD NOLAN: Perhaps I might, just before Sir Sigmund speaks, remind those who were here earlier and mention for the benefit of those who were not that—this is right, isn't it?—the Institute of Business Ethics, I think almost alone in the organisations which have given evidence to us, has a specifically Christian inter-faith background which has brought you together and which underlies your work.

NEVILLE COOPER: Yes. Its origins did come from a very specifically religious approach. When we founded it, we decided we wanted it to be firmly business-based. The qualification is that people who are on its executive shall be practical businessmen, because any change should come from within, but we didn't want to cut ourselves off from philosophical and theological interpretations, so we invited the Cardinal, the Archbishop of Canterbury, the Moderators, the Chief Rabbi and the Imam of the London Central Mosque to be joint patrons, and they all accepted with alacrity. We do write to them and we do ask for their input on various things and we do get it. We receive good advice from that quarter. But I have to emphasise that basically we are business-based. One of the first recommendations of one of the bishops on our council is that we should remove the religious patrons from the top and put them on the bottom, to make it clear that we were business people first. Having said that, can I ask Sir Sigmund to outline his point about the basic source of codes.

LORD NOLAN: If you please. Yes, Sir Sigmund.

SIR SIGMUND STERNBERG (Member of the Advisory Council, Institute of Business Ethics): Thank you very much. As someone who is very actively involved in interface work, which broadly means building bridges between various faiths and having dialogue—or I should really say "trialogue", because we have Christians, Jews and Muslims—I should like to bring to the committee's attention the fact that the Old Testament makes enormously stringent demands of openness from public officials, far more demanding than anything that has ever been suggested. The emphasis is that one is expected not only to act rightly but also to be seen to act rightly, which I found always very difficult, because when I was appointed a magistrate drummed it into me "It is not enough that you believe that you act rightly; it must be seen that you act rightly", and this always created a problem, but thereby instilling public confidence, because that is the only way you can have public confidence. These biblical traditions are particularly significant because they balance the demand for highly ethical standards with a pragmatic approach to commerce and public affairs.

A number of organisations are currently actively involved in efforts to disseminate such religious teaching as applies to the modern world of commerce and in public life. These include the Catholic Van Hugel Institute in Cambridge, Interfaith, led by Sir Evelyn de Rothschild—if you want to question me on that, I should be very glad to answer you—the Institute of Business Ethics and the Jewish Association for Business Ethics. The last two organisations have together broken new ground in initiating a special moral education programme for sixth-form students. This is so very important, because how can people know anything about business ethics unless they learn it in school or universities? There ought to be some teaching in the curriculum of business ethics. It is so obvious in some of the Iron Curtain countries which have no idea how private business works, and here is something where we can be of great help. When I was invited to China last year the government didn't know anything about business ethics quality control and they would like to learn from us.

It is relevant to point out that the Jewish committee has established its own association, which focuses on translating timeless biblical teaching into the modern context, with the hope that it will be a model for other minority faith groups. So that is exactly what we would like to see. That would be my opening statement.

LORD NOLAN: Thank you very much indeed.

NEVILLE COOPER: Thank you so much. If I may, therefore, Chairman, we will take your other questions and, in a word, state our superficial answers and ask you to probe us further on what might interest you. I would ask Stanley Kiaer, our director, to take the first one: why do we think there has been a growth of interest in company business codes of ethics?

STANLEY KIAER (Director, Institute of Business Ethics): There are four reasons I would give, in a nutshell, to this. The first one has been the growth of public interest in what business is doing, due to there being many more shareholders in privatisation and, secondly, to the interest of the press being shown in it. I think the second thing has been the campaigns that have been conducted. Certainly the Institute of Business Ethics, ourselves, have been in touch with a lot of companies recommending codes of practice, and of course the Cadbury Committee also suggested that each company should have a code of business ethics. I think the third thing is that companies have had the desire to be the best in their field and regard their reputation as their most priceless asset, so they have gone for it for that reason. Fourthly, there is an element of self-interest in that they attract good staff by telling their employees what they stand for and what they expect from them, and also that any newcomer joining a company is protected from exploitation, in that, if half-way up the company in the search for extra profit or something he is pressurised, at least he has a standard to measure that behaviour against and knows what to do about it.

NEVILLE COOPER: Thank you very much. Your next point was that the public sector has a long history of having rules and procedures and so on. Has the tendency in business been to have more general principles or specific and detailed rules? I shall ask Stanley again to comment on that one.

STANLEY KIAER: I think I would say both—general principles in terms of having a mission statement of what they believe in and stand for, but then also finding that it's necessary to have detailed principles to make it realistic and stick.

NEVILLE COOPER: Thank you. Certainly it makes clear to everybody what the company policy is: it is a yardstick against which to measure. If you don't know what you're aiming at, you don't know how well or badly you are achieving it, and in some respects, for example operating in difficult situations, the definition of what the company regards as presents or tips or bribes and how it will handle it, in detail, is most important. Otherwise the company chairman says "We will have nothing to do with doubtful payments", but then he doesn't say what is doubtful, and locally somebody says "Well, that's all right. We've always done it", rather than saying "This far we will go". There is one company which has gone very far in saying "This far we will go. There we will not go."

I will take the next two myself—confidential hotlines. Certainly no anonymous hotlines—I think that is a recipe for abuse. A number of companies in this country do have them, and more in the States. I was for many years executive director in STC, which is a large company of some 30,000 in telecoms. We introduced a code in 1974, so we had quite a long period in which to see how it worked—or how it didn't work. We said that anyone who doubted that we were living up to our code, which was published, could write to the chairman or write to me and it would be investigated. It was not the cases where they were wrong, but the cases where we said "You're absolutely right. We're sorry, and here's the money back", or something, which made them really interested. But now people have taken it further. I think you have to involve everybody in the drawing up of the code, and it is good to involve them in the review of it. For example, Esso have a much more proactive stance. They don't wait for people to phone them. They gather groups of employees regularly and say "Here is our code. Are we living up to it? Do you know cases where we have fallen down? Is it still relevant? How should we update it?" In other words, they take an initiative.

On the next one, the ethics compliance officer, I think there is a bit of a distinction between the ethics compliance officer, who is popular in the States, often for protective reasons because of legislation and requirements. That is important. I have been a vice-president of IIT (UK), where we all had to sign each year that we and our staff complied. That is a little different from the managerial task of promoting a constructive code and involving people in it. I think it has a slightly different feel. It is much more prevalent in the States than here, but it does tend to attract some very honourable people to be appointed as vice-presidents for this purpose.

1924. LORD NOLAN: Is it—dare I say?—largely confined to compliance with particular statutory or other governmental regulations?

NEVILLE COOPER: Not only, because some companies have decided, particularly when they have got into trouble, to review all that they do—for example, that there shall be no political contributions, even if they are legal, and so on and so on—so the compliance is really compliance with the company's own standards, which can be audited.

On the last one, and then we must make good our undertaking not to take too long, rule of thumb on gifts and hospitality, I shall ask Stanley to say a word.

STANLEY KIAER: We made various points on this one. I think the first one was what we call the "sleep well" factor, or another old-fashioned word would be "conscience". The second one is openness—that you tell your boss about what you have been offered and that you declare any interest that you may have, and basically that you'd be willing to have it publicly known what you have received. The final one is: does it make a difference to your usual standard of living? In this one we quoted the police code, whereby you are allowed to offer a policeman on the beat a cup of tea, but you mustn't give him supper, on the ground that you wouldn't normally expect to do so. So those are a few rules of thumb, as it were.

NEVILLE COOPER: Thank you very much.

SIGMUND STERNBERG: May I come in on that, because it is a very difficult one. For many years I have been engaged in international trading, and people sometimes offer an inducement. We make it a rule in our company that we do not pay commission, we can't do anything like that, and of course in many cases we have lost business. But there is a very narrow line between what is a bribe or an inducement and what isn't. To someone

who asks whether paying a commission to a director in Switzerland is a bribe, to my mind of course it is a bribe. Unless you pay the person directly, it is a bribe, but some other countries see it quite differently. Therefore, some of our companies who have got these high moral ethics are at a disadvantage.

NEVILLE COOPER: I think we could summarise by saying that we feel that the rules should be very specific. You can either accept a gift worth £15 or no gift or £50 or whatever, and also that declaration, whether it is gifts or interests, should not be left too much to individual interpretation but should again be quite specific.

1925. LORD NOLAN: I don't want to anticipate the questions, but Sir Sigmund touched on experience abroad. Does one find similar standards of probity in all countries—it is rather a naive and broad question—or do you find that there are greater difficulties in some other countries than there are in this country?

NEVILLE COOPER: I think in practical terms we all find, don't we, that in some countries there are things that are "old Spanish customs"? I think, however, you have to differentiate between what is accepted morality and what is practised. I think both are important. We sometimes say that people of other faiths, for example Muslim countries, have a different attitude. It was interesting that the Duke of Edinburgh's joint work on a Jewish-Muslim-Christian code came out absolutely specifically on all sides against any kind of bribery and corruption, though in all our nations we don't always live up to our principles. So I don't think there's a difference in perception, though I think there's a difference in custom. One of the companies which have been most specific does not have a perfect policy, but it is interesting. It says: "We will give no money and no favour to get business. We will try to avoid, even where it is customary, tipping people to do their job", like public officials. "If it is considered quite essential, then it shall be recorded. It shall only be of a reasonable amount which is normal, and it shall be to induce the official to do his duty and not to do something other than his duty." That's the way they have handled it. We don't say it's a perfect solution, but it's better than saying "We do nothing" and then doing something.

SIGMUND STERNBERG: I would like to add to that. As someone who has done international trading for many years, I must tell you that in this country, whatever you read in the papers about individual cases, there is very high moral conduct in people on the whole, and I think we should be proud of ourselves and our moral conduct.

LORD NOLAN: Thank you very much. I am now going to ask Sir Martin Jacomb, who is of course a very experienced and senior businessman, to take up the questions.

1926. MARTIN JACOMB: You have really answered all the questions, so I am going to keep mine to a very, very few. Just to pick up the last point that Sir Sigmund made, before I get on to the things I really wanted to ask you, would you think British business as a whole has lost business as compared with some of our American, European or Japanese competitors because of the adherence to high standards in not giving bribes, which in my view is entirely correct?

NEVILLE COOPER: Yes, my own gut feel is that we probably have, and of course the Americans feel it even more strongly because of their legal restrictions. So it is rather difficult to say specifically. But we could always point to other countries which we feel do worse.

1927. MARTIN JACOMB: But those legal restrictions, which were relatively recently brought in, I think, as a result of Lockheed or something like that, were brought in because the situation was so bad, weren't they?

NEVILLE COOPER: Yes, that's right. I think some American executives say that they are so draconian that they almost stop you doing anything. But I was trying to answer the question of who we think is worse, and I really don't know.

1928. MARTIN JACOMB: Could I go on to how you came into existence, because those of us who are familiar with your work obviously admire it a great deal, but I should just like to go back to its origins. Could you say whether you think it was necessary because of a decline in the standard of business ethics or a decline in the standard of ethics and morals generally?

NEVILLE COOPER: I feel sure they are interrelated, although of course in some respects public conscience and the conscience of young people and so on is stronger than it was before. It's rather variable. In other ways it is worse. I don't think we had any particular view as to what was the origin of the need to do it. It was obvious that it was desirable to promote and encourage higher standards of business ethics, but also we were very keen to show people that good ethics, good business and good common sense are not only reconcilable but must be reconciled. So our strategy was not to join in retailing the latest horror story, but to research the best practice and thinking and to promulgate that, to do two or three things: one, to encourage the people who were doing it right; secondly, to give ideas to other people on how to do it, because very often people think "We should do this, we should have a good environmental policy, but where do you start?", so we publish what others do'; and, thirdly, to show the public that actually there is a strong core of highly ethical and responsible businessmen in the country who actually do want the same things as they do. We believe that businesses' standards as a whole are probably as high as or higher than in many other walks of life, but unfortunately it is only the Maxwells and things who get the maximum publicity.

1929. MARTIN JACOMB: Raising peer group behaviour among business was an essential part of what you were doing?

NEVILLE COOPER: It was, yes, and obviously to encourage the people who did have right motivation but thought "We're rather a minority" or "We're alone", to show they weren't.

1930. MARTIN JACOMB: I think you have been successful in that. Is there any way of measuring your success?

NEVILLE COOPER: No. If we wish to, we can make claims, but they are always dubious. When we started out, only one in six of the major companies had a reasonable code or statement of principle. Now it is one in three and, with those in the pipeline, is coming up to one in two. People tell us we have made a contribution to this, but goodness knows how large that is and goodness knows how much is simply public pressure on the rest. But I think

we have made a contribution to that, and that's how we measure it.

1931. MARTIN JACOMB: Yes, that's fair enough. Could I go to something a little bit more specific, which is what I think you called internal hotlines. The difficulty with anonymous hotlines you have referred to, and you are not pursuing those. The difficulty with non-anonymous hotlines is the risk to the career of the person who uses them.

NEVILLE COOPER: Yes.

MARTIN JACOMB: You mentioned Esso, who have found a way of getting over this.

NEVILLE COOPER: Yes.

MARTIN JACOMB: Is there any other way of getting over this?

NEVILLE COOPER: Of course you are in all this wholly dependent upon the genuineness of the top management. In the case I mentioned from personal experience we made darn sure that there was absolutely no discrimination as a result of this. Had we been even careless about that, we would have let them down very badly, so it is not a thing that you can lightly do or encourage people to take part in, unless they have that confidence.

One of the difficulties here is this. You have asked just what might be relevant to public life. The reason for the hotline is that you can jump over your immediate superior if he is trying to block you—that is bluntly it—whereas in terms of Parliament I suppose MPs don't have an immediate superior, so it is a little bit different, but I think the principle that you should be able to have recourse directly to some body, which will be bound to take your point seriously and investigate it, might be one which would have application.

1932. MARTIN JACOMB: No, I think it is tremendously relevant to the Civil Service and to quangos and other bodies. The difficulty is replicating the situation which you had, but I won't pursue it, because I think others might want to.

Could I just ask one final point, which you might have an observation on? It is absolutely clear, and indeed you gave it as the fourth of the reasons to the first question you posed, that business has a tremendously strong self-interest in high ethical standards: if you want to ensure that your buyer of components gets the best possible price and quality, you want to ensure that he is not subject to influence through entertainment by component suppliers—a very strong self-interest. How would you comment on the fact that that strength of self-interest is not present in the public sector?

NEVILLE COOPER: I suppose only in saying obviously you must be right. There's not the same in strength of pecuniary interest. Therefore, I suppose that is one motivation which might have to be replaced by another. Of course we are aware that in public life standards of propriety and so on have probably in the past been taken more seriously than in some aspects of business and there is a tradition and so on there, so maybe something like that can help to replace it. But whatever the system, it does need these days buttressing and sharpening, and again I come back to the whole code question: I think it makes generalisations specific, and you can't say "Well, I didn't know you meant that".

MARTIN JACOMB: Thank you very much.

SIGMUND STERNBERG: Can I add to that? What one would like to see is in company accounts reference made to "We adhere to a code of conduct", not necessarily that it would injure the business, but that shareholders and others should know that this company has a code of conduct and adheres to it. It would be quite interesting not only for shareholders but for the public in general to know that therefore we are governed. Of course to your first question, people have lost business through adhering to a certain standard, but they accept it. People accept it because "This is the way we want to do business", and that's it, and they will lose it, but in the long run it comes right.

MARTIN JACOMB: Of course. No, I quite agree with you. Thank you.

LORD NOLAN: Mr Tom King, would you like to take up the questions?

1933. TOM KING: We are concerned about standards of conduct in public life and generally, and I wondered if you had any comments on whether you saw problems emerging from what could be seen as the great divide in our country at the moment, which is between what might be seen as the telephone number earnings at certain levels in the City and the whole of the rest of the population, with huge, huge inducements being offered to move from one company to another and to people of quite different ages and in quite different activities.

NEVILLE COOPER: Yes. One has to add from one football club to another and pop group and so on, but it doesn't take away from the fact that it happens. Yes, we do have concerns, on two grounds. I don't think it is very easy for people to prescribe absolutely in social engineering terms what should be the differential between top and bottom, even if you take it after tax or pre-tax. You are getting into a managed state if you do too much of that. Nevertheless, there are two things which concern us. One, a gut feel that in certain enterprises the additionally onerous aspects of the job haven't really justified the additional remuneration, and that's a popular perception—in other words, the idea, which many of us share, that some people are taking themselves too big a share. It is a bit subjective and so on, but it is a feeling and a strong feeling.

I think the thing on which there can be no doubt, however, is that the extent of total remuneration and the way in which it is determined should be much more transparent. We gave a submission to the Cadbury Committee in which we suggested a little more openness in accounts than there now is. We suggested that in terms of remuneration committees it might be revealed who was on which boards to avoid the feeling of "You scratch my back and I'll scratch yours", because people obviously didn't always have confidence in this. But our basic proposition would be that there should be a proper remuneration committee, there should be a known basis for remuneration, which would be revealed to shareholders, and that what should be given should be both justifiable and transparent. Unfortunately, when you've done all that, you will never stop some people being greedy in any walk of life, and this causes problems.

SIGMUND STERNBERG: I anticipated this question and yesterday I phoned up the Institute of Directors and I asked what their view is, and hot off the press is "The Remuneration of Directors", which sums it up admirably. I think you can't do better than that and I agree with every word written in this document, and it does refer to what Neville Cooper said about the committee. If you haven't got a copy, I shall hand it to you, and it saves me explaining to you what it is all about. But of course this is a burning issue, because unless justice is seen to be done, the social fabric is going to suffer, because people just will not understand what is going on, especially when the tabloid press prints articles, some of which do not make any sense.

NEVILLE COOPER: Could I ask Stanley to comment, although I would like to make one remark in passing? I think that the ethical issue is that something may be legally justifiable, or you may be able to find a justification for it, but there is an element called leadership and example, and that also is important.

STANLEY KIAER: I am in that wonderful situation where my chairman has actually said the magic word, which I think is crucial in this. In the same way as in the Army you have somebody leading, you have to have good leadership at the top. If you have an enormous differential between those who lead and those who are led, then it's totally wrong and doesn't work, and part of the reason for all the outcry is, I think, bad leadership, basically.

1934. WILLIAM UTTING: There is an assumption in some quarters that the importation of commercial values into the public service has actually contaminated the public service. I don't wholly go along with that rather crude view myself, because it seems to me that part of the trouble may arise from public servants getting into commercial activities without the support of the kind of ethical code that you have been talking about. The public service code is perhaps different in certain respects from the business ethical code.

What I wanted to ask you was whether, in enabling and encouraging business to adopt ethical codes, you have a proforma or specimen that contains the essentials that ought to be in this code which you are able to offer any business inquirer.

NEVILLE COOPER: Yes. We have a document called "Codes of Business Ethics: Why companies should develop them and how". It is very brief. There have been two previous reports which give a great deal of background material and examples reprinted from specific company codes, because it is useful to say "Well, they did it in a published booklet. Let's do it the same way and let's use that typeface." The first chapter is why codes are necessary, which deals with many of the plausible objections. The second is a checklist of some 64 subjects, so you can go down that and see if you cover them. Then there is an illustrative code, which is not one which we think should be prescriptive. It is taking in fact the best and most far-reaching elements from all the company codes—100 or more—that we have analysed and saying "That's best practice. It may not all be applicable to you, but if you run down that and you have covered those reasonably well, you're doing all right." In practice many people have lifted whole sentences and paragraphs, so it has proved to be quite useful.

1935. WILLIAM UTTING: So what you have got there is something that's much fuller than simply saying "Don't take bribes from people when you're doing business with them".

NEVILLE COOPER: Oh, absolutely, yes.

WILLIAM UTTING: And you approach issues of delivering value for money to your customers, for example——

NEVILLE COOPER: Surely.

WILLIAM UTTING: —issues of responsibility to employees, responsibility to local communities, responsibility to interest groups beyond the narrow group of your shareholders.

NEVILLE COOPER: Sure. We build it around what it is fashionable to call the stakeholders—the suppliers of the money, the employees, the customers, I was going to say, the suppliers and those with whom they have business dealings and the community.

SIGMUND STERNBERG: And of course you go further with the environment of staff practice, which is of course a very important part of our work.

NEVILLE COOPER: Yes, this is right.

1936. WILLIAM UTTING: I suspect that when I see this code, and I see that we actually have got copies of it, there may not be, to my eye, a great deal of difference between what one would call a public service code and this specimen code that you have produced. I'll be interested in looking to see if there are differences.

NEVILLE COOPER: I think a number of the elements probably would be common, as you say. Referring to the earlier question, obviously there is a difference in many ways between a nationally run enterprise or a department run by civil servants with their own disciplines and a commercial one, in timescales, disciplines, constraints and all the rest of it. So I would say that one of the difficulties of introducing certain market standards where they have not been before is people's unfamiliarity with the process, and there isn't really enough time to do it before you are confronted with knotty problems. How you allocate your health services on a basis of certain rigid or otherwise financial criteria and so on is obviously an immensely difficult task, and we sympathise, because businesses find it hard enough when they've been brought up to it for years.

WILLIAM UTTING: Thank you. That's very helpful.

1937. ANNE WARBURTON: I'm one of the lucky ones who have got a copy of your document. I promise I didn't conceal it from others. You came today, obviously, because you saw that there might be things to be learnt from your experience in the business world and our efforts in the public world. One of the things that strike me is that, in your world and in your recommendations, you urge very much that individual companies should work out

their own code of ethics. You offer perhaps a core, but you say "Make your own adaptations". We have had recommendations from some of the people who have come to talk to us on similar lines, that there should be a general code which can be adapted to suit the different organisations. The thing that strikes me as being perhaps a problem there, and I wonder what you think of it, is that it might not be so easy to get the individual bodies in the public world to work out their own.

NEVILLE COOPER: Yes. Can I answer this perhaps on the basis first of personal experience rather than of our corporate institute experience? As I say, the company I was with did this in 1974 and there wasn't much to go on, we had to learn as we went along, but I think one of the first points was this. There are three stages, each of which is important and valuable. The first is the drawing up of the code and the way it is done, and many people say that, if you do that right because it includes all the right people, you could almost stop there; the second is the code itself, which, as I said, has certain advantages; and the third, and this is something we are now studying in depth, is the application of the code—what you do when it goes wrong, discipline, retraining, whatever happens to enforce the code.

On the first point the company I was with decided that it was worthwhile literally to consult with 30,000 employees on this. It had to be done in a very structured way. There were small group meetings with trainers and psychologists who knew how to do it, to have discussions to draw out what was important to people, and it did come out very clearly that the things our employees as a whole mentioned most often were that the primary thing was to be efficient and profitable and give a good service, and the second was that we should be straight and honest in our business dealings, which we never knew they thought highly about, and the third was to treat everybody with respect and enable them to grow and develop, and the fourth was to be open and participative—rather general, but we said "OK. Then we will build the whole policy around those four principles". As a result, people felt included, they felt it was their own. We had the resources to put into it, and it was expensive. I wouldn't recommend that everybody did quite the same, but I do recommend that, whatever the body concerned, some way is found of getting people's individual inputs, so they feel they have had a real share in drawing it up. Otherwise I think you have lost out before you start. But before you can do that, you must have absolute unanimity on your board or management committee or whatever the group is that that's what you want to do and that you're going to live with it, because if there's half-heartedness in the management, it won't work.

1938. ANNE WARBURTON: Against that background I have to go on to ask what you would think of the concept of a statutory code.

NEVILLE COOPER: I would have thought, and I shall invite my colleagues to comment if they have any ideas, that there was room for both: in some respects you may wish to make things statutory; in others you may wish to have something which is supplemental and specific to that organisation. With both, you need to review and update pretty regularly, because things change. Sigmund, do you have any additional comment?

SIGMUND STERNBERG: Yes. This is a very difficult question, because there cannot be an answer. You see, you cannot legislate for people to be honest. You can't do it. Either you are or you are not, and no statutory code can take care of that. But I think it would be worth while looking into it. This is an area which we ought to look at. We ought to strengthen not only the code of conduct but also company law. This is something which ought to be strengthened, something ought to be looked at. For many years I served on the Labour Party's company law reform group, and from time to time new company laws were enacted, but it all had to be updated, because business changes to such an extent. Now we are in a global business, companies are multinational companies, and this has a great deal of difficulty. It is certainly something which we ought to look at very carefully to see what can be done statutorily and what cannot be done.

If I may say so, I am not being a commercial, because I mentioned it before. The Rotary Club is an organisation which has over 1 million members in 167 countries, and every club has a vocational service committee, which puts high standards of conduct into practice of Rotarians in their business and professional lives. There are not only Rotary Clubs but other service organisations, like the Lions, and we ought to encourage their activities. Rotary stopped at the time when the second world war broke out in some of the countries in Eastern Europe, but now it has come back, and I was charged by Rotary International with forming Rotary Clubs in countries like Romania. Even Albania now has a Rotary Club, and talks are going on about having a Rotary Club in China. If people knew what these organisations were doing, it would be very beneficial. Incidentally, I can say it quite easily, because I am not looking for members. You cannot apply to join a Rotary Club; you have to be invited. But this is an area where a great deal can be done.

1939. LORD NOLAN: One problem which we as a committee have to consider is the movement from the public sector to the private sector of senior civil servants and Ministers. As you know, there are rules for civil servants; in the case of Ministers there is a general, what one might say, guidance and appeal to their integrity. To the question whether Ministers should be subjected to some sort of regime similar to civil servants, on the one hand it is said that there is no real evidence that the appeal to integrity has ever failed, and on the other side it is said that, nevertheless, because of setting a good example, because of leadership, because of public perception, because of fairness to the individuals, there should be some procedure that can be adopted. Have you, as an institute, any views you could offer us on that?

NEVILLE COOPER: No, we have not debated that as an institution at all. If you want off-the-cuff comment, I would have thought that it might well be desirable to have some minimum requirements in terms of time or other criteria, so that at least it isn't just totally open, if that was felt to be desirable. The difficulty, as we know, is that you can cut off your nose to spite your face: you may be denying the country business and other advantages by having some rigid rule to try to appear to be right. So I would have thought that you wanted some minimum rule for good form but ask people to use their conscience and also leadership again in terms of seeing how far they could extend it. But I'm afraid we don't have a view, and couldn't have a view, because we know something about business when we don't know much about these matters.

LORD NOLAN: Thank you very much.

STANLEY KIAER: Could I add two points, sir? First of all, on the question of openness, I think one has to face the fact that there has been a great change in outlook, if you like, between the older generation and the younger generation. I think we were taught to accept authority and the younger generation have been taught to question everything. Therefore, if you want to satisfy most of the population, you have not only to do it but to show that you're doing it, and I think this is a new factor that we have to take into account. The second one is that you can no longer rely on people's home or schooling or the fact that they may or may not have gone to church to enable them to make a moral judgment. Therefore, there is a greater need today, particularly with new people entering a particular field, whether it be the public sector or the private sector, to spell out, for the first time if you like, what is expected and what they can expect.

The other point I would like to make is that the experience in business is that it takes about two years to change the culture of a company as regards business ethics. It has to start at the top, and if it doesn't start at the top, you haven't a hope, but once started at the top, it takes at least two years for that culture to permeate the company, with the great deal of consultation, feedback and talk-back that is necessary.

1940. PETER SHORE: You have mentioned the Cadbury Committee report on one or two occasions. From the point of view of the promotion of business ethics, what did you feel was most helpful in the Cadbury report?

STANLEY KIAER: I was going to say that one of the most helpful things was that they suggested that every company should have a code of business ethics, and this is the first time that that had ever been stated in the business arena, one might say.

NEVILLE COOPER: Not unrelated to the fact that two members of our council were on the committee and they suggested it to the rest, who agreed.

1941. PETER SHORE: And the committee saw that, of course, as a voluntary rather than a prescriptive one?

NEVILLE COOPER: Yes, indeed.

1942. PETER SHORE: We could have a very long and interesting debate on the matters you have touched on. I just want to put one or two points to you. The first one is this, following what I think Sir Sigmund said to us earlier on. There really are, are there not, whole markets in the world where the application of strict business ethics would exclude yourselves? Has one simply to recognise that or does one modify the practice according to the circumstance?

NEVILLE COOPER: I think the whole question of corruption, fortunately, is beginning to enter the public arena more and more. What were accepted as ancient practices aren't any longer accepted. I think it's been a shock to some people in Italy to find that what was accepted isn't accepted, and now they find themselves in jail, whereas some time before they might be heroes, and I have heard that it's the same in East Africa in at least one instance and in other places. There seems to be this popular feeling "No, enough is enough". It is immensely complex. It is rather like, I think, fighting cancer. It is not just "Are we going to cure it next year?", but "Are we actually fighting and making progress and pushing it back?", because you're not going to cure corruption next year. It demands considerable joint action, because there are two sides to bribery: there's the extortion side and there's the giving side. I think that one organisation which is trying to tackle this from a very small beginning is a thing called Transparency International, which is starting at the governmental level and trying to get different governments to declare against their officials demanding bribes. This is extremely helpful to business, because of course if people don't demand, there is less incentive to give, although it's not the whole story, because some people are prepared to outbid each other, whether it's demanded or not. So I think it is enormously complex. We must drive it back, and by imaginative means.

There is one company in India which published a half-page in the paper congratulating a number of government departments on having ceased to demand bribes from them and saying how many miles of road, how many permits and so on had been given from different departments without bribes, but the sting in the tail was the departments they didn't mention. We, to be frank, in one of our publications published the names of all the major companies we knew who had acceptable codes, so people could say "Wait a minute, my company isn't there". So I think it is going to be a long task that has got to be intelligently done. We don't feel able to go to specific companies and say "Look, are you giving any doubtful money? If so, stop now." We know personally, all of us, whole sectors of business where it is the accepted practice, but we want to drive it back and, as Sir Sigmund says, the experience of many people is that when you adopt a policy of doing the business straight, you often in the long run get more business. But what I think is important is that we should have the joint governmental business campaign.

LORD NOLAN: Gentlemen, we are very grateful to you all for giving us so much of your valuable time and for the written material as well as the oral evidence that you have given to us. Thank you very much indeed.

SIGMUND STERNBERG: Before I go, I brought this morning the Archbishop of Canterbury's speech yesterday in Madras and I am going to leave it with you, because it deals with some of the topics discussed.

LORD NOLAN: Thank you very much.

TUESDAY 21 FEBRUARY 1995

Members Present:

The Rt. Hon. The Lord Nolan (Chairman)

Sir Clifford Boulton GCB
The Rt. Hon. Tom King CH MP
The Rt. Hon. Peter Shore MP

The Rt. Hon. The Lord Thomson of Monifieth KT DL
Sir William Utting CB
Dame Anne Warburton DCVO CMG
Diana Warwick

Witnesses:
Jack Straw MP, Shadow Home Secretary
Robert Gunn, Chairman, and Sir William Stubbs, Chief Executive,
the Further Education Funding Council
Leif Mills, President, John Monks, General Secretary, and David Lea,
Assistant General Secretary, TUC

1943. LORD NOLAN: Today we begin our last week of oral evidence before getting down to the task of assimilating all the comments made and preparing our recommendations.

Our second group of witnesses today will continue the theme of quangos, which we have been pursuing for the last few days. They are Mr Robert Gunn, Chairman, and Sir William Stubbs, the Chief Executive, of the Further Education Funding Council for England, which has a budget of some £3 billion a year. A report in *The Times* on 6th February said:

"The Further Education Funding Council has taken the initiative in a way that may become a model for the Nolan Committee's recommendations for public bodies",

and we shall be exploring that proposition with them today.

Our other two groups of witnesses are dealing with more general matters, as we move into the closing stages. The Trades Union Congress, headed by Mr John Monks, its General Secretary, will, we hope, have views both on Members' of Parliament financial interests and on public bodies. These are both areas in which it has taken a close interest.

First, however, we are pleased to welcome Mr Jack Straw, opposition spokesman on home affairs, who will give evidence on behalf of the Labour Party. We have already heard from Mrs Ann Taylor as Shadow Leader of the House, but I understand that Mr Straw will cover the whole spectrum of our studies. Mr Straw, I hope that is right, and am I right in thinking that you have prepared an opening statement which you are going to start us off with?

JACK STRAW MP

JACK STRAW MP (Shadow Home Secretary): I have, Lord Nolan, thank you, and thank you very much for the invitation to appear before you.

I think that among the central questions before your committee is whether there has been a decline in standards of conduct in public life and, if so, why. There are those who would wish the committee to believe that nothing much has changed in the last few decades. In this view, some failure to meet accepted standards of conduct, some corruption and sleaze, is an inevitable consequence of the exercise of power, and the last 15 years have been

no better and no worse than any other comparable post-war period.

This is not a view, however, which in our belief is consistent with the facts. Of course it is true that some departure from accepted standards of conduct in public life has occurred during every administration since the Northcote-Trevelyan reforms, but in our opinion the departure from these accepted standards which has increasingly occurred over the past 15 years is of a wholly different character from what has gone before. This decline has arisen principally because of profound changes in the nature of the public service and its relationship with the private sector, which have not been paralleled by changes in the rules and conventions governing public life.

As to evidence of decline, your committee will have received an enormous amount of detailed evidence, and we can always add to that, if required, from the large number of surveys which have been undertaken. But we believe that three things highlight the fact that there has been a change in the magnitude of the departure from accepted standards.

First, there was the report of the Public Accounts Committee in January of last year. Considering that this is an all-party committee with a government majority, its conclusion was as damning as it was remarkable. It said:

"In recent years we have seen and reported on a number of failures in administrative and financial systems and controls within departments and other public bodies which have led to money being wasted or otherwise improperly spent. These failings represent a departure from the standards of public life which have been established during the past 140 years."

Secondly, there is the establishment of this committee itself, which plainly would not have been set up had senior members of the government not accepted that there were indeed very well-founded causes of complaint. Thirdly, there is the government's reaction since the establishment of the committee. Taken together, the proposals which the government has already made in respect of a code of conduct for the Civil Service and appointments to quangos are much less than adequate, but the timing and the fact of the concessions at all speak volumes about the scale of the problem. Those concessions amount in our view to an admission by the government of our case that civil servants have not been adequately protected from undue pressures from Ministers and that the system of appointments to quangos has been characterised by secrecy and bias.

There is then the question as to why this decline has occurred. The Northcote Trevelyan reforms of the last century were part of a sustained effort by the mid-Victorians to develop a concept of public money and public service which was distinct from private profit and the private sector. Over time this meant that the boundary between these two sectors became relatively narrow, clear and at arm's length. But over the past 15 years the interface between the public and private sectors has changed hugely. That interface is now much broader, less clear and more intimate. Many of the old conventions constraining the behaviour of Ministers, Members of Parliament and government appointees have, as a result, broken down. The policy of "rolling back the frontiers of the state" has led to a paradox: whilst the numbers directly employed in the public sector have indeed shrunk by nearly 50 per cent since 1979, the amount spent by the state has not. Public spending as a proportion of national income was just over 44 per cent in 1979 and is just over 44 per cent today.

The reduction in the numbers employed directly by the state has not, therefore, led to a corresponding reduction in the functions of the state. Instead, these functions, previously provided directly by the state, are now provided by government contractors through the process of privatisation, compulsory competitive tendering and market testing. This has led to an enormous increase in the number of private firms and individuals wholly or largely dependent upon the state for their profit and their livelihood.

But even this is to understate the degree to which the private sector is now intimately involved in the operation of the state, in two respects. First, the programme of privatisation has meant that fees from advising and underwriting privatisation issues have become extremely important to the profits of many merchant banks and other City institutions. Second, there has been a vast expansion in consulting work paid for by the taxpayer but undertaken by private consulting firms, often arms of multinational accountants. In some cases there are now whole divisions in such accountancy firms dedicated not just to public sector work but to gaining contracts from individual departments. We gave, Lord Nolan, in the written evidence which we submitted to you, a detailed breakdown at paragraph 41, showing how this income from the government to management consultancies grew from £35 million in 1985 to £209 million in 1993. Alongside the straight transfer of functions from the state to the private sector there have been two related developments which have in practice reduced the accountability of government—the introduction of Next Step agencies and the great extension in the role of executive quangos.

The great increase in the number of high income earners wholly or mainly dependent upon the state has led to a corresponding increase in the demand for information and influence within government. The changes which have led to this have also resulted in a significant increase in Ministerial power and discretion. Individuals and firms have a vested interest not just in whether a particular service is market tested or put out to contract but in how this is done. One form of market-testing and out-sourcing

may favour their skills and experience, another that of a competitor. Getting to Ministers and those who may influence them—officials, other MPs, the media and think tanks—as early as possible and securing the maximum advance information is often crucial to success. In this climate the exponential expansion in parliamentary lobbyists and in MPs on their pay-roll is wholly explicable, but it too has helped significantly to corrode the previous ethic of the public service.

To earn their fees, lobbyists and consultants have had to develop close relationships between themselves, Ministers, Members of Parliament and senior officials. At a time when insider trading has become a criminal offence for those trading on the Stock Exchange, inside information about government traded for cash—much the same thing—has become the central commodity of those involved in "government relations".

There is another factor which has acted further to alter the climate of the public service, in our view. This is the knowledge that an "inside track" within the Conservative Party machine will almost always secure a competitive advantage. The packing of quangos with Conservative appointees is there both as a reward for services and donations rendered and as a warning to those who do not accept the new environment. For example, any firm wishing to trade with the new "NHS" will quickly spot the connection between the local Conservative establishment and those running trusts and associated bodies. It may be—it usually is the case—that the trust will operate entirely within the rules when it actually decides which tender it will accept for a particular service. But whether it decides in the first place to out-source a service and what is specified will often depend upon who has influenced trust members in the first place. We believe this is doubly true at a national level.

This leads me on to the critical issue of the funding of political parties. I well understand, sir, that you feel constrained by your terms of reference from inquiring generally into the financing of political parties, into issues like the source of funds, the balance between private and state funding and whether any limits should be imposed both on the size of individual donations and on the total expenditure of parties at election time. But it seems to us, with respect, that your committee cannot fully meet its terms of reference, especially that part of them which refers to "including arrangements relating to financial and commercial activities", unless it examines the issue of openness, or lack of it, in the funding of political parties.

After all, at least one of your committee's members has spent some time inquiring into the relationship between trade unions and the Labour Party. However, I must draw attention to the fact that, by law with the trade unions and by choice with the Labour Party, our funding is extraordinarily open, as is that of the Liberal Democrat Party. This is in stark contrast to the Conservative Party, which does not publish complete accounts of the source and destination of its funds and uses a variety of front organisations, like the so-called "river companies" and various other organisations, to fund itself.

This issue of the secrecy of the funding of political parties is of supreme importance, in our view, to your work, because of the subtle way in the British political tradition that favours are obtained. It is very unusual for payments for favours to be made direct to any individual, although not unheard of. What is far more common is a subtle, triangular arrangement, in which, for example, a substantial donation to the Conservative Party coincides, or just precedes, an appointment to a quango and the success of a company or individual in relation to an award of a contract or other government decision. The suspicion of these arrangements is now notorious, the circumstantial evidence in their support overwhelming. If standards of conduct are to be raised, I respectfully suggest that new rules of openness on large donors to all political parties, and their front organisations, are required.

The suspicions generated by the present secrecy are well illustrated by the increasing difficulty which my parliamentary colleagues have in gaining information about government contractors and their fees. One of the many consequences of the increasing use of government contractors has been that information that would have been obtained were these services provided direct by government departments is not now provided by government Ministers.

Six months ago Ministers were giving information about the fees paid to consultants advising about rail privatisation. Now exactly equivalent questions from my colleague Glenda Jackson have been blocked on the wholly spurious ground of commercial confidentiality. Four of the companies concerned have financial or personal links with the Conservative Party. Surely the public have a right to know the exact nature of those links and are unlikely to have much faith in the current arrangements for securing probity unless they do.

There is an extraordinary contrast between the rules long established which apply, say, in respect of the award of a contract to construct a building and those which apply in respect of contracts for the supply of consultancy services. Where there is a contract for the erection of a building, the tendering process is open and the amount paid to the tenderer is made public at the time of the tender. I can see no reason why that system should not apply in respect of fees paid to consultants in the City, but it does not. What grounds for secrecy are there here, especially as no similar grounds appeared to exist just six months ago?

In oral evidence we set out our case for a comprehensive, as well as comprehensible, Governance of Britain Act. I should of course be happy to take questions on any aspect of that evidence, but I should like in closing to mention just three matters. The first is on executive quangos. We do not believe that the government's proposals deal with the problem, which has been fully identified before this committee. There has to be a full disclosure of political affiliations and financial interests and a much more open system of appointments, with an independent element involved.

The second point is to draw the committee's attention to our evidence in respect of the government statistical service. The political process in a democracy cannot operate unless there is complete faith in the integrity and independence of the government statistical service. That is not the case at the moment, as the retiring director-general of the government statistical service himself drew attention to in an interview which he gave in *The Independent* in December. We strongly believe that the government statistical service should be established as an autonomous service, with a relationship to Ministers and to Parliament similar to that of the National Audit Office.

The third point is to confirm the evidence of my parliamentary colleague, Mr Chris Mullin, that we believe that membership of the freemasons and similar organisations should be declarable by all elected and appointed public officials.

LORD NOLAN: Thank you very much. That has covered a very wide area in some detail. We will go straight on, if we may, to the questions, and Diana Warwick, whom I think you know, will take the lead with them.

1944. DIANA WARWICK: Perhaps I should declare an interest, in that Jack Straw, my Lord, was the paid political adviser to my old union, the Association of University Teachers, for several years. I think I can confirm that he was always helpful, but also always independent.

Can I take you to the evidence that you have given us? You have urged us to look at the hard evidence of an increase in corruption and sleaze, but in fact when we have looked at the problem there seems to be an issue of reality versus perception. We have been told that the public believe that there is a very large amount of corruption, and yet government Ministers, who asked us to look at the experience of other governments, and, perhaps even more relevant, journalists who have given us evidence have suggested that in fact there isn't as much corruption as the public perceive. Can you comment on that?

JACK STRAW: First, I don't think that this country wishes to be compared with other countries. We were always proud, from the middle of the last century onwards, that we had a much higher standard of conduct in public life than most other countries, and I think the comparison should be with the standards that have existed and applied in the past in this country and not with what is going on in other countries.

Secondly, Ms Warwick, I sought to deal with the evidence in my opening statement. Of course this is an area where absolutely hard evidence of a decline in standards is bound to be difficult to obtain: it is going to be circumstantial. But I think the most comprehensive and authoritative assessment of that evidence was in the Public Accounts Committee report in January last year. Those who have served on the PAC or have watched its operation and also know the personality of the current chairman of that committee, Robert Sheldon, know that it is very judicious and careful in its approach. For it to have published such a damning report, a unanimous report supported by, as I understand it, all the Conservative Members of that committee, charting what they believed was the decline in standards of conduct which have obtained since the Northcote-Trevelyan reforms, is, I think, evidence enough, but it can be added to. It is not only of corruption and sleaze, although there is, I think, sufficient of that, and we have published our own documents drawing together evidence of declining standards in the operation of quangos; there is also evidence of undue influence exercised in the appointment to quangos and their pursuit of agendas which are not necessarily in the public interest and too often in the Conservative Party's own interest.

1945. DIANA WARWICK: Could I turn to your evidence and deal with it in the way that you have presented it and perhaps ask a couple of questions about quangos and then move on to Ministers and civil servants? One of the things that you place an enormous amount of stress on in relation to quangos is that appointments are being made for political reasons. One of our difficulties has been getting at hard evidence, and I wonder whether you think the Labour Party has contributed to the problem by abandoning any effort to make appointments to quangos. I think that you only recently decided to make such appointments.

JACK STRAW: By the way, Lord Nolan, I forgot to introduce my colleague, Ben Lucas, who works as my political adviser, for which I apologise.

DIANA WARWICK: Did you shoot yourselves in the foot?

JACK STRAW: We haven't shot ourselves in the foot, because, with respect to you, the assumption behind your question is inaccurate. There has been no restriction on members of the Labour Party serving on quangos. I am actually living proof that wherever there is an opportunity to serve on a quango, however modest, members of the Labour Party take it. I have served as a member of the governing body of Blackburn College for the past four years. I began as a member nominated by the local authority and I continued when the college became part of the Further Education Funding Council, with the full support of the Labour Party. As you might imagine, I would not have taken that post, even though it is a relatively modest post and, I may add, wholly unpaid, unless that had had the support of the Labour Party.

The second point to make is that, if you take the health service, where this issue has been most acute, the government removed Labour councillors from health authorities in 1988 and sent out a very clear signal that they didn't want Labour councillors or Labour appointees on those health authorities. Indeed, I was present at a conference of the Audit Commission in March 1993 when Kenneth Clarke, then the Home Secretary, was asked why he had behaved in this way, why he had removed councillors from the health authority. I think that his response was really very revealing. He said "I have to say that when we started the change in the health service I took local authorities as of right off the health authorities, because frankly the meetings of the health authorities were being turned into party political debates for the benefit of the local newspaper about things that had nothing to do with the day-to-day running of the health authority." He then said "I then reappointed quite a lot of councillors, but I reappointed the ones who had an interest in the health service and could contribute to it. The difference was that when I appointed them they weren't mandated any longer by the local authority." He said that with his characteristically rumbustious self-confidence: he wasn't interested in these people from the local authority being there as of right, representing the people who had elected them, but he was going to determine who was going to go on these health authorities, and it is known that most of the people appointed came from the Conservative Party.

I want to make two last points on this. One is that Baroness Denton, in an interview which she gave to The Independent, also in March 1993, told her interviewer, who asked her whether she had ever appointed anybody with a Labour Party connection, that in over 800 public appointments in which she had been involved "I have never knowingly appointed a Labour supporter". The message that has come through from the Conservative Party, in the last six or seven years particularly, has been that Labour supporters should not apply, but there has been no ban on them at all.

The very last point I want to make is this. Looking, as I have done, with great care at the evidence which David Hunt gave and at the changes which Virginia Bottomley has issued about appointments to the health service quangos, I think that there is a fiction at the heart of that evidence, a disguise, which is that the government has been intent all along on making appointments without regard to people's political affiliations. In democratic public life this seems to me to be utter nonsense. First of all, we know, and Mr Hunt hints at this, that all serious appointments are vetted by a network of the government Whips' Office, special advisers in government and Conservative Central Office, so they are vetted for their political affiliations: it may not be for membership of the Conservative Party, but it is certainly for their political sympathy.

Secondly, not all people but most people in public life do have political sympathies and affiliations, and it seems to us that these ought to be known. I draw a very sharp contrast between the system which Ministers have said they are following, but manifestly have not followed, and now say they wish to put in place, where they say are going to be blind and deaf to people's political affiliations, with a system which has worked pretty well in respect of appointments to the magistrates' bench. It is very important that when people go on to the magistrates' bench they do not take political considerations into account in making their judicial judgments, but the way the advisory committees for JPs have worked is to accept the reality of local public life, that people do have political affiliations. They invite nominations from the political parties; it comes up in the general management committee of the Blackburn Labour Party as to who we wish to nominate; there is no pretence that we are going to get away from politics, and the advisory committees then try to secure a balance, and there is very rarely any criticism that benches have operated in a partisan way. The value of that is that the benches in each area on the whole have the confidence of local people and local political institutions.

1946. DIANA WARWICK: Clearly you are not opposed to quangos, because under both governments there have been numbers of quangos and they have often increased, again under both governments, but I am quite interested in this idea of how you ensure that political sympathy plays no part in appointments. You have suggested that we should follow the system of appointments to the magistracy. I wonder if you could expand on how you would see such a system working for the huge range of quangos with which we have to deal.

JACK STRAW: If I may say so with respect, we don't at any stage suggest or imply that political sympathy and affiliation should play no part. Indeed, it ought to play a part. One of the reasons why the Conservative Party is in such a jam now is that it has sought to maintain a pretence that political affiliations have played no part, when manifestly they have played every part. That was why Ken Clarke, who at least has the merit of being frank about his method, explained why he had removed councillors, and in the main had removed Labour councillors, from health authorities. We believe that systems of appointment ought to follow reality.

Previous governments, Labour and Conservative, took account of political affiliations in making appointments to various quangos; of course they did. The difference, however, and this is partly a consequence of one party being in power for a long time, is also to do with the way in which the former Prime Minister, Lady Thatcher, worked, with her initial test of "Are they one of us?" The difference is that the present government has operated a sort of "winner takes all" approach. I worked as a political adviser in the last government, and I ought to declare another interest: I worked, for a very happy period, for Peter Shore as his political adviser and, before that, for Barbara Castle. As I recall, when appointments to quangos were being made it was well known what the political affiliations were of the various people who were coming forward, but if you check back on that record and the record of the Heath, Wilson, Douglas-Hume, Macmillan governments before, you will see that an effort was made, which was translated into action, to secure a balance. There was not a "winner take all" approach and there was a great involvement of local authorities. So we want a system that recognises the political reality.

In terms of the way in which an independent element would operate, one of the points where I do agree with David Hunt in his evidence is that a system of proportionality should operate. Some executive quangos are much more important than others, they spend more money, they have a higher profile. You need to develop different systems for different quangos. But in terms of an independent element, there is no reason, for example, so far as appointments to the health service are concerned, why you should not have people who are wholly independent, which is not what Mrs Bottomley is suggesting for a moment, drawn in respect of, for example, the advisory committees for JPs, and who are then required to produce a political balance on the health authorities as well as to ensure that people of high standing are appointed. I can't see anything wrong with that. Indeed, I think it would greatly improve public confidence in the system.

1947. DIANA WARWICK: Don't you think that that might lead just to a devolution of the possibilities of patronage? I didn't hear the word "merit" enter into your comments.

JACK STRAW: I am sorry, I think I did use the word "merit" at the end of what I just said.

1948. DIANA WARWICK: And where would the people come from who would be appointed on their merit as opposed to according to their political sympathy?

JACK STRAW: It doesn't follow that people who have political sympathies are without merit, not for a moment. These are public bodies which are spending large amounts of public money. Overall our view is that many of the decisions for the functions of quangos ought to be put back either directly or indirectly in the hands of elected people, but of course there will continue to be some executive quangos. The people running them should be visible, their political affiliations should be known, there should be an effort to secure political balance. Of course there should be people of no political persuasion on those bodies as well, but that should be known.

1949. DIANA WARWICK: So can you confirm that, were there to be a Labour government, Ministers would be quite happy to surrender the powers of patronage that they have at the moment?

JACK STRAW: Yes. It would not be a surrender; it would be producing a much more open system. If Ministers are required by statute to make appointments, they have to make them and they are accountable to Parliament for them, in the same way as the Lord Chancellor and the Chancellor of the Duchy of Lancaster are responsible for making appointments to the benches in England and in the Duchy of Lancaster. But it is the system by which names are brought forward, the criteria that are taken into account, which in our view is extremely important, and the lack of a system and the essential contradictions are among the reasons why public confidence in people who serve on quangos and in the operation of quangos is now extremely low.

1950. DIANA WARWICK: I wonder if I can turn briefly to the question of Ministers. In your evidence you have suggested that there ought to be a long quarantine period for Ministers moving to outside posts. What evidence we have suggests that a fair number of the appointments about which there has been publicity have all taken place after the Civil Service period of two years. Do you envisage a longer period for Ministers than the Civil Service period?

JACK STRAW: We have an open mind on this. We didn't specify a precise period, because frankly we were unable to come to a firm view on this and we thought we would wait until we received your recommendations about this. It may be extraordinary for a political party to do this, but we thought we should, as we were not in full possession of all the evidence.

I think that one of the issues here is to determine a starting time. Is the starting time the point at which a Minister stopped being directly involved, in a departmental sense, in those issues or the time at which he stopped being involved as a Minister? To take the example, since it has been made public, of Lord Wakeham, it is quite some years since he was Minister for Energy; it is, however, very recent since he ceased to be a senior member of the government, I think serving, although I stand to be corrected, on the Cabinet committees which were dealing with electricity and gas privatisation. My instinct is that you have to take the starting time from the point at which he ceased to have influence over those decisions rather than the point at which he ceased to have departmental responsibility for them.

1951. DIANA WARWICK: Would you, though, use the Civil Service rules to determine whether it was appropriate for a Minister to make such a move, because they are actually quite restricted? They apply to those who have had direct dealings with the company concerned or where the person might have knowledge that could give competitors an advantage. You seem to be suggesting that any connection with a company might be regarded as suspect.

JACK STRAW: I don't think any connections, but in view of what you have said your committee may certainly want to think about wider criteria than those which apply to civil servants. The fact that rules exist for civil servants but not for Ministers is very suggestive of the need for such rules to apply to Ministers, who often have more power over these matters than do civil servants, but I accept the implication, I think, of your question that the rules should be tailored to take specific account of the position of

Ministers, who after all have ultimate responsibility for these decisions in a way that officials do not.

1952. DIANA WARWICK: Could I then ask you about the point you make in your evidence about codes? You recommend that there should be statutory codes of conduct for public servants, and indeed for Ministers. I wonder if you could elaborate on that and tell us why you think they should be statutory.

JACK STRAW: I am just getting the government's response to the Treasury and Civil Service Select Committee report, which also discussed this issue. We say in our evidence that initially we accept that many of these changes could be made, and ought to be made, effectively by use of prerogative powers. The reason why we believe, however, that they ought to be brought together in what we have described as a Governance of Britain Act is that, if they are in statute, they are much open, they have been the subject of infinitely more detailed parliamentary scrutiny in being prepared, and it then becomes impossible for Ministers who wish it to change those codes, except by reference to Parliament. I was interested that the government half accepted this point in the discussion which they enter into towards the end of their response to the TCSC report about the use of prerogative powers versus statute. I am trying to turn up the exact reference. It is paragraph 2.15 on page 8. It says:

"It follows that it is for Ministers alone to issue instructions concerning the management of the Civil Service and it follows that they do not require parliamentary authority to do so."

I think that is an extremely dangerous statement indeed, because Ministers are responsible to Parliament for the operation of the Civil Service. The government has already accepted that the Civil Service owes duties to the Crown and to Parliament and, as it were, to the public above and beyond the day-to-day duties which it owes to the Ministers who occupy the seat of a Minister for the time being. So for them to assert that the issuing of instructions is solely a matter for Ministers seems to me to be a) inconsistent with the whole gravamen of their evidence and b) very dangerous. I hope that explains why we think that it ought to go into statute.

1953. DIANA WARWICK: I would like to ask you a little more about what might be included, but I wonder if I can ask whether, if the Labour Party has given some thought to that, they could let us have those thoughts?

JACK STRAW: Yes. Let me say so far as the issue of codes is concerned that I consider—we consider—that this document represents a very substantial advance on what was the government's position before, because for a great many years they resisted any suggestion of having a code, or certainly that it should be placed on any kind of formal basis. So this is an advance and we are happy to give them credit for accepting the need for such a code. Let me say, both to restore the confidence of the Civil Service in Ministers and the confidence of the public in the operation of the public service, that I have looked at the government's helpful annotated amendments to the TCSC code, I have some detailed comments to make on them, but will happily let you have a note on them.

1954. DIANA WARWICK: Thank you. I wonder if I can turn to another issue that has occupied the headlines,

and that is the question of the accountability of Ministers for policy matters as opposed to operational matters, particularly in the context of Next Steps agencies. I wonder whether, if I can put it this way, you accept the principle that the dropping of a bedpan in a National Health Service hospital should be heard in the Secretary of State's office. Would you go so far?

JACK STRAW: No, I don't. The test of that is that during the great public interest in the prison riots and escapes from prisons, which took place last month, I resisted all suggestions, which, let me say, were many and various, especially from the tabloid newspapers, that I should call for the Home Secretary's resignation because of what had happened. I never did so. But I happen to believe that the distinction that the Conservative Party makes between policy and operations and between accountability and responsibility is an artificial one which is not based upon reality.

Let me deal with these two things in turn. The myth behind the establishment of the Next Steps agencies is that it is possible wholly to separate operations from policy, that you can describe in a framework document a policy and then require the chief executive of that to get on with operating the policy, for which he and not Ministers is then responsible. This is based upon a myth that somehow policy is some abstraction, whereas in the real world the only test of a policy is how it operates in practice. To deal with your bedpan analogy, if someone drops a bedpan—although I dare say they are all plastic these days—and it breaks, then for sure that is the operational responsibility of the person holding the bedpan. If it turns out that there is a shortage of bedpans, or sheets—in Blackburn not so many years ago there was a shortage of sheets, and paper sheets had to be dished out to the patients—it seems to me that it is fair for questions to lie to the Minister as to how and why this has occurred, because the public want somebody who is visible to be accountable for this. The public also know that Ministers of all parties—and this applies to Tom King too—are only too happy to claim credit for the successful operation of policy. Given that that is the case, they have to accept the contrary.

I think the public are perfectly capable of understanding that direct responsibility for things like bedpans dropping does not necessarily lie at the Minister's door, but what they don't want, and what I think the public felt was pretty incredible, is to see Ministers trying to evade responsibility for what is happening in, say, the prison service under the guise that this is an arm's length agency, because that reduces the parliamentary accountability of Ministers. We have a ludicrous situation now in respect of, say, the prison service, where, if I, as I do often, ask a question of a Minister about what is happening in the prison service, it is not the Minister who replies, except to attach a little rubric: he attaches a letter from the director general of the prison service. I think that is reduced accountability. There is still a Minister of prisons and he is a talented man: Mr Michael Forsyth has virtually nothing to do, because his job, which was to gain experience about how the prison service operated and then relate that to Parliament, has now been by-passed by Mr Derek Lewis.

The other point I wanted to raise was this distinction which Ministers have made between accountability and responsibility, a distinction which was exploded by the Treasury and Civil Service Select Committee report which led to this response. Again, making that distinction is to secure an evasion of responsibility: if Ministers are accountable to Parliament for what happens within a service, in our judgment they ought also to be responsible to Parliament, and Parliament and politicians will make their own fair judgments about whether the responsibility of Ministers is such as to involve culpability. That is not always the case.

1955. DIANA WARWICK: Could I ask one final question? I think you are the only former special adviser to come before us, and I would just to like to pick that up, because we have heard that special advisers to Ministers are targeted by the lobbyists, to which you have also referred, as people with access to Ministers and therefore very useful. They are not subject to the business appointments rules, which may be something we should look at. But I wonder if you can tell us: what was it about the job you did that you could take away that people would have paid you for?

JACK STRAW: Well no one did pay me for it, let me tell you, so it may not have been anything. I am sorry, but as a piece of light relief, I am reminded of when Barbara Castle introduced Brian Able-Smith, who was a distinguished professor of social administration and myself to a visiting professor from another country. She introduced Brian Able-Smith as her senior policy adviser and me as political adviser. This chap asked Barbara what the difference was. She said without hesitation or deviation, "I've appointed Brian for his brains and Jack for guile and low cunning". Whether that was a marketable quality, I do not know. Later on, by the way, I developed some policy sense, let me tell you. This was early on, and I was simply there for guile.

What I took away from the three-and-a-half very happy years in which I served as a political adviser was a great knowledge about the way government and the civil service operated from a unique standpoint, halfway between Ministers and officials, admiration for the two senior politicians I worked for and a good deal of understanding of the political process at a senior Cabinet level. I suppose that might have made me marketable, but I then went off to work for Granada Television for two years as a researcher and have been in the House of Commons ever since.

1956. DIANA WARWICK: But do you see special advisers as a useful conduit for lobbyists? Are they perceived in that way in the House?

JACK STRAW: I think they are now. I thought your question was going to be, was I ever contacted by a lobbyist or taken out to lunch by one. My recollection was that in the three-and-a-half years in which I worked for Ministers I was only once approached or taken out to lunch by lobbyists, and I think it turned out to be rather a waste of a lunch for them, although fulfilling for me. In the past 15 years there has been a huge increase in the number of lobbyists, for reasons that I tried to explain. I think now, obviously, their information and their connection with Ministers is of great importance and very marketable.

LORD NOLAN: I think it is likely that all members of the Committee will have some questions they would like to ask you. May I start with Sir William Utting?

1957. WILLIAM UTTING: Thank you, Chairman. I have yards of questions that I should like to ask you, Mr

Straw, but I shall sense my colleagues on the Committee starting to shuffle if I go on too long, so I shall try to restrict myself to two general areas. The first of these is the question of the interests of Members of Parliament and the ways in which Parliament regulates the conduct of Members. I think these matters occupy a rather lower profile in your written evidence than some of the questions that Diana Warwick has been putting to you. I happen to think that they are pretty important and perhaps central to our work, so I should be delighted to hear from you about the kind of paid activities that you consider is improper for MPs to take on in addition to their parliamentary duties and whether or not you have views about the ways in which Parliament regulates the conduct of its Members might be improved.

JACK STRAW: Thank you, Sir William. The only reason why I did not deal with that at any length is because Mrs Taylor has dealt with it separately. We agreed within the Shadow Cabinet that we would divide the task between matters directly relating to Members of Parliament, which Mrs Taylor properly took on as Shadow Leader of the House, and the wider issues, which I took on. I endorse the evidence that she gave.

I think there is a distinction, which has been flagged up in this Committee, between advice and advocacy. As you know, I had a modest role with the Association of University Teachers, for which I was paid, I think, £1,250, rising to £1,500, which went into my office fund. During that period I gave advice to the Association of University Teachers. I do not recall that I ever advocated anything on their behalf, and indeed, during the five years that I was Shadow Education Secretary—and if it was a debate, I would declare the interest—no Conservative ever criticised me for seeking to speak up for the AUT, because I did not see that as my role and I did not do it. As Miss Warwick suggested, I sometimes gave the AUT advice which they did not want to hear; but that seemed to me to be my role. I think there is a major distinction between advice which one might well give -and does give—to bodies with which one has no paid relationship and advocacy, which I think is really unacceptable, because it cuts across a Member of Parliament's role. When one sees people standing up in the House, even if their role as advocate is well known, there is always the question in the back of one's mind, are they doing this because this is their judgment or because it arises from their role as a paid consultant.

The second point you asked, Sir William, was about the method by which Parliament regulates these matters. I think it is unsatisfactory; that view is now widely shared in the House and publicly. I do not think that the Committee of Privileges is working properly. It is a partisan body and its current inquiry into the so-called "payment for questions" and the parallel inquiry being undertaken by the Committee of Members' Interests are both likely to come to rather partisan grief. In her evidence, Mrs Taylor raised the possibility of there being an independent body, which would be—this is a slightly overdone analogy, because it would be very much smaller—in a similar relationship to the NAO. This body could act to give independent advice and opinion about whether the rules had been followed. Ultimately, of course, it would have to be a matter for Parliament to decide; there is no other way of doing it. I think that this independent scrutiny would greatly improve the current system.

1958. WILLIAM UTTING: Good. One small supplementary to that, the question of the richness that extra-parliamentary work is argued as bringing to the business of Parliament itself.

JACK STRAW: I think that extra-parliamentary work is important, but it does not have to be paid. I have extra-parliamentary work as a visiting fellow of Nuffield College, a governor of Blackburn College, a parent governor at Pimlico School, and I have an attachment with Barclays Bank through the Parliament and Industry Trust. None of these is paid. They all enrich my experience as a Member of Parliament. But there is no need for these relationships to be paid—indeed, I think that if they are paid, it can undermine the independence of judgment which as a Member of Parliament one is supposed to make.

1959. WILLIAM UTTING: Thank you. If I can move on to Quangos, your paper says a great deal about the movement of power and resources, in particular, from local forms of government to centralised Quangos. I take it that you are not philosophically totally opposed to non-departmental public bodies, but if you were in power, you would want to be looking at Quangos on a category by category or case by case basis, to see how best those services should be provided. Are you in fact thinking of some of them going back under local democratic control?

JACK STRAW: "Quangos" is a word which I suppose we have been partly responsible for bringing into public use, but it covers three distinct categories of body, does it not? There are those that exercise quasi-judicial functions, which almost by definition should not be full of people who are elected, but people who are appointed. There is the Health & Safety Commission, various quasi-judicial commissions, and tribunals. There has not been a great deal of criticism, by the way, of appointments to those bodies.

WILLIAM UTTING: No. We have not heard very much.

JACK STRAW: Although I think there is a case for having some of them scrutinised by the appropriate Select Committee. They ought always to be above board.

There are also advisory committees—usually expert advisory committees. When the Government claim that they have cut down the numbers, it is the Advisory Committee on Beekeeping in Norwich—or things like that—that on the whole have been reduced in number. It really made no difference whether they existed or not. But there are advisory committees. People appointed to them should be appointed for their expertise. Again there has been no serious criticism of them, although I can think of one or two cases where there has been.

The key focus of this Committee is on executive Quangos, those that have power to spend public money. We do not argue that there should be no executive Quangos, but our starting point is that public money ought to be spent by elected individuals, unless there are good reasons for it not to be spent by people who are elected directly or indirectly. For that reason, among many others, we have wholly opposed the incremental changes, for example, in the Health Service, which have occurred where control over funding has shifted from partly elected bodies to wholly appointed bodies. We are examining on a case by case basis how to get back an elected element into each of these Quangos, or in some cases simply to transfer responsibility back to central or local government.

WILLIAM UTTING: Thank you. Thank you, Chairman.

1960. CLIFFORD BOULTON: Can I ask you a detailed question about the jobs that Ministers take after they have left office? How do you visualise a system of control working? What is the sanction? There are former Ministers of all kinds, and over the past few months we have been collecting different ways of leaving the Government. There can be a general election which clears the lot out. How do you see a system working that applies to each individual case?

JACK STRAW: We have not anticipated that there would have to be a statutory sanction for this, although if there was plain abuse of a recommendation that someone should not take a post, I suppose we should have to bring these rules into statute. On the whole we have worked on the basis that if there were clear rules, which were known in advance when Ministers took a position, they would accept and abide by those rules. If there was a suggestion that that was not the case, these rules would have to be wrapped into the law—among other things, the criminal law. In terms of direct need to sanction, Sir Clifford, it would be possible, I guess—although it is a matter for lawyers rather than me—for this to be part of a contract between Ministers and the Crown, although it would be an odd kind of contract.

In terms of the process, it would have to be a similar process to that which applies to the civil service. There would have to be a body—a group of people—who would assess in individual cases how particular rules should apply. They would have to have a considerable degree of discretion.

1961. CLIFFORD BOULTON: So the Minister would end up almost with a certificate stating that it was okay, which would be helpful to him to have, in order to be able to say to people, "I've had this cleared", if there is public criticism?

JACK STRAW: Yes.

CLIFFORD BOULTON: Because sometimes former Ministers feel that they are unfairly criticised.

JACK STRAW: Yes, it would. I can well understand that some Ministers do feel unfairly criticised. It is easy to anticipate that some Ministers may have had nothing whatever to do with a particular policy area, but have been subject to criticism for the fact that they have moved to a post that has aroused these criticisms—all the more reason for having clear rules that ensure that those who could be in a position of exercising judgments that brought in information which they had gained as a Minister in an unacceptable way were excluded from jobs, but equally ensure that those who had had no such access to information were able to take on such jobs without criticism.

1962. CLIFFORD BOULTON: Can I now look at appointments to Quangos for a moment? You quoted a snippet from Baroness Denton, who said:

"I can't remember knowingly appointing a Labour supporter".

That does have to be understood, does it not, in the context of paragraph 55 of your paper, in which you say:

"Ministers have consistently refused formally to register the political affiliation of those appointed to Quangos and claimed that they are not told by officials what are the political sympathies of those who are recommended for appointment"?

Presumably it is in the context of that claim that she said that she did not knowingly appoint Labour supporters? Your memorandum is followed by another paragraph, which can best be described as "hollow laughter", I think, because you accept the Government's position, but that was the position, as I understand it. What about Mr Kenneth Clarke's comment that if people appointed otherwise from local authorities or whatever turn up on these bodies mandated and cease to operate as individuals? Is there anything in that? Could it best be addressed by a code of conduct for Quangos or some such rules of that sort?

JACK STRAW: Let me deal with those in turn. You gave my answer to your first point, because paragraph 55 is followed by paragraph 56, which describes the claim by Ministers as disingenuous nonsense. It is true that when minutes come through from officials with lists of people who might be appointed, there is no symbol on them about their political affiliations, unless they are notorious. These names are then fed into the Government Whips' Office special advisers' and central office network and, as Mr Hunt was kind enough to admit, the Whips' Office arrangement is far more formal and extensive than even I had anticipated. By the time Ministers come to make their decisions, they know exactly the political affiliations or sympathies of the people they are appointing; that is evident from the plain political sympathies of the people who have been appointed. What I do not understand is why this fiction that Mrs Bottomley above all maintains, that they never take into account political affiliations, is sustained, when everybody knows—and she knows—that it is sustained. What purpose is she trying to secure by sustaining such nonsense?

CLIFFORD BOULTON: Of course she says that they are not being put on to perform as political animals.

JACK STRAW: I think she may say that.

CLIFFORD BOULTON: I was just trying to make sense of what you say is preposterous.

JACK STRAW: Yes. I think she may say that, but of course they are there explicitly for a political purpose. The appointments that are made to Trust bodies—and the latest proposed changes of Mrs Bottomley—have to be seen in the context of the politics of the NHS. Mr John Maples—God bless him!—wrote a memorandum, which then happily got covered in the Financial Times, which talked about the problems facing the Conservative Party. He said in respect of the NHS:

"The best result for the next 12 months would be zero media coverage.".

That is the overwhelming political imperative for the Conservatives, to have no coverage at all on the NHS. If one wants to achieve a situation of no political coverage on the NHS, one has to make damned sure that the people who are serving on the NHS Trusts and other bodies are people who will assist in that project. That is why the Conservative Party cannot afford to put on to these bodies people who are likely to kick over the traces or to stress, for example, what is happening in my constituency. The Blackburn public have just been told that the casualty department is no longer available to "inappropriate referrals". Since it is a long way from the centre of town to Blackburn Royal Infirmary, people on the whole do not go there on a fool's errand. It is not like the siting of the casualty department at St Thomas's. Nobody from the health authority has spoken out against this.

1963. LORD NOLAN: What is an "inappropriate referral"?

JACK STRAW: An "inappropriate referral" is someone who ought to go to their GP. My one experience of going to the casualty department at Blackburn Royal Infirmary is that a Chadwickian principle of less eligibility applies. People have to wait a lot longer there than at their GP's. One has to work on the basis that people who turn up there on the whole have a reason for being there other than wasting doctors' time. I make this point as a small vignette. No one in the Health Authority or the Health Trust has complained about this, I think, so no one on the Health Trust is representing people.

On your point about politics ———

CLIFFORD BOULTON: It is the mandated point.

JACK STRAW: There used to be a joke which applied in the educational world, where people who pay me carried blue rosettes in their handbag. It was suggested that they were saying, "I'm not a Conservative, I'm apolitical". There was this view that those in the Conservative Party could be apolitical, anybody of any other political persuasion was bound to be entirely partisanly political. That was inherent in Mr Clarke's claim that he wanted to put on to Health Authorities people of no politics. The Health Service is a highly political issue and will be at all times, however it is organised. One cannot divorce politics from its operation, nor should one, in a democracy.

I accept that it is pointless to have endless party political rows which are off the agenda in any kind of body, but one can do it by codes of conduct, by saying that people should not be mandated. On the whole people were not mandated, but were going to the Health Authority and complaining about cuts. My experience of bodies on which I serve has been of a school governing body where there are Conservative councillors and also of the governing body of Blackburn College, where we all know what people's politics are. On the whole people act reasonably and do apply themselves to the agenda. There is no reason why that should not be reflected in a code.

CLIFFORD BOULTON: Thanks.

1964. PETER SHORE: Really on the same point about appointment, we have had witnesses before us who have really justified the political imbalance on the grounds that unless the appointee has an enthusiasm and a commitment to the policy, it will not be properly carried out. What is your comment on that?

JACK STRAW: I understand that point of view. It is certainly possible to envisage Quangos under either Government which have a partisan role and only Conservative or Labour Members should apply. If that is the case, it should be made known publicly. This is now the ex-post facto explanation for the exclusion of signed-up Conservatives from the initial operation of Trusts. At the time Trusts were being established, the claim was being made that the people being put on them were entirely of non-political character, appointed—to use Ms Warwick's word, only for their "merit". There may be a partisan job to do; if there is—I do not exclude that possibility from either Government—that should be known: it should be said, "This is a partisan job and we are only going to appoint these people. The prior question is, are they one of us."

In terms of the expenditure of public money, however, there needs as a general rule to be political bias and having such partisan vanguards should only be used in extremely limited circumstances.

1965. PETER SHORE: Presumably you take the view about people being appointed to Quangos who are known to have a political view, but that political view would not disqualify them from contributing to the public service job that they had to perform?

JACK STRAW: Not at all. I find this mythology-because that is what it is—that the only people who can serve on public bodies are those without politics or those whose political affiliation should not be known quite extraordinary. I do not deny for a moment that there are people of the highest repute serving on your Committee, Lord Nolan, whose political affiliations are not known and have formed no part of their public persona. They have an important contribution to make, but that applies equally to those who do have political affiliations. We live in a democracy where people are offered political choices. It seems to me crucial that, whenever public money is being spent, the public should be able to watch how political choices—with a small and a big "p"—are being made.

1966. PETER SHORE: Yes, but the first and overriding consideration—I think you answered this point before—is the merit of the candidate who is appointed.

JACK STRAW: Yes, sure. But, as I said, that does not follow just because one is a politician.

1967. PETER SHORE: Can I ask you what you think about the latest proposals for NHS authorities? I think the scheme that Mrs Bottomley announced was that in each region of the country -about eight regional bodies are to be created shortly—there would be a panel set up, consisting of three chairmen of local Regional Health Authorities, who would have the job of advising the Secretary of State on what other appointments she should make. Do you think that would give greater independence? Would that meet the requirement of improving Quango appointments?

JACK STRAW: I do not think it would. I have Mrs Bottomley's detailed proposals in front of me. She said that the sifting would be conducted by a panel

"consisting of at least three local Chairmen or non-Executives, not from the same Board. It might also include an independent member of a local Community Health Council, JP, local employer or voluntary agency.".

I do not believe that there will be any but marginal change in the appointments that Ministers make to the NHS. That is because of this overriding political imperative in the mind of Mrs Bottomley, which is shown by her track record in ensuring that she has Trusts and Health Authorities which do the Conservatives' bidding. It is Mr Maples's imperative that so far as possible the NHS is taken off the agenda that is the overriding consideration.

The other point I would make, Peter, is that they talk in this document and in Mr Hunt's about the use of the Public Appointments Unit. My parliamentary colleague Tony Wright published last week a very well written pamphlet entitled Beyond *The Patronage State*, Which at the end draws attention to how little used the Public Appointments Unit has been. He was able to identify that in 1992 only 84 public appointments that were made were from nominations from that unit out of total of 50,000—not in only one year—I guess that in any one year the total would be between 5,000 and 10,000. Frankly, these arrangements are at the moment risible and take no account of the reality.

1968. PETER SHORE: Moving to another part of your evidence, I was struck by paragraph 19, where you talk about the very enhanced role that lobbyists and consultancy firms played in recent years. You go on to say:

"At a time when insider trading has become a criminal offence for those trading on the stock exchange, inside information about government traded for cash... has become the central commodity of those involved in 'government relations'.".

That is a very striking comparison. What kind of measures would you have in mind to limit the influence of people trying to benefit by insider trading of government information?

JACK STRAW: I accept that it is a reasonably striking comparison. As I was writing this evidence, it was one that came to me and I was struck by the fact by the connection between the way in which the financial markets now work and the way in which the political markets work. After all, not so many years ago insider trading was the meat and drink of City institutions. It was how people earned their fees. Now, there is an extraordinary compliant system—and a very expensive and rather admirable one—to prevent insider trading between City institutions. This is an area where the financial markets are well ahead of the political markets. How does one deal with that? By, I think, a panoply of changes that are before your Committee, which would exclude altogether advocacy by Members of Parliament of causes outside. Payments by consultants to Members of Parliament would require very much greater openness, particularly on the issue of political funding. It is an issue that applies principally to the Conservative Party, because its funding is not open, just as very great care is taken by Ministers and officials—it is an interesting point when we come to the issue of open government—not to release information selectively, so that it cannot be traded in an inside way, but information is either closed and kept within the confines of government or is out in the open.

1969. PETER SHORE: Is not the problem to some extent inherent in the practices?

JACK STRAW: Inherent in the current practices?

PETER SHORE: Yes.

JACK STRAW: Yes, it is, and it has got much worse. When talking to colleagues of your generation, I was struck by a colleague who served with you at the Ministry of Defence, who said to me that during the whole of the time he was serving as Minister for Defence Procurement he had never been lobbied by any arms company. I doubt whether that is the experience of people in the Ministry of Defence today, either as an official or at Ministerial level. Lobbying has taken on a much more American character.

1970. PETER SHORE: My last area of questioning is what is really implicit throughout your paper, the desirability of much greater openness of procedures. You make a point towards the end of your evidence in paragraph 27 that information that was previously supplied to Members of Parliament through questioning about the fees paid to consultants has now been blocked. What is your understanding for what is clearly a very odd change of policy?

JACK STRAW: I assume this is an entirely political decision which has been made by Mr Mawhinney, who I think took his post—although I may be wrong about this—since 14 July, when the previous questions were answered. The comparison is stark. On 14 July 1994, I put these papers before you sir, Mr Dobson, who was then Shadow Transport Secretary, asked the Secretary of State for details of consultancy fees paid in respect of rail privatisation. Roger Freeman, the then Minister, answered with a detailed list. It was very straightforward: he provided information. Ms Jackson then asked a similar question on 14 February and was told by the Junior Minister, Mr Watts, that information about fees paid by the Department to individual contractors was commercially confidential. The total payment to date to these contractors amounted to £17 million. It is unusual to get such a stark example of where the Government are reducing the amount of information being made public, yet here it is. They say it is commercially confidential, but it was not commercially confidential six months ago. Some of the firms are the same who were content to have their fees published. In any event, I do not understand what should be commercially confidential about the fees paid to a government contractor. As I said, if Tarmac, Bovis and John Laing bid for a contract to put up a new building, the amount of the tender accepted is known—indeed, they are the first people to issue a press notice about it. There is no argument about it; of course it should be known. Surely the same should apply here. I can only assume that the reason why the Government want to close down scrutiny is that, for tactical reasons, they wish there to be less scrutiny of the costs of rail privatisation, because they are worried that a number of these firms in the City have direct connections with the Conservative Party and because behind the global fees that these institutions are paid lie exorbitant hourly fees on a scale that would in some cases dwarf the payments made to the Chief Executive of British Gas. Their reluctance is unacceptable, but in the current political climate, I suppose, comprehensible.

1971. PETER SHORE: Your message really is that lack of openness anyway feeds suspicions.

JACK STRAW: Lack of openness feeds suspicion. The other message is that, contrary to the claims that Mr Hunt made in his evidence where he talked about the development of Next Step Agencies and arm's length Quangos as consistent and, indeed, supporting the Government's "aim for greater openness"—that was

exactly the phrase he used—the practice of having more and more public services provided by government contractors is to reduce the amount of information available to Members of Parliament under the guise of commercial confidentiality. It has led to greater secrecy, not greater openness.

1972. PETER SHORE: Yes. That applies also to your plea for openness with political contributions.

JACK STRAW: Yes, because, as I say, the British political system of favours is a subtle one; it has none of the vulgarity of the Italian system or of the system that may have obtained in this country in respect of football transfers. "Bungs" are very unusual in politics—certainly no one has ever offered me one, and I doubt whether anyone else here has been offered one. When people like Mr Asil Nadir pay £400,000 to the Conservative Party, I assume they think they are going to get something back for their money. There are other people who make payments like this from abroad. People within the country have made very large payments to the Conservative Party, but we do not know exactly who they are, how much they paid. The Conservative Party runs River Companies, which I think are run out of an office in north Northumberland. There are people like the British Union of Industrialists. There is a whole nexus of funding arrangements, all designed to deceive. The British public no longer want to be deceived about the funding of political parties. Our funding is open, and over the past 15 years the financial arrangements of the trade unions have become much more open. We have no objection to that, but we wish to see some symmetry.

PETER SHORE: It is only fair to add to your point that Mr Nadir is now a refugee from British justice.

JACK STRAW: He is indeed.

PETER SHORE: I will finish with that.

1973. LORD NOLAN: We are running a little short of time, so I will try to keep my three questions as short as possible. The first arises out of what you were saying about the system of appointing Justices of the Peace. My experience, like yours, is that it seems a very good system that works well and one gets a political balance. This would seem to me to be the sort of approach that should equally be adopted for tribunals, which account for a lot of appointments. Are there not quite a lot of Non-departmental Public Bodies, or Quangos, where it would be inappropriate? Take the Prison Service, which you must have had much opportunity to think about: if the Minister decides that prisons should be privatised, that may be regarded as a very good decision or a very bad decision, but it is a legitimate political decision which then has to be carried into effect. It would not be necessarily helpful, would it, to strike at a political balance in the membership of the senior branches of the Prison Service, if that was the policy? I think you accept that.

JACK STRAW: Yes.

LORD NOLAN: I think you did earlier. There are certain types which could be identified and defined as not calling for a balanced political approach. Are there not others, though—this is really my point, a point put by Mr Kalms, amongst others ———

JACK STRAW: By whom?

LORD NOLAN: Mr Kalms, the Chairman of Dixons.

JACK STRAW: Mr Kalms, yes.

LORD NOLAN: Who is on a Health Service Trust. He said that political ideas are really irrelevant when one is running a hospital properly. I wondered if there too might be a danger of striving for a balance of politics, ages and sexes which actually was inimical to producing the best people to do the job.

JACK STRAW: May I deal with those points in turn? In most cases the model of advisory committees for JPs could apply, especially to local Quangos. If you take NHS Trusts and Commissioning Authorities, Health Authorities, it would be very sensible and make for the better administration of the Health Service, if the people on those bodies were politically balanced, because if they were, then, as with the magistrates' benches, they would inspire all-round public confidence. They would not be seen as partisan forces, as they are, frankly, at the moment.

As I think I indicated in answering earlier questions, I accept that there may be some appointments where one needs a partisan job done. I will offer you another example. There is a Funding Agency for Schools. We wholly opposed the establishment of grant maintained schools. It is an issue of partisan politics. I therefore understand the reluctance of Ministers to put on to the Funding Agency for Schools people other than signed up Conservatives. But Ministers ought to admit that that is what they are; to some extent they are not doing so.

On the Prison Service, it is certainly a fact of life—and I think it is well known—that Mr Derek Lewis was appointed in preference to Mr Joe Pilling, because Mr Pilling was regarded by Mr Kenneth Clarke as being unenthusiastic about privatisation, while Mr Lewis apparently thought that it was a good idea. The reverse could apply, of course. That is the real world. I want to see a system of appointments that reflects political reality, but does not make pretence of arrangements.

As to Mr Stanley Kalms, he makes my point. Mr Kalms is a partisan Conservative. He is an engaging fellow, but he is a Conservative. He goes into one body after another saying he is politically impartial and that political ideas are irrelevant. They are not, and he knows it, if he will think about it for a moment.

The Health Service is supremely political. Of course it should not be the subject day by day of political argy-bargy, but, frankly, whether my constituents are going to have full access to a decent casualty service in the Blackburn Royal Infirmary is a political issue. They would wish to hear members of the Health Authority and Health Trusts speaking up for them, because they do not at the moment.

1974. LORD NOLAN: Secondly—this is really a request for more information—as you know, we have taken the view that, although party funding as such is outside our terms of reference, we are naturally very closely interested in any evidence of political contributions being associated with patronage, with a deal being done. We are short of hard evidence. If you have any, will you please let us have it.

JACK STRAW: We will let you have large amounts of hard evidence.

1975. LORD NOLAN: Finally, we have been impressed from the start of this inquiry by an early figure put before us by Professor Ivor Crewe. It was a Gallup Poll showing that 64 per cent of the people who answered the poll thought that most Members of Parliament were more interested in making gain out of their position than serving their constituents. Do you accept that view?

JACK STRAW: I think that the opinion poll is unquestionably correct. For the vast majority of Members of Parliament it is not true, by the way. I had to send a cheque to the Fees Office today to cover a deficit out of my salary on my secretarial allowance and, since the letter I received from the Fees Office was cyclo-styled, I think that I am one of a large company of people in a similar position. I also notice that there is a difference in public perception between politicians generally and politicians whom they know. They are going to be much more discriminating about the politicians whom they know.

1976. LORD NOLAN: Have you any ideas about how we are going to get the good news across as well as the best good news that we have?

JACK STRAW: By openness, is the answer, and, I think, by full disclosure of the fees that people receive. I have told you how much I receive from the Association of University Teachers and where it went. I have no objection personally to MPs publishing accounts relating to their work as MPs, so that all the money in and out is accounted for. It has nothing to do with their family finances, but their work as a Member of Parliament. If they happened to own a farm when they came into the House, that is different. It would relate to their operations as a Member of Parliament and things that arise from that. I think that the more openness there is, the more we can restore public confidence.

LORD NOLAN: A bit of what the Americans call "Government in the sunshine"?

JACK STRAW: If you say so, sir.

1977. ANNE WARBURTON: Mr Straw, you told us a great deal about your views and ideas on Quangos, but I still have two little questions I should like to put to you. First of all, political reality: you say for that reason that there should be declared political affiliations from members of Quangos. Does this imply, in your view, that the top posts might be liable to change on changes of government?

JACK STRAW: Are you talking about posts of Quangos or posts of senior officials?

ANNE WARBURTON: Yes. You are right. I am talking about public servants other than civil servants.

JACK STRAW: I would hope not. When we last went into government in 1974, there were very few changes in people running Quangos at a senior level, nor had there been in 1970, when the Conservatives went into government. It is important to put on record how much Lady Thatcher changed the climate with this "one of us" test, which preceded any test of merit. There will be pressure on some Ministers, if there is a Labour Government, to invite some members of Quangos to seek a career elsewhere, shall we say. In most cases, I think, there would be agreement about this. Before the last election, I talked to somebody—there is no need to mention his name—who is heavily involved in the education world, with whom I got on well personally, but there was a political difference. It was accepted by both of us that it would not be possible for him, given the position that he had held in the past, to carry on serving as confidential adviser to a Minister. We want political affiliations to be made known, but we do not want to see an American system where things are turned upside down every four or five years—or even every 16 years.

1978. ANNE WARBURTON: Thank you very much. My other question concerns local authorities. We have heard quite a lot from all sides really, about the relationship, or lack of relationship, between Quangos and local authorities and it seems to me perhaps it may be one of the most difficult things to solve. Have you ideas on how it could be solved?

JACK STRAW: I do. Again, it is something which many Conservative councillors now greatly regret and it is interesting that Dame Elizabeth Anson, who used to be Chairman of the Association of District Councils and may be known to some members of the Committee, herself made some very critical comments, which I have referred to in our evidence, about the use of Quangos. So people in Conservative local government are also rather hostile to what has happened. It is paragraph 52 of our written evidence and talking about Quangos says nobody knows who they are, they do not know to whom they are accountable and yet they are spending more money than the whole of local government put together. There is real bitterness in local government fields about the fact that people who serve on Quangos as a whole receive quite substantial fees whereas those in local government do not. That those in local government are subject to very tough rules of surcharge and disqualification whilst those in Quangos are not. There is also bitterness about access. How do you change it?

You change it partly by structural improvements so that you have a system by which councillors do serve on these Quangos and they are there as a right without being mandated.

Secondly, you send out a signal that you wish to involve them and I notice that when Mrs Bottomley issued her suggestions about who should serve on these local panels, there is no mention made that a local councillor might be appropriate when, in my judgment, a local councillor or two might be most appropriate drawn from each party. They would know who was, as it were, the local political establishment and who might be not only active party people but people who are active in public life in the area. In Blackburn, to use an example because I happen to know it best, the leader of the Labour group, the leader of the Conservative group, or the leader of the Liberal group, know all the people in public life in Blackburn and they would, together—and they would work co-operatively—make a very good panel for advising on these appointments. Why should they be excluded in this way?

The third point is that some local authorities have established arrangements—Harlow, Stevenage, Watford, Kirklees are four—by which they monitor the work of Quangos, particularly the health, training and employment. Harlow has produced a very good directory of Quangos in their area and what is interesting, because I have talked to people, is that on the whole the people

running the Quangos do not regard this as hostile. They actually regard it as very helpful in improving their accountability. We can certainly let you have further evidence about that if you wish.

ANNE WARBURTON: Thank you very much.

1979. LORD THOMSON: Can I explore briefly just a little further your thinking about the kind of rules that might be applied to Ministers leaving office and going into the private sector. The differences that there might be between these rules and those applied to civil servants. One of the major points in time when there are a lot of Ministers in this position, is of course at the time of a change of Government in a General Election. Would it in your view be appropriate, in these circumstances, that it should be the new Prime Minister who should adjudicate on it, just as it is the Prime Minister who deals with senior civil servants? Or would it be adequate that it should perhaps be the Advisory Committee that deals with civil servants but advises the Prime Minister, should be the final decision-making body?

JACK STRAW: Well I think that in practice the decision should be made by an advisory body. I say in practice, there may be a matter of some theory about who makes the final decision which perhaps Sir Clifford can advise, but I think it would be an unwise Prime Minister, coming into office in a new Administration, who sought, as it were de novo, to exercise control over the destination of Ministers, some of whom will certainly have lost their Ministerial position and may well have lost their seats as well. So I think you have to in practice.

1980. LORD THOMSON: You are also speculating, quite rightly, on how a timetable might be applied. In a change of Parliament and a change of Government, would it not be wholly appropriate that the timetable should be very different from inside a Parliament, the ongoing Government?

JACK STRAW: I think the different considerations would apply on a change of Government. Let us go back to base on this. The reason why there is this concern is because there is a sense that former Ministers may be making money out of their position as a former Minister. Or may be assisting their employer to make money, by using inside information; it boils down to that. I think the quarantine period should be measured against that test. It is a self-evident truth and if there is a change of Government the opportunities for influence, certainly in respect of privatisation plans, are going to be rather less.

1981. LORD THOMSON: Finally a slightly personal question relating to the past anyway, do you think redundant political advisers ought to have the same rules applied to them as civil servants?

JACK STRAW: Not necessarily the same but similar rules, yes, I do. Indeed, I am quite sure they should because of the very sensitive position which many are in.

LORD THOMSON: Thank you.

TOM KING: It is a great privilege to have somebody here who has such a long history of political experience and I think immortalised as the original special adviser on television.

JACK STRAW: So what is coming next Tom, after the flattery?

1982. TOM KING: Very good. I would just like to say this because obviously I have listened to what has been unashamedly, and you are entitled to make it, a party political presentation on behalf of the Labour Party of your position. That is what you sought to do, it has contained a considerable amount of smear and innuendo. It includes phrases such as the "suspicion of these arrangements", suggesting conspiracy taking place in Government or in a political party. "Suspicion of these arrangements" is now notorious and you have played a major part in helping to create that suspicion and I recognise that as a perfectly legitimate political campaign, however much I dislike it.

From the point of view of accuracy, you have used an interesting phrase about appointments to Quangos, in saying, what is happening now is quite intolerable, the phrase about "winner takes all". And I wondered if you could think of anybody, in recent times, who has held as many appointments as Chairman of the River Authority, Chairman of a passenger transport authority, member of two development corporations, Chairman of the Joint Regional Airport Committee and Chairman of the Police Authority. Can you think of anybody who has as many appointments as that, and do you think it helped the fact he was also a member of the Labour National Executive, that he got those appointments?

JACK STRAW: I will happily take your challenge, Tom, and I will come up with an answer.

1983. TOM KING: You made the point, you went back to Macmillan and Wilson and you said that standards now are quite different and there had never been the degree of preferment in previous times under these golden years and distinguished gentlemen that you identified now. I only make this point because I am not aware of anything beginning to equal the gentleman in question, you know to whom I am referring, I will not mention his name, but the amount of appointments that he had as a result of a Labour Administration.

JACK STRAW: First of all, on the smears and innuendo, I wholly reject that suggestion. We have put forward very careful studied evidence, which is based in turn on an enormous amount of evidence about the connection and the coincidences between donors to the Conservative Party, recipients of honours, membership of Quangos and those who end up as Government contractors, and I am happy to send further evidence on this but it is repeated in this pamphlet by Tony Wright, that television recently made reference to the fact that one of the large clearing banks had a very large number of its board members involved in Quangos whilst the co-operative bank had nobody. There are plenty of other examples as well.

It is interesting—it was not, as it were, we who started this—how much public attention there is now about the Quango state. This has arisen out of real concern. That is the first point I want to make.

Funnily enough, I do not know who you were talking to—I am trying to guess—but I take your word for it that this person exists. I am quite sure there are people of equivalent appointments.

I have never denied, and we do not deny in our evidence, that the Labour Government between 1974 and

1979, which I have most knowledge of, and the one before that, made appointments on the basis of people's political affiliations, and so did the previous Conservative Governments.

First of all I say two things, one is that these appointments were out in the open, it was known that they were political appointments, no pretence that they were not political appointments. Secondly, there was a considerable effort made to secure balance. Yes, on some of the Quangos a majority but it is usually a bare majority of people, would be for the Government Party. What you did not have, Tom, and what you have had now, is a clear out. It was not either the Heath Government, nor the Wilson or Callaghan Governments, which just removed altogether the right of local elected people to serve on health authorities. It was Ken Clarke and he was quite unashamed about why he was doing it; he wanted to get rid of Labour people.

1984. TOM KING: Can I just go on. What I mean by this sort of general smear or general allegation, whether it is substantiated. You made an interesting remark about the Further Education Funding Council and you made the comment that because, I believe, the Labour Party are opposed to the provisions—is this correct?

JACK STRAW: I was talking about the Funding Agency for Schools.

1985. TOM KING: Are you in favour of the work of the Further Education Funding Council?

JACK STRAW: I am in favour of the work of the Further Education Funding Council.

1986. TOM KING: Are Labour people willing to support?

JACK STRAW: Let me just explain that because I led for the Opposition on the Further Education Funding Council. We were not in favour of removing control over Further Education Funding from local authorities to the Further Education Funding Council and we voted against the Bill which I think was before the House in 1991, for what I thought were good reasons. I was a member of the governing body of Blackburn College, which is a further education college. We have sought to make the system work and as I reported earlier I was then appointed to what is, effectively, a Quango thereafter in, I think, 1992 and we have done our best to make the system work.

I have got lots of criticisms of the way the Further Education Funding Council operates, although I have very high regard for somebody I think you are going to take evidence from, William Stubbs, who is now the Chief Executive.

1987. TOM KING: I only make that point as it is interesting looking at this because they just happen to be going to give evidence after you. Looking at this—the Vice Chancellor of the University of Sunderland; the Principal of Newcastle College; the Senior Partner of Grant Thornton, Past President, Institute of Chartered Accountants; the President of the Royal Institution of Chartered Surveyors; two Principals of two colleges; Head of Croydon Continuing Education and Training Service; Principal of Exeter College, Devon, there are not any local government people in there—I get the feeling that is a pretty heavyweight lot, with an awful lot of experience in education and the point that Diana Warwick asked you, is the word merit sometimes missing from some of the recommendations you make?

JACK STRAW: No, the word merit is not missing. I think that, with Bill Stubbs, the Further Education Funding Council has probably made greater efforts than almost any other centralised Quango, to improve its accountability, and I am pleased to say that I have sometimes talked to Sir William about this and about how it should be done. That is the first point.

The second is that funding for Further Education is less intensely partisan than say of the Health Service and it is therefore understandable that the "are they one of us" test has been less rigorously applied to those people than it has been to many in the field of the Health Service.

The third point I would make, which is something you may want to take account of, is that the establishment of these Further Education Funding Councils has wholly changed the work of the governing bodies of Further Education colleges. Our agenda is determined, by the Further Education Funding Council which, in turn, is determined by the Department for Education.

Just to give you one example, again from Blackburn, and I think it illustrates the point very neatly, the College took into its estate an Adult Education and Community Centre called Four Lane Ends Centre in the north part of Blackburn and it serves adult education in that area; it has nothing directly to do with the mainstream work of the College. Because of the funding arrangements, the College Governors now feel obliged to sell this building—it is in need of repair—not in order to provide another building for similar service but in order to buy a different building in the centre of town to provide business education.

Now this is something I am arguing about with my colleagues on the governing body, but the whole politics of this would have been different had it been within the local authority field and we could have an open debate about it. So do not assume this is just about who is on these bodies, it is also about the environment in which they work.

1988. TOM KING: I make this point because it is very easy to make these assertions that because local authority people have come off, may be in certain areas the majority of them were Labour, that it has immediately been replaced in these bodies by a lot of Conservatives, and what has actually happened in many of these cases is that they have gone from people with range and experience, that can really benefit and basically have the capacity to take on the scale of task involved.

Are you actually suggesting—because I know it is not necessarily a party political point, is not very popular, as you made clear, that it is Conservative Councillors as well as Labour Councillors who like these positions as well—that you would reinstate local government representatives on the scale that they were present before on these bodies?

JACK STRAW: Yes, in principle I am suggesting it.

1989. TOM KING: You are going back to a system of local authority representation?

JACK STRAW: Mrs Beckett has been making this point during the passage of the Health Services Bill and I think it would be a good thing, and it would be a good thing for your party Tom, as well as ours for all sorts of reasons.

I believe in "representative democracy". I think that if you take something as central to people's lives as the running of the Health Service, which is a national service but it is locally administered and on which there is a great deal of local discussion, it is of crucial importance that people should have confidence in the way it is being run at a local level and they should hear people speaking up for them.

The point I make about my experience as a member of a Further Education governing body is that when you change the systems and personality, it not only involves an exclusion of locally elected people but it also involves a change in the role of the people administering these services. If you take the members of health authorities, whereas before they saw themselves, as it were, representatives of Blackburn to the Minister, now they see themselves as representatives of the Minister to Blackburn.

LORD NOLAN: I am very sorry to interrupt. It is always bad luck coming last but we are running heavily into overtime.

TOM KING: I know my Lord Chairman, but as you know the main thrust of this is a criticism of Conservative conduct in Government and I am sure you will allow me time to ask the questions.

LORD NOLAN: Yes, indeed, I think you have put that point very clearly to Mr Straw.

1990. TOM KING: Thank you. Can I then move on to the point about the "bedpan" story. When you talk about the Secretary of State and being answerable and accountable, who is the Secretary of State. Obviously it is not for example Secretary of State for Health, Virginia Bottomley on her own, but it is Virginia Bottomley with sufficient officials, advisers, civil servants, to enable her to discharge whatever accountability and responsibility is deemed appropriate under the system.

Now one of the benefits that have been about some of the delegation of authority, the Next Steps Agencies, is some reduction in staff centrally. Now if you go back to what I understand you are suggesting, you are advocating the rebuilding of a very substantial staff of civil servants and officials, who will have to discharge that. It is not a question obviously of a single Minister, you know this from your own time working within Government. But it will be the scale of staff involved to be able to discharge that sort of accountability.

JACK STRAW: No. Tom, you are making assumptions about what I said which I do not think I reflected in my evidence. I did not say that we had plans "holus bolus" to turn the Agency system upside down because frankly, if we do go into Government there will be enough to do without pulling up all the plants by the roots to see whether they are still growing.

My personal view about Agencies is that it depends on their function. I think there is very little argument that it is sensible to put the passport service into an Agency, or the issues of vehicle licences, because it is a very clear administrative task, without any political discretion involved and you can set those people targets and let them get on with it, and then judge them by it. But let me say also, no Government has ever been brought down by delays in issuing passports.

If you come to an area, a key operation of Government, for example the Prisons, or Child Support, I think very different considerations apply and they apply to Ministers as well. It was very interesting, the rows at Christmas about the Prison Service. When Mr West was found hanged in his cell, Michael Howard's initial reaction was to leave this matter to the Director-General of the Prison Service. Then there was one riot at Everthorpe and again he left it—this was I think on the Monday or Tuesday after the New Year—to Mr Derek Lewis. The moment there were two riots and then an escape, Mr Michael Howard assumed operational responsibility for what was happening in the Prison Service, because that reflected a political reality.

TOM KING: The point I am making is there has to be a balance.

JACK STRAW: Yes, of course.

1991. TOM KING: May I just ask you as a last point because you referred in your paper to me inquiring into the relationship between trade unions and the Labour Party?

JACK STRAW: Yes.

TOM KING: I was not doing that, I was inquiring into the relationship between trade unions and individual Members of Parliament and that is a different matter. You have rightly said and the phrase you use, raising this issue about advice and advocacy and the difference between them, and when somebody stands up and speaks, you ought to know, "is it his own judgment"—this is the phrase you use, I wrote it down—or "is it because he's paid?".

Now, Diana Warwick, at the very start of the exchange, very properly declared the fact that you worked together before because you were I think paid, you declared here today the amount of money that you got, for being sponsored, or working as advising the AUT. And you were doing that while I believe you were shadow spokesman for Education. And that is the issue that I think does raise very real issues for us. We have had trade union leaders sitting here, telling us that they actually pay Members of Parliament an annual sum and for that they expect Members of Parliament to table Parliamentary questions for them. Now that was given in evidence here to this Committee. And the issue I really raise, others have suggested on this Committee, do you think that money might more appropriately be given to the Labour Party, as opposed to being given to individual Members because does it not lay you open? And it was said also that the Shadow Health team are actually paid a substantial sum, a much bigger sum than you receive, from COHSE, as a Health Service union, and if they come into Government they will do so in the knowledge that they will receive, in the years of Opposition, a very substantial amount of money from one union who has a very direct interest in what is happening in the Health Service. Do you think that that is an arrangement that probably does need to be reconsidered?

LORD NOLAN: Now Mr Straw, before you answer Mr King, he said that is his last point and I am afraid we must, because we have got a lot of important evidence to get through, make this your last answer. You and he will, of course, have other opportunities elsewhere to pursue these matters.

JACK STRAW: Yes, let me make it clear I have never personally profited from the modest sum I have received from the Association of University Teachers, nor from my sponsorship by the General Municipal Boilermakers' Union, nor from the fact that UNISON pays for research assistants for me, all of which are declared. There is a crucial difference it seems to me, first of all between people who make personal profit and add to their own income and those of us in the Shadow Cabinet who have to, because of the inadequacy of funding of Shadow Cabinet members, seek whatever income we can to fund our offices.

Now, in principle, Tom, I think you are right to say that it would be better if the money was paid to the Labour Party and then re-allocated; that would be a better system. I also say—I do not wish to finish on a partisan note but some may judge that I am—that if members of the Shadow Cabinet simply received the same money that members of the Cabinet receive for their political advisers, we would not have to seek funding of our offices in the way that we do.

LORD NOLAN: Thank you very much. You have been very helpful and we have detained you for a lot longer than we expected to. We are most grateful to you as all of our witnesses.

JACK STRAW: Thank you very much indeed.

1992. LORD NOLAN: And now we are very happy and particularly grateful to see Mr Robert Gunn and Mr William Stubbs. I am afraid we do have a regrettable tendency, however hard we try, to overshoot a little and although, of course, one must never exclude the introduction of a party political element, I am afraid it has led us this morning to run late. So let us begin without more ado. Have you prepared an opening statement which you wanted to make before going into the questions?

ROBERT GUNN AND SIR WILLIAM STUBBS

ROBERT GUNN (Chairman, Further Education Funding Council): Yes I have.

LORD NOLAN: Would you be kind enough to give it to us.

ROBERT GUNN: May I start by thanking the Committee for its invitation to contribute to its work. You will note from the written material which we have given to your secretariat that the Council attaches importance to the question of accountability, and to assuring those with an interest in its work that its procedures and practices are open and fair.

It may assist your Committee to note that the Council is an executive body whose major responsibility is the distribution of almost £3 billion of public money. In so far as it considers policy questions, these are matters of policy relating principally to the operation of its funding and securing the provision of effective facilities for further education in England. Its concern is to operate in a way which supports its main purposes and which gains the confidence of the sector and the public.

Throughout its relatively brief existence, the Council has sought to apply high standards to its work. However, there can be no complacency and the Council has recently published a circular setting out proposals formalising its existing arrangements for the conduct of its business, and taking these further. Copies of this are with your secretariat. It may be helpful if I comment briefly on the themes in the document.

The first theme relates to accountability. While the Council accepts responsibility towards the public, it does not for the most part deliver services direct to individuals. The main relationship between individuals, especially students, and further education is at the local college level. The Council's responsibilities are to Parliament, the Secretary of State and to colleges. In relation to the public, its responsibilities are mainly to do with assuring the public that it is properly exercising the duties given to it by Parliament.

The second theme is how the Council conducts it business. In my involvement with the Council I have been impressed by the high standards of conduct of both its members and its staff. I have received no evidence of any concern about the integrity of the Council, its members, or its staff. But, as I have just outlined, the Council does wish to ensure that it has taken all suitable steps to satisfy the public about its conduct of business. Accordingly, in the circular I have referred to, there is raised the conduct of both the Council as a whole and the individual members of the Council. We are proposing a public register of interests and published rules on the declarations of interest. This register is intended to give reassurance that Council members and senior staff do indeed separate their private interests and public duties. While no system can guarantee honesty, such arrangements will put considerable pressure on Council members to operate with due regard to propriety.

The third theme of the circular refers to openness. This is in some ways a difficult issue to deal with. Arrangements must balance the public interest with the efficient despatch of business. The Council has proposed arrangements which, in its judgement, strike such a balance.

We are proposing arrangements for providing access to information which the Council holds. We are intending to make available, publicly, minutes of Council meetings in addition to the bulletins which are already published and circulated widely after each meeting. We are also proposing arrangements whereby institutions may complain about our decisions and seek an independent review of possible maladministration through arrangements similar to those provided by the ombudsman in other parts of the public service. We are also suggesting that there would be benefit in a mechanism whereby those with questions about any aspect of the Council's work may have an opportunity to have those questions answered publicly, without necessarily having to disclose their identity.

Chairman, that sets the scene against which we have addressed the two specific questions which your Committee addressed to us: that of how to achieve high standards of conduct and appointments to bodies such as the Council.

We have already provided you with information about how we believe high standards can be achieved in bodies such as the FEFC. What we would wish to bring to your attention this morning are two specific aspects of conduct on which your Committee may have a view. The first raises the question of whether there should be some external means of scrutinising compliance with any code of conduct which a public body has put in place? The Council has not come to any answer to this question, but is aware of the view that the confidence of the public might be increased further if such an arrangement were to be put in place. The second question relates to the arrangements which the Council has in place to deal with the arrangements for seeking Council business from firms in which a Council member has an interest. The Committee may have views on whether the FEFC's arrangements are sufficient in this area.

On the question of appointments to the Council, Parliament gave responsibility to the Secretary of State. We have in the list of key points, which we provided to you, commented from our experience as to how this arrangement has worked.

Thank you, Chairman, that is all I would wish to say at the outset, and both the chief executive of the Council and I will be pleased to answer any questions from your Committee.

LORD NOLAN: Thank you very much. That statement does help us to focus the questions we would like to ask. I am going to ask Sir William Utting to begin please.

1993. WILLIAM UTTING: Thank you, Chairman. Mr Gunn you said that the Council spends nearly £3 billion of public money. Could you say just a little more about the kind of organisation it is and the tasks that it has to perform?

ROBERT GUNN: The Council has headquarters in Nottingham and has nine regional offices. It was set up under the 1992 Further and Higher Education Act and our duties are described within that Act, in the main.

We have, in addition to the normal administrative and finance staff in the Council, a very substantial inspectorate which we have set up from scratch. There are in all about 70 full-time inspectors and several hundred part-time inspectors, all of whom have had to be trained.

Each college is inspected fully every four years and a document is published giving the results of that inspection.

1994. WILLIAM UTTING: And you said there are 457 colleges in all for which you are responsible?

ROBERT GUNN: 457.

1995. WILLIAM UTTING: And technically you are a Non Departmental Public Body?

ROBERT GUNN: Yes we are.

1996. WILLIAM UTTING: You referred in the note you gave us to the fact that both you and Sir William had previously been members of the Polytechnics and Colleges Funding Council?

ROBERT GUNN: Yes.

1997. WILLIAM UTTING: Was that the predecessor body to your FEFC?

ROBERT GUNN: No. The FEFC deals with Further Education and as I say was set up in 1992, when the Colleges were about to become independent co-operations, which they did on 1st April 1993. Now some years before, in 1988 to be precise, the Polytechnic Colleges became independent, but these are Higher Education institutions.

WILLIAM UTTING: Yes.

ROBERT GUNN: And the Polytechnics have now become the new Universities and the Polytechnics and Colleges Funding Council ceased when it was amalgamated with the Universities Funding Council to become the Higher Education Funding Council, on which I actually served for a couple of years as well.

1998. WILLIAM UTTING: As we heard in previous evidence it sounds as though your Council was actually taking over some responsibilities previously discharged by local authorities and there is a degree of sensitivity on that score.

ROBERT GUNN: That is absolutely right. All these Colleges were within the power of the Local Education Authority before.

1999. WILLIAM UTTING. Good. Thank you. You provided us with a very helpful note of main points of evidence and I wanted to look at arrangements for appointing members of Council in particular, and take up a couple of issues there. But, first of all, could I ask how potential members are actually identified and recruited and whether you and Sir William play a part in that process?

ROBERT GUNN: In the setting up of the Council itself you mean?

WILLIAM UTTING: In the identification of members of the Council.

ROBERT GUNN: The responsibility for appointing the members of the Council is with the Secretary of State.

WILLIAM UTTING: Quite.

ROBERT GUNN: The Department for Education therefore identify potential nominees for that Council. They did consult with Sir William and myself about what the membership should consist of and what the balance should be on that Council. And we were very anxious, although it is defined that there should be educationalists and also people from business and commerce etc, that we had a very broad Council base and we suggested that we would like to have from business, for example, representatives of finance and accountancy, personnel, property and one other which escapes me at the moment.

WILLIAM STUBBS (Chief Executive, Further Education Funding Council): The adult education.

ROBERT GUNN: The adult education side. But we also wish to have a balance of different types of college

principal because the sector is very diverse. It has very small colleges, very large colleges, it has sixth form colleges, further education colleges, agricultural and horticultural colleges etc, so that we wanted to ensure that we had a proper balance of principals from further education, from sixth forms, adult education etc. We also wished to have the regional spread of where people came from because they are delivering the education in the different regions. We also wish to have a balance of men and women and we would have preferred to have a balance of ethnic minorities etc.

But these were all considerations that we decided, in the first place in collaboration with the Department, of what the balance of the Council should be. It was therefore very important that when these people were being appointed we did not just look at them solely as individuals but also what they would contribute to the balance, and I think we actually succeeded very well. We have had a very successful first two years.

2000. WILLIAM UTTING: Have you played a significant part in establishing the balance of membership as well as in the appointment of individuals?

ROBERT GUNN: Yes. Either Sir William or myself were present at the interviews which took place in the Department of the potential members of the Council.

2001. WILLIAM UTTING: It is what you have to say about the balance of the Council that attracted my particular interest because in your note to us you said there is also a public expectation that the Secretary of State will have regard to the appropriate balance between men and women, different parts of the country, desirability of including persons from ethnic minorities—I would myself add to that, and disabled people, but I am absolutely delighted to see this in there. I take it that the Secretary of State wholly accepts that this public expectation is legitimate and you have the support of the Secretary of State in making these appointments.

ROBERT GUNN: Yes.

WILLIAM UTTING: The other interesting thing is that you go on to say that in making appointments it is the overall composition of the Council that counts. You are looking for that as a body to represent all the interests and strengths that you need?

ROBERT GUNN: Yes.

2002. WILLIAM UTTING: You are not looking to clone one particular type of person, or one particular collection of attributes around 14 or 15 people?

ROBERT GUNN: No.

2003. WILLIAM UTTING: In a sense you are implying that issues like gender, regionalism, whether or not one is from an ethnic minority, these are issues to be considered in the context of merit for the job?

ROBERT GUNN: Absolutely.

2004. WILLIAM UTTING: Thank you very much. Could I move on to this extremely interesting consultative circular you have issued to your constituency, and could I just ask, since this is a consultative circular, if, so to speak, it has been trailed in front of the Secretary of State and the Department for Education before it has gone out?

WILLIAM STUBBS: Thank you Chairman. It would be part of our normal business, when bringing forward matters of major consultation with the sector, to share that with civil servants in the Department and that we did in this case.

2005. WILLIAM UTTING: Again, delighted to hear it because there is a radical and progressive element to this document but one is delighted to hear that it is tolerated and perhaps positively encouraged by the Department for Education.

There is one point in it that I wanted to bring up particularly and that is that at various points and also in your Draft Code of Corporate Responsibility, you emphasised responsibility to the public as well as to the Secretary of State and Parliament. Would you say something more about how that kind of general responsibility to the public is going to be discharged? You have mentioned, for example, these arrangements you propose for access to information on the part of the public. Are there other ways in which you are going to discharge this general accountability?

ROBERT GUNN: I think that we believe that "openness" is really the solution to a lot of the problems of Quangos and if we can be as open as we possibly can then we believe that the public has every opportunity to find out what we are about, and I have to disagree with one point that Jack Straw made, I think people know who we are. We publish an annual report, that gives the full accounts, it gives the distributions that we make to colleges, all the cash we give to colleges, that is all published. We give the names of all the people on our Advisory Committees as well as the Council itself. So I think we are being as open as we can be.

We are proposing in the document, as you can see, that we are intending going rather further than that but I think that we are trying, by being as open as possible, to help the public understand what we are about.

2006. WILLIAM UTTING: And you are proposing quite open systems for dealing with complaints and possibly an independent review of maladministration.

One final area in this document. I note that your proposed register of interests requires very extensive declaration on the part of people connected with your Council. Extending to the interests of spouses, partners, close family and including relevant unpaid interests. I think that goes a bit further than many of the suggestions that have been made to us about declaration of interests in other areas and I wondered why you went as far as you have gone in those proposals.

ROBERT GUNN: Again I think we want to be as open as we can be. I do not think it is enough to have declaration of your own interests if your family interests are being affected. I think it is very much better if we are quite clear as to what the interests of spouses are as well. There has been a suggestion made to us, in terms of gifts for example, the way round the code of practice is to make sure that it is always your wife that gets the gift, and I think we would certainly not wish to be accused of anything like that, but

we did discuss this at great length in the Council. Perhaps you would like to add to that?

WILLIAM STUBBS: The main thrust Chairman is the Council wishes to see its constituency so to speak having confidence in it, and if by concealing such information that confidence was weakened, then the Council would be concerned. The members certainly felt they were content with these arrangements. So it was not something that caused much difficulty.

2007. WILLIAM UTTING: So the public interest requires departing from what one might call conventional ideas about the privacy of one's own interests and one's own business?

ROBERT GUNN: Well it is mainly paid employment. It is only we have said relevant non-paid employment. You do not have to declare every interest you have got.

WILLIAM UTTING: Thank you very much. Thank you Chairman.

2008. DIANA WARWICK: May I first of all compliment you on the comprehensive and clear circular that you are sending round to your constituents and I would like to ask you two questions: one is to follow up Sir William's point about the declaration. Given that the main area of concern that has been expressed to us about quangos generally has been political appointments to quangos, for political favours effectively, is one of the things you expect, or would like to see declared, where there is a business appointment to a quango or to your non-departmental public body, where a firm has made a political contribution?

ROBERT GUNN: The appointed council member, you mean—his firm has made a political contribution?

DIANA WARWICK: Yes.

ROBERT GUNN: His firm is bound to have made a declaration in their annual accounts if they made a political donation, are they not?

2009. DIANA WARWICK: But would that be known? I am getting really at the point that was made about the number of political appointments that have been made to quangos. Would you expect that to be declared?

ROBERT GUNN: I would have no difficulty with that. I would just make the point that in my time on the Polytechnic and Colleges Funding Council, Higher Education Council and now the Further Education Funding Council I have never been asked once what my political affiliation is. I have no doubt that somebody may guess or may have drawn a conclusion but I have never been asked and I have certainly never said what it is. I was Chairman of a company for a number of years—I was a director for fifteen—and that company never made any political donations at all, because we felt it was inappropriate to do so. So I don't think in my particular case that there has been any suggestion that it is because I am a contributor to the Conservative Party. In fact I would go so far as to say that the person who asked me to take the job on was Kenneth Clarke, whom I knew as a local MP, but also with whom we did battle many a time when he was at the Ministry of Health.

2010. DIANA WARWICK: But your view is that declaration through annual reports is perfectly adequate in these circumstances?

ROBERT GUNN: Yes.

2011. DIANA WARWICK: Could I ask you a very different question? You have emphasised openness in the Further Education Funding Council's decisions and the code of practice which you are recommending is about the operation of the council. But there are criticisms of secrecy and lack of openness in the governing bodies of further education and indeed other educational institutions, and I wonder, in the light of events, for example at Wilmorten in Derby, whether your council has any duty to scrutinise the structure and codes of practice of the institutions you fund?

ROBERT GUNN: I seem to be doing all the talking. I will let Sir William answer in a moment, but if I can just start by saying that these colleges are independent corporations and we are there to ensure that they spend public money satisfactorily and for the purpose for which the money is provided. It is not up to us to run these colleges or to tell them how they should run their own affairs. We have welcomed the fact that they are, many of them, producing their own codes of practice and their associations are also consulting on that matter. We have issued guidance where we think it would be helpful and in fact we have issued a Guide to Governors, which is a quite substantial document, giving them advice on how we think they ought to operate. Nevertheless we don't believe we can go further than that—they are independent corporations.

2012. DIANA WARWICK: Could I then ask who does have the duty—if they are independent who has a duty to scrutinise the appointments to Boards of Governors of colleges? I just don't know.

ROBERT GUNN: They themselves.

DIANA WARWICK: Right.

WILLIAM STUBBS: If I may add to that, Chairman, there is an Instrument of Government for each college that has been approved by the Secretary of State and it will have within it a framework specifying categories of membership and it is within that that the governors must act.

DIANA WARWICK: Thank you.

2013. LORD THOMSON: Could I just follow that up briefly? Since we keep saying that we are dealing with problems of perception as well as of reality, would it not in fact be prudent to have some form of scrutiny of the nature of the appointments that go to the governing bodies of the institutions for which you are responsible? A central register, or some kind of survey of it?

ROBERT GUNN: The governing bodies of the colleges, you mean?

LORD THOMSON: Yes.

ROBERT GUNN: I don't think we can take any action on that. I don't think that it is within our sphere of competence.

2014. LORD THOMSON: Would you not then perhaps feel that there may be problems of perception, that at the end of the day you may quite unfairly be blamed for?

ROBERT GUNN: Yes, I think that is absolutely true, but I do think that—you have mentioned Wilmorten and the Birmingham College—the fact that we were able to act reasonably quickly in these two cases and to advise the Secretary of State that there had been mismanagement in both and that the governors should be removed I think is an indication that if there is serious mismanagement we can act and advise the Secretary of State accordingly.

2015. LORD THOMSON: What sort of duty do you have in relation to the financial administration of the institutes that come under the central Funding Council?

ROBERT GUNN: May I ask the accounting officer to answer that?

WILLIAM STUBBS: Thank you, Chairman. That is the first responsibility—that as chief executive of the Council I have been designated accounting officer and therefore responsible for the funds voted by Parliament and the Council itself and its relationship in financial terms with the individual colleges are scrutinised by the National Audit Office. Indeed, they are our external auditors. And, indeed, within the last month I have published a report on the Council's work so we certainly feel open to scrutiny in terms of how we use the money voted by Parliament. So we are responsible for that to the Public Accounts Committee.

2016. LORD THOMSON: You will have noticed, I am sure, that the Public Accounts Committee has, in fact, been dealing with a case relating to your former body, the Higher Eduction Funding Council—or it was part of your former body—and there there has been criticism, has there not, that the Higher Education Funding Council failed to keep a check on university spending in a particular case? I am not asking you, nor are we commenting on a particular case, but are you reasonably sure that with the statutory provisions and the duties that are laid on, you would give your reasonable hope of avoiding that kind of situation?

WILLIAM STUBBS: That is a question, Chairman, to which the giving of a completely satisfactory answer might lead one into difficulty in the fullness of time as colleges develop, but at the present state the Council—I as accounting officer and, indeed, the National Audit Officer—are satisfied that the arrangements put in place will be sufficient to stand up to the tests of time. We have over 450 colleges, they are independent, they will choose their own destiny in slightly different ways, but Parliament, I think, can be satisfied that the arrangements for looking after its money are under close scrutiny. You mentioned before while speaking about confidence in the membership of the governing body of colleges—it may help you to know that there is a requirement in each governing body that it shall publish its membership, make known those, and also publish the minutes of each meeting of the governing body of each college. That is within the Articles of Government of every college.

LORD THOMSON: Thank you very much.

2017. ANNE WARBURTON: Could I follow up a little on the National Audit Office? You told us in your papers that it is your external auditor. First of all I would say that works well, does it, as far as you are concerned? And do they also audit all the bodies which you fund?

WILLIAM STUBBS: No, Chairman, it is the responsibility of each governing body to appoint its own internal and external auditor. The Council, for its part, has given them detailed advice as to how they might go about that, including the appointment within each governing body of an audit committee.

2018. ANNE WARBURTON: So the National Audit Office is not in a position to keep you informed of audits made elsewhere?

WILLIAM STUBBS: It itself can look at and examine the accounts and the books and the papers of each college—it has the opportunity to do that—but it itself is not the external auditor of each college. For one body that would be a very large task.

2019. ANNE WARBURTON: And would it come back to you if it found something it was worried about?

WILLIAM STUBBS: Oh, yes, yes.

2020. ANNE WARBURTON: Could I then ask—it looks at value for money as well as strict financial questions. You say in one of the papers—perhaps it was in your remarks, Mr. Gunn—that one of the questions you hope perhaps we will be able to advise on is what form of monitoring of code of conduct, for example, would eventually be the best. Would you see the NAO in that sort of role—potentially, I mean?

ROBERT GUNN: It is one possibility. I think there are a number of ways of overseeing a code of conduct but, of course, it is very difficult to audit a code of conduct if people are not declaring an interest for example. It is very difficult to find that out. I think it is the sanction at the end of the day when it becomes known that they have not declared an interest that is much more likely to have an effect. I think an auditor is one way of looking at the matter. But I think there are others that could be investigations by the Department for Education, for example. We have not actually considered it fully yet.

ANNE WARBURTON: So you would not want to go on down the line? Thank you very much.

2021. LORD NOLAN: I wonder if I could ask you a question in the same area? You say in paragraph 7 of your opening note this morning:

"We are also proposing arrangements whereby institutions may complain about our decisions and seek an independent review of possible maladministration through arrangements similar to those provided by the ombudsman in other parts of the public service...."

—and the ombudsman idea, if I may say so, seems to be helpful as we have found—as others found—in many areas. You continue:

"We are also suggesting that there would be benefit in a mechanism whereby those with questions about any aspect of the Council's work may have an opportunity to have those questions answered publicly, without having to disclose their identity."

Have you carried that any further?

ROBERT GUNN: No, it is part of our consultation.

LORD NOLAN: Yes. It is obviously a very sensitive one and, again, it has been suggested in a number of areas and, again, one knows in some areas, like ChildLine, undoubtedly it resulted in an enormous amount of upheaval and dismay and no doubt some totally unfounded accusations but equally led to a great many genuine cases ———

ROBERT GUNN: I think that is one of the dangers and that is what we are interested to hear from people about.

LORD NOLAN: Yes. Thank you very much, that is all I wanted to ask. Peter?

2022. PETER SHORE: The two examples, or the two instances that you mentioned, were they Wilmorten College and St. Philip's?

WILLIAM STUBBS: Yes.

PETER SHORE: I am right about that. What were the principal defects, as it were, in the administration of these two bodies which was taken up by the Minister?

WILLIAM STUBBS: Complaints were being made about the running of both colleges—different types of complaints—occasionally to the Funding Council but more frequently latterly to the Secretary of State, and as a result of that the Secretary of State asked the Council to investigate, the Council appointed an independent investigator in each case and gave them facilities to carry out an investigation. They published a report and the findings of those separate reports are on the public record. In the case of St. Philip's there were a number of matters that caused concern but perhaps the most common one was the inability of the governors, or some of the governors, to leave the executive of the college to assume its own responsibilities and encroach too heavily into the detailed day to day running of the college. There were other matters but that was one. That was largely peculiar to St. Philip's.

In the case of Derby Wilmorten the matter there was that the proper conduct of the governing body's business, particularly with respect to the declaration of personal interests, had not been properly adhered to. But, again, there were other matters causing concern as well.

2023. PETER SHORE: Who brought the complaints into the public domain?

WILLIAM STUBBS: In the case of Derby Wilmorten the members of staff of the college and to a lesser extent members of the community. In the case of St. Philip's it was, I believe, largely members of staff of the colleges. But it may also have been some members of the community as well.

2024. PETER SHORE: And in the first instance those complaints came to your Council?

WILLIAM STUBBS: In the instance of both colleges complaints came to our Council and then also started to come to the attention of the Secretary of State.

2025. PETER SHORE: Yes, thank you. You have told us really that you are limited to giving guidance to colleges, so they are basically, these 457 colleges, self-governing, both in terms of the composition of their managing boards and in terms of the rewards that are paid to the people on the boards?

WILLIAM STUBBS: Yes, that is true, except that in addition to the guidance we give them on certain matters we have a financial memorandum with each college between the college and the Council and we can put into that financial memorandum conditions attached to the money which we give to them, and one of these conditions in the financial memorandum is that they must declare what their senior staff are paid and that must be published in their annual accounts. That was not the case with the Higher Education Funding Council at the time.

2026. PETER SHORE: So this is really an indirect way in which you can hope to discipline at least the rewards paid to employed staff?

WILLIAM STUBBS: Yes. Can I just make clear for the record that it is not open to a governing body to pay a salary to a member of the governing body itself. The governing body may reimburse them for their expenses incurred, for example, but may not pay them a salary or make any other form of similar payment. That is within the requirements laid down by the Secretary of State.

2027. PETER SHORE: Yes. What is your impression of the general direction of rewards and salaries since the Funding Council was set up and since the colleges themselves ceased to be part of local government and became independent?

WILLIAM STUBBS: We have no detailed or systematic collection of information that would enable me to give a reliable answer to that question. Any impression I have—and the Chairman—would be from the reports we see in the Press from time to time.

2028. PETER SHORE: Thank you for that. My last area of questioning—unusually you have added to your paper you submitted to us an actual list of the members of the F.E.F.C. and, again, even more unusually it is possible to identify the political connections of at least two of the Council members. Well, now, there are, apart from yourselves as Chairman and Chief Executive, twelve members on the board. Two of those members appear to be (1) an ex-Conservative MP and (2) a current Conservative Birmingham Councillor. Has the appointment of these two Councillors been critically referred to in your knowledge and can you say that the same criteria for appointment were applied to them and no political element entered into it as was applied to the other members of the F.E.F.C?

ROBERT GUNN: I think that would be very difficult for me to answer because in the final event, after we had interviewed various candidates, the nominations were in the hands of the Secretary of State and we don't quite know exactly at the end of the day how he made his final choice.

PETER SHORE: Yes.

WILLIAM STUBBS: For the record, those two members you referred to were also invited to take part

and did take part in interviews as for the other members, in other words with a Minister in the Department, with a deputy or senior civil servant and with either the Chairman or myself, before going to the Secretary of State for decision.

PETER SHORE: Thank you.

2029. CLIFFORD BOULTON: Just very quickly —how many days a year normally does the ordinary Council member put into this work?

ROBERT GUNN: We have eight or nine Council meetings a year plus a strategy meeting, which is an overnight meeting. But in addition to that some of the Council members serve on committees, for example I chair the Reorganisations Committee and that meets about every six weeks, for example. It varies form member to member depending on which committee they are on.

2030. CLIFFORD BOULTON: And there is remuneration, is there, for serving on the Council?

ROBERT GUNN: There is a flat honorarium of £4,000 a year.

CLIFFORD BOULTON: Thank you very much.

LORD NOLAN: Well, thank you both very much indeed for coming along and for giving us clear and helpful advice. We are most grateful to you.

ROBERT GUNN: Thank you.

2031. LORD NOLAN: Now, gentlemen, I have to say not so much "Good morning" as "Good afternoon" and I am very sorry indeed that we are starting twenty minutes late. We, for our part, will willingly go as long over 1 o'clock as is needed for you to say what you want to say. I only hope that we are not putting you to great inconvenience by this twenty minute late start.

LEIF MILLS, JOHN MONKS AND DAVID LEA (TUC)

LEIF MILLS (President, TUC): No problem.

LORD NOLAN: Thank you very much. Now, is Mr. Leif Mills the President, Mr. John Monks the General Secretary and the third member of the party?

DAVID LEA (Assistant General Secretary, TUC): David Lea, Assistant General Secretary.

2032. LORD NOLAN: Thank you very much. I believe that both you, Mr. Mills, and you, Mr. Monks, have prepared short opening statements which you would like to make. Would you like to do that straight away, please?

LEIF MILLS: Thank you, Lord Nolan. We welcome the opportunity to give oral evidence. You will have received our written evidence. I think it is fair to say, as well as being true to say, that the TUC in the United Kingdom and the trade union movement generally is the largest and most representative non-governmental organisation in the country. And as you and your colleagues will know the TUC is also the oldest trade union centre in the world and it is a voluntary organisation. We have a very direct interest in the work of the Committee and its impact upon our members and upon the society in which we operate. And so we welcome the opportunity. We have, of course, a very difficult role in many ways in trying to balance different interests across society, but we reckon we do that in the fairest and best manner.

My own trade union, Chairman, just as an example, which is in the Financial Sector, is now not untypical of a trade union which is not affiliated to the Labour Party, we do not have a political fund but we do have many people active who are involved in work outside their sector employment, whether they are on local councils or on the wider stage. You might be interested to know that my own union, as an example, does make a financial contribution to two Members of Parliament and also two members of the European Parliament, one from the governing party in the case of the House of Commons and one from the main opposition party, and I would be very pleased to amplify that if necessary.

I think, Chairman, it would be true to say—and it is certainly our view—that one political party has been in power in the UK for a very long time and, whatever view one takes of politicians, it is also I think true to say that the party in power has perhaps been insufficiently tested by effective opposition parties for at least some of the period during which it has been in power. That inevitably leads, in our view, to a certain arrogance that Government can in essence get away with anything. And over a period the lack of effective opposition I think has contributed to that arrogance. What is most regrettable from our point of view is that the concept of consensus, or even to use what is now regarded as an old-fashioned concept but still very true in our view, the "One Nation" concept, seems to have become anathema to a number of people. Now, obviously politics are adversarial by their very nature but it seems to us that in a whole range of public life there is less respect and less account taken of the other point of view.

We see that there has been in recent years a systematic centralisation of power and what were the traditional checks and balances in a healthy democratic society have been eroded. Just as an example, a combination of capping of local authority expenditure, a reduction in the local tax base and restrictions upon the way local authorities can operate perhaps have contributed to that.

In our written submission we do outline a number of particular causes of concern. There has been, Chairman, in our view a decline in the standards of managing public finances. We are concerned at the growing award of contracts to the private sector for consultancy and tasks that were once performed and regarded as part and parcel of the job in the public sector and operated by a public sector ethos are now shipped out to consultants. The presumption of that is that it is cheaper and more efficient to do so, but there is little evidence of that.

Secondly, we have seen the growth and abuse of patronage and I understand that rightly one of the subjects of your committee is the growth of the quasi non-governmental organisations. We see there that the old pluralistic approach of appointing people onto these bodies is becoming a thing of the past and it has been replaced by what we would call in shorthand the "cult of the businessman", as if the businessman is the only person who is qualified to play a part in what are important organisations. Also there has been a rapid movement of Government Ministers onto the boards of companies with whom they had dealings as Ministers and that does raise

the question in the eyes of our members about what favours are expected in return for such movement.

There is also, in our view, a threat to the traditional impartiality of civil servants as a party in power for so long begins to blur the difference between the interests of the party and the interests of the State. Now, we are concerned as trade unionists by these changes for a number of reasons. I mean, one of them is that our affiliated unions represent many of those in the public sector who have been most affected. But more importantly trade unions collectively represent those who on their own have virtually no influence or power. We are a collective organisation of voluntary people to represent their interests and obviously our sphere of activity is the work place but political decisions have a great impact on our membership.

We want to see the UK society take account of the interests of the majority of citizens who do depend on effective regulation, high quality public services and the rule of law, and any weakening of democracy which we have detected—well, not really detected because it has been fairly obvious in recent years—gives more power to those who exercise existing power in an unaccountable manner for their own benefit rather than in the public interest.

We have referred to those items, Chairman, in our written submission but very very briefly in a couple of minutes, what can we do? The General Secretary of the TUC will make a number of detailed points and some broader points after I have just finished.

First we believe that Members of Parliament should declare all the gifts, payments and earnings they received and there should be sanctions for those who do not do so. Clearly the existing voluntary system of self-regulation is insufficient.

Secondly, Members of the House of Lords should also be covered by a Register of Interests. Like councillors they should not be able to vote on issues where they have a direct influence or involvement.

Thirdly, lobbyists should have to register as they do in the United States of America and declare all their clients.

Fourthly, there should be an increase in the office support for Members of Parliament and the Register of Interests of Members' staff should also be made public.

The legal rules that apply to trade unions about political involvement should also apply to companies. There seems an extraordinary asymmetry between the way in which trade unions are dealt with and the way in which companies are dealt with. For example, we believe that shareholder approval should be secured from the appropriate company before political donations can be made and, indeed, as trade unionists have the right to opt out of the political levy where it exists, so shareholders should have the right to opt out of political donations. It seems to us that the balance of fairness is very much against the trade union movement. And there should be, as the Houghton Committee recommended, a modest degree of state aid to political parties.

The same rules that apply to civil servants when they leave the public service and apply for jobs in the private sector should also apply to those former Ministers.

You have already received, Chairman, the evidence from the Council of Civil Service Unions—their emphasis on the code of ethics. We very much support those at the TUC and indeed approve of their proposals.

That, in essence, is the summary of what we wanted to say, Chairman, but I know that the General Secretary of the TUC would like to make some additional points. Thank you.

LORD NOLAN: Yes, please, Mr. Monks.

JOHN MONKS: (General Secretary, TUC) If I may, Lord Nolan, just briefly add really one particular, what I regard as a central point, and that is: what is the essence of the debate that the Committee is dealing with and your establishment, in a sense, has acted as the catalyst for? It is not just about the contention that politicians' standards are in question, nor is it just about the relationship between Ministers and civil servants and it is not just about the lack of balance in recent years in appointments to quangos.

Important though all of these issues certainly are, certainly the more I have thought about it in preparation for today the more I am struck by the parallels from the last century, which led to the emergence of a strong, independent public service and a distinctive ethos of public service which has stood this country very well over many years. By that standpoint, under those rules, every financial opportunity that comes the way of an individual is not exploited, the ethos of self-interest is subjugated to the common interest and it has been a great strength of British public life and it is still a great strength of British public life in very many areas and I think in a sense the challenge to the Committee is to rehabilitate the concept of Public Service.

I use it in a very broad sense. I include in it people giving up their time at a very local level to be school governors, without remuneration. People who sit on the myriad of advisory committees of all sorts, again, often without remuneration. I mean people who take part in public life at every level, because they want to put something back into the society and into the community.

I think this rehabilitation of the concept of Public Service lies at the roots and the base of rehabilitation of politics and recent events have done it some damage. We would like to see a broader understanding of this—looking back to the Fulton Committee. We argued then for the creation of a National College for the public services, broader than the Civil Service College, which would involve industry and unions and others in it and in terms of rebuilding a concept of public service which would span the community we still think there is considerable merit in that idea.

On quangos, an area which for certainly the war—for instance since the Second World War the TUC has been a major part of many of the quangos in the employment, economic and industrial field—we believe that balance of political and industrial representation is vital for confidence that these are impartial bodies and bodies which have got some scope for genuine independence. We still have on our files correspondence going back to Mr. Attlee and Sir Vincent Tewson—we have got successive Prime Ministers—and my predecessors about the procedures governing different types of public bodies and boards on which trade unionists should sit and would be invited to sit and the procedures which would be adopted.

Now, those procedures stood the test of time for many years—not without some criticism, but no one doubted at that time that employers were there in equal numbers and that other interests were properly represented. No one doubted that you needed political balance to produce a sense of common purpose, some common standards and agreed actions. All the stakeholders were represented and worked together on strategy formulation and implementation. That has not been the case with the Training and Enterprise Councils, for example, and it has not been the case with the NHS Trusts. There are other examples that I could quote as well. I hope we can get back to the older concepts and, to put it another way, that the forces of integration in society should command public support and that we ensure that we help each other to achieve that process.

That is the broader canvas for the Committee, Lord Nolan, that I believe you need to paint your picture on. It is rebuilding the concept of public service and the ethos, as I say, which has stood and which stands this country well, but which is in need of rehabilitation.

LORD NOLAN: Thank you both very much. You may have noticed that both in the foreword and in the final chapter of our paper on Issues and Questions we did touch on the broader picture. We have a passage called Common Threads at the end and you will have noticed, too, that the working method we have adopted—because you have to start somewhere—is to single out three particular areas of concern. Work rather as the common law does on individual cases of concern and then see what you can build up from that and that is what we have been doing. But your broader canvas, if I may say so, speaking for myself, certainly has a very wide appeal and we shall consider it carefully. Now to more detailed questions may I ask Sir Clifford Boulton to take over?

2033. CLIFFORD BOULTON: Thank you very much. I would like to concentrate on the specific aspects of your paper but could I just first ask you in general terms how bad the situation is in your view and what is it in particular that is the anxiety because obviously however grubby the bath water is we don't want to throw the baby out with it and we do want to make sure that we don't cause damage by over-reacting unnecessarily in areas which maybe require more ability for public scrutiny than actually providing examples of actual corruption. I mean, it was said rather unkindly that

"The British had an empire on which the sun never set because God couldn't trust us in the dark"

and it could be that your attitude is that you don't trust the establishment in the dark and what you are really wanting to see is more light in dark places. Now, if we were able to switch the light on how much really deep damage would we find—would we find lots of corruption, would we find the whole thing was rotten? You did say at the beginning of your paper perhaps we had been set up too late to do much good. How bad is it?

LEIF MILLS: There are a number of mixed metaphors, if I may say so, in that! I don't think that Britain as a country, the United Kingdom, is wallowing in a sea of corruption at all and we don't seek to make that point, but we do make a very serious point that it seems that the standards of public service, and the expectation of people as to what that public service should provide, has declined and I think the perception of people is that public service is just a job, if they can do well out of it personally, so be it. The standard of Members of Parliament I don't suppose has ever been terribly high, even looking back three hundred years, as you know, and I know there is always a temptation as you get older to think that things are not as good as they were when you were younger. But there is no doubt that in the minds of our people, if you look at the degree of public expenditure that is now controlled by non-Governmental organisations, i.e. the quangos, the appointment of people who determine the allocation of that expenditure on the quangos, the political background or the political interest they represent, and if you look at the concept of the individual and that the individual must make progress—and the examples of pay awards of Captains of Industry is an obvious example of that—I think there is growing disillusion that there is something wrong somewhere. Not that corruption is endemic but the attitude to public service, the attitude to honesty and openness, has declined substantially. As I say an obvious example is a disbursement of what is, what, £55 billion by quangos now—42,000 jobs on quangos? I think one of the Government Ministers, Baroness Denton said in evidence, I think, to the Treasury Committee, she had "never appointed a Labour Party member to her knowledge on any of those quangos". I think the Chairman of the Conservative Party used rather more colourful language, saying he was "not going to stuff such bodies full of socialists". I don't think that attitude towards what is in a sense in essence and what should be worthwhile accountable open duties on behalf of society—I don't think those attitudes do anything else than reflect the obsession with individual greed, personal advancement and to hell with public service.

2034. CLIFFORD BOULTON: And is there any one principal thing that we could do to turn this round?

LEIF MILLS: Yes, I think one of the things is the actual method of appointment to quangos, who determines them, what are the criteria, are they selected, appointed and who does that? I mean, that is one example. There is, of course, the wider example of the actual number of quangos that there are and the powers that they have. I recall as I am sure that you do, Sir Clifford, in 1979 the political party which then became the Government launched a big campaign about "how dreadful to have all these quangos, there were far too many of them, we are going to get rid of them" and, of course, there has been a quantum leap in their number and the amount of public expenditure they are responsible for. So I think as one example it is the method of appointment of people who are responsible for disbursing what is a huge slice of public money and the accountability of those people.

2035. CLIFFORD BOULTON: You do very fairly say that there is a proper role for quangos and one can be over-simplistic by calling all these bodies quangos anyway—they all have different kinds of role. But when we talk about the nomination and the make-up of the quangos sometimes it is felt that nominated members who come from identified groups end up appearing to be mandated by the body that recommended them and that they cease to be individuals and operate as individuals, that it does not make towards a happy co-operative team if you are getting members nominated from interest groups. Do you think that there could be a problem about that?

LEIF MILLS: Theoretically there could be, yes, of course, but in practical terms I think there is very little evidence of this. Just to take an example, ever since 1946 the Bank of England had a trade union person on the Court of Directors. Now that person did not go armed with congress policies and motions but that person was put on by Government at that time ever since 1946 until a year ago to express views from the constituency from whence he came—perhaps views that would not be immediately available to the other members of the Court of Directors. That worked well. He was not a delegate, he was not a representative—he was a person with a background. Now, for reasons which I find quite extraordinary the current Government have decided that they will not continue with that. It is not what the Bank of England wanted but it is the Government for some peculiar reason. I think you can look at any number of organisations which did have trade unionists involved—they were not delegates, they were people from a background and from a constituency who could speak with a different experience.

2036. CLIFFORD BOULTON: On the methods of appointment—again they would have to be many and various because the range is enormous—but there are some appointments which are actually made by Ministers and required to be made by Ministers by statute. You do refer to those in your paper and you say

"Where Ministerial appointment is appropriate such appointment should be subject to approval and review by a relevant House of Commons Select Committee".

How far do you want the Select Committee to get involved in this before the appointments are actually made? I mean, most of the Select Committee work consists of judging the actions of the Minister rather than sharing responsibility for them. You are not suggesting these committees should get into the business of actually sharing responsibility for making appointments, are you?

JOHN MONKS: No, we are saying that they should scrutinise what Ministers do in a more purposeful way than perhaps they do at the moment.

2037. CLIFFORD BOULTON: But within their terms of reference, what you are saying is you would like to see it done more often and so it would be more light cast on effectively making the Secretary of State explain to somebody why he made that appointment?

JOHN MONKS: Quite correct, yes.

2038. CLIFFORD BOULTON: Do you have any other specific further down the line ways of increasing accountability and openness in these appointments? Do you have any specific suggestions of advertising, or whatever it might be that you——

JOHN MONKS: Well, if I may, President, just say that we have noted some of the changes that have been introduced and in effect I suspect prompted by your appointment in some areas of Government and I think our primary concern is with balance and of harnessing people with stakes in particular areas behind programmes of common purpose. I am not against advertising these positions but it does look a little cosmetic against the present political background and the way the Government have certainly treated the trade union constituency pretty consistently over the last fifteen years.

I don't think there would be too many trade unionists who applied who would have very high hopes of actually being appointed, having answered an advert in the *Times* or *Sunday Times* or whatever it might be.

2039. CLIFFORD BOULTON: So you think really that there ought to be areas where the Government would feel that, as a matter of practice, they always ask for nominations or let it be known that appointments are coming up and be a bit more active in seeking nominations.

JOHN MONKS: Yes, there still are and I do not want to overstate the case to the extent to say there are not any. I serve on the Council of the Advisory Conciliation Arbitration Service as an example, but the number of areas where the tripartism still reigns in the industrial field has shrunk markedly, and the number of areas where business men and women have filled virtually all the seats on particular organisations has increased markedly and I think that is wrong. I look for a balance of representation of those with a stake in a particular area.

2040. CLIFFORD BOULTON: Can I just switch to the Civil Service now and the Government's acceptance of the Treasury and Civil Service Committee's recommendations for a code of conduct with certain amendments. Do you have any comments about that? Are you pleased about this code of conduct. Do you generally approve it?

JOHN MONKS: We certainly think it is a welcome step in the right direction and, again, it is one of these areas where we certainly acknowledge the contribution the Nolan Committee has already made. I think the Government's ready acceptance of that report was prompted by public concern and by the committee's work. Our particular concern at the moment is to try and prompt the discussions between the employees of the Government and the Civil Service in particular who have some concerns about the proposals of the proposed code with the Government. We are seeking through the Council of Civil Service Unions to see some talks take place about the final details of that, but in general terms we welcome the proposals and we think they are a considerable step forward. A bit late, but a step forward.

2041. CLIFFORD BOULTON: What about the situation for local government staffs? Are they in need of a code both as to regulate their own conduct and/or conduct of those who employ them?

JOHN MONKS: Many authorities do have codes and we note the very active work of the Audit Commission in the local authority sector, and the role of the district auditor and so on. Yes, certainly, we would support the view really that large organisations should have codes governing the conduct of managers and employees in terms of levels of conduct, so local government is a very major employer, a great deal of public money involved and it certainly should have the highest standards.

2042. CLIFFORD BOULTON: You pointed to some of the dangers of outside contractors being brought in to areas of expenditure at all levels, but that has been very strongly in local levels hasn't it?

JOHN MONKS: Yes.

2043. CLIFFORD BOULTON: Is that something that is different in kind? Does it need more control or a new

kind of supervision to allay public anxiety? One of the things that was actually mentioned almost in passing in evidence some time back was anxieties that have arisen in local government employees setting up their own companies to do business with contractors, or as contractors, and that there have been some anxieties about conduct in that area. Is there anything specific you wanted to say about that?

LEIF MILLS: I think there is some anxiety. As I understand it the policy of hiving off some of the functions, or some of the work, to the private sector is because there is this assumption that the private sector is good, the public sector is inefficient. Lord Nolan's Committee will be well aware there are examples of inefficiency in some of the local authorities. There are examples of some mismanagement I am sure, there is bound to be in any human organisation, but we would strongly question whether the financial control of a lot of functions which are hived off from local authorities is sufficient. If I could just take it slightly wider, one of the things we are very interested in as a trade union movement are the Training and Enterprise Councils. Some of them are good, some of them are well run, some are very poorly run, one has gone bust. Without being silly about it, the chairman of that Training and Enterprise Council is the chairman of a major management consultancy firm in the United Kingdom. I think there is a bit of difference between theory and practice. So certainly, yes, there should be tighter control.

CLIFFORD BOULTON: There should be some machinery in operation to keep an eye on these things.

LEIF MILLS: Correct.

CLIFFORD BOULTON: It just needs sharpening up.

LEIF MILLS: Not sharpening up. If you take the Training and Enterprise Council, there are 82 of them in England and Wales, there are 22 local enterprise companies in Scotland, they are nominally responsible to the employment department. When I say "nominally" I do not mean that in any pejorative sense, but although there is some degree of control one must question why it happened that one of them was allowed to go bankrupt without knowledge or awareness. It touches on a slightly wider area for you, Chairman, about who was responsible for governmental policy in terms of training anyway, but we would say that is an example of where you can get a wide variety of efficiencies and inefficiencies and no real necessary public authority that can control it.

2044. CLIFFORD BOULTON: Can I just shift briefly to members' interests. You mentioned that your own union has two Members that it has a relationship with and in fact it was in page 4 of the document. You talk about consultancies which some unions have with Members. You say——

"When payment is made it is considerably less that what appears to be the current market rate".

You do not pay the going rate but you are not making a merit out of this. That is the housemaid's baby excuse, isn't it. I mean, you are not making a merit of the fact that you do not pay them startling sums. The principle of it you are saying is that you do not see anything intrinsically harmful in having such a relationship. Presumably the terms and expectations of it are right and everybody knows what is involved. Would you have any objection to actually having a written understanding with the Members that you have this relationship with and for that being published so that everybody could see what it amounted to?

LEIF MILLS: I think that would be a very good idea. For example, in our own particular case—there is absolutely no secret about it because we publish the details in our own annual report that goes throughout my organisation—we pay the princely sum of £850 a year to one Conservative MP, one Labour MP, we do the same for the two members of the European Parliament, and I know that the two Members of Parliament declare this in the Register in the House of Commons. We find it useful. I think they find it useful to keep in touch with a particular part of the economic industrial scene. It is perfectly open. We have had this system for 20 years and we think it works well. I think if it were laid down that there should be something on the lines you suggest, Sir Clifford, that would be fine.

2045. CLIFFORD BOULTON: Presumably it is a two-way flow of information. They give you ideas of what is cooking and what is relevant to your interests, and you in turn draw their attention to things that are going on in the world of your union that you feel as parliamentarians they would usefully know.

LEIF MILLS: Absolutely. For example, we had a lobby of Parliament of our disabled members to lobby for improved facilities for disabled people. Both our MPs were very helpful in actually arranging the lobby, and I think some of the examples we were able to give about lack of facilities for disabled people in the financial sector was of news to them and obviously of interest.

2046. CLIFFORD BOULTON: When the Disabled Persons Bill came up, and if one of those Members had got up and said "I happen to know through my contact, which is well-known and registered and I declare it, that there are particular problems in this industry and I think the House ought to be aware of them and they are very relevant to this Bill" you would not be shocked by the fact that they had spoken even though they had a financial interest?

LEIF MILLS: Not at all because everybody would know what their interest is, that is the point. But equally, Sir Clifford, it is not part and parcel of our scenario to say that because we pay this princely sum to them they must do as we ask them to do. That would be quite wrong.

2047. CLIFFORD BOULTON: Yes, but this is a very significant area of our examination of what is called "paid advocacy" because I think we all accept that no Member should accept an instruction as to how he should vote or how he should speak. The idea that he should be silent because he has the kind of interest we are talking about is equally problematical because should a Member ever undertake anything that shuts him up in the House. I was just interested in the distinction that we are making between advocacy which is acceptable and that which is not.

LEIF MILLS: Yes, there is a distinction. There was a debate in the House of Lords a few years ago about the report of the Monopolies Commission on the supply of beer, a matter in which I have a personal interest, and I was absolutely amazed at the number of Members of the House of Lords who got up and said they had better declare that they were a director of a brewing company. There seemed to be more directors of brewing companies in the House of Lords than anything else. Perfectly proper that they should express their interests and express a view. What would be absolutely wrong, and I do not think in that case there was an example, is if the person who paid them the retainer or paid them the non-executive director's fees said, right, you will vote in this appropriate way. That would be entirely improper.

CLIFFORD BOULTON: Just as it is for a union to tell its sponsored Members how they are to vote.

LEIF MILLS: Absolutely. I entirely agree.

2048. CLIFFORD BOULTON: It is irksome for you to have sponsorship equated with consultancies because I know no money goes into the Member's pocket, but you do not see anything intrinsically wrong with sponsorship so long as there is, again, absolutely no obligation placed on the Member who is sponsored to do anything in particular.

LEIF MILLS: Correct.

2049. PETER SHORE: In your evidence of the TUC, Mr Mills, when you reach the recommendations you start off by saying——

"We share the concern of the growing number of consultancies and other sources of income acquired by MPs".

There certainly has been a growth, but do you feel that the concerns that you have expressed there can be simply met by fuller disclosure of information about sources of pay and consultancies?

JOHN MONKS: We certainly think that is the main way and we are conscious, in a sense, of the role of Parliament in all this as well. We think that at the end of the day you will make proposals. Parliament, we hope, will accept those proposals and that transparency will be the central theme of what is going on. In a way it is a bit like top executive pay, a different issue but one in the news at the moment, that the oxygen of publicity is perhaps the biggest check of the lot on what is going on, and exposing some things to public gaze is perhaps the best regulatory authority of the lot.

2050. PETER SHORE: May I point out that there has been a Register of Members' Interests now for some years, and although amounts are not stated certainly the interests which are being represented—a Member of Parliament having a consultancy with a firm or with a PR firm—that is generally stated, but that apparently has not been sufficient either to allay public anxieties about standards of conduct or, in fact, to greatly discipline conduct itself.

LEIF MILLS: Yes, I think one of the reasons, and I think you touched on it, Mr Shore, it is generally stated, there are examples where it is not stated, and it is not revealed to the extent of the sponsorship involved. I am quite sure that in a number of these consultancies there are vast sums of money, but equally there is unease and there is anxiety about sums of money being paid which in some cases only a few are not declared and be amounts which could be quite considerable.

2051. PETER SHORE: Sums of money do not necessarily affect the principle of the thing as we have already heard, but they do obviously affect, or are likely to affect, the conduct of Members. Do you think that amounts should be declared then as part of the Register of Interests?

JOHN MONKS: Yes.

LEIF MILLS: Yes, certainly and amounts not just for the Members of Parliament but I think equally those, as we put in our evidence, of their wives or husbands and children should be declared as well. There have been cases apparently of people trading on the name of their parents in order to get arrangements with consultancy companies, and I think that is quite wrong.

2052. PETER SHORE: Thank you for that. Do you think there are not some activities which are peculiarly open to Members of Parliament that should not be curtailed because they are in receipt of large sums of money in consultancies? For example, do you think it is all right for an MP who is being paid a substantial sum by a big firm to be present on a Standing Committee and able to move amendments to a bill? All right, he would have declared his interest, but would you feel that that was an action in Parliament which really went beyond what was acceptable?

JOHN MONKS: I personally would not think that was unacceptable. I am drawing a parallel, say, from the union side that if there was a sponsored MP from the Engineering Union and there was a bill about shipbuilding or something going through, I would not like to think that that person was muzzled in some way from perhaps bringing their particular expertise and their perspective to bear on what was going on. I think it would be equally true for a company, but the important thing is that everybody should know in a sense where that person is coming from as is stated I know when interventions are made now, but I think adding in the amount is an important extra ingredient.

2053. PETER SHORE: Your acceptance of a Member's freedom of action who is sponsored by a particular firm would extend presumably to access to Ministers, arranging private meetings with Ministers?

JOHN MONKS: Yes.

2054. PETER SHORE: Thank you very much. Can I just switch now to quangos. I thought the phrase "the cult of the businessman" was a very vivid one in describing obviously one of the great themes that have been formed, decisions as to appointments of quangos in recent years. Clearly you are in favour of an additional element of representativeness of the community being taken account of on boards, and that would include presumably local councillors as well as trade unionists?

LEIF MILLS: Correct.

2055. PETER SHORE: Say the issue of representativeness had been satisfied, as for the remaining members of the quango appointment do you feel that there should be some independent element apart from the Minister's own judgment helping to determine who should be appointed to those other seats on the quango board?

LEIF MILLS: It is a very interesting point if I may say so. I understand, Lord Nolan, that on Thursday you have

the Chairman of the Monopolies and Mergers Commission coming here and he would explain to you how that happens. My understanding of the position is that if they come across somebody who they think might be suitable for the task they can advise the Secretary of State. Equally, other organisations should have the right to feed in, should have which they do not. For example, on the MMC there is no formal contact with the TUC about who they should be. As it happens there are a small number of trade unions on it, in fact two at the moment, possibly three, and when I was on it there were four of us, but that was not formal it was partly accidental. Unless I have got you wrong, Mr Shore, if apart from the Secretary of State and the organisation itself there should be some third body, it is an interesting point but I do not know who that third body could be because the issue then would be who appoints the third body, wouldn't it?

2056. PETER SHORE: Indeed. It could be perhaps something like a public appointments unit, not quite like the thing we have today but something with some influence.

LEIF MILLS: That is an interesting point, yes, and I think certainly worthy of consideration.

2057. LORD NOLAN: Just one question. Would you distinguish in the matter of acceptable consultancies between the kind that you yourself are concerned with, that is to say an open engagement of two Members of Parliament on the one hand and on the other hand consultancies with a firm of professional lobbyists, or multiple consultancies—one Member acting like a gun for hire and taking on a large number of consultancies for different people? Is there a line to be drawn there?

LEIF MILLS: I think it is a wavy line actually, Chairman, that is the problem. As we put in our written evidence, all lobbyists should be declared above board, we should know who they are, what their interests are, and I understand that is the situation in the United States. Certainly over there it does not stop the growth of lobbyists; it is a big growth industry, as you know, but at least it appears to be fairly open. I think our concern about consultancies is tied up with several other points we have made. To take an entirely hypothetical example, if somebody was a lobbyist for a defense company, then became a Minister, officially severed his connection with that defense company, then ceased to be a Minister and then got a job back with the defense company for which he had been previously lobbying, I think that somehow is wrong. How you stop that is very difficult. You have to have open declaration and all the rest of it, and you also have to have a period of time between when a Minister can do that, sort of jumping out of Parliament straight into bed with a company.

LORD NOLAN: That is a rather separate issue though, isn't it?

LEIF MILLS: Indeed it is.

LORD NOLAN: I was more concerned with whether there was a distinction to be made between one type of consultancy and another. I think your answer is, well it is a very difficult distinction.

LEIF MILLS: It is very difficult.

2058. ANNE WARBURTON: In your first recommendation there are two little points I would like to ask about. First, you distinguish between peers and Members of the House of Commons as to voting on matters where they have a direct interest. I do not want to take you into a long discussion but I just wondered why.

DAVID LEA: I think we probably had in mind the hereditary element and some of the issues that come up to do with fishing rights or something like that. There seem to be a very direct interest in the House of Lords in many of these examples, and I think that is the sort of example we had in mind.

2059. ANNE WARBURTON: But in the House of Commons you would not think that Members needed to be kept back from voting?

DAVID LEA: I think that was the distinction we had in mind.

LEIF MILLS: It is the hereditary point in a sense.

2060. ANNE WARBURTON: I see. Then you say that you do not think that self-regulation of Members' interests in the House of Commons has been a success. Have you gone beyond that to think what would be a better form of regulation?

LEIF MILLS: What we have said, Dame Anne, is that there should be some sanction to ensure that the declaration of interests is fully complied with. There have been cases, as you would know, of some Members of Parliament proudly proclaiming they will never fill in the Register. I think it should be filled in, we covered the point earlier about the amounts of money involved.

2061. ANNE WARBURTON: Are you meaning that there should be statutes on this point, or are you thinking that there should be some agency, some element, outside Parliament which has a role in ensuring compliance?

LEIF MILLS: We are not going to suggest that we should have a quango to look at quangos, the whole thing becomes terribly incestuous. I suppose the short answer is, yes, there would have to be some statutory basis for that, but who does the statutory implementation is a different question.

2062. ANNE WARBURTON: The other thing I have been interested to hear about is in Mr Monks' statement, a reference to your testimony to the Fulton Committee on the National College for Public Services and also for industry and trade unions. I just wondered, as I do not know whether I could find that, if it is easy for you to get at the testimony you have put in I would be interested what has really developed.

JOHN MONKS: We would be happy to send that in.

ANNE WARBURTON: Thank you.

2063. LORD THOMSON: I suppose we are a quango to look at quangos. Could you help us either now or

maybe with a note afterwards by giving us any sort of order of magnitude of the drop in the number of appointments that trade union people are faced with in terms of voluntary service on various public service bodies?

LEIF MILLS: Certainly.

LORD THOMSON: It would be very helpful.

2064. DIANA WARWICK: It has been said to us in relation to support by unions of MPs that really the time has come perhaps for unions to make straightforward donations to the party either at local level or at national level. I wonder if I might direct my attention at Mr Mills. Do you think that ordinary trade union members would welcome that, and would it be appropriate for those substantial numbers of unions who are not affiliated to a political party?

LEIF MILLS: No I do not think it would be helpful, in my view it would be wrong.

2065. DIANA WARWICK: So you stick very much with your idea that it should at least be an option for unions to make a donation to an individual MP?

LEIF MILLS: It is up to them. Providing that they have the authority under their own constitution and organisation, providing they tell everybody about it, and provided that the MP concerned tells everybody about it, that is up to them.

2066. DIANA WARWICK: Could I ask you in relation to declaration of payment of monies received by MPs, do you include all income in that? I think Jack Straw drew a distinction immediately before you to money which might be earned from an occupation not connected with Parliament. Do you think such a distinction can be drawn and, indeed, do you think it should be drawn in such a declaration?

JOHN MONKS: We do think a distinction can be drawn. I know there are distinctions. In practice you can see particular people are earning a living which has absolutely nothing to do with their parliamentary interests, but there is also quite a grey area in between the two as well. I think an open disclosure is the only way in a sense to build confidence and allay some of the suspicions that are around at the moment.

2067. DIANA WARWICK: Do you think that would include things like journalism or writing of political thrillers?

JOHN MONKS: I think so, yes.

LEIF MILLS: Absolutely. The two are the same, aren't they? [Laughter]

LORD NOLAN: On that uncontroversial note, thank you all very much for giving us so much of your time and your trouble with these written papers, we are very grateful to you.

WEDNESDAY 22 FEBRUARY 1995

Members Present:

The Rt. Hon. The Lord Nolan (Chairman)

Sir Clifford Boulton GCB

Sir Martin Jacomb

Professor Anthony King

The Rt. Hon. Tom King CH MP

The Rt. Hon. Peter Shore MP

The Rt. Hon. The Lord Thomson of Monifieth KT DL

Sir William Utting CB

Dame Anne Warburton DCVO CMG

Diana Warwick

Witnesses:

Robert MacLennan MP, President, Liberal Democrat Party

Professor Jack Mahoney, Professor of Business Ethics and Social Responsibility, London Business School

Dafydd Wigley MP, President, Plaid Cymru

Rt. Hon. The Lord Howe of Aberavon

2068. LORD NOLAN: Today is our second last day of oral evidence. I am glad to say that for it we shall have, when Mr Tom King joins us, a full turnout of the Committee. We look forward to hearing from three politicians of different parties and from a distinguished academic. Our second witness, Professor Jack Mahoney, is Professor of Business Ethics and Social Responsibility at the London Business School. He has been at the forefront of the development of business ethics in the United Kingdom. He is also a Jesuit priest.

Dafydd Wigley is the Plaid Cymru president and Member of Parliament for Caernarfon. He is interested in Quangos in Wales and has also submitted to us the written guidelines for Plaid Cymru MPs' Standards of Service.

Lord Howe of Aberavon is former Deputy Prime Minister, Leader of the House, Chancellor of the Exchequer, Foreign Secretary, Minister for Consumer Affairs and Solicitor General. As our final senior Conservative witness, no one could be more experienced across the whole range of our work than Lord Howe.

But first we welcome Mr Robert MacLennan MP, who will give evidence on behalf of the Liberal Democrat party. Mr MacLennan is of course a parliamentarian of great experience and authority and, as well, is a former party leader. Mr MacLennan, welcome, and thank you very much for coming along. Is it right that you have an opening statement that you would like to make?

ROBERT MACLENNAN MP

ROBERT MacLENNAN MP (President, Liberal Democrat Party): Thank you, Chairman. I am grateful to the Committee for inviting me here today to give oral evidence on behalf of the Liberal Democrats. I am the elected President of the party and also spokesman on constitutional reform.

Members will be aware of written evidence submitted earlier this week, which will form the basis of my remarks this morning.

We have set our recommendations in the context of views about constitutional reform which we hold, but which we recognise go beyond the scope of your remit. Although we advocate constitutional reform, and believe that among the reasons for its justification is the need to raise the standard of conduct in public life and provide effective checks and balances within the system,

nonetheless the recommendations which we make to you stand on their own merits and are not contingent upon the implementation of these wider measures.

Liberal Democrats welcome this inquiry, as do all those who value the democratic tradition in this country.

The corruption of any system of government is always a disfigurement of its ideals, but in a democracy the injury is doubly wounding. In a system such as ours, the corrupt politician or public servant diminishes not only himself, but the trust upon which his position—and ultimately democracy itself—depends.

Our current position in this country is a curious one. Public concern about falling standards in public life is reflected in opinion polls which indicate the low esteem in which politicians are generally held. Numerous exposés daily confirm these impressions. Yet voter turnout has increased in each of the last three general elections. Unlike the United States, therefore, disaffection with politicians has not yet translated itself in this country into disengagement from democracy itself. That time is yet to come. Only firm action now can avoid it.

If it were possible to abolish corruption with a stroke of a pen, it would have been done many centuries ago. Furthermore, corrupt people do not distinguish between professions. It is for professions to discriminate against corruption. Malpractice is, therefore, always possible. What matters is how difficult it is made.

The pure self-regulation of Parliament which has pertained for several centuries functions by making individual Members the guardians of their own conscience. What guidelines there are tend to be obscure and imprecise. No guidelines or sanctions can ever stand in the way of the determined offender. But the disagreements that currently exist between politicians themselves over what is, and is not, ethical behaviour suggest to us that in many cases the offender may not know he has stepped over the line until someone calls him out.

The lines of good behaviour therefore now need to be drawn. They should be interpreted and policed independently of Parliament itself.

The central recommendation which our submission makes to the Committee is the establishment by statute of an independent Standing Commission on Public Ethics. It would be to good behaviour in public life what the National Audit Office is to good accounting. This body would have the duty of overseeing the development and implementation of ethical codes for all public bodies and roles. In respect of Parliament, this Commission would supplement, rather than replace, self-regulation. It would act, in other words, as the public's guarantor.

In one respect only do we consider this an insufficient means of establishing a known and respected ethical standard, sufficiently monitored. That is the question of bribery of Members of Parliament. It is not, in our view, enough to leave bribery—which in all other circumstances is a criminal or civil offence -within the remit of regulation alone. As the law currently stands, a man may, with legal impunity, bribe a Member of Parliament to vote against a particular piece of legislation which he finds onerous, and the Member may accept. Yet if the same man successfully bribed a policeman not to charge him with an offence under the same law, both are liable to a prison sentence. The bribery of politicians offends against everything democracy is supposed to achieve, which is rule by popular consent, not by private money. It is rightly a matter for the criminal courts, and we recommend to the Committee that it be made so.

I also wish to draw the attention of the Committee to our recommendations on the disclosure of Members' interests. Common sense dictates that openness is the best protection against malpractice, but it can also serve positively to enhance public faith in their Members of Parliament if it is properly done. The present register does not meet that standard. It is opaque, the facts revealed being often too imprecise.

For example, a Member who declares that he is paid by a commercial lobbyist, which serves any number of different interests, has given, in some sense, less information than a Member who declares a consultancy for a manufacturing company which has only its own corporate interest to look after. In the latter case, at least the interest which the Member of Parliament is serving can be known from the declaration. In the former, the interest is not revealed. We would wish to see the rules on declaration amended to ensure that more precise and useful information is given which allows the public to determine what work was done, for whom and for what reward.

Where we may appear radical, it is because we consider the problem deep; where we are moderate, the problem slight. But we have proposed only what we consider to be the minimum changes necessary to ensure the maintenance of the highest standards in public life.

LORD NOLAN: Thank you very much. If I may say so, that was admirably clear and succinct. As you know, I think, we take it in turn to have the first chance to ask questions. This morning it is Professor King's turn. I will ask him to take up the questioning, please.

2069. PROF. ANTHONY KING: Your party's evidence is very wide-ranging and I shall ask you only about some parts of it. Could we start by talking about MPs and their outside interests? At one point you say on behalf of the Liberal Democrats,

"We are particularly concerned, as is the public, about the extent to which Members may surrender their independent judgment as a result of being paid as advocates or lobbyists for particular organisations."

When I read that sentence, I expected your evidence to go on to say that certain restrictions should be placed on MPs acting as paid advocates or lobbyists. That in fact was not the line that the Liberal Democrats' evidence took. I was rather surprised by that. Could you explain why you did not take that line?

ROBERT MacLENNAN: Yes. As we say in the next sentence,

"We are unable to see a clear distinction between a Member offering advice as a consultant to such organisations and acting as an advocate for their interests, nor are we able to draw a clear line between a Member offering his or her services as a consultant to an organisation with many clients and offering services to a single interest.".

My judgment is that there are very, very fine lines to be drawn between advocacy and advice. The experience I have had as a consultant to a particular company, of counsel to an American law firm for nine years, as someone who was approached by one of the leading firms of accountants to act as a spokesperson in Parliament, have given me a clear view that those who employ MPs in these roles do not themselves draw a clear distinction between the functions. It may be that on some occasions one is asked to offer straightforward legal advice; certainly that has been true in my case. It may be that one is asked to advise about the climate of political opinion, or what is coming down the pipe in the way of proposed amendments to the law. It may be that one is asked, either on behalf of a particular client or in the general, wider interest of the firm of accountants or lawyers, to recommend that a particular change in the law that is being proposed should be resisted. One may be asked to resist it oneself or asked how most effectively it could be resisted by others. I think in those circumstances it is clear that it is very difficult to draw a line between advocacy and advice.

2070. PROF. ANTHONY KING: Although it is difficult to draw the line, all of us are in the business most of the time of drawing difficult lines. On the face if it, it would not seem impossible, even if there were some cases that straddled the borderline, between examples of giving advice—you have just give a whole long list of them—on the one hand and on the other hand speaking in Parliament, asking Parliamentary Questions, seeking access to Ministers, organising entertainment at the House of Commons on behalf of the organisation, and so on. It is a difficult line to draw, but is it impossible? Is it so difficult to draw that one should not even think of drawing it?

ROBERT MacLENNAN: I am not really sure that there is any great point in seeking to draw the line. What is of public importance is that it should be known that the MP is engaged in offering services to particular clients for money and that the nature of the advice or advocacy can be recorded. That is why a core recommendation we make is that codes—in particular, that for MPs—should require the nature of the service provided to be stated specifically, so that if it were in the form of arranging Ministerial meetings, tabling questions, arranging hospitality or offering general advice, that would be known. I see no particular advantage in seeking to make it more complex for MPs to seek to decide precisely what role they are playing, whether it falls on one or other side of a line which, in my judgment, could very easily be blurred.

2071. PROF. ANTHONY KING: Could I ask you therefore about the second of the two sentences,

"nor are we able to draw a clear line between a Member offering his or her services as a consultant to an organisation with many clients and offering services to a single interest."?

Certainly it has been put to us frequently that it is one thing for somebody to sign up to Age Concern, Scottish whisky distillers or whatever, and quite something else for someone to be a cab at a rank for hire—that is to say, working for an organisation which may have multiple clients, not all of which are known to the MP before he or she signs up with the firm.

ROBERT MacLENNAN: If one is representing the interests of a particular public company, it is likely that that information of itself will reveal quite a lot. If one is working for a firm of accountants with many clients, it may reveal very little to say that one is working for a particular firm of accountants. It might be thought that in giving the service to the accountancy firm, one is giving advice about accountancy or about projected changes in the tax system that might affect the accountants' firm generally. But it seems to me that, although on the face of it it is clear that if one is speaking and acting for a company, the public may think it understands what service is being offered, it may in fact be not very different from the kind of advice that one would offer to an organisation representing a multiplicity of clients. It might also be concerned with general questions of the changing of tax regimes or the tightening up of competition policy generally. The important thing is transparency about the work actually done, not about how the work is described in broad, general terms, with assumptions being made by the public about what might be expected of someone who was serving a particular client's interests for money.

2072. PROF. ANTHONY KING: So you very much want to go down the transparency road rather than the prohibition road?

ROBERT MacLENNAN: Yes, I do. I favour that, because I believe that the work done by MPs for outside bodies can be very enlightening in their discharge of their Parliamentary role. It enables them to speak on terms to a range of people affected by what Parliament is doing, which might not be so easily open or comprehensible to them if they were not so engaged.

2073. PROF. ANTHONY KING: Could I ask you about bribery? In your opening statement this morning and also in this document, you lay great stress on the undesirability of bribery and indeed on the desirability of its being made a criminal offence. My problem is simply this. Why is it so awful for a Member of Parliament to accept, say, £1,000 for asking a question in the House of Commons, but perfectly acceptable for that same Member to accept, say, £50,000 for acting as an organisation's paid advocate in the House of Commons, which activity might well include asking Parliamentary Questions? Where does "retail bribery" end and "wholesale bribery", as one might think of it, start?

ROBERT MacLENNAN: If the declaration of interests indicating the relationship with a particular

company shows that the financial nexus is there and shows that the service rendered is asking a Parliamentary Question, then there can be no question of bribery. It is open, it is clear; it is an assertion of the interests of a particular client, and it is one which is not clandestine. Many questions are tabled by people for many reasons, to elicit information for individual clients or individual members of the public. It is well understood, for example, that the Police Federation, which employs currently a Labour Member of Parliament and a Conservative Member of Parliament, will table Parliamentary Questions to elicit information about current thinking in the Home Office about matters affecting the police. That seems to me to be perfectly understandable and acceptable. An individual accepting money for a particular planted question in respect of a particular company's interests is not transgressing, in my opinion, morally or ethically if that interest is known and if the financial nexus is declared.

2074. PROF. ANTHONY KING: So if somebody declares publicly that he has bribed a particular MP to vote in a particular way, so long as the declaration has been made public, it is perfectly all right. That is what you seem to be saying.

ROBERT MacLENNAN: The essence of bribery is that it is clandestine and if the interest is not known to exist, it is buying without declaring that one is buying the services of a Member.

2075. PROF. ANTHONY KING: Could we pursue transparency for a moment? This is more ad hominem in form than it is meant to be, but in the Members' Register of Interests, you offer as "remunerated employment, office, profession etc."

"employed by Enclyclopaedia Britannica as a consultant.".

My question is simply, under the Liberal Democrats' proposals for a new-style Register of Members' Interests, what would your own entry under that heading have to say?

ROBERT MacLENNAN: It would probably say that I had given the company advice about the progress of thinking on the Net Book Agreement, about the attitude of Ministers to the removal of the zero rating of VAT on books. It might indicate that I had had communication with the Office of Fair Trading to consider whether they were likely to introduce new rules on distance selling—matters of that kind, which affect the company's policy and thinking. If I had thought it necessary to table a Parliamentary Question to elicit any of that information or to have written letters or had meetings, I think it would be proper to declare that.

2076. PROF. ANTHONY KING: So the Register of Members' Interests would come to have a somewhat historical property, in the sense that it would describe what MPs had done; it could not, as you described it, necessarily give a very detailed account of what Members were currently doing or might do at some time in the future.

ROBERT MacLENNAN: Well it depends on how frequently and effectively the Register is brought up to date. With modern communications technology, I do not think it should be too difficult to revise the Register much more frequently than it is at present.

2077. PROF. ANTHONY KING: How dissatisfied would you be with the idea that has been put to this Committee that it would really be enough for people who are working as consultants to outside organisations to register, not the details of what they had actually done, but a fairly detailed contract, setting out the relationship between the outside body and the Member and giving a pretty clear indication of what the outside organisation expected the Member to do?

ROBERT MacLENNAN: I think the actual services given are probably more important than the general language of the contract for services between the Member and the firm employing him.

2078. PROF. ANTHONY KING: Can I ask one question which arises out of another of your suggestions in connection with the Register of Members' Interests, that is, for the sums of money that would be required to be registered? You say here as an illustration that

"Annual payments from individual organisations or individuals above a value equivalent to one-third of a Member's basic salary should be declarable".

That struck me as an astonishingly high threshold, because as I read that suggestion, somebody could be working for two organisations, be making £10,000 a year from each, and not have to declare the sum involved.

ROBERT MacLENNAN: Yes. I attach no particular importance to the level of the threshold. It was merely an illustrative suggestion. I think there probably should be a threshold rather than a precise sum which is declarable, partly for the reasons that I set out, which include the work that is done by MPs for an outside interest, which may very well not be related to his value to the organisation qua Member of Parliament. He may be engaged qua lawyer. Although that may say something about the amount of time he spends on parliamentary business or his angle of vision, or something of that sort, it does not seem to me that it touches upon the question of impropriety, which I what I understand this Committee's interest to be principally concerned with. Therefore if the amount of money is relatively small and may be the reward for professional skills rather than a reward for being employed qua Member of Parliament, the broad bands of payment are probably more properly indicative of the significance of the work that is being done.

2079. PROF. ANTHONY KING: You refer to "relatively small" sums of money. One of the things I have been struck by in the evidence we have been hearing is people's conception of what a small sum of money is. In many lines of work, £10,000 may not be very much money, but it is in fact roughly half the average annual income of the people of this country. Ought one not perhaps to be requiring disclosure of sums considerably smaller than that?

ROBERT MacLENNAN: I think there is certainly a case for that, although I think that members of the public might be surprised by the relatively modest work that is done for sums of the kind you mention. It might give a quite wrong impression as to the extent of the commitment of the individual Member. It will be known to the Committee what are the sorts of rewards for non-executive directorships and also how much time that takes. Many members of the public might be surprised by the levels of remuneration for the amount of time. It may

be said that the remuneration is a reward for the responsibilities and quite onerous duties of a non-executive director under contemporary conditions rather than the commitment of time. Anything the Committee can do to clarify these matters will obviously be helpful.

2080. PROF. ANTHONY KING: My own fear would be that many members of the public do indeed suspect what you say they might be surprised to hear, that some MPs are taking home relatively large sums of money for doing very little work.

ROBERT MacLENNAN: They might be.

2081. PROF. ANTHONY KING: Can I ask you straightforwardly about pay? In the Liberal Democrats' evidence there is a reference to the pay of Members of Parliament. I take it that I am to infer from that reference that you believe that MPs are not paid enough?

ROBERT MacLENNAN: The terms of reference of your Committee—and indeed the document Issues and Questions—explicitly says that you are not charged with looking at Members' pay. The purpose of that reference was simply to draw attention to the fact that there does seem to be a relationship between Members' perception of the calls upon their income and their need for additional employment. These things cannot be approached totally disjunctively. I do not think that it is pure greed that makes MPs seek additional outside employment. I certainly think that the whole subject of Members' pay needs to be looked at again.

2082. PROF. ANTHONY KING: What do you think the relationship is? Suppose that MPs doubled their own salaries: do you think that the incidence of MPs being paid to act on behalf of outside interests would decline substantially?

ROBERT MacLENNAN: I think that many MPs would stop searching for outside employment. I could not possibly hazard a guess as to what its impact would be in quantitative terms, because many MPs value, for the reasons I mentioned earlier, their employment by outside bodies for the light it may throw on the work they do as MPs and for the opportunity to meet people whom they might not otherwise meet if they had to rely simply upon contacts with their constituents or building up their own personal networks of friends.

2083. PROF. ANTHONY KING: Can I ask you about your recommendation of a Speaker's Committee on Members' Ethics? Which existing institutions would that replace? How do you see the new committee operating?

ROBERT MacLENNAN: I think it would take over some of the functions of the Committee on Members' Interests, clearly—indeed all of those functions—and some of the functions of the Committee on Privileges. I also have noted that when allegations of corruption or impropriety have been made in the past, the House has on occasion felt it necessary to appoint ad hoc committees to look at these matters. I am thinking of the inquiry into Robert Boothby in 1941 and the Poulson inquiry in 1976. These were, I recall, ad hoc inquiries. It seems to me that one of the disadvantages of the ad hoc inquiry is a lack of procedural regularity. I am not advocating that the committee be turned into a court of law, but I should want to see much greater clarity about rules of evidence. I should also want to see much greater resources put into the investigatory work than is available, I believe, under the ad hoc arrangements, which is why I recommend that the resources of the National Audit Office, among others, might be looked to for assistance in considering cases of this kind.

What I am recommending may seem like the construction of rather an elaborate apparatus to deal with a relatively minor problem, but much of what I am recommending is intended to deter bad behaviour, not solely to deal with evidence of bad behaviour when it arises.

One might also say about the ad hoc arrangements that there has been some evidence, I think, that the House of Commons as a whole has been reluctant to go so far as to accept all the recommendations of these ad hoc inquiries in respect of those alleged to have been acting improperly. An upgrading of the standard of the committee is required. If the committee was chaired by the Speaker, that would give it the sort of authority to ensure that its findings and recommendations were effectively those of the House of Commons.

2084. PROF. ANTHONY KING: You say that you would not want this committee to be a court of law. I am bound to say that, reading the document, that is the impression given: there is to be a code of conduct, the contents of which are not specified, and built into that code of conduct penalties for breaching the code of conduct. There is then to be quite an elaborate procedure, with both MPs and outside assessors involved in investigation and adjudication. If that is not a court of law, what is?

ROBERT MacLENNAN: I envisage that the proceedings could be quite informal, that the rules of procedure guide, rather than constrain, the working of the committee. The committee would not be a court of lawyers nor a court of judges, although I suggest that it should be assisted by two legal assessors, who would be charged with the investigative role in the first instance. I suggest that they should be drawn from the ranks of the judiciary or nominated by a panel from the legal professions. I do believe that such an apparatus of inquiry would fortify Parliament in dealing with the problems that have erupted from time to time to the disfigurement of Parliament.

2085. PROF. ANTHONY KING: Suppose we were, as a committee, to pick up your ideas and simply include them as stated here in our report, how do you think those ideas would be regarded by your colleagues in the House of Commons? How acceptable would they be?

ROBERT MacLENNAN: I suspect that some might claim that the setting up of the Commission on Public Ethics might constitute some kind of infringement of Parliamentary sovereignty, but I am bound to say that, as I regard that as a theoretical constitutional arrangement which has been largely damaging to public life, that would not disturb me greatly. Parliamentary sovereignty has been eroded to some extent by a number of happenings, which seem to me to have been perfectly acceptable, over the past 20 years. I think it has become a shield behind which it is possible for people to hide and for standards to be eroded.

There is in the Public Accounts Committee, to which I belong, as it happens—I have served on it for a substantial

number of years—since 1980—a sense that one is dealing there with a quasi-judicial body. It considers evidence brought before it, usually of some malpractice or failure of judgment, and indeed in recent years, as we have pointed out, these tendencies have been strengthened. That committee is serviced by the National Audit Office. I am greatly influenced by the effectiveness of that work in putting forward the recommendations I do. I am not suggesting that we should create a new office comparable to that of the NAO to deal with what would by any test be a relatively small number of cases, but the sorts of procedures which the Public Accounts Committee has—reliance on the advice of the Comptroller and Auditor General, the availability of that advice, the availability of the Treasury Officer who services the committee—seem to me to professionalise the inquiry of that committee in a way which puts it on a different level of effectiveness from that of some of the other Select Committees and certainly of the other ad hoc committees which have looked at these problems in the past.

2086. PROF. ANTHONY KING: Could I ask you briefly about Ministers and their interests? Right at the beginning of your document—indeed in the very first paragraph—you referred to

"the movement of Cabinet Ministers into private companies whose interests they advanced in office".

Do you have evidence that Ministers have in fact "advanced in office" the interests of companies or other bodies for whom they have subsequently gone to work?

ROBERT MacLENNAN: Well I think in my mind there was the number of Cabinet Ministers who went into companies which they had privatised; in a senior role they had gone to them after the event. These are well known examples. The Ministers were dealing in the course of the privatisation developments with members of the company which became the private company which they joined in another capacity.

2087. PROF. ANTHONY KING: You propose that the rules relating to civil servants be adapted to cover the case of Ministers, and you propose a quarantine period of two years to be placed on Ministers before they take up private sector employment. Can you say a little more about the form the quarantine would take and how it would be policed?

ROBERT MacLENNAN: Yes. I think it should be a presumption against taking up jobs of that kind, which could be displaced on application to the Standing Commission on Ethics which we propose. It would clear that the role was one which was limited in kind, although I must say that I think it would be rare for it to be appropriate to displace the presumption against employment, because of the difficulty of drawing lines, to which I referred in an earlier context, between the kind of work that is done for a client, the difference between what is purely the corporate, non-political work that is done and the work that is directly political.

2088. PROF. ANTHONY KING: You seem to be saying that, were the Conservatives to lose the next election and therefore some 70 or 80 Ministers to lose their jobs, they would remain unemployed for two years—indeed, should remain unemployed for two years.

ROBERT MacLENNAN: There is a balance to be struck here. Let me recall that my Conservative opponent at the last election, who failed to unseat me, was appointed within a year Chairman of the local Health Trust, which the Secretary of State for Scotland indicated in advance he would have it in mind to do if, following the consultation, he set up the Health Trust. He thought it right that the public should know about this. This is not quite on the point you are making, but it has to be said that a number of other Scottish MPs, who had been Ministers, or Conservative candidates who have achieved some prominence have lost no time in being appointed to bodies with which they had a connection. One Minister, who currently is a Minister again as a Peer, was appointed following the loss of his parliamentary seat in Argyll to be the Chairman of the Sea Fish Industry Authority. It almost came to seem as though there was an automatic reward for trying; one did not have to win, but only try. I do not feel punitive about these matters, but I do not think it brings the public service into favour when that sort of defiance of the democratic decision takes place.

The question of the quarantine does not arise from that sort of instance. It is important to avoid insider knowledge being used for the interest of a particular body or company. The connections that have been made in government being put to the commercial advantage of a particular outside body is unacceptable.

2089. PROF. ANTHONY KING: But how would you meet the specific point that a Minister who lost office perhaps through no fault of his own—perhaps through the collective fault of the Government—would be made unemployable for years afterwards?

ROBERT MacLENNAN: No. I do not think so at all. The Minister might have been engaged in one of the Health Departments and take up office as a director of a public contracting company or some other firm whose interests were not in any way connected.

2090. PROF. ANTHONY KING: So the quarantine is specifically on jobs related to the job that the person was doing as a Minister?

ROBERT MacLENNAN: Yes.

2091. PROF. ANTHONY KING: May I ask you one last point about the behaviour of Ministers? It says at one point in your document:

"Questions of propriety in relation to individuals would be referred to the Public Ethics Commission for determination. The Commission would have the power to determine whether or not breaches of the code by Ministers had occurred and to make judgments as to their gravity.".

That seems on the face of it—this may be what you intend—to be taking away from the Prime Minister one of his or her most important powers and giving it to this autonomous Public Ethics Commission. Is that what you intend?

ROBERT MacLENNAN: Yes, it is what I intend. In practice, it appears that the Cabinet Secretary is the man who makes the judgment as to whether or not there has been a transgression. The Cabinet Secretary, to take an example that came to the attention of the Public Accounts Committee recently, had to look at the question of the propriety of spending public money on the ejection from the Chancellor of the Exchequer's premises of an

undesirable tenant. It was the Cabinet Secretary. I do not think it would be appropriate for the Prime Minister to decide whether what had been done had been properly done. It would be invidious for the Prime Minister to have to get involved in that kind of issue. It would be extremely helpful to have a body which had clearly no axe to grind to come to a view about this. The Cabinet Secretary is in the awkward position of being the servant of the government, having to give a recommendation or a judgment about the behaviour of some of its members, so, yes, I do think that that is a proposal of some importance.

2092. PROF. ANTHONY KING: So, in practice, the Prime Minister would find himself in the position of having to decide himself whether to sack a Minister against whom a fairly public report had been laid by this Public Ethics Commission, is that right?

ROBERT MacLENNAN: I read the evidence of Robert Sheldon on the point, with which I was in some agreement, that Prime Ministers would have to act in any event and form their own judgments and it would only be in the rare case of there being some contest, as it were, and some doubt in the Prime Minister's mind about whether to dispose of the services of a particular Minister that the matter would be referred.

I recall the example given of Attlee in the 1945 government quite summarily dismissing Ministers for relatively minor matters it might be thought now in the climate of opinion that has developed in the past decade and a half. There is also, I think, a need to recognise that allegations are sometimes made against Ministers who deny them. I am thinking particularly of the recent case of Mr. Neil Hamilton. He chose to resign but he might have chosen not to resign. It seems to me that in a case of that kind it would greatly assist the Prime Minister to be able to refer the matter to a distinguished, small standing body which is able, through continuous consideration of these questions of ethics in public life, to bring the weight of its own independent authority to bear upon particular allegations of transgression.

2093. PROF. ANTHONY KING: Finally, on the specific point of the Public Ethics Commission do I have it right that you see the Public Ethics Commission being both in effect the Law Commission keeping the existing codes of conduct under review and as the House of Lords acting in its judicial capacity taking up individual cases and, in a sense, adjudicating on those. Is that right?

ROBERT MacLENNAN: I do. I do not see the body as, in a sense, a legislator. I think it is important to retain the responsibility for drawing up these codes of practice with those who are being governed by them so that they take direct responsibility for their own behaviour. That is extremely important to emphasise, that they cannot put into commission their own responsibilities. But to have some oversight of how these codes of practice are working in practice, and also to receive views from the public as to possible changes that might be appropriate as circumstances develop, I think that would be a very healthy role. That is, if you like, the Law Commission role certainly.

LORD NOLAN: Thank you very much. In the last 50 minutes you have covered a great deal of the central area of our enquiry but I am sure that the other members of the committee in the time remaining would be glad to supplement the questions you have been asked. Sir William?

2094. WILLIAM UTTING: If I could pick up one or two points about quangos, Mr. MacLennan—as you say in your evidence, a vast and complex field and one about which it is difficult to generalise satisfactorily. Do you base your recommendations on quite simple general principles——

"believing that those providing public services must be accountable to democratically elected bodies and local people."

You say——

"we want to see a reduction in the number of quangos, the abolition of unnecessary bodies and the transfer of their powers wherever possible to elected bodies."

It is the last point I want to pursue with you; really, to enquire whether the transfer to elected bodies is code for saying that a lot of these functions ought to go back to local government?

ROBERT MacLENNAN: Yes, it is. It is not a very heavily disguised code but we have a structure of government proposed—I notice that Mr. Jack Straw referred to it also in his evidence—for regional government which we would advocate. In some circumstances it might be that if our ideal constitutional arrangements were in place the regional tier would also take over responsibility from regional quangos.

There will be an irreducible minimum of bodies—advisory bodies, executive bodies—which will not be capable of being transferred to these elected authorities and which have ad hoc roles in some cases or standing roles in others. Therefore, it seems to me that openness and accountability must be secured in those areas and I would attach particular importance to our recommendations, which are very much in line with the Comptroller and Auditor General, about ensuring that the National Audit Office has of right the power to see the accounts of non-departmental public bodies. As you will have heard, I think about one third of them are beyond purview of the National Audit Office save with the agreement of Ministers which is often difficult to obtain.

That seems to me to be unacceptable when such vast sums of public money are being handled by these bodies. That is a very important aspect here because we have seen in the work of the Public Accounts Committee transgressions and departures from standards, standards the public has a right to expect in these bodies—I think you have already taken a deal of evidence on this and I need not repeat it—but it seems to me that that would be one of the most powerful ways of enhancing Parliament's control over what has been in some cases frankly corrupt behaviour.

2095. WILLIAM UTTING: The NHS strictly speaking is not a quango but are you including the NHS as one of the bodies that would be subject to more locally elected control?

ROBERT MacLENNAN: Yes.

2096. WILLIAM UTTING: Thank you very much. Political patronage you refer to and we get a variety of answers to this question about political patronage. The most familiar one is that, of course, governments have to have confidence that these bodies will carry through the policies of the Government and, surprise, surprise, if it is a Conservative government you therefore get lots of Conservatives on these bodies and if it is a Labour government you, understandably, get lots of Labour people on these bodies. There seems to be a kind of inevitability about political patronage on the policy function.

ROBERT MacLENNAN: I have mentioned in my written evidence my awareness that there was some political patronage of that kind before the present Government took office. I was, myself, a junior Minister in the last Labour government. I had personal responsibility delegated for making 600 appointments a year in consumer advisory jobs and was heavily consulted about many of the more senior appointments, including such as the Chairman of the Monopolies and Mergers' Commission, the Chairman of the Price Commission, and so forth.

I have to say that politics did come into it. I certainly considered the politics of members of the bodies which I was appointing very carefully and I tried to ensure that there was a balance. It seems to me to be a change in the practice which has developed over the past 15 years which has led to the notorious statement of Baroness Denton that she had——

"never knowingly appointed a socialist"

in 800 appointments that she had made. I certainly appointed Conservatives to important positions; I appointed Liberals, as they then were; I appointed people on the left of the Labour party who were regarded by some of my colleagues as too left to be acceptable for these jobs. I also appointed people on the right of the Labour party. What I would never have claimed was that politics did not play a part. Politics did play a part because very often people who are actively engaged in politics are active in the public service and are interested in public service.

What I think is important is to know what their interests are, to have them openly declared and the tissue of disingenuiness, let me say, about this which has been spread before your committee seems to me to suggest that some people are neither as grown up nor as wise in the ways of the world as I would have expected from their seniority.

2097. WILLIAM UTTING: I am starting to feel sorry for Baroness Denton because of the number of times that remark has been quoted to us. I almost wish I had £10 for every time it has been put to us. I have to say that for all I know she may have followed that up by saying that she had not knowingly appointed any Conservatives to non-departmental public bodies either.

ROBERT MacLENNAN: I think what was distinguished about Baroness Denton was that she said what we know to be the case about very many other Ministers.

2098. WILLIAM UTTING: Can I pursue your recommendation for dealing with this, which is to establish a statutory framework governing the creation, appointment, operation and accountability of any of these bodies that remain outside democratic control. The problem about that seems to me to blur the directness of accountability to the Secretary of State for the operation of these businesses. Once you put in an intermediate body of this kind, removing from the Secretary of State some of the discretion for appointments, does it not mean that that body almost becomes accountable itself for the operations of the quango?

ROBERT MacLENNAN: So it should, in my judgment. With the Next Steps agencies development in government and the devolution of responsibility for administration from Ministers it seems to me extremely important that these bodies should be seen to be accountable in a way they are not at present. We are getting the worst of both worlds. We are having Ministers denying responsibility for the day-to-day operations of these bodies and others not taking up the responsibility.

I do not know whether the point has been made already but we have as many Ministers today as we have ever had in Britain but we also have a huge proliferation of people who are conducting the executive roles that Ministers formerly had but those people are not clearly accountable to Parliament. Questions may be tabled about their work and they will be answered by the Minister saying, "I have referred that enquiry to the chairman concerned". There is no way in which Parliament can call these people to account as they stand and, to boot, if they are strongly politically partisan it makes it the more difficult to get access to what is going on to call these people to account.

WILLIAM UTTING: I wish I could pursue the issues of accountability and responsibility with you but my time is long expired and I must pass you on to other members of the committee.

LORD NOLAN: Sir William's questions have brought out the subject of quangos which was, I think, about the only area that you had not covered in answer to Professor King. I am, I am afraid, having to exercise my all too frequent function of curbing the enthusiasm of my members but I would like to go round the table because there may be important matters which would justify us going into overtime. Sir Clifford?

2099. CLIFFORD BOULTON: As you are speaking on behalf of the party it is very helpful for us to clear up certain matters of detail. If I may just quickly ask you one in connection with Members' interests. You said there is nothing intrinsically wrong in advocating the cause of an interest with which one had a relationship but, clearly, it would be wrong to put oneself in a position where one had to take instructions on that cause. Advocating under instructions is not a proper activity, is it?

ROBERT MacLENNAN: I would agree.

2100. CLIFFORD BOULTON: Therefore, there is scope for definition of acceptable and unacceptable advocacy. You will recall the Speaker, in the statement which we used in our Issues and Questions Paper, said that there was a tendency of Members, or temptation of Members, to think that registration cured everything and that once you had registered it must be all right.

You have resisted the suggestion that the terms of the arrangement that one had come to with an outside interest

should be deposited. If the terms of that arrangement were to be deposited would that not assist this officer that you have in mind who could advise and help Members on propriety; would it not help him to help the Member to get the nature of his interest right and could there not be benefit in the registration of the terms of an arrangement?

ROBERT MacLENNAN: The first point I would make is that it is plainly unsatisfactory that the mere interest is registered without any revelation of what it means. It is, I think, probably possible to satisfy the requirements of the declaration, even of an interest which was illegal, by simply indicating that one is a non-executive director of the company which was pursuing an illegal function. It may be unlikely perhaps but it is an oddity.

Yes, I think the reason I was cautious about the contractual document is that I fear that it would be couched in language of such generality as to be rather unrevealing of what in fact was being done and that it would beg questions so that people would not actually have the kind of guidance that you feel they might be assisted by. Yes, I was aware of the Speaker's drawing that to our attention and it does very much fortify the case for some codification beyond the generality which we have. I think that is a difficult job. I make no bones about that. I think it is extremely difficult to do it effectively and that is why it is sensible that we should have a stab at it in the Commons itself and why we should have a body standing outside of the Commons looking at what is being done and casting an eye over it, seeing how it works in practice and whether it is taking account of the concerns of the public and of the new temptations, if you like, the new possibilities of adverse pressure on Members.

The general rubrics which the Speaker referred to about considering how one behaves leave Members a little bemused. I can point specifically to the reaction of Mr. Albert Roberts in the Poulson case who said that he did not know where he stood—I do not quote him exactly—but he made it plain in his speech on the debate of the Select Committee that he felt unassisted by the very generality of the inhibitions on certain types of behaviour. I do not think Mr. Roberts was misleading the House when he said that. I think he was reflecting a general lack of consensus about what was appropriate and what was not. He might have taken a more extreme view than others but there would have been different views.

CLIFFORD BOULTON: Thank you.

2101. PETER SHORE: With great self discipline, I will ask one question. How would the Speaker's Committee on Members' Ethics differ from, and in what ways would it be an improvement upon, the present Privileges Committee?

ROBERT MacLENNAN: It would be different in that it would be serviced by two legal assessors. It would have a wider ambit of operation. It would have both a legislative role and an investigative role. It would have, I believe, perhaps comparable authority but because of its wider remit and because it is presided over by the Speaker, the kind of unimpeachable authority that would make it extremely improbable that the House of Commons would recoil from implementing its recommendations.

2102. LORD NOLAN: Very briefly, on the law of bribery you commend, in effect, the recommendations of the Salmon Commission which were never debated, let alone acted upon, in this respect. It would take some time, would it not, to get Statutes through which brought that law up to date and reconciled it with the position of Members of Parliament. Do you think it would be possible for the House of Commons in the shorter term—because we are faced, we are told, with the problem of urgency—would it be possible for the House of Commons, if it thought right, to go towards the process of an independent element in the regulation of its affairs short of bringing in statutory machinery, whether it is the Ethics Commission or the criminal law?

ROBERT MacLENNAN: First, I think it is anomalous as it stands and there is also some dubiety, as I read the authorities, about what the law actually is. Therefore, it seems to be desirable to clarify and reach agreement to put it beyond doubt. I would be reluctant to take the view that anything short of that could be wholly satisfactory, particularly because one recognises that when procedural changes are made and suggested there is always a body of opinion that says, "Let's give this time to work. Let's see how it comes out in practice and let us not trouble with the difficulties."

There may be theoretical difficulties of the kind which I referred to about sovereignty of Parliament but they seem to me not to be practical difficulties and in a matter of this kind I would be very happy if advice was sought from a body like the Law Commission and that a Bill would be introduced with all-party support, maybe in your Lordships' House where fine legal minds could be brought to bear upon the issue and be seen to be analysing the problems in a way that would command respect.

LORD NOLAN: I would hope to see your House, the House of Commons, taking the first step if a step is to be taken in this direction, but there it is, that is perhaps for the future. Martin?

2103. MARTIN JACOMB: I just have one question going back to the question of Ministers going into the private sector after leaving office where you want a two-year quarantine period. You say that you would not apply that where the activities were not related to their Ministerial responsibilities, but if you take a Ministry like the Department of Trade or the Foreign Office concerned with promoting British exports their responsibilities cover virtually the whole business scene. This is the question. How are you going to get any person of decent quality to accept a precarious position of being a Minister, particularly a junior Minister where the pay is not great, under those conditions?

ROBERT MacLENNAN: Having experienced that I am quite sympathetic to it.

MARTIN JACOMB: What is the answer to it then?

ROBERT MacLENNAN: I think the answer is that it is not impossible to find suitable employment having been a precarious junior Minister underpaid. I also think that the safety valve which I recommended of dispensation from the rule would enable a judgment to be made by an independent body as to whether it was a risky course to take. For a Minister, shall we say, in the Department of Defence to take over a position in Ferranti's might be thought to be inappropriate but for him to take over a position in a retailing company, a non-executive director

of Sainsbury's, would seem to me perhaps not to raise the same questions.

I can draw broad categories and broad lines but if there are difficulties in applying them I think it is right that there should be a process for analysing a particular case and assisting Ministers back into properly remunerated employment for the reasons you give. I think one wants to have high quality people and, certainly, if they were unable to be employed that would have a very devastating effect but I am not convinced that they would.

2104. MARTIN JACOMB: So they would just have to chance their arm on what the body might say?

ROBERT MacLENNAN: I think the body would be likely to develop a corpus of jurisprudence which might act as an indication of what was acceptable and what was not.

MARTIN JACOMB: Thank you.

2105. DIANA WARWICK: Could I just ask a question about the Register. You say that self-regulation by Members of Parliament has not worked satisfactorily and no longer enjoys public confidence. Because you place so much emphasis on transparency and on the Register being more accessible particularly through Internet, do you envisage penalties being associated with non-compliance, with changing the register?

ROBERT MacLENNAN: Yes.

2106. DIANA WARWICK: What sort of penalties do you have in mind?

ROBERT MacLENNAN: Penalties of sufficient severity to make compliance more likely. It might be a pecuniary penalty, loss of pay.

2107. DIANA WARWICK: And given that you are also concerned about the Register becoming out of date, do you envisage any changes in the statements to the House or declarations to the House or in Select Committees, for example, that might ensure that particular interests that might not have been registered would nevertheless be obvious to the House?

ROBERT MacLENNAN: I am sorry, I am not sure that I followed that question.

2108. DIANA WARWICK: You were concerned that because there might be delay in registering a change in outside interests that the Register would become out of date. We have also had concern expressed that Members of Parliament are not always aware of interests of colleagues. Do you envisage any changes in the way in which declarations are made in the House or in Select Committees?

ROBERT MacLENNAN: No, not really. I think it is clumsy to ask Members to do much more than they do at present by way of declaration of their interests. Those who are engaged as spokespersons for the Police Federation invariably declare it, although everyone knows who they are, in the course of debates on Criminal Justice Bills for example. I think that rule works quite well.

I think a greater accessibility to the public of the document is quite important and, as I say, Members of

Parliament are now, by modern communication methods, connected to the Library of the House of Commons and are able to bring up information on their office screens quite readily. This kind of thing, updated, could be at the fingertip control of Members of Parliament if they wanted it.

DIANA WARWICK: So, there would be no excuse for them not doing it?

ROBERT MacLENNAN: No, none at all.

DIANA WARWICK: Thank you.

ANNE WARBURTON: I think I have forfeited by coming late.

2109. LORD NOLAN: We are very grateful to you. We have kept you far longer than we had warned you and we thank you very much for the care you have taken to present us with both written and spoken material that is so clear. Thank you very much.

Would Professor Mahoney be kind enough to come now to the chair. Professor, may I begin by asking whether I have pronounced your name correctly?

PROFESSOR JACK MAHONEY

PROFESSOR JACK MAHONEY (Professor of Business Ethics and Social Responsibility, London Business School): I regret, Chairman, that your first statement is incorrect. The Scottish pronunciation is different but I will settle for yours.

2110. LORD NOLAN: I will ask you to forgive me for that. Have you prepared an opening statement that you would wish to make to us?

JACK MAHONEY: Yes, I have made available a one-page series of notes.

LORD NOLAN: Thank you very much. A list of headings in effect?

JACK MAHONEY: Yes.

LORD NOLAN: Would you be good enough to develop that for us. We should be very grateful if you did.

JACK MAHONEY: Thank you. I have been researching and teaching ethics for about 30 years, both general and applied in various fields, and in the past eight or so years I have been specialising in business ethics and, more latterly, in private sector ethics and so it is logical to ask whether ethics in general, or business ethics in particular, has anything to say to the questions which are being faced by this committee.

I have jotted down here various considerations of principle. It is a rather dense document; it is more a sort of aide-memoire than an argued piece of presentation but I suggest the points I make here have material implications. So, first of all, ethical norms for the public sector contrasted with the private. I am a great believer in Aristotle's beginning everything by saying, "What is it for?" and if one can work out what the purpose or the role of a particular thing or position is then one can begin to say what is going to promote it in its activities and what is going to prevent it in its activities.

This is basically what I am saying here: starting from the role in society, identify the duties and then uncovering the inner moral values which are at work and at play and then, from that, principles can be generated which will commend some types of behaviour and deprecate others. That applies in every area of human activity for ethical consideration.

In the public sector I think there are two special features which I have identified. One is the ethics of service and the implications of that and, secondly, the fiduciary relationship, the special trust which is involved there between the parties and the necessary values which would emerge as means to discharge one's role and one's duty would include particularly the ones I have mentioned —honesty, transparency, impartiality, competence—and to that I would add, having thought a little bit more about it, moral courage.

Codes of conduct in public life: this is clearly something which the committee has been considering both in its deliberations and in the evidence and a lot of work has been done in business ethics in the whole field of codes of conduct. What I have done there is identify some of the features which may throw some particular light on to the remit of the committee. For example, the aims—to inform, reassure and win the support of the public and then also for its subscribers to inform them, to guide them, to encourage them, to protect them from undue influence both from above and from below and to deter them should they have any behaviour in mind which would be not in accordance with that.

Then the dynamic form is, once again, the same thing: stating the purpose, leading to values which will promote that and then resulting in citing examples, illustrative of behaviour which would exemplify or negate those values.

The third point in which I think you may be interested is how to encourage and monitor organisational ethical standards. Here, clearly, there are personal means and there are institutional means. In personal means one cannot entirely avoid the magic word "integrity" and practising it and rewarding it, remembering of course that integrity means wholeness, it means an all-rounded ethical character, and raises the whole question of whether ethics in the life of any individual is a seamless role between, say, private life and public life. Integrity, I think, is a very threatening word if it is used properly, not simply a formality.

Individual and corporate consistency is of enormous importance providing example then as a colleague or a role model or as a mentor, giving authoritative guidance and then looking to particular qualities in the recruitment and promotion of individuals. Then there are the institutional means and this is standard material in all the studies in business ethics in the private sector and I have simply listed them, starting with the code of conduct evidently which has to be authoritatively enjoined—in other words, it has to have some authority behind it pushing it—but it also has to be widely "owned" for its internal authority and, therefore, the greater participation there is in composing a code of conduct, or in revising it, then the more likely it is to be successful and to appeal on its internal merits and not simply on the sponsoring authority.

Seriously applied and sanctioned it is common practice that a code of conduct which does not have teeth is worse than useless. It simply creates disillusionment or bad faith. Therefore, a code of conduct is the beginning of a process or ethical review and ethical concern; it is not the end of a process. It is really a blueprint for action.

Then, other features in addition to the code of conduct would be the anonymous helpline or a hotline in a company for employees who have particular worries or perhaps conscientious difficulties or something of that nature; a counselling facility for those who may have ethical dilemmas or quandaries; an Ombudsman; an ethics committee, and this is of increasing interest, either a particular committee or a sub-committee of the board in a company which has a particular remit to look at the ethical behaviour. One of the important things there is that an ethics committee should contain some independent membership, such as non-executive directors or something of that nature, along the lines of the Cadbury Report on Corporate Governance.

An ethics compliance officer is becoming quite popular in the United States, so much so that there is now a Professional Association of Ethics Compliance Officers. It has obvious merit. It has the demerit of saying, "Let's leave all the ethical problems to Joe; he can solve them, it is not our problem". I have mentioned independent directors, then there is ethics awareness induction and training programmes and then corporate self-evaluation. These are in-house methods used by an increasing number of businesses to encourage and monitor their standards.

Finally, the much larger question of developing and inculcating ethical standards in society and in large organisations. Here, of course, there is really no substitute for self-direction on the part of the individual. In a sense, the problem is how to help the individual to become the sort of person who will be self-directed or who will be conscientious. Moral education is obviously preferable to detailed instruction and yet some form of socialisation seems necessary, some form of training or induction. As I see it, one problem is that traditional carriers of moral values and agents of moral education in society are now weakened in their authority and their acceptability. I think of the family, of the religion—the churches and synagogues—and I think of the educational system. So, there is some need within any society, and particularly ours, to look for some sort of remedial ethical education in order to try to help to enhance and raise the standards of ethical behaviour in society at large and not simply in various sectors.

This means that influential agents in society—and I include here, obviously, public figures—should, to use a phrase, try harder. There is a tradition going back to, I think, the 17th century that the conduct of business is a humanising influence, that it is certainly preferable to warfare, and one might go on to say that possibly politics, although this is perhaps a rather daring comment to make, should see itself as a moral educator and introduce a humanising influence. I think, for example, of the deplorable example which is frequently given in the House of Commons which is much less than being a positive influence for ethical conduct in society at large.

The final point I would want to make is looking at the strengths and interior resources of the individual there is a lot to be said for the classical idea of the virtues as ethical skills developed through practice and disposing their

owner to appropriate responses. The classic ones are justice, self control, practical wisdom and moral courage. The problem then arises of how are these to be introduced and inculcated and reinforced and that takes me back to what I have already suggested in the way of personal and structural arrangements in society.

LORD NOLAN: Thank you very much indeed, that is very clear. I am now going to ask Sir Martin Jacomb—himself, of course, an experienced businessman —to take up the questioning.

2111. MARTIN JACOMB: Thank you very much for that opening statement, it was very, very interesting. You have been looking at this question for a long time, particularly business ethics for the past eight years. Could you just tell us something about how over that period you have seen the need for the teaching of this subject. Have you seen the need for that increasing greatly?

JOHN MAHONEY: Yes, indeed.

2112. MARTIN JACOMB: Has it always been there or is it a new discovery, or what?

JOHN MAHONEY: I like to talk about modern business ethics, to distinguish between, say, the post-1960s phenomenon. This started basically in the United States after Watergate, the various scandals there, the bribery of foreign governments and local officials, and so on, and then the whole Civil Rights campaign for blacks and then the womens' movement, the environmental movement, the product safety movement—all this ferment in the 60s and 70s led to a renaissance of business ethics in the United States and comparable experience in other societies—including, for example, in Britain, the whole Poulson affair, the discovery of environmental damage, and so on—all of these led to comparable developments in other countries but it has to be said, I think, that the United States, both in business and in its educational system, led the field in the new development of modern business ethics.

2113. MARTIN JACOMB: So, a need was perceived to be growing?

JOHN MAHONEY: Absolutely. Then, as the demand was met, it increased.

MARTIN JACOMB: Appetite grows with the eating.

JOHN MAHONEY: Absolutely.

2114. MARTIN JACOMB: Over that period, could you tell us something about progress or, indeed, regress in ethical standards in business?

JOHN MAHONEY: It is rather difficult to distinguish between procedures put in practice by businesses and whether they have, in fact, been successful.

MARTIN JACOMB: That is what I am asking you about. That is the very point I am asking you about.

JOHN MAHONEY: Exactly so. For example, I teach business ethics to MBA students and the question has to be asked, do I make any difference to their perception. A lot of academics are concerned about this and, on the whole, they tend to say, "Well, maybe eventually, yes"; in other words, they may not be particularly interested as they are beginning their career, as they are moving up the ladder, but as they get increased responsibility, as they get older, perhaps they begin to think a little bit more that maybe there are other values in addition to the bottom line. That is one line of answer.

I think what one can see from business itself and not simply in the academic world is a distinct growing interest in business ethics, not just through the media and not just through scandals but as a matter of internal reflection and development within companies, partly from shareholders, partly from management itself, partly from the general public. The corporate responsibility of business is a new phenomenon which recognises that businesses have certain responsibilities to society—certainly economic obviously, also legal—and, in addition to that, some ethical responsibilities about treating people fairly and honestly, with impartiality, and so on.

Businesses themselves are becoming increasingly aware of this and the most evident proof of this is the growing popularity of codes of conduct and codes of behaviour, both within business companies and within some of the professions. I am a member of the Professional Practices Committee of the Institute of Management and two years ago we helped to produce a totally revised code of conduct for the Institute of Management in the United Kingdom. This reflects the growing interest in many other companies.

2115. MARTIN JACOMB: Would I be right in detecting from that that although there is no way of measuring it even in general terms you feel that the standards now applied in business, and now aimed for, are better than they were when you started?

JOHN MAHONEY: Yes, now applied and now aimed for. Whether they are actually discharged is a matter for debate.

2116. MARTIN JACOMB: Right. You mentioned the introduction of codes and, indeed, in your opening statement you dealt with the distinction between generalised codes and detailed codes. Could you develop that a bit and tell us some of the limitations which you see if one tries to have a very detailed code?

JOHN MAHONEY: Yes, indeed. One can see three stages in the development of a business's self expression in society. First, the mission statement, which may be a sentence or a paragraph, just saying what they are about. Then a values statement, which can be as long as they want because everyone is in favour of apple pie and motherhood and patriotism. Where it begins to bite is when it goes on to say—and in the light of all this there are certain types of behaviour which we would commend and there are other types of behaviour for which we simply would not stand. Of course, this inevitably includes the whole area of conflicts of interest, but it also includes honesty, fairness, reliability and so on.

The disadvantages of a written code of conduct are that it can encourage legalism—if it is not in the code then it must be all right. It can encourage, what shall we say, barrack room lawyerism, which is partially the same sort of thing. There are many older companies who feel that this is trying to capture something intangible—the ethos or the culture of a firm, perhaps it started as a family

business—and they feel that this is becoming de-personalising and surely a person's word is their bond and there are certain values we can rely upon, intangible and inexpressible perhaps. There is still a certain amount of support for that view.

There is also the view, of course, that if you publish a code of conduct you are providing the public with an instrument to beat you over the head with, just as if you publish a series of public charters you are giving hostages to fortune. There are several disadvantages but on the whole it seems as if the case in favour of a code of conduct is winning and my impression is that in the United Kingdom, for example, about a quarter to a third increasing of public companies have such a code in place.

2117. MARTIN JACOMB: Yes. Could I just then go quickly to the question of a compliance officer because that could be seen simply as a way of getting easy absolution, could it not?

JOHN MAHONEY: Yes, indeed.

2118. MARTIN JACOMB: Any further comments on whether that is really a satisfactory route or whether it is not much better to say that this must come from senior management?

JOHN MAHONEY: Yes. I would prefer to say the latter. It must come from senior management in consultation with all levels within the company so far as that is possible. I think the idea of an ethics compliance officer, which is really by analogy with a legal compliance officer or the company secretary and an environmental compliance officer, has certain disadvantages. One is that it appears to exonerate everyone else. It would only be of importance, I think, or of help if the ethics compliance officer was seen as the focal point for helping to increase ethical sensitivity throughout the company but certainly not as a sort of ethical "Mr Fix It" of any kind.

2119. MARTIN JACOMB: Other people have mentioned this question of the hotline as being another aspect of this in order to ensure that people of all levels can adopt the highest standards of integrity, even if their immediate superiors do not.

JACK MAHONEY: Yes.

2120. MARTIN JACOMB: Does a hotline really work in your view?

JACK MAHONEY: I think it can and does work. The extreme position there is the whole idea of whistle-blowing, where someone's discomfort has reached such a peak that this cannot be satisfied internally and therefore they must to an outside agency. I am on record as saying that the company which suffers from justifiable external whistle-blowing has only itself to blame. In other words, it should have put in place methods for handling difficulties, including the possibility of individuals raising problems, perhaps anonymously in the first instance, and seeing whether they can be helped in some way or other. That is why I prefer a help line to the idea of a hotline, which injects a note of panic; I prefer to see this as something rather more routine.

2121. MARTIN JACOMB: Can I switch now to the area of the difference between standards in business here and abroad.

JACK MAHONEY: Yes.

MARTIN JACOMB: Where do we come out on that comparison?

JACK MAHONEY: My impression is that standards of business here are high and, if it does not sound patronising, that the vast majority of business people are trying to do a decent job of work. Therefore we should not have too many misgivings about that.

If one is looking elsewhere, to other countries or cultures, the big example which leaps out in almost every business conversation is the question of bribery and corruption elsewhere. I used to suspect that in Britain when we spoke about that there was an element of racism hidden in it because we thought this was what the lesser breeds without the law got up to. Then, of course, we discovered the Poulson network in this country, the situation in Italy and Japan, there is something blowing up now in Belgium and Germany and so on. It is clearly problem that is central to business as a whole and it is incumbent upon it to take what steps it can.

If there are practices such as bribery that have to be accepted, however unethical they may be, particularly if one is dealing abroad, there is a considerable amount of analysis that can help one to realise that there are ethical ways through the minefield of bribery, nepotism, kickbacks and so on in other countries. For example, there are two major distinctions between bribing someone to do what they should be doing and to do what they should not be doing. There is also a difference between offering someone a bribe and extortion—in other words, not being able to get one's business done or one's goods moved from the jetty and so on unless one pays some sort of money. When the Chairman of Olivetti took his dossier to the magistrates of Milan about two years ago at the beginning of the scandals in Italy, he said this was not bribery, but extortion. Whether that was true is open to debate, but as a distinction it was ethically interesting. In other words, it may be an inevitable expense, which one has to pay reluctantly, just to run a good business.

2122. MARTIN JACOMB: Do people ever come to you and say "We're trying to sell this enormous order of hardware abroad and we are in competition with people from other countries, with lower standards in relation to bribery. We are a British company; what do we do about that?" Do they come and ask you that?

JACK MAHONEY: It has happened on one or two occasions. I do not claim to have a vast experience of business, I am more of an academic, but I would say that we can begin to analyse it along the lines. I have mentioned, but then the question of international bribery is being dealt with by a number of bodies. The United Nations is looking at it, OECD is working on it, the International Chamber of Commerce has produced various guidelines on this and I say to any company which raises this question "Are you big enough to fight this?"—in other words, "How powerful are you; will you simply succumb to this sort of thing or have you the track record, power and influence simply to decline or refuse to succumb and to win through on your own merits and make a fuss while you're at it?".

2123. MARTIN JACOMB: Thank you very much. I must restrain myself, although I find the subject very interesting obviously. I just wanted to get you back from the question of the application of business ethical standards and procedures on which you have been concentrating so far, to the public sector.

JACK MAHONEY: Yes.

2124. MARTIN JACOMB: In the private business sector there is the overwhelmingly powerful touchstone of what is good business. There is every reason why a business wants high ethical standards if it wants to do good business and stay in business permanently or for a long time.

JACK MAHONEY: Yes.

2125. MARTIN JACOMB: That central touchstone is not available in the public sector. What analogue can one look for in the public sector?

JACK MAHONEY: The ultimate touchstone in the public sector is public esteem and profile. That is the ultimate and it is very similar to consumer satisfaction. How one discharges the duties of one's role and office with transparency, openness and so on seems to be the ultimate touchstone in the public sector. One cannot commercialise it and say "The customer is king—the sovereignty of the consumer.", but if public sector standards fall below what is expected by the general public, one has first a judgement that one is simply not discharging the duties of one's position, and secondly, an incentive to do something about it and to do it hard and soon.

MARTIN JACOMB: Thank you very much.

LORD NOLAN: Dame Anne?

2126. ANNE WARBURTON: I hope I shall be allowed more than one question: can I start by asking you whether you can help us in the matter of reconciling parliamentary sovereignty and privilege with effective compliance?

JACK MAHONEY: There is a certain amount of rhetoric attached to the idea of parliamentary sovereignty. First, I always want to raise the question of sovereignty against what or whom? I suppose one can say, it is sovereignty of Parliament initially over against the Crown, through say, the Bill of Rights, Magna Carta and so on. It is surely not sovereignty over the electorate because Parliament is ultimately subject to the electorate and to its wishes. The development of mandates and party manifestos is to a certain degree an acknowledgement that the sovereignty of Parliament is perhaps not as absolute or as sacrosanct as has been thought.

Secondly, the sovereignty of Parliament as I understand it (and I am in no sense a political theorist) refers to a body, not necessarily to each individual Member of Parliament. If one goes on to ask how Parliament can best discharge its sovereignty and privilege, the answer may be through some form of self-regulation or statutory regulation.

My third point is that if Parliament is sovereign in terms of legislation, then presumably it is open to Parliament to pass legislation to control and regulate itself, even drawing upon independent figures and bodies to enable it to discharge its sovereignty.

2127. ANNE WARBURTON: Thank you very much. You may recognise that the way to proceed in these matters, perhaps by formulating a code, is to identify abuses because that is easier than taking a positive approach—discuss!

JACK MAHONEY: Yes. I think that is true. It may be no coincidence that most of the ten commandments are in the negative. It is easier to identify abuses. I find it interesting to say to students that if they want to identify what fairness is, they should examine examples of unfairness and through the absence of certain characteristics and features, may begin to draw up a profile of what fairness consists of.

Looking at malfeasance, misbehaviour and so on is helpful to clarify the mind in order to be able to ask what it is we are looking for which is not this. But then I would want to go on and say, when one presents some form of instrument such as a code of conduct, that it must be put in a positive, affirmative way. If it is simply put as a series of negatives, it is not sufficiently proactive, but it has to be realistic in order to be able to take note of the abuses (sometimes very gross) that can take place.

ANNE WARBURTON: Thank you, Professor.

2128. DIANA WARWICK: I wonder if I could take you back to the point you made about public esteem. Could you help me with the problem we face of perception and reality. We are told—and this is a statistic to which we keep coming back—that 64 per cent of the public believe that MPs are feathering their nests from their parliamentary work and yet those who are either engaged in Parliament or who comment as journalists on Parliament, have told us that things are nothing like as bad as that really and there is no evidence that helps us very much. Do you have any light to cast on that discrepancy?

JACK MAHONEY: Not a lot, I have to say. To some extent I share the discomfort. I do not think it is a plot on the part of the media for example. The public are not fools—they can draw their own conclusions, even though they may draw the wrong ones. I am not sure. Is what we have seen and what has been disclosed in terms of sleaze and various other abuses, the tip of the iceberg or is it simply a remote part of parliamentary life? I have no means of knowing whether that is the case, but I would incline to say that a matter of such importance and public esteem is such a difficult animal to keep in captivity, that one should lean over backwards in order to ensure that fairness, honesty and all these other values are seen to be the case.

2129. DIANA WARWICK: You have come down pretty much in favour of codes of conduct. Can I put to you thoughts put to us by a senior Minister as an antidote to codes. This is a question to an MP or a Minister: would you feel happy to see all the relevant facts of any transaction or relationship fully reported on the front page of your favourite newspaper? The second is, if in doubt, cut it out. Are these adequate ethical considerations?

JACK MAHONEY: No. First, the idea related to the front page of the newspaper has a variety of forms—would you like your children to know, would you like to see this as a headline on the paper and so on. That could lead to infantilism in ethical analysis and consideration. There are many situations that are extremely complex and need a

very nuanced approach. Therefore it is extremely difficult to capture that and communicate it and certainly not to one's children. One would have to say, for example, "How old are the children?" or "What sort of paper are we talking about? Are we talking about the tabloid with its banner, one-word headline, or one of the more respectable newspapers?". That seems to me to be too simple.

Also it is a brutal sort of maxim and we are looking for something much more nuanced and calibrated to meet the complexity of the problem, which is the behaviour of individuals in public life. Therefore I return to the idea of the code of conduct as something which is indispensable, with the caveat that I have already made, that it is only a beginning. It has to have teeth and be revised regularly and it has to be owned by as many people as possible.

This is why I am extremely interested to see the sort of suggestions coming through (more than these cosy maxims), which say that something has to be done by way of legislation. I think of the recommendations of the Salmon Committee and certainly for local government—the code of conduct there was excellent; the new Civil Service code, which is long overdue, and which is excellent; the Irish Bill "Ethics and Public Office" which is going through the Dáil at the moment, which is largely on conflicts of interests; and the movements in Canada and the United States and various other legislatures which say that the whole question needs a thorough sifting by Parliament and some steps need to be taken to reassure the public and lean over backwards in order to dispel any fears or misgivings that there are murky or dark areas around. "Transparency", if one was looking for one word, would be preferable to any newspaper headline.

DIANA WARWICK: Thank you, Professor.

2130. LORD THOMSON: Professor Mahoney, some of the fears that have been expressed to us in the six weeks we have now been sitting have been on the impact of the culture of business on standards in public life. We are just about to receive some evidence from Mr Wigley, the President of Plaid Cymru and MP for Caernarfon, who will tell us that the traditions of public service in the professions are now substituted for those of language incentives and penalties of private sector business management. We have heard the very respected Chairman of the Public Accounts Committee telling us that some of the worst cases that they have had to deal with of misbehaviour in the financial management of quangos arise out of businessmen bringing their business culture into the quango and being unaware of the ethics of public service. What do you say to that?

JACK MAHONEY: I think that is too bland to be true for a start. The introduction of economic and business values into public life seems to me to be long overdue in terms of efficiency, profitability and so on, and those are ethical values. The best use of resources is an ethical value, as are proficiency, value for money and so on.

I deplore as much as anyone some of the terminology that has been introduced.

LORD THOMSON: That includes the best use of human resources.

JACK MAHONEY: Yes and that itself shows the danger of depersonalising because one is talking about human resources by parallel with material resources and so on. Something I find interesting is that whereas on the one hand there is the attempt to introduce business values into public activities, on the other hand I sense a movement in the business community itself towards an increasing professionalisation and the idea of adopting the ethos of service, trust and so on. I would not like to see the public and private sectors passing each other in the night and taking up different places, but there is a certain symbiosis going on between them at the moment.

2131. LORD THOMSON: In teaching ethics to your MBA students, do you teach them the advantages as good citizens, as well as businessmen, of giving some of their time for public service?

JACK MAHONEY: I talk about that as the philanthropic aspect of business which, in my book, is the lowest of the priorities for an ethical business.

LORD THOMSON: The lowest of the priorities?

JACK MAHONEY: Yes. The top priority for any business is not intentionally to do harm to anyone. The second is more positive and that is to run a decent business. Third, I would say, (and I would honestly see it as more of an extramural activity) is to be generous, philanthropic and so on in business.

One of the big debates in business ethics, as you may know, arises from an article by Milton Friedman in the *New York Times Magazine* in 1970 when he asserted roundly that the social responsibility of business is to make a profit. I would say "Two cheers for Milton Friedman.". There is a danger of the social contribution of business, as business, being dislodged in the public mind and within the business community by the idea that you must be a good citizen, you must be philanthropic and so on. If you wish to do that as an optional extra, that is fine by me, but no amount of public generosity, seconding staff or aid to urban regeneration schemes and so on will act as a substitute for running an ethical business.

2132. LORD THOMSON: So you do not think that the great nineteenth century traditions of the Rowntrees and the Cadburys are relevant today?

JACK MAHONEY: Yes, I do, as philanthropy, but I would also have to say that appeals to business philanthropy sometimes seem to me to cloak political ideology of being unwilling to go in for public spending and of confusing corporate philanthropy with social justice.

LORD THOMSON: Thank you.

2133. LORD NOLAN: I am going to introduce the Nolan code of no more than one question each. Mine will be this. In your opening remarks, under the heading of *developing and inculcating ethical standards*, you spoke (and I noted the phrase because it is a strong one) of the deplorable example of the House of Commons. What precisely did you have in mind?

JACK MAHONEY: I have in mind the conduct of the House of Commons at Question Times and at other times.

LORD NOLAN: Their behaviour as seen on the television screen by the public?

JACK MAHONEY: As seen by the public—but of course that is an indication to the public of the deplorable standards which exist, whether or not they are being televised. I hope I do not sound pompous, but I find it deeply offensive that the elected representatives of this democracy should comport themselves with such verbal violence. It is something I would associate more with the terraces than with the Back Benches and even more it is an appalling example to young people in our society—I do not mean children, but teenagers and students. If the supreme legislature in the country conducts itself in that way in debating and arguing out subjects of enormous public importance, what hope have students and youngsters got of trying to improve things?

I took the liberty of linking that to my final point, that in a sense people in public life should try harder. Certainly the House of Commons should clean up its act.

LORD NOLAN: Thank you very much.

2134. PROFESSOR ANTHONY KING: If you had to choose, what single recommendation would you most like this Committee to make?

JACK MAHONEY: An independent ethics committee to oversee standards of behaviour in public life.

2135. WILLIAM UTTING: Could I just ask you about sanctions. I assume that if in the public service the rewards are public esteem, then the punishments are the withdrawal of public esteem so that public disgrace and humiliation would be sufficient sanctions for people who broke codes of public conduct.

JACK MAHONEY: Not necessarily. I could perhaps experience that and then emigrate with my ill-gotten gains and lead a very comfortable life elsewhere. Public disgrace is important, but not sufficient.

WILLIAM UTTING: So the Tower of London would still fulfil a valuable purpose?

JACK MAHONEY: No I think not—I would draw the line at that! It is not for me to lecture Parliament on this, but it has a series of sanctions already, does it not, from reprimand to suspensions, fines and so on. But what you say, public obloquy or disgrace, has an importance because this is part also of the philosophy of punishment. I think it was Lord Denning's great view of punishment that the public denunciation of the harm done is already a punishment to the individual. But may be it should be a bit more practical and pragmatic when it comes to individual Members who are guilty, perhaps, of favouring their own interests—that they should somehow or other not be allowed to enrich themselves in any way through what they have done.

WILLIAM UTTING: Thank you.

2136. LORD NOLAN: Thank you very much indeed. You have been of great help to us and we have very much enjoyed your evidence, as well as benefiting from it.

Mr Wigley, I am just in time to greet you with "good morning" instead of "good afternoon". We are a little late, I am afraid, and I am sorry to have kept you waiting. To you, as to all of our witnesses, we are very grateful for your help and I shall begin as I always do by asking if you have an opening statement that you would like to make.

DAFYDD WIGLEY MP

DAFYDD WIGLEY MP (President, Plaid Cymru): Thank you very much, Lord Nolan, and may I thank you and all the Committee for the opportunity to appear before you. I do so as a rare breed—a party leader, a permanent Back Bencher and 25 per cent of my party's parliamentary strength. The evidence I give on behalf of our parliamentary party draws on the 21 years that I have had as a Back Bench MP and also, I hope, on the formula that I and my colleagues have used, I think fairly successfully, in serving our constituencies and the way in which we have tried to carry out our public duties and managed to get support with us.

The written evidence which I submitted to you in December deliberately dealt with two specific aspects of your work. We do, of course, have views on many of the other matters under your scrutiny and I would like to touch very briefly on a couple of these before returning to the main points in the documents we put to you.

First, on the question of cash for questions: in the 21 years I have spent in the House of Commons, during of which I have been amongst the top twenty of question askers in the House, I have never been offered cash for tabling a question, nor am I aware of any parliamentary colleagues, not only in my own party, but in other parties, that have had that offer. I believe that the reports grossly exaggerate the issue. Clearly it would be totally wrong to take money for such a purpose and MPs must understand that.

Secondly, I do not believe that MPs should be employed by professional lobbying companies. There should be specific rules on that matter. Thirdly, I do not believe that former Ministers should take on paid employment with companies with whom they have been dealing directly in their ministerial capacity, so as not to open the accusation of carrying departmental secrets into commercial board rooms for personal gain.

Having said that, I do not believe that these are the main issues that have caused the public to question the standards of conduct of MPs. Much of the emphasis of the evidence that has been given to you has related to an agenda of "Thou shalt not". It is equally important, to say the least, to address the issue of a positive perspective with regard to the work of MPs. That is the background to the charter we submitted in our written evidence. It is a copy of the guidelines which we, as Plaid Cymru MPs, drew up for our own use for the standard of service. This is a document we drew up last year for internal purposes, but I suggest it is relevant to your work. I say this because first, and I quote, "disillusionment with established institutions", and that is the phrase used in paragraph 11 of the Introduction to Issues and Questions, is just as likely to arise from neglecting to do what we as MPs should be doing as it is from specific actions or activities that are unacceptable.

Secondly, you ask, in paragraph 13 of the Introduction to that document, about the:

"extent to which rules and conventions underlying the various aspects of public life are adequate in modern circumstances".

Our guidelines, I submit, are relevant in that context.

Thirdly, in paragraph 22 of Chapter 1, you ask about the time MPs spend on parliamentary and constituency work and again I believe our guidelines address this point. In paragraph 29 of the same chapter you ask whether there should be a "published code of conduct for MPs". We would say "yes" and that it should be a positive statement.

Could I highlight three or four points from those guidelines. We feel strongly that MPs should have their main home in their constituency. The very least that constituents should have the right to expect is that their MP lives amongst them. To refuse to do so is to sow the seeds of alienation.

We believe that every MP should have a full-time constituency office, open normal office hours to serve constituents and staffed by full-time paid employees. After all, we have an office cost allowance of over £40,000 a year and there is no conceivable excuse for not sustaining such a service. Personally, I believe that there should be an office of the MP in every constituency analogous, if you like, to the Mayor's Parlour or the Town Clerk's office. It should be a public building and the MP, whoever the incumbent is, should move into it.

We also believe that MPs should not be ex-directory with regard to their telephone availability. Their homes, office and House of Commons phone numbers should be publicly available. I see nothing wrong in that at all and it would help with regard to contact.

We believe that there should be a minimum requirement by way of holding surgeries—we suggest at least 50 a year. Gone are the days that MPs could refer to their monthly surgery. That is just not acceptable.

These are examples of how we believe MPs can work in closer harmony with their constituents and in doing so, minimise the risk of alienation. The whole premise of this paper is that those who take decisions on behalf of constituents or who can make representations on their behalf, should be openly available and accessible to the people in their area and that brings me, Lord Nolan, conveniently onto the issue of quangos—the epitome of bodies which are inaccessible and remote from the public.

You clearly recognise the significance of the growth of quangos. You have a whole chapter dedicated to them in *Issues and Questions*. My experience as an MP has been that quangos, more than any other aspect of public life, are a source of mystery, suspicion and frustration to the general public. Constituents come to my surgeries, concerning perhaps a problem with, say, a hospital or, increasingly these days, the collapse of the NHS dental service or a question of water charges, although that now is with a privatised quango, and they do not know how to follow up their problems. They say they have been to the local district councillor who says he cannot do anything to help, to the county councillor who cannot help and they ask me if I can raise the problem specifically in Parliament. Most often I cannot raise a detailed specific problem in Parliament because it is not a matter that has direct parliamentary answerability.

Quangos are faceless, unaccountable and unapproachable bodies and their growth is a major irritant for the public and represents a failure to provide an open, democratic and user-friendly service in the areas of their responsibility. We in Wales have had more than our share of these bodies. Many of the functions that used to be democratically answerable, such as health, aspects of housing and education, river control, come under all-Wales or regional quangos. There are now about 88 all-Wales quangos, that number has doubled since 1979, according to *The Western Mail*. They have 1,377 quango members at the last count, running very important aspects of our day-to-day lives. According to *The Western Mail* on Monday there are as many as 350 quangos in Wales, if one counts the local ones as well.

The Secretary of State appoints 761 of these 1,377 quango members to run the bodies for him and the quangos are responsible for overseeing the spending of about £2.7 billion out of the Welsh Office budget of £6 billion. When the new unitary authorities come into being in Wales next year, there will be fewer elected councillors in Wales—1,273—than people appointed to work on the quangos, a large majority of whom are appointed by the Secretary of State.

There are a number of serious problems relating to government by quango. The basic problem is that they are unrepresentative of the public and unanswerable to them. In Wales this has a party political dimension in that we in Wales have not elected a majority of Tory MPs since 1868 when we had some sort of popular vote. In the past 15 years we have had Tory government, in the past 7 years we have had Secretaries of State who have not even been elected by Welsh constituencies. These Secretaries of State appoint people to carry out their mandate—one which has not emanated from those who are being served by these bodies. A Secretary of State will appoint people who will do his bidding, understandably—that is human nature—but that causes the problem.

These are often people who have a direct involvement with the Tory party, and this seems particularly true if I may say so in the health sector. It represents to my mind the worst aspect of patronage. Only yesterday I was approached by a BBC reporter trying to do a story on quangos in Wales. It was impossible for that reporter to get members of quangos to speak out on what was going on. I was told that they were obviously constrained by the requirement not to upset the Secretary of State—they would not bite the hand that feeds them.

The system of government by quango in Wales has to end and in conclusion I would ask what we should do to replace them. Many of the all-Wales quangos should be answerable, as you would expect us to say, to an all-Wales Parliament or assembly. Local quangos should come under the elected local authorities or joint committees of those authorities. There are a very small number of quangos which may need to remain at arm's length—such as the Broadcasting Council or the Arts Council—but these are the exception rather than the rule and I would be happy to go into more questions on that if you wish.

We have seen that things can go wrong in quangos in Wales. We have had some sad sagas within the Welsh Development Agency for example. We hope that your Committee can make a strong recommendation on the need to move away from government by quango for these reasons. I am grateful for the opportunity to give those comments, as well as the papers we presented to you.

LORD NOLAN: It gives us a very clear lead and I think you have already dealt with some of the questions

we had in mind. I will ask Lord Thomson to begin the questions.

2137. LORD THOMSON: Mr Wigley, thank you very much. I read, as a former MP with a certain sense of awe, your guidelines for the behaviour of your MPs. I am not sure whether when I was an MP up in Dundee I could ever quite have lived up to all of them. Do you monitor the behaviour of your colleagues? Do you check or is there a compliance officer?

DAFYDD WIGLEY: We do not designate a compliance officer, although our whip, and we have one even in a small party of four, has the responsibility for organising us. I have monitored myself, for example, the hours that I worked—and I do not for a moment pretend that this is greater than the hours worked by MPs of all parties—during two periods. I monitored myself for a two-monthly period in separate years and it came out to 68 to 70 hours a week. I am sure that is a pattern followed by most MPs who are doing a full-time job.

Looking positively on the responsibilities that an MP has, if he or she is doing the work, and the work is there to take those hours up, there is not an awful lot of time left to be doing other extraneous activities.

2138. LORD THOMSON: Could I ask you about your own personal position. I think you list in the interests, Diagnostics Products as a client and you mention research assistance from European public policy advisers. Could you tell us something about those.

DAFYDD WIGLEY: Yes, I will tell you a little about both those points. My background is in manufacturing industry, with three supranational corporations and in the early 1980s a friend of mine and I set up a small company in the constituency making electronic medical equipment. I was the non-executive chairman for the entire life of that company and my colleague put in most of the hours; I used to put in a couple of hours on a Sunday morning to help develop the thing. It grew from nothing to employing almost 50 people eventually and it merged with the company that is quoted in the declaration of interests, at which point of course I stopped being the chairman and for a period of time I have had a consultancy interest to help the changeover.

I do not believe there is anything at all wrong in having an interest like that in the constituency which helps to create work there, providing that it does not cut across the requirement to do a Member of Parliament's job and it did not—if it had, I would not have done it.

With regard to the other matter that you mention, some of our work on parliamentary committees can be very heavy indeed. I serve on European Committee B, which in fact was sitting this morning. We have yards of paper—running to several hundred pages every week—to be analysed.

LORD THOMSON: That sounds a bit like the Nolan Committee!

DAFYDD WIGLEY: Yes, I can well imagine it. In order to do justice to the work, I find that it is helpful to have support from somebody who is an expert in European affairs. There happens to be a consultancy that is willing to give me that research back-up, if I can tell them what is going on with regard to these matters in the Committee. It is simply an exchange of expertise, but it enables me to make a much better contribution to the work of that Committee, because I could not afford to have a full-time researcher doing the work.

2139. LORD THOMSON: That is very helpful information. Could you then extrapolate from that the general position of your party and yourself about MPs' outside interests. You mentioned I think in your opening remarks that no MP should be employed by lobbyists.

DAFYDD WIGLEY: Yes.

LORD THOMSON: You put a total prohibition on that?

DAFYDD WIGLEY: Yes.

2140. LORD THOMSON: How would you draw the line between legitimate outside interests for MPs and unacceptable outside interests?

DAFYDD WIGLEY: I think that it is unacceptable for MPs to be paid and to be using their position in Parliament to further a private interest. I think that would be absolutely wrong. Also MPs must be constrained by the requirement to put in the hours that are necessary to undertake their work. We mentioned in our paper a requirement of 60 hours a week and if, over and above that, MPs have interests and prefer to be, say, farming a few acres of land rather than going to a pub on a Saturday or Sunday, that is fair enough, provided it is never compromising their need to put their first commitment to their constituents and to put in the time that is necessary to do the job in Parliament as well as in the constituency.

2141. LORD THOMSON: Do you think that the present Register of Members' Interests is an adequate safeguard, or what sort of reforms or changes would you like to see?

DAFYDD WIGLEY: I would be totally relaxed to see that changed to take on board the amount of money that is received by MPs for their various activities. There are of course items that are listed in Members' Interests from which MPs may not have any income whatsoever. For example, if one holds more than 1 per cent of the shareholding of a company one lists it. One may have that in a very small company in order to facilitate things, whether in one's constituency or elsewhere. One may not even expect to see the money coming back. I was a shareholder by guarantee of Caernarfon Town Football Club for a number of years and I did not expect to see any benefit whatsoever coming from that, but one is required to put down those shareholdings.

If one also noted how much income comes, if any, from those, it would put some of these matters in perspective.

2142. LORD THOMSON: Do you think that the present arrangements for MPs regulating themselves are satisfactory? Is the sovereignty of Parliament absolute in your view, or do the ideas that have been put to us by various people that parliamentary machinery might be supplemented by some outside assessors or an outside ethics committee appeal to you?

DAFYDD WIGLEY: I was very interested in hearing a moment ago the talk about the sovereignty of Parliament. I am afraid I am a little bit of a revolutionary, if not a reformer, in these matters and I would regard sovereignty as emanating from the people. Our legitimacy comes from the people and therefore, in safeguarding their interest, it is helpful to have such a committee, I would be happy about that.

I was impressed by the evidence that Jeff Rooker gave to you a short time ago with regard to such a committee and I think it could be very helpful to MPs to know more clearly where the line is drawn and, if necessary, even to be able to make approaches to have clarification on matters on which they may be a bit uncertain; that is something I would welcome.

2143. LORD THOMSON: One of the things that interested me in your guidelines for MPs, which includes such things as a weekly schedule of all movements reported back to your constituency party, is that there is nothing which could be distinctively said to be an ethical requirement of MPs. Is that because in Plaid Cymru you do not feel any need for underlining the importance of good ethical behaviour?

DAFYDD WIGLEY: I heard a moment ago the discussion of the content of the term "ethical" and I would regard giving the comprehensive service to the constituency in line with what we have been appointed to do and for which we were elected as constituency MPs, as an ethical issue in itself. Of course one takes for granted that one is not caught with one's hand in the till or trying to make personal gain out of one's job. The guidelines that were drawn up here were not, of course, for the purpose, primarily, of this Committee, but for our own activities, to make sure that we were giving a commitment and using our time and organising ourselves in a way that gave the best possible service to constituents.

I repeat, I believe that in order to ensure that the public have a high regard for their representatives in Parliament, it is important that this sort of service is carried out. In particular I would stress the need and requirement that every single MP should have a full-time constituency office, open normal hours to the public. There is no excuse at all why MPs do not have that and more than anything that is something that can improve our performance and acceptability to the public.

2144. LORD THOMSON: Do you think that there should be an ethical code for MPs and would you like to see other parties adopt and perhaps adapt your guidance to your Members for theirs?

DAFYDD WIGLEY: I think that other parties may work to the same guidance we have, but we would not be aware of that. Each party no doubt has within its organisation its code of practice. Constituencies themselves may have requirements they have drawn up which are not clear cut. But ethical guidelines by all means, to the extent to which there is a problem. I believe, however, that we must address the positive agenda here as well as the negative one.

2145. LORD THOMSON: Thank you. Can I move on to quangos because of course, in Wales, as you have said, there is perhaps a distinctive dimension to the quango problem. I want to explore with you some of your ideas about dealing with these problems. First, can we take the point you made that the Conservative party is weak in parliamentary numbers in Wales and yet we have a Conservative Government of the United Kingdom. There is a dilemma, is there not, as to whether that Government, in terms of its various public bodies, is entitled to at least ensure that they are under a leadership that supports the policies of the elected Government. How do you respond to that dilemma?

DAFYDD WIGLEY: As you can well imagine I would respond by saying that there is a democratic deficit in Wales and that is the base problem that we have. And it exists in Scotland, of course, to a very large extent as well, and it may well exist in the northeast and northwest of England at a regional level. I believe that where decisions can be taken close to the people they should be taken close to the people. This is the subsidiarity principle extended further than just a dipole from Brussels to London but right through. If Government in its widest context is to be acceptable to the people then they should feel that it is responding to their needs. If one has a structure of quangos where there is a writ that is imposed on the people that may not be what they see as their priorities, and that there is non-answerability and an inability even to influence the agenda, there is bound to be a divergence between the feeling of the public and the bodies that have so much power. I believe that has to be addressed. Part of it can be addressed by making local government more democratic in future than it has been in recent years, there has been a taking of powers away. Equally, there is a need to fill the democratic vacuum on the all Wales level where we have a tier of government, there is an all Wales tier of government, the Welsh Office with £6 billion of expenditure, the quangos in Wales—I have given the details of those—govern all aspects of large parts of our day to day life in Wales and yet they are not answerable to the people of Wales in a realistic manner.

2146. LORD THOMSON: As Robert MacLennan was telling us in evidence earlier this morning, he also put some very general views about major constitutional change for the United Kingdom but recognised that that is outside our remit, so we have to look at the quango situation within the present constitutional arrangements and to consider whether there are improvements in it that we could recommend.

One point that has been put to us what that in the past there was a tradition in making appointments to quango-type bodies that the government of the day, whatever its political complexion, did ensure, no doubt while its main policies were preserved, that there was a political balance in quango appointments. Do you see possibilities for improvement on that particular line in Wales?

DAFYDD WIGLEY: Yes I do. There is considerable scope for being more even handed and perhaps trying to seek a balance of representation on the quangos that reflects political balance in Wales. One of the things that I believe should be done while the quangos persist in their present form is that every member of a quango should be required to indicate whether or not they are or have been members of a specific political party, and that should be public knowledge in the same way as we have declarations of interest in Parliament. That should be required of quango members, and that would be very revealing I suspect if that was the case in Wales. Whether or not the system of advertising quangos and inviting people to join makes any difference I am not sure. It will depend to what extent that is a facade and the Secretary of State just carries on then appointing the people that he wanted to in

the first place having given others the opportunity to make themselves known to him. It is not an acceptable system. It is not open and there is not that answerability. I realise that this is stretching your own remit, but there is the question of the standing in which the public sector in general is held amongst the electorate and the population. If one feels that decision taking mechanisms on things such as health, which are literally vitally important to people in their everyday lives, that they cannot get at the people who have responsibility and they cannot get their complaints into the system in a satisfactory manner, that is alienating people from the system and I believe that it has to be taken on board. That is quite apart from any question of sleaze on quangos, that is another area. If you do not have scrutiny, openness and a need to be accountable, there will always be a greater temptation to try and get away with things, and I think that is human nature. That, again, is why we need a better system.

2147. LORD THOMSON: The evidence that we had from the Chairman of the Public Accounts Committee tended to indicate that the most serious cases of sleaze, if one likes to use that word but I rather regret using, the worst cases of problems of financial mismanagement quangos had occurred in Wales. Is there any special reason for that?

DAFYDD WIGLEY: I have no reason to believe it is worse in Wales other than the extent that we have more quangos in Wales and they seem to cover more aspects of our everyday lives. There have been well reported instances with regard to certain bodies, and of course people have appeared before the Public Accounts Committee, and changes have been undertaken as a result of that. Of course, that highlights the fact that because they had to appear before a parliamentary committee they felt obliged to make changes. Because there was no general answerability on a month by month basis that would have ensured that those changes would have happened and there would have been a built in self-monitoring procedure that would have ensured that these questions came to the forefront of the agenda. I believe that the fact that there have been those instances highlights the weakness of the system.

2148. LORD THOMSON: If there are problems with quangos are there not also problems with local government? Is not a one party rule in a local government situation also open to abuse in the way that sometimes quango administration has proved to be?

DAFYDD WIGLEY: Yes it is. We have not submitted our evidence as yet with regard to the local government part of your work and no doubt we will be wishing to do so.

LORD THOMSON: That is for the future.

DAFYDD WIGLEY: That is for the future. I was a local elected representative on a county borough council for a couple of years before entering Parliament in an area that was dominated by one party and I saw examples of that, yes. I think that in any structure where there is a one party rule going on for decades or even generations, then there is a danger of people shortcutting the system. The decisions being taken in caucuses rather than in open meetings where the press and the public have access, and I think that that would be the case whichever party was in permanent long-term control and that is why one needs to ensure that there is an adequate opposition that can get itself elected to being a governing party in all the areas where we have the democratic ridge running. I think that is a question that goes, again, possibly into the second part of your enquiries.

LORD THOMSON: Thank you very much, Mr Wigley.

LORD NOLAN: I am afraid we have to introduce rationing. Sir Clifford.

2149. CLIFFORD BOULTON: Our last witness suggested that loudly expressed support and dissent, or even incredulity in the House of Commons was in itself in some way unethical. I think members of the public who only see the House of Commons on the snippets provided by the television might think that Parliament spends all its time in that kind of atmosphere. Do you want an opportunity to say a word in defence of noise or was it a fair cop?

DAFYDD WIGLEY: We all tend to be a little noisy when there are matters that are very close to our hearts that arise, matters that cause great passion, and I suspect the construction of the Chamber of the House of Commons, adversarial as it is, facing each other, perhaps accentuates that, and the nature of the Chamber, timbered as it is, perhaps magnifies the sound that arises, but I do not think this is anything new. I think perhaps the impression that is gained by the general public is based on Prime Minister's Question Time, quarter of an hour twice a week, when that in reality is a very small proportion of the work of the House of Commons. The best work of the House of Commons, to my mind, goes on in committees, and very rarely do you see that sort of outburst in committees. It would perhaps be a good idea if there was more coverage of that. Clearly we have to be careful how we behave, and when there is feedback from constituents to tell us that the place is too noisy then perhaps we should be having a little bit of greater self-control and self-denying ordinance on ourselves even during those most controversial times on the floor of the House.

CLIFFORD BOULTON: Thank you.

2150. PROF. ANTHONY KING: One question to follow up something that Lord Thomson asked, you said in your opening statement and again in reply to Lord Thomson's questions, that you thought there was a kind of activity on the part of MPs that ought to be prohibited, and at one point you used the phrase "commercial relations with lobbying companies". Later, in response to a question from Lord Thomson you used the phrase "private interest". What exactly is it that you want to prohibit?

DAFYDD WIGLEY: With regard to the lobbying I do not think that any MPs should be purchasable by organisations whose main objective is to get change in decisions taken in Parliament and to use MPs by virtue by buying them up in order to secure that change. I think that is absolutely wrong and that should be totally black and white. Secondly, I do not believe that MPs themselves should be seeking to make private profit out of undertaking the work for which they are paid a salary after all to undertake on behalf of their constituents. If there are any other interests, whether it is a solicitor with an interest or whether it is somebody who has an interest in a small business outside, that is something that should be totally separate from Parliament and it should not cut across the working of an MP in the House of Commons or the hours that are available to serve the constituents and

parliamentary work. It may well be that we do need to go further, that we need to contemplate having the sort of rules that apply to Government Ministers as rules for all Members of Parliament. That would be a black and white way of doing it. If there is no way of drawing the line short of that, I certainly would accept that if necessary.

2151. PROF. ANTHONY KING: How does your own interest as receiving research assistance provided by European Public Policy Advisers UK Limited fit in to the rubric you have just been describing?

DAFYDD WIGLEY: It was the case that I mentioned in reply to Lord Thomson that I do not get any money and no money passes at all, but I do get the help of a person who is employed by that company on research into the papers that arise from the European Community, very voluminous papers, and a summary brief of those papers given to me. In return for that I keep them informed of what is coming up in the committees with regard to European matters which is obviously of importance to them. That facilitates me to undertake my parliamentary work on that committee. It would be very difficult indeed for me to do justice to that committee without a researcher to support me, and my research budget is already committed with regard to the other responsibilities that I have.

2152. PROF. ANTHONY KING: A charitable organisation might come to a Member of Parliament and say, "We would like your help. We need your advice but we also need our cause advocated in Parliament", and the MP might reply, "But this is going to take up a great deal of time if I am to do the job for you properly", and the charity might respond by saying "Well, we'll give you a small honorarium to help you buy a research assistant" or whatever. Would that fall foul of your set of procedures?

DAFYDD WIGLEY: I think that if there is a provision of research assistance it has to be declared in the way that I have declared the matter there. I have links with a number of charitable organisations, mainly in the world of disability, organisations such as MENCAP and the Spastics Society, or SCOPE as it now is, and quite clearly if one is undertaking significant work on an agenda such as a disability agenda it can take up a lot of hours. The support that we are given from these organisations is very valuable indeed. Sometimes it is necessary or helpful to provide parliamentary passage, for example, for people from those organisations that are helping us with our work on the disability agenda, and that, again, is something which I think you have been addressing in earlier sittings of your committee. Clearly, if there is research support being given with regard to something like a disability campaigning organisation it would have to be declared. I do not believe that that is something that should be prevented. Nonetheless, that should not lead us to being in a position to be taking decisions or undertaking our work in a manner different to that which we would have had that not existed, and that has to be absolutely clearcut and my friends in the disability world know that that is very much the line I take.

2153. PETER SHORE: Quangos appear to be very obviously unbalanced in terms of their political composition in Wales, perhaps the evidence there is stronger than it is elsewhere in the country. When you consider the justification that is put to us for this imbalance, that is to say that Ministers must appoint people who will do their bidding or who they can rely upon to pursue their policy, do you find that really convincing? When I think of a quango like the Welsh Development Agency I would have thought, whatever other defects it may have, it was really concerned with developing commonly of an industry in Wales and that was the overriding purpose, whether people liked a particular Minister and his party political connection or not. Would you not agree with that?

DAFYDD WIGLEY: Yes, I would like to take the opportunity to pay tribute to the work the Welsh Development Agency has done in Wales. We have had four times as much inward investment in Wales than the UK on average and that is largely thanks to the Welsh Development Agency, and therefore it is very important indeed when criticisms are made of bodies such as the WDA or of the quangos that we do not throw the baby away with the bath water. It is important that these bodies are helped to do a better job, to be more effective rather than undermined in the work that they do. There is a point that arises with regard to undertaking their responsibilities where there can be a clash between the interests and needs of Wales, and the wishes of those running the Welsh Development Agency, and the wishes of the Secretary of State himself. Take, for example, the funding of the Welsh Development Agency. They are now required to sell off their capital assets in large proportions in order to fund their budget over the next two years without any guarantee that there will be the revenue income that has previously been available. Now I have reason to believe that may not have been the first choice of those who are in an executive position in the Welsh Development Agency, but nonetheless, because that was the wish of the Secretary of State, they had to follow that.

2154. PETER SHORE: A very vivid example of the point that I am making that even when people are obliged or required to do things which they find basically rather objectionable, like selling off the asset, nevertheless they would do so. Surely the same thing is true of National Health Service Trusts and other bodies. People who are appointed to those bodies can be relied upon to do their utmost for the Health Service in their area and will not constrain their efforts because they dislike the particular policies being pursued by the Minister himself.

DAFYDD WIGLEY: But they will have to work within the structure of those policies that are imposed upon them. They will do their best within that structure no doubt for their area and for the Health Service in general according to their rights, but they will be constrained by what is imposed upon them and they are there to do the bidding of the person who does the imposing and that may not necessarily be in line with what is wanted in the area, needed in the area, or even analysed on the basis of areas of Wales or Wales as a whole, or, as I say, Scotland or areas of England.

2155. PETER SHORE: I am really making the case that there is no reason why the composition should be politically tilted in a certain way when you know perfectly well that the people who you do appoint, regardless of their political allegiance, will do their utmost to carry out the policies on behalf of the people they serve.

DAFYDD WIGLEY: Yes, although of course individuals do have a different perspective of what is in the interests of the area that they are serving, and some may feel that that is better achieved by bringing in more commercial elements into areas such as Health Care, that that actually delivers a better service is something I do not personally agree with, but they may well genuinely believe that and undertake the responsibilities imposed on them or requested of them by the Secretary of State on that agenda, but it may well not be the emphasis or the direction which a majority of the people in their area would want them to take.

2156. PETER SHORE: One further question on appointments. You obviously favour the extension of democratic control over quangos, but there will be a number which frankly are not suitable for direct democratic control. In your paper I think you make the suggestion that the system of appointment of members of quangos should become far more democratic than it is at present. This implies that it should be taken away from Ministers deciding on their own. What have you in mind there as a procedure, as it were, preceding the Minister's appointment?

DAFYDD WIGLEY: In a structure such as the current structure of government where we have the Welsh Office Minister there may well be a need for the Minister to be advised by people and that there is a body set up for that purpose to advise so that there is an arms length involvement at least in screening people and making sure that the appropriate people come forward and that all considerations are taken on board. Of course, I would like to see a change in a system of government, as I mentioned earlier, where more decisions are being taken by those who have been elected whether on the all Wales level or in local government for that matter, and that some of these powers are repatriated to such democratic bodies.

2157. DIANA WARWICK: Could I just ask one question. Am I right in that your view would be that the Register of Members' Interests should contain the amount of time and the remuneration received by an MP for all outside activity?

DAFYDD WIGLEY: Yes.

2158. DIANA WARWICK: Could I ask you then, when you were talking about the role of your research assistant it did seem to me to be very similar to the arrangements made by trade unions and others to provide research assistants but not directly financing. How would you reflect that if you were required to put a monetary value to it? Would you see a monetary value being attached to such assistants?

DAFYDD WIGLEY: Yes, it could be done quite easily on the basis of the time that is put in on the work. If it is a day a week or a day and a half a week in undertaking the work that can be quantified, and I would be perfectly happy to see that being a requirement of the Members' Register of Interests.

2159. LORD NOLAN: Thank you very much indeed. You will not be surprised to hear that there has only been one day, I think, when we have begun our last witness on time, but that is because the previous witnesses have been so interesting and so helpful. Thank you very much indeed for all your help.

Lord Howe I am afraid that we on this committee, for the reason I have just mentioned, have become accustomed to going beyond the one o'clock deadline. I hope it will not inconvenience you too greatly if we do so in your case because we would be very sorry to cut you short.

RT HON. LORD HOWE
OF ABERAVON, QC

RT HON. LORD HOWE OF ABERAVON, QC: Lord Nolan, I am entirely happy. It is your misfortune to be late for lunch every day, it is mine only today.

LORD NOLAN: You have been kind enough to send us a statement which has been enormously helpful. It is one of some considerable length and fullness covering aspects of our enquiry. I hope you will read it out for us now in full, at the same time accepting that we shall need to devote more time to it than this morning to exploring all its implications, but it will be a very great help to us, I think, if you could read it to us now.

LORD HOWE: You would like me to read it now. I thought I might short circuit that, but if you wish me to do so.

2160. LORD NOLAN: I would welcome the whole statement and I think members of the committee would. So would you please?

LORD HOWE: If you please, yes. I begin by acknowledging that there is certainly a case to answer, not only against MPs, Ministers, Government, but also against business and the City, law and the judiciary, organised sport and the media. The existence of this Committee (only 20 years after the 1975 Salmon Commission) is evidence enough of that.

I have the impression that in the second half of the nineteenth century, growing awareness of "sleaze" led to an improvement of standards. Whether that was true or not—and my historical insight could easily be wrong—it seems clear that the second half of the present century has been characterised, perversely, by a simultaneous crescendo of concern and diminuendo of standards. Why, I ask, has contemporary anxiety apparently been so ineffective against contemporary abuse? Have we all been rubbishing each other too much, and thus diminishing mutual respect, expectations and so performance?

If so, again I ask, can we somehow reverse that trend, not by mutual whitewash but by greater willingness to encourage a more positive view, even to recognise virtue where it does exist? I echo what Ann Taylor said to this Committee about the negative impact of much of the media. The very existence of this Committee is rightly seen as evidence of deterioration of standards. By the same token, the positively engaged way in which you have been conducting yourselves could (if I may be disrespectfully bold) point the way towards part of the treatment.

My first point, please do not expect too much by way of salvation from detailed legalistic provision. I attached a note giving some quotations which illustrate the importance of what I describe as the domain of "Obedience to the Unenforceable" where people do right although there is no one and nothing to make them do right but themselves.

Please try not to regard legal hoop-leaping as the answer. If I amplify that as I make the point. If one looks at

the impact of the Financial Services Act, for example, of the Cadbury Committee Report, of the rituals one used to have to go through appearing before Brewster Sessions of the licensing Justices, where witnesses said that water was equally available with acholic refreshment in their restaurants and so on. One can too easily be led to think that things have been rightly done by compliance with a whole series of rules rehearsed by rote, so I think it is very important not to go too far down that road.

Codification, if you cannot resit a move in that direction, should be illustrative and not exhaustive. I offer three very simple general propositions. First, echoing but not quite verbatim what Ann Taylor said: it is crucially important to maintain the public trust that should accompany the privileges of public office. The idea of seeking or securing personal reward or advantage as a consequence of using any of the powers or procedures of office must be seen as entirely inadmissible.

If that statement is set out clearly and loudly and emphatically time and time again it will have more enlightening effect than almost a host of detail.

Secondly, a question to ask oneself. Would you, whether MP or Minister, feel happy to see all the relevant facts of any transaction or relationship fully and fairly reported on the front page of your favourite newspaper?

Thirdly, if in doubt, cut it out. (That is a paraphrase of paragraph 103 of Questions Procedure for Ministers).

Then on outside interests. I support very strongly the case for outside interests. Indeed, if possible, of a career outside Parliament. This approach helps to maintain the independence as well as the worldly wisdom of Parliament and its Members. So too does acceptance of their earning capacity before and after their time in public service (which should itself in any case be better rewarded). It is hard to believe that there is no connection between anxiety about a possible decline in the integrity of politics and the parallel drop in compensation for service in posts of great public responsibility. I attach an article which amplifies the point in a slightly fanciful fashion perhaps.

On scrutiny, again, we must take care not to load the prospect of public service with bureaucratic and other scrutiny on a scale calculated absolutely to deter candidates of self-respecting quality. We should hesitate a long time before contemplating a Washington-style public circus, so please take seriously the warnings set out in paragraphs 2.13 and 3.20 of your own discussion document. If I may echo there a phrase used by the present American Ambassador to the Court of St James when he said that——

"In my country today a man or woman is presumed innocent until he is appointed to public office by the President".

I think to see a reproduction for membership of the House of Lords Judicial Committee of the procedure adopted in relation to the Supreme Court might not merely cause discomfort to the people concerned but also lead to a reduction in the quality of people filling those offices.

Please try to maintain a similarly hands-off approach to entertainment and overseas travel. I am not discounting the importance of that at all. Openness is important here, but Ministers are constrained by the fact that their diaries are public property. And for Members, registration (but only of substantial matters) should be sufficient. Frankly, if one knows that a Member has made his third visit in 18 months to Bophutania, or wherever it may be, one is ready enough to discount the value of his testimony in relation to that thereafter, but it is important for the facts to be registered. I have never felt discomforted by the range of hospitality I have received either at home or abroad. Perhaps I ought not to say that. On occasions, certainly, it has been disconcertingly magnificent, even pleasant. At other times it has been discomfortingly spartan, even positively dangerous. As Chancellor of the Exchequer I could have been overwhelmed by so much competing hospitality that the process was entirely self-cancelling. Overseas there was never any difficulty in coping with what I call Bocassa-type gifts, particularly if, as was often the case, they had come originally from Bond Street. At the other end of the scale, some pettiness of existing restrictions was often irritating, and I can illustrate both those points if you would like me to.

On employment of ex-Ministers, I hope you may encourage a similarly grown-up attitude (and again I do not mean a lax or louche attitude, but a mature attitude) towards employment after service as a Minister. Our country derives great advantage from the comparative earliness of the retirement age of 60 imposed upon our civil servants and diplomats (by contrast with, for example, the French equivalent of 65). Many of them achieve (from a well-pensioned base) what is almost a second career of often fully paid service to the country (often, of course, voluntary as well) as a consequence of their liberation from public service. Existing scrutiny procedures for their post-retirement employment (lightly and discreetly applied as I think) have worked reasonably well. So I have been tempted to believe that ex-Ministers could be similarly treated, if only for their own protection. And yet, and yet, and yet .... I ask myself whether that should be adopted as your conclusion because there are important differences to take into account.

Most Ministers leave office (whether at the hands of the electorate or of the Prime Minister) at a time and in circumstances not of their own choosing. I was, myself, an exception to that rule. Many will be well short of pensionable age, will have been earning well below their market value, will have children still in full time education, and will need a job and soon. In such circumstances the imposition of even a short period of waiting time could cause real hardship, and even a purely qualitative restraint would be hard to define and operate.

Some of these people, particularly the self-employed, will leave office with their earning capacity enhanced: former law officers, journalists, bankers, broadcasters, accountants, academics, to name but a few. Are all these to be banned and, if so, for how long from returning to their chambers, their partnerships, their firms, their papers, their studios and their classes? Are bankers and accountants to be free to return to their professions so long as it is not from the Treasury because there will be a continuity of interest? Businessmen and industrialists to return to their firms so long as not from the DTI? Academics and teachers to their classes so long as not from the D of E? Does it make sense to insist that round pegs should serve only in square holes and vice versa? What effect would all this have on MPs willingness even to take on junior ministerial appointments at all?

My guess is that the three General Elections of 1983, 1987 and 1992 witnessed the departure from Parliament of some 400 MPs and from office of some 50 or 60 Ministers—that is an estimate, particularly the last figure, but I think that is about right—all, unusually for such a long period, from the same party. A small handful of these may have achieved substantial, if sometimes short-lived, rewards in the media and not many more may have found their way into newly privatised board-rooms. That may have been unwise, but similar opportunities are unlikely to occur frequently. It is worth thinking, I suggest, long and hard before trying to design the wrong kind of door for the wrong stable when the bolting pony is already almost out of sight. Hard cases—perhaps heedless of the unwritten law—are not the best foundation for new, more formal, restrictions.

Oversight of alleged parliamentary misconduct. So far as oversight, investigation and assessment of alleged misconduct by MPs is concerned, I agree about the need for a system that is fair as well as effective. I echo as well Antony Newton's call for more thought than has so far been given to methods of improving present procedures. They are certainly less expeditious and less compatible with the rules of natural justice than I should like.

The locus classicus of those rules, in this context, is in the report of the earlier Salmon Commission of 1966. If, as I believe is inevitable and right, final decisions have to be left to Parliament itself, some shortfall from what I call "perfect Salmon" may be inescapable. But careful study of the case of John Browne, with which I was closely concerned as Leader of the House, does make apparent the case for some reforms. The design of precise alternatives will require very careful and deliberate consultation. I believe there may be a role here for independent participants in the proceedings, both in the investigation and presentation of matters for consideration and in the pre-final adjudication. I join with what Alex Carlisle said in inclining towards as much informality as possible.

If I can just mention two points that occur to me. First, in addition to the suggestions you have had of an Ombudsman or Comptroller and Auditor General type supplement to the parliamentary machinery, one has other possible parallels in the Interception and Communications Act and the Secret Service Act in the form of commissioners or tribunals or independent people who can play a role alongside the parliamentarians.

Secondly, I felt there was rather a ragged frontier between the role played by the Privileges Committee and the Committee of Members' Interests in approaching the same questions from two different points of view, but I do not have a detailed prescription to offer.

Finally quangos. Quangos have a useful, indeed an indispensable, role. That may be all the better fulfilled if quango membership does include "outsiders" with what I call a more adventurous experience than the treadmills of political or public service. My particular experience as Minister for Consumer Affairs when I had responsibility for the appointment of a small army of consumer councillors and was constantly scavenging the nation for people of sufficient usefulness and diversity and vitality to fill these places, reminds me that the problem is often to find anything like enough people of appropriately energetic and activist disposition. So, while I could certainly go along with the case for some system of responsive oversight of what I call "croneyism" or other impropriety, because it is important that there should be some safety valve, I should attach as much importance to openness of recruitment and evaluation of new Members. For some at least of the senior posts I commend for possible consideration the procedures widely adopted in recent years for the selection and appointment of lay magistrates: advertisement of vacancies, interviewing of applicants and so on. If I may draw there on my wife's experience, she served on the Lord Chancellor's Committee for the appointment of magistrates for Inner London in the mid-1960s under the Chairmanship of Lord Denning, and at that time it was quite unusual to do other than receive nominations from the two or three political parties. They changed the system in Inner London and it spread more widely round the countryside so as to advertise their existence. Lord Denning broadcast on the radio, which had been practically unheard of in those days, to advertise for vacancies and applications and to interview applicants before they appointed them. One of the questions they had to consider was, do they ask about the politics of the applicants or not? They felt they had to be informed about that, not because they were seeking to generate a politically dominated or politically even-handed bench even, but because they wanted to avoid having one that was inadvertently out of balance the wrong way. So they had to have that information as part of the material they needed to draw on in getting a reasonable outcome.

If I may use that, if you like, Chairman, as a reason for saying a word about spouses in the context of quangocracy, because spouses do sometimes have the misfortune of being treated merely as appendages of their spouse rather than as people in their own right. If I take my own wife's case, with her permission but no doubt with some dismay, her first role in voluntary work sprang, I suppose, from her membership of the Bow Group and that landed her with the misfortune of doing voluntary work in the part of London represented by Peter Shore. So in that Tory dominated area she found herself coming forward for nomination for various school governing bodies and management committees, and in due course to the Juvenile Magistrates Bench in the early 1960s I think. Her first "quango-type" jobs were as membership of the Inner London Magistrates Committee and as a member of the Legal Aid Committee, and as a member of the Briggs Committee on the nursing profession, to all three of which she was appointed by fearful right wing characters like Lord Gardner and Richard Crossman. Her next round of experience was appointment in 1975 as deputy chairman of the Equal Opportunities Commission, again by that enormously right wing character Roy Jenkins. Subsequently, when I became Chancellor of the Exchequer, she felt she had to give up that particular job because of the risk of conflict between her holding that particular office which might bring proceedings against the Government of which I was a member. Oddly enough she was criticised for having done that as being unfaithful to her principles as suggesting she did not believe in living in a household where there were two people drawing two incomes, which was an absurd insight. Then subsequently she has been appointed by the Hansard Society to chair one thing while the Local Government Management Board chaired another, and most recently by the Archbishops of Canterbury and York to preside over the commission on cathedrals which is scarcely a corrupt activity. When she took on her present single public sector

paid job as chairman of the Broadcasting Standards Council I venture to think that probably the only handicap that stood in her way was being married to me.

2161. LORD NOLAN: I am very glad you made that account. Thank you very much for the whole of your paper. I wonder if I could take you back to paragraphs 4 and 5 where you urge us not to expect too much by way of salvation from detailed legalistic provision, and this with me at least strikes a very sympathetic cord. You then go on to the question of codification and put forward three very simple propositions, the first of which is what might be almost the first sentence of a short general code of behaviour. The second is a guiding rule that you ask yourself would you feel happy to see all the relevant facts of any transaction fully and fairly reported on the front page of a newspaper, a precept which in the days when I practised at the Tax Bar and people would sometimes contemplate the most extraordinary bogus transactions I found was a very helpful question. You say, more generally, it is a salutary question for people in a doubtful situation to ask themselves

I wonder this. There must be, mustn't there, a few rules, preferably simple, certainly clear, and essentially accepted, and if they are not accepted, enforceable against those to whom they apply?

LORD HOWE: Clearly whatever code or set of rules is in force needs to be respected and, if necessary, enforced, there is no doubt about that. One can see how easy it is to be drawn down the road of detailed provision in relation to everything, and that can sometimes happen simply by case law. If you look either at the old rules of conduct provided by the Bar Council that was a mountain of detail that became almost impenetrable. So I think my inclination is that if you are going to go beyond those very general propositions then try to do it by example. It is often useful advice but disregard it in relation to statutory draughtsmanship. We are very reluctant to have draughting by example, but I think if you have four, five or six very clear cases against a powerful statement of principle that may be more useful than a mountain of detail.

2162. LORD NOLAN: The Bar, like many professions, does now have a code of conduct which barristers undertake to obey, and it is, I think, something that has worked quite well, it is relatively simple and clear.

Against that background, when we were set up it was at once apparent, because we were asked to consider Members of Parliament and their financial interests, that a crucial area of our enquiry was the Register of Members' Interests. Is that clear, is it accepted, and is it enforceable?

LORD HOWE: I think that the Register is very important. I do not know how far it is enforceable in the sense that I have not had all that much direct experience of it. My impression is that Members probably would be helped by having access more openly and more readily than happens now to advice about the registration of particular things, and that that is the way to go rather than going into much, much more detail about what has to be registered. Certainly you do need such a thing and therefore it does need to be enforceable.

2163. LORD NOLAN: The evidence we heard from Mr MacLennan earlier this morning criticised the rules governing the Register as being very vague and sometimes quite confusing to those who were bound by them, and also criticised the present committee procedure for enforcing them. You, indeed, in paragraph 14, after referring to the Salmon Commission and the case of John Browne, say that made apparent the case for some reforms. You go on, and if I may so, speaking for myself, it must plainly be so that the design of precise alternatives will require very careful and deliberate consultation. You believe there may be a role for independent participants in the proceedings. You rather alarm me by referring to the possible precedent of the Interception of Communications Act and the Commissioner under that Act because that (I do not know whether you know it) is me and I am not volunteering for any further job.

If it did combine simply with a view to exploring the facts, something of the role of the Comptroller and Auditor General and the Ombudsman if it was an officer or servant of the House or appointee of the House appointed by the House, answerable to it, would that be the sort of thing you had in mind?

LORD HOWE: Well, I think that one would certainly look at that as a possibility. I think, for example, the rules I am not now familiar with in sufficient detail to know whether they are adequate or not, but I do know that at the time of the case I refer to there we invited the Committee on Members' Interests to examine the adequacy of the rules and look at them in more detail. There clearly was a very unsatisfactory situation of uncertainties there and one therefore does need to address that matter. That is no doubt something that you are looking at closely. Again, I would say I hope not to produce a massively detailed code.

As far as investigation of alleged misconduct thereafter is concerned I am sure you need somebody in the role adopted, for example, by the Treasury Solicitor in relation to a tribunal enquiry under the 1921 Act—someone who gathers together the material for it to be considered by whatever body is then going to adjudicate on it. That need not be a parliamentarian who does that himself. So somebody like the C & A.G. or an ombudsman might be the appropriate investigative person, if only for the facts as alleged in correspondence or a newspaper article to be sorted out so that they can be looked at tidily by the adjudicating body. Then I think the adjudicating body, which would be something like the Committee of Privileges or conceivably the Committee on Members' Interests——that is why I say that one needs to look at both those alongside each other to reach the right answer——I am not sure that that as at present constituted comes as close as it should do to giving the Member whose conduct is being investigated notice of the charge. I would stop short of commending full legal representation and cross-examination—I think there are many professional bodies of a less than front-row kind that have informal procedures for the investigation of misconduct in a way that complies with the rules of natural justice. But I think that even at that stage—the adjudication stage—again the Committee of Members (whichever it was) might well be helped by having somebody alongside the Chairman of the Committee in the role of the assessor, the GMC Disciplinary Committee, or something of that kind, so that independence can be introduced both in the investigative process and in the adjudicating process. I do not think, though, that the final decision on "sentence" could be taken other than by the House itself. That is not because I have any romantic or absolutist view of sovereignty but

because I think that in relation to membership of the House the House of Commons is the right final adjudicating body.

2164. LORD NOLAN: It is the only possible final adjudicator?

LORD HOWE: Yes.

2165. LORD NOLAN: Thank you very much. There is just one other subject I wanted to raise with you, although you have made very clear points in your paper, and that is paragraphs 9 and 10 when you talk of the employment of ex-Ministers. You say you are tempted to believe that ex-Ministers could be treated in the same way as senior civil servants in whose case, from what we hear, the rules have worked pretty well. You say "and yet, and yet, there are important differences." Now, one factor in favour of introducing something like the same system for Ministers as for civil servants was put to us strongly by Mr. John MacGregor and Sir Norman Fowler and that is justice to the wrongly accused ex-Minister himself—they have been through the mill of what they regarded as desperately unfair public criticism for taking up jobs in which they said no possible conflict of interest arose and that in their case, if they had been able to point to an umpire's decision, there was no reason at all why they should not have done what they did.

LORD HOWE: That is why I include the sentence that I do—"So I have been tempted to believe that they could be similarly treated—if only for their own protection". That is the heart of the matter. But then if one contemplates the actual process of designing rules—I give examples in my paragraph 11—that becomes very difficult—if one contemplates the process of designing an institution that might one day, long after the Greek calends, have to cope with the departure of eighty Ministers at the same time, for example. One wonders then quite what the structure can be for dealing with it. I am very anxious to avoid the introduction of any inhibiting delays and so on because the situation could be very urgent and one can think of X Ministers in all parties and walks of life who have found it actually quite hard to secure fresh fields and pastures new. So all I think I am really saying is that I fully understand the importance of the point you make—I set it out in my own draft—but I beg you, please, to look very very carefully at the other side of the equation.

2166. LORD NOLAN: Indeed we shall. May I just take a little further your comparison with Ministers leaving office and going back to self-employment as journalists, bankers, barristers? Is not the fear of this, with the senior civil servants and in some cases with Ministers, that there is an actual or perceived potential link between the office they have held and the employment they will be going to? There is a possibility that in office they may have been instrumental in Company X obtaining a valuable contract—clearly it must be as undesirable for a Minister, as for a civil servant, then to go to Company X——

LORD HOWE: Yes, that is the central reason for anxiety and to some extent it demonstrates the lack of complete validity of the examples I have given because in each of those cases the person is returning to his old haunts, as it were, and the impropriety that one is concerned about is to find someone leaping to a commercial perch which he would not have done had it not been for his Ministerial service, either because of his interest in that particular leap or because of the poacher's interest in securing his arrival. That I think is the anxiety one is concerned to address. So that is why I say no time barriers but there may be a necessity for some kind of scrutiny for qualitative links. Again I say that with hesitation because one could so easily see such a system becoming inhibiting in an unhealthy fashion. I think it is very important to have Parliament as full as possible of people with wide experience both ways. I strove as hard as I could when I was a member of the Government to promote more interchange between the Civil Service and Industry and the City and so on. But I agree that that kind of interchange is very closely scrutinised for impropriety. So that I think is the area one has to look at.

2167. LORD NOLAN: And, of course, one recognises that Ministers may be in a financially totally different position from retired civil servants. That can't unfortunately, though, allow the principle of avoiding conflict of interests to be relaxed in their cases, can it, in the type of situation which one sees as——

LORD HOWE: No, it can't possible. I mean Ministers quite consciously, with their eyes open, often accept long periods when they are earning below their market earning capacity and then they return to the market thereafter free, I hope, to do what they can to remedy that in the short time left. But it is of crucial importance that that should not be accompanied by any suspicion of impropriety. That, I think, is the issue that——

LORD NOLAN: Sir Michael Quinlan—and I think others—have drawn a broad analogy with the commercial area where I think if an employer has a restrictive covenant included in his contract he would expect to get half pay. This is not really a matter for us but one does see the justice for Ministers—and Ministers are entitled to justice like everybody else—of perhaps some recognition being given to their special situation. But I think you have answered the questions I asked you about the principle. I, for my part, am happy to leave it there. Thank you very much. May I go round the table now starting with Dame Anne?

2168. ANNE WARBURTON: Thank you very much. We have had a great deal of evidence emphasising openness and transparency and the need for it in virtually every angle, every aspect of public life, and quite a lot of the evidence has come out in favour of codes of conduct of which you have already spoken and also of a solution in the form of some kind of an ethics office, or ethics commissioner. I noted your hesitations about the code of conduct. I wonder what you would think of an ethics commissioner?

LORD HOWE: Well, I think for example, the role of someone who could give advice more obviously in relation to what should be registered and what should not be registered, someone to whom a Member of Parliament could go for clarification of that. It might well be useful there.

2169. ANNE WARBURTON: I was thinking—and I think they were thinking—in a wider context, perhaps with a remit also for NDPBs appointments and things like that.

LORD HOWE: Yes. I would not close my mind to that. I would suggest something of that kind in relation to

appointments to senior Quango offices. I think some structure or person to whom that question might be referred for advice. I think that in the last resort if a Minister is seeking advice about the appointment of somebody it is his responsibility to make the appointment. That is why the Lord Chancellor's Advisory Committee on Magistrates is a useful parallel, because it is advisory and the Lord Chancellor takes the decision. I think one could have the same kind of thing. If a Member or a Minister goes to this creature for advice, then in the last resort the decision, the responsibility, would have to be that of the person seeking advice and not the person giving the advice.

ANNE WARBURTON: Thank you.

2170. TOM KING: I think your first answer to Lord Nolan—I am not quite clear whether you agreed that if you had a system of some sort of scrutiny for Ministers on leaving office that it should somehow be enforceable. I was not quite clear—I may have misunderstood that—because you referred to the civil servant's position and working reasonably well. It does, of course, actually have no enforcement—there is no sanction, as I understand it. There is a sanction perhaps that if a civil servant goes, for instance, from the Defence Department to a major contractor against the wishes of the Committee, that that may raise questions about the suitability of that contractor and in other words there is that sort of hidden sanction and therefore not observed. But do you think there can be any sanction actually on a Minister who has lost his seat and his post and is, as it were, out in the sort of civilian life?

LORD NOLAN: Perhaps while Lord Howe is contemplating that I should make it clear. No, I was talking about enforceability solely in connection with the Register of Interests——

LORD HOWE: Right. Well, yes, that is what I had in mind. I was addressing myself to that only.

TOM KING: But on the point—I am sorry the point still rests—do you think actually there is any——

LORD HOWE: Well, I haven't myself ever asked myself what sanction there is for the enforcement of the Carlisle Committee Rules. As far as I know there is none but it is a very good example of an area where we still do comply with the unwritten law. And I think one wants to hang on to that all the time. There are many areas of our life that can only be regulated by a sense of integrity and a sense of decency, collectively enforced. And this is one of them.

2171. TOM KING: And who, if you did have this protection of Ministers that has been described and it was a pretty instant procedure of some kind so it avoided delay, who actually do you think should do it?

LORD HOWE: Well, I think that some kind of body, a kind of cross between the Carlisle Committee and this Committee, if you like, but shrunk to the size of about two or three. In other words, some judicial or quasi-judicial figure or at least legally qualified figure, and some politically experienced figure, or public service experienced figure. That kind of thing. I think that Lord Nolan's point to me that something of this kind would confer benediction upon something which would otherwise be open to unfair criticism is the area which—it may sound a rather self-serving motive but I think that the public and the participant has that much interest but it must be something that doesn't introduce a factor of delay.

TOM KING: Thank you very much.

2172. DIANA WARWICK: Lord Howe, you say right at the start of your evidence to us that there is certainly a case to answer. But going through what you have said and listening to you you seem to be saying to us "not too much law, not too many codes, don't restrict outside interests too much, hands off on scrutiny, hands off entertainment, make oversight in investigation informal." I don't think that is over-characterising what you have said and yet if we are going to try and address both the case that you identify as needing an answer and the amount of public concern, as well as one of the most persistent criticisms that we have that Parliament has not really been capable of adequately scrutinising itself, if you were to choose one aspect of change that you thought might answer those, what would you choose?

LORD HOWE: You are as difficult as Lord Goddard used to be and he always asked counsel appearing before him "Mr. Howe, what is your best point?" and I honestly don't know. I think in a way my most important point is the not too much law point because it flavours all my answers. It is certainly not meant to indicate a laxity or lack of concern on my part about any of these matters but I think that it is so tempting to believe that detail and close interwoven oversight is the answer. I have been concerned with quite a lot of legislation, including a lot of fiscal legislation, or the Consumer Credit Act, for example, all of which——the Companies Act, I was advised to include 200 provisions in a schedule to the Companies Act—we have gone law-mad and before we came into office in 1979 I made a speech entitled "Too much law?", mercifully including a question mark in the title. In fact in the last three years of the Government of which I was a Member we were enacting three times as many pages of primary legislation as in the last three years of the Government that we replaced. Now, that is the temptation and my advice can be given in two ancient Greek words "μηδὲν ἄγαν—nothing to excess". I am not dismissing your agenda at all—it is crucially important—but somehow refrain from too much of that.

2173. DIANA WARWICK: But if we follow your other maxim we ask ourselves, how would what we do look reported on the front page of our favourite newspaper? Would the words "whitewash, kicking into touch" possibly be reflected there?

LORD HOWE: Yes. That is why I emphasise and, indeed, underline in my observation there "fully and fairly reported". And it is one of the strange features—if I may draw on one other bit of personal experience—I conducted a long time ago an enquiry into alleged misconduct in a mental subnormality hospital in Wales and it was a matter of intense difficulty, as you could imagine, and I was equipped with advisers, with fellow tribunal members of great sensitivity, and we went to great care in writing our conclusions in each paragraph about each of the people concerned, to give a fair judgment. In the newspaper reporting of our tribunal in the news pages that fair judgment was pretty well reflected but in the headlines, the headlines screamed "The Horror

Hospital", "The Cruel Hospital" and there were pictures of barbed wire around the hospital which was nothing at all to do with the case, so that the bus crews in the City of Cardiff who took people to work in this hospital declined to accept them on their buses because of the sensationalised treatment of our report. Now, you must be familiar with that from other experiences and that is my anxiety, fully and fairly reported. So please don't be too afraid of full reporting of your conclusions, even if you have less confidence that they will be fairly reported.

2174. MARTIN JACOMB: Could I just go back fairly briefly to the question of the employment of ex-Ministers? We do have a big problem of perception—there is a real problem, obviously, and there are some cases——you yourself referred to some cases having been unwise——but there is a much bigger problem of perception and I think in France, for example, it would not only be considered a bad thing for a Minister who had been associated with the Ministry of Defence going into a defence contractor, it would be seen as a good thing for France because it would be seen as an advantage for a French company competing for arms orders against other international companies. So we do have a problem of perception here. If we tried to find a way of scrutinising Ministers going into the private sector, could we look for a better way of getting a better perception of it through more openness, do you think? Through more openness than applies in the case of civil servants?

LORD HOWE: I don't get the impression that lack of openness is the problem. It seems to me that these transactions are now scrutinised you know by the Press very very closely. I don't think that one is concerned at them not being known to the public.

2175. MARTIN JACOMB: You do not feel that because—let us take the analogy of civil servants—because that committee works in private and its conclusions are never published that people are always willing to assume that there is some kind of whitewash or some hidden advantage which is not made public?

LORD HOWE: Yes, I see the point now a little more clearly. I think that I have assumed, perhaps too easily, that there is public confidence in the Carlisle Committee procedures for former civil servants. My impression is that that is still the case. One gets some examples of criticism but not very many. So I don't think that openness of that procedure is a necessary——In other words, you know, a public hearing, or public presentation of all the facts is a necessary component of a proper system. People would want to know that a system exists, I think, rather than that every blow should be publicly conducted.

2176. MARTIN JACOMB: So we have really just got to live with this public perception of tremendous readiness to criticise?

LORD HOWE: No, you haven't. I mean, I can't answer your question, if I may say so, because I haven't been living with it for as long as you have and I see that you have to balance these factors and I can see why you are most anxious to come to a conclusion that persuades people that you have addressed the issues and come to a proper conclusion. But I hesitate to say "yes" to your question without thinking about it more.

MARTIN JACOMB: Yes, thank you very much.

2177. LORD THOMSON: Before we finish, could you give us the benefit of your experience on the difficult question of how to investigate complaints against Ministers, if it is not to be the Cabinet Secretary—and that procedure has been the subject of a good deal of criticism during our proceedings—who else should it be? Law Officers, Chief Whip—who? Any ideas?

LORD HOWE: Well, again, I haven't thought about it a great deal but looking back over occasions in the past I was inclined to think that the Law Officers and Chief Whip would be the best way of doing it, although one hesitates to come to any conclusion because that didn't produce the right answer in relation to John Profumo But one can't say it got less close than the Cabinet Secretary would have got. So I think I would incline in that direction faut de mieux.

2178. PETER SHORE: You spoke, Lord Howe, about Parliamentary misconduct and the possibility of introducing an independent element for investigation and presentation of matters which would be helpful to the Committee. We have had quite a lot of evidence on our present procedures for dealing with alleged misconduct and among the criticism we have heard was Lord Callaghan saying that the Privileges Committee is nothing like as effective today as it was some years ago—when the Leader of the Opposition served on the Privileges Committee it was smaller and more authoritative. From your experience if we had the additional help of investigative and presentational assistance that you envisage, what other reforms would you wish to make in the way we handle, through the Privileges Committee, allegations of misconduct?

LORD HOWE: Well, again, as you will know, I had experience of it myself only for a very short time, twelve months. I think my main anxiety is in relation to this uncertainty of jurisdiction between the Privileges Committee and the Members' Interests Committee because as I recollected, the John Browne case was investigated by the Members' Interests Committee rather than the Privileges Committee which was perhaps unusual. I think one wants to sort that out and be clear whose function it is.

2179. PETER SHORE: Perhaps merge them?

LORD HOWE: Possibly. Quite possibly, or have a sub-committee looking at the detail of Members' Interests which ought to be cleared up fairly quickly because to draw up the rules is one thing but to apply them and enforce them is another, so merger might be the right thing. I would not like to comment on the rank of the members of the committee—I should have thought that in today's age to expect the Leader of the Opposition to take part in that would be unreasonable and my impression for what it is worth is that it did have Members who were senior, respected and that the committee did not suffer from lack of rank, so to speak. But that is just an impression.

2180. PETER SHORE: What would you say about the age-old practice of reflecting the composition of a committee of that kind according to the actual strength of the different parties in the House?

LORD HOWE: I can't see any very easy alternative to that quite honestly. I think that I might incline to the inclusion of a larger representation of the smaller party, so to speak, and that might be heresy—I haven't thought about it for a long time. But not much more than that. I think one has to try and find the best combination of well-respected wisdom and on the whole I think there is an attempt to achieve that anyway.

2181. PETER SHORE: Yes. Could I just switch you now to Quangos and appointments? You make one interesting suggestion, I think on page 7 of your evidence—for some at least of the senior posts, you say, you commend for possible consideration the procedures widely adopted in recent years for the selection and appointment of lay magistrates. I am not familiar with that—can you tell us what would be the particular advantages of following such a procedure?

LORD HOWE: Well, I think there are three things; one is that there is an advisory body, other than the Minister himself who advises and which therefore conducts the surveillance. The second is that the existence of that body is publicly known, the third is that it advertises its role and says "we are now considering appointments of so many whatever it is" and the fourth is that it interviews the people whom it is considering appointing. So it is a very open process. Now I can't possibly see one adopting that for every member of every consumer council but for some positions it may be worth considering. I am not sure. Even then the last responsibility has to rest with the appointing Minister.

2182. PETER SHORE: But such an advisory body would be a permanent body?

LORD HOWE: I am just trying to see—I thought I had a phrase here that——Yes, I said "Some system of responsive oversight". So I am not sure that one should necessarily put every such application or appointment through such a committee. But it might be a body to which one might resort in cases of particular difficulty or where criticism was advanced. In other words there are two alternative suggestions for you. A kind of appellate scrutiny or preemptive surveillance. I don't know which you would prefer.

PETER SHORE: Thank you.

2183. PROF. ANTHONY KING: Lord Howe, one of the more thoughtful people who wrote in to us distinguished between a scrutiny code on the one hand, which would be very detailed, and on the other an honour code, which would be of the kind I think you have in mind under your general principle of not too much law. Do you accept that if one has in a situation of the kind we are in, an honour code, then a corollary of that is that transgressions of the honour code must lead to dishonour, that the penalties in fact may be more severe under the kind of arrangement that you have in mind and I wonder whether you think that Members of Parliament who have over the last few decades behaved dishonourably have in fact themselves been punished severely enough?

LORD HOWE: It is a very difficult question that. If you read the debates on the John Browne case, as I am sure you have, you will find some agonising analyses of what is severity and several people suggest that the penalty there proposed and imposed of a twenty-day suspension was lighter than a reprimand given with full magisterial authority of the speaker. I think the truth is that for a Member of Parliament any one of those things in fact is a powerfully discouraging conclusion. But there are one or two exceptions who perhaps take it quite lightly. But on the whole I should have thought that that kind of penalty is a powerful one and can be reflected in his subsequent career. But, again, I have not considered it in close detail and I probably support your general principle that if you are expecting good behaviour on the grounds of honour then bad behaviour requires people to fall on their swords. I would not put it quite as high as that but——

2184. PROF. ANTHONY KING: Just a question about the first of what we will now think of as "Lord Howe's rules" which reads:

"The idea of seeking or securing personal reward or advantage as a consequence of using any of the powers or procedures of office must be seen as entirely inadmissible."

Does "office", for this purpose, include being a Member of Parliament?

LORD HOWE: I think so, yes.

2185. PROF. ANTHONY KING: Is there any specific activity which is now admissible which you think in practical terms, applying your rule, should become inadmissible?

LORD HOWE: Well, I don't think any proper activity. That is the difficulty when one is logic-chopping. I think that most of the things that have been presented and regarded as questionable would fall if you applied these rules to them. If one takes quite different examples of——No, I am not going to get drawn because it is too detailed.

2186. PROF. ANTHONY KING: But, for example, it is quite clear from the Register of Members' Interests, perfectly properly compiled, that there are quite a few Members of Parliament who are in some sense taking advantage of the fact that they are Members of Parliament to augment their income by working for people who would not employ them if they were not Members of Parliament and I was not quite sure from your first rule whether you regarded that kind of behaviour as inadmissible.

LORD HOWE: I think that—again one has to get drawn back to particulars and I think that engagement as a lobbyist, for example, would seem to me to fall foul of the same rules that existed in 1947, was it, prohibiting the use of one's position for promotion or advocacy of something for an outside interest. I have always been ambivalent about something like the Police Federation representation because in a sense that, in my mind, has fallen into the Bophutania category—that if one knows that X or Y is the spokesman for the Police Federation, provided he is doing the job honourably one aims off a win but one doesn't take him off so as to discount altogether. It is a very difficult evaluation to strike—that is why I am anxious to try and avoid too much codification. I am half-ducking your question but that is why I am against too much law.

2187. PROF. ANTHONY KING: But under your first rule you do seem to have some doubts about Members of Parliament working for lobbying organisations?

LORD HOWE: Yes, working for lobbying organisations—because that is so directly related to promoting particular interests. The very word "lobby" implies promoting a cause in the lobby. It seems to me it is a very difficult parallel relationship to regard with enthusiasm.

2188. CLIFFORD BOULTON: Hitherto when a Member of Parliament's conduct has been investigated and there is no specific rule that has been broken the test that has tended to be applied is "conduct inconsistent with that which the House is entitled to expect of its Members". Are you really saying to us that if you get some objective report on the facts of a matter the House can still be trusted to recognise conduct inconsistent with the standards entitled to expect without us having to invent a lot of new school rules to try and think of everything that might go wrong?

LORD HOWE: Well, I wasn't clear in my own recollection that the judgment was "which the House is entitled to regard as inconsistent with is own standards" because if you compare that with Military or ecclesiastical conduct the test there is "conduct unbecoming an officer and a gentleman" which is an objective judgment, not necessarily one endorsed by the Officer's Mess, I think. And likewise under ecclesiastical law there is an offence of committing conduct unbecoming a priest—I forget the exact formulation. That decision, incidentally, in the ecclesiastical courts is taken by a panel of assessors, two clerics and two lay members of the church, under guidance from the registrar of the Chancery Court. So there is an objective element in that—in that judgment. I think that given a degree of objectivity then it can be left to a general judgment of the House.

2189. WILLIAM UTTING: I thought that conduct prejudicial to good order in military discipline might actually well be adapted for Parliamentary purposes in view of some of the criticisms we have heard this morning of the way Members behave.

LORD HOWE: I think that is perfectly fair!

2190. WILLIAM UTTING: I wanted, if I might, just to ask you about *Questions of Procedure for Ministers* which seems to be an extremely important document and it is invaluable to have it in the public domain. My particular point was the amount of discretion that Ministers have in interpreting the guidance in questions of procedure. There is a key sentence in the introduction:

"It will be for individual Ministers to judge how best to act in order to uphold the highest standards"

While I can appreciate that this may be there to bring home to Ministers the extent and nature of the individual responsibility they have got, it also seems to me to offer a loophole for Ministers to exercise that judgment in such a way that it overrides this guidance at particular points when perhaps they ought to follow it. Do you have thoughts about that?

LORD HOWE: I think as a matter of drafting you may be right, yes, but as a matter of reality Ministers have so many decisions about their personal conduct they have to take, on which they have to make the judgment themselves—often quite quickly—and it must be for them in many such circumstances to make that judgment for themselves. You might perhaps add the rider, which is one of my own rules "but watch it, because it might get onto the front page of the *Sunday Times* next week". And I think that is a necessary caution. But you can't say Ministers have to go to somebody else to get it decided for them surely?

2191. WILLIAM UTTING: No, but there is a paragraph, such as paragraph 27, about responsibility and accountability to Parliament where one would have thought that Ministers' discretion should actually be limited and that they should regard this as an absolute to be followed. I quite accept that there are other parts of this which are practical tips about how to carry on your business where one could accept a great deal of discretion on the part of a Minister.

LORD HOWE: I think it really comes back to my central point, does it not, that there are certain things that are clearly identified for which Ministers are customarily accountable to Parliament and could as a matter of routine expect? There are others where they are accountable in the first instance and hopefully for ever and it is for themselves and their conscience and their own sense of integrity. But all those may in the last resort be scrutinised in public opinion. I think that is the only thing one can say. It may be that the drafting you have identified gives Ministers an undue sense of comfort and say "Oh, this is up to me". If that is the impression it creates then it is the wrong impression because there are very few things which are up to Ministers in that sense.

WILLIAM UTTING: Thank you.

LORD NOLAN: Well, I am sure I speak for the whole Committee in saying how very much we appreciate the care and thought you have taken to giving us the benefit of all your experience. We cannot even offer you a free lunch—I am afraid we have almost deprived you of lunch! But thank you very much indeed.

LORD   HOWE: Thank   you   very   much.

THURSDAY 23 FEBRUARY 1995

Members Present:

The Rt. Hon. The Lord Nolan (Chairman)

Sir Clifford Boulton GCB
Professor Anthony King
The Rt. Hon. Tom King CH MP
The Rt. Hon. Peter Shore MP

The Rt. Hon. The Lord Thomson of Monifieth KT DL
Sir William Utting CB
Dame Anne Warburton DCVO CMG
Diana Warwick

Witnesses:

Graeme Odgers, Chairman, and Jane Richardson, Senior Legal Adviser, Monopolies and Mergers Commission
Tony Wright MP
Earl Russell, Professor of British History, King's College, London, and Liberal Democrat spokesman, House of Lords
Professor Dawn Oliver, Professor of Constitutional Law, Dean and Head of the Department of Laws, University College, London

2192. LORD NOLAN: On this, our last day of oral evidence, I intend to make some closing remarks, so I shall keep my opening remarks even shorter than usual.

Our second witness this morning is Mr Tony Wright, Member of Parliament. Mr Wright was unable to come earlier because he was unwell. He has written a very thoughtful piece about quangos, and we shall be discussing that with him.

Our third witness is Earl Russell, who is the Professor of British History at King's College, London. He describes himself as a seventeenth century historian. Although he takes the Liberal Democrat Whip in the House of Lords, it is as a constitutional historian that we talk to him today.

Our final witness is also a constitutional expert. Professor Dawn Oliver is the Professor of Constitutional Law and also Dean of the Law Faculty at University College, London. She is one of our leading, younger constitutional lawyers. So, as on our first day, we end with a constitutional perspective, I hope today looking forward as well as back.

But, first, we are pleased to welcome the chairman of the Monopolies and Mergers Commission, Mr Graeme Odgers, supported by Ms Jane Richardson. The MMC, because of the nature of its work, has some of the strictest rules in government circles on conflicts of interest, and it is in this area that we shall particularly want to listen to Mr Odgers today. So thank you very much for coming to talk to us, Mr Odgers. Am I right in thinking that you would like to make a short opening statement?

GRAEME ODGERS AND JANE RICHARDSON (MMC)

GRAEME ODGERS (Chairman, Monopolies and Mergers Commission): I do not have a formal statement, but if you would like me very briefly to run over how the Commission works and particularly how the problem of conflicts of interest impinge on our work, I should be very happy to do that.

LORD NOLAN: That would be most helpful.

GRAEME ODGERS: Thank you. The MMC has been in existence since 1949, and I suppose we could therefore be regarded as one of the oldest of the quangos. We are part of a tripartite system of regulation of

competition, and there is a broad separation of functions between what one might call the prosecution, which is the Office for Fair Trading, the OFT, the quasi-judiciary, which is ourselves, the MMC, and then the executive, which is the Secretary of State for Trade and Industry. So we as a body are independent of government, we are independent of the OFT, but the inquiry is always referred to us by other parties, by the Director-General of Fair Trading or the Secretary of State or one of the various utility regulators, and in most instances we have to come to our judgments on the basis of the public interest, which is defined within the Fair Trading Act. Many of the inquiries that we handle are complex and difficult, and they are very often also very contentious.

The MMC consists of about 32 members, including myself, the chairman, and three deputy chairmen. All except myself are part-timers, and that is important. The members are appointed by the Secretary of State for Trade and Industry and they come from a great variety of different backgrounds—from the professions, from academia, from business, from the trade unions—and because these are all men and women of affairs whose principal incomes derive from non-MMC sources, that makes the problems of actual or potential or perceived conflicts of interest an important matter for us to be concerned with.

When a new inquiry comes in from the DGFT or the Secretary of State or one of the utility regulators it is my job, as the chairman of the MMC, to appoint a group of members, usually between five and seven, to handle that particular inquiry, and it is this group of members, not the MMC as a whole, which comes to the judgment that is contained in the MMC report, which is always published. So the setting up of these groups is important to us, and I seek always to have an appropriate breadth and a balance of background and experience on each one of these inquiry groups that is set up, as well as the particular expertise that is needed to deal with the issues that are likely to come up on the inquiry.

In approaching individual members to participate in a group, we always ask them specifically at the time of the approach about possible conflicts of interest—these may relate to directorships, to business dealings, to investments, to family relationships—and if there is a perceived or a potential conflict of interest, or an actual conflict of interest, it will mean that that individual cannot participate in that inquiry. We remind people on an ongoing basis during the course of an inquiry that, if some new facet comes up which may constitute a conflict of interest, that needs immediately to be advised to me or my senior staff, and that will usually mean that the individual has to step down from that inquiry.

So you can see that this is a very important aspect to our handling of our affairs. It is very important that we be seen on an on-going basis as an unbiased and independent body. Thank you very much.

LORD NOLAN: Thank you very much. Now I am going to ask Mr Tom King to take up the questions.

2193. TOM KING: Thank you very much. Mr Odgers, it was very interesting for me to read the reports that you so kindly provided, because I must admit that your profile is low, maybe deliberately so, and yet you deal with some very sensitive matters, and in financial terms your decisions can have enormous implications and represent a very substantial financial benefit for individuals or companies or what have you. How do you think you have done? People have disagreed with your decisions, but have you had complaints that decisions have been influenced by the fact that the Commission has not been even-handed or has been biased in some way?

GRAEME ODGERS: Certainly people are unhappy on a pretty regular basis about our decisions, because, as I said, many of the matters that come to us are controversial and there tend to be different parties involved for and against, for instance. When we come to a conclusion, those who in a sense are the beneficiaries of our particular decision walk away rather smugly, usually rather quietly: they may think it has taken an inordinately long time to reach an obvious conclusion. But of course the other side can often be quite vocal about it, and they could say that we're unprofessional or biased or what have you. I don't think I have ever come across a case where people have said that the particular background of an individual or his or her particular financial interest has affected the decision in any way, so I think that the procedures that we go through help very substantially to avoid that kind of feeling that there has been bias.

2194. TOM KING: I don't think we have heard a body before us where the decisions of its members can result in such huge financial gain to the party or other that comes before them. Have you, as a result of that, ever had any attempts at corruption?

GRAEME ODGERS: Not as far as I know. Really not as far as I know at all, not the vaguest smell of it.

2195. TOM KING: Can I then ask you about the method of appointment? You said that it is by the Secretary of State and you have this large list of ladies and gentlemen, which is a sort of part-time panel from which you draw.

GRAEME ODGERS: Indeed.

TOM KING: Does that system work?

GRAEME ODGERS: Well——

2196. TOM KING: I add this point—because they are part-timers, of whom you suddenly ask, for some of these inquiries, a very considerable amount of work often in quite a short time. Is that correct?

GRAEME ODGERS: That's absolutely right, and we don't pay them a great deal of money either—or they are not paid a great deal of money either. The system of appointment is that it is the responsibility of the Secretary of State and his department. I suppose I get involved in that to the degree that I am consulted from time to time as to the kind of people that should be approached for membership. This is very important to me, because the breadth, as I said, and the balance of these groups is hugely important, so I want to be able to draw on a range of different background, a range of different skills. I also want of course to be able to draw on women as well as men. We have at the moment five women; I would like to see more women on our Commission. But that breadth of background is hugely important, and therefore I am consulted by members of the staff of the DTI, and indeed by Ministers, as to the kind of background that I would like. From time to time I make my own suggestions as to who might be an appropriate member to be considered, and from time to time the DTI consult me about a particular person that they have in mind, but I am advised that what they are looking for in the detailed procedures that they go through is similar to what I am looking for, which is a variety of professional background.

The degree to which any politics enters this thing is something which is outside of my particular knowledge or remit. I do not know whether political views in any way affect the decisions on the appointment to MMC members. What I can say is that my own appointment was handled in a very professional manner: professional consultants were appointed to seek out in the market place. The first time I ever met the Secretary of State was when I was interviewed by him. I have no political affiliations myself. So it was handled in a completely professional manner. I would hope that that is applicable to all other members as well.

2197. TOM KING: The post wasn't advertised?

GRAEME ODGERS: In that particular case I believe it was not advertised. At the moment we are seeking a replacement for one of our deputy chairmen, who will be retiring towards the end of this year. The deputy chairmen are very important to the MMC, because the chairing of the individual groups is done either by myself or by one of my three deputy chairmen, so they are hugely important positions. We are seeking a replacement to one of our deputy chairmen who is retiring.

2198. TOM KING: Is that a full-time job?

GRAEME ODGERS: That's a three-and-a-half-days-a-week job. That one is both being handled by the executive recruitment consultants and it is being advertised—both of those tacks are being used—but I must say that my experience, and I have had a long experience of recruitment in a variety of different ways, is that when you get to the level of appointment we are talking about here, the kind of standing of the people we are talking about, most of those kinds of people will not respond to an advertisement as such, and while I do see that there is some point in making a public advertisement in order to ensure that the net is complete, I think that many people of the sort of standing we are looking for would not respond to an advertisement; they would, however, be prepared to discuss on an informal bias with consultants or indeed on a direct approach from Ministers.

2199. TOM KING: Do you have an input into the Secretary of State's choices of people he suggests to join the Commission?

GRAEME ODGERS: Yes, I do suggest people from time to time. At the moment I understand that a couple of my suggestions—I might have made 10 or 15 over the two years I have been in the current post—are being considered, but only along with a whole range of other people. So it is only a very modest input.

2200. TOM KING: What views do you have of the routes by which the other people come?

GRAEME ODGERS: I think that, if you wanted to get into this, you ought to talk to the Ministers, because it is not something that I am directly involved in. I do encourage members of the Commission to let me know if they have particular people who they think would be helpful, and if they do feel that that is the case, I simply pass on that information to the Department of Trade and Industry.

2201. TOM KING: I suppose the Secretary of State can avoid the charge of biasing the Commission by the range of people that he makes available to you. Then on you and whom falls the real responsibility for ensuring that the particular group that does a particular inquiry is above suspicion?

GRAEME ODGERS: That very much is a matter for the MMC, and the responsibility is mine, because I am responsible, under the Act, for actually appointing the members to that particular group, and the group, as I said, is the one that makes the decision, not the MMC as a whole.

2202. TOM KING: Is that the total group?

GRAEME ODGERS: That is the group of five to seven members that is set up for this particular inquiry, and it is that group that actually makes the decision. If I am not on that group, I can be consulted by the group about any views I might have.

2203. TOM KING: I am so sorry, I didn't mean to interrupt, but the key point I am on is this: who does the choosing of the people on the group that does the inquiry?

GRAEME ODGERS: It is I who make that decision.

2204. TOM KING: Alone?

GRAEME ODGERS: Alone. I am supported, obviously, by my staff, because if we have a large range of ongoing inquiries, as we have at the moment—I think we have 10 to 12 inquiries on-going—we are extremely busy, and of course only a limited number of people are available. I am assisted greatly by my staff in terms of who might be available, making the initial approaches and so on.

2205. TOM KING: And what considerations do you take into account, if I can give you some thoughts on this?

You obviously look at somebody's career—the companies they have been with or the activities they have been in—to see if there is a manifest and patent conflict or prior interest in the area being covered. Do you worry about what their wives do?

GRAEME ODGERS: Yes. Family interests are important. If I have a new inquiry group——

TOM KING: Or spouses, I should say.

GRAEME ODGERS: Or partners. I think we use the word "partners".

TOM KING: I apologise.

GRAEME ODGERS: When the inquiry group has to be set up, first of all I am looking for a balance of backgrounds. Ideally, I will want an economist on, I will ideally want a lawyer on, I will want a business person on, I will want a trade unionist on, so that is important, and I will be looking, in some cases, for very particular expertise. For instance, if matters of return on capital are important, as they would be on utility company references, for instance, I would look for somebody with an accounting background, so that just sets the scene, as it were. But then when the individuals have been identified as potential members, first of all we will see whether they have any on-going relationships. Are they, for instance, members of the board of a company in that particular industry? Out. Do they have any financial interest in the sense of shareholdings in the company? Any substantial financial interest—out. What about their spouses, their partners? Any financial interest, anything substantial—out. What about family relationships? Is there a child or a family member who actually works for the company? Now that is more difficult.

TOM KING: Not "out"? I didn't hear the word "out".

GRAEME ODGERS: No, it may influence. It depends on the relationship. If, for instance, one were dealing with a banking situation and a child of a member who is grown up, maybe a 35-year-old, happens to be an executive in the merchant banking side of the banking company, would that exclude or not? I think you must say it depends. If one could in any way perceive that relationship to influence the individual, then it's out. So my tendency always is to be cautious rather than the other way round.

2206. TOM KING: But you are just changing the rules, I gather. Is that right?

GRAEME ODGERS: We are looking at the rules again.

2207. TOM KING: Why do you need to do that?

GRAEME ODGERS: For instance, the guidance rules that we have sent out so far say that any substantial financial interest, say a shareholding, would mean that the individual could not participate, but what about a small financial interest? What if the person has, say, a couple of thousand pounds' worth of investment in a company that comes before us—say, a utility company—and many people, because of the nature of the privatisation exercise, have shareholdings? Would a small shareholding exclude the individual? In the past we have said that a small shareholding might not exclude the individual, provided there is appropriate disclosure to the companies or the parties involved. I think now we would take a slightly tougher view. I think we would take the view that we simply would exclude the individual, even if they have a very small shareholding. That is the view we would take. We would also take that view in the case of shareholdings by the family. We would also take the view in the case of the utility company that, if there is a shareholding in another company within the industry, that would exclude the person, so we are toughening up on these lines.

2208. TOM KING: So what is accepted, I think—I don't want to put words in your mouth—is that you have people on the Commission who could have conflicts of interest.

GRAEME ODGERS: Indeed.

TOM KING: So you have to choose the ones who don't.

GRAEME ODGERS: Indeed.

2209. TOM KING: And the full responsibility for that rests entirely on you, and you have not actually had, as far as you are aware, any complaints that this hasn't been properly discharged.

GRAEME ODGERS: I have not had any complaints. I have from time to time, when I have made appointments, had representations—this happens very rarely, but it has happened—from parties concerned, who say "Look, I don't think it would be helpful or proper for Mr or Mrs X to sit on this inquiry" for this, that and the next reason. I have then heard what the individual or the party has to say, taken it into account and on a number of occasions I have said that this perceived possible conflict of interest means that we should exclude that individual, and we have excluded that individual.

TOM KING: So there's a consultation procedure in a sense.

GRAEME ODGERS: I wouldn't call it a consultation procedure, but I am open to approach from parties concerned and I feel it is very important that I should be open to approach. On the other hand, I don't want to be brow-beaten, in the sense that anybody can feel that they can come in and tell me how to set up the panel that I feel is the right panel.

TOM KING: Thank you very much.

LORD NOLAN: Sir William, would you like to ask any questions?

2210. WILLIAM UTTING: I should just like to follow up the issue of non-financial interests. In talking to Tom King, you got into the area of the sort of jobs one's children may be doing becoming relevant and you implied that when you were exercising your own personal judgment you would take, or could take, non-financial interests into consideration. I am being increasingly struck by the fact that you don't actually need to bribe people all the time in order to influence them; you can do that through being a member of a network, fellow club people, "went to the same school" sort of thing. Are these the kinds of non-financial considerations that you take into consideration?

GRAEME ODGERS: They could be included, but the sort of thing that does happen and has happened over the last year or so is the question of commercial relationships. For instance, if, say, British Gas come before us, what about a customer of British Gas? Is that a conflict of interest? No, because everybody is a customer of British Gas. But, on the other hand, if a regional water company comes before us and an individual happens to have a residence in the area concerned and there is a fairly substantial bill going between the individual and that particular regional company, in that case we have excluded those individuals. So in one case a customer relationship is important; in another case it wouldn't be. Take a banking relationship again. If a person simply has a modest current account, that probably would not be regarded as a significant relationship. If, on the other hand, there is a significant overdraft facility, that may well be a situation.

All our people are people of affairs, as I said earlier on. They need to circulate, they need to go to functions. They may, for instance, have invitations to go to Wimbledon or Twickenham, or whatever. We wouldn't want to discourage people from doing that. Having said that, however, we do not want a situation to develop where the judgment of the individual on his or her MMC affairs can be, or can be seen to be, influenced at all by these relationships with outside parties. If, for instance, an inquiry comes before us and the individual does participate in Wimbledon or whatever it is with that particular party, we would expect that individual to advise us, and if it is of any substance, I will say no; I will choose somebody else.

2211. WILLIAM UTTING: So there is an honour system as far as they are concerned, which is monitored by you as the chairman.

GRAEME ODGERS: That's correct. What we don't have is a register of interests, because the problem with a register of interests is that it can't be inclusive, not if we are dealing with complex matters of the kind that I am talking about here. It is bound not to cover all the matters we want. So it is much better, when the particular situation arises where an appointment is to be made to a particular group, that I and my staff say "Now are there any particular or potential conflicts of interest? Think about it, think about it hard." It's an honour system in that sense, yes.

WILLIAM UTTING: Thank you.

LORD NOLAN: May I take Professor King out of turn, if you don't mind, Dame Anne, because I know that he may have to go out for a few minutes? Would you like to go next, Tony?

2212. PROF. ANTHONY KING: Yes. Can I just ask one question? You said quite emphatically in response to a question from Tom King that there had been, to your knowledge, no instance of an attempt to corrupt a member of the MMC? Have there been instances where the government has leaned on the MMC to come up with one decision rather than another?

GRAEME ODGERS: No, not in that sense. Of course the government may well be one of the parties involved. In terms of putting evidence, it may be very important that the government's views be taken fully into account. There are on-going inquiries at the moment where the government has a very significant interest to put in, and we will have hearings—the feel of the hearings is not much different from these hearings here, where a government department is actually sitting on the side of the table—and they will be trying to persuade us of their particular view, but that is not what I call leaning. All our parties have particular points of view that they want to put across, but in no way would there be what I would call improper leaning on us by the government—absolutely not. This business of having the tripartite system, the separation of the powers—the prosecution, the OFT, the judiciary, ourselves, the MMC, and the executive, the government—won't work if the parties are not seen to be independent.

Remember that the decisions that we make can ultimately be overturned in some ways by government. If we come to a view that a situation is not operating against the public interest, then our decision is final. If, on the other hand, we decide that a situation is working against the public interest, then we will make that judgment and we will make recommendations. It is then up to the government to decide whether to accept our recommendations or not. Normally they will do so, but in some cases they overturn it. So in the last resort, if there is a substantive change to be made in a particular industry, that decision lies with government. I actually think that that is proper: government is there to govern, under Parliament of course, but they have the final say, as it were, and maybe in that sense the inclination to lean is less severe than it might otherwise be.

2213. PROF. ANTHONY KING: So there has been no instance of impropriety at all, from your experience?

GRAEME ODGERS: Not in the two years I've been in the chair, correct.

2214. ANNE WARBURTON: Mr Odgers, we have been looking at so many questions of appointments, and so often it is a question of openness, of transparency. Is there any published list of the criteria which are applied in choosing members of the MMC itself, the whole body?

GRAEME ODGERS: Not as far as I know, but really you ought to approach the Department of Trade and Industry for that.

2215. ANNE WARBURTON: But their names are published?

GRAEME ODGERS: Oh, of course. If you look at the Annual Review, everybody is clearly indicated and their backgrounds, and we have taken the rather unusual step of actually publishing the photographs of the groups of people. This has been a bit controversial, because I don't think everybody likes to have their photographs published, but my feeling was that we didn't want to be, in a sense, faceless bureaucrats; we wanted to be seen as individuals operating in groups, who put their signatures to their individual reports, and that is why we did it in this last annual review.

2216. ANNE WARBURTON: Yes. Do you think that your methods, and particularly perhaps the appointment of sub-groups, would be readily applicable in other, shall we say, less eminent bodies than your own?

GRAEME ODGERS: I think that in a sense our situation is somewhat unique, in that we use only part-

timers, that the inquiries that come up cover a tremendous range of different situations, and one never knows when that situation and what situation is going to come up. So it is inevitable that we have to follow the kind of tactics that we do on this one. If there are other bodies that face the same kind of problems, it is possible that the same kind of methods would be applicable.

2217. ANNE WARBURTON: One last question. I almost wanted to ask you: are you under-manned—or womanned, or whatever? You said that you have 10 to 12 inquiries going on and 35 members. It looks as though you might want some extra support sometimes.

GRAEME ODGERS: Yes. This business of handling the level of business that comes in is extraordinarily difficult, because we have no control whatsoever over what comes in: the references are made by other parties. In the middle of last year we had a relatively light business load and, as a result of that in part, I dropped down the level of staff; also we dropped down the numbers of members. Suddenly in comes a huge flow of new inquiries, and we are somewhat pushed. So we are working with the department at the moment in terms of increasing that number. But, in addition to our on-going staff, we are using external consultants now, and we have set up a panel of 28 consultancy arrangements, so that when there is pressure we can bring on these consultants to help us. The problems of conflict of interest of course apply just as much with consultants as with our own members. In every instance, once again, we go through exactly the same procedure when we are thinking of appointing consultants: are there potential conflicts of interest, are there actual conflicts of interest? There are very precise rules as to what business they can take on when they are working with us on an assignment. But in terms of having the ability to do the work at any point in time, whatever is thrown at us, we have to use these external consultants; otherwise the size of our membership would be too high, and we have to establish the right core levels.

ANNE WARBURTON: Before you told Sir William that you had no register of interests, I was going to ask you what people had to declare, because it obviously would be extremely detailed, but in the light of what you have just said I shall leave that question for others to raise.

2218. PETER SHORE: Very large interests are involved in and affected by the decisions that you reach in your sub-groups. Do you find that when an inquiry is established you are the target of a lot of pressure groups and lobbying activity?

GRAEME ODGERS: Yes, I think that is correct. There are lobbying groups, who have an entirely legitimate role—for instance in consumer affairs—and they would seek to make sure, first of all, that they have appropriate information and representation coming in to us, and of course if it is a significant representation, we will have a hearing with the party concerned. But we do find that the parties very often talk to the press at the same time in order to make sure that the general public know what they are saying. Sometimes people have actually published the representations that they put into the MMC. So there is this kind of external pressure, I suppose in a sense attempting to affect our thinking. But frankly, when it comes to an individual inquiry, there are so many powerful views being put in, and we seek always to make sure that the parties concerned have absolute ability to put forward their views in the way that they want to put them forward. In other words, we really want to understand their particular point of view, we want to understand the essence of the situation. The judgment between these various, often conflicting, points of view is not an easy one. Indeed, during the course of an inquiry you might have these five or six men and women who have rather different views as to how the thing is developing.

The very important thing as far as Members are concerned is that they have to do two things at the same time, which is sometimes not all that easy. They do have to bring to bear their own individual expertise, their background, in a sense their predilections, their personalities, their personal qualities—it is very important to bring those to bear on that inquiry—but in the last resort it is the group that comes to the decision, and therefore they need to participate in a collegiate decision.

2219. PETER SHORE: Those representations are very open, and indeed are often formal, but what about less open pressures, because there must be a great temptation to engage in behind-the-scenes activities? Do the Members of your panel go into a sort of purdah in terms of informal contacts with possibly interested groups?

GRAEME ODGERS: Yes, yes, that would be correct. That doesn't mean to say that they won't attend dinners where other parties happen to be, although they may do that. For instance, when I am invited to small, informal gatherings, I will normally seek to find out before the dinner happens who else will be there. That doesn't mean to say that I will necessarily refuse the invitation if somebody is an important party on one of our inquiries at the moment, but it will be absolutely clear to me, and also to the party who is at the dinner, that we don't talk shop at all. It is absolute purdah from that point of view—very important.

PETER SHORE: Thank you.

2220. LORD NOLAN: I wonder if I may ask two personal questions, not in any impertinent spirit, but because if you feel able to answer them, they will be useful information for the qualifications that other people with roles of great responsibility might be asked to adhere to. What was your background when you were appointed? You have told us how you were approached and professionally interviewed. What had you been doing beforehand?

GRAEME ODGERS: I was the chief executive of one of the major construction groups, Alfred McAlpine Plc. I had been the managing director of British Telecom prior to that and I had been managing director of Tarmac Plc prior to that. So I had that industrial background. I had at an earlier stage actually spent some time working at the Department of Industry, as it then was—this was in the mid-70s—running a unit called the Industrial Development Unit. I had been on secondment at that time and I was there for three and a half years. This unit was involved in the handling of aid to companies that got into problems or that were regionally oriented. I loved that job, I absolutely adored it. It was at the interface between government and industry, and I have always been fascinated by that particular interface.

When I was approached out of the blue, on the telephone, I was approached by the consultant saying that

Mr Heseltine was looking for somebody, ideally with an industrial-type background to do this particular job. I knew immediately that I was very, very interested in it, because clearly the MMC job is one of the key interfaces between, if you like, government on the one hand and industry and commerce on the other, so there was never any doubt in my mind, even though it meant an enormous reduction in income as a result, that if I was asked to do the job, I would do it. I would hope that, for positions like this, people would have the same kind of reaction: that they would like to take the job on because it is of enormous interest to them.

LORD NOLAN: You brought to it exceptional experience of business, as seen from both the public and the private side.

GRAEME ODGERS: Unusual, I suppose, in the sense that I had both the governmental and the private sector experience.

2221. LORD NOLAN: Secondly, may I ask you this? Do you have to accept limitations upon, for example, the investments that you can make or the other interests that you can pursue?

GRAEME ODGERS: The formal arrangement I have with the DTI is that I have to let them know every year my own investments and those of my wife, and that I do. In practice what I have done, with the exception of two very small shareholdings, I have eliminated all my investments in individual companies and put them entirely into government bonds, because it makes it so helpful not to have that financial interest.

2222. LORD NOLAN: Finally, do you have a legal representative on each of the working party committees that carries out the various investigations and makes the reports?

GRAEME ODGERS: There is always the legal input. Jane Richardson is our senior legal adviser and she has an assistant. They don't sit in on all of the meetings, but they do tend to sit in on the important meetings. The legal input is very important indeed, because all our action is governed by statute of one kind or another, and we have to get it right. We have been subject to judicial review on 10 separate occasions. In every single case I am very pleased to say that we have won, but I don't enjoy it at all, and we want to avoid that if at all possible. The business is complicated enough as it is without getting involved in that sort of thing.

LORD NOLAN: Thank you very much.

2223. CLIFFORD BOULTON: I see your budget is about £7½ million a year. Is that right?

GRAEME ODGERS: Yes. This year I think it is £6.8 million.

2224. CLIFFORD BOULTON: And you have to get that money out of the DTI?

GRAEME ODGERS: Yes.

2225. CLIFFORD BOULTON: Everybody would like more money, but do I gather you are not actually complaining about the way the system works for getting the level of your finance?

GRAEME ODGERS: We have to do whatever work is sent to us. By statute we have to do it. The arrangement that we have with the DTI is that prior to the beginning of each year we go through with them, with some care, what the likely cost structure is going to be. Clearly we are put under pressure, quite properly, and we put ourselves under pressure, to ensure that costs are reduced as far as possible. But we cannot really know what the ultimate cost will come out at, because if we have a very heavy workload, it will cost more. But the key thing that we do is that if there is likely to be an over-run on the budget, we will at a very early stage put the DTI on notice that that is likely to be the case, and in consultation with them we will come to an agreement.

2226. CLIFFORD BOULTON: Who is the accounting officer for your expenditure?

GRAEME ODGERS: The accounting officer is the Commission Secretary, who unfortunately cannot be with us today. That is Tony Nieduszynski.

2227. CLIFFORD BOULTON: And are you audited by the National Audit Office?

GRAEME ODGERS: No, we are not audited by the National Audit Office. I think that's correct.

MS JANE RICHARDSON (Senior Legal Adviser, Monopolies and Mergers Commission): I am not sure—at the moment.

GRAEME ODGERS: Not at the moment, but I think the likelihood is that we will be so in the future, and clearly we would be quite happy with that situation.

2228. CLIFFORD BOULTON: Have you or your predecessor ever been asked to go before one of the House of Commons Committees?

GRAEME ODGERS: Yes, indeed. I was before one of the House of Commons Committees yesterday, so this is old hat for me today.

2229. CLIFFORD BOULTON: It shows how one loses track. I ceased to be an Officer of the House last autumn. But the Secretary of State, presumably, feels himself answerable in general terms for your performance in the House. Is that correct?

GRAEME ODGERS: I am not sure that that would be the case. The Secretary of State is required to make the appointment, subject ultimately to prime ministerial approval, as I understand it, but once he has made that appointment, I am independent of the Secretary of State. It is quite clear that from time to time we have our disagreements, in the sense that he turns down certain recommendations from the MMC, and I would not in any way see the MMC as being subordinate to the Secretary of State. The budget of course is ultimately covered by the DTI budget.

2230. CLIFFORD BOULTON: This is why I carefully said "in general terms", because if the House wanted to complain that you were being run down, they would

complain to the Secretary of State, and he would have to say "No, they're in perfectly good condition". That is the kind of general responsibility you would accept?

GRAEME ODGERS: Yes.

2231. CLIFFORD BOULTON: But no accounting officer in his department is responsible for the way you actually spend your money: you have your own accounting officer.

GRAEME ODGERS: We have our own accounting officer, who will consult with the DTI officials in terms of the setting up of the budget.

CLIFFORD BOULTON: Yes. Thank you.

2232. DIANA WARWICK: I am interested, first of all, in the question of informal influences. Do you keep a record of the statements or admissions that members make about things like Wimbledon, Twickenham, Glyndebourne or whatever, so that any accusations of croneyism can be rebutted?

GRAEME ODGERS: No, we don't. If people have a particular relationship with a particular company that may at some time come before us, I like to know about it, just to be careful, just to have it in the back of my mind, because it is important that the members be seen not to be subject to any kind of external influence, but we don't keep a register, no.

2233. DIANA WARWICK: And has it, in your recollection, ever been appropriate to ask about the political affiliation of members for particular inquiries——

GRAEME ODGERS: No.

DIANA WARWICK: - or about the membership of particular clubs? I think of masons, for example.

GRAEME ODGERS: No. No.

DIANA WARWICK: Never?

GRAEME ODGERS: Not as far as I am concerned. I would not regard political affiliation as relevant, frankly, to the kind of work that we have to do, because the judgments that are made by the individual members, and therefore the groups, are within the outline set within the Fair Trading Act. The public interest is quite clearly defined there, and it is that that defines how they come to their judgments. Political affiliations are not included in the Fair Trading Act and I would not expect them to be behind the judgment of the individual.

2234. DIANA WARWICK: And you said in your presentation that you were not aware of any criticism of political bias. I wondered whether you had ever been concerned because of a lack of commitment to the work, and it is quite a considerable time commitment, that you might have been foisted off with a place man.

GRAEME ODGERS: We have two different types of members. One is called an ordinary member who commits himself or herself to one and a half days a week on average to our affairs and the other is called the reserve member who commits himself or herself on the basis of availability to an average of one day a week. If somebody has a problem in terms of time availability they will come in on a reserve basis rather than an ordinary basis.

If an individual is an ordinary member and is not prepared to do the work then I might want to have words with the individual but it is very rare. If there is a problem like that what happens is that the individual will come and consult with me. There have been occasions where an ordinary member has said, "For the next 12 months I would like to move to reserve status if I may" and I have said that that is fine. That is the way it works.

People actually like the work. It is very demanding but it is very interesting and people feel that it is of some significance and so they really like to spend the necessary time on it. Obviously, if they are heavily involved in their ongoing other affairs there are occasions when they have to miss meetings. I am very upset if an individual misses a major hearing with one of the main parties because it is very important that they are sitting on one side of the table when the key people involved in that enquiry are on the other side of the table.

2235. DIANA WARWICK: You have said it is very demanding and it is not particularly well paid. Do you regard it as a public service?

GRAEME ODGERS: Very much so, very much so, yes.

2236. DIANA WARWICK: Could I then ask you about the involvement of consultants because one of the issues that we have been dealing with has been the difference in ethos between the public sector and the private sector and the role of consultancies and lobbying groups and so on. Do you think a firm of consultants might gain a substantial advantage by being involved in some of your enquiries that could be of commercial benefit subsequently?

GRAEME ODGERS: Yes. I think that the experience that they gain in working for the MMC will be valuable experience for them in doing other work associated with the public sector. I think the fact that they are a client of the MMC is a sort of feather in their cap they can certainly use on the other side. Of course, when it comes to actually establishing and negotiating the terms and conditions of the assignment we might put pressure to bear on them that would it not be appropriate actually to have a discount on their normal fee structure because of these kinds of advantages or the attractiveness of the work to them from their point of view.

2237. DIANA WARWICK: So, they are paid on a different scale at a different level, are they, the consultants?

GRAEME ODGERS: They may be. If we can negotiate a good deal we will negotiate a good deal, that is for sure. On the question of conflicts, however, we have to be very, very tight and very, very careful if there are any problems, and there are problems. For instance, on this last round of negotiation with the consultants as to whether they were prepared to help us and be part of a panel, some of the leading consultants said, "Look, we deal with such a wide range of firms as it is that to work with the MMC is actually going to make it impossible for us to carry out our normal business because of potential conflicts of interests, so we will not actually put ourselves forward." A number of companies have done precisely that. It is a matter of balance really.

DIANA WARWICK: Thank you.

2238. LORD THOMSON: Tom King mentioned to you that as a major public institution you achieve a remarkably low public profile. I think after the six weeks we have been sitting here hearing complaints about lack of political balance and quangos and so on one might say, "Happy the quango that has a low public profile". Have you, over the years, had controversies about particular appointments to the MMC?

GRAEME ODGERS: Not about appointments to the MMC as far as I am aware. We do, of course, have great controversy over our decisions. For instance, we had an investigation into Recorded Music, into CD's, last year which I personally chaired and there was a general perception which was that the prices of CD's in this country was higher than in other countries. We looked at the thing in great detail. We came to our judgment in that particular case that the situation was not working against the public interest.

There was a lot of furore as a result of that because people did not like the answer and when people do not like answers that we come up with there often is attack and one has to be pretty thick-skinned but, on the whole, I think our feeling is that provided we answer the criticism as necessary in a sensible way and hopefully get people to understand the way in which we carry out our business which is designed to get a thorough investigation and a fair decision making I think, on the whole, one can deal with those kinds of criticism.

2239. LORD THOMSON: I know from my own experience that your decisions are often highly public decisions and disputed decisions. I was concentrating really on the fact that you seem to be relatively immune. I wonder if you could confirm it, from the arguments that have applied to other quangos, about the overall balance of appointments to the Commission?

GRAEME ODGERS: I believe that there has not been a lot of controversy on that score, yes.

2240. LORD THOMSON: You have trade union members, do you not?

GRAEME ODGERS: We do.

2241. LORD THOMSON: Are the numbers the same as they have always been or have they reduced over recent years?

GRAEME ODGERS: I am not sure going back in history. When I joined there were two members. We lost one, Alex Ferry, who was absolutely magnificent, a wonderful man; he died. We now have his replacement, Roger Lyons, who has just come on. David Jenkins is our other member. David is a very valued member. I really do feel that it is very important for us to have solid representation—not representation but people who come from that kind of background. It is important that the members, when they come to us, they are not actually representing particular interests, they are coming with a particular background, with particular experience, particular expertise, so they are not representatives of the trades unions but they come from a trade union background.

2242. LORD THOMSON: You obviously have a very heavy workload. I just wondered whether there is any sort of information consultation with you from those who have the right to make references to you, either the Secretary of State or the OFT or the utilities. Do they consult with you informally in advance as to whether a particular reference is appropriate given your workload?

GRAEME ODGERS: Not whether it is appropriate, certainly not. We will not in any way influence whether an inquiry comes to us, that is not our function, absolutely not our function. In a sense the judiciary is largely our function and if we are in any way involved in what I might call "prosecutory zeal" it might affect our judgment so we do not get involved at all in the decision as to whether to refer or not.

However, we have an ongoing consultation with the OFT in terms of what is in their particular pipeline and it may be that if they have a number of things which are variable in terms of the timetable that they might be able to push the thing to us we might say, "Well, if we could have a delay for a month or two, that would be quite helpful." There is also a thing called the Mergers Panel on the merger side of our business where we sit in on that Mergers Panel and we might give technical advice but we do not participate in terms of urging that the thing comes or does not come.

LORD THOMSON: Thank you.

2243. LORD NOLAN: Thank you very much indeed for coming along. You have been very helpful and clear. We are most grateful to you.

Now, we have Mr. Tony Wright, Member of Parliament. Good morning, Mr. Wright. Thank you very much for coming along. I am sorry we are making a slightly late start with you but, as you know, our enthusiasm often overruns our time when it comes to questions. Do you have an opening statement which you would like to make before you submit to questions?

TONY WRIGHT MP

TONY WRIGHT MP: Perhaps I will make a very short one, if I may. I have not written it down and submitted it but I have submitted what was the draft of what has now become a pamphlet by the Fabian Society called, "Beyond the Patronage State".

LORD NOLAN: We are very grateful for that and that we have all read with profit.

TONY WRIGHT: Right. You have the draft of that and I think all you lack is the preface to the pamphlet.

If I could just make very quickly perhaps just three points. One is that I would like to suggest to the Committee that there is a large theme surrounding the particular issue of patronage that I have looked at and I think this would explain why the Committee may be grappling with the notion of whether Parliament can regulate itself. In some ways that theme was best expressed for me by Enoch Powell many years ago when he said——

"There is no such thing as Parliament. All there is is Government and Opposition."

There is wisdom in that remark and if you reflect on it you get to understand how Parliament works and why it is

not very good at regulating itself. He also said, of course, in relation to registers——

"I am having nothing to do with them unless Parliament passes a law to make me."

Again, that goes to the heart of the question of self-regulation. I saw recently from the House of Commons Library a list of all Privileges Committee recommendations in the past 30 years. The last column in that list said——

"Action taken"

and the recurring phrase on the right-hand side was——

"No further action taken".

I think that very much explains to you why, even when you have recommendations made, they get lost in the system and I suspect other people have said that to you. My conclusion from that, to finish off this first point, the lesson I learn from that is that where Parliament is most useful and effective is when it puts in place mechanisms to do jobs that it cannot do very well itself. The examples of that would be the National Audit Office in the early 1980s which has made a massive contribution to British government and the Ombudsman, established in the late 1960s.

I have recently been looking at the debate surrounding the establishment of the Ombudsman and what is remarkable there is how many people were saying that this would undermine the constitution as we know it; indeed, that was the line of the official Opposition at the time, led by the man who became Lord Hailsham, who said——

"This will erode the relationship between Ministers and Members of Parliament, will undermine ministerial responsibility, will cut away the foundations of Parliamentary life."

Of course, that was far from the truth and I suspect that with some of the things that are being said to you now it may be worth just remembering some of those earlier things.

Those mechanisms have been effective. They have not undermined Parliament, they have added to Parliament's armoury and, therefore, I would conclude that insofar as the Committee is exploring ways of finding new bits of equipment which will be independent and service Parliament that is a fruitful path to explore.

The second point that comes more directly out of the evidence and the pamphlet that I have submitted relates to that insofar as you have to ask why it is that over the years Parliament has never become active in relation to the question of ministerial patronage. Why is it that Parliament has not taken this in hand over the years? The answer is that it is in the interests neither of Government nor of Opposition to do it because it is an extraordinary reservoir of power that both governments and putative governments want to have. In a sense it shows the deficiencies of Parliament as a regulating instrument.

I would simply quote very quickly something which I quote in the evidence to you. For me, it is extremely fruitful just to think about the conclusions of a study in 1960 by PEP, Political and Economic Planning, that great old organisation. Looking at government by appointment, as they called it then, they state——

"The growth in appointment amounts almost to a new patronage"

and they said——

"The time has come to examine it, to document it, to regularise it and to establish for it public standards of propriety and good practice."

That was 1960 and, of course, nothing at all has happened on that front since. Even more alarming is the only study that has been done of patronage in Britain on a large scale which was by the political scientist, Peter Richards, in 1963 called "Patronage in British Government". One sentence from that study bears reflection. It is a very conventional book. It does not make any radical suggestions but it says——

"At present the abuses are not grave due to adequate ethical standards in the conduct of public business. Perhaps the greatest danger for the future is the possibility that one party will exercise uninterrupted power for too long a period. Temptations would grow as security bred carelessness."

I think there is much to mull on in that remark if you want to understand what has happened over the past 15 years. I do not make that as a narrow, partisan point, I make it in as dispassionate way as I can. What we have to address is why is it acceptable that Ministers should be allowed to make somewhere between—we are not sure what the figure is—between 40,000 and 50,000 appointments, 10,000 annually, without any proper scrutiny or accountability. That has been identified in the past, indeed in terms of previous government reviews, as the central anomaly inside the system. I think it is the central anomaly inside the system, which is why I have argued for an independent element in this case of a public appointments commission. That is the line I would like to ply to you.

Finally, very quickly, the third point is that amongst the many words which have been used to you in discussing this whole area one that possibly bears a little more attention is "legitimacy" because no system of government is going to be durable and command respect unless it has legitimacy. I give the best evidence I can find in the evidence that I have given to you on the analysis of this in terms of what has happened to the abuse of patronage in this period is that what it does is undermine legitimacy. People no longer feel that the government is to be trusted and it is not to be trusted because it has been packed with people for a variety of reasons who are not traditional public servants. That is, for me, the most profoundly disturbing part of this whole story.

LORD NOLAN: Thank you very much. I am now going to ask Professor King if he would please take up the questions.

2244. PROF ANTHONY KING: What evidence do you have, if any, that the scale of ministerial patronage has increased over the past 10, 20, 30 years?

TONY WRIGHT: I think the general answer is that insofar as the trend has been towards appointive

government and away from elective government, and one can point to many areas -training, further education, education generally, the Health Service, I suppose, most conspicuously—where this has happened, insofar as that has been a major trend then, obviously, it will reflect itself in the growth of appointive government and, therefore, in the problem of appointment.

The one thing I would add to that is that it is extraordinarily difficult to get precise figures. I think in the Government's evidence to you it could not actually produce precise figures. It acknowledged that the figures on appointments that came from public bodies were not full figures because they only count the appointments that are made to public bodies. The big figure, we know, is somewhere between 40,000 and 50,000. From answers, I have made it between 43,000 and 44,000.

2245. PROF ANTHONY KING: And you suspect the number has increased over the years but you have no hard data bearing on that point?

TONY WRIGHT: If you went through institution by institution, area of government by area of government ...

PROF ANTHONY KING: But you do not have it?

TONY WRIGHT: But if you are asking for a figure, I would be very loath to try and produce a figure.

2246. PROF ANTHONY KING: You referred in your opening remarks to an abuse of patronage and in the Fabian pamphlet I do not know that you used such a crude term but you certainly draw attention to the "packing" of quangos with Conservative supporters. What hard evidence do you have bearing on that point? Could you prove to a disinterested person that the evidence suggested that the Government was deliberately putting an awful lot of Conservatives, far more than supporters of other political parties, on these bodies?

TONY WRIGHT: As a dispassionate, truth-seeking, former political scientist, all I did as a preliminary to making the argument, and in a sense I was more interested in the argument than that in that, I simply went around and tried to find every bit of evidence that had been done. There is a whole range of studies and surveys, mostly of a journalistic kind I have to say but that is the nature of the case because of the lack of available public information.

I would ask the members of the Committee to look at the first section of the pamphlet where I have sought to bring together all the evidence that I know bearing upon that question. In some ways the best summary of it still comes from a piece that the Financial Times did looking at the Chairs of all these major bodies and then comparing back with the late 1970's position. Their conclusion from that is——

"If there is a new elite running Britain's public services it appears the best qualifications to join are to be a businessman with Conservative leanings."

I think that is the best overall description of the volume of evidence that different studies have unearthed.

2247. PROF ANTHONY KING: Let me ask you the obvious follow-up question which is, so what? A government consciously sets up a large number of quangos, many of which are executive agencies. It wants those executive agencies to pursue government policy. Therefore, it naturally appoints to those executive agencies people who will actively and enthusiastically support government policy and execute it in the way the government wants. What is the problem with that?

TONY WRIGHT: Yes. I think that broadly was the line that the Chancellor of the Duchy of Lancaster gave to you when he came. As a citizen, I do not find that a tolerable answer. I want public servants to perform public services. I do not want them to be clients of the regime. That is a perfectly possible model to have. It is a model that we would be affronted by in relation to the rest of the public services and I am affronted by it in relation to this whole chunk of public bodies. That is my straightforward answer.

2248. PROF ANTHONY KING: Would you be affronted by it if a Labour government were in power and Labour was behaving in exactly the same way, as indeed it did a good deal of the time when it was in power?

TONY WRIGHT: Absolutely. Indeed, if you read the stuff I have put in you will see that I emphatically argue that, which I also said at the beginning, that maybe in the past there has been a conspiracy on this between governments and putative governments that there are great weapons here to be deployed if one can get away with it. Certainly, if Parliament is supine and will allow you to get away with it then get on with it, but, of course, it is unacceptable.

What has changed though is the scale—your first question—that clearly has changed but the character of it has changed too. Back in the 1970's it was far more bipartisan, it was far more a question of taking nominees from external organisations to sit on public bodies than making appointments. That has been the change from a nominee system, which also has some infirmities, to an appointments system.

I have quoted in the evidence I have given to you from the 1989 Cabinet Office Review of the Public Appointments System. They note two things. They note the anomaly between the way that Civil Service appointments are made and appointments to public bodies are made. They say that is how it is but there is an anomaly. They go on to use the phrase, quite interestingly——

"but there is also now a move away from a consensual approach"

Their conclusion was that Ministers need to be far more "hands on" because they want bodies to do things for themselves.

2249. PROF ANTHONY KING: You said a moment ago that you were offended by the way in which the present Government has been using its patronage power and you said, equally emphatically, that you would be offended if a Labour government used its patronage power in the same way. Could you spell out in a little more detail why you are offended? What, in your view, is the objection to the system and the way in which it now operates?

TONY WRIGHT: Yes. I think it discounts any serious notion of public interest. I think it is possible to specify, to

give a framework, to public bodies to say what you want them to perform, the parameters within which they will operate, but then, as one does with Civil Service appointments, one gets people to do that job. I do not really understand the argument -I know that David Hunt gave it to you—that people may not accept this framework, they may not accept the framework of resources and policy.

I find that to be an expression of the kind of politics that has entered our thinking in the past 10 or 20 years. That is an alien presence and I would like to expunge it because I think public service takes place within a framework set by government but then public servants perform it.

2250. PROF ANTHONY KING: Could I then ask you the following. The people who have appeared before us have put forward two solutions to this problem and they are quite different. One solution might be called the "old fashioned party balance" solution that when you are choosing members for quangos of course there will be Conservatives on the quangos but there also ought to be Labour people. That is one way of approaching the problem, the party balance way.

But there is another way and that is the "non political way"; taking it out of politics, regarding quango appointments as really being much more akin to appointments in the Civil Service. Which of these two roads would you personally want to see us go down?

TONY WRIGHT: Emphatically the latter. The first view is very much that Enoch Powell view that there is no such thing as Parliament, there is only government and opposition and they should carve the system up between them. If there are appointments going they should carve appointments up between them. I am also outraged by that.

I take the notion of public service rather seriously. Here we have 50,000 appointments going. If we were simply to do it on the basis of party affiliations, first of all you recruit from an appallingly narrow base given the fact that party membership is minuscule and is never going to get massive again. You disenfranchise the vast majority of the population from taking part in public life at all. I think we should see this as a challenge, that there are thousands of public bodies doing all kinds of important, interesting and difficult things and we have millions of citizens, many of whom potentially can contribute to this system. So, instead of thinking how we can divide it up between the parties because we control everything else, we should see it as a great opportunity to go out, recruit, advertise and bring new participants into public life.

2251. PROF ANTHONY KING: So, you clearly prefer the non-political, public service model. How would you like to see that model institutionalised? What do you actually want us to recommend?

TONY WRIGHT: I may be the only person who is saying this to you, I do not know, but I am advocating that we take the principles of open competition, merit and independence that comes through the Civil Service Commission way of doing things and apply it to this area of public body appointments. Specifically, therefore, I argue for a Public Appointments Commission that would simply do that job. As I also say, it would enable Ministers to say what they wanted from posts, to define job descriptions. It would enable them to float candidates. All these things would be possible, but it would do it within a framework of independent, public appointment. Just to pick up the point I made earlier, that would do everything for the legitimacy of this system.

2252. PROF ANTHONY KING: So, in effect, members of quangos would become, at least in terms of their recruitment, effectively civil servants?

TONY WRIGHT: They would become public servants which I hope they see themselves as being.

2253. PROF ANTHONY KING: And the Minister's role in your scenario would simply be that of advising your Public Service Commission and indicating what his or her wishes were but going no further. The Minister would no longer make the appointments?

TONY WRIGHT: That is what I am arguing, that it is the issue of who makes the appointment that is the crucial thing. The technical things we can talk about but the issue of principle is who makes the appointment. As I understand it, the Government is coming along, as it has done many times before, and saying "We'll make it a bit more open, we'll have a bit more advertising here, a bit more advertising there, a bit more consistency among departments, but there will be no infringement of the essential principle which is that Ministers inside departments will decide." I think simply that issue of principle has to be negotiated.

2254. PROF ANTHONY KING: Is there any role for the House of Commons? Again, some of the people who have come before us have indicated that it might be useful if Select Committees of the House of Commons had some role if not in the choice of then perhaps in the validation of appointments to the Chairs of quangos?

TONY WRIGHT: I have to say that in the past I have been of that view. When I first entered Parliament after 1992 I introduced a Ten Minute Rule Bill—I think it was called the Ministerial Patronage (Parliamentary Scrutiny) Bill—precisely built on that argument, that key public appointments ought to be validated by House of Commons Select Committees. I must say that having experienced two or more years in the House of Commons I am not persuaded that in its present state of un-reform it is in any position to perform that role. I am afraid I would want to look outside.

PROF ANTHONY KING: Why not?

TONY WRIGHT: For the reasons I gave earlier.

PROF ANTHONY KING: The Enoch Powell reason?

TONY WRIGHT: I think I put it this way in the pamphlet. Its partisan character will always triumph over its collegiate character. Because that is so, I do not think it is the mechanism that can do this job.

2255. PROF ANTHONY KING: Can I ask you finally, on a completely different topic, self-regulation of the House of Commons. You said in your opening statement that the House of Commons, in your view, needed a new bit of equipment. What would that new bit of equipment look like?

TONY WRIGHT: That comes from the point about why is it that the Privileges Committee has never been effective, as it were. My argument is that when new bits of independent machinery have been established they have worked very well. Self-regulation has worked badly and that is the model upon which to build.

I mentioned the Ombudsman earlier. I sit on the Select Committee on the Ombudsman which has been a great success story of British government. There were great worries when it was set up, as I said, but here is an officer of the House of Commons. If the Committee is looking for a model here that would somehow make it all right in Parliamentary terms, I think the model, both of appointment and role, of the Comptroller and Auditor General and of the Parliamentary Ombudsman may be the models.

There you have the Ombudsman whose job it is to investigate maladministration in government. In a sense this is what we are talking about. He has access to every bit of paper, apart from Cabinet papers. He does not have the power to enforce recommendations but has never had a recommendation turned down by government because of the force of the office and is backed by a Select Committee of the House which gives that collegiate character to an independent report. I would suspect that that kind of model is one which, on some of the fronts you are looking at, may turn out to be helpful.

PROF ANTHONY KING: Thank you very much.

LORD NOLAN: Lord Thomson?

2256. LORD THOMSON: I want to explore your solutions for the future here. You gave a very prophetic sentence from a book written in 1982 which suggested that until then the patronage system had been tolerable because there had been some kind of bipartisan background to it but if you had somebody in office for too long it might very well erode.

Do you feel that perhaps the matter might be simply dealt with by the process of a General Election and a change of government creating a different situation? Is that going to be an adequate solution?

TONY WRIGHT: I am tempted to say that it would certainly help but that is not the kind of answer that I should properly give. The system depends on two things, perhaps more than two but two I can readily think of. One is that there should be regular transfers of power, which is your point. That shakes the system up. It stops prolonged packing of systems, so it would certainly help. There is no doubt that one party rule has had an effect on this system, particularly though, I have to add, not just one party rule, it has been one party rule allied to the fact that you also wanted to make a revolution in British government at the same time, changing the character of British government towards appointment and away from election and wanting to bring people in of a new kind particularly business folk who did not have a public service background. It is that constellation of factors together which has produced the big change. So, a shakeup, yes.

The second thing the system has always relied on is what I would call a "play the game" culture, that the chaps will play the game. We have a system of government that is notoriously lacking in formal restraints but somehow the chaps will play it by the rules, albeit informal rules. I suspect we have also seen a breakdown of that and that is why I am really interested in trying to think of new, more independent mechanisms that do not depend simply upon the chaps playing it right.

2257. LORD THOMSON: You talk about the "taming of patronage" and you produce the flattering but, in my judgment, rather inadequate proposition that perhaps the perpetuation of the Nolan Committee might be a major contribution to that. Would you allow me to say that it seems to me that what you have been proposing in answers to Tony King to the problem of an excessively quango State is an appointments system that would be done by a super quango.

TONY WRIGHT: Yes, I am very conscious of that charge. Whenever one recommends a new piece of independent machinery that is the charge that comes. I am fully aware of it and I reflected upon it but I come back to the point that I think we suffer grievously in all kinds of areas from the fact that we do not have mechanisms to protect public administration—indeed, to protect the constitution—outside Parliament armed with sovereignty. I have come to that view and I think in all kinds of areas, therefore, we have to start developing such mechanisms. They are not unknown elsewhere.

LORD THOMSON: Thank you.

2258. DIANA WARWICK: I wonder if I could ask you whether you believe that your analysis, which is detailed and quite comprehensive, will influence your party should it come to power. You say that patronage offers the power to use public appointments to change the character and direction of public bodies and that a change of government might certainly diminish the importance of patronage, but surely a new government is going to want to do precisely that, to change the character and direction of public bodies, and probably want to do it quite quickly?

TONY WRIGHT: Yes. I think there are two instincts at work here certainly on our side of politics. One is to say, "Let's get their lot out and put our lot in" because that is the reservoir of power that one has and it is understandable. The more one is confronted by the sheer abuse of the system, the more one wants to do that.

My argument to you and, indeed, in the written evidence is that that would be an inadequate and flawed response, however understandable. It is always through the demonstration of abuse that reform comes. One of the great merits of this whole period and process is that because of the abuse of patronage in this last period, because those earlier warnings happened the culture did not work to stop them happening. Out of that will come the impetus for reform. I am interested in seeing a new government—clearly a Labour government—engineer really quite a radical process of constitutional reform, of which this would be a part.

2259. DIANA WARWICK: The words "culture", "ethos", "public service", you have used them a lot. One of the things that has been said to us about the recent changes in the Civil Service, even in relation to those bodies which are very close to the Civil Service like Next Steps agencies, is the fear that that public ethos, that public service element, is being lost. I ask you, if you are going to push down the appointments process, or push out

the appointments process, to a very much wider range of the public and of all interests is it feasible to hope to maintain that Civil Service, that public service ethos in the face of those sorts of criticisms and concerns?

TONY WRIGHT: Whether the Civil Service ethos and the public service ethos are the same I am not so sure about, nor do they necessarily have to be. The notion of public service and what it means to be a public servant should be constant. The Government has been exercised in thinking about its reforms to the Civil Service and wanting to bring new people in from the outside at higher levels, how it could do it in a way which preserved the public service ethos. What is very interesting there is that if you look at the Civil Service White Paper it states——

"Appointments will continue to be made on merit through fair and open competition overseen by the Civil Service Commissioners."

It says that because it wants to insert a public service guarantee while bringing in new kinds of people. What I am saying to you is that if that kind of public service guarantee is necessary when you bring in people from the outside to the higher reaches of the Civil Service it is also necessary when one brings in all kinds of people to run assorted public bodies.

2260. DIANA WARWICK: Do you think the recent proposals made by Mrs. Bottomley, for example—I do not know if you have had a chance to look at them—do they address the issues that you are most concerned about?

TONY WRIGHT: Not that I feel I ought to say this as a party person, they clearly do not. They have to be taken alongside the Government's general latest review of all this which says that here there is a political problem which has to be sorted out and reassurances must be given. Various new processes will be gone through, more advertising, more transparency and, in the case of the Health Service, there will be these regional sifting boards. But that does not go to the heart of the issue. It does not go to the heart of the ability of Ministers to appoint who they want subject to these new mechanisms of floating names to them.

Can I give one example just to make the point and say why I feel outraged by much of this. A few months ago I went to visit the Mental Health Trust in my constituency. I had not met the chairman before, I met him for the first time, a nice decent man, a nice man to have as a neighbour, cuts his grass, that kind of thing. I asked him how he became chairman of the Mental Health Trust. He said that he was wanting to retire from his timber business and hand over to the next generation. I said that was very interesting but what did that have to do with running a Mental Health Trust. He told me he had a friend who was a consultant and that he had asked him if it would be a good idea and was told that it would be a good idea to do it but he then thought could it be right that mental health services in his part of the world were being run as a kind of occupational therapy for a retired timber merchant who happened to be chairman of the local Conservative association.

This is outrageous. It should not happen. It has been happening and it undermines the legitimacy of a major public service and it has to be attended to.

2261. TOM KING: You have talked about methods of appointment and here in your paper you talk a strong case for an independent public appointments commission to take over the entire activity. You talked about the problem with Tony King of what is a quango and how many there are, that they take many different forms and, as I take your argument, this is the entire activity of appointments, is that correct?

TONY WRIGHT: Yes.

2262. TOM KING: Obviously, what we are seeking to do out of this procedure is to do things that genuinely improve and do not damage the performance of public life in our country. I just look at this idea of an officially manned, sort of civil servant body and I think about the areas where I have been.

I think about the man who is responsible for the biggest procurement programme the Government runs, some £10 billion a year of public expenditure, who is in charge of the Chief of Defence Procurement. We have had two outstanding holders of that office in recent years and neither of them could possibly have been appointed through a system that was run by officials who would have come to the safe conclusion and undoubtedly the two appointments made in the shape of Sir Peter Levene and Mr. Macintosh. One of them was the chairman of a defence contractor which might have ruled him out under certain rules but Michael Heseltine had the courage to appoint him. Mr. Macintosh was an Australian civil servant who we brought in because we thought he had considerable experience and capability in that field. I think Sir Humphrey would certainly have described both those appointments as "courageous" and that would have been sufficient to damn them.

I worry that your proposal will lead to a safety first system of proposal. I am saying this now with the limited experience I have had as a Minister. Very often with the appointments that are made the list that comes up through the official net will be what your committee would like and will be all safe choices but very often, regardless of political affiliation, we have looked for somebody with a bit of gumption, a radical approach and a bit of energy to really wake the place up and get some life into a particular body. I think your system would guarantee that would not happen.

TONY WRIGHT: I find myself in entire agreement on your substantive point about the need to have an interesting range of public appointments, absolute agreement there. The last thing one wants is the Sir Humphrey moral. What I do not understand or accept is your idea that it is not possible to invent an independent public appointments system that cannot deliver interesting appointments. That clearly cannot be right.

The Government does not believe it in relation to the Civil Service and in bringing new people in. There it thinks that it has to underpin it with a role for Civil Service Commissioners to guarantee the integrity of the system. I am arguing that we have to follow the same path. We have, yes, to encourage—indeed, I want to encourage more, that is my line.

2263. TOM KING: Can I take you on from that because Tony King drew you out on this point about were you going back to some form of balance and put in the political balance and then you would meet this point about integrity and you said "No, no, I don't want that, I want

the other solution". Now, actually inherent in what you are putting forward and the points you have just made about integrity is you do actually want to go back to balance. I make this point because you sneer at the idea of saying you are more likely to get appointed—you quoted the *Financial Times* line——

"If you are a businessman with Conservative leanings."

Now, the reality is that what the Government has done in many areas is actually to take politics out, take this awful business of equal shares of local Government counsellors, Conservative and Labour balanced, on some big authority which previously under the arrangement, handling huge sums of public money, because they were not professional, they were not experienced, they were there because of their political background—I am not making party political points, it is true of Conservative counsellors as well as Labour counsellors—it meant the whole thing was run by the chief executive with a huge body of people who were theoretically the board or the authority but actually were not in charge. Now, this is the point I am making to you: Margaret Thatcher was sneered at for bringing in people from Marks and Spencers, but actually it is hugely in the public and national interest that some of the big quangos, as called, which handle huge sums of money and are required to give a public service, do actually have some of the features of management that Marks and Spencers have manifestly demonstrated in their commercial activity. Do you agree with that?

TONY WRIGHT: Yes. First of all I am a great believer in Marks and Spencers and all kinds of parts of my body attest to that! But, I think, again we are on the same confusion. I want to share all the positive things you say about bringing new people in, don't be hide-bound, look wider—all those things—that interests me, that is what I want to do, I want to get away from the old arid party, ministerial appointment model. You are saying you can only do that if you keep that old model. I am saying for goodness sake invent a model that gives guarantees about independence, impartiality, and yet does the things that we want to do in terms of widening the net.

2264. TOM KING: I suppose the point I am making is that I am suggesting to you that if you exclude the Ministerial input, from whatever party it comes from, and I believe that Ministers have made a major contribution in finding people, people who they have seen and identified, who would not have been found through official nets—and you can look at that and you can see over the history of Governments, because you analysed that, you know that has happened—and I am very worried that your proposal to cut out any Ministerial role will not be in the national interest.

TONY WRIGHT: Could I just make one final response: it is very difficult—one, I accept the thrust of what you want—it is very difficult looking at the evidence, frankly. I do not just trade anecdotes about Health Authority chairmen but if you just look dispassionately at the evidence that exists on the nature of the appointments system during a period of heavily ideological government, wanting to change the character of government itself, there were some very very peculiar appointments made and they were made—I quote from the Times in 1992 about Mrs. Thatcher saying "one of us" and, indeed, the Times arguing then in the wake of Mrs. Thatcher's departure, for what it called "a more tolerant use of patronage". Now, it is that that I want to get away from, frankly.

LORD NOLAN: Could we move on now. Clifford?

2265. CLIFFORD BOULTON: You face up to the fact in your paper that there are types of Quango, many and various, and there might be no one answer to how they should be manned up, and I had great fun speculating what this might mean:

"For example, it would be worth exploring how lot or random selection might be developed as a way of representing people on some public bodies."

You are not going to find your Chairman of your Mental Health Board that way, are you? Could you just give me some examples of what you meant by that?

TONY WRIGHT: Yes. Well, again, this, if I may say so, I think reinforces my answer to a previous question, which is that I am clearly not interested here in political fixing, I am interested in exploring a variety of ways in which people may come to exercise public office and I think we have to think more interestingly about it. On that particular point, because I am talking about how people come to occupy public offices I did just remind anybody who was reading it that, of course, in Classical Athens, election was felt to be a rather undemocratic device because only those people who had money, who were powerful, would win and that there are other ways of doing it. No, I don't think it is at all inconceivable that—particularly locally—if you are looking to represent people as users, consumers, on a range of public services, that one way of finding such people might be to do it through ways other than either election, old election, or straight party appointment, that it may be possible to explore other ways. For example, school governing bodies. It would not be at all outrageous for me to think that one way of finding parents, some of whom are very reticent in coming forward, to engage in the business of school government, would be to do it through some kind of lot system mixed with other kinds of systems. I mean, we have an appalling, I think, lack of imagination in thinking of ways in which we can represent people in public life. That is the point that I was trying to make.

2266. CLIFFORD BOULTON: Could I just suggest another reason why select committees might not be appropriate bodies to join in the examination of candidates for these posts, other than the one you have expressed that you don't trust them to be impartial in this, and that is that one of the glories of the "winner take all" system is that the Minister takes responsibility and everybody knows who to blame. Now, if you have a select committee sharing responsibility for these things and then the appointment is a failure, has the Minister not got a "cop-out" and is it not better, really, for us all that we know who to praise and who to blame?

TONY WRIGHT: Yes, I half agree. I don't want to sign up to the idea that ministerial responsibility to Parliament is the answer to all these questions. I mean that is the official constitutional line. I don't believe it to be true, I don't think ministerial responsibility on a day to day basis is very effective. It is what we call often the lack of real accountability. But where I think you are absolutely right and I would want to agree is that I think the role of Select Committees, far more than it has been in

the past, ought to be to keep an eagle eye on public bodies and I think they have been extremely remiss in not doing this. They need to enforce a kind of accountability in relation to extended Government that they have not done before and it would be very hard to do that if they were contaminated in the appointments process.

CLIFFORD BOULTON: Thank you.

LORD NOLAN: I am going to forego my question because you have been very clear and covered the points I wanted to raise. Peter, have you any?

2267. PETER SHORE: Yes, I have one or two. I was very struck by two tables that appeared at the end of your paper, both covering the period April 1992 to December 1993, which is a twenty-one month period, if I have got my arithmetic right. You list there the number of public appointments that were actually advertised and seeing this against a background, I suppose, of several thousand appointments a year, the number advertised was thirty according to your table 2 and the number of people in table 3 who were actually head-hunted, which is an alternative way which Mr. Kalms before us greatly favoured, was only sixteen. It is extraordinary that. The Government has come forward recently, when we had the Chancellor of the Duchy of Lancaster before us, placing a great emphasis upon the role of advertising. Given this background where there has been so little in the past, do you think actually that advertising, if it is really used for public appointments, would have a significant improving effect upon future appointments?

TONY WRIGHT: I think you are right to look at those tables with interest. In fact I perhaps would invite you to look at the next table, too, which extends the picture even further, looking at the role of the Public Appointments Unit which is much talked of in this context and what is extraordinary there is that in all the period covered by the publication Public Bodies 1992—all the appointments in that year—only eighty-four emerged from the Public Appointments Unit, which is this central body created to service this system and to provide names. So if you take together the paucity of advertising and the other things that you mention, you know, we have been round this circle before and reading the previous reviews that had been done in the Cabinet Office 1974-1989 they all talk the same language. They all talk about the need for more advertising, more openness, all these things. My conclusion is—and we are having the same thing in the Government's review now—it has not changed the system, which is why I want to argue now for the failure of that system, the inherent failure of that system. It cannot work unless we move to a quite different model. So instead of saying again that we need more consistency amongst departments I think we need a different kind of system.

2268. PETER SHORE: Let me turn with you to the alternative model. I do not share Tom King's great concern about the inevitable, as it were, conformism of the people who would be doing the appointing—I think you could have rather different bodies. But thinking of the sheer scale of numbers who are being appointed every year, do you really see this as a job that can be done by a single public commission or do you see that its job would be rather to lay down guidelines and oversee other bodies who would be actually doing the appointments?

TONY WRIGHT: Yes, of course. As with the Civil Service Commission and the Civil Service

Commissioners—they don't do it but what they do is they ensure that the system works on public service lines. They are the guarantors of the system and I think what we lack at the moment are similar guarantors of the system in relation to appointments to public bodies. And that is what I would be looking for. There is—and I think I do mention it along the way—there would be another model, which was to say "Let's simply think about abuses—if that is the issue let us think about abuses, as we did with the Honours System in the wake of Lloyd George's 'Sale of the Century'" and so in 1925 we set up the Political Honours Scrutiny Committee. So for potentially dubious appointments one has a separate little bit of mechanism to look simply at those and that would be a model that maybe people may be interested in. Myself I would not be—I would rather move to a system which, as I say, underpins the integrity of the whole system through something analogous to Civil Service Commissioners who, of course, would not do it, but they would preside over a system that made sure it happened in the right way.

2269. PETER SHORE: And are you actually suggesting—am I right to infer this from your earlier remarks—that you think a Select Committee in the House of Commons could be, as it were, a body that oversaw special responsibility for looking at appointments to quangos?

TONY WRIGHT: I think there are issues to be thought of here as to how wide the remit of such a committee would go. I mean, I talked about it earlier in relation to the issue of Members' Interest, which I know is not the thing that I am here to particularly talk about but where we simply do have a problem and we lack an investigatory device of an independent kind which is why I was floating the idea of the ombudsman there reporting to a Select Committee. Now, it may be that one could envisage a select committee, to be called whatever, that had a remit that picked up a number of these areas, serviced by something like an ombudsman to do the investigatory work and the reporting work that does not take place now.

PETER SHORE: Thank you.

2270. ANNE WARBURTON: If I can very briefly, Chairman, come back to the paragraph that Sir Clifford referred to, which I would call your "futuristic" paragraph, that is to say he spoke of the "lot or random select" idea. You also suggested that schemes of functional representation might be looked into. I really want to say that looking for answers to the sorts of problems we have about quangos and local perceptions I saw some interest in following this up and I rather wondered how you thought this could be best explored—another Fabian Pamphlet by Tony Wright, perhaps?

TONY WRIGHT: Well, I don't want to range too widely and the Committee does not want me to and I apologise for those flights of imagination, but there are a number of people around now who are seriously wanting to explore ways in which we can escape from just the kind of old models of governing that we had and particularly want to bring new people in, to represent users in different ways. Much of this is going on, I think, in the world of local government, which I think has understood that local government and local democracy can be different things and are looking for ways to represent users of services

really quite differently, looking at forms of group representations through people performing certain functions—and I mentioned the "lot" idea. I think, you know, would that the Committee could solve all these problems, too, but I flag it up as a way of escaping from some of the old categories.

2271. WILLIAM UTTING: I just wanted to pursue one of the points that has already been made by other members of the Committee about the feasibility of the concept of the Public Appointments Commission. I think it has been suggested to us by other people that really the body of Quangos need fairly extensive surgery before one can get round to applying any uniform system of appointment to them. One suggestion is that at one end certain of their functions should become the prerogative of elected bodies, possibly local government, but at the other end it is quite proper to persist with the current practice in which the accountability is directly to a Minister. You are then left with a group in the middle to which some different form of appointments could be applied and it is this middle group which in my eyes is becoming a more attractive category for the kind of Public Appointments Commission that you are suggesting. Is that something that you think is a runner?

TONY WRIGHT: Well, I think we have, as a matter of principle, to be sure that all appointments made by Ministers cease to be discretionary and potentially open to abuse and follow certain procedural rules. I think I am absolutely clear about that. What I think is a much wider question which is not, again, perhaps the remit for me just now, though I have got views on it, is what we do about the whole world of appointed Government. Now there—again I wouldn't want to think this was a question simply of abolishing quangos, reintegrating with local government. I think the approach will differ, as you are suggesting, very much between kinds of bodies. Some may very properly sit within a more elective structure again. Some, I think, can be composed—back to the previous questions—in more interesting ways than we compose them, seeking to represent people in more interesting—— You know, these are not just two models—the idea of straight election or straight appointment—there are mix and matches here that may be appropriate in relation to all different kinds of bodies, but I would want my Public Appointments Commission to oversee the appointed side of all this, to guarantee integrity.

2272. WILLIAM UTTING: I have a particular concern about the National Health Service, which seems to me to be so big an institution, so important to the nation and consuming so many resources that appointments, certainly at senior levels in the National Health Service, must be a matter of direct concern for the Secretary of State. Would you agree with that?

TONY WRIGHT: No problem with direct concern, of course, for the reasons that we talked about earlier on and one would expect Ministers to have views upon the kinds of people—first of all setting the descriptions of the job, that is, you know, "what kind of role do we want to be performed here?", certainly having names to suggest about the kinds of people who might perform that job as specified. But I come back to the point that I would want that to be underpinned though by a procedure for actual appointment that was procedurally fair and independent. I think for me that is the bottom line of principle in all this.

2273. WILLIAM UTTING: So the NHS would come within a Public Appointments Commission in your view?

TONY WRIGHT: Well, it may sit—it could well sit—as a separate arm of a Public Appointments Commission——

WILLIAM UTTING: Yes.

TONY WRIGHT: —— concerned with Health Service appointments. That would simply be a mechanism for making sure that the system worked.

WILLIAM UTTING: Good. I am most grateful.

2274. LORD NOLAN: We are all grateful to you for the trouble you have taken, both in writing and today by word of mouth, to present your views so clearly. They have been extremely interesting and helpful. Thank you very much.

Earl Russell, thank you very much indeed for coming along to give evidence to us. We have, of course, read with gratitude the written matter that you have sent. I wondered if you had anything in the way of an opening statement that you would like to make to get this part of our morning going?

EARL RUSSELL

EARL RUSSELL (Professor of British History, King's College London and Liberal Democrat spokesman House of Lords): I think really the central point I want to make is that I think the present doctrine of parliamentary privilege, like quite a lot else in the theory of our Constitution, rests on a set of presumed facts that have not really been true since the reign of William III. It assumes that Parliament and Executive are two opposed and largely separate bodies whereas, of course, the degree of interaction and overlap is really very considerable indeed. I think the paradigm case which would illustrate this—and I stress that I am speaking entirely hypothetically—is a breach of a backbencher's privilege by a Government whip, by means, shall we say, of use of force, blackmail, or anything else that ought not to go on within the precincts. That is just the sort of exercise of executive power that parliamentary privilege was originally meant to protect us against, but, of course, if it is done by a representative of the Parliamentary majority it is extremely hard to use the doctrine of Parliamentary privilege as a protection against it.

Also, of course, it does present Parliament, as all internal disciplinary tribunals do, with a conflict of interest. I can remember one case in Parliament of 1945 when an MP was found guilty of bribery and if my memory is correct—and I have not been able to check it—he was sent to the Tower. If he had done the same thing in the Parliament of 1964 I don't believe he would have received the same sentence. That, I think, really puts the point of conflict of interest in a nutshell.

It is argued sometimes that any restriction on Parliamentary privilege would infringe Parliamentary sovereignty. I think that is a misunderstanding of what sovereignty is. Sovereignty is the supreme power to make the law; it does not confer an immunity to break the law. That is a point which goes back, I think, to the due process clause of Magna Carta. It was brought to the attention of our kings in a long, long series of conflicts—finally very reluctantly accepted. I think saying that Parliament is sovereign and saying that Parliament must keep the law are not incompatible propositions and I agree with Aristotle that whoever makes the law ought then to be subject to it and bound to keep it. I do not see any contradiction there.

LORD NOLAN: Thank you very much. That has got us off to a good clear start and I am going to ask Dame Anne Warburton to take up the questions.

2275. ANNE WARBURTON: Lord Russell, I would like to say first that I think all of us found your paper very stimulating when we received it a couple of months ago already. It is good to be able to talk to you about it. You have begun on the subject of privilege which, in a sense, might have been the thing to work up to, but could I, as we have started there, ask you—the view that you take about Parliamentary privilege is one which perhaps not everybody in Parliament would subscribe to. What can be done about Parliament's attitude if this were something which we were to pick up?

EARL RUSSELL: Now, here we are up against the problem of Parliamentary sovereignty. I do not see that one can change the doctrine of Parliamentary privilege except by legislation because there is no other way I know of effectively changing the law. So it is a matter of creating a climate of opinion in which Parliament might see it as being in its interest to make such a change. I do not see how it could otherwise be done.

2276. ANNE WARBURTON: It would be a long-term process?

EARL RUSSELL: That I think we would have to wait to discover.

2277. ANNE WARBURTON: Could I then ask about actions which are short of crime—and the lifting of Parliamentary privilege makes it quite clear—but when it is not a matter of that sort of consequence how do you see the regulation of conduct in Parliament—how should it be assured?

EARL RUSSELL: I think there has to be an area within which every body is capable of regulating its own conduct. An outside control, I think, is much easier to impose where it is a matter of breaches of the criminal law than where it is a matter of breaches of the convention of an institution. It is very much the same problem that you have with the relation between, say, universities and the courts. You call in the courts where breach of the criminal law is involved. I do not think one can get an extreme degree of outside regulation because convention is something which is forming itself and reforming itself almost in every day's experience.

2278. ANNE WARBURTON: You yourself instance three reasons why it does not necessarily satisfy the whole situation. You mentioned that Parliament might fail to follow a due process, it might wish to cover up wrongdoing and Members might suffer from a conflict of interest. I think in our Committee we would perhaps want to add another point to that and that is that public perception might not be satisfied by self-regulation. We have been looking at mechanisms which could be brought in.

EARL RUSSELL: Now that ultimately, since the House of Commons is elected, is the one case where outside power of persuasion can be brought to bear. They are ultimately answerable to the voters and were there to be a very strong demand from among the voters for a change I think they would be under considerable pressure to listen to it.

2279. ANNE WARBURTON: Thank you. Can I then take up the question of outside income. You kindly followed our paper and in talking about that you suggested that perhaps the way to proceed here might be to identify legitimate payment to services rendered outside the Chamber and apart from Parliamentary duties. That would be one way around it—we have looked at various possibilities—another one is not to start from the legitimate payment side but to start from the illegitimate side. I wonder if you would like to develop that thought?

EARL RUSSELL: I think any direct payment for services rendered inside the Chamber has to be regarded as illegitimate. For one thing, if that is accepted, it does confer an immense advantage in Parliament on those who are able to make such payments and therefore, to an extent, deprives those who cannot make them of due representation. I think everybody is agreed that direct payment for a particular act inside the Chamber is improper. The marginal case, I think, is a permanent consultancy to look after the interests of a particular body in Parliament. That has hitherto been regarded as legitimate and I think myself that ought to change because, again, it does tend to deprive those who cannot make such payments of due representation. The Committee of Vice-Chancellors and Principals could make such payment, though it does not, and the National Union of Students could not. That, I think, does make the point about inequality. Anyone, I think, who has spoken in Parliament to a brief from an organisation with which he was connected must have the right to leave out particular paragraphs, to adapt other paragraphs, because they do not coincide with his or her judgment of the national interest. One must be speaking in Parliament to the national interest as well as the interest of one's own group and if there is no give and take, no fretting along the edges of the jigsaw pieces, then no ultimate resolution emerges. But as soon as one accepts payment from an organisation then as soon as one wants to leave out or adapt one of the paragraphs in its submission one does get into a situation of conflict of interest, especially if the income should be big enough to be important to paying one's mortgage. It is the sort of temptation to which I think one should not really be subject.

2280. ANNE WARBURTON: Earlier in our discussions we heard quite a lot, discussed quite a lot, the distinction between advising and advocacy in Parliament—looking for this rather hard to define line between legitimate and illegitimate activities. Is this a thought that attracts you, that one might say that offering advice, selling advice, selling your expertise, is allowed but when it comes to the point of advocating that it is not allowed to do that for payment?

EARL RUSSELL: It is not, I think, a line that particularly attracts me but it might be technically feasible. It cannot be an offence, I think, to repeat public information and there is an awful lot of information available in the pages of Hansard which could be of interest to outside bodies, but outside bodies do not really know where to look for it, and they do not know who has particularly strong feelings about what or where the Parliamentary corns' are. Now, I do not like people paying for access to that sort of expertise—I think if you are interested you ought to be prepared to do the work—but I can see that you could in theory make such a distinction. But it does not follow that because I think you could I would particularly like to do it.

2281. ANNE WARBURTON: Understood. Thank you very much. On quangos you talk about various points

and the one I would like to take up with you is where you say that—you question, really, whether corruption is the right label to put on, as you would say, "the enforcement of partisan policies through quangos, or is that more a question of political un-wisdom?" That left me feeling that perhaps you would have views about how appointments to quangos might best be managed.

EARL RUSSELL: I don't think one can say exactly the same things about every quango. If I look at some of the quangos in my own field what really worries me is that if I were to be offered an appointment on one of those I would not be able to take it because I could not possibly bring myself to co-operate in enforcing the policies which it is bound to conduct. So I do not think it is the Government's fault that they have not appointed me—I think it is that I would not take it if I were asked. And I think the same goes for a very great many of my colleagues. Where it is inherent in the purpose and the nature of the quango that people with one of the major political outlooks in the country cannot take office, there it necessarily becomes a reward system for the Government's friends, even if they did not so intend it. It is really, I think, part of the price of revolution and like Richard Cobb, I really do not awfully like revolutions—I think they cause a lot of harm. One cannot, I think, say that Governments can never follow revolutionary policies, I think one can only say that they are not to be taken in hand lightly, wantonly or unadvisedly.

2282. ANNE WARBURTON: It sounds rather like solemn undertakings given in marriages! Would you see a role for some sort of independent body which might look at appointments to make quango appointments more acceptable?

EARL RUSSELL: Yes, I think that could be a good idea and I think it could look at the obvious competence to undertake the job. I think it could look at any possible link that there might or might not be between rewards of various sorts and services rendered. And, of course, there are cases when suspicion may be cast on an appointment—as it turns out undeservedly—and one ought to be thinking of the possibility of clearing people's reputation as well as of finding something wrong. I think in that way it might, like the Political Honour Scrutiny Committee, be useful. It would not deal with the problem of extreme partisan policies.

2283. ANNE WARBURTON: Thank you very much. You—particularly in a later paper—have raised with us a question which is not on our agenda and I think you recognised that, the question of payment by results and its possible effects. Would you like to put that on the record here—we will have an after-life and we would be interested to have it on our record, I think?

EARL RUSSELL: Yes, I would like to put it on the record and I do have a very uncomfortable sense that performance-related pay may on occasion have some of the characteristics of a corrupt payment, because there always is a possible conflict between the performance indicator and the performance. Suppose I look at a conference paper I have just given and I know that the finances of my department are likely to benefit if I send that paper to Press. I also know that ten years ago I would have said that that paper would benefit from being put away in a bottom draw while I saw whether it stood up or not. I am there put in a situation of conflict of interest and

I must recognise it as such. I don't think I should be. And if police performance indicators are influenced, say, by a detection rate, there are a lot of ways that a detection rate can be fiddled, there is a temptation. Take, for example, a case which I mentioned in my submission, of somebody who went to a police station to notify a pick-pocketing. Now, I am not identifying the station because I am not taking up individual cases, I am making a general point. The police said that they were very busy and that they would accept the notification of the pick-pocketing if the complainant would wait at the police station until half past twelve that night to do it. Very naturally she said she would not bother. So that will not go in their list of undetected crimes which is a great pity because she could have given an exact physical description of those who did it. I think that illustrates the temptation that performance-related payments may put people under.

ANNE WARBURTON: Thank you very much.

LORD NOLAN: Sir William?

2284. WILLIAM UTTING: I would like to seek your views on the value of the Register of Members' Interests in the House of Commons. We have had views expressed to us that it is a bad thing to have to have this kind of register, that having it means that MPs feel relieved of the need to consider whether their actions are proper or not because the mere fact of recording them seems to make them proper. On the other hand we have had views expressed that the Register of Members' Interests ought to be dramatically extended to cover partner, spouse, children and almost everybody else one could think about.

EARL RUSSELL: I would have more sympathy with the second view than the first though obviously, as you illustrate, it is capable of getting out of hand. It is, I suppose, possible the existence of a register might tempt people to think they have done it all but the point of a register is that it enables other people to make the judgment for themselves which, of course, brings us on to the question of my own House—I do not know how far we are considering that today. I would be entirely in favour of my own House having a register of interests. The only difficulty I see which I have not thought my way round yet is what actually should be done for sanctions.

LORD NOLAN: This, of course, at the moment is being looked at, is it not, by a sub-committee of the Procedures Committee with Lord Griffiths in the Chair? Please do not let me stop you but it is something that I am sure we will hear about much more later in the year.

EARL RUSSELL: Well, I would be perfectly happy to wait for the judgment of that Committee, with which I might well agree.

WILLIAM UTTING: Thank you.

2285. PROF. ANTHONY KING: Could I bring you back to the question of Members of Parliament's outside interests? You said in effect, in response to a question from Dame Anne, that in your best judgment Members of Parliament ought not to be allowed to accept money for acting as consultants to outside interests and that is a view that I am sure a lot of people find attractive. It poses for me this kind of problem: you say elsewhere in your written submission that in your view it is perfectly all right for people who are MPs to continue to follow their profession

or business, provided they declare their interests. Now, a bill having to do with the regulation of the banking industry comes before the House of Commons and there are people in the House of Commons who are by profession bankers. Provided they declare their interest they can pursue the interests of the banking industry as they see fit. But on the basis of your own account of what should happen, the trade union representing bank employees could not itself hire, as a parliamentary consultant, a Member of Parliament not previously associated, I take it, with the trade union. That would seem to raise precisely the kind of inequality that you were worried about when you made your original suggestions.

EARL RUSSELL: But it is perfectly possible for a member of the banking union to stand for election to Parliament on the ticket of one of the major parties and possibly even to get elected.

2286. PROF. ANTHONY KING: But suppose that has not happened does that place the interest group—and it might not be an organisation as large as a banking trade union, it might be a relatively small group of people—at a systematic disadvantage from the people who are better off and better organised?

EARL RUSSELL: I would not have said it was a systematic disadvantage because on the whole Members of both Houses of Parliament are really quite ready to listen to representations and an opposition Member presented with a large amount of ammunition against a Government bill, even without any payment, will not necessarily refrain from using it. It is, of course, actually a problem which, with education bills in the House of Lords, I have personal experience of and I have obviously had to think for quite a long time about it. What I was told when I arrived by my Whip's office was "you can never declare an interest too often" and I have always tried to act on that. I think Members of the House are in no doubt of my interest. I have occasionally been attacked from the other side of the Chamber because of it and the House has been told that therefore it can ignore what I say. The House has every opportunity to make that judgment if it wants to and I think that is all right.

2287. PROF. ANTHONY KING: Could I ask you just one quick question about quangos? You tell us that with regard to appointments to quangos "arsonists should not be eligible for jobs in the Fire Service"—and I am sure we are grateful for that observation. You go on to say:

"The difficulty is that the placing of an overwhelming weight of patronage at the disposal of a partisan view may have a corrupting effect even where there is no corruption in intention..."

And you go on to spell out that argument. Do you think that in practice the way in which patronage in connection with quangos has been used over the past decade or so has had in practice a corrupting effect?

EARL RUSSELL: I think it has been certainly close enough to it to be worth serious thought and the question is in the end philosophical not historical. It depends how one describes and defines a corrupting effect. There is certainly always an incentive to people to adopt a line which tends to lead to their own advancement and if, shall we say, in the Government of the Health Service or of universities, attachment to particular views tends to lead to advancement, there are always and will always be people who tend to incline in that direction. Yes, I think one could describe it as having a potentially corrupting effect and I keep thinking of the system developed by Sir Robert Walpole.

2288. PROF. ANTHONY KING: My question was has it actually had a corrupting effect as distinct from potentially having had.

EARL RUSSELL: I think what I am saying is that it has had an effect which, if one were feeling unfriendly, one might choose to describe as corrupting.

PROF. ANTHONY KING: I will leave it at that.

2289. PETER SHORE: I come back to the question of a legitimate and illegitimate payments to Members of Parliament. I think you said that payments for services rendered inside the chamber are illegitimate. That presumably includes all the things that one can do in Parliament as a Member, including speaking on the issues—on issues involved?

EARL RUSSELL: Yes, I think payment for speaking is improper and that is what one draws one salary for in one House or one's attendance expenses in the other.

2290. PETER SHORE: So you would forfeit the right to speak, in other words, if you did engage in a consultancy that covered work inside Parliament?

EARL RUSSELL: Yes. And a question for written answer I think has to be construed to be inside the Chamber which by legal fiction I think it is.

2291. PETER SHORE: Yes. Would that also cover representations to correspondence with Ministers?

EARL RUSSELL: It is subject to qualified privilege which I think is a good test for saying "yes".

2292. PETER SHORE: Thank you. Well, then, if one was to accept this approach, which is certainly a very severe restraint upon what Members of Parliament can do, how would you see it being enforced? Would it be a code of conduct?

EARL RUSSELL: I think it would actually have to be a statutory crime to take money for Parliamentary services, other than in the form of one's salary. A code of conduct might do it but I would prefer to see it have plain statutory effect, which would leave no doubt of Parliament's own view of the matter.

2293. PETER SHORE: So you are really equating it virtually with bribery or corruption?

EARL RUSSELL: Yes.

PETER SHORE: Thank you very much.

2294. LORD NOLAN: That is an area of the law, is it not, which was recommended for clarification by Lord Salmon when he made his report—a report which, alas, was never even debated in the House let alone to any significant extent acted upon. Would you agree that it is an area of the law that whatever views one might take about current problems needs clarification?

EARL RUSSELL: Yes, it does. I was fascinated by what you said about that in your first report. I have not had the time to follow it up because I have been otherwise occupied but I am interested in it.

LORD NOLAN: Thank you very much. Well, we shall follow it up perhaps with your help at some stage.

2295. CLIFFORD BOULTON: Could I just explore a little bit how much of Parliamentary privilege you would like to salvage because you want to salvage freedom of speech in Parliament, which I would regard as probably the most significant and substantial privilege that Parliament has. Presumably you would also want to retain the power of the House and its committees to summon persons, papers and records?

EARL RUSSELL: Yes, I would.

2296. CLIFFORD BOULTON: So we are then left with the possible protection that Members might enjoy from the criminal law. But they, of course, can only claim that in respect of Parliamentary proceedings. I do not think a Member has actually been imprisoned by the House, or anybody else for that matter, since about 1880 but, of course, Members have been imprisoned for breaches of the criminal law and indeed if you wanted immunity you would have to say that you were engaged in a Parliamentary proceeding. It is quite difficult. You were talking about violence in the Chamber. I do not think that two Members who engage in fisticuffs in the House of Commons are immune to the operation of the criminal law. But, of course, there is a concurrent jurisdiction—they are busy committing a contempt and so they might be subject to proceedings in two places and I think that may have sometimes led to a diffidence by one tribunal or another in proceeding in both ways. In fact, I think we might agree, mightn't we, that the area of doubt is only concentrated on criminal acts which are part of proceedings.

EARL RUSSELL: Yes, I would agree entirely with that. I am interested in what you say about the case of fisticuffs in the Chamber. I have discussed this with one retired judge who strongly took the view that the judges could not investigate a case of fisticuffs in the Chamber, because they would be questioning a proceeding in Parliament that is forbidden by the Bill of Rights. I think the disagreement between two authorities so eminent perhaps suggests a need for clarification.

2297. CLIFFORD BOULTON: Well much thought is given to this in *Erskine May* itself. Anyway, I was wanting to make it clear because you made a very general statement at the beginning about the enemy having changed because the sovereign power moved into the House and took it over, but I wanted you to agree really that there are still enemies without and the House does still have to be protected by something which unfortunately is called "privilege".

EARL RUSSELL: Yes I would agree with that.

CLIFFORD BOULTON: Thank you very much.

2298. DIANA WARWICK: One of the things that we have been wrestling with is this whole question of whether it is possible to draw a line between appropriate and inappropriate behaviour in the House. You have made clear your views about payment for services inside the Chamber, but, of course, there are all sorts of other ways in which MPs, whilst MPs, can earn additional money besides their parliamentary salary. You have talked about the importance of the public and of other MPs being able to make a judgment about MPs' special interests. Do you think there is enough information currently in the Register for them to be able to do that? You talked about if income is important enough to pay the mortgage, and I ask specifically—do you think that the amount of money that MPs earn from outside interests should be declared?

EARL RUSSELL: I think I would regard that as desirable. Before I said it was necessary I would want to be able to think a great deal longer. As for what is not in the Register, it is not my House, I obviously do not have the sort of knowledge I have in my own House. I would not like to give you a binding answer on that at the moment.

2299. LORD NOLAN: We are very grateful to you for an instructive and most interesting set of papers, and for the care and thoughtfulness with which you have expanded on them in your remarks to us. Thank you very much indeed, Earl Russell.

Professor Oliver, we are starting only five minutes late which, by our standards, is almost a record but I am sorry to have kept you even that long. We are very grateful to you for coming to give evidence to us, and for the paper which you prepared and which we have all read with great interest. I wonder, though it is entirely a matter for you, since the paper goes into some detail and is naturally fairly lengthy, whether it would be helpful if you were to begin by perhaps reading the first two pages or so which set the scene against which you then comment on particular topics.

PROFESSOR DAWN OLIVER

PROFESSOR DAWN OLIVER (Professor of Constitutional Law, Dean and Head of Department of Laws, University College London): Yes, I am happy to proceed in that way.

LORD NOLAN: Thank you very much. Please do so.

DAWN OLIVER: The question how the standards of conduct of Members of Parliament can and should be regulated raises sensitive questions of parliamentary privilege, and it is these issues that I would like to consider. It is, as we all know, a long established principle that the Houses of Parliament, and not the courts, take cognisance of their own procedure and the two Houses have asserted exclusive privilege of dealing with breaches of privilege and contempts of Parliament, so those are not supposed to be for the courts. So any suggestion that there should be an independent element in the formulation and then the supervision of the operation of standards of conduct for Members of either House would appear on the face of it to challenge that long established set of principles. My own view is that this is not in reality as much of a challenge or constitutional innovation as may be thought, and that it is highly desirable that there should be independent elements in the supervision of standards of conduct. The question is how, legally, this can be achieved.

An obvious possibility, and one that would not pose legal problems, would be legislation which might, for example, transfer these functions to a body outside Parliament or establish a new Officer of the House of Commons or the Lords having that sort of role. But I appreciate that it is not easy to separate law from politics in this area, and it is far from clear what would be politically acceptable. Of course, this is an important matter since any legislation would have to be passed by the Houses of Parliament who are so intimately involved.

I think it is helpful to bear in mind what the rationales of the privileges of the House are. They are, broadly, to protect the Houses collectively and their Members against outside interference, and the reason that this is important is to enable them to carry out their constitutional functions effectively. The two Houses have, over time, justified the special rights, powers and immunities conferred by privilege as being necessary for the welfare of the nation. So I think it is clear that the privileges are not, and are not supposed to be, for the benefit of the Members of the Houses or the Houses themselves, but they are meant to be promoting much broader public interests which the Houses are supposed to be concerned with.

I think looked at in this way it is legitimate to ask whether the operation of parliamentary privilege in the matters we are looking at has actually acted or operated in such a way as to promote general public interests. My own view is that it is not because the operation of the rules relating to lobbying, advocacy, consultancy etc have, at the very least, undermined public respect for the House of Commons and its authority. That is my strong feeling. It has also undermined the ability of MPs to discharge their parliamentary functions, as they should, free from conflicts of interest and according to their own judgments of what is right and wrong and in the public interest, and their judgments of what is in the interest of their constituents and their constituencies and the general public. I cannot really see how it can be plausibly suggested that it is positively for the public benefit that some of the activities which are being raised and questioned should be carried on as they have been. I think at the most one could say that there is no harm in them, and personally I do not agree, and one could argue from that that it would be wrong to interfere with the freedom of Members to do what they like with and for whatever contacts they have, but I do not find that convincing.

I think we need to consider how the maintenance of proper standards of conduct in the House of Commons could be enhanced, and then the implications of certain changes that I know are being considered for parliamentary privilege and its rationales. My view is that things cannot continue as they are and I do not find helpful the thought that I know is held in some quarters that if only the Committee of Privileges and the Committee on Members' Interests and the House generally were more conscientious in performing their functions, there would be no problem. The point is that there are reasons why the Committees do not operate effectively. One point that has been made in an article by Mancuso is that there seems to be a genuine degree of what is called "ethical lassitude" amongst many MPs. I am really not convinced that widespread wishful thinking about the Committee of Privileges and the Committee on Members' Interests operating more effectively is really going to help. I think something more institutional needs to be done.

2300. LORD NOLAN: I wonder if I might begin by asking you a quite general question. From the circles in which you move in the university and, indeed, in private life, can you tell us whether you find this feeling of unease widely shared about the working of Parliament?

DAWN OLIVER: I would say, yes, I think there is a very widespread degree of cynicism about Members of Parliament and Parliament generally. That is something I get from students and generally I think it is in the air, and I think it is born out by some of the evidence that Ivor Crewe produced which is to do with public opinion polling.

2301. LORD NOLAN: You have already indicated in the passage that you read that the Register of Interests seems an imperfect medium for regulating the outside interests of Members. What precisely are the criticisms that you would make of it?

DAWN OLIVER: First I do not think it contains sufficient information. I do think it would be helpful if it disclosed both the amount of money that was changing hands and also the quid pro quo that Members were expected to give for the arrangement, their duties. I think the other problem is, and one cannot expect Registers of Members' Interests to do this, is that it does not at all seek to articulate what the standards of conduct of MPs are, and it is quite easy for people to assume that just because they registered an interest it is therefore proper for them to do whatever they feel should be done for the body with whom they have the relationship.

2302. LORD NOLAN: It rests, does it, on an assumption of certain shared values which are not explicit?

DAWN OLIVER: Yes, I think so.

2303. LORD NOLAN: Should they be explicit? Should there be, do you think, some sort of code which would set out as simply as possible the underlying values upon which the behaviour of Members should rest?

DAWN OLIVER: Yes I do. I think this is a real problem that many Members quite simply do not know because it is not written down anywhere coherently, or in an easily accessible form what is and is not regarded as acceptable.

2304. LORD NOLAN: I suppose up until now it has been assumed, and until recently not questioned, that it was too obvious to need writing down, but we have heard a great deal of evidence from others about the need for codes and the apparent success of codes in areas such as the Civil Service and the professions and the Armed Forces. Is Parliament, do you think, in the same position as those from this point of view?

DAWN OLIVER: Yes I think so. I think life has got much more complicated, relationships are much more complex than they were 20, 30, 40 years ago, so it would be helpful to have the rules spelt out.

2305. LORD NOLAN: How would you see it being put into place? By resolution of the House, or would there be a need for legislation?

DAWN OLIVER: I think that would tie in with the method of enforcement, using the word "enforcement" fairly neutrally. I think it would be quite possible,

obviously work would have to be done on drawing up the standards for it to be adopted by a resolution of the House, but what would happen then if the standards were not met would be a question, whereas if it was put into statutory form one would expect there to be some kind of a mechanism for monitoring and enforcement to go with that.

2306. LORD NOLAN: Are we envisaging certainly some specific rules on the lines of those at present governing the Register, perhaps clarified and expanded in the manner that you have suggested, coupled with a set of principles contained in a code by which the seriousness of any particular failure to meet the rules could be judged?

DAWN OLIVER: Yes. I know they are interlinked, but I think there are two issues; one the Register of Interests and what it should be disclosed and so on, and secondly a Code of Conduct which, of course, is not entirely covered by registration of interests, they are not the same thing.

2307. LORD NOLAN: First of all, starting with the present methods of enforcing breaches of the rules of the House, are those, in your view, sufficient for this purpose? I think you have indicated that you think not.

DAWN OLIVER: No. The first difficulty is that the rules are not clear so a complaint is made, referred to the Committee of Privileges and then the facts are looked at and some sort of rules, hitherto unwritten, are formulated in the Committee's report and then that is debated by the House. I think it would be much more helpful if the rules were set out first so that the Committee of Privileges, if that were the body dealing with it, had clear criteria against which to measure the alleged misbehaviour, or whatever it was is being complained of. I think then there is a problem about what becomes of the report of the Committee of Privileges because these will often, in fact, be very carefully drawn up with findings of fact and formulations of what is and is not appropriate. Then the House debates the matter and a resolution is passed which will not necessarily, or probably almost never, follow very closely the recommendations in the report of the Committee of Privileges and you end up not quite knowing what the rule is or what is right and what is wrong.

2308. LORD NOLAN: It has been suggested, and you suggested it in your paper as one possibility, that there should be some independent element of review introduced into the consideration of accusations against Members if they have broken the rules. What do you see as the best way of approaching that?

DAWN OLIVER: Ideally I would like to see an independent body outside Parliament dealing with this. Personally I would not necessarily exclude the Committee of Privileges also having jurisdiction, but in some situations it would be appropriate for that to be looked at by an independent commission which I think would have to be established by statute, which could either be concerned simply with matters to do with Members of Parliament and their relationships with outside bodies, or else—and I know this goes beyond your present area of enquiry—it could be something to do generally with standards of conduct and so it would be looking at other matters in completely different areas.

2309. LORD NOLAN: Set aside for the moment the criminal law which plainly would be a matter for the courts, do you think that the courts have any role to play in the regulation of what might be called internal Parliamentary proceedings?

DAWN OLIVER: No I do not. The election courts are involved in elections, but apart from that I do not see an increased role for the courts.

2310. LORD NOLAN: One can see there would be a very, very strong arguments indeed in keeping the separation of powers intact and maintaining a respectful distance between the courts and Parliament.

DAWN OLIVER: Yes.

2311. LORD NOLAN: What else might there be? What about a new Officer of the House which is one of the headings which you consider?

DAWN OLIVER: Yes, on the surface this is an attractive idea and one could follow the model of, say, the Comptroller and Auditor General who is an Officer of the House, or the Parliamentary Commissioner for Administration, both of whom are established by statute with statutory functions, and both of whom are servants of the House reporting to the House and to particular committees of the House. The difficulty I see, though, is that both the Comptroller and Auditor General and the Parliamentary Commissioner for Administration are concerned to assist the House in the discharge of its function of scrutinising Government, so the Parliamentary Commissioner is to do with assistance in the resolution of citizens' grievances, and the Comptroller and Auditor General to do with the way in which public money has been spent. Generally, as I understand it, the House does in those functions recognise a bit of a separation between the functions of the House of Commons as the legislature and the Government. The difficulty with having a statutory Officer of the House charged with looking at breaches or otherwise of a code of conduct is actually it would not be looking at what the Government was doing, the Officer would be helping to monitor the House itself and would be a servant of the House. I see a rather ambiguous role there for such an Officer.

2312. LORD NOLAN: Would it require legislation to set up such an Officer with sufficient powers, or could it be done by resolution of the House?

DAWN OLIVER: I think it would depend what powers it was felt the Officer should have. Just to take an example, if an Officer were investigating an allegation about a Member of Parliament having done something in breach of a code and the Member of Parliament was reluctant to appear before the Officer, I do not think that there is anything an Officer could do unless there was legislation. At the moment I think it is for committees of the House who complain about people not being willing to attend to refer the matter to the House, and then the House has to pass a resolution and then it goes back to the committee. I think it would be very difficult to give the Officer that sort of coercive power.

2313. LORD NOLAN: Really I suppose it would not have to be by the consent of the Members of the House. Of course, I am a child of these matters, but I understand that by and large if a committee asks a Member to come and give evidence there is no question of it having to issue

a subpoena or anything of that sort, he comes. But you are envisaging there might be difficulties in pursuing a detailed factual investigation without some sort of statutory power behind it?

DAWN OLIVER: Yes, and I think there could also be difficulties about getting the attendance of outsiders if it was necessary to look at people with whom the MP is supposed to have had an arrangement.

2314. LORD NOLAN: One other suggestion that was floated by Lord Howe yesterday, amongst others, if, indeed, the House thought it right to introduce an independent element, would be the appointment of independent members to the Committee of Privileges. Is that something that you considered?

DAWN OLIVER: I have thought about it. As far as I know it would be a complete innovation. I do not know of non-Parliamentarians sitting as members of Parliamentary committees. If the independent Members had a vote, if it comes to that, or very strong input into any recommendations, I can see there being concerns about whether these were really recommendations of a committee of Parliament as opposed to of a mixed body that was not really rooted in Parliament.

2315. LORD NOLAN: I suppose one possibility would be that the independent Member or Members would have no vote but would have the right to register dissent and have their reasons published, or something of that sort.

DAWN OLIVER: Yes, that might be possible. I think it rather a weak way of stiffening up the system myself.

2316. LORD NOLAN: I wonder, since I am sure the others will have questions to ask, if I could bring you to your conclusions which, again, we find in your paper at the end. Are you happy with those, so to speak, as written because, if so, again it might be helpful if you were to read them out for the benefit of our listeners.

DAWN OLIVER: Yes. I have written this in rather a rush but perhaps I will read out my conclusions.

I think that Members of Parliament should be, if they are not already, and that is a moot point as far as the law is concerned, subject to the criminal law of bribery. I think there should be—I have said statutory but I would not go to the stake about that—a Code of Conduct for Members of Parliament and for their sponsors. I think the Register of Interests should disclose information about the sums paid under the arrangement and the duties of the Member to the sponsor. There should be an independent extra-Parliamentary body to investigate complaints and breaches of the Code of Conduct and breaches of registration requirements and report—I said to the Speaker but I do not feel I know enough about the House to know to whom the report should be made.

For me, the very second-best variation would be a new independent statutory Officer of the House with power to investigate complaints, make findings of facts and recommendations to the Speaker. But, as I have said, I see legal difficulties about that and ambiguous relationship.

LORD NOLAN: As you indicate in your closing words, this is, of course, entirely a matter for the House. You seem to suggest some lack of optimism.

DAWN OLIVER: I am afraid I am a bit pessimistic. I think it very important that something should be done and I am not sure that it will be, or that the right thing will be done.

LORD NOLAN: Thank you very much. I will now ask a very experienced parliamentarian, Lord Thomson, to begin the questioning.

2317. LORD THOMSON: In your Code of Conduct, where would you draw the line between what are legitimate outside paid interests and unacceptable outside paid interests?

DAWN OLIVER: I cannot give you a detailed answer obviously in the time available and I would want to write it down. I do not, myself, have a problem with Members of Parliament being journalists or carrying on their professions and that kind of thing. I would draw the line when the arrangement becomes a very specific one, or involves very specific obligations on Members to speak in certain ways, vote in certain ways. I am not even very happy about arranging access to Ministers and so on. I cannot be terribly precise about where you draw the line, but the more precise the obligation tying the independence of the Member the less acceptable it is.

2318. LORD THOMSON: There are two distinctions we have been debating, and since you are our last witness and a very special one it would be very interesting to have your judgment on. One is to draw a distinction between consultancy and advocacy. The question is, do you think that is a sustainable difference? The second is to draw a distinction between somebody who is paid to look after a particular industry or a trade association or something of that kind as being acceptable, but what would be unacceptable is somebody who is paid by a multi-client, a lobbying firm whose clients change all the time, any of which he might be expected to further their interests in the House irrespective of its merits. What do you think?

DAWN OLIVER: I am not at all happy with the idea of being paid by a multi-client consultancy firm. I think that is really selling your soul to an anonymous devil.

2319. LORD THOMSON: That is an MP for hire, is it?

DAWN OLIVER: Yes, I do not accept that at all. Consultancy, obviously it depends what the terms are, but I do not find it too unacceptable that Members of Parliament should meet with certain bodies with whom they have an interest and discuss what the climate in politics is and that kind of thing. I suppose the amount of money that changes hands, or if any money changes hands, would obviously be very relevant there.

2320. LORD THOMSON: If the consultancy contract specifically laid it down that the Member was free to speak and, of course, vote in whatever way his conscience told him and that he was not in any way tied in that way, and that was published in the Register of Interests, would that be a help?

DAWN OLIVER: It would be a help, but you can write things down and then life might be rather different.

LORD THOMSON: Thank you.

2321. DIANA WARWICK: Mine is not a constitutional question. I was much struck by the strength of feeling in your evidence to us about the lack of willingness on the part of the House of Commons to regulate itself and what you called "ethical lassitude", and the severe degree of pessimism that it was possible to put this right despite the very widespread concern that you acknowledge as existing. We have, however, received some evidence from a long serving Member of the House of Lords who said to us that some evils need drastic remedies, and the commercialisation now rife in Parliament should be cleaned out of the system. He went on to say

"What I am very sure about is that Parliament has become so frightened that it has put itself in the hands of the Committee ..."

that is our Committee

"...and it will expect to get a pretty severe message back".

Do you think that is the case?

DAWN OLIVER: Are you asking me whether I think the Committee should give Parliament a strong message, or whether I think that Parliament feels that it needs a strong steer? I am not quite sure what you are asking.

2322. DIANA WARWICK: I am asking you whether you think that Parliament has, in fact, made the decision to accept a severe message if we choose to give it?

DAWN OLIVER: I cannot say that I am privy enough to what people are saying in Parliament to give you an answer. I would very much hope so, but I am an optimist in most things but I am a pessimist on this.

2323. CLIFFORD BOULTON: Thank you very much for your paper which I only saw this morning a quarter of an hour before we came in, so I am sure it deserves much closer study than I have been able to give it. I will only just raise a couple of things and then go away and read it properly.

The extent to which one could helpfully draw up a code which Members would find useful and could be held to, I wonder if there are limits to that because what we are talking about really is letting the side down, either yourself or damaging the House by your conduct, which is in the nature of a contempt. I do not think the courts have attempted to make a list of all the different ways in which you could commit contempt of court, have they, and then say every citizen if he reads this will know how to behave in court? Is it not something that is much woollier than that and draws on a sense of propriety and a sense of what is acceptable which one has to assume people in public life who have been elected to the House of Commons will feel in their bones?

DAWN OLIVER: I do not think the parallel with contempt of court is really a fair one. The sort of behaviour that might be contempt of court is often quite extreme, and anyway people are so rarely before the courts that it would not be very helpful to write it down. You hardly ever have an opportunity to be in contempt of court. I do think that it would help enormously to try to write down certain standards of conduct. It would not be too difficult; many of them are already there in resolutions of the House and reports of the Committee of Privileges and many of them, I am sure, are very widely held if one could get a discussion going about it.

2324. CLIFFORD BOULTON: I think it is one of the areas that the Speaker asked the Committee of Privileges to attend to shortly before we were actually appointed, which was to seek greater clarification of these things. I notice that you say the report on the W.J. Browne case was much clearer than the subsequent resolutions which, of course, tended to harp back to some of the 17th century resolutions appearing to ban all payments. But the House did not intend that, did they, because they clearly straight from then on did not ban all payments. What they were banning in the W.J. Browne case was people seeking to give directions to a Member as to how he should behave and the Member being prepared to accept such directions. Both of those are offences, and continued to be offences. There was no attempt at that time to prohibit any financial nexus with someone outside Parliament; it depended what the terms of the contract or understood or written were, is that not the case?

DAWN OLIVER: Yes, I think that is true. I think one of the difficulties is that because Members' salaries were provided for so late and, of course, are not very generous, it has just happened. One absolutely understands why it has come about that MPs rely on outsiders for support of various kinds. The W.J.Browne case was 1947 and unless there is legislation it is not easy to turn the clock back.

2325. CLIFFORD BOULTON: But neither in 1947 nor any time since has the House actually prohibited Members having financial relationships with outside interests which could involve them speaking up for that interest so long as they were not speaking under instructions, and therefore there is not some falling away that has occurred. We are not trying to go back to the golden age of W.J. Browne, are we, because what has happened is that the literal words of the resolutions that were passed then and in the 17th century have then been contrasted with the rules for registration and declaration, and it appears that there is some falling off of standards. There might have been a falling of standards but that fact does not illustrate it, I do not think, is that not right?

DAWN OLIVER: No, I think practices have changed, that is part of what has happened since 1947. The W.J.Browne case was to do with a trade union sponsorship arrangement and my impression is that in the last 15 years or more these other arrangements to do with consultancy and lobbying firms and so on have proliferated. It is difficult to say whether standards have fallen away or not because there are new things possible that were not actually being done before.

2326. CLIFFORD BOULTON: Apart from the alleged "cash for questions" issue which we are not considering because somebody else is and it is a specific case, nobody has given us, as I recall, any evidence that anybody has sought to give directions or instructions for money to a Member of Parliament. Are you aware of any cases where Members have bound themselves improperly?

DAWN OLIVER: I am not aware of any recent cases though I do remember the National Union of Mineworkers' case and the National Union of Public Employees' case in the 1970s where rather indiscreet trade union officials did rather seem to be demanding that their Members of Parliament should do what the union wanted them to do.

CLIFFORD BOULTON: It was in breach of the undertaking.

DAWN OLIVER: Absolutely.

CLIFFORD BOULTON: So it was not the sponsorship arrangement which was at fault, it was the way somebody was seeking to administer it.

DAWN OLIVER: And presumably the union did not realise what the rules were.

CLIFFORD BOULTON: One region had to be told by headquarters, yes.

DAWN OLIVER: I think it would be very helpful, not just for Members of Parliament but also for those with whom they deal, if there was a Code of Conduct of some kind that just made quite clear what is and is not acceptable.

CLIFFORD BOULTON: Thank you.

2327. PETER SHORE: Is the problem one of instructing Members of Parliament or, in fact, the temptation of accepting money to do things?

DAWN OLIVER: I suspect there is not much instructing, or probably virtually none. I think the unions misunderstood in those cases so I am not really conscious of that.

2328. PETER SHORE: So really it is not a question of worrying about the possibility of Members of Parliament being instructed to do things by outside bodies. The problem is, if it is a problem and how big it is we are deciding, of people paying Members of Parliament to do things, and paying is a form of persuasion not a form of instruction.

DAWN OLIVER: I have no particular reason at all to believe that there is a problem of instruction, but I do not know. I do not frequent the corridors of the House of Commons and I do not know, but I have no reason to think it happens.

2329. LORD NOLAN: I wonder before Professor King takes over I could raise a suggestion which I think was first made by Sir Clifford about the registration of engagements and what they did and did not expect a Member of Parliament to do. If the whole contract had to be in writing and registered and showed how much was paid, would that not give a fairly clear indication of the degree of commitment involved?

DAWN OLIVER: It probably would; that is assuming it is all written down.

LORD NOLAN: True.

2330. PROF. ANTHONY KING: This is really a point rather than a question, and I am making it to you simply because you are our last witness. I have been very struck and a little amused and a little dismayed by the very large number of people who have either written to us or come before us to say there ought to be a Code of Conduct without actually offering us a draft Code of Conduct, let alone the rationale that would underlie it. I am struck by the fact that people seem to think there are standards out there that Members of Parliament ought to adhere to, that those standards are agreed and that all this Committee has to do is, as it were, systemise and draw together in one place that which right thinking men and women everywhere believe to be proper. It ain't like that.

DAWN OLIVER: Perhaps I can just comment that lawyers are quite used to the idea of principles evolving on a case by case basis, and that is why I have drawn attention to the past reports of the Committee of Privileges and Resolutions of the House which I would have thought would provide quite a rich source of standards of conduct. I do not imagine they would provide everything but there is that material.

PROF. ANTHONY KING: They may not provide the standards of conduct that you would like.

DAWN OLIVER: I have not done the research yet, but maybe not.

2331. ANNE WARBURTON: Professor Oliver, can you confirm what has been said to me quite early in this proceeding that this is the first outside committee ever to be licensed to examine the workings of Parliament, and if that is correct does that have implications for the ambition we should show in our forthcoming report?

DAWN OLIVER: I do not know of any other equivalent committee having been appointed, but I do not feel that I am an authority, particularly on history. Assuming it is it seems to me it is a very important opportunity for further guidance and serious thought to be given to a very important problem.

ANNE WARBURTON: Thank you for your help in formulating it.

2332. WILLIAM UTTING: I am an enthusiast for codes of conduct because it seems to me that life has become too complex for people in business or Government or the professions to manage without an easy external frame of reference. The particular difficulty about the Code of Conduct for Parliament seems to me to be that in general, to use the jargon, people have to "own" or "internalise" these documents before they are of much practical use to them, which means that they themselves have got to be constructively engaged in their formulation. In view of your rather pessimistic views earlier making me doubt the feasibility of actually being able to engage Members of Parliament sufficiently to come up in the end with a worthwhile code. The worst thing would be an attempt to impose upon them a code constructed by other people who could be written off as lot of ignorant busy-bodies. Do you have any helpful suggestions about how we might go forward with this? You have made the suggestion that we may have some role to play in this. Oh help!

DAWN OLIVER: I do take that point. I come back to one source which is a Parliamentary source and that is the Committee of Privileges' and House's previous resolutions. Those are definitely the House's own creation over many, many years, although I dare say many Members are not conscious of it. I do not think those values would be regarded as some outsiders imposing things on the House. To the extent that that set of sources does not cover some of the current problems that we are looking at, clearly it would be very helpful if a joint group

were established of Members of Parliament and maybe this Committee. I really had not thought it through. I quite take the point that it is important to have Parliamentarians very much involved so that "own" it is a good word. Without some outside participation I am not sure how far they would get.

2333. WILLIAM UTTING: Yesterday we had evidence from Plaid Cymru which included a list of practical points for their Members to abide by in delivering good service to their constituents. I suspect that there are other sources of guidance from other quarters to Members of Parliament about what they should do and how they should behave if they are to fulfil their responsibilities both to constituents and to the effective workings of the House. Would you see those as being suitable for inclusion in codes of conduct?

DAWN OLIVER: I do not know whether you are referring to the rules of the political parties. If there are other sources, possibly, but I am not quite sure what other sources there are.

2334. WILLIAM UTTING: Do you think "How to be a Good MP" is something that ought to go into a Code of Conduct in addition to "Be careful about who you take money from"?

DAWN OLIVER: Yes, that could be very constructive because it would make the document not seem an entirely restricting and punitive document. It could be a positive, constructive, up-beat set of ideas and not simply a do's or don'ts.

WILLIAM UTTING: Good. Thank you.

LORD NOLAN: Thank you very much. I know we came upon you at quite an exceptionally busy time even by your standards, and I know that you have gone to great trouble to put before us this very thoughtful and detailed paper which we shall keep and record amongst our archives and return to, so we are most grateful to you, as to all our witnesses. You finish up as we hope to finish up with an objective view of the position as seen by a constitutional lawyer. Thank you so much.

DAWN OLIVER: I am very glad to have had the opportunity.[15]

LORD NOLAN: Now we have ended our public hearings, as we began, with impartial evidence from witnesses who are experts on the constitution of this country. I speak for all members of the Committee when I say how grateful we are to all of our witnesses for volunteering to come forward and for the care and thought which they have devoted to putting their points of view clearly before us.

During the course of our eighteen hearings we have listened to a total of 72 witnesses or groups of witnesses. Given more time we should like to have heard a much greater number. I believe, however, that we have been able to examine most, if not all, of the main streams of prevailing thought upon the issues which we are addressing. I am satisfied that any ground which has not been covered in the public hearings is fully dealt with in the huge volume of letters and written submissions—nearly 2,000 at the last count—which we have received since we started work at the beginning of November. Our gratitude to witnesses who have given

---

[15]Professor Oliver's oral evidence should be read with her letter to Lord Nolan of 23 February, see Evidence pp. 535–536.

evidence is equalled only by our gratitude to all of those individuals and organisations who have given us their views in writing, views in many cases buttressed by the results of invaluable study and research.

But I must stress that by far the greatest number of our correspondents have been ordinary members of the public, the men and women in the street. It has not been practicable to include them amongst our witnesses from whom we have taken oral evidence, but they should be in no doubt that we have taken careful account of their views and that the members of this Committee fully share their pride in this country and their concern that the highest standards of conduct in public life should be observed. In due course we propose to make all the letters and written submissions which have been sent to us available for inspection by the public, save for those which are unsuitable for publication.

We are very conscious of the burden placed upon us to produce recommendations of a quality which will meet the anxieties of the public and at the same time be realistic and practicable. We shall do our best. We are, of course,

simply a committee of ten individuals. The final responsibility will rest, as it should, upon the elected Members of Parliament.

We are now going to retire from the public gaze, consider all of the evidence which we have received, and set to work upon the writing of our first report. Since this is due in early May, we must ask that any further letters or written submissions relating to the three subjects which it will cover—that is to say in short Members of Parliament and their outside interests, Ministers and civil servants, and quangos should be sent to us by 28 February.

In conclusion, the members of the Committee wish to join me in extending our warmest thanks to the management and staff of Central Hall, to the media and their technicians and to our own staff for all of their willing and highly efficient cooperation in making our public hearings so enjoyable and trouble free. And may I add how much pleasure it has given to see a number of the same faces in this room every day following our proceedings with a most encouraging interest. Thank you all.

THE COMMITTEE ON STANDARDS IN PUBLIC LIFE SUPPLEMENTARY MEMORANDA RELATING TO TRANSCRIPTS OF ORAL EVIDENCE

The principal documents necessary to understand evidence given by witnesses in the transcripts of oral evidence are included at the end of this volume. Copies of all other submissions received by the Committee may be consulted at the Public Records Office in Kew, the Public Record Office of Northern Ireland in Belfast, the Scottish Public Records Office in Edinburgh, and the National Library of Wales in Aberystwyth.

Letter from the Rt Hon Lord Callaghan to the Chairman of the Committee

I fear that in my answers to Professor Anthony King and to yourself, I failed to give a clear or accurate indication of my views and I should like to correct what I said then.

I wish to put a limited case for remuneration of a Member who, prior to entering Parliament, has made his career in a particular industry (say, shipping). As that has been his lifetime's work, such a Member will have a specialised knowledge of the problems of his industry and it seems to me quite defensible that this should be put to use by his industry in seeking advice, for which he might be remunerated, on how best to make its case to Parliament. I also think it not unreasonable for such a Member to speak in debates as his background and his expertise will be well known to other Members. It would probably be better for him to abstain from voting in Parliament, nor should he actively lobby Ministers, especially if he is a Member of the governing party.

You will see that I draw a distinction between such a Member and one who has no connection with an industry or a firm before entering Parliament but who is approached with an offer of remuneration to represent an industry only after he has entered Parliament and probably because he is a Member of Parliament.

Incidentally, this illustrates the difficulty in drawing up exact rules. If I may revert back to the grievances of the Police, forty years ago, they were in a position where they were obviously underpaid, their remuneration was settled by Local Authorities and the Home Office jointly, they were not allowed to join a Trades Union, they had no staff able to negotiate with their powerful opposite numbers in the Local Authorities and the Police on equal terms. Without outside help, their genuine grievances would have continued to remain largely unknown and possible uncorrected.

There might be other instances today where a similar situation could arise.

31 January 1995

Memorandum from the Rt Hon John MacGregor, OBE, MP

I promised to send you a note on an issue which I raised at the end of my evidence, in relation to the procedures of the Select Committee on Members' Interests. I enclose the note, which I hope will be helpful.

23 February 1995

Procedures of the Select Committee on Members' Interests

1. At the end of my evidence to your Committee, you asked me to do a note on a specific and limited point I made, namely that I had become concerned about the extent to which the Select Committee on Members' Interests is asked to be "detective, interrogator, judge and jury all in one" in certain cases which might be so serious as to affect a Member's total career.

2. I was interested to see that Sir Geoffrey Johnson-Smith in his evidence expressed uneasiness about fulfilling all these roles in relation both to the John Browne case and a current investigation (the latter also involving a writ for libel). He went on to argue that when a complaint is made against a Member "the complainant inevitably has the initiative. He may be selective in the range of documents he brings to our attention and the burden of proof can be placed to an unfair extent on the Member concerned, who has no legal representation or power of cross-examination of his accuser. And there are moments of doubt as to whether one is fulfilling the best principles of justice and fairness..."

3. I would like to emphasise that the cases I have in mind are extremely rare. Over the last 30 years there probably are only two. Nevertheless when they do involve an individual's whole life and career, it is important that proper rules of justice are applied. I have serious misgivings as to whether the present Parliamentary procedures achieve that.

4. Interestingly, the 1966 Salmon Commission dismissed Select Committees as unsuitable bodies for investigating allegations of public misconduct; I accept that in the majority of cases which come before the Privileges Committee or the Select Committee on Members' Interests, normal judicial procedures would be inappropriate. I have also opposed in the past putting the Register on a statutory basis, which would have involved more formal legal procedures too. But I do feel that in very specific cases involving serious allegations we need to think again. When a Member's career is at stake, it seems to me that the "cardinal principles" identified by Salmon, that witnesses should be entitled to legal representation, informed beforehand of allegations made against them, and allowed to cross-examine those making such allegations need to be applied.

5. As I understand it, the Select Committee on Members' Interests sets out its own rules each time. Both parties can be allowed to have their legal representatives with them if the Committee agrees, but for technical purposes only and in the preparation of papers. There is no ability to examine the other party, complainant or Member, either directly by the party concerned or by his legal representative. There are also severe constraints on whether both parties can hear what the other says. If both complainant and complainee are MPs, then both can attend if the Committee agrees. Where the complainant is not an MP, it is likely that both would be excluded.

6. There is no direct analogy with the Professional Conduct Committee of the General Medical Council. But it is relevant in the sense that in extreme cases the GMC procedures involve a doctor's suspension or erasure from the Register. Similar penalties can happen to MPs. In such cases before the PCC both complainant and doctor usually attend the hearing, both are usually legally represented, cross-examination does take place and legal expenses are provided.

7. It is entirely capricious whether there are experienced lawyers on the Select Committee to ensure that the proceedings are properly conducted in a legal sense; but even then I doubt whether it is appropriate that such a lawyer or lawyers should be asked to fill that role as well as be Members of the Committee. The Attorney General does serve on the Select Committee on Privileges, but again he is a Member of the Committee and may well play a leading role in cross-examining the witness. Speaker's Counsel can be asked to advise on strictly legal issues, but again I wonder whether that is enough.

Recommendation

8. I would, therefore, suggest that in case involving serious allegations which may lead to suspension or expulsion, and where the Member complained of specifically requests it:—

(a) Legal representation should be available and expenses met.

(b) Cross-examination should be permitted.

(c) All documents should be made available to the Member complained of beforehand.

(d) Both complainant and complainee should be allowed to attend all hearings.

Consideration should also be given to having available to the Committee a legal adviser who would assist the Chairman on the judicial aspects of the enquiry, but who would not have a vote.

9. I would like to stress again that this procedure would only be required in rare and grave cases. In most cases a Member is responsible ultimately to his or her electorate and therefore normal judicial processes would be inappropriate. But when between elections Parliament itself could totally affect a Member's future, that Member is entitled to the full legal processes that apply to others.

Other Issues

10. A question also arises, as in the case of the General Medical Council, as to whether proceedings should be in public. I am inclined to agree with Sir Geoffrey Johnson-Smith that it is better to have the proceedings in private but the report made publicly available, on the grounds as he said that if the proceedings were in public they would be treated like a Select Committee, in particular with the media covering it like a news event "with all the selectivity and sound-bite reporting that that entails". The Member against whom the complaint is made would be subject, therefore, to speculation which, as the enquiry proceeded, could turn out to be totally untrue. The first impressions created by selective reporting could have serious repercussions for the Member with his constituents, even if they were shown later to be totally untrue.

11. I think there is some blurring and uncertainty as to the roles of the Select Committee on Members' Interests and the Select Committee on Privileges in these matters. I note that Professor King suggested a Committee on Standards of the House to deal with both issues of the Register and contempt of the House if those occurred. There may be a case for a single Committee to deal with such issues affecting a Member's conduct. But the two Committees could not be combined as such, given that the Select Committee on Privileges also has to deal with much wider issues not involving the Register itself.

Memorandum from Public Relations Consultants Association

CODE AND REGISTER FOR PROFESSIONAL PARLIAMENTARY ADVISERS

Scope and Interpretation

1. This Register and the associated Professional Charter and complaints and arbitration procedure applies to professional Parliamentary Advisers within membership of the PRCA. Accordingly, any company (or partnership, or

an individual person) engaged in parliamentary or public affairs consultancy or work of a similar kind, and which lobbies Members of Parliament (or their staff) for reward on behalf of clients or which provides information or advisory services to clients to assist them to lobby on their own behalf shall place an entry upon a Register which shall be kept by the PRCA.

2. For the purposes of the Register "Lobbying" consists of representations made to any member of Parliament or to any member of his or her staff on any aspect of Government policy, or on any measure implementing that policy, such as contracts, appointments, loans or grants, or planning decisions, or any item of legislation, or any matter being considered, or which is likely to be considered, by either House of Parliament or any Committee of either House.

Arrangements for Registration

1. The PRCA shall cause the Register to be published annually and, prior to publication, every person or firm entered upon the Register shall notify the PRCA in writing of any change, or shall confirm in writing that there is no change, in the entry.

2. Registration shall not give the right to any preferential access to the House or to any services or facilities of the House, or to Parliamentary Papers unless Parliament determines otherwise.

3. It shall be the duty of all those who register to ensure that their entries are clear and accurate and are kept up to date on a rolling basis.

Rules

1. Any entry in the Register shall contain the following information:

a. Full name and business address (or addresses).

b. In the case of a company, whether the company is public or private; the name (when relevant) of any parent company; the names of any associated or subsidiary companies and the names of all directors.

c. The names of all clients identifying:

    i. those clients to whom a lobbying service as been provided.

    ii. In any case where the client is not the ultimate beneficiary of any service provided the name of such beneficiary.

d. In any case of a company or partnership, the name of any member of Parliament with a pecuniary interest in, or receiving pecuniary benefit from, the company or partnership (not being a shareholding purchased in the normal way).

2. In the case of a company, the directors of that company, or in the case of a partnership, all partners, and in other cases the individual person or persons submitting the entry shall be responsible for the accuracy of the information that entry contains.

3. Those who register thereby bind themselves to observe a Code of Conduct and to obey any associated disciplinary procedure, both of which may be amended from time to time.

CODE OF CONDUCT

Preamble: Scope of the Code

1. This Code of Conduct allies to all who register. Any firm or partnership one of whose directors or partners knowingly causes or permits a member (whether a full-time or part-time member) of its staff to act in a manner inconsistent with this Code is party to such an action and shall itself be deemed to be in breach of it. Any member of staff of a company or partnership, as the case may be, who acts in a manner inconsistent with this Code must be disciplined by the employer.

2. This Code is intended to co-exist with other professional Codes of Conduct to which signatories to the Register already subscribe. However, in the event of any conflict arising, or appearing to arise, the obligations of the Register, this Code of Conduct, and the related disciplinary procedure are paramount.

3. All those who register have the positive duty to observe the highest professional standards particularly in their dealings with members of Parliament; with Members' staff, with public servants, with fellow professionals and with clients.

4. All those who register shall uphold this Code and co-operate with Parliament and with other signatories of the Register in exercising vigilance in order to ensure the maintenance and enforcement of the Code.

General Conduct

5. All those who register shall:

a. Comply at all times with the rules relating to the Register;

b. Conduct their professional activities in accordance with the public interest;

c. Have a positive duty to respect the truth;

d. Not disseminate false or misleading information knowingly or recklessly; and shall exercise proper care to avoid doing so inadvertently;

e. Ensure that the actual interest of any organisation with which it may be professionally concerned is fully declared;

f. When working in association with other professional persons, identify and respect the codes of those professions;

g. Honour confidences given in the course of professional activity;

h. Avoid any professional conflict of interest;

i. Neither propose nor undertake any action which would constitute an improper influence on the organs of Government or legislation or on the media of communication;

j. Neither offer, nor give, nor cause a client or an associate to offer or give, any inducement to any Member of Parliament, or any other person holding public office, or any public servant, or any member of any statutory body or organisation with intent to further their interest of any client (except that a director, executive or retained consultant of any firm in question shall be entitled to receive proper remuneration).

k. Not receive any commission from a client which involves only payment by result (ie "continency payments", or "success fees").

6. No person to whom this Code applies may indicate directly or indirectly to a client; to a prospective client, or otherwise, that entry in the Register in any way constitutes approval by Parliament. However, it shall be permitted to draw the attention of any person whatsoever to the commitments that have been entered into by every signatory of the Register, in particular to the terms of this Code.

Conduct towards Members of Parliament

7. Any person to whom this Code applies shall have the duty:

i. To inform any Member of Parliament who is approached on behalf of a client of the name of the client, the reason for the approach, and the name of any company or partnership employing that person;

ii. To inform any Member of Parliament, or any member of his or her staff, or any member of staff of the House of Commons, from whom information is sought relating to any proceeding of Parliament of the reasons for seeking that information;

iii. While within the precincts of the House, to conduct themselves full in accordance with the rules laid down by the authorities of the House.

8. Any person to whom this Code applies, and who is in possession of a Palace of Westminster access pass in any other capacity than a Member of the House, or as a Member of the House of Lords, shall not use any facility of either House to which that person has access in order to make any representations or otherwise to assist clients (either his or her own clients or the clients of his or her employer).

Conduct towards Clients

9. All those who register shall:

a. Safeguard the confidence of both present and former clients and shall not disclose or use these confidences to the disadvantage or prejudice of such clients or the financial advantage of the member firm unless the client has released such information for public use, or has given specific permission for its disclosure; except upon the order of a court of law or of either House of Parliament.

b. Inform a client of any shareholding or financial interest held by that firm or by any member of that firm in any company, firm or person whose service it recommends.

c. Inform a client of any fees, commissions, or other valuable considerations offered by any persons other than the client; which are relevant in any way to the interests of that client.

d. In no way misuse any information regarding a client's business or any other "inside" information for financial or other gain.

e. In no circumstances directly invest in a client's securities without prior written permission of the client.

f. In no circumstances serve a client under terms or conditions which might impair that client's independence, objectivity or integrity.

g. In no circumstances represent conflicting or competing interests without specific consent of the clients concerned.

h. In no circumstances guarantee the achievement of results which are beyond the practicable possibility of achievement.

Conduct towards other signatories of the Register

10. All those who register shall:

i. Adhere to the highest standards of accuracy and truth, avoiding extravagant claims or unfair comparisons.

ii. Refrain from any comment or action which would be liable to inure the professional reputation of others in the profession.

COMPLAINTS AND ARBITRATION PROCEDURE

1. The main purpose of the complaints procedure is to provide a mechanism for the enforcement of the Code of Conduct.

2. Like the Code of Conduct the complaints procedure is intended to be co-existent with any professional Code of Conduct and disciplinary procedure to which signatories to the Register already subscribe. In the event of a conflict arising or appearing to arise; this Code of Conduct, complaints procedure and any arbitration procedure that may subsequently be established shall be paramount.

Complaints

3. A complaint may be made:

i. Any Member of Parliament in respect of paragraphs 5 to 8 of the Code of Conduct.

ii. Any company or other organisation or person, whose name has appeared in the Register for not less than six months in respect of paragraphs 5 to 10 of the Code of Conduct.

iii. Any client in respect of paragraphs 9 and 10.

4. All complaints shall be investigated by the PRCA Professional Practices Committee which shall consist, in part, of representatives of firms who are registered.

5. Matters that are currently the subject of legal action will not normally be subject to the complaints procedure, except when, in the case of a civil action, it is the opinion of the Professional Practices Committee that there has been an unwarrantable delay in bringing the matter before a Court of Law.

6. The Professional Practices Committee operates an arbitration procedure in respect of such matter.

Memorandum from Mr Peter Preston

I am keenly interested in all the areas of the Committee's concern and anxious to contribute across the spectrum as required. I very much welcome the appointment of this Committee and the prospect that the framework of rules and conventions governing British public life may be reformulated. That seems to me a necessary response to the new pressures on the system from the outside world - for example, from mushrooming growth of political columnists.

There is only one central core of particular concern I would share with the Committee. That is that the best framework in the world must lose its force and respect if there is no open and accountable way of delivering it in specific cases.

Two brief examples, I feel, demonstrate the problem in my mind. I am not here to reopen the controversy that arose last year between Mr Jonathan Aitken and my paper. I quote only from three letters to make a point of principle.

On 20th January 1994, picking up an earlier suggestion of my own, Mr Aitken wrote: "You may be surprised to know that given the impasse which our correspondence has reached, I would be entirely happy for your allegations to be referred to the appropriate higher authority. It is for you to decide whether you wish to approach the Chief Whip or the Prime Minister, but in my view the most appropriate authority would be the Cabinet Secretary, Sir Robin Butler, as he is the arbiter of the Ministerial Rules of Procedure".

I readily agreed and wrote in detail to Sir Robin—separately telling the Prime Minister what was happening. On 18th February, Mr Aitken wrote to me to let me know that he had received advice from the Cabinet Secretary on the facts set out in our recent correspondence. "In the light of that advice I am entirely confident of my position in relation to the Questions of Procedure for Ministers, namely that no breach of them has occurred".

A letter of the same date from Sir Robin said "I have made it clear to Mr Aitken that while I am happy to give him my views on the circumstances he has outlined to me, I am not prepared to have that advice made available to you. As with other advice given by officials to Minister, my advice is confidential and must remain so. Contrary to some popular belief, I am an adviser not an arbiter on these matters".

Briefly, I then wrote to the Prime Minister saying that if Sir Robin was not the arbiter that Mr Aitken had thought him, I assumed that the Prime Minister must be that person. A letter from the Prime Minister's office on 29th March said that "In the light of Mr Aitken's assurances and the Cabinet Secretary's advice to him, the Prime Minister regards these as private matters for Mr Aitken and sees no grounds for what you describe as 'inquiry' or 'arbitration' on his part".

The simple matter for this Committee, I think, considering Questions of Ministerial Procedure, is to note that no one seems to know quite where a final decision and final accountability lay. Mr Aitken thought that Sir Robin was the arbiter. Sir Robin didn't think he was the arbiter. It is, I would suggest, very unsatisfactory, in principle, for any outsider or member of the public wishing to raise a matter under the published code of Questions of Procedure for Ministers not to know who decides on what and whether the complainant, hopefully a public spirited one, will ever be given any reasons why his or her complaint is not being progressed. If Sir Robin can only advise Ministers in confidence there can be no openness. I think this most important as a text for the delivery of any framework as it affects people with ministerial authority.

In just the same way and much more briefly, I am keenly aware that the House of Commons' own self-regulatory mechanisms in contentious cases can be pretty mystifying to anyone caught up in them. Many months ago, as you may dimly remember, I was roundly assailed as a "whore from hell" and other things in the House of Commons and the matter in question was referred to the Privileges Committee. That Committee hasn't yet given me any date for any hearing and has still, I understand, to resolve the matter of the two MPs and the cash-for-questions raised by the Sunday Times last summer. Can I politely say that I cannot think that the delays and politicisation of the process gives either the feeling or the reality of justice being done. And I say that neutrally. Graham Riddick and David Tredinnick are the two MPs involved in the Sunday Times question and they should have had the opportunity to lay out their version of events long before now. It is political argument that has got in the way - just as it is political argument that stopped in the implementation of the Select Committee of Members' Interests reports from 1991 on the regulation of lobbyists within the House of Commons.

In all cases, in the eyes of the ordinary person looking from the outside, openness and accountability are lacking. Within the framework of self-regulation there is no independent influence working for openness and the rapid delivery of a conclusion. As Members may know, I used to be a member on the Press Complaints Commission - a body much derided by many MPs. But I would remind members of your Committee, Sir, that that Commission has for some time had a clear majority of lay and independent members sitting on it in order that the delivery of self-regulation may not be seen to be in the control of those it effects. I would, with respect, very much think that some similar mechanism urgently needs to be included in any framework of rules you may recommend.

19 January 1995

Memorandum from Mr Stuart Bell, MP

1. In my view, it is neither possible nor desirable to exclude a Member of Parliament from having paid outside interests.

2. One thing is clear: to take up an appointment as a paid adviser to a Parliamentary lobbying firm, to be a director or shareholder of such firm, does not fall within the defining or articulating of the national interest.

3. A Member of Parliament should be able to pursue an outside interest where it falls within the purview of his knowledge, where he has an interest in a specified subject, and where that paid outside interest is of some national significance or importance, however minor that may be.

4. Such paid outside interests should not extend beyond more than three categories.

5. A Member of Parliament, when he enters Parliament, should be given a Code of Conduct by which he is expected to abide; just as there is a Code of Conduct for the Bar of England and Wales.

6. A more specific Ethical Parliamentary Practice Code should also be drawn up and attached to each contract covering a paid outside interest, specifying what public affairs role is expected of the Member.

7. Those who work outside the House, in the City or at the Bar, or who have interests in Lloyd's or farming, or have other interests built up over the years, such as ownership of property, should register these interests as they do at present.

8. The House should set up its own Scrutiny Committee to oversee privilege and outside interests, thus merging the present committee on privilege and outside interests.

9. It would be unwise for the House to transfer its authority over the conduct of members to an outside body that cannot understand the ways of Parliament.

10. If the Committee were so minded to recommend outsiders to a Scrutiny Committee these should be drawn from Privy Councillors, former Commons members now in the Lords, or former Clerks to the House; or those associated with the House and have expertise on how the House works.

11. The Committee might wish to recommend that a Member does not place any questions on the order paper on behalf of a paid outside interest; rather that the government should create its own agency for the response to such questions; and where the response can be charged at cost.

Where on the spectrum, from total freedom to a total ban, should the line be drawn for MPs paid outside interests?

1. In my view, it is neither possible nor desirable to exclude a Member of Parliament from having paid outside interests.

2. A Member of Parliament is not employed in the sense he has no employer; his salary is paid out of Treasury funds but he does not work for the Treasury.

3. He is in fact retained on behalf of the nation to conduct the nation's affairs and whilst this involves work on behalf of the citizen through his constituency, and in accordance with his conscience, as pronounced by Edmund Burke, his interest is the national interest and how best this may be defined and articulated.

4. The definition and articulation of national interest may vary from Member to Member.

5. Winston Churchill had no track record as a constituency MP; but in the thirties his articulation of national interest lay in the domain of foreign affairs and defence. Other MPs devote their Parliamentary time to areas such as health, education, trade, industry, finance, law, children, to name but a few.

6. All Members bring knowledge and experience to their role, coming as they do from all walks of life. Some have interests which they would wish to continue, others find new interests; some have interests which are personally driven by their own life experience.

7. It is the bringing together of this experience and knowledge in the House of Commons that makes the Commons what it is, a forum for the nation's affairs, the defining and articulating of the national interest, in health, education, finance, as well as the loftier of foreign affairs and defence.

8. To seek to limit the role of the MP in relation to his paid outside interests would be fair on some and unfair on others.

9. Writers and broadcasters feel theirs is a legitimate outside interest that can be pursued and which neither discredits their Parliamentary life nor impinges upon the rights which their constituents have upon their time.

10. Our national life would be the poorer if Roy Hattersley and Tony Benn, to name but two, were precluded from publishing their writings or their diaries.

11. Similarly, the House of Commons would be the poorer if Ivan Lawrence, Alex Carlile, John Morris and Gerry Bermingham, *inter alia*, were not able to bring their expertise in legal affairs to the floor of the House.

12. Or that Sir Peter Tapsell should be precluded from his affairs in the City of London when he can and does add so much knowledge on financial matters.

13. But if it is fair for the write and broadcaster and professional man to continue his paid outside interests is it not unfair on those other Members, in the overwhelming majority, who have none of their talents or qualifications?

14. The question, therefore, to my mind, is not whether there should be a paid outside interest but how best that outside interest can be declared; and how best it can be defined as a genuine outside interest and not an escape hatch for those Members interested in making money rather than participating in defining and articulating the national interest.

15. One thing is clear: to take up an appointment as a paid adviser to a Parliamentary lobbying firm, to be a director or shareholder of such firm, does not fall within the defining or articulating of the national interest.

16. Rather, it reduces a Member to a role no greater than soliciting. It adds a burden upon other Members who often respond on the basis of friendship and politeness, and takes away the time individual members should be spending on their own Parliamentary work.

17. Therefore, a Member of Parliament should be able to pursue a paid outside interest where it falls within the purview of his knowledge, where he has an interest in a specified subject, and where that paid outside interest is of some national significance or importance, however minor that may be.

18. In any event, such paid outside interests should not extend beyond more than three categories.

Should MPs be given more detailed guidance on what is and is not acceptable?

19. A Member of Parliament, at the beginning of each Parliament, or when he arrives at the House after a by-election, should be given a Code of Conduct by which he is expected to abide; just as barristers-at law are given a book on etiquette on the night of their call. And just as there is a Code of Conduct for the Bar of England and Wales.

In what form and detail should outside paid interests be declared?

20. A more specific Ethical Parliamentary Practice Code should also be drawn up and attached to each contract covering a paid outside interest and signed by both parties to the contract. This should specify what public affairs role is expected of the Member.

21. The Ethical Parliamentary Practice Code and the contract should be lodged with the House and should be available to a new Scrutiny Committee in the event of complaints about a Member.

22. These should not be public documents, but any paid outside interest should be properly registered on the Register of Interests, though not the remuneration, unless the Member so wishes.

23. Non registration of remuneration means that a Member entering upon a paid outside interest will not be placed at a disadvantage with those practising a profession who are not required to state their earnings.

24. Those who work outside the House, in the City or at the Bar, or who have interests in Lloyd's or farming, or have other interests built up over the years, such as ownership of property, should register these interests as they do at present.

25. Members of Parliament should continue to inscribe in the register of interests foreign travel or gifts above a certain value as they do at present; or other interests which they feel they should register in accordance with the Code of Conduct which they will have seen on becoming a Member.

Should the procedures for investigating and taking action on alleged malpractice be changed in any way, and if so should there be any role for persons other than MPs?

26. The House should set up its own Scrutiny Committee to oversee privilege and outside interests, thus merging the present committees on privilege and outside interests.

27. The role of the Committee is to ensure that the Code of Conduct and the Ethical Parliamentary Practice Code are fully abided by; and that any alleged transgressions can be fully and quickly dealt with.

28. Recommendations of the Committee should be referred to the whole House for consideration. The Committee should meet in private and only its recommendations published.

29. The Committee should have power over persons and paper.

30. Parliament has in the past transferred some of its powers to the courts: The Parliamentary Elections Act 1868 transferred any dispute on election to the High Court of Justice. The determination of the Judge is notified to The Speaker and is entered upon the journals of the House.

31. It would be unwise, however, for the House to transfer its authority over the conduct of members to an outside body that cannot understand the ways of Parliament. It is for the House to preserve the reputation of the institution in relation to the public.

32. If the Committee is minded to recommend an extension of a Scrutiny Committee beyond Members of Parliament from the Commons, this extension should be limited to Privy Councillors, former Commons members now in the Lords, or former Clerks to the House, or those associated with the House and have expertise on how the House works.

33. Appointments to the Scrutiny Committee from outside the House should be made by the Prime Minister after consultation with other Party leaders.

34. No recommendations should be envisaged where the Scrutiny Committee is composed in its entirety of other than Members of Parliament.

General

35. The Committee might wish to recommend that a Member does not place any questions on the order paper on behalf of a paid outside interest; rather that the government should create its own agency for the response to such questions; and where the response can be charged at cost.

Codes of Conduct

1. A Member of Parliament must understand that he has been elected by his constituents to serve in the House of Commons, that he represents all his electors, and that his duty is to serve them as he serves his country; that there are matters where he can and should exercise his conscience; and that he is elected to serve rather than rule.

2. A Member should act at all times as a Member of Parliament, respecting the dignity of the House and the institution, understanding that to fall below the appropriate standards bring not only the Member but also the entire House into disrepute.

3. A Member must set for himself the highest standards of Parliamentary and individual behaviour consistent with the traditions of the House and essential to the furtherance of the national interest during the time he is a Member.

4. A Member must master the rules of the House and its standing orders so that his behaviour and comportment on the floor of the House will add to its reputation and a Member's own and inspire confidence in the electorate and in a Member's constituents in particular.

5. A Member must understand that improper behaviour is not in the country's interests and certainly in not in his own.

6. A Member must bring to his Parliamentary work a strong sense of integrity and ethics as well as responsibility.

7. A Member must understand that by his own efforts, his work, his responsibility and his comportment, he must be an example to others.

Ethical Parliamentary Practice code

1. If a Member wishes to accept a paid outside interest he should first ask to see the Ethical Business Practice Code for the interest which seeks to retain him, and if there is no such document he should insist that one be drawn up.

2. This Ethical Business Practice Code should be attached to a contract which a Member should sign with his paid outside interest.

3. His own contract should specify the advisory role which he proposes to play in relation to legislation or other public affairs matters.

4. The Code of Conduct of the House which a Member shall have should also be attached to the contract.

5. A Member entering into such a contract to cover a paid interest shall be personally responsible for its adherence, for upholding the Code of Conduct and for upholding the Ethical Parliamentary Practice Code.

6. The Ethical Parliamentary Practice Code shall state that a Member should not seek to influence either Ministers of the Crown nor civil servants nor other Members of the House in furtherance of the paid interest.

7. The Ethical Parliamentary Practice Code shall state that a Member should not seek to place questions on the order paper of the House nor prepare nor sign early day motions on behalf of the paid outside interest.

8. A Member shall be personally responsible for upholding the Code of Conduct of the House and the Ethical Parliamentary Practice Code.

Letter from Mr Stuart Bell, MP to the Secretary of the Committee

I am referring to my appearance before the Nolan Committee yesterday.

As I indicated during the session, I have received permission from Merck Sharp & Dohme to submit their Ethical Business Practices Code to the Committee and I am therefore sending you a copy herewith.

26 January 1995

CORPORATE POLICY: ETHICAL BUSINESS PRACTICES

Policy Statement

Corporate conduct is inseparable from the conduct of individual employees in the performance of their work. Every Merck employee is responsible for adhering to business practices that are in accordance with the letter and spirit of the applicable laws and with ethical principles that reflect the highest standards of corporate and individual behaviour.

Since only such behaviour is consistent with Merck's traditions, and since such behaviour is essential to the success of its business endeavours, the Company will not accept anything less. Like integrity of product, integrity of performance is a Merck standard wherever we do business, and ignorance of that standard is never an acceptable excuse for improper behaviour. Neither must improper behaviour be rationalised as being in the Company's interest. No act of impropriety advances the interests of the Company.

No illegal payments of any kind are to be made to any local, state, or Federal government officials of this or any other nation, at any time or under any circumstances. Beyond legality, it is contrary to Merck policy for Company funds or other assets to be paid directly or indirectly to government officials or persons acting on their behalf for the purpose of influencing government decisions or actions with respect to Merck's business. Employees who may be undecided about whether contemplated actions are within the limits of legality or propriety should seek guidance from higher levels of management before the actions are taken.

All transactions shall be accurately reflected in the Company's books and records to permit their audit and control. Managers at all levels are responsible for the completeness of the documentation and for ensuring that funds are spent for the described purposes. There shall be no undisclosed or unrecorded fund or asset of the Company or any of its subsidiaries. There shall be no false or misleading entries made in the books or records of the Company or any of its subsidiaries. Strict compliance with corporate accounting methods and controls is expected, as is co-operation with internal and external auditors.

Acceptance of a Merck executive or management position at any level includes acceptance or responsibility to uphold the Company's policies governing ethical business practices. It also includes acceptance or responsibility to inculcate proper ethical behaviour among sub-ordinates and to act with the assurance that the Company is unwilling to seek any business advantage that involved unethical conduct.

Memorandum from the Rt Hon Tony Benn, MP
INDEX OF SECTIONS

A. Introduction—The issue of democracy

1. I welcome the decision of this Committee to hear evidence in public, and since there is no valid case for holding discussions, within the Committee, behind closed doors, I hope that it will also decide to deliberate in public so that those who read the recommendations in the Report will be able to understand the reasoning that lies behind them.

2. This paper is based upon the submission that I would have made had I been able to remain a member of the Committee of Privileges, and it is my intention to make it available to that Committee.

3. It is based on my conviction that the real issue that needs to be examined is the relationship between the standards in public life and the democratic process itself.

4. Public pressure for the extension of the franchise over the centuries has been motivated by a growing and proper demand by the whole population and to gain an effective say in the conduct of public policy and acquire the power to hold those in Parliament to account for their actions.

5. Edward I summoned the first Parliament in 1295, exactly 700 years ago this year, but until the Reform Act was passed in 1832, only 2 per cent of the population—all men and all wealthy—had the vote and it was they, and those whom they elected, who ran the country.

6. They legislated in their own interests, in secret, a system that inevitably encouraged and concealed corruption and this fact needs to be borne in mind before Britain boasts of having "long enjoyed a reputation for the honour and integrity of its public institutions."

7. It was not until 1928—less than 70 years ago—that the universal adult suffrage was conceded to men and women at the same age (then 21) thus conferring on them some countervailing power, through the ballot box, to use the House of Commons to check abuse and realise their political aspirations.

8. If it were now to be widely believed that powerful economic interests, operating in secret, could by-pass the will of the voters, by purchasing the services of those who have been elected to represent them, the result could be to undermine confidence in democracy, and in the House of Commons.

9. This could lead to growing public apathy, or even to civil unrest, to draw attention to injustice, which often took place before the general public had the ballot box at their disposal.

10. What is at stake therefore is more than the maintenance of high standards of personal conduct by those who occupy positions of authority—important though that is—it is whether power through the ballot box is to continue to enjoy public confidence.

11. I believe that this fundamental constitutional question is much more important than the supposed behaviour of some individual Members of Parliament which has received a great deal of publicity in the media.

12. It should be remembered that the media have their own particular interests in stories of this kind which can boost newspaper sales or the ratings of broadcasts, and these interests do not necessarily correspond with the public interest.

13. Similarly, criticisms of particular Members of Parliament, for alleged improper conduct, that come from their political opponents, may be motivated by a desire to secure some party political advantage, and this is not the best way to discuss the real question.

14. It would not be right to shuffle off the responsibility for what has happened on to a few scapegoats when the real problem is that the House of Commons sets such low standards for its own members, and what is required is a raising of those standards, underpinned by new legislation.

15. In short, a desire to muck-rake, whether by the media or other parliamentarians is not the right way for these matters to be handled.

B. The roots of the present problem

1. Two related developments need to be noted if we are to understand why this issue has recently come to public attention.

2. The first is the emergence of a whole new group of companies, loosely called Lobbyists, which have been established on a commercial basis, to promote the interests of their clients, and some of these companies appear, in the past, to have regarded it as perfectly proper to pay certain MPs either to join the boards of those companies or to employ them for a fee to promote the interests of those clients.

3. The second is the prevailing culture of the times in which we live, namely that market forces are, and should dominate our lives, and determine our conduct.

4. Such a philosophy can be used as a justification for anyone, including an MP, to sell, for money, anything he or she may possess which a customer may wish to buy at the market price.

5. The marketable service which MPs may be thought to possess is influence, and the customers for that service are those companies that wish to purchase that influence for their own financial fain.

6. The logical conclusion of this could even be that seats in the House of Commons should no longer be won by election, but go out to public tender, with the candidate who put in the highest bid being awarded the seat when the bids were opened.

7. Unless the whole philosophy of putting profit before service, and the culture of secrecy, are challenged and completely rejected in public life, the whole fabric, both of democracy and society, could be undermined.

C. The rights of the electors in a democracy

1. If public confidence in democracy is to be maintained, the rights of the electors must be safeguarded and these rights may be summarised as follows:-

   a. The right to elect whomsoever they wish, and for whatever reason, to represent them.

   b. The right to expect that those whom they have elected will regard their work in Parliament as a public service and not as an opportunity to make more money by the sale of their influence to anyone who is prepared to pay.

   c. The right to know what their representatives have done while they have been there.

   d. The right to remove those whom they have elected, for whatever reason, at subsequent elections.

2. If these rights are accepted as fundamental it must follow that the only body of persons who have a moral and democratic right to elect, or remove, and MP are his or her constituents, unless and until an MP is convicted of a breach of the law, carrying with it the penalty of disqualification.

3. This consideration would necessarily limit the powers of the House of Commons, or of any independent body that was proposed, if it was intended that they should control the conduct of members, acting within the law, since MPs are not primarily responsible either to the House or to some 'watchdog', but solely to those who put them there, namely their own electors.

D. Disclosure—The greatest safeguard against abuse

1. In my submission, the greatest safeguard against improper conduct is that there should be complete disclosure by all candidates for Parliament and all Members of Parliament as to the nature of their own commercial or financial interests.

2. For this reason, I believe an extended, and more comprehensive Register of Members' Interests should be established, put on a statutory basis and be extended to all parliamentary candidates.

3. This declaration should include all the sources from which an MP receives money, beyond his or her parliamentary salary, to allow electors to assess the likely impact that these sources might have on the Members parliamentary work.

4. All returning officers should, therefore, be required, by law, to obtain from all parliamentary candidates a declaration of their interests and should circulate this information to all electors with the poll cards which they now issue.

5. In this way, every elector would know, before they vote, exactly what other interests all candidates have.

E. Legislating to control commercial lobbyists

1. Another change that needs to be made is to legislate to make it an offence, in law, for any person to offer to pay, or for any Member of Parliament to accept payment, for the use of influence to obtain a commercial or financial advantage for either party to such a transaction.

2. In addition it should also be accepted as rule of the House of Commons that all pass-holders should sign a declaration to the effect that they are not in any such contractual relationship with a commercial lobbyist.

3. Breaches of this law by any member of parliament, or any lobbyist, would then fall within the jurisdiction of the Courts.

4. Such a law would not prevent, or hamper, campaigners working for policy changes on behalf of any organisation, but it would make it illegal for commercial lobbyists to employ MPs or pay them for specific purposes designed to advantage their clients.

F. The case for a Code of Conduct

1. Quite apart from statutory declaration of interests, there is a case for establishing a Code of Conduct based on the principle that service in Parliament is a public service and this Code should be drawn up and agreed by the House itself.

2. One, very early statement of what is expected of us is contained in the Prayers for Parliament read by the Chaplain of which reminds us of the moral aspects of this matter by call upon all members to lay aside:

3. " ..all private interests, prejudices and partial affections.."

4. There is also, in existence a Code of Conduct which applies to Ministers called "Questions of Procedure for Ministers" issues by all Prime Ministers to each member of his or her administration.

5. My own copy, Number 21 issued on April 26 1976 by Mr James Callaghan, just after he became Prime Minister, contains these words:

6. "It is a well established and recognised rules that no minister or public servant should accept gifts, hospitality or services from anyone which would, or might appear to place him under an obligation .... It is a principle of public life that ministers must so order their affairs private interests and their public duties".

7. I believe that those principles should be at the heart of any new Code of Conduct for all Members of the House.

8. Where breaches of the Code of Conduct or of the proposed statutory Register of Members Interests are alleged, the matter should be investigated and dealt with by the House of Commons itself, possibly through a strengthened Committee of Privileges.

G. The possible extension of disqualification

1. But apart from these measures, the policing of which, I submit belong properly to the House itself, there is a case for strengthening the law in relation to disqualification from election to, or service in, the House of Commons.

2. Certain classes of persons have long been declared ineligible including peers, lunatics, minors, convicted felons, judges, civil servants, officers, members of certain public authorities, bankrupts, ordained priests in the Church of England or the Roman Catholic Church.

3. Similarly, those holding, or taking up an office of profit under the Crown, including the Steward or Bailiff of the Chiltern Hundreds, certain Government contractors, and those guilty of corrupt practices are covered by the House of Commons (Disqualification) Acts.

4. It should now be considered whether this list of disqualifications should be extended to include those who have received money for political services, regardless of whether such transactions have been declared in the Register of Interests.

H. An extension of the jurisdiction of the Election Courts

1. If such a change in the law were to be made then cases arising from alleged breaches of it would have to go to a court for trial.

2. The precedent for this is the system of Election Courts which were set up in the 19th century to hear Election Petitions based upon alleged breaches of election law.

3. Before 1770 the House itself tried and determined controverted elections, as mere party questions, and this was followed by the handing over of these decisions to a Tribunal made up of its own Members, so that it was not until 1868 that the jurisdiction of the House, in respect of Election petitions, was transferred, by statute, to the courts of law.

4. An Election Court, under the 1949 Representation of the People Act, consists of two judges, sitting alone, without a jury, who then hear the case and report their judgement to the House which has the responsibility for executing them.

5. The House is required to take notice of any legal disabilities affecting its members, and to issue writs in the rooms of Members judged incapable of sitting.

6. Where corrupt practices may be brought to light, these are dealt by a different legal procedure and provision is made for the punishment of offenders.

7. In this connection it should be noted that any candidate who offers money to an elector in return for his or her support would be guilty of a corrupt practice and immediately disqualified from election.

8. That being the law now, it is hard to resist the conclusion that the same disqualification should apply to any Member who receives money to perform a political act on behalf of some commercial organisation.

9. I believe this precedent provides the best basis for enforcing the implementation of any new statute dealing with Disqualification.

I. Other work undertaken by Members of Parliament

1. It is sometimes argued that this whole situation could best be resolved by requiring, by law, that all Members of Parliament should work exclusively and full-time as members, just as civil servants do, and should undertake no other work.

2. I do not share that view because those MPs who also work in or for, say, charities, the trade unions, voluntary organisations, business firms, the professions, the Arts, or as writers, broadcasters, teachers, or local councillors, and receive research assistance for that purpose, often acquire valuable experience which helps with their parliamentary work, and there is no comparison between that and secret financial arrangements leading to improper influence.

3. So long as the electors know what these activities are, as they would do from the Register of Interests, sent to them in all elections, it is for them to decide whether they regard such activities as constituting a reason for not electing them.

J. Contributions to political campaigns

1. Though I understand that the terms of reference of this Committee do not include a requirement to examine the payment of contributions to political parties, it is necessary to mention this question because such money may pass in a way that appears to benefit individual candidates, and thus might be seen as a form of personal payment, in advance, for specific political services, to secure some personal financial advantage on behalf of individuals who have made those contributions.

2. This issue needs to be clarified because if contributions, of both money or people, by trade unions or businesses or other charitable or other organisations which have a direct interest in the policies which they wish to see carried through parliament, were to be regarded as illegal, it could undermine the voluntary funding of political campaigns which is both legitimate and desirable because they sustain the democratic process.

3. Elections, and other open political campaigns, are expensive, funds are necessary to pay for them and these funds must be raised by appeals for money from those who support the policies to which candidates or MPs are pledged.

4. But all contributions for political campaigns, both during, and between, elections should be required to meet the following conditions:

  a. They should always be paid to organisations and not to individual Members and the figures should be published.

  b. All contributions made to candidates, above a certain amount, should be reported in the Declaration of Election expenses, and should be declared in the Register of Members Interests, where a candidate, or member has made use of such funds in pursuit of the campaigns in which they are involved, and published, nationally, by all parties which have put up candidates.

K. Ballots for political campaign funds by organisations

1. There is also a very strong case for saying that when money is paid by organisations to assist political campaigns, such organisations must have first established a political fund, by a ballot of all those members of those organisations in exactly the same way as trade unions are now required to have a ballot before a political fund is set up and with the right for individuals to opt out.

2. This would mean that all organisations including companies and associations of all kinds would have to consult their shareholders and/or their members for authority from them to establish such a political fund.

L. Summary of points made

1. The importance of seeing these issues against a proper historical perspective of the development of democracy.

2. The contemporary culture that puts personal gain above public service.

3. The overwhelming importance of safeguarding the rights of the electors.

4. The key role of disclosure in preventing abuse.

5. The need to legislate to control commercial lobbyists.

6. The case for a Code of Conduct for Members.

7. The possibility of extending the law of disqualification.

8. A possible extension of the Jurisdiction of Election Courts.

9. Consideration of other work undertaken by Members of Parliament.

10. Clarification of the rules governing contributions to political campaign funds.

11. The case for ballots for political campaign funds by organisations.

M. Conclusions

I hope that all the issues touched on this paper will be considered carefully by this Committee, and that when its Recommendations are published, they will be accompanied by a full transcript of its own deliberations.

20 January, 1995

Supplementary Memorandum from the Comptroller and Auditor General

When I appeared before the Committee on 1 February I promised to provide a note on my current powers of access to various bodies receiving public money and how I would like to see these powers improved. I am pleased to submit the enclosed paper which sets out the main weaknesses in the current audit and inspection arrangements for executive Non-Departmental Public Bodies and other bodies receiving money. It also considers the weaknesses in my rights of access to records of contractors carrying out departmental functions.

I hope the Committee will find the paper of value in their consideration of current accountability arrangements.

National Audit Office Access to Organisations receiving Public Money
Note by the Comptroller and Auditor General to the Committee on Standards in Public Life

Part 1:   Introduction

1.1 During his evidence to the committee on 1 February 1995, the Chairman of the Committee of Public Accounts expressed his concern about limitations on the Comptroller and Auditor General to provide Parliament with a complete audit of bodies receiving money from central government and, in pursuance of these responsibilities, to follow the destination of public money in a comprehensive fashion. I was asked to submit a note on these matters.

1.2 In recent years there have been major changes and increasing diversity in the way government services and programmes are delivered. Government departments have encouraged a more entrepreneurial approach on the part of their staff and they have delegated more clearly defined responsibilities to Executive Agencies, which remain directly accountable to their Secretary of State. They have also devolved more responsibilities to:

- **Executive Non-Departmental Public Bodies,** operating at arms length from central government and with corporate responsibility for all their activities;

- **other bodies,** delivering specific government programmes (sometimes, like housing associations and Training and Enterprise Councils, these are private sector in form); and

- **private sector contractors,** handling an increasing share of departments' mainstream functions under the Government's Competing for Quality initiative.

The boundary line between public and private sectors is likely to become even less distinct as private finance is increasingly brought in to supplement the funding of government projects.

1.3 The Government have stated that the fundamental purpose of their programme of reform is to strengthen the management of the public sector so that waste is reduced and those who manage public services are more accountable for their actions. And they have agreed with the view of the Committee of Public Accounts (in their Eighth Report of 1993–94) that effective programmes for economy and efficiency must be combined with a proper concern for the sensible conduct of public business and care for the honest handling of public money.

1.4 A major task of the National Audit Office is to provide Parliament with the information it requires to hold government departments accountable for their performance in ensuring that public money is spent properly and wisely. To do this, the National Audit Office need access to the records of those organisations which spend the money provided by government departments and voted by Parliament.

1.5 There are three main ways in which the National Audit Office help Parliament enforce accountability:

- by providing an annual certificate on the accounts of all government departments, executive agencies and some Non-Departmental Public Bodies that the money spent has been applied for the purposes authorised by Parliament and that the accounts properly present the transactions of the organisation;

- inspecting selectively the records of other organisations to establish that the money has been spent for the purposes and in the ways intended;

- carrying out selective examinations of the value for money with which government departments and other bodies have used their resources.

1.6 It is a particular feature of the National Audit Office's financial audits and inspections that they include considerations of:

- **regularity** ie the requirement for all items of expenditure and receipts to be dealt with in accordance with the legislation authorising them, any applicable delegated authority and the rules of Government Accounting;

- **propriety** ie the further requirement that expenditure and receipts should be dealt with in accordance with Parliament's intentions and the principles of Parliamentary control, including the conventions agreed with Parliament (and in particular the Public Accounts Committee).

1.7 The Exchequer and Audit Departments Acts of 1866 and 1921 provided the Comptroller and Auditor General with the statutory authority to undertake financial audit of government departments and with the rights of access necessary to do this. The National Audit Act 1983 provided authority and rights of access to carry out value for money audits at government departments and some other bodies.

1.8 The legislation which governs the Comptroller and Auditor Genoral's activities could not envisage the changes introduced in recent years and there are now gaps in his statutory rights of access. The Comptroller and Auditor General does not audit all Executive Non-Departmental Public Bodies and he does not have access to some other bodies receiving significant amounts of public money and contractors delivering contracted out services.

1.9 In line with his undertaking to the Committee on 1 February this note sets out the current audit arrangements for Executive Non-Departmental Public Bodies; other bodies receiving public money, and contracted out functions. Appendix A illustrates the level of central government expenditure handled in this way, and Appendix B indicates the audit arrangements for Non-Departmental Public Bodies .

Part 2: Non-Departmental Public Bodies

Background

2.1 A Non-Departmental Public Body is defined as a body which has a role in the process of national government but is not a department or part of one, and accordingly operates to a greater or lesser extent at arm's length from Ministers.

2.2 There are three main categories of Non-Departmental Public Bodies:

- executive bodies—bodies with executive administrative, regulatory or commercial functions;

- advisory bodies—bodies which are set up by Ministers to advise them and their departments;

- tribunals—bodies whose functions are, like those of courts of law, essentially judicial.

The Government have published a full list of these in Public Bodies 1994.

2.3 Advisory bodies and Tribunals do not account separately for their spending, they are funded from within the Departmental Vote and are subject to audit by the Comptroller and Auditor General as part of the annual audit of the departments' accounts.

Financial accountability at Executive Non-Departmental Public Bodies

2.4 Executive Non-Departmental Public Bodies operate at arms length from departments and have their own statutory boards, employ their own staff and have their own budget and accounts. The scale of their activities can vary, from the Higher Education Funding Council which spends some £2.8 billion per annum, to the Fleet Air Arm Museum which spends less than one million pounds per annum. There are 294 Executive Non-Departmental Public Bodies which spend in total some £18 billion per annum, as set out in Appendix B.

2.5 The accounts of Non-Departmental Public Bodies are normally laid before Parliament, and therefore come within the remit of the Committee of Public Accounts. The senior full-time officials of the Non-Departmental Public Bodies are responsible for the propriety and regularity of the bodies' activities and all other matters relating to the stewardship of public funds.

2.6 The Comptroller and Auditor General is the auditor of the 157 Executive Non-Departmental Public Bodies listed in Appendix B(1). The remaining Non-Departmental Public Bodies listed in Appendix B(2) are audited by private sector auditors appointed by the responsible Secretary of State.

2.7 For Executive Non-Departmental Public Bodies audited by private sector firms, it is normal for the Comptroller and Auditor General to have a right of inspection. The purpose of inspection rights is to enable the Comptroller and Auditor General to bring to the attention of Parliament any departures from accepted standards governing the use of public funds or from any conditions attached by the sponsor department to the use of granted money. Generally he can also report on the value for money achieved by the body.

Conclusions

2.8 The Comptroller and Auditor General's powers in relation to Non-Departmental Public Bodies are not entirely unsatisfactory. However, there are two main weaknesses in the current arrangements:

a) Where the Comptroller and Auditor General audits the annual accounts, Parliament benefits from an annual opportunity to consider a report from an independent Officer of the House about the financial affairs of the Non-Departmental Public Body. And the National Audit Office are able to draw on the results of their financial audit to consider whether a more in-depth investigation of the body's affairs is called for. Where this is not the case, there is not the same systematic and annual scrutiny on behalf of Parliament of regularity, propriety and value for money. To draw attention to this gap in Parliamentary scrutiny is not to impugn in any way the professional work of the private sector auditors who currently carry out this work under the terms of their contracts with the bodies who appoint them.

b) Unless inspection rights are specified by statute, the Comptroller and Auditor General has to agree them with the organisation. This is not always straightforward. For example, the Housing Corporation received some £1.8 billion of public funds in 1993–94 but the Comptroller and Auditor General is not the appointed auditor and his rights of inspection are not set out in statute. The National Audit Office's rights of inspection are in practice subject to agreement and the sponsoring department, the Department of the Environment, have yet to agree to the need for annual inspections.

2.9 These weaknesses might be overcome by providing for the National Audit Office to audit all Executive Non-Departmental Public Bodies, or by providing for the National Audit Office to supervise the allocation of such audits to private sector firms and to have statutory inspection rights to those bodies not audited.

Part 3: Other public and private sector bodies

Background

3.1 There are other public and private bodies involved in the delivery of major programmes of public expenditure, which do not fit within the definition in paragraph 2.1 above and which are not therefore classified as Non-Departmental Public Bodies. Significant examples in the fields of health, education, housing and employment training are considered below. In many cases, the National Audit Office's access rights to these bodies are satisfactory. In others they are not.

National Health Service Bodies

3.2 There are 746 health bodies which are listed in "Public Bodies 1994". They spend over £27 billion per annum and include Regional Health Authorities, NHS Trusts and a range of other bodies. The accounts of these bodies are audited by the Audit Commission (or in Scotland by auditors appointed by the Secretary of State). The accounts of individual bodies are then consolidated to form the summarised accounts of the health departments and these are audited by the Comptroller and Auditor General. The Comptroller and Auditor General has inspection rights at all NHS bodies and can also report to Parliament on any significant weaknesses found by the Audit Commission.

Higher and Further Education Institutions

3.3 In England there are now 457 further education institutions and 128 higher education institutions. In 1993-94 these bodies will spend some £5.6 billion. The Comptroller and Auditor General is the auditor of the Funding Councils which distribute this money, and he has statutory inspection rights to all these institutions which have enabled him to report to Parliament on a wide range of issues covering value for money and matters of propriety.

Grant maintained schools

3.4 There are currently nearly 1,000 grant-maintained schools in England and Wales receiving grants totalling over £1.9 billion. Under the terrns of the Education Reform Act 1993 the accounts of all grant-maintained schools are open to inspection by the Comptroller and Auditor General, and he is required to report annually to the House of Commons on the results of examinations he has undertaken. The first of these reports was presented to Parliament in August 1994 and the findings included failures in financial control, shortcomings in budget management, scope for improving arrangements for procurement, and the need for governance procedures to be regularly reviewed.

Training and Enterprise Councils

3.5 The Training and Enterprise Councils were set up as private sector companies. In 1993–94, the 75 Training and Enterprise Councils in England received payments from the Department of Employment totalling over £1.4 billion. Each Training and Enterprise Council enters into an annual contract with the Department which provides for the Comptroller and Auditor General to have access to each Training and Enterprise Council for the purpose of auditing the Department's accounts. These contracts do not provide the Comptroller and Auditor General with the right to undertake value for money examinations of the Training and Enterprise Councils but he can examine value for money aspects of the Department of Employment's use of the funds given to the Training and Enterprise Councils.

Housing Associations

3.6 Housing associations are essentially private sector bodies which play a major part in the delivery of the Government's housing policy. In 1993–94, some 500 associations received central government grants and subsidies totalling £1.8 billion and they have played an increasingly important role in the supply of homes for people in housing need. These funds are allocated by the Housing Corporation, to which the National Audit Office have a degree of access.

3.7 The National Audit Office do not have rights of access to housing associations, which are audited by private sector auditors and subject to the oversight of the Housing Corporation. They are therefore unable to undertake systematic examinations on the lines set out in paragraph 1.4 and 1.5 above of the regularity and propriety with which associations have spent the money provided by the Housing Corporation, funded by the Department of the Environment and voted by Parliament. They have been able to undertake periodic value for money examinations but only to those associations which volunteered to be examined.

3.8 In their Twentieth Report of 1993–94, the Committee of Public Accounts considered that it was only by the National Audit Office's examination at housing associations that the propriety and regularity of expenditure could be directly and independently examined on Parliament's behalf. They recommended that inspection rights for the National Audit Office should be made a condition of grant to associations which receive a significant part of their resources from public funds. In their response, the Government did not consider that such a general provision for access would be appropriate.

Other miscellaneous bodies

3.9 Government departments also provide grants to a wide range of organisations to help them discharge their functions. For example, the Foreign and Commonwealth Office gives grants totalling over £7.5 million to 28 bodies. The Comptroller and Auditor General is the auditor of three of these bodies, the Commonwealth Institutes of London and Edinburgh and the Anglo-German Foundation. The other recipients include bodies such as the British Youth Council and the Commonwealth Trust, and in all cases the Foreign and Commonwealth Office provide in the grant for the Comptroller and Auditor General's right of access to the body.

3.10 Sometimes, however, where grants have been to a body which takes a private sector form, as in the case of Local Enterprise Companies in Scotland and Regional Development Organisations funded by the Department of Trade and Industry, departments have been reluctant to concede inspection rights to the National Audit Office.

Conclusions

3.11 The position on the National Audit Office's access to the bodies considered in this part of the note is mixed. The National Audit Office's rights of access at NHS bodies, further and higher education institutions and grant-maintained schools are generally satisfactory. The main weaknesses in relation to other organisations are:

a) The National Audit Office are unable to carry out annual checks of the regularity and propriety with which housing associations have spent money provided by Parliament for the implementation of major housing programmes.

b) There are limitations on the National Audit Office's ability to undertake value for money investigations at Training and Enterprise Councils, which are largely financed out of public funds and which deliver public programmes of employment training.

c) The negotiation of inspection rights for all the individual bodies in receipt of significant departmental grants and subsidies is a time-consuming process, and departments have sometimes been reluctant to concede such rights.

Part 4: Access to contracted out functions

Background

4.1 Government departments have always needed to procure goods and services from private sector contractors. The implementation of the "Competing for Quality" programme, however, has led to a significant increase in the scale of government contracting, with traditional departmental activities and functions being contracted out to private sector suppliers. The programme began in April 1992 and by September 1994 competitive tendering had taken place for 664 activities with external suppliers winning 345 of these contracts. In total £1.18 billion of work was awarded to external suppliers.

4.2 The contracts awarded under this initiative vary in both the scale and the nature of the service provided. A significant example of such a contract is that for the provision of Inland Revenue Information Technology services, with an estimated value of £1 billion over ten years. Other activities and functions contracted out include catering, cleaning, engineering and maintenance, estates and facilities management, office services, financial and legal services, and debt management.

Implications for Parliamentary accountability

4.3 Guidance to departments on Market Testing by the Cabinet Office requires departments and agencies to ensure that, where functions are contracted out, the Comptroller and Auditor General continues to have access to documents to enable him to carry out financial audits and value for money examinations of the department or agency concerned (The Government's Guide to Market Testing, 1993, paragraphs 10.6–10.8, is reproduced at Appendix C). More detailed guidance from the Treasury, however, is more restrictive. It requires that access clauses should only be included in those contracts which relate to "finance-related functions" and that other cases should be considered individually in consultation with the Treasury.

4.4 Only 40 per cent of the contracts which have been won by external suppliers since April 1992 have provided the Comptroller and Auditor General with access rights to the contractors' papers and records. For the rest, the Comptroller and Auditor General must base any examination on the information held by the department or agency for monitoring purposes.

Conclusions

4.5 Although the central guidance provides for the National Audit Office to have access to relevant contractors' records in some cases, there are significant weaknesses in the current arrangements.

a) Parliament has a right to expect the same high standards of probity, regularity and value for money in the use of public funds however these are spent, whether a function is performed in-house by departmental staff, or by a private contractor.

b) The functions that are now being contracted out require increasingly complex contracts. The monitoring information held by departments and agencies will not necessarily be sufficient to ensure full public accountability, and will not provide the first-hand evidence which the Comptroller and Auditor General requires.

c) Except for those cases where the nature of the contract is such that it is possible to examine goods or services at departmental premises, it is likely that the National Audit Office will need access to relevant documentation and information at contractors. The criterion of whether functions are "finance-related" does not clearly define all the cases where access is necessary.

d) Parliamentary accountability for financial rectitude rests on the Comptroller and Auditor General's examination and certification of departments' accounts. It is unsatisfactory that the National Audit Office's ability to discharge this role effectively should be dependent on having to negotiate with departments on the inclusion of access clauses in agreements with contractors.

4.6 For the avoidance of all possible doubt the Comptroller and Auditor General should have a suitably drafted statutory right of access to contracted out functions based on the Cabinet Office guidance quoted above, so that there is no need to negotiate clauses on individual contracts. It should be possible to draft legislation in such a way that rights of access are not created in relation to those contracts for goods and services where audit access is not needed, and such access would not of course relate to the contractors' own mainstream business. Such a statutory right would give the Comptroller and Auditor General access rights in line with those of similar institutions in the United Kingdom and abroad. These include the Audit Commission, the Parliamentary Commissioner for Administration, and the European Court of Auditors, who have greater powers in this regard than the National Audit Office to examine expenditure in the United Kingdom financed by the European Community.

4.7 As legislative change may not be possible in the short term, an immediate solution would be for the Government to issue clear guidance to all departments, agencies and other centrally funded bodies that appropriate National Audit Office access clauses should be included in contracts for contracted out functions in accordance with the Cabinet Office guidance quoted above.

Part 5: Summary

5.1 In recent years, there has been a significant increase in the volume of central government business devolved to bodies at arm's length from government departments. Arrangements have been made aimed at enabling the National Audit Office to audit or inspect the regularity, propriety and value for money of expenditure on such activities but there are deficiencies.

5.2 The main weaknesses are:

a) a reduced level of coverage where the National Audit Office do not audit the financial accounts of Non-Departmental Public Bodies (paragraph 2.8(a));

b) the lack of an enforceable general right to undertake inspections (paragraph 2.8(b), 3.11(a), 3.11(b) and 3.11(c));

c) the lack of a general right of access to the relevant records of contractors carrying out functions for departments (paragraph 4.5).

Public Funds spent by Executive Non-Departmental Public Bodies, Other bodies and contractors 1993–94

		£ billion	£ billion
1.	**Executive Non-Departmental Public Bodies** **Appendices B(1) and B(2))** including		14.9
	Housing Corporation	1.8	
	National Rivers Authority	0.1	
	Legal Aid Board spending	1.0	
	Higher Education Funding Council	2 8	
	Further Education Funding Council	2.7	
	British Council	0.3	
	Scottish Enterprise	0.4	
2.	**Other bodies receiving significant public funds**		37.0
	● 746 health bodies	27.0	
	● 585 further and higher education institutions	5.6	
	● 75 Training and Enterprise Councils	1.4	
	● 500 Housing associations	1.8	
	● 829 Grant-maintained schools	1.2	
3.	**Contracting out** (Activities to the value of a further £1.1 billion will be reviewed under the Governments Competing for Quality initiative in 1994–95)		1.2

Total departmental spending for 1993–94 was some 232 billion *(Financial Statement and Budget Report 1995–96 (Table 6.5) Summary and Conclusions)*

Note. Funds are provided by departments to Executive Non-Departmental Public Bodies who in some cases further distribute them to other public bodies. For example most of the Housing Corporations funds are passed on to housing associations and therefore appear in the above table under both Executive Non-Departmental Public Bodies and Other Bodies

Executive Non-Departmental Public Bodies which produce independent accounts audited the C&AG

	Gross expenditure 1993/94 £m	Funded by government 1993/94 £m
Ministry of Agriculture, Fisheries and Food		
Royal Botanic Gardens. Kew	20.5	14.9
Ministry of Defence		
Fleet Air Arm Museum	0.8	0.4
National Army Museum	3.7	3.7
Royal Naval Museum, Portsmouth	1.1	0.6
Royal Air Force Museum	3.9	2.9
Royal Marines Museum, Southsea	0.5	0.5
Royal Navy Submarine Museum, Gosport	0.4	0.3
Department for Education		
Funding Agency for Schools (Note 1)		
Further Education Funding Council	2,682.5	2,682.5
Education Assets Board	0.8	0.8
School Curriculum and Assessment Authority	16.9	16.9
Higher Education Funding Council for England	2,793.0	2,793.0
Employment Department Group		
Advisory, Conciliation & Arbitration Service	22.6	22.6
Commissioner—Rights of Trade Union Members	0.3	0.3
Commissioner for Protection Against Unlawful Industrial Action	0.1	0.1
Equal Opportunities Commission	6.0	5.8
Health & Satety Commission	0.4	0.4
Health & Safety Executive	219.6	174.1
Department of the Environment		
Audit Commission	82.6	—
Countryside Commission	45.6	45.5
Nature Conservancy Council for England (English Nature)	40.2	38.8
Rural Development Commission	38.3	19.4
Foreign and Commonwealth Office		
British Council	402.2	266.1
Commonwealth Institute London & Edinburgh [2 bodies]	3.2	3.9
Crown Agents Holding & Realisation Board	0.1	—
Marshall Aid Commemoration Commission	1.3	1.3
Department of Health		
Central Council for Education and Training in Social Work	43.5	42.2
Human Fertilisation & Embryology Authority	1.1	1.0
National Biological Standards Board (UK)	12.4	11.5
National Radiological Protection Board	14.0	6.2
Public Health Laboratory Service Board	118.3	65.2
Home Office		
Commission for Racial Equality	15.1	15.1
Gaming Board for Great Britain	3.0	2.9
Criminal Injuries Compensation Authority	182.5	181.4
Office of the Data Protection Register	3.6	3.4
Police Complaints Authority	4.0	4.0
Department for National Heritage		
Arts Council of England	225.6	225.6
British Library	105.1	72.1
British Museum	44.3	33.2
British Tourist Authority	48.0	32.2
Broadcasting Standards Council	1.5	1.5
English Tourist Board	18.9	13.9
Imperial War Museum	18.0	10.8

Executive Non-Departmental Public Bodies which produce independent accounts audited the C&AG

	Gross expenditure 1993/94 £m	Funded by government 1993/94 £m
Department for National Heritage (continued)		
Millenium Commission	0.1	0.1
Museums & Galleries Commission	9.4	8.9
Museums & Galleries Merseyside	17.0	13.9
National Gallery	26.1	17.9
National Heritage Memorial Fund	10.6	10.6
National Maritime Museum	11.6	10.6
National Museum of Science & Industry	26.2	21.9
National Portrait Gallery	11.4	4.8
Natural History Museum	41.2	28.4
Registrar of Public Lending Right	5.0	5.0
Royal Armouries	6.6	5.8
Sports Council	54.0	50.6
Tate Gallery	21.8	17.1
Victoria & Albert Museum	32.9	31.7
Wallace Collection	2.2	2.0
Northern Ireland Office		
Police Authority for Northern Ireland	600.0	600.0
Probation Board for Northern Ireland	10.1	10.1
Police Complaints for Northern Ireland	0.7	0.7
Office ot Public Service and Science		
Economic & Social Research Council	55.6	53.2
Medical Research Council	288.3	262.7
Natural Environment Research Council	185.3	140.3
Engineering and Physical Sciences Research		
Particle Physics and Astronomy Research Council	766.9	692.9
Biotechnology and Biological Sciences Research Council		
Scottish Offfice		
Accounts Commission—Scotland	6.0	—
Highlands & Islands Enterprise	78.6	61.9
National Galleries Scotland	9.2	8.4
National Library Scotland	19.5	19.4
National Museum Scotland	17.7	17.1
Royal Botanic Garden, Edinburgh	8.0	6.4
Scottish Arts Council	23.3	23.0
Scottish Enterprise	451.0	379.0
Scottish Higher Education Funding Council	415.2	415.2
Scottish Homes	480.2	320.2
Scottish Natural Heritage	36.9	36.9
Scottish Sports Council	12.9	10.4
Scottish Tourist Board	17.1	13.7
Department of Trade and Industry		
Design Council	11.4	8.0
National Enterprise Board	0.0	—
National Research & Development Corporation	0.0	—
The Simpler Trade Procedures Board	1.6	0.8
United Kingdom Atomic Energy Authority	377.0	—
Department of Transport		
Northern Lighthouse Board } General Lighthouse Authorities	21.8	—
Trinity House	31.2	—
Welsh Office		
Arts Council of Wales (set up.30.3.94)	0.0	—
Countryside Council for Wales	19.9	19.8
Curriculum and Assessment Authority for Wales	1.7	1.7
Development Board for Rural Wales	24.9	16.3
Further Education Funding Council for Wales	143.1	143.1
Higher Education Funding Council for Wales	179.0	179.0

Executive Non-Departmental Public Bodies which produce independent accounts audited the C&AG

	Gross expenditure 1993/94 £m	Funded by government 1993/94 £m
Welsh Office (cont.)		
Land Authority for Wales	12.3	—
National Library of Wales	6.5	6.0
National Museum of Wales	16.8	14.4
Sports Council for Wales	8.6	6.4
Wales Tourist Board	13.8	13.7
Welsh Development Agency	151.7	69.6
Welsh Language Board	0.1	0.1

Note 1 The Funding Agency for Schools W2S established on 1.4.94 under the provisions of the Education Act.1993. In 1994/95 the Agency is estimated to spend £2.237 million.

There are also 56 bodies which do not produce separate accounts but whose expenditure (in total some £38 million) is audited by the C&AG within the audit of the sponsor departments' Votes.

Executive Non-Departmental Public Bodies where the C&AG has inspection rights

	Gross expenditure 1993/94 £m	Funded by government 1993/94 £m
Ministry of Agriculture, Fisheries and Food		
Apple & Pear Research Council	0.4	—
Food from Britain	9.2	5.1
Home-Grown Cereals Authority	8.3	0.1
Horticultural Development Council	3.6	—
Horticultural Research International	23.9	16.6
Meat and Livestock Commisslon	41.8	—
Regional Flood Defence Committees [9 bodies]	0.0	—
Sea Fish Industry Authority	7.9	0.7
Wine Standards Board of the Vintners Company	0.1	0.3
Ministry of Defence		
Oil and Pipelines Agency	1.6	1.3
Services Sound & Vision Corporation	48.0	30.7
Department for Education		
Centre for Information on Language Teaching Research	1.4	0.9
Further Education Unit (Note 1)	3.8	3.8
National Council for Education Technology	11.7	5.6
National Youth Agency	2.3	1.9
Teaching as a Career Unit	1.2	1.2
Employment Department Group		
Investors in People UK	0.9	0.9
Construction Industry Training Board	115.2	—
Engineering Construction Industry Training Board	10.5	—
National Council for Vocational Qualifications	9.4	3.8
Remploy Limited	200.5	89.2
Department of the Environment		
British Board of Agrement	3.8	0.9
Commission for the New Towns	114.9	27.8
English Partnerships (Urban Regeneration Agency)	21.7	21.7
Housing Action Trust: North Hull	26.9	26.5
Housing Action Trust: Waltham Forest	33.2	29.1
Housing Action Trust: Liverpool	19.9	16.6
Housing Action Trust: Tower Hamlets	8.4	8.4
Housing Action Trust: Birmingham Tower Vale	2.4	2.0
Housing Corporation	1,843.2	1,794.8
Letchworth Garden City Corporation	5.6	—
London Pensions Fund Authority	240.0	—
London Residuary Body	3.3	—
National Rivers Authority	404.0	114.0
UK Eco-Labelling Board	0.8	0.7
Urban Development Corporations [12 bodies]	457.6	352.9
Foreign and Commonwealth Office		
Commonwealth Scholarship Commission	0.1	0.1
Great Britain—China Centre	0.3	0.2
British Association for Central & Eastern Europe	0.3	0.2
Britain—Russia Centre	0.3	0.2
Westminster Foundation For Democracy	2.0	2.0
Department of Health		
English National Board for Nursing, Midwifery, & Health Visiting	152.7	145.5
UK Central Council for Nursing Midwifery, & Health Visiting	8.6	—
Home Office		
Alcohol Education & Research Council	0.5	—
Community Development Foundation	1.8	1.0
Fire Services Examinations Board	0.4	0.4
Horserace Betting Levy Board	48.8	—
Horserace Totalisator Board	30.7	—
Police Promotions Examinations Board	1.5	—

Executive Non-Departmental Public Bodies which produce independent accounts audited the C&AG

	Gross expenditure 1993/94 £m	Funded by government 1993/94 £m
Lord Chancellor's Department		
Authorised Conveyancing Practicioners Board	0.1	0.1
Legal Aid Board	1,278.0	1,021.0
Department for National Heritage		
British Film Institute	27.2	15 0
Broadcasting Complaints Commission	0.5	0.5
Crafts Council	4.6	3.4
English Heritage (Historic Buildings and Monuments Commission for England)	114.3	100.2
Football Licensing Authority	0.9	0.9
Greater Manchester Museum of Science and Industry	4.1	2.1
Geffrye Museum	1.2	0.9
Horniman Museum	2.5	2.5
Museum of London	13.6	4.2
National Film & Television School	3.8	1.8
National Film Development Fund	0.8	—
Sir John Soane's Museum	0.9	0.7
Northern Ireland Office		
Training Schools Management Boards (Rathgael and Whiteabbey) [2 bodies]	3.9	3.8
Office of the Rail Regulator		
Rail Users Consultative Committees [8 bodies]	0.7	0.7
Scottish Office		
Animal Diseases Research Association	5.3	4.2
Cumbernauld Development Corporation	43.1	15.0
East Kilbride Development Corporation	60.6	11.9
Edinburgh New Town Conservation Committee	1.4	0.9
General Teaching Council for Scotland	0.6	—
Glenrothes Development Corporation	43.2	15.1
Hannah Research Institute	3.9	3.2
Irvine Development Corporation	26.5	11.7
Livingston Development Corporation	62.9	27.2
Macaulay Land Use Research Institute	8.5	6.2
National Board Nursing Midwifery & Health Visiting for Scotland	3.7	3.7
Police (Scotland) Examination Board	0.1	0.1
River Purification Boards [7 bodies]	13.9	—
Rowett Research Institute	9.5	7.7
Scottish Community Education Council	1.1	0.6
Scottish Conveyancing & Executory Services Board	0.1	0.1
Scottish Council for Educational Technology	3.4	1.4
Scottish Crop Research Institute	10.2	7.9
Scottish Examination Board	9.8	—
Scottish Film Council	1.2	0.9
Scottish Hospital Endowments Research Trust	1.3	—
Scottish Legal Aid Board	152.6	126.2
Scottish Seed Potato Development Council	0.3	—
Scottish Vocational Education Council	7.5	1.3
Scottish Further Education Unit	1.4	0.6
Department of Trade and Industry		
British Hallmarking Council	0.8	—
Gas Consumer's Council	2.8	2.8
Hearing Aid Council	0.1	—
National Consumer Council [4 bodies]	3.4	3.2
Policyholders Protection Board	6.7	—
Department of Transport		
Central Rail Users' Consultative Committee	0.3	0.3
Traffic Director for London	9.1	9.0
Welsh Office		
Cardiff Bay Development Corporation	47.5	45.2
Housing for Wales	161.2	159.7
Wales Youth Agency	0.4	0.4
Welsh National Board Nursing Midwifery & Health Visiting	1.2	1.1

Note: 1. From 1.4.95 the Further Education Unit will be replaced by the Further Education Development Association.

Extract from 'the Government's Guide to Market Testing, 1993'

Access for National Audit Office (NAO)

The NAO's role is to provide information, assurance and advice to Parliament on the way Government Departments, Agencies and some other Public Bodies account for and use taxpayers' money.

10.6 The contracting-out of services does not in any way reduce the accountability of Departments' or Agencies' Accounting Officers to Parliament for their use of public funds. The NAO's role is to provide information, assurance and advice to Parliament on the way Government Departments, Agencies and some other public bodies account for and use taxpayers' money. They achieve this through the certification audit of accounts and by examining the economy, efficiency and effectiveness of projects, programmes and activities.

Departments and Agencies should ensure that the NAO continues to have access to documents to enable it to carry out financial and value for money audits.

10.7 Departments and Agencies should ensure that the NAO continues to have access to documents to enable it to carry out financial and value for money audits. Departments and Agencies may themselves hold these documents even though the work has been contracted out. However, where such documents are no longer held by the Department or Agency the NAO will need to have a right of access to the relevant papers and records held by the contractor and this should be provided for in the contract. If in doubt on this, Departments and Agencies should consult the Treasury. (TOA1 Division).

Whatever rights of access are needed for NAO they must be limited to papers and records which relate to the Department or Agency: they will not report on the supplier's own financial affairs, or conduct a value for money examination of his/her business.

10.8 Whatever rights of access are needed for NAO, they must be limited to papers and records which relate to the Department or Agency: they will not report on the supplier's own financial affairs, or conduct a value for money examination of his/her business. In those cases in which NAO has access rights, it is likely that they would have to be exercised for the purposes of financial audit on a regular basis and that access for value for money audits would only arise in the context of specific studies.

Memorandum from Lord Armstrong of Ilminster

I should like to make the following points in relation to Lord Wakeham's appointment as a non-executive director of N M Rothschild & Sons Limited:

1. It is nearly three years since Lord Wakeham ceased to be Secretary of State for Energy.

2. It is over six months since Lord Wakeham ceased to be a member of the Government.

3. Lord Wakeham has made it clear that he does not intend or expect to return to ministerial office.

4. N M Rothchild & Sons Limited never advised Lord Wakeham, when he was Secretary of State for Energy, or the Department of Energy, on electricity privatisation matters. They advised the Regional Electricity Companies, and they advised Hanson PLC on its bid for PowerGen.

5. Rothschild did not advise the Secretary of State for Energy or the Department of Energy during Lord Wakeham's time as Secretary of State on coal privatisation. During that time Rothschilds were commissioned to do a study of the options for the future of the coal industry. This study was commissioned in May 1991, after the Government had declared that it would not be privatising the coal industry until after the then forthcoming General Election.

It is of course impossible to say what advice would have been given to the Prime Minister, if Lord Wakeham's appointment had been referred to some such body as the Carlisle Committee. If I may express a personal view, it would be that such a committee, on its present criteria, would have been unlikely to recommend a delay of more than six months after his leaving government office before his undertaking such an appointment.

More generally, it is clear as important for former ministers as for former civil servants not to accept industrial or commercial appointments which are or might reasonably be thought be to be in some sense improper in relation to their previous public employment (which in my view Lord Wakeham's directorship of N M Rothschild & Sons Limited is not). But it would be in nobody's interests, and certainly not in the wider public interest, to have rules so strict as in effect to make it impossible, even when there is no hint of impropriety, for the talents and general experience of such people to be employed to the benefit of the industrial and commercial life of this country after their departure from public service. Indeed, if the rules were too draconian, that could (given the unpredictable changes and chances of ministerial office) be a deterrent to the willingness to accept such office of people whose abilities were otherwise well suited to it.

I should like to believe that anyone who has held ministerial office in this country could be expected to behave responsibly and sensibly, consulting the Prime Minister or others as appropriate, in deciding what (if any) appointments he or she can properly take up after leaving public service. But it is clearly desirable to avoid nor merely the reality but also the appearance of impropriety in these matters, and I think that it could well be useful for the Prime Minister to appoint a committee to provide advice, analogous to that provided by the Carlisle Committee in the case of civil servants, on proposals by former ministers to take up paid industrial or commercial employment after leaving public service. The criteria for the committee's recommendations could well be similar to, though not necessarily exactly the same as, those to which the Carlisle Committee works. Such an arrangement could give reassurance to the public and a degree of protection to the former Ministers concerned.

2 February 1995

Letter from Lord Armstrong of Ilminster to the Chairman of the Committee

I wish to make a supplementary point, more for clarification than anything else, relating to an answer to Mr Tom King.

It was (I think) implied in Mr King's comment, and was explicitly stated in a leading article in The Guardian on the morning of 6 February, that the Chief Whip's judgement on an allegation of impropriety or misconduct on the part of a Minister would carry no credibility ("he would say that, wouldn't he?"). It seems to me that neither the Chief Whip nor any other Minister who was asked to investigate and express a view on such an allegation would in practice be able to get away with a "whitewashing" job, or could afford to try to do so: he would be well aware that his own political and public reputation would be at stake, and that an outcome which was widely seen as incredible would be the subject of intense scrutiny by investigative journalists. It would be very much in his own interest to make his inquiry searching and thorough.

7 February 1995

Letter from Richard Mottram, CB to the Secretary of the Committee

In the course of my evidence with Mr Fox to the Committee on 8 February, Lord Nolan raised the question of whether some kind of Ombudsman might be established to investigate allegations of improper appointments. Reference was made to the Parliamentary Ombudsman, although it then became clear in the discussion that Lord Nolan had a different arrangement in mind. For completeness, it may be helpful if I clarify the position in relation to the Parliamentary Ombudsman.

The Parliamentary Ombudsman does not have powers to investigate appointments. Under Schedule 3, 10(1)(c) of the Parliamentary Commissioner Act 1967, the Parliamentary Ombudsman cannot investigate action taken in respect of appointments made by Ministers. The Ombudsman has interpreted the legislation as meaning that his jurisdiction excludes all aspects of selection and appointments procedures. Most of the complaints about appointments could be expected to concern discretionary decisions which are outside the Ombudsman's remit.

As well as being unable to investigate the merits of discretionary decisions taken without maladministration, the Parliamentary Ombudsman cannot conduct investigations into matters where legal remedies exist, or where there is a right of recourse to a tribunal (unless in the circumstances of a particular case the Ombudsman considers it unreasonable to expect the complainant to resort to such matters). Other significant exclusions to his jurisdiction are the whole of the "personnel" area (appointments, removals, pay, discipline, superannuation); the commencement or conduct of civil and criminal proceedings; and matters relating to contractual or other commercial transactions.

13 February 1995

Letter from Dr Chris Robinson to the Secretary of the Committee

It occurred to me that it might be of some help to you and the members of the Committee if I gave you the attached copy of a flow chart I prepared to explain how we saw the process working and how the two sets of the committees that I referred to in my evidence would function. If there are any questions in relation to it please do not hesitate to contact me. I would be only too happy to clarify any points.

27 February 1995

NAHAT proposals for the revised appointments process for Trust and Health Authority Boards

Independent Regional Authority Panel

Composition: Leading public figures from within Region plus minority of NHS senior figure/s.

Role: Oversee appointment process—advising Regional Policy Board Member both on process and its probity. Agree regional criteria for Trust and Purchaser Board appointments if no national ones? Advise RPBM on the appropriateness/balance of the recommendations being submitted by the RPBM to the Secretary of State. Select independent Chairman for Appointments Panel.

Appointments Panel

Composition: Independent Chairman (leading public figure) selected by Independent Advisory Panel, and either one or two each of the Purchaser and Provider Trust Chairmen in that Region selected by Policy Board member.

Role: Selection, from spectrum of nominations obtained by various processes, of those candidates who are deemed to be above the line/suitable for Board membership. Indication as to whether those candidates will be more suitable in either a commissioning or a providing Board.

Flow chart

Self nomination   Other ways (organisations, MPs etc)   Chairmens Nominations

———————————————— Appointments panel ————————————————

Pool of suitable names

Local Trust or Commissioning Authority Chairman

Recommendation for Board
membership plus alternatives
in priority order

RPBM   (+/– Regional Advisory Panel)

Checks nominations for balance etc

Secretary of State

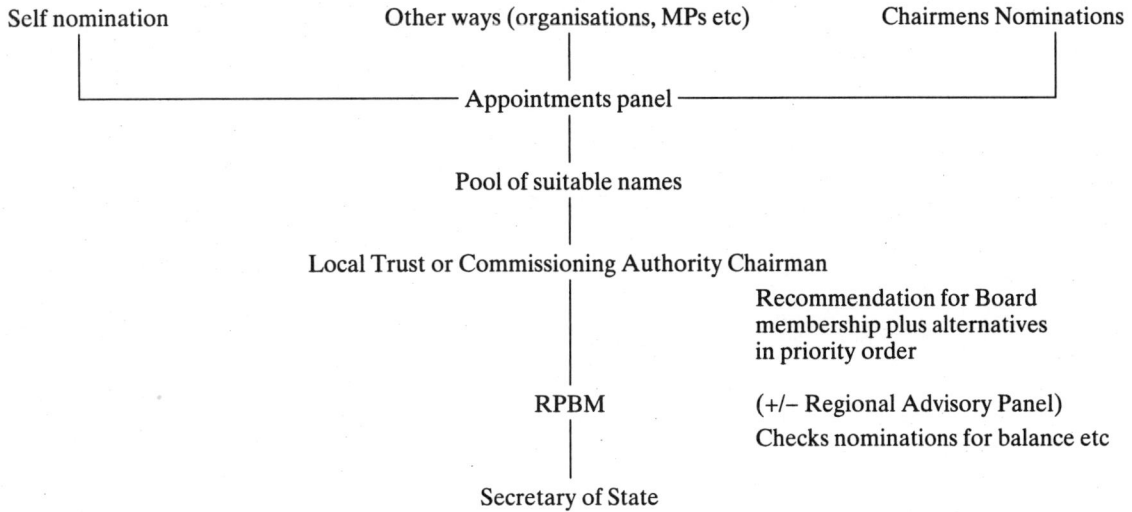

Letter from Derek Day to the Secretary of the Committee

I apologise for not writing to you before but on re-reading our oral evidence and the suggested outline arrangements for future appointments of chairman and non executive director/members, there is one aspect which needs clarification.

You will recall that both in the oral evidence given in the outline appointments arrangements we submitted, reference was made to establishing a smaller appointments advisory committee in each of the regions to oversee the appointments of activities and ensure that the processes are open, transparent and fair. However, neither in our oral evidence nor in the note did we spell out the suggested composition of that committee or how it was appointed.

We would envisage each of the committees consisting of five eminent, respected but independent people drawn from the community or public life, the business sector and NHS professional interests. So far as appointing the membership is concerned, we would see this as either the responsibility of the Secretary of State or alternatively if a national committee (parliamentary or otherwise) were set up to oversee appointments arrangements then by that body. An alternative would be for the Secretary of State to make the appointments, with vetting being undertaken by that body.

23 March 1995

Letter from Sir Ronald Hampel to the Secretary of the Committee

I hope that the answers which Anthony Weale and I gave the Committee on Wednesday were helpful to your Inquiry. Towards the end of the session, in answer to a question from Sir William Utting, I mentioned that ICI does have a publicised Business Ethics Policy and promised to send you a copy. This I now do, and draw your attention particularly to Page 7 (righthand column) which covers a question asked by Dame Anne Warburton relating to ICI's policy on the acceptance of hospitality and gifts.

I should perhaps have mentioned that every year we require all our senior managers of all ICI operations worldwide to sign what we call a "Letter of Assurance". This is basically a signed confirmation that they have behaved properly through the previous year in a number of specific and sensitive areas. I thought you might find it helpful to have a copy of this undertaking; section 2 refers to Business Ethics.

17 February 1995

LETTER OF ASSURANCE

I am writing on behalf of the ICI Board to seek your annual assurances with regard to internal controls for the Businesses/Services for which you are responsible. Internal control is defined as:

The whole system of controls, financial and otherwise, established in order to provide reasonable assurance of:

1. effective and efficient operations.

2. internal financial control.

3. compliance with laws and regulations.

This letter of assurance forms part of the systems for safeguarding the ICI Group's assets and reputation. It serves to formalise and confirm ongoing business responsibilities and allows for the identification of areas of concern and for the sharing of experience.

The letter of assurance should cover the areas set out below and should, if this is appropriate to your circumstances, follow the format given in Appendix I.

1. Internal financial control

This is described in more detail in Appendix II which covers:

i. Definition of internal financial control

ii. Responsibility for internal control.

iii. Notification of

* non-compliance with Group policy or
* breaches of internal control

iv. Group accounting requirements

I seek your assurance that internal financial controls are adequate for the entities (ie subsidiary undertakings and accounting units) for which you are responsible and to advise me of any major weaknesses which cannot be corrected immediately.

I should remind you that responsibility for internal control to entities also includes controls relating to the management of retirement plans provided by subsidiaries. You should be satisfied that there is compliance with "Guidelines for Good Management Practice of Retirement Plans" issued on 9 November 1988 by Mr Hampson (copy attached as Appendix III together with authorities list).

The power to establish and modify pension or retirement benefit schemes is expected to become a "Reserved Power" and, in this event, next year's Letter of Assurance will require compliance to be confirmed in the terms set out in the document establishing these.

Confirmation of coverage of pension funds related to Group subsidiaries is outlined below (see "Coverage of Response")

2. ICI Group statement on "Business Ethics"

At the end of 1993 Secretary's Department issued a statement of ICI's policies on ethical standards in the conduct of the Group's business activities in a booklet entitled "Business Ethics", a copy of which is enclosed. You are asked to confirm that a process is in place which ensures that all employees are made aware of the policies detailed in this booklet and that copies are made available to them.

3. Internal control—other

You are being asked to confirm that your system of controls provides you with assurances on the effective and efficient management of your operations.

You are also being asked to confirm that the entities for which you are responsible have complied with the laws and regulations of any country in which they are doing business and in particular with the following policies which are referred to in the "Business Ethics" booklet:

(a) Policy on compliance with competition laws (see "Compliance with Laws" section—page 5)

(b) Policy on payments to government officials and employees of state organisations (see "Business Practices" section—page 7).

(c) Policy on "Political Contributions" (see section so identified—page 8).

As last year, Group Internal Audit will prepare summaries of their internal audit reviews. After discussions with you, your Internal Auditor will send a copy of the audit summary directly to the Group Chief Internal Auditor who will use it for preparing his report to the Audit Committee on the adequacy and effectiveness of internal controls in the ICI Group.

Coverage of Response

At a time of significant organisational change, being managed by "Project Triple A", it is particularly important that control is not weakened by lack of clarity on the responsibility at the boundary between businesses, or between businesses and territories and service organisations.

A list is enclosed of the managed entities and pension funds related to those entities which Controller's Department has recorded as being under your responsibility. If you believe that any of the entities or funds concerned is wrongly attributed to your responsibility, or if there are any omissions, please let me know by 28 October where you believe it falls. The list of entities have been prepared taking account of boundaries being established by "Triple A". In some cases these have yet to be finalised and therefore there may be entities incorrectly attributed to your responsibility. In the case of pension funds, this is the first occasion that a comprehensive list has been compiled. It has been derived from memorandum information held by Group Pensions Department so it is possible that this list may not be complete: please advise me of any changes to this which you believe are necessary.

Please note that for entities listed as dormant or in liquidation the only requirement is to confirm their status.

Recipients of this note are entitled to assume that I receive adequate assurance from the entire circulation (attached). I would expect that, in general, users of services will feel able to rely on this central request for assurance and will not therefore need to request direct assurances themselves.

In order to avoid conflict with the intensive year end period I am asking for your letter of assurance to cover the period from the date to which you last reported until 30 September 1994 ie, 12 months. Please will you ensure that your letter of assurance reaches me not later than 5 December 1994. To the extent that your business has not had its 1994 internal audit review meeting by that date (I understand those meetings are scheduled up to the end of December), I will be happy to receive a supplementary note covering any further issues to emerge from those meetings.

[No enclosures]

Letter from Professor Dawn Oliver to the Chairman of the Committee

I was very pleased to have the opportunity to give evidence to the Committee today and I found it a very stimulating and encouraging experience. I look forward to publication of your report.

I wonder if I could take the opportunity to add to a couple of my answers?

First, Sir Clifford Bolton's questions about parallels between contempt of court and contempt of Parliament. This was not a matter that I had considered and I am conscious that I was not able to give a very convincing answer

I am, as I indicated, not sure that the analogy with contempt of court is a close one. But I think that it is relevant that those participating as 'insiders' in the proceedings of the courts (ie those with whom the strongest analogies with MPs could be drawn) are barristers, solicitors and judges; the first two of these are governed by elaborate codes of professional conduct, (partly with a statutory underpinning). Judges, as former barristers and solicitors, will also have absorbed the ethos of the courts from the professions' rules. The codes for barristers and solicitors are enforced partly by bodies with independent representation. I do think this parallel between MPs and members of the liberal professions is a helpful one, and reinforces the case for a code of conduct for MPs.

To purpose the analogy with contempt of court further, some of those who might be found in contempt of court are 'outsiders'—witnesses, litigants, members of the public—and it is true that the rules relating to them are not embodied in a code. But the proper analogy there with contempt of Parliament (if it is an appropriate analogy) is with parliamentary outsiders—sponsors, witnesses before select committees and members of the public. For none of these categories, in court proceedings or in Parliament is there a code of practice. But, for the reasons I gave this morning, I think it would be helpful if a code were drawn up for the guidance of sponsors of MPs as well as MPs. I do not see the need for such guidance for others appearing in the courts or Parliament.

Another point I would like to add to was that of Sir William Utting about Parliament 'owning' a code of conduct. I do think that it is important for codes to be owned if possible by those governed by them, and this principle is reflected in, for instance, Notes of Guidance for Ministers and a number of other 'codes' and handbooks in government which have been built up over the years by ministers etc. In the light of experience.

On the other hand the 'Osmotherly Rules' which govern the conduct of civil servants appearing before select committees, are imposed on civil servants by government, despite the fact that the civil servant is, at the higher levels at least, arguably a member of a liberal profession. The proposed new civil service code has been drafted by a select committee and amended by the government, and will not be 'owned' by the civil service, though the FDA has been involved in its elaboration. So there does not seem to be general recognition that codes of practice will not be effective unless 'owned' by those whom they bind.

I would not argue from this that any code of conduct for MPs should or should not be imposed upon them, only that we need to be careful of enunciating principles about the imposition of codes that do not apply generally.

I thought Sir William's suggestion that a 'code of conduct' could be part of a positive set out guidelines about 'How to be a Good MP' was very interesting. A handbook of this kind could cover a much wider range of matters than relations with sponsors etc, and it could also include information about procedures in the House etc that would be of particular use to new Members. The handbook idea chimes with the current fashion for elaborating 'best practice' standards in many areas of activity. But I think that the elements of such a code that governed standards of conduct would need to have the special status and mechanism for independent supervision that the Committee has been considering, whereas other 'good practice' points would not need special status.

23 February 1995

The following list includes all organisations and individuals who contributed written evidence which we considered in our work. Evidence which concerned individual cases, or which has been found to be potentially defamatory, has been excluded.

Members of Parliament, Members of the European Parliament and Members of the House of Lords

Graham Allen MP
Lord Armstrong of Ilminster GCB, CVO
Tony Baldry MP
Lord Bancroft GCB
Harry Barnes MP
Spencer Batiste MP
Hugh Bayley MP
Rt Hon Alan Beith MP
Stuart Bell MP
Rt Hon Tony Benn MP
Rt Hon John Biffen DL, MP
Dr Gordon Brown MP
John Butterfill MP
Rt Hon Lord Callaghan of Cardiff KG
Dale Campbell-Savours MP
Alex Carlile QC MP
Rt Hon Lord Carlisle of Bucklow QC
Winston Churchill MP
Michael Colvin MP
Quentin Davies MP
Robert Dunn MP
Alan Duncan MP
Angela Eagle MP
David Evans MP
Sir Nicholas Fairbairn QC, MP (dec.)
Derek Fatchett MP
Barry Field MP
Dudley Fishburn MP
Rt Hon Sir Norman Fowler MP
Glyn Ford MEP
Nigel Forman MP
Sir Peter Fry MP
Sir John Gorst MP
Rt Hon Jeremy Hanley MP
Andrew Hargreaves MP
Lord Harris of Greenwich
Rt Hon Roy Hattersley MP
Sir Peter Hordern MP
Rt Hon Lord Houghton of Sowerby CH
Rt Hon Lord Howe of Aberavon QC
Rt Hon David Howell MP
Rt Hon David Hunt MBE, MP,
    Chancellor of the Duchy of Lancaster
John Hutton MP
Baroness Jay of Paddington
Hon Bernard Jenkin MP
Lord and Lady Kennet
Archy Kirkwood MP
Lord Lester of Herne Hill QC
Ken Livingstone MP
Peter Luff MP
The Earl of Lytton CB
Rt Hon John MacGregor OBE MP
Robert Maclennan MP
Denis MacShane MP
Max Madden MP
Sir David Madel MP
Michael Meacher MP
Rt Hon Lord Merlyn-Rees
Alan Milburn MP
Austin Mitchell MP
David Mitchell MP
Chris Mullin MP
Emma Nicholson MP

Mike O'Brien MP
Christine Oddy MEP
Phillip Oppenheim MP
Richard Ottaway MP
Rt Hon Sir Geoffrey Pattie MP
Tom Pendry MP
Jeff Rooker MP
Andrew Rowe MP
Earl Russell FBA
Michael Shersby MP
Alan Simpson MP
Nigel Spearing MP
Rt Hon Lord Stewartby
Jack Straw MP
Anne Taylor MP
Peter Thurnham MP
John Townend MP
Paul Tyler MP
Rt Hon Lord Wakeham
Nigel Waterson MP
Sir Jerry Wiggin MP
Brian Wilson MP
David Winnick MP
Nicholas Winterton MP
Tony Wright MP
Lord Wyatt of Weeford
Rt Hon Lord Younger of Prestwick KCVO, TD, DL

Local Government etc.

Arfon Borough Council
Association of County Chief Executives
Association of County Councils
Association of District Councils
Association of District Secretaries
Association of Metropolitan Authorities
Avon County Council
Bedford Borough Council
City of Bradford Metropolitan Council
Brent Liberal Democrats
Cambridgeshire County Council
City of Cardiff Council
Chesterfield Borough Council
Cleveland County Council
Colchester Borough Council
Commission for Local Administration in England
Commission for Local Administration in Wales
Coventry City Council
Dartford Borough Council
Derby City Council
Devon County Council
Droitwich Spa Town Council
Enderby Parish Council
Forest of Dean District Council
London Borough of Greenwich Labour Group
London Borough of Hackney
Hereford & Worcester County Labour Party
Histon Parish Council
Isle of Wight County Council
Leicestershire County Council
Leicestershire County Council Liberal Democrat Group
Lewisham Borough Council
Lincolnshire County Council
Local Government Information Unit
Milton Keynes Borough Council
Newark & Sherwood Disrict Council
Newbury District Council Liberal Democrat Group
Newport Borough Council

Norfolk County Council
　Social & Liberal Democrat Group
North of England Assembly
Norwich City Council
City of Nottingham Council
Nottinghamshire County Council
Oswestry Branch Labour Party / Oswestry
　Borough Council Labour Group
Oxfordshire County Council
Reading Borough Council
Rochford District Council
Rotherham Metropolitan Borough Council
City of Salford Council
Sheffield City Council
Society of County Secretaries
Society of County Treasurers
Society of Local Authority Chief Executives (SOLACE)
Society of London Treasurers
South Norfolk Council
Stevenage Borough Council
Borough of Thamesdown
Uttesford District Council Liberal Democrat Group
Wansbeck District Council
Warwickshire County Council
Western Isles Islands Council
West Midlands Joint Committee
West Sussex County Council

NDPBs (Quangos) and Health Service Bodies

Bedfordshire and Hertfordshire Ambulance
　and Paramedic Service
Birmingham City Hospital NHS Trust
Bury Community Health Council
Camden & Islington Community
　Health Services NHS Trust
Design Council
Royal Devon and Exeter Healthcare NHS Trust
Dorset Health Commission
East Wiltshire Health Care NHS Trust
English National Board for Nursing, Midwifery
　and Health Visiting
Equal Opportunities Commission
Further Education Funding Council
London Pensions Fund Authority
Medical Practices Committee
Mid Kent Healthcare Trust
Monopolies and Mergers Commission
National Association of Health Authorities
　& Trusts (NAHAT)
NHS Executive
National Health Service Trust Federation
Newcastle & North Tyneside Health Authority
North Western Regional Association of
　Community Health Councils
School Curriculum and Assessment Authority
Scottish Arts Council
Scottish Film Council
South Manchester Community Health Council

Universities and Colleges etc.

Association of Teachers and Lecturers
Association of University Teachers
University of Birmingham
Cambridge Centre for Business & Public Centre Ethics
　(Director, Dr Rosamund Thomas)
Colleges Employers' Forum

De Montfort University, Leicester
University of Essex
University of Exeter
Royal College of General Practitioners
Manchester Metropolitan University
　(Faculty of Management and Business)
University of Oxford
　(Centre for Criminological Research)
University of Reading
　(Centre for Ombudsman Studies)
Robert Gordon University, Aberdeen
University of Sheffield (Faculty of Law)
University of Southampton (Department of Politics)
St. Philip's Sixth Form College, Birmingham
University & College Lecturers' Union
University of Strathclyde
University of Wales School of English Studies,
　Communication & Philosophy
　(Centre for Applied Ethics)

Other Organisations and Groups

Action for Justice
Action for London
Amanda Society
Article 26
Association of British Chambers of Commerce
Association of British Insurers
Association of Chief Police Officers of England,
　Wales and Northern Ireland
Association of First Division Civil Servants
Association of Professional Political Consultants
Audit Commission
Bath & District Charter 88 Group
Birmingham Chamber of Commerce and Industry
British Association of Social Workers
British Medical Association
British Sikh Federation
Campaign Against Drinking and Driving
Campaign for Real Education
Certification Officer for Trade Union and
　Employers' Associations
Chalkwell Ward Labour Party
Chartered Institute of Public Finance
　and Accountancy (CIPFA)
Chartered Insurance Institute
Charter 88
Cheethams
Chideock Society
Christian Conventions
Christian Socialist Movement
Clifford Chance Public Policy Group
Commission for Local Democracy
Common Campaign Limited
Community Voice
Comptroller and Auditor General (Sir John Bourn KCB)
Confederation of British Industry
Conference on the needs of the Muslim Child
　in the State School
Consumers in Europe Group
Co-operative Party
Council for Academic Freedom and Academic Standards
Council of Civil Service Unions / UNISON
Decision Makers Ltd
Democratic Left (South West England)
Demos
Doctors Save Barts Campaign
Dyson Bell Martin
East Birmingham Pensioners
Egham Riverside Residents' Association
European Public Affairs Consortium

European Public Relations Confederation
Family Charter Campaign
Farm and Food Society
Federated Union of Managerial
 and Professional Officers
Forty Plus
Freedom to Care
General, Municipal & Boilermakers' Union (GMB)
General Synod of the Church of England
 (Board of Social Responsibility)
Government Policy Consultants
Government Relations Unit
Guild of Editors
Heathrow Association for the Control
 of Aircraft Noise
ICI Pontypool Retired Employees' Association
Imperial Chemical Industries plc
Institute of Business Ethics
Institute of Chartered Secretaries & Administrators
Institute for Global Ethics
Institute of Internal Auditors
Institute of Management
Institute of Public Relations
Institute of Public Service Administrators
International Relief Friendship Foundation
Kent Jones and Done
Labour Party
Land Value Taxation Campaign
Lewes Charter 88 Group
Liberal Democratic Party
Lovell White Durrant
Maldon District Green Party
Manufacturing, Science & Finance Union (MSF)
Market Access International Ltd
Metropolitan Police (Fraud Squad, Public Sector
 Corruption Unit)
Midland Pensioners' Convention
Kings Heath Branch
Mid Yorkshire Chamber of Commerce
 and Industry Ltd
Museums Association
National Association of Citizens Advice Bureaux
National Council for Christian Standards
National Federation of Housing Associations
National Youth Agency
Natural Law Party
New Britain
Nithsdale Coalition of Disabled People
Parliamentary and Scientific Committee
Penwith Labour Research
Plaid Cymru
Politics Association
Profile Corporate Communications Ltd
Prowess
Public Concern at Work
Public Health Alliance
Public Relations Consultants' Association
Queen Mary & Westfield Public Policy Seminars
 (University of London)
Queens Park Rangers Loyal Supporters'
 Association
Recall
Religious Society of Friends (Quakers)
Royal Institute of British Architects
Royal Society of Chemistry
Salvation Army
Scottish National Party (Crieff Branch)
Scottish Police Federation
Scouts Association
Shadwell Keenan Ltd

Society of Motor Manufacturers
 and Traders Limited
South London Link Travellers' Association
Southport Constituency Labour Party
Stratford Promoter Group
Trades Union Congress
Transparency International and Transparency
 International (UK)
Transport and General Workers' Union
Transport Salaried Staffs' Association
UNISON
UNISON Northern Region
UNISON Scotland
UNISON Strathclyde Region Branch
United Pensioners of Wales
United Reformed Church
Values, Education, Consultancy, Training,
 Organisational Research (VECTOR)
Wales Assembly of Women
Welsh Liberal Party
Westminster Strategy

Individuals

A

Walter J Ablett Esq
G J Adams
J R Adams Esq
Mrs S C Adamson
Tony and Jackie Adamson
Prof Geoffrey Alderman
Len Aldis Esq
R Allen (Corby)
R Allen Esq (Colwyn Bay)
Rev Roy C Allison MA
G Andrews Esq
Dr James Andrews
V Annells Esq
W F H Ansell
Derek A Archer Esq
W J K Arnold
Victor C Arundell Esq FCA, F.Inst.D
Prof John R Ashton
Derek Asker Esq
Janet Askew
M G de St V Atkins
Rodney E B Atkinson Esq
Allan Auty Esq
Geoffrey and Judith Ayres

B

D E Baddeley
R E J Bailey Esq JP
J T Baker
S J Baker
Dr Robert Baldwin
Christopher Balfour Esq
M A Ballard
Alma Banks
Mrs A Barge
Mira Bar-Hillel
Anthony Barker Esq
Malcolm J W Barker Esq
Charles Barren Esq
Donald Barton Esq
Mrs Barbara A Bashford
N K Basu Esq
Reginald Bayne Esq
Mrs D A Beach

Douglas Beach Esq
W Beadle
Stephen Beard Esq
Dr J H Beaven
F G Beck
Mrs P Beck
S Robert Beech Esq
Mrs Lesley J Beggs MA, CA
Gordon Bell Esq
Robert Bell Esq
B J Benjamin
Nicholas Bennett Esq
David Benny Esq
H C Bentley
H W Bentley FCII
A W Berry
Dr Sebastian Berry
Dr L Bevan
G Bewes Esq
Michael Bichard Esq
Les Biek Esq
Jack Biggs Esq BEM
N Biggs
G B Binns Esq
Prof J M Bishop
Len Bishop Esq
Bernard Black Esq
Peter Black Esq
A Blackhurst
Cllr Roger Blackmore Esq
W D Blake
R Bloom Esq
S W Blunt
Vernon Bogdanor Esq
Mrs K Bonds
J D Booker
W Booth Esq
J Bowbanks Esq
Mrs Persis M Bower
John R Bowers Esq
Sir Jeffery Bowman
John Boxall Esq
S Boxall BSc(Hons), MSc
Prof R D H Boyd
Capt H H Bracken CBE, RN(Rtd)
John and Valerie Bradley
Stanley R Brand Esq
R Branner Esq
Prof Rodney Brazier
Ian Brennan Esq BA, FCCA
Daniel, Frances and Carl Bridgeman
Simon Bridgen Esq
N K Brierley Esq
R Brissenden
R Broad Esq ACIB
Mrs M D Brodie
J H Brooks Esq
Kenneth R Brooks Esq
Mrs Judith Brown
J W Brown
A Browne
Peter Browning Esq
J Michael Buchanan Esq
Miss Y E Buckoke
J W and V A Bull
C R Bullen Esq
J N Bunker
D C Burgess Esq
S B Burke Esq
William T Burke Esq

Geoffery P Burn Esq
Brian D Burrage Esq
John G S Burton Esq
Norman E Butcher Esq
David Butler Esq CBE
Phil Butler Esq
C J Buttery
Barrie Buxton Esq

C

M H Cadman
Anne S Caldwell
Rita Calvert
George Calvin Esq PhD
K C Campbell
Jeremy N H Campbell Grant Esq
J D Cannon
Most Rev and Rt Hon George Carey,
    Archbishop of Canterbury
Hugh Carlisle Esq QC
Ann Carlton
Marian E Carnick
Ralph Carpenter Esq
Biddy Casselden
S Caudwell
T H Caulcot Esq
John D Chadwick Esq
Simon Chandler Esq
Mrs Amy Charman
Paul Charman Esq
J Chesters Esq
J K Chuchla Esq CEng, FIEE, MBCS
Mr and Mrs D G Church
R Church Esq
Mrs Betty Clark
Don Clark Esq
George Clark Esq OBE
R J Clark Esq
Thomas J Clark Esq
E Clarke
C G Clayton
Len Coates Esq
Stephen Cochrane Esq
Alan Cocker Esq
Arthur D Cole Esq
Frederick Coles Esq
J P Coles Esq
Stanley A Colk Esq
Edward Collier Esq
Barbara H Collins
Ron Collins Esq
Tony Collins Esq
M Colton
H K Compton Esq FCIPS
A Condrad Esq
E F Cook Esq
Raymond Cook Esq
J M Cooksey Esq
John W Cooper Esq
John Cope Esq
Sir Alcon Copisarow
J L Corbett Esq
Derek S Cordery Esq
L W Cottell
E C Courtney
Peter A Cowan Esq
Michael Cox Esq CEng FIEE
Rodney J Cox Esq
A K Crackett

R D Cramond Esq CBE, MA, FIMgt
Charles Crebbin Esq
Frank-Cilla Cresswell Esq
Frank A Crewe Esq
Charles E Crisp Esq
Philip Critchley Esq CB
R F Crook MBE
Derek J Crow Esq DipEE, CEng, FIEE, MCIBSE
K Crow Esq BM
R Cullen Esq
Trevor Curnow Esq
George Curtis Esq
O A S Cutts Esq

D

A D Daters DipTP, ARICS, MTPI
Miss Shelley Davey
Ian Davidson Esq DPA, MSc
David R Davies Esq
Frank Davies Esq
Hugh Davies Esq
K C Davies
Linda A Davies
W T Davies
David Davis Esq
Miss Suzanne Davison
C Deadman Esq
Conrad Dehn Esq QC
David Denby Esq
G T Denton
A Devlin Esq
R Dickinson Esq
Stephen Dillon Esq
Jill Dimmock
David A Diprose Esq
W D W Dodd BA, FCA
J G Doel
Mrs Diana M Donald
S P Doody Esq
Pamela J Dowling BA, Dip.Soc.Ad., Dip.S.Wk
Mr J and Mrs E Downs
Ernest Dowson Esq OBE and Olive Dowson
Douglas J Drane Esq BA, BSc
Dan W Draper Esq
Dr Peter Draper FFPHM
N T Drew Esq
D C Duckworth
S Duncliffe Esq
Neil Dunkin Esq
Malcolm C Dunlop Esq

E

R G J M Earl Esq
C W Earnshaw
Martin Easteal Esq
B J Easterbrook Esq
Janet Elizabeth Edge
H D Edmunds
Dr H D Edwards
A Egan Esq
J S Elkington Esq MA, MB, BChir, FRCS
E R Ellen OBE
James Philip Elliott Esq
Cllr Brian Ellis Esq
Capt J G G P Elwes
Michael English Esq
P L Erbe Esq
Chris Evans Esq
J L Evans

Maureen Evans
Mrs Mavis Evans
Roger Warren Evans Esq BA, FCIOB
J P M H Evelyn Esq
Harry Ewings Esq

F

D L Fanning
David E R Faulkner Esq CB
J Fawens Esq
John Fay Esq
V C Fay
Andrew Fidler Esq
H R Fidler
John R Finlow Esq
Derek A Firth Esq
John Fisher Esq
Dr Justin Fisher
G A Fitzpatrick Esq
M C Fitzpatrick
Caroline Flint
Mrs Jane Fond
Mrs V A Foote
Andrew Footner Esq
Patrick M Forman Esq MA, LLB
A S Foster
J H Foster ARICS
Roy Foster Esq
I W Fotheringham Esq TD, MA(Oxon), FCA, FCMA
Mrs Anne Foulds MA
Mrs A Fowler
Neil Fowler Esq
Roy Frankland Esq
John A Franks Esq
Alan Fraser Esq
Simon Frazer Esq
A J French
J Frood
Rev R Michael Frost
John C W Fulbeck Esq RIBA, FRSA
Janet Fulford
John Fuller Esq

G

Mrs Anne Galbraith
J W Garbutt
John Garrott Esq
Roger Gartland Esq
R C Geall Esq
Peter Geliot Esq
John Geraghty Esq
E Gerres Esq
P J D Gething Esq
Edward Gibbon Esq
Michael Gilbert Esq CEng
Martin Glaser Esq
Clive Glover Esq
Jeffrey Goh Esq
Philip Goldenberg Esq
W A Goldfinch
Mel J Goldie
J John Goodman Esq
D B Goodrick Esq
Arthur S Graham Esq
A T Gray
Canon Donald Gray
V Gray
Mrs E Green
David Green Esq (Castle Morris)

David Green Esq (Shillington)
Joan Greenaway
Colin B Greenstreet Esq
P R Gregory
John Samuel Griffiths Esq
Simon G Griffiths Esq
Irene M Grisedale MRCVS
Peter A B Guenin Esq
W Guy Esq

H

S A Hall Esq
Margaret Hallett
James Hamilton Esq
Kenneth Hamilton Esq
G J Hammett Esq
Sir Ronald Hampel
B R Hanby Esq
David Hands Esq
Mark Hagger Esq
John and Cecily Hallett
George Harding Esq
Kenneth P Hardy Esq
Mrs C Harford
David Harries Esq
A E Harris
E G Harris Esq
S P Harris
A R Harrison
Dennis Harrison Esq LL.B
D Harrison Esq
James J H Harrison Esq
Kathleen M Harrison
Tony J Hart Esq
Philip Harwood Esq
O P Hassell Esq
Mark Hatcher Esq
Dr J Hawgood
A Hawker
David Hayes Esq
John W Hayes Esq
Peter R D Hayes Esq
Mr A N Haynes and Mrs M M Haynes
T R Hayward Esq
H Heimer CEng, FIEE, FIM
Richard Heller Esq
John Henderson Esq
Douglas M Henly Esq
Stanley E K Hewitt Esq
Barrie Hibberd Esq
E C and P E Hickford
Penn Hicks Esq
Cdr M B S Higham Esq
Kenneth Hill Esq CEng, MIM
Ted Hill Esq AMIPR
Councillor Lesley Hinds
Rev Dr Michael Hinton
Dr Peter Hitt
Anna B Hodgetts
Walter Hoffman Esq
Mark Hollingsworth Esq
D K Holmes
Mrs J Homer
Michael Honey Esq
J R Hooley DL
C V Horie
W G Horn BSc Eng(Chem Eng), ACGI,
    MIChemE, FInstP
Mrs Adelina Horsey

James V Hose Esq
Ivor R Hosgood Esq
Peter Household Esq
Mrs M M Hubner
John Hudman Esq
John N F Hudson Esq ACIS, ATII
Wg Cdr T F H Hudson
Mrs I Hughes
Patrick Hughes Esq
T C Hughes Esq
His Eminence Cardinal Basil Hume,
    Archbishop of Westminster
S J Humphreys
W Humphries Esq
C A Hunt
G Hunt Esq
Michael E Hunt Esq
Muir Hunter Esq QC
M E Hurden
B E Hurle BSc, CENG, FIMECHE
B C Hurley
D Hussey Esq MISM, MInst AM
George Huxley Esq Hon.Litt.D
D G Hyde
Frederick Hyde-Chambers Esq

I

P R P Ingram
Mrs Thelma Ireland
Dr D H Irvine
Arthur R Ivatts Esq

J

Dennis Jackland Esq
Michael R Jackson Esq
P A Jackson
H B Jacobs
E A Janes
Ram Jatan Esq
S G Jefferson
Diane M Jeffrey
Paul Jeffreys Esq
Diane Jenkins and Mark Jenkins Esq
Simon Jervis Esq
Stanley John Esq
Colin Johnson Esq
Dr M Johnson
Nevil Johnson Esq
R Johnston Esq
Bernard Jones Esq
J C Jones
Mrs Joyce Jones
Peter Jones Esq
Richard Jones Esq
R J Jones Esq
Cllr Steve Jones Esq
F D Judd Esq
M E Judd

K

Stanley Kalms Esq
Mrs Susan Karnik
Mrs A N Kayser
Robert A Keatley Esq
Sir Curtis Keeble
Bernard Keeffe Esq
Mark Kelly Esq
A Kembery

Sir Peter Kemp
C E Kendall Esq
Mrs Doreen Kendall
George Kendall Esq
J M Kendrick Esq
Prof Alexander Kennaway
Kevin Kilduff Esq
Mr A and Mrs B J Kilmartin
Capt P R D Kimm OBE, RN(Rtd)
Peter Kinderman Esq
T J King Esq MA
Anthony G Knight Esq
Mrs D Knight
Richard B M Knight Esq
Rita Knight

L

T R Lacey Esq
J Laflin
Michael Lambert Esq
C Lanfear Esq
F J Langfield
Mary Large
Richard W E Law Esq
W H Lawler Esq
Dr Richard Lawson MB, MRCPsych
Dr Alan Lawton
Anthony Lawton Esq
Robert A Lay Esq
D A Lee Esq
Alexander Leigh Esq MA, FIL
Nigel J Lemon Esq
Cllr Christopher Leslie Esq
C P T N Leslie Esq
Dewi Lloyd Lewis Esq
Sir Kenneth Lewis DL
Sue Lieberman
B Littman Esq
Bruce Lloyd Esq
D E Locke Esq
Frances Locker
E S Lomax
Miss Bridget Loney
D H Long Esq
R H Long
Brian Love Esq
K Lowe Esq
A R Lucas Esq
Raymond E Luke Esq FInst, LEx
David Lunn-Rockcliffe Esq
David A Lyle Esq MA, LLB, NP

M

Stewart McArdle Esq
Jim McBrearty Esq
Miss Sheila T McBrearty
R G McBurnie Esq
Hugh McCartney Esq
William M McClure Esq RIBA, ARIAS
Arthur and Victoria McConnell
Dr John F McEldowney
Charles McGinnis Esq
Stanley McGlenn Esq
Mrs A E M McGraa SRN, SCM, MTD, DN
Matthew J McGuire Esq
The Very Revd Canon J F McHugh
G McKay Esq
Kathleen McKenna

Ewan L S McLay Esq
W McMellon Esq
Mrs Alison McNair
D E McNamara Esq
Eddie McParland Esq
R MacDonald
Ian B Macleod Esq
W MacPherson Esq
P A Macrow Esq
Prof Jack Mahoney
John Malin Esq
Prof Maureen Mancuso
Cllr Roy Manley Esq
Anthony F Mapleson Esq
W S Marble Esq
Mrs M A Marfell
R G Markey
Stacy Marking
Mrs Leslie Marks
Dr Edmund Marshall
Michael E Martin Esq
R Martin
S W Martin
D B Maycock
Tony Mayer Esq
Denis Meehan Esq
W H Melly Esq
Kenneth Merry Esq
Petre I Metanie Esq
S H Metcalf Esq
Peter Methuen Esq
David A Millard Esq
Hugh Miller Esq
Sue Miller and Alan Palmer Esq
J K Milner
Sir Godfrey Milton-Thompson KBE, FRCP
Frank Mitchell Esq LLB
Philip G Mitchell Esq
J W R Mizen
J A Moakes
George Mogridge Esq
M Mohin
Kevin Moloney Esq
Philip Monger Esq BA(Hons)
J F Montgomerie MA, CEng, MIEE, MRAeS
Dr D P Moody
J S Moore
James Moran Esq
Mrs A Morant
Ian H Morgan Esq
Mrs J Morley, A G Morley Esq
and J R Morley Esq
T C Morrice
G Morris
Owen Morris Esq
P J Morris Esq
Martin Morton Esq
Diana Moss
Harry Moss Esq
Jack Moss Esq
J Mottram Esq
John Mowles Esq
K Mudd Esq
Janet Muir
Robert Muir Esq
Nigel J R Mullan Esq
A W Murdoch
Dr Louis Murray
M H Murrell Esq (Maj Rtd)
Gordon Mustoe Esq

N

Owen Nankivell Esq MA (Econ)
G K Naylor
M A Naylor
Dr Ralph Negrine
Mrs Anne-Marie Nelson
Edward Montague Nelson Esq
L M Nerva Esq
Mrs Daphne Newbould
G B Newman Esq MA, CStat
Joseph Nicholas Esq
D and J Nicholson
J A Nightingale CBE
Brian Nixon Esq
Dr Pippa Norris
David Northmore Esq

O

Dominic O'Callaghan Esq
B O'Connell MD, MRCP, MRCP(E), DCH
Prof James O'Connell
James Odgers Esq
J O'Donnell
Patrick O'Keeffe Esq ARIBA
C F Old
Prof Dawn Oliver
M O'Malley
George Paul Orechoff Esq
J C Overton
Robert Owen Esq

P

A P Paddington
J W Page Esq
John Palmer Esq CB
Mrs Rosemary Papaeliou
Colin Park Esq
Cllr Michael W Parkin Esq
Thomas Parkinson Esq
John Parry Esq
Jack Parsons Esq
L M Parsons
Mrs Alice Patterson
Cllr Edward Pawley Esq
Andrew Payne Esq
Barry Arnold Payton Esq
Edward Pearson Esq
Ronald Pearson Esq MA, PhD and J L Pearson MA
A A Pelling Esq
A H Pengelly
Robert W Perceval Esq
K R Perrin Esq
Cllr N Perrott Esq
Cllr Kevin Peters Esq
K E Pheasant
Dr W M Philip
A A Phillips
Mr and Mrs E P Phillips
R H Phillips
Dr Mark Philp
Miss J M Pick
D H Pickett
John Pickin Esq
Anthony Piepe Esq
F L Pitt
Malcolm Pitt Esq
R Pitt
John R Plummer Esq

John D Pollock Esq
Alex Pomeroy Esq
David W Powell Esq
George Powell Esq
R G Powell
Phillip E Preedy Esq
Peter Preston Esq
Prof T A Preston MA(Cantab), FMS, FRSA
Greville Price Esq
Mrs Mary Proctor
Michael J Pulman Esq
R H Purshouse
Andrew N Pykett Esq

Q

Sir Michael Quinlan

R

Francis Radcliffe Esq
A Ramskill Esq
P L Rankin
Adam Raphael Esq
Noel Ratcliffe Esq
J Michael Rawcliffe Esq
Dr George Read
John P Read Esq
George H Readman Esq
John Rebecchi Esq
Philip Redfern Esq CB
E Redgrave
Alexander Redhouse Esq
    RIBA, MRTPI, ACIArb, MBAE
P J Rewcastle
John Reynolds Esq
A Richardson
Frank Richardson Esq
Mr and Mrs S Rickard
J D Riddiough Esq
S Ridpath Esq
Dr R M Ridsdill Smith MA, FRCGP
Dr Vicky Rippere
G Risoli Esq
Peter G Roads Esq
Philip Roberts Esq
P Roberts
R G Roberts Esq
Trevor Roberts Esq
David Alexander Robinson Esq
John Robinson Esq
J R Robinson Esq
K Rogers Esq
B P M Rooney
D J Rose Esq
Stephen Rosen Esq
Euilleam Ross Esq
George Ross Esq
George W Ross Esq
Cllr Michael Ross Esq
Andrew Roth Esq
Thomas Rothwell Esq
Brian Rowland Esq QPM
Mrs Sue Rowlands
Michael Rule Esq
Michael Rush Esq BA, PhD, FRSA
Mrs Sylvia Russel
Michael Ryle Esq

S

C D Samuel
Mrs Janet Sandilands
Neil Sandilands Esq
Sailendra Sarker Esq
F/Lt F A Saunders
Kate Saunders
Dr Chris Saville FRSA, FIPD
T E Scales
Stephen Schlich Esq
Peter Schofield Esq
I B Scholefield
Robert James Scidler Esq
Frank G Scott Esq BA, MHSM, MIPD, FIWO
Lionel F Scott Esq FAPA
Margaret Scott
Mavis Scott
Mrs C Scrivner
Dr Paul Seabright
Barry E Sealey Esq
Dr Lily M Segerman-Peck
B H J Segrott Esq
Victor Serebriakoff Esq
Mrs P M Sharp
Tony Sharp Esq
H C W Shaw Esq
H A Shearing
John H Shedden Esq
Brian Sheehy Esq
John Shemilt Esq
D M Shephard Esq JP, BA, Dip LS
D Shepherd
Gordon J Sheppard Esq
P J Sherfield Esq
David K Sheridan Esq DMA, MIPD, LLB
Derek J Shields Esq
Barry Shooter Esq
Lawrence Sicard-Askey Esq
James E Siddeley Esq MA, JP
Ruth Silcock
Donald Sime Esq
Charles Simeons Esq
Paul Sims Esq
L F Smale
Douglas G Smart Esq
Dr Harry W Smart
The Venerable Rev B John Smith
D J W Smith
Geoffrey R Smith Esq Dip.Arch. Oxford, RIBA
G M Smith
Graeme S Smith Esq
Larry C Smith Esq
Nick Armand Smith Esq
Dr P J A Smith
S L Smith Esq
Duncan Smyth Esq
Stan Smyth Esq
B C N Snelling Esq
Owen H Speirs Esq
Richard Spencer Esq
Ivor Stanbrook Esq
L C Stanford
Mrs Beryl Stangoe
Peter Stangoe Esq
David Starkie Esq
Robert C Steed Esq
B Stenhouse
Peter Stephens Esq
Mrs G P Stevens
Robert Stevens Esq

Robert Stevenson Esq
David F Stewart Esq
Alvin Stockmarr Esq FCCA, IPFA, FCIS, FIMgt
J C G Stocks
Stephan Stockton Esq
Ms M Stoklosinski
B Stott
Miss Catharine Straker
Peter Street Esq
Geoffrey Streets Esq
Richard Strong Esq
Oliver Stutchbury Esq
Helen Style
Brian T Sutcliffe Esq
Eric Sutherland Esq F.Inst.D
V Sutton-Vane
J A Svendsen PhD
Peter Swaby Esq IPFA, ALCM
Christopher Swain Esq
Pamela Swaine
Shelagh Sweeney
Clifford Swindells Esq
Dr P Symmons
Tim Symonds Esq

T

F P Taylor
R J Taylor
Mrs J K Terry
R L Terry
Mrs Renee Marie Thackrah
Bronwen Thomas
Cllr Gareth Thomas Esq
Michael J Thomas Esq
Prof Noel B W Thompson PhD, CEng
H G Thomson
Harold John Thorn Esq
E W Thornhill
James Thorp Esq
Alan Thorpe Esq
R B Thrower
A R Tidball
Tony Tigwell Esq
R Tilleke Esq
John Tincey Esq
Bryan G Todd Esq
P Todd
Sarah M Tooze
Helen Trafford DSc, SRN
D J Treagus
Cllr Edward G Trevor Esq FRICS
Mr and Mrs A Truder
Winifred Tumim OBE, JP
C E Turnock
Ian Tweedie Esq
Ken Twentyman Esq
Paul Hadleigh Twyman Esq MScEcon,
    FIMgt, MCIT, FRSA

U

Miss Beryl Urquhart OBE
D I Urwin FIPD, MIMgt

V

George Stuart Varley Esq
Richard Venable Esq
G B Vickery
Prof Gerald Vinten

W

Prof Sir William Wade QC, LLD, FBA
Cdr B H Wainwright OBE, MNI, RN (Ret.)
John Wainwright Esq
David Wakeford Esq
Jenifer Wakelyn
Douglas A Walker Esq
Mrs M Walker
Tim Walker Esq
J W Wall Esq
Daniel Wallace Esq
Jim Walton Esq
P J Ward MA(Cantab)
Robin M Wardrope Esq
Mrs Valerie Waring
Mrs M P Warke
Mike Warner Esq
Norman Warner Esq
John W Warren Esq MSc, PhD
R Warrior
W E Watson Esq
Donald T Watts Esq
Peter Watts Esq
Dr Nick Webb
Sir Michael Weir
P P Wells Esq
John Westcombe Esq
R J Westmarland FCCA
E Wheeler
Ben Whitaker Esq
D Whitehouse Esq
David Whiteley Esq
Mark Whittet Esq
Brian Whittle Esq
R A Wiersma Esq
Mrs A Wilks
Dr Edward M A Willhoft BSc, PhD, FIFST, AKCC
David L Williams Esq
E P Williams
F L T Williams Esq

Gareth Williams Esq
J Williams Esq
Dr Olwen Williams
Robert Williams Esq
Ron Williams Esq
William Clemant Williams Esq
Robert Williamson Esq
Rt Rev Roy Williamson
Steve Willis Esq
A J Wills
John B Wilson Esq
John H Winn Esq
Garth Wiseman Esq MSc, DMS, Dip Int Econ, MCIM,
    MIEx, MInstD, FFA, FRSA
John Witherow Esq
W O Wittering Esq
Mrs Wolkonskij-Karpoff
Charles Wood Esq
Peter J Wood Esq
Patrick Woods Esq
Duncan J Woolard Esq CEng, MIMechE
Paul Woolf Esq
R W Wordley
Royston Worthing Esq
A H Wright
Roger Wright Esq
M Wrightson
D J Wyatt
Jean A Wyatt

Y

Andrew Yale Esq
D A Yates Esq
Mrs Frances M L Young
Mary Young BEd (Hons),
    Adv.Dip.Ed. Counselling & Guidance
Neville Young Esq
Mrs Ruth Young

Printed in the United Kingdom for HMSO
Dd 5064129   5/95   C25   3398/4   65536   o/n 321335   15/32581